INTELLECTUAL PROPERTY:

PATENTS, COPYRIGHT, TRADE MARKS AND ALLIED RIGHTS

Fourth Edition

By

W. R. CORNISH, Q.C., LL.B., F.B.A.

*Herchel Smith Professor of Intellectual Property Law,
University of Cambridge*

LONDON
SWEET & MAXWELL
1999

First Edition 1981
Second Impression 1982
Third Impression 1984
Second Edition 1989
Second Impression 1990
Third Impression 1991
Fourth Impression 1993
Fifth Impression 1994
Sixth Impression 1995
Third Edition 1996
Second Impression 1997
Third Impression 1998
Fourth Edition 1999

Published by
Sweet & Maxwell Limited of
100 Avenue Road
Swiss Cottage
London, NW3 3PF
http://www.smlawpub.co.uk

Laserset by
LBJ Enterprises Ltd
Aldermaston and Chilcompton
Printed in England by
Clays Ltd,
St. Ives plc.

British Library Cataloguing in Publication Data
Cornish, W. R. (William Rodolph), 1937—
Intellectual property: patents, copyright,
trade marks and allied rights. – 2nd ed.
I. Great Britain, Intellectual property Law
I. Title
334'1064'8   1002115094

ISBN 0—421—635401 (pb)
ISBN 0—421—635304 (hb)

PREFACE TO THE FIRST EDITION

The various branches of intellectual property law—patents, trade marks, registered designs, copyright, confidence and so on—confer legal exclusivity in the market-place. The right to prevent others from using ideas or information to their own commercial advantage is not easily delineated. Legal techniques of some sophistication are called for and this has until recently made intellectual property a somewhat esoteric specialism. But, particularly in industrial, free-market economies, these intangible property rights are becoming increasingly valuable in the fight to secure and retain shares of a market. A widening circle of people need some knowledge of what they involve.

This book deals with the British law of intellectual property, in the new setting provided by EEC membership and a growing encrustation of international conventions. I have not written it for the person who understands the main characteristics of the law: specialist lawyers and professional advisers, such as patent and trade mark agents, are well supplied with detailed practitioners' texts. I am seeking rather to help the relative novice who wants something more substantial than a purely introductory account of the subject.

I have, indeed, had three types of reader in mind. First, students in universities and polytechnics, whether they are studying law in general or specialising in business law or training for one of the intellectual property professions. In Britain and the Commonwealth, an increasing number of students are tackling the subject each year. For them, I have described not only the current state of British law but have sketched in the political and economic debates which always surround the subject.

Secondly, there are lawyers, business executives and civil servants who come in contact with the field in the course of their careers and need to look at its structure systematically. Thirdly, there are specialists in the subject abroad who are looking for a relatively succinct presentation of United Kingdom law. International negotations about intellectual property proliferate; but legal protection is still at base a matter for the domestic laws of national states. As trans-national business grows so does the expert's need to have some acquaintance with the intellectual property laws of all major industrial countries. Within the EEC, with its special market objectives and its great interest in securing Community-wide or harmonised regimes of intellectual property, there is a real need to understand the British legal position. Both the independent development of the common law and Britain's long industrial history have given the country a distinctive experience which deserves to be better understood among our continental collaborators.

W.R.C.

October, 1980

PREFACE TO SECOND EDITION

This book has had to wait more than eight years for revision, even though a great deal has happened to the subject in the interim. Throughout the period, the British government has been considering how it should revise U.K. copyright law and the parasitical growth upon it relating to industrial designs. In 1983, the Green Paper by Sir Robin Nicholson, *Intellectual Property Rights and Innovation,* broadened an already wide prospect for reform by questioning the capacity of the current types of protection to foster scientific and technological progress in British industry. Out of the domestic debates has come the Copyright, Designs and Patent Act 1988 and suddenly the need for this second edition has shifted from pending to urgent.

The Act restates general copyright law in various ways, adds something to the panoply of moral rights, seeks to foster the collective enforcement of copyright in face of new, much-enhanced technology and, above all, creates a new, complex scheme for industrial design. The Act also contains changes relating to patent and trade mark agents, patent litigation, the compulsory licensing of certain pharmaceutical patents, and trade mark piracy, but it does not touch the heart of patent or trade mark law. Accordingly revision on those fronts has been more interstitial than in relation to copyright and design. Nonetheless there has been a flow of important case-law, so there is new material at many points of the book.

On the European scene, progress has been made towards the institution of an E.C. Trade Mark, but final issues (including siting of the Community Trade Mark Office) are still in the balance. Implementation of the scheme, as of the Community Patent Convention, now becomes part of the drive to 1992. They are mentioned in the book as important developments for the future.

In international fora, the impetus behind the New International Economic Order, so fervently desired by developing countries, has faltered. The tensions generated by this movement have meant the abandonment of attempts to revise the Paris Industrial Property Convention. More recently, reaction against it has taken the form of pressure within the current round of GATT negotiations to secure a much improved level of recognition and enforcement of intellectual property rights. Something of this rather abrupt reversal, led by the United States, finds its way into these pages. But it is early yet to see much of its potential effect upon legal practice.

My thanks once again to those who have provided research and secretarial assistance and to the publishers for the despatch with which they have processed the necessary work.

W.R.C.

May, 1989

PREFACE TO THIRD EDITION

Intellectual property is in demand as never before. Those who undertake scientific and technological research, those who create and interpret works of learning, culture, entertainment and information, those who devise the marketing of products and services—all look to legal protection against competitors, as a way of sustaining the value of their skill and labour or their investment in what is distinctively theirs. In biotechnology, computing, telecommunications and many related arts, the scale of production of new, individual material is such that their case has to be conceded; rights have to be created or enchanced.

More than ever, it becomes crucial to study intellectual property as an overall phenomenon: hence the breadth of this book. It is necessary to distinguish between the objects and the forms of the different types of right. Only then is it possible to understand the bearing which each may have on any particular subject-matter. Cumulation of different rights is now increasingly characteristic: most of intellectual property seems to bear on the task of providing proprietary protection within the global communications structures that are presaged by the Internet.

Certainly the pace of legal change, much of it basic, is far greater than even a decade or so ago. One driving force is international, and arises from the insistence of the major producing countries that intellectual property rights should become one ground rule of liberalised world trade within the GATT. Hence, the Trade Related Intellectual Property Agreement (TRIPs) included at the end of the Uruguay Round in April 1994. Equally assertive has been the pressure to complete the internal market of the European Communities. This has now given us a new regime for trade mark registration, operating at both the Community and national levels; it has produced a splay of strategic Directives to harmonise copyright law, covering computer software, rental rights, neighbouring rights, satellite and cable, and the duration of rights. Now databases are to be protected by a mixture of copyright and a producer's right in their content. Virtually every other field of intellectual property either has Community law, which already reshapes it, or it stands to undergo such alteration soon enough.

It has accordingly been very difficult to complete this edition. Much has had to be altered in course of production and the publishers have had to show continuing forbearance. The British Government is behind on its timetable for implementing the Directives on copyright. Elsewhere, litigants in our courts are presenting British judges with the chance to be first past the post in interpreting the new law on trade marks. The results are certainly to be applauded, but they are the outcome of British heats in E.C. championships which will be finalised in Luxembourg. Again, the E.C. Commission and other Community organs continue to further their various law-making projects. Little can be predicted about outcomes in the various fields, save that a further edition of the book is going to be needed in an all-too-short space. For it the author will try to garner the energy.

W.R.C.

May, 1996

PREFACE TO FOURTH EDITION

The first three editions of this book followed upon transforming legislation in a major section of intellectual property. The first edition dealt with the Patents Act 1977, the second had to wait for the Copyright, Designs and Patents Act 1988 and the third for the Trade Marks Act 1994. In 1996 I also planned to include British implementation of the first phase of the European Community's drive to harmonise copyright law by Directive. That process, however, proved to need an extended gestation and some parts of it had to be held over.

Eventually the United Kingdom government did implement the outstanding parts of the Rental, Lending and Related Rights Directive, the Cable and Satellite Directive and the Duration Directive, so far as it judges legislative change to our own law to be needed (a judgment not always shared by Commission officials). It has also made a beginning on a second phase of copyright reforms with implementation of the 1996 Database Directive.

The first purpose, accordingly, of the present edition is to keep the text up-to-date with these changes in current legislation. A second is to report developments of case law. Every element in the new machinery for trade mark registration seems to be under test before tribunals and courts, both at the national and Community levels. The scope of the patent system has been reviewed in decisions on claims to computer program applications and on new uses and knowledge of known substances. Britain's distinctive contribution to the protection of technical design—the unregistered design right of 1988—has been given clearer outline. Cross-border patent litigation, mainly within the EEA, has raised a whole range of novel difficulties which may be only a foretaste of things to come in a world of globalised commerce and communications.

A third purpose is to keep watch over the bubbling cauldron of law reform. The European Commission is preoccupied with the digital revolution. It has proposals for Directives on copyright in the Information Society, and more generally on electronic commerce, both of which are of considerable importance for the future of intellectual property. It is still considering the introduction of a lesser form of patent or utility model and it continues to examine a range of other extensions of protection. The World Intellectual Property Organisation is increasing its regular reviewing of developments thought to be needed at the international level, including protection for databases. It has yet to be seen whether the World Trade Organisation, deeply involved in the staged implementation of the TRIPS Agreement, will engage in a review of the contents of that document as early as the year 2000. Its gains for rightholders in the international arena represented such a dramatic advance that many are reluctant to hazard again so quickly. Calculating where the intellectual property world will be in even a few years is a fool's game. Authors of texts will be praying for respite and consolidation.

W.R.C.

July, 1999

CONTENTS

PART II: PATENTS

PART III: CONFIDENCE

PART IV: COPYRIGHT AND DESIGNS

PART VI: THE EUROPEAN DIMENSION

APPENDICES

TABLE OF CASES

1

TABLE OF STATUTES

Foreign Statutes

TABLE OF STATUTORY INSTRUMENTS

TABLE OF EUROPEAN AND INTERNATIONAL LEGISLATION

RULES OF SUPREME COURT

TABLE OF CONVENTIONS

Conventions

TABLE OF TREATIES

TABLE OF ABBREVIATIONS

Annand and Norman	=	R. Annand and H. Norman, *Blackstone's Guide to the Trade Marks Act 1994* (1994)
Bellamy and Child	=	Common Market Law of Competition
Benyamini	=	Patent Infringement in the European Community
Berne	=	Berne Convention for the Protection of Literary and Artistic Works
Brussels Judgments Convention	=	Convention on Jurisdictions and the Enforcement of Judgments in Civil and Commercial Matters
Budapest Treaty of 1977	=	International Recognition of the Deposit of Micro-organisms for the Purposes of Patent Procedure 1977
CA 1956	=	Copyright Act 1956
CDPA 1988	=	Copyright, Designs and Patents Act 1988
CISAC	=	Confedération Internationale de Sociétés des Auteurs et Compositeurs
CLA	=	Copyright Licensing Agency
Copinger	=	*Copinger and Skone James on Copyright* (14th ed., 1999, with supps.), Garnett, J. Rayner James and G. Davies
COPAC	=	Common Patents Appeal Court
CPC	=	Community Patent Convention 1975, revised 1989
CTM	=	Community Trade Mark
EPC	=	European Patent Convention 1973
EPO	=	European Patent Office
Fellner	=	C. Fellner, *Industrial Design Law* (1995)
IFRRO	=	International Federation of Reproduction Rights Associations
ITC	=	Independent Television Commission

Kerly	=	T.A. Blanco White and R. Jacob, *Kerly's Law of Trade Marks and Trade Names* (12th ed., 1986, with supp.)
Laddie *et al.*	=	H. Laddie, P. Prescott and M. Vitoria, *The Modern Law of Copyright* (2nd ed., 1995)
Madrid Protocol	=	Protocol (1989) to the Madrid Agreement concerning the International Registration of Marks
MCPS	=	Mechanical-Copyright Protection Society
OHIM	=	Office for the Harmonisation of the Internal Market (Trade Marks and Design)
PA 1977 Rules	=	Rules under the Patents Act 1977
PACT	=	Producers Alliance for Cinema and Television
Paterson	=	*The European Patent System* (1992, with supps.)
PCT	=	Patent Co-operation Treaty 1970
PCT Rules	=	Rules under Patent Co-operation Treaty
PIP	=	Paris Convention for the Protection of Industrial Property
PLR Scheme	=	Public Lending Right Scheme (*see* Public Lending Right Act 1979)
PLRA 1979	=	Public Lending Right Act 1979
PRT	=	Performing Right Tribunal
Reid	=	*A Practical Guide to Patent Law* (3rd ed., 1998)
Ricketson	=	S. Ricketson, *The Berne Convention for the Protection of Literary and Artistic Works 1886–1986* (1987)
Rome	=	Rome Convention for the Protection of Performers, Phonograms and Broadcasting Organisations of 1961
Rothnie	=	W. Rothnie, *Parallel Imports* (1993)
Singer	=	R. Singer, *The European Patent Convention* (2nd English ed., 1995)
SPC	=	Supplementary protection certificate
TMA 1994	=	Trade Marks Act 1994

TMA 1994 Rules	=	Rules under the Trade Marks Act 1994
TRIPS	=	Agreement on Trade-Related Intellectual Property Rights including Trade in Counterfeit Goods
UCC	=	Universal Copyright Convention of 1952
UPOV Convention	=	Convention for the Protection of New Varieties of Plants
WIPO	=	World Intellectual Property Organisation
WTO	=	World Trade Organisation

Part I

COMMON GROUND

CHAPTER 1

STARTING POINTS

1. GENERAL

(1) "Intellectual property"

Patents give temporary protection to technological inventions and design **1–01** rights to the appearance of mass-produced goods; copyright gives longer-lasting rights in, for instance, literary, artistic and musical creations; trade marks are protected against imitation so long at least as they continue to be employed in trade. These and similar rights in United Kingdom law are the subject-matter of this book. There is no single generic term that satisfactorily covers them all. "Industrial property" is not infrequently used in the common law world, but many would hold this to exclude copyright, particularly if they want to emphasise the special importance and vulnerability of the creative artist. "Intellectual property" is the term used in this book for the whole field. The term scarcely describes trade marks and similar marketing devices; but it has now acquired international acceptance.[1] "IP" or "IPR" is indeed becoming a fashionable description of research results and other original ideas, whether or not they fall within the ambit of what the law protects. As a title, the term may sound rather grandiloquent. But then, at its most serious, this is a branch of the law which protects some of the finer manifestations of human achievement.

The various aspects of the subject differ in purpose and in detailed rule. Nonetheless there is good sense in studying them together. Each is concerned with marking out, by means of legal definition, types of conduct which may not be pursued without the consent of the right-owner. The rights thus delimited are enforced in similar ways[2] and all are dealt with by broad analogy to property rights in tangible movables.[3] Frequently the

---

[1] As in the title of the UN organ, World Intellectual Property Organisation (WIPO) and in the Agreement on Trade-Related Intellectual Property Rights including Trade in Counterfeit Goods (TRIPS), which forms part of the GATT Round completed in April 1994. In older Continental usage, intellectual property referred to the protection of works of authorship.

[2] See Chap. 2, below.

[3] An analogy that nonetheless is not straightforward: see, *e.g.* the discussion of damages for breach of confidence in para. 8–47, below.

objective of controlling the activities of competitors and licensees is achieved by use of a number of forms of intellectual property conjointly. Where their deployment comes in conflict with other policies, such as has happened under the impact of E.C. law, comparisons between the different forms of intellectual property need to be made.[4]

(2) Organisation of the material

1–02 The main branches of intellectual property each have a Part devoted to them in the course of the book. Those concerned with the protection of ideas and information—patents, breach of confidence and copyright—are treated before those which deal with trade marks, trade names and the like. Before reaching this stage, however, there are a number of themes that can usefully be pursued in common and they are explored in this introductory Part.

In the remainder of this chapter four distinct topics are raised: the roles of national, regional and international law in the development of intellectual property law; the use of statute and judicial decision as a means of defining intellectual property rights and the interrelation between these two sources of law; basic economic considerations underlying the objectives of the law; and certain relevant principles of the European Community. Chapter 2 deals with matters more immediately practical: the remedies and procedures generally available in the enforcement of intellectual property rights.

1–03 The subject has grown in a variety of directions over recent years. Its increasing economic significance for countries with any degree of industrial development is making it both more international and more complex. To contain it within a single book has called for a considerable measure of selection. This has involved a number of strategic choices, which it is worth listing at the outset:

(1) Each of the subjects has spawned enough detailed law to merit very substantial texts for specialist practitioners. This book does not try to cover all the detailed points of statute or case law to be found in them. Some attempt has been made to include cross-references to them where they carry a point further.[5] Beyond this the reader in search of all the available knowledge must be prepared to refer to them without explicit guidance from this book. In particular, the account here tends to concentrate on substantive rules rather than on matters of procedure, both in the acquiring and the enforcement of rights.

---

[4] See further, paras 1–51—1–57, below, and the references given there to other parts of this book.

[5] Most are referred to in abbreviated forms: see the Table of Abbreviations.

(2) The major statutes on British intellectual property have been subject to very substantial revision in the last two decades. Of particular importance have been the Patents Act 1977, the Copyright, Designs and Patents Act 1988 and now the Trade Marks Act 1994; and there is a continuing stream of further measures, the most significant of which today come from the European Community. For the most part, the existing subject-matter has been brought within the changed law by transitional provisions which will be alluded to in the course of the text. The issue has been most complex in relation to the patent law changes in 1977. However, the last of the "old patents" will expire in the next few years, so the law affecting them is left to specialist works.

(3) Of the lesser intellectual property regimes, the protection of registered and unregistered designs is closely entwined with artistic copyright and the 1988 Act regime in the field is dealt with in Chapter 14. That discussion also extends to the special protection given to semi-conductor chip topographies.[6] Public lending right is treated as an adjunct of copyright.[7] Plant variety rights, however, are assigned to Appendix 3.

(4) With membership of the European Community, the rules of competition and allied principles in the Treaty of Rome have come to play a prominent role in the whole subject. This difficult and often imprecise field of law deserves study as a whole and on its own. Here all that can be examined is the impact of competition and free movement rules on the different types of intellectual property. To this end: (a) the relevant policies of the European Community are outlined in this introductory Part[8]; (b) the impact of these policies (together with certain provisions of British statute law) is discussed in the Parts on patents, copyright and trade marks and in a final chapter[9]; (c) Appendix 1 gives some further crucial clues to the administration of E.C. competition policy; and (d) the same Appendix says something about native British competition law, which has had a less dramatic impact upon intellectual property rights.

(5) The law contained in this book is largely based on statutes applicable to the United Kingdom as a whole. By contrast, most of the case law has been decided in English courts. Nonetheless there are three separate jurisdictions to which litigants may on occasion resort. While the procedures and remedies available in Northern Ireland closely resemble those of England and Wales, the Scottish system is

---

[6] See paras 14–48—14–51, below.
[7] See paras 13–101—13–102, below.
[8] See paras 1–48—1–58, below. There is also a brief introduction to Community law-making in paras 1–26, 1–27, below.
[9] See paras 7–30—7–40, 12–59—12–62, 17–120, 17–121; Chap. 18, *passim*.

often distinct in substance or in nomenclature. The special characteristics of Scottish litigation, however, are not pursued here.

(6) For readers who come to this subject without much legal background, it is important also to say that knowledge of the general
structure of both the English legal system and that of the E.C.
(within the European Union) is assumed.

2. TYPES OF INTELLECTUAL PROPERTY[10]

1–04 Intellectual property protects applications of ideas and information that are
of commercial value. The subject is growing in importance, to the advanced
industrial countries in particular, as the fund of exploitable ideas becomes
more sophisticated and as their hopes for a successful economic future
come to depend increasingly upon their superior corpus of new knowledge
and fashionable conceits. There has recently been a great deal of political
and legal activity designed to assert and strengthen the various types of
protection for ideas.

One characteristic shared by all types of intellectual property to date is
that the rights granted are essentially negative: they are rights to stop others
doing certain things—rights in other words to stop pirates, counterfeiters,
imitators and even in some cases third parties who have independently
reached the same ideas, from exploiting them without the licence of the
rightowner. Some aspects of intellectual property confer positive entitlements, such as the right to be granted a patent or register a trade mark
upon fulfilling the requisite conditions; but these are essentially ancillary.

The fact that intellectual property gives a right to control the activities of
others has a number of implications, often inadequately understood. The
rightowner does not need the right in order to exploit a market for its
goods or services: a patent is not a pre-condition to exploiting one's own
invention. By way of corollary, the right gives no liberty to ignore the rights
of other individuals (including their intellectual property) or to override
public liabilities: a trade mark registration does not justify its use to
advertise illegal goods. Nor does intellectual property confer on the
rightowner's products any privileged position in international trade, rendering them exempt from prohibitions or quotas which a country would
otherwise apply to them: the fact that films embody copyright does not
mean that they cannot be subject of programming limitations designed to
favour national culture. Of course, it would be possible to adopt a new
approach to these matters, and arguments for doing so are made from time
to time. However, if they were ever to succeed, fundamental assumptions
about the role and purpose of intellectual property would also shift, with
consequences which might be very hard to predict.

---

[10] For the evolution of the concept, see Ladas, *Patents, Trade Marks and Related Rights*, vols I,
II, (1975); Sherman and Bently, *The Making of Modern Intellectual Property Law* (1999).

Apart from this shared characteristic, the three central types of intellectual property right—patents for inventions, copyright for literary and artistic works and associated products, and trade marks and names for the goodwill attaching to marketing symbols—cover distinct subject-matter and have different objectives. The law on each accordingly varies in strategic ways and these need to be compared at the outset.

(1) Patents (Chapters 3–7)

Patents are granted in respect of inventions, *i.e.* technological improve- **1–05** ments, great and small, which contain at least some scintilla of inventiveness over what is previously known. To take the standards now operating in much of Europe, they are typified by the following:

— they issue from a state or regional patent office after a substantial examination of their validity;
— they last for a maximum of 20 years from application; and
— they require that the invention be publicly described in the patent specification.

The right which they accord is to prevent all others—not just imitators, but even independent devisers of the same idea—from using the invention for the duration of the patent. That core conception reveals a great deal about why invention patents are the most basic, the most valuable, and, to others, potentially the most dangerous, of all intellectual property—the category which demands to be studied above all others.[11]

The practical applications of scientific knowledge which make up "technology" are rooted in objective information. Inventions are discoveries about the inherent capacities of matter, and in a sense are waiting to be made. Inventors may proceed by all sorts of routes, but those addressing the same problem are after essentially the same knowledge. A first discovery in a particular field may well be followed by further research results which all competitors in an industry will need to embody in their products if they are to keep in the market.

A stage will be reached where further inventions produce both advantages and disadvantages over other ways of making and doing things, at which point product developers will have alternatives to hand. But whether a patent is for a primary breakthrough or for some subsequent development, it will only have industrial value to the extent that it covers all embodiments of its inventive concept. Otherwise there will be ways of

---

[11] Elements of personal, even arbitrary, choice may enter the design of embodiments of the invention and some of these may come to define industrial standards—the gauge of railway track, the dimensions of couplings and other "interfaces"; but these are not a part of the invention itself.

taking the idea over without infringing the right and any patent will be good only against simple imitators. A patent system must above all strive to ensure that it gives rights over all applications of the invention revealed but over no more than this—a balance which can be remarkably difficult to achieve.[12]

The special potential of a patent is accordingly that it may be used to prevent all others from including any form of the invention in their products and services; and where real breakthroughs are patented this potential is occasionally so considerable as to render the competition obsolete. More regularly, a patent poses serious difficulties for competitors. This is why patents are not freely available for all industrial improvements, but only for what is judged to qualify as a "patentable invention".

(2) Copyright (Chapters 9–13)

1–06 Copyright, by contrast, is a right given against the copying of defined types of cultural, informational and entertainment productions. Classically, these have been (in international jargon) "literary and artistic works"—the creations of authors, playwrights, composers, artists and film directors.[13] At least the outstanding works in each of these categories are marked by their individuality—that distinctness which results from the creator's myriad choices made in the course of constructing the work in the chosen medium. Because aesthetic productions are endlessly different, and therefore the protection, quite properly, operates only against copying, the right has come to have a very substantial duration: typically, the author's life and 50 years thereafter—or 70 years as it is now becoming in the E.U.[14]

In this century, the range of copyright has been complicated by the addition of certain analogous rights given to performers and to the producers of sound recordings, films, broadcasters and other entrepreneurs, for somewhat shorter periods (sometimes labelled "related" or "neighbour-ing" rights as distinct from "authors' rights"). At this introductory stage it can be taken that these rights share many of the characteristics of the authors' copyright. They are, however, somewhat closer to industrial property in the relative shortness of their duration.

The basis of copyright lies in the personal character of the subject-matter in issue. It is the particular expression making up a work which is protected, rather than the idea behind it. It is *St. Joan* or *Jeanne d'Arc au bûcher* that is copyright, rather than any play or oratorio on the historical story of Joan of Arc. Copyright law must strive, therefore, to give meaning and a sense of

---

[12] See paras 6–28—6–31, below.
[13] While the work of film directors is included within the Berne Convention on Literary and Artistic Works (for which see para. 9–24, below), it is only now that it is to be given direct recognition in British copyright law: for the complex development, see paras 10–23—10–25, below.
[14] See paras 10–43ff., below.

proportion to the often amorphous distinction between "expression" and "idea". It is a difficulty which becomes acute when copyright is extended to an utilitarian subject-matter and nowhere more so than in treating computer programs as "literary works" within copyright.[15] Yet without some such distinction, the right would be of unconstrained breadth. It would then be very difficult to justify the long term attached to it.

(3) Trade marks and names (Chapters 15–17)

Trade marks and related aspects of trading goodwill (get-up, trade names **1–07** of businesses, etc.) are protected as symbols needed by consumers to distinguish between competing products and services in a market economy. As long as they continue to be used in trade these signs are a prominent part of goodwill and rights in them cannot be subject to any maximum duration. In the British and many other systems, rights are conferred either by virtue of formal registration or else because of a reputation generated by actual trading (mainly through the action against passing-off).

By association with a successful product or service, or by persistent advertising or even the vagaries of fashion, a mark may be built into an asset of prime value to a business; witness the household names of five continents—Levis for jeans, Mercedes for cars, Panasonic for televisions, Outspan for oranges, Fosters for lager. Nonetheless, marks do not by themselves have the capacity to prevent a competitor from entering any market with his own products or services; they merely prevent him from annexing the protected mark in order to facilitate his market entry. Accordingly there is no policy reason for imposing any limit on the duration of rights of this type. At least, this will remain so provided that marks are not allowed to become barriers in the way of marketing products or services themselves.

(4) Other aspirants

These three types of intellectual property may be regarded as setting the **1–08** models to which aspirants will turn for the protection of other ideas, information and "trade values". Throughout the period of industrialisation there have been claimants who seek either to fit a new subject-matter within one of the model systems or else to have a new regime created to protect it.

(a) *Industrial designs (Chapter 14)*

The longest standing of these has concerned the design of industrial **1–09** products. Legal responses remain as much a problematic hybrid today as they have long been. Many countries have a design registration system, but

---

[15] See paras 13–25ff., below.

they differ in the extent to which the right granted is akin to patent protection (in the form of a full monopoly) or to copyright (requiring copying). Some use artistic copyright itself to give protection of the designs of industrial products, often with some modification of its scope. This may raise awkward questions about whether the two types of protection can be cumulative. Others again may add a right that is *sui generis*, as the United Kingdom did in 1988 with its unregistered design right for the shape of products, both technical and non-technical.[16]

(b) *Trade secrets and other confidential information (Chapter 8)*

1–10 Over much the same period, there have been claims to rights over secret business information—technological know-how (whether inventive or not), ideas for new products and markets, commercial information about customers, finance, employment and many other things. To this countries have responded in various ways, some confining protection to general civil remedies affecting contract, tort, property and perhaps unjust enrichment; some building specific provisions into their law of unfair competition; some (notably common law jurisdictions) generating a form of *sui generis* protection that is akin to but is not quite a form of property right. Countries in this last tradition (such as the United Kingdom) have tended to place the protection of trade secrets in a broader conceptual frame which also encompasses governmental secrets and personal confidences. This approach avoids the need to define limited categories, but it means that cases which may demand very different responses will fall to be considered under a single rubric. However the protection of secrets is formulated, the rights given are likely to be unlimited in time and also to be effective against unjustified uses and disclosures of all kinds. Hence the reluctance to give them the absolute character of "property".

(c) *Further demands*

1–11 In more recent times, an increasing number of countries have thought that industry needs a system of short-term rights protecting minor technical advances, which supplements the patent system and is particularly valuable where know-how cannot be kept secret. Known variously as petty patents, short-term patents and utility models, they depend upon an official grant of rights for a term of six to ten years. The basis on which they are granted, the subject-matter they may cover and numerous other elements vary from country to country. The case for this form of protection has so far been rejected in Britain.[17]

---

[16] See paras 14–33 *et seq.*, below.

[17] The E.C. Commission is now discussing possible systems for the whole Community: see paras 3–30 *et seq.*, below.

To turn to more specific fields, there have been claims from breeders of new plant varieties which numerous countries have now met with patent or *sui generis* protection. Latterly they are being followed by the developers of new animal breeds. Both spheres now work partly by genetic manipulation techniques and their activities are one aspect of a whole complex of issues about the future of intellectual property in the sphere of biotechnology.[18]

For more than a century, new technology has constantly invaded the copyright worlds of culture, education and entertainment, bringing in succession sound recording, film, broadcasting, cable and satellite transmission and the modern wonders of copying technology. All these have created immense pressure for expansion of copyright, the creation of "neighbouring rights", and the protection of entertainment ideas, as well as for the improvement of the legal machinery against piracy and the collective administration of rights.[19] The arrival of the computer, and the demand for protection of programs, electronic databases and computer output, at least against copying, have imposed very considerable strains on traditional conceptions of intellectual property. Indeed, the current coalescence of computer technology and advanced systems of telecommunication is heralding a multi-media revolution which may wear down current notions of intellectual property beyond serviceable endurance. Alongside these developments of central economic significance have run an unending miscellany of other claims: for type-faces; folk-songs and other indigenous culture; the format of media game-shows; "look-alikes" to products and their get-up; character merchandising; merchandising of sport, exhibitions, festivals, universities and film sites; the use of personal characteristics (name, voice, appearance) in publicity—and these are but examples.

3. Pressures for Development

Much of this book is concerned with the extent to which these demands **1–12** have been met. The position varies from country to country and our attention will be centred on the United Kingdom as a core within the wider frame set by the E.U.

Virtually no country favours conferring on the creator of an idea a perpetual property in it against imitators. The political and economic implications of such a privilege would be remarkable. Instead a set of limited forms of protection are fashioned against some types of exploitation by others. The root issue is whether the balance achieved by this approach is broadly appropriate to the economic needs of the country and to the prevailing sense of what is just. While the legal protection that is provided varies for the different types of subject-matter, there are some useful preliminary points to make: about the way, historically, that developments

---

[18] See paras 5–70 *et seq.*, and App. 3, below.
[19] See Chaps 10, 13, below.

have occurred; about the kinds of justification for adopting one or other course of action; and about the foundations from which arguments about ends and means ought to proceed. These are taken up in what follows.

(1) Specific rights and unfair competition

1-13 As a regime is developed for protecting a form of intellectual property a number of basic decisions have to be made: What types of subject-matter are to be included? Is the right to be conferred only upon application to a government office? How long is it to last? Is it to be a right good only against imitators (as with copyright and unregistered designs), or is it a "full monopoly" that even affects independent devisers of the same idea (as with patents for inventions, registered designs and trade marks)? The operative rules vary because each type of subject-matter calls for a different balance of public and private interests—the interests of the society as a whole in its economic and cultural development, and the interest of the individual to secure a "fair" value for his intellectual effort or investment of capital or labour.

The marked tendency under modern conditions is to reach answers about the proper scope of protection by political decision expressed primarily in legislation. Partly this is because the interest groups concerned are expected to make out their case sufficiently to a responsible body; and partly because a complex set of rules is required which cannot satisfactorily be fashioned from the vagaries of litigation.

1-14 Hence, in Britain, the majority of intellectual property rights have a statutory basis. The patent system had its origins in royal grants under the prerogative, which, from the Statute of Monopolies 1624 onwards, came to be conditioned by legislation.[20] In the complex evolution of the copyright system a strategic decision was reached in 1774: to the extent that Parliament had entered the field, copyright under the Statute of Anne 1710 was not to be supplemented by more embracing common law rights.[21] And in the modern period, the ability to adhere to the principle of legislative creation has been much enhanced by the willingness of Parliament to use "copyright" as a catch-all for the protection of new subject-matter, such as records, films, broadcasts, cable-casts and published format, and to act with expedition enough for the judges to reserve their creative urges mainly for ancillary matters, such as remedies.[22]

But this is not the unvarying history. In the early industrial period the judges fashioned the tort of passing off to meet an evident commercial need; and when Parliament did introduce a system for registering trade marks this was regarded as a supplement, and not a displacement, of

---

[20] See paras 3-03—3-09, below.
[21] *Donaldson v. Beckett* (1774) 2 Bro. P.C. 129.
[22] See para. 9-09, below.

common law rights.[23] More recently the courts have extended the action against breach of confidence unassisted by legislative intervention and in response to another strong demand that the law should act against certain kinds of unacceptable business practice.[24]

In all these developments there are distinctively British characteristics, **1–15** which are the product of a particular economic development and political history. What is perhaps most striking of all, however, is the absence of any basic conception that "unfair competition" or the "misappropriation of trade values" should be treated as an underlying principle of liability by which the judges can extend protection to new types of subject-matter and business relationships as they see fit.

In 1918 a majority of the United States Supreme Court in principle adopted a misappropriation doctrine. The well-known *INS* case[25] arose out of the French government's refusal to allow facilities to the Hearst press to report the war in Europe. So one way in which the Hearst news agency procured its war reports was from first editions of Associated Press's newspapers on the American East Coast. It telegraphed the information to its West Coast papers in time for reports to appear in competition with Associated Press newspapers there. This keen bit of acquisition was held a tortious form of competition even though it lay outside the confines of statutory copyright. Noting that "the news has an exchange value to one who can misappropriate it", Pitney J. characterised the defendant's conduct thus:

> "Stripped of all disguises, the process amounts to an unauthorised interference with the normal business operation of complainant's legitimate business precisely at the point where the profit is to be reaped, in order to divert a material portion of the profit from those who have earned it to those who have not; with the special advantage to defendant in the competition because of the fact that it is not burdened with any part of the expense of gathering the news."[26]

Significantly, however, Holmes J. would have restricted relief so that it covered only the implied misrepresentation that the news was Hearst's own (through failure to acknowledge source); and Brandeis J. insisted that legislation alone was the proper medium for fashioning new legal rights in information.

Some years later Dixon J. summarised developments elsewhere in the **1–16** common law world in a way that showed a close affinity to Brandeis J.'s position:

---

[23] See paras 15–08; 16–36ff., below.
[24] See paras 8–01, 8–02, below.
[25] *International News Service v. Associated Press* 248 U.S. 215 (1918). See further, paras 16–36 *et seq.*, below.
[26] 248 U.S. 215 at 240 (1918).

"[The courts] have not in British jurisdictions thrown the protection of an injunction around all the intangible elements of value, that is value in exchange, which may flow from the exercise by an individual of his powers or resources whether in the organisation of a business or undertaking or in the use of ingenuity, knowledge, skill or labour. This is sufficiently evidenced by the history of the law of copyright and by the fact that the exclusive right to invention, trade marks, designs, trade names and reputation are dealt with in English law as special heads of protected interests and not under a wide generalisation."[27]

The evidence for this lay in a succession of decisions. For instance, the House of Lords had refused to subject untruths in comparative advertisements to the discipline of civil action, save in extreme cases of malicious falsehood.[28] Another of its decisions apparently prevented misrepresentation about the quality of one competitor's goods from being actionable at the suit of a rival.[29] In the case being discussed by Dixon J., it was no tort for a broadcasting station to run a commentary on a race meeting from a stand erected outside the course but looking onto it.[30]

1–17   The contrast lay not only with the emergent misappropriation doctrine in the United States (which did not prosper, particularly in its early years) but also with most countries of Western Europe. There, starting either from general provisions on tortious liability in civil codes[31] or from separate proscriptions of unfair competition,[32] the judges tended to develop a broadening series of precedents concerning unfair business practices in the market place. Under such a rubric, advertisements that made, or even implied, comparisons were treated as actionable; and various types of seller's enticements, such as additional "gifts", were treated as unfair ploys. There was also some tendency to consider slavish copying of the details of products as a form of actionable misappropriation—notably when new

---

[27] *Victoria Park Racing v. Taylor* (1937) 58 C.L.R. 479 at 509, HC (Aust.); firmly reiterated in *Moorgate Tobacco v. Philip Morris* [1985] R.P.C. 219 at 236–240, *per* Deane J., HC (Aust.); *cf.* Ricketson and Macchi [1997] E.I.P.R. 128.

[28] *White v. Mellin* [1895] A.C. 154, HL See also *Hubbuck v. Wilkinson* [1899] 1 Q.B. 86, CA; *Alcott v. Millar's Karri* (1904) 21 T.L.R. 30, CA; and generally, paras 16–48 *et seq.*, below. These cases put a stop to the more generous attitude suggested in *Western Counties Manure v. Lawes* (1874) L.R. 9 Ex. 218.

[29] *Native Guano v. Sewage Manure* (1891) 8 R.P.C. 125 (alleged representation that "native guano"—human excreta converted into a fertiliser—was made by the plaintiff's process, when it was not). See also *Cambridge U.P. v. University Tutorial Press* (1928) 45 R.P.C. 335. The decision in the *Guano* case has now been deprived of much of its effect by remarks upon it in the "Advocaat" case [1980] R.P.C. 31 at 408–409, 418.

[30] See n. 26, above. This, however, was one of the earlier instances of "misappropriation" admitted in the U.S., under the *INS* doctrine: *Pittsburgh Athletic Club v. K.Q.V. Broadcasting* 24 F.Supp. 490 (1938).

[31] As in the case of France: see, *e.g.* Krasser, *Répression de la concurrence déloyale: France* (1972); Plaisant [1979] J.B.L. 83; Kaufmann, *Passing Off and Misappropriation* (1986).

[32] As in the case of Germany: see, *e.g.* Reimer, *Répression de la concurrence déloyale en Allemagne* (1978); Kaufmann (above, n.30); Fammler [1994] E.I.P.R. 448; Steckler [1996] E.I.P.R. 390.

technology, such as the apparatus which made it possible to copy records and broadcasts, allowed piracy that fell outside the scope of existing copyright laws.[33] Protection against the direct imitation of products began to assume the character of a sub-species of intellectual property.

Whenever this occurred, the ability of competitors to engage in "reverse engineering" or "reverse analysis" of a novel product or service was proportionately diminished. They could, in other words, be prevented or hindered from breaking a product down into its component parts to see how it was put together or composed. Yet one of the most fundamental assumptions about a competitive economy has been that once a producer enters a market, exactly that type of imitation needs to be present, at least as a potentiality. For no other mechanism will so efficiently secure the welfare of consumers as the prospect of such competition. The intellectual property rights in ideas (patents, copyright, etc.) exist by way of limited exception in order to encourage the mental effort and productive invest-ment which will procure new products and services. To add to their scope by a right against misappropriation or unfair imitation is to place an amorphous further impediment in the way of competition by imitation and that is an inherently controversial step. It is important for the law to preserve a freedom to engage in reverse engineering unless there are convincing reasons against it. The issue will recur at numerous points throughout this book, for many people now consider that they have exactly such reasons.

It is worth trying to divine why British common lawyers resisted a **1–18** demand from business litigants that was being met in comparable countries—places indeed whose industrial and commercial development had only followed the British. A complex set of justifications and underlying motives seem to have been at work. To have adopted a broad principle such as "unfair competition" would have been foreign to the traditional caution of the common law courts. Their long-implanted preference for development only by close and necessary analogy had formerly been expressed through the forms of action, and even the abandonment of that technique in the judicature reforms of the 1850s and 1870s had done little to modify the basic attitude.[34] The nineteenth century had given flesh to one great (indeed over-broad) generalisation, the concept of contract. But the sanctity of bargains, so much a part of the Victorian *Zeitgeist*, was

---

[33] Unfair competition doctrine in the U.S. expanded for the same reason and at much the same time: *e.g. Waring v. WDAS*, 327 Pa. 433 (1937); *Jackson v. Universal*, 36 Cal. (2d) 116 (1950); *Metropolitan Opera v. Wagner-Nichols*, 199 Misc. 786 (1950); *Capitol v. Mercury*, 221 F. (2d) 657 (1955).

[34] With the conjoint system of judicial administration introduced by the Judicature Act 1873 rather more contact came about between the traditions of common law and equity. But where equity's penchant for large moral generalisations produced results that would make "mercantile men cry out" (Lord Bramwell, *Derry v. Peek* (1889) 14 App. Cas. 337 at 350) its excesses were curbed. For our purposes, note the tendency to confine breach of confidence to liability in contract: paras 8–06, 8–07, below.

inimical to legal obligations imposed *ab extra*, as distinct from those reached by voluntary agreement. Large generalisations about rights—unjust enrichment, the right to privacy and unfair competition, just as much as the duty to one's neighbour to take care—found little favour.

1–19   Another recurrent fear was of a flood of litigation[35]—a matter of serious concern to a court system (with its underlying professional structure) in which a small number of superior judges held the power to make law through precedents. In the case of unfair competition, this threat was linked with a concern that the courts should not become a forum for justifying the advertising claims of one business competitor against those of another.[36] At the same time, the emergence of Parliamentary democracy provided new reason for the judges to appear as objective administrators of established law, rather than as wholesale makers of new principle; the more so in the various fields of intellectual property where the legislature was increasingly active.

1–20   How far, then, were the judges also expressing a clearly reasoned preference for freedom to compete, even if it involved making use of the ideas or goodwill of others? Did they, in particular, consider that the public interest in an improved economic future was best served by as little legal interference as possible, and that accordingly rights of intellectual property should be confined to the exceptional categories marked out in the existing law? Whatever their ultimate motives may have been, it is hard to find evidence that they worked out their decisions explicitly from such a premise. If they had felt strongly the need to encourage competition they ought to have been active in turning the law against a different form of unfair business practice from the "excessive" competition in which we are primarily interested. They should have been ready to refuse to enforce agreements amongst competitors not to compete but rather to link together in cartels and other restrictive agreements that would preserve to each his existing market share.

Yet in a succession of judgments, they showed considerable reluctance to intervene.[37] The watchword was provided by Fry L.J.: "to draw a line between fair and unfair competition, between what is reasonable and unreasonable, passes the power of the courts."[38] In truth, in the quarter century before the First World War, free-trade Britain, facing the growing competition of protectionist Germany and America, had reason to think

---

[35] See, *e.g. White v. Mellin* [1895] A.C. 154 at 164, HL.

[36] *ibid.*

[37] See especially *British United Shoe v. Somervell* (1906) 95 LT. 711; *USM Canada v. Brunet* [1909] A.C. 330, JC; *A.-G. for the Commonwealth v. Adelaide Steamship* [1913] A.C. 781, JC; *North Western Salt v. Electrolytic Alkali* [1914] A.C. 461, HL; *English Hop Growers v. Dering* [1928] 2 K.B. 174, CA *cf. Evans v. Heathcote* [1918] 1 K.B. 418, CA; *McEllistrim v. Ballymacelligott Coop.* [1919] A.C. 548, HL Note also the refusal to hold tortious a cartel's indirect pressure upon an outsider: *Mogul Steamship v. McGregor Gow* [1892] A.C. 25.

[38] *Mogul case* (1889) 23 Ch.D. 598 at 625–626.

that there was competition enough.[39] Her judges could afford to place themselves apart for the sorts of motive mentioned earlier. In a world that was having to accept enterprises of the size and strength of the modern business corporation, they showed little desire to become embroiled in the obviously political business of settling the rules of competition.

Over recent decades there has been some modification of the courts' **1–21** approach, but when compared with developments of unfair competition doctrine in parts of Western Europe and the United States,[40] the continuing attraction of late Victorian attitudes remains apparent. Most developed economies have responded to "consumerism" and the fear of business coalitions by introducing anti-trust laws which draw considerably on the American inspiration. Likewise they have tried to improve the standards of information and legal protection that traders must meet in advertising and selling goods and services. In some countries,[41] it has been possible to adapt the action for unfair competition so as to allow competitors and consumer groups equally to enforce these standards. The particular advantage of these civil proceedings is that they make available the potent weapon of injunctive relief.

In Britain, as we shall see, over much of the field, criminal law sanctions and administrative enforcement alone perform the same tasks. Civil obligation has expanded only fitfully. On the one hand, in its *"Advocaat"* decision,[42] the House of Lords offered some encouragement towards a broader conception of unfair competition.[43] At the same time, that very decision, with its emphasis on the need to show damage, underscored the limits of tort law. Cases soon followed which conveyed a lively concern for the dangers of "monopoly" inherent in extensions of exclusive trading rights.[44] The judges of the 1980s proved as sensitive on the issue as their predecessors a century before.

The first Parliamentary interventions in the creation of intellectual pro- **1–22** perty—the Statute of Monopolies 1624, the Copyright Act 1710 and their successors—left much for the courts to work out in terms of principle. Over

---

[39] Attitudes in Britain, France and Germany contrasted strongly with those in the U.S.: see Cornish in *Law and the Big Enterprises in the 19th and early 20th Centuries* (Horn and Kocka eds., 1979), p. 280.

[40] But in the U.S., there was a significant "liberal" reaction against uses of the misappropriation doctrine: see *Sears-Roebuck v. Stiffel*, 376 U.S. 225; *Compco v. Daybrite, ibid.,* 234 (1964). Argument centred upon the constitutional power of state legislatures and courts, but it carried more general overtones. In turn the full effect of this has been tempered: see especially *Goldstein v. California*, 412 U.S. 546 (1973); *Kewanee v. Bicron*, 416 U.S. 470 (1974). But the pendulous movement continues: *cf. Bonito Boats v. Thunder Craft Boats*, 103 L. (2d) 118 (1989).

[41] Germany is a significant example.

[42] *Erven Warnink v. Townend* [1980] R.P.C. 31; *cf. Moorgate* [1985] R.P.C. 219.

[43] See para. 16–03, below.

[44] Three of the most striking, since affected by legislative changes, were *"Holly Hobbie"* T.M. [1984] R.P.C. 329, HL (registration of a mark for merchandising not permitted); *Coca-Cola T.Ms.* [1986] 421, HL (bottle shape not a trade mark); *British Leyland v. Armstrong* [1986] R.P.C. 279, HL (copyright in car exhausts not assertable against spare parts).

the past century, as legislation has become broader in range and more complete in content, judicial influence has increasingly been felt through the interpretation of statute. In earlier decades of this century, the attitudes of the judges have much in common with their caution towards the creation of new common law rights. The preference for taking the meaning of a statute apparently expressed by Parliament, rather than searching for some "true" intent; the refusal to fill in gaps in legislation; the readiness to insist that it is for Parliament to remedy unsatisfactory results—these are all part of an approach which abjures obvious intervention in the political process.

It is an approach in no way peculiar to intellectual property, and its consequences in this field have, as we shall see, been varied. What should be appreciated is the effect of the general approach upon the style of statutory draftsmanship practised in the United Kingdom and countries which follow its lead. The tendency to proliferate detail and to make complicated cross-references has a long history. It is rooted in the assumption that the judges cannot, will not or should not, work out the implications of statutory directives for themselves. We shall have occasion enough to wrestle with provisions that neglect the statement of general principle in favour of dealing elaborately with relatively special circumstances.[45]

Today, however, there are influences at work—and nowhere more so than in the intellectual property field—that are inducing change.[46] To these we shall return under the next heading.

(2) Enhancement of intellectual property

(a) *Demands for greater protection*

1–23 The expansion of trade competition since 1950 has brought ever-increasing advantages to those in the van of innovation. Intellectual property rights, which help to sustain the lead of those with technical know-how, with successful marketing schemes, with new fetishes for pop culture, have come to foster immense commercial returns. The increasing numbers of patents granted and trade marks registered, particularly in industrial countries, and the upsurge of publishing, record-producing, film-making and broadcasting, stand as some measure of this development. But in some of these fields particularly, success has been accompanied by advances in copying techniques which make piracy possible on a scale that is just as new. The resources of existing legal techniques are under considerable strain. This is

---

[45] Lord Diplock found occasion to remark upon the "unhappy legacy of this judicial attitude" (*Fothergill v. Monarch Airlines* [1980] 2 All E.R. 696 at 705). See further, para. 6–05, n. 16, below.

[46] Their influence has given both the Copyright, Designs and Patents Act 1988 and the Trade Marks Act 1994 a novel clarity of organisation and expression.

one reason why today there is a profusion of different and sometimes conflicting demands, some for new and some for improved rights.

The growth of international organisations, particularly within the frame of the United Nations, has provided one forum for the discussion of such claims. In particular, the World Intellectual Property Organisation (WIPO) (situated in Geneva) administers and fosters the Paris Convention on Industrial Property, the Patent Cooperation Treaty, the Berne and Rome Conventions on copyright and neighbouring rights and the Madrid Agreements on trade mark registration, as well as various others, which are in existence or in the making.[47]

Now there is a new development. The General Agreement on Tariffs and Trade (GATT — not a UN organ), through the completion of its Uruguay Round in April 1994, has created a World Trade Organisation (WTO) (also situated in Geneva) which, among other things, will administer a highly significant instrument, the Agreement on Trade-related Aspects of Intellectual Property Rights, including Trade in Counterfeit Goods (TRIPS). All states which subscribe to the WTO become bound to a mutual recognition of intellectual property rights at a high level of protection, in various respects going beyond the range of international obligation achieved in the Conventions mentioned in the previous paragraph. The ramifications of TRIPS are considerable and we accordingly return to them later in this Chapter.[48]

Industries and professional experts have produced a plethora of interest **1–24** groups which seek to further their own political ambitions at the national and international level. At the same time, other pressures for change have been at work. The expansion of bureaucracies, such as national patent offices, has brought in its train plans for rationalising their activities. Partly this goes to standardising procedures such as classification for indexing purposes, but it also aims to reduce overlaps in the work that they do.[49] Thus it is a basic object of the Patent Co-operation Treaty that the acceptance, searching and even examination stages of applying for a patent should be conducted on an international basis before proceeding to the grant of national patents.[50]

In Western Europe it has been possible to link this desire to eliminate repetitive waste with the desire to strengthen the bonds of the Economic Community and associated free trade area (now together entitled the European Economic Area—EEA). One result has been the opening of the

---

[47] See paras 1–29—1–32, below. In addition, UNESCO administers the Universal Copyright Convention. For the role of UNCTAD, see para. 3–17, below.

[48] See para. 1–29, below.

[49] The urge to rationalise is all the greater when budgetary overseers notice that an office is being run as a service below cost. As recent experience of the British Patent Office shows only too clearly, the other weapon against this sort of extravagance is a steep increase in official fees.

[50] See paras 3–01, 3–19—3–22, below.

European Patent Office, another the Convention (signed, but still not implemented) for a unified Community patent.[51] In the field of trade marks, the drive by E.C. authorities to eliminate distortions in the Common Market has resulted in a Community-wide system of registration.[52] Harmonisation of copyright within the E.C., which is proceeding step-wise, has now been the subject of successive Directives of very considerable importance; more is to come, particularly to deal with digital communication.[53] A Community Plant Varieties Office has been instituted and a Community designs regime is in prospect, an attendant Directive on the harmonisation of national designs law being already in place.[54] There has already been Community legislation on semi-conductor chip design, supplementary protection for pharmaceutical and like inventions, misleading and comparative advertising, databases; and, after long and acrid debates, biotechnological patents.[55] The plan for a Directive on Utility Model protection has advanced somewhat during 1998.[56]

(b) *Sources of United Kingdom law*

1–25 The end product of much of this activity must be domestic legislation, particularly given the rule which requires the authority of a Parliamentary act to turn the international obligations of the United Kingdom into municipal law. This may be done either by re-enacting a convention in a paraphrase which a British draftsman deems suitable for legislation here, or it may be done by making the convention text itself part of United Kingdom law. It is the latter technique which is applied to the E.C. Treaty of 1957 and Community legislation under it in the form of regulations.[57] The British enabling statute is then no more than a conduit pipe for texts which will likely have been drafted with a Continental preference for the statement of general principle—relatively uncomplicated in language, but more or less indeterminate in scope. The former technique may be adopted at least partly in the belief that British courts must be provided with more specific guidance than the convention text affords.[58] If not, they may be led by their traditional approaches to interpretation into destructive readings that would do little for comity between the contracting states concerned.

---

[51] See paras 3–01, 3–23—3–29, below.
[52] See paras 15–16—15–18, below.
[53] See paras 9–17—9–19, below.
[54] See paras 4–26, 5–82ff., 13–50—13–52, 14–52—14–67, 17–107, below.
[55] See paras 14–48—14–50, 14–26, below.
[56] See paras 1–27, below. The Directive on artists' resale rights has, however, been blackballed: see paras 13–103—13–104, below.
[57] Under the European Communities Act 1972. For specific examples, see PA 1977, s. 86 (CPC); TMA 1994, ss. 51, 52 (CTM).
[58] In taking over principles of the PCT and EPC, the PA 1977 provides numerous examples of this approach. This seems particularly curious in an Act which (see previous note) also adopts an E.C. convention in virgin form.

The fear is not without foundation. The courts' preference for literal interpretation in the past gave rise to the rule of construction that, unless a British statute is ambiguous, its meaning must be accepted, however much this results in inconsistency with the convention from which it derives.[59] But the point at which ambiguity is considered to arise is itself a matter of judgment. Certainly once the meaning of a provision is deemed uncertain, the courts have shown a new willingness to resort to the convention text (or texts, if more than one language has been used).[60] In searching for the most acceptable meaning in such a case, the House of Lords has indorsed the adoption of a purposive approach to interpretation, rather than a literal one.[61] Equally, the House is willing to take account of the decisions of foreign courts on the convention's meaning, the writings of experts on the subject and even (with caution) the *travaux préparatoires* which led to the agreement of the final text, at least if they have been published[62] and were intended to resolve doubts about its meaning. Indeed, as part of the shift in perception, the House of Lords has ruled that, in certain limited circumstances, judges should take account of explanations offered in the course of British Parliamentary proceedings about the intended meaning of a particular provision, if to the court it appears ambiguous, obscure or absurd. This allows reference to be made to any clear statement by the Minister or other promoter of the Bill, if it discloses the mischief aimed at or the legislative intention.[63]

Purposive interpretation and the aids to it are evidently important in dealing with law that comes from the E.C. British courts heed the

---

[59] *Ellerman Lines v. Murray* [1931] A.C. 126, HL; *Soloman v. Commrs. of Customs and Excise* [1967] 2 Q.B. 116 at 143, *per* Lord Diplock; *Warwick Films v. Eisinger* [1969] 1 Ch. 508. *cf. Buchanan (James) v. Babco Forwarding* [1978] A.C. 141 at 153, *per* Lord Wilberforce. But note also the tendency to stress that, if there is room for manoeuvre, a court will strive to achieve consistency between statute and convention: *e.g. Post Office v. Estuary Radio* [1968] 2 Q.B. 740; *The Jade* [1976] 1 All E.R. 920 at 924, *per* Lord Diplock; *Smith Kline and French v. Harbottle* [1980] R.P.C. 363; *E's Applications* [1983] R.P.C. 231.

[60] The House of Lords has refused to accept that a foreign text may only be referred to if expert evidence about its meaning is led; there are no precise rules and a judge may rely on his own knowledge of the foreign language, dictionaries or expert opinion, when it is appropriate to do so: see Lord Wilberforce, *Buchanan* case [1978] A.C. 126 at 152, HL; Lord Fraser of Tullybelton, *Fothergill* case (n. 60, below) at 709–710.

[61] *Fothergill v. Monarch Airlines* [1980] 2 All E.R. 696.

[62] In enacting measures, the E.C. Council and Commission may record Minutes of Understanding. Though often in circulation they are not public documents. They cannot, therefore, be cited as guides to interpretation in an English court: *Wagamama v. City Centre Restaurants* [1995] F.S.R. 713. For moves permitting greater publicity in future, see *Carvel v. E.U. Council* (CFI, October 19, 1995) and new Council rules: Gielen [1996] E.I.P.R. 83 at 86. It is hard to see that such changes should affect Minutes prepared on the basis of confidentiality. See further para. 17–95, below.

[63] *Pepper v. Hart* [1993] A.C. 593. This draws counsel into careful monitoring of *Hansard*, a task which, in relation to modern intellectual property statutes, can be formidable. Hundreds of amendments stood in the paths through the legislature of the Patents Bill 1977, the Copyright, Designs and Patents Bill 1988 and the Trade Marks Bill 1994. Even before this development, the courts were prepared to consider the reports of official commissions and committees with the same end in view: *Fothergill* case (n. 60, above) at 705–706. For the implementation of E.C. directives, see para. 17–01, n. 3, below.

European Court of Justice's approach to the interpretation of legislative texts. This is characterised by Lord Diplock as teleological rather than historical, seeking "to give effect to what the Court conceives to be the spirit rather than the letter of the treaties; sometimes, indeed, it may seem to the exclusion of the letter".[64] This, as we shall see, is likely to be equally important whether the text has become United Kingdom law in its original form, or whether it has been adapted to the purpose by the British draftsman.[65]

(c) *Sources of European Community law: general*

1–26 Since Community law is now the most fecund source for change in British intellectual property law, the status of its legal acts—and in particular of regulations and directives—deserves to be outlined.[66] Neither the E.C. Treaty of 1957, nor the constitutional arrangements which have amended it and added to the European Union (the Single European Act (1985), the Maastricht Treaty (1992), the Amsterdam Treaty (1997)), have given a direct power to the Community institutions to enact laws relating to intellectual property rights. Moreover, as Article 222 insists, the Treaty "shall in no way prejudice the rules in Member States governing the system of property ownership."[67] Accordingly, they have to seek the necessary authority in more general law-making provisions now to be outlined.

Under Article 189 of the Treaty of Rome, the Council, together with the European Parliament,[68] has power to make regulations having general application and to issue directives to Member States.[69] Regulations by their very nature are directly applicable in all Member States, both in relations between individuals and the Member States and, where appropriate, in relations one with another. This consequence is secured in United Kingdom law by the terms of section 2 of the European Communities Act 1972.

A regulation under Article 235 of the Treaty of Rome has, for instance, been the means of establishing the E.C.'s own Community Trade Mark and

---

[64] *R. v. Henn and Darby* [1980] 2 All E.R. 166 at 196.

[65] Note, in particular, the appreciation of the need to bring uniform interpretation to the EPC and its national derivatives, demonstrated on the "second medical use" question: paras 5–74 *et seq.*, below.

[66] See generally, *e.g.* Wyatt and Dashwood, *European Community Law* (3rd ed., 1993), pp. 66–88. For procedures, and for the current status of interventions in intellectual property matters, see each month's issue of the E.I.P.R.

[67] For the very limited impact of Art. 222 upon E.C. plans for intellectual property, see below, para. 1–28.

[68] E.C. Treaty, Art. 189, as amended by the Treaty on European Union 1993 (Maastricht Treaty), Art. G(60). When acting under E.C. Treaty, Art. 235, the Council has only to consult the European Parliament, but when acting under Art. 100a, the co-decision procedure instituted under Art. 189b must be followed.

[69] Of the other law-making powers of Community institutions, we should note the Commission's power to issue decisions, particularly in implementation of the Rules of Competition, and equally the power of the Community Trade Mark Office in dealing with applications for rights.

the Office in Alicante which operates as its registry.[70] Article 235 is the residual provision which empowers the Council to take appropriate measures, over and above those provided for in the Treaty, which are "necessary to attain, in the course of the operation of the common market, one of the objectives of the Community".[71]

As the name implies, a directive binds the Member States which it **1–27** addresses but gives them a choice as to implementation and indeed sometimes as to extent. In our context, of particular significance is the power of the Council and the Parliament under Article 100a to issue directives "for the approximation of the provisions laid down by law, regulation or administrative action in Member States which have as their object the establishment and functioning of the internal market".[72]

Under this Article, directives have now required the partial harmonisation of both national copyright and national trade mark law.[73] Incorporation of their contents into national law necessarily varies because the relevant legislation differs from country to country. A directive requirement may already be part of national law by legislative statement or case law and so will not need restatement. Directives can also include non-mandatory provisions, which accordingly leave an express choice to the Member States.[74] This is an important procedure when otherwise it would not be clear whether a directive was, or was not, intended to preclude a Member State from (say) giving additional rights to those provided by E.C. law.[75] Whether a state has adequately implemented a directive can ultimately be tested by proceedings before the European Court of Justice, brought either by a Member State or the Commission.[76]

A directive, being addressed to Member States, does not have the same direct effect on the rights and obligations of individuals which may follow from a regulation, but, in certain circumstances, it may be relied upon against a state which has failed to implement it (but not against an individual[77]). This, for instance, can occur if a state fails to enact a provision

---

[70] See para. 15–16, below. Regulations have introduced the Community Plant Variety Right (paras A3–02 *et seq.*, below) and the Supplementary Protection Certificate for pharmaceutical and similar inventions (para. 4–26, below), and are likely also to establish the Community Design (paras 14–52 *et seq.*, below). The Community Patent is to be introduced through a convention which has already been separately negotiated (para. 3–26, below).

[71] The consequential effect of adopting a treaty obligation with external states under Article 228 is discussed in relation to TRIPS: para. 1–31, below.

[72] The Commission must propose, the Economic and Social Committee must be consulted; and (in the post-Maastricht world) the Council, if it is to act by qualified majority, must obtain the assent of the Parliament under Article 189b. Despite formal conciliation arrangements, this procedure led in 1994 to rejection of the politically sensitive Directive on Patent Rights in Biotechnology (see para. 5–72, below).

[73] Also the protection of semi-conductors chip layouts (see paras 14–48 *et seq.*, below) and databases (see para. 13–49, below).

[74] Whether there is then power under the European Communities Act 1972 to take up this permission in delegated legislation is doubtful.

[75] See, *e.g.* the scope of rights permitted in national trade mark laws: para. 15–17, below.

[76] Under the Treaty of Rome, Arts 169, 170.

[77] *Marshall v. Southampton Area Health Authority* [1986] E.C.R. 723.

relating to the invalidity of a trade mark under the relevant harmonisation directive.[78] If on the other hand, non-implementation means that one person has been deprived of a right against another, it would be for the state which was in default to make good the injury by compensation—a principle introduced by the Court of Justice in *Francovich v. Italy*[79]—out of despair at the inability of some Member States to implement directives timeously. This, however, is only so where (1) the directive itself is intended to grant a right to individuals, (2) it defines the content of the right, and (3) there is a causal link between breach of the state's obligation and the damage suffered.

Beyond this, a directive may also have an indirect effect, in that its terms are to be applied, where relevant, in resolving ambiguities in the interpretation of national law. In its controversial *Marleasing* decision,[80] the European Court of Justice held that this principle can even affect the law operative in a state before the directive is due for implementation. The better view[81] is that it does so only as a principle of preferable interpretation when the previous law is unsettled; and this ambiguity may arise either because statutory wording is unclear, or because case law is in conflict or is of uncertain scope. In other words it is not a rule which *requires* the old law to be overridden retrospectively.

(d) *The E.C. Treaty and Intellectual Property*

1–28 Regulations on Community intellectual property rights and Directives for the harmonisation of national rights have in practice to be made under the non-specific provisions of Article 235 or 100A. Proposals and legislative texts accordingly begin with a recital of the grounds for intervention which are considered to justify reliance upon the relevant provision. In respect of intellectual property, the assertions of Community need most frequently refer to the efficiencies of having a Community-wide right or to the need to eliminate differences of national law which may have a consequential effect on the free flow of goods within the internal market. These assertions result from the lobbying for legislative change from sectors of European industry and the consultations which the Commission, the European Parliament and other institutions make in the course of responding to such pressure. They

---

[78] *"Mister Long" T.M.* [1998] R.P.C. 401; and for the supremacy of a Community Directive over a contradictory national law: *Konsumentombudsmannen v. De Agnostini (Svenska) Förlag AB* [1998] 1 C.M.L.R. 32. See the limitations imposed in *Van Gend en Loos v. Nederlandse Belastingensadministratie* [1963] E.C.R. 1, and developed in subsequent case law: Wyatt and Dashwood (n. 65, above), pp. 58–63.

[79] [1991] I E.C.R. 5357; *Faccini Dori v. Recreb* [1995] 1 C.M.L.R. 665; Wyatt and Dashwood (n. 65, above), pp. 84–87.

[80] *Marleasing v. Comercial Internacional de Alimentacion* [1990] I E.C.R. 4135; *Wagner Miret v. Fondo de Garantia Salarial* [1993] I E.C.R. 6911; *Silhouette v. Hartlauer* [1998] I E.C.R. 729, 737, ECJ; and see *Webb v. EMO Cargo* [1995] 4 All E.R. 577, HL.

[81] See, *e.g.* Wyatt and Dashwood (n. 65, above) pp. 172–173.

remain no more than assertions. As a new proposal makes its way forward, questions have often enough been raised about the legal authority for it. This was particularly true during the course of the Community Trade Mark Regulation, since it set up a completely new Community organ—the eventual Office for Harmonisation of the Internal Market (Trade Marks and Designs) (OHIM), whose cumbrous title reflects the constitutional sensitivities.[82]

On one major occasion, the issue has been raised before the European Court of Justice. An E.C. Regulation, enacted under the harmonisation provision, Article 100A, has provided a mechanism for extending the term of pharmaceutical and agro-chemical patents, where government testing has delayed commercial introduction of the invention.[83] Previously the term of patents had been a matter for national law, as harmonised in Conventions beyond the scope of the E.C. Spain objected that the E.U. Council had no power to create such a Regulation, relying most fundamentally upon the guarantee of "systems of property ownership" in Member States which is given by the E.C. Treaty, Article 222.[84] Whatever the scope and purpose of this provision,[85] the Court refused to employ it in order to invalidate the Regulation. A general consequence appears predictable. Only in most unusual cases will the Court find that the enhancement of intellectual property on a Community-wide basis cannot be justified. On most essential issues of legal policy in the field, the Union is empowered to pursue its unifying and harmonising objectives as it may decide.

(e) *Legal issues across state boundaries; international conventions*

Intellectual property rights have been introduced by nation states in response to economic demands and ideas of moral value which have focused particularly on their own territories and nationals. The rights accordingly arise primarily under national law. Obligations between states in this field, whether regional or wholly international, operate to shape and condition national laws, but not for the most part to displace them. **1–29**

One strain within the moral arguments for intellectual property is universalist in character, stressing the peculiar value to mankind of invention and aesthetic creation. But attractive as such notions may be, they have to be set against the high levels of jealousy and suspicion which are all

---

[82] See below, para. 15–16.
[83] Below, para. 4–20
[84] *Spain v. E.U. Council* [1995] I E.C.R. 1985. The Spanish government also argued that, by requiring Member States to grant extensions, the Community was introducing a tool which might be used only in some states and so might increase the barriers to movement between member states. But some states had already introduced their own extensions of patent term, and there was a much greater risk of differential treatment if no uniform provision were made across the E.U., a counter-argument which the Court had no difficulty in upholding.
[85] One view is that Art. 222 exists to prevent the E.U. from compelling Member States to adjust their particular apportionment of public and private ownership.

too readily generated when industries of one country demand intellectual property protection for their trading and licensing activities in other countries. Such tensions run high in the relations between the great producer countries and developing countries. However, they can be equally acute between the largest economies, particularly where one country believes that over decades it has been the subject of sophisticated and highly successful imitation by another (which is a common attitude of Americans towards Japan). Moreover, as the most recent re-negotiation of the GATT has shown, intellectual property has become one important factor in the demand for greater mutual access to markets in international trade.

1–30   One way of expressing the close association of national policy and legal right lies in the principle of "territoriality". While this characteristic is often attributed to the major forms of intellectual property, there is less accord on its implications. The territorial nature of the rights *may* be treated as having at least four potential ramifications:

(1) The right in each country is determined by the law of that country and is independent of equivalent rights governing the same subject-matter (invention, work, trade mark, etc.) in other countries and neither stands nor falls with them.

(2) The right only affects activities undertaken by others within the geographical territory for which it is granted. This area is normally defined by the boundaries of the state concerned, with possible extensions for cross-border, sea, air and space activities connected to it.

(3) The right may be asserted only by nationals of the country for which it is granted and such others as the law also includes.

(4) The right may be asserted only in the courts of the country for which it is granted.

Civil rights of action in general (concerning tort, property, contract, etc) are not considered to have such wide-ranging associations with territoriality, though they are likely to have some, particularly in relation to the first two attributes just mentioned. Most rights of action are not restricted by reference to the plaintiff's nationality, domicile or residence. Moreover, as we shall note later, in most countries there is a principle of private international law allowing actions to be brought for torts committed abroad in accordance with certain jurisdictional and choice of law rules.[86]

A good measure of the peculiarly territorial character of intellectual property is this: it is conceivable that nations would agree to treat inventors and authors as having personal rights to patents or copyright which are

---

[86] See paras 2–71—2–87, below.

determined by their country of origin. In principle, then, they would be able to carry their rights thus defined to other countries and demand recognition and enforcement there. Thus, an author from country A which gives copyright for the author's life and 50 years would be able to demand that period of protection in country B, even though its local law is limited to a copyright of (say) 56 years. The same would be true of the range of material protected and the scope of the rights granted. In the early period of industrialisation, the political unacceptability of this approach was soon enough appreciated and instead the territorial character of intellectual property became widely accepted during the nineteenth century.

Thanks to the third aspect of territoriality, states have needed to **1–31** negotiate reciprocal recognition of rights for their citizens. By the late nineteenth century, they were devising multilateral conventions, which became early versions of those now administered by WIPO. In them each state undertakes to accord intellectual property rights to the nationals of the other participants:

— In the sphere of industrial property, which includes patents for inventions, industrial design rights, trade marks and names and unfair competition protection, there has since 1883 been a basic international agreement, the Paris Convention for the Protection of Industrial Property (PIP).[87] Beside it have developed a host of further initiatives, notably on international applications for patents and trade marks; on micro-organism deposits for patents; on design registration; appellations of origin; and semi-conductor chips. They have succeeded in varying degrees; the United Kingdom is not party to them all. Beyond them there are agreements at regional level (the United Kingdom having particular investment in those for the E.C. and Europe more generally) and bi-lateral accords, often as part of wider trade negotiations.

— In the sphere of copyright, authors' rights have since 1886 been the subject of the Berne Convention for the Protection of Literary and Artistic Works (Berne), and to a lesser extent to the Universal Copyright Convention of 1952 (UCC); while so-called "neighbouring" or "related" rights are partly covered by the Rome Convention for the Protection of Performers, Phonograms and Broadcasting Organisations of 1961 (Rome).[88] As with industrial property there is a phalanx of further international, regional and bi-lateral arrangements of various kinds and degrees of success.

---

[87] In 1998, the Paris Convention had 156 contracting states. See Bodenhausen, *Guide to the Paris Convention for Industrial Property* (1968); Ladas, *Patents, Trademarks and Related Rights* (1975).

[88] In 1998, the Berne Union comprised 131 states. See Ricketson, *The Berne Convention 1886–1986* (1987); Geller and Nimmer, *International Copyright Law and Practice* (1987 ff.); Nordemann Vinck, Hertin and Meyer, *International Copyright and Neighbouring Rights Law* (1990); Stewart, *International Copyright and Neighbouring Rights* (2nd ed., 1989).

— The inclusion within the Accord finalising the latest (Uruguay) Round of the General Agreement on Tariffs and Trade of an Agreement on Trade-Related Aspects of Intellectual Property Rights including Trade in Counterfeited Goods (TRIPS), adds significantly to all previous international arrangements by including provisions on all the major forms of right. The new World Trade Organisation (WTO) will administer TRIPS.[89]

To date, the states in the conventions administered by WIPO can require other state parties to comply with their obligations by reference of the dispute to the International Court of Justice. While there have been allegations enough of non-compliance, this has never led to such cumbrous proceedings. A prime advantage which has been secured in the TRIPS Agreement concerns enforcement. Breach by a state of its often detailed and onerous requirements may lead to the GATT dispute settlement procedure and, if necessary, to sanctions withdrawing GATT advantages.[90] These could include the suspension of concessions in the same sector or even cross-retaliatory measures such as the imposition of quotas or other exclusions on a country's export of goods or services.[91]

TRIPS thus has a potency of a novel order in the intellectual property world.[92] Only WTO states will be able to use its procedures, but governments may well be willing to help their major industries, or even individual firms, by acting against other states which can be held responsible for a TRIPS breach. On occasion this may provide an alternative mode of attack when actions to enforce individual rights have given no satisfaction. As a result, WIPO is seeking to add specific provisions on inter-state dispute settlement to its conventions, but it is by no means clear that this initiative will be accepted by countries which want the advantages of GATT counter-retaliation.

1–32   All these conventions seek to achieve reciprocity, while at the same time allowing for the fact that national laws may differ in scope. The main

---

[89] For the significance of TRIPs within the WTO system, see Blakeney *Trade Related Aspects of Intellectual Property Rights* (1996), Chap. 1; Drahos (1995) 13 Prometheus 6; Gervais, *The TRIPS Agreement* (1998); Ricketson (1995) 26 I.I.C. 872; Reichman (1996) 29 Vand. J. Trans. L. 345; Katzenberger and Kur in Beier and Schricker, p. 1; Abbott in Petersmann (ed.), *International Trade Law and the GATT/WTO Dispute Settlement System* (1997) Chap. 14; and in Abbott and Gerber, *Public Policy and Global Technological Integration* (1997), Chap. 4.

[90] See Lee and von Lewinski in Beier and Schricker, p. 278. For the constitution and work of the Panels under the GATT Dispute Settlement Understanding, see Heduc, *Enforcing International Trade Law* (1993); Pescatore, Davey and Lowenfeld, *Handbook of GATT Dispute Settlement* (1991ff.); Petersmann (1991) 31 C.M.L.R. 1157.

[91] There are evident difficulties in withdrawing intellectual property rights by way of sanction against other GATT breaches, since the rights are conferred on individuals: see Cottier (1992) 79 Aussenwirtschaft 97, 100–102.

[92] So exorbitant are its demands that only 35 states have been bound from the start by its requirements; others are permitted transitional delays of 5 or 10 years. For criticism of the whole Agreement, Hamilton (1926) 29 Vand J. Trans. L. 613.

technique for accommodating differences between laws is the principle of national treatment which operates as a ground rule of PIP, Berne and the UCC, and now in TRIPS[93]: each Member State is obliged to grant nationals of the other members the same rights as it accords to its own nationals.[94] National treatment is thus the corollary of the territoriality of intellectual property rights.

In addition, where reciprocity is considered vital, as occurs particularly with copyright, the conventions strive to set minimum standards which all members must meet. They may also introduce exceptions to national treatment, such as the "rule of the lesser term" in Berne.[95] Where reciprocity is not of the same order of significance, as with patents, some convention states may not even limit the right to apply for protection to persons of any particular nationality.[96]

(f) *International Treaties; Authority and Applicability*

The major interventions of the E.U. into the realm of intellectual property **1–33** have important legal consequences in the international framework. The negotiation of the TRIPS, as one element in the WTO regime, was conducted by the Community, in tandem with the governments of Member States and that raised a major question over which institutions were the proper signatories of the agreements reached. The European Commission argued that the Community alone should sign, since it was exercising its authority to foster a common commercial policy with non-E.U. states.[97] The E.U. Council, however, took the view that the Member States retained competence in respect of many matters and so were properly also signatories. With this the European Court of Justice agreed.[98] So far as concerns intellectual property and TRIPS, there are clearly major issues concerning the administration and enforcement of national rights which are still governed purely by national law. The Commission's exorbitant view was thus rightly rejected. The consequence is that national governments continue to retain a degree of independent standing in future GATT negotiations.[99]

---

[93] PIP, Arts 2, 3; Berne, Art. 5; UCC, Art 2; Rome, Arts 2, 4–6; TRIPS, Art. 2; Evans [1996] E.I.P.R. 149.

[94] The TRIPS Agreement (Art. 3) also requires most-favoured-nation treatment. This is the result of certain bi-lateral agreements with the U.S. which offer U.S. nationals better treatment than home nationals (notably the so-called "pipeline" provisions to secure future patent rights once a national office is established for present inventions). It may have unintended consequences: see para. 10–56, below.

[95] See para. 9–25, below.

[96] As, for instance, with the European Patent Convention: para. 4–06, below.

[97] Under the E.C. Treaty, Tit, VII, esp. Art. 113.

[98] *Advisory Opinion, No. 1/1994* [1994] I E.C.R. 5267. Only in respect of border controls at E.U. frontiers (TRIPS, Arts 51–60) was the Community solely competent; see Drexl in Beier and Schricker, p. 18.

[99] Giving each Member State and the Commission a seat at inter-governmental conferences, a consequence to which the U.S. administration has roundly objected.

Since the Community has at least a shared competence in negotiating international agreements over intellectual property, the status of those agreements in Community law, once they are ratified, becomes of considerable importance. The common law countries belong to a bloc of Member States which adopt a strict dualism towards international law obligations, which is treated as a necessary consequence of the doctrine of Parliamentary sovereignty.[1] Even where the purpose of a treaty is to confer individual rights upon citizens, this cannot occur until it is carried into national law by statutory authority. Other Member States, however, treat treaty obligations of this character, which are specific in content and do not need further elaboration in municipal law, as directly applicable by individuals in litigation. This approach has various consequences. It reduces pressure on such a country to enact the necessary implementing law; and where there is national legislation, but it is not in precisely the terms of the treaty, it renders the treaty text a second, possibly superior, legal source.

1-34   In the context of ensuring that the international obligations of the E.U. are absorbed into law across the Member States, the European Court of Justice has proved ready to adopt the latter approach as the appropriate doctrine for Community law.[2] In our field, that brings two second order questions. First, can the WTO in general, and the TRIPS, in particular, be regarded as directly applicable? The preceding GATT agreement was held by the Court of Justice not to have this effect.[3] In *ex parte Lenzing*,[4] Jacob J. has reached the same conclusion for the WTO, pointing to the basic terms in which the Agreements are couched and to the fact that outside partners, such as the U.S. have plainly declared that the WTO does not have direct effect in their law. That position is likely to attract wide support in most Member States, not just those with common law backgrounds; but the German government for one has taken the contrary view.

There is in any case a second question: in dealing with Article 177 questions from a national Court, will the Court of Justice interpret the WTO Agreements in order to establish what the international obligation of a Member State is? The Court has undertaken such a task on a matter of procedural detail in the TRIPS Agreement. In *Hermès v. FHT Marketing*,[5] it has held that, under Article 50(6), an order made under the Dutch abbreviated civil procedure, the *kort geding*, must be followed within a

---

[1] See *Allen & Hanburys v. Controller of Patents* [1997] F.S.R. 1 (HC Ire.): Irish legislation required implementation of TRIPS: provision of Irish Patents Act 1964 inconsistent with Art. 27(1) (limitations upon compulsory licences) no longer valid.

[2] *HZ Mainz v. Kupferberg* [1982] E.C.R. 3641; Wyatt and Dashwood, pp. 76–77.

[3] *International Fruit v. Produktschap voor Groenten en Fruit* [1974] E.C.R. 1219.

[4] [1997] R.P.C. 245; and see *Palmaz's European Patents* [1999] R.P.C. 47 at 58; to the contrary, Drexl (above, n. 98); McCormick [1997] E.I.P.R. 205.

[5] [1999] R.P.C. 107, ECJ; Wooldridge [1999] I.P.Q. 124. The case concerned infringement of the Benelux Trade Mark Law, and so arguably raised an issue for which the Benelux countries were the competent signatories of the TRIPS—not a matter which caused the ECJ any hesitation.

reasonable period[6] by proceedings to try the merits of the case or else the order must lapse. The decision leaves the Dutch government uncertain whether it must positively alter its procedural law for intellectual property cases, and the Court of Justice is being asked further questions.[7] Such issues are part of private litigation. Regrettably, each answer that the Court gives draws it towards saying that TRIPS is, in many of its provisions, directly applicable.

(3) Challenges to intellectual property: political

As on the one hand the demand for increased protection has arisen, so on **1–35** the other has the level of suspicion and criticism of intellectual property protection. Some of this has come from English judges specialising in intellectual property, speaking on public platforms rather than through judgments.[8] This adds significantly to a long-standing British readiness to ask whether extensions of protection are justifiable. More comes from two outside sources.

First, the developing countries, which are only beginning to exploit intellectual property of their own, often find themselves with an inheritance of "protectionist" laws from colonial days. These can all too easily appear a legal pretext for foreign industry, technical and cultural, to cream off scarce resources in royalty payments. Yet in the race for development, there is a real need to acquire technology from the advanced nations and there is often strong popular demand for products bearing the allure of Western prosperity. Patent, copyright and trade mark laws therefore tend to be kept because they give the security that will continue to attract foreign enterprise. But their operation may well be modified. There may be compulsory licence requirements, curbs on the manner in which royalties may be paid, or official examination of the terms on which foreign right-owners establish their own local operations or grant licences to local enterprises.

For two decades, the developing countries strove to secure the international acceptability of such derogations from unfettered rights of "property". They based their claim upon their need for freer access to technical and educational materials and for self-sufficiency and independent initiative for national business concerns. Of this movement, which had its first major impact during the revision of the Berne Copyright Convention in Stockholm in 1967 and continued particularly at the meetings of UNCTAD, and the abortive attempts to revise the Paris Industrial Property Convention, there will be more to note at later stages. It undoubtedly makes more remarkable the counter-offensive, led by the United States, but strongly

---

[6] This is specified in the Article to be the period set by the Court, or else 20 working or 31 calendar days.

[7] See references (October 30, 1998) in *Assco v. Wilhelm Layher* (Dutch SC).

[8] Jacob [1993] E.I.P.R. 312; [1997] I.P.Q. 1; Laddie [1996] E.I.P.R. 253.

supported by the European Community and Japan, for the Uruguay Round re-negotiations of the GATT, which have now seen the acceptance of TRIPS as an international guarantee of respect for intellectual property. The depth and breadth of that accord, which a decade before would have seemed the purest fantasy, has been possible because of an overwhelming change of attitude among developing countries. In part, unquestionably, this is the product of single-minded pressure from an America haunted by trade deficit, but in part also it derives from the alluring example of the rapidly industrialising states of the Pacific Rim and more generally from the extraordinary shifts in political organisation and allegiances across the world. For a host of reasons, old antagonisms have for the present given place to a faith in "property rights" as major keys to technological development and national prosperity. It is, however, a faith that is going to be continuously tested against results.

1–36   Secondly, there is the tendency, amongst the developed capitalist states, led by the United States, to limit the monopolistic tendencies of successful private enterprise by anti-trust laws (or competition laws as they are known in the E.C.). Intellectual property rights have often enough been one basis for powerful anti-competitive collaborations. Since their very purpose is to confer rights to exclude competitors, it is inevitable that they should have been combined into wider accretions of market power. But legislatures, competition authorities and courts have felt the need to impose restrictions upon at least the most evidently excessive arrangements of this kind: patent pools, copyright collecting societies, international or regional divisions of marketing territories achieved by the splitting of rights and the suppression of the initiative and independence of licensees.

As we shall see later,[9] the competition law sketched out in the Treaty of Rome for the E.C. has been read in tandem with the basic principle of the free movement of goods within the Common Market. The consequence has been that traditional ways of using intellectual property rights to divide up markets country by country has been severely curtailed; and licensing agreements, particularly when exclusive, have been subjected to detailed scrutiny which has aroused considerable controversy.[10]

(4) Challenges to intellectual property: technological

1–37   Intellectual property rights are constantly destabilised by technological advance. Patent law, evolving primarily around machines and chemical processes, has had to absorb the emergence of electrical engineering, computer construction, atomic energy, microbiological production techniques and now biotechnology. Copyright, initially a rather belated response to the printing press, had then to address the performance of

---

[9] See paras 1–48—1–58, below.
[10] See paras 7–30 *et seq.*, below.

plays and music, photography, sound recording, film, broadcasting and now the extraordinary prospects of digital recording and transmission.

As the pre-history of copyright makes plain, the demand for new forms of protection is dependent upon many factors, including the expansion and liberation of an economy to a point where new entrants to a market can no longer be excluded by local cartels in the form of guilds and corporations. When the London stationers found in the later seventeenth century that they could no longer control what was printed and sold in the capital, they were obliged to press their authors' case for a copyright in what they published and they procured the world's first copyright statute in 1710. Their earlier position was undermined by improvements in typesetting, which cheapened the costs of imitation, and improvements in transportation, which made it possible to ship copies in to the capital from around the kingdom.

In other words, it is not the initial technology so much as the technology of imitation which stimulates the strongest demands for intellectual property. The early computer industry was content with contract and secrecy as the legal weapons of its development; but the opening of mass markets made possible by micro-computer technology and its astonishing ability to copy programs, rapidly reversed such perceptions. The greater the differential between initial development costs and those of easy and accurate imitation, the more exigent the case for legal protection becomes.

Intellectual property rights are the result of idealistic and utilitarian **1–38** perceptions. In some traditions, aesthetic and cultural values are held to justify these rights (or some of them—particularly the rights of authors, performers and inventors) quite apart from any role which they may have as incentives to production and so to economic expansion and enhanced consumer choice. These non-economic values also express the wrongness of allowing one person to take over and reap rewards from the intellectual or the marketing efforts of another. "Reaping without sowing" declare those with a strong sense of the injustice. "But the sower's seed came from the crops of others before her", answer those who would preserve a sense of moral proportion in the matter. And so the law must establish regimes which offer market exclusivity to an extent that will rectify the most evident cases of undue appropriation of intangible value, while preventing them from giving protection against the effects of competition which is quite disproportionate.

Today's great advances—in computing, telecommunications, biotechnology and so on—require very considerable investment indeed in order to be made, but are often taken over by others quickly, efficiently and cheaply. This makes the case for some intellectual property protection very hard to resist. It explains why in the 1980s the copyright system was roughly manipulated so as to provide a degree of protection for computer programs, and why semi-conductor layouts acquired their own form of right. It explains why there is currently a strong drive to protect database compilations, multi-media works, new forms of electronic distribution and even DNA structures whether uncovered in a natural state or varied by genetic engineering. Now, as perhaps never before, policy-makers are having to react to demands for new or adapted protection before there is real time to contemplate desirable conditions and qualifications. As the sleigh careers forward, one can only look anxiously for the restraining hands on the reins.

4. PROPERTY AND MONOPOLY: ECONOMIC APPROACHES

1–39 No serious student of intellectual property law can today afford to ignore the economic arguments for and against the maintenance of these rights. Patents, copyright and trade marks each have a different form of economic impact, so a good deal must be reserved for later discussion.[11]

Underlying them all, however, are theoretical approaches to two matters: the justification for conferring private property rights and the nature of monopoly power in a market. Full analysis must be sought in a textbook on economics,[12] but a word of non-technical explanation may at least be suggestive.

(1) Property Rights

1–40 Intellectual property operates mainly as a form of legal exclusivity in free enterprise markets. While Eastern bloc countries remained in the grip of socialist planning, patents, copyright and trade marks had only vestigial meaning in their internal economies. For them the rights acted as an ancillary attraction to foreign trade. It was during the latter stages of the great battle of economic systems, that, in the West (and hence the world), these rights came regularly to be treated as "property" and labelled "intellectual property".

At that period, economists who strove to analyse the virtues of liberal capitalism as practised in the United States, Western Europe, Japan and other newly industrialising states, were turning afresh to theories of private property rights. They argued that only with firm legal recognition of individual ownership would the full value of society's resources come to be realised. Property, with a functioning regime of contract law as its necessary corollary, would maximise exploitation. A synergy of individual transactions would enable the economy to grow and diffuse its riches to an increasing range of its population. Classic theories enjoyed new favour: John Locke's justification of property entitlements as stemming from the labour of the

---

[11] See especially paras 3–36—3–54, 9–45—9–55, 15–24ff., below.
[12] Particular help may be derived from Lipsey, *An Introduction to Position Economics* (5th ed., 1979), Pt IV, especially Chap. 20; Samuelson, *Economics* (11th ed., 1980), Pt III, especially Chap. 25; Scherer and Ross, *Industrial Market Structure and Economic Performance* (3rd ed., 1990), especially Chaps 2, 14–17.

person in cultivating and producing; Adam Smith's prescription for economic health in the freedom of individuals to pursue their manifold, differing self-interests.[13]

Ideas of private property have evolved around tangible things—land and **1–41** movables. Their physical existence inevitably constrains the uses that can be made of them. If that use is to be shared—by joint or common entitlement, by successive interests in time (life interests, leases, hiring), by division up of uses (easements, profits)—each exploiter is constrained in his use by the need to preserve the interests of others. Property rights theorists argue for the efficiency of undivided, absolute ownership and have seen its vindication, first and foremost, in the collapsing Communist regimes of the 1980. Equally the claims for property rights have been set against much less complete systems of social co-determination. Thus they underpin the current retreat across the world from governmental ownership or control of staple elements in free enterprise economies, such as power supply, transport, communications, housing, health, social protection and even education.

A degree of theoretical adjustment is needed if intellectual property is to be fitted within the justifications for property rights in general. The information which these rights protect is not a restricted resource in the same sense as physical property. On the contrary, information which one person discovers, creates or publicises will not be lost to him because it comes to be used by others. In that sense, it is open to divided use without limit. When the law intervenes to insist, artificially, that only one person has the right to deploy categories of information in certain ways, it does so, not as a support for the physical reality of possession, but in order to create out of nothing an equivalent exclusivity. It can certainly be argued that this fencing off of intangible subject-matter fulfils an economic function equivalent to that of ownership of physical property, because otherwise the incentive to optimise the value of the information will be impaired or destroyed. Those who would be innovators will wait instead to be imitators and the dynamic processes which would have generated new ideas will disappear; in the end there will be little or nothing different to imitate.

Nonetheless, the analogy remains incomplete. If A appropriates B's **1–42** invention, both remain able to use it. A does not preclude B from competing in the same measure as when he has appropriated the axe which B previously used for tree-cutting. Information has an inherent capacity to be taken over by all who can get access to it and used by them all, for competitive and non-competitive purposes alike. Plainly, competition can enhance the welfare of consumers by reducing prices to them and providing greater choices; so much so that in general there is a presumption in its favour unless there is a sufficient case to the contrary.

---

[13] See Hughes (1988) 77 Georgetown L.J. 287; Hettinger (1989) 18 Phil. & P.A. 31; Paine (1991) 20 Phil & P.A. 247; Palmer (1989) 12 Hamline L.R. 261; and further, below, para. 9–33ff.

Intellectual property rights are therefore granted to the extent that competition involving the unauthorised use of the rightholder's work or invention or mark evidently prejudices that person's exploitation of it and therefore his willingness to engage in the mental and associated activities which brought it to light in the first place. Nonetheless the greatest differences among economists over intellectual property now lie between those who would stress the virtues of conferring protection in the form of property; and those who would calculate with scrupulous care the degree of protection needed to procure new production of material. The first group adopts a relaxed view of the growth of these property rights and is ready to extend them by analogy so as to capture as much intangible value of economic activity as is not overridden by sufficient countervailing arguments. The latter regards them with suspicion and would limit the categories of protectable material, keep a tight rein on their term, introduce qualifications to reflect other basic values, such as further experimentation and freedom of expression, and ensure that they cannot be used to exert market power over and above that intended by the strictly limited nature of the right.

This book is about the ways in which the United Kingdom and the European Union choose, through their law, to resolve this unending tension. Some of the arguments turn upon a degree of familiarity with economic analysis of monopoly and competition and to this we must turn.

(2) Monopolist behaviour

1–43 The typical circumstance in which monopoly power is acquired concerns a commodity which the consumer already needs or desires: a monopolist's power can be thought of in terms of his ability to restrict the supply of the commodity; this has a consequential effect on its price. Everyday experience of prices for (say) petrol, food or land suggests the effect of cutting down the quantity of such a commodity on the market. Some purchasers will be prepared to devote more of their resources to buying what there is of it. If, therefore, a supplier is in a position to reduce the quantity of something that the public wants, he will be able to effect an increase in its price: he then behaves as a monopolist. If, on the contrary, he has competitors enough it will not avail him to reduce his output, because they are likely to be able to expand their output to fill the shortfall that he would otherwise bring about. And of course to raise his prices unilaterally would be merely to invite his customers to take their business to a cheaper competitor. This is equally true whether the competitors offer precisely the same products or things more or less similar which the public will treat as substitutes.

The profit that any trader makes depends upon three principal factors: the number of things sold, their price and their cost per unit to produce. Assuming that unit costs do not vary significantly, there is a relationship between number and price which is crucial to an understanding of why a monopolist may benefit from selling fewer units at higher prices. Suppose that the first producer of a video cassette recorder is setting his price for a year in which he can expect no competition from other manufacturers. He knows that if he limits his production run to a given number, he should be able to increase his price to the level that this number of purchasers is willing to pay. (How far the level of demand will regress as price increases is something that he will have to guess from such market indicators as he can amass.) But he must appreciate that, if demand can be accurately forecast, there is an optimum number and correlated price to find. Suppose the calculation looks like this:

Number	Price per unit	Cost per unit	Profit (total revenue less total cost)
	£	£	£000's
1,000	700	400	300
2,000	600	400	400
3,000	550	400	450
4,000	500	400	400
5,000	475	400	375
6,000	450	400	300

A rational producer under these conditions will market 3,000 at £550.

(3) The presumption against monopoly

In any economy which is to a substantial extent unplanned by government, **1–44** there are good reasons for fearing the market power of the monopolist, or at least for making sure that there are countervailing justifications, general or specific. Four arguments may be mentioned:

(1) The basic theoretical objection taken by economists concerns those who were not prepared to buy at the monopoly price, though they would have paid the competitive price or something in between. These consumers are left by the monopolist's behaviour to buy something else less valuable to them and in this sense there is a "misallocation of resources": too little of society's resources by this criterion are being put into the production of the goods monopolised. This objection is in fact a complex argument turning upon a number of assumptions: in particular that competition, or conditions equivalent to it, prevails in the market for similar or connected goods. Such qualifications are enough to make some economists doubt the relevance of this theory to the problem of monopoly.

(2) Compare with this the common objection—socio-political rather than economic in nature—which looks rather at the position of those who do pay the monopolist's price. The latter thereby acquires his monopoly profit at their expense. A redistribution of wealth takes place which may be regarded as unjustifiable.

(3) The monopolist is able to determine factors about goods in addition to their price: the kinds of service supplied, continuity of supply, the number of different versions, the amount of research and development into future products or services. This may have deleterious effects, immediate or consequential, for the consumer.

(4) The monopolist loses the incentive to keep down costs that comes from competition. For only if his costs are constantly pared can a competitor hope to maintain or enhance his market share against those of his rivals.

Monopoly, or at least some measure of market power, nonetheless has its advocates. At one extreme lie cases where economies of scale are such that the most efficient production will be procured from a single source. Few people would argue against the advantages of this sort of "natural monopoly", but if it is to remain in private hands it may be desirable to make it in some way publicly accountable. We shall see that copyright collecting societies present a special instance of such a phenomenon.[14] More equivocal are cases where, for instance, it can be said that only with the security of monopoly profits will a firm make sufficient investment in research to secure the really advantageous break-throughs for the future.[15] This sort of consideration becomes particularly germane to the justification of the patent system.

Advanced industrial societies engage in a continuing debate about the advisability of taking steps to curb or restrain the dangers set by monopolists, oligopolists and cartels within the private economic sector. The current growth of "anti-trust" laws is an indication of an increasing concern over the scale of profit and economic power of private enterprise. The tendency in these laws to treat certain manifestations of market power as at least prima facie unjustifiable demonstrates the force that experience gives to the theoretical objections to monopoly; equally, the provision that is made to allow firms to justify their practices is some admission that there may well be a countervailing case to be made out.

(4) Intellectual property and monopoly

1–45 All intellectual property consists in the exclusive right to perform some defined activity, in the main productive or commercial. But this is not at all the same thing as the ability to exert monopoly power within a market.[16] A market for goods has to be conceived in terms of all the goods that

---

[14] See paras 12–51—12–62, below.
[15] See paras 3–32—3–37, below.
[16] See Kitch (1986) 8 Rsch. in L. & Econs. 31; Bouckaert (1991) 13 Harv. J.L. Pub.Pol. 775; Palmer, *ibid.*, 817; MacKaay, *ibid.*, 867; Meiners and Staaf, *ibid.*, 911; Lehmann (1989) 20 I.I.C. 3.

consumers will treat as substitutes for one another: will they switch from one to another if, for instance, the price of the first is raised? The extent to which purchasers want the product that is the subject of intellectual property and not some alternative is often difficult to determine. It may depend on the technical advance that has been made (particularly in the field covered by patents), or upon the dictates of fashion (as with many of the most popular copyright works), or upon the effect of repeated advertising (as with well-known trade marks).

The degree of market power that may be secured in these different areas by the deployment of intellectual property is a matter that we will take up topic by topic. Here it is appropriate merely to bring out two underlying considerations.

First, the fact that much intellectual property has very little capacity to **1–46** generate market power leads to considerable difficulty in arguments over the proper scope of rights. On the one hand there is the potential disadvantage of power over a market in the few really successful cases—a power which may sometimes be unjustifiably great even given the special public policies (such as the encouragement of invention) which may underlie the creation of the right in the first place. On the other hand, if the investment of resources to produce ideas or convey information is left unprotected, it will be prey to the attentions of a competitive imitator who will not be obliged to pay anything for what he takes. There will accordingly be little incentive to invest in the ideas or information and the consumer may be correspondingly the poorer. The only way out of this dilemma is, on the one hand, to make the best practicable estimate of the dangers that unjustified monopolies may produce; and, on the other hand, to assess the degree to which the claimant's investment will be open to dissipation if he is not accorded his right.

Secondly, to the extent that intellectual property is capable of generating **1–47** market power, it offers its owner (and his associates) the opportunity to reduce output and raise prices. What it does not bring about is the condition in which the monopolist behaves as though he were the only competitor on the market. Yet the more naive arguments in favour of one or other exclusive right often imply that this alone will be the effect of according the right sought. This intermediate condition can indeed be aimed at: through mechanisms such as direct price control, or through one or other of the forms of statutory or compulsory licensing. Accordingly it is no surprise to find that economists who doubt the justifiability of unconstrained intellectual property turn to the compulsory licence as a moderating technique.[17] In theory at least it provides machinery for obliging the right-owner to accept a return (the royalty officially set under the licence)

---

[17] Good instances are the Economic Council of Canada, *Report on Intellectual and Industrial Property* (1971), Chap. 5; Penrose, *The Economics of the International Patent System* (1951). And see Scherer, *The Economic Effects of Compulsory Patent Licensing* (1977).

at a rate below that which he would have accepted if left to exercise his market power unfettered (hence the need for compulsion). Whether in practice this mechanism can be made to work without creating a disproportionate run of administrative expense depends on the legal form in which it is clothed. We shall have occasion to study a number of different examples in the course of this book.[18]

5. DIVISION OF MARKETS AND THE EUROPEAN ECONOMIC AREA

(1) Dividing markets

1–48 The European Economic Area (EEA) to which this section and later discussion refers was constituted in 1994–95 to establish free trade obligations between the European Community and certain former European Free Trade Area States. Since Austria, Finland and Sweden joined the E.C. in 1995, the states in this free trade association are Iceland, Liechtenstein and Norway (Switzerland having refused to join). The principles of free movement and the rules of competition, described in the following paragraphs in their E.C. embodiments, now apply equally to EEA relations though in rather complex ways.[19]

The obvious purpose of intellectual property is to give protection against rival enterprises which would otherwise sell goods or provide services in direct competition. In international trade, however, these rights have acquired a separate significance. In many cases, by adopting the appropriate legal technique, goods produced by a single organisation or associated enterprises can be prevented from moving from one territory to another; a barrier of private rights can be set up against imports or exports which is as effective as an embargo or tariff imposed by a state.[20] The procedure is often more effective than limitations on movement imposed only by contract.

Accordingly a middleman (known in Community jargon as a "parallel importer") cannot buy A's goods in cheap State No. 1 and transport them to expensive State No. 2 for resale at a profit. But A's ability to discriminate in his pricing between different territories is only one reason for restraining parallel importing. In countries other than his home territory it may be economically desirable, or sometimes legally necessary, to manufacture and sell through the medium of a local licensee, or at least to sell imported goods through a local distributor. Difficulties with the local language, local contacts or local labour relations may be overcome by such arrangements. It may, however, be hard to find a local licensee or distributor unless he can

---

[18] See, *e.g.* paras 7–41—7–50, below.

[19] See Oliver, *Free Movement of Goods in the European Community* (3rd ed., 1996), Chap. 14.

[20] The customs authorities of a state may be used to arrest the importing of goods that infringe an intellectual property right: for the British position, see para. 2–23, below.

be assured of exclusive rights to market in his own territory; for he will have his own investment in promoting a foreign product to protect. An intermediate case is the transnational corporation which has reasons (often involving taxation and foreign exchange) for operating in different territories through national subsidiaries. Again, each may be given exclusive rights to restrain imports of products emanating from the others—in order to protect price differentials, or to monitor performance comparatively within the group.

(2) Exhaustion of rights

The manner in which intellectual property can be deployed to divide **1–49** markets varies with the kind of right held, the question is accordingly one to which we must return at later points.[21] But one general concept can usefully be introduced here. In every intellectual property law it is necessary to decide which steps in the chain of production and distribution of goods require the licence of the right-owner: manufacture; first sale by the manufacturer; subsequent sales and other dealings; export and import; use. In the past, legislators have often left the answer to the courts. In many cases, both in British and in foreign laws, the rights are "exhausted" after first sale by the right-owner or with his consent. But often this is confined to first sales within the territory covered by the right—it amounts to a principle of domestic, rather than international, exhaustion. Accordingly, national rights that are subject to such limitation can still be used to prevent the importation of goods sold abroad by the national right-owner or goods which come from an associated enterprise.

In Britain, the relation between rights and distribution of goods has not in the past been dealt with by any general concept of exhaustion. The approach has varied with the subject-matter. In the case of patent law (in contrast with other major patent systems), the British traditionally adopted the contrary position to "exhaustion": in principle, subsequent uses and sales continued to require the patentee's licence. This, as we shall see,[22] is an approach that is in process of being dismantled in all save exceptional cases. For this, basic policies of the E.C. are primarily responsible.

(3) The idea of a common market

A common market is the product of a political decision to promote trade **1–50** competition without the interposition of legal or fiscal barriers. It is a

---

[21] The discussion of exhaustion is taken up at paras 6–15—6–16, 7–34—7–35 (patents), paras 11–27—11–29, 12–28—12–32 (copyright) and para. 17–120, below (trade marks). As regards E.C. law in general, see Chap. 18, below.
[22] See paras 6–15—6–16, below.

41

normal consequence of political unification (the United Kingdom) or federation (the United States, Canada, Australia) and it may be established by independent states that are concerned with economic integration (as originally with the European Economic Community). How far legal measures are introduced to help in achieving a common market has varied with time and place. But as far as intellectual property rights are concerned, it has been usual to work towards a unified law for the whole territory.

In the E.C., the absence of political union has made any movement towards unified or harmonised laws of patents, copyright and trade marks a complex business.[23] Yet in the past, intellectual property rights have played a major role in preventing the movement of goods from one part of Common Market territory to another. In the eyes of Community authorities the need to put an end to this has correspondingly been urgent. Indeed this was initially seen as the prime reason for studying the unification of intellectual property laws. However, action has not waited upon the outcome of these investigations. The European Court of Justice and the E.C. Commission have interpreted provisions of the Treaty of Rome as limiting the scope of national intellectual property laws in certain circumstances where they give rise to a conflict with policies expressed in the Treaty. Basic provisions, such as the outlawing of discrimination on the ground of nationality, may accordingly apply.[24] Beyond these, two aspects of the Treaty have had persistent importance: the elimination of restrictions upon the free movement of goods between Member States, and the establishment of a system to prevent distortions of competition in interstate trade.[25] The provisions of the Treaty which give specific content to these objectives are Articles 30–36 (free movement of goods) and Articles 85–90 (competition). At this stage, these provisions can be introduced in general terms, while leaving their effect upon the different types of right to later chapters.

Both sets of provisions are directly enforceable and so may generate rights and obligations in individuals, as well as in Member States, which may be enforced or pleaded in defence in litigation before national courts.[26] Accordingly, it should be noted that decisions on the content of E.C. law may reach the ultimate court of reference, the European Court of Justice, by way of appeal from the Commission—for example in respect of a violation of the rules of competition; or by way of Article 177 reference in the course of national litigation—as where the enforcement of an intellec-

---

[23] See paras 1–26 *et seq.*, above.
[24] Art. 6 (formerly Art. 7). See esp. *Collins v. Imtrat* [1993] 3 C.M.L.R. 773: para. 18–01, below.
[25] Other policies of the Treaty—notably the freedom to provide services and the right of establishment—contain some potential for conflict with intellectual property. See para. 1–46, below.
[26] For the extent to which the provision afford direct rights of action to individuals, see para. 18–03, below.

tual property right is allegedly in conflict with the free movement of goods policy or the rules of competition.

(4) Free movement of goods

Article 30 of the Treaty prohibits quantitative restrictions on imports "as **1–51** between Member States", and all measures having equivalent effect. The European Court of Justice has held that national industrial property rights may amount to "measures having equivalent effect" when they are directed to preventing acts of importation.[27] Accordingly actions for the enforcement of such rights should not be allowed to succeed unless justified by Article 36. This permits prohibitions or restrictions on imports if they are justified on various grounds, including the protection of industrial and commercial property. But this exemption itself does not apply where the "prohibitions or restrictions . . . amount to a means of arbitrary discrimination [or] a disguised restriction of trade between Member States".[28]

As we shall see, there are a wide range of circumstances in which the Court of Justice has ruled that national intellectual property rights should not be used to restrain parallel importing so as to defeat the free movement of goods policy. Article 36 has not been allowed to stand in the way, any more than has Article 222 which provides that the Treaty is no way to prejudice the rules in Member States governing the system of property ownership. The Court has characterised some assertions of these rights as going to their very existence (and therefore properly made), while other assertions have been labelled mere exercises of the right (and therefore not within the exemption of Article 36).[29] The distinction has been made to turn upon a "definition" of the specific subject-matter of the particular right.[30] But, as with the basic dichotomy between existence and exercise, these definitions have the appearance of being formulated only in the wake of a policy decision to give preference to community policies over some assertions of national rights. All of this may seem an exercise in legal obscurantism, but the basic intent is not hard to grasp: intellectual property rights are properly exercised when used against goods that come from independent competitors in trade; but they are not to be used against the movement from one Member State to another of goods initially connected with the right-owner.

---

[27] But not when the right applies to some other action within the territory (*e.g.* hiring or selling), irrespective of whether the articles in question are of local manufacture or are imported from another Member State.

[28] See the final sentence of Art. 36. See further Wyatt and Dashwood, *The Substantive Law of the EEC* (3rd ed., 1993), Chap. 7.

[29] The distinction was first applied in connection with the competition policy (from the *Consten/Grundig* case onwards); but it was treated as equally relevant to free movement of goods (from the *Deutsche Grammophon* case (para. 18–04, n. 13, below) onwards).

[30] This refinement was first introduced, for trade marks, in the *Hag I* and *Winthrop* cases and for patents, in the *Sterling Drug* case: paras 18–04, 18–05, below.

1–52   Intellectual property is not the only form of legal embargo that can affect the free movement of goods. The Court of Justice has been equally strict in appraising other forms of legal barrier, some of which have related objectives. Thus regulations under the German Wine Act 1971, which allowed "Sekt" and "Weinbrand" to be used only on German sparkling wine and brandy, were held equivalent to a restriction on imports. In Germany at least, the words were not specific designations or indications of origin but simply general descriptions of types of goods, and as such not within any exemption provided by Article 36.[31] One permitted ground within that Article is the protection of life and health, but still the measure must be a matter of imperative necessity.[32] A Dutch Decree which had the effect of restricting importation of a drug to the enterprise which secured its clearance from the Dutch health authorities was deemed in this respect unduly restrictive.[33]

The conjoint policy concerning the free provision of services, outlined in the Treaty of Rome by Articles 59 to 66, may also have an impact upon intellectual property rights, as for instance in the broadcasting or cable-casting of copyright material. Article 59 has required the abolition of restrictions on the freedom to provide services within the Community "in respect of nationals of Member States who are established in a State . . . other than that of the person for whom the services are intended". The Articles do not explicitly refer to justifiable exceptions; there is no provision equivalent to Article 36. Nevertheless, the Court of Justice interprets these provisions as open to reasonable limitation.[34]

(5) Rules of competition

1–53   The Rules of Competition in the Treaty that apply to private undertakings hang upon two pegs. Article 85 deals with restrictive practices between enterprises, Article 86 with abuse by one or more firms of their monopolistic position. A particular commercial practice could well be prohibited under both heads. Without these rules there would be little point in lowering customs and other barriers to trade imposed by states. They are vital machinery in insisting that resources should be allocated by market forces—forces that will cause efficient firms and sectors to expand at the expense of others.

---

[31] *Re German Sparkling Wines and Brandies* [1975] 1 C.M.L.R. 340.

[32] See esp. *Rewe v. Bundesmonopolverwaltung für Branntwein* [1979] E.C.R. 649 ("Cassis de Dijon"); paras 18–13 *et seq.*, below.

[33] *Officier van Justitie v. De Peijper* [1976] 2 C.M.L.R. 271. For a similar decision that regulations were unduly restrictive of parallel imports, even though their object (protecting the genuineness of "Scotch" for whisky) was proper: *Procureur du Roi v. Dassonville* [1974] E.C.R. 837, [1974] 2 C.M.L.R. 436. *cf. E.C. Commission v. Belgium* [1979] E.C.R. 1761; *E.C. Commission v. Ireland* [1982] E.C.R. 4005 ("Buy Irish").

[34] *Coditel v. Ciné Vog (No. 1)* [1980] E.C.R. 881, paras 13–57ff., below.

Article 85(1) prohibits agreements between undertakings, decisions of associations of undertakings and concerted practices "which may affect trade between Member States and the object and effect of which is to prevent, restrict or distort competition within the Common Market".[35] An agreement which falls within this prohibition may nevertheless be exempted for a limited period where it can be economically justified: if it contributes towards improving the production or distribution of goods, or towards promoting technical or economic progress, whilst allowing consumers a fair share of the resulting benefit; provided also that it does not (1) impose on the undertakings concerned restrictions which are not indispensable to the achievement of these objectives, nor (2) afford them the possibility of eliminating competition in a substantial part of the products in question. The E.C. Commission, which is the body chiefly charged with the enforcement of the rules of competition, alone has power to grant such an exemption under Article 85(3).

In its formative decision on the impact of Article 85, the Court of Justice **1–54** had to consider whether the electrical manufacturers, Grundig, could divide the markets for its products among distributors which each had different Member States of the Community as their exclusive territory. As well as settling that such vertical restrictions fell within the scope of the Article, the Court also held it offensive to add a separate mark, "Gint", to the products and have that mark registered in each state in the name of the exclusive distributor there.[36] The special purpose of this technique was to furnish each distributor with its own intellectual property repellent against the parallel importing of genuine "Grundig" products from other countries. It could not be saved by exemption under Article 85(3).

Article 86 prohibits any abuse by one or more undertakings of a dominant position within the Common Market (or a substantial part of it) in so far as it may affect trade between Member States.[37] There is here no explicit power to exempt a practice for its countervailing benefits, but this is implicit in the requirement that the deployment of dominant position be abusive.

To re-emphasise: some basic points about the enforcement of the competition rules are contained in Appendix 1. Their impact upon the exploitation of the various forms of intellectual property is taken up in later Parts relating to the different rights, and again in general in Chapter 18.[38]

---

[35] A list of examples is then set out. Art. 85(2) declares such agreements and decisions to be "automatically void".

[36] *Consten and Grundig v. E.C. Commission* [1966] E.C.R. 299.

[37] Again a list of examples is attached.

[38] See paras 7–30—7–40, 18–14—18–16, below.

(6) Relation between the two policies

1–55 The policy of securing the free movement of goods between Member States is an objective distinct from that sought by the rules of competition. Accordingly there are two basic differences in the scope of the relevant provisions of the Rome Treaty which call for mention at once.

(a) *Trade between Member States*

1–56 The provisions on the free movement of goods relate specifically to the import and export of goods between one Member State and another. They do not apply where the goods are being moved between a non-Member and a Member State. In *EMI v. CBS*,[39] the Court of Justice held that trade mark rights in any Member State could be used to prevent the importation of goods from the United States without offending Article 30. But in the rules of competition, the requirement that there be an effect on trade between Member States need only be consequential. Thus, if the reason why imports of CBS's records from America could be kept out of any E.C. country by virtue of trade mark rights was that the various E.C. marks had been put into EMI's hands in pursuance of an agreement, the object and effect of that agreement would have to be examined. If it brought about a significant distortion of competition in the Common Market by keeping out goods that otherwise would be sold somewhere within it, Article 85(1) would be offended.[40] It seems that in applying this Article it is not necessary to ask for proof that the goods would, if sold in part of the market, have been purchased for resale in another part; this may instead be assumed.[41]

(b) *The economic counter-balance*

1–57 From another perspective, the free movement of goods policy, when it does apply, may be more categorical. The competition rules of Articles 85 and 86 allow the economic impact of an apparently impermissible practice to be viewed as a whole, since an analysis is required of the market or markets which it affects. If there are countervailing benefits, it may nevertheless be permitted—under Article 85(3) by way of exemption, under Article 86 by finding the deployment of dominant position not, after all, to be abusive. By contrast, the manner of reading Article 36 that was initially developed did not take account of economic justifications for using industrial property rights in ways that may result in division of markets within the totality of

---

[39] [1976] E.C.R. 811, [1976] 2 C.M.L.R. 235, see Judgment, paras 8–12; See also *Re Tylosin* [1977] 1 C.M.L.R. 460 (West German, SC); Hay and Oldekop (1977) 25 Am.J.Comp.L. 120.
[40] Judgment, paras 25–39.
[41] *cf.* Judgment, paras 28–29 with the observations of Warner, A.-G. [1976] 2 C.M.L.R. 235 at 258–259.

the E.C. More recent decisions, however, bring a greater measure of differentiation to this task. National laws of intellectual property and unfair competition are examined to see whether their application affects imports from another Member State disadvantageously in comparison with domestic products, thus showing the "arbitrary discrimination" referred to in Article 36,[42] and to determine whether the exploitation is a normal means of realising their economic potential.

(7) Overview of the parallel importation problem

The extent to which territorially limited intellectual property rights should **1–58** be an instrument to prevent the international movement of "legitimate" goods is an issue of great political moment, yet one which is wracked with conflicting policy demands. We are concerned at various points in the coming chapters with questions of present and of future law, as well as of underlying rationale. We shall return to the position from an E.C. perspective in the final chapter. In the meantime, the following pointers should be absorbed.

First, "parallel importation" normally refers to the activity of an independent entrepreneur who acquires "legitimate" goods in one country (normally the cheaper) and transports them for sale in another (normally the dearer). It is a distinct phenomenon from exclusive rights to manufacture or distribute in a particular territory. The latter is a consequence of business strategies in which the developer of products finds his best hope of market penetration in an exclusive collaborator: save at egregious extremities, there is economic advantage in leaving the developer of a product or service to choose the channels of exploitation. With parallel importation, however, the initial marketing choices have already been made and price differentials (for a host of reasons) have emerged which apparently disadvantage one group of consumers. That is why legal rules which prevent parallel importation require special justification.

Secondly, within the EEA, the policy of a unified market demands the free movement of goods and the elimination of price differentials which is part of that unification process. Accordingly intellectual property rights (and rights against unfair competition, etc.) have become subject in Community law to a wide-ranging doctrine of exhaustion. It takes effect not only upon release of relevant goods in one Member State by the right-owner itself, but equally where there is any legal or economic connection between the first marketer and the right-holder. Contracts which attempt to restrict any consequent parallel importation will be void and may lead to penalties under the Rules of Competition.

---

[42] See paras 17–35ff., below.

1–59   Thirdly, at the outer perimeter of the EEA, where parallel imports are being brought in from third countries, there may be no exhaustion of right. The legal position needs careful examination, since it may depend on any of the following:

(1)   Unless the E.C. has adopted an effective rule of Community law on the matter, the applicable rule is determined by the law of the country of import. In the view of the E.C. Commission, regulations and directives on particular rights, which prescribe an internal exhaustion throughout the Community necessarily imply a rule of "non-exhaustion" at the EEA's external boundaries. However, that opinion is both controversial and, even if correct, of uncertain scope.

(2)   How far it is correct may depend upon the basic scope of the right itself. In particular, external non-exhaustion may apply to intellectual property which exists as an incentive to the creation and commercialisation of new ideas (patents, copyright, etc.). However, it may have no relevance to a trade mark or similar right. Arguably a mark which is used on genuine goods cannot be infringed, since there is then no misstatement about their origin. (What should count as "genuine goods" in this context is then a matter of dispute, and will be complicated by differences in quality between the goods put out in different countries). If there is a rule of external exhaustion for trade marks, the policy is of general impact, since a much wider range of consumer products bear marks than embody protected inventions, works or similar subject matter.

(3)   A rule of non-exhaustion must be subject to the contrary intention of the right-holder in the country of importation. If that right-holder has marketed elsewhere (or consented to that marketing) on terms, express or implied, that the goods may then be moved to other countries, this ought to be determinative. In practice, the issue becomes whether a sale without express restriction on subsequent movement should be understood as carrying authorisation to move. The question ought to be treated as of secondary importance, since, if an impeding notice is required, trans-national corporations will make sure it is given. Accordingly, it is a way of introducing protection against parallel importation under partial disguise; and because the parallel importation issue is politically so controversial, it is very tempting to accept this blurring compromise as a technique of resolution.

(4)   Despite the current upsurge in favour of international free trade, countries are deeply uncertain about the issue of parallel importation in relation to intellectual property. None wishes itself to introduce international exhaustion unless it can secure a reciprocal move from countries with which it trades. None relishes explaining to its own consumers why internationally available goods are less expensive in other countries; nor that this differential is maintained

because intellectual property rights cut out the levelling effects of bringing in the cheaper goods.

Yet, on the other hand, industrialised countries may wish to encourage their industries to set up production in de-socialising or developing countries, and will be able to do so only if there is some guarantee against consequent parallel importation from markets that will (at least initially) be cheaper. To do this by the "private" route of intellectual property barriers, rather than a public policy of quotas, has an obvious attraction (hence the E.C. Commission's bullishness on the issue). In the end, TRIPS explicitly refrained from addressing "the issue of exhaustion of intellectual property rights"[43]; but it will remain on the agenda at the WTO, WIPO and similar fora.

---

[43] Art. 6—unless the issue can be dressed up as concerning national treatment or most-favoured-nation treatment (Arts 3, 4). "Exhaustion" is not defined and could have various meanings; see Heath (1997) 29 I.I.C. 623; Verma (1998) 29 I.I.C. 534.

CHAPTER 2

THE ENFORCEMENT OF RIGHTS

This chapter deals with the forms of relief available to the owner of **2–01** intellectual property rights and with a variety of procedural factors affecting their enforcement. Although there are variations between the different specific fields, there is enough common ground to justify treating these matters in one place: a good deal of repetition can be dodged and various comparisons pointed up.

There is a more basic reason for prefacing the discussion of the different rights with some consideration of how they are turned to practical account. Most commercial law is facilitative in character. It determines the effect of consensual dealings between individuals and limits their freedom of contract only where some exception of public policy is overriding. Accordingly, for much of the time, commercial law provides a safety-net for the execution of contracts. When the net is needed, it is frequently the contract which provides one party with a self-help remedy. Intellectual property rights are, of course, the basis of many contractual dealings. But their fundamental characteristic is their power to constrain those who have no relationship with the right-owner. They are rights that depend for their effectiveness, to a peculiar degree, upon the speed and cheapness with which they can be enforced. This explains why, so often in the modern law, it is cases in this field that test the procedures and remedies provided by the courts. In Britain, these are matters typically within the province of the judges, who receive only a modicum of direction from Parliament. Many of the issues raised in particular cases have large implications.

The remarkable advances in information storage and copying technology **2–02** mentioned in the last chapter have made piracy and counterfeiting a major and highly unscrupulous trade in many parts of the world, as well as inducing unauthorised reproduction on a very considerable scale in enter-prises, organisations and the home.[1] The challenges to intellectual property rights at so many levels has prompted the courts to expand their repertoire of civil procedures, while Parliament has been active in increasing the range and severity of criminal law in this field.

---

[1] See, *e.g.* the European Commission's Green Paper, Combating Counterfeiting and Piracy in the Single Market, November 1998.

To give one plaintiff a more effective method of proceeding is to give it to all who can claim to be in comparable case. Amongst them must be reckoned those whose claims are dubious or downright false—a particularly telling consideration where the rights are intangible and may depend on complex value judgments. Accordingly there are delicate balances to be struck in most of the issues that call for examination.

In some countries, the degree of piracy has been threatening to deprive intellectual property of any meaning at all. The music, film, computer, pharmaceutical and luxury goods trades have had to set up joint organisations dedicated to combatting infringement on a commercial scale. They have had rough treks uphill—wrestling with conspiracies of silence, official uninterest, courts unable or unwilling to understand or assist, fly-by-night copy-dens, stark thuggery—in their battles for their own rights and protection of their licensees and distributors. Much of the effort which currently goes into inter-governmental negotiation on the recognition of intellectual property is concerned with this unrefined, but severely threatening, aspect of the whole complex.

2–03 The TRIPS Agreement, indeed, settles a new consensus on the measures which must exist in the legal systems of WTO countries in order to give effective meaning to substantive rights.[2] In a book on United Kingdom law it is not necessary to detail the long set of TRIPS Articles on the subject, because they read as an international ratification of so much of what this country, particularly over the last 20 years, has striven so determinedly to put into place. Overall, TRIPS calls for enforcement procedures which permit effective action against intellectual property infringement, "including expeditious remedies to prevent infringements and remedies which constitute a deterrent to further infringement"; at the same time the measures must avoid being barriers to legitimate trade and provide safeguards against abuse.[3]

Under TRIPS, civil process must be provided which may lead to injunctive as well as compensatory relief and delivery up for destruction of infringing material and means for producing it.[4] It is permissible to require information about the source and distribution of infringing goods or services.[5] It is mandatory to have provisional procedures for preventing infringement of intellectual property rights and preserving relevant evidence.[6] Against the importation of counterfeit trade mark goods and

---

[2] See Dreier in Beier and Schricker, p. 248.

[3] TRIPS Agreement, Art. 41, which, with Arts 42, 43 and 48, specifies a number of due process requirements: fairness and equity; no undue cost, complexity, time-limits or delays; right to be heard and to give evidence; right to a prompt, reasoned, written decision; judicial review; written notice of claims; legal representation; protection of confidential information; discovery of evidence held by the other side; indemnification against undue enforcement.

[4] *ibid.*, Arts 44–46.

[5] *ibid.*, Art. 47.

[6] *ibid.*, Art. 50, providing at the same time a set of specific safeguards against abuse: after *ex parte* proceedings a prompt right for the defendant to be heard, speedy procedures for determination of the allegations, compensation for unjustified relief.

pirated copyright goods, there must be arrangements for customs seizure.[7] The activities must be treated as serious criminal offences, with accompanying measures for seizure, forfeiture and destruction.[8]

1. TYPES OF PROCEEDING

This section takes up some basic characteristics of the different methods of **2–04** protecting intellectual property. It treats in turn civil actions, criminal proceedings, administrative procedures and measures of self-help. Of these, civil actions are the most central and many additional aspects of them are dealt with elsewhere in this book. The other three categories have resonances only occasionally at later points.

(1) Civil causes of action

For the most part, the acts of infringement with which we are concerned **2–05** are treated as tortious invasions of property.[9] Questions accordingly arise about which people have title to sue, whom they may proceed against and which courts they may use. These are dealt with first. Then some consideration is given to the more general economic torts, particularly where they may help plaintiffs who otherwise have no sufficient basis for action.

(a) *Owners and licensees of intellectual property*

The obvious person to bring proceedings for infringement of one of the **2–06** statutory types of intellectual property is the owner at law (or one of them). A person with a purely equitable title (under a trust or a specifically enforceable contract) is permitted to bring a motion for interlocutory relief, but he may not proceed further without joining the legal owner.[10] A person lacking title when he institutes an action cannot cure the defect by subsequently taking an assignment.[11]

Where the right is the subject of a grant by the state, the fact that the proprietor is not registered as such may introduce complications. In the case of patents and marks, the true owner is entitled to sue but risks failing to secure damages or an account of profits through not registering.[12] In the case of registered designs, registration of an assignment of title is a prerequisite.[13]

---

[7] *ibid.*, Arts 51–60 (and see also PIP, Art. 9; Berne Convention, Art. 16).

[8] TRIPS Agreement, Art. 61. Other infringements may be the subject of criminal procedure, "in particular where they are committed wilfully and on a commercial scale".

[9] Breach of confidence, however, requires special consideration: see Chap. 8, below.

[10] *PRS v. London Theatre of Varieties* [1924] A.C. 1; *Baxter International v. NPLB* [1998] R.P.C. 250; but note the modern rules on the assignment of future copyright: para. 12–12, below.

[11] *Israel Makor v. ABC News* [1994] E.I.P.R. D-30.

[12] PA 1977, s. 68 (see para. 7–17, below); TMA 1994, s. 25(4).

[13] RDA 1949, s. 7(1).

In the case of patents, registered marks, copyright and unregistered design right, an exclusive licensee is entitled to bring the proceedings, joining the proprietor as a defendant if he will not be joined as plaintiff.[14] In other cases, licensees cannot themselves sue for infringement of intellectual property,[15] but must rely upon their licensors to take action. This can be difficult and cumbersome, particularly for an organisation which exists to provide right-owners with collective protection.

A representative action may be pursued, for instance, against a defendant who has allegedly been selling pirated tapes of copyright sound recordings. The association of British record producers, British Phonographic Industries Ltd, could proceed in the name of one member, suing on behalf of itself and all other members. In the circumstances, the Court would order not only an injunction but an inquiry as to damages suffered by all the members.[16]

(b) *Defendants*

2–07 The law relating to each form of intellectual property defines the nature of the exclusive right in terms of content and business activity. For instance, the invention that is the subject of a patent is defined principally in the claims of the patent specification; it is then an infringement to make, sell or use this invention in the various ways prescribed in the Patents Act 1977.[17] A person who performs such an infringing act is liable in respect of it and anyone else who collaborates in a common design to do the act will be liable as a joint tortfeasor.[18] This is today a principle of growing importance in securing process and relief against all the parties involved, including those who themselves may be doing nothing within the jurisdiction.[19] A person, who, in supplying an infringing article or some essential component of it, acts solely outside the jurisdiction, will not thereby be infringing a

---

[14] PA 1977, s. 67; TMA 1994, s. 31; CDPA 1988, ss. 101, 102, 234, 235 (but, oddly, not registered designs). The licence must exclude even the licensor and must exist when the writ is issued: *Procter & Gamble v. Peaudouce* [1989] 1 F.S.R. 180, CA In the case of copyright and design right, it must comply with the formalities prescribed in CDPA 1988, ss. 92, 225. Beyond this it is a matter of interpreting each licence to decide whether, and if so in what respect, it is exclusive: *Morton-Norwich v. Intercen (No. 2)* [1981] F.S.R. 337; *Biotrading & Financing v. Biohit* [1998] F.S.R. 109 CA. In each case there are provisions concerning the assessment of damages; in the case of copyright and design right these are elaborate.

[15] They may, however, be able to sustain an action for the tort of unlawful interference with trade: *PCUK v. Diamond Shamrock* [1981] F.S.R. 427. For an exception, see TMA 1994, s. 30.

[16] *EMI Records v. Riley* [1981] F.S.R. 503. Equally an action may be pursued against a represented class in which an *ex parte* interlocutory injunction and associated relief may be ordered: *EMI Records v. Kaidhail* [1985] F.S.R. 36.

[17] See paras 4–37 *et seq.*, above.

[18] A director of a company will be personally liable for torts committed on the company's behalf where he has ordered or procured their commission: see *Clerk and Lindsell on Torts* (17th ed., 1995) para. 4–49.

[19] See para. 1–30, above.

British intellectual property right. However, if he is collaborating with a person in the United Kingdom, he becomes jointly liable for the latter's infringement.[20] Because of their common design, he will not merely be facilitating but will be procuring the doing of the act.[21]

In order to begin English proceedings against a defendant, the Court **2–08** must have jurisdiction and this is determined by complex and changing rules.[22] Provided the requirements for jurisdiction are satisfied, a defendant must respond with a defence which, by the measure of fair and reasonable probability, can be seen to be real and bona fide.[23] Failing that, the defendant faces the prospect of an order for summary judgment, which will normally include orders of the same kind as are made after full trial of an issue: injunction, inquiry as to damages, etc.[24]

In addition an employer is vicariously liable for torts committed by an **2–09** employee in the course of his employment,[25] but a person who commissions work from an independent contractor is not normally placed under the same responsibility.[26] The distinction is often important where the production of some species of intellectual property is concerned. Many authors, composers and artists, and some inventors, work in some degree of independence from those who take up their ideas for exploitation. In the field of copyright, as we shall see, the absence of vicarious liability in such cases is compensated for by other means: to "authorise" an act of infringement is there treated as itself amounting to infringement.[27]

It is not always easy to determine whether a person is employed, nor whether he is acting within the course of his employment. Employment may be a part-time, as well as a full-time, relationship. Traditionally the governing characteristic has been that the employer is entitled to control the work that is done in detail. But many types of work relationship are now treated as employment, even though the employee exercises managerial or professional skills under no regular supervision. In those cases other indicators are relied upon. Typical attributes of employment today

---

[20] *Unilever v. Gillette* [1989] R.P.C. 583 at 608, *per* Mustill L.J.; *Mölnlycke v. Procter & Gamble* [1992] R.P.C. 21 at 29, *per* Dillon L.J. *Cf.* the case of successive infringment down a distribution chain, where nonetheless there was no common design: *Def Lepp v. Stuart-Brown* [1986] R.P.C. 273. See further para. 2–75, below. A parent company must engage in furthering a common design to be jointly liable for infringements committed by a subsidiary: *Mead Corp. v. Riverwood Multiple Packaging* [1997] F.S.R. 484.

[21] *Belegging Lavender v. Witten* [1979] F.R.S. 59 at 66, *per* Buckley L.J.

[22] See below, para. 2–72ff.

[23] RSC O. 14. See *Microsoft v. Electro-Wide* [1998] F.S.R. 580: filed evidence will not be taken at face value if it passes belief.

[24] *ibid.* In the case of a default judgment, see *PPL v. Maitrou* [1998] F.S.R. 749.

[25] Vicarious liability of the employer in no way exempts the employee from his personal liability. There may be consequential questions of ultimate liability between employer and employee, for which see *Clerk and Lindsell on Torts* (17th ed., 1995), paras 4–66, 4–67.

[26] For the exceptional cases (not of significance to intellectual property), see *Clerk and Lindsell*, Chap. 5, Pt 4.

[27] See paras 11–18—11–20, below; *cf.*"indirect" infringement of a patent, paras 6–17—6–19, below; and the general tort of incitement or procurement, para. 2–14, below.

are: payment of regular sums as a wage or salary, rather than lump sums for given jobs; income tax deductions under Schedule E on the P.A.Y.E. basis; joint contribution to a pension scheme; and joint national insurance contributions as for an employed person.[28] Much is accordingly determined by the relationship that the two sides set out to establish. Tribunals have to settle the issue where the practical arrangements still leave ambiguities. A composer who is obliged to supply a music publisher with one song a month will be an independent contractor if his return is to come solely from royalties and none of the other attributes of employment are present. But the contrary will likely be the case if he receives a monthly salary subject to P.A.Y.E. and national insurance deductions, even though he is entitled to copyright royalties in addition.

What an employee does in the course of his employment is determined by what he is employed to do. The employer may not restrict the scope of vicarious responsibility by instructing the employee not to commit torts in the course of those duties.[29] If a broadcasting organisation employs a commentator who makes a slanderous statement, the organisation remains liable however firm its rule against defamation. However, as we shall see, not everything that a journalist or business executive writes is done in his employment, nor is everything that a doctor does to improve treatment of patients.[30] There must be sufficient connection between his job and what he has written.

(c) High Court and County Court

2-10 In England and Wales civil proceedings for the enforcement of intellectual property have traditionally been brought in the Chancery Division of the High Court, patent matters being required to go before the Patents Court within that Division.[31] It is from this superior jurisdiction that plaintiffs have been able to secure the range of interlocutory and final relief which makes civil process their usual resort.

2-11 At the same time the County Court jurisdiction in tort, traditionally limited in amount, has been used for a few intellectual property matters.[32] This has changed in two ways, one general and the other specific:

> (1) County Court jurisdiction levels have much increased,[33] making them the normal place of resort for actions valued at up to £25,000,

---

[28] On the question generally, see *Clerk and Lindsell* (n. 21, above), Chap. 5, Pt. 2; *Sweet & Maxwell's Encyclopedia of Employment Law*, I B, Chaps 1, 2.

[29] *Clerk and Lindsell*, Chap. 5, Pt. 3.

[30] See paras 7–04, 12–05, 12–06, below. The same question arises in deciding whether intellectual property belongs to an employee or his employer.

[31] For patent infringement, revocation and related claims, see para. 6–23, below. The position in the jurisdictions of Scotland and Northern Ireland should be sought in specialist works on the various rights. For the effect of impending reforms, see Lubbock [1997] E.I.P.R. 385.

[32] *e.g.* for obliging pubs and restaurants to pay for performing copyright music.

[33] High Court and County Courts Jurisdiction Order 1991, S.I. 1991 No. 724.

and of equal standing up to £50,000.[34] County Courts in general have power to grant interlocutory and other injunctions, though not *Mareva* injunctions or *Anton Piller* orders.[35]

(2) Having regard to the notoriously high cost of full-fledged litigation over patents and similar rights,[36] a Patents County Court with a specialist judge has been established in London, with jurisdiction to try patent and design issues, and ancillary questions.[37] It does have power to grant *Mareva* injunctions and *Anton Piller* orders. There are (as yet) no limits on monetary awards or special restrictions on costs related to such awards.[38] Not without difficulty, the new Court has sought to restrict recoverable costs and to advance the preparation of actions. Its small flow of business enables it to act promptly.[39] Its existence has undoubtedly acted as a spur to the High Court, which has done much, in advance of the general "Woolf Reforms" of April 1999, to control the course of patent and other intellectual property proceedings in the interests of efficiency.[40]

(d) *General torts covering economic loss*

The common law developed a number of heads of liability which are **2–12** usually grouped together as economic torts. Two of these—passing off and injurious falsehood—are directly germane to our subject and are dealt with in Part V.[41] Here, however, mention must be made of torts which may effectively broaden the range of people who can be held responsible when someone interferes with intellectual property or proposes to do so. In particular, the torts have some capacity to go beyond the rules on plaintiffs and defendants which have just been discussed. Their general characteristics are that the defendant must be acting intentionally or recklessly; that the plaintiff must suffer (or be about to suffer) damage; and that they will not apply if some ground of justification is open to the defendant.[42]

---

[34] In special circumstances, the amount may be even more. There are certain cases, such as seizure orders on material infringing copyright, designs and trade marks, where there is no jurisdictional limit in any County Court.

[35] County Courts Remedies Regulations 1991, S.I. 1991 No. 1222, allowing limited transfer to the High Court for such orders.

[36] See Intellectual Property Rights and Innovation (Cmnd. 9117, 1983), pp. 20–22. Report of the Oulton Committee on Patent Litigation (1987).

[37] CDPA 1988, ss. 288–291; Courts and Legal Services Act 1990, s. 2(1); Patents County Court (Designation and Jurisdiction) Order 1994, S.I. 1994 No. 1609. On jurisdiction, see *McDonald v. Graham* [1994] R.P.C. 407, CA; *Chaplin Patents v. Group Lotus, The Times*, January 24, 1994, CA.

[38] As well as barristers and solicitors, patent agents have rights of audience before it, a fact which may influence the High Court in ordering transfer to the lower jurisdiction: *Memminger-Iro v. Trip-Lite* [1992] R.P.C. 210.

[39] See Nott [1994] E.I.P.R. 3; Adams [1995] E.I.P.R. 497; Ford [1996] CIPA 464.

[40] See Rackham (1992) 74 JPTOS 445. The TRIPS Agreement obliges WTO Member States to provide fair and equitable civil procedures (Art. 42), which are prescribed in considerable detail (Arts 43–50): para. 2–03, above.

[41] See Chap. 16, below.

[42] No attempt can be made to present a systematic analysis of the torts that are mentioned. Good descriptions can be found, *e.g. Clerk and Lindsell* (n. 21, above), Chap. 23.

2–13 (i) **Conspiracy.** It is tortious for two or more people to combine together with the purpose of injuring the plaintiff and so cause him damage. However, the conspirators must either mean to use unlawful means (the narrow form of the tort), or else intend to act without employing any such means, but having as their predominant motive to injure the plaintiff, rather than to pursue their own selfish interests (the wider form).[43] Thus, under the narrow form, it is tortious for two or more people to agree to secure the commission of an infringement of intellectual property, as of other unlawful acts.[44] This may occur equally if one or more of the conspirators is to perform the infringing act or if a third party is to be induced to do so.[45]

2–14 (ii) **Inciting or procuring commission of a tort.** While there has been recent recognition that such a basis for liability exists,[46] it appears that it is not a conception appreciably wider than that of joint tortfeasance.[47] It is necessary to show more than that the defendant facilitated the doing of an act. He must, generally speaking, induce, incite or persuade a specific infringer and must identifiably procure a particular infringement.[48]

In the *Amstrad* case, a company was manufacturing and selling a twin-deck tape-recorder, knowing the likelihood of its use for home-taping which would infringe copyright. The company was nonetheless not a procurer of any infringement,[49] any more than that it was a joint tortfeasor, or a person who incited the commission of crime.[50]

We shall see that in the law of copyright there is a statutory proscription against "authorising" and "permitting" types of infringement[51]; and in the Patents Act 1977 there is now a rather elaborately defined notion of "indirect" infringement.[52] In their particular fields, these act as extensions of the strictly limited common law conception.

2–15 (iii) **Inducing or procuring breach of contract.** It is tortious for a defendant, D, to induce T to break a contract which D knows he has with a

---

[43] The wider form has no special relevance to intellectual property matters; but see *Jarman & Platt v. Barget* [1977] F.S.R. 260 at 277–282, CA.

[44] For what may constitute "unlawful means", see *Clerk and Lindsell*, paras 23–85—23–90. There is authority that abuse of confidence is one form: *Spermolin v. Winter, The Guardian*, June 22, 1962.

[45] For the application of this tort where the wrong is infringement of a patent, see para. 6–17, below.

[46] *Law Debenture v. Ural Caspian Oil* [1995] 1 All E.R. 157.

[47] For which, para. 2–07, below.

[48] *Lavender BV v. Witten Industrial Diamonds* [1979] F.S.R. 59 at 60, *per* Buckley L.J.; *Dow Chemical v. Spence Bryson* [1982] F.S.R. 397, CA; *Kalman v. P.C.L. Packaging* [1982] F.S.R. 406; *Cadbury v. Ulmer* [1988] F.S.R. 385.

[49] *CBS Songs v. Amstrad* [1988] 2 All E.R. 484 at 496–497.

[50] *ibid.*, at 497.

[51] See paras 11–18—11–20, below. In the *Amstrad* case (n. 49, above), the selling of the tape-recorders did not amount to "authorising" infringement.

[52] See paras 6–17—6–19, below; but there was already some authority concerning the common law tort in the patents field: *ibid.*

plaintiff, P, so as to cause P loss. This could occur, for instance, if a licensee of intellectual property were persuaded to depart from the limits of his licence and so to infringe. It is also a form of liability that may affect indirect recipients of confidential information.[53] The tort has developed so as to cover the case where D indirectly procures the breach of T and P's contract, for instance by getting S not to supply T with the materials necessary for performance. It has also been extended to inducements to T to break the contract without realising, and not to perform it where, because of a limitation of liability in it, T will not be responsible for making good P's loss.[54]

(iv) **Unlawful intimidation, fraud, etc., resulting in damage.** A defendant, **2–16** D, who, by unlawful conduct or threat of it, induces T to do or refrain from something which causes loss to a plaintiff, P, P has a right of action; it does not matter that T's act or omission is not itself unlawful, but D's unlawful conduct must be aimed at causing P's loss. Early instances involved a threat to injure T physically, causing him to do business with D rather than P.[55] Subsequently, the tort also arose where D threatened to break contracts with T, for instance, by strike action.[56] Equally the liability arises if D tells T lies which induce T not to deal with P.[57]

(v) **Wrongfully interfering with business relations by unlawful means.** The **2–17** tendency of the torts summarised under heads (iii) and (iv) gradually to spread their wings, has led some courts to recognise, as a separate basis of liability, the wrong of interfering with the plaintiff's trade or business by unlawful means which aim to cause loss to the plaintiff.[58] The defendant's unlawful act may consist of a tort or breach of contract. Thus, an importer of illicit recordings of copyright music committed the tort of infringement against the copyright owner; but equally he could be sued by the collecting society which licensed legitimate recordings of the music and took a contractual commission on the licence fees.[59]

It is less clear how far the unlawful means may consist of any crime or breach of statutory duty. At a time when the only express protection given against the unauthorised recording of a performance was by criminal law, the Court of Appeal was prepared to hold that the consequent injury to the

---

[53] For its relevance in that field, see para. 8–06, below.

[54] *National Phonograph v. Edison Bell* [1908] 1 Ch. 335, CA; *Merkur Island Shipping v. Laughton* [1983] A.C. 570, HL; and where the plaintiff's loss is still potential: *Law Debenture v. Ural Caspian Oil* [1995] 1 All E.R. 157, CA.

[55] *Tarleton v. McGawley* (1794) Peake 279.

[56] *Rookes v. Barnard* [1964] A.C. 1129, HL.

[57] *Lonrho v. Fayed* [1990] 2 Q.B. 479, CA, and see [1992] 1 A.C. 448, HL.

[58] See *Merkur Island* (n. 54, above); *Indata Equipment Supplies v. ACL* [1998] F.S.R. 248, CA. For what constitutes sufficient intent to injure, *cf. Lonrho v. Shell* [1982] A.C. 173, HL, with *Fayed* (n. 57, above).

[59] *Carlin v. Collins* [1979] F.S.R. 548.

expectations of the performers' recording company justified interlocutory relief.[60] However, later the same Court held that it was not enough to show that a contract had been rendered less valuable because of criminal activity. The crime must be one intended by Parliament to give rise to civil responsibility to the plaintiff. The Performers' Protection Acts were interpreted as giving this protection to performers, but not to the recording companies with which they had exclusive contracts.[61]

2–18 (vi) **Duties of care.** In addition to the discussion of intentional economic torts the sphere of our subject, there have also been attempts to argue that failure to prevent others from infringing intellectual property amounts to the tort of negligence. They have not met with success. A printer who produced labels for a skin cream to the order of a customer without knowing or inquiring about the latter's proposed use of them, would be liable for any infringement of copyright; but he did not have an additional duty to discover whether the customer would engage in passing off skin cream as the plaintiff's.[62] Likewise, in the twin-deck cassette recorder case, Amstrad owed no duty to ensure that those who purchased its tape-recorders did not make infringing copies on them. Those who merely facilitate infringement by others, without controlling what they do or positively encouraging it, are not to be made liable by this route.[63]

(2) Criminal proceedings

2–19 It is a distinctive characteristic of the English judicial system that civil and criminal modes of redress are largely kept separate.[64] In our field of interest, most claimants make use of the civil process, partly because its technique and atmosphere are appropriate to the assertion of private property rights amongst businessmen, and partly because the types of remedy—in particular the injunction (interlocutory and permanent) and damages—are more useful than punishment in the name of the state.[65]

---

[60] *ex p. Island Records* [1978] Ch. 122. See also *Gouriet v. Union of Post Office Workers* [1978] A.C. 435, HL; but *cf.* the criticism in *Shell* (n. 54, above), at 187, *per* Lord Diplock.

[61] *RCA v. Pollard* [1983] Ch. 135; *Rickless v. United Artists* [1987] F.S.R. 362 for the present protection of performers, see paras 13–88 *et seq.*, below.

[62] *Paterson Zochonis v. Merfarken Packaging* [1983] F.S.R. 273, CA.

[63] *Amstrad* case (n. 49, above) at 497–498. See also *Western Front v. Vestron* [1987] F.S.R. 66.

[64] If anything this tendency became more marked from the late nineteenth century onwards. There is now some movement back. Under the Powers of Criminal Courts Act 1973, ss. 35–38 (as amended by the Criminal Justice Act 1988, s. 72), a Court, on convicting an offender, may order him to pay compensation in respect of personal injury and other loss or damage. Magistrates' Courts may order up to £1,000 compensation and a Crown Court has the alternative of making a criminal bankruptcy order (ss. 39–41). Compensation orders have been made with some regularity in favour of consumers misled by false trade descriptions. In *R. v. Thomson Holidays* [1974] Q.B. 592, it was held that a series of orders could be made in favour of different customers misled by the same travel brochure.

[65] The decision to prefer criminal proceedings, where they are open, remains with the right-owner, not the Court: *Thames & Hudson v. DACS* [1995] F.S.R. 153.

The very power that civil remedies generate has been one reason for circumspection in conferring civil rights. Accordingly there are some activities on the periphery of our sphere where the relevant statutes only specify criminal sanctions.[66] This remains true of various forms of mis-descriptive advertising and labelling that may be injurious to competitors as well as consumers (and constitute offences under the Trade Descriptions Act 1968 and allied legislation).[67] In this connection it is worth noting the competence of any citizen (in England and Wales, and Northern Ireland) to institute criminal proceedings.[68] Under the Trade Descriptions Act this means that a competitor, who objects to a misdescription on a rival's product, may institute a prosecution, just as may a consumer, a police officer or a trading standards inspector.

There are some criminal offences that cover the same ground as rights of intellectual property. In these cases the right-owner usually prefers the civil route—for the reasons already mentioned, and because of two further factors:

(1) There is no possibility in criminal procedure of securing an interim order to desist from conduct pending the trial (which will take weeks or months to mount); nor are there pre-trial procedures, such as discovery, for the extraction of information from a defendant.

(2) There is a high burden of proof on the prosecution in criminal proceedings: the defendant must be shown to be guilty beyond reasonable doubt, and not merely (as for most civil issues) on a balance of probabilities. This quantum of proof may be specially hard to demonstrate if the type of offence requires proof of *mens rea* in the defendant, for example that he knew, or had reason to believe, that he was committing an infringing act or other offence.

(a) *Offences specifically concerning intellectual property*

Offences are most prominent in relation to infringement of trade marks **2–20** and of copyright, where there is a long history of conferring special remedies against pirates.[69] The Copyright, Designs and Patents Act 1988, creates a series of summary offences concerning infringements of copyright. These cover the same sphere as "secondary infringement" of copyright, and in the case of the more serious instances may now be prosecuted either

---

[66] For the unauthorised recording of performances, see para. 2–17, above.

[67] Discussed para. 16–03, below.

[68] But some crimes are exceptional in requiring the consent of the Attorney-General or Director of Public Prosecutions. The Law Commission is provisionally of the view that this should apply to all prosecutions under the CDPA 1988 and any which might in future become available for wrongful use or disclosure of trade secrets: Consultation Paper No. 149 (1997); Harbottle [1998] E.I.P.R. 317.

[69] See para. 9–03, below.

summarily or on indictment.[70] Likewise, the trade marks legislation now provides a similar set of offences against the counterfeiting of registered trade marks, both on goods within the registration and even, in cases of improper dilution, on other goods.[71]

While such offences do not cover everything that is actionable as infringement in civil proceedings, their ambit is much wider than anything applicable to patents, registered designs or confidential information.[72] Since these latter are forms of protection which depend upon official grant or registration, there are specific offences relating to this procedure. It is in each case an offence to secure false entries in the register[73] and to make an unauthorised claim to the right.[74] However, no criminal liability attaches specifically to the activity of an infringer, as is equally the case with unregistered design right.

(b) *Conspiracy to defraud*[75]

2–21 To some extent the lacuna just noted may be filled by the general crime of conspiracy to defraud.[76] This may be committed not only where those agreeing together are proposing to acquire property dishonestly, but also when they seek to obtain some other pecuniary advantage or try to deceive a person into acting contrary to his duty. Thus in *Scott v. Metropolitan Police Commissioner*[77] there was a conspiracy to defraud the owners of film copyright by bribing cinema employees to hand over films so that they could be surreptitiously copied and returned. The House of Lords confirmed that the owners were defrauded by this practice, even though no one was deceived by the operation.[78] The decision does not depend upon the fact that the actual copying was itself a summary offence,[79] and so it might apply if the subject-matter were some form of intellectual property other than copyright.

---

[70] CDPA 1988, ss. 107–110, and see para. 11–29, below.

[71] TMA 1994, ss. 92 *et seq*. It is no longer a defence to show that other matter dispelled any potential in the mark to deceive or cause confusion; so it would now be an offence to sell a product as a "brand copy", giving the brand; *cf. Kent C.C. v. Price* (1993) Tr.L.R. 137.

[72] As to the last, see below, para. 8–61.

[73] See PA 1977, s. 109; TMA 1994, s. 94; RDA 1949, s. 34.

[74] See PA 1977, s. 110 (s. 111 covers false claims to have applied for a patent); TMA 1994, s. 95; RDA 1949, s. 35. There are also offences connected with secrecy directions in PA 1977, ss. 22(9), 23(3); RDA 1949, s. 34.

[75] See generally, *e.g.* Ashworth, *Principles of Criminal Law* (2nd ed., 1995) Chap. 11.4, 11.5; A. Smith, *Property Offences* (1994) Chap. 19.

[76] For the preservation of this common law form of conspiracy, see Criminal Law Act 1977, s. 5.

[77] [1975] A.C. 819. See further Cornish (1975) 6 I.I.C. 43 at 57.

[78] Relying upon a line of authority, especially *Welham v. DPP* [1961] A.C. 103 at 123–124.

[79] Conspiracy to commit this offence was also charged: it would now rank as a statutory form of conspiracy (Criminal Law Act 1977, s. 1(1)), and could only be charged with the consent of the DPP (see s. 4(1)).

There is some doubt where the subject-matter is confidential information.[80] In *DPP v. Withers*[81] the accused conspirators induced bank officers to provide information about their customers by pretending to be acting for another bank; they then supplied the information to their own clients. This may be chargeable as a conspiracy to defraud, either if the information is itself treated as close enough to property to be in the line of *Scott's* case, or because persons are being actively deceived into breaking a duty. However, it is not clear whether the latter approach extends beyond deceiving public officers and covers deceiving those acting for private institutions such as banks.[82]

(c) *Crimes and civil relief*

As already noted the mere fact that a person is the victim of a crime does **2–22** not entitle him to civil relief such as damages or an injunction.[83] While accepting that the Trade Descriptions Act 1968 gave no civil causes of action, Lord Diplock nevertheless encouraged the judges to look to the range of the criminal law in determining the scope of equivalent civil redress—in this instance, the extent of the tort of passing off.[84]

A further possibility should be noted. If the criminal offence is imposed in order to confer a "public right", the Attorney-General may secure an injunction to restrain its commission. He has an unfettered discretion over intervening, which the judges will not review; it makes no difference whether the Attorney-General considers the case upon his own motion or at the relation of some interested person.[85] Thus he refused to intervene in order to protect the interests of particular performers under the Performers' Protection Acts.[86] But under the Trade Descriptions Act, where there is a threat to the interests of consumers in general, the chances of obtaining his co-operation could be greater even where the relator is an interested competitor.

---

[80] See also para. 8–34, below.

[81] [1975] A.C. 842, HL. The prosecution failed because the accused were charged with conspiracy to effect a public mischief, an offence held to be unknown to the criminal law.

[82] In *Scott* [1975] A.C. 819, HL, Lord Diplock thought that, if there was no element of economic loss, a public officer must be deceived; but other members of the House were more equivocal.

[83] See, in relation to injunctions, *Emperor of Austria v. Day* (1861) 3 De G.F. & J. 217; *Springhead Spinning v. Riley* (1868) L.R. 6 Eq. 551; *CBS Songs v. Amstrad* [1987] R.P.C. 429, CA.

[84] See para. 16–03, below.

[85] See especially *Gouriet v. Union of Post Office Workers* [1978] A.C. 435, HL. For repeated breaches of the criminal law an injunction may be granted: *Att.-Gen. v. Harris* [1961] Q.B. 74, CA.

[86] See *ex p. Island Records* [1978] Ch. 122, CA.

(3) Administrative procedures

(a) *Customs prohibition*[87]

2–23 Appropriately enough, the possibility of arresting the movement of pirated and counterfeit goods[88] through the intervention of customs officials at borders has become a matter largely for E.U. legislation.[89] What is more, the dismantling of customs controls between member states has meant that the main impact of such procedures is now at the external boundaries of the Community.[90] Council Regulation 3295/94[91] is the second attempt to secure an adequate regime for this purpose and is itself the subject of revision and expansion.[92] Each State must nominate a single service within its customs authority to receive and decide on applications for border protection, and a limit is placed on the amount of information which can be demanded from rightholders. Once pirated or counterfeit goods are identified in accordance with the notification, the Customs authority will refuse to release them to the importer. However, the rightholder owes the authority a duty to indemnify it against any liability or expense. There is some evidence that this system is beginning to be used, though more in Germany than elsewhere around the E.U.

(b) *Trading standards authorities*

2–24 The measures of consumer protection that have been developed under the modern law are now enforced principally by the trading standards departments of local authorities. In particular a positive duty to act was placed upon these authorities by the Trade Descriptions Act 1968. To this end

---

[87] See generally Wordsall and Clark, *Anti-Counterfeiting* (1998) Chap. 7; Arsie (1995) 18 World Comp. 75; Clark [1998] E.I.P.R. 414.

[88] Counterfeiting adds imitation of marks and packaging to pirated copies of products, with the intention of deceiving purchasers completely.

[89] Pirating is not a term of legal art, but refers to the illicit production and marketing of products copied from a source protected by certain types of IP: as with films and records, photocopies, objects bearing designs, etc. At present, the E.C. regime does not extend to patented products, and there is controversy over adding them: see Clark, above, n. 86.

[90] U.K. legislation continues to prescribe the procedure for seeking action by the Commissioners of Customs and Excise and it now forms the basis for U.K. implementation of the 1994 Regulation: see S.I. 1995 Nos 1430, 1444 and 1445; CDPA 1988, ss. 111, 112; TMA 1994, ss. 98–91; *Commissioners of Customs v. Top High* [1998] F.S.R. 464. The TRIPs Agreement, Arts 51–60, requires WTO states to maintain such controls of imports. The considerable detail of these provisions is satisfied in the E.U. and U.K. arrangements discussed here.

[91] [1994] O.J. L314/8; For further reforms, see the Commission's Proposal [1998] O.J. C198/63. As to reform of practicalities, see the E.C. Green Paper, *Combatting Piracy and Counterfeiting* (1998).

[92] The initial legislation, Regs 3842/86, became fully effective only after a long period, and in several countries could operate only upon an order being first obtained from a court or tribunal.

they are armed with powers to make test purchases and to seize goods and documents for the purposes of the Act.[93] The extent to which the criminal offences contained in that Act may protect competitors against unfair practices has already been noted. The executive powers of the local authorities may sometimes provide a lever in the process of securing evidence or in informally putting a stop to some relatively minor injury.

(c) *Supervision of broadcasting*

The content of television and radio advertising on the commercial channels **2–25** and stations is supervised by the Independent Television Commission and the Radio Authority. Each administers a detailed code on a great variety of matters, including such points of concern to competitors as comparative advertising and sponsorship.[94]

(d) *Advertising Standards Authority*

Outside the field of broadcasting, the advertising industry has averted the **2–26** creation of a public body to supervise it by setting up a voluntary organ of its own, the Advertising Standards Authority, half of whose members are drawn from outside the industry. Complaints about the content of advertising may be made to the Authority, and these are judged against the British Code of Advertising Practice which is drawn up by the industry. The proponents of the system claim for it the advantages of co-operation and quick action that are certainly possible within an organisation of this kind. However, there have been criticisms of the effectiveness of the A.S.A., to which we shall come later. The system is mentioned here in order to point the contrast with the public institutions that work in cognate fields.

(4) Self-help

Those entitled to possession of chattels have a right of recaption which **2–27** entitles them to take their things, using no more force than is reasonably necessary.[95] The rights in intangible property which we are discussing give rise to no equivalent remedy by self-help, with one exception. The Copyright, Designs and Patents Act 1988 creates such a power, subject to specified conditions, which is exercisable against the lowest rung in the piratical heirarchy, but only in relation to copyright and rights in performances.[96] The right-owner, or anyone whom he authorises, may seize and

---

[93] Trade Descriptions Act 1968, s. 26(1). See generally, Cornish (1974) 5 I.I.C. at 82–85, where the role of the Office of Fair Trading in this field is also discussed.

[94] For details, see Nelson, *Law of Entertainment and Broadcasting* (1995), paras 23.22—23.27, 29.17, 29.18.

[95] *Clerk and Lindsell on Torts* (17th ed., 1995), para. 29–11.

[96] As originally introduced, the power was to have been much broader.

detain infringing copies that are "exposed or otherwise immediately available for sale or hire", provided, first, that a local police station is duly notified and, secondly, that the seizure is in a public place or is on public premises from a person who does not have a permanent or regular place of business there.[97] Notice of what has been seized has to be given in the prescribed form.[98] No force may be used,[99] so, if the police will not accompany, the remedy is probably only good against the feeblest suitcase-salesman. The seller will mostly be committing a relatively minor offence, which is non-arrestable. However, a police officer present may be able to use his discretionary power to arrest, on the ground, for instance, that he cannot ascertain the name, or the true name, of the offender.[1]

2. REMEDIES IN CIVIL ACTIONS

2–28 The precise value of a right must be measured in terms of the remedies that lie for its enforcement. The range of relief provided by civil courts for the protection of property is wide and that is one of the most significant consequences of characterising patents, copyright, trade marks and the like as property. The forms of intellectual property now embodied in statute now list the forms of remedy available, and to some extent regulate the detailed law.[2] However, the subject must be approached with a weathered eye upon history. Before the mid-nineteenth century reforms which culminated in the Judicature Acts, the award of damages (assessed by a jury) was the remedy of the courts of common law. Remedies such as the injunction, which laid constraints upon a defendant beyond the mere payment of money, were developed by the Chancellor in equity. In addition, some causes of action arose at common law, others in equity. Each attracted the remedies available in its own court. Furthermore, while purely equitable actions could not lead to an award of common law damages, equity might supplement the relief in a common law action by granting an equitable remedy. However, Chancery judges would frequently require that the opinion of a common law court first be taken on the substance of the matter.[3]

2–29   In the 1850s, statutes began the process of making the remedies of each jurisdiction available more readily in the other. In particular: courts of common law could award equitable forms of relief including injunctions[4]; courts of equity were to grant injunctions for breach of common law rights

---

[97] CDPA 1988, ss. 100, 196.
[98] *ibid.*, s. 100(4).
[99] *ibid.*, s. 100(3).
[1] See Police and Criminal Evidence Act 1984, ss. 24, 25.
[2] See PA 1977, ss. 61, 62; CDPA 1988, ss. 96–100, 195, 229–233; TMA 1994, ss. 15–19; see below, paras 6–25—6–27; 11–58—11–60.
[3] Not that the Lord Chancellor necessarily considered himself bound by the jury's verdict.
[4] Patent Law Amendment Act 1852, s. 42; Common Law Procedure Act 1854, ss. 79 *et seq.*

without first requiring a common law trial[5]; and by Lord Cairns' Act 1858, damages might be awarded in a court of equity "in lieu of or in addition to" an injunction (and other equitable relief).[6] This cross-fertilisation laid a basis from which to achieve the coalescence in administering civil law that was brought about by the Judicature Acts.[7]

The main intellectual property rights, whether they arose out of statute **2–30** or judicial decision, were early in their existence accepted as rights enforceable at common law. This meant that damages were available, although, as the jury was gradually dropped from the trial of civil actions,[8] their assessment fell to the judge trying the action. But as the consequence primarily desired by most right-owners was the cessation of the competing wrong, an injunction was commonly sought, even in the days when it was necessary to pursue the case through two courts. Only the action for breach of confidence does not conform to this straightforward pattern. It grew as a comparatively recent manifestation of equity's power to put down impropriety by means of injunction, and its exact status is still in some measure opaque. To this special case we shall return later.[9]

(1) Injunction

An injunction looks to the future. It is an order of the court directing a **2–31** party to litigation to do or refrain from doing an act.[10] Wilfully to disobey is contempt of court, punishable by fine, imprisonment or sequestration of assets.[11] The law of injunctions is beset with over-general propositions that require qualification in particular areas of application. In the intellectual property field an injunction is almost always prohibitory (as opposed to mandatory) since it enjoins the threatened commission[12] or continuance of

---

[5] Chancery Procedure Act 1852, ss. 61, 62; Chancery Regulation Act 1862, ss. 1–3.

[6] The jurisdiction established by Lord Cairns' Act continues in force, though by a somewhat circuitous route: see 24 *Halsbury's Laws of England* (4th ed.), para. 934, n. 3.

[7] But substantive rights were not in consequence expanded or altered in nature. Thus an attempt to argue that the Acts gave a house-owner a new right to an injunction to restrain his neighbour from calling his house by the same name was firmly rejected: *Day v. Brownrigg* (1878) 10 Ch.D. 294.

[8] Because of the length and difficulty of patent actions, the right of a party to a jury was restricted in 1873.

[9] See Chap. 8, below.

[10] The order may restrain the defendant by its directors, employees or solicitors from doing the prohibited act: the latter, and any others who deliberately engage in the conduct, will be liable in contempt: *Seaward v. Paterson* [1897] 1 Ch. 545, CA; *Marengo v. Daily Sketch* [1948] 1 All E.R. 406, HL; *Att.-Gen. v. Newspaper Publishing* [1987] 3 All E.R. 276, CA. *cf. Chelsea Man v. Chelsea Girl (No. 2)* [1988] F.S.R. 217.

[11] *Director General of Fair Trading v. Smith's Concrete* [1991] 4 All E.R. 150, CA Sequestration is the form appropriate to contempt by a company. And see *Hospital for Sick Children v. Walt Disney* [1968] Ch. 52, CA.

[12] An injunction may be granted *quia timet* against a proposed course of action that will infringe the plaintiff's rights, if there is a strong probability that harm will occur. It may include, where appropriate, an injunction concerning future rights.

wrongful acts. It can be granted after a trial establishing infringement of the plaintiff's right, when it is called "final" or "perpetual". However, it may also be sought in "interlocutory" form, not to enforce an established right, but to maintain the status quo until a trial of the merits can take place. A cause of action is however a necessary precondition of this form of relief.[13] This latter type of injunction contributes a great deal to the practical efficacy of intellectual property rights and we shall discuss it first.

(a) *Interlocutory injunction*

2–32 (i) **Preconditions.** An interlocutory injunction, ordering the defendant not to continue or not to embark upon a course of action until the trial of the issue with the plaintiff, is a rapid and relatively cheap way of procuring temporary redress.[14] Its effect against a business competitor may be to cut off for good the road to commercial success. Even without this, business-men frequently treat the outcome of the interlocutory proceedings as settling the matter in dispute.

Whether such an injunction should be granted has always been a matter of discretion.[15] The motion to procure it must be brought as soon as the plaintiff learns of the alleged infringement of his rights; even short periods of delay may debar interlocutory relief if there is no reasonable explanation.[16] An injunction will normally be granted to a plaintiff, other than the Crown,[17] only if he gives a cross-undertaking to make good any damage suffered by any defendant from the injunction, should the plaintiff fail at the trial.[18] The interim period will inevitably be a matter of months and, in a patent action, probably two years or more. The defendant's competitive losses over such a period may well be considerable. The cross-undertaking cannot be lightly given.

The injunction granted is typically in the form that the defendant be restrained from infringing the plaintiff's right as asserted. This will cover variations of what the defendant has been doing if they too would amount to infringement.[19] It is open to the defendant to obtain a declaration that

---

[13] *The Veracruz* [1992] 1 Lloyd's Rep. 353 at 357, 359, CA, abandoning a view of Lord Denning's to the contrary.

[14] Exceptionally the injunction may be mandatory, requiring action of the defendant: *Lockoll Group v. Mercury Communications* [1988] F.S.R. 354 CH.

[15] *Series 5 Software v. Clarke* [1996] F.S.R. 273. It is a discretion difficult to challenge on appeal: *Elan Digital v. Elan Computers* [1984] F.S.R 374 at 384, 386.

[16] cf., e.g. *Bourjois v. British Home Stores* (1951) 68 R.P.C. 280, CA; *Versil v. Cork Asbestos* [1966] R.P.C. 76; *Quaker Oats v. Alltrades* [1981] F.S.R. 9, CA.

[17] The cross-undertaking will not usually be required of the Crown where it seeks the injunction to enforce the law: *Hoffmann-La Roche v. Secretary for Trade* [1975] A.C. 295.

[18] See *Harman Pictures v. Osborne* [1967] 2 All E.R. 324 and 24 *Halsbury's Laws of England* (4th ed.), paras 1072–1078. The cross-undertaking does not found an independent cause of action, but is a discretionary order: *Cheltenham and Gloucester Building Society v. Ricketts* [1993] 1 W.L.R. 1545.

[19] This assumes that the right as alleged can be substantiated at the trial: *Spectravest v. Aperknit* [1988] F.S.R. 161; but note Scott J.'s doubt whether such an assumption can properly be made: *Staver v. Digitext Display* [1985] F.S.R. 512. cf. *Video Arts v. Paget Industries* [1988] F.S.R. 501.

his altered product is outside the injunction; and he will protect himself better if he chooses that course rather than putting the variation on the market without telling the plaintiff.[20]

(ii) **Assessment:** *American Cyanamid.* Beyond this, the usual approach was, **2–33** until 1975, first to consider whether the plaintiff has made out a prima facie case of infringement, taking account of the apparent merits of any defence that the defendant proposed to establish at the trial.[21] Each side normally supported its case with written evidence in affidavits.[22] If a prima facie case was established, the court then considered whether the balance of convenience lay in favour of restraining the defendant until the trial or in leaving the plaintiff to recover damages at the trial for any infringements by the defendant in the intervening period.

In *American Cyanamid v. Ethicon,*[23] the House of Lords modified this **2–34** approach. It did so in patent litigation, insisting, however, that the new principles were in no way special to this field. According to Lord Diplock, the correct approach is as follows: The court must first be satisfied that there is a "serious question to be tried".[24] Thereafter, it should not try to assess relative merit by looking for a prima facie case in the affidavit evidence; it should instead turn at once to the balance of convenience.[25] If it appears that damages awarded at the trial will adequately compensate the plaintiff, and that the defendant is likely to be able to pay them,[26] interlocutory relief should not normally be granted. If damages will not be adequate to compensate the plaintiff, it becomes necessary to consider whether, on the other hand, the defendant would be adequately compensated by damages upon the plaintiff's cross-undertaking, should the plaintiff not make good his claim at trial; if these damages would be adequate, the injunction will be granted. Where there is doubt about the adequacy of damages to one or both,[27] any factor which may affect the balance of convenience is brought into account—in particular, whether the defendant

---

[20] *Spectravest v. Aperknit* (n. 19, above).

[21] For an instance, see *Hubbard v. Vosper* [1972] 2 Q.B. 84, CA.

[22] Witnesses were summoned to give oral evidence only when it appeared crucial to test their credibility at this preliminary stage.

[23] [1975] A.C. 396, [1975] R.P.C. 513.

[24] *i.e.* that the claim was not "frivolous or vexatious" or that it "disclosed no real prospect of [the plaintiff] succeeding in his claim for a permanent injunction at the trial". Lord Diplock used all three phrases, apparently as synonyms, and subsequent Courts have varied in their understanding of the standard which the plaintiff must satisfy: see Megarry V.-C. in *Mothercare v. Robson* [1979] F.S.R. 466 at 471–474, in whose own view the plaintiff must show more than "an honest but hopelessly optimistic case". (This, however, is what "frivolous or vexatious" means when an order to strike out an action is being sought under RSC, O. 18, r. 19(1)).

[25] A weakness of the judgment is that it did not deal with *Stratford v. Lindley* [1965] A.C. 269 or with the *Hoffmann-La Roche* case (n. 14, above), in both of which the House of Lords adopted a "prima facie" case approach: see *Series 5 Software v. Clarke* (n. 27, below).

[26] See, *e.g. Belfast Ropeworks v. Pixdane* [1976] F.S.R. 337, CA.

[27] *Walker (John) v. Rothmans* [1978] F.S.R. 357; *Combe v. Scholl* [1980] R.P.C. 1.

has not yet started on his allegedly infringing course of action[28] (it being "a counsel of prudence . . . to preserve the status quo").[29] If the balance remains substantially even, some account can ultimately be taken of the relative strength of each party's case as revealed by the affidavit evidence. "This, however, should be done only where it is apparent upon the facts disclosed by evidence as to which there is no credible dispute that the strength of one party's case is disproportionate to that of the other party."[30]

2–35 How substantial a reorientation was effected by this judgment has long been open to question.[31] Because a court has no longer to consider whether, if the case went to trial on the affidavit evidence, the plaintiff would probably succeed, it can cut short any invitation to evaluate rival contentions presented in elaborate affidavits.[32] Accordingly, substantial trials-before-trials can be eliminated. But short of this, because so many cases that are fought at the interlocutory stage involve substantial uncertainties, it is difficult for the court to exclude all consideration of relative merits—the factor given such prominence in the former "prima facie case" approach. Thus some considerations that previously went to the prima facie case may be given weight in deciding whether there is a serious case to be tried[33]; and they may appear equally relevant to the adequacy or otherwise of damages. Whether the defendant's trade mark or name is close enough to the plaintiffs' to constitute passing off often affects the likelihood of damage.[34] In other cases again, because the adequacy of damages remains in doubt, some judges have taken advantage of the statement that as a last resort they may balance the merits.[35]

---

[28] See *Beecham Group v. Bristol* [1967] R.P.C. 406 at 416, CA; *ibid.*, [1968] R.P.C. 301, HC (Aust).

[29] Where there is a delay between issue of the writ and its service, it is at the latter date that the status quo falls to be considered: *Graham v. Delderfield* [1992] F.S.R. 313, CA.

[30] [1975] R.P.C. 513 at 542. This cautious approach was directly challenged as unduly restrictive by Laddie J.: *Series 5 Software v. Clarke* [1996] F.S.R. 273 at 285, 286; Phillips [1997] J.B.L. 486.

[31] Judges have varied in their readiness to follow the changed approach religiously. Lord Denning M.R. and Pennycuick V.-C. were early doubters: see *Fellowes v. Fisher* [1976] Q.B. 122; *Hubbard v. Pitt* [1975] 3 All E.R. 1 at 10; and see *Dunford v. Johnston* [1978] F.S.R. 143 at 150. It has however stood the test of time. The Court of Appeal has since insisted that it applies both to restraint of trade and passing-off cases: *Lawrence David v. Ashton* [1989] F.S.R. 87; *County Sound v. Ocean Sound* [1991] F.S.R. 367. *cf.* now, *Series 5 Software v. Clarke* (n. 27, above).

[32] *American Cyanamid v. Ethicon* posed just this threat: see [1977] F.S.R. 593, CA.

[33] Thus an important question of law was decided under this rubric in *Revlon v. Cripps & Lee* [1980] F.S.R. 85; see paras 17–114 *et seq.*, below. See also *Mothercare v. Penguin Books* [1988] R.P.C. 113; *Mail Newspapers v. Express Newspapers* [1987] F.S.R. 90.

[34] *Sirdar v. Mulliez* [1975] F.S.R. 309; *Walker (John) v. Rothmans* [1978] F.S.R. 357; *Morning Star v. Express* [1979] F.S.R. 113, DC; *Newsweek v. BBC* [1979] R.P.C. 441; *Marcus Publishing v. Hutton-Wild Communications* [1990] R.P.C. 576, CA; *Antec International v. South Western Chicks* [1997] F.S.R. 278.

[35] *Constable v. Clarkson* [1980] F.S.R. 123, CA; *Quaker Oats v. Alltrades* [1981] F.S.R. 9, CA; *Mirage Studios v. Counter-Feat Clothing* [1991] F.S.R. 145. If the result of the interlocutory proceedings is likely to dispose of the dispute, the court will consider the relative chances of success: see Lord Diplock, *NWL v. Woods* [1979] 3 All E.R. 614 at 625–626; applied in *Athletes Foot v. Cobra Sports* [1980] R.P.C. 343; *BBC v. Talbot* [1981] F.S.R. 228.

(iii) **Balance of convenience.** *American Cyanamid* has given greater promi- **2–36** nence to the balance of convenience, although no appreciable change has been needed in the manner of assessing it. Three factors in particular are of recurrent importance. First, is the degree to which plaintiff and defendant are successfully established in business: for loss of market share during the interim period until trial may well be thought to have wide-ranging effects that cannot be easily quantified in damages. If the defendant has not yet set up in production, but the plaintiff is already on the market, the balance may well be in the latter's favour.[36] If both are marketing and the plaintiff is struggling to gain a foothold with a new product, again the special danger to him may lead to grant of the injunction. The contrary may well apply if he is already well-established and the defendant is unlikely to offer major competition in the interim.[37] In such cases, it is generally easier to assess the loss to the plaintiff from actual sales by the defendant than loss to the defendant by being enjoined from competing.[38]

Secondly, if either party appears to lack the financial ability or backing to meet any ultimate liability in damages this may operate against him.[39] Thirdly, unnecessary delay on the plaintiff's part will weigh against him, at least if the defendant has materially altered his position in consequence.[40]

Beyond this, for all its alleged universality, the manner in which the *American Cyanamid* rule is applied needs to be separately considered in relation to particular intellectual property rights.[41]

(b) *Final injunction*

Even after the plaintiff has established his right at trial of the action, an **2–37** injunction is said to be subject to two considerations: it lies in the discretion of the Court; and it is available at the instance of a private litigant only if he has some proprietary right or interest to protect. As regards intellectual property the following can be said in amplification:

(1) Against proven infringement of patent, design, copyright, trade mark and any other right that has acquired the status of "property" at

---

[36] *Belfast Ropework v. Pixdane* [1976] F.S.R. 337, CA; but see n. 40, below.

[37] *Catnic v. Stressline* [1976] F.S.R. 157, CA. *cf.; e.g. Parfums Givenchy v. Designer Alternatives* [1994] R.P.C. 243, CA. If the dispute is worldwide the damage to each must be considered in that context; where the plaintiff has been unable to secure interlocutory protection through his patents in other countries, this may militate against a grant in England: *Polaroid v. Eastman Kodak* [1977] F.S.R. 25, CA. If the effect of an injunction would be to deprive the defendant of his usual means of earning, this weighs against grant: *Raindrop Data v. Systemics* [1988] F.S.R. 354. Likewise, if the effect will be to put the defendant out of business: *Cayne v. Global Natural Resources* [1984] 1 All E.R. 225, CA; *Entec v. Abacus Mouldings* [1992] F.S.R. 332, CA.

[38] It is no argument that failure to grant the injunction effectively licenses invasion of the right: *Hunter v. Wellings* [1987] F.S.R. 83, CA.

[39] *Standex v. Blades* [1976] F.S.R. 114, CA.

[40] *Sirdar v. Mulliez* (n. 31, above); *Radley Gowns v. Spyrou* [1975] F.S.R. 455; *cf. Belfast Ropework* case (n. 33, above).

[41] See paras 6–24—6–27, 8–41—8–43, below.

common law, an injunction will be granted in the absence of something special in the case—such as imminent expiry of the right, no likelihood of repetition by the defendant, or some conduct on the plaintiff's part that leaves him with unclean hands, such as a representation that he would not seek an injunction.[42] In the general run of circumstances, to leave the plaintiff to a remedy in damages[43] would in effect be to compel him to license his right to all comers.

(2) To protect confidential information, injunctive relief is more evidently at the court's discretion. The relevant case law is discussed later.[44]

(3) There is no right to an injunction in order to protect against irrecoverable loss, *e.g.* loss of sales to other companies linked to the plaintiff only indirectly and not as subsidiaries.[45]

(4) A private party may not procure an injunction against violation of the criminal law unless he has a special interest in its enforcement greater than that of the ordinary citizen.[46] Even if he has this interest, the statute creating the offence must not have been drawn with the intention of restricting its enforcement to criminal law procedures.[47]

(2) Delivery up

2–38 In order to ensure that injunctions are properly effective, courts of equity and their successors maintain a discretion to order delivery up of infringing articles or documents for destruction, or else to require their destruction under oath by the defendant, or some equivalent step such as erasure of a trade mark.[48] In a breach of confidence case, however, the defendant was ordered to deliver up when he was not trusted to destroy under oath.[49] In the case of copyright and unregistered design right this jurisdiction is now governed by statute and extends both to infringing copies and to apparatus, etc., specifically designed to make infringing copies.[50] Here the court's

---

[42] *cf. Banks v. EMI Songs* [1996] E.M.L.R. 452. An intermediate possibility is for the court to give the plaintiff leave to apply for an injunction should it prove necessary in future.

[43] Whether by refusing an injunction under the general discretion or under Lord Cairns' Act.

[44] See paras 8–41 *et seq.*, below.

[45] *Polaroid v. Eastman Kodak* [1997] R.P.C. 379 at 394–5, 397; *Peaudouce v. Kimberley-Clark* [1996] F.S.R. 680.

[46] See para. 2–22, above.

[47] See para. 2–11, above.

[48] See, *e.g. Mergenthaler Linotype v. Intertype* (1927) 43 R.P.C. 381; *Slazenger v. Feltham (No. 2)* (1889) 6 R.P.C. 531 at 538 (trade mark); *Peter Pan v. Corsets Silhouette* [1963] 3 All E.R. 402. *cf. Ocular Sciences v. Aspect Vision Case* [1997] R.P.C. 289 and 420: relief refused because it would be disproportionately damaging to defendant.

[49] *Industrial Furnaces v. Reaves* [1970] R.P.C. 605 at 627–628.

[50] CDPA 1988, ss. 99, 230. There is in general a time limit on such an order of six years from making the article. In criminal proceedings for copyright infringement similar orders may be made: CDPA 1988, s. 108; and for forfeiture orders concerning trade marks, see TMA 1994, ss. 97, 98.

discretion is wider than in general, for, in order to compensate the right-owner, it may forfeit the things to him rather than order destruction or other disposal.[51]

(3) Damages

(a) Bases for assessment

The normal aim of an award of damages is to compensate the plaintiff for **2–39** the harm caused him by the legal injury.[52] In the case of breach of contract, damages generally seek to put the plaintiff in the position that he would have occupied had the contract been carried out; and so (subject to the exclusion of losses that are unforeseeably remote) he may recover profits that he anticipated making from the contract.[53] Damages in tort (again subject to exclusion of the unforeseeably remote)[54] aim to put the victim back to his position before the tort, the victim being able to recover for any loss which was foreseeable (i.e. not too remote), caused by the wrong and not excluded from recovery by public or social policy.[55] Generally, if a tortious action is also a breach of contract, the law allows the claim to be put on either basis; and occasionally the different assumptions for calculating damages may make this significant.

Contrary to the older view, exemplary damages may not be awarded to punish the plaintiff for wrongful conduct, however aggressively or insultingly deliberate. But there is an exception where the defendant's conduct has been calculated by him to make a profit for himself which may well exceed the compensation payable to him by the plaintiff; for "it is necessary for the law to show that it cannot be broken with impunity".[56] However, it is still open to courts to award aggravated damages, adding compensation for injury to the plaintiff's feelings or reputation to a sum for the breach which otherwise may only be nominal.[57]

---

[51] CDPA 1988, ss. 114, 231. See also *Industrial Furnaces v. Reaves* [1970] R.P.C. 605 at 627–628.

[52] Not from some other cause: see *United Horse Shoe v. Stewart* (1888) 5 R.P.C. 260 at 267. But it is no excuse that the defendant might have injured the plaintiff as much by some non-infringing act: *ibid.*

[53] See, *e.g. Chitty on Contracts* (27th ed., 1994), Vol. I, paras 1551 *et seq., McGregor on Damages* (15th ed., 1988), paras 24–47, 175–207.

[54] This concept is *semble* somewhat narrower in contract than in tort: *Koufos v. Czarnikow* [1969] 1 A.C. 350 at 422–423, HL.

[55] *Gerber v. Lectra* [1997] R.P.C. 443, CA; see further below, para. 2–45, *cf.* also *Cambridge Water v. Eastern Counties Leather* [1994] 2 A.C. 264; *Claydon Architectual Metalwork v. Higgins* [1997] F.S.R. 475.

[56] *Rookes v. Barnard* [1964] A.C. 1129 at 1220–1231, *per* Lord Devlin. The other recognised exception concerns the acts of government servants. See also *Cassell v. Broome* [1972] A.C. 1027, HL; *Morton-Norwich v. Intercen (No. 2)* [1981] F.S.R. 337.

[57] Notice also the power in a copyright or unregistered design case to award additional damages: CDPA 1988, ss. 97(2), 229(3); para. 11–61, below.

2–40   In arriving at the measure of damages in the various fields of intellectual property, Courts have to deal with recurrent circumstances. The similarities are often of broad outline rather than of detail. Accordingly statements about the proper approach to assessment provide general guidelines, not strict rules. In particular the judges resist being saddled with any single test for all cases.[58] The fact that a particular assessment is difficult and must be rather rough-and-ready is not a reason for refusing to attempt it.[59]

There are many ways in which particular copyrights and patents may be exploited. A starting point in assessing damages is accordingly to ask whether the plaintiff and defendant are in actual competition.[60] Where this is so, the next question is whether the defendant might have had the plaintiff's licence if only he had sought it. Then the measure of damages will likely be what the plaintiff would have charged for a licence.[61] The award for infringements already perpetrated may well be based on a royalty for each infringement.[62] However, the plaintiff is not normally under any compulsion to grant licences.[63] If he would not have done so, the Court will look to his losses through the defendant's competition. It is only where the plaintiff's and defendant's anticipated profits are the same in the same market that the defendant's gain will be the plaintiff's loss. To take an obvious example: the plaintiff may be exploiting his copyright by selling small numbers of high-priced hardback books, and the defendant may infringe with large quantities of low-priced paperbacks. The issue is the loss to the plaintiff, and this may include not only the lost profits on hardback sales (taking account of any price reduction forced on him by the defendant's conduct),[64] but also the damage to his future prospects—his chance of putting out paperbacks, the loss of ancillary supplies or services[65] and possibly even the fact that infringement has enabled the defendant to build up a strong position in other competitive lines.[66]

---

[58] *Meters v. Metropolitan Gas* (1911) 28 R.P.C. 157 at 161, 163, CA; *Watson, Laidlaw v. Potts Cassels* (1914) 31 R.P.C. 104 at 117–118, HL; *Interfirm Comparison v. Law Society* (1975) 6 A.L.R. 445 at 446–447, S.C. (N.S.W.).

[59] *Chaplin v. Hicks* [1911] 2 K.B. 786; *Watson, Laidlaw* case (n. 58, above) at 118. See also *Ricketson* [1980] E.I.P.R. 149.

[60] Taking account of competition by the plaintiff's licensees, if any.

[61] *General Tire v. Firestone* [1976] R.P.C. 197 at 212 *et seq.*, HL.

[62] A plaintiff who has fought his case to judgment may not then be bound by the royalty rate that he gave before the validity of his right was established: it depends on whether the rate was a standard one or not: *General Tire* case (n. 61, above); and see *Caxton v. Sutherland* [1939] A.C. 178 at 203, HL. If no injunction is to be granted for the future, damages may take the form of a capitalised royalty. See also *British Thompson-Houston v. Naamloose* (1923) 40 R.P.C. 119 at 127–128, IH.

[63] As far as trade marks and the like are concerned, he may indeed jeopardise his own rights, if he grants a licence, unless certain conditions are complied with: see paras 17–12 *et seq.*, below. At the other extreme, *cf.* the possibility of compulsory licensing for patents and designs: paras 7–41, *et seq.*, below.

[64] See *Meters* case (n. 58, above) at 48; *Manus v. Fullwood* (1954) 71 R.P.C. 243. *cf. United Horse Shoe v. Stewart* (n. 52, above).

[65] *Gerber Garment v. Lectra* [1997] R.P.C. 443, CA.

[66] *cf. Alexander v. Henry* (1895) 12 R.P.C. 360 (trade mark); *Khawam v. Chelaram* [1964] R.P.C. 337 at 342–343, PC (registered design).

When it comes to non-competitive infringements, the courts have held **2–41** that a reasonable royalty for non-competing use will be awarded upon a principle "of price or of hire".[67] Otherwise the right might be invaded with impunity.[68]

A different question also goes to the nature of the "property". Suppose that the infringement (even if competing) is only one contributory factor in the profit that the defendant has made: a copyright work has been included in a larger compilation; an invention forms one part of more complex plant; or it is a machine or process that is used in making a non-patented article. In which of these cases, if any, is the plaintiff only entitled to some proportion of the whole amount otherwise arising under the principles just discussed? If the damages represent lost sales to the plaintiff[69] he is entitled to the whole lost profit.[70] Where this is not so a royalty may be the appropriate basis of calculation at a rate which takes into account the proportional contribution of the right infringed.[71]

(b) *Innocence*

Normally, rights that rank as common law property are enforceable even **2–42** against those who unwittingly interfere with them. However, this aspect of the property analogy in our field has not always appealed to Parliament and the courts. They have not, it is true, refused injunctions against the continuance of an infringement simply on the ground that a defendant in all innocence expended money on a production system—a change of position that will bring him loss if he is then obliged to desist. But there has been some reluctance to oblige him to pay damages for infringements committed during a period of "innocence". Thus, in the Acts relating to patents, designs and copyright it is explicitly provided that no damages are payable for a period in which the infringer did not know, and had no reasonable grounds for supposing, that the right existed.[72] However a genuine belief that there was no infringement or that the right had been properly licensed is not an excuse.[73] The requirement of reasonableness, moreover, means that a defendant who copies a new product ought to

---

[67] Lord Shaw, *Watson Laidlaw* case (n. 58, above) at 119–120; and see Fletcher Moulton L.J., *Meters* case (n. 58, above) at 163–165.

[68] ". . . what would have been the condition of the Plaintiff, if the Defendants had acted properly instead of acting improperly?": Page Wood V.-C., *Penn v. Jack* (1867) L.R. 5 Eq. 81 at 84. For the possible application of this approach to trade mark infringement, see *Dormeuil v. Feraglow* [1990] R.P.C. 449.

[69] Because the plaintiff would have produced an end product competing with the defendant's.

[70] *United Horse Shoe v. Stewart* (1888) 13 App.Cas. 401, 3 R.P.C. 139 (patented machine saved expense in making nails).

[71] *cf. Meters v. Metropolitan* (n. 58, above).

[72] PA 1977, s. 62(1), RDA 1949, s. 9(1), CDPA 1988, ss. 97(1), 233 (also affecting "secondary infringement").

[73] See, *e.g. Byrne v. Statist* [1914] 1 K.B. 622 (belief that someone other than plaintiff owned copyright did not excuse).

inquire whether it is patented,[74] and one who copies a literary work or the like should look for any indications that it is in copyright.[75] Where statute has not intervened there is less certainty. Innocent infringement of a trade mark, whether registered or unregistered, gives rise to damages,[76] though a discretionary remedy such as an account might be refused.

We shall see that the uncertain status of confidential information—is it property, and if so is the property legal or equitable?—is bound up with the question whether any form of relief should be given against "innocent" defendants.[77] In this connection the comparison with the rules for the established forms of intellectual property needs to be remembered; it has sometimes been ignored in the past.

(4) Account of profits

2–43 Equity never trespassed so directly upon the prerogatives of the common law courts as to award damages for common law wrongs.[78] However, as a corollary of the injunction, it might order a defendant to account to a plaintiff for profits made from wrong-doing such as the infringement of an intellectual property right.[79] This is not a notional computation as with damages, but an investigation of actual accounts,[80] which may incidentally afford the plaintiff a sight of customers' names and other information about the defendant.[81] Nonetheless it is a laborious and expensive procedure and is infrequently resorted to. If the protected subject-matter is part of the article sold, or a mark used to sell it, the plaintiff is entitled to the whole profit on each infringement.[82] If the defendant's wrong merely enables him

---

[74] *Lancer Boss v. Henley Fork-Lift* [1975] R.P.C. 307. But note the provision that (in the case of patents and registered designs) it is not enough to mark goods "patent", "registered", etc., without adding the number.

[75] *Byrne v. Statist* (n. 73, above).

[76] *Spalding v. Gamage* (1915) 32 R.P.C. 273; *Gillette v. Edenwest* [1994] R.P.C. 279.

[77] See paras 8–49 *et seq.*, below.

[78] Equity did, however, order payments to rectify equitable wrongs, such as breach of trust. This jurisdiction is now being claimed as the basis for equitable damages: see para. 8–46, below.

[79] This was treated as accepted by Lord Eldon, *Hogg v. Kirby* (1803) 8 Ves.Jun. 215 at 223.

[80] It is thus a personal remedy against unjust enrichment: see esp. *A.G. v. Observer* [1990] 1 A.C. 109 at 262, 265–267, 288, 293–294.

[81] There is a discretion to order discovery concerning infringing acts in relation to damages as well as an account: *Smith Kline & French v. Doncaster Pharmaceuticals* [1989] F.S.R. 401; and see *Minnesota Mining v. Jeffries* [1993] F.S.R. 189, FC (Aust.).

[82] *Peter Pan Manufacturing Corporation v. Corsets Silhouette* [1963] 3 All E.R. 402; *Potton v. Yorkclose* [1990] F.S.R. 11; *Celanese Int. v. BP Chemicals* [1999] R.P.C. 203. In a trade mark case, the plaintiff is entitled to the profit on each item wrongly sold—he does not have to prove that the sale was to a deceived customer: *Lever v. Goodwin* (1887) 36 Ch.D. 1, CA; if necessary the number may have to be reached by approximation: *My Kinda Town v. Soll* [1982] F.S.R. 147; *House of Spring Gardens v. Point Blank* [1985] F.S.R. 327 at 345. For expenditure properly deductible in calculating the defendant's costs, and the entitlement of the plaintiff to lost opportunity profits, see *Dart Industries v. Decor* (1993) 179 C.L.R. 101, HC (Aust.); *Zupanovich v. Beale* (1995) 32 I.P.R. 339.

to save expense in production, the plaintiff may only be entitled to the amount by which the saving increases the profit.[83]

In principle, the account will give a better recompense than damages when the defendant has been making profits that the plaintiff would not himself have made,[84] but if the case is an exceptional one, exemplary damages may achieve much the same result.[85] It used to be said that the plaintiff must elect either for damages or an account, upon the theory that by seeking an account the plaintiff adopted the defendant's acts as his own,[86] but this explanation is now dubious.[87] The better principle is merely that in respect to any one infringement the plaintiff should not be entitled to be both reimbursed and compensated.[88]

A modern view of account is that it is restitutionary in character, aiming **2–44** to put paid to an unjust enrichment to the defendant at the plaintiff's expense. It is only a personal, not a proprietary, remedy, such as would give the plaintiff title in equity to particular funds or property representing the profit.[89] To achieve such an outcome, it would be necessary to impose a constructive trust. While equitable interests may be called in aid to give effect to the intended arrangements concerning the ownership of intellectual property (as may, for instance, be the proper implication to be drawn from a commission to create a copyright work), a trust is not imposed by way of remedy attaching to the tortious profits of infringing intellectual property. But here the equitable character of breach of confidence makes for complications. Given in particular the proximity of that obligation to fiduciary duties, it is conceivable that constructive trusts may form part of the court's remedial armoury for protecting trade and similar secrets.[90] It is hard to see why this should be so where technical know-how has been misappropriated yet not so when a patent is infringed. The law's strongest incentives go to inventions which qualify for patents.

---

[83] *United Horse Shoe v. Stewart* (n. 52, above) at 266–267. *cf.* the calculation of damages on the basis of actual sales lost, where the plaintiff can claim the whole of his own lost profit: see para. 2–40, above.

[84] As far as the innocent defendant is concerned there are curious differences: the patent infringer is protected to the same extent as he is from paying damages, whereas the opposite applies in the case of copyright and unregistered design right: *Wienerworld v. Vision Video* [1998] F.S.R. 832. Since an account is discretionary, the innocence of the defendant may always be a reason for refusing it: *e.g. Seager v. Copydex (No. 1)* [1967] 2 All E.R. 415, but *cf. Edelsten v. Edelsten* (1863) 1 De G.J. & S. 185.

[85] For the conditions, see para. 2–39, above.

[86] *e.g. Neilson v. Betts* (1871) L.R. 5 HL 1; *De Vitre v. Betts* (1873) L.R. 6 HL 319; *Sutherland v. Caxton* [1936] Ch. 323 at 336. See also para. 11–61, below.

[87] *cf.* the House of Lords' rejection as fictitious of the same theory for waiver of tort: *United Australia v. Barclays Bank* [1941] A.C. 1; Street, *Law of Damages* (1962), pp. 263–266.

[88] This appears to follow from the formula in PA 1977, s. 61(2).

[89] And identified if necessary, by equitable tracing rules.

[90] See para. 8–51, below, esp. for the difficult *Lac Minerals* case.

(5) "Franking"

2–45 Intellectual property rights relate to a series of stages in the commercial life of products—their creation and preparation for sale, their distribution down the chain to ultimate users; and in some cases also to their use, their resale second-hand, etc. The question accordingly arises whether monetary payments for infringement, paid on goods in respect of an early step in the chain, "franks" them as legitimate thereafter. It has been held, both in relation to damages and an account of profits for patent infringement, that no such legal effect is brought about. Actions may be maintained in relation to later wrongful acts.[91] Where there has been a settlement, any payment will not be understood to "frank" infringement unless this is an agreed term.[92]

(6) Remedies for acts which are not themselves infringements

2–46 Frequently the acts which infringe intellectual property have come to be defined in terms first of a primary act or acts and then secondary acts. The latter may take the form of preparation for completion of a primary act (for example providing parts for making a patented invention[93]) or they may consist of consequential acts, for example importing or marketing goods which fall to be treated as infringements or as bearing infringing marks.[94] In those circumstances, legislation settles that the law should extend its remedies against these surrounding activities. However, though in some cases there will be no liability, or remedies will be limited, unless the defendant is shown to know or to have reason to believe that infringing goods were involved.[95]

Intriguing questions arise about the extent to which legal or equitable remedies may encompass acts or events which do not themselves constitute primary, contributory or consequential infringement.

> In *Chappell v. Graphophone Co.*,[96] according to the law then in effect, it was infringement of musical copyright to copy sheet music but not to record the work from it. A defendant who did both these things was held liable to deliver up the records it had made for destruction. This form of relief was not confined merely to the sheet music.[97]

---

[91] *Catnic Components v. Evans* [1983] F.S.R. 401; *Codex v. Racal-Milgo* [1984] F.S.R. 87.
[92] *Lewis Trusts v. Bamber Stores* [1982] F.S.R. 281; *Rose Records v. Motown Records* [1983] F.S.R. 361.
[93] See paras 16–17 *et seq.*, below.
[94] See para. 17–86, below.
[95] For instance, see para. 11–29, below.
[96] [1914] 2 Ch. 745, CA See also *Crossley v. Derby Gas-Lights* (1838) 3 My. & Cr. 428 (injunction); Prescott (1991) 54 M.L.R. 451.
[97] *cf.* the decompilation of a computer program: paras 13–37 *et seq.*, below.

In *Gerber v. Lectra*,[98] the infringer of a patent for automatic cutting machines was held liable (*inter alia*) for the "associated" damages arising from lost profits on computer-aided design systems sold with the machines, on spare parts for them, on servicing contracts, and for putting itself, through infringement, in a position to make sales after expiry of the patent.

As already noted, the latter decision was based on the concepts of foreseeability and causation, but was made subject to considerations of public and social policy.[99] Policy in intellectual property matters has always been to balance a fair scope for the right-owner against a general freedom of competitors to imitate what is not within the bounds of the right. It is this policy which should remain the governing consideration.[1] It should not become wrongful to write a non-infringing sequel to a novel by virtue merely of having made a single copy of the novel from which to work; nor wrongful to make a non-infringing variation of a patented invention by virtue merely of having made commercial use of the invention once.

3. SECURING EVIDENCE OF INFRINGEMENT

Intellectual property litigation is mostly governed by the general principles **2–47** of civil procedure[2] and no attempt can here be made to review the whole gamut of relevant rules.[3] But given the great significance of the law's machinery in this field, two things can be attempted. In this section, attention is given to procedures developed to help the plaintiff in amassing evidence for his case. Often enough it is difficult for him to know whom to sue or to discover what a particular competitor or pirate is doing. In the next section we look from the opposite direction—by considering what a defendant can do against a plaintiff who turns litigation into a war of nerves.

This section, then, is concerned with three aspects of the plaintiff's armoury. It concentrates particularly on recent developments designed to increase the strength of his position.

---

[98] [1997] R.P.C. 443, CA; Moss and Rogers [1997] E.I.P.R. 425. As to post-expiry damages, see also *Union Carbide v. BP Chemicals* [1999] R.P.C. 409; *Generics v. Smith Kline* [1997] I E.C.R. 3929, ECJ.

[99] Above, para. 2–39.

[1] As seems well-recognised in cases not applied in *Gerber: Polaroid v. Eastman Kodak* [1977] R.P.C. 379 at 394; *Corruplast v. George Harrison Agencies* [1978] R.P.C. 761 at 764, 765; *Catnic Components v. Hill & Smith* [1983] F.S.R. 512. See generally, *McGregor on Damages* (15th ed., 1988), paras 1707–1716.

[2] It should be noted, however, that patent and registered design actions receive their own treatment in the Rules of the Supreme Court; see especially RSC, O. 104.

[3] Reference should be made to the standard texts on the various intellectual property rights.

(1) Search order for inspection and other relief: Anton Piller order[4]

(a) *Requirements for the order*

2–48 In *Anton Piller v. Manufacturing Processes*,[5] the Court of Appeal approved a procedure that is of major practical importance to some owners of intellectual property rights. The plaintiff applies to the High Court or Patents County Court[6] *in camera* without any notice to the defendant, for an order that the defendant permit him (with his solicitor) to inspect the defendant's premises[7] and to seize, copy or photograph material relevant to the alleged infringement. The defendant may be required to deliver up infringing goods,[8] keep infringing stock or incriminating papers,[9] and even to give information, for instance, about his sources of supply, or the destination of stock passing through his hands. An injunction against infringement may be part of the order. The procedure, now to be known as a search order, is given statutory force by the Civil Procedure Act 1997, s. 7.[10]

The order will be made if the plaintiff (1) provides an extremely strong prima facie case of infringement, (2) shows that the damage, actual or potential, to him is very serious, and (3) provides clear evidence that the defendant has in his possession incriminating documents or things and that there is a real possibility that this material will be destroyed before any application *inter partes* can be made.[11] There are certain safeguards which

---

[4] See S. Gee, *Mareva Injunctions and Anton Piller Relief* (2nd ed., 1990); M. Dockray, *Anton Piller Orders* (1992); R.N. Ough and W. Fenley, *The Mareva Injunction and Anton Piller Order* (2nd ed. 1993).

[5] [1976] Ch. 55, [1976] R.P.C. 719; approving *EMI v. Pandit* [1975] 1 All E.R. 418. A slender line of earlier precedent existed: *e.g. East India Co. v. Kynaston* (1821) Bli.P.C. 153; *Hennessy v. Bohmann* [1877] W.N. 14.

[6] The jurisdiction given to all county courts in 1984 was removed in 1991: County Court Remedies Regulations 1991, S.I. 1991 No. 1222, reg. 3. As to the Patents County Court jurisdiction, see *McDonald v. Graham* [1994] R.P.C. 407.

[7] Orders covering any premises under the defendant's control are made only in exceptional circumstances: *Protector Alarms v. Maxim Alarms* [1979] F.S.R. 442. Orders have sometimes been made against those who have no premises, or whose names are not known: *EMI Records v. Kudhail* [1985] F.S.R. 36; *Tony Blain v. Splain* [1994] F.S.R. 497, SC (N.Z.); Barron [1996] E.I.P.R. 183. Against some of these, there is a self-help remedy available in copyright cases: see para. 2–27, above. Being an *ex parte* procedure, an *Anton Piller* order is not enforceable in other E.C. countries under the Brussels Judgments Convention, Art. 24: *Denilauler v. Couchet Frères* [1981] 1 C.M.L.R. 62. As for aid towards foreign proceedings, see, *e.g.* Dockray (n. 98, above) at 5.28.

[8] *Universal City v. Mukhtar* [1976] F.S.R. 252.

[9] *EMI v. Sarwar* [1977] F.S.R. 146, CA.

[10] See also the Civil Procedure Rules 1999, Part 25.

[11] *Anton Piller* case (n. 5, above).

are said to distinguish this sort of order from a search warrant[12]: the plaintiff's solicitor, who is an officer of the court, must attend,[13] and so in most cases must a supervising solicitor from another firm[14]; the defendant must be given time to think and must be informed of his right to consult his own solicitor and to apply to discharge the order.[15] The plaintiff must also give a cross-undertaking in damages. Subject to these, the defendant's refusal to allow the inspection is contempt of court (as well as in itself being evidence against him) and will be dealt with according to the circumstances.[16]

(b) *Dangers in the process*

"*Anton Piller*" orders have been a response to growing concern over the **2–49** current volume of sound recording, video and other copyright piracy and the counterfeiting of popular trade marks, but they are equally available for instance, in breach of confidence cases.[17] Although the reassurance was at first given that the orders would be rare,[18] the procedure is regularly used, and it has considerably increased the speed and effectiveness of civil process. Yet it raises the spectre which in former times made the courts so fearful of the general warrant to search. The proceedings turn upon the plaintiff's evidence alone and they occur *in camera*. If a single judge is satisfied prima facie that there is infringement and a likelihood of serious injury, the plaintiff through his solicitor is empowered to launch his own attack on the defendant. Those executing the order are likely to believe that

---

[12] Ormrod L.J., *Anton Piller* case (n. 5, above), R.P.C. 719 at 726; and see Lord Denning M.R. (at 752) who adds that the inspection must do no real harm to the defendant or his case. On the basic requirements, note also the *Island Records* and *Carlin* cases (para. 2–16, above). It seems unlikely that *ex parte* orders concerning premises out of the jurisdiction (even in Scotland) will be made: see *Protector v. Maxim* (n. 7, above); *Altertext v. Advanced Data* [1985] 1 All E.R. 395; but *cf.* the *inter partes* proceedings in *Cook Industries v. Galliher* [1979] Ch. 439.

[13] *Anton Piller* case (n. 5, above), at 724, 726.

[14] As now provided for in the Practice Direction (Mareva Injunctions and Anton Piller Orders), July 28, 1994 (text with annexed draft Orders: N.L.J., August 12, 1994, p. 1134); Hall [1995] E.I.P.R. 50. It is also required that, where the premises are likely to be occupied by an unaccompanied woman, one of those attending must be a woman, and certain other restrictions are imposed: see (B) 2, and Annex 1, Terms of Order. For the preceding criticism, see para. 2–50, below.

[15] Normally the defendant will have two hours during which he can prevent the search from starting (though not entry): Practice Direction, Annexes 1, 3. An *ex parte* application to discharge the order will not, however, be granted in the absence of strong evidence: *Hallmark Cards v. Image Arts* [1977] F.S.R. 150, CA. As to an appeal against the order, see *Bestworth v. Wearwell* [1979] F.S.R. 320.

[16] Even a defendant whose contempt is not very serious may have to pay the plaintiff's costs on the application on an indemnity basis: *Chanel v. Three Pears* [1979] F.S.R. 393. *cf.* the *Hallmark* case (n. 15, above).

[17] *Anton Piller* itself concerned copyright and confidential information in a machine. See also *Vapormatic v. Sparex* [1976] F.S.R. 461—confidential list of customers ordered to be removed.

[18] Ormrod L.J., *Anton Piller* case [1976] R.P.C. 719 at 725.

right is on their side and that they must put on a show of aggression if they are to secure what their client needs and deserves. In the tensions generated by the surprise service of the order, a defendant will need considerable temerity if he is to seek legal advice and challenge the basis on which the order was made. As a measure of "privatisation" the order is remarkable: a non-state agency is employed in a direct infraction of personal liberties; and, more than that, those executing the order act for the very person who can least be expected to preserve a measure of objectivity and sense of proportion.

2–50 Because of its inherent unfairness, the *Anton Piller* order became the subject of increasing concern in the later 1980s.[19] Many of the criticisms went to the undue eagerness with which it was sometimes executed. A double threat would be produced by having the police simultaneously execute a search warrant procured on suspicion of criminal conduct such as dealing in obscene material. This practice was challenged under the European Convention on Human Rights, Article 8, which contains a guarantee of respect for private life and the home.[20] Since Article 8 allows for exceptions where public authority acts "in accordance with the law" and (*inter alia*) "for the protection of the rights and freedoms of others", the European Court of Human Rights found that the *Anton Piller* process was in principle justifiable, case law having substantially delimited its scope. The Court was critical of the execution of the order in the particular case,[21] although it did not in the end find this "disproportionate to the legitimate aim pursued" against a commercial infringer of film copyright. Nor did it accept an argument that the order could only be legitimate if executed by, or in the presence of, a court official.

The tenor of that judgment was reflected in Hoffmann J.'s call for

> "careful balancing of, on the one hand, the plaintiff's right to recover his property or to preserve important evidence against, on the other hand, violation of the privacy of a defendant who has had no opportunity to put his side of the case . . . To borrow a useful concept from the jurisprudence of the European Community, there must be proportionality between the perceived threat to the plaintiff's rights and the remedy granted."[22]

---

[19] See esp. Scott J., *Columbia Pictures v. Robinson* [1986] 3 All E.R. 331 (describing the process as "draconian and essentially unfair"); Hoffmann J., *Lock International v. Beswick* [1989] 1 W.L.R. 1268 at 1281; Nichols V.-C., *Universal Thermosensors v. Hibben* [1992] 1 W.L.R. 840 at 854. In its first flush, some 500 *Anton Piller* orders were being made a year, but as criticism grew this number fell considerably. By 1992 it was a tenth of that number: see the Consultation Paper (n. 14, above). The reduction in numbers must also have reflected its success as a weapon.

[20] *Chappell v. United Kingdom* [1989] F.S.R. 617.

[21] As had been the Court of Appeal on a motion for contempt of the undertakings in the *Anton Piller* order by those executing it, a motion which likewise did not on balance succeed.

[22] *Lock International v. Beswick* (n. 19, above).

In 1992, Nicholls V.-C. showed such concern over the effects of carrying **2–51** out the order[23] that the Lord Chancellor's Department issued a Consultation Paper[24] and from this followed the Practice Direction of 1994.[25] The Direction obliges the judge making the order either to require a private watch-dog in the form of the supervising solicitor already mentioned, or else to state why this is not appropriate. The added cost which this entails was considered to be an unavoidable burden.[26]

(c) *Challenges to the order*

Accordingly the courts strive to be watchful for plaintiffs who go to excess, **2–52** seeking, for instance, a means of shutting out the defendant from all business, legitimate as well as illegitimate. There is now a mandatory return date, when the court examines the execution of the order. The ground on which defendants have regularly challenged orders is the plaintiff's failure fully to disclose all material circumstances. This, it has been said, should err on the side of excess; for it is for the court, not the plaintiff's advisers, to decide whether the order is justified.[27] It is no answer to a charge of inadequate disclosure that enough was shown to justify the making of the order.[28] Moreover, if business records have been seized, they should not be retained until trial, but should be returned after necessary information has been extracted from them; and where infringing material has been seized it should be handed over to the defendant's solicitor, once he is on the record, upon his undertaking to keep it in safe custody and produce it, if required, at the trial.[29]

Even if the order is open to challenge, for instance because of inadequate **2–53** disclosure, it is for the court, not the defendant, to decide whether it should be discharged.[30] One objection which the Court will not accept is that if a defendant is obliged to reveal information he risks personal violence from criminal associates.[31] Accordingly it remains contempt of court to refuse to

---

[23] *Universal Thermosensors v. Hibben* (n. 19, above), which accepted the uncompromising criticisms of Dockray and Laddie (1990) 106 L.Q.R. 601, including their proposal for a supervising solicitor. See also Davenport (1992) 109 L.Q.R. 555; Russell [1992] E.I.P.R. 243.

[24] *Anton Piller Orders* (No. 181, 1992).

[25] See n. 14, above; Davies [1996] Civ.Just.Q. 17. The supervising solicitor must make a report on execution, to be returned to the Court.

[26] But the role of this person is problematic: Willoughby [1999] Civ. Just. Q. 103.

[27] See esp. *Lock International* (n. 19, above); *Naf Naf v. Dickson* [1993] F.S.R. 424; *Intergraph v. Solid Systems CAD Services* [1993] F.S.R. 617.

[28] *Wardle Fabrics v. Myristis* [1984] F.S.R. 263.

[29] *Columbia Picture Industries v. Robinson* [1986] 3 All E.R. 338 at 371. It is also wrong to procure wider seizure than the order allows without the defendant having a solicitor's advice.

[30] *ibid.*, at 372–375. Even if a wrongly obtained order has been executed, it will be discharged: *Booker McConnell v. Plascow* [1985] R.P.C. 475, CA unless that would amount to an empty gesture without practical effect: *Columbia Picture Industries*, at 377–379. It remains in the court's discretion to decide whether to restrain use of implicatory information wrongly obtained: *Naf Naf* case (n. 27, above).

[31] *Coca-Cola v. Gilbey* [1996] F.S.R. 23, CA.

comply with the order.[32] The defendant is protected by the discretion on costs and the plaintiff's cross-undertaking in damages. If the order was not justified or its execution was oppressive—whether or not it is subsequently discharged—the defendant will be entitled to compensatory damages for injury to his business; and possibly also to aggravated damages for the "contumely or affront" in the way the proceedings were used against him, and even to exemplary damages. The last are justified under the special case concerning wrongs committed by government servants, given that the plaintiff's solicitor is acting as a court officer.[33]

(d) *Self-incrimination*

2–54 The acute difficulties of balancing efficacy against fairness have surfaced equally over the element of "instant discovery"[34] in any *Anton Piller* order which requires answers on sources of supply or customers. Since these answers would in many cases furnish evidence of criminal conduct, defendants at first sought to plead in response a privilege against self-incrimination. The House of Lords upheld this plea in any case where there was more than a remote or fanciful chance that a serious charge, attracting heavy penalties, might result.[35] This meant that the privilege was available to those who ran substantial piracy operations and so were likely to be charged with conspiracy to defraud, as distinct from (say) a summary offence under the copyright or trade descriptions legislation, which might be appropriate against a street trader. Because the upshot was to offer a haven to those apparently most culpable, Parliament proved willing to intervene. Under section 72 of the Supreme Court Act 1981, in proceedings for infringement of intellectual property rights[36] or passing off, a defendant may after all be compelled to answer a question or comply with an order which would tend to expose him or her to proceedings for a related offence or recovery of a related penalty.[37] It is, however, not possible to use any statement or admission so procured in any equivalent criminal proceedings.[38]

---

[32] *Wardle* (n. 28, above); *Columbia Picture Industries* (n. 29, above) at 368.

[33] *Columbia Picture Industries* (n. 29, above) at 379–380; *Universal Thermosensors v. Hibben* [1992] 1 W.L.R. 840 at 854. The judge has power, on the return date, to assess damages at once: Practice Direction 4.

[34] Bridge L.J., *Rank Film v. Video Information* [1980] 2 All E.R. 283.

[35] *Rank Film v. Video Information* [1982] A.C. 380.

[36] This, the first statutory use of the term, encompasses "patent, trade mark, copyright, registered design, technical or commercial information or other intellectual property": Supreme Court Act 1981, s. 73(5). The privilege may still be claimed in other cases: see *Cobra Golf v. Rata (No. 2)* [1997] F.S.R. 317.

[37] The privilege is taken away more generally where proceedings are being brought against apprehended infringement, rather than against acts which have already occurred: s. 73(5); *Universal City v. Hubbard* [1984] R.P.C. 43, CA. But it seems that documents wrongly seized, where the privilege should still have been upheld, do not have to be returned: Cumming-Bruce L.J. at 47–48.

[38] *i.e.* such proceedings as are no longer a justification for upholding the privilege against incrimination by virtue of the section.

With such a patchwork of exceptions, the privilege itself is not easily **2–55** justified as a general rule; yet it still applies in cases of fraud outside the scope of the statutory exceptions, and notably where a defendant is likely to be prosecuted for conspiracy to defraud.[39] Where it applies, it has a perverse effect: it protects most readily when the evidence against the person concerned is really damning and is therefore likely to result in prosecution for a serious offence.[40] Either it should be restored as the general rule in a real sense, or it should be replaced by the approach now used in the exceptional cases: the incriminating answers must be given (and other facts revealed), although the information may not then be used as evidence in criminal proceedings.[41]

(2) Freezing injunction for the retention of assets: *Mareva* injunction[42]

The development of the *Anton Piller* order has coincided with another, **2–56** more general evolution in interlocutory procedure. The *Mareva* injunction—now to be known as a freezing injunction—is directed, not to the uncovering and preserving of "fragile" evidence, but to the retention of assets belonging to the defendant which may be needed to satisfy judgment in the action, particularly if they may otherwise be removed from the jurisdiction.[43] Orders are frequently made which contain both *Anton Piller* and *Mareva* terms.[44] These may relate to bank accounts and other financial assets.[45] Equally, there have been orders directed to the seizure of specified valuables, such as cars, in which, according to evidence, the proceeds of infringement have been invested. Just as a defendant is permitted an allowance for living expenses out of financial assets that are subject to a *Mareva* order, so also, where the order relates to other assets, he will not be deprived of things needed for living and conducting legitimate trade.[46]

As with *Anton Piller* orders, the courts tended to relax the requirements **2–57** as they became more familiar with their use. To begin with, they required proof of an extremely strong prima facie case, but that later became a

---

[39] *Tate Access Floors v. Boswell* [1990] 3 All E.R. 303; and see *Societdad Nacional (Sonangol) v. Lundqvist* [1991] 2 W.L.R. 280.

[40] See, *e.g.* Lord Templeman, *Istel v. Tully* [1992] 3 W.L.R. 344 at 350, HL.

[41] This approach is favoured in the Lord Chancellor's Department's Consultation Papers on Self-Incrimination and *Anton Piller* Orders.

[42] Civil Procedure Rules 1999, Part 25. See the works by Gee, Dockray and Ough and Fenley (n. 4, above); Zuckermann (1992) 109 L.Q.R. 560.

[43] A number of cases have manifested a desire to aid a plaintiff in searching for the defendant's assets world-wide: *Babanhaft v. Bassatne* [1989] 2 W.L.R. 232, CA; *Republic of Haiti v. Duvalier* [1989] 2 W.L.R. 261, CA; *Derby v. Weldon (No. 1, Nos. 3 and 4)* [1989] 2 W.L.R. 276 at 412, CA; *Grupo Torras v. Sheikh Fahad Mohammed Al-Sabah* [1995] 1 Lloyd's Rep. 374, Q.B.D. See also Collins (1989) 105 L.Q.R. 262; Capper (1991) 54 M.L.R. 329.

[44] Equally they may well contain an interlocutory injunction.

[45] In order to ensure efficacy, the court may allow cross-examination on affidavits in defence: *House of Spring Gardens v. Waite* [1985] F.S.R. 173, CA.

[46] *CBS United Kingdom v. Lambert* [1983] F.S.R. 123, CA.

"good arguable case"[47]; the need to identify the defendant's assets in advance was by-passed, as was the need to show that he was likely deliberately to dissipate his assets.[48] There is so far no requirement that a supervising solicitor be appointed, but the court does not itself supervise the continuance of the order with any great attention. Yet the effect of such an order, going as it does to the defendant's assets as a whole, and giving the applicant some real opportunity to convert an entitlement into a preferred claim, is capable of inflicting very considerable harm. A strong case has been made for it also to be curbed.[49]

(3) Discovery of names: *Norwich Pharmacal* action

2–58 Sometimes the only lead that a right-owner can pick up about infringing goods is that they are passing through the hands of some person in the course of transit. That person may, however, not be infringing and may not even know that others have infringed or are likely to do so. The court may order such a person to disclose the names of the consignors or consignees responsible, if this is the only way for the plaintiff to discover whom he should act against and if the person against whom the order is made is shown (however unwittingly) to be facilitating the wrongful acts.[50] In *Norwich Pharmacal v. Commissioner of Customs and Excise*,[51] an order was made against the Commissioners of Customs and Excise to reveal the names of importers of a patented drug, which their published records showed to have been imported. The order, which is discretionary, is not confined to such circumstances.[52] For instance, a television company was ordered to reveal the name of a "mole" within British Steel, who was acting in admitted breach of confidence in revealing how the Board was acting against strikers. The admitted purpose of the proceedings was to procure the mole's dismissal, not to sue him.[53] Where goods are involved which are still being held, an injunction restraining their removal may also be granted.[54]

---

[47] See Lord Denning M.R., *Rasu Maritima v. Perusahan* [1978] 1 Q.B. 644 at 661.

[48] See *Nimenia v. Trave* [1983 1 W.L.R. 1412.

[49] Willoughby and Connal [1997] E.I.P.R. 479.

[50] *Jade Engineering v. Antiference Window Systems* [1996] F.S.R. 461; *CHC Software v. Hopkins & Wood* [1993] F.S.R. 241.

[51] [1974] A.C. 133, [1974] R.P.C. 101, HL; *Jade Engineering (Coventry) Ltd v. Antiference Window Systems Ltd* [1996] F.S.R. 461. The costs of the proceedings may be recovered as damages from the infringers thus exposed: *Morton-Norwich v. Intercen (No. 2)* [1981] F.S.R. 337. An importing or exporting agent might equally be subject to such an order: see *Orr v. Diaper* (1876) 4 Ch.D. 23; *Upmann v. Forester* (1885) 24 Ch.D. 231. Information obtained against one person may be used in the pursuit of others: *Levi Strauss v. Barclays* [1993] F.S.R. 179.

[52] It will not be granted if unduly prejudicial: *Sega Enterprises v. Alca Electronics* [1982] F.S.R. 516; *cf. AIRC v. PPL* [1993] E.M.L.R. 181 at 244; *Romeike & Curtice Ltd v. Newspaper Licensing Agency* [1999] E.M.L.R. 142.

[53] *British Steel v. Granada* [1981] A.C. 1096.

[54] See Buckley L.J., *Norwich Pharmacal* case [1972] R.P.C. 743 at 771.

(4) Discovery, interrogatories, inspection

English courts have generally been careful to protect defendants against **2–59** speculative suits that are no more than "fishing expeditions"—proceedings begun to find out what, if anything, might really be claimed.[55] Accordingly, in our field, infringement actions cannot be launched effectively unless the plaintiff can specify in his statement of claim particulars of at least one act of infringement.[56] If he does not give them and does not comply with any order for further and better particulars he will be unable to defend himself on a motion to strike out pleadings or action.[57]

Provided that he can show enough to repel attacks on his pleadings, the **2–60** plaintiff will carry his case forward to the stage of pre-trial preparations. As in other types of civil litigation, discovery of documents and the administration of interrogatories are steps which on occasion may provide important evidence or admissions.[58] In the United States of America such steps have been inflated into a form of discovery that allows wide-ranging preliminary cross-examination of party by party.[59] That has yet to occur in England, but some expansion has occurred of the range of documents which must be made available during discovery in a complex patent action.[60] If the documents discovered contain confidential information, the other party may be restrained from using the information for purposes such as revelations in the press[61] or further litigation.

---

[55] While power exists to order discovery before delivery of a statement of claim, it will not be exercised readily (*RHM Foods v. Bovril* [1983] R.P.C. 275; *Lubrizol v. Esso* [1993] F.S.R. 64); likewise with inspection (*Smith Myers v. Motorola* [1991] F.S.R. 62; *Dun & Bradstreet v. Typesetting Facilities* [1992] F.S.R. 320).

[56] Equally if a defendant ripostes with a defence or counterclaim which turns on issues of fact, he may be required to give particulars of allegations; for instance, that the plaintiff's alleged trade mark is in fact common to the trade. If his response in a patent suit is to seek revocation of a patent he will be obliged to give particulars of his objections to validity: see Ency. PL, para. 10–107.

It has been said that a plaintiff who brings a motion for interlocutory relief is entitled, on seeing the defendant's evidence, to apply to stand the motion over until trial of the action without costs being immediately awarded against him: *Jeffrey v. Shelana* [1976] F.S.R. 54. But this may invite a form of fishing and a later Court has held that the award of costs is always a matter of discretion: *Simons Records v. W.E.A. Records* [1980] F.S.R. 35 at 36. See also *Rockwell v. Serck* [1988] F.S.R. 187.

[57] Equally he will not be permitted to seek discovery or deliver interrogatories: *AG für Autogene Aluminium v. London Aluminium* [1919] 2 Ch. 67.

[58] Discovery concerning the whole of a defendant's trading operation, in order to secure evidence going purely to his credit, is oppressive and will not be allowed: *Ballatine v. Dixon* [1975] R.P.C. 111; *E.G. Music v. S.F. (Film Distributors)* [1978] F.S.R. 121; *cf. Mood Music v. de Wolfe* [1976] Ch. 119.

[59] For the impact of this procedural development in patent actions, see White, *Patent Litigation: Procedure and Tactics* (1979), paras 5.01—5.06.

[60] *American Cyanamid v. Ethicon* [1977] F.S.R. 593 at 602, CA.

[61] *Distillers v. Times Newspapers* [1975] 1 All E.R. 41; *Home Office v. Harman* [1983] A.C. 280; *Wilden Pump Engineering Co. v. Fusfield* [1985] F.S.R. 159, CA This applies equally to prejudicial material uncovered under an *Anton Piller* order, which carries an implied

2–61 Beyond this there are special procedures for cases involving industrial techniques. The plaintiff may need to discover what the defendant is doing; but the defendant may fear that inspection by him will reveal the defendant's own secrets—a fear that, in the race to get ahead, is sometimes acute. The Court has power to order inspection even against this sort of objection.[62] But while it will not require first to be satisfied prima facie that the defendant is infringing,[63] it may need to be shown that there are "formidable grounds", rather than a mere suspicion.[64] It may try to alleviate the defendant's anxieties by requiring an independent expert to make the inspection.[65] If such a person could not make a properly informed inspection, then it may have to be done by the plaintiff and his advisers; but possibly on condition that nothing is copied or taken away and that all involved are placed under obligations to respect confidence.[66]

4. DELAYED AMBUSH AND SELECTIVE ACTION

2–62 In the main it is not isolated acts of infringement but runs of production that provoke the owner of intellectual property rights into taking action. Accordingly, a defendant's stake is likely to be high; and it may well become higher if proceedings against him are delayed until he has established commercial production and tied himself to distribution arrangements. While there are incentives that will induce right-owners in many circumstances to move as quickly as possible (in particular, the chance to secure interlocutory relief)[67] these may for some reason have little or no force. Not only may there be tactical advantages in delay, it may also seem more damaging to proceed not against the manufacturer who is the source of the alleged infringement, but against his wholesale or resale distributors or even the ultimate users or consumers. In all this, the legal limitations upon a plaintiff's freedom of action can have great importance, and the most important of these limitations, many of them matters of general law, deserve to be sketched in.

---

undertaking not to use it for a collateral purpose; but the court has an ultimate jurisdiction in the matter: *Crest Homes v. Marks* [1987] F.S.R. 305, HL; *CCE v. Hamlin Slowe* [1986] F.S.R. 346. *Cobra Golf v. Rata (No. 2)* [1997] F.S.R. 317. It is proper to use the material to arrest assets in another jurisdiction: *Bayer v. Winter (No. 2)* [1986] F.S.R. 357; but see *Grapha Holdings v. Quebecor Printing* [1996] F.S.R. 711; *Chiron v. Evans Medical* [1997] F.S.R. 268.

[62] *Medway v. Doublelock* [1978] 1 All E.R. 1261; *Riddick v. Thames Board* [1977] 3 All E.R. 677, CA.

[63] *British Xylonite v. Fibrenyle* [1959] R.P.C. 252, CA. To hold that there was a prima facie case might embarrass the trial judge.

[64] *Wahl v. Buhler-Miag* [1979] F.S.R. 183; and see *Electrolux Northern v. Black & Decker* [1996] F.S.R. 595.

[65] cf. *Printers & Finishers v. Holloway* [1964] 3 All E.R. 54 (inspection of plaintiff's plant for defendant: elements claimed to be secret must be pointed out).

[66] *Centri-Spray v. Cera* [1979] F.S.R. 175; *Roussel Uclaf v. ICI* [1990] F.S.R. 25.

[67] See para. 2–32, above.

(1) Limitation of actions

The question here is: within what period after a particular infringement has **2–63** been perpetrated must a writ be issued? The various infringement actions in our field, being tortious in character, must normally be begun within six years of the wrongful act.[68] The same applies to actions based upon breach of contract. Only the action for breach of confidence may differ (when not founded in contract) because of its equitable origin: probably the only principle is that a period of too great a delay (*laches*) must not be allowed to lapse.[69]

An action which is commenced within the limitation period, but then allowed to stagnate, may be struck out for want of prosecution. Under current practice, this will only be done if there is real prejudice to the defendant as well as inordinate delay.[70] Such prejudice might arise if witnesses in a patent action would have to testify to the state of an art which has receded a considerable distance in time.[71]

(2) Acquiescence

Beyond the limitation periods for particular wrongs lies a further question: **2–64** if a defendant has been left to pursue a course of infringement for a substantial period of time, can the right-owner be taken to have consented to its continuance? If so, no part of the defendant's activity, even the most recent, is actionable. This consent may be expressly given or it may be implied from the circumstances; it may occur before, at the time of, or after the infringing act. Conduct alone can create an implied licence in some circumstances. Where the plaintiff represents, expressly or impliedly, that the defendant's conduct is not an infringement, he will thereafter be estopped from asserting his right.[72] A party may not deny that which, knowingly or unknowingly, he has allowed or encouraged another to assume to his detriment.[73] In such a case there is no need to show any element of delay.

At least when the question is whether an injunction should be granted in support of a legal right, it may be enough to prove delay by itself if the delay is "inordinate"; or delay coupled with "something . . . to encourage

---

[68] Limitation Act 1939, s. 2(1). There are exceptions for cases of mistake and fraud: see generally, 28 *Halsbury Laws of England* (4th ed.), paras 16 *et seq.* The rule applies to amendments alleging additional acts of infringement: *Sorata v. Gardex* [1984] F.S.R. 81.

[69] See para. 2–64, below.

[70] *Birkett v. James* [1978] A.C. 297, HL; *Compagnie Française de Télévision v. Thorn* [1978] R.P.C. 735, CA; *Bestworth v. Wearwell* [1986] R.P.C. 527; *Department of Transport v. Smaller* [1989] A.C. 1197, HL.

[71] *Horstman Gear v. Smiths Industries* [1979] F.S.R. 461.

[72] Cotton L.J., *Proctor v. Bennis* (1886) 36 Ch.D. 740 at 758–761.

[73] Oliver J., *Taylor Fashions v. Liverpool Victoria* [1982] 1 Q.B. 133; *Film Investors v. Home Video Channel* [1997] E.M.L.R. 347.

the wrongdoer to believe that he does not intend to rely upon his strict legal rights, and the wrongdoer must have acted to his prejudice in that belief".[74]

(3) Estoppels of record (*res judicata*)[75]

2–65 In order to give finality and to prevent a person from repeatedly asserting either an unsubstantiable right or the freedom to act in contravention of another's right, estoppels of record may be raised against him in various circumstances. Three kinds should be distinguished.

(a) *Judgment in rem*

2–66 Certain types of judgment bind all persons and not merely the parties to the action. In our field, an order revoking a patent, registered design or registered trade mark—the rights that depend upon grant—may be relied upon by all the world against the former right-owner. By contrast a decision that a plaintiff has no copyright, that a patent is valid or that a trade mark is properly registered can only have a binding effect on the other parties to the action and their privies.[76] The judgment is *in personam* and falls for consideration under the next heads.

(b) *Cause of action estoppel*

2–67 If A sues B alleging a particular cause of action upon pleaded facts and he loses, he will subsequently be estopped from suing upon the same cause of action. Suppose, for instance, the action is for passing off and A fails to provide sufficient evidence that the public was likely to be deceived by the defendant's acts into believing that it was getting goods of the plaintiff; or he unsuccessfully claims a reputation with the public as manufacturer when he might have succeeded on a claim to be known as a distributor; or a general rule of law is held to preclude his claim. In each of these circumstances, a second case based on the same facts would be precluded, if

---

[74] Goff L.J., *Bulmer v. Bollinger* [1978] R.P.C. 79 at 134–136, referring especially to *Electrolux v. Electrix* (1954) 71 R.P.C. 23; *Cluett-Peabody v. McIntyre* [1958] R.P.C. 335. In *Vine Products v. Mackenzie* [1969] R.P.C. 1 at 25–26, Cross J. held that the defence might arise, even though the plaintiff did not appreciate that the law afforded him any civil remedy; but *cf. Willmott v. Barber* (1880) 15 Ch. D. 96. For acquiescence as a reason for refusing an account of profits, see *International Scientific Communications v. Pattison* [1979] F.S.R. 429.

[75] This is a complex subject. See generally, Spencer Bower and Turner, *The Doctrine of Res Judicata* (2nd ed., 1969); 15 *Halsbury's Laws of England* (4th ed.), paras 1527 *et seq.* The term *res judicata*, commonly applied to one or other aspect of the subject, is here avoided because of its ambiguous meaning.

[76] But certificates of contested validity may be granted for patents and registered designs and marks: PA 1977, s. 65; RDA 1949, s. 25; TMA 1994, s. 73. An unsuccessful challenge subsequently risks an award of solicitor-and-client costs (designs and marks), or even solicitor-and-non-client costs (patents).

the first judgment was final and not interlocutory.[77] Thus this category of estoppel may debar attempts to put the same case more persuasively, whether in point of evidence or legal argument; but it operates only where the cause of action is the same.[78]

(c) *Issue estoppel*

If a Court of necessity decides an issue of fact and gives a final judgment, **2–68** the loser is estopped from raising the issue a second time even upon a different cause of action.[79] In the case of such an issue estoppel, both the initial parties and their privies will be bound. The range of this "privity" is not wide. Where a number of enterprises are engaged in the evolution of a product from conception to marketing, and a question of (say) copyright infringement arises, the successors in title and the employees of any business will be treated as its privies, and probably also an assignee of its rights. But a design-creating firm and the manufacturer which it commissions to execute its designs are not privy.[80]

The manner in which issue estoppel may go further than cause of action **2–69** estoppel is illustrated by this: if it were decided that A and not B is the successor in title to a business by proceedings to establish ownership, in subsequent passing-off proceedings by A against B for misappropriation of the marks of the business, B could not reopen the question of A's ownership. But the issue must have been raised and not allowed to go by default—in this respect issue estoppel is narrower. In its wider aspect, issue estoppel has special importance for intellectual property. In this sphere, defendants frequently repeat the allegedly infringing act in the course of producing or marketing goods. Each new act may give rise to a distinct cause of action, so the cause of action estoppel may be too narrow to achieve the objective that the law sets itself.[81]

---

[77] Decisions in the course of examining a patent application (including third-party oppositions) have been held not to be final: see below, para. 4–29. Arguably, the same would apply to applications to register trade marks.

[78] In general, any matter is *res judicata* which is raised on the pleadings and falls within the terms of the order; but exceptionally, an explicit qualification in the judgment may be taken account of to limit the scope of the estoppel: *Patchett v. Sterling* (1954) 71 R.P.C. 61, CA.

[79] *Carl Zeiss v. Rayner & Keeler (No. 2)* [1967] 1 A.C. 853; *Chiron v. Organon Teknika (No. 14)* [1996] F.S.R. 701, CA; *Kirin-Amgen v. Boehringer Mannheim* [1997] F.S.R. 289, CA; *Hodgkinson & Corby v. Wards Mobility Services (No. 2)* [1998] F.S.R. 530, CA. Under the law before 1978, the conditional character of a decision to allow a patent application to proceed to grant despite opposition (see para. 4–22, below) meant that it was not final (see *Bristol Myers v. Beecham* [1978] F.S.R. 553 (Israel S.C.)). Now that a third party may challenge only after grant it may well be that an unsuccessful attack on validity before the Comptroller or in an EPO opposition would raise an estoppel. On the difficult questions which may arise when only one issue is appealed, see the *Bristol Myers* case (*cf.* at 562–563, 568–571).

[80] *Gleeson v. Wippell* [1977] F.S.R. 301; see also *Kirin Amgen* (above, n. 79).

[81] For an instance, see *Form Tubes v. Guinness* [1989] F.S.R. 41.

2–70   Both cause of action and issue estoppel may be raised in English proceedings upon the judgment of a foreign Court.[82] As intellectual property grows in significance as a supra-national commodity, so does the impact of this rule: litigating the same issue in several jurisdictions can be just as harassing as litigating it several times in one. Equally, the Courts are likely to approach this form of issue estoppel with caution, taking care to see that the issue was a basis for the foreign decision, rather than being merely collateral or obiter, and avoiding prejudice to a party who found it impracticable to fight the issue properly in the foreign jurisdiction.[83]

2–71   As already noted, the main intellectual property rights are territorial in character.[84] A French judgment, therefore, on (say) infringement of a French patent or copyright cannot give rise to a cause of action estoppel between the same proprietor of the equivalent British rights and the same defendant who is performing equivalent acts in England. Whether it might found an issue estoppel is less certain: the question remains unexplored in the case law.[85] Since the actual activities must be different, the issue would be concerned with the application of the law to equivalent facts. A finding of estoppel could scarcely be made unless the court was satisfied that the same legal principle fell to be applied. Given such arrangements as the European Patent Convention, it may now be possible to meet this criterion in some circumstances (for example, on the validity of patents granted by the European route in light of a prior publication or use).

(4) Actions concerning foreign intellectual property[86]

(a) Foreign infringements

2–72 English Courts have in the past refused to hear actions based on claims for alleged intellectual property infringement occurring in other countries. This was justified both by a jurisdictional rule of public policy and under the choice of law rule which called for "double actionability".

(a) The rule of public policy (the *Moçambique* rule)[87] abrogated jurisdiction over foreign torts where their character was "local" as opposed

---

[82] *Carl Zeiss* and *Bristol Myers* cases (n. 79, above).

[83] *Carl Zeiss* case at 917–918, *per* Lord Reid; and see at 948–949 (Lord Upjohn), and at 972 (Lord Wilberforce).

[84] See paras 1–30 *et seq.*, above.

[85] The Israel SC in the *Bristol Myers* case (n. 79, above), however, assumes the possibility in appropriate circumstances.

[86] See Wadlow, *Enforcement of Intellectual Property in European and International Law* (1998); Fawcett and Torremans, *Intellectual Property and Private International Law* (1998); Ginsburg, *The Private International Law of Copyright in an Era of Technological Change* (1999); *cf.* Ulmer, *Intellectual Property Rights and the Conflict of Laws* (1978). As to patents, see Stauder, von Rospatt (1998) 29 I.I.C. 497 at 504, 509.

[87] *British South Africa Co. v. Companhia de Moçambique* [1893] A.C. 602; applied in patent matters by the Australian High Court: *Potter v. Broken Hill Pty Ltd* (1906) 3 C.L.R. 479; *Norbert Steinhart v. Meth* (1960) 105 C.L.R. 440.

to "transitory." The primary category of "local" rights were those pertaining to land; but increasingly intellectual property was also treated as having the same close connection with its own territory.[88]

(b) The "double actionability" rule in private international law concerned torts in general. It arose because English courts chose to apply their own tort law to wrongs occurring abroad and therefore required as a condition that the action should also be wrongful by the law of the place where it occurred.[89] While that remained the general rule, in *Red Sea Insurance v. Bouygues* the Privy Council latterly admitted an exception under which, where an issue between the parties had its most significant relationship with an occurrence in another country, then the law of that country should be applied to it.[90] This qualification was in effect transformed into the prima facie rule by the Private International Law (Miscellaneous Provisions) Act 1995, Part III.

In a table-turning decision, *Pearce v. Ove Arup*, the Court of Appeal has **2–73** accepted a reversal of both the traditional rules concerning actions over foreign intellectual property.[91] The public policy rule, having already been abolished by statute in relation to land,[92] was held no longer to apply to intellectual property either. Alongside this, the "double actionability" rule was to be taken as abrogated by the *Red Sea* case: it was particularly appropriate to apply the local law to the foreign intellectual property wrong because of its territoriality. The position in the *Red Sea* case has in effect been affirmed by the Private International Law (Miscellaneous Provisions) Act 1995, section 11, which has effect from May 1, 1996.[93]

Provided that this decision holds up in future, it has become permissible to bring an action in England in respect of the infringement abroad of foreign intellectual property rights, no matter whether the country concerned is or is not a Member State of the E.U. or of the European Free Trade Agreement ("EFTA"). We shall, nonetheless, consider the position

---

[88] See esp. *Mölnlycke v. Procter & Gamble* [1992] R.P.C. 21 at 21, CA, *per* Dillon L.J. Because of it, the Brussels and Lugano Conventions (for which see below, para. 2–74) were previously regarded as introducitng an exception, which would opereate only as between states party to the Conventions: see *Pearce v. Ove Arup* [1997] F.S.R. 64 (Lloyd J.), *Coin Controls v. Suzo* [1997] F.S.R. 660 (Laddie J.); *Fort Dodge Animal Health v. Akzo* [1998] F.S.R. 222 at 226–227 (Laddie J.) and, by implication also the CA: *ibid.* at 239 ff.

[89] *Dicey and Morris on the Conflict of Laws* (12th ed., 1993) Rule 203, deriving from *Phillips v. Eyre* (1870) L.R. 6 Q.B. 1 at 28–29; *Boys v. Chaplin* [1971] A.C. 356.

[90] [1995] A.C. 190; the exception was foreshadowed in *Dicey and Morris*, Rule 203.

[91] [1999] F.S.R. 525. Since this appears to represent a dramatic reversal of attitude, it could always be reversed in the HL.

[92] Civil Jurisdiction and Judgments Act 1982, s. 2(1).

[93] The wrongful activity in the *Pearce* case occurred before this date: it was the infringement of copyright by erecting a building in Holland in accordance with architectural plans actually drawn in England. Hence the Court's decision was determined exclusively by the position at common law.

between EU/EFTA states first, since that is governed by the special arrangements of the Brussels and Lugano Conventions.

(b) *Jurisdiction: the Brussels and Lugano Conventions*

2-74 The Brussels and Lugano Conventions on Jurisdiction and Enforcement of Judgments in Civil and Commercial Matters operate between the E.U. and EFTA states. The Brussels Convention was first agreed in 1968 as a separate instrument by the six Member States of the European Economic Community. In the case of the United Kingdom it was given effect by the Civil Jurisdiction and Judgments Act 1982.[94] The Lugano Convention of 1989 extends the same arrangements to the EFTA countries outside the E.U.[95] and is put into municipal law by the Civil Jurisdiction and Judgments Act 1991. The purpose of the Conventions is to determine the international jurisdiction of courts in Community countries, so as to facilitate recognition and to introduce an expeditious procedure for securing enforcement of judgments, authentic instruments and Court settlements—this indeed is what the Convention's Preamble specifies. It is designed accordingly to ensure the equality and uniformity of rights and the persons concerned with them, in pursuit of the principle of legal certainty.[96]

As experience with cross-territory patent actions has now shown, the Conventions fall demonstrably short of this aim. The structure of the two Conventions is best understood by first looking at the three bases of jurisdiction which they allow:

(i) the preference for suit in the E.C. State of the defendant's "domicile", where such a connection exists;

(ii) the additional jurisdiction arising in the place of tortious harm; and

(iii) the exclusive jurisdiction over validity and associated matters where the right requires registration—which is reserved to the granting country.

Then come three further qualifying factors;

(iv) the rule concerning co-defendants;

(v) the rules on priority of jurisdiction in cases of *lis pendens* and related actions; and

(vi) the ability of other jurisdictions to take provisional measures.

---

[94] Note that the rule is in no way dependent on the domicile of the plaintiff; so it may be taken advantage of by a non-E.C. plaintiff.

[95] At present, Iceland, Norway and Switzerland. Lugano is in the same terms as Brussels and its Articles bear the same numbers. The Conventions contain provisions for interpretation by the ECJ under references equivalent to those of the E.C. Treaty, Art. 177.

[96] *Duijnstee v. Goderbauer* [1985] 1 C.M.L.R. 220, ECJ (a case concerned with entitlement to patents.

(i) **General jurisdiction: defendant's "domicile" in an E.C. State.** The first 2–75
principle of the Convention, specified in Article 2, is that an E.C. defendant
can be sued in a civil or commercial matter in the courts of his, her or its
"domicile". Unless an exception arises under some other Article, this is the
sole basis of jurisdiction.[97] "Domicile"—a matter for the law of the relevant
state[98]—in the United Kingdom means:

(i) in the case of an individual, that he or she is resident in, and has a
substantial connection with, the U.K.;

(ii) in the case of a company, the state in which it has its seat.[99]

This root provision has had a dramatic effect, in particular, upon patent
cases: actions for cross-border injunctions and other extra-territorial relief
have become regular features of life in some of the states concerned. If
there is only one defendant, or if all defendants share the same domicile,
the courts of that domicile have jurisdiction over an action claiming
infringement in any other EU/EFTA state and the principle of territoriality
will oblige them to apply the law of that other state to the question. The
Court may determine all such claims; hence Article 2 gives the widest
jurisdiction under the Conventions. Unfortunately, as we shall see, in more
complex cases that desirable end is easily subverted and the parties may
well perceive very different advantages for themselves in having the case
dealt with in one jurisdiction rather than another.

(ii) **Special jurisdiction: place of tortious harm.** An exception by way of 2–76
addition arises under the Convention, Article 5(3), allows an action to be
brought, "in matters relating to tort, delict or quasi-delict, in the courts of
the place where the harmful event occurred". This affects intellectual
property infringement and threats actions, since both involve torts within
the broad (phraseology of the exception.[1] It thus allows jurisdiction in
patent matters in accordance with the rule which used traditionally to be
applied in English courts.[2] Where this is the basis of jurisdiction, relief is
likely to be limited to infringements occurring within the jurisdiction.

(iii) **Exclusive jurisdiction: registration and validity of a patent.** An 2–77
exclusionary exception arises under the Convention, Article 16(4), which
contains a reservation of jurisdiction, regardless of "domicile", to the

---

[97] Note that the rule is in no way dependent on the domicile of the plaintiff: so it may be taken
advantage of by a non-E.C. plaintiff.

[98] The original six members of the Convention use the term to mean "habitual residence".

[99] Convention, Arts 52, 53; 1982 Act, ss. 41, 42. By s. 43(2) and (6), a company has its seat
where it is incorporated or where it has its "central management and control." To this,
other provisions in s. 43 add certain qualifications.

[1] It is likely also to extend to actions for declarations of non-infringement.

[2] See *Modus Vivendi v. Sanmex* [1996] F.S.R. 790, a passing off case, in which it was held that
the place where the harmful event occurred was where the passing off was effected. See also
Shevill v. Presse Alliance [1995] E.C.R. I–415, ECJ (defamation jurisdiction).

following courts: "in proceedings concerned with the registration or validity of patents, trade marks, designs, or other similar rights required to be deposited or registered, the courts of the Contracting State in which the deposit or registration has been applied for, has taken place or is under the terms of an international convention deemed to have taken place."

Thus in the realm of patents, exclusive jurisdiction is plainly applicable to proceedings in national courts for revocation of the patent or similar registered right for invalidity, for a declaration of validity, or for amendment of the patent specification.[3] A major difficulty arises, however, when an attack on the validity of a patent is mounted as a counterclaim or defence by the defendant to an action for its infringement. In Community States other than Germany proceedings for infringement and invalidity may be integrated, thus allowing the specification to be interpreted by a single tribunal which will have regard both to the prior art and the specific allegation of infringement. In *Fort Dodge Animal Health Products v. Akzo Nobel*,[4] the Court of Appeal has accepted that, where a substantial issue of invalidity is to be raised in response to an allegation of infringement, the exclusive jurisdiction of Article 16(4) applies to both elements in the proceedings. Article 19 requires a court in one Contracting State to deny its own jurisdiction where it is "seized of a claim which is principally concerned with a matter over which the courts of another Contracting State have exclusive jurisdiction by virtue of Article 16". The Court has decided that both claim and counterclaim are "principally concerned" with an Article 16(4) question.

2–78 Courts in Holland reached the opposite interpretation of Articles 16(4) and 19 and for a short period a major conflict of interpretation threatened which would have demanded a resolution of the issue by the European Court of Justice.[5] In the event, the Hague Court of Appeals modified the basis for assuming jurisdiction over foreign infringement elements in the quasi-interlocutory proceedings, known as the *kort geding*, which are a special feature of Dutch civil procedure.[6] An action for patent infringement is not to be pursued in that country, so far as it extends to acts carried out in other Community States and alleged to be infringements of the equivalent patents in those states once the validity of the patents has been put in issue. The only exception to this would arise when it was immediately clear that the invalidity proceedings were without merit.[7]

---

[3] The exclusive jurisdiction does not cover proceedings concerning entitlement to the right: *Duijnstee v. Goderbauer* [1985] 1 C.M.L.R. 220, ECJ.

[4] [1998] F.S.R. 222, following *Coin Controls v. Suzo International (UK)* [1997] F.S.R. 660.

[5] Questions for a reference under the E.U. Treaty, Art. 177, were formulated and referred to the ECJ in *Fort Dodge* and an associated case: see *Pearce v. Ove Arup* [1999] F.S.R. 525, CA. In the event, these and equivalent Dutch proceedings were settled before the ECJ began any hearing.

[6] For the acceptability of the *kort geding* as a provisional measure under TRIPs, Art. 50(6), see *Hermès v. FHT Marketing* [1999] R.P.C. 107.

[7] *Expandable Grafts Partnership v. Boston Scientific* [1997] F.S.R. 352, refusing relief even in respect of the Dutch patent, because there was merit in the challenges to validity.

(iv) **Co-defendants.** The principal provision of the Conventions which **2–79** undermines their intention to eliminate forum shopping is Article 6(1): where there are a number of defendants, a defendant may be sued in the courts where any one of them is domiciled.[8] In Britain, when this is crossed with the new acceptance that actions may be brought for foreign infringements, applying the *lex loci delicto*,[9] a bewildering variety of circumstances may present themselves, all of which require a distracting factual investigation before jurisdiction is properly established. At one extreme, there are cases where an English domiciled defendant is allegedly infringing the British rights, and the other related defendants (typically, local subsidiaries in various E.U. states) are also contributing to the British infringement. At least where the English defendant is principally responsible, this must be a straightforward case for applying Article 6(1).[10] At the other extreme, the English defendant may be the only infringer of the British rights, the attack on the other subsidiaries being that each infringes its local rights. In such a situation, the Court of Appeal has refused to allow the foreign subsidiaries to be joined, relying on the legal consequence of territoriality: there can be no danger of irreconcilable judgments because each right has effect only over its own domain.[11]

In a patents case, *Expandable Grafts v. Boston Scientific*,[12] the Court of Appeal of The Hague accepted that in such cases Article 6(1) stands to controvert the very essence of the Brussels Convention unless some constraint is placed upon it.[13] It accordingly agreed (in line with the English Court of Appeal) that, because of the territoriality of national patents, including those forming an E.P.O. bundle,[14] a judgment on the patent of one country is not capable of being irreconcilable with a different judgment on the patent of another country. It held, moreover, that, in the case of a group enterprise with different national subsidiaries, a Dutch Court should take jurisdiction over the infringement of patents in other Member States only when the head office for Europe is in The Netherlands.[15] The head

---

[8] Art. 6(3) provides for jurisdiction on a counterclaim arising from the same contract or facts on which the original claim was based, in the court in which the original claim is pending.

[9] Above, para. 2–73.

[10] So held in *Mölnlycke v. Procter & Gamble (No. 4)* [1992] R.P.C. 21 CA, applying, as the test for joinder, that there be a good arguable case against each defendant.

[11] *Fort Dodge Animal Health v. Akzo Nobel* [1998] F.S.R. 222 at 243.

[12] [1999] F.S.R. 352.

[13] The Court therefore placed emphasis on remarks of the ECJ stressing the exceptional character of Art. 6(1) in the scheme of the Conventions: see esp. *Kalfelis v. Bankhaus Schröder* [1988] E.C.R. 5505; *cf. The Tatry* [1994] I–E.C.R. 5439. It also drew attention to the Court's restrictive interpretation of cross-border jurisdiction arising out of Art. 5(3) to be found in *Shevill v. Presse Alliance,* [1995] I–E.C.R. 415.

[14] For this procedure, see below, para. 3–25.

[15] Under Dutch private international law, it was the place of registration of a corporation which determined this issue—even if purely fiscal considerations had determined this— rather than the place of actual business operation. For the English position, see para. 2–75 above.

office—the so-called "spider in the web"—is described as the office "which is in charge of the business operations in question and/or from which the business plan originated". This interpretation is likely to commend itself across Europe[16] and should, it is submitted, be accepted by the ECJ. Even so, it will remain complicated and expensive to administer; and ultimately it will prove impossible to apply to all the cases which can arise.[17]

2–80 (v) **Lis pendens.** If proceedings may be commended on the basis of a single defendant's domicile, the domicile of any one among connected defendants or the place or infringement, conflicts of jurisdiction are an inevitable consequence. Article 21 of the Judgments Conventions gives the first court to be seized strict primacy, where more than one set of proceedings involving the same cause of action and between the same parties are brought. Where, however, related actions, *i.e.* actions which risk resulting in irreconcilable judgments, are brought in courts of different states later courts may cede precedence but, under Article 22, do not have to do so.

So far as the strict rule in Article 21 is concerned actions to enforce patents for different Member States, even when they are granted for the same invention and in common form from the EPO and are asserted against equivalent acts, are not for the same cause.[18]

2–81 As to the Article 22 question of related actions, the principal factor to be taken into account—the danger of irreconcilable judgments[19]—is the test which courts have also used to judge how far jurisdiction under the Conventions may be assumed upon the basis of the domicile of any one co-defendant (Article 6(1)). The Hague Court of Appeal has now agreed with its English counterpart that causes of action for infringement of equivalent patents in different Convention states are separate because of the territorially distinct nature of each patent.[20] On this strict view, judgments from two Contracting State courts, relating to the patent for the same invention in each of their jurisdictions, would not be treated as irreconcilable and the later court would not be called upon to decide whether to stay the action before it. That is a rather unsatisfactory outcome since it

---

[16] The judgment represented a striking modification of previous Dutch practice, but it is coming to be followed at the District Court level in The Netherlands.

[17] Where the defendant has no head office within the territories of the Conventions, they have no application. National law will determine whether there is a sufficient basis for assuming jurisdiction. For an example of the complexities which can arise, see *Sepracor v. Hoechst, The Times*, March 1, 1999.

[18] Art. 21 requires the later court of its own motion to stay its proceedings until such time as the jurisdiction of the court first seized is established, and thereafter to decline jurisdiction. The discretion given by Art. 22 to the later court is to stay proceedings for a related action while proceedings at first instance are pending in the court first seized. For its basis, see *The Tatry* [1994] E.C.R. I–5439.

[19] The factor is explicitly mentioned in Art. 22(3); *cf.* Art. 6(1).

[20] *Supra*, at n. 12; *cf.* Fawcett and Torremans (above, n. 86) 36–37, proclaiming the courts' view "old-fashioned".

precludes a court from considering what is the appropriate outcome in a case which alleges only parallel infringements.

(vi) **Provisional and Protective Measures.** Article 24 provides that a court which does not have jurisdiction over the substantive matter may nonetheless impose provisional or protective measures. In the view of The Hague Court of Appeal, these can only relate to activities within the jurisdiction and not to foreign infringements.[21] This additional jurisdiction is conferred because the local court is best placed to judge the circumstances of the application[22]; it should not therefore employ the Conventions to grant injunctions or preservation orders relating to events beyond its territory.

(c) *Recognition and Enforcement: the Conventions*

A judgment given in accordance with the Brussels Convention in one **2–82** Contracting State is to be recognised in others without further proceedings; and (after registration, so far as the United Kingdom is concerned) such terms as require it are to be enforced.[23] It may be for an injunction as well as for monetary relief.[24] It is not to be recognised if (*inter alia*) it conflicts with Article 16(4)[25]; nor if it is contrary to substantive public policy,[26] or is irreconcilable with a judgment given in a dispute between the same parties in the State in which recognition is sought.[27] These limitations, as already noted, are not adequate to deal with all conflicts which may arise between judgments finding infringement and judgments finding invalidity or ordering revocation. In the end, the Convention will be made to apply satisfactorily to the range of disputes which can arise over patents only if courts engage in some highly purposive interpretation of its text.

(d) *Foreign Defendant from outside E.U. and EFTA*

In *Pearce v. Ove Arup*, the Court of Appeal has apparently surrendered all **2–83** the law's former caution over hearing actions for infringement of the intellectual property laws of another country, whether or not the country is party to the Brussels and Lugano Conventions.[28] Those Conventions lay down a series of rules which not merely entitle, but require, the courts of a given country to assume jurisdiction. One object of the Conventions was to leave these courts no power to refuse after all to hear a case because some

---

[21] *Expandable Grafts v. Boston Scientific* [1999] F.S.R. 352.
[22] *Denilauler v. Couchet Frères* [1980] E.C.R. 1553.
[23] Arts 26, 31.
[24] For interlocutory relief, see Encyc. P.L., para. 10–505.
[25] Art. 28, first sentence.
[26] Arts 27(1)(a), 28, third sentence.
[27] Art. 27(3).
[28] *Pearce v. Ove Arup* [1999] F.S.R. 525, CA.

other more suitable jurisdiction was being sought by one of the parties. Unlike the United Kingdom and Ireland, Continental countries had not adopted any doctrine of *forum non conveniens*. The desire for certainty which underlies this approach means that a court may not sidestep the Conventions' paths in order to reach a fair solution in complex cases.

Where, however, the defendant or defendants are all from outside the EU/EFTA countries, English procedural law determines the matter. In particular, in determining whether there can be service of the writ out of the jurisdiction, the fact that another country is available to provide a more convenient forum is likely to lead to a refusal.[29] The Court of Appeal has held that *forum non conveniens* may equally be applied where the defendant is domiciled in England and the alleged wrong occurred abroad (in that case, in Argentina).[30] The Conventions were found to be applicable only in respect of wrongs in other contracting states, so that no Article 2 jurisdiction arose. That remains the law at present; but the issue has yet to be tested in the context of intellectual property infringement.[31]

(e) *Foreign transactions*[32]

2–84 Intellectual property acquires its value partly through the pursuit of infringers but even more through voluntary transactions. These are contractual agreements which incorporate within them the grant of a proprietary interest or licence and they raise their own issues of private international law.[33] To formal questions concerning assignment and licensing, the law of the country of grant will be applicable.[34] To questions of the interpretation and execution of agreed terms, English law will apply its rule for contractual conflicts, which normally refers the issue to the proper law, that is the law of the country with which the contract has most connection, if it has not

---

[29] The doctrine is relevant to the discretion arising under RSC, Ord. 11, r. 1; in the context of an alleged assignment of patent rights, see *GAF Corp. v. Amchem Products* [1975] Lloyd's R. 601, CA.

[30] *Re Harrods (Buenos Aires) Ltd* [1992] Ch. 72, CA.

[31] One conundrum concerns proceedings for invalidity of (say) a U.S. patent. The exclusive jurisdiction of Art. 16(4) relates only to patents granted for other contracting states. If therefore the Conventions apply, Art. 2 jurisdiction might have to be adopted in any Convention state where the patentee-defendant was domiciled. This suggests the wisdom of *Re Harrods*.

[32] See Wadlow (above, n. 86) Chap. 7; Fawcett and Torremans (above, n. 86), Chap. 11; *Dicey and Morris on the Conflict of Laws* (12th ed., 1993), Rule 177.

[33] So far as concerns jurisdiction in litigation, the principles of the Brussels and Lugano Conventions may be applicable. An outline of those principles has been given in relation to infringement claims (para. 2–73, above); note also the jurisdiction based on place of performance of a contract; Art. 5(1). Any valid jurisdiction clause in an agreement will prevail in an action as to the validity and enforcement of the contract: Art. 17; *Benincasa v. Dentalkit* [1997] E.T.M.R. 447.

[34] An appropriate rule which could nevertheless have awkward consequences for intellectual property dealings which cover world rights or regional rights. In practice, these consequences seem to be avoided.

been expressly selected.[35] Many difficulties can, however, arise. Only two of them can be identified here.

First, the right to grant an assignment or licence may turn on an issue of **2–85** ownership of the intellectual property. Notions of territoriality would lead one to expect that ownership of a right will be determined in accordance with local law. In each jurisdiction, this law may be complex, varying sometimes from right to right, and certainly varying country by country. Yet those dealing with a set of national rights in the same invention, work or other subject-matter need the security of knowing that they have accomplished the proprietary grants which are the whole purpose of their dealing. There is accordingly a pressing need, unless very strong policy interests dictate to the contrary, to ensure that a single law settles substantive questions of entitlement,[36] for instance, between employer and employee or between commissioner and person commissioned. In particular circumstances this is procured by legislation.[37]

Secondly, where the proper law is not that of the country where the **2–86** relevant rights arise, that country may have a rule of public policy limiting freedom of contract. This is particularly apparent in the field of copyright, where countries in the European tradition of authors' rights may have rules highly protective of authors. It will be necessary to examine the rule to determine whether it is mandatory for all transactions affecting the local right, or is only a rule affecting contracts governed by local law or affecting persons with a personal attachment to that country.[38] It will be necessary to examine whether in the place of performance executing the contract would be unlawful; and if that place is England, whether it would be contrary to any public policy.[39]

It has been held, for instance, that the proper law alone determines **2–87** whether an ex-employee's undertaking to respect trade secrets and otherwise refrain from competition is enforceable, so that it is irrelevant what the law of, for instance, the forum is; likewise, the question whether a trade-mark dispute can be settled by a binding undertaking not subsequently to attack the validity of the registration.[40] By contrast, where the British patents legislation rendered a patent unenforceable so long as an agreement existed under which a licensee was obliged to obtain starting material from the patentee, that principle prevailed in Britain; it was irrelevant that the proper law of the licence did not prohibit such a tying arrangement.[41]

---

[35] As now modified to some extent by the Contracts (Applicable Law) Act 1990, implementing the Rome Convention 1980, with its Brussels Protocol giving interpretative jurisdiction to the E.C. Court of Justice: see *Dicey and Morris*, Rule 174, esp. at pp. 1191–1211.

[36] Questions of form must remain with the local law.

[37] See para. 4–08, below (entitlement to European patents), paras 7–08 *et seq.*, below (employed inventor's right to compensation).

[38] See further para. 12–08, below.

[39] See *Dicey and Morris*, Rule 177.

[40] *Apple Corp v. Apple Computer* [1992] F.S.R. 431.

[41] *Chiron v. Organon Teknika (No. 2)* [1993] F.S.R. 567, CA.

(5) Making others responsible

2–88 A defendant to an action who wishes to establish the responsibility of another solely or jointly for the alleged wrong may do so by issuing him with a third party notice.[42] If two or more defendants in an action are liable in respect of the same damage and one meets the liability he will have a claim to contribution from the others.[43] The same is true where the second and subsequent persons have not been sued by the victim of the tort.[44] The amount of contribution due is that found to be just and equitable having regard to the person in question's responsibility for the damage.[45]

2–89 A contract to indemnify for loss suffered through legal liability will displace this principle. These indemnities are common in intellectual property dealings: for instance, where an inventor assigns the rights in what he claims to be his invention, or where an author, in entering a publishing agreement, undertakes that he infringes no one else's rights. The obligation to indemnify is indeed implied in some contracts. If a person purchases a machine and is then obliged to pay damages for its use because it infringes a patent, the vendor will be in breach of his implied warranty of quiet possession[46] and accordingly obliged to make good the loss. Where one person commissions another to carry out work for him and the other thereby unwittingly commits a patent or copyright infringement, there is arguably a similar implied undertaking to indemnify for any loss through liability; but the matter has never been decided.

(6) Establishing freedom from liability

2–90 A person who fears that he will be sued can only have the issue brought to a head if: (1) he has some countervailing right; (2) a procedure exists for annulling the right on which the other party may eventually claim; or (3) the claim against him is imminent.[47] In the case of patents, statutory procedures exist for attacking the validity of the right, and these are open

---

[42] RSC, Ord. 16. Equally a manufacturer may intervene in proceedings against his customer under RSC, Ord. 15, r. 6(2): *Tetra Molectric v. Japan Imports* [1976] R.P.C. 547, CA.

[43] Civil Liability (Contribution) Act 1978, s. 1. The legal basis of liability may be tort, contract, trust or otherwise: s. 6(1).

[44] When the victim's action against the orders has become time-barred the payer may still seek contribution: *ibid.*, s. (3). But there is also a limitation period for the contribution claim: see Limitation Act 1963, s. 4. For the subject in detail, see, *e.g.* Goff and Jones *Law of Restitution* (4th ed., 1993), pp. 232–235; *Clerk and Lindsell on Torts* (17th ed., 1995), para. 4–61.

[45] Law Reform (Married Women and Tortfeasors) Act 1935, s. 6(2).

[46] Sale of Goods Act 1979, s. 12(2)(b). But to the extent that this obligation is limited in accordance with s. 12(3) and (5), the responsibility will be reduced.

[47] In *Vine Products v. Mackenzie* [1969] R.P.C. 1, it was assumed that, after an exchange of letters before action, the person threatened with liability could himself institute the proceedings for a declaration of freedom from liability. *Bulmer v. Bollinger* [1978] R.P.C. 79, CA, followed the same course.

to competitors and others with sufficient interest to bring them.[48] Even then, the question whether a person is infringing lies outside these procedures: the alleged infringer must proceed by way of an action for a declaration that he is not doing so.[49]

In intellectual property litigation generally, this possibility is a recent development. In the case of patents, special provision was made earlier. A person may apply in writing to a patentee[50] for an undertaking that a particular act does not infringe the patent.[51] If this undertaking is not forthcoming he may seek a declaration from the Court to the same effect.[52] In the course of the proceedings questions of the patent's validity, as well as of infringement, may be raised.[53]

(7) Threats to sue

If a potential plaintiff chooses to do what damage he can merely by **2–91** threatening to sue, again those affected may find it difficult to force his hand. Apart from instituting revocation or rectification proceedings in the cases mentioned under the last head, a person who suffers by the threats may not be able to prevent them, save in exceptional cases. In general the common law has not limited the freedom to institute claims or to threaten that they will be begun. Rather it insists that those who choose to succumb to a claim instead of fighting must abide by the consequences of their faint-heartedness. If the claim was in fact groundless, they are not in general permitted to re-open the controversy by having the settlement rescinded, by claiming back money paid or by suing for loss suffered because of their submission.[54]

The same approach applies in general even where the threats cause injury indirectly. For instance, A, a promotion firm, imported toy bricks to be used as free gifts in a campaign being organised for a client, B. C threatened B with an action for infringement of rights in their design if the campaign went ahead. In consequence B refused to participate, leaving A with the stock of toys on its hands. An action by A against C for wrongful interference with contractual relations was struck out as disclosing no cause of action.[55]

---

[48] See PA 1977, s. 71; *Filhol v. Fairfax* [1990] R.P.C. 293. *Auchinloss v. Agricultural & Veterinary Supplies* [1997] R.P.C. 649. For certificates of contested validity, see n. 76, above.

[49] As in the cases mentioned in n. 47, above.

[50] Or exclusive licensee.

[51] He is not obliged to show the alleged infringement to the patentee, only to describe it: *Plasticisers v. Pixdane* [1979] R.P.C. 327.

[52] PA 1977, s. 71.

[53] This is a change introduced in 1977.

[54] For these rules and exceptions to them, see, *e.g.* Goff and Jones *Law of Restitution* (4th ed., 1999), especially pp. 53–55.

[55] *Granby Marketing v. Interlego* [1984] R.P.C. 209.

2–92   However the tort of injurious falsehood will lie for the *malicious* statement that a right of action exists and will be sued upon.[56] Malice will be present if the threatener knows that his claim is groundless; likewise, if he draws attention to his success in proceedings against another defendant without saying that the court saw fit to stay the injunction pending an appeal.[57] Nonetheless the requirement of malice severely limits this form of tortious relief.

2–93   In the case of patents, where the expense and uncertainty of infringement and validity proceedings is acute and the threat to sue is accordingly grave, an exception has long existed by statute. In the version included in the 1977 Patent Act, a person aggrieved by the threat that he himself or someone else (such as a customer) will be sued for patent infringement may claim relief in civil proceedings in the form of a declaration that the threats are unjustifiable, an injunction against their continuance and/or damages for any loss that they cause (for example because a customer switches his orders to the threatener).[58] But threats relating either to making or importing a product for disposal, or to using a process, are outside the scope of this special provision.[59] Similar provisions have also been introduced in relation to registered and unregistered design rights, and mostly recently in relation to registered trade marks.[60] The result is an odd patchwork, still leaving out copyright, confidential information and those marks and names protected only at common law. Since copyrights are often administered by powerful collecting societies there is a strong case for extending protection against threats into that field.

2–94   To avoid liability the threatener may show either that what he said did not amount to a threat, or that the threat was justified.[61] The patentee is entitled to draw attention to the existence of his patent.[62] To go further is to court danger.[63] It is actionable, for instance, for a patentee to say to a

---

[56] The scope of injurious falsehood is discussed in detail, paras 16–48—16–56, below.

[57] *Mentmore v. Fomento* (1955) 72 R.P.C. 157, CA.

[58] PA 1977, s. 70. For orders restraining the institution of vexatious proceedings against customers, see *Landi den Hartog v. Sea Bird* [1976] F.S.R. 489; *Jacey v. Norton* [1977] F.S.R. 475.

[59] *Nield v. Rockley* [1986] F.S.R. 3; *Cavity Trays v. MRC Panel Products* [1996] R.P.C. 361, CA; *Brain v. Ingledew (No. 1)* [1996] F.S.R. 341, CA. The PA 1977, s. 70(4) permits threats against acts of importing that are allegedly acts of indirect infringement (for which see s. 60(2)): *Therm-a-Stor v. Weatherseal* [1981] F.S.R. 579, CA; *Bowden Controls v. Acco* [1990] R.P.C. 427.

[60] RDA 1949, s. 26; CDPA 1988, s. 253; TMA 1994, s. 21. For the threats which are not caught: see RDA 1949, s. 26(2A); CDPA 1988, s. 253(3); TMA 1994, s. 21(1) *cf. Prince v. Prince Sports Group* [1998] F.S.R. 21.

[61] *e.g.* he may show that the threat concerned infringement of a valid patent. But the patent must have been granted: *Brain v. Ingledew (No. 2)* [1997] F.S.R. 271.

[62] PA 1977, s. 70(5) and see RDA 1949, s. 26(3); CDPA 1988, s. 253(4); TMA 1994, s. 21(4).

[63] A solicitor's letter before action can frequently amount to a threat. However, once a writ is actually issued, consequential losses are normally attributed to it rather than the preceding threat: *Carflow v. Linwood Securities* [1998] F.S.R. 691; *Symonds Cider v. Showerings* [1997] E.T.M.R. 238 (Irish HC).

competitor's customers that he is going to apply for an injunction against the competitor and that the customers are to see that there are no further infringements.[64] In the case of circulars to customers or notices in trade journals (common ways of giving notice of rights claimed) a person suing for threats must show that potential customers of his would understand the circular or notice to be referring to his goods.[65]

A threat can be justified only if the threatener shows that the acts of which he complains do constitute infringement of some patent (or other right), and the person suffering by the threats cannot establish that the relevant patent claim is invalid.[66] Thus, in the case of a serious fight, the threat gives the alleged infringer a springboard equivalent to an action for a declaration of non-infringement from which to launch the contest.

---

[64] *Berkeley & Young v. Stillwell* (1940) 57 R.P.C. 291. Note, however, the obligation under the Civil Procedure Rules 1999 to set out claims and defences fully in pre-action correspondence: *Unilever v. Procter & Gamble, The Times*, March 18, 1999.

[65] *Reymes-Cole v. Elite Hosiery* [1965] R.P.C. 102 at 120, CA.

[66] Frequently these issues are raised by counterclaim for infringement and counter-counterclaim for revocation of the patent.

Part II

PATENTS

CHAPTER 3

GROWTH AND PURPOSE OF PATENTS

1. THE NEW DEAL OF 1978

With the Patents Act 1977, the British patent system received the largest **3–01** culture shock in its history. The Act introduced machinery for collaborating in three supra-national ventures:

(1) Since June 1, 1978, it has been possible to secure a patent for the United Kingdom either by the traditional route of an application to the British Patent Office or by applying to the European Patent Office (EPO), established under the European Patent Convention 1973 (EPC). The EPO grants a bundle of national patents in common form, of which one may be a European patent (U.K.).[1] Its headquarters are in Munich, its Search Branch in The Hague.

(2) From the same date it has been possible to initiate international patent applications in a number of countries throughout the world by a "one-stop" procedure under the Patent Cooperation Treaty 1970 (PCT). The PCT system provides for a single application and search, and in some cases a single preliminary examination; but thereafter it transmits applications to national offices for them to decide upon the grant of a patent for their territories.[2] It is administered by WIPO, Geneva.

(3) From a date still to be fixed, an application to the EPO for a patent in an E.C. country may mature into a single Community patent covering the whole Common Market. The main provisions of this scheme are contained in the Community Patent Convention 1975 (CPC), which has been the subject of substantial revisions, agreed between 1985 and 1989.[3]

In addition to all this, the substantive and procedural law governing **3–02** patents for the United Kingdom was extensively altered by the 1977 Act. This was for various reasons. The EPC arrangements require each contracting state to treat a European patent granted by the EPO for that territory

---

[1] See paras 3–23—3–25, 4–01—4–05, below.
[2] See paras 3–19—3–22, 4–01—4–02, below.
[3] See paras 3–26—3–29, below.

in accordance with standard rules on basic matters such as term, validity and scope of protection. There was a strong case for subjecting patents granted by the national system to the same substantive regime and for modelling the application procedure on similar lines to the European granting system.[4] The Report of the Banks Committee on the British system also awaited implementation[5]; and the government had plans of its own on the subject of inventions by employees.[6]

3–03   The resulting edifice is byzantine in complexity. At least it can be said that the building blocks from which it is constructed are not themselves a novelty. These have been formed out of the experience of national patents; and in their turn national systems are a characteristic by-product of a country's "take-off" into industrialisation. In private enterprise economies a patent system represents a judicious compromise. On the one hand it is a recognition that technological innovation, which is seen as the key to economic growth and social prosperity, cannot be left to the stimulus of market competition alone. On the other hand it leaves the added incentives to be determined by demands of the market rather than by the apparatus of the state, through rewards or grants of some kind. But because the idea is a compromise on a vital ground, it has long been the subject of controversy—particularly in the mid-nineteenth century and again in our own time. Indeed the arguments today are an appendage to larger questions: about the possibility and desirability of pursuing innovation, and the need to avert its more damaging consequences for people and their environment.

This chapter accordingly contains, first, an historical sketch of the British patent system and its relations with those of other countries. This leads to an account of the international developments that stand behind the 1977 Act. Finally, there is some introduction to the range of current debate about patent systems, national and international.

2. THE BRITISH PATENT SYSTEM: HISTORICAL DEVELOPMENT

(1) Beginnings

3–04 The idea of conferring a market monopoly as an incentive to innovate has old roots.[7] In England, as in other parts of Europe, it emerged as one minor form of state patronage.[8] James I was partial to rewarding his political

---

[4] See paras 4–01, 5–01, below.

[5] *The British Patent System*, Cmnd. 4407 (1970).

[6] The government's plans were developed in a White Paper, Cmnd. 6000 (1975) and accompanying Consultative Document (Green Paper).

[7] The growth of guilds and boroughs with exclusive trading privileges was to some extent connected with the desire to introduce and support new industries: see, *e.g.* Fox, *Monopolies and Patents* (1947), Chap. 2: Davenport, *The United Kingdom Patent System* (1979).

[8] A Venetian law of 1474 went so far as to establish a positive system for granting 10-year privileges to inventors of new arts and machines: Mandich/Prager (1948) 30 J.P.O.S. 166, (1960) 42 J.P.O.S. 378. See generally, Penrose, *The Economics of the International Patent System* (1951) pp. 2 *et seq.*; Phillips [1983] E.I.P.R. 41.

creditors with trading monopolies granted by letters patent. For this there were precedents enough from the illustrious hand of Elizabeth I.[9] But James lacked her command. In 1624 Parliament sought to declare these exercises of royal prerogative void.[10]

The Statute of Monopolies which it enacted suggests not only the **3–05** growing significance of trade in the country's economy and the beginnings of the long political campaign to favour competition at the expense of monopoly[11]; it also shows the readiness of the political forces represented in Parliament to challenge policies of convenience to the Crown. In its own way it reflects some of the conditions which gradually coalesced to make England the first country to leap forward into industrial production.

Section 6 of the Statute of Monopolies, which exceptionally allowed patent monopolies for 14 years upon "any manner of new manufacture" within the realm to the "true and first inventor", has its own character. The English were already feeling their relative technical backwardness—in comparison with France and Holland—and an "inventor" was accordingly understood to cover not only the deviser of the invention but also one who imported it from abroad. The appeal of patent systems to countries that are set to catch up in the race for technology is a continuing one and one that makes the international aspects of patents, if anything, more important than domestic considerations.

Section 6 also expressed the desire to impose some qualification upon the system in the name of higher public interests. The protected manufactures were not to be "contrary to the law nor mischievous to the state, by raising prices of commodities at home, or hurt of trade, or generally inconvenient". The difficulty of finding either criteria or language that could more precisely curb excesses in the system remains as perplexing today. More generally the terms of the section make it plain that an act of economic policy was intended: the objectives were the encouragement of industry, employment and growth, rather than justice to the "inventor" for his effort. The patentee's "consideration" for the grant was that he would put the invention to use and the 14-year period may well represent two cycles of seven-year apprenticeships.

---

[9] Even she, at the end of her reign, had to face considerable pressure which led to her issuing the Proclamation concerning Monopolies of 1601. Subsequent litigation declared the invalidity at common law of a patented monopoly granted by her in playing cards; expediently, the case was not brought to judgment until after her death: *Darcy v. Allin* (1602) 11 Co.Rep. 846. See also Fox (n. 7, above), Chaps 7, 8; Davies (1938) 48 L.Q.R. 398.

[10] This was the culmination of a battle on the subject that ran throughout James's reign and continued against his successor, Charles I: see Fox, Chaps 8–10.

[11] The idea is more completely expressed in the case of the *Cloth Workers of Ipswich* (1615) Godb.R. 252. See further, Fox, pp. 219–232.

(2) The coming of industrialisation

3–06 The seventeenth century provided no more than a germ of a functioning patent system.[12] Even the patent specification, the kernel of today's practice, made its appearance only in the early eighteenth century. Then patentees started to enrol statements of their inventions with the Court of Chancery. Initially this practice may have been a device to help prove against infringers what the protected invention was.[13] A half-century later the courts were requiring the patentee to make a sufficient statement of his conception as "consideration" for the monopoly granted to him.[14] In the pre-industrial world, the notion that patents should be used as a regular source of technical information was not an obvious one. As long as competition in international trade remained primitive, each country might hope to keep its technical advances to itself. Britain was to be first in learning the economic rewards of exporting technology, but not before she had attempted a policy of national conservation[15] which accorded ill with the notion of patents as a source of technical information. But the requirement of an adequate description was often pressed,[16] not only because patents could then teach an industry what its liveliest members were doing, but because it provided competitors with ammunition against the patent; the sufficiency of the disclosure could itself be attacked, and also the usefulness of the invention. There was a correlative shift in the conception of novelty which would justify the patent grant: the question had been whether anyone was already practising the invention in the country; now another issue was added, did the trade already know of it through publication?[17]

3–07 These changes of emphasis coincide with the first steps towards mechanised factory production and with a decisive increase in the number of patents.[18] Probably these concerned many more home-grown inventions

---

[12] For a detailed study of the eighteenth-century system, see McLeod, *Inventing the Industrial Revolution* (1988).

[13] Hulme (1897) 13 L.Q.R. 313; but *cf.* Adams and Averley (n. 14, below) at 158–160.

[14] Hulme (1902) 18 L.Q.R. 280, claiming Lord Mansfield's judgment in *Liardet v. Johnson* (1778) to have been decisive; but *cf.* Adams and Averley (1986) 7 J.Leg.Hist. 156. See also Adams (1987) 8 J.Leg.Hist. 18.

[15] A succession of Acts (not completely repealed until 1843) forbade the export of British machinery, parts or plans and the emigration of skilled workers. Arkwright attempted to defend the obscurity of one specification by claiming that the invention was kept from foreigners: Mantoux, *The Industrial Revolution in the Eighteenth Century* (1961), pp. 227–228.

[16] As in *Arkwright's* case; see n. 21, below.

[17] A doctrine also propounded in *Liardet v. Johnson* (n. 14, above). Half a century later it seems to have been thought that one act of communication to a third party, without any condition of confidence, would rank as an anticipation: Select Committee (n. 25, below) at p. 9. This became firm law later: see para. 5–13, below.

[18] In the 1750s fewer than 10 patents a year were being granted: in the 1760s that number more than doubled. By the 1810s the average was 110 p.a. and in the 1840s 458 p.a. The figures are tabulated in Boehm, *The British Patent System: 1. Administration* (1967), pp. 22–23: later periods: pp. 33–34.

than before, but the role of the patent system in this first remarkable stage of industrial development was somewhat tangential, if not as irrelevant as some economic historians have supposed.[19] Among the famous, Boulton and Watt secured large sums from their steam-engine patents, but these came partly from a special extending Act.[20] Arkwright's main patent threatened the whole industry but proved to be too obscurely drawn to survive the attack on its validity.[21] Crompton had to be given a parliamentary reward of £5,000 since he had virtually no commercial return from his spinning jenny.[22] It is likely that patents provided equally sporadic encouragement for those with less celebrated improvements.[23]

Part of the explanation must lie in the inefficiencies and uncertainties **3–08** that surrounded the procedures for securing and enforcing patents.[24] Despite vociferous complaints to a Select Committee in 1829,[25] the process of patenting was to remain one of those obscure pockets of grasp, if not graft, which were able to resist longest the demands of bureaucratic reform. Change finally came just as the Great Exhibition of 1851 marked the vast commercial success of Britain's technical pre-eminence. The reforms in the patent system were earnest of purpose rather than complacent. The rifts in industrial society were to be filled by providing the working man with every opportunity for self-improvement; and what more significant contribution could there be than to help finance his inventive schemes?[26]

The new patents system,[27] cheap and simple in concept, was designed to **3–09** attract capital for the small ventures and out-of-the-way ideas being generated on the fringes of industry, as much as at its centre. For reasonable fees,[28] an applicant could in effect secure grant merely by registering his specification; and he might take advantage of the new arrangement for first filing a provisional, and then within a year, a complete

---

[19] H. Dutton, *The Patent System and Inventive Activity during the Industrial Revolution 1750–1852* (1984) is an admirable assessment of the evidence.

[20] And after laborious litigation: *Boulton v. Bull* (1795) 2 Hy.Bl. 463; *Hornblower v. Boulton* (1799) 8 T.R. 95.

[21] See *R. v. Arkwright* (1785) 1 W.P.C. 64. Subsequently, Arkwright considered publishing all the details of his machine so that foreigners could have it as well: Fitton and Wadsworth, *The Strutts and the Arkwrights 1758–1830* (1958), p. 88.

[22] See Mantoux (n. 15, above), pp. 237–238.

[23] See Boehm (n. 18, above), pp. 22–26.

[24] Separate patents had to be secured for England, Ireland and Scotland (until 1852) and a large number of officials had to give their approval. There were some (inevitably) who thought this disincentive a useful filter, but active reform groups kept up agitation. Dickens provided some telling parodies of the inventor's lot (*A Poor Man's Tale of a Patent; Little Dorrit*). See Dutton (n. 19 above), Chaps 2, 3; Phillips, *Charles Dickens and the "Poor Man's Tale of a Patent"* (1984).

[25] B.P.P. 1829 (332) III.

[26] The same motivation impelled a contemporaneous movement for companies with limited liability.

[27] Introduced by the Patent Law Amendment Act 1852; and see the Report of the Select Committee on Patents, B.P.P. 1851 (486) XVIII.

[28] The initial cost of securing U.K. protection was reduced from some £300 to £25.

specification, thus gaining time to work out his ideas more fully. The amount of patenting activity at once increased markedly.[29] Perhaps it was invention at a relatively minor level that was particularly encouraged—it has often enough been said that this is the point where the system has most impact.

But easy patenting had other, less happy consequences. Patent litigation had always been notably protracted and costly. This might deter the genuine inventor from seeking protection, but it left the swashbuckler plenty of room to brandish dubious patents, hoping that competitors would find it simpler to treat shadow as if it were of substance. In the high age of economic liberalism, one school of thought reacted by demanding abolition of the whole system, another by proposing that the alleged invention should, at least in some measure, be the subject of an official examination before any patent was granted.[30]

3–10 Even so modification only came slowly. In 1883,[31] the modern Patent Office replaced the Commissioners of 1852 and it began to examine applications, mainly for formal defects and for sufficiency of description.[32] Successive governments remained reluctant to create a bureaucracy that would search the prior literature and examine against the search results; and this despite the fact that the United States Patent Office had done so since 1836. It was not until 1901, when the Fry Committee demonstrated that 40 per cent or more of the patents granted were for inventions already described in earlier British specifications, that the change became irresistible.[33] The Office began to search British specifications of the previous 50 years in 1905,[34] but the examination (contrary to the United States example) was confined to the issue of novelty. From this point outwards novelty is generally to be understood in its limited modern sense—as separate from any inquiry into the obviousness of the alleged invention. But equally, it is by this time accepted that a patent once granted might be

---

[29] Net sealings: 1852—891; 1854—2,113: see Boehm (n. 18, above).

[30] The critics had opportunities to put their cases before a Royal Commission (B.P.P. 1864 [3419] XXIX) and then a Select Committee (B.P.P. 1871 (368) X, 1872 (193) XI); and a bill imposing very severe constraints on the system was even passed by the House of Lords; see Bafzel [1982] Bus. Hist. 189; Oppenheim [1998] I.P.R. 400. A similar anti-patent movement arose elsewhere in Western Europe. It lost headway in face of the adoption of the German Patent Law of 1877 and the movement for international patent co-operation: see Machlup and Penrose (1950) 10 J.Econ.Hist. 1.

[31] Patents, Designs and Trade Marks Act 1883. Again the initial fees were reduced and the number of patents granted rose from under 4,000 p.a. to some 9,000 p.a.: Boehm (n. 18, above).

[32] The new Comptroller-General was also given a limited power to hear third-party oppositions to applications for patents, a jurisdiction somewhat expanded in 1902. Right of appeal was to the Solicitor- and Attorney-General until 1932, when the Patents Appeal Tribunal (consisting of a Chancery Division judge) was established.

[33] B.P.P. 1901 [Cd. 506, Cd. 530] XXIII.

[34] See Patents Act 1902.

attacked for its obviousness or lack of inventive step.[35] This additional criterion, which casts such a miasma of uncertainty around patents, is one expression of concern over the consequences of making patents "too easy" to obtain.[36]

Two other changes in 1883 are linked: juries were excluded from trials of **3–11** patent actions in favour of a single judge[37]; and patentees were obliged to include in their specifications at least one claim delineating the scope of their monopoly.[38] The question whether the defendant was infringing, so often marginal in contested cases, ceased to be weighed upon a private moral balance in the jury-room and was instead subjected to that nice form of linguistic inquiry so natural to the Chancery mind. Buoyed up by a certain suspicion of monopoly grants, the judges soon insisted that claims marked out the full range of protection: alternative embodiments outside the scope of the words used in the claims were not covered,[39] any more than were the separate parts of machines claimed as mechanical combinations.[40] As we shall see, this use of claims as "fence-posts", rather than as "guidelines", affects a great deal else in the basic law of patents. It is a development which has not been paralleled in the same manner in some other industrial countries. Even today, when defining claims are much more the norm, there are still crucial differences of attitude towards their significance.[41]

With these developments, the essential features of the modern admin- **3–12** istrative system were settled in a way that was not to be disturbed until the events of the 1970s. The statutory revisions of 1907, 1919, 1932 and above all 1949, put the law more in the form of a code and altered it in many details, but attempted nothing really drastic. Apart from certain international considerations dealt with below, events worth recording were the restrictions upon claims to chemical substances that were introduced in 1919 and removed again in 1949 as having little real value[42]; and the introduction in 1949 of obviousness as a ground of pre-grant opposition— an objection which, however, it proved very difficult to substantiate in these proceedings.[43]

---

[35] Fox (n. 7, above). Part II traces the beginnings of this doctrine (which it is his object to denounce) to *Crane v. Price* (1842) 1 W.P.C. 393 at 411. By the end of the century Brett M.R. could treat it "generally with amused contempt" (*Edison Bell v. Smith* (1894) 11 R.P.C. 389 at 398; and see him also in *Hayward v. Hamilton* (1879–81) Griff P.C. 115 at 121). But thereafter the doctrine was at most looked at with suspicion, *e.g.* by Fletcher Moulton L.J. in *British Westinghouse v. Braulik* (1910) 27 R.P.C. 209.

[36] Obviousness secured an earlier foothold in U.S. law (see *Hotchkiss v. Greenwood* 52 U.S. 248 (1850)), but patents were then more readily available in that country.

[37] Complaints about the difficulty of presenting technical matters to juries can be found in the various Parliamentary investigations.

[38] Patents, etc, Act 1883, s. 5(5): "a distinct statement of the invention claimed".

[39] *Nobel v. Anderson* (1895) 12 R.P.C. 164, HL.

[40] *British United Shoe Manufacturers v. Fussell* (1908) 25 R.P.C. 631, CA.

[41] See paras 4–37 *et seq.*, below.

[42] See paras 4–47—4–48, below.

[43] See paras 5–39 *et seq.*, below.

3. The "International" Patent System

(1) Foreign impact upon national systems

3–13 Many countries have been attracted to introduce a patent system by the hope that it will act as a lure to foreign technology. The same concern has induced them to open their systems to foreign applications. The United States, for instance, allowed foreigners to apply for patents well before it offered copyright to foreign authors.[44] Equally the patenting countries of the nineteenth century were led to a modest union, under the Paris Industrial Property Convention of 1883,[45] which guaranteed the nationals of each Member State the same treatment in the others as was given to their own nationals.[46] The union also established the system of Convention priority, under which an application in one of the Member States gave a period (eventually 12 months) in which to pursue an application in any of the others; this would bear the same priority date as the first.[47]

3–14 In this century, the international exchange of technology became the chief point of maintaining patent systems in countries whose socialised economies provided little reason for offering market power as a reward to domestic inventors. Within a planned economy it was logical to encourage innovation by systems of state rewards[48]—the very notion which is most often posed as the alternative to a patent system even for capitalist countries.

3–15 As in seventeenth century England, any country which offers patents to foreigners will want the invention to be exploited to the advantage of its own economy. It may indeed take measures to make the patent more than a cover protecting the import of foreign-made goods. If it has a domestic industry that competes with the foreign patentee there may be particular cause for jealousy. This certainly was the motive force behind the introduc-

---

[44] In 1836 and 1891 respectively. The British, having greater interest in securing rights for themselves abroad, were in both fields prepared to extend protection to foreigners; even so, in copyright it took reciprocal agreement to establish that publication in another country could found British copyright: see paras 9–06—9–08, below.

[45] Subsequently revised in 1900 (Brussels), 1911 (Washington), 1925 (The Hague), 1934 (London), 1958 (Lisbon) and 1967 (Stockholm). The U.K. ratified the latest version in 1969. For the debates leading to the Convention see Ladas, *The International Protection of Industrial Property* (1930); Penrose, *The Economics of the International Patent System* (1951), Chap. 3. In 1996, the Convention had 123 members of its union. See generally Beier (1984) 15 I.I.C. 1.

[46] The point of this formula was that countries without a patent law could join the Union and get benefits for their own nationals abroad. On this basis the Netherlands and Switzerland joined and the strategy proved useful in getting them to adopt patent systems of their own. The present provisions (Arts 2, 3) provide equal treatment on a basis of domicile and place of business as well as nationality.

[47] See paras 4–10—4–13, below.

[48] For such inventors' certificates see, *e.g.* Soltysinski (1969) 32 M.L.R. 408; Boguslavski (1979) 18 Ind.Prop. 113; they have disappeared from the new patent laws of Central and Eastern Europe.

tion into the British system of provisions allowing the grant of compulsory licences on the ground that the invention was not being worked domestically[49]: the success of the German and Swiss chemical industries in the late nineteenth century was built to a substantial degree on the holding of key patents.[50]

The French originally went even further, making revocation of the patent the penalty for importing patented articles from abroad; lifting this draconian sanction was made a precondition of membership of the Paris Convention.[51] The majority of patenting countries now have some form of compulsory working requirement,[52] which the Paris Convention allows to be sanctioned by compulsory licensing once three years have elapsed from grant[53]; and by revocation if compulsory licensing fails after two years to produce the required result.[54] Provisions of this kind in national law are not only offensive to notions of international comity supposedly underlying the Convention; they are also economically unsound in any case where efficiencies of scale demand production in one place for international markets.

(2) Hostility to patents

Countries which are well enough organised to bargain hard for the foreign **3–16** technology that they buy, and technically advanced enough to build for themselves upon what they learn, are likely to be reasonably satisfied with what they get out of patents. By keeping their patent systems alive, Comecon countries created some sense of security for Western enterprises selling them technology. To some extent they appreciated that the system has a potential for underpinning the transfer of technology. If receivers are adept in building upon their local strengths, they may secure access to industrial development in ways denied to state economic planning and expropriation. Today's developing countries are coming to appreciate the same message.

It was in countries where the patent system remains part of an unplanned or partly planned economy that its effects upon the international trade of the state have been more persistently called in question. To take two very different examples among common law countries: in Canada, the patent system came under careful, but sceptical scrutiny from a team of econo-

---

[49] Tentatively introduced in 1883 without reference to foreign working, the provisions were made much more specific in 1907. As elsewhere, they did not lead to frequent applications: see paras 7–41 et seq., below.

[50] Haber, *The Chemical Industry during the Nineteenth Century* (1971), pp. 166–167, 198–204.

[51] See Penrose (n. 45, above), pp. 74–77; PIP, Art. 5A(1).

[52] But the U.S. has always, by geography and economic position, been able to remain aloof from this sort of requirement.

[53] Or four years from application if this is longer.

[54] PIP, Art. 5A(2)–(5).

mists.[55] To them it seemed to operate largely as a shield for the imported products of foreign owners (mainly from the United States), while doing very little to encourage the development of home-based industry. However, plans drastically to curtail the scope of the patent monopoly in the wake of these criticisms met with hostile reception from industry there and abroad—some measure at least of the very considerable value that substantial owners do attach to patents.[56] In India, where the government became intent on rapid intervention in industrial ownership and policy, wide powers were actually taken to grant compulsory licences on "reasonable" terms.[57] One result was a marked reduction in the amount of patenting by foreign enterprises in that country.

3–17 For countries even less advanced, the disadvantages may seem still graver. Yet they are now under indomitable pressure from industrialised countries and trans-national enterprises to have a patent system, whether or not one has been inherited from a colonial past. Over the last quarter-century developing countries have been searching for a *via media* by which they can use patents to attract foreign technology, while at the same time influencing by bureaucratic intervention the terms on which their own firms collaborate with foreign enterprises. In the 1970s a number of experiments were made in domestic legislation, particularly in Central and South America.[58] In international circles there was increasing discussion about acceptable models. This focused particularly on two negotiations: one was the formulation of UNCTAD's Code of Conduct for the Transfer of Technology, which was a practical expression of the search for a New International Economic Order. The other was the Revision Conference of the Paris Convention, which also grew out of UNCTAD criticisms of the current operation of patent systems internationally. The Transfer of Technology Code was taken by 1980 to a point where detailed drafts existed; but it was a point of high controversy, with different versions being preferred by the Group of 77 (developing countries), the industrial countries and the socialist countries.[59] It was never settled whether any final

---

[55] Economic Council of Canada, *Report on Intellectual and Industrial Property* (1971) (with additional background studies); Firestone, *Economic Implications of Patents* (1972). For a similar appraisal in Australia, see Manderville, *et al.* (para. 3–36, n. 22, below).

[56] Working Paper on Patent Law Reform (1976).

[57] Patents Act 1970 (India); Vedaraman (1972) 3 I.I.C. 39; Kunz-Hallstein (1975) 4 I.I.C. 427 at 438–440.

[58] Following, in particular, resolutions of the Andean Pact countries in 1970 and the Argentine law on technology transfer of the same year: see, *e.g.* Soberanis (1977) 7 Georgia J.Int.L. 17 (on Mexico).

[59] For these developments, see, *e.g.* Anderfelt, *International Patent Legislation and Developing Countries* (1971); *Vaitsos* (1972) 9 J.Dev. Studies; Penrose (1973) Econ.J. 768; Lall (1976) 10 J. World Trade Law 1; Kunz-Hallstein (n. 57, above); Laird (1980) 9 CIPA 276; Wilner and Fikentscher in *Legal Problems of Codes of Conduct for Multinational Enterprises* (Horn ed., 1980), pp. 177, 189; Fikentscher, *The Draft International Code of Conduct on the Transfer of Technology* (1980); Cabanellas, *Antitrust and Direct Regulation of International Transfer of Technology Transactions* (1984); Blakeney, *Legal Aspects of the Transfer of Technology to Developing Countries* (1989).

form of the Code would have legal effect or would be regarded as a voluntary code of good practice. Immediately after this, the Revision Conference of the Paris Convention held three sessions, but then adjourned *sine die* in 1982. The eventual sticking point proved to be demands from the Group of 77, for example, that their countries have power to impose *exclusive* compulsory licences on patentees in respect of failure to work the invention in the national territory.[60]

Against such revisions, the United States took a particularly strong **3–18** position, urging the importance at the least of maintaining the Convention's existing standards of protection.[61] The stalemate incited the United States to take intellectual property into the frame of inter-governmental trade negotiation, making it a prominent part of bilateral agreements with countries such as Korea and Brazil and using its Trade Act powers to block imports into its territory where a country did not come up to scratch on the intellectual property front. In the field of inventions, the greatest pressure has been to secure the extension of patent systems to chemical and/or pharmaceutical products *per se.*[62] The success of the tactic has led to the incorporation of intellectual property protection in the new GATT as the TRIPS Agreement (to which we come back under the next head). The United States is by no means content with the remarkable bouleversement of the state of affairs a decade ago. Alongside TRIPS and its dispute settlement procedures, the United States' government intends to continue pursuing individual countries with import sanctions, wherever they offend its sometimes myopic sense of propriety in intellectual property matters.

(3) Co-operation in patenting: world-wide linkages

Before 1977, there was nothing that could be called an international patent **3–19** system, at least in legal and organisational terms. The Paris Convention was largely restricted to basic principles for securing readier access to the national systems maintained by the different Member States.[63] It made no arrangements, beyond its priority system, for standardising or simplifying the process of applying for patents and it required the substantive law to conform to its standards only on such collateral matters as the compulsory licensing requirements.[64]

---

[60] On this particular campaign compare, P.A. 1977, s. 49(3), now quietly removed by CDPA 1988, Sched. 5, para. 13.

[61] It stood alone in resisting demands that the present unanimity rule for amending the Convention become a qualified majority rule.

[62] Where this has been allowed as a guarantee in future, a "pipe-line" down which U.S. inventions can pass in order to gain priority for applications which will be accepted only later. In some cases this treatment was offered preferentially to Americans, and it was this which led to the Most-Favoured-Nation provision in TRIPS: for which, see para. 1–31, above.

[63] On the principle of national treatment as it affects patents, Evans [1996] E.I.P.R. 149.

[64] See para. 3–15, above.

The experience of many industrial countries has been that unexamined patents lead to nuisance. The answer to this was to institute some form of pre-grant examination of the substantive merits of the case in the light of a search of earlier technical literature. Serious examination is not cheap; and, as the number of countries demanding an examination rose, so did the cost. The applicant seeking a patent in several countries saw his case processed in a roughly similar way, but subjected to a search of a varying range of literature and judged according to varying criteria, in a series of offices operating quite independently. Accordingly patentees (whatever the interests of their patent departments and professional advisers) and governments (whatever the bureaucratic pretensions of their patent offices) began to appreciate that "internationalising" the patenting process might increase efficiency and reduce costs.

3–20 On a world-wide basis,[65] the system of international patent applications under the Patent Cooperation Treaty (PCT) (Washington, 1970) was put into effect from June 1, 1978, its central administration being provided by WIPO in Geneva.[66] The Treaty is of interest to any country which is not content to have a pure registration system but instead opts for some form of examination. Its main chapters provide, after the submission of a single international application designating the PCT countries in which patents are wanted,[67] for two things. Chapter I creates an international search conducted by one of a handful of international search authorities (the Australian, Japanese, Russian and United States Patent Offices, the European Patent Office and, to a more limited extent, the Swedish and Austrian Offices)[68]; Chapter II establishes an International Preliminary Examination. Participating states are not obliged to adhere to both chapters[69]; nor is an applicant obliged to have the Preliminary Examination.

3–21 The Treaty is not founded upon any international agreement about the grounds of validity for a patent. The Preliminary Examination accordingly leads to a report on a number of basic questions (patentable subject matter, novelty, inventive step and industrial applicability) in accordance with criteria that are defined only generally in the Treaty.[70] Nevertheless, for countries which have no examining system, the report may provide a basis upon which a national patent office, applying its own law, can decide

---

[65] Another collaboration of importance is the Strasbourg Convention concerning the International Patent Classification 1971 (not yet ratified by the U.K.).

[66] Records of the Diplomatic Conference are published. See generally Pfanner (1979) 1 E.I.P.R. 98.

[67] National or regional patent offices are appointed receiving offices for applications from given countries.

[68] The range of material open to search is broadly defined: PCT, Art. 15(2), PCT Rules, r. 33; but each search authority will work upon a different body of material, depending upon its collection and linguistic capacity.

[69] The Member States adopting Chapters I and II, the search authorities and examining authorities at any time may be ascertained from the latest number of the PCT Gazette.

[70] PCT, Art. 33, PCT Rules, r. 64.

whether or not to grant a patent. In the hope of opening this opportunity to developing countries, it was hastily decided to introduce the second Chapter along with the first in 1978.[71]

Apart from this, the main advantage of the Treaty is practical: it allows an applicant to institute applications in numerous countries by a single procedure; and to delay his final decision to apply in a number of countries (with the official fees, agents' fees and translation costs that this entails) for a period of 20 months (or, where Chapter 2 can be employed, for 25 months) after his priority date.[72] What the Treaty does not provide is an "international patent", since in the end each national office, or regional office such as the EPO, decides what patents to grant for its own territory.

In 1995, 78 states were participating in the PCT. Over its first decade in operation, the Treaty attained a moderate degree of success with users: in 1987, over 9,000 international applications were filed and numbers have grown since then.

By way of contrast, the TRIPS Agreement is set to standardise substantive **3–22** patent law and procedures for its enforcement to a much greater extent than ever before. The influence of the European model on its provisions is plain, and therefore it will not require major amendment to United Kingdom or European patent law.[73] The provisions on patentable subject-matter and on adequate disclosure bear a family resemblance to the EPC, though they are not always so explicit.[74] Likewise the provisions on the patent term and on the rights conferred derive from the EPC and CPC, but rights do not have to be defined by reference to claims in the patent specification.[75] There are, however, quite extensive provisions designed to inhibit the granting of compulsory licences and equivalent depreciations of the exclusive right, including exceptions for the benefit of governments and those they authorise. The impact of these on United Kingdom law will be considered later.[76]

A current may now be running in favour of a truly international patent system. Alongside the TRIPS negotiations have been two other potentially significant discussions. A WIPO initiative for a world-wide treaty harmonising essential substantive rules began with publication of a first draft in 1990.[77] By its side, the largest patent offices—those of the United States and Japan, together with the EPO—entered tri-partite discussion toward standardisation of application procedures.[78] Neither has made easy progress, since they have had to confront both philosophical differences and

---

[71] Accordingly a number of African states from the start took advantage of both Chapters.
[72] See para. 4–03, below.
[73] See Straus in Beier and Schricker, p. 16; cf. McGrath [1996] E.I.P.R. 398; Verma (1996) 27 I.I.C. 331.
[74] TRIPS, Arts 27, 29 and 32 (revocation).
[75] TRIPS, Arts 28, 30, 33, 34 (reversed burden of proof).
[76] See para. 7–42, below.
[77] For a most useful summary of issues and debates, see Wegner, *Patent Harmonisation* (1993).
[78] *ibid.*

professional jealousies of considerable proportions. Nonetheless by the end of the century, some parts at least of this work may come to fruition.

Meanwhile the shifting economic fortunes of the third world have to an extent displaced the direct antagonisms for the 1970s with a more complex set of concerns. The environmental concern to preserve the diversity of natural resources is driven partly by a desire to traditional forms of pre-industrial existence, but also by a desire to manage changes in production and life-style in a way which ensures that local communities benefit from new opportunities. Where, in particular, pharmaceuticals and other products are developed from plants or other resources of a particular country, a demand is being voiced for a share of the revenue stream being generated internationally, equivalent to the royalties which come from the extraction of minerals. This, however, is a claim being made on behalf of communities and other groups, mainly in traditional societies. How it can be accommodated within the individualistic scheme of reference which is the basis of intellectual property rights is a very difficult question. The answers to it deserve extended debate.[79]

(4) Co-operation in patenting: Western Europe[80]

3–23 Europe's industrial renaissance after the Second World War pointed up the considerable differences that existed in the systems of patent administration in the different countries. West Germany, Holland and Switzerland, for instance, undertook extensive examination of patents before grant and permitted third-party interventions; but the first two countries had introduced arrangements allowing this to be deferred for up to seven years.[81] France, Belgium and Italy had registration systems, though in the French Law of 1968 a search, with examiner's commentary, was introduced.[82] Britain occupied a mid-way position, providing for a limited search and examination, together with the possibility of third-party opposition on somewhat wider grounds.

3–24 It was appreciated very early in the life of the EEC that patents would pose a substantial barrier to intra-Community trade in "legitimate" goods.[83] In 1959, a working group was convened to consider solving the problem by instituting an EEC patent. Its plan for the purpose[84] was put aside in the

---

[79] Contrast, *e.g.* Straus [1993] 24 I.I.C. 602; Wells [1994] E.I.P.R. 111; da Costa e Silva [1995] E.I.P.R. 522; Blakeney [1997] E.I.P.R. 298.

[80] Leith, *Harmonisation of Intellectual Property in Europe* (1998).

[81] See para. 4–18, below.

[82] This "documentary report system" survived in the 1978 legislation which gave effect to the new conventions, but the opportunities for intervention have increased: Vianès (1979) 18 Ind.Prop. 220; Lecca (1979) 9 CIPA 282.

[83] See para. 1–50, above.

[84] The "Haertel Draft" of 1962. This was followed by the Strasbourg Convention on The Unification of Certain Points of Substantive Patent Law (Council of Europe, 1963), which has proved of great influence in settling the law of validity in the EPC and CPC. Its entry into force was, however, delayed until 1980 (the U.K. being one of the initial ratifying states). For the history of the European Conventions, see further Van Empel (n. 80, below), Chap. 1; Banks Report (Cmnd. 4407, 1970), Chap. 3.

wake of Britain's first failure to secure entry to the EEC; for the desirability of having the British in such an enterprise was widely acknowledged. When, however, the United States took the lead in promoting the Patent Cooperation Treaty, France sought refuge in a revival of the Community plan. With only the beginnings of an examination system, she found reason to fear the advent of international applications for France which would carry the impress of a PCT search and preliminary examination.

The revived negotiations now involved a double package: first, a conven- **3–25** tion for a single granting system through a European Patent Office; second, a convention for a Community patent which would be one product of this system. The first convention was concerned, not with freedom of E.C. trade, but with providing a less wasteful, but nonetheless substantial, examination of applications. It was accordingly to be open to a wider range of West European states, including the United Kingdom. A successful applicant would secure at the end of the process a bundle of national patents, normally in common form, for such participant countries as he designated in his application. The system would only provide an alternative route to a patent in those countries, each of which would be left free to maintain its own national system.[85] On this basis the European Patent Convention (EPC) was signed at Munich in 1973.[86] That city became the headquarters of the European Patent Office (EPO),[87] which opened its doors for applications on June 1, 1978.[88] In 20 years of operation, it has granted over 400,000 patents, having received nearly one million applications, of which some 700,000 required examination. In 1998, 113,343 applications were made and 82,087 patents granted (these being for applications made at earlier dates). A high proportion of the applications originated in the United States and Japan, the leading EPC state being Germany.[89] There are now 18 countries participating in the system, the E.C. States plus Switzerland and Liechtenstein.[90]

The second part of the arrangement, the Community Patent Convention **3–26** (CPC), was signed two years later in Luxembourg by the EEC States (including, by then, the United Kingdom). Its principle is that, at the end of the European granting procedure, if a patent is sought for any EEC State, a

---

[85] Proceedings of the negotiations have been published and form a source which is considered in deciding how to interpret the EPC.

[86] See Van Empel, *The Granting of European Patents* (1975); Paterson, *The European Patent System* (1992).

[87] The main sub-branch is at the Hague where the Search Division of the EPO is situated: the Office took over the former International Patent Institute there.

[88] Originally the fields in which it would examine were restricted, but progress towards the complete range was completed by December 1, 1979; see EPC, Art. 162.

[89] EPO, Annual Report, 1998, which contains much else by way of interest on the European system.

[90] Eight East European states have been invited to seek accession on July 1, 2002. Some of them and others already have arrangements for the extension of European patents to their territories.

single patent for the whole Community will be granted.[91] This Community patent will thus come in the "bundle", together with national patents for such non-EEC States as are also designated.

3–27   There have been various reasons for the long delay in introducing the CPC. The chief advantage of the single Community patent would be the ability to enforce it throughout the Common Market by a single main proceeding.[92] But since such a process would involve national courts, the matter is inevitably complex and was left by the original Convention for further discussion. An Agreement on the subject was negotiated in 1985 and signed in 1989.[93] This provided that, for an indefinite period, certain national courts[94] would have jurisdiction to consider both the infringement and validity of a Community patent. Alternatively, validity could be raised before a special Revocation Division of the EPO.[95] In addition, a Common Appeal court (COPAC), with judges from all Member States, would act as the effective appeal court from the national Courts and the Revocation Division.[96] The European Court of Justice would only consider references involving possible conflicts with the Treaty of Rome and on questions of jurisdiction arising under a special Protocol which will determine the Member State in which proceedings may be launched.

3–28   Other problems have been political. Since the CPC is a Convention distinct from the Treaty of Rome, Community organs possess no power to impose its terms on Member States. Until quite recently, Denmark and Ireland both faced serious obstacles in securing the national mandate necessary to ratify the Convention and its proposed amendments.[97] It was so much hoped that the CPC would form an element in the unified internal market of "1992" that the 1989 Agreement allowed its introduction first for those states able to join it—a step which in the circumstances would have been a wry compromise.

3–29   In the event, while the Danish and Irish constitutional problems were eventually overcome, other hazards emerged to prevent the CPC from

---

[91] CPC, Art. 3. The Community Patent is to be "unitary" in the sense that it can be granted, transferred, revoked or allowed to lapse only in respect of the whole Common Market: Art. 2(2). It seems, however, that an applicant will retain the right to opt for national patents.

[92] This would include the possibility of interlocutory orders having Community-wide effect. Note, however, the possible development of cross-border judgments in national patent litigation: para. 2–74, above.

[93] Together with a revised version of the CPC itself and its Implementing Regulations, the various aspects of jurisdiction are contained in the Agreement relating to Community Patents of 1989, which has Protocols on Litigation, on Privileges and Immunities for COPAC and on the Statute for that Court: see Paterson, App. 19.

[94] There was agreement that in some countries the range of Courts able to hear these proceedings would be much more restricted than for national patents at present. See generally, Groves [1987] 8 Bus.L.R. 170; Paterson, Chap. 12.

[95] Originally, after a transitional period, invalidity was to be restricted to the Revocation Division (and above it a Revocation Board, now abandoned).

[96] In appeals from national Courts, overall conduct would be in the hands of a second instance national court, which would be required to refer questions of infringement and validity to the COPAC.

[97] This created consequential difficulties with states which had subsequently joined the E.C.

starting in January 1993. In particular, a majority of states have insisted that upon grant a Community patent must be translated into their national languages. This is only one instance of the Babel crisis which threatens the very future of the E.U., but it is a significant illustration of it. Without limitation upon translation requirements (restricting them, for instance, to the claims of the specification), a cost saving is lost which would otherwise be a main key to the success of the Community patent. Among those concerned with the efficiency of patent systems, there is widespread agreement that a CPC should be introduced under either a single language regime (which would mean that the language was English) or with a (translation requirement to cover only the three official languages of the EPO—English, French and German.[98] It must remain doubtful whether this can be made to carry against national feeling in disfavoured Member States.

The Community Patent is wanted by leading industries because the EPC **3–30** "bundle" of national patents is now seen as a slow and costly way of securing complicated rights for a range of small to medium-large countries. Criticism is currently being channelled through responses to a E.C. Commission Green Paper.[99] Majority opinion among users still favours the Community Patent as an alternative to national patents granted through the EPO or national offices. The principle of unity should not be compromised; otherwise the great advantage of securing Court orders against infringers for the whole Community would be dissipated.[1]

However, there is strong insistence that EPO procedures to be made swifter, cheaper and more respectful of due process. The delays which are widely claimed to dog examiners' objections, appeals and oppositions need to be reduced. Costs at the EPO currently run much higher than at the U.S. or Japanese patent offices. For a CPC, they should be reduced to an equivalent level. Great concern has been expressed over the lax manner in which oppositions and appeals are on occasion managed, it being alleged that, in various ways, cases are not seen to be decided on the basis of submissions which the parties have had adequate opportunity to make or comment upon. An English court felt compelled to the conclusion that it could not entertain judicial review proceedings over EPO opposition proceedings which resulted in (*inter alla*) a European Patent for the United Kingdom being granted.[2] This is because, as a matter of international

---

[98] See the Papers referred to in n. 99.

[99] *Promoting Innovation through Patents* Com(97) 314. Prepared by DG XV and preceded by the DG XIII Paper by Straus, *The Present State of the Patent System in the European Union (1997)*. Responses to the DG XV Green Paper up to November 1997 are collated in a Commission Report of Findings (Paper 115, 1998). Not included therein is H.L. Paper 115/1998 (S.C. on the E.C.), expressing British reactions, but these are upon similar lines.

[1] European opinion runs in favour of the trial of both infringement and validity issues before a single Court.

[2] *ex p. Lenzing* [1997] R.P.C. 245; Cook [1997] R.P.C. 245.

treaty, the EPC creates a separate judirical structure, which cannot be amenable to supervision by an English tribunal. The complaint which had raised the issue was, however, taken to be a serious one, which must, at the very least, be addressed in settling the judicial structure for administering the Community Patent.[3]

(5) A second tier right for Western Europe?

3-31 A separate question of unified or unitary rights within the E.C. has recently come into prominence. A majority of Member States supplement their patent system with a secondary form of formal protection for technical advances.[4] These go by various names—short-term patent, petty patent, utility model (an awkward translation of *Gebrauchsmuster*), *certificate d'utilité*—and may together be labelled "second-tier protection". The variety of names is a first indication of the considerable differences in these rights from country to country. Inevitably, the variations and the lack of such protection in some states, have led the E.C. Commission to study prospects for an E.C. right and/or national harmonisation.[5]

3-32 The special position of the United Kingdom lies in the distinctive route which it has followed in order to provide a second tier of protection for technical ideas: by introducing industrial copyright and then by modifying it into unregistered design right, it has provided a wholly informal means of protecting the shape of industrial articles; and at the same time it has extended this protection indiscriminately to technical and to aesthetic shapes of products.[6] The systems provided elsewhere in Community countries all adopt a formal process of some kind, making application to a national office a necessary pre-condition. It is primarily this difference which seems to put the unregistered design right beyond the range of possible models for a European future.[7]

3-33 Of the various schemes now operating in West Europe, none is subject to any substantive examination of validity before grant.[8] As a balance for this

---

[3] See Brinkhof, Bossung, Krieger (1996) 27 I.I.C. 225, 287, 855.
[4] All save Sweden, Luxembourg and the U.K. Under the Paris Convention, "utility models" must be given national treatment and six months' priority. This is extended to WTO countries by TRIPS, Art. 2(1), but the latter Agreement does not require second-tier protection (it is not part of the U.S. world-view).
[5] Green Paper on Utility Model Protection in the Common Market (July 19, 1995, COM(95) 370). In preparation the Commission obtained two Reports from the IFO-Institut which show some industrial opinion in favour of an utility-model system, but the Green Paper itself is extremely cautious. Compare the much more forthright proposal for an E.C. utility model by the Max Planck Institute for IP Law, Munich (1993); Kern [1994] 25 I.I.C. 627.
[6] See paras 14–43 *et seq.*, below.
[7] See further, paras 14–52 *et seq.*, below.
[8] There may, however, be a search before grant (*e.g.* in Austria, or optionally in Germany) or a search before infringement proceedings (*e.g.* in France and Ireland). The Japanese system used to be the best-known utility model with a patent-like examination; in 1994, however, this was dropped. The number of applications there has plummeted.

relative informality (and cheapness), the rights endure for a maximum, which in many states is now 10 years from application.[9] The chief differences concern two matters: the extent of subject-matter within the system; and the test of necessary advance over the prior art.

Some variants have adopted a modest range, operating in the sphere of technical design and relating only to the functional shape of articles.[109] Such a "utility model" system became well-known in Germany (until it was expanded in 1990) and passed from there to Greece, Italy, Spain and Portugal, where it remains in force. In contrast, Austria, Ireland, Belgium and France all permit second-tier rights in any patentable subject-matter[11]; and Germany (since its reform) permits everything save processes, as does Denmark.

So far as the element of technical advance is concerned, almost all countries seek to lower the threshold of admissibility, compared with the inventive step requirement of modern patent law. There may be no requirement other than novelty (as in Austria, Italy and Greece) or some differentiating phrase may be adopted, such as the Spanish *superevidencia— utter obviousness.*[12]

The typical case which countries have had in mind when introducing **3–34** second-tier schemes is the inventor of modest workshop improvements, perhaps in his own or some other small business which lacks the resources to engage in full-scale patenting.[13] This meritorious image has made the development a particularly attractive one recently in smaller E.C. States. Where the system is confined to technical design (utility model protection in the true sense), it probably fits this modest aim reasonably well. It is when the schemes are extended to all patentable subject-matter, at the same time as lowering the threshold of technical advance, that real danger is to be anticipated. Patent systems, after all, were obliged to introduce the expensive and time-consuming business of substantive examination in order to cut out the belligerent claimant to a dubious invention from doing a great deal of damage by threatening litigation. Yet a wide-ranging second-tier right actually entitles the holder to claims of a breadth which may well not be sustainable under a patent system. He may indeed acquire this extensive, unexamined protection for his first 10 years and then, for the second decade, get a patent for as much as he can actually justify.[14]

---

[9] In fine isolation, Portugal allows indefinite renewal!

[10] Thus at this point providing some affinity here to the U.K. unregistered design right.

[11] In one significant respect, Austria goes further, allowing this form of protection for the logic underlying a computer program (Act of 1994, Art. 1(2)): this appears intended to by-pass the exclusion of computer programs as such from the patent system: paras 5–63 *et seq.*, below.

[12] Another limitation may be that novelty takes account only of the national state of the art (at least for prior use). This may lead importers of inventions to secure second-tier protection. The Commission appears to favour a test of absolute, rather than relative, novelty in its Green Paper (n. 5, above). It would also want a 12-month grace period.

[13] Smaller countries with less advanced technological bases feel a natural interest in such schemes. See, *e.g.* Parkes (1994) 25 I.I.C. 204 (discussing the Irish short-term patent).

[14] See Tootal [1994] E.I.P.R. 511; Llewelyn, *Utility Models/Second Tier Protection* (1996).

3–35   The British have had the historical experience and commonsense to hold back from any development on such a scale, arguing instead for improved efficiency in the patent system itself.[15] At the same time, by creating the Patents County Court, and by reforming High Court procedure, they have taken steps to reduce the enormity of patent litigation.[16]

Where the argument will end is hard to prognosticate. As its most recent step, the European Commission has published a Draft Directive for a moderate form of standard "utility model" to be adopted by all E.U. states.[17] It is proposed as a harmonising measure that will enhance competitiveness in the Community, in particular, by encouraging the innovative efforts of small and medium firms. A right would be granted for a maximum 10 years[18] without any preceding examination of the substance. The applicant would merely have the right to require a search to be conducted for prior art.[19] The right would be for an "invention", which, like a patentable invention, would have to be novel, inventive and industrially applicable.

Despite the borrowing of these concepts from patent law, on the all-important question of "inventive step", only a lower threshold would need to be satisfied: compared with the prior art, the invention must show either, particular effectiveness in terms of, for example, ease of application or use; or a practical or industrial advantage.[20] This could, at one and the same time, establish a very low threshold of inventiveness for a utility model and push up the requirement in patent law. It could indeed herald a return to the opaque concept of the former German law which required a sufficient "level" of inventiveness in a valid patent. Because some major industries object to the inevitable insecurities that this will introduce in the kernel of protection, they would be omitted from the plan. The right would not be available for biological inventions, chemical or pharmaceutical substances or processes, or "inventions involving computer programs".[21] That only makes the distinction between the two rights more obscure in the remaining industrial fields. The proposal accordingly remains highly controversial.

---

[15] The concept of a "registered patent" was fostered in the Nicholson Green Paper (*Intellectual Property Rights and Innovation* (Cmnd 9117, 1983), paras 220–222) but rejected in the Government's White Paper (Cmnd. 9712, 1986), paras 15–18. For attempts to keep the idea alive in the U.K., see Lees [1993] CIPA 79 and subsequent report, *ibid.*, at 150; Chartered Institute of Patent Agents, *Second Tier Protection* (1994).

[16] See para. 2–10—2–11, below; Nott [1994] E.I.P.R. 3; Jacob [1997] I.P.Q. 3.

[17] [1998] O.J. C 36/13.

[18] The right will be granted for six years, renewable twice for two-year periods.

[19] A member state would be entitled to require a search before any litigation to the utility model was brought—not much comfort to a defendant already working within its bounds.

[20] Art. 6. Double-talk pervades the loose drafting of this provision. It is said that the *applicant* has to satisfy this test "clearly and convincingly" (to what level of proof?): of course, it is only a right-owner who has to do so. That is the nub of the difficulties.

[21] Art. 4. Biotechnical inventions have received their own dispensation in the Directive 98/44, which is discussed at various points below. *cf.* the much narrower exclusion from the patent system of computer programs *as such*: below, para. 5–63ff.

4. JUSTIFYING THE PATENT SYSTEM

(1) Basic objectives

In the course of time, both "individual" and "public" justifications have **3–36** played prominent roles in the arguments in favour of patents for invention, as for other kinds of intellectual property.[22] At various periods the idea of a patent as an instrument of justice to the inventor has proved attractive, and the power of this sort of argument is by no means exhausted.[23]

Yet rewarding inventive ingenuity may seem little more than an incidental consequence of modern patent systems. They do not protect each inventor who conceives an invention. Only the first-comer is entitled—in most systems, indeed, it is the first to apply for a patent, rather than the first to invent, who is given priority. The protection is then good not only against those who derive their information from that patentee but also against those who work it out independently. The period of protection, moreover, is very short compared with other forms of "property". If a major object were to give the inventor his just reward, a system more closely akin to copyright—with its "property"-like duration and its protection of all original creations, but only against copying—would seem more appropriate. In this connection, the intrusion of artistic copyright into the sphere of industrial production after 1968, and its major modification twenty years later, provides a telling comparison.[24]

Today the debate over patent systems tends to concentrate upon their **3–37** role as a "public" instrument of economic policy. Patents are looked upon to provide two kinds of aid towards the technical efficiency, and hence the growing wealth, of the community as a whole. They are intended to encourage the making of inventions and the subsequent innovative work that will put those inventions to practical use; and they are expected to procure information about the invention for the rest of the industry and the public generally, which otherwise might be withheld, at least for a period

---

[22] What follows builds upon the ideas introduced above at paras 1–32—1–47. The best-known modern discussion of the justifications for patent systems, sceptical in tone, is Machlup, *An Economic Review of the Patent System* (U.S. Senate Committee on the Judiciary, Sub-Committee on Patents, Trademarks and Copyrights, Study No. 15). And see Plant (1934) 1 Economica 30; Nordhaus, *Invention, Growth and Welfare* (1969); Scherer and Ross, *Industrial Market Structure and Economic Performance* (3rd ed., 1990), Chap. 15; Economic Council of Canada, *Report on Intellectual and Industrial Property* (1971), Chaps 3, 4; together with Hindley, *Background Study on Economic Theory*, Chap. 1; and Firestone, *Economic Implications of Patents* (1971); Taylor and Silberston, *The Economic Impact of the Patent System* (1973), Chap. 2; Bowman, *Patent and Anti-trust Law* (1973), Chap. 2; Kitch (1977) 29 J. Law & Econ. 265; Manderville, Lamberton and Bishop, *Economic Effects of the Australian Patent System* (1982); Kaufer, *Economics of the Patent System* (1989); Hall, *Innovation, Economics and Evolution* (1994); Arup, *Innovation Policy and Law* (1993).

[23] For instance, the introduction of compensation for employee-inventors reflects this attitude: see paras 7–08—7–14, below.

[24] See Chap. 14, below.

that could be crucial. These incentives and informational objectives deserve separate consideration.

(2) Patents as incentives to invent and innovate

3–38 Discussion about the efficacy of incentives has a practical, utilitarian flavour which is lacking when the argument is about the demands of justice for the individual. Even so, it is very difficult to measure or assess the effects (if any) that a patent system is producing. It is widely felt that some sort of intervention is needed if inventions are to be made and introduced at anything like an optimal rate. Whether this should be done by a patent system, rather than by giving legal protection against breach of confidence or copying, or by direct investment on the part of the state, is more controversial. If it is to be by a patent system, there are many questions about its exact nature which may affect its performance.

Modern patent systems, it should be observed, offer a standard formula to all who have "inventions" to protect. They contrast with systems of research grant and reward, whether funded by the state or private organisations.[25] These usually depend upon a decision by the paymaster to concentrate resources upon particular objectives. Assessing a patent system, accordingly, means taking a view of its effects across the board—and that adds considerably to the difficulty. Two aspects of its range which make useful starting points in the discussion are the types of inventor for whom today it provides its incentive; and the types of invention to which it is applied.

(a) *Types of inventor*

3–39 One persistent argument against patents in the nineteenth-century controversy was this: since inventions are there to be discovered, industries that have progressed to a certain point will inevitably make them, and so artificial aids are unnecessary.[26] It was a line of argument that carried some conviction when the bulk of inventions concerned relatively simple mechanical contrivances that were often worked out as a by-product of ordinary manufacturing. In the face of increasingly systematic organisation of research and development, and the extensive process of education which precedes it, this point of view is harder to maintain.

---

[25] Compare also proposals for systems of "innovation patent" and "innovation warrant", both of which require a state office to play a decisive role in determining the term and other incidents of the right granted: Kronz [1983] E.I.P.R. 178, 206; Kingston (ed.) *Direct Protection of Innovation* (1987).

[26] See Machlup and Penrose (para. 3–09, n. 30, above). Further, it could be said that there was injustice in giving the reward to the man who stumbled upon the solution first, since he probably owed a great deal to what he had learned from his precursors. Note in this connection the refusal of a patent to a genetic engineering firm because it merely won a race to a known goal by known methods: para. 5–47, below.

If anything, the development of this characteristic of modern industry **3–40** turns the issue on its head: is the pertinent question now whether patents are needed to produce the optimal degree of investment in research and development organised on a "corporate" scale? It seems not. One perceptive account of the historical record suggests that the individual inventor, and the small organisation centred around individuals of outstanding quality, continue to contribute a significant, even perhaps a disproportionate, number of the most important inventions that have been made over recent decades.[27] This type of inventor certainly cannot be ignored in any assessment of patents.

In any case, there is no clear evidence that corporations are not **3–41** influenced in their research and development decisions by their chances of securing and taking advantage of patent protection. Invention, and its subsequent development, still occur across the whole spectrum of industrial organisation from giant troop to one-man band. One of the more attractive arguments for a patent system is that, because of this very diversity, a range of different incentives is desirable.[28] Patents then have their place as the technique aimed at those who feel the attraction of market rewards.[29]

(b) *Levels of invention*

Patent systems protect a wide variety of technical novelties, from break- **3–42** throughs that will found new industries, to quite minor improvements in established products. The chance of behaving to any striking degree as a monopolist is in fact reserved to a tiny proportion of all patentees.[30] Two characteristics of the invention will determine how far this is possible: the extent to which it fulfils a demand from consumers that was previously not met at all, or met only by something much less satisfactory (television in place of sound radio); and the degree to which it is cheaper or leads to more efficient operations in comparison with the substitutes which preceded it (power-driven tool replacing one hand-operated).

Occasionally, as with a drug that had no real precursor, a patentee may be able to withhold supplies so as to charge the price which will give him

---

[27] Jewkes, Sawers and Stillerman, *The Sources of Invention* (2nd ed., 1969), Chap. 9; Mansfield (1986) 32 J. Pol. Sc. 175; Schankerman and Pakes (1986) 96 Econ. J. 1052. It does not follow that individual inventors are necessarily spurred by the patent system. In the past academic scientists, for instance, have been moved more by the desire for knowledge and the recognition that invention may bring. That attitude is now changing, but serious tensions are the result. See Eisenberg (1987) 97 Yale L.J. 177.

[28] Jewkes *et al.* (n. 27, above).

[29] There is some evidence that the expenditure of really large firms on R & D does not produce proportionately as much invention as that of smaller firms: see esp. Kamien and Schwartz, *Market Structure and Innovation* (1982) pp. 49–104. But it is hard to weigh the significance of this, since it requires an evaluation of the merits of different inventions; nor, even if it is true, has it any clear consequence for the future of patent systems.

[30] See also paras 1–45—1–47, above.

the largest return from estimated demand. So also when he is able to cut costs of production so much that he can still reach this level of profit at a price below that at which competitors can sell any substitute products and stay in business. More often, however, he cannot achieve so drastic an effect. His room for manoeuvre is then limited by the need to sell at a price just enough below that of competitors to cut into their market shares.[31]

3–43   Some of this century's most significant inventions were only put to productive use long after their discovery, which suggests the system is not always a noticeably efficient mechanism for procuring commercial innovation.[32] But equally the long gaps indicate the need for some artificial intrusion into the competitive process. The barriers that may stand in the way of introducing completely new ideas, however striking their ultimate commercial success, are numerous. The difficulties may be innovative—the investment and time needed to arrive at a viable product may be unpredictable. The problems may be financial—the cost of setting up new plant, and often of writing-off old, or the cost of persuading distributors to stock and consumers to buy, may seem forbidding. The inhibitions may be organisational—the very size of an enterprise may mean that risky ideas are abandoned in face of well-reasoned argument from one or other quarter.

Of course there are industries where the leading firms become seized by a determination to innovate. Pharmaceutical producers are one outstanding recent example, the computer industry another. But in others again, major technical change may be held up until individuals with flair and determination can secure the independence (within or outside a larger organisation) that they need to override the well-meaning caution of others less adventurous. In particular, if the dominant firms in an industry are few, there is a danger of complacent sluggishness; of this a number of illustrations exist.[33]

3–44   Patent systems ought to help in lowering the psychological barriers to major innovation, particularly since the limited period of protection imposes a penalty for being dilatory. But the practical operation of the system introduces elements which diminish this impact. An innovator who is successful either demonstrates that there is a new market to be tapped, or he begins to cut substantially into the market shares of established competitors. No one is more obviously exposed to envious imitation. It becomes vital for competitors to examine the innovator's patents for

---

[31] This puts in very summary form some crucial conclusions to be drawn from the standard economic analysis of the patent system: for which see, *e.g.* Baxter (1966) 76 Yale L.J. 267, 358–370 (Appendix); Kitch (1986) 8 L.R. Econ. 31.

[32] Individuals or industries have an obvious motive for suppressing highly efficient inventions of the long-lasting razor-blade variety. However, there is not much evidence that this object can actually be achieved: that it can be brought about by patenting, as distinct from swearing all concerned to secrecy, seems highly unlikely, though it is sometimes suggested.

[33] *e.g.* Jewkes *et al.* (n. 27, above), pp. 166–168 on the extraction of iron from laconite; Merges and Nelson (1990) 90 Col. L.R. 839, 884 *et seq.*; David in Wallerstein *et al.*, *Global Dimensions of Intellectual Property Rights in Science and Technology* (1993).

weaknesses. Since the protection a patent gives depends primarily on the language used to define the claims in the specification, a rival may well spend a good deal on finding other ways of doing much the same thing, which the draftsman of the specification did not contemplate (and did not inadvertently manage to cover). Any competitor with fight in him must be expected to look for methods of "inventing round" the specification.[34]

As far as the validity of a patent is concerned, the difference between **3–45** making the invention and succeeding in innovation is crucial. There may have been various suggestions in the literature and practice before the patent which reached more or less the same invention. Even if none of these led to successful production, they may nevertheless provide a plausible basis for attacking the patent.[35] A patentee who appreciates this when he is deciding whether to manufacture may be obliged to treat his exclusive right as a weapon that can be tested only in prolonged and exhausting legal skirmishes.

In terms of objectives, the implications are straightforward: if the patent **3–46** system is to provide a useful incentive for the making and commercial introduction of major inventions, it must give sound rights of clear scope. The current movement to strengthen the examination procedures of patent offices should not be allowed to slacken. If in consequence a few significant inventions are mistakenly refused protection, this should be accepted as an inevitable risk in the pursuit of a greater good. Regrettably, the creation of competing patent offices, such as has occurred in Western Europe, has the effect of making them "applicant friendly". While this may be a desirable reversal of the past attitude of some national offices, it can easily be carried too far.

Looking across the whole range of industry, however, a measure of doubt must continue to surround the role of patent systems in encouraging the exploitation of major inventions. Even with pharmaceutical products, where patents do appear to provide a significant amount of protection, it is evident that this strength arises from a combination of forces: in particular, the fact that many countries now require lengthy testing of new products substantially increases the "lead-time" of a novel drug over the substitutes and alternatives that competitors may then develop. It may well be that the incentive effect of patents is of more significance when it comes to marginal ideas—concepts that do not hold hope of more than minor improvements in the existing art. Although a patent cannot in such a case promise a major run of monopoly profits, nonetheless it offers the chance to explore and exploit free of direct imitation; and competitors may not feel the same compulsion to find equivalents or to attack validity. With major inventions,

---

[34] "Inventing round" a patent, and the patentee's counter-ploy of himself fencing off all alternatives, may sometimes produce valuable information. But this is scarcely a rational way to allocate scarce resources: see Plant (n. 22, above) at 21; Machlup (n. 22, above) at 51.

[35] See further, paras 5–29 *et seq.*, below.

moreover, the advantage of being first in the field may well be a perfectly adequate incentive, whereas lesser improvements may well be neglected in the absence of a protective stimulus. Of course, there is no telling when something that looks small will turn out big.

3–47 One practical question which stems from such considerations is how to define the minimum inventive content that will justify the grant of a patent. Should the general patent system adopt a requirement of inventive step (or "non-obviousness"), and, if so, how should its level be set? Most modern patent systems (including the British) have such a test, and we shall discuss later the search for verbal formulae which seek to specify the elusive quality in question.[36] Here it should be emphasised that the issue creates uncertainty about the validity of many patents and is one significant cause in lowering the practical value of the system as an incentive to invention and innovation.

"Second-tier" schemes are sometimes advocated as a means of reducing this problem. As already suggested they may result in an even wider margin of uncertainty.

(c) *Optimum term for patents*

3–48 The consensus in the European convention negotiations was that patents deserve to last for 20 years from filing. A single period for all patents has an arbitrary appearance[37]; but the British experience of granting extensions in deserving cases demonstrated the practical hurdles in the way of introducing individual variations. If one term must be chosen as a maximum how can the most desirable be ascertained? The answer must be given in terms of incentives, and in particular of the encouragement needed for inventions of commercial importance enough to last for the whole period. It may be that the recent increase in the British period from 16 to 20 years is large enough to have real impact on the willingness to spend on invention and innovation of this potential kind. Nonetheless the present value of a return of investment from a point so far in the future is small.[38] Additions even of this magnitude to the term can have little predictable effect on incentives. Yet each year that is added increases the social cost of having the invention available only through the channel of the patent monopoly. Certainly any further extension should be made only after most careful consideration.

---

[36] See para. 5–32, below.

[37] Hence the growing campaign of the pharmaceutical and agricultural industries, already in some measure successful in the U.S. and the E.C., for an additional term to compensate for the delay imposed by official testing of novel drugs and crop products: see para. 4–26, below.

[38] For a technical demonstration of this, see Machlup (n. 22, above) at 66–73; *cf.* Nordhaus (above, n. 22); Scherer (1977) 62 Am.Ec.R. 422. Priest (1986) 8 Rsch. in L. &. Econ. 19.

(3) Patents as an information system

In Britain the policy of making the patent system a source of technical **3-49** information has been deliberately pursued since the early industrial revolution.[39] For many years the results have justified treating this aspect of the system as more than a useful by-product. Patents do make available a large quantity of information about the latest technical advances, and they are regularly consulted by those concerned with development in many industries. Nevertheless exaggerated expectations need to be avoided. If the inventive concept is one that has to be embodied in a marketed product, the patent may give earlier access to the information and perhaps a more explicit statement of what the invention is. Only if the invention is one that need never be revealed to the rest of the industry in the course of exploiting it does the patent provide a clear long-term gain in terms of publicity. But this, of course, is the case where secrecy offers a real alternative—a route that, despite the danger of leaks, may seem simpler and cheaper to pursue.

The information aspect of patents is not a policy that is altogether easy to **3-50** implement.[40] There is an obvious temptation to any patentee to omit from his specification information that may seem incidental but is in fact useful or important to commercial success. When this effect can be achieved, the patent system is reduced to an index of sources from which further information may be had on application and payment. This leaves the policy-maker, whether legislator, patent office administrator or judge, with a choice: either to recognise that the system cannot hope to provide more information, or to insist that it should by declaring such patents invalid. Countries with examining offices have arrived at rather varied results in their approach to this dilemma. The typical American specification is noteworthy for its dogged attention to pedestrian detail; a German specification may be hazy about practical steps but is more likely to reveal basic concepts. One decision of the English Court of Appeal leans in the former direction: it holds that a specification about basic ideas in a new technology should teach its principles to second-rank technicians rather than to leading researchers in the field.[41] This sort of insistence carries with it the danger that really significant developments may be the subject of invalid patents. Yet to give up any real effort to police the disclosure requirement may be to surrender the one public advantage of the patent system that remains relatively uncontroversial.

The notion of patent collections as an index of where to apply for more **3-51** information at least gives some clue to the businessman's continuing interest in the patent system. Of course specifications are read by competi-

---

[39] See para. 3-06, above.
[40] See generally, Beier and Straus (1977) 8 I.I.C. 387; Eisenschitz and Oppenheim in Phillips (ed.) *Patents in Perspective* (1985) Chaps 5, 6; Koenig (1983) 12 Res. Pol. 15; Mansfield (1985) 34 J. Ind. Econ. 217.
[41] *Valensi v. British Radio* [1973] R.P.C. 337; and see generally, paras 5-93 *et seq.*, below.

tors who are at roughly the same stage of advance and who then seek licences in order to avoid impediments in the way of their own development work. But a great deal of licensing is of an information package to a firm which lacks the background to set up production for itself. In this sort of case the basic concept is frequently patented, while much crucial incident exists only as know-how that has to be transmitted under terms of confidence. For this sort of case, the patent system may alert potential licensees about people who have interesting ideas on offer; and the licensor will be interested in having a patent, not only for the publicity that may follow but also because it may provide a measure of security. If his only protection lies in confidence obligations, he has to ensure that all personnel have given adequate undertakings and he may well have to contemplate proceedings against them if they appear to be in breach. Resources ought not to be devoted to ensuring that people keep their bargains whenever this can be avoided.

(4) Adapting the patent system: new technology

3–52 The emergence of each major technology produces adjustments in the patent system, and is, therefore, likely to stir up arguments about underlying rationale and specific policy objectives. The coming of computers, as already noted, first activated symptoms of denial, with a series of moves to place computer programs beyond the reach of the system; latterly, there has been growing industrial pressure to take the opposite position.[42] Over a much longer period, the well-known resistance to the idea of a monopoly over something as fundamental as a chemical substance (particularly where it is a pharmaceutical) has gradually given way.[43] A set of rules on the disclosure requirement have enabled claims of commercially significant breadth to be made, and at the same time for biological material to be made available through culture collections.[44]

A generation after Crick and Watson's uncoiling of living structures, techniques of genetic manipulation have undergone a series of remarkable advances. Once uncovered, each procedure has been rapidly taken over by laboratories everywhere, spawning quantities of competitive research. In particular medical applications of biotechnology have attracted a rash of new businesses, often spinning-off from academic teams. There have been rushes to patent, accompanied by demands for very wide claims modelled on those of the initial master patents by now familiar in organic chemistry. Patent offices and tribunals have reacted slowly and cautiously to this.[45]

---

[42] For details, see paras 5–63 *et seq*., below.
[43] The TRIPS Agreement marks a strategic triumph: see para. 3–22, above.
[44] See para. 5–98, below.
[45] See further below, paras 5–50, 5–70ff., 5–102.

Only a decade after some of the first applications were filed did attempts to enforce them produce indignant responses and so litigation.[46]

In Britain the resulting case law has demonstrated how very chancy some **3–53** of the early work was, and how patent advisers nonetheless acted upon first signals of success to seek protection for the ultimate end in sight. The courts have shown themselves responsive to arguments that one competitor has been seeking to oust his rivals to an extent that the limited range of his "invention" simply cannot justify. If patentees of biotechnology could have such a weapon the incentive effect of the patent system would be mightily enhanced. If one of them were entering new territory without rivals, no doubt he could be treated as if he were being given a licence to prospect for minerals.[47] What that generous analogy in the theory of property rights fails to appreciate is that, often enough, the lure of gold will have brought several prospectors onto the territory before anyone of them is in a position to show a superiority which alone ought to entitle him to an exclusive licence.

The biotechnology experience underscores how the justifications for the **3–54** patent system are not independent. Rather they are cumulative, and each imposes its limitations. Out of competition in the production of goods and services, consumers benefit from the range of alternatives presented to them and the resultant capping effect on prices. Even to encourage the generation and commercialisation of new products, patent rights are limited to technological invention, and the rights ought to preclude competitors in proportion to the scale of that invention. In order to measure that scale, the invention must be described, and thus the disclosure requirement is not just an economic benefit in opening up vital information. It is an essential element in determining whether and what there is that deserves state-supported curtailment of competition at a point where competition is likely to be intense.

The justification for this balance can be put in economic terms: it may be said to offer incentives to invent and then to innovate at a level which secures a considerable measure of action, while providing the industry concerned with highly useful information and some chance to stay in the technology by making improvements and variations.[48] At the same time,

---

[46] The issues of adaptation are rendered complex by the provisions of the EPC which limit the scope of biological subject matter which may be patented. The meaning to be attached to them has become one focus of ethical campaigns against technical interventions in human, animal and plant development. The area embraces such emotive practices as in vitro fertilisation, animal and human cloning, animal testing and genetically modified foodstuffs. To a limited extent, the E.C. Commission has been able to modify the provisions deriving from the EPC in a Harmonisation Directive on the Legal Protection of Biotechnological Inventions (98/44 [1998] O.J. L.213/13.), which is discussed later (below, paras 5–70ff). Its rather limited terms were procured only after extended negotiations on a number of fronts, during which the opposition sometimes looked insurmountable.

[47] The "prospect" theory was advocated by Kitch (1977) 20 J.L. & Econ. 283; criticised esp. by Beck, 5 Res. in L & Econ. 193 (1983).

[48] See esp. Merges and Nelson (n. 33, above).

there is no denying the moral sense of propriety which insists that invention alone justifies any reward by exclusive right, and then only a proportional reward. To depart from this root impulse—for instance, by saying that the commercial development of any novelty should be the basis for exclusivity—will replace the incentives with other, probably less desirable alternatives, and will also be felt to lead to unfair preferences which could ultimately return us to Queen Elizabeth's patent over playing cards.

5. The Patents Act 1977: Structure and Interpretation

3–55 This chapter ends with a bridge passage. The international and European antecedents of the Patents Act 1977 make it a complex measure which deserves a more technical outline than has yet been given. Part I sets out the new domestic law. So far as this is concerned with the making and processing of applications, it only affects applications to the British Patent Office as such[49]; European applications are governed by the EPC so long as they are being dealt with by the EPO (that is up to grant and during post-grant opposition before the EPO). The other main provisions apply to British patents granted by either route. These concern patentability,[50] term, restoration and surrender[51]; property rights and employees' inventions[52]; abuse of monopoly and Crown use[53]; infringement, revocation and associated issues[54]; and amendment.[55]

3–56 Part II provides the incorporative machinery for the EPC, CPC and PCT. International applications under the PCT may evolve into applications to the British Office under the Act by virtue of section 89. By section 77, European patents which designate the United Kingdom fall to be treated as patents under the 1977 Act from publication of the mention of grant in the *European Patent Bulletin*; and there follow a number of consequential provisions on European applications, authentic texts, conversion into a national application, jurisdiction over the right to apply for a European patent, professional representation and evidence for EPO proceedings.[56]

By contrast, if and when the CPC takes effect, Community patents will be governed by that Convention. The main purpose of section 86 of the 1977 Act is therefore to make the Convention itself part of United Kingdom law and to give the Secretary of State an implementive power to make regulations. It is important to note that a Community patent will not

---

[49] See PA 1977, ss. 14–21; to this s. 13(3) is an exception. The provisions on secrecy (ss. 22, 23) can affect European and foreign applications generally.
[50] *ibid.*, ss. 1–6.
[51] *ibid.*, ss. 24–29.
[52] *ibid.*, ss. 30–43.
[53] *ibid.*, ss. 44–59.
[54] *ibid.*, ss. 60–74.
[55] *ibid.*, ss. 75, 76.
[56] *ibid.*, ss. 78–85.

become a patent under the 1977 Act and so will not be governed by the provisions of Part 1 which affect a European patent (U.K.). Thus infringement of a Community patent will be determined by the CPC's provisions, not the Act's[57]; and the rules on patentability will be the relevant Articles in the EPC since these are incorporated into the CPC. But because there is still no immediate prospect of the CPC being implemented, the law governing Community patents will be mentioned only incidentally in the following chapters.[58]

Part III deals with a variety of general matters: legal proceedings, **3–57** including the creation of the Patents Court within the frame of the Chancery Division[59]; criminal offences[60]; patent agents[61]; administrative provisions[62]; the power to make Patent Rules[63]; a provision attempting to elucidate what is meant by the scope of a patented invention (taking account of the Protocol to the EPC, Article 69)[64]; and interpretation.[65] Sections 127 and 128 and associated Schedules[66] determine how far "old" patents—that is those already granted on June 1, 1978, or resulting from applications for which a complete specification had been furnished before that day—are still governed by the Patents Act 1949. Few now survive.

Some parts of the new domestic law have been inspired in a general way **3–58** by legal developments elsewhere. Thus the restructured application system in the British Patent Office is to a considerable extent modelled on the arrangements for the PCT and the EPO. Yet the derivation is not direct in the sense that provisions of the Patents Act use the same language as the international and European conventions. Yet strangely section 130(7) of the 1977 Act declares that they are "so framed as to have, as nearly as practicable, the same effects in the United Kingdom as do the corresponding provisions" of the EPC, CPC and PCT in the territories to which they apply. These provisions concern: patentability and the requirements for description and claims of the specification; revocation at the behest of the person properly entitled to grant; non-working as a ground for granting a compulsory licence; infringement and the extent of monopoly; grounds of revocation; and certain supplemental provisions.

The legacy of strict, grammatical interpretation by British Courts led the draftsman of the Act to make many variations of expression in the hope

---

[57] *cf.* the *Harbottle* case, n. 70, below.
[58] PA 1977, Pt II also provides machinery for declaring countries to be Convention countries for the purpose of the Paris Convention arrangements on priority (s. 90(1)) and on evidence, judicial notice and other matters in relation to the more recent conventions (ss. 91–95).
[59] *ibid.*, ss. 96–108.
[60] *ibid.*, ss. 109–113.
[61] *ibid.*, ss. 114–115.
[62] *ibid.*, ss. 116–123.
[63] *ibid.*, s. 124.
[64] *ibid.*, s. 125.
[65] *ibid.*, s. 130.
[66] *ibid.*, Scheds 1–4.

(presumably) of giving British judges directions that would unambiguously produce the legal result aimed at by the Convention text.[67] But there are two dangers in this technique. One is that the draftsman may not spot ambiguities in his revised version and so introduce his own uncertainties.[68] The other is that if a variation in language produces a clear difference in meaning, this may, despite section 130(7), be treated as intentional.[69]

3–59   There have now been numerous occasions on which the terms of section 130(7) have been used in order to reach an interpretation of the Act which is considered consistent with a convention text.[70] Whitford J. remarked that "it is of the greatest importance that in this jurisdiction we should take note of the decisions of the EPO and that, so far as may be possible in all those countries which are now bound by the common interest created by the Convention, an attempt should be made to give the same meaning to relevant provisions, whichever the jurisdiction which is being invoked".[71]

The significance of that statement lies in the fact that there is no ultimate Court of Appeal to which questions of interpretation can be referred for final settlement. Within the E.C. this will to a large extent be rectified once the amended CPC is brought into effect, since this will create a Community Patent Appeal Court (COPAC).[72] But even so, this will not provide a complete solution for the whole network of authorities established through the Conventions. For this, COPAC will hear appeals from national Courts trying proceedings for infringement or revocation of Community patents. However, it will not be a Court of Appeal from decisions of the EPO taken in the course of its granting procedure. These will continue to go to the EPO Boards of Appeal, with ultimate reference to the Enlarged Board of Appeal.[73] Nor will it have jurisdiction over tribunals in the non-E.C. states (Liechtenstein and Switzerland) which have dealt with the equivalent European patents for their country.[74] Accordingly, even at that stage, Whitford J.'s spirit of co-operation will remain hard to achieve. It is currently fostered by biennial meetings of judges concerned with patent matters from the EPC States, which began in 1982.

3–60   Over time the judges' willingness to collaborate may be tested, for one reason in particular. It is widely considered that a meeting to revise the EPC would be a complex and unpredictable event, only to be undertaken when it proves unavoidable.[75] This accordingly places considerable strain

---

[67] See para. 1–25, above; and Ellis in M. Vitoria (ed.) *The Patents Act 1977* (1978), pp. 21–34.

[68] For an example, see para. 5–16, below, on the disclosure of information in breach of confidence.

[69] Note in this connection the authorities on the interpretation of statutes derived from convention texts, para. 1–25, above.

[70] *e.g. Smith Kline v. Harbottle* [1980] R.P.C. 363; *Schering's and Wyeth's Applications* [1985] R.P.C. 545.

[71] *B. & R. Relay's Application* [1985] R.P.C. 1 at 6.

[72] See para. 3–27, above.

[73] EPC, Arts 106–112; Paterson, Chap. 2.

[74] On the need for harmonisation, Gall [1988] E.I.P.R. 38.

[75] However, the EPO has held a hearing (Report, published December 20, 1995) soliciting views on its strategies.

upon the judiciary concerned to read the existing text in a manner which will allow for reasonable adaptation. Already there are a number of points at which the decisions embodied in the text of 1973 seem no longer to fit the needs and wishes of particular industries.[76] Somehow the present edifice must be kept in position without an appellate keystone to its vaulting.

[76] See para. 5–75, below.

CHAPTER 4

THE PATENT: GRANT AND CONTENT

1. OBTAINING A PATENT

(1) General

(a) *Parallels*

A patent may now be secured for the United Kingdom either through the **4–01** British Office or the EPO; with the additional possibility of entering either system by means of an international application under the PCT. In 1977, native British procedures were substantially remodelled to resemble the new European granting system. Accordingly the major steps through which an application proceeds to the stage of grant in each office can be represented in a common diagram (see p. 126).

A European patent designating the United Kingdom falls to be treated as a patent under the Patents Act 1977 as if it had been granted by the British Office.[1] For a variety of purposes the European application ranks as if it were a British application.[2] But there remains one significant difference: the European patent as a whole is open for a limited period to opposition proceedings before the EPO, and the European patent (U.K.) will be subject to revocation proceedings before British tribunals. Obviously a patent granted by the British Office can be subject only to the latter form of attack.[3]

(b) *Competition between the systems*

The new international arrangements have provided a measured competi- **4–02** tion which ought to benefit patenting industries. The greater efficiency that is their chief attraction turns on a number of variables. As far as the PCT is concerned much depends on the trust that is accorded to the international search.[4] At present a measure of mutual suspicion remains. The EPO, for

---

[1] PA 1977, s. 77.
[2] *ibid.*, s. 78.
[3] See paras 4–27 *et seq.*, below.
[4] PCT Rules, r. 34 lays down the minimum documentation that an international search authority must cover.

instance, currently makes its own search (with extra fee) to supplement international search reports emanating from most of the other PCT search authorities.[5]

4–03 Within the EPC States the choice between application routes is more complex. For the applicant with a strong case, confirmed perhaps by a private search in advance, the single procedure before the EPO will look more attractive if cover is wanted in three or four participant countries (or more). It is at this point that the considerable fees and other expenses of a European application begin to fall below the cost of national fees and the other costs of separate applications.[6] But if the expenditure of patenting is justified at all, it is worth paying for the course that is more likely to give the desired protection. The EPO route, moreover, has an all-or-nothing outcome in terms of geographical coverage. The EPO examines applications in a reasonably helpful spirit.[7]

The choice may well turn on the countries for which protection is most needed: thus the possibility of deferring examination in the Netherlands and Germany for seven years may in some cases be important, or the absence of any examination in Belgium or Italy or of a power of rejection in France. In some cases, it will be considered worthwhile pursuing both European and national patents. The only consequence of covering an invention to the same extent by both procedures, as far as the United Kingdom is concerned, is that the Comptroller must then revoke the patent granted by the British Office.[8]

(c) *Languages*

4–04 One particular advantage offered by the international conventions concerns languages. This is not just a matter of saving translation costs, considerable though these often are. In an art so tied to linguistic skills, every translation is fraught with dangers of error and inaccuracy. What the PCT provides is the longest chance to delay preparing translations during the crucial months after an initial application has been lodged.[9] The international application

---

[5] EPC, Art. 157; EPO Official Journal, 1979, p. 50. This supplementary search takes place during the six months in which the applicant has to decide whether to ask for examination: see Ency. PL, para. 11–101; see also PA 1977, s. 18(3A), introduced in 1988.

[6] Notably the costs of professional representation and translation: for the latter, see paras 4–04—4–05, below.

[7] The aim has been to achieve a standard mid-way between the severity of the Dutch and the lenience of the Austrian and British approaches: the German standard was thought to be "about right": Van Benthem and Wallace (1978) 9 I.I.C. 297 at 298; see also Pagenberg (1978) 9 I.I.C. 121; Casalonga (1979) 10 I.I.C. 412.

[8] PA 1977, s. 73(2) (as amended by CDPA 1988, Sched. 5, para. 19). The British patent must be "directed to the same invention": see *Maag Gear's Patent* [1985] R.P.C. 572; *Marley Roof's Patent* [1994] R.P.C. 231, CA.

[9] See also n. 12, below.

must be in the appropriate PCT language[10]; but translations are not needed until the application is transferred into the national (or regional) offices: normally after the international search (up to 20 months from the priority date)[11] or (if applicable) after the international preliminary examination (up to 30 months from the priority date).[12]

In the EPO an applicant may proceed in any of the official languages, **4–05** English, French, or German.[13] When his application is published, he will need to translate the claims, as they then stand, into the languages of his designated states if he wants to secure protection from then until grant[14]; and when his patent is accepted for grant he must translate the claims into the other official languages.[15] All the participant states except Luxembourg and Germany require translation of the whole specification into their own language.[16] The authentic text remains that of the language of the proceedings before the EPO; but some protection is provided for a person misled by a narrower translation.[17]

(2) Persons entitled to grant

The Paris Industrial Property Convention ensures that nationals of any one **4–06** Union country have the same right to secure patents in each other Union country as do nationals of the latter.[18] Both the United Kingdom and the EPC systems go further, making access open to all without consideration of nationality, residence or other status.[19]

---

[10] *i.e.* the language that is used by the international search authority to which an application from the particular receiving office will be referred: English, French, or German where the EPO will search, English for the U.S. Patent Office, Japanese for the Japanese Patent Office and so on. The search report and abstract will be translated into English, if in another language: PCT Rules, r. 48.3.

[11] PCT, Art. 22.

[12] This is possible only for a country which has adopted the PCT, Chap. 2; and the request for the international examination must be made within 19 months of the priority date, if the need to start the national examination within 20 months is to be averted: PCT, Art. 39(1); and see PCT Rules, rr. 46.1, 52.1, for the time allowed for making voluntary amendments.

[13] EPC, Art. 14(1). Nationals of states (such as Italy) which do not have English, French, or German as an official language are entitled to file in their own language and supply a translation, the original document being treated as the document filed, in cases of variance: see Art. 14(2), (4) and further, Ency. PL, paras 11–301—11–304.

[14] If this is not done, states are permitted to treat the application as not giving rise to any intermediate rights: EPC, Art. 67(3). Most have done so, but not so far the U.K. (note the power given by PA 1977, s. 78(7), (8)).

[15] EPC, Art. 97(5), EPC Rules, r. 51(4).

[16] EPC, Art. 65 leaves the matter optional. Power to require this translation is to be found in PA 1977, s. 77(6)–(9) and was exercised in 1987.

[17] See PA 1977, s. 80; EPC, Art. 70.

[18] PIP, Art. 2(1).

[19] See EPC, Art. 58; *cf.* PCT, Art. 9: PCT Rules, r. 18 (resident or national). There was a stage in the EPC negotiations when the exclusion of foreign nationals was seriously contemplated. This was intended as retaliation against the U.S.: foreign applicants there were considered to suffer certain disadvantages in comparison with domestic applicants. Nobler sentiments prevailed: see Van Empel, *The Granting of European Patents* (1975), pp. 72–80.

In the new British system, the right to be granted a patent[20] is given to the inventor or the inventors[21] unless: (1) at the time when the invention is made a general rule of law or an enforceable agreement gives that right to someone else[22]; or (2) the person entitled when the invention was made (under head (1)) later assigns his right, or it has been otherwise disposed of to a successor in title (through death, bankruptcy, winding up, etc.[23]). Under head (1) the most likely person to supersede the inventor by virtue of a rule of law is his employer[24]; this is a matter treated more fully in Chapter 7.[25]

4–07 The 1977 Act creates a presumption that the applicant or applicants are the persons entitled to be granted the patent.[26] But it provides channels through which someone else may claim to be properly entitled—alleging, for instance, that he revealed it to the applicant without transferring any right to secure grant of a patent or that they made the invention together. Such questions of proprietary right can always be raised in declaratory or other proceedings in the High Court.[27] In addition the Comptroller is given special jurisdiction to decide upon the right to be granted not only the British patent, but also European and foreign patents and allied rights, provided that the question is referred to him before the relevant patent is granted.[28] He can also entertain references concerning the right to be granted the United Kingdom patent even after its grant (by either route).[29] Neither the Court nor the Comptroller may resolve a dispute concerning

---

[20] Formerly, the limitations were placed upon the right to apply, but that is now unrestricted: PA 1977, s. 7(1); this follows the EPC approach, see para. 7–01, below.

[21] *i.e.* the actual deviser of the invention: *ibid.*, s. 7(3). The hallowed notion of the importer of an idea as inventor (see para. 3–05, above) finally disappeared with the 1977 Act. Its only recent value had been in overcoming formal difficulties that could affect applications from abroad.

[22] But "the whole of the property (other than equitable interests)" must be given to the preferred person; which may lead to complications where there are joint inventors.

[23] PA 1977, s. 7(2). But the applicable rule may arise by foreign law, treaty or convention (s. 7(2)(b)), because this is the appropriate rule to apply by virtue of the private international law of the British jurisdiction invoked: see further n. 35, below.

[24] *ibid.*, s. 39.

[25] See paras 7–03 *et seq.*, below.

[26] PA 1977, s. 7(4).

[27] s. 72(1)(b) and 72(2) together permit a patent to be revoked, at the behest of such a claimant, on the ground that it was granted to a person not entitled. The jurisdiction appears to have been limited in curious ways by s. 74(4). But, given the equivalent provisions in the EPC, Art. 138(1) and CPC, Art. 56(1), these sections have been read so as to allow such claims to be made either where an exclusive entitlement or a shared entitlement is in issue: *Henry Bros. v. Ministry of Defence* [1997] R.P.C. 693.

[28] *ibid.*, ss. 8, 12. Note that the question can be raised before any application has been made, leading to a declaration over entitlement to grant, and to consequential arrangements such as the grant of an exclusive licence: *Goddin and Rennie's Application* [1996] R.P.C. 141, Ct. of Sess.

[29] *ibid.*, s. 37 (as amended by CDPA 1988, Sched. 5, para. 9). A reference received before grant by the British office is treated as continuing under this section: PA 1977, s. 9. The Comptroller may refuse to act on the ground that the Court is a more suitable tribunal: ss. 8(7), 12(2), 37(8).

rights in a granted patent by revoking it, unless the proceedings were begun within two years of grant, or a person registered was shown to know of the defective title at grant or on assignment to him.[30]

If a challenger shows that he has a proper entitlement in the patent, for **4–08** all or some part of the subject-matter covered by the specification,[31] the tribunal has a wide discretion to do what it thinks fit.[32] The proper claimant may be allowed to join in, or take over, the existing application[33]; or, if the patent has already been granted, to be registered as proprietor. Or he may be allowed to start afresh, taking for himself the date of filing of the displaced application (provided that he does not add to its disclosure),[34] but after grant this course is open only if proceedings are begun within two years.[35] There is also power to grant and transfer licences, and to register transactions and instruments relied upon by the claimant.[36]

As far as European applications are concerned, the EPO does not undertake investigations of entitlement[37]; that is left to national tribunals.[38] So long as the EPO has not granted the European patent, the proper forum for deciding who is entitled to the grant is dealt with in a special protocol to the EPC.[39] Once the patents have been granted, however, the question is one for each designated country. Where a challenge is successfully made to a European application, the challenger may, in appropriate circumstances, continue the application, have it withdrawn, or file his own application (as

---

[30] PA 1977, ss. 37(5), 37(9), 72(2); but *cf.* s. 37(8).

[31] The jurisdiction conferred on the Comptroller also allows him to deal with disputes where one co-applicant is objecting to the transfer or granting of any right to any other person. In addition, there is a separate power to give directions to joint applicants if they cannot agree upon how a British application is to proceed: *ibid.*, s. 10.

[32] For examples of how the jurisdiction has been exercised, see Ency. PL, paras 8–107A, 8–107B.

[33] Where the rights of licensees may be affected, they are afforded at least some measure of protection: see *ibid.*, ss. 11, 38.

[34] *Semble*, he may not also annexe any earlier priority claimed for the original: *Georgia Pacific's Application* [1984] R.P.C. 469.

[35] See PA 1977, ss. 8(2), (3), 37(2), 37(9). In the case of "non-British" applications—apart from the special cases dealt with in s. 12(6)—the Comptroller is left to determine the question as far as he is able and makes such order as he thinks fit: see s. 12(1). The Court's jurisdiction and the jurisdiction to order revocation on the ground that the patent was granted to a person not entitled are similarly limited in time: ss. 37(9), 72(1)(b) (as amended by CDPA 1988, Sched. 5, para. 18), PA 1977, s. 72(2); *Dolphin Showers v. Farmiloe* [1989] F.S.R. 1; Thorley [1995] CIPA 104.

[36] PA 1977, s. 37(5).

[37] EPC, Art. 60(3); see Ency. PL para. 13–102.

[38] In the EPO the application will, on request and subject to limitations, be stayed: see EPC Rules, rr. 13, 14. British applications are not stayed in the same way: see n. 29, above.

[39] This Protocol on Jurisdiction and Recognition gives jurisdiction first to the Contracting State agreed by the disputants; if not agreed, then, in employer-employee disputes, to the state where employed (see Art. 60); and in other cases, to the applicant's state; or otherwise to the clairmant's state; and if none of these tests provides a Contracting State, then to Germany. PA 1977, s. 82 (jurisdiction) and s. 83 (recognition) give effect in the U.K. to this Protocol. See further Ency. PL, para. 8–111; *Kakkar v. Szelke* [1989] F.S.R. 225, CA.

to the whole or a part), with a claim to the earlier priority date if he is adding nothing of substance.[40]

(3) Patent specification

4–09 It should by now be plain that the crucial document in the whole process of securing and relying upon a patent is the specification. In the British and European systems it has two main parts[41]: the description (which may be accompanied by diagrams or drawings) and the claims. The former must disclose the invention sufficiently for it to be performed by an appropriately skilled person, the latter will mark out the scope of monopoly rights. Where the invention involves use of a micro-organism, it may be necessary to deposit a sample with a recognised culture collection.[42] There will be a good deal to say about both aspects of the specification. The reader who has not had an opportunity to study specifications would do well to look at a representative sample.[43] In particular, it is useful to note how far the draftsman has referred to the "prior art" in an effort to bring out the character of the invention; the degree to which specific examples are used to give explicit description of how the invention can be performed; the generalisations used in the claims (particularly the broadest); and the manner in which a succession of claims cover increasingly specific areas (for fear that the wider may prove invalid).

(4) Priority

4–10 Today more than ever, those engaged in research may be competing to solve a scientific or technical problem. The "first-to-file" basis of most patent systems exacerbates the pressure to reach the patent office as soon as feasible.[44] It may be necessary to file a series of applications as, on the

---

[40] EPC, Art. 61.
[41] It must also have a title and name the inventor. The abstract, which is used for patent office search purposes and to notify the public at once of the fact and nature of the application, is separate: this notification is made in the issues of abstracts that accompany the *British Patent Office Journal*, the *EPO Bulletin*, or the *PCT Gazette*.
[42] See para. 5–98, below.
[43] If no other source is ready to hand, the reported case law often sets out in full the specification in dispute. Good examples for beginners: *Carroll v. Tomado* [1971] R.P.C. 401 at 402–404 (clothes horse); *Reeves v. Standard Fabrics* [1972] R.P.C. 47 at 48–62 (bonding polyurethane foam); *Bugges Insecticide v. Herbon* [1972] R.P.C. 197 at 198–202 (weedkiller); *Minnesota Mining v. Bondina* [1973] R.P.C. 491 at 493–503 (scouring pads); *Illinois Tool v. Autobars* [1974] R.P.C. 337 at 339–351 (nestable cups for vending machines); *Procter & Gamble v. Peaudouce* [1989] F.S.R. 180, CA (nappy holders).
[44] The EPC regimen takes a severer attitude than ever before on the need to reach the patent office without prior publication, yet with an application complete enough to support the eventual patent: the elements that are compounded in this attitude are considered together in paras 6–28—6–31, below. On the comparison with a "first to invent" system, see Nicolai (1972) 3 I.I.C. 103; Kingston [1992] E.I.P.R. 223.

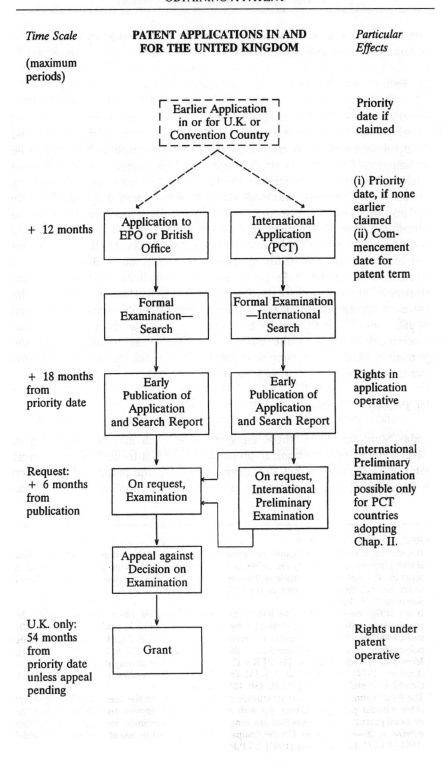

Time Scale

(maximum periods)

PATENT APPLICATIONS IN AND FOR THE UNITED KINGDOM

Particular Effects

Earlier Application in or for U.K. or Convention Country

Priority date if claimed

+ 12 months

Application to EPO or British Office

International Application (PCT)

(i) Priority date, if none earlier claimed (ii) Commencement date for patent term

Formal Examination— Search

Formal Examination —International Search

+ 18 months from priority date

Early Publication of Application and Search Report

Early Publication of Application and Search Report

Rights in application operative

Request: + 6 months from publication

On request, Examination

On request, International Preliminary Examination

International Preliminary Examination possible only for PCT countries adopting Chap. II.

Appeal against Decision on Examination

U.K. only: 54 months from priority date unless appeal pending

Grant

Rights under patent operative

one hand, more is discovered about how the invention works, and, on the other, more is appreciated about alternatives that might be deployed by competitors outside the scope of the initial application. On top of this, the question of which foreign patents to pursue imposes its own pressures, since foreign applications often involve collaboration with patent agents abroad and the making of translations.

4–11   This brings us to the initiatory steps on the Table (p. 126). It has long been recognised that an applicant should have some room for manoeuvre in these matters. Within one year, he is given a limited opportunity to amplify his application without losing his priority. Equally, through the machinery of the Paris Convention, he is able to keep the priority of his first application for other applications filed within a year in or for other Convention countries.[45] Most countries of any industrial significance belong to this Convention and the European system is also within its net.[46] To secure this advantage, then, the earlier "informal" application need only satisfy the basic requirements for a filing date: an indication that a patent is sought, identification of the application, a description of the invention, and, for a European or international application, at least one claim and the designation of at least one state.[47]

4–12   The "priority date" of a patent is the date on which it is tested against "the state of the art"[48]; and it is the date on which it, or any application claiming priority from it (provided that it is subsequently published), becomes part of the art, when assessing the novelty (but not the obviousness) of later applications.[49] This crucial date will be the filing date of the application unless the date of an earlier application in the United Kingdom, the EPO, or a Paris Convention country is claimed.[50] As already noted, the earlier application must have been made within the previous 12 months. And so far as the British Act is concerned, it must "support" the invention in the later application by the matter it discloses.[51] Generally also it must be

---

[45] For the tendency nonetheless to favour national applicants at the expense of Convention applicants in some Member States, see Wieczorek (1975) 6 I.I.C. 135; Gansser (1980) 11 I.I.C. 1.

[46] For the relation of the EPC to PIP, see Paterson, Chap 8 B.

[47] PA 1977, s. 15(1); EPC, Art. 80; PCT, Art. 11. For the full requirements of a "formal" application, see para. 4–16, below. It is possible to claim priority from a utility model or utility certificate; but not from a registered design application: *Agfa-Gevaert's (Engelsmann) Application* [1982] R.P.C. 441, CA; *Arenhold* [1981] O.J. EPO 213.

[48] See para. 5–03, below.

[49] See paras 5–14, 5–15, below.

[50] PA 1977, s. 5(1), (2); EPC, Art. 7(1)–(3), and note Art. 89.

[51] EPC, Art. 87 has been similarly read by the EPO Enlarged Board of Appeal: *Priority Interval* [1994] E.P.O.R. 521. That case settles that the EPC creates one particular difficulty for an eager applicant: suppose he puts in a first application, publishes the content and then makes a second application from the first but cannot sustain his priority, his second application will be anticipated. It has been held that the same must apply in U.K. law, despite the presence of PA 1977, s. 6: *Beloit v. Valmet* [1995] R.P.C. 705 following *Priority Interval* [1994] E.P.O.R. 521 (Enl.B.A.).

the applicant's first disclosure of the invention in a patent application.[52] So a priority issue may involve examining the content of applications made both during and before the relevant 12-month period.

In either case, the question is essentially the same: has there been an "enabling disclosure" of the invention? Would the skilled person to whom the description is addressed have been able to perform it without engaging in independent invention? The previous, looser practice looked only at whether there had been a description. The new rigour has had beneficial effects throughout the corpus of the law. This is because the same test also determines whether an earlier description has anticipated a patent claim and settles whether an applicant has made a sufficient disclosure of the invention for which the patent claims protection.[53] The House of Lords so held, finding that the terms of a claim may be used to amplify the expressed or implicit meaning of descriptive matter, but cannot stand in place of that description.

The case in point, *Asahi Kasei Kogyo's Application*,[54] which raised interrelated questions of priority and novelty, concerned the effect of an application for the protein, human tissue necrosis factor (HTNF), when produced by genetic engineering. It gave the DNA-structure of HTNF but did not disclose how to make it, at a time when it was exactly this which competitors were seeking to discover.[55] It could not, therefore, confer the priority necessary to cause one application to anticipate another. The date for determining whether an enabling disclosure has been made in a patent specification is that at which priority is claimed, not the date at which that specification is later published.[56]

The 1977 Act allows an applicant to claim multiple priorities, based on **4–13** different earlier applications, not only for different claims but even for different aspects of a single claim.[57] If, for example, a first document discloses molten metal cathodes, a second document other cathodes and

---

[52] Disclosures in a first application can be disregarded only if that application was unconditionally withdrawn, abandoned or refused without having been made available to the public before filing of a second application from which it is sought to derive priority and the first was not the basis of any claim to priority: PA 1977, s. 5(3), EPC, Art. 87(4), giving effect to PIP, Art. 4C(4); *cf.* Beier and Straus (1990) 21 I.I.C. 593; Wegner (1992) 23 I.I.C. 184; Harden (1993) 24 I.I.C. 729.

[53] For these issues, see paras 5–18, 5–102, below.

[54] [1991] R.P.C. 485. See also *Biogen v. Medeva* [1997] R.P.C. 1, HL; *Chiron v. Murex Diagnostics* [1996] F.S.R. 153, CA; *Evans Medicals' Patent* [1998] R.P.C. 517. This conclusion is in line with EPC, Art. 88(4), despite its different wording. PA 1977, s. 130(3), which makes reference to the content of claims as well as description, does not alter this. For the same approach in the EPO, see *ICI/Herbicides* [1987] O.J. EPO 5; *Collaborative Research/Preprorennin* [1990] O.J. EPO 250; Paterson, paras 8–25—8–38.

[55] The case concerned anticipation by a prior unpublished application, under the special conditions of PA 1977, s. 2(3), for which see paras 5–14, 5–15, below.

[56] *Biogen v. Medeva* [1997] R.P.C. 1, HL.

[57] PA 1977, s. 25(2); EPC, Art. 88(2), (3). This reverses the restrictive approach concerning convention applications apparently adopted in *Union Carbide's Application* [1968] R.P.C. 371; and see *SCM's Application* [1979] R.P.C. 341, CA.

the application or suit in one claim refers to the two classes separately, then the different priority dates can easily be assigned. But if the cathodes are claimed only in general the claim must be split into separate parts.[58]

The system of priorities eases the pressure of an applicant to decide whether in Europe to proceed in the EPO or in national offices, since he may use an application in any one office to give priority in the others. It is not necessary to designate (say) the United Kingdom in a European application in order to secure priority for a subsequent national application in the United Kingdom.[59]

(5) Secrecy: national interest

4–14 Applications under the EPC and PCT may be lodged with the United Kingdom Patent Office. One purpose of this arrangement is to allow the national office, in collaboration with the Ministry of Defence, the Atomic Energy Authority and other government departments, to vet applications in the interests of national security and public safety. British residents, indeed, are obliged (under criminal law sanction) to lodge applications with the British Office six weeks before applying abroad.[60] If the Comptroller considers that any application contains information prejudicial to the defence of the realm[61] or the safety of the public he may make a secrecy direction.[62] So long as it remains, the application cannot be sent on through the EPC or PCT routes,[63] and foreign applications may be made only through restricted arrangements, for instance within NATO.[64] It may be processed in the British Office, but without any publication, to the point where it is ready for grant. No patent will be granted, but the applicant is entitled to compensation for any Crown use[65]; and—as a matter of departmental favour—he may also be compensated for hardship resulting from the secrecy direction: taking account, for instance, of lost commercial opportunities and foreign patent rights.[66] The government department involved must review the need for secrecy from time to time.[67]

---

[58] For the requirement of unity of inventive concept, see para. 4–15, below, and *Biogen v. Medeva*, para. 5–102, below.

[59] It would in practice be unusual to use a European application in order to secure priority for national applications.

[60] PA 1977, s. 23; the Comptroller's permission may be sought to file abroad without filing first in Britain. See generally, Ency. PL, paras 6–118—6–120.

[61] By reference to a list of subject-matter supplied by the Ministry of Defence.

[62] PA 1977, s. 22(1); and for the muddled and muddy history, see O'Dell, *Inventions and Official Secrecy* (1994).

[63] Provided that the U.K. is a designated country, an EPC application may be converted into a British application; a PCT application is similarly treated: see EPC, Arts 75(2), 77(4), (5); PCT, Arts 11(3), 12(3); PA 1977, s. 81(1)(b).

[64] PA 1977, s. 23(1)(b).

[65] Following the general rules: see paras 7–49—7–50, below.

[66] PA 1977, s. 22(7).

[67] PA 1977, s. 22(5): *i.e.* on the making of the secrecy direction, then at least at the ninth month from the filing date and annually thereafter.

(6) Unity and division

Two patents are not to be had for the price of one. One invention per **4–15** patent, moreover, simplifies the classification of specifications and the process of searching which is the reason for classifying. Accordingly, as the EPC has it, an application must "relate to one invention only or to a group of inventions so linked as to form a single general inventive concept".[68] It is possible to have claims for a process, the apparatus to operate it and its products; or for products, processes for making them and use of the products.[69] Beyond this what will be allowed is a matter of judgment, and one that is left to the examiner(s) of the patent office in question.[70]

An applicant may cope with an objection that he is seeking to patent more than one invention by dividing his single application into two (or more). Provided that he adds no new matter and keeps to the prescribed time schedule, he may keep his priority date for the "new" applications.[71] Division is permitted even where there is no objection to unity: it may be requested, for instance, where new claims are wanted which might give rise to an objection to unity.[72]

(7) Formal examination

If the applicant does not ask for a preliminary examination and search the **4–16** only value of an application will be that it may found priority for a later application. But, once the request is made (and fee paid), the office will make its preliminary examination to ensure that there is a request for grant; a description and one or more claims; any drawings referred to; identification of the applicant(s); identification of the inventor(s); an abstract of the invention described; and compliance with various formalities.[73] In the EPC, the states for which a patent is sought have also to be designated: these designations may afterwards be withdrawn but never added to.[74] An

---

[68] EPC, Art. 82; PA 1977, s. 14(5)(d) (omitting "general"). See, *e.g. Bayer's Application* [1983] O.J. EPO 274.

[69] EPC Rules, r. 30; PA 1977 Rules, r. 22.

[70] In the past the Appeal Tribunal in Britain has been exceedingly reluctant to interfere with the British Office's discretion. And it is no objection to a granted patent that it lacks unity: PA 1977, s. 26. In the EPO, where Search and Examining Divisions are separate, and only the latter may refuse an application, the Search Division may require a second fee to search parts of an application which it considers separate; with power in the Examining Division to remit the fee if it finds unity: EPC Rules, r. 46 (note also r. 45; search not possible, as a whole or in part).

[71] For EPO practice, see esp. *Advanced Semiconductor Products* [1995] E.P.O.R. 97 (Enlarged B.A.).

[72] For time limits, see Ency. PL, paras 6–111, 13–202.

[73] PA 1977, ss. 14(1)–(3A), 17(1)–(3); EPC, Arts 78, 90, 91. Only in relation to drawings is there a special rule in effect allowing post-dating. If drawings referred to are not provided, reference to them can be deleted; or they may be filed within a limited time, the date of filing being postponed until this is done.

[74] EPC, Art. 79. A mistaken failure to designate may, however, be remedied under EPC Rules, r. 88: [1980] O.J. EPO 293.

4. THE PATENT: GRANT AND CONTENT

application will, of course, normally be drawn to meet the much more stringent standards of the substantive examination, and these will be discussed later.

The inventor or inventors must be named as a matter of "moral right".[75] Now that employee-inventors are entitled on occasion to "compensation", there may be considerable evidential value in being named as an inventor.[76]

The abstract is required as an aid to those conducting searches, giving them preliminary assistance in deciding whether a specification is relevant to their investigation. Its terms may ultimately be settled by the patent office concerned, and it is disregarded when treating the specification as part of the art. Probably it is not to be used in interpreting the claims.[77]

(8) Search and examination

(a) *Introductory*

4–17 At the heart of the European and the new British systems lies a compulsory examination before grant, not only of the novelty but also of the inventiveness of the alleged invention. To this there are three important preliminaries: (1) a substantial search; (2) "early publication" of the application in the form that it has by then reached; and (3) the opportunity within a short period after that for the applicant to decide whether or not he wants his application to proceed to examination.

British practice under the 1949 Act was very different: the Patent Office's examination only went to novelty and prior claiming, judged against a search of British specifications for the previous 50 years. It took place without the applicant's first considering the search result and before the industry was acquainted with the content of the specification. The detailed content could be kept dark for as much as four years from the priority date. Before grant, obviousness could only be brought in issue by an outside party in separate opposition proceedings, but upon whatever prior art he put to the tribunal. However, this ground of opposition was narrower than that available in post-grant attacks on the validity of the patent before the High Court; and the same restriction applied in "belated oppositions" launched before the office within one year of grant.

Under the EPC approach, both the British Office and the EPO examine for obviousness as a matter of course in proceedings before grant that are *ex parte*.

4–18 Neither the European nor the new British system has adopted the technique of deferred examination. This was introduced into the "full

---

[75] PA 1977, s. 13; PA 1977 Rules, rr. 14, 15; EPC, Arts 62, 81; EPC Rules, rr. 17–19 in implementation of PIP, Art. 4*ter*. For the concept of "inventor", para. 4–06, above. See *Nippon Piston Ring's Application* [1987] R.P.C. 120.
[76] See para. 7–08—7–14, below.
[77] PA 1977, s. 14(2); PA 1977 Rules, r. 19; EPC, Art. 85; EPC Rules, r. 33.

examination" systems of the Netherlands, West Germany and Japan in order to lift some of the burden on their patent offices in the great patenting boom of the 1960s. Quite apart from bureaucratic considerations, this arrangement has one advantage. Many patents that are applied for prove to have no lasting commercial value; even if granted they would be allowed to lapse. Delaying examination for up to seven years, while allowing a provisional form of protection after publication of the application, means that this swill of unwanted patents can filter away without wasting resources on examining the applications.[78]

In the councils where the EPO was negotiated, however, a different principle triumphed. The importance of trying to ensure that an industry was saddled only with valid patents was held to require a rapid pre-grant examination.[79] Accordingly, the applicant was given only six months from early publication in which to decide whether to seek examination. It should be noted, however, that neither the Dutch nor the Germans have got rid of deferred examination in their own systems. This remains one factor which may attract an applicant in Europe to the national systems, particularly if he is not sure how he will fare under examination or if he doubts the commercial potential of the patent.

(b) *Search*

A search undertaken by one of the PCT authorities, or by the EPO for **4–19** itself, will cover a considerable body of patents from major patenting countries and a range of the most important technical literature.[80] If the British Office is searching for itself, the material covered is narrower,[81] even though the British system now is concerned with the prior art throughout the world (and not only in Britain, as formerly.[82])

(c) *Early publication of application*

The new systems aim to publish the application, for the benefit of outsiders, **4–20** 18 months from the priority date.[83] References to the prior art cited in the search report are also published.[84] From this point in time the patent-office

---

[78] See, *e.g.* Hoffmann (1972) 3 I.I.C. 423; Webman (1995) 77 J.P.T.O.S. 921.
[79] The Banks Committee's firm rejection of deferment was influential: Cmnd. 4407, 1970, paras 100 *et seq.*
[80] For the range covered by the EPO, see its Guidelines B IX.
[81] It is still largely confined to prior British specifications.
[82] See para. 5–03, below.
[83] PA 1977, s. 16; PA 1977 Rules, rr. 27, 28; EPC, Art. 93; EPC Rules, rr. 48–50; PCT, Art. 21; PCT Rules, r. 48. Until publication, the application may be withdrawn without jeopardising the novelty of its contents. In the U.K. Office, this may be done until allotment to a printing contractor and collection: *Intera's Application* [1986] R.P.C. 459, CA.
[84] In the European system, if the search report is not available at the date of early publication, it may be published later; in which case the time for requesting examination is extended: EPC, Art. 93(2); *cf.* PCT Rules, r. 48.2(g).

file (subject to a variety of exceptions) falls open to inspection[85]: outsiders may thus trace how an applicant has reacted to the results of the search and objections that examiners may subsequently put.[86]

If at this point an applicant using the PCT does not opt for the International Preliminary Examination,[87] his application must pass into the national systems (or the EPO).[88]

(d) *Amending during prosecution*

4–21 In the successful prosecution of an application, much may turn on the degree to which a specification and claims originally filed can be amended and the points in time at which this can be done. The applicant is offered his largest opportunity in the period after receiving the search report and in his response to the first report of the examiner; thereafter, amendments require leave.[89] Even when making amendments of his own volition, however, the applicant is constricted by general rules. As far as the description of the invention is concerned, he may not add to his original disclosure; if he does, the examiner may reject the amendment, or subsequently (even if the examiner allows it) the patent may be revoked.[90]

Equally with claims: although they may be broadened in the course of prosecution, they must continue to be supported by the description—as well as being clear and concise. As we shall see, objections to claims can be raised after grant only indirectly.[91] So examiners ought to take this requirement particularly seriously. But without the stimulus of outside criticism, it will be tempting for them to let the applicant's drafting stand.

(e) *The course of examination*

4–22 The purpose of the examination is to decide whether the application meets all the criteria for the grant of a patent: whether the subject-matter is within the patentable field; whether, in the light of the search report, the invention is novel and inventive; whether there is a sufficient description and the claims meet the criteria mentioned above. Examining the application in the light of the search report proceeds with relative informality. The examiner in charge sets forth any objections in a letter and states the time within

---

[85] PA 1977, s 118; PA 1977 Rules, rr. 92–96; EPC, Art. 128; EPC Rules, rr. 92–95; PCT, Art. 30 (but note Art. 38—confidential nature of International Preliminary Examination).

[86] For the significance of this, see para. 4–45, below.

[87] Or cannot do so, because a country has not ratified Chap. II.

[88] PCT, Art. 20; PA 1977, s. 89 (requiring a translation into English if necessary); EPC, Art. 158 (requiring a version in one of the three official languages). For supplementary search in the EPO, see para. 4–02, above.

[89] PA 1977, s. 19, PA 1977 Rules, r. 36; EPC, Art. 123(1), EPC Rules, r. 86; PCT, Arts 19, 28, PCT Rules, rr. 46, 52.

[90] Amendment is considered further paras 4–30—4–35, below.

[91] See para. 5–101, below.

which amendments may be submitted in order to overcome the objections. If applicant and examiner cannot agree, the issue may be raised in a formal hearing—in the United Kingdom Office before a senior examiner, in the EPO before the full Examining Division[92]; in either case, with a right of appeal.[93] Formal proceedings at this stage are infrequent in the British system, even with obviousness now on the agenda.[94]

Although outsiders have no right to present a case in opposition to grant before it takes place, they may make observations on patentability, drawing attention to prior art or even prior use which may not be known to the office.[95] Even though there are enhanced opportunities for competitors to monitor the progress of applications after early publication,[96] this remains an occasional strategy. Its tactical disadvantage is that the competitor cannot put a case on how the information should be regarded.

(f) *Time limits*

The EPO and the British Office and Courts have seen a procession of cases **4-23** about failure to comply with the requirements of the application system within due time. The fact that such errors occur with frequency is one measure of the complexity of the whole structure.[97] Thus a noticeable proportion of those arising in Britain have concerned the process of converting an international application under the PCT into a national application, either after search or after preliminary international examination.[98] Where the default is in part a consequence of a failure in communication from the patent office concerned, the tendency has been to discount it.[99] In the EPO there may be further help under the arrangements for restitution of an out-of-time application where due care has been observed.[1] However, there are some dates crucial to the whole procedure—

---

[92] *i.e.* three examiners of whom one has been primarily responsible from the outset.

[93] *i.e.* in the British Office, to the Patents Court and in some cases to the Court of Appeal (PA 1977, s. 97); in the EPO, to a Board of Appeals: EPC, Arts 106(1), 21(3); Paterson [1987] E.I.P.R. 221; Stephens-Ofner [1990] E.I.P.R. 215.

[94] Unless an appeal is pending, the period for completing the examination in the British Office is 4¹/₂ years from priority: PA 1977, s. 20, PA 1977 Rules, r. 34. The EPO has no such prescribed limit. The price of the EPO's success has been a serious backlog, which has attracted harsh criticism: *e.g.* Jacob [1993] E.I.P.R. 312. Statistically at least, performance is now improving.

[95] PA 1977, s. 21; EPC, Art. 115.

[96] See para. 4-20, above.

[97] For details, see, *e.g.* Ency. PL, paras 6-002, 13-005.

[98] See, *e.g.* *E's Applications* [1983] R.P.C. 231, HL; *Mitsui's Application* [1984] R.P.C. 471; *Matsuda's Application* [1987] R.P.C. 37; and see also PA 1977, ss. 89, 89A, 89B (as amended by CDPA 1988, Sched. 5, paras 24, 25). For equivalent questions in the EPO, see Gall [1984] E.I.P.R. 302.

[99] See PA 1977 Rules, r. 100; *M's Application* [1985] R.P.C. 249, CA; *Mills' Application* [1985] R.P.C. 339, CA; *Université Laval* [1995] O.J. EPO 831.

[1] EPC, Art. 122. If the mistake is made by a professional representative, he must show that it was an isolated error in a normally satisfactory system: *Motorola* [1987] O.J. EPO 362; see Paterson, paras 6-20—6-42.

such as the six-month period for requesting examination—to which that special concession does not apply. These require the most scrupulous watching.

(9) Grant and renewal

4–24 The patent grant is formally effective from the date when notice of it is officially published.[2] The maximum term for which it may last is 20 years from the filing date,[3] the effective period for a claim to damages running from the date of early publication.[4] Grant is also the point at which the European application matures into a bundle of patents for the designated contracting states (including, once the CPC is brought into operation, a Community patent).

4–25   A patent continues for the full 20 years only upon payment of the annual renewal fees. In the United Kingdom these start with the fifth year and increase with age: the one official price of success. The fees may be paid up to six months late under penalty.[5] After that time the patent will lapse for non-payment, but may be restored within a further prescribed period subject to a measure of protection for those who in the meantime begin in good faith to work within the patent.[6] If the Comptroller finds it proper, a patentee may formally surrender his patent.[7] He may also secure a 50 per cent reduction of renewal fees if he has the patent indorsed "licences of right"[8]; in which case he must license all-comers on terms which, if they cannot be agreed, will be fixed by the Comptroller.

4–26   Patented pharmaceuticals cannot today be marketed until there has been substantial safety testing by government authorities. So their introduction may be delayed for years during which the patent runs towards its close. Intensive lobbying by the drug industry procured it a form of patent extension, the "supplementary protection certificate (SPC)".[9] This cumbrous name indicates the convoluted networking of legislation which creates the right. The power to grant SPCs lies with national patent authorities.[10] So far as concerns E.C. countries, these authorities are

---

[2] When the patent is in order, the fees due must be paid; in the case of the EPO, the Examining Division has also to notify the applicant of the final terms of the grant. Translations of the claims into other official languages have to be filed; see EPC, Art. 97(5); EPC Rules, r. 51(4); see also Teschemacher [1986] E.I.P.R. 149.

[3] See para. 4–10, above. This is the term now required by the TRIPS Agreement, Art. 33.

[4] EPC, Art. 63; PA 1977, s. 25(1). The EPC allows general extensions on account of a state of war or similar emergency conditions; and the 1977 Act gives a rule-making power that would include such cases.

[5] PA 1977, s. 25(3)–(5), Sched. 1; PA 1977 Rules, r. 39.

[6] PA 1977, ss. 28, 28A. The liberalising amendments introduced by CDPA 1988, Sched. 5, paras 6, 7, were a response to a set of difficult cases about failure to renew on time.

[7] PA 1977, s. 29. The surrender would likely not be accepted if it prejudiced a licensee; *cf.* CPC, Art. 50.

[8] PA 1977, s. 46, which contains further conditions.

[9] The demand first succeeded in the U.S.

[10] Where the patent was originally granted by the EPO, the EPC, Art. 63 (by amendment: [1992] O.J. EPO 1) confers this authority.

required by a Council Regulation of 1992[11] to grant SPCs for patented products which have been authorised for marketing as a medicine under control procedures.[12] In the United Kingdom at least, an SPC is governed by the existing patent legislation.[13] The scheme is relatively straightforward to administer, though there are certain grounds on which a grant can be challenged by outsiders.[14]

The term of an SPC depends upon the period of delay between the date of patent grant (that is the date of filing the application) and the date of authorisation. A delay of six years gives a right to a year's supplement; and each additional year's delay gives a further year's supplement up to a maximum of five years. Thus a delay of ten or more years qualifies for a five-year SPC. Hostility from patient groups and drug imitators put an end to the demand for a maximum of ten or more additional years of protection.

(10) Objections to validity after grant

The EPC, drawing inspiration from the "belated oppositions" of the former **4–27** British procedure, allows an outsider to launch an opposition in the EPO within nine months of grant.[15] Objections may be taken on three grounds[16]—unpatentable subject-matter,[17] inadequate disclosure[18] and unallowable amendment.[19] If it succeeds, the whole "bundle" of European patents will be revoked, or granted only in amended form, save in exceptional cases.[20] So the procedure offers an outsider a unique chance of

---

[11] 1768/92: After considerable debate, extended to agro-chemicals by Regulation 1610/96; and see S.I. 1992 No. 3091, S.I. 1996 No. 1320. For the validity of the Regulation in E.U. Law, see above, para. 1–28.

[12] Thus it applies to national patents granted either by the EPO or the national office. See further: *Biogen v. Smithkline Beecham* [1998] R.P.C. 833; *Yamanouchi v. Comptroller-General* [1998] R.P.C. 844.

[13] See the Patents (Supplementary Protection Certificates for Medicinal Products) Regulations 1992, S.I. 1992 No. 3091, reg. 5. No special provision regulates licences during the extended period. Grant may be subject to authorisation to market the product: *Yamanouchi Pharmaceutical v. Comptroller-Gen. of Patents* [1997] I E.C.R. 3251, ECJ.

[14] The EPO and some national patent offices (including the British) take the view that the legislation covers the case where the patent is for a compound in its acid form and the medicine licence is for one of its esters or salts: see Adams [1995] E.I.P.R. 277. It does not apply to new formulations of known drugs: *Draco's Appln.* [1996] R.P.C. 417.

[15] EPC, Arts 99, *et seq.* The opponent need establish no special interest to oppose. Even after the time for launching an opposition has expired, any person who has been sued or threatened with infringement proceedings personally may intervene in an opposition: Art. 105. See generally, Paterson, paras 4–33—4–121.

[16] EPC, Art. 100.

[17] See paras 5–54—5–91, below.

[18] See paras 5–93—5–100, below.

[19] *i.e.* that the amendment extends the subject-matter beyond the application as filed: see para. 4–31, below.

[20] If the state of the art differs for different states, because prior applications do not designate them all (as to which see para. 5–14, below), a patent may be available only in some; alternatively, it may be granted subject to amendment for some. Or if proprietors differ, amendments may vary from state to state.

attack and is therefore being used more than the old British opposition. Because of the thorough consideration now given at the application stage, an opposition based on the material in the search report and nothing else is not likely to succeed.

4–28   Contrary to the British "accusatorial" tradition, which applied as much to oppositions as to Court proceedings, Opposition Divisions of the EPO are expected to play a more directive part in resolving issues raised before them—deciding what evidence to take, and possibly securing information from sources not nominated by the parties, appointing experts to give opinions and conducting inspections.[21] Even if an opponent withdraws, the Opposition Division should continue where it is convinced that the patent cannot be supported, at least in its granted form.[22] Since British proceedings will allow questions of infringement and invalidity to be tried together, a Court may well refuse to stay them pending an EPO opposition—an approach which the United Kingdom is not alone in adopting and which reflects impatience with the slowness of EPO procedures.[23]

4–29   The British system continues to offer the outside party an opportunity of attacking a patent[24] by a largely documentary procedure originating in the Patent Office[25]; this is intended to be cheaper and more expeditious than a challenge to validity in the Patents County Court or the High Court.[26] This chance does not arise until after grant, but it is then available throughout the life of the patent and the grounds are the same as those on which an attack may be launched in Court proceedings. It is an alternative to the latter, rather than an intermediate course.[27] Accordingly the applicant for revocation ought not to face any specially high standard of proof, though he must still make out his case.

A particular question of issue estoppel can arise in this connection. An objection may be raised to an application: for instance, the invention may be said not to be novel, or to involve no inventive step, on the basis of particular documents which contain relevant prior art. A decision during

---

[21] But adequate notice of them must be given as a matter of due process: *Atotech* [1998] E.P.O.R. 135. See further, Gall (1983) 14 I.I.C. 229; Stephens-Ofner [1997] E.I.P.R. 167.

[22] *ICI* [1989] O.J. EPO 412. An opponent may not add new grounds during an appeal: see, *e.g.* G 1/95 and G 7/95 [1996] O.J. EPO 615, 626 (Enl.B.A.).

[23] *Amersham v. Corning* [1987] R.P.C. 53; *Pall v. Commercial Hydraulics* [1988] F.S.R. 274; *cf. Beloit v. Valmet* [1996] F.S.R. 715, CA, and see [1988] O.J. EPO 357–362 (cases from France, Netherlands, Switzerland).

[24] Including, of course, a European patent (U.K.). If the patent is also being opposed in the EPO, the British proceedings are likely to be stayed: see Ency PL, para. 12–102.

[25] PA 1977, s. 72; as to amendments in such proceedings, see paras 4–31—4–34, below.

[26] See Ency. PL, paras 6–201 *et seq.*

[27] As indicated by this: if the Comptroller refuses to revoke, the applicant may apply to the Court only with leave: PA 1977, s 72(6). The Comptroller may always certify that the case would be more suitably determined by the Court: s. 72(7). The Court will in its discretion decide whether proceedings before it ought to be stayed in favour of those in the British Office: *Hawker Siddeley v. Real Time* [1985] R.P.C. 395; *cf. Gen Set v. Mosarc* [1985] F.S.R. 302.

the application stage (including in this an EPO opposition) may determine the issue in favour of the applicant and the patent is granted. In Britain, however, decisions on the application have traditionally not been treated as involving a final judgment, and the Court of Appeal has held that this applies to United Kingdom patents granted under the 1977 Act.[28] The patentee may thus be left to face the same battle twice. The approach has been thought justified because the true assessment of such issues deserves to be tested with the full evidence that can be presented in a challenge to the validity of the granted patent (above all on issues of inventive step). It is conceivable that, if in future the national and European patent offices gain real standing, at least a cause of action estoppel might arise from the initial decision to allow the patent.[29]

More generally, some have argued that there is too great an imbalance between the position of the patentee and that of competitors who challenge validity. If a patent applicant fails to survive Office examination and loses on appeal, he has no subsequent opportunity to justify his case; yet if he then succeeds he may still face third party objections at the opposition stage, and equally thereafter. The fact remains, however, that it is patentees and not opponents who are seeking exclusive rights. An improvement in the "balance" could arguably be achieved if procedures in the EPO, both during examination and opposition, were capable of final appeal to a highly experienced Court which was plainly positioned outside the Office.[30]

2. AMENDMENT

(1) Introductory

The fact that a specification may be amended adds finesse to the art of **4–30** patenting. In the course of securing the grant, the description, the claims or both may be substantially rewritten, either to take account of prior art or some other objection to validity, or to reflect the growing understanding of the invention by those prosecuting the application. Nevertheless amendments have to comply with important ground rules and these can conveniently be set forth here. Some illustrations of what can be achieved by amendment will, however, be found in the discussion of validity in Chapter 5, below.

The legal provisions in point distinguish two cases: (1) alterations that are intended to introduce new ideas, or at least new expression of existing

---

[28] *Buehler v. Chronos Richardson* [1998] R.P.C. 609, CA.
[29] *i.e.* an estoppel between the same parties on the same allegation: see above, paras 2–67, 2–68.
[30] See Von Morzé and Van Zant [1998] I.P.Q. 117; and, for an interim proposal Jacob [1997] E.I.P.R. 224; Brinkhof, *ibid.*, 226.

ideas; and (2) on the other, corrections that remove mistakes in expressing what was originally intended. The bulk of amendments, proposed and allowed, are of the first kind. But the two categories are not always easy to distinguish, and there may be advantages in trying to justify a change under the second head. This is discussed below.

(2) Amendment: general

(a) *Legal requirements*[31]

4–31 The rules governing amendment distinguish between alterations in the description of the invention and in the claims. The description must not be amended so as to introduce matter extending beyond that disclosed in the specification as filed.[32] This applies whether the amendment is sought during the application or after.[33] If such an amendment is improperly allowed after grant, this may ground a suit for revocation of the patent, in whole or in part.[34]

If the claims are amended during application, they must not notionally add something new to the description in the body of the specification. Thus, a claim including a "mechanical compression spring" was not allowed to be changed to a "mechanical spring", because this added a whole range of springs not included in the previous unambiguous language.[35] Moreover, the amended claims have still to satisfy the basic rules that they must be clear and concise, be supported by the description and satisfy the requirement of unity of invention. But it is primarily for the patent office concerned to see that this principle is observed.[36] Amendments that are themselves sought after grant[37] may not alter the claims so as to extend the scope of protection; if wrongly admitted, they may provide cause for revocation.[38] If they are proper, they have a retroactive effect.[39] In the

---

[31] See generally Ency. PL, Chap. 7; Paterson, Chap. 5; Wheeler, Laddie, Brinkhof, Rogge (1997) 28 I.I.C. 822ff.

[32] PA 1977, s. 76(2) (as amended by CDPA 1988, Sched. 5, para. 20); EPC, Art. 123(2); Opinion 93/89 [1993] O.J. EPO 117. For circumstances in which cross-referencing is permissible, see *Raychem/Event detector* [1993] O.J. EPO 616. See also *Hsiung's Patent* [1992] R.P.C. 497, CA.

[33] PA 1977, ss. 19, 27, 75; and see para. 4–30, above.

[34] PA 1977, s. 72(1)(d); EPC, Art. 100(c); *Liversidge v. British Telecommunications* [1991] R.P.C. 219. The content of the claims constitutes a distinct disclosure: PA 1977, s. 130(3); *Southco v. Dzus Fastener* [1990] R.P.C. 587; *Edwards v. Acme Signs* [1992] R.P.C. 131, CA.

[35] *Protoned's Application* [1983] F.S.R. 110.

[36] How far the content of the claims is open to challenge after grant is considered in paras 5–101—5–108, below.

[37] Either in the course of proceedings for infringement or revocation (PA 1977, s. 75); or, if none are pending, in an application to the Comptroller to amend (s. 27); or in opposition proceedings before the EPO (EPC, Art. 123(2), (3)); see Decision G 1/93 [1994] O.J. EPO 169. S. 75 jurisdiction will prevail over that of the EPO so far as concerns the British patent. *Petrolite Holdings v. Dyno Oil* [1998] F.S.R. 190; but *cf. Palmaz's European Patents* [1999] R.P.C. 47.

[38] PA 1977, s. 72(1)(e) and see EPC, Arts 123(3), 138(d): *Raychem's Application* [1986] R.P.C. 521.

[39] PA 1977, ss 27(3), 75(3).

course of seeking amendments after grant, the patentee cannot be required to amend his original claims so as to render them fairly based on the description.[40]

In many cases the aim of an amendment is to cut down the scope of what is claimed, because a piece of prior art is discovered which makes the original claim cover unjustifiably broad territory. Sometimes this can be achieved by amending the claims alone: the broadest may have to be deleted; or features of subsidiary claims may have to be added to it; or claims for different aspects of the invention may have to be coalesced. In a well-known example,[41] the broadest claim originally related to a tool for crimping together electrical wires and connectors, which had a ratchet and pawl device to prevent premature release of the tool before crimping was complete. In order to side-step prior art, the patentee was allowed to add to this a device that was mentioned in the description incidently as an additional feature—a stop designed to prevent crimping from going too far. Within this general principle, it is permissible to change a product claim to a claim to its use.[42] **4–32**

If the description must also be amended, the issue may be nicer. In the crimping tool case,[43] if the stop device had not originally been mentioned, to add it by amendment would in most circumstances be barred as "extending" the matter disclosed. The same would probably apply if originally a particular kind of stop was mentioned and the amendment sought to refer to all kinds of stop. Again, suppose that stops were mentioned in general and the amendment sought to refer to one particular kind of stop. It may be objected that this is to give prominence to something not previously pointed up in the description.[44] **4–33**

(b) *The discretion*

Amendment in the course of application is frequent; after grant, much less so. But if leave to amend is sought from the Comptroller or the Court after grant, not only must the applicant show that it is within the legal requirements just discussed; he must also satisfy the tribunal that it should in its discretion allow the amendment to be made.[45] **4–34**

---

[40] *Chiron v. Organon Teknika (No. 11)* [1995] F.S.R. 589, CA—a decision related to a more general problem, discussed para. 5–95, below.

[41] *Amp v. Hellerman* [1962] R.P.C. 55, HL; and see *Edwards v. Acme Signs* (above, n. 34); *Mölnlycke v. Procter & Gamble (No. 5)* [1994] R.P.C. 49, CA.

[42] *Mobil/Friction reducing additive* [1990] O.J. EPO 93 (Enlarged B.App.); and see *Moog* [1988] O.J. EPO 386.

[43] See n. 41, above.

[44] See *Ward's Application* [1986] R.P.C. 54. The EPO Guidelines C VI 5.3–6 direct the examiner to consider whether there has been an overall change in the content of the application; and he is to object to greater specificity (*e.g.* "mounted on helical springs" in place of "resilient supports") unless the substitution is an obvious one.

[45] PA 1977, ss. 27(1), 75(1); leave to amend may be conditional, requiring possibly that no proceedings be brought for past infringement (but note the relevance here of s. 62(3) (restriction on damages)). See Krasser (1992) 23 I.I.C. 467.

In the past, the discretion has been used to subject the patentee's conduct to critical scrutiny. This contrasts with the approach to most other issues, where the applicant or patentee is obliged to meet specific requirements but not in addition to show that he has behaved properly, honestly and candidly.[46] Patentees who have delayed their application to amend for long periods after appreciating the need, or who have insisted first in maintaining an invalid claim, have been denied leave.[47] To some extent, the new willingness to see virtue in the patent system[48] seems to have made the judges and the Patent Office reluctant to refuse amendments that fall within the legal requirements. But still judgments are given which insist that the onus that the applicant has to discharge is a heavy one and that he must put before the Court the whole story leading to the application to amend.[49]

(3) Correction of errors

4–35 The British Office and the EPO each has power itself to correct errors of translation, transcription, clerical errors and mistakes in all documents.[50] But in the case of specifications, the correction has to be obvious in the sense that it is immediately evident that nothing else would have been intended than what is offered as the correction. This is a severe limitation. The Enlarged EPO Board of Appeal requires that a skilled person be able to appreciate the true intention directly and unambiguously from the document itself and common general knowledge, without additional evidence. Moreover, errors in the description, drawings or claims can be altered only if there is in consequence no extension to them over the subject-matter originally filed.[51]

4–36 Errors of translation are particularly liable to occur. However, the rule seems to allow little scope for their correction, since so often translations leave obscure what the original must have meant. Only in the case of European patent applications may a special rule apply. If the United Kingdom at any time requires the claims of the published application and the whole of the granted patent to be translated from French or German into English,[52] these can be corrected so as to achieve the meaning of the original.[53] There is, however, intermediate protection for those who rely on

---

[46] But *cf.* the duties associated with the requirement of disclosure: see paras 5–93 *et seq.*, below.

[47] For examples, see Ency. PL, para. 7–205.

[48] Put in these terms by Salmon L.J., *Ethyl Corp's Patent* [1972] R.P.C. 169 at 193, CA; *cf. ICI's (Small) Application* [1979] F.S.R. 78.

[49] *S.C.M. Corp's Application* [1979] R.P.C. 341, CA; *Smith Kline & French v. Evans* [1989] F.S.R. 561, CA; *Procter & Gamble v. Peaudouce* [1989] F.S.R. 614, CA.

[50] PA 1977, s. 117; PA 1977 Rules, r. 91(2); EPC Rules, r. 88. In the EPO there must first be a request (though not necessarily from the proprietor of the patent).

[51] Opinions G 3/89 and 11/91 [1993] O.J. EPO 117; and see *VEB Kombinat's Application* [1987] R.P.C. 405; *Holtite v. Jost* [1979] R.P.C. 81, HL.

[52] *i.e.* making use of powers in PA 1977, ss. 77(6), 78(7); see para. 4–04, above.

[53] PA 1977, s. 80, following EPC, Art. 70(3), (4).

the earlier version.[54] Claims of the European patent have to be translated into the other official languages; but it is the original which governs[55] and in this case there is no special protection for a person who relies on a more narrowly formulated translation.

3. CLAIMS

(1) Claims and infringement: an introduction

In Britain, the United States and countries which have taken their patent **4–37** laws from these sources, the purpose of claims in the patent specification is to delimit the scope of the monopoly. "Fence-posts" are set up, most often by the use of words, but commonly also by chemical and mathematical symbols; sometimes by reference to drawings. Activities within the territory thus defined require the patentee's consent if they are not to infringe.[56] Whether activities which all but fall within the area also infringe has been the subject of some flux in British case law. There was a period in the 1960s when the House of Lords seemed intent on keeping the patentee strictly to his claim, at least when the invention consisted only of a modest improvement over what was already known.[57] During the European Convention negotiations, this undoubtedly aroused a mistrust of the British way of doing things. Using the claims in this way has two crucial consequences. First, draftsmen must perfect the art of legitimate generalisation—in part this is an exercise in imagining alternative forms for the inventive idea, in part in finding descriptions that will cover all the variants concisely. Secondly, disputes about the interpretation of claims become of central significance, both in deciding what constitutes infringement and in determining the validity of the patent itself.[58]

"Fence-post" claiming is to be distinguished from the "sign-post" **4–38** claiming which has been favoured by some patent systems. "Sign-post" claims aim to specify the essential inventive concept in the specification: an important part of this accordingly is to distinguish what is new from what is old, and the claims are generally put into a form which is designed to achieve this.[59] The relation between claim and protected territory is then less direct: to some extent it is left to the Court to work out the proper scope of the monopoly from the description of the invention, the claims

---

[54] PA 1977, s. 80(3), (4).
[55] *ibid.*, s. 80(1), following EPC, Art. 70(1).
[56] The concept of infringement is dealt with in detail in paras 6–01 *et seq.*, below.
[57] For these cases, see para. 6–04, below.
[58] For the general principles of construction, see paras 4–41—4–42, below.
[59] The influence of this thinking is to be found in the form that European patent claims are to be given "wherever appropriate": the features shared with the prior art must first be described, and then the inventive additions emphasised in a phrase starting "characterised by . . .": EPC Rules, r. 29(1).

merely showing what the patentee considers is his inventive step. In the more extreme applications of this approach the Court is in effect deciding whether, given the description of the invention, a "fence-post" claim could have been written that would cover the alleged infringement.

4–39   With the introduction of the EPC and PCT examining arrangements, this difference of emphasis suddenly became something much more immediate than an occasional trap in patenting across a spectrum of countries. For it affects not only infringement but also questions of validity. In the new European system, so far as statutory texts go, the "fence-post" approach has been preferred. By Article 69(1) of the EPC, the extent of protection is determined by "the terms of the claims", using the description and drawings to interpret them; and this formula is in effect repeated for United Kingdom patents in section 125 of the 1977 Act.

4–40   Even so, qualification looms, in the ungainly form of the Protocol on the Interpretation of Article 69.[60] This requires Article 69 to be read as defining a middle position which combines a fair protection for the patentee with a reasonable degree of certainty for third parties. Two extremes are disapproved: using the strict, literal meaning of the claims to define the scope of protection, with resort to description and drawings only to resolve ambiguities (a caricature of the former British approach); and using the claims only as a guideline, the scope of protection covering "what, from a consideration of the description and drawings a person skilled in the art, the patentee has contemplated" (an exaggeration perhaps of the old German approach). While the Protocol has not had explicit effect on British attitudes to interpretation,[61] there has come in the last few years to be a new emphasis on "purposive construction" which seems in result to honour its directive.[62]

If it achieves anything at all, the Protocol may help Courts in other countries to realise that they ought not to mark out their own bounds for the monopoly; and it may stimulate patent draftsmen in other countries into imagining alternatives and drafting claims to cover them. For if Britain or another EPC country with a similar approach to claims is among those designated for a European patent, the claims must be drawn to meet their more exacting standards.

(2) Interpretation of specifications

4–41 Since the claims are the principal determinant of the scope of the monopoly, how they are to be interpreted is frequently the nub of a dispute. In so far as this goes to infringement, the patentee will generally be arguing

---

[60] The Protocol also applies to the principle in the PA 1977 that the patented invention is that specified in a claim, as interpreted by the description and drawings, and the extent of protection is to be determined accordingly: see s. 125(1), (3). On the whole question see Winkler (1979) 10 I.I.C. 296; Sijp. *ibid.*, 433; Armitage (1983) 14 I.I.C. 811; Stauder (1992) 23 I.I.C. 311; Beton [1994] E.I.P.R. 276; Chisum *et al.*, *International Perspectives on the Legal Interpretation of Patent Claims* (1995).

[61] See para. 6–08, below.

[62] For this notion, see para. 6–05, below.

for a wide construction. However, if it goes to validity, he may well want a narrow reading. Sometimes he finds himself pinioned upon this dilemma: the defendant will allege that what he is doing is something anticipated in the prior art or obvious from it. In which case, if the claim covers the activity, it is bad; if not, there is no infringement.[63]

The construction of claims is not something that can be considered in isolation from the rest of the specification. Claims are intended to be pithy delineations of the scope of monopoly, and they are drafted in light of the much more detailed text of the description.[64] A specification must always be read as a whole, just as any other document is.[65] It must moreover be read as having been addressed to a person acquainted with the technology in question. So it must take account of his state of knowledge at the time. Terms which then have a special meaning in the art, or are given a special definition by the specification, will be read in their particular sense. Otherwise they will be understood in their ordinary meaning.[66]

The direction in Article 69 of the EPC that description and drawings are **4–42** to be used to interpret the claims[67] simply reflects British practice. It has not been proper to construe claims in isolation unless and until some ambiguity emerges in the course of doing so. What British Courts have insisted on is that the claims are there to mark out the monopolised territory; Article 69 says the same. If they clearly do mean one thing, arguments that they nevertheless mean something else will be rejected. It is in this sense alone that Lord Russell of Killowen's well-known dictum is to be understood:

> "I know of no canon or principle which will justify one in departing from the unambiguous and grammatical meaning of a claim and narrowing or extending its scope by reading into it words which are not in it; or will justify one in using stray phrases in the body of the specification for the purpose of narrowing or widening the boundaries of the monopoly fixed by the plain words of a claim."[68]

As will be emphasised later, claims are to be construed purposively, to determine how they would be understood by those skilled in the relevant art as indications of the scope of monopoly claimed.[69] This modern approach is apposite not only when the question is whether it is infringed, but also on issues of validity, such as novelty and adequate disclosure.[70]

---

[63] This is the so-called "Gillette" defence, after Lord Moulton, *Gillette v. Anglo-American Trading* (1913) 30 R.P.C. 465 at 480. It requires strict proof: *Hickman v. Andrews* [1983] R.P.C. 147.

[64] See Lord Russell, *EMI v. Lissen* (1939) 56 R.P.C. 23 at 40–41.

[65] *ibid.*; and see *Ransburg v. Aerostyle* [1968] R.P.C. 287 at 297, HL.

[66] See Lord Russell, n. 64, above.

[67] See para. 4–40, above.

[68] See n. 64, above.

[69] *Catnic v. Hill & Smith* [1981] F.S.R. 60.

[70] See *Dow Chemical v. Spence Bryson* [1982] F.S.R. 397, CA; *Van der Lely v. Ruston's Engineering* [1985] R.P.C. 461, CA; *Warin Pipe v. Hepworth Iron* [1984] F.S.R. 32.

(3) The addressee of the specification

4-43 The complexity of some modern technologies, and the fact that some fields—notably organic chemistry[71]—have lost the precision of earlier, simpler days, makes the task of interpreting specifications increasingly difficult. Some assumption, however, has to be made about the persons to whom it is addressed. As we shall see, essentially the same question arises when assessing whether the invention is obvious and whether the disclosure is adequate,[72] though in those cases there is likely to be more concern over what conclusions the reader would draw from what he is told, and whether he would likely be misled by positive misstatements and misleading implications.

4-44 In *Valensi v. British Radio*,[73] the Court of Appeal felt constrained by venerable authority to hold that, even in a new and still experimental field (colour television in 1939), a specification must be looked upon as addressed to skilled technicians, rather than to leading experts (that is, those in the few research teams then tackling the problem) or to manual workers. But they did find that such an intermediate group must have existed in fact and that it would have included representatives from the different technical fields whose knowledge was being pooled in the research.[74] If specialist and highly skilled workers are the only ones who exist at the priority date, the specification may, it seems, be treated as addressed to them.[75] The judges have been careful to preserve the general rule that they interpret the words of a document.[76] However, expert witnesses may be asked what technical words, phrases and even sentences mean in context to them.[77] It is the general responsibility of the judge, before he construes the claim, to acquaint himself with the art concerned as it would have been understood by the notional addressee at the priority date.[78]

---

[71] See Satchell (1970) 1 I.I.C. 179, on the serious practical problem of defining inventions in macro-molecular chemistry. See also *Fernholz's Application* [1984] O.J. EPO 555; *Bayer's (Wagner) Application* [1982] O.J. EPO 149.

[72] See paras 5–39 *et seq.*, 5–96, below.

[73] [1973] R.P.C. 337. See further paras 5–97 *et seq.*, below.

[74] *ibid.*, at 375–377.

[75] *American Cyanamid v. Ethicon* [1979] R.P.C. 215 at 245–246.

[76] See especially Lord Tomlin, *British Celanese v. Courtaulds* (1935) 52 R.P.C. 171 at 196; *Glaverbel v. British Coal* [1993] R.P.C. 90; [1994] R.P.C. 443. In origin, construction of documents was a matter for literate judges, not jurors of uncertain education. The same attitude is not maintained in respect of drawings and photographs: *Van der Lely v. Bamfords* [1961] R.P.C. 296 at 306, CA, [1963] R.P.C. 61 at 71, HL.

[77] See Lindley L.J. *American Cyanamid v. Ethicon* [1979] R.P.C. 215 at 251–255.

[78] *Boyd v. Horrocks* (1892) 9 R.P.C. 77 at 82, HL; *British Dynamite v. Krebs* (1896) 13 R.P.C.190 at 192, HL; but it has been firmly denied that the specification should be construed specifically in the light of an alleged anticipation in the prior art, with an eye to avoiding it: *Dudgeon v. Thomson* (1877) 3 App.Cas. 34 at 53–54, HL; *Molins v. Industrial Machinery* (1938) 55 R.P.C. 31 at 39, CA. Equally, no account is taken of the alleged infringement: *Dudgeon v. Thomson* (above); *Nobel v. Anderson* (1894) 11 R.P.C. 519 at 523, CA.

(4) The application file

In the course of prosecuting an application, substantial amendments are **4–45** frequently made.[79] In the past, outsiders were not entitled to inspect the official file and so could not know of amendments before publication.[80] Now they may do so at the EPO and the British Office.[81] This may well provide evidence, for instance, of why a claim was limited in a particular way, or what construction the applicant said ought to be put upon a claim when he persuaded the examiner to drop an objection. Such "file-wrapper" estoppels are used as an aid to the construction of claims in the United States.[82] It has also been accepted in English proceedings that if an applicant relied on a narrow meaning of a term in order to secure grant, he cannot subsequently argue for a wide view of the same term.[83]

(5) Types of claim

(a) *General*

In modern patent systems a certain amount turns on the kind of claim in **4–46** question. The basic distinction is between, on the one hand, product or substance claims and, on the other, process, method or use claims. The first of these categories comprises claims to things. Such claims are infringed primarily by making, selling or using the things claimed. The second category concerns procedures for conducting activities. Here infringement consists primarily of performing the activity. There are overlaps. Consider a claim to an article which is some form of mechanical apparatus: since the monopoly includes using the apparatus, it must cover a process. Conversely, we shall see that a process claim may be infringed by dealing in its products in certain circumstances.[84] There are also refinements: a "product-by-process" claim gives a monopoly in an article only when made by the defined process.[85] But the basic distinction is the one to watch: a claim to a thing gives a monopoly over it whatever it is to be used for—and is correspondingly broad; when the prior art precludes such a claim, it may still be possible to secure a method claim to protect the invention of a particular use for the known thing—but then the monopoly is restricted to that use alone. Sometimes claims are drawn in such a way that it is difficult to decide which kind they are. This has to be settled by interpretation.[86]

---

[79] See paras 4–31—4–32, above.

[80] Publication previously took place after examination and acceptance by the British Office.

[81] EPC, Art. 128, EPC Rules, rr. 93–95; PA 1977, s. 118, PA 1977 Rules, rr. 93–95. There are various exceptions and procedural requirements.

[82] See Chisum, *Patents* (1978) IV, para. 18.05; the judges have differed in their willingness to look beyond amendments to the reasons for requiring, proposing or resisting them.

[83] *Fürr v. C.D. Truline* [1985] F.S.R. 553.

[84] See para. 6–14, below.

[85] Such a claim can be allowed only when the product is itself patentable: *IFF/Claim Categories* [1984] O.J. EPO 309.

[86] For instance, claims to a thing "for" a purpose: see paras 5–26, 5–27, below.

(b) *Chemical inventions*

4-47 The distinction just made is particularly important in the application of the patent system to chemical inventions—rather more so than in the case of mechanical inventions. Indeed, the adaptation of the patent system so as to accommodate the various branches of the chemical industry has proved a difficult matter, and one on which some international consensus has been slow to emerge.[87] Speaking very broadly, inventive activity in the chemical field sometimes consists of making or in analysing compounds whose existence could not even have been theoretically predicted in advance. More often it involves devising ways of making substances more successfully or cheaply. But the largest part of the ground is concerned with searching for the values that substances may have in use. This sort of work is frequently concerned either with substances which are new (in the sense of never having been made before) but can be made from known starting materials by known methods; or with substances which are known, either as laboratory playthings or as functional products, and which are then tested for initial or further practical uses.

4-48 The first difficulty in the chemical field is whether patents should ever be granted for a chemical substance itself. Substances may prove to have a variety of values: well-known examples are dyestuffs which prove to have valuable pharmaceutical properties.[88] (By contrast, mechanical things less readily assume new functions, at least without adaptation.) Accordingly, many systems have at some time required chemical claims to be for "substance-by-process". The British system contained such a constraint between 1919 and 1949.[89] But it was found, as in other countries, that this only introduced a game of seeing whether the patentee could think of all the possible processes for producing the substance and therefore claim them. This still left him with the difficulty of showing that the defendant was using one of them.

In Britain from 1949 onwards, and now elsewhere in EPC States,[90] it has been accepted that claims to chemical substances of all kinds, including pharmaceuticals, are admissible. It seems that they may be validly granted whenever the substance itself is not part of the prior art.[91] This is then treated as any other article claim: the patentee's permission is needed to make the article for any purpose. If a second use for the substance is found during the life of his patent, his permission is needed just as much to make,

---

[87] *cf., e.g.* the papers by Satchell (n. 71, above) and Robinson and Nastelski (1972) 3 I.I.C. 139, 267; Lawrence (1973) 2 CIPA 385; Gaumont (1982) 13 I.I.C. 457; Klöpsch (1982) 13 I.I.C. 457.

[88] See for instance the adventures of the phenothiazines: *Olin Mathieson v. Biorex* [1970] R.P.C. 157 at 185 *et seq.*

[89] See Final Report of the Swan Committee (Cmd. 7206, 1947), paras 92–95.

[90] See Michaelis (1983) 14 I.I.C. 372; Gruber and Kroher (1984) 15 I.I.C. 588 at 726.

[91] But see further para. 5–104, below.

sell and use for that purpose as for the purpose that he worked out. This is not so overweening as it may sound, because there are ways in which the second inventor can secure patents, by means of use claims or through the special rules for "selection".[92] In the main, therefore, the first patentee is given the chance of a share in the monopoly for the second discovery, provided that it comes during the life of his patent.[93] Any injustices arising from this compromise have not aroused chemical industry circles to major protest.

A second problem concerns the breadth of monopoly allowable.[94] Much **4–49** investigation into the properties of organic substances involves testing a few substances in a family of compounds that may have thousands or millions of members. The basic structure of the family has a defined molecular form which can be varied by attaching atoms or chains at particular positions of the molecule. Experience shows that in many cases, the whole group of compounds will have similar characteristics, though in different degrees and with different consequences. The dilemma then is this: if the patentee is restricted to claims upon the substances that he has used in his experiments, his rival is free to take up the next nearest in imitation. If, however, he is given a claim to the whole family of compounds, his monopoly may appear unduly wide. Authorities in different countries have reacted with greater or less caution in seeking some compromise, looking in the main at the degree of certainty with which it can be predicted that the whole class will share the discovered advantages. On a strict view, for instance, it can be insisted that either end of a range of compounds be tested, together with a representative sample of those in between. But it is difficult to reach a formula like this which seems reasonable in every case.[95] In Britain, by contrast, it has been held that it is enough, in the absence of positive proof that some members of the class do not work at all,[96] to base a claim to the class simply upon a sound prediction that all members will show the advantageous property in some degree.[97] The test finds a place in the EPO Guidelines; and it has been espoused by the Supreme Court of Canada in place of an earlier, more grudging approach.[98]

Chemical patents present a number of other difficulties. With the macro- **4–50** molecular substances that play such a part in modern plastics and other chemistry, there are major obstacles to finding a sufficiently clear descrip-

---

[92] See paras 5–23—5–25, below.
[93] Should he obstruct the second application by refusing permission, a compulsory licence could be secured: see para. 7–41, below.
[94] See Roberts [1994] E.I.P.R. 371; Brandi-Dohrn [1994] I.I.C. 648; Wibbelmann [1997] E.I.P.R. 515.
[95] An attempt by the German Patent Office to require this was rejected by the courts: see Nastelski (n. 87, above).
[96] Whether this factor remains of any significance under the new law is questionable, since inutility is no longer a distinct ground of objection to validity: see para. 5–53, below.
[97] Graham J., *Olin Mathieson* case (n. 88, above) at 193: see para. 5–104, below.
[98] EPO Guidelines, CIII 6.2; *Monsanto's (Coran and Kerwood) Application* [1980] F.S.R. 50.

tion for a claim.[99] There is a problem when the substance claimed has itself no use but may prove a useful intermediate in the production of something that does turn out to be valuable.[1] The continued preclusion of patents for methods of human and animal treatment poses problems which are growing with the current expansion of biotechnology.[2] These are particular difficulties which can be left for later discussion. But they are symptomatic of a larger truth.

[99] See para. 4–43, above.
[1] See para. 5–53, below.
[2] See paras 5–70 *et seq.*, below.

Chapter 5

VALIDITY

This Chapter investigates the substantive law of validity of patents. A **5–01**
number of ideas introduced in the last Chapter form an essential background. First, the challenges that may be made to validity, and the persons
who may make them, differ for applications and granted patents. Secondly,
if a patentee seeks to enforce his rights, he may be met by the defence that
his patent is invalid or a counterclaim for its revocation. Thirdly, the claims,
which define the monopoly, are the starting point of various issues about
validity.

European patents must meet the criteria of validity specified in the EPC;
but a national state for which a European patent is granted may not add
further requirements by its own law.[1] The Patents Act 1977 accordingly
adopts the EPC grounds of invalidity for United Kingdom patents whether
granted by the European or the British Office.[2] But to some extent the
language of the EPC is revamped, with attendant uncertainties.[3] In outline
the grounds are these:

There must be an "invention" (a concept which is not defined[4]) and
that invention must be patentable; that is:

(1) it must be novel (or not "anticipated");
(2) it must involve an inventive step (thus escaping the taint of
"obviousness");
(3) it must be capable of industrial application; and
(4) it must not fall "as such" within any of the categories of subject-
matter specifically excluded.[5]

The specification must satisfy the "internal" requirement of adequate
disclosure,[6] and during the application stage the claims must meet a
number of standards.[7]

---

[1] One basic limb of the so-called "maximum" approach adopted in drafting the Convention:
see EPC, Art. 138.
[2] PA 1977, s. 72.
[3] These difficulties are, if anything, compounded by *ibid*., s. 130(7): see para. 3–58, above.
[4] But which is a logical prerequisite with important consequences, according to the Court of
Appeal: para. 5–54, below.
[5] EPC, Arts 52–57; PA 1977, ss. 1–4, para. 5–03, below.
[6] EPC, Arts 83, 100(b); PA 1977, ss. 14(3), 72(1)(c), paras 5–93 *et seq*., below.
[7] See paras 5–101 *et seq*., below.

There are certain other objections relating to the right to grant and to unallowable amendments.[8]

The grounds of invalidity are formulated in general terms. Yet the issues that are hardest fought often lie at their perimeters. There remains much for the Courts and other tribunals to do in determining the precise application of law to particular cases.

5–02 There is now a considerable body of case law, from national Courts and even more from the EPO, which interprets the provisions of the Patents Act 1977, other national legislation and the Articles of the EPC from which they derive.[9] Decisions under the former British law must be treated as suggestive rather than authoritative, for they were concerned with statutory texts that were differently formulated.

An important objective of the present regime is that patents should be granted only after a more extensive examination than previously. The former British approach deliberately and rather indiscriminately set a low standard for applicants to satisfy before grant: if doubt existed about an objection it was to be resolved in the applicant's favour, full investigation being reserved for proceedings after grant.[10] We shall see that there are inherent reasons for taking a cautious approach to some objections, notably obviousness, at an early stage in the life of an invention. But a firmer hand may be applied at that stage to other questions, such as whether categories of subject-matter (computer programs, micro-organisms, etc.) fall within the system or not. For these are issues of policy and interpretation that do not depend on evidence in the particular case.[11] We shall, however, reserve consideration of them until we have dealt with novelty and obviousness.

1. NOVELTY[12]

(1) Introduction

5–03 No system grants valid patents for inventions that are already known: that would be to encumber industry with constraints upon the use of information without any sufficient return. Accordingly, the present law requires a patented invention to be new in the sense of forming no part of the state of the art, that is it must not be found at the priority date in any "matter (whether a product, a process, information about either, or anything else)

---

[8] See paras 4–30—4–36, above.
[9] If and when the CPC takes effect, the European Court of Justice and the proposed Community Patent Appeal Court will also have jurisdiction.
[10] The approach stemmed from the *R. v. P.A.T., ex. p. Swift* [1962] R.P.C. 37, DC
[11] For examples, see paras 5–54 *et seq.*, below.
[12] See generally Ebbink [1995] Pat. Wld. 25; Rogge (1997) 28 I.I.C. 443; Crespi (1997) 28 I.I.C. 603.

which has at any time been made available to the public (whether in the United Kingdom or elsewhere) by written or oral description, by use, or in any other way."[13]

This concept draws no distinction between information published by the inventor and by someone unconnected with him: if the inventor were protected from prejudicing himself, he might delay his patent until it was commercially most advantageous to apply.[14]

In most cases the assessment of novelty is relatively straightforward. Here **5–04** are a few examples which illustrate the nature of the inquiry and point towards some of the problems requiring further discussion.

(1) (*Van der Lely v. Bamford*[15]: mechanical product.) The patentee claimed a hayraking machine in which the rake-wheels were turned not by an engine but by contact with the ground. The patent was held to have been anticipated by a photograph in a journal which showed a hayrake with this feature (the issue was whether the photograph was clear enough to reveal the invention to an informed person. It was found to do so).

(2) (*Fomento v. Mentmore*[16]: mechanical process/product). The patentee claimed a ball-point pen in which the housing around the ball had a groove running in a ring below the equatorial plane of the ball; this produced a smooth flow of ink. One alleged anticipation (a patent specification[17]) was found to describe a method of enclosing the housing around the ball by "peining", that is by hitting the open housing with a tool shaped like a candle-snuffer. Before there could be anticipation, however, it was necessary to show that peining would inevitably produce the desired ring-like groove in the correct position; and the earlier document, it was held, only gave instructions that "might well" produce this effect.[18]

(3) (*Opinion: Availability to the Public*[19]: chemical combination). A chemical composition was marketed before the priority date of a patent claiming that substance. It could be analysed and reproduced by a person with the appropriate skills. The claim was therefore anticipated.

---

[13] PA 1977, s. 1(1)(a), s. 2(1), (2), based upon EPC, Arts 52, 54. For the special problem of prior patent applications subsequently published (PA 1977, s. 2(3), EPC, Art. 54(3)), see paras 5–14—5–15, below.

[14] But see para. 5–07, below.

[15] *Van der Lely v. Bamfords* [1963] R.P.C. 61, HL For anticipation in a drawing, see, *e.g. Charbonnages' Application* [1985] O.J. EPO 310.

[16] [1956] R.P.C. 87, CA.

[17] In which at least one plaintiff had an interest.

[18] There was also a prior use point: para. 5–13, below.

[19] Enlarged Board of Appeal [1993] O.J. EPO 277.

5–05   From these examples it may be seen that novelty involves an essentially factual investigation: has the same invention already been made public? There is comparatively little room for the sort of evaluation that arises where the issue is obviousness: is the step over what is already known significant enough to be called inventive? There are circumstances in which, if an anticipation cannot be shown, there is no room for an attack on the grounds of obviousness. Equally, "what is hidden may still be obvious".[20] It is therefore important to know what counts as lack of novelty. It is worth introducing some of the problems in historical and comparative terms.

(2) Publication and use

5–06 The British patent system originally treated prior use as the principal objection to the validity of a patent, the first purpose of the system being to encourage the introduction of inventions into British manufacture.[21] Even when prior publication evolved as a distinct ground of objection, prior use kept its independent status—for instance, in the principle that even a secret use was in some circumstances a ground of invalidity; and in the rule that a prior use which did not reveal the invention to the world but which involved no deliberate secrecy could found an objection under the general provision relating to novelty, rather than the more limited secret use provision.[22]

5–07   In the current law, use has lost its independent status as an objection to validity. An invention is new if it does not form part of the state of the art; and the state of the art comprises all matter made available to the public before the priority date of the invention "by written or oral description, by use or in any other way".[23] Use founds an attack on novelty if it effects a public release equivalent to publication. The issue is whether a skilled worker, by observation or analysis, could discover and reproduce the invention.[24] But to make batches of one chemical substance that are then mixed with others so as to be undetectable when the mixture is sold[25] would not be to "publish" the substance. Under the new law, novelty is concerned with the patent system as a source of information, not as a stimulus to use nor as protection to those who have already used the invention.[26] The prior user who does not reveal his invention is confined to a limited measure of protection against being held an infringer.[27]

---

[20] *Mobil/Friction-reducing additive* [1990] O.J. EPO 93.
[21] See paras 3–04, 3–05, above.
[22] See PA 1949, s. 32(1)(c), (e); Frost [1996] E.I.P.R. 18; Aúz Castro (1996) 27 I.I.C. 190; Törnroth (1997) 28 I.I.C. 800.
[23] There is no distinction between the two forms of anticipation: Opinion G1/92: [1993] O.J. EPO 277 (Enlarged Board of Appeal); *Quantel v. Spaceward* [1990] R.P.C. 83.
[24] *Stahlwerk Becker's Patent* (1919) 36 R.P.C. 13, HL, held that to market a steel was to publish its composition, since this could be deduced by chemical analysis. See also *Opinion* (n. 18, above).
[25] As in *Bristol Myers' (Johnson) Application* [1975] R.P.C. 127, HL.
[26] For difficulties in applying this principle, see below, para. 5–20.
[27] See paras 6–21, 6–22, below.

While prior use was a distinct objection, it was not open to an inventor of **5–08** a secret process first to use it until it became a success and then to patent it at the most advantageous moment. If he can do so, the patent system suffers as an incentive to early revelation in the very case where it ought to have greatest effect. However, the devisers of the EPC chose not to provide separately against this danger. Certainly in a system which is strictly "first to file", an inventor who intends to patent can risk delay only if he sees no serious hazard of others publishing or applying for a patent before he does.

(3) Material available for consideration

A patent system has to define the material which it will take into **5–09** consideration in assessing novelty, using broad criteria relating to time, place and form. Each element can be separately considered:

(a) *Temporal factors*

The British system has long taken the priority date of the patent as the **5–10** point in time for deciding whether there has been an anticipation and this (subject to fewer exceptions than before[28]) continues to be the rule: there is no general period of grace.[29] The special difficulty created by applications with earlier priority, which are published only after the later priority date of another application, receives new treatment as far as British law is concerned: the earlier specification is added to the state of the art for purposes of novelty but not obviousness. To the problems that this may cause, we return subsequently.[30]

(b) *Territorial factors*

Traditionally the British system, with its emphasis on the encouragement of **5–11** national industry, only looked at anticipations within the United Kingdom.[31] Other countries have taken greater account of the growing internationalism of technical knowledge. But in the various solutions adopted, there has been some tendency to distinguish between anticipations by documentary publication and by use: in some systems the former is

---

[28] For the present exceptions, see para. 5–16, below. Previously no account was taken of the content of patent specifications more than 50 years old, but that limitation does not apply under the 1977 Act.

[29] Periods of grace covering material published by the patentee (or deriving from him) have been found in various systems. Disregard of material published or used within a period before the priority date, is typically associated with the "first to invent" system of the U.S. and Canada: see Chisum, *Patents* I, paras 3.04—3.07. There is now much discussion of the need to introduce more extensive grace periods into the European systems: see Wegner, *Patent Harmonization* (1993), Chap. 9.

[30] See para. 5–14, below.

[31] See paras 3–04, 3–05, above.

considered upon a worldwide purview, while the latter has to take place within the territory.[32]

The EPC and the 1977 Act pursue an uninhibited internationalism in the matter, apparently imposing no territorial constraints at all. The British Act refers specifically to material "made available to the public (whether in the United Kingdom or elsewhere)".[33] But this liberality offers temptations to the unscrupulous to produce instances of anticipation from highly obscure foreign sources. If a British Court or tribunal has doubts about the genuineness of the evidence, it may find that the attacker has not sufficiently proved his case. Alternatively, it may be attracted to hold that the anticipation must have been made available to a public which includes at least some persons from British industry. Certainly on this basis material could be disregarded which, because of a legal embargo in a foreign country, could not be consulted by a British technician or research scientist; more doubtfully in the case of material which could only be obtained by such a person after laborious and expensive persistence.

(c) *Form*

5–12 In the past, prior publication of an invention has normally been found in a document, while prior use has required proof that the use has taken place. The current law admits prior matter irrespective of its form. It may be made available to the public "by written or oral description, by use or in any other way".[34] While this makes clear that the essential inquiry is the same in respect of publications and actual embodiments or uses, the very fact that in the latter category the information has to be capable of discovery by some means other than reading does pose additional considerations, to which we come below.[35]

(d) *Degree of dissemination*

5–13 Underlying the rules about place and form is a general question of degree. How far must information have been communicated, or at least put at the disposal of others, before it can be said to be available to the public? As under the 1949 Act, the law calls only for a minimum that is, in a sense, artificial: it was enough that information about the invention (or the means of discovering it from a concrete embodiment) is put in the hands of a single person who may use it as he likes, free from obligations of confidence

---

[32] For countries which prefer this "relative" novelty, those which allow "absolute" novelty and those which adopt the "local" novelty formerly found in British law, see Baxter, *World Patent Law and Practice*, paras 4.01, 4.02.

[33] PA 1977, s. 2(2). The EPC, Art. 54(2) has nothing equivalent to the phrase in brackets.

[34] See EPO Guidelines, D V 3 1. Demonstrating in specialist training courses or on television are given as examples of "other ways".

[35] See para. 5–19, below.

and similar duties.[36] Likewise it suffices that a document was placed in a library or other place in the United Kingdom for consultation as of right by any person with or without paying a fee[37–38].

These liberal rules not only simplified an attacker's task in procuring evidence; they also side-stepped the difficult question: how much publicity would make a thing "known"? So long as novelty was confined to anticipations within the United Kingdom, and the Patent Office made only a limited search as the basis for its *ex parte* examination, the artifice of the rule had its merits. But, as already remarked, the "absolute novelty" of the new law leads to the citation of much more obscure documents, to say nothing of oral communications and uses.[39] If the actual circulation of them, or the potential availability of information from them, is very limited it is possible that they may be discounted.[40] But at least it must be assumed that the contents of patent specifications, no matter where or when published,[41] belong to the art.

(e) *Matter in prior specifications*

If competitors make the same invention at much the same time (by no **5–14** means an uncommon phenomenon in today's race for innovation) there is a special aspect of the principle under which the first to secure a priority date is preferred. Once the earlier applicant has his specification published, it becomes part of the state of the art. But without special provision it would not have that character in the period between securing the priority date and publication of the specification. Yet if nothing is done, "double patenting" may result, and that has long been thought unacceptable. Previously, British law sought to deal with the problem in the way that would least jeopardise the chances of the later patentee: by preventing him from also claiming protection for inventions within the claims of the earlier patent, provided that they were valid. But under the 1949 Act this process of comparing

---

[36] *Humpherson v. Syer* (1887) 4 R.P.C. 407 at 413–414, CA; *Fomento v. Mentmore* (n. 15, above) at 99; *Monsanto's (Brignac) Application* [1971] R.P.C. 127; *Télémechanique/Power supply unit* [1993] O.J. EPO 646: *cf. Macor/Confidence agreement* [1994] O.J. EPO 713. Claims that a communication was not confidential will be critically examined: *AT & T's Applicn.* [1998] O.J. EPO 131. Private conversations between scientists are likely to be treated as a secret: *Visx v. Nidex* [1999] F.S.R. 406.

[37–38] PA 1949, s. 101(1). PA 1977, s. 130(1) "published". Display on the same day anticipates; but mere proof of posting beforehand does not suffice: *IBM/Ion Etching* [1991] O.J. EPO 18; nor does a mere contract to publish; *Bilfinger/Sealing screen* [1999] E.P.O.R. 192.

[39] See *Stahlwerke Peine-Salzgitter/Hot strip* [1997] E.P.O.R. 371; a lecture will be presumed to be the same as a subsequent text only if the latter is published shortly afterwards; and see *Kanegafuchi* [1999] E.P.O.R. 270.

[40] *cf. Badowski v. U.S.* 118 U.S.P.Q. 358 (1958) (Russian document available only through diplomatic channels is not an anticipation). An EPO Board of Appeal has recently said that proof of the prior use must be beyond reasonable doubt: *Sekisu/Shrinkable sheet* [1998] E.P.O.R. 432; and see *AT&T* [1997] E.P.O.R. 509.

[41] Unlike the former rule which discounted U.K. specifications more than 50 years old.

claims in order to exclude overlap bred highly recondite judicial decisions which militated against continuing this approach.[42]

Instead, the material in a patent specification is now given a priority date, which is determined in the same way as the priority date of a claim. Provided that it is subsequently published, it is treated as having formed part of the state of the art in the intervening period for the purpose of assessing the novelty of later inventions; but not, let it be stressed, for ascertaining inventive step.[43] In applications to the British Office this applies to the contents of prior British applications[44]; in the EPO to the contents of prior European applications, but only to the extent that the same states are designated in the earlier and later applications[45] (hence the European patents granted for various states may differ). Correspondingly, after grant of a British patent by either route, the Comptroller or Court must take account of earlier applications for United Kingdom patents by either route.[46] It is not required of applications that they must mature into granted patents, a pre-condition which would conjure echoes of "prior claiming".[47]

5–15 This "whole contents" approach applies not only between rival applicants but also to successive applications by the same person. Hence the danger of "self-collision", which is particularly apparent in the case of mechanical inventions. In that field, one piece of research may produce a succession of broadly interrelated inventions, each of which calls for a separate application either as a matter of tactics or because of the requirement of "unity of invention".[48] Each application will need a sufficient description and this may well call for mention of the other parts of the whole concept. If the applications are not filed on the same day, it is only too easy for the first to describe matter for which the second seeks protection. It was just this hazard that the old "prior claiming" approach avoided; but by making the

---

[42] For the debate, see the Banks Report (Cmnd. 4407, 1970), Chap. 10. See now Rogge (1997) 28 I.I.C. 794.

[43] PA 1977, s. 2(3); EPC, Art. 54(3). The Banks Committee had proposed the contrary (Chap. 10) but this was not accepted for the EPC or the PA 1977. Switzerland is one EPC member which continues to adopt a "prior claiming" approach in its own law: see EPO Bulletin 1979, p. 14.

[44] As far as the PA 1977 is concerned (see s. 78(1), (2)), this could also include prior European applications designating the U.K.; but no regular machinery exists for searching these applications. A third party "observation", however (see para. 4–22, above), could provide the notification.

[45] EPC, Art. 54(3), (4); and see *Mobil Oil* [1992] O.J. EPO 117, refusing to allow amendments in EPO opposition proceedings which would take account of national prior applications; Paterson, para. 9–33.

[46] PA 1977, ss. 2(3), 78(1), (2). (This is a matter for national law: see EPC, Art. 139). PA 1977, s. 73(1) gives the Comptroller special power to revoke upon his own initiative, in order to take account in particular of late information about prior European patents (U.K.). Under s. 73(2) and (3), a British-granted patent will be revoked if a European patent (U.K.) for the same invention bears the same priority date.

[47] See now PA 1977, s. 78(5A), inserted by CDPA 1988, Sched. 5, para. 22.

[48] See para. 4–15, above.

earlier material part of the art only for novelty and not for obviousness (until it is actually published) the danger is to some extent reduced.

(f) *Special exclusions*

A patentee faces the risk of anticipation from two sources: from indepen- **5–16** dent inventors and from those whose information comes from the same inventive source as his own. In a modern business organisation risks of the latter kind may arise because its research staff are eager for recognition, because an employee has turned disloyal, or because an outsider to whom the invention was revealed in confidence breaks his undertaking. Against such hazards as these, the 1977 Act affords some measure of protection, but it is more limited than under the old law. For instance, inventors are no longer free to describe the invention in a paper to a learned society.[49] So it is crucial to keep their natural desire to share ideas with colleagues under rein until all relevant priority dates have been secured.[50] Now that academic researchers are driven increasingly to contemplate the commercial prospects of their work, these severe requirements cause considerable aggravation. The case for a general grace period of, say, six months continues to be hotly debated.

In two circumstances, according to the British Act, a disclosure does not count in determining novelty for a period of six months after it is made[51]:

(1) if the information was obtained unlawfully or in breach of confidence; or if it was disclosed in breach of confidence.[52]

(2) if the disclosure resulted from display by the inventor at a prescribed "international exhibition" and the applicant files proper notification of this.[53] Only exhibitions to educate the public (not trade fairs) are within the exception and they must last between three and 26 weeks and must occur no more than once in every 20 years.[54]

---

[49] As in *Palmaz's European Patents* [1999] R.P.C. 47 at 83. *cf.* PA 1949, s. 51(2)(d) and note the other exceptions in ss. 50, 51.

[50] Because of the equivalent position under the EPC, PA 1977, s. 6, provides no effective protection for the applicant who is not able to maintain expected priority and publishes in the interim: para. 4–12, above.

[51] Whether the six months run between disclosure and the actual filing date, or (more sensibly) the priority date, has been the subject of conflicting decisions in the E.P.O. and is being considered by the Enlarged B.A.: *University Patents* [1999] E.P.O.R. 211.

[52] PA 1973, s. 2(4)(a), (b). This abbreviates highly elaborate provisions, covering various possible situations. On the burden of proof, see *Dunlop's Application* [1979] R.P.C. 523, CA.

[53] PA 1977, s. 2(4)(c). The exhibition has to be one within the Convention on International Exhibitions 1928: see PA 1977, s. 130(1), (2). For the notification required, see PA 1977 Rules, r. 5; EPC Rules, r. 23.

[54] Unlike the more generous provisions in the previous law: see Ency. PL, para. 5–122; [1979] O.J. EPO 159; Vitoria [1978] October E.I.P.R. 29; note the attempt to read in an additional "common law" exception for reasonable public experimentation: *Prout v. British Gas* [1992] F.S.R. 428, dismissed by Jacob [1993] E.I.P.R. 312 at 315; and see *Lux v. Pike* [1993] R.P.C. 107.

These exceptions do not follow the equivalent EPC provisions,[55] apparently because "it will not do"[56] to have English judges wrestle with the Convention's vague language ("evident abuse in relation to the applicant or his legal predecessor"). One consequent difference is that the British provisions appear to exempt the disclosure of an invention even if it has also been made by an inventor who is quite independent of the applicant or his predecessor, and the information comes from this separate source.

(4) Relations between anticipation and invention in suit

(a) *The comparison*

5–17 Novelty involves a comparison between the invention, in any of its embodiments, and the thing that is revealed by the prior publication or use. Under the old law at least, the question was whether anything within the claims has already been published or used. Or, standing the question on its head: would the earlier thing fall within the later claims for purposes of infringement (assuming that other conditions for infringement were fulfilled)?[57] For instance, in *Van der Lely v. Bamfords*,[58] if the photographed hayrake were made in the United Kingdom after publication of the patent application, would it fall within the terms of any claim? If it would, then the photograph was an anticipation. Given the new emphasis on the purposive construction of claims, the result may be a correspondingly enlarged scope for anticipation.[59] Thus a claim to a windsurfer of the familiar modern type of board included as one element, "a pair of arcuate booms", by which was meant the wishbone-shaped grip held by the surfer. An earlier model made by a young amateur and used publicly, had a pair of straight booms. Since in use these deformed flexibly into arcs, they were held to anticipate.[60]

(b) *The anticipation: clarity and sufficiency of a document*

5–18 Not infrequently a question of anticipation centres on whether the prior document does sufficiently disclose the later invention. This may be so when the alleged anticipation is "unintentional"; but the issue is by no means confined to such cases. For instance, in *Fomento v. Mentmore*,[61] actual examples were put in evidence of pens produced according to the

---

[55] EPC, Art. 55; Paterson, paras 9–22—9–30.
[56] J. C. H. Ellis, in *The Patents Act 1977* (Vitoria ed.), p. 23.
[57] See, *e.g. Harwood v. GNR* (1865) 11 HLC. 654 at 681; *General Tire v. Firestone* [1972] R.P.C. 457 at 486, 496, CA.
[58] See para. 5–04, example (1), above.
[59] See para. 4–41, above.
[60] *Windsurfing International v. Tabur Marine* [1985] R.P.C. 59, CA. See also *Dow Chemical v. Spence Bryson* [1982] F.S.R. 397, CA.
[61] See para. 5–04, example (2), above.

allegedly anticipatory instructions. Virtually all showed the crucial deformation of the housing of the ball. Yet the Court of Appeal still found, on the evidence as a whole, that, while this "might well" occur from following the instructions, yet it would not do so "necessarily", or "inevitably", or "in 99 cases out of a hundred".[62]

This then is the test: if the claim is for a method of use or a process, the anticipation must give "clear and unmistakeable directions to do what the patentee claims to have invented".[63] If it is for an article, apparatus or substance, the qualified reader must be enabled "at once to perceive and understand and be able practically to apply the discovery without the necessity of making further experiments".[64] If instructions are given for carrying out a chemical process with such precision that a particular substance must result, there cannot thereafter be a claim for that substance; it makes no difference that the later work establishes more information about its structure or other characteristics.[65] Instructions or descriptions may, however, anticipate even if they fall short of the detailed description that it would be needed to support a valid patent.[66] But—and here obviousness must be distinguished—it is not permissible to read two documents together if one does not positively cross-refer to the other.[67]

In the case of a publication describing a new substance but not how to make it, if common general knowledge in the industry would not permit a skilled person to select or secure the starting material or make intermediate products, there has been no sufficient description of the invention and accordingly there is no anticipation. To satisfy these criteria, there must be an enabling disclosure in the sense required by the House of Lords in *Asahi KK's Application*.[68] Not least in its biotechnological context, this case has

---

[62] A statement, later shown to be incorrect, that something would not work can scarcely be an anticipation: see *Nestle's Application* [1970] R.P.C. 88; but a statement that something has been tried and did not work is more doubtful; a statement that something works for a purpose when it does not anticipates a claim to the thing, even though it is found to have a different advantage: *Shell's Patent* [1960] R.P.C. 35; but see paras 5–26, 5–27, below.

[63] Parker J., *Flour Oxidising v. Carr* (1908) 25 R.P.C. 428 at 457. Subsequently much cited, *e.g.* Lord Dunedin, *Metropolitan Vickers v. British Thomson-Houston* (1927) 45 R.P.C. 1 at 22–23; *Beecham Group's (Amoxycillin) Application* [1980] R.P.C. 261; *Evans Medical's Patent* [1998] R.P.C. 517 at 560–561, CA. "A signpost, however clear, upon the road to the patentee's invention will not suffice. The prior inventor must be clearly shown to have planted his flag at the precise destination before the patentee": Sachs L.J., *General Tire v. Firestone* [1972] R.P.C. 457 at 486.

[64] Lord Westbury, *Hill v. Evans* (1862) 4 De G. F. & J. 288 at 300; cited in *Van der Lely v. Bamfords* [1963] R.P.C. 61 at 71, HL.

[65] *Bayer/Diastereomers* [1982] O.J. EPO 296; *Mobil* (n. 97, below); *cf. Du Pont/Copolymers* [1989] O.J. EPO 491.

[66] Lord Watson, *King Brown v. Anglo American Brush* (1892) 9 R.P.C. 313 at 320; cited *Ransburg v. Aerostyle* [1968] R.P.C. 287 at 299, HL.

[67] See para. 5–42, n. 52, below.

[68] [1991] R.P.C. 485, H.L; see above, para. 4–12—a test deriving from *ICI/Pyridine herbicides* [1987] O.J. EPO 5 and *Collaborative/Preprorennin* [1990] O.J. EPO 250. Applied subsequently, *e.g.* in *Lux v. Pike* [1993] R.P.C. 107 and *Merrell Dow v. Norton* (below n. 75); and see *Genentech Human t-PA* [1996] O.J. EPO 564.

imposed a significant constraint on attempts at pre-emptive patenting where analysis has run ahead of practical production.

(c) *The anticipation: appreciation of significance of an embodiment*

5–19 For a prior use of the invention to constitute anticipation, it is only necessary for another person (not under any obligation of confidence[69]) to be able to secure, from the thing or the process, the knowledge necessary to make or perform it himself. But in what sense must it have been possible to carry out the necessary observation or analysis? Must there have been some indicator which would induce a skilled worker to undertake the analysis? Would his analysis have revealed the advantage which the subsequent patentee has demonstrated?

The Enlarged Board of Appeal (EPO) requires that a skilled person must have been able to discover the composition or the internal structure of a product and also to reproduce it "without undue burden".[70] A particular DNA sequence could, in principle, be made public if deposited in an appropriate gene bank; but it is not enough to show that it was there in a "library" of fragments and could only be detected by probing tens of thousands of samples.[71]

As to the likelihood or otherwise of the analysis being carried out, some EPO decisions required that there must be sufficient reason to conduct the analysis, including consideration of whether it was financially worthwhile. However, the Enlarged Board has rejected these.[72] It has preferred the relatively mechanical and straightforward approach to the question, long followed in the United Kingdom,[73] which inquires only into the feasibility and not the likelihood of the investigation. As a consequence, some anticipations have an entirely notional character: but straightforward advice can be given on the matter.

As to knowledge of advantages, we reach difficult and shifting terrain which will take some considerable exploration. At the outset, let us note that the former law took a plain attitude: if a thing or a process had been used or described publicly, then it could not be claimed again, even when an important new purpose was found for it. A way would have to be sought for claiming something that was physically different.

In *Molins v. Industrial Machinery*[74] the patent concerned a way of ensuring an even distribution of tobacco in cigarettes formed on a

---

[69] As to which, see para. 5–13, above.

[70] *Availability to the Public* [1993] O.J. EPO 277; applied in *Merrell Dow v. Norton* (n. 72, below). "Without undue burden" relates only to the ability to reproduce the subject-matter: *Packard/Supersolve* [1995] O.J. EPO 755.

[71] *Biogen/Alpha-interferons* [1990] O.J. EPO 335.

[72] *Opinion* n. 18, above; not following, *e.g. Hoechst/polyvinyl ester dispersion* [1992] O.J. EPO 718; *Heidelberger Druckmaschinen* [1993] O.J. EPO 295.

[73] See para. 5–07, above.

[74] (1938) 55 R.P.C. 31, CA.

high-speed machine: the trick lay in giving the tobacco a preliminary push in the same direction as the paper in which it would be wrapped. Bonsack's much earlier specification, dealing with a low-speed machine, described a device which would give this movement. Accordingly it anticipated, although it was not directed to solving the patentee's problem.

There may well be a way of respecting this principle while allowing an amended claim which will give adequate protection to the later discovered advantage. In the *Molins* case, an amendment restricted the claim to high-speed machines, leaving a process which was not obvious in light of Bonsack's patent.

If the rule on anticipation were otherwise, there could be further patents **5–20** for discovering how something which is already known to work actually does so. In *Merrell Dow v. Norton*,[75] the House of Lords refused to contemplate such a prospect.

> The plaintiff had already benefited considerably from a patented antihistamine drug, terfenadine. Before expiry of the first patent, the plaintiff discovered that in the liver terfenadine was metabolised to produce an acid metabolite of terfenadine. This was a previously unidentified, chemically distinct, substance which was largely responsible for the drug's effectiveness in the treatment of asthmatic disorders. By patenting the acid metabolite, the plaintiff extended its overall period of protection substantially.[76] The first patent, which clearly disclosed use of the substance claimed, terfenadine, in order to treat the conditions also covered in the acid metabolite patent, was held to anticipate the second; its claim would include the metabolite as produced in the liver, and the steps neccessary to produce the metabolite had been described in the first patent even though the nature of the chemical reaction had not then been identified.[77]

The House of Lords would not rule out a claim to the metabolite, when made outside the human body, because that would be physically different from the state of the art.[78] Equally, it distinguished the case where a new advantage is discovered for a known thing, a matter on which the EPO has recently shown a novel generosity. This we must reserve for later consideration.[79]

---

[75] [1996] R.P.C. 76; Karet [1996] E.I.P.R. 97.

[76] A competitor marketing terfenadine was alleged to be infringing "indirectly" by supplying "essential means" for making the acid metabolite (see para. 6–17, below).

[77] Both patents had to be for the pharmaceuticals, since use claims could have been excluded as methods of medical treatment (see paras 5–73 *et seq.*, below). It made no difference whether the two patents were held by the same or by quite separate patentees. Had there only been use, and not disclosure, of terfenadine, by itself this would not have constituted anticipation, and the user could have been stopped from doing what he had already done.

[78] The patent has since been amended to this effect.

[79] See paras 5–26, 5–27, below.

In *Merrell Dow*, the House refused to find anticipation from actual administration of the drug to patients, as distinct from publishing the specification which disclosed doing so. It is perhaps hard to see why doing and describing the same thing should be differently treated in the law of novelty. The House, however, considered that it must give some scope to the 1977 change which prevented account any longer being taken of prior unwitting use or prior secret use. In *Evans Medical's Patent*[80] Laddie J. was at pains to stress the special application of doctrine which arose on the facts of *Merrell Dow*: the person taking terfenadine was not put in a position to conduct an analysis which would reveal the substance subsequently patented—the metabolite. The actual giving of terfenadine itself did not provide the means of discovering the invention claimed in the second patent. The case was therefore different from one in which an article capable of analysis in order to discover the invention was placed in a third party's hands in non-confidential circumstances. The latter continues to be a form of anticipation.

(5) Things and their uses

(a) *New thing with an advantage*

5–21 It has long been a basic assumption of our own and many other patent systems that the discovery of a use for a previously unknown thing or substance may found claims to the thing or substance itself, whatever it is subsequently used for.[81] As justification it has been asserted that:

> if product *per se* claims could only be enforced in relation to uses known at the time of the patent application, much of the incentive to invest in original research would disappear.[82]

How far this is true is guesswork. There are many who are obliged by the existence of prior art to settle for mere use claims. It is pure conjecture that they are less willing to undertake research because they will not enjoy the benefits of later, unsuspected inventions.

The present approach is nonetheless acceptable for its simplicity, so long as one assumes that for the most part first discoveries represent the most important breakthroughs. About this, however, there are now serious

---

[80] [1998] R.P.C. 517 at 573–568.

[81] Indeed, if a phrase of the type "for use as . . ." is added this will be interpreted as meaning that the thing is suitable for that use; but the exclusive right extends to production, distribution or use for any purpose.

[82] Armitage and Ellis [1990] E.I.P.R. 119. Drawing on the Kitch metaphor (para. 3–53, n. 47, above), they add: "It is rather like asking someone investing in a gold mine to limit his return to what he knows about at the time of the investment and to forgo any additional benefit if the mine later struck it rich". Certainly he should have the rewards from gold-findings, even if unexpectedly large. But also from diamonds, if they turn up unbeknownst? At least, beware metaphor.

doubts. In medical and other biotechnology, the initial description and discovery of use for a gene or some smaller sequence of DNA is comparatively straightforward. The real difficulties lie in subsequent work on the stimulation and control of externally created genes and their operation in the circumstances of actual treatment. Some sources, particularly in Italy, have suggested that the European patent system should adopt a more discriminating approach either to the drafting or the interpretation of claims to the first use of a substance or thing.[83] The issue deserves most careful monitoring in the coming years.

The next paragraphs consider the ways in which consequential inventions can in general be claimed. At this juncture, we should note that the field of pharmaceuticals forms a special case, which we will deal with after we have taken account of the special exclusionary principle, which places outside the system claims to methods of medical treatment of humans and animals.[84]

(b) *New use of an old thing*

The principle, that once a thing has been made public no one may have a **5–22** patent for it, must be understood as a ground rule to which a number of qualifications are admitted. These certainly go some way towards giving patentees a monopoly commensurate with the novelty of their invention. But not in every case; for the system does not aim to reward merely for creative effort.

Many of the difficulties in the basic rules arise from the fact that an inventor may discover a new use for something already known. He may, for instance, discover that a well-known chemical can be added to water in a boiler so as to reduce scaling. To allow him to claim the chemical as a substance would give him a monopoly over all its uses, not just in boilers; this would be more than he is entitled to. But if no one has found a use for the chemical in boilers before, he is entitled to claim "a method for preventing scale in boilers in which. . . ." Such a claim limits his monopoly to what he has discovered: only those who use the chemical in this way, or who induce its use, will infringe.[85]

(c) *Selection patents*

In certain types of case, mainly concerned with chemical substances and **5–23** mixtures,[86] claims to a selection have been allowed.[87] Where a class of things is already known from a general description of some kind, it has

---

[83] See Marsico [1990] E.I.P.R. 397; *cf.* Armitage and Ellis (n. 82, above); Jacob, Paterson (1996) 27 I.I.C. 170, 179.

[84] Below, para. 5–73ff.

[85] The exclusion of methods of medical treatment (see previous note), limits the possibility of using use claims in pharmaceutical and veterinary patents. That is why special techniques developed to expand their scope: below esp. para. 5–75.

[86] Only occasionally is selection possible in a mechanical case.

[87] The EPO, sometimes with knotty convolution, has accepted a similar approach: Paterson, paras 9–55—9–57; Spangenberg (1997) 28 I.I.C. 808.

been possible to claim specific things within that class, or a sub-class, provided that these latter are stated to have an advantage over the class as a whole. This special approach is of considerable value, particularly since recent decisions have shown some willingness to apply the idea flexibly in favour of patentees.

Du Pont's (Witsiepe) Application[88] concerned a co-polymer comprising three elements, including as its second 1,4-butanediol, was claimed for its quality as a rapidly hardening plastic. A much earlier I.C.I. specification had claimed a similar plastic for its capacity to absorb dye. Its second element had to be one of a list of nine possibilities, including 1,4-butanediol; but this was named only as a prospect on paper, the experiments recorded having been with other substances on the list. The House of Lords refused to treat this disclosure as one which precluded the possibility of selection of Du Pont's co-polymer for the newly discovered purpose. It is by such a response that the patent system has adapted to fit the needs of the chemical industry.[89]

5–24   The special treatment of selections needs to be viewed in light of the rules discussed in the previous paragraphs. First, the need for selection only arises if the earlier description does disclose the later subject-matter sufficiently. It is not enough that the later thing in a sense fits within earlier language that is too general to describe any clear result. It has been common practice, when a novel chemical substance (or a few related substances) are shown to have a particular use, to refer to derivative and analogous compounds (sometimes totalling millions in number) which may be expected to show similar characteristics in some degree.[90] This is treated as revealing the whole class sufficiently to raise prima facie an objection of novelty against claims anywhere within the class.

Those members of the class which have been specifically named as the subject of experiment may not be claimed again as substances even if an advantage previously undetected has been discovered for them; only if this advantage calls for the substance to be put to a new use can a claim to the new method be secured. But because, apart from these specific cases, the earlier reference to the class has been general, the "selection rules" allow

---

[88] [1982] F.S.R. 303, HL, approving the classic formulation of the requirements for a selection patent: Maugham J. in *IG Farbenindustrie's Patents* (1930) 47 R.P.C. 289 at 321. See also *Shell's Patent* [1960] R.P.C. 35 at 53, CA; *Beecham Group v. Bristol Laboratories* [1978] R.P.C. 521 at 579, *per* Lord Diplock.

[89] Lord Keith and Lord Simon expressed some disquiet that the result would keep I.C.I. from using one of its named alternatives. However, they did not insist that Du Pont's claim be limited to the new use: [1982] F.S.R. 303 at 316; *cf. Beecham Group's (Amoxycillin) Application* [1982] F.S.R. 202, where the New Zealand CA required that a pharmaceutical selection patent be restricted to a composition for oral administration to humans; see para. 5–74, below.

[90] If, however, specific compounds or sub-classes have alone been mentioned and a later patentee is concerned with other compounds or sub-classes, the only issue normally is obviousness: a well-known instance of the problem is *Sharpe & Dohme v. Boots* (1928) 45 R.P.C. 153.

claims to be made to substances (or sub-classes of the whole) and not merely to methods, and this by virtue of the advantages as such and not only because the advantages result in a new use. So where selection is possible, it is free of the difficulties of proving infringement of a method claim. In the field of human and animal treatment, where a method claim is not possible, the ability to secure a selection claim is often essential in order to get any patent at all.[91]

The "selection rules" allow the anticipatory effect of general revelations **5–25** to be discounted where special advantage is stated by way of quid pro quo: this is the "consideration" and so goes to the sufficiency of the disclosure. Equally it may be looked upon as the quality which provides the incentive subject-matter. Selections, accordingly, are one occasion upon which a patentee is obliged to state the usefulness of his idea over the prior art. The current law calls for both adequate disclosure and inventive step, and so this aspect of the "selection rules" seems likely to survive. In their "classic" form, it was also required that substantially all the selected group should show the special advantage, and that substantially only those selected should show it.[92] In *Shell's Patent* the Court of Appeal showed little inclination to attach any precise meaning to the latter[93]: probably the rule is only that the advantage must not be one shared by virtually the whole class.[94] As to the former requirement, now that the objection of inutility has been abandoned, there may be a rather generous tendency to excuse the inclusion of some examples which do not have the advantage[95]: but claims that go too far in this direction would undoubtedly appear grasping; the selection would likely be disallowed for its failure to tell others when they will get the alleged advantage.

(d) *New advantage of old thing*

The selection patent rules do not directly create exclusive rights over a **5–26** thing or activity which is specifically known, because they apply only to selection from a class other members of which have been the subject of specific disclosure or use. But the EPO has now decided to step in where the selection rules refrain from treading.[96] It treats as novel a claim to a

---

[91] For this, see paras 5–73 *et seq.*, below. PA 1977, s. 3(6), now admits a significant qualification.

[92] See Maugham J., *IG Farbeninstrie's Patents* (n. 88, above).

[93] The patentee's Claim 2, after amendment, covered proportions of ester up to two "theories" (a proportional measure). It was admitted that the new advantage would attach to mixtures up to four theories; but this was not allowed to prevent the selection; the Court's sympathy was with a deserving patentee faced with an apparently valueless anticipation. See also *Du Pont* (n. 88, above); and in the EPO, *Hoechst's Application* [1985] O.J. EPO 209.

[94] If it were, the claim would come under the edict against allowing a claim to a substance merely for having found it a new advantage: paras 5–22—5–24, above.

[95] For this, see further paras 5–96, 5–97, below.

[96] Stimulus for this development has come from the sphere of medical treatments: see below, esp. para. 5–75.

known way of using a known thing where it is shown that this has a novel advantage (which must also be non-obvious):

> A claim was upheld to the use of a specified lubricant for the reduction of friction in engines, even though it has previously been used as a rust inhibitor. Likewise a claim was allowed for a given compound as a regulator of plant growth, when previously it had been used as an insectide.[97]

In both cases, the physical acts within the claims would be exactly the same as the steps taken during the previous use. The circumstances thus differ from the new use of an old thing, where the earlier use can continue unobstructed by the later patent because it is not within the new claim. The Enlarged Board of Appeal has felt the distinction nonetheless to be artificial and so one that ought no longer to be drawn.

5–27   Being solely a granting office, the EPO does not have to decide what activities will constitute direct or indirect infringement of a claim to use a thing for a new purpose, as distinct from use by a new physical act. To anticipate the issue on that front: if the scope of the right can be limited so as to cover only the making, using and commercial supply of the thing (or its essential elements) specifically for the new purpose, then the freedom of other users can be to some degree assured.[98]

Even so—and despite the virtues of comity within the ranks of EPC countries—national Courts may yet consider that the Enlarged Board is wrong to introduce distinction of purpose into the law of novelty in the way that it has. As we have seen, the House of Lords indignantly rejected what looked like an attempt to obtain a second patent monopoly on a drug for having found out more about how it worked.[99] That may be a special and distinguishable case, but it shows the difficulties of the way ahead. Some of these the EPO is having to face for itself.

> Two components were known for use in an agent which would sequester the ions of certain elements. It was not permissible to re-claim them for this same use purely on the basis of showing that they were together more effective than the use of either component by itself.[1]

A substance was first described as a food additive for flavour control and as a thickening agent; it was subsequently claimed as an emulsion stabiliser. If this last effect had previously been hidden, it could, according to the Technical Board of Appeal, be found novel.[2]

---

[97] G 2/88: *Mobil Oil/Friction-reducing additive* [1990] O.J. EPO 93; G 6/88: *Bayer/Plant growth regulating agent* [1990] O.J. EPO 114; Paterson, paras 9–72—9–77. Both severely criticised by Floyd [1996] E.I.P.R. 480; Doble *ibid.* 511.

[98] See paras 4–40, above, 6–20, below.

[99] See n. 75, above.

[1] *Dow/sequestering agent* [1994] E.P.O.R. 1.

[2] *Mars II* [1994] O.J. EPO 192 (although "hidden", the invention was nonetheless found obvious).

(6) Exclusion by amendment

Where one of the alternatives covered by a claim is anticipated by a **5–28** previous description, it may be possible to save the rest if the particular case is disclaimed by amendment. The amendment, giving what is often referred to as an "n-l" claim, will not, however, be allowed if the result would still be objectionable.[3] In most cases, if one alternative has been described, others are likely to be held obvious. But if the earlier description covered the later only by chance and not as a result of an effort to solve the same problem, the objection of obviousness will not arise: hence the amendments allowed in such examples as *Molins*.[4]

2. INVENTIVE STEP

(1) Introduction

Patents are constantly sought for inventions which vary from the known **5–29** only in some more or less minor detail. For instance, when a new kind of material is put on the market, claims will likely follow which attempt to patent the making of well-known articles out of the material (plastics, for instance, provided a welter of examples).[5] Sometimes at the outset the applicant will know that he is seeking protection for a thing that is not greatly different from what is known already. Sometimes he is pushed into that position by the unearthing of prior art which he did not appreciate. The difficulty is increased by the need to mark out broad "fence-post" claims.

It is in order to draw a line excluding some claims of this kind that many patent systems have come to require the presence of an inventive step.[6] In the EPC and the 1977 Act, an inventive step[7] is considered to be present if, having regard to the state of the art, the invention is not obvious to a person skilled in the art.[8] The state of the art is the same broad conception that operates in assessing novelty,[9] save that no account is taken of any prior specifications subsequently published.

---

[3] Now that obviousness is a regular objection in patent office proceedings, there is less scope for amendment by the exclusion of numbers of particular anticipations, resulting in claims for "n-m".

[4] See para. 5–19, above.

[5] See para. 5–47, below.

[6] See para. 3–11, above.

[7] Which is a requisite of "patentability": EPC, Art. 52(1); PA 1977, s. 1(1). See generally, Beier (1986) 17 I.I.C. 301.

[8] EPC, Art. 56; PA 1977, s. 3.

[9] See para. 5–03, above. The exclusions (PA 1977, s. 2(4); EPC, Art. 55) probably apply to inventive step as well.

5–30   The evaluative issue that this introduces is the largest single cause of uncertainty about the validity of patents and hence a frequent inflator of the scale and length of patent disputes. The assessment it calls for is often labelled a jury question[10]; which means, amongst other things, that firm rules (such as define the factual comparison called for in determining novelty) are replaced by a vaguer, qualitative yardstick.

Measuring with it involves the four "stages" identified by Oliver L.J. in *Windsurfing International v. Tabur Marine*[11]:

(1) the Court must identify the inventive concept embodied in the patent;

(2) it must assume the mantle of the normally skilled but unimaginative addressee in the art at the priority date and impute to him what was, at that date, common general knowledge in the art in question;

(3) it must identify what, if any, differences exist between the matters cited as being "known or used" and the alleged invention;

(4) it must ask itself whether, viewed without any knowledge of the alleged invention, those differences constituted steps which would have been obvious to the skilled man or whether they required any degree of invention.

In seeking to describe in more detail how the yardstick is deployed, we must first take a number of introductory points.[12] With them in position, we can then turn to the essence of the inquiry.[13]

(a) *Terminology*

5–31   It has become customary to treat "inventive subject-matter" and "non-obviousness" as largely synonymous with "inventive step". But cases occur where what the patentee is suggesting is pointless (at least at the time). If there is no reason for it, the step is scarcely an obvious one to take: yet if nothing useful is being added to the sum of human knowledge there ought to be no inventive step.[14]

---

[10] *e.g.* Jenkins L.J., *Allmänna Elektriska v. Burntisland Shipbuilding* (1952) 69 R.P.C. 63 at 69; *Johns Manville's Patent* [1967] R.P.C. 179 at 491, 496, CA.

[11] [1985] R.P.C. 59. This approach has since been much reiterated as giving structure to the issue under PA 1977, s. 3: *e.g. Hallen v. Brabantia* [1991] R.P.C. 195 at 213, CA; *Mölnlycke v. Procter & Gamble (No. 5)* [1994] R.P.C. 49, CA; *PLG Research v. Ardon International* [1995] F.S.R. 116, CA; *Unilever v. Chefaro* [1994] R.P.C. 567; the second and third steps are not to be compounded: *Beloit v. Valmet* [1997] R.P.C. 489, *per* Aldous L.J.

[12] See paras 5–31—5–37, below.

[13] See paras 5–38—5–52, below.

[14] *cf.* Lord Shaw, *British Thomson-Houston v. Duram* (1918) 35 R.P.C. 161 at 184; Jenkins J., *May & Baker v. Ciba* (1948) 65 R.P.C. 255 at 281; Lloyd-Jacob J., *Anxionnaz v. Rolls-Royce* [1967] R.P.C. 419 at 467.

(b) *Paraphrases*

Oliver L.J.'s steps are essentially a procedural strategy; they do not attempt **5-32** any verbal paraphrase of the concept of "obviousness" or "inventive step". It is currently accepted that verbal variations of these expressions generate heat, rather than light.[15] In particular, phrases which suggested that the addition to knowledge had only to be slight—such as "very plain" or "lacking a scintilla of invention"—are no longer considered helpful. The same is true of the question, does the patent disclose something sufficiently inventive to deserve the grant of a monopoly?[16]

But paraphrase is difficult to keep entirely at bay. The Court of Appeal has recently looked to see if the inventor has produced "a novel insight or discovery".[17] This has been linked with another phrase which has some tendency to raise the standard of an inventive step: would a person versed in the art assess the likelihood of success as sufficient to warrant actual trial?[18] Was it "obvious to try"? Or, as the EPO chooses to put it: would the skilled worker be likely to use it, as distinct from could he have done so (the "would . . . could" test)?[19] It would be easy to carry this a long way.[20]

It will be apparent from this how difficult it is to establish a consistent line on the degree of severity which is to be brought to the testing of obviousness. Amongst the countries now collaborating in the EPC, a particularly stringent test of "inventiveness" seems previously to have prevailed in the Netherlands and Switzerland; while in Germany talk of a "level of invention", together with the separate protection of utility models (a form of petty patent) that in theory at least need not reach the same inventive level, creates an impression that there too rather more has been required.[21] The EPO has indicated that it aims for a middle level (roughly equivalent to that of German practice), rather than adopt the particularly favourable attitude towards applicants that has characterised British pre-grant procedure under the 1949 Act.[22]

(c) *Objective test*

The comparison called for is between two objective conditions: the state of **5-33** the art and what the patentee claims to have invented. It is not an inquiry into how easy or difficult it was for him personally to take the step. The

---

[15] *Mölnlycke* (n. 11, above) at 112; *PLG Research* (n. 3, above) at 136.

[16] *Mölnlycke* (n. 11, above) at 112.

[17] *Biogen v. Medeva* [1995] F.S.R. 4 at 56.

[18] Lord Diplock, *Johns-Manville's Patent* [1967] R.P.C. 479 at 494 (at the same time warning against the dangers of general paraphrases; and see at 496); Lord Reid, *Technograph v. Mills & Rockley* [1972] R.P.C. 346 at 356; *Genentech/Human t-PA* [1996] E.P.O.R. 275.

[19] See Paterson, para. 10–30; *Japan Styrene/Foam articles* [1994] O.J. EPO 154.

[20] See further, paras 5–49, 5–50, below.

[21] On the nuances that may attach to EPC, Art. 56 in its various linguistic versions, see Pagenberg, (1974) 5 I.I.C. 157.

[22] See para. 5–02, above, para. 5–37, below.

patent system makes no attempt to exclude protection for accidental, lucky or sudden inventions.[23] Equally it is of no relevance to consider whether the person responsible thought that he had made an invention[24]: he may well have worked out independently what others knew already. Nonetheless it is relevant to the ultimate assessment to know how the alleged inventor reached his result and accordingly discovery may be ordered of notes and other documents concerning his research. This may assist the defendant in cross-examining the inventor and other witnesses, in obtaining expert evidence of what a skilled man would or should have done, and in comparing what was actually done with the state of the art at the priority date.[25]

(d) *Advance in the art*

5–34 There is no distinct requirement in the new law, any more than in the old, that an invention should show "technical progress" over the prior art, that is, that it should in some practical sense be a better way of doing things.[26] However, considerations of technical advance, as of commercial value, become points of reference in the search for an inventive step. For if the idea is a real step forward in technique, yet it is an obvious one, why was it not made before?[27] And in the case of "selection" from a larger class, the particular advantage which the specification must describe and which alone avoids the objection of anticipation, must also be one that is not obvious: the selection must be more than a mere verification that particular properties would be found in the sub-group.[28]

"Technical progress", which was previously a requirement of German patent law and which has been actively debated in the United States, in fact involves two sorts of consideration: substantive (whether there is any advance at all, whether it is so large that there must be invention), and formal (whether the specification must describe the advance). Accordingly it is an issue to which we turn again when discussing sufficiency of description.[29]

---

[23] *Crane v. Price* (1842) 1 W.P.C. 393 at 411. See further paras 5–40, 5–41, below.

[24] Fletcher Moulton L.J., *British United Shoe Manufacturers v. Fussell* (1908) 25 R.P.C. 631 at 652; *Allmänna Elektriska v. Burntisland* (1952) 69 R.P.C. 63 at 70.

[25] *SKM v. Wagner Spraytech* [1982] R.P.C. 497, CA; *Hoechst Celanese v. BP Chemicals* [1997] F.S.R. 547.

[26] But *cf.* Warrington L.J.: "a step which is useful and not merely one which results in some immaterial and futile improvement": *Teste v. Coombes* (1923) 41 R.P.C. 88 at 104, CA.

[27] See, *e.g. British Vacuum v. L.S.W.R.* (1912) 29 R.P.C. 309 at 328–330, 333. In *Moulinage de Chavonoz's Application* [1961] R.P.C. 279 at 295, Lloyd Jacob J. distinguishes between the perception of the advance in the art and its evaluation in terms of inventive ingenuity. The former, being "susceptible of reasonably precise expression" is more readily open to review on appeal.

[28] For the rules concerning selection patents, see paras 5–23—5–25, above. They need to be considered not only in relation to obviousness but also in relation to sufficient disclosure: see next note.

[29] See paras 5–93—5–97, below.

(e) *New advantage and new use*

The discovery of a new advantage in a thing already known does not in **5–35** general save it from objection. So equally a thing that it is obvious to make for one purpose should not become the less so just because a further, unexpected, advantage is discovered.

> A patentee claimed a self-pulling type of corkscrew in which the screw element had a non-stick coating of the kind commonly found on saucepans. The coating produced a surprising improvement in extracting the cork. Because it was predictable that the coating would help to insert the screw, it was obvious to add it; whether there was any commercial merit in doing so was not relevant.[30] The additional advantage could only become the subject of a valid patent if it could be claimed as a new use or as a selection.[31] In this way, the patentee could be confined to a monopoly proportionate to his real invention.

(f) *Perception of problem*

The inventive step may lie in seeing that a particular solution to a problem **5–36** should be adopted: it does not have to be found in the technical means that are then employed.[32] Consider, for instance, "the problem of indicating to the driver of a motor vehicle at night the line of the road ahead by using the light from the vehicle itself. As soon as the problem is stated in this form the technical solution, *viz.* the provision of reflective markings along the road surface, appears simple and obvious."[33]

(g) *Onus of proof*

Since obviousness has become a matter for patent office examiners to judge **5–37** upon the material arising from the search (and their own general knowledge), much is likely to turn on the onus and quantum of proof employed during the examination stage. The past practice of the British Office and tribunals was to resolve doubts about an inventive step in the applicant's favour,[34] because, although these proceedings had to arise out of

---

[30] *Hallen v. Brabantia* [1991] R.P.C. 195, CA; but *cf. Cleveland Graphite v. Glacier Metal* (1930) 67 R.P.C. 149, HL.

[31] A new use claim was not open in the "corkscrew" case; equally the patent had not been drafted as a selection: [1991] R.P.C. 195 at 217–218.

[32] *Hickton's Patent Syndicate v. Patents & Machine Improvements* (1909) 26 R.P.C. 339, CA (inventive to see that a process of "shogging", already used in net machines, could be used in lace machines for the purpose, there important, of equalising the bobbin threads).

[33] EPO Guidelines, C IV 9.4(i). The whole chapter is full of useful examples.

[34] See para. 5–02, above. "At this stage in the lifetime of an application there exists in addition to the two verdicts, so to speak, of obviousness and non-obviousness, an interim stage of non-proven": Lloyd-Jacob J., *Bakelite's Application* [1958] R.P.C. 152 at 160.

the opposition of an outside party, the evidence was not tested as thoroughly as it would be in Court, where oral witnesses would be examined as a matter of course.[35] In the new law this procedural difference remains in essence, even when the legal tests have become the same.

(2) Assessing obviousness[36]

(a) *The notional skilled worker*

5–38 The tribunal assessing obviousness is expected to trace out the mental processes of a determinedly prosaic individual—one who, according to British case law, has the following characteristics[37]:

(1) He is a skilled technician who is well acquainted with workshop techniques. "Technician" may probably be contrasted both with the highly-qualified research staff who in industry today are set to solve many of the more complex technical problems; and also with the "ordinary workmen" who frequented the earlier case law.

(2) He will read the relevant literature carefully,[38] showing an unlimited capacity to assimilate it but none in making even a "scintilla" of invention from it.[39] Such indefatigable but uninspired individuals do not wittingly give evidence themselves; for the most part, tribunals are left to make their own assessment after hearing what cleverer people have to say.

(3) Where research is normally conducted by a team—as typically today in much pharmaceutical and biotechnological work—a notional group will replace a single individual as the Court's starting-point.[40] Where it is obvious to call in special expertise, the notional skilled workman will have it.[41]

---

[35] *General Electric's Applications* [1964] R.P.C. 413 at 452–453, treating the differently worded standards of obviousness before and after grant (PA 1949, ss. 14(1)(e), 32(1)(f)) as merely reflecting the difference of approach necessitated by the different procedures. The 1977 Act no longer draws this verbal distinction but that is not the governing consideration.

[36] See generally, Asquith (1978) 8 CIPA 19; Reid, pp. 34–48.

[37] See Lord Reid, *Technograph v. Mills & Rockley* [1972] R.P.C. 346 at 355; followed in *General Tire v. Firestone* [1972] R.P.C. 457 at 504.

[38] See paras 5–39—5–44, below.

[39] He bears considerable resemblance to the ordinary skilled worker by whose powers of comprehension the adequacy of disclosure is tested: see para. 5–44, below. But it has been doubted whether, in determining obviousness, his powers of perception must be regarded as quite so limited: *Genentech v. Wellcome Foundation* [1989] R.P.C. 147, *per* Mustill L.J., at 280 for Mustill on some inventiveness.

[40] *Boehringer Mannheim v. Genzyme* [1993] R.P.C. 716 at 727.

[41] *Fives-Cail Babcock/Conveyor cleaner* [1982] O.J. EPO 225; *NI Industries/Filler mass* [1992] O.J. EPO 725; *cf. Richardson-Vick's Patent* [1997] R.P.C. 888, CA.

(b) *The uninventive technician's knowledge*

Like novelty, obviousness is judged by the state of the art, excluding, it must **5-39** be supposed, the same material published in breach of confidence and at international exhibitions.[42] Accordingly, the notional technician will be taken to have in mind, first, the common general knowledge of his art at the priority date and, secondly whatever he would learn from the existing literature when seeking an answer to the problem at issue. Frequently a case of obviousness is built up by referring to specific documents (such as patent specifications, learned articles, and items in the general press) and to specific instances of use; and generally these belong to the second category. Common general knowledge (which may be shown from such sources as standard texts and used throughout an industry)[43] is then used to explain why it would be obvious to take the patentee's step from the specific sources that have been cited.[44]

In one instance,[45] the patent was for a steel tip to a shoe heel so made **5-40** that the bottom of the heel fitted the tip, thus solving the problem of aligning the two parts. At the time, this seemed inventive to shoe repairers. But shoe manufacturers were already using very similar heels, which were thus part of the trade's general knowledge. In addition, some of these heels were illustrated in cited documents. The attack might well have succeeded even if one or other class of evidence had not been available. Note, however, that the general knowledge arose from actual use of the interlinking tips. It is much more difficult to show that a "mere paper proposal" is part of the ordinary technician's standard mental equipment. Even as specific citations, unworked proposals—mere "laboratory toys"—are treated with suspicion.[46] Occasionally they may form the basis for a finding of obviousness, perhaps because they come very close to being an anticipation.[47] But they demand answers to the standard questions: Are they addressed to the same problem which the patentee solved? If so, why did they not lead to earlier discovery of his solution?

---

[42] This is not made explicit in the relevant provisions; see para. 5-29, n. 8, above.

[43] Common general knowledge is what is generally known and regarded as a good basis for further action by the bulk of those who are engaged in the particular art: Luxmoore J., *British Acoustic Films v. Nettlefold* (1936) 53 R.P.C. 221 at 250, as modified in *General Tire v. Firestone* (above n. 37); and see *Beloit v. Valmet* [1997] R.P.C. 489, CA; *Buhler v. Satake* [1997] R.P.C. 232; *Union Carbide v. BP Chemicals* [1998] R.P.C. 1; and *Raychem's Patent* [1998] R.P.C. 31.

[44] Common general knowledge is not pleaded: *Holliday v. Heppenstall* (1889) 6 R.P.C. 320; *British Thomson-Houston v. Stonebridge* (1916) 33 R.P.C. 166. Since the state of the art is not limited to what is known and used in the U.K., common general knowledge should be similarly judged: *cf. Lucas v. Chloride Batteries* [1979] F.S.R. 322, Fed.Ct. (Aust.).

[45] *Colburn v. Ward* (1950) 67 R.P.C. 73. See also *Fives Babcock's Application* [1982] O.J. EPO 225: if a problem concerning a suitable substitute material for making scrapers would have been put to a materials specialist, the issue must be judged from his perspective.

[46] Basic scientific principles may attract rather different treatment: *Sonotone v. Multitone* (n. 72, below).

[47] See paras 5–46, 5–47, below.

197

5-41   Now that patent offices regularly examine the question of an inventive step, it is important to step back from the applicant's view of what he has invented. The specification is likely to have been drafted in light of the prior art known to the applicant. The question to be addressed, however, is whether objectively there is an inventive step over the prior art produced by the search. The EPO has accordingly favoured a "problem-and-solution" approach in which the examiners, having identified the closest prior art, formulate the technical problem to be solved in reaching the claimed invention and then judge whether that solution is obvious.[48] The viewpoint must be forward from the prior art, not backward from the invention, otherwise the judgment will be infected by hindsight. The British practice is not formulated in these terms but equally insists upon the importance of objective assessment.

In this connection, Buckley L.J. has drawn a useful distinction.[49] There will be the situation where the uninventive but skilled man has a particular problem or need in mind, in which case the testing carried out by him may amount to no more than obvious verification, though it could be inventive if the result is unexpected in kind rather than degree. Equally there will be the case where the skilled man has no particular problem or need in mind. Then, selecting a particular course for further research which provides unexpected results is likely to be inventive, for he is then on "a voyage of discovery" rather than "a mere exercise of ingenuity". In *Beecham Group's (Amoxycillin) Application*,[50] Buckley and Browne L.JJ. were prepared to classify the case before them as falling within the second of these categories, even though the prior art indicated that work should be done on six further substances in the search for better semi-synthetic penicillins. Accordingly the applicant was entitled to a patent for one of them, upon making the anticipated discovery of its outstanding ability for absorption into the blood-stream.[51]

(c) *"Mosaicing"*

5-42   Obviousness is judged by viewing the invention as a whole[52] against the state of the art as a whole.[53] Cited documents do not have to be treated in isolation (as normally they would be when assessing novelty). They may be

---

[48] *Bayer/Carbonless Copying Paper* [1981] O.J. EPO 206; *BASF/Metal Refining* [1983] O.J. EPO 439; Paterson, paras 10–04 *et seq*.; Szabo (1995) 26 I.I.C. 457; but *cf*. Alcan [1996] O.J. EPO 32; Cole [1998] E.I.P.R. 214 at 267.

[49] *Beecham* case [1980] R.P.C. 261 at 291; and see *Pfizer/Sertraline* [1999] E.P.O.R. 286.

[50] [1980] R.P.C. 261; and similarly in New Zealand: [1982] F.S.R. 218.

[51] Contrast the assessments of later Courts of Appeal in the *Genentech* and *Biogen* cases: para. 5–50, below.

[52] A combination should not be picked apart into its components: Lord Romer, *Non-Drip v. Strangers* (1943) 60 R.P.C. 135 at 145, HL.

[53] Lord Simonds, *Martin v. Millwood* [1956] R.P.C. 125 at 133–134; *Illinois Tool v. Autobars* [1974] R.P.C. 337.

read in the light of one another—but only if it is obvious to do so.[54] Even so, James L.J. disparagingly called this making a "mosaic of extracts",[55] and it remains difficult to build up such a case. Again doubts surface which are hard to refute. Why, if it is obvious to combine two pieces of knowledge, has no one done so before? Is the case not one where the precursors were able to think out everything except the crucial bridge from failure to success? It is in this context that some judges have been particularly hard on paper proposals.[56]

(d) Obscure sources: publication

Obviousness calls for inquiry into whether the invention in suit could have **5-43** been straightforwardly derived from what was already known. Accordingly, difficult problems are set by the fact that a prior publication or use would have been hard for the average skilled worker to find, or understand.

On the difficulties of unearthing sources: on the one hand it is possible to treat the state of the art as being the same for obviousness as it is for novelty (save for the special case of subsequently published specifications)—that is, anything made freely available to even a single person will be treated as published.[57] On the other hand it is possible to limit the state of the art for obviousness to whatever a diligent searcher would have uncovered.

In the case law on the 1949 Act each approach had its adherents, Lord Diplock emerging as protagonist of the former, Lord Reid of the latter.[58] The former approach had the merit of not attributing different meanings to the same statutory formula.[59] It also eliminates one dimension of evaluative judgment—a dimension which it may be particularly difficult for patent

---

[54] "... a mosaic which can be put together by an unimaginative man with no inventive capacity": Lord Reid, *Technograph v. Mills & Rockley* [1972] R.P.C. 346 at 355; and see *GE/ Polycarbonate compound* [1997] E.P.O.R. 341.

[55] *Von Heyden v. Neustadt* (1880) 50 L.J. Ch. 126 at 128; and see Fletcher Moulton L.J., *British Westinghouse v. Braulik* (1910) 27 R.P.C. 209 at 230. In the EPO, where there tends to be less reliance on common general knowledge, there is greater willingness to read documents together. Sometimes this is done in order to show a trend pointing away from the invention: see *e.g. BASF* (n. 48, above); *Solvay/Olefins* [1985] O.J. EPO 166; *Britax* [1987] O.J. EPO 112.

[56] *cf.* Gratwick (1972) 88 L.Q.R. 349, Blanco White (1973) 89 L.Q.R. 16. But in *Allmänna Elektriska v. Burntisland* (1952) 69 R.P.C. 63 at 68–69, the Court of Appeal refused to hold that there could never be a mosaic of documents, as distinct from actual uses; and proceeded (surprisingly) to read together descriptions different in date and language.

[57] See para. 5–13, above.

[58] *Technograph v. Mills & Rockley* [1972] R.P.C. 346 at 355, 361. (In the Court of Appeal [1969] R.P.C. 395 at 408), Sachs L.J. even suggested that the searcher might confine his reading of prior specifications to the claims and perhaps the drawings; Lord Diplock specifically disapproved this and certainly Lord Reid did not go so far. See also *General Tire v. Firestone* [1972] R.P.C. 457 at 499, CA; *I.C.I.'s (Pointer) Application* [1977] F.S.R. 434.

[59] *i.e.* previously "known or used ... in the United Kingdom"; now "the state of the art", as defined.

office examiners to handle on a regular basis. The latter approach aims to make the inquiry into the activities of the unimaginative technician somewhat more realistic; but it may be doubted whether, even on its own terms, it helps much. For the diligent searcher still has to be treated as having found some things that in reality would have been unlikely to have reached him by the priority date: for instance a description in a patent specification published only a few days before[60]; or, given the definition of "the state of the art", a use which has occurred only in a remote place. There seems little point in striving to decide what revelations are so exceedingly remote that they should be discounted.[61]

(e) *Obscure sources: comprehension*

5-44 In *Woven Plastics v. British Ropes*, it was accepted by counsel that utility model specifications, available only in Japanese and apparently never worked, were to be treated as known. Harman L.J. regretted that such "recondite" publications should have to be brought into account.[62] In the new world of supra-national patenting, however, the notional technician presumably has acquired, at least passively, the gift of tongues.

Language difficulties aside, the notional technician's reading of the literature will be "careful".[63] If after this it appears that a document expresses its ideas obscurely, it is unlikely that obvious inferences are to be drawn from it. But there is the further case where, although (with hindsight, particularly) a highly suggestive reference can be found in a prior document, it is for some reason masked, perhaps by the abundance of other documentation, or by prevailing opinion that other avenues of inquiry would be much more hopeful. These are factors which have weighed against a finding of obviousness.[64] Thus, even if it is proper to treat the technician as having read everything in the state of the art,[65] these further considerations may modify the effect of particular documents.

(3) **The basic comparison**

5-45 We may now return to the crux of the issue: was it for practical purposes obvious to the appropriate skilled technician, armed with all the specific information and general knowledge deemed relevant, that he could or

---

[60] As in *Du Pont's (Holland) Application* [1971] R.P.C. 7.

[61] Consider, for instance, the prior patent specification that has been inadequately indexed. In *Asea's Application* [1978] F.S.R. 115, this was held to be no reason for disregarding it when assessing obviousness.

[62] [1970] F.S.R. 47 at 48; and Widgery L.J. said that it went "beyond the bounds of reason" (at 58).

[63] See *Johns Manville* [1967] R.P.C. 479 and *Technograph* [1972] R.P.C. 346. It will, however, be by a person "oriented towards practicalities" who may only see narrower implications than would an inventor: *Boehringer/Diagnostic Agent* [1987] O.J. EPO 413.

[64] See, *e.g.* Whitford J., *I.C.I.'s (Pointer) Application* [1977] F.S.R. 434 at 454.

[65] *i.e.* accepting Lord Diplock's view (n. 58, above). *cf.* Whitford J. (previous note) who, despite a nod in Lord Diplock's direction, appears in substance to favour Lord Reid's approach.

should do what the patent proposes?[66] Part of the answer may depend on the proximity of the idea to the prior art, part on the extent to which the idea is a technical or a commercial success. Each of these factors deserves exploration.

(a) *Proximity to the prior art*

Novelty and inventive step are different questions. Even so, the fact that **5–46** an idea escapes being anticipated only by the shortest remove will often jeopardise the chances of its being found inventive. Indeed, if the claimed invention is a "mere collocation"—where two known devices are to be placed side-by-side without any working inter-relationship—it will be more likely to be treated as a claim to discrete things separately anticipated. The traditional example of such a case is the "sausage-machine patent": a claim to a known cutting-machine and a known filling-machine placed in juxtaposition.[67] Another example is a pill containing two known therapeutic substances which have no interactive or heightened effect when taken together.[68]

Beyond this point, "near anticipations" have to be considered for **5–47** inventive step.[69] They may well fail the test, being discounted under one of the following axioms:

(1) There can be no patent for the analogous use of a thing or process; or, as it is sometimes put, for the mere new use of an old thing. For instance, it was held unpatentable to coat boot eyelets with celluloid when this was already done to hooks and studs[70]; or to keep drinks hot or cold in vacuum flasks when they had already been used for liquids in laboratories.[71]

(2) There can be no patent for the mere application of a known principle to a use or subject-matter admittedly within its scope.

---

[66] This derives from the "Cripps question", first formulated by Sir Strafford Cripps (as counsel) in *Sharpe & Dohme v. Boots* (1928) 45 R.P.C. 153 at 173, CA, and reformulated by Oliver L.J. in *Windsurfing* (para. 5–30, above). The question does not allow for two cases: (1) where it was allegedly obvious to do the thing for a different purpose (see para. 5–35, above); (2) where at the date of the prior art, what was proposed in it had allegedly no usefulness at all (as in *Killick v. Pye* [1958] R.P.C. 366, CA). See further, Ency. PL, para. 5–213.

[67] *Williams v. Nye* (1890) 7 R.P.C. 62: in fact there was just enough interrelation of parts for the CA to deal with the question as one of inventive step. See further Ency. PL, para. 5–107.

[68] *cf.* also *Beecham Group's (Amoxycillin) Application* [1980] R.P.C. 261 (selected substance not anticipated (or obvious) when claimed as a pharmaceutical composition).

[69] A typical example is *Seiller's Application* [1970] R.P.C. 103: toy bells—the new version differing from its predecessors only in a minor detail of construction which could amount only to a theoretical scientific advantage bearing no practical relationship to the purpose for which the invention was intended.

[70] *Riekmann v. Thierry* (1897) 14 R.P.C. 105, HL.

[71] *Thermos v. Isola* (1910) 27 R.P.C. 388.

Thus, there was no invention in applying a basic principle of electrical amplification to bone-conducting hearing aids, even though this had not previously been suggested in the considerable period since the principle's first formulation.[72]

(3) There can be no patent merely for verifying previous predictions. Where it was already known that polyesters for electrical insulation could be made from reagents that were members of a chemical series, it was not inventive to demonstrate that satisfactory results ensued from substituting other members of the same series.[73] The particular choice "would sooner or later inevitably have attracted attention" and no unexpected result was demonstrated which might have justified a selection. Likewise in genetic engineering: where the substance to be made is known through its occurrence in the human body, and the relevant procedures of recombinant DNA technology are also known, there is nothing inventive in working them through, even though this involves considerable labour by specialists in a new field, and specific knowledge is procured in the course of the work. The person or team which first produces a successful result has only won a race down an established track to a known goal.[74]

5-48   These should be regarded today as no more than ways of stating emphatically that no inventive step has been taken.[75] Like most such aphorisms, they have their counter-propositions—for use in cases that are considered to fall on the other side of the evaluative line. Thus, a use is not a mere analogy, or the mere application of a principle, if it calls for some ingenuity to overcome a practical difficulty in the adaptation or application.[76] For instance, to adapt a suction pump for the purpose of supplying petrol in an engine from fuel tank to carburettor was held to involve more than merely putting a well-known thing to a new use.[77] Likewise, a patent covers more than mere verification if others have been able to do everything except take the last crucial step.

(b) *Obvious to try: chemical and biotechnological inventions*

5-49 The test, "obvious to try?", appeals to tribunals in many situations where pre-existing information falls only a little short of what is claimed to be inventive. However, in its turn it demands an assessment of how compelling

---

[72] *Sonotone v. Multitone* (1955) 72 R.P.C. 131, CA; but *cf. BASF's Application* [1989] O.J. EPO 74.

[73] *General Electric's Application* [1964] R.P.C. 413 at 436, CA; and also *Sharpe & Dohme v. Boots* (n. 58, above).

[74] *Genentech v. Wellcome Foundation* [1989] R.P.C. 147, CA.

[75] Formerly there was some distinction (not easily identified) between whether something was a manner of new manufacture and whether it involved an inventive step. The Patent Office itself had power to refuse an application if it could be said to involve new manufacture.

[76] See especially Lindley L.J., *Gadd v. Mayor of Manchester* (1892) 9 R.P.C. 516 at 524; *cf. Lister's Patent* [1966] R.P.C. 30 at 35–37, DC; *Mutoh's Application* [1984] R.P.C. 85.

[77] [1956] R.P.C. 125, HL.

the case for investigation must seem, and on what grounds. In the search for novel pharmaceuticals, a breakthrough with a new class of drugs, by working on one or a few of the large range within the class, may make further investigation a relatively straightforward choice of one out of a number of laborious paths.

In one sense it may be obvious to try them all, but the Courts drew back from too extensive a view from this perspective. If there was nothing to mark out the line of research actually pursued by the patentee as the path to follow first, a case of inventive step might well be sustained, it being asked: 'Would the notional research group at the relevant date, in all the circumstances . . . directly be led as a matter of course to try [the particular alternative selected by the patentee] in the expectation that it might well produce a useful alternative to or better drug than [the previously known substance] or a body useful for any other purpose?"[78] In any case the test is relevant only where those in the art have a particular problem in mind.[79]

The median thus struck proved an acceptable dividing line in the **5–50** pharmaceutical industry as it developed in the post-war decades. As applied to biotechnological work, however, the test has proved much more controversial. The work of microbiologists, geneticists and cell biologists has advanced the manipulative techniques of biotechnology in a series of remarkable leaps. Yet after each bound it has been possible to apply the new technique to all sorts of subject-matter without more than a degree of persistence and luck. Where patents are sought on successful results of such work, English Courts have adopted a sceptical attitude towards claims of an inventive step. They have taken the view that, once the desired objective is known, and standard techniques are applied to test whether a particular route will reach it, it is merely a commercial decision whether to take the chance of success. Mustill L.J. likened the choice to a bet on a race.[80] Later, however, Lord Hoffmann contemplated the possibility that there could be invention in such research by attempting something which a man less skilled in the art might have regarded as obvious, but which the expert would have thought so beset by obstacles as to be not worth trying.[81]

(c) Technical advantage and commercial success

Patents that provoke litigation concern successful ideas—novelties which **5–51** apparently generate substantial demand because of their technical superiority or their propensity to cut costs. Where an idea is proving to attract

---

[78] Graham J., *Olin Mathieson v. Biorex* [1970] R.P.C. 157 at 187; and see *American Cyanamid v. Ethicon* [1979] R.P.C. 215 at 266–267; *Hoechst Celanese v. BP Chemicals* [1997] F.S.R. 547; *cf. Brugger v. Medic-Aid* [1996] R.P.C. 635 at 661.

[79] *Beecham's (Amoxycillin) Application* [1980] R.P.C. 261 at 290.

[80] *Genentech's Patent* [1989] R.P.C. 147 at 281.

[81] *Biogen v. Medeva* [1997] R.P.C. 1: in the event, he assumed an inventive step and found against validity for lack of disclosure: see below, para. 5–102.

business, it impels the question, why was so desirable a thing not discovered and introduced before? Indeed in such circumstances, if the solution is disarmingly simple, this tends to confirm its inventive character.[82]

Commercial success can help to demonstrate inventive character only if the invention is the cause of the success. There may well be other explanations: in *Martin v. Millwood* the success of the patentee's ball-point pens was found to turn not upon the patented nib construction but upon the discovery of an adequate ink reservoir, which was not the subject of the patent[83]; in *Parkes v. Crocker* the patentee's clip device became a sudden success some 11 years after the patent grant because all the railway companies agreed to adopt it and more than a million were then sold.[84]

Because other causes may exist, Courts have said that they will take account of commercial success only if the need for the patentee's invention has long been felt, "so that men's minds were likely to have been engaged upon a mode of remedying" the pre-existing defect. The vigour with which Lord Herschell makes this point in *Longbottom v. Shaw*[85] would suggest that the person attacking validity is not obliged to show some other explanation of the patentee's commercial success so long as the latter has not clearly demonstrated the "long-felt want" to which his invention is the answer.[86]

5–52   Such caution continues to be much in the mind of today's Court of Appeal. Primary evidence on the issue of inventive step comes from properly qualified experts[87]:

> "who will say whether or not in their opinions the relevant step would have been obvious to a skilled man having regard to the state of the art. All other evidence is secondary . . . [T]he importance, or weight, to be attached to it will vary from case to case. However, such evidence must be kept firmly in its place. It must not be permitted, by reason of its volume and complexity, to obscure the fact that it is no more than an aid in assessing the primary evidence."[88]

---

[82] *BASF/Triazole derivatives* [1989] O.J. EPO 74; and see *Southco v. Dzus* [1990] R.P.C. 587 at 619, dealing with the situation where the inventor and the skilled technician both have the same "tool box of knowledge"; if the former discovers a commercially successful solution it is probably not obvious.

[83] [1956] R.P.C. 125 at 139.

[84] (1929) 46 R.P.C. 241, CA.

[85] (1981) 8 R.P.C. 333 at 336, HL.

[86] *cf.* the balanced version of the same idea propounded by Tomlin J. in *Parkes v. Crocker* ". . . once it has been found . . . that the problem has waited solution for many years, and that the device is in fact novel and superior to what had gone before, and has been widely used, and used in preference to alternative devices, it is, I think, practically impossible to say that there is not present that scintilla of invention necessary to support the Patent": (1929) 46 R.P.C. 241 at 248.

[87] Note that, in Aldous J.'s view, the evidence of a Nobel prize winner, especially one not working in the relevant field at the priority date, may not provide much clue to the state of the appropriate skilled worker's mind at the time: *Chiron v. Organon* [1994] F.S.R. 202.

[88] *Mölnlycke* [1994] R.P.C. 49 at 113.

That is a highly salutary attitude in a world where high-powered teams compete to solve similar problems, and the granting of a wide patent to one of them, therefore, needs clear justification. The others should not be put out of business upon loose assumptions that the patentee must have invented something important because it captured a striking market share.[89] At the stage of application (when today patent offices must examine for an inventive step in every case) there will rarely be decisive evidence of commercial success. Not surprisingly the EPO has tended to stress technical assessment rather than market reaction.[90]

3. INDUSTRIAL APPLICATION

The requirement that a patentable invention be "susceptible" or "capable" **5–53** of industrial application had no direct counterpart in previous British statutes.[91] In part, the concept is concerned with the categories of subject-matter that fall within the sphere of the patent system.[92] It is used to indicate that agriculture is an industry for patent purposes; and to exclude methods of medically treating humans and animals.[93] The fact that they concern a product consisting of or containing biological material, or a process by means of which biological material is a product is not of itself a reason for finding no industrial application.[94] To these we shall return in the next section.[95]

The capacity of an invention for industrial application raises other questions. Can objections that used to be dealt with under the notion of inutility[96] instead be treated as showing lack of industrial applicability? The EPO uses the concept for the purpose of excluding some aspects of the lunatic fringe: attempts to patent ideas which evidently do not achieve the claimed ends, such as machines to produce perpetual motion.[97] In the past

---

[89] Note the tendency of some recent U.S. decisions to move in this direction, strongly criticised by Merges (1988) 76 Calif. L.R. 805.

[90] See Paterson, paras 10–31—10–34.

[91] EPC, Art. 52(1); PA 1977, s. 1(1)(c).

[92] This was apparently considered its main function during the drafting of the EPC; for this and its origins in German law, see Ullrich, *Standards of Patentability in European Inventions* (1977), pp. 7–9.

[93] EPC, Arts 52(4), 57; PA 1977, s. 4(1); *Wellcome/Pigs I* [1989] O.J. EPO 13. In contrast, other ways of treating humans and animals (weight-reduction, cosmetic improvement) are industrially applicable: *Du Pont/Appetite Suppressant* [1986] O.J. EPO 301. The E.C. Directive on Biotechnological Inventions ([1998] O.J. L213/13) requires that products containing biological material, and associated processes, be treated as susceptible of industrial application: Art. 3.

[94] Biotechnology Directive 98/44, Art. 3(1); and see para. 5–59, below. Nor is a patent excluded for biological material, if it has been isolated or produced by a technical process, merely because it previously occurred in nature: Art. 3(2).

[95] See paras 5–54 *et seq.*, below.

[96] For this objection under the 1949 Act, see Blanco White, paras 4–401 *et seq.*

[97] EPO Guidelines, C IV 4.1. Note the connection with inadequate disclosure: a claim to the machine without reference to its purpose would be disallowed by the EPO on this latter ground, which is discussed in paras 5–93—5–97, below.

the British system, partly because of its approach to claims, found occasion to deploy inutility much more extensively. The objection aroses not only when the patentee's basic idea did not work, but also when one of the variants specifically pointed to in a claim proved ineffective. This sanction was rejected in 1977 as unduly severe[98]; after all a claim to something unusable does not directly incommode anyone else.

Nevertheless there is one important sense in which the patent system ought to be constricted: it ought not to apply to scientific information for which there are no practical applications as yet ascertained. The Court of Appeal has now so held. A claim could not be sustained to an almost infinite number of polypeptides, mostly without any known purpose or use. Only some among them would encode the hepatitis C virus or the antigenetic determinant to the antibodies produced by exposure to that virus.[99]

4. PATENTABLE SUBJECT-MATTER

5–54 Patent law has to define the types of subject-matter to which it accords protection. The issues of policy involved are varied. Nice distinctions seem unavoidable. Decisions in particular cases have to be left to the Courts and patent offices. But there is still the question, how far can they be guided by general propositions laid down in legislation or case law?

In Britain, before the 1977 Act, the judges dealt with the matter, guided only by the Jacobean catch-phrase, "manner of new manufacture".[1] Increasingly in recent years, this was treated as an invitation to decide what properly fell within the scope of the patent system, rather than the occasion for investigating the real meaning of "manufacture".[2]

In the 1997 Act there are lists of things which are not to be granted patents, or are not "as such", to be taken as inventions, or are not to be taken as capable of industrial application.[3] This stems from a list in the EPC which represents a fairly conservative consensus of European opinion on the subject in 1973. In large measure, the list involved no departure from previous British understanding. It is in very general terms, so the earlier case law provides suggestive illustrations. The continued applicability of these decisions, however, turns on whether or not the new statutory provisions are found to have introduced some change.

---

[98] It was not included in the EPC and it was rejected by the Banks Committee: Report (Cmnd 4407, 1970), para. 376.
[99] *Chiron v. Murex Diagnostics* [1996] F.S.R. 153 at 176–178. For the significance of this, see para. 5–59, below.
[1] See generally, Blanco White, para. 4–901.
[2] This became especially true after the judgment of the High Court of Australia in *NRDC's Application* [1961] R.P.C. 134; see *CCOM v. Jeijing* [1993] F.S.R. 314.
[3] PA 1977, s. 1(2) (with power to extend by order: s. 1(5)), ss. 1(3), (4), 4; EPC, Arts 52(2)–(4), 53.

The Act does not define "invention", but may be read to imply that "patentable inventions" are but one type in a broader class. According to one view, Courts may conclude that an idea is not an "invention" on a ground distinct from those set out in the specific exclusions just mentioned.[4] As an approach this adds to the judicial armoury for repelling disproportionate claims. However, the scope of such a power is inherently obscure, and so the interpretation may well be rejected in subsequent decisions.

Two main ideas recur in distinguishing the categories of subject-matter **5–55** that may and may not be patented. One is that intellectual conceptions become patentable only to the extent that they have been embodied in technical applications. The other is that techniques which relate to living organisms, animal or vegetable, may call for special treatment: either because the public interest demands that their use should not be restricted or because a special legislative regime is needed for their protection. We shall first consider the specific cases associated with these two ideas, and then turn to general issues of moral and social value.

(1) Intellectual conceptions

(a) *Discoveries*

The list of things excluded from invention in the 1977 Act starts with **5–56** discoveries, scientific theories and mathematical methods[5]; but these are excluded only to the extent that the patent relates to the conception "as such". The distinction is well-known in many patent systems: discovery is the unearthing of causes, properties or phenomena already existing in nature; invention is the application of such knowledge to the satisfaction of social needs.[6] For instance, in an internal combustion engine, the idea of putting a cushion of air in the cylinder between the fuel and the piston in order to cushion the explosive effect of ignition was said not in itself to be patentable; but a machine devised to do so was.[7]

At this point we meet a question of interpretation that is strategic for all the exclusions discussed under this head: must the excluded subject-matter be disregarded in assessing whether there is invention in a claim involving an application of it in (say) a production process or a machine. In relation to a claim for an application of a computer program, Falconer J. held that

---

[4] See Mustill L.J., *Genentech v. Wellcome* [1989] R.P.C. 147 at 262; Hobhouse L.J., *Biogen v. Medeva* [1995] R.P.C. 25 at 88 (the latter being under appeal at the time of writing).

[5] For the evolution of this in the EPC, see Kolle (1974) 5 I.I.C. 140 at 147–148; *IBM/ Document retrieval* [1990] O.J. EPO 12.

[6] Kolle (n. 5, above). And see Buckley L.J., *Reynolds v. Smith* (1913) 20 R.P.C. 123 at 126: "Discovery adds to the amount of human knowledge, but it does so . . . only by disclosing something . . . Invention necessarily involves also the suggestion of an act to be done." *cf.* also the use of "mere discovery" to preclude from patentability the discovery of a new advantage for an old thing": para. 5–22, above.

[7] Jessel M.R., *Otto v. Linford* (1882) 46 L.T. (N.S.) 35 at 39.

invention must be found in some aspect of the application apart from the program.[8] However, in *Genentech v. Wellcome Foundation* the Court of Appeal ruled that approach to be incorrect.[9] Discoveries concerning the structure of the DNA of a given protein could contribute the element of inventiveness in a claim to the employment of that knowledge in producing the protein by genetic engineering: patentability of the discoveries was excluded only "to the extent that" they are claimed "as such".

5–57   In chemical research the matter raises an issue of general importance: is it more than discovery to make a substance without also finding a use for it? It might be said that to give a new thing to the world is in itself sufficiently useful to merit protection; and that argument will doubtless seem stronger where technical difficulties are overcome in order to produce it.[10] Moreover, if mere making is not invention, yet discovery of one use allows a patentee to claim the substance itself in all its uses, an evident imbalance results: only if the first identifier of a use can patent for that use alone would it seem reasonable to deny any protection to the first maker of the substance.[11]

5–58   In the bulk of cases where discovery and invention can be distinguished, the two stages are part of a single development by one person or team. Even so, as invention has become less the product of trial and error on the job and more a matter of systematic research, the possibility of the two steps being taken by different people has increased. It is likely to have practical consequences, first between individuals, since only "inventors" are entitled to an employee's rights in an invention[12]; and secondly, between commercial rivals, as in the case where one is first to discover but only second to invent.

The case in favour of treating the conceptual stages in research and development as involving "invention", rather than "discovery", is broadly that these are the points at which the system should do more: by encouraging "pure" rather than "applied" work and by affording early protection that will stimulate the investment for innovation.[13] But unless all theoretical work is to lead to patents for whatever practical uses may subsequently be found for it, the approach raises formidable difficulties.

---

[8] *Merrill Lynch's Application* [1988] R.P.C. 1 at 12.

[9] [1989] R.P.C. 147; repeated in the *Merrill Lynch* case on appeal [1989] R.P.C. 561 and re-affirmed in *Chiron v. Murex Diagnostics* [1996] F.S.R. 153; both decisions are in line with the EPO's approach (adopted just before) in *Vicom* (para. 5–66, n. 53, below).

[10] It may also seem stronger where the substance is an intermediate which may be useful in making further substances, even though they are at the time of unknown usefulness. *cf. Smith's Applications* [1971] R.P.C. 31, where it was said that the question of the value of the ultimate products was irrelevant to the assessment of obviousness; but the more fundamental issue was not addressed.

[11] See also para. 5–53, above.

[12] For which, see paras 7–07—7–14, below.

[13] See Neumeyer (1975) 14 Ind. Prop. 348; Beier (1975) 6 I.I.C. 367; *cf.* Kitch (1977) 20 J. Law & Econ. 265 at 288; Beier and Moufang (1994) 43 Revista. di Diritto Ind. 340.

How would it be possible to characterise information coming close enough to practical application to be patentable? And unless further requirements were built into the system, it might result in information about practical applications never being made publicly available.[14]

The rapid advance of biotechnology has produced an industry in which **5–59** many academic researchers have been drawn into close partnership with commercialisers of results. The very high cost of the initial research is such as to make scientists, research institutions and funding bodies (charities, government and industrial collaborators) all acutely aware of the need to make the most of intellectual property potential in the results. This in turn has induced patent applications at the earliest stage that could conceivably produce protection. The Human Genome Project—collaborative research on an international scale which is mapping the human genetic structure— began as an objective exercise in which results would be shared and academic renown would provide the true reward.

Soon enough, however, United States participants began applying for protection of thousands of specific genes or gene elements (expression tag sequences); and British and other partners made their own applications, essentially in retaliation. Before the question whether, in any given instance, such information has sufficient practical relevance to constitute "invention" could be considered by tribunals in any country, the applications were withdrawn. That seems a prescient decision so far as British law is concerned. It has since been held, as already noted, that the requirement of industrial applicability demands that the claimed invention be made or used in trade or manufacture; it must, in other works, have a known use. Without such a test, the applications in question would have resulted in patents for very wide subject-matter. These patents would go, moreover, to researchers pursuing relatively mundane (but highly competitive) courses of inquiry, while allowing only secondary derivative patents for very difficult inspirational work needed to transpose basic genetic knowledge into products and procedures of practical value.[15] The Biotechnology Directive now provides that a patent application must disclose the industrial application of a gene sequence or partial sequence.[16]

---

[14] As to this *cf.* the U.S. Supreme Court's requirement that there be "specific utility" before scientific information is patentable: *Brenner v. Manson* 383 U.S. 519 (1966). Douglas J. (at 534): "Until the process claim . . . has been reduced to production of a product shown to be useful, the metes and bounds of that monopoly are not capable of precise delineation. It may engross a vast, unknown and perhaps unknowable area. Such a patent may confer power to block off whole areas of scientific development without compensating benefit to the public."

[15] See generally, Eisenberg (1992) 257 Science 903; Maebius (1992) 74 J.P.T.O.S. 651; HUGO, *Intellectual Property in Genome Mapping Projects* (1993).

[16] Dir. 98/44, Art. 5(3); see also *Howard Florey/Relaxin* [1995] E.P.O.R. 541.

(b) *Schemes for performing mental acts; presentation of information*

5–60 Similar in essence to the previous category is the exclusion "as such" of schemes, rules or methods for performing mental acts, playing games or doing business; likewise presentations of information.[17] There have been many instances of attempts to patent ideas which involve some association between a technical device and the collation, interpretation or deployment of information.[18] In such cases the usual inquiry has been whether the novelty or usefulness lies in the former or the latter aspect.[19] If the latter, the idea is likely to be labelled a "mere scheme or plan" and placed outside what is patentable.

Contrast the following[20]: colouring fertilisers in order to distinguish them from one another (unpatentable),[21] and colouring a squashball a particular shade of blue to make it specially visible (prima facie patentable)[22]; a system of marking buoys in a channel in order to show ships where to go (unpatentable),[23] and a system of devices on vehicles which would co-operate on approach to avoid dazzle (patentable)[24]; the rules of a new game (unpatentable), and new card-packs and similar equipment for a game (patentable)[25]; a record on which the music is new (unpatentable), and a new way of forming grooves on a record so as to transmit stereophonic sound (patentable)[26]; printed forms for a "home shopping club" (unpatentable),[27] and a new way of printing a newspaper so that it could be folded crossways as well as longways (patentable).[28]

On the whole, the existing British decisions have looked to the essence of the matter, not taking account of the form in which the invention is claimed. Thus a scheme for arranging the supply of water, electricity and other services to a set of houses was held to be merely a layout plan not affecting the technical means of supplying any of the things; it made no difference that the rejected claim read: "In an underground installation for

---

[17] PA 1977, s. 1(2)(c), (d); EPC, Art. 52(2) (c), (d). "Presentations of information" comes from PCT Rules, rr. 39.1(v) and 67.2(v) and needs to be read in a limited sense: see Kolle (n. 5, above) at 152–153; *Merrill Lynch's Application* (n. 54, below). For board games see Doble [1997] E.I.P.R. 587.

[18] Cases where there is no technical aspect are clearly not patentable: for instance, methods of musical notation (*C's Application* (1920) 37 R.P.C. 247) or of learning a language (see EPO Guidelines, C IV 2.1); *cf.* however *Pitman's Application* [1969] R.P.C. 646 (material printed in a form suitable for use in a reading machine).

[19] The distinction is common to most patent systems: Kolle (n. 5, above) at 150.

[20] For the many other examples, see Ency. PL, para. 5–234.

[21] *Johnson's Application* (1930) 47 R.P.C. 361.

[22] *ITS Rubber's Application* [1979] R.P.C. 318.

[23] *W's Application* (1914) 31 R.P.C. 141; *cf. de Beers' Application* [1979] F.S.R. 72, CA.

[24] *F.M.M.'s Application* (1941) 58 R.P.C. 115.

[25] See Official Ruling 1926 (A) 43 R.P.C. 1; *Cobianchi's Application* (1953) 70 R.P.C. 199.

[26] See EPO Guidelines, C IV 2.1.

[27] *Littlewood's Application* (1954) 71 R.P.C. 185.

[28] *Cooper's Application* (1902) 19 R.P.C. 53; and see *Fishburn's Application* (1940) 57 R.P.C. 245.

distribution of utilities ... the improvement characterised by ... [a specified layout]."[29]

Mostly the judicial decisions that distinguish between novelty in schemes **5-61** and novelty in means offer by way of explanation the merely reiterative statement that the concern of the patent system is with technical advances alone.[30] The real justification for the distinction seems to lie partly (as with "discoveries") in concern lest monopoly powers of potentially great scope may be conferred, partly in the belief that the encouragement of industry through a market monopoly is an effective medium only in the sphere of industrial production, and partly in a fear that it would be difficult to determine what constitutes anticipation and infringement if the range of the system were broadened.[31] The effect of the current approach can be measured by what is excluded: in particular, new ways of organising businesses and of testing their efficiency are not patentable even though they are often the subject of considerable investment in today's economic conditions. They may be copied by others, save to the extent that contract or confidence operates to the contrary.

(c) *Aesthetic creations*

The exclusion "as such" of literary, dramatic, musical and artistic works and **5-62** any other aesthetic creations[32] can be justified by the existence of copyright and industrial designs protection.[33] The kinds of distinction already discussed pertain equally here. Where the element of creativity lies in the aesthetic ideas expressed there is no room for patent protection.[34] Thus, it was not patentable to claim disk jackets the only novelty of which lay in the colours given to them.[35] The contrary will apply where a new technical process or article is devised for its pleasurable appeal—for instance, a new method of making candles,[36] or a novel perfume.

---

[29] *Hiller's Application* [1969] R.P.C. 267; *cf.* also *Quigley's Application* [1977] F.S.R. 373.
[30] Formerly this was expressed in the proposition that a "manner of manufacture" required the making, improvement or repair of a "vendible product", an approach in effect abandoned after the *NRDC* case [1961] R.P.C. 134.
[31] See on these factors, Lloyd Jacob J., *Rolls-Royce's Application* [1963] R.P.C. 251 at 255.
[32] PA 1977, s. 1(2)(b); EPC, Art. 52(2)(b); *cf. Tetra Molectric's Application* [1977] R.P.C. 290, CA.
[33] There has been much recent discussion of the extent to which technical designs should be protected by copyright (see Chap. 14, below) but none of whether the patent system should offer protection to the essentially aesthetic. The registered design system, however, offers comparable monopoly protection; *cf.* the U.S., where the same kind of protection is actually incorporated within the patent system.
[34] Where they take the form of instructions (plays, music) they are methods of performing mental acts in the sense discussed in the previous paragraph.
[35] *Fuji/Disk Jacket* [1990] O.J. EPO 395.
[36] *cf.* the German decision to this effect: 1972 Mitt. 235, BGH.

(d) *Computer programs*[37]

5–63 The electronic hardware of computing technology is a natural subject for patentable invention and from its inception the industry has been sustained by such patents. Software, however, poses considerable problems.[38] In 1973, it was decided, against the pleas of some interest groups, specifically to exclude programs for computers "as such" from the ambit of what is patentable under the EPC.[39] "Computer program" is a term that may describe a wide range of phenomena, from basic algorithms capable of application in an indefinite number of more specific uses[40] to detailed instructions for the solution of particular problems.[41] A different complication is this: the result of actually using a programmed computer is to produce information which may be taken for itself, or may immediately be put to some further use, as where a computer controls a step in the operation of a production process.[42] To add to the complexities, there is, for instance, the possibility that principles which might be written into programs are instead given expression in the circuitry of the computer, and the possibility of writing programs that will bring about the co-operation of a network of computers.[43]

5–64 A computer uses mathematical instructions to select information from "input" data and, frequently, to perform mathematical manipulations with what is selected. It goes through processes that could theoretically be undertaken by the human brain unaided. If what is claimed to be patentable is a way of making a known machine operate upon data to produce desired results, then in essence it seems that nothing other than an instruction about how to perform intellectual tasks is being given. But the case is not a precise analogy to the instruction to the pilot to fly a plane in a certain way in order to reduce noise.[44] For no human interprets the instructions each time a computer uses its program. Computer programs

---

[37] See Bandey, *Intellectual Property in Computer Program Technology* (1996); Blakemore [Nov. 1995] Pat. Wld. 21; Rau and Watkin (1996) 27 I.I.C. 447; Van Raden [1996] E.I.P.R. 384; Hart (1997) 13 C.L. & S.R. 147; Newman [1997] E.I.P.R. 701; Davies [1998] E.I.P.R. 429; Harris [1999] CIPA 214.

[38] For copyright in programs and associated instructions, see paras 13–22, 13–39, below.

[39] EPC, Art. 52(2)(c); hence PA 1977, s. 1(2)(c) to the same effect. For the evolution, Kolle (n. 94, above) at 150–152.

[40] Some of the cases presented to test the patentability of programs have involved ideas of this type: *Slee & Harris's Applications* [1966] R.P.C. 194 (claim to computer as programmed accepted in the U.K.); [1968] F.S.R. 272 (refused in Australia). *cf. Gottschalk v. Benson* 409 U.S. 63 (1972) (algorithm for conversion of binary code into pure binary: refused).

[41] In the U.S. Supreme Court's view, if the only novelty in the process is the added efficiency brought about by the way the computer is programmed, the case fell to be treated as if it were a claim to a program without the technical consequence: *Parker v. Flook* 437 U.S. 584 (1978); for the growing liability of the U.S. Courts today, see *Re Alappat* 33 F. 3rd 1526 (1994); Karjala (1998) 17 John Marshall J.C.I.L. 41.

[42] This at least is more than a computer program "as such".

[43] As in the *Burroughs* case (n. 46, below).

[44] Held unpatentable in *Rolls-Royce's Application* [1963] R.P.C. 251.

accordingly lie exactly at the boundary of what previously has been thought to separate the patentable from the non-patentable: to some, even the most detailed operational programs remain nothing else than instructions for performing intellectual exercises; to others, the conversion of the operation into a technical process capable of constant repetition carries it over into the patentable sphere.[45]

In Britain, under the 1949 Act, claims to methods of programming a **5–65** computer were allowed to reach grant by reasonably liberal analogy to cases where new contrivances have been held patentable.[46] The computer with its special instructions was regarded as a different machine from one without, and that made it patentable, whether the claim was for a computer as programmed, means for programming (tape, cards, etc.), or a method of programming it.[47] Among EPC countries, France by statute apparently excluded such patents[48] and in other countries the Courts showed themselves reluctant to adopt so favourable a position as in Britain.[49] With the introduction of the EPC provisions excluding computer programs as such from patentability, the question has required consideration in the EPO and under the revised national legislation. The patent frontier has become increasingly significant, as the industry has discovered the limitations of copyright, contract and trade secret protection for programs and associated material.

A willingness to explore accommodations within the Convention frame- **5–66** work was indicated by the EPO when it amended its Guidelines in 1985.[50] The change made it clear that that Office would allow claims involving use of a program if overall the invention made a contribution to an art that was technical. The scope of what is still excluded may be judged by contrasting the following examples:

(1) (*Koch and Sterzel*[51]: program governing the operation of a technical device). A claim to X-ray apparatus controlled by a computer program so as to secure optimal exposure without overloading the X-ray tube was held patentable by an EPO Board of Appeal. It sufficed that "technical means" were involved as well as the mathematical method or algorithm, which was characterised as "non-technical". It was not necessary to show that invention lay exclusively or largely in the former domain.[52]

---

[45] See the *Burroughs* case (n. 46, below) at 159–160.
[46] *Burroughs' (Perkins) Application* [1974] R.P.C. 147.
[47] The first cases attempted to draw distinctions between different ways of formulating claims. This approach was abandoned in *Burroughs* as pure casuistry.
[48] Patent Law of 1968.
[49] See generally, Pagenberg (1974) 5 I.I.C. 253.
[50] Guidelines, C IV 2.2. See Sherman [1991] E.I.P.R. 85, and for wider comparisons, Hoffmann *et al.* [1988] E.I.P.R. 355, [1989] E.I.P.R. 7.
[51] [1988] O.J. EPO 19.
[52] See also *Sohei Ford Management System* [1996] E.P.O.R. 253.

(2) (*Vicom's Application*[53]: computer operating program in a industrial technique). Likewise a claim is patentable to a computer so programmed (or provided with hardware) as to be able to process digital images in accordance with a given mathematical procedure expressed as an algorithm. The program had been developed for the computer-aided design (CAD) of engineering and similar products, and the application was upheld once the claim was amended so as to cover only uses which started with a computerised image; the original claim was for less specific methods of using the algorithm. This, the EPO's leading decision on the whole subject, was allowed because the claim went to the general functioning of the computer, rather than to an application designed to execute particular tasks. With this amendment the Board of Appeal could accept that it was sufficiently "directed to a technical process". At root, what mattered was that CAD is a widely used and most valuable aid to product design.

(3) (*Merrill Lynch's Application*[54]: application program for analysing data). The claimed program could be used in an automated market for shares and similar securities. It analysed customers' orders to buy and sell against given criteria; those which met the criteria were then carried out. The Court of Appeal held this unpatentable under the 1977 Act. The program could be introduced into any suitable computer in any encoding language, causing data to be acted upon so as to carry out legal transactions, rather than technical production in any ordinary sense.

(4) (*Gale's Application*[55]: new method of calculation). The applicant's essential discovery was of a method of calculating square roots in the binary functioning of a computer by eliminating division and restricting multiplication to specified binary functions. This could be given form in the electronic circuitry of a read-only memory (ROM) and the claim was to a ROM carrying the relevant controls. Aldous J. was prepared to accept the claim; but the Court of Appeal refused the application for its very apparent reference to mathematical procedures for producing numbers. The Court refused to accept in such a case that embodiment in a ROM made the program patentable, where it would not be if expressed purely in mathematical terms or was contained on a floppy disk for insertion in a computer.

---

[53] [1987] O.J. EPO 14.

[54] [1989] R.P.C. 561.

[55] [1991] R.P.C. 305. Similarly, in the EPO a claim was refused for a program to run on conventional hardware which would replace difficult expressions in a text with comprehensible synonyms: *IBM/Text Clarity* [1990] O.J. EPO 384; *cf. Kearney* [1998] E.O.P.R. 236; *IBM/Computer Programs* [1999] E.P.O.R. 301. German and Australian Courts have refused a word-processing program which enabled a user to write Chinese characters: see *CCOM v. Jiejing* [1993] F.S.R. 315; XZB 29/89 (1993) 24 I.I.C. 124.

(5) (*Fujitsu's Application*[56]: *physical analysis*. The Court of Appeal rejected a claim to a computer programmed to convert data concerning the structure of two crystals into data representing the physical layout of the crystal structure that would have been obtained by combining the original two structures in such a way that the two selected atoms were superimposed, the two selected *lattice-vectors* and the two selected crystal-faces were superimposed. This was held unpatentable because the claim left it to the operator to select what data to work on, how to work on it, how to assess the results and which, if any, results to use. The process was abstract and the result of the use of it undefined. What was produced was not an inevitable result of taking a number of defined steps but was determined by the personal skill and assessment of the operator. This amounted to a method of performing mental acts which involved no sufficient technical contribution.

The distinction between the first two and the last three of these examples is rationalised by differentiating between the securing of a technical effect and the mere production and manipulation of information. It has been introduced in order to confine the exclusion of computer programs as such within a limited compass, itself an approach founded on a belief that the patent system should be open to "technology" in a broad sense, and one that implies criticism of the cautious drafting of the EPC.

As with any attempt to define the boundaries of intellectual property at **5–67** all precisely, the technical/non-technical dichotomy has its arbitrariness. It is being deployed to strike some compromise between a wide and a narrow interpretation of the exclusion of computer programs from patentability. Wide exclusion would follow from the view expressed at first instance by Falconer J. in the *Merrill Lynch* case: if the inventive step was stated to lie in the computer program it could not be patented. But this interpretation (which could have been applied equally to other exclusionary categories, such as mathematical methods and discoveries) was rejected by the EPO in *Vicom* and then by the Court of Appeal in *Genentech*[57] and *Merrill Lynch*. Fletcher Moulton L.J.'s classic dictum was called in aid:

". . . invention may lie in the idea, and it may lie in the way in which it is carried out, and it may lie in the combination of the two; but if there is invention in the idea plus the way of carrying it out, then it is good subject-matter for Letters Patent."[58]

This however implies a eviscerating interpretation of the statutory exclusion, for it appears to lead to the conclusion that a computer as

---

[56] [1997] R.P.C. 608, CA.
[57] For which, see para. 5–56, above.
[58] *Hickton's Patent Syndicate v. Patents & Machine Improvements* (1909) 26 R.P.C. 339 at 348.

programmed (in the various forms of claim in which this might be dressed) is always patentable. Aldous J. at first instance in *Gale* appeared to be reaching this position, as had the patent judges under the 1949 Act. But this equally was not acceptable to the Court of Appeal, and one is left to determine what is patentable by the uncertain touchstone of sufficiently technical "means" or "effect" or "connection".

5–68   The sphere in which it is most difficult to apply this notion is that of computer technology of and for itself. On the one hand, there has been hostility towards claims, however presented, for mathematical procedures in programming which would have general application: programs for the calculation of square roots; for the conversion of binary decimal numbers into pure binary numbers; for the compilation of a source program in high-level language into object code. If concepts of this type prove to be major breakthroughs, their use in programming will have immense commercial value.

5–69   At the other extreme, there are cases concerned with networking of computers which are linked together physically, the claim being in essence to program instructions which bring about the efficient co-operation of the various stations. These are readily allowed.[59] Networking has the "feel" of larger technology. But how is it in principle different from a single computer programmed to operate in accordance with given instructions? The case law to date records an unresolved tussle between extremes: compromise reigns in the place of certainty. If resolution is to come it will be because the industry continues to press for program patents, sensing that in the end Courts will have to follow Fletcher Moulton L.J.'s logic, as Aldous J. proposed to do in *Gale*. If this step is eventually taken, discussion can then focus on the novelty and inventiveness of the particular program. In all likelihood it is the position into which Europe will in the end be driven,[60] as has recently occurred (without the same statutory impediment) in the United States[61] and Australasia.[62]

(2) Biological subject-matter

5–70 The boundaries of the patent system are re-drawn (almost always by widening) as industries which are used to working with patents extend their ambit of operation. In their campaigns for novel patents, they are likely to

---

[59] *IBM/Data processing network* [1990] O.J. EPO 5; *Wang's Application* [1991] R.P.C. 463.

[60] In the latest decisions of the EPO (T0935/97 and T1173/97, Tech BA), while the requirement of technical effect is still insisted upon, it is held unnecessary to restrict claims to the program when recorded on a carrier, such as a disc. This may prove to have a considerably broadening effect in the practice of the Office and potentially therefore on national courts.

[61] For the position after *Re Alappat* (n. 41, above), see Ayers and Goodman *et al.* (1994) 76 JPTOS 741, 771; Turkevich (1994) 11 Comp.L.1.

[62] *IBM v. Commissioner of Patents* (1994) 25 I.I.C. 109. Pressure for such a change has been recorded by the European Commission, Report of Findings on Green Paper (DGXV Paper 115, 1998). See Newman [1997] E.I.P.R. 701.

succeed except where they meet persistent and implacable opposition from some other interest group. The pragmatic nature of this expansive process is nowhere better illustrated than in relation to patents which involve living matter.

Some "industrial" processes have traditionally used the capacities of living matter to make products, as with yeasts in brewing and baking. At least in Britain there has accordingly never been a general embargo on patents which involve living matter. Yet, for a long period, agriculture was not thought to be a proper sphere for patenting. Eventually, in the decades after 1945, agriculture, horticulture and animal production adopted increasingly artificial procedures, in which natural growth was affected by chemical additives, such as fertilisers and herbicides, and to special physical conditions, such as alterations of light, temperature and humidity. It was only then that the Courts began to accommodate these techniques within the patent system. At the same time, plant breeders won a special regime of plant variety rights.[63]

Advances in microbiology were introducing production techniques for pharmaceuticals and other substances which depended upon the use of micro-organisms in controlled reactions. In Britain their patentability was accepted with little argument.[64] The question of a deposit system for new strains proved of greater concern. The EPC and the 1977 Act, created a special system to deal with the latter and thereby confirmed the place of this technology within the patent firmament.[65]

In the United States the basic issue had to be taken to the Supreme **5–71** Court. That Court's decision in favour, *Diamond v. Chakrabarty*,[66] made the sweeping generalisation that "anything under the sun", apart from a human being, should be regarded as patentable. It sent a crucial signal to the world that patenting must be made available in any country which sought to join the race for commercial returns on biotechnological research.

To this there has been a complex set of reactions, not least in Western Europe, where the EPC has set particular puzzles for those who would advance the patent frontiers in this field. The campaigns of these advocates have in their turn brought determined opposition, which gives expression to a whole range of environmental and moral discontents. In particular, the attempt to remould the EPC formulae by the curious expedient of a Biotechnology Directive, dealing with the content of *national* patent laws in

---

[63] See paras 5–82—5–85; App. 3, below.
[64] *American Cyanamid v. Berk Pharmaceuticals* [1976] R.P.C. 231.
[65] See para. 5–98, below. Preceding this development, had been the 1949 extension of the system as a whole to cover chemical (including, above all, pharmaceutical) substances *per se*: see paras 4–47, 4–48, above.
[66] 65 Law Ed. (2d) 144 (1980).

E.C. countries, was halted for three years in 1995 and only became law in modified form in 1998.[67]

5-72 Biotechnology promises many advantages in the cultivation of foodstuff and other natural products, in combatting illness and generic disorders in humans and animals, the effects of which may, in particular, benefit less developed countries. The new Directive may enhance the contributions of the patent systems of E.U. states to these ends, but is likely to do so only in modest ways. Much will continue to depend on the attitudes of patent offices and Courts. The very lifeblood of the EPO is the granting of patents. But that Office has been made uncomfortably aware by lively demonstrations of opposition, outside its doors as well as in its hearing divisions, that a continuing advance of the system should not be taken as an unquestioned good in the realm of biotechnology. Until there is clearer evidence that, in the great run of cases, the benefits of genetic manipulation plainly outweigh any dangers, many will continue to question the advisability of employing the patent incentive in at least some parts of this sphere.

There are three exclusions from patentable subject-matter which in the Patents Act 1977 derive directly from the EPC: (1) methods of treating the human and animal body; (2) plant and animal varieties and essentially biological methods for their creation; and (3) inventions contrary to *ordre public* or morality. Each will be treated in turn.

(a) *Methods of treating the human or animal body*

5-73 An invention that has to be claimed as a "method of treating the human or animal body by surgery or therapy or of diagnosis practised on the human or animal body" is unpatentable.[68] The 1977 Act deems these activities to be incapable of industrial application. The rule gives formal expression to a public policy favouring the dissemination of new medical techniques unimpeded by claims to exclusive rights.[69] In Britain such claims have long been refused.[70] In the prevailing view, the patent system should not intrude into the realm of a leading liberal profession where expectations of renown

---

[67] Directive on the Legal Protection of Biotechnological Inventions [1998] O.J. L213/13 (to be given effect in Member States by July 30, 2000); Llewelyn [1997] E.I.P.R. 115; Nott [1998] E.I.P.R. 455; Bostyn [1999] I.P.Q. 1. Its constitutional validity has since been challenged by the Netherlands government: Scott [1999] E.I.P.R. 212.

[68] PA 1977, s. 4(2), (3); EPC, Art. 52(4). For the history in Europe and an argument against continuance, see Moufang (1993) 24 I.I.C. 18; and Panchen (1991) 22 I.I.C. 879. Common law jurisdictions which have abandoned the exclusion include Israel (*Wellcome v. Plantex* [1974] R.P.C. 514), and Australia (*Anaesthetic Supplies v. Rescare* (1995) 26 I.I.C. 399).

[69] See *Wellcome/Pigs I* [1988] E.P.O.R. 1; *Visx v. Nidex* [1999] F.S.R. 406 at 465.

[70] As regards human treatment, the U.K. Patent Office followed the practice of exclusion for decades before it was upheld by an appellate Court: see *Upjohn's (Robert) Application* [1977] R.P.C. 94, CA. The exclusion of animal treatment, new in 1977 so far as the U.K. was concerned, was introduced by the EPC on the basis of ethical considerations which, it seems, were not clearly articulated.

and reward have traditionally taken quite different forms from those which flow from exclusive rights over commercialisation.[71] The spectre of a single doctor reserving the performance of the most satisfactory, possibly life-saving, operation to his or her own team and extracting therefrom monopoly profits on the scale of a successful pop-star seemed to put the matter beyond argument.

With the movement in medicine towards drug therapies, however, this abstemious approach has had to confront pharmaceutical producers avid for patent protection. In the second half of the twentieth century, patent law in every industrial state has had to develop in ways which mediate this conflict. A mixture of legislation and litigation has given the pharmaceutical industry much of the protection which it has sought (though by no means all). One question which now hangs in the air is whether an exclusion of "methods of medical treatment", such as is to be found in the present European laws, makes any real sense. We shall return to that question after reviewing the ways in which, as a legal concept, the exclusion has been kept in confinement.

The legal limitation of the exception turns upon the technical distinction **5–74** between types of claim which we have already met in general terms in considering novelty: a new substance or composition—one that has had no previously known use—may be claimed "as such". It, therefore, does not come with the exclusion of *methods* of medical treatment. The same applies to the selection of a specific substance or composition from a generally known class, because the discovery of a special quality justifies a claim to that thing.

It is only with a thing already known to have a use that claims must be confined to a method and the exclusion of medical treatment begins to bite. The first demand of the pharmaceutical industry has been for patents covering newly constituted substances and on the success of such patents the profitability of leading producers has depended. Here at least the system has worked in archetypal fashion. The monopoly profits of one patented success have allowed extensive research to be supported in the hope of finding a further winner which can come on stream in time to continue the flow of revenue.

Because of this crucial significance of patenting to pharmaceutical production, the case for further concessions has been diligently pursued and politicians have listened with some sympathy. It is hard to see why work on a new substance, including one specially selected, should bring a patent, while work on the properties of things already known should not be patentable in the sphere of medical and veterinary application. Inventions of the latter kind may be relatively hard or relatively easy to achieve. If they are excluded from patenting, then the industry must feel itself directed to

---

[71] It was once said that "the whole subject is conceived as essentially non-economic": *NRDC* case [1961] R.P.C. 134 at 145.

investigate new substances. Yet it cannot be claimed that, as a category, research of that kind is necessarily of greater human benefit than work to improve existing products.

5-75   Thinking on these lines led to an important exception in the EPC and its derivatives to the law of novelty as it had previously applied. An invention consisting of a substance or composition for use in an excluded method of medical treatment remains novel, despite the fact that the substance or composition is itself known, "provided that its use in any [such] method . . . is not comprised in the state of the art".[72] The natural meaning of this special exception is that only for the first discovery of a medical use for a known product can a claim be made to it for that use which will be regarded as novel. So, left to itself, would the Patents Court have read it.[73] But the Enlarged Board of Appeal of the EPO, faced with numerous applications for second and subsequent discoveries of medical use, showed its determination to confine the medical treatment exception strictly to what it described as "non-commercial and non-industrial medical and veterinary activities". In *Eisai's and other Applications*,[74] it decided that in addition to the exception for first medical use, it was legitimate to recognise claims to use of a substance for making up into a medicament for pharmaceutical administration in pursuit of a subsequently discovered use,[75] provided that the new treatment has been tried and tested.[76] In the interests of common progress, the Patents Court proceeded to accept the same casuistry.[77]

5-76   The potency of these decisions as precedents was soon enough realised. As already indicated, the EPO Enlarged Board of Appeal went on to hold valid a claim to a known article for a novel non-medical purpose, even where the new purpose involves only an already known physical use.[78] What part of these developments is going to become settled law throughout the EPC countries is quite unpredictable. At least in relation to the case of subsequent medical uses, here under discussion, it can be said that the general exclusion of methods of medical treatment puts an exception in this sphere in a category of its own.

The decisions on subsequent medical applications limit the exception for methods of medical treatment, but they by no means deprive that exception

---

[72] PA 1977, s. 3(6); EPC, Art. 54(5).

[73] See *Schering and Wyeth* (n. 77, below).

[74] [1985] O.J. EPO 64; and see *Duphar's Application/Pigs II* [1989] O.J. EPO 24; White [1984] E.I.P.R. 62.

[75] This is known as "the Swiss form of claim", the Swiss Patent Office being the first perspicacious enough to appreciate its potential; *cf.* the earlier, wider decision of the German Supreme Court (*Hydropiridine* [1984] O.J. EPO 26) which was not followed. For different Swiss claim formulations, see *Thérapeutiques Substitutives* [1998] E.P.O.R. 417.

[76] *McManus' Applicn.* [1994] F.S.R. 558. There is no need to show a new manufacturing process: *MA/Trigonelline* [1996] O.J. EPO 430.

[77] *Schering's and Wyeth's Applications* [1985] R.P.C. 545 (in banc).

[78] See paras 5–26, 5–27, above.

of significance. For instance, more efficient or less harmful dosages in known treatment,[79] the administration of a bacterium to secure immunity from a disease[80] and the employment of known medical equipment for new treatments, still remain unpatentable.

At the margins there are certain possibilities of avoiding the prohibition. **5–77** If the method can be shown not to constitute surgery, therapy or diagnosis it will not be caught. Therapy covers non-surgical treatment designed to cure, alleviate, remove or lessen the symptom of, or prevent or reduce the possibility of contracting any malfunction of, the human or animal body.[81] Before the 1977 Act, the view was taken in England that oral administration of known substances in reduced dosages in order to prevent conception was not *medical* treatment and that is still the law.[82] The EPO has accepted claims to treatment for a cosmetic or other non-therapeutic purpose, such as an appetite suppressant (for slimming).[83] But these did not include the removal of plaque from teeth because it was a way of preventing dental decay. Nor can the prohibition be side-stepped by showing an additional non-medical advantage.[84]

Diagnosis, according to the EPO, must involve an examination of the body to establish symptoms which lead to a diagnosis. On this basis, preliminary tests, providing results which may be taken into account in reaching a diagnosis, are not excluded from patenting.[85]

Under the 1949 Act, the Patent Appeals Tribunal once allowed a "pack **5–78** claim" as a way of patenting the discovery of an improved dosage: the claim was for a pack giving the daily dosages of two pharmaceuticals (oral contraceptives) together with instructions about the days on which each should be taken in relation to the female menstrual cycle.[86] The need to convey this specific information was held to justify a claim to the particular

---

[79] *Bristol-Myers Squibb v. Baker Norton* [1999] R.P.C. 253: it is not within the "second medical use" exception to claim a medicament so formulated that it would release the drug taxol over three hours instead of 24, thus reducing its side-effects.

[80] *Unilever's (Davis) Application* [1983] R.P.C. 219; *Duphar/Pigs II* [1988] E.P.O.R. 10.

[81] *Salminen/Pigs III* [1989] E.P.O.R. 125.

[82] *Schering's Application* [1971] R.P.C. 337; *General Hospital* [1995] E.P.O.R. 446; *Baxter* [1998] E.P.O.R. 363. See also *Joos v. Commissioner of Patents* [1973] R.P.C. 59, H.C. (Aust.) (treatment to improve condition of nails and hair). *cf. Wellcome/Pigs I* [1988] E.P.O.R. 1 (treatment of pig mange caused by parasites: unpatentable); *Telectronics/Pacers* [1996] O.J. EPO 274 (method of operating heart pacer by inserting in body and taking measurements during exercise: not patentable).

[83] *Du Pont* [1987] E.P.O.R. 6; see Paterson, paras 7–30—7–42.

[84] *General Hospital* (n. 82, above) (therapeutic as well as contraceptive treatment). *cf. Roussel-Uclaf* [1986] O.J. EPO 295 (skin cleanser patentable although also an acne treatment). A disclaimer of the medical treatment may save a twin-purpose claim: Panchen, Moufang (n. 68, above).

[85] *Bruker/Non-invasive measurement* [1988] O.J. EPO 398.

[86] *Organon's Application* [1970] R.P.C. 574; *Blendax-Werke's Application* [1980] R.P.C. 491; *cf. L'Oréal's Application* [1970] R.P.C. 565, where a reason (putting creases in material) existed for wanting to combine the two chemicals which the applicant claimed in a pack for a different purpose (treating human hair); accordingly the claim was refused.

type of packaging. It can, however, be said that the pack only conveyed information designed to direct the course of human conduct; certainly the Court of Appeal has prevented the proliferation of "pack claims" where the method of display does not help particularly in transmitting the new information.[87]

5-79   To return to less marginal issues: the exception covering methods of medical treatment may be regarded as a last redoubt against the sweep of the patent system into the territory of health care. Previously many countries precluded patenting for chemical substances as a whole, or pharmaceutical substances. The obligation in the TRIPS Agreement to allow such patents is a tribute to the lobbying power of the pharmaceutical industry world-wide.[88]

5-80   Now only the procedures followed by doctors and veterinary surgeons are beyond the range of a patent claim; but in the EPC countries that exception is fixed in the legislation and so is not just a matter of judicial determination.[89] While it may no longer make much sense to exclude the patent system from this one rather limited area of medical and health practice, it is not likely that the EPC will be amended so as to remove the provision. At last, suddenly, there is a considerable lobby against the "patenting of life". This emotive but vague expression certainly covers procedures (including DNA manipulation) directly involving the human body; and for many protesters, the animal body as well. Since the patenting of medical procedures would also generate considerable mistrust among professionals and health administrators, the exception is unlikely to be dislodged. If there were ever to be a change, there would be a strong case for subjecting medical treatment patents to compulsory licensing.

5-81   These current sensivities are acknowledged in the TRIPS text: it requires patents to be available in all fields of technology. But it allows developing countries a ten-year transitional period in which to achieve this for product patents; and it allows the exception under discussion to be maintained in all systems, alongside exclusions "necessary to protect *ordre public* and morality, including to protect human, animal or plant life or health or to avoid serious prejudice to the environment".

(b) *Plant and animal varieties; certain processes for their production*

5-82   The field of "industrial application" includes agriculture and, will under the Biotechnology Directive include products containing biological material and associate processes.[90] In consequence, the scope of such patents are

---

[87] *Ciba-Geigy's (Dürr) Application* [1977] R.P.C. 83; and see *Wellcome Foundation's Application* [1981] F.S.R. 72, HC (Aust.). The importance of "pack claims" in catching infringers has been reduced with the introduction of indirect infringement: see paras 6–17, 6–19, below.

[88] See para. 3–22, above.

[89] *cf.* para. 5–73, n. 68, above.

[90] PA 1977, s. 4(1); EPC, Art. 57; Biotechnology Directive 98/44, Art. 3.

both extended and, as with the "farmers exception," limited.[91] Thus patents continue to be granted for those uses of chemical substances in the production of plants and animals for commercial purposes which were first given patentable status in the 1960s.[92] There is, however, a restricted exception which excludes patents for plant and animal varieties, and essentially biological processes for the production of plants and animals other than micro-biological processes and the products thereof.[93]

Such a tangle of words needs dividing. We shall consider separately its three main concepts—"variety", "macro-biological process" and "micro-biological process"—while bearing in mind that each may have a different impact in relation to plants and to animals. In each case the legal issue starts from the type of claim. A claim to a living thing raises the question, is this a "variety"? A claim to a procedure for making live material raises the question, is this a biological process? If so, does it concern macro- or micro-biology?

(i) **"Variety".** As is discussed elsewhere, in the 1950s and 1960s various **5–83** countries (including Great Britain) introduced a special plant variety right (PVR). At least in Western Europe, PVRs were designed to cover the production of new varieties by standard methods such as cross-pollination, hybridisation and grafting.[94] The regime was open to adaptation for different species, and (for instance in the United Kingdom system) rights were available only where a scheme had been set up for a species. Twenty-eight PVR Schemes were carefully shaped to give exclusive rights in particular varieties and their names.

The notion of a plant variety was not unproblematic, but the system as practised in West Europe involved official testing to determine that an alleged new variety was sufficiently distinctive in its detailed characteristics (shape, height, colour, habit, etc.) and was also homogenous and stable. The characterising of varieties thus became an established procedure. While the rights were limited in scope, at the same time they side-stepped requirements of patent systems, such as inventiveness and adequate disclosure. They were considered by the plant breeding industry to leave no room for patents as an alternative; hence the exclusion in the EPC.[95]

By contrast, no such regime applied to the production of new animal **5–84** breeds and the exclusion of "animal varieties" from patenting seems merely to have reflected traditional expectations. The expression animal varieties is

---

[91] See below, para 6–14.

[92] A leading example was *NRDC's Application* [1961] R.P.C. 134 (use of chemical as weedkiller).

[93] PA 1977, s. 1(3)(b); EPC, Art. 53(b); and see Biotechnology Dir., Art. 4(1), 4(3).

[94] See further, App. 3, below; Greengrass (1989) 20 I.I.C. 622; Byrne, *The Scope of Intellectual Property Protection for Plants and Other Life Forms* (1989); Christie [1989] E.I.P.R. 394; Crespi (1992) 23 I.I.C. 168; Moufang (1992) 23 I.I.C. 328.

[95] The exclusion was originally formulated in the Strasbourg Harmonisation Convention of 1963, Art. 2.

an artificial one in any EPC language; and indeed the term in German may well refer to an entire animal species, but in French and English only to a subspecies.[96] The exclusion was adopted without animal breeders having experience of exclusive rights of any kind. This helps to explain the curious drafting.

The increasingly artificial manipulation of plant and animal forms, from recombination of genetic elements in DNA upwards, has been a striking characteristic of industrial development in the two decades since the EPC was written. The new techniques may yield much larger quantities of a substance, having a purity and uniformity which are very hard to achieve by extraction from nature. These products moreover have uses not only in farming and horticulture but in other forms of food production, medical diagnosis and therapy and indeed in other spheres. In a broad sense, the techniques arouse images and understandings of technology, and that makes it harder to say that it is still a sphere from which patent incentives should be debarred wholesale.

5–85   After a decade of operation, the EPO was called upon to decide the scope of the exclusions of plant and animal varieties, and the other factors in Article 53(b). One principled view is that, despite the reference to varieties, the provision operates to prevent patents for plants or animals in a general sense. A claim relating to all the plants of (say) a genus, can be regarded as a claim to each of the members of the class (and hence to all the varieties)—just as with a claim to a class of chemical substances. This would leave the sphere of plants to the PVR system, and that of animals free of any intellectual property incentive.

At first, in relation to animals, one Examining Division took this line, but then other counsels prevailed based upon the unspecific proposition that any exception to the range of the EPC system should be narrowly construed, the following plant patents were granted:

(1) *Ciba-Geigy/propagating material*[97]: a claim to seed of any kind dressed with a defined chemical in order to make it resistance to certain weedkillers.

(2) *Lubrizol/hybrid plants*[98]: a claim to hybrids produced in accordance with a staged sequence of selection of parent plants (one of which had to be heterozygous) and then of cross-testing, evaluation, and further multiplication.

---

[96] See *Harvard/Oncomouse* (n. 99, below).
[97] [1984] O.J. EPO 112.
[98] [1990] O.J. EPO 59.

(3) *Harvard/Oncomouse*[99]: a claim to a mouse or other non-human mammal genetically manipulated so as to insert an activated oncogene, which could then be used in cancer research was held not to be for an animal variety.

In the first two cases the Board of Appeal confined the exclusion of "plant **5–86** varieties" to claims to individually characterised plants which would have the detailed differences of taxonomy and the reproductive capacity which is required in general for a PVR. In *Oncomouse*, "animal variety" was taken to refer to a particular subspecies and nothing more general.

Since these pragmatic decisions, however, the Board has reverted to the more principled stance. In *Plant Genetic Systems*[1] it has refused to allow claims to all plants which (in lay terms) have been transformed by genetic engineering so as to contain foreign DNA capable of negating the effect of certain weedkillers. Since this includes plants in which the inserted characteristic will be transmitted through generations of plants, these are taken to have the character of a "plant variety" within the UPOV Convention. The Technical Board of Appeal has thereby excluded from the EPO system a considerable range of biogenetic invention upon plants. Presumably the same should apply to patents for the genetic alteration of species of animals, but that is as yet untested. Now, in a second decision refusing a claim to the treatment of plants—*Novartis*—a set of questions have been raised before the Enlarged Board of Appeal, which are intended to resolve the issue at the highest level available in the EPO system.[2]

The Biotechnology Directive seeks to impose the second approach on the patent systems to which it applies, *i.e.* the national systems but not the EPO granting system. It provides that patents shall be available for inventions which concern plants or animals, provided the claims are not technically confined to a single plant or animal variety.[3] If this is interpreted as the drafters intend, then it will leave greater scope for patents obtained through national patent offices than through the EPO. Practical politics lead to a very strange way of resolving this product of the grave tensions in public opinion over biotechnological research.

---

[99] *Harvard/Oncomouse* [1990] O.J. EPO 476; for the disclosure issue, para. 5–98, below. For the acceptance of animal patents in U.S. law, see *ex p. Allen* 2 U.S.P.Q. (2d) 1425 (polypoid oysters). On the questions raised by animal patents, see esp. Bent *et al. Intellectual Property, Rights in Biotechnology Worldwide* (1987) pp. 50 *et seq.*; Curry, *Patentability of Genetically Engineered Plants and Animals* (1987); Lesser (ed.) *Animal Patents* (1989); Moufang (1989) 20 I.I.C. 823; Peace and Christie [1996] E.I.P.R. 213; Kinkeldy (1993) 24 I.I.C. 777; Di Cerbo (1993) 24 I.I.C. 788.

[1] [1995] O.J. EPO 545; criticised by Schrell [1996] E.I.P.R. 242.

[2] [1999] E.P.O.R. 123; see Nott [1999] E.I.P.R. 33.

[3] Art. 4(2) and see Recitals 29–33. Art. 12 provides for compulsory cross-licensing in consequence.

5–87 (ii) **"Macro-biological process".** The exclusion of essentially biological processes (other than micro-biological) for the production of plants and animals is evidently related to the exclusion of varieties. Claims to methods occur alongside those to their products in the examples just considered. However, the exclusion of processes is in terms stated to apply to the production of plants and animals, and not mere varieties of them. This appears to introduce a significant distinction, given the restricted interpretation now imposed upon "variety".

The process exception was drafted in an age before biotechnology. The intended difference was probably between steps which rely upon natural development and those which involve artificial human intervention. Under the 1949 Act, it was, for instance, held that a method of improving the breeding of poinsettias by subjecting them to artificial regimes of light and dark was not patentable. Production of the plants still depended substantially on processes of growth.

However, in its *Lubrizol* decision,[4] the EPO held that intervention in breeding processes, such as the steps there specified of selection, crossing and re-crossing, could be the subject of valid claims to the method of proceeding. There was said to be enough human intervention to count as technical alteration of natural occurrences. This carried it beyond "known biological and classical breeders' processes" and so it was no longer "essentially biological". The difference from ordinary plant breeding was nonetheless only in the complexity of sequence, not in the nature of what was done. The decision must be regarded as controversial, even by those who most sympathise with its determination not to confine the patent system by marginal limitations of uncertain purpose.

On the animal front: in the case of the *Oncomouse*, the process involved was something quite distinct from the ordinary workings of the animal's biological system. The oncogene had to be inserted artificially into a vector, and this was then micro-injected into the recipient animal for incorporation in its genome. Claims to this process, therefore, avoided the prohibition. In addition claims to animals which had been subject to the treatment were held not to be caught by the exclusion of essentially biological processes because they were product-by-process, rather than process, claims.[5] But if that is correct, the prohibition on essentially biological processes would appear to have evaporated, since it could generally be subverted through a product-by-process claim.

5–88 (iii) **Micro-biological process.** Even if claims are made to an essentially biological process for the production of plants or animals, they are

---

[4] See n. 98, above.

[5] The Board of Appeal gave this answer, so as not to have to address a difficult issue: the product-by-process claims covered both the originally injected mice and subsequent generations which inherited the oncogene. It was argued that the latter were produced by the essentially biological process of reproduction. Even so the Board of Appeal indicated an unwillingness to accept this argument on its merits.

patentable if the process is micro-biological. This counter-exception acknowledges that micro-biological production techniques have been so long within the patent fold that, even when used for plant and animal production, they must be treated as patentable. That may have been a rough assumption for three decades, but its meaning is opaque, since there is no scientific line between micro- and macro-biology. This is well-illustrated by the EPO's decision that a genetically manipulated plant variety is not as a whole the product of a microbiological process, where the insertion of DNA (itself microbiological) is followed by breeding up of plants containing the genetic insertion.[6] However, if the *Lubrizol* and *Oncomouse* decisions do find acceptance in contracting states, the distinction will not have to be drawn often, because so little of the exclusion of "essentially biological processes" will remain.

The exclusion of varieties and essentially biological processes in part expresses ethical objections to human intervention in the generation of animals and plants—objections which may equally be raised on the moral and public policy grounds to which we come below. But this exclusion has its basis primarily in the expectations of the traditional industries and professional expertise of plant and animal breeding. Those industries now find themselves participating in biotechnological and similar grand-scale, high-investment strategies, for which innovators and their financiers expect protection against competition and look towards the broad range which the patent system is most likely to provide. The EPO's interpretation of the exclusion, which was to have been entrenched in E.C. national laws by the proposed Biotechnology Directive, goes as far as it can to accept this new development. Even without the Directive, it is quite likely that, in individual states, Courts and offices will prove reluctant to depart from the emergent European line on such matters.

(c) *"Ordre public" and morality*

Finally we reach a provision which was long thought to be of utterly **5–89** marginal relevance but which, in the tide of environmental concerns, has suddenly been washed mid-stream. The 1977 Act excludes the patenting of inventions the publication or exploitation of which would be generally expected to encourage offensive, immoral or anti-social behaviour.[7] The EPC's version refers to inventions, the publication or exploitation of which would be contrary to *"ordre public"* or morality; and adds that mere

---

[6] *Plant Genetic Systems* (n. 1, above). The *Novartis* case (above, n. 2) addresses to the Enlarged Board the question whether this is correct.

[7] PA 1977, s. 1(3)(a). Since the patent system aims to advance the spread of technical information, it is right that this prohibition should in principle go to publication as well as exploitation of the invention. If the unacceptable idea also has defence implications (*e.g.* a new form of germ warfare), the secrecy arrangements of s. 23 may be used to prevent circulation: para. 4–14, above.

prohibition by law or regulation in some or all of the participant states is not enough for the provision to come into play.[8] Both the E.C. and Britain have a variety of regulatory bodies which determine directly whether scientific, technical or medical practice should be prohibited in the interests of ethical, health, safety or environmental concerns, or should be carried out only according to specific standards, or in limited amounts, or under controlled conditions.

Since patents give only the right to prevent the activities of others, and impose no obligations on the patentee in relation to its own activities, the grant or refusal of a patent cannot be any direct substitute for these controls. Many would argue (and in particular those with commercial interests in the relevant technology) that moral and public policy objections should play no part in the question of grant.[9] At least, so it is said, patent office examiners lack any expertise to form the appropriate judgment, so some other body should do so.[10] Moreover, it is pointed out that applications concerning inventions with considerable potential for the relief of human suffering can become embroiled in costly and long-lasting proceedings which reflect bitter, irresoluble conflicts of ideology. These, so the case goes, would be better avoided, leaving the patent system to the technical business of protecting novel inventions.

5–90   Convenient as this outcome would be to those looking to recoup large investments in research and development, it is quite disingenuous to view the patent system as some morally neutral form of state aid in recognition of the cleverness of inventors. Patents provide an effective incentive to the introduction of novel technology within a generally competitive economy: that is why they survive. The state, as granting authority, cannot disclaim responsibility for the inventions for which it grants protection. It cannot hide behind the negative character of the patent right in order to avoid deciding whether a particular idea is inherently too repellant or dangerous to deserve this form of incentive. The power to refuse a patent on grounds of morality or public policy may need to be used cautiously. It is an appropriate step only where all the significant uses of the information are

---

[8] The concept of *ordre public* has proved untranslatable (hence the reformulation in the 1977 Act) but refers broadly to grounds of public interest or policy: *cf.* Beyleveld and Brownsword, *Mice, Morality and Patents* (1993) and *Patenting Human Genes* (1997); Moufang (1994) 25 I.I.C. 407, (1995) 26 I.I.C. 487; Straus (1995) 26 I.I.C. 920. Armitage and Davis, *Patents and Morality in Perspective* 1994); Ford [1997] E.I.P.R. 315; Sherman and Bently in Bently and Maniatis (eds) *Intellectual Property and Ethics* (1998) 109; Varma and Abraham (1997) I.P.L.R. 83.

[9] *e.g.* Nott [1993] E.I.P.R. at 85–86; so also the initial decision in *Oncomouse* (n. 12, below).

[10] So far as the EPC structure is concerned, decisions are open to wide-scale review before and after grant by the EPO. Further flexibility is added by the fact that any designated country can reject the consequent national patent on grounds (possibly religious) which seem sufficient within that territory. Thus, judges may be involved as much as technical examiners, and they form judgments on a great range of moral and social issues within general rules of law.

objectionable, and not only where some are. But the objection is rightly contained in the law and Courts should not interpret it out of existence.[11]

The *Harvard/Oncomouse* proceedings before the EPO brought the issues into sharp focus. The application claimed a mouse or other non-human mammal, genetically manipulated to make it abnormally sensitive to carcinogeic substances and stimuli; its use lay in cancer research. The Board of Appeal required the Examining Division to balance the moral and environmental factors involved by a utilitarian calculus.[12] The Division then held that the patent should be granted.[13] Of the objections to grant,[14] it was acknowledged by the Board that the experimental animals must suffer; on the other hand there was little danger in this case of incalculable environmental damage since the animals could not reproduce their artificial genetic make-up.[15] Of the advantages of the invention, the animals were considered highly useful in a form of experimentation indispensable to medical research. It was the importance of this consideration which justified the patent grant.

The outcome seems an honest attempt at resolving a difficult and sensitive issue.[16] It has been strengthened by the appellate decision in *Plant Genetic Systems*,[17] which rejected an opposition by Greenpeace to a patent for the genetic encoding of crops with a resistance to certain weedkillers. The decision accepted in principle that the protection of the environment fell within the concept of *ordre public*.[18] But the Board of Appeal required that there be sufficient evidence that the environment would be damaged. The suggestions that crops might be transformed into weeds, that the herbicide resistant gene might be spread to other plants or that the ecosystem might be damaged, had here raised only possible hazards.

As to objections on the ground of morality, it was necessary to show that **5–91** publication or exploitation of the invention would be contrary to conventionally accepted standards of culture inherent in European society and civilisation. Survey and opinion evidence among particular groups (here, Swedish farmers) would not necessarily settle the question; nor would the

---

[11] See further, Beyleveld and Brownsword (1993) (n. 8, above).

[12] [1990] O.J. EPO 476; *cf.* Beyleveld and Brownsword (1993) (n. 8, above).

[13] [1992] O.J. EPO 589.

[14] Various objectors filed observations (para. 4–22, above) for consideration during examination. Many of their views are being canvassed again in the opposition proceedings currently before the EPO.

[15] The opposite is already true of some biotechnological advances—and accordingly an issue of concern for the future.

[16] A provision to much the same effect was proposed in the ill-fated Directive on Biotechnological Patents.

[17] *Plant Genetic Systems* [1995] E.P.O.R. 357; a great improvement on the decision below, criticised by Cornish in (1994) 2 Hume Papers on Public Policy, No. 3, 41 at 53–54.

[18] At the same time, the Board stressed the necessity of regulatory bodies with the responsibility of testing the safety and environmental acceptability of new substances and processes; and it made plain that the patent system cannot be regarded as a substitute for such investigative procedures.

fact that some EPC states permitted exploitation of the invention. Certainly, the mere fact that genetic manipulation was used did not render an invention immoral. Traditional selective breeding also brought about genetic alteration and both must be treated as acceptable.

5-92   The most emotive issues, inevitably relate to human tissue and its manipulation. In *Howard Florey/Relaxin*,[19] the EPO allowed a patent for the genetic engineering of DNA from a pregnant woman's body so as to produce human H-2 relaxin. This was opposed on moral grounds of sweeping generality: that the procedure involve the patenting of human life, the abuse of pregnant women, the return of slavery, the sale of women piecemeal to industry, etc. The objections were held insufficient. In particular, DNA was characterised, not as "life" but as a substance carrying genetic information which can be used to produce proteins that are medically useful.

In the hope of drawing a more precise line around the range of the patent system in relation to human and animal life forms, the Biotechnology Directive now prescribes that they shall not be granted for:

(i) processes for cloning humans;
(ii) processes for modifying the germ-line genetic identity (*i.e.* the inheritable gene characteristics) of humans;
(iii) uses of human embryos for industrial or commercial purposes, and
(iv) processes for modifying the genetic identity of animals which are likely to cause them suffering without any substantial medical benefit to man or animal, and also animals resulting from such processes.[20]

These exclusions were long-fought-over, but go very little beyond the current law and widespread public opinion. Whether they will prove to be a serious dampener to valuable biotechnical developments in future, it is impossible to say. The Commission's European Group on Ethics in Science and New Technologies is charged by the Directive to keep these and all ethical aspects of the subjects under review,[21] a process which could lead to future amendments of these and other provisions. We can assume that, before the law is again altered in either direction, there will be the same

---

[19] [1995] E.P.O.R. 541 at 551.

[20] Art. 6, and see Recitals 35–45.

[21] Art. 7, and see Recital 44. Note also the duties of reporting given to the Commission: Art. 16. The European Group may, in particular, have to deal with two well-known ethical difficulties: the position of the person whose biological material is used as the basis for a technical development (as in the case of *Moore v. University of California*, 793 P. 2d 479 (1991)); and claims of indigenous peoples to rights in techniques developed from natural material in their regions, particularly when they were taken up for experimentation because of traditional knowledge of their therapeutic value—rights which are recognised in some degree by the Rio Convention on Bio-Diversity. Both these claims find an echo in the Biotechnology Directive's Recitals (26 and 27) which are not the subject of requirements specified in the Articles.

heated debates which have surrounded the generation of the Directive and the hearing of cases on the subject in the EPO.

5. CLEAR AND COMPLETE DISCLOSURE

(1) General

The specification must disclose the invention clearly enough and completely **5–93** enough for it to be performed by a person skilled in the art.[22] There must be the same "enabling disclosure" as that which justifies a claim to priority and which may amount to an anticipation.[23] It must do so at the date of filing, not when the application is first published.[24] It is this requirement that aims to extract the essential "consideration" for the patent grant— revelation of the invention for the information of the rest of industry and any others interested. When the invention consists of a step forward that then needs only routine development to make it a commercial success, the question of disclosure is usually straightforward. But where a succession of inventions is needed, as in the evolution of most new technologies, the issue is more complex. Obviously it would be wrong to reserve the patent for the person lucky enough to take the last step towards the most successful version of the article or process. Witness to the contrary the long-settled practice of granting patents for "basic" inventions and then for improvements upon them and selections within their range. But if there are to be patents for inventions on the road to ultimate success, they must be kept for steps that are not only non-obvious, but also which work well enough to contribute something useful to what is already known; and this the instructions for performance must reveal. How the law seeks to do this we consider under the next sub-heading.

Beside these considerations arise two associated problems. First, is the **5–94** patentee to be bound by obligations of good faith—bound for instance to reveal the best way of performing his invention at the time of his application? It is by no means clear how far this is a requirement of the present law.[25] Secondly, how much broader may the claims be than the specific examples of the invention that are described, given the special function of claims in the specification? This relationship we shall consider when we turn in the next section to the criteria governing claims.[26]

---

[22] PA 1977, ss. 14(3), 72(1)(c); EPC, Arts 83, 100(b) (ground of opposition).

[23] See above, paras 4–12, 5–18, referring in particular to *Asahi's Applcn.* [1991] R.P.C. 485.

[24] *Biogen v. Medeva* [1997] R.P.C. 1, HL: in that case, the tardiness of the EPO procedure meant that there were seven years between the two dates and common general knowledge had progressed the all-important distance in the interim. At the earlier date the specification was insufficient.

[25] See paras 5–95—5–100, below.

[26] See paras 5–101—5–105, below.

The former law contained a number of specific requirements covering the sorts of issues just mentioned: sufficient and fair description, utility, disclosure of best known method, fair basis for claims.[27] Now, after grant, the only relevant objection, apart from those going to amendment,[28] is absence of complete and clear disclosure. There are indications that this provision is to be read in a broad sense, covering much of the former range of objection within its ambit.[29]

(2) Making the disclosure

5–95 In the case of mechanical contrivances, the patentee normally seeks to fulfil his obligation of disclosure by describing at least one embodiment of his concept, giving details about how it is to be made wherever that is not obvious. He may, of course, resort to such abbreviations as "any suitable material" or "general methods", whenever these will be readily understood by addressees. Likewise in a chemical case he will provide at least one example of the procedures involved in his invention. One embodiment may suffice if it contains a feature present in one or other of all the claims. Where alternatives are claimed, other examples may well be necessary.[30]

In his examples, the patentee will often use specific measures: of size, weight, volume temperature and so forth. But in cases where nothing turns on finite limits, he may confine his description to general relationships between component parts. This is permissible if it will take only simple experiments for someone else to carry out the invention successfully. In the classic case, the invention was a "smokeless ashtray" consisting of a receptacle with a tube at the top and a deflector at the bottom, so placed that butts would give off smoke only into the enclosed space above. This was properly described in terms of interrelationships that would produce the desired result (and claims in equivalent terms were also allowed).[31]

The danger inherent in such descriptions and their attendant claims is that they will merely state desiderata; that they will, in other words, disguise problems still awaiting solution and pre-empt the chances of those who later find the answers. Recently, in the rush to procure wide claims for techniques of biotechnology, the courts have found reason to be suspicious of sanguine generalisations. Thus, both the EPO and the House of Lords have come to insist that it is not necessarily enough to describe in detail

---

[27] See especially PA 1949, s. 32(1)(g)(i).
[28] See paras 4–30 *et seq.*, above.
[29] See para. 5–102, below.
[30] It has never been an absolute requirement of British practice that even one example be provided. In the case, for instance, where the invention consists in discovering a use for a new material that is made from known materials by known methods, an example to illustrate its making may be superfluous. But in the EPO detailed description of at least one way of performing the invention is required, and more examples may be needed in many cases claiming a broad field: EPC Rules, r. 27(1).
[31] *No-Fume v. Pitchford* (1935) 52 R.P.C. 231, CA.

one embodiment of the invention claimed; there must be sufficient information for the skilled addressee in essence to perform everything within a claim without himself having to invent anything.[32]

Whether disclosure is sufficient has always been treated as a question of **5–96** fact.[33] A Court must judge the issue from evidence about how the skilled addressee would have understood the specification at its date of filing.[34] The purpose is not to instruct the uninitiated in the whole art. Those who have been working in a field soon build up a web of assumptions and understandings about how things can be made to work which will not be shared by outsiders. Their common general knowledge does not have to be rehearsed in the specification.[35]

A typical issue about disclosure concerns the failure to specify a limiting condition that is crucial to success. For instance, suppose that a chemical reaction will work only in an iron autoclave, but this the patent fails to require.[36] In such a case, the patentee will seek to argue that the notional addressee would have known to use the right vessel; the objector to the patent will claim that there was no such understanding. He will, moreover, emphasise any passages which appear to suggest that any autoclave will do; for positive suggestions that something can be done which will in fact not work are likely to be fatal.[37] Since patent office examiners and patent agents tend to share a similar level of expertise, they are likely to take much the same view of what can be assumed and what must be spelled out.

It is when the matter goes into Court (and particularly before non- **5–97** specialist judges on appeal) that this sort of issue becomes chancy. Much may depend on the Court's picture of the proper addressee. It was in considering sufficiency of description that the Court of Appeal held a "pioneer" patent in the field of colour television to be addressed to skilled technicians rather than to members of leading research teams. What is more, those technicians could not be expected to make "prolonged study of matters which present some initial difficulty".[38] These are high standards

---

[32] See para. 5–102, below.

[33] *British Dynamite v. Krebs* (1896) 13 R.P.C. 190 at 192, HL.

[34] See para. 5–93, above.

[35] Lloyd L.J., *Mentor v. Hollister* [1993] R.P.C. 7 at 10; *Chiron v. Organon Teknika* [1996] R.P.C. 535, CA.

[36] Example drawn from *Badische Anilin v. Usines de Rhône* (1898) 15 R.P.C. 359, CA, where the patentee did not in fact appreciate the significance of iron to the reaction; even so, the instructions were held insufficient.

[37] Likewise, positive suggestions that a selected sub-group has a particular advantage (subject to *de minimis* exceptions). For the requirement that a selection patent must state as part of its disclosure the special advantage involved, see paras 5–23—5–25, above. However, an erroneous explanation of why an invention works will not be objectionable, unless it is misleading to someone trying to achieve performance: *"Z" Electric v. Marples* (1910) 27 R.P.C. 737, CA.

[38] *Valensi v. British Radio* [1973] 3 R.P.C. 337 at 377, CA. *cf. Genentech's Patent* [1989] R.P.C. 147 at 215 (in an advanced technology the skilled addressee has "a degree of inventiveness"). If technicians with different skills are addressed, it is assumed that they will work together: *"Z" Electric* case (n. 37, above). See generally, paras 4–43, 4–44, 5–93, above.

which pursue a categorical view of the patent system's informational role. In other circumstances, Courts have treated specifications as addressed to leading research teams who are taken to have the most advanced apparatus.[39]

(3) Micro-organism deposit

5–98 A special scheme deals with the disclosure requirement for a micro-biological process or its product, if it involves the use of a micro-organism which is not available to the public and cannot be described so as to enable a skilled person to carry out the invention. The scheme requires the deposit of a sample of the micro-organism with a recognised culture collection.[40]

Most of these depositories operate under the Budapest Treaty of 1977 on the subject.[41] Samples have then to be made available to outsiders from the date of early publication of the application.[42] It is the only case where a competitor, in addition to receiving such information about the state of an application, also becomes entitled to starting material for performing the claimed invention. Since this possibility becomes available before the applicant knows whether or not he will succeed in securing his patent, the procedure is highly controversial. Contrast it with the U.S. approach, where there is no early publication of applications, and release of deposited strains can occur only upon grant.

Until the application is withdrawn, refused or granted, any requester of a sample must undertake not to transfer it to others and only to use it for experimental purposes. In order further to modify the risk to the applicant, the EPO has added an "expert option". Under it the applicant may insist that during the same period, the disclosure be to a nominated expert—that is, a person approved either by the applicant or by the President of the EPO.[43] It is striking testimony to the demand for pharmaceutical and related patents that, in relation to material which might well found a secret production process, many prefer to take the risks inherent in the European type of deposit.

---

[39] *Genentech's Patent* [1989] R.P.C. 147.
[40] PA 1977, s. 125A, PA 1977 Rules, r. 17, App. 2; EPC Rules, rr. 28, 28A; Notices [1981] O.J. EPO 358; [1986] O.J. EPO 269. The deposit must be made by the filing date, but details do not have to be included in the application for 16 months after the priority date; for difficulties which this raises, see Paterson, paras 3–37—3–38.
[41] Treaty on the International Recognition of the Deposit of Micro-organisms for the Purposes of Patent Procedure 1977. For a list of the collections, see Ency. PL, EPC Rules, r. 28. For equivalent rules in the British Patent Office, see PA 1977, s. 125A, Patents Rules 1995, r. 17, Sch. 2.
[42] For excusal by the EPO of temporary failures to make available, see Paterson, paras 3–48—3–52.
[43] The Biotechnology Directive, 98/44, requires all Member State patent systems to adopt an "Expert Option"; Arts 13, 14.

(4) Good faith in disclosing

It is only to be expected that some patentees may try to secure effective **5–99** patent cover and at the same time keep to themselves crucial pieces of information about how the invention works best. How to make a patentee describe his invention sufficiently was a preoccupation of the early case law, and pronouncements that he must act in utmost good faith, that he must be "fair, honest and open" have been repeated often enough.[44] This attitude used to be reflected in the statute law, which required the description to be fair and to disclose the best method known to the patentee.[45] Now all that is called for is that the disclosure be clear and complete.

To prove an objection that the best method had been withheld was never easy. But, given the necessary proof, how would a Court now react? If it found that the disguising had taken the form of deliberately obscure passages in the description, it would doubtless hold the disclosure insufficiently clear or complete.[46]

> In *Hakoune*,[47] a European applicant claimed a step of etching stone by cathode bombardment. It was not known how to do this in the art, and the applicant admitted that it had not described the necessary steps in order to prevent them from being copied from the specification. There was found to be no sufficient description.

But suppose that the description leads to a perfectly acceptable, but not necessarily optimal, version of the invention, and the patentee knew this at the date of the application. The current law allows him to do just this.

Arguably, under conditions of modern research, patentees can no longer **5–100** be expected necessarily to give full instructions for performance. Instead it should be enough if they indicate clearly the problem to which they have found some solution, and upon which they are likely to be pursuing further research; the patent then names the person to whom application can be made for further information and the patentee is left free to keep his extra knowledge for his own "head-start" or to sell it as know-how.[48] This modification has a certain attraction if one thinks in terms of a single technological leader and a circle of dependant exploiters. However, as the disturbing conditions of biotechnology have so forcibly shown, the patent system operates in competitive conditions and exists to heighten them. A system which does not insist upon adequate disclosure (as well as upon demonstration of a technical effect and of an inventive step) risks reward-

---

[44] See, *e.g. Morgan v. Seaward* (1836) 1 W.P.C. 170 at 174; *Vidal Dyes v. Levinstein* (1912) 29 R.P.C. 245 at 269, CA; *Raleigh v. Miller* (1948) 65 R.P.C. 141 at 147, HL.

[45] PA 1949, s. 32(1)(h).

[46] See *Biogen v. Medeva* [1995] R.P.C. 25 at 86–87.

[47] [1986] O.J. EPO 376.

[48] On this see, paras 5–58, 5–59, above, esp. the arguments of Beier and Kitch (para. 5–58, n. 13, above); Brandi-Dohrn (1994) 25 I.I.C. 648; Barton (1995) 26 I.I.C. 105.

ing not those who win the race but those who jump first into the water.[49] Accordingly recent case law has been much concerned with disclosure and in particular—as explored under the next heading—the symbiotic relationship between the information provided about the invention and the claims to which this can properly lend support.

6. REQUIREMENTS FOR CLAIMS

(1) Claims and disclosure

5–101 The claims of the specification, so crucial to the whole patenting process under a "fence-post" regime, must comply with four criteria: they must (1) define the protected matter, (2) be clear and concise, (3) be supported by the description, and (4) be related to one invention.[50]

During the application stage, the examiner must consider all these. Unity of invention has always been a matter which cannot afterwards be brought in question.[51] It is required in the interests of orderly classification and it is something which has simply to be settled one way or other at an early stage. But the other requirements are fundamental. Under the former British law, they could be raised throughout the life of a patent on the discrete ground that the claims were not fairly based on the description. That ground of objection was not contained in the EPC, either in relation to EPO oppositions or subsequent invalidity proceedings in national Courts, and the British Act of 1977 was in the same terms.[52] Accordingly our Courts at first considered, with considerable misgiving, that the proper scope of claims was not a matter that could be raised after grant.[53] However, the House of Lords has now said that the issue can be raised as an objection to the adequacy of the disclosure, because of the requirement that claims be supported by the description.[54] The EPO now adopts the same approach.[55]

5–102 Thus the crucial issue has become what is a sufficient description to justify a given claim—and the answer has to be guided by the modern requirement of an enabling disclosure. Through a series of evolutionary decisions, both the EPO and British Courts have reached the following propositions:

> (1) if there is a single invention in a straightforward sense, then a description of how to perform one instance of it will suffice to

---

[49] *cf.* Beier and Moufang (1994) 43 Revista di Diritto Ind. 340, with Beier (previous note).

[50] PA 1977, s. 14(5); EPC, Art. 84.

[51] See para. 4–15, above.

[52] EPC, Arts 100, 138(1); PA 1977, s. 72(1).

[53] *Genentech v. Wellcome Foundation* [1989] R.P.C. 147.

[54] *Biogen v. Medeva* [1997] R.P.C. 1; Colston [1997] I.P.Q. 521; Cripps [1997] C.L.J. 262; Spence (1997) 113 L.Q.R. 368; Warren [1997] J.B.L. 575; McInerney [1998] E.I.P.R. 14.

[55] *Genentech/t-PA* [1996] E.P.O.R. 275; *Mycogen/Modified plant cells* [1998] E.P.O.R. 114.

support a claim to other instances in which predictably it will work. Thus, where a patent claimed a general principle for enabling plasmids to control the expression of polypeptides in bacteria, and there was no reason to believe that it would not work equally well in any plasmid, bacterium or polypeptide, there was sufficient disclosure[56];

(2) in such a case, it will not be enough to attack such a claim that a few marginal instances cannot be made to work[57];

(3) the contrary will be so, if a substantial proportion of the claimed embodiments do not work or cannot be made to work merely by reliance on common general knowledge and routine trial[58];

(4) in consequence, if a claim covers a number of discrete methods or products, it may be necessary to provide the skilled addressee with sufficient instructions in respect of each of them.[59]

(5) equally, if a general claim is to a product, irrespective of how it is made, the specification reveals only one way of making it and there is evidence that there are other ways, the description will not be regarded as adequate to support the general claim.

The final proposition, still to be distinctly adopted by the EPO, is the major conclusion of *Biogen v. Medeva* in the House of Lords.[60] The crucial claims were to genetically engineered DNA molecules containing an insert needed to produce a crucial protein for a vaccine against the hepatitis B virus. The virus itself consisted of an outer protein envelope (the surface antigen), an inner protein core (the core antigen) and DNA genome within the core. Because of this, DNA molecules had to be constructed with inserts for the surface antigen and the core antigen. The House was satisfied that there was an adequate description of one procedure for achieving this difficult task. Subsequently, it became clear that there were other routes which could be followed.[61] Since the contribution to the art lay in solving the problem of producing the vaccine by recombinant DNA techniques, it was not permissible to claim all ways of doing so.

---

[56] *Genentech I/Polypeptide expression* [1989] E.P.O.R. 1; and see *Quantel v. Spaceward* [1990] R.P.C. 275; Morritt J, *Mölnlycke v. Procter & Gamble* [1994] R.P.C. 49 at 99.

[57] *Genentech v. Wellcome Foundation* [1989] R.P.C. 147; this avoids the former strict notion of inutility, whereby a claim which covered any non-workable instance was bad (as in *Mineral Separations v. Noranda* (1952) R.P.C. 81 at 95, JC).

[58] *Agrevo/Triazole sulphonamides* [1996] E.P.O.R. 171; *Hymo/Water-soluble polymer dispersion* [1997] E.P.O.R. 129; *Evans Medical's Patent* [1998] R.P.C. 517.

[59] *Biogen v. Medeva* [1997] R.P.C. 1; and see generally *Mycogen* [1998] E.P.O.R. 114. In *Biogen* the CA's view of the facts (for which see the next paragraph) provided a pertinent illustration of this proposition: the Court found that the claimed vaccine required the production of both a "surface" antigen and a "core" antigen; and that there were instructions only for making the former and not the latter—hence insufficiency. With this finding the HL disagreed.

[60] [1997] R.P.C. 1.

[61] The House was careful to stress that this distinguished the case from *Genentech I* [1989] E.P.O.R. 1.

5–103　Consider these further illustrations. The invention may lie in proposing a new thing (reflecting cat's eyes as guides to night drivers[62]) or in improving an old thing (better reflectors). The first inventor should be allowed to claim all ways of reaching his "idea", for that is what is inventive; the second should be confined to his particular technique and not permitted to claim all ways of reaching the result.[63]

5–104　Rather similar to the conception of an "idea" is the discovery of a principle. In this case, the discoverer ought to be allowed to patent the practical embodiments of the principle. His new theory supplies a measure for the proper scope of the claim.[64] Contrast with this the empirical discovery, where experiment shows that particular instances give useful results. One success, say with a new chemical compound or micro-organism, will suggest, even to the uninventive, that closely related alternatives may be as good or better. There would thus be little value in a patent confined to the examples worked upon. Yet if the inventor is to be allowed to generalise, it is not easy to suggest any rational basis for settling the scope of his claims. As already noted, it has been held that a claim to a very large class of organic substances is justified, whenever a sound prediction can be made from the experiments on a few members, that all the class will have the beneficial property discovered (in some degree); beyond this a claim will be disallowed as merely speculative.[65] For want of anything better, this has seemed a usable test in a number of patent systems and it has been adopted by the EPO.[66] Because those who carry out further work on different members of the class will be able to have selection patents for the non-obvious successes, the result will frequently be to give the initial inventor a share in subsequent improvements, while his patent remains alive.

5–105　More difficult are the cases where the thing is not so evidently "new" as is a class of previously unmade chemical substances. Consider first, a claim to synthetic rubber, that is to a polymer however synthesised whose chemical structure was already known from the natural product. Where the difficulty was to discover a reaction that would achieve the synthesis and the inventor disclosed one catalyst that would work, the High Court of Australia held a claim to the rubber too broad.[67] It amounted to a claim to all ways of reaching a desired, but previously unattainable result. The patentee was rightly confined to claims involving his reaction.[68]

Consider next, the claim in *Mullard v. Philco*[69] to a radio valve with three auxiliary electrodes, in which that nearest the anode was connected to the

---

[62] For this example, see para. 5–36, above.
[63] See Ency. PL, para. 3–404.
[64] *cf.* para. 5–22, above.
[65] *Olin Mathieson v. Biorex* [1970] R.P.C. 157 at 192–193.
[66] *e.g.* see para. 4–49, above.
[67] *Montecatini v. Eastman Kodak* [1972] R.P.C. 639.
[68] *Firestone's Patent* [1966] F.S.R. 366, was decided the other way; criticised by Blanco White, para. 4–303.
[69] (1936) 53 R.P.C. 323, HL.

cathode. When used in a radio as the final amplifier in a series, this produced an unexpected advantage, and there could be no objection to a claim limited to this deployment. The actual adjustment in the valve involved no technical difficulty, once a reason for making it had been found (in this case the patent was concerned with an "idea" invention. But even so, it was not permissible to have a monopoly good against others who might want to put the valve in this novel form to uses other than that for which the design was being suggested. The House of Lords accordingly held that the claim was too broad.

(2) Ambiguous claims

The requirement that the claims define the invention and that they be clear **5–106** should be read in the same sense as the similar objection under the old law.[70] Their essence is disciplinary; they insist that the draftsman should not use language that is avoidably obscure and ambiguous. While this is supposed to apply whether the obscurity was deliberate, careless or simply the result of lack of skill, a Court is most likely to take offence at attempts unnecessarily "to puzzle a student and frighten men of business into taking out a licence".[71] The advance of science has brought increasing difficulties of definition. The old precision with which chemical formulae could be used to define the structure of substances, for instance, can no longer always be used for macro-molecules of today.[72] Where the difficulty is genuine, a draftsman who does the best the case admits of will not be penalised.[73]

The Courts have not insisted, in the name of precision, that patentees **5–107** adopt strict dimensional and other limits, if to do so would likely offer competitors a simple route around the patent and they will not be seriously embarrassed in trying to decide whether or not they are performing within the claims. Thus, claims limited by result (such as for the "smokeless ash-tray" mentioned in connection with sufficient disclosure)[74] are allowed if only simple experiments with the feature called for by the claim will determine what works. In similar vein, patentees may be permitted to use general words, that are comparative in import, like "large". Thus, in *British Thomson-Houston v. Corona*,[75] a claim to a new type of electric light filament was held valid even though one characteristic required in the relevant claim was that the filament should be "of large diameter". This was read in the light of knowledge about filaments previously in use and was

---

[70] PA 1949, s. 32(1)(i).
[71] See especially Lord Loreburn, *Natural Colour Kinematograph v. Bioschemes* (1915) 32 R.P.C. 256 at 266, 269; *Lubrizol v. Esso Petroleum* [1997] R.P.C. 195 at 206.
[72] For the considerable difficulty that these present, see para. 4–43, above; for a simpler instance, *Nihon Nohyakul* [1998] E.P.O.R. 333.
[73] For the assorted dicta, see Blanco White, para. 4–702.
[74] See para. 5–95, above.
[75] *British Thomson Houston v. Naamloose* (1922) 39 R.P.C. 49.

sufficiently clear to allow an informed worker to know when he was achieving the invention.

5–108   Judges have not been unanimous about how hard to strain in the search for definite meaning in a claim. On the whole, modern Courts have proved readier to find some meaning rather than none, and indeed to prefer meanings that will avoid absurd results.[76] This will not necessarily redound in the patentee's favour: for if he is trying to make his case by having his claims read in an unexpected sense (by virtue perhaps of some passage in the body of the specification) he may find the "plain" meaning preferred.[77] Altogether it has proved more difficult than in the past to sustain an attack based on the ambiguity of claims. There is no reason to suppose that this reflects a rise in standards of draftsmanship; indeed, the current readiness to be accommodating positively invites imprecision. Rather it is that patents are no longer looked upon with that suspicion of monopoly which underlay all the insistence upon accuracy in claiming.

---

[76] See especially, *Henriksen v. Tallon* [1965] R.P.C. 434, HL (claim to ball-point pens with "jumbo" and "capillary" tubes read so as to exclude variants that would not work).

[77] See, *e.g. Mineral Separations v. Noranda* (1952) 69 R.P.C. 81 at 93–94, JC; *Scanraegt v. Pelcombe* [1998] F.S.R. 786 at 797.

CHAPTER 6

SCOPE OF MONOPOLY

1. INFRINGEMENT

(1) Introduction

Two sorts of patent infringer may be regarded as typical: the enterprise **6–01** which through ignorance or stupidity, imitates the patentee's own product and so falls within the core of the monopoly; and the concern which, by independent effort or determination to find a way round the patent, works (if at all) only in the penumbra of the claims. A patent which does not provide substantial protection against the second kind of infringer is generally not worth much. Yet if it is for an invention of real value, its precise scope is likely to be the subject of constant questioning. Hence the importance, in a system of patent law, of how this question of extent is determined.

The British law before the 1977 Act, with its "fence-post" approach to the definition of monopoly, in fact combined scrupulousness over the question of who was infringing with a wide view of the scope of the rights affecting acts that did fall within the claims. The initial scrupulousness was found in the rule that, primarily but not quite exclusively, the monopoly was determined by the scope of the claims; and equally in the rule that a person who only contributed towards infringement could not for that alone be held liable. The subsequent breadth was to be found particularly in the principle that all sales and uses of patented goods required the patentee's licence; so that if he himself sold goods on terms restricting their resale or use, those who knowingly broke the conditions would infringe.

This highly individual blend of severity and generosity has been substantially changed in the European deal. A contributor may now be held responsible for "indirect infringement"; and a doctrine of exhaustion of rights will in future curb the possibilities of limited licensing. Both of these changes we shall discuss in due course.[1] At the same time, somewhat more interstitially, the former British approach to the question of what constitutes "direct infringement" has altered, and this must be the first subject for investigation.

---

[1] See paras 6–15—6–19, below.

(2) The role of the claims

6–02 The "fence-post" approach of the British System to the claims of the specification expresses a preference for certainty, however arbitrary it may sometimes seem, over the inevitably vaguer merits of "fair" protection to the patentee in the light of his disclosure. It is the approach which in principle has been accepted in EPC, Article 69,[2] and accordingly no radical redirection of British practice has been called for. The essential question over the scope of the monopoly remains whether an activity falls within the scope of a claim. This continues to make extent turn upon construction of the claim, in accordance with the rules already mentioned.[3] An article with the attributes called for in the claim remains an infringement, even if further things are added to it and even if those things make it more successful. Likewise it remains an infringement even though further work by the infringer enables him to select the best version of all the alternatives covered by the claim.[4] But a thing will cease to be within a claim if one or more of the essential elements is omitted or substituted by something different—by something which does not fall within the description used in the claim.[5]

Accordingly, the question often in doubt is whether a defendant who is acting in the shadows of meaning on the periphery of a claim still falls within it. In answering this, recent decisions have responded, albeit cautiously, to the injunction not to take too severe an interpretative approach, which is one element in the Protocol to EPC, Article 69.[6]

6–03 Before the 1977 Act, English case law did not in fact insist that a person was free to perform any act which did not fall exactly within the language of a patent claim properly construed. It was always law, as the recent leading cases have emphasised, that while an infringer must take each and every one of the essential integers of a claim, "non-essential" integers may be omitted or replaced by mechanical equivalents.[7] That oddly mixed metaphor—taking the "pith and marrow" of the invention—was to be understood in this sense and not as introducing some broader catch-net.[8]

---

[2] But while the English version says that extent is to be determined by the "terms" of the claims, the other versions use words ("teneur", "Inhalt") which may well convey a looser idea to those likely to use the French or German.

[3] See paras 4–37 et seq., above.

[4] Even if the selector secures his own patent for his selection, this gives him no right to ignore a still subsisting patent for the wider class from which he selects: see paras 5–23—5–25, above.

[5] See, e.g. Birmingham Sound Reproducers v. Collaro [1956] R.P.C. 232 at 245, CA; Van der Lely v. Bamfords [1963] R.P.C. 61, HL; Rodi & Wienenberger v. Showell [1969] R.P.C. 367, HL.

[6] The content of the Protocol is described in para. 4–40, above.

[7] Parker J., Marconi v. British Radio (1911) 28 R.P.C. 181 at 217; and see the cases cited n. 5, above.

[8] The phrase was used by Lord Cairns in Clark v. Adie (1877) 2 App.Cas. 315 at 320; and see Lord Reid, Van der Lely case (n. 5, above) at 75; Lord Upjohn, Rodi case (n. 5, above) at 391.

There was, however, considerable argument over what differences could be ignored as "insubstantial", "immaterial", "non-essential" (the three adjectives appear interchangeable).

In the 1960s the House of Lords decided two cases concerning mecha- **6–04** nisms where invention lay merely in a new combination of known parts. Both ideas were useful, but not major advances of technology. In *Van der Lely v. Bamfords*,[9] the claim in issue was for a mechanical hayrake with given characteristics in which the hindmost set of rakewheels could be moved forward in parallel with the foremost rakewheels, so as to cover wider areas of ground in some operations. The defendant's hay-rake had means for moving its foremost rake-wheels back in line with the rearmost, which produced no different effect; but a majority of the Court refused to consider this infringement: if a claim stated that an integer should have a given characteristic, then this was essential because the patentee had chosen so to describe it.[10] Similarly in *Rodi & Wienenberger v. Showell*[11] an expandable watch-strap was required by the claim to have two layers of links which were connected on each side by "U-shaped" bows. The defendant instead used "C-shaped" bows which extended from one side of the strap to the other, thus amounting to a combination of two U-shaped bows. A bare majority of the House of Lords took the view that there was no infringement in this substitution, inclining to the opinion that some material change in function had been introduced.[12]

However, in *Beecham Group v. Bristol Laboratories*, a claim to a semi-synthetic penicillin was infringed by importation and sale of a chemical substance which did not have the claimed formula but which would nevertheless be converted in the human blood-stream into the claimed substance. The infringing "bio-precursor" was treated as being the claimed substance "temporarily masked".[13] In this case the patented invention was of basic importance, the result of a major research initiative. There was moreover no apparent advantage in using the defendant's bio-precursor form (though in some cases, administration of a drug through a bio-precursor may reduce harmful side-effects).[14]

---

[9] See n. 5, above. The plaintiff was reduced to relying upon this subsidiary claim because the main claims were anticipated (see para. 5–04, above). The first filing was in the Netherlands where less exacting standards prevailed towards claims. The case was an object lesson to those charged with British applications to use greater imagination in thinking through obvious alternatives.

[10] Particularly where the claim was a subsidiary one, relating to something more specific than what had gone before: see Lord Radcliffe, at 78; Romer L. J., *Submarine Signal v. Hughes* (1932) 40 R.P.C. 149 at 175; Buckley L.J., *Catnic v. Hill & Smith* [1979] F.S.R. 619 at 633.

[11] See n. 5, above.

[12] And see n. 17, below.

[13] [1978] R.P.C. 153, esp. at 200, 202.

[14] The discovery of this fact in an appropriate case could give rise to a separate patent: *cf. Beecham Group's Application* [1977] F.S.R. 565.

6–05 If this suggested that some liberalisation over the attitude of the 1960s was beginning, it has been confirmed by subsequent events. In the last leading case under the 1949 Act, *Catnic v. Hill & Smith*,[15] the House of Lords speaking through Lord Diplock, shifted emphasis in the construction of patent claims. True, his speech first insisted that interpretation is the sole issue, and that there is no separate question of "non-textual infringement". Equally he underscored the importance of "purposive", rather than "purely literal" construction. He disapproved of "the kind of meticulous verbal analysis in which lawyers are too often tempted by their training to indulge" and preferred the understanding of "persons with practical knowledge and experience of the kind of work in which the invention was intended to be used". Would they read a particular descriptive word or phrase as making strict compliance an essential element, excluding any variant, even though it could have no material effect upon the way the invention worked?[16]

The case concerned a lintel for placing over doors and windows in the construction of buildings. It was made of reinforced steel plates formed into a box girder with a hollow inside. By replacing solid joists made of concrete and other materials, this invention provided a lighter, more manipulable substitute and was accordingly an immense success. The issue in infringement proceedings came to turn on a single adverb, "vertically". The claim required that one of the pieces of steel extend vertically down one side of the lintel. Following expert advice, the defendant's product varied the angle of the relevant piece, so that it ran either six per cent or eight per cent from the vertical. This produced no known advantage of its own and it was held still to infringe: a builder would treat the side as vertical for his purposes; and the specification was addressed to him, not to a geometer.

6–06 Lord Diplock's approach was applied equally to cases arising under the 1977 Act which involved such variants from a strict interpretation of a claim; and in *Improver v. Remington*,[17] Hoffmann J. restated the issues systematically, as two questions of fact and a third of construction:

> "(1) Does the variant have a material effect upon the way the invention works? If yes, the variant is outside the claim.[18] If no—
> (2) Would this (*i.e.* that the variant had no material effect) have been obvious at the date of publication of the patent to a reader skilled in the art.[19] If no, the variant is outside the claim. If yes—

---

[15] [1982] R.P.C. 183. See also Pendleton [1982] E.I.P.R. 79; Walton [1984] E.I.P.R. 93.

[16] [1982] R.P.C. 183 at 242–243. For dislike of undue meticulousness, see also Lords Reid and Pearce, dissenting in *Rodi* case (n. 5, above) at 378, 388.

[17] [1990] F.S.R. 181 at 189.

[18] For instances where such differences led to a finding of non-infringement, see *Heath v. Unwin* (1800) 2 W.P.C. 296; *Deere v. Harrison McGregor* [1965] R.P.C. 461, HL; *Rodi & Wienenberger v. Showell* (n. 5, above), particularly as regards the second allegation of infringement in that case.

[19] This does not raise any inquiry into whether the variant was itself obvious. The question is whether the absence of any material difference in effect was obvious.

(3) Would the reader skilled in the art nevertheless have understood from the language of the claim that the patentee intended that strict compliance with the primary meaning was an essential requirement of the invention. If yes, the variant is outside the claim."[20]

As in *Catnic*, the *Improver* case turned on the meaning of a single expression. The invention, the "Epilady", was a popular gadget for removing body hair which used an electric motor to spin a coiled spring while it was bent. The spring thus opened and shut rapidly, trapping hairs and pulling them out. The defendant's "Smooth & Silky" substituted for the spring a rubber tube with a series of cuts going through almost from one side to the other—rather as if it were a comb. This was said to avoid the plaintiff's claim, which called for a "helical spring". Reaching his third question, Hoffmann J. agreed, finding that a skilled reader would expect there to be a spring, not some substitute for it which would operate in a similar manner.

This litigation provided a striking test of the meaning to be attached to **6–07** the EPC, Article 69, Protocol, since similar actions on "Epilady" patents, all deriving from a single EPO grant, were brought in several other participant countries. Both in Germany and Holland, the plaintiff went as far as trial and succeeded.[21] In those countries the Courts followed precedents which required the wording of the claims to be taken as the "decisive basis" of protection, rather than to "what the patentee has contemplated". Nonetheless, it is apparent that, approaching the matter from an opposite tradition to the British, there remained scope for the Court to decide that the defendant was employing the patentee's inventive concept through some measure of equivalence to what had actually been claimed.[22] This point is put in some cases in convoluted phraseology,[23] and in others in simple terms.[24] Either way, there seems little room for the linguistic scruple which is the essential point of Hoffmann J.'s third question.

The difference of approach having been highlighted so incontrovertibly, **6–08** the Court of Appeal did in one case indicate that the *Catnic* test should be "left to legal historians" and the matter approached purely by reference to

---

[20] Rubbing in the grammatical niceties of the exercise, for inclusion of a non-literal meaning within claim language, Hoffmann J. would require the use of an expression as synecdoche (part for a whole: "face in the crowd") or metonymy (attribute for a thing: "the Crown").

[21] For the principal "Epilady" decisions, see (1993) 24 I.I.C. 803 at 823.

[22] Note esp. the German decisions, *Formstein* [1991] R.P.C. 24; *Ion Analysis* (1991) 22 I.I.C. 249; and the Dutch decision, *Meyn v. Stork* (1992) 23 I.I.C. 529—first brought to common law attention in the Hong Kong "Epilady" proceedings: [1990] 1 H.K.L.R. 33.

[23] As when the Bundesgerichtshof asks whether "the average person skilled in the art would have been able to discover the embodiment deviating from the wording and literal sense of the patent claim by proceeding from the invention as it is defined in the patent claim": *Handle Cord for Battery* (1991) 22 I.I.C. 104.

[24] As in the blunt insistence in the Netherlands upon broad "interpretation" of the claims: *Improver v. Beska* (1993) 24 I.I.C. 823; *cf.* Brinkhof (1990) 21 I.I.C. 488. There are now signs that this attitude may be moderating in that country.

the Protocol.[25] But, with the aid of the patent judges, it has thought again and reinstated the three "Catnic-Epilady" questions.[26] For the present, British Courts refuse to accept the uncertain quantity of a doctrine of equivalents, choosing thereby to remain distinct from both the jury-centric United States and the juristic Continent.[27]

Perhaps by way of compensation, "purposive construction" has occasionally been broad. In *Kastner v. Rizla*,[28] the Court of Appeal, dealing with a cigarette paper machine, was prepared to treat as infringing a machine which replace five distinct claim features (out of nine) with a single essential function.[29] Nevertheless, where there is an apparent limitation in a claim, given Lord Hoffmann's third question, the Court is unlikely to disregard it, even when the reason for its inclusion is not apparent.[30] One motivation for introducing the limitation may undoubtedly have been the avoidance of prior art during the prosecution of the application. That possibility is one which British courts refuse to investigate.[31] Countries with an equivalence doctrine, by contrast, find themselves obliged to search in the application file for evidence of proposed amendments which are designed to avert a finding of anticipation or obviousness. If it is there, the evidence creates (in American jargon) a "file wrapper estoppel", which operates against a broad interpretation of the claim. The search is often difficult and sometimes inconclusive, so there is sense in avoiding it.

Where there is a numerical limit, it is likely to be taken as meaning what it says, subject to small variations which a skilled person might be expected to encompass. European patents designating the United Kingdom have accordingly to be drafted to meet the scrupulous attention to claim language demanded by British courts in the name of that "certainty for third parties" required by the Protocol. Were the CPC to introduce a unifying patent jurisdiction for the E.C., no doubt equivalence would carry the day and

---

[25] *PLG Research v. Ardon International* [1995] R.P.C. 287; this in face of a long line of cases holding that the *Catnic* test determined the effect of the Protocol under the 1977 Act. The judgment made substantial reference to the German case-law cited above.

[26] This result has followed from Aldous L.J.'s elevation to the Court of Appeal where he has declared *PLG* to be *obiter*: *Kastner v. Rizla* [1995] R.P.C. 585; *Beloit v. Valmet* [1997] R.P.C. 489; *Minnesota Mining v. Plastus Kreativ* [1997] R.P.C. 737; *Auchinloss v. Agricultural and Veterinary Supplies* [1997] R.P.C. 397, CA; *Union Carbide v. B.P. Chemicals* [1999] R.P.C. 409, CA.

[27] In the U.S., despite the role of the jury in some respects, it continues to decide infringement questions with the aid of a now rather restrained doctrine of equivalence: see *Warner-Jenkinson v. Hilton Davis*, 117 S. Ct. 1040 (1997); see MacKernan and Stern [1997] E.I.P.R 375; and for its relevance in Europe: Van Engelen [1998] I.P.Q. 149.

[28] Above, n. 26. Criticised by Oliver [1996] E.I.P.R. 28 and see Cole [1997] E.I.P.R. 617.

[29] For a case in which a "plurality of projections" was interpreted to include a single flap with a relief hole having the same function: *Mabuchi Motors' Patent* [1996] R.P.C. 387; contrast the equivalent German proceedings: *ibid.*, 411.

[30] Thus it is certainly not open to a court to ignore whole features in a claim: *Palmaz's European Patents* [1999] R.P.C. 47 at 77.

[31] Stressed by Hoffmann L.J. in *STEP v. Emson* [1993] R.P.C. 513 at 521, and relied on in several cases since, including *Beloit* (above, n. 26).

courts might more readily come to the rescue of deserving plaintiffs who found themselves foisted with ill-drafted claims. That, however, may be so long coming, that claim drafting practice may have come truly close to the British tradition. It must be remembered what a complex change our European partners have faced in measuring up to the implications of Article 69 and its Protocol. Among other things it has applied to patents which were drafted for less scrupulous regimes and these are only now ceasing to be in force. Opinion could continue to shift towards the precision and certainty which comes with adherence to the claims and their interpretation.

(3) Types of infringing activity[32]

A defendant infringes only if he performs certain kinds of activity, normally **6–09** industrial or commercial. These are now defined in section 60 of the Patents Act 1977, which draws upon CPC, Articles 25 to 28, but does not always say the same thing.[33] The bulk of patents are concerned with things manufactured or processes of manufacture; accordingly the prohibited acts may usefully be considered under three heads: acts performed during manufacture, acts after and acts before. These are rough divisions and have to be related to the type of claim which the patentee has been able to obtain. Bear in mind that in general a claim to a product (a machine, a substance, a compound) is first infringed *directly* at the moment when a product is made which contains all the essential features claimed; while a claim to a process (manufacturing procedure; use of a known substance) is first infringed *directly* when the process is carried out.

In all cases there are three qualifications to observe: **6–10**

(1) **Territoriality:** a British patent is infringed only by acts done in the United Kingdom, its territorial waters and "designated" continental shelf.[34] A patentee who wishes to sue for acts done in (say) France must sue upon a French patent and will normally bring the action in French courts.[35]

(2) **Licence:** nothing done with the patentee's consent is an infringement; the act is then licensed. With one exception, "direct" infringement occurs even where the user of the invention does not know of the invention, believes the use to fall outside the claims or believes

---

[32] See, in particular, Benyamini (1993).

[33] But remember the injunction to conform contained in PA 1977, s. 130(7): see, *e.g. Smith Kline & French v. Harbottle* (n. 58, below).

[34] The U.K. includes the Isle of Man but not the Channel Islands. For the designation of seabeds, important in an age of off-shore extractions, see the Continental Shelf Act 1964; *cf.* generally, Stauder (1976) 7 I.I.C. 470; Benyamini, Chap. 10. There is now developing a need to provide for the patenting of inventions in space, *e.g.* on satellites: see Beier and Stauder, *Space Stations* (1985); Meyer (1988) 70 JPTOS 332.

[35] For jurisdiction under the Brussels and Lugano Conventions to sue for foreign infringements, see paras 2–71 *et seq.*, above.

that there is a sufficient licence.[36] Occasionally the question may arise whether the patentee in effect consents either by standing by in silence or by some positive misstatement to the defendant: delay, acquiescence and estoppel have been discussed already.[37]

(3) **Additional liability at common law:** while the statute now specifies activities which constitute both "direct" and "indirect" infringement, the general law of tort can give additional aid. A patentee may be able to proceed against persons whose auxiliary activities fall beyond the range of the statutory acts: liability as a joint tortfeasor, or tortious liability for conspiracy or for inducement to wrongdoing—conceptions which often overlap—may provide this additional legal armoury.[38] In addition, there is old authority favouring the grant of an injunction against persons, such as warehousers, prohibiting them from handling infringing goods, even though they themselves would not be tortiously liable for doing so.[39]

(a) *Infringement during manufacture*

6–11 Making a patented product and using a patented process head the list of infringing acts.[40] Most of the problems here concern the issue already discussed: is the defendant's activity within the terms of the claims (or some extension beyond them allowed by law)? Suppose that a patented device (a windsurfer, to take a much litigated example) is claimed to comprise an assembly of four distinct elements. Is it "direct" infringement within section 60(1) of the Patents Act 1977 to supply a complete kit of the parts which can be assembled without difficulty by a purchaser? Occasionally courts have so held.[41] If one of the claimed elements is left out, a patentee is thrown back into the more limited realm of an action for preliminary, "indirect" infringement (under section 60(2)) or for a common law tort.[42]

A different borderland is reached over repairs and replacement of parts.[43] A person who obtains a patented product from a legitimate source

---

[36] The exception is the case of offering a process: para. 6–17, below. Indirect infringement also has a knowledge requirement: para. 6–18, below.

[37] See paras 2–63—2–71, above.

[38] See paras 2–12 *et seq.*, above.

[39] *Washburn v. Cunard Steamship* (1889) 6 R.P.C. 398 at 403. For declarations of non-infringement, see para. 2–90, above.

[40] PA 1977, s. 60(1); CPC, Art. 25; Benyamini, Chaps 6, 7.1.

[41] *e.g. Rotocrop International v. Genbourne* [1982] F.S.R. 241 at 257–260; but see the doubts expressed in *Lacroix Duarib v. Kwikform (U.K.)* [1998] F.S.R. 493.

[42] See paras 6–17—6.19, below.

[43] The same considerations apply, if the issue is considered as indirect infringement under PA 1977, s. 60(2). Previously this was regarded as turning on the extent of the patentee's licence to use the invention, which was to be implied from unconditional sale. In future it may be better regarded as a limit upon the scope of the doctrine of exhaustion (see para. 6–15, below); and consider also the doctrine of non-derogation from grant: see para. 14–06, below.

may repair it or have it repaired; but he may not go so far as to make the product anew.[44]

The Act creates exceptions to the range of infringing acts: two of these are general, the rest particular.[45] The general exceptions cover:

(1) **Private use:** acts done privately and for purposes which are not commercial.[46] Note the conjunctive "and": activities of governmental, educational and charitable organisations may not be commercial, but they are not likely to be private.

(2) **Experimental use:** acts done for experimental purposes relating to the subject-matter of the invention.[47] This exception has proved increasingly controversial in connection with patents over successful pharmaceutical products. Many systems traditionally admitted such an exception for the non-commercial activities of the research scientist in a university or government laboratory. Recent development in the EPC countries show that the exception may also apply to commercial research. Nonetheless a distinction has to be drawn between work which seeks to improve or modify the invention and other activities. It is not justifiable to use the invention for experiments on unrelated subject-matter. If for instance, a medium is wanted in order to grow a particular micro-organism, and the medium is patented, then a licence for its use will be necessary.[48] Nor does it cover trials to see whether a person can produce commercially according to the patent.

Three situations on the borderline may be identified:

(i) *Testing by a defendant to procure authority to market a pharmaceutical or agro-chemical product already marketed by the patentee.* Towards the end of a successful patent's life, generic producers will be preparing to enter the market as quickly as possible and securing

---

[44] *Solar Thomson v. Barton* [1977] R.P.C. 537 (design right may present a different problem); *Sirdar Rubber v. Wallington* (1906) 22 R.P.C. 257 at 266, (1907) 24 R.P.C. 539 at 543. A person who supplies replacement parts for an *infringing* article may well be an indirect infringer: see para. 6–18, below. A person who merely carries such repairs out, although he helps to prolong the article's life, is less likely to be caught (but does he "keep" the invention—s. 60(1)(a))? *cf. Aro Mfg. v. Convertible Top* 377 U.S. 476 (1964).

[45] Amongst the particular exceptions, the one relating to manufacture covers "extemporaneous" preparations by pharmacists from prescriptions: s.60(5)(c), *cf.* CPC, Art. 27(c). See generally, Benyamini, Chap. 11.

[46] PA 1977, s. 60(5)(a); CPC, Art. 27(a). This includes an experiment for legal proceedings: *Smith Kline v. Evans* [1989] R.P.C. 513. It must be permissible to test a specification for the adequacy of its instructions.

[47] PA 1977, s. 60(5)(b); CPC, Art. 27(b). See in particular, Gilat, *Experimental Use and Patents* (1995); Eisenberg (1989) 56 U. Chi. L.R. 1017; Grossman (1990) 30 Idea 243; Cornish (1998) 29 I.I.C. 735.

[48] For another example, see *Smith Kline* case (n. 58, below).

regulatory authority in these fields is a requirement which patentees have no wish to see speeded up. In Europe it is almost universally accepted that the experimental use defence does not permit such testing to take place in advance of expiry.[49]

(ii) *Testing by a defendant in the wake of its independent discovery of beneficial properties of a substance which falls within the plaintiff's patent but which differs from the product which the plaintiff markets.* In this case, experiments genuinely to discover further information about the properties of the defendant's substance will be permissible, whereas tests to provide further evidence of already known qualities will not. In *Monsanto v. Stauffe*,[50] the Court of Appeal allowed a defendant in such a situation to continue its in-house experiments, but disallowed external field tests because they sought only to reaffirm what was known. They had the twin purposes of satisfying regulatory authorities and demonstrating advantages to customers.

(iii) *Testing for new uses and further information about properties of a patented product including conduct of clinical trials with patients.* This situation has yet to be considered in the United Kingdom. In Germany two leading judgments have held that such trials fall within the exception, provided either that they have, as one real motivation, a search for further medical applications or for more information about the effects and the tolerability of a drug which incorporates the patented substance.[51] The decisions are firmly based upon the public interest in ensuring that the patent system does not act as a block on genuine research developments—the cases arose because patentees were not prepared to grant licences for the work.[52] As precedents they are likely to be persuasive throughout Europe.[53]

Particularly in the realm of biotechnology, basic research and practical applications of it are not easily distinguishable. Experimentation to further general understanding must continue in this rapidly advancing science. The importance of keeping this process to some degree free of patent constraints is expressed by the experimental use exception. It is hard to judge whether it now sets a satisfactory dividing line. Gilat suggests as a touchstone that the exception should only operate in those cases where licences of the existing

---

[49] See esp. *Ethofumesate* (1991) 22 I.I.C. 541, BGH; *Auchinloss v. Agricultural and Veterinary Supplies* [1999] R.P.C. 397, CA; *Generics v. Smith Kline & French* [1997] R.P.C. 801, *per* Jacobs A.-G., ECJ. In the U.S., the Hatch-Watchman Act has reversed this approach, to the fury of major pharmaceutical producers. See also the *Clinical Trials III* decision of the Japanese S.C., April 16, 1999.

[50] [1985] R.P.C. 515; and see [1984] F.S.R. 559, [1987] F.S.R. 57.

[51] *Klinische Versuche I (Interferon-gamma)* [1997] R.P.C. 623, BGH; *Klinische Versuche II (Erythropoetin)* [1998] R.P.C. 423, BGH.

[52] Indeed, in the second case, the defendant had (quite exceptionally) procured a German compulsory licence to market the drug.

[53] See below, para. 6–12 for the curious effect of PA 1977, s. 60(6), on "indirect" infringers.

patent are unlikely to be given—as where a patentee is seeking to monopolise further experimentation. That at the very least should fall within the exception.

(b) *Infringement after manufacture: general provisions*

The list of infringing acts also covers: disposing of, offering to dispose of, **6–12** using, importing, and even keeping for disposal or otherwise, either the patented product or a product "obtained directly by means of a patented process".[54] The range of defendants made possible by this extensive list is considerable. Where infringing goods pass down a chain of distributors each person becomes liable: as a "keeper", then as a "disposer". Even the ultimate recipient may be a "keeper", if he is not a "user".[55] A person who acquires or imports goods for the purpose of exporting them to sell abroad will thus infringe, as he did under the previous law.[56] Both sides to a simple hiring agreement will in turn be "keepers".[57] But a mere carrier has not been treated as a keeper.[58] However, a person who negotiates with a view to selling an article after expiry of a patent covering it "offers to dispose" of it.[59]

Again, in addition to the licensing by the patentee of "acts", there are exceptions. For instance, the exclusion from infringement of private, non-commercial acts and experimental acts[60] apply in this post-manufacture phase, but only to protect those who perform the specified acts. The exceptions do not give cover for subsequent "acts" that would otherwise infringe: if infringing apparatus is sold once in a purely private sale, this does not justify its resale in a business deal.[61]

Where the chain of distribution originates abroad, a person who com- **6–13** pletes a sale by transferring property in the products in another country does not infringe (because of the restriction to acts done in the United

---

[54] PA 1977, s. 60(1); note that there are a number of trying variations here from the language of CPC, Art. 25: for instance, the former uses "disposes of", etc. in place of "puts on the market"; and see the following footnotes. When Community patents are eventually introduced, their precise scope may differ somewhat from U.K. patents.

[55] In contrast with (1) the previous law (see, *e.g. British United Shoe Manufacturers v. Collier* (1910) 27 R.P.C. 567); and (2) CPC, Art. 25—to which the old authorities on "use" seem relevant (see Ency. PL, para. 3–216.)

[56] Here the different language of PA 1977, s. 60 and CPC, Art. 25, seems to lead to the same result. And see *Hoffmann-La Roche v. Harris* [1977] F.S.R. 200; *British Motor v. Taylor* (1900) 17 R.P.C. 723.

[57] Under the CPC, hiring out is covered, if at all, by "putting on the market". This phrase is also used in the CPC's definition of exhaustion of rights: see Arts 28, 76. It is a common assumption that if something is hired out a patentee can continue to control its use: but that may be open to question, once this version of exhaustion takes effect. See paras 6–15, 6–16, below.

[58] *Smith, Kline & French v. Harbottle* [1980] R.P.C. 363; *McDonald v. Graham* [1994] R.P.C. 409, CA

[59] *Gerber Garment v. Lectra* [1995] R.P.C. 383.

[60] S. 60(6). See para. 6–11, above.

[61] For special exceptions covering uses connected with land, sea and air craft, see PA 1977, s. 60(5) (d)–(f); CPC, Art. 27 (d)–(f); Ency. PL, para. 4–310.

Kingdom),[62] but the subsequent importer will. Even if the foreign exporter at some stage writes to the British purchaser about an order, he will not thereby be offering to dispose.[63] However, if he positively solicits orders from British customers, he is likely to be infringing on this ground, or as joint tortfeasor or as one who procures infringement.[64]

6-14   It is in such cases that infringement of a process patent by dealing in its *direct* product becomes specially important.[65] The commercial value of a process patent can obviously be impaired if the process can be carried out abroad (where there may be no patent) and the product sold in competition in Britain.[66] In the pre-1977 law, English courts had gone some distance in holding a claim to a process to be infringed by the importation of the subsequent product, requiring not that the product be the immediate result of the process (for there might be intermediate steps in which the first product changed its composition or other attributes)[67] but only that the contribution of the process to the final product be important (the "Saccharin" doctrine).[68]

Under the EPC and the 1977 Act, however, the connection between process and product must be "direct." *Pioneer Electronics v. Warner Music*[69] holds that this precludes infringement where there are intervening steps which deprive the first product of its essential characteristics. So in the production of compact discs, a process for producing the so-called "father" disc at a particular pressure was not infringed by importing the final discs; in between there had to be conversion into "mothers", then to "sons" and then, by injection moulding, into discs.

This limited interpretation has implications both for the production of pharmaceuticals by standard techniques and through genetic manip-

---

[62] See para. 6–10, above.

[63] *Kalman v. P.C.L. Packaging* [1982] F.S.R. 406; *Badische Anilin v. Johnson* (1897) 14 R.P.C. 919. Not all West European countries take so restrictive a view; the issue may have to be reconsidered: see Benyamini, pp. 251–257.

[64] See paras 2–07, 2–13, above.

[65] Note that the EPO will grant "product-by-process" claims only where the product is itself novel: *BICC/Radiation processing* [1986] O.J. EPO 261. This does not, however, apply to a process which improves a thing (*e.g.* tenderising meat): *Mobil Oil Friction reducing additive* [1990] O.J. EPO 93; Paterson, paras 9–58, 9–59.

[66] It is possible, of course, to take the strict view of the Banks Committee (Cmnd. 4407, 1970), para. 297, that if a patentee wants appropriate cover he must secure a product-by-process claim; which is all very well if he knows all the relevant products when he applies for his patent. This approach has not been adopted in the 1977 Act.

[67] *Saccharin Corp. v. Anglo-Continental Chemical* (1900) 17 R.P.C. 307.

[68] Tomlin J., *Wilderman v. Berk* (1925) 42 R.P.C. 79 at 86; *Beecham Group v. Bristol Laboratories* [1978] R.P.C. 153 at 201, 203, 204.

[69] [1997] R.P.C. 757, CA; Hurdle [1997] E.I.P.R. 322. The wording derives from Germany, and British courts have paid attention to one view from that country: Bruchhausen [1979] GRUR 743 (who is critical of more liberal German authority); and see *Pfizer* (CA Hague, June 10, 1983) (The Adv.-Gen. in the latter, however, gives examples close to those of Tomlin J. (n. 68, above)). *cf.* Van Benthem in Pennington (ed.) *European Patents at the Crossroads* (1976) pp. 125–126; Benyamini, Chap. 8.

ulation.[70] The Biotechnology Directive seeks to expand the scope of protection given to product claims in that one field so as to cover material derived by propagation or multiplication[71]. What effect this will have is hard to predict. So too with the provision concerning patents on products containing genetic information, which extends to all material in which the products are incorporated, save (it seems) the human body,[72] Thanks to the long disputed "farmer's exception", these provisions do not apply to his own use of seed or breeding of animals.[73]

(c) *After manufacture: exhaustion of rights*[74]

Patents used to be the field of intellectual property where in British law no **6–15** notion of exhaustion of rights applied. As noted already, even when the patentee made or authorised a sale of patented goods, restrictions on their further sale or use could still be imposed as part of the patent right: these would bind not only another contracting party but all recipients of the goods with notice of the restrictions.[75] It is, however, necessary to show not only that the first recipient, but all those who precede a defendant, had the requisite knowledge, otherwise the necessary chain is broken.[76] This may create a considerable obstacle for the patentee.

Where the British patentee himself markets patented goods abroad he will be able to prevent their import into Britain only if he attached a clear and express embargo.[77] Where, however, the sale abroad is by a licensee under the foreign patent, the goods cannot enter Britain unless there is a licence (express or implied) from the British patentee.[78]

---

[70] For the importance of the issue in biotechnology, see Byrne (1985) 16 I.I.C. 1; Beier and Straus (1986) 25 Ind. Prop. 447 at 456; Christie (1989) E.I.P.R. 394 at 402.

[71] 98/44, Art. 8 and note the movement exception in Art. 10. There will be no problem where a claim has been allowed to the derivative product. Although the EPC will not itself be altered by the Directive, the EPO will doubtless take account of its change in deciding what claims are justifiable.

[72] Arts. 9, 10.

[73] Art. 11.

[74] On this important and difficult subject in relation to patents, see esp. Demaret, *Patents, Territorial Restrictions and EEC Law* (1978); Benyamini, Chap. 12; Rothnie, Chap. 3. Compare the position in respect of copyright: below, para. 12–15.

[75] *A fortiori*, where the claim is to an intermediate "indirect" product, as distinct from an intermediate process. Even in the *Beecham* case, the House of Lords were doubtful about the former: (n. 61, above) at 200–204. Any subsequent taker who knows that conditions exist will be bound: *Dunlop v. Longlife* [1958] R.P.C. 473; and see *Goodyear v. Lancashire Batteries* (1958) L.R. 1 R.P. 22 at 35, CA.

[76] *Roussel-Uclaf v. Hockley International* [1996] R.P.C. 4431; but *cf. Gillette Industries v. Bernstein* [1942] Ch. 45, CA; Wilkinson [1997] E.I.P.R. 319.

[77] *Betts v. Willmott* (1871) L.R. 6 Ch. 239; *Smith Kline v. Salim* [1989] F.S.R. 407, H.C. (Malaysia); attacked as illogical by Walton and Laddie, *Patent Laws of Europe and the UK*, paras 948–950; *cf.* Laddie *et al.* paras 18.19ff.

[78] *Beecham v. International Products* [1968] R.P.C. 129; *Minnesota Mining v. Geerpres* [1973] F.S.R. 113. These cases rely heavily on *S.A. des Glaces v. Tilghmann* (1883) 25 Ch.D. 1, CA, even though it is concerned with direct exportation to the U.K. by a foreign licensee. Its strong emphasis on territoriality seems essentially at odds with *Betts v. Willmott*: Rothnie, *Parallel Imports* (1994) 125–142.

6–16   This principle, which began to be modified by legislation such as the Resale Prices Act 1964, is now in the process of virtual annihilation. Two stages are involved:

(1) **Limitation by the Treaty of Rome.** Until the CPC takes effect, the former British principle continues in operation. But as well as the qualifications upon it in British legislation, it has been affected since 1973 by the twin doctrines of the Treaty of Rome: the free movement of goods and the rules of competition. Thus in 1972 it was held that where patented drugs were sold on condition that they were not to be exported from the United Kingdom, a sub-purchaser who knew of the restriction could be enjoined from infringing by exporting.[79] So far as such a condition applied to exporting to other Common Market countries, it would now be bad; the same would be true of a condition that the goods could be exported only to part of the Common Market.[80] Each of these constraints inhibits the free movement of goods within the Community.[81] But the old British principle upholds restrictions preventing exports to non-E.C. countries; likewise with a condition attached to a sale in a non-E.C. country that goods are not to be imported into the United Kingdom. To these the free movement of goods policy has no application[82] and the question is whether any aspect of the Community's competition rules is offended.

(2) **Operation of the CPC.** If and when the CPC is put into effect, it will introduce a specific doctrine of exhaustion affecting both Community and national patents within the E.C.[83] This provides that once patented goods have been put on the market in any part of the E.C. by the patentee or with his express consent,[84] the rights conferred by the patent or other national patents within the E.C. can no longer extend to them, unless Community law admits some special exception. If the ownership of national patents for the same invention has been divided up among patentees economically associated, so that a different legal person must license the initial sale in the different countries, the rights will still be treated as exhausted.[85]

Because these principles of Community law, current and anticipated, directly affect the scope of patent infringement they are mentioned here in

---

[79] *Sterling Drug v. Beck* [1973] R.P.C. 915.
[80] For the evolution of the whole doctrine, see Chap. 18, below.
[81] Accordingly they would constitute a measure equivalent to a quantitative restriction on imports (Treaty of Rome, Art. 30) which, as a "mere exercise" of industrial property rights operating as a disguised restriction upon intra-Community trade, could not be absolved by Art. 36: see para. 1–51, above, paras 18–04 *et seq.*, below.
[82] See *EMI v. CBS*, para. 1–56, above.
[83] CPC, Arts 28, 76; with specific exception for the case where the goods are first marketed by a compulsory licensee (including in Britain someone within the Crown use exemption): Arts 45(1), 76(3). PA 1977, s. 60(4) makes this the rule that will govern U.K. patents.
[84] For the significance of "express" consent, see para. 18–07, below.
[85] Art. 76(2); see further, paras 18–02 *et seq.*, below.

brief. But they need to be seen in broader context. This has been introduced in general already and its impact on patent deployment and licensing is dealt with in the next chapter.

We should note that the scope of "exhausted" rights is not free from doubt. Suppose X has a patent claiming (1) chemical Y and (2) the use of Y in process Z. If X or a licensee sells Y, X ought arguably to be able to control the use of Y in process Z: but, if the two claims are in the same patent, a literal reading of the exhaustion rule suggests that he cannot.[86]

(d) *Before manufacture: "indirect" and other infringement*[87]

The former law showed great reluctance to treat as a "contributory **6–17** infringer" someone who assisted in preparations for acts within the claims, but did not himself perform the acts. Only if the "assister" ordered the full performance,[88] or participated in a conspiracy or common design to secure performance,[89] or knowingly induced another person to perform,[90] would any liability in tort be imposed. In other cases, the Courts' caution obliged the patentee to proceed against the actual performer.[91] For one thing he might well deny infringement, claim that the patent was invalid, or claim a licence or Crown authority. The approach had some attraction, particularly where the patentee was attacking a small "assister" who supplied to a larger "performer".[92] But in the contrary case of a large "assister" supplying materials towards infringement by small "performers", the patentee could be placed in considerable difficulty.

Following other patent systems and the CPC, the 1977 Act has introduced general principles of contributory infringement.[93] As one special case of "direct" infringement, it is impermissible to offer a process for use, knowing that the user will have no licence from the patentee and that the use will be an infringement.[94] In strictly territorial vein, both offer and use must be in the

---

[86] Perhaps "Community law" would admit an exception for this case: see Arts 28, 76. It ought to do so, unless the arrangement is part of some larger anti-competitive agreement.

[87] Benyamini, Chaps 7.2, 9.

[88] *Sykes v. Howarth* (1879) 12 Ch.D. 826.

[89] *Morton-Norwich v. Intercen* [1976] F.S.R. 513.

[90] *Innes v. Short* (1898) 15 R.P.C. 449; *Belegging v. Witten* [1979] F.S.R. 59 at 66–67, CA; and see generally paras 2–12 *et seq.*, above.

[91] *Dunlop v. Moseley* (1904) 21 R.P.C. 274, CA.

[92] A good illustration is provided by *Slater Steel v. Payer* (1968) 55 C.P.R. 61, Ex. Ct. (Canada).

[93] The expression, "indirect infringement", is used in the CPC, Art. 26.

[94] A paraphrase of PA 1977, s. 60(1)(b); *cf.* CPC, Art. 25(b). Neither is happily drafted. The offeror must know (objectively) that use of the patent without the proprietor's consent would be infringement. This may excuse the offeror (1) who could not have known of the patent; or (2) who could not have known that the process would be used in an infringing way; or (3) who could not have known that the user did not have the licensee's consent or other authority. The last does not easily fit the language used, but would probably be read in; *cf.* s. 60(2), para. 6–18, below. It is not within this provision to direct use in a non-infringing way when it would not be obvious to use the process in an infringing way: *Fürr v. C.J. Truline* [1985] F.S.R. 553; see also *Kalman v. PCL Packaging* [1982] F.S.R. 406.

United Kingdom; and the offeror's knowledge is judged objectively, taking account of what is "obvious to a reasonable person in the circumstances".

6–18 It has also become "indirect" infringement to supply (or to offer to supply) "means relating to an essential element of the invention, for putting the invention into effect" to someone not licensed or authorised to work it, knowing that the "means" are suitable for putting, and are intended to put, it into effect.[95] Again the supplier is treated as knowing what is obvious to a reasonable person in the circumstances.[96] Clearly, this type of infringement may arise in cases where the "means" have non-infringing as well as infringing uses. If, accordingly, they constitute a staple commercial product, there is no infringement unless the supply is for the purpose of inducing the person supplied to infringe directly.[97]

For there to be indirect infringement, both the place of supply and the place where it is intended to carry out the invention must be in the United Kingdom. This excludes the foreign supplier of materials or parts which are brought into Britain by the "direct" infringer; and also the British manufacturer who makes up kits of the parts needed for completing manufacture or operating a process abroad.[98] Arguably, in the latter case, a doctrine of indirect infringement ought to cover such an obvious way of assisting towards infringement that is so essentially connected with production in the United Kingdom.[99] But to treat it as a common law tort, such as conspiracy or inducement,[1] would be to subvert an apparent limitation in section 60(2) of the 1977 Act and Article 30(1) of the CPC.

6–19 The former British approach made it important to secure claims, where possible, to parts of mechanical combinations, to intermediates in chemical production, and to the substances that would be applied in methods and processes. There are marks of this upon the inherited law of novelty, obviousness and patentable subject-matter.[2] Under the new law focus shifts

---

[95] PA 1977, s. 60(2), CPC, Art. 26(1). Not every person supplied has to use the thing in an infringing way: *Chapman v. McAnulty* (1996, unreported). One person does not escape being an "indirect" infringer by supplying essential means to another who acts within the exceptions for private use, experiment or pharmaceutical preparation: PA 1977, s. 60(6)—a most surprising limitation: Benyamini, pp. 182–185. The provision presumably does not apply to a person who collaborates in the direct infringement, for instance, by helping to set up clinical trials.

[96] Presumably the reasonable person (who is mentioned specifically only in the PA 1977 text) is someone in the supplier's position: see Ency. PL, para. 4–204.

[97] PA 1977, s. 60(3); CPC, Art. 26(2). Where the enterprise supplied knows, or must be taken to know, the patent position and makes its decision to act as it does independently of anything that the supplier does (as, *e.g.* in the *Slater* case (n. 92, above)), there would be neither inducement nor conspiracy.

[98] These limitations do not apply if what is done constitutes direct infringement: for the kit-of-parts question, see para. 6–11, above.

[99] *cf.* Stauder (1972) 4 I.I.C. 491; Kerr (1974) 26 Stanford L.R. 893.

[1] See paras 2–13, 2–14, above.

[2] For instance in the importance attaching to article claims, as distinct from method-of-use claims (paras 4–46 *et seq.*, above), and in the attempts to secure "pack" claims (para. 5–78, above).

to the question, have the conditions for "indirect" infringement been fulfilled? Whether material or apparatus is a "staple commercial product" is likely to depend on whether there exists at least one alternative way in which the product as sold could ordinarily be used. Far-fetched or purely experimental alternatives will doubtless be discounted.[3] On the question of whether a supplier ought to have known that "means" would be put to an infringing use, consider the case where a client orders a particular part to be made up from his specifications. The maker may well not be in a position to know how the part will be used. It is presumably his (objective) state of mind that is relevant, not that of his client.[4]

Indirect infringement (together with additional tortious liability) strengthens the patentee's position by giving rights against those who are essentially involved, in a preliminary way, in bringing about complete infringement within the claims. These forms of liability delimit the extent to which a patentee can legitimately require a licence to be taken by those who supply things which are not in themselves infringing. Beyond their bounds, a licensor is in the territory of restrictive "tie-ins" and may face the strictures of E.C. Competition Law.[5]

(e) *New medical and other applications of known substances*

A substance may be claimed for its first known medical use and a **6–20** composition including it may be claimed for subsequently discovered medical uses.[6] Moreover the EPO has decided to make claims in such form available to non-medical subject-matter.[7] If the claim covers the substance or composition "for" its medical use then only those who administer it or who make or market it for its medical purpose would infringe. If a claim has been allowed to the substance *puro*, proof of the earlier knowledge ought either, for once,[8] to cut down the claim's scope so as to confine it to use in or towards the medical purpose, or amendment by the addition of a "for" phrase ought to be required. If claims are in this instance to be read as limited by the discovered use, why not in other cases? Should claims to entirely new things also be read as limited by the useful application described for them in the specification? This would be one solution to the nagging problem posed by *Mullard v. Philco.*[9]

---

[3] U.S. patent law contains a similar distinction (Patents Act, s. 271(c)) and much case law to this effect: see Chisum, *Patents* (1978) IV, para. 17.03[3]. Thus if the alternative use calls for sale in much larger quantities than the defendant is putting on the market, his commodity will not be treated as staple: *Johnson v. Gore* 195 U.S.P.Q. 487 (1977).

[4] PA 1977, s. 60(2) leaves the matter uncertain; *cf.* n. 85, above.

[5] For which see para. 7–37, below.

[6] See para. 5–105, above.

[7] For this still contentious development, see para. 5–26, above; Vossius [1998] Bio-Sc.L.R. 19.

[8] Whether suppliers would be direct or indirect infringers is unclear, and could be important: for if "indirect" and the product is a "staple", the limitations in PA 1977, s. 60(3) will apply.

[9] It has never been suggested in English courts that the doctrine of equivalents could be used to cut down the apparent scope of claims: *cf. Graver v. Linde*, 339 U.S. 605 at 608–609 (1950).

(4) Prior use and commencement of infringement[10]

6–21 If a person uses an invention in a way that makes it public before the priority date of a patent for it, his anticipation will render the patent invalid.[11] As well as this, he has a defence against infringement, should he continue to use the invention after the patentee's rights take effect.[12] This defence is also open to people who have not provided material for attacking the patent's validity—prior users whose activities have not made the invention available to the public,[13] and those who have in good faith made effective and serious preparations to use the invention (or to do some other act in the list of infringements).[14] The preparations must be so far advanced that the infringing acts are about to be done.[15] The defence, however, is limited: the act done or prepared for before the priority date may be continued[16] or done afterwards by the person concerned, a partner of his or an assignee of the relevant business,[17] but not by a "licensee".[18] While the person concerned may not expand into other products, he is not confined to making things which are absolutely identical or to following a process to the letter. He can go on doing what in substance he was doing before.[19]

6–22 The earliest point in time at which infringement can occur is the date of publishing the application—normally some 18 months from the priority date. But proceedings for the period between then and the grant can only be brought after grant; and the defendant's act must infringe not only the claims finally included but those in the published application.[20] There is the difficulty, however, that the claims of the early publication may be clearly objectionable. A potential infringer may have no idea whether the application will ever pass examination so as to leave claims that he will infringe. If it would not have been reasonable to expect this outcome, the Court or Comptroller is given a discretion to reduce damages.[21]

---

[10] Monotti [1997] E.I.P.R. 351.

[11] See above, para. 5–19.

[12] PA 1977, s. 64 as substituted by CPDA 1988, Scheds 5, 17; the CPC, Art. 38, follows whatever national law allows for national patents: see Østerborg (1981) 12 I.I.C. 447.

[13] Formerly, if their use was "secret", in certain circumstances this formed a ground for attacking validity. Now the principle is that an anticipation must be published rather than merely used: see paras 5–06—5–08, above.

[14] Previously such people went unprotected.

[15] *Lubrizol v. Esso Petroleum* [1998] R.P.C. 727 at 770, CA.

[16] Although the wording is not completely clear, this must include the ability to continue repeating a production process.

[17] *ibid.*, s. 64(2). Articles thus produced may be dealt with as if disposed of by the patentee: s. 64(3).

[18] *i.e.* anyone to whom the prior user attempts to transfer or license his freedom to continue doing the act, without assigning the business.

[19] *Lubrizol* (above, n. 13) at 770. He does not have a general licence to alter a process from what he was doing before.

[20] PA 1977, s. 69(1), (2); Benyamini, Chap. 11.

[21] PA 1977, s. 69(3). This is somewhat more precise than the alternative allowed by EPC, Art. 67(2) under which compensation reasonable in the circumstances may be provided for in national legislation.

In the period between priority date and publication of a patent application, it is possible for another person to start his preparations and production of something in the claims. Not only will his production after publication be actionable; equally articles which he has made before this date will infringe if sold, used or kept by himself or another person after the date. In these circumstances, a seller will then be in breach of his contractual warranty either that he has the right to sell or that his buyer will enjoy quiet possession.[22] These rules constitute a fortuitous hazard, which scarcely seems necessary, to the patent system.

(5) Proceedings concerning the infringement and validity of patents[23]

Proceedings for infringement, revocation and such associated matters as **6-23** relief from threats to sue for infringement and declarations of non-infringement,[24] are brought either in the Patents Court,[25] the Patents County Court,[26] or, in certain cases, before the Comptroller (with appeal first to the Patents Court).[27] The Comptroller's jurisdiction in revocation proceedings is now co-terminous with that of the Patents Courts.[28] This marks a considerable extension of his powers. Formerly he could entertain a belated opposition to the grant of the patent only on limited grounds, provided that it was commenced within twelve months of grant.[29] But the nature of the proceedings has not changed, the Comptroller's decision is still normally upon documentary evidence, with lower scales of fees.[30] Attackers who want an exhaustive investigation of the merits, with oral examination of witnesses, should still bring proceedings in court.[31] Questions of infringement can be referred to the Comptroller only by the agreement of both parties[32]; but his power to grant declarations of non-infringement is not conditioned in this way.[33]

---

[22] *Microbeads v. Vinhurst Road Markings* [1976] R.P.C. 19, CA. The warranty now arises under Sale of Goods Act 1979, s. 12, which allows for the undertaking to be given in conditional form. Apart from this, liability cannot be excluded: Unfair Contract Terms Act 1977, s. 6(1).

[23] For a comparison (German, France, Italy, England): see Stauder (1983) 14 I.I.C. 793.

[24] For these, see paras 2–90—2–94, above.

[25] Created as a part of the Chancery Division of the High Court by PA 1977, s. 96; for Scottish equivalents see ss. 97(4), (5), 98. The Patents Court consists of one or more patents judges (ss. 96(2), 97(2)) and there is power to appoint scientific advisers (s. 96(4); RSC, Ord. 104, r. 11). In the past this was not used: but the appellate courts now do so under equivalent powers.

[26] For which, see paras 2–10, 2–11, above.

[27] PA 1977, s. 97(1); further appeal only lies in certain cases to the Court of Appeal: s. 97(3).

[28] PA 1977, s. 72. The Comptroller also has certain powers to revoke upon his own initiative: see para. 5–14, n. 43, above.

[29] See PA 1949, s. 33. The Banks Committee recommended that the Comptroller be given wider jurisdiction: (Cmnd. 4407, 1970) paras 181–188.

[30] *i.e.* lower fees for both initial proceedings and any appeal to the Patents Court.

[31] The difference is marked by the rule that the Comptroller's decision creates no issue estoppel against subsequent court proceedings: PA 1977, s. 72(5), but note s. 72(6).

[32] *ibid.*, s. 61(3)–(6). He has no jurisdiction over threats.

[33] In each case, invalidity may be raised as a defence: *ibid.*, s. 74(1). If revocation is sought under s. 72, the proceedings would be heard at the same time. See also para. 4–29, above.

6-24 We have already noted some general techniques that exist in intellectual property actions to preserve or elicit evidence of what the defendant has been doing. When, however, the patent is for a process, and the alleged infringements are imported, there may be no means of discovering or inspecting how they are made. In such a case it may be that a court will find against a defendant who refuses to explain himself, upon proof of a bare prima facie case of infringement.[34] There is also a statutory presumption that a new product is made by an infringing process.[35] But "new product" can only mean one not previously known for novelty purposes; and in such cases, product claims are allowed. So the provision appears to cope with a spectral difficulty.

6-25 In proceedings for infringement, the validity of the patent can be put in issue.[36] This may be done purely as a matter of defence, or by way of a counterclaim for revocation: the former will save expense, the latter is more final.[37] There are cases when the two questions are closely related: as where the defendant alleges that what he is doing is anticipated or obvious.[38] And more generally there is a feeling that a broadly just outcome can be reached only if what the plaintiff has tried to annex is set against how the defendant has acted, whether with the patent in mind or in ignorance of it.

But this traditional approach is controversial. Two E.C. countries—Germany and the Netherlands, each with strong examining offices—generally require validity to be raised before specialist tribunals, while leaving infringement to ordinary civil courts.[39] For Community patents, the draft CPC originally adopted this division of functions; there was a fear that non-expert tribunals in some countries would not handle revocation questions satisfactorily. But in the light of British objections, the revised version of the Convention will allow the practice to continue without limit of time.[40]

The length, complexity and cost of patent infringement actions have long been notorious. One consequence has been the introduction of special procedures for the protection of potential defendants—the action for a declaration of non-infringement and the action against threats, which were dealt with in Chapter 2.[41] Other aspects of procedure and remedies affecting patent suits are dealt with there, and the reader is reminded

---

[34] See para. 2–59, above.
[35] PA 1977, s. 100; there is a saving clause protecting defendants against "unreasonable" disclosure of secrets.
[36] Likewise both issues may be raised in actions for threats and for declarations of non-infringements; and invalidity may also be raised in disputes about Crown use: see PA 1977, s. 74.
[37] Even if there is no counterclaim the Court probably has power to order revocation in the public interest: Whitford J., *Norprint v. SPJ Labels* [1979] F.S.R. 126.
[38] See para. 4–41, above.
[39] For the German position, see Pakuscher (1979) 10 I.I.C. 671; *cf. Formstein* [1991] R.P.C. 24.
[40] See CPC, Arts 56–63, 68–73, 78, 90.
[41] See paras 2–86—2–90, above. Note also PA 1977, s. 61(1), (2).

particularly of the guidelines that are used to assess damages and the problems of apportionment that may arise where the infringement contributes to the making of a loss or profit for which damages are being awarded or an account taken.[42]

The one issue that deserves special comment at this stage is the **6–26** availibility of interlocutory injunctions in patent infringement suits. Because of the grave implications of deciding to carry an action to its full term, much of the real effectiveness of a patent may turn on whether the Court will intervene at this early stage. Before *American Cyanamid v. Ethicon*,[43] the patentee could rarely hope to succeed. He had to make out a prima facie case and against this the defendant could usually set up a sufficient barrier by averring the invalidity of the patent, particularly on the ground of obviousness. On such an issue it is intrinsically hazardous to form a preliminary view. Accordingly, success was reserved to patents for exceptionally significant or widely acknowledged inventions.[44]

The *Ethicon* case, however, has transferred emphasis to the balance of **6–27** convenience.[45] This means that the substantive dispute between the parties is demoted and prime weight is given to their relative commercial positions, with particular stress on the use that each is making, or is intending to make, of the invention covered (actually or allegedly) by the patent. Either party will boost his case, for instance, by showing that this is most or all of his business.[46] A patentee will make ground out of showing that he is struggling to secure a market position for the invention and would be impeded by the defendant's direct competition.[47] A defendant will fall back if he has not yet started manufacturing and has not expended much in preparations for doing so,[48] or if he only imports and so has not committed capital to production plant.[49]

---

[42] See paras 2–39—2–46, above.

[43] [1975] A.C. 396, [1975] R.P.C. 513, HL For the new approach to the granting of interlocutory relief established by this case and for its application to intellectual property cases in general, see paras 2–32—2–36, above.

[44] See Blanco White (1974), para. 12–113.

[45] See paras 2–34—2–37, above. The plaintiff's need first to show a serious case to be tried can usually be satisfied in a patent infringement action: questions of law might, however, be decided under this rubric. *cf.* Cole [1979] E.I.P.R. 71.

[46] *e.g. Netlon v. Bridport-Gundry* [1979] F.S.R. 530, CA; *Potters-Ballotini v. Weston-Baker* [1977] R.P.C. 202, CA (breach of confidence). The counter-argument that the defendant started production knowing that he was likely to be sued may weigh against him: *Belfast Ropework v. Pixdane* [1976] F.S.R. 337, CA. But the argument that, even if a defendant is enjoined, he will be able to open up other lines of business has been discounted: *Condor v. Hibbing* (1978) [1984] F.S.R. 312, CA.

[47] *cf. Catnic v. Stressline* [1976] F.S.R. 157, CA. If a patent is nearing the end of its life, the Court of Appeal has been reluctant to refuse an injunction where to do so would provide the defendant with a bridgehead against both the patentee and other competitors: *Corruplast v. Harrison* [1978] R.P.C. 761 at 766.

[48] *Hepworth Plastics v. Naylor*, CA (see Cole, n. 45, above) at 13.

[49] *Belfast Ropework* case (n. 46, above).

A defendant in a small way, moreover, may have difficulty in showing his ability to pay any damages ultimately awarded.[50] One line of argument that may well be to a defendant's advantage, however, is that, if he is allowed to continue, his sales will normally form a reasonable basis for assessing competitive losses to the plaintiff,[51] whereas if he is stopped, what he might have made will remain speculative.[52] There are, of course, many other such considerations which may affect the outcome of particular cases.[53]

The danger of the *Ethicon* approach is that a particular patent's value comes to depend too much on commercial position.[54] Statistically at least, the chance of securing interlocutory relief has undoubtedly improved under the new principles. This is likely to foster the general impression that patents in Britain have become more damaging weapons in competitive industry than was previously the case.

2. THE SPECIFICATION IN LIGHT OF THE LEGAL REQUIREMENTS

6–28 Patent specifications are drawn to deal with conflicts. Even where they form the basis for licensing, their real significance arises only when the collaboration begins to turn sour. A specification must strive to provide protection against those looking for ways of side-stepping it; at the same time, it must not break any of the validity rules. The basic principles, which we have now looked at in some detail, interact in a complex manner. We have reached the point where it is useful to summarise some crucial points in these interrelations.

(1) The description

6–29 There are a variety of pressures upon the draftsman to include in his description of the invention a fair amount of detail, going beyond the minimum that may satisfy the requirement of a complete and clear disclosure:

(1) There is the danger that if particular versions of the invention are not mentioned, room may be left for a competitor to secure an

---

[50] *e.g. Belfast Ropework* case (n. 46, above), where even a bank guarantee of £15,000 was not enough to satisfy the Court of Appeal.

[51] Refusal of an injunction may "snowball" by inducing other competitors to follow the defendant: but the Court of Appeal has been reluctant to take this into account: *Condor v. Hibbing* (n. 46, above).

[52] *Polaroid v. Eastman Kodak* [1977] R.P.C. 379, CA; *Brupat v. Sandor Marine* [1983] R.P.C. 61, CA; *cf. SKM v. Spraytech* [1982] R.P.C. 497.

[53] Particular difficulties arise with patented pharmaceuticals. The patentee may argue that doctors and patients may be seriously put out if, after learning to use the defendant's product, they see it removed from the market after the trial: *American Cyanamid v. Ethicon* [1975] R.P.C. 513. But if there is some difference between the plaintiff's and defendant's products the latter may argue that the public should not be deprived of his version, particularly if it could be life-saving: *Roussel-Uclaf v. Searle* [1977] F.S.R. 125.

[54] See Cole, n. 45, above.

improvement or selection patent at the very point where the patentee wants himself to operate; whereas specific description will put paid to this possibility from the moment that the application is filed, provided that the application (or one claiming priority from it) is later published.[55]

(2) There is the need (at least before the patent office) to show support in the description for the claims, particularly the broadest.[56]

(3) A case must be developed to support the presence of an inventive step; where the subject-matter is an improvement over known art, rather than a breakthrough with a mechanical principle, chemical substance, or new micro-organism, this means spelling out the advantage that gives inventive character.[57]

(4) The limitations upon amendment condition the possibility of introducing changes during prosecution of the application[58]; the governing rule that there must be no new disclosure over the contents of the specification originally filed makes it crucial to start with all that may later be needed. It is important to put enough into any "informal" application to ground priority round the world.[59]

(2) The claims

The aim is to cover all imaginable alternatives, while avoiding the inclusion **6–30** of things that are anticipated or obvious. In the United Kingdom in the past, this has meant that if, for instance, the inventor has found a way of making a material that is then used in a production process, it has been desirable to include claims for making the material, the material itself, and its use in the subsequent process. To some extent, the introduction of "indirect" infringement[60] has reduced the importance of doing this. However, it is more secure to cover the matter directly. At the other end, the rule that a process claim covers only its direct products[61] is stricter than the former British approach; so where, for instance, a series of chemical syntheses are involved, it is important to cover those at the end as well as those at the beginning.

(3) Pitfalls of saying too much

So much for the pressures to be as complete as possible: now consider the **6–31** dangers inherent in this course.

---

[55] See paras 5–14, 5–15, above.
[56] See paras 5–101—5–105, above.
[57] In the case of a selection, advantage is also necessary to disclose what makes the invention novel; see paras 5–14, 5–15, above.
[58] See paras 4–31—4–34, above.
[59] See paras 4–10—4–13, above.
[60] See paras 6–17—6–19, above.
[61] See para. 6–12, above.

A would-be patentee may endanger his own chances by any sort of publicity: we have already noted the severity of the new European concordat in the matter of "periods of grace".[62] Equally there are dangers that one of his specifications will prejudice others that come later, whether they are attempts to cope more successfully with what is essentially the same invention or they deal with some distinct improvement. It is worth drawing together the points at which earlier applications tell against later:

(1) The arrangements for according priority are limited by the requirement that the later application or applications be made within 12 months of the first application to disclose the invention. The only exception discounts earlier applications that are totally abnegated without having been published.[63]

(2) If an application is made for patent protection in the United Kingdom (to either the British Office or the EPO) and the application reaches the stage of being published, its content is treated for novelty purposes as forming part of the art from the priority date claimed. So before the applicant allows this publication to take place, he must consider whether he is prejudicing any of his own later applications, not claiming the same priority, which attempt to patent any invention disclosed in the published form of the application. Gone is the confinement of this issue to a question of prior claiming. But it does not, for this interim period, matter that the later invention is obvious in the light of the earlier.

(3) Once an application is published,[64] like any other publication, it joins the state of the art for all purposes. Improvements that are obvious in the light of its revelation cannot be patented. No longer is there the old patent of addition, which allowed the engrafting of improvements even though they marked no inventive step over the main patent.

All in all the patent system calls for acute awareness of the hazards and the highest attention to getting the whole thing right from the outset. More than ever, it is a game that only the highly professional can hope to play with much success.

---

[62] See para. 5–16, above.
[63] See para. 4–12, n. 52, above.
[64] As to this, see Burnside (1980) 9 CIPA 266.

CHAPTER 7

PROPERTY RIGHTS AND EXPLOITATION

This Chapter draws together a number of themes concerned with the **7–01** ownership of patent rights and the exploitation of those rights through consensual dealings. The question of initial entitlement to a patent arises from the making of the invention onwards. It may be important before any application is made, during the application and after grant. The person or persons thus entitled may deal with their rights, disposing of them by assignment or permitting others to act within the scope of the monopoly, by giving them a licence to do so. These two aspects of property rights in patents are considered in the first part of this Chapter. The second part deals more specifically with the content of patent and allied licences and takes account of the competition law criteria which they must now meet, particularly the requirements of E.C. law. The third part is closely related to this, since it deals with the application of Community law to the importation of patented products. The last two parts move on to other public policy considerations—the provisions seeking to correct under-exploitation by allowing for the grant of compulsory licences, and the provisions which allow for Crown use upon payment of compensation.

1. INITIAL ENTITLEMENT AND PROPERTY DEALINGS

(1) The right to grant: general

In contrast with the former law, the 1977 Act allows anyone to apply for a **7–02** patent but restricts those to whom a patent may be granted.[1] At the moment of invention, section 7(2) confers the right to be granted a patent upon one of three categories of persons: (1) the inventor or co-inventor[2]; or (2) the employer of the inventor when the invention is made during

---

[1] PA 1977, s. 7(1), following EPC, Arts 58, 60(1); PA 1949, s. 1, by contrast, defined the classes of persons entitled to apply.

[2] "Inventor" means actual deviser: PA 1977, s. 7(3); see para. 4–06, above. A person who contributed one of two main ideas in an invention is a co-inventor: *Norris' Patent* [1988] R.P.C. 159; likewise one who contributed an idea thought by the collaborators to be essential, without regard to whether it was known or obvious: *Viziball's Application* [1988] R.P.C. 213; and see Lloyd (1979) 8 CIPA 11.

employment[3]; or (3) where foreign law"[4] applies by virtue of private international law rules,[5] the person entitled by that law.[6] Whoever is given this initial entitlement to the patent can assign it; or it may devolve upon a successor because of death, bankruptcy and the like. An assignee or successor is then entitled to the grant in place of his predecessor. The right to an assignment may be implied from the circumstances in which an invention was made.[7]

(2) The right to grant: employees[8]

(a) *Common law rules*

7–03 In free-market economies it is an assumption, by now largely unremarked, that the products of labour belong to the owner of the business. Even so, it took some time for the first industrial countries to apply this assumption to intellectual property rights without some measure of reserve. In England it was left to Lord Simonds, in the age of corporate capitalism, to declare that "it is an implied term in the contract of service of any workman that what he produces by the strength of his arm or the skill of his hand or the exercise of his inventive faculty shall become the property of his employer".[9] Before that, emphasis tended to be placed on the need to show either a positive contract in the employer's favour or an implied duty of trust.[10] Indeed, it was said that the invention might be the employee's even though made in the employer's time and with his materials.[11] The tendency

---

[3] An employer who is only entitled to part of the property right—for instance, because his employee has worked with an outsider to make the invention—should, it appears from PA 1977, s. 7(2)(b), take an assignment from his employee so as to acquire a right under s. 7(2)(c).

[4] Including rights created in foreign law by treaties or conventions (in countries where, contrary to English law, international obligations may take effect directly upon ratification).

[5] This could be the law of the place of invention, or that governing the inventor's contract of employment. Such a question has never been explored in English private international law; but see para. 7–10, below.

[6] The mention in PA 1977, s. 7(2)(b) of entitlement by virtue of a "pre-invention" agreement seems meaningless, as far as English law is concerned, since such an agreement can only be to assign future property rights and that can at most create an equitable interest: yet the paragraph specifically excludes equitable interests.

[7] *Goddin and Rennie's Application* [1996] R.P.C. 141 (C. of Sess.).

[8] See also Cornish in Vitoria (ed.) *The Patents Act 1977* (1978) p. 79 and [1992] E.I.P.R. 13; J. Phillips and M. Hoolahan, *Employees' Inventions in the United Kingdom* (1982); J. Phillips (ed.) *Employees' Inventions: A Comparative Study* (1981); Chandler and Holland, *Information, Protection, Ownership, Rights* (1993), pp. 128–129.

[9] *Patchett v. Sterling* (1955) 72 R.P.C. 50. Who is an employer in this context is left to be judged by common law tests, which are discussed in connection with copyright: paras 12–05, 12–06, below. An express agreement not to treat a person as an employee is binding: *SJD Engineering v. Baruch Sharon* [1994] E.I.P.R. D-51.

[10] See *Marshall and Naylor's Patent* (1900) 17 R.P.C. 553 at 555; *Edisonia v. Forse* (1908) 25 R.P.C. 546 and 549, both citing *Frost on Patents*.

[11] *Worthington v. Moore* (n. 18, below) at 48; *Mellor v. Beardmore* (1927) 44 R.P.C. 175 at 191, I.H.

to increase the presumption in favour of his employer probably grew as cases arose in which employees were trying to stop their employer from using the invention in his own business. The implied term adopted by English courts may be contrasted with the handling of similar problems by United States courts. There, in cases where the employer's claim to entitlement is doubtful, he is given only a "shop right": he is entitled to a free licence to use himself, but has no general power to stop the employee from licensing his invention to others.[12]

In English law, there have been two kinds of case in which, commonly, an **7–04** employee has been obliged to hold his invention for his employer. First, where the employee was employed to use his skill and inventive ingenuity to solve a technical problem—where he was "employed to invent". Thus an engineering draftsman who was instructed to design an unlubricated crane-brake was obliged to hold a resulting patent on trust for his employer.[13] An assistant engineer employed to design linings for colliery tunnels was sent at his own request to a particular colliery and in consequence produced an inventive solution to its problem: the arrangement of the visit was held to place him under a duty to make over the consequent patent.[14] But a man employed purely as manager to sell valves and to deal with customer problems in the first instance was not obliged to hold an invention concerning the valves for his employers. They referred serious difficulties to the Swiss firm from whom they acquired the technology.[15] Equally, a hospital registrar employed by a health authority to treat patients was held to be under no duty to his employer to devise improvements to ophthalmic equipment. It made no difference that, in doing so, he was using associated university facilities in pursuit of an academic career.[16]

Secondly, where the employee occupied a senior managerial position and so owed a general duty of fidelity to his employer.[17] Thus, in *Worthington v. Moore*, an American pump manufacturing corporation put a man in charge of its English business at a high salary and commission and made him a vice-president of the corporation; he was held liable under an obligation of good faith to account for patents relating to developments in pumps.[18]

---

[12] See Stedman in Neumeyer, *The Employed Inventor in the United States* (1971) Chap. 2. An attempt to introduce an apportionment of benefits into the same "grey area" (PA 1949, s. 56(2)) was held to have no effect in the absence of a contractual agreement to divide: *Patchett v. Sterling* [1955] 72 R.P.C. 50.

[13] *British Reinforced Concrete v. Lind* (1917) 34 R.P.C. 101.

[14] *Adamson v. Kenworthy* (1932) 49 R.P.C. 57.

[15] *Harris' Patent* [1985] R.P.C. 19 (decided under PA 1977, s. 39—see n. 25, below); and see *Spirroll v. Putti* (1976) 64 D.L.R. (3d) 280.

[16] *Greater Glasgow Health Board's Application* [1996] R.P.C. 207; Chandler [1997] E.I.P.R. 262.

[17] Not easily distinguished in scope from the duties imposed in equity upon fiduciaries, such as company directors, to account for profits where there has been a conflict of personal interest and duty: see now *Canadian Aero v. O'Malley* (1973) 40 D.L.R. (3d) 371, S.C. (Canada); and as to the duty of a managing director to exploit all new opportunities: *Fine Industrial Commodities v. Powling* (1954) 71 R.P.C. 254 at 258.

[18] (1903) 20 R.P.C. 41. Note that there was evidence that the defendant was patenting the work of other employees.

More recently, an employee who was a chief technician, employed *inter alia* to give technical advice on the design and development of soda syphons, but not to design the particular kind of syphon that he actually invented, was held accountable.[19] But the manager of a lampshade business (not a director of the concern) was held entitled to keep a patent for a method of coating wire frames, an idea which amongst other uses could be applied to lampshades.[20]

The employee's duty under either head applied to rights in the invention from its conception onwards. Until a patent application had been filed, his obligation coincided with his duty to keep confidential any information about his employment which was more than mere general knowledge and skill.[21]

7–05 The common law principle operated as a presumption within a regime of free contract; express agreement could alter its operation. Recently, however, to exclude it there had to be a positive contract and not a mere "understanding".[22] One common practice was for employers, both industrial and governmental, to require employees to give over rights in all inventions made during the time of the employment, rather than just in its course, at least if the invention related to the employer's business. But such a term has been held ineffective as being in unreasonable restraint of trade: a vacuum cleaner company could not require a senior storekeeper to surrender rights in an invention made at home, even though it consisted of an adapter for vacuum cleaner bags.[23]

(b) *The changes in the 1977 Act*

7–06 If the only purpose of the patent system in a private-enterprise economy is to stimulate that economy, it may be logical to exclude employed inventors from the benefits of employment patents: one has simply to accept that the incentives—towards instituting research, development and publication—will only affect the employer. In other words, the bait of a patent or patent share is unlikely to incite the employed inventor to greater effort. As an assumption this may seem more or less plausible. However, the shift of

---

[19] *British Syphon Co. v. Homewood* [1956] R.P.C. 225 at 231:
"Now, would it be consistent with good faith, as between master and servant, that he should in that position be entitled to make some invention in relation to a matter concerning a part of the Plaintiff's business and either keep it from his employer, if and when asked about the problem, or even sell it to a rival, and say: 'Well, yes, I know the answer to your problem, but I have already sold it to your rival'?" Roxburgh J. held not.

[20] *Selz's Application* (1954) 71 R.P.C. 158. It was emphasied that the manager had not tried to keep knowledge of the invention or patent application from his employer.

[21] See para. 8–30, below.

[22] *Patchett v. Sterling* (n. 12, above).

[23] *Electrolux v. Hudson* [1977] F.S.R. 312. The Banks Committee (Cmnd. 4407, 1970) had recommended legislation to similar effect, though it wanted no further compulsion to be placed upon employers: Chap. 16; see now PA 1977, s. 42(2), para. 7–12, below.

opinion in the employee's favour has not turned upon this sort of psychological calculation. Rather it expresses a resurgent feeling for the demands of natural justice—a belief that an inventor should not go unrewarded for the fruits of his intellectual endeavour. This inspiration has coalesced with the recent tendency to cast legal protection around contracting parties who as a class may well not appreciate the unfavourable consequences of their bargains.

The "new deal" in the 1977 Act is, however, a strictly limited concession to the demand for fairness towards the inventor. Just what has been given is in any case still obscure, since much of the hard decision-making is left to the courts and the Comptroller.[24] What the Act does is to lay out a framework of rights, which can nevertheless be replaced if certain provisions of the scheme are observed.

(c) *Basic entitlement under the 1977 Act*

Section 39 in effect codifies the common law principles which determine **7–07** whether employer or employee is initially entitled to an invention.[25]

The employer takes the invention (1) when made either in the course of the employee's normal or his specifically assigned duties, provided that an invention might reasonably be expected from carrying them out[26]; and (2) where the employee has a special obligation to further the interests of the employer's undertaking "because of the nature of his duties and the particular responsibilities arising from the nature of his duties".[27] This reflects the two types of case where the decisions held employers entitled, and they are likely guides to future decisions. In all other cases the employee has the initial rights in his own invention.

(d) *Compensation and employers' inventions*

Where the invention belongs to the employer, the inventor may neverthe- **7–08** less have a statutory right to what is called "compensation", that is a special bonus. This arises when (1) the patent for the invention is of outstanding benefit to the employer,[28] and (2) it is just that compensation should be

---

[24] This is in striking contrast with the statutory scheme in Germany, whose detailed regulations lay down methods of weighting and calculation. From these there is much of interest to be learnt: see, *e.g.* Schade (1972) 11 Ind. Prop. 249 and [1979] Ann I.P.L. 169; Schippel (1973) 4 I.I.C. 1.

[25] In *Harris' Patent* [1985] R.P.C. 19, however, Falconer J. refused to accept that this statutory provision necessarily embodied the common law.

[26] PA 1977, s. 39(1). The invention must accordingly be one expected to be achieved by carrying out the employee's duties: *Harris' Patent* (n. 25, above).

[27] PA 1977, s. 39(2). By amendment in 1988, the employee entitled to a patent may use material in support of his application in which the employer owns copyright or design right: s. 39(3).

[28] "Outstanding" implies a superlative, and so means more than significant: *Memco-Med's Patent* [1992] R.P.C. 403 The onus is in general on the employee, which makes the test hard indeed to satisfy: *ibid. cf. GEC Avionics' Patent* [1992] R.P.C. 107; *British Steel's Patent* [1992] R.P.C. 117.

awarded; in assessing which, tribunals are under the ambiguous instruction to have regard, among other things, to the size and nature of the employer's business.[29] It is the patent, not the invention, which must be of outstanding benefit, and a patent is a right to prevent others from infringing; so the prime issue is, how much has the employer made, or how much could he have made, from licensing the patent? This may be difficult to assess, but perhaps explains the sense in which the size and nature of the employer's own business are to be considered relevant.[30] If there are no competitors, or if competitors would use some alternative to the patented invention, then there may well be no outstanding benefit from the patent. If the employer supplies the patented product to a single firm with which it has long had an established relationship, the sales may be explained by that relationship, rather than by the patent.[31]

Once this basic test is satisfied, the 1977 Act directs that the assessment of compensation is to allow the employee "a fair share (having regard to all the circumstances)", treating for the purpose dealings between the employer and a person connected with him as if an "arm's-length dealing" had taken place between them.[32] A number of factors are specified to which the tribunal must have regard, but only among other things: (1) the employee's duties, remuneration and other advantages from employment or "in relation to" the invention; (2) the employee's effort and skill; (3) the effort and skill of others—co-inventors, whether employees or not, other employees who give advice and assistance; and (4) the employer's contribution—by the provision of advice, facilities and other assistance, the provision of opportunities, and managerial and commercial skill and activities.[33]

(e) *Compensation and employees' inventions*

7–09 Where the patent is the employee's, the employer will be entitled to use the invention only if he has acquired rights from the employee by assignment or licence. "Compensation" falls to be paid by the employer when the consideration for this transaction is inadequate in comparison with the benefit derived by the employer from the patent, and it is just that it should be paid.[34] The general principles for the assessment of compensation are the same as those for employers' inventions. But the list of factors to be

---

[29] PA 1977, s. 40(1).

[30] The *Memco-Med* judgement offers no elucidation of this mysterious factor. An invention which provided 2–3% turnover of a small company is not of outstanding benefit: *Garrison's Patent* [1997] C.I.P.A. 297 (device for joining snooker cue).

[31] *Memco-Med* (n. 28, above): patent for lift-entrant detectors all sold to a major lift manufacturer: no outstanding benefit proved.

[32] PA 1977, s. 41; and note, in PA 1977, s. 41(3), the further provision governing free licences by the Crown and Research Councils.

[33] *ibid.*, s. 41(4).

[34] *ibid.*, s. 40(2).

brought into account differs somewhat: while account must be taken of the contribution of any co-inventor and the employer, the employee's own employment is not relevant; but conditions in licences (granted, presumably, by the employer) are.[35]

(f) Scope of the provisions

The compensation provisions apply to inventions[36] made after June 1, **7–10** 1978[37] by a person who is an employee[38] mainly employed in the United Kingdom.[39] They appear to apply only between the employer and the employee at the time of making the invention—something that is likely to cause difficulty, given the lapse of time before a claim is made.[40] They do require that benefits received under foreign patents and equivalent protection be brought into account.[41]

(g) By-passing the Act: collective agreements

A collective agreement may replace the statutory scheme for compensation **7–11** if it is made by or on behalf of a trade union to which the employee belongs and by an employer or an employer's association to which the employer belongs and the agreement is in existence at the time of making the invention.[42] The agreement does not have to procure any particular level of benefit to the employee in order to be effective. The broad definition of "trade union" allows a temporary group (for example a research team) to negotiate a collective agreement. This possibility may enable a shop agreement to be reached where (as may well be the case) the research employees are not members of a regular union.[43] With the spread of white-collar unionism, such collective agreements may become commoner. They may well seek to spread bonus moneys amongst all the staff concerned with the development and marketing of the invention.

---

[35] PA 1977, s. 41(5).

[36] *i.e.* "inventions for the purposes of this Act", and so not the "things" in *ibid.*, s. 1(2).

[37] For the question, when is an invention made? see *Dupont's Patent* [1961] R.P.C. 336, CA; *Bristol Myers v. Beecham* [1978] R.P.C. 521.

[38] Not an independent contractor, nor a director without a service contract: *e.g. Parsons v. Parsons* [1979] F.S.R. 254, CA; see paras 2–07—2–09, above.

[39] Or if not mainly employed anywhere, or it is not possible to determine where he is employed, but he is attached to a U.K. place of business of the employer: PA 1977, s. 43(2). This follows the formula in EPC, Art. 60(2) for determining which national law shall decide employer-employee questions over European patents. If such a connection does not exist with the U.K., but (exceptionally) English law applies to the question, the common law rules will apply.

[40] Benefits to the personal representatives of the employer must be brought into account; and the personal representatives of the employee may claim in his shoes: PA 1977, s. 43(4), (5); but these exceptions serve to show that other substitutions are not to be made.

[41] *ibid.*, s. 43(4).

[42] *ibid.*, s. 40(3), (6).

[43] The definition of "trade union" is that in the Trade Union and Labour Relations Act 1974: see ss. 28, 29.

(h) *By-passing the Act: individual agreements*

7–12 As with the latter-day extension of the public policy considerations in common law doctrine,[44] the Act renders unenforceable contractual terms which diminish an "employee's rights in inventions . . . or in or under patents for those inventions or applications for such patents".[45] The contracts covered are those that he makes with his employer or any third party at the employer's request or in pursuance of the contract of employment, before the date on which the invention was made.[46] This provision is beset with uncertainty, but, given the extension of common law doctrine, it may well be generously construed. It clearly applies to a provision in an employment contract requiring an employee in advance to give up his rights of initial ownership where there is no distinct consideration for this.[47] But if (say) a reasonable sum is to be paid for these rights, it might well be held that they were not "diminished" (if the sum to be paid were an undervalue, it could in any case be the subject of "compensation").[48]

More importantly, can the inventor make a pre-invention contract to surrender his rights to compensation when the patent belongs initially to the employer? The Act says he may not, if by doing so, he diminishes his rights "under" the patent; and arguably this is the case. A contract made after the invention is not affected by the statute and so by implication would seem a matter of free bargaining. Certainly, if the invention belongs to the employee he cannot make a contract with his employer, before or after the invention, which deprives him of "compensation" which would adjust the price paid to him.[49]

(i) *By-passing the Act by not patenting*

7–13 Where the employer has initial ownership of the invention under section 39 of the 1977 Act and chooses not to patent it, it would seem that the employee is deprived of any right to "compensation". The only hope of arguing to the contrary is by way of a generous construction of the reference in section 43(4) to "other protection": if this were to include the protection of the invention as confidential information or through design right, the result might be achieved.[50] A Court might be tempted into such a

---

[44] See *Electrolux v. Hudson* (n. 23, above).
[45] PA 1977, s. 42(2).
[46] *ibid.*, s. 42(1), (2). Duties of confidentiality owed by employee to employer must be respected: s. 42(3).
[47] Equally, an employer could not require the employee to seek his consent to any patent application. However, it would not diminish the employee's rights if he were required to notify the employer of the invention and any patent application.
[48] PA 1977, s. 40(4).
[49] *ibid.*
[50] The "other protection" would certainly include foreign protection through utility models and the like.

construction if faced with an employer who had set out deliberately to do his employee down by not patenting.

(j) *Administration*

Issues between employer and employee—over ownership or **7–14** "compensation"—can be heard by the Patents County Court or the High Court or upon a reference to the Comptroller. They may order "compensation" in the form of a lump sum or periodic payments.[51]

Obviously the scope for disputes is very considerable. This potential can only be reduced if at all stages an acceptable record of events is kept concerning: (1) who instituted the research, (2) the making of the invention, and (3) its subsequent development and commercial exploitation.[52] At the same time the definition of duties in the contract and employment needs to be clear and to be kept under review.

(3) Dealing in rights

A patent is a right of personal property; so is an application.[53] Both can be **7–15** dealt with by assignment, mortgage, licence and the like. The 1977 Act indeed provides a code of basic rules about such dealings, introducing at the same time certain modifications of the pre-existing law.

(a) *Formalities*

The grant of a licence is not required to be in any particular form. **7–16** "Licence" covers everything from occasional permission to exclusive licence, and it is only right that an informal oral licence should be legally effective.[54] However, assignments or mortgages of patents, applications and rights in patents (including, for example assignments of patent licences) are in law void unless in writing signed by or on behalf of the parties (not just the right-giver).[55]

(b) *The Register*

In the 1977 Act, the system of maintaining a register of all legal interests in **7–17** a patent is carried over from the previous law, but with some differences. There is no statutory obligation to register transactions and the like, and

---

[51] See PA 1977, ss. 8, 12, 37, 41(6), (8). There is also power to vary, discharge, revive or suspend the order and to hear an application despite previous lack of success: see s. 41(7), (9)–(11).

[52] Where research is successful and patents are obtained the records should be kept at least for the life of the patent.

[53] PA 1977, s 30(1). They are not however, things in action; though why not, is a mystery.

[54] See *ibid.*, s. 30; and for Scots law, s 31. Note that even an exclusive licence does not have to be in writing in order to give the licensee his entitlement to sue for infringement: see ss. 67, 69 and note s. 58.

[55] See *ibid.*, s. 30(6). A written assignment signed only by the assignor has been treated as an agreement to transfer which in equity entitles the assignee, as equitable proprietor, to institute infringement proceedings, provided that the assignor is later made a party: *Baxter International v. NPLB* [1998] R.P.C. 250.

indeed, registration only provides prima facie evidence of the things registered.[56] There are two sanctions for failure to register which are intended to provide greater incentive to do so than in fact has been the case in the past:

(1) The person with the unregistered right may lose priority to the holder of an inconsistent later right.[57] Where, for instance, the proprietor executes assignments of his title to different people, or the proprietor grants an exclusive licence and then assigns his title, the rule is that the person taking under the later of the grants is to be preferred unless at that time the earlier was already registered (or notified to the Comptroller in the case of an unpublished application) or the person taking the later right knew of the earlier.[58] This varies the rule which otherwise would have applied to legal proprietary rights in patents: that once granted they would be good against all who take later interests even in all innocence.[59]

(2) A proprietor or exclusive licensee who does not register within six months cannot claim damages or an account of profits for infringements between his entitlement and registration.[60]

The relationship between equitable interests and the requirement to register is not clear. The Comptroller is not to enter notice of trusts—express, implied or constructive—on the register.[61] Where, therefore, the legal owner of a patent is constituted trustee of the beneficial interest for others,[62] it would seem that the ordinary rules relating to equitable interests apply: their interests are enforceable against all save a person who acquires an inconsistent right in good faith for valuable consideration without actual or constructive notice. But where a contract is made to transfer a legal interest in property and is supported by consideration, this also creates an immediate equitable interest in the property. In the case of patents such an interest has in the past been held registrable.[63]

---

[56] *ibid.*, ss. 32(2)(b), 35(1), PA 1977 Rules, r. 46; *Brown's Application* [1996] S.T.C. 483; Karet [1996] E.I.P.R. 404.

[57] *ibid.*, s. 3.

[58] Probably each joint assignee falls to be considered separately.

[59] PA 1977, s. 33 deals only ambiguously with cases where subsequent dealings follow the inconsistent transactions; as where A assigns to B, and subsequently assigns to C; then B assigns to D; is D entitled to rely upon being the latest in time, or can C claim under the later of the initial transactions? See Ency. PL, para. 8–103.

[60] Unless exceptionally he can claim to be excused: PA 1977, s. 68. It has long been the practice, in order to avoid revealing the scope and extent of an entire commercial transaction, to follow an agreement which *inter alia* assigned patents with a second short-form assignment of the patents alone for the purpose of registration. This practice may set a trap for the patentee: *Coflexip Stena's Patent* [1997] R.P.C. 179 at 194.

[61] *ibid.*, s. 32(3).

[62] For instance, where an employee secures a patent to which his employer has the better right under *ibid.*, s. 39 (see para. 7–07, above), or vice versa.

[63] *Stewart v. Casey* (1892) 9 R.P.C. 9, CA.

(4) Co-ownership

Joint entitlement to ownership of a patent can arise either initially (where **7–18** there are co-inventors) or through subsequent dealings.[64] Joint owners are each entitled to operate under the patent by themselves; but they may not transfer, mortgage or license their interest to third parties without seeking the consent of other co-owners.[65] A co-owner who has the capacity to set up as a manufacturer himself is thus in a comparatively strong position.[66] He may have an outside business supply him with components for a thing covered by the patent without the outsider becoming liable as an indirect infringer to other co-patentees,[67] and, more generally, he may act together with agents in a non-technical sense.[68] He may also use and deal with patented articles made by him as if he had been the sole proprietor, though he may not supply parts for others to use in completing manufacture.[69] He is under no liability to share with his co-patentee what he earns from permissible exploitation. By contrast a co-owner without any manufacturing capacity can only import and sell.[70]

2. Licences of Patents and Allied Rights[71]

(1) Traditional approach

In obeisance to freedom of contract, English courts have generally left the **7–19** parties to patent licences and assignments to determine the scope and extent of obligations by mutual agreement between themselves. Whatever they included in their contract the courts would enforce, resolving any ambiguities by reference to the likely intention of the parties and reading in only such additional terms as might be reasonably necessary to give the agreement business efficacy. In 1875 it was held that the assignor of a

---

[64] Where a patent is granted to two or more persons, they are entitled, in the absence of contrary agreement, to equal undivided shares—*i.e.* they take as tenants in common, rather than as joint tenants. So the interests of each survives his death as part of his estate: PA 1977, s. 36(1). See also *Florey's Patent* [1962] R.P.C. 186 at 188.

[65] PA 1977, s. 36(2), (3). If one alone is registered as proprietor, he must accept registration of the other, rather than, say, seeking revocation: *Henry v. Ministry of Defence* [1999] R.P.C. 442, CA.

[66] The Crown's power in such a situation is particularly wide—an unsatisfactory position: *ibid*, at 450.

[67] *ibid.*, s. 36(4).

[68] *Henry v. Ministry of Defence* [1997] R.P.C. 694.

[69] Note the provisions concerning infringement suits by a co-patentee: *ibid.*, s. 66; for disputes between joint applicants and patentees, see ss. 8, 10, 12, 37; Ency. PL, para. 8–203.

[70] Purchasers and others who acquire patented products, directly or indirectly, from one co-owner are treated as having acquired from a sole registered proprietor: *ibid.*, s. 36(5).

[71] For technical treatment of this complex subject, see *e.g.* Melville, *Forms and Agreements on Intellectual Property and International Licensing.*

patent must honour his undertaking to assign subsequent patent rights covering improvements to the technology. Any public disadvantage in thus discouraging him from further invention was outweighed by the policy that "contracts when entered into freely and voluntarily shall be held sacred and shall be enforced by courts of justice".[72]

Accordingly, a licence gave each party what he was strong enough to demand, or canny enough to include. Because typically it concerned technical procedures that would be used with modifications over a substantial period of time, there was the chance that one or other party would find himself benefited or disadvantaged in an unanticipated fashion: for instance, because a problematic invention licensed for a modest lump sum proved unexpectedly successful; or because a licensee found himself bound not to use alternate technology. There has been no regular technique for adjusting agreements in the name of "fairness,"[73] nor did statute intervene, save exceptionally,[74] to prevent abuse of monopoly.

(2) Types of licence

7–20 As a matter of law, there is only one distinction of importance between the different types of patent licence. The exclusive licence, by which the licensor undertakes voluntarily not only to grant no other licences but also not to manufacture or sell within the licensee's province himself,[75] puts the licensee in the special position of being able to sue infringers.[76] In actual business life, the terms of licences vary greatly. It is vital to understand something of this real world, not only because it forms so significant a part of the lawyer's business in industry but also because licences have to meet exacting criteria developed by competition law. Accordingly, this section first sketches the kinds of consideration that the parties to a manufacturing licence will want to cover if left to their own self-interested concerns. After this, we can turn to the constraints upon them now imposed in the name of public interest.

(a) *Interests at the start*

7–21 The value of what the licensor has to offer varies greatly from case to case. If the licensor has not already put the invention into production, the licensee may have no sure means of judging whether the idea is commer-

---

[72] Jessel M.R., *Printing and Numerical v. Sampson* (1875) 19 Eq. 462 at 465. See also, *Jones v. Lees* (1856) 1 H. & N. 189 (royalty payable on non-patented item); *Brownie Wireless' Application* (1929) 46 R.P.C. 457.

[73] For possible modification of this attitude, see *Schroeder v. Macaulay* and ensuing case law (discussed in paras 12–29—12–33, below).

[74] See para. 7–31, at n. 97, below.

[75] See PA 1977, s. 130(1), which defines an exclusive licensee as one whose rights exclude all others, including the proprietor. Where both have rights, the licence is called "sole".

[76] PA 1977, s. 67.

cially or even technically viable: this may well be so where he is dealing with an individual inventor or an organisation devoted to research. If the licensee is an enterprise which also has its own research and development resources, it may be keen to restrict its obligations towards an outside licensor; then its own team remains free to explore ideas beyond and to the side of the patent.

If licensor and licensee are both manufacturing organisations, the purpose of the licence may simply be to transfer rights in one direction, because the licensor alone holds the technical knowledge; but it may be that each has technology to exchange—patented or unpatented, competing or complementary. The latter circumstance may have grown out of collaboration in a joint research programme (not infrequently organised by creating a joint subsidiary for the purpose), or a mutual agreement each to conduct research only in complementary fields.[77] The pooling of patents by cross-licensing may be one consequence of a decision to deploy joint strength in the battle against outside competition. What follows is primarily concerned with "one-way" manufacturing licences, where at the outset the technology is all on one side. But it should not be forgotten that the more complex cases of cross-licensing and pooling will raise many of the same issues for the parties, and the mutual restrictions that they are likely to contain will appear more obviously anti-competitive.

(b) *Rights in the technology*

Where an invention has been worked out into a system of production, the **7–22** licensor is likely to have on offer not just the invention described in his patent specification but additional information—anything from knowledge of how to adapt the invention for particular tasks to merely incidental tricks that help in putting the invention to best use. If he is selling a whole process, the licensor may collect this know-how into an operations manual; in addition he may provide technical staff to get the plant operating properly and to teach the licensee's staff how to keep it going. In such cases the know-how is likely to be imparted upon terms of confidence which will be legally binding.[78] There may be legal reasons for keeping the know-how licence separate from the licence of associated patents: the former may carry fiscal advantages or may avoid provisions directed against abuse of monopoly. But because patents and know-how are so frequently associated in licensing we shall consider aspects of both in this discussion.

It should be added that other forms of intellectual property have often to be included also in licences: the licensee may well want the licensor's

---

[77] Joint ventures in R & D and specialisation agreements have attracted their share of attention from the E.C. Commission's Competition Directorate: see further Bellamy and Child, Chap. 5.
[78] The legal basis of breach of confidence is dealt with in Chap. 8, below.

designs, whether protected by registration or through unregistered design right, and use of his trade marks. Sometimes the licensor will want to compel the licensee to use either designs or trade marks as part of a strategy for building long-term goodwill with the public.

(c) *Exclusivity*

7-23 Particularly when the licensor is seeking to get a technical process used in a new geographical area by finding a manufacturing source there, a basic issue is likely to arise over exclusivity: whether the licensee is to be guaranteed that neither the licensor nor other licensees will manufacture or sell, directly or indirectly, in his territory. The licensee will be interested in shoring up the investment that he will have to make: on the manufacturing side, the plant that he must install and the labour that he must employ; on the selling side, the outlets that he may have to set up, the advertising that he may have to put out, the spare parts and servicing that he may have to provide. If risks such as these are heavy and the licensor is not prepared to help in shouldering them, the licensee may well hold out for complete exclusivity: protection even against potential price differences between territories and the parallel importing that these may induce.

If a licensee is given the security of exclusivity it is frequently on condition that he will respect the exclusivity of others—licensor or exclusive licensees—in their territories. Unlike the restrictions on the licensor mentioned in the previous paragraph, which must be made a term of the licence, the licensee can be kept to his own territory simply by not granting him manufacturing or sales licences under the patents of other territories.[79] This is, of course, protection only so long as the country of import neither treats a first "legitimate" sale beyond its borders as exhausting patent rights, nor assumes that sale abroad by one licensee implies a licence to export to other countries where there are parallel patents. But it has been normal for national patent laws to give the necessary protection. It may, therefore, be difficult to use rules of competition to object to this form of exclusivity, since there may be no contractual term on which they can bite. Only in the E.C. does the doctrine of free movement of goods[80] qualify patent law at this point. There at least contract is the sole mode of achieving the kind of limitation under discussion (and such an agreement will likely offend the competition rules).

Mutual exclusivity in sales may, of course, be achieved indirectly. If the licensor has power to dictate prices, maximum quantities of production or

---

[79] But a determined competition authority such as the E.C. Commission may treat absence of a licence as the equivalent of an undertaking not to sell in the territory concerned: see *AOIP* case (n. 1, below), and *cf. Chemicals Wavin v. TERI* [1977] F.S.R. 181, CA.

[80] Or of Community-wide exhaustion, as it will become with the introduction of the CPC: see para. 6–16, above.

even the types of goods for which the technology can be used, this may in practice lead to territorial protection.

(3) Particular terms in licences

(a) *Basic obligations*

If the licensor undertakes no more than to give the licensee permission to **7–24** manufacture under his patent or patents, he acquits himself by making the grant.[81] If he is to provide "know-how", then he must make available whatever information has been described in the contract. Giving an adequate description of "know-how" for this purpose can be a difficult business. Since in practice much of it may have to be made known in the course of negotiations, the wise potential licensor insists on a preliminary contract that anything revealed will be kept confidential and used only in accordance with such contract as may be agreed. If the licensee is seeking not just a chance to work under the patent or to use the know-how, but instead wants a fully operative package, he must secure undertakings from the licensor that this is what will be provided, with escape clauses leaving him free of obligation if it is not.

Unless for some reason the licence is to be free, the licensee's first obligation will be to pay for what he has received. This will likely take the form of a lump sum, or a royalty on articles produced (normally calculated as a proportion of their net selling price) or both. If there are special risks in the project—particularly because more technical development needs to be undertaken—a profit-sharing arrangement may prove attractive.

(b) *Duration*

Equally basic will be the duration of the licence, and the definition of **7–25** circumstances in which either party is to have power to terminate it. If a patent licence is properly determined while the patent remains in effect, the former licensee falls to be treated like any other stranger.[82] More difficult issues arise upon the ending of a know-how licence; for (subject to public policy) the contract between the parties will settle whether the licensee must give up his use of the information, while continuing to keep knowledge of it from outsiders. If this is provided for expressly, it may well be coupled with an obligation to return all relevant documentary information. If it is not, it will not necessarily be implied, particularly when the information was given in order to get a business established.[83]

---

[81] Unless he guarantees the validity of the patent expressly, the agreement will be taken to be the licence of a risk and so to survive revocation: *African Gold Recovery v. Sheba* (1897) R.P.C. 660; *IMH Investments v. Trinidad Home Developers* [1994] F.S.R. 616.

[82] But there may be difficulties about the obligations which one side owes to the other at the date of termination, *e.g.* to make over rights in improvement patents: *National Broach v. Churchill Gear* [1965] R.P.C. 61.

[83] *Regina Glass Fibre v. Schuller* [1972] R.P.C. 229, CA; *cf. Torrington v. Smith* [1966] R.P.C. 285.

In the past, strong licensors have tied their licensees to long-term arrangements by such techniques as requiring the continuance of royalties after expiry of the patents[84]; or requiring royalties on articles whether or not made under any licensed patent; or requiring them whether or not the patent is valid.[85]

(c) *Improvements*

7–26 Since novel technology is generally subject to further development, it is important to decide whether new information is to be fed around—from licensee to licensor as well as vice versa. And if additional intellectual property rights are acquired by one, the other is likely to want at least a non-exclusive licence under these rights. It is common practice for the patentee of a basic invention to set up a net of "one-way" manufacturing licences, country by country. Since each licensee will be likely to discover improvements, traditionally the patentee has sought to keep control over the developing technology by requiring not only "feed-back" of information for distribution to the other licensees but also "grant-back" in the form of an assignment of consequent patent and allied rights acquired by the licensee; or if not this, then at least an exclusive licence, with or without power to grant sub-licences to others within the network. Each licensee will find this arrangement to its advantage only to the extent that it feels that it is getting at least as much as it is giving. Not only may it try to drag its own feet in the matter of revelations, it may not make much effort to find improvements.

(d) *Ties*

7–27 The licensor may well want to insist that the licensee acquire non-patented goods from him alone as a condition of the patent or know-how licence. If a process is being licensed, he may in particular want the exclusive right to supply the starting materials to be used in it. Sometimes there are technical reasons for this: his material alone may be good enough to make the process function satisfactorily. For one reason or another such "ties" have, traditionally, been common.[86] There may also be "ties" in distributing the licensee's product.[87] The licensor may insist that it be marketed through his own distribution channels. This may be so even though the licensed patent

---

[84] Or requiring royalties so long as any patents relating to the subject-matter of the licence are in force—including those subsequently taken out on improvements.

[85] See para. 7–39, below.

[86] Despite legislation (from 1907 onwards) treating "ties" and exclusions of competitive technology as abuses of monopoly: for repeal, see para. 7–31, below.

[87] A special case for mention here is the "sub-contracting" out of work on parts for a machine to be completed by the licensor, as to which see the E.C. Commission's Notice on Sub-contracting Agreements [1979] 1 C.M.L.R. 264.

only contributed to the course of production and no patent rights apply to the final article.

(e) *Protection for the licensor*

In exclusive licences for royalties, the licensor needs particularly to ensure **7–28** that the licensee gets the invention into production. If he can negotiate a minimum royalty or minimum production clause, this will give him the guarantee of specific amounts. Beyond this he may seek an undertaking that the licensee will use his best endeavours to exploit the invention. The Courts read this to mean what it says, unqualified by any notion of "reasonableness",[88] but the licensor may face grave difficulties in actually establishing that the licensee has not been as assiduous as he might have been. Closely allied to this, the licensee may undertake not to employ competing technology,[89] thus explicitly surrendering one aspect of his capacity to compete to his own best advantage.

A different hazard for the licensor is that, because the licensee becomes closely acquainted with the invention he is in a peculiarly strong position to discover weaknesses in the patent: reasons, for instance, for saying that the disclosure was inadequate or that its subject-matter is obvious in the light of prior art.[90] Even if the licensee cannot mount a sure attack he may be able to cause enough trouble to secure variations of the licence in his own favour. Accordingly, it has been traditional practice for the licensor to require an undertaking that the licensee will not challenge the validity of the patent or know-how during the currency of the licence; or to require the payment of royalties, whether valid or not.[91]

(f) *Protection for the licensee*

The exclusive licensee acquires a position of some independence from his **7–29** licensor.[92] The non-exclusive licensee, on the other hand, may well be concerned that he is having to pay for permission that others are getting cheaper or for nothing. Against the danger of more favourable licences, he may seek a clause which will reduce his obligations to the best terms at any time granted to any other licensee. To meet the danger that the licensor

---

[88] *Terrell v. Mabie Todd* (1952) 69 R.P.C. 234; *IBM v. Rockware* [1980] F.S.R. 335.

[89] See n. 86, above.

[90] Likewise he may be able to show that know-how has become public knowledge from an independent source.

[91] An express "no challenge" clause is arguably invalid as being in unreasonable restraint of trade and so contrary to public policy: see, *per* Clauson J., *VD Ltd v. Boston* (1935) 52 R.P.C. 303 at 331; *cf. Mouchel v. Cubitt* (1907) 24 R.P.C. 194 at 200. If this is good law, it may be questioned whether there is room for any implied estoppel, based on the notion (borrowed from landlord and tenant law) that a licence must not "approbate and reprobate".

[92] Particularly by his ability to sue infringers: PA 1977, s. 67, para. 7–20, above.

will simply fail to pursue an infringer, he may seek power to withhold royalties for any period of inaction.

(4) Competition law criteria[93]

7–30 Modern business history knows examples enough of agreements amongst leading firms in an industry which uses the licensing of intellectual property rights as a basis for anti-competitive liaisons—arrangements that will keep out or drive out competition by price, by product, by advertising, or in a host of other ways. A "pool" by leading firms under which they and they alone can use inventions patented by them individually or after joint research can prove a very efficient instrument for such manifestly horizontal links. Pools may increase geometrically the potential market power of the individual patents and there is widespread agreement that competition policy should be used against such "expansions" of patent rights, especially where they cover the competing ways of making a product. Accordingly they find no special exemption from either United Kingdom[94] or E.C. competition law.

Patent and know-how licences such as those described in preceding paragraphs, however, are frequently concerned with fostering the use of the licensor's technology in the competition against the same and similar products in the market. By themselves, they do not limit "inter-product" competition. If competition authorities are to subject them to critical scrutiny it is because of their inhibiting effect upon the "intra-product" competition that could otherwise exist between licensor and his licensee or licensees. But the use of competition policy to this end is controversial for an obvious reason. A patent is a decision to allow the patentee to behave as a monopolist to the extent that the market admits. When he licenses his rights, albeit on terms that limit the licensee's or his own freedom of action, he would seem prima facie to be doing no more than realising the potential of his economic power. A rational patentee will not grant licences if his best chance of extracting monopoly profits from the market lies in exploiting the patent himself. Accordingly, if a term in such licensing agreements is to be regarded as invalid, there must be an acceptable explanation in economic terms of how it increases the anti-competitive effect of the initial monopoly grant beyond what was intended.

7–31 In the early years of the Common Market, "intra-product" competition became of great moment to those directing the E.C. Competition Policy. The prime importance of breaking down barriers to free marketing within

---

[93] See further Bellamy and Child, *Common Market Law of Competition* (4th ed., 1993); Korah, *An Introductory Guide to E.C. Competition Law and Practice* (5th ed., 1994); Whish, *European Competition Law* (3rd ed., 1993); Anderman, *EC Competition Law and Intellectual Property Rights* (1998).

[94] For their treatment in U.K. law, see App. 1, below. For comparison with U.S. Guidelines, Fogt and Gotts Knable [1996] E.C.L.R. 327.

Community territories made the E.C. Commission critical of exclusive selling rights wherever they occurred, and whether they are created directly or as a consequence of some other restriction, such as a maximum production limit in a technology licence. Accordingly, any restrictive licence having significant impact on interstate trade within the Community was subjected to detailed regulation.

As we shall see, this original severity has gradually been replaced by a greater readiness to accept that vertical limitations agreed between businessmen may have a healthy impact on inter-brand competition between businesses. That has been reflected in changes of attitude over the permissibility of restraints in technology licences. Further concessions may be in the wind, since the Commission is in the process of reassessing its policies on vertical restraints in general.[95]

The competition law of the United Kingdom, as developed after the Second World War, took a much less aggressive attitude towards vertical restraints in general and intellectual property licensing in particular. Now that law is undergoing a renovation, since in the Competition Act 1998 it has been restated in terms derived from the Community's Rules of Competition. Only when the coming transition has progressed some distance will it be possible to see how closely our new law is developing in line with its regional model.[96] The Competition Act will not be separately treated here. It may be noted, however, that it repeals two isolated provisions in the Patents Act 1977 which were directed against particular "abuses" of monopoly in patent licensing.[97]

(5) Development of E.C. Commission policy on patent licences

As early as 1962, in a non-binding notice (the "Patent Notice"),[98] the **7–32** Commission reserved its position on patent pools, cross-licences and similar forms of mutual horizontal restraint.[99] But it indicated that it would not regard certain limiting terms in "one-way" licences as falling within the prohibition of Article 85(1) of the Treaty of Rome.[1] Even so there were indications that some clauses (non-essential "tie-ins", exclusive "grant-

---

[95] However its Green Paper of January 1997 on the subject does not relate to technology transfers through patent and know-how licences.

[96] The main body of the Act will be brought into force in 2000.

[97] PA 1977, s. 44 (collateral "tie-ins") and s. 45 ("tie-ups" beyond the duration of initial patents); to be repealed by Competition Act 1998, s. 70; *cf.* below, paras 7–37, 7–40.

[98] Announcement on Patent Licensing Agreements, December 24, 1962 (hence known to initiates as the "Christmas Message")—now withdrawn.

[99] In *Video Cassette Recorders Agreements* [1978] F.S.R. 376, the Commission found a patent pooling aspect of the licences in question to be restrictive of competition because any member of the pool was to surrender its rights upon leaving the pool but was obliged to allow continuing members to retain their rights in its patents.

[1] For the main content of Arts 85, 86, see para. 1–53, above; for a note on their implementation, Appendix 1.

backs", post-patent obligations) might go too far and towards these Commission policy remains unchanged. But within a decade, the Patent Notice clauses ceased to be a reliable guide (particularly over exclusivity in manufacturing or sales, and maximum production limits). In the 1970s a number of test decisions by the Commission took a severer (and so more controversial) line.[2] Agreements that at first were thought to be outside Article 85(1) were instead treated as needing exemption under Article 85(3); and in the matter of sales exclusivity this has proved particularly difficult to justify.

In consequence of this shift, the Commission eventually, in 1984, formulated a Block Exemption on Patent Licences that specifies the conditions under which a licence need not be individually justified before exemption. To some extent the industrial and governmental objections raised against the drafts of this Block Exemption[3] induced a softening in the Commission's approach, which was indicative of a more general shift away from restrictive regulation under the competition policy. This was followed four years later with a similar Block Exemption for technical know-how licences.[4]

7–33 The two are now amalgamated into a single Block Exemption for Technology Transfer.[5] This contains a further significant measure of deregulation.[6] Article 1 is primarily devoted to defining the extent to which exclusivity provisions may protect the licensee, the licensor and licensees in other territories; Article 2 comprises a newly lengthened "White List" of permissible clauses; and Article 3, comprises of an etiolated "Black List" of impermissible clauses, some of them in direct contrast to clauses on the White List. It is to be remembered that an agreement which does not come within the terms of the Block Exemption may still be the subject of an individual exemption granted by the Commission, and today such treatment

---

[2] See especially *Raymond/Nagoya* [1972] C.M.L.R. D45; *Davidson Rubber* [1972] C.M.L.R. D52; *Burroughs/Delplanque and Geha* [1972] C.M.L.R. D72; *Kabelmetal/Luchaire* [1975] 2 C.M.L.R. D40; *Bronbemaling v. Heidemaatschappij* [1975] 2 C.M.L.R. D67; *AOIP/Beyrard* [1976] 1 C.M.L.R. D14; *Vaessen v. Moris* [1979] F.S.R. 259.

[3] The change in attitude is easily seen by comparing the final version with the initial draft, as given in [1977] 1 C.M.L.R. D25.

[4] See Regulations 2349/84 and 556/89.

[5] Regulation 1996/240 (referred to below as "Block Exemption"); text, with introduction [1996] 4 E.I.P.R. Supp.; and see Korah, *Technology Transfer Agreements and the EC Competition Rules* (1996); Robertson [1996] E.C.L.R. 157; Saltzmann [1996] E.I.P.R. 506; Kerse [1996] E.C.L.R. 331. The Exemption covers only manufacturing licences, not sales distribution agreements (governed by Regulation 1983/83), franchising agreements (Regulation 4087/88) or joint ventures: see further Regulation 1996/240, Art. 5.

[6] In applying to patents, it also covers utility models and their equivalents, SPCs, plant breeders' certificates and applications (Art. 8): and to know-how as defined in Art. 10, though not to other intellectual property licensing. For other details, see Art. 6 and the definitional provisions of Art. 10.

is by no means beyond hope.[7] There is also an interim case: the Exemption provides an opposition procedure in respect of agreements within its subject-field which have provisions restrictive of competition that are not within those exempted, but are not on the Black List: if such an agreement is notified and the Commission does not oppose exemption within four months, the Block Exemption applies to it.[8] And as a further qualification, the Commission retains power to withdraw the benefits of the Block Exemption in particular cases which are incompatible with Article 85(3) of the Treaty of Rome.[9] The threat to use it had previously forced a dominant manufacturer of drink cartons to amend an exclusive licence of patented technology so as to admit further licensees.[10] The future of the Block Exemption will be affected by the Commission's review of its policies on vertical restraints in general.[11]

The content of the Block Exemption will be treated in rather more detail under two main heads: provisions relating to exclusivity; and terms restricting the licensee's freedom of action.

(6) Exclusivity

In its decisions of the 1970s on patent licences, the Commission's starting **7–34** point was that undertakings to ensure the exclusivity of territories were restrictive of competition in the sense of Article 85(1) of the Treaty of Rome, since they necessarily involved a surrender of freedom.[12] This applied to the licensor's undertaking not to manufacture or sell in the licensee's territory and not to grant licences to others to do so; and it even applied to the licensee's undertaking not to manufacture or sell in a territory which the licensor reserved to himself, or was licensing to another exclusive licensee. The latter was particularly controversial since, but for the licence to him, the licensee would have no entitlement to use the patented technology at all, and so would be even more constrained. The Commis-

---

[7] Shortly before adopting the Know-how Block Exemption in 1989 the Commission issued a number of individual decisions which indicated how far it was prepared to go on various issues: *Boussois/Interpane* [1988] O.J. 69/21; *Mitchell Cotts/Sofiltra* [1988] 4 C.M.L.R. 111; *Rich Products/Jusrol* [1988] 4 C.M.L.R. 527; *Delta Chemie/DDD* [1988] O.J. C152/2; Korah (1989) (n. 3, above).

[8] Art. 4.

[9] Cases where this may in particular occur are listed (thus constituting a "storm grey" list): absence of effective competition from other equivalent products, particularly where the licensee's market share exceeds 40 per cent; refusal to meet unsolicited demand unjustifiably; best endeavours and minimum quantity clauses keeping the licensee from competing technology; no right to terminate exclusivity after five years of non-use by licensee.

[10] *Tetra-Pak (No. 1)* [1990] 2 E.C.R. 309.

[11] For which see Riley [1998] E.C.L.R. 483.

[12] See esp. *Davidson Rubber, Raymond/Nagoya*, and *Kabelmetal/Luchaire* (n. 2, above). It should be remembered that in the last two of these cases, the Commission took the view that licences for manufacture outside the E.C. could infringe Article 85(1) if they excluded a realistic prospect of the licensee selling into the Common Market: see also *Davide-Campari Milano's Agreement* [1978] 2 C.M.L.R. 397.

sion, however, considered that the ultimate objective of unifying the internal market justified treating a licence to manufacture in one country of the Community as a licence to sell in all.

However, proceedings concerning a licence of plant variety rights in a new form of maize seed, to which the Commission applied its approach, were taken on appeal to the European Court of Justice.[13] The developer of the new variety, a French research organisation, INRA, had granted an exclusive manufacturing and sales licence for Germany to, Nungesser, a German firm. The Court accepted that, so far as this agreement sought to impose *absolute* territorial protection on Nungesser, by requiring that even a parallel importer should be prevented from obtaining the seed in France and exporting it to Germany, it was bad under Article 85(1) and could not be saved by exemption.

The parallel importer is a prime mover in operating the Common Market. But so far as the agreement only secured *open* exclusivity—undertakings that neither INRA nor its French licensees would themselves export to Germany—the matter must be judged in light of the prevailing circumstances in the particular market (in American parlance, by "rule of reason").[14] Given the "specific nature of the products in question", to introduce the newly developed seeds involved such risks in cultivating and marketing that a potential licensee might have been deterred by the prospect of direct competition in the same product from other licensees. Accordingly competition would be prejudiced by the licensor's inability to offer exclusive rights. It was not even a question of exemption; there was no infraction of Article 85(1).

7-35   The decision constitutes a *via media*. Open exclusivity may be useful where price differentials between different parts of the Common Market are not substantial, or where transportation costs or other factors serve to inhibit parallel importation. But there will be circumstances where the insistence that opportunities for the parallel importer be preserved may prevent the initial producer from supplying a cheap market at all with his product, to the detriment of consumers there. The Court has insisted that such a risk has to be taken, both here and (as we shall see) in relation to the free movement of goods between Member States.[15]

The "Maize Seed" decision undoubtedly curbed the Commission's vehemence against exclusivity provisions. In the 1984 Block Exemption it gave up its attempts to limit certain types of exclusivity clause to the protection of small enterprises. Instead it was provided that, in most cases, undertakings to preserve exclusivity are exempted, even where they do not

---

[13] *Nungesser v. E.C. Commission* [1982] E.C.R. 2015; Korah (1983) 28 Antitrust Bull. 699.
[14] On the distinction between absolute and open exclusivity, see Hoffmann and O'Farrell [1984] E.I.P.R. 104.
[15] See para. 18–04, below.

fall completely outside Article 85(1) of the Treaty of Rome.[16] In 1996, this approach has been continued. Article 1 of the Block Exemption may apply for the duration of patents licensed and, in the case of know-how, for 10 years from first E.C. marketing by a licensee.[17] Article 1 covers:

(1) the licensor's undertaking not to exploit the invention in the licensee's territory either by his own activities or by licensing others—though this, following *"Maize Seed"*, will be no infraction of Article 85(1) if it is needed in order to get new technology introduced;

(2) the licensee's undertaking not to exploit the invention in territory explicitly reserved by the licensor for himself; and

(3) the licensee's undertaking not to manufacture in the territory of another licensee or to engage actively in selling there (for instance, by setting up a branch or depot, or by advertising)[18]; but, so far as concerns passive selling (responding to unsolicited orders from the other licensees' territories), such exclusivity can last only for five years from the first putting of the licensed product by one of the licensees on some part of the Common Market.[19]

In support of the Court's disapproval of "absolute" elements in exclusivity, the Block Exemption places on the Black List terms requiring parallel importers to be refused supply or calling for difficulties to be placed in their way, unless an "objectively justified reason" can be given.[20] The major tightening which the Commission sought to introduce in the Technology Transfer Block Exemption has been to place a ceiling on the exemptions of exclusivity in terms of the licensee's market share (restricting it to 40 per cent). But in face of loud industrial resistance, this has become merely an exceptional reason for withdrawing the Block Exemption's protection in particular cases.[21]

---

[16] The Commission's Competition Directorate (DG IV) has shown no enthusiasm for the *Nungesser* outcome, though its existence has had to be acknowledged in the Block Exemptions. DG IV naturally prefers an approach through limited exemption (E.C. Treaty, Art. 85(3)), which it may then monitor and control.

[17] Block Exemption, Art. 1.2–1.4.

[18] It is true that the *"Maize Seed"* case does not deal directly with exclusivity between different territorial licensees, so it cannot be said with certainty that its reasoning applies equally to such cases; but it may well place some exclusive licences outside, Art. 85(1).

[19] This last limitation is reinforced by Block Exemption, Art 7.1.

[20] Block Exemption, Art 3.3. Blocking the movement of television sets into a country which has a different operating system would, for instance, be justified.

[21] See n. 8, above. Exemption under Art. 85(3) does not prevent a finding of abuse of dominant position under Art. 86: *Tetra-Pak Rausing v. Commission* [1991] II–E.C.R. 309.

(7) Restrictive Terms

(a) *Restrictions on production and sale*

7-36 According to the Black List, it is not justifiable to restrict the licensee's freedom, or the licensor's, in reaching certain basic decisions about marketing products made under the licence—in particular, about sale price[22] or their corollary, maximum quantities of production.[23] Nor is it permissible, directly or indirectly,[24] to divide up the customers that each may serve.[25]

However, the Commission has accepted that there is sufficient justification in allowing the licensor to restrict the types of application open to the licensee: for patents the licensee may be confined to "one or more technical fields of application" or to "one or more product markets".[26] It has also accepted that an exclusive licensor must be able to build in incentives to ensure himself an adequate return. He may require a minimum quantity of production by the licensee, or the payment of a minimum royalty.[27] Equally he may impose a requirement that the licensee use his best endeavours to exploit the licensed technology, though he must not go so far as directly to prohibit the production, use or distribution of a competing product, or other forms of competition.[28] Inevitably it must be doubted whether the "black-listing" of non-competition clauses has much effect, given the scope of what may be included.

(b) *Technical adequacy versus unwanted ties*

7-37 The licensor of a new technique has a legitimate interest to ensure that it is adequately used by any licensee. He may, for instance, insist that the licensee should have no power to sub-license or assign the licence to another. In *Erauw-Jacquéry v. La Hesbignonne*,[29] the Court of Justice has recognised the propriety of such an objective, and the White List includes such a clause.[30] The licensee may be placed under an obligation (a "tie-in") to procure goods or services from the licensor or his nominee so far as is necessary for a technically satisfactory exploitation of the invention or know-how; to the same end he may be placed under minimum quality specifications and have to undergo checks to see that they are observed.[31] It

---

[22] Block Exemption, Art. 3.1.
[23] *ibid.*, Art. 3.5.
[24] Indirectly: *e.g.* by reference to distribution systems or types of packaging.
[25] Block Exemption, Art. 3.4: but the parties must previously have been competing and the restriction must be within the same technological field of use.
[26] *ibid.*, Art. 2.1.8.
[27] *ibid.*, Art. 2.1.9.
[28] *ibid.*, Art. 3.2.
[29] [1988] E.C.R. 1919.
[30] Block Exemption, Art. 2.1.2.
[31] *ibid.*, Art. 2.1.5.

is also proper for the licensor to require that products be sold under his trade mark or with his get-up, provided that the licensee is not deprived of his ability to indentify himself as manufacturer.[32] But an opposition may be raised against a term obliging the licensee to accept further licences, or other tied goods or services which he does not want[33] (if that can be established, given that he has in fact accepted them).[34]

(c) *Further technical advances*

Manufacturers ought to perfect what they are producing: to this end the **7–38** patent system and the legal protection of know-how act as lures. If therefore a licensee must hand over to the licensor any rights in his improvements, the incentive may be substantially dampened.[35] Hence from the outset, the E.C. Commission has objected to "grant-back" clauses which require assignment to the original licensor.[36] Even a clause which obliges the licensee to give information and non-exclusive rights is likely to be objectionable if it does not impose a reciprocal obligation on the licensor.[37] Unless such a mutual exchange is agreed, the policy insists that each party should compete with the other in the matter of improvements.[38]

(d) *Duration and termination*

No licence is necessary, if the patent in question is invalid or the know-how **7–39** is not capable of protection. A person who nevertheless takes a licence will be working the technique and so will be in a particularly strong position to discover reasons why the rights are in fact invalid. Against that prospect arising to upset the established relationship under the licence, traditional practice was to require the licensee to undertake not to challenge the validity or existence of the rights during the term of the agreement. The Commission was formerly steadfast in disapproving of "no challenge" clauses, as seeking to maintain the extraction of royalties where none are properly justified.[39] In general, this approach is supported by the Court of Justice.[40] But, it has held, in an agreement compromising a genuine dispute

---

[32] *ibid.*, Art 1.1.7.

[33] *ibid.*, Art. 4.2(a), and note the example given in the Treaty itself—Art. 85(1)(e).

[34] The complicated provision against "tie-ins" to dealings with British patents, contained in the Patents Act 1977, s. 44, will be repealed under the Competition Act 1998, s. 70. It had become an occasional trap for the unwary.

[35] Even more so, if the licensee must grant over rights in competing technology.

[36] Patent Notice, 1962, ID IV. Now "black-listed": Block Exemption, Art 3.6. This approach has been adopted by the Court of Justice: *Royon* v. *Meilland* [1988] 4 C.M.L.R. 193.

[37] For permissible feed-back and grant-back, see Block Exemption, Art. 2.1.4.

[38] See also *Davidson Rubber* and *Kabelmetal/Luchaire* (n. 2, above).

[39] See, *e.g. Davidson Rubber, Kabelmetal/Luchaire* (n. 2, above).

[40] *IMA v. Windsurfing International* [1984] 1 C.M.L.R. 1; *Royon v. Meilland* [1988] 4 C.M.L.R. 193; Venit (1987) 18 I.I.C. 1.

over the validity of a patent, that a clause may be included to prevent the licensee from reopening the issue which has been compromised.[41] Accordingly, in the 1995 Block Exemption, no challenge clauses are only subject to the four-month opposition procedure.[42] The Commission also looks attentively at settlements of disputes and at the findings of arbitrators, to ensure that they do not dress up what is really an amicable market-sharing arrangement between competitors.[43] Inevitably it may be slow and costly to decided on which side of the line the "compromise" falls.

7–40 The Technology Transfer Block exemption permits the inclusion of a term by which the licence may be for less than the full duration of a patent or patents, or the period in which the know-how remains secret. In consequence it is permissible to require the licensee not thereafter to exploit the patents (so long as in force) or the know-how (so long as still secret).[44] By way of corollary, it is permissible to continue royalty arrangements even after expiry of a patent, if the licensee has been obtaining wider technical advantages under the agreement.[45]

In the Block Exemption, there is no longer any black-listing of a term allowing the licensor to prolong the licence by adding in licences of further patents and know-how. This change raised a tension with a provision of the Patents Act 1977, but this is now being abolished.[46]

3. Compulsory Licences

7–41 A wholehearted patent system will contain nothing that fetters a patentee's power to act as a monopolist if the market allows it: he will be able to hold production of his invention down to the level of maximum profit. But many countries have felt the urge to qualify this full potential in the name of some other political objective, such as local working of the invention or the satisfaction of consumer demand.[47] The technique for this is generally some form of compulsory licence, which will prevent the patentee from acting as sole producer. He will be obliged instead to face direct competition subject only to a royalty or other fee on the licensee's sales, assessed by an outside arbitrator under some criterion of reasonableness.[48] Pressure for this sort of

---

[41] *Bayer and Hennecke v. Süllhöfer* [1988] E.C.R. 5249; Korah [1988] E.I.P.R. 381.

[42] Block Exemption, Art. 4.2(b).

[43] *Bronbemaling* (n. 2, above); *Sirdar/Phildar* [1975] 1 C.M.L.R. D93 (trade mark dispute); *cf. Penney's T.M.* [1978] F.S.R. 385 (settlement of trade mark war, parts of which are documented in the report).

[44] Block Exemption, Art. 2.1.3. This too is a matter on which the Commission came only slowly to its present view.

[45] *Kai Ottung v. Klee & Weilbach* [1989] E.C.R. 1177.

[46] PA 1977, s. 45, repealed once the Competition Act 1998, s. 70 takes effect.

[47] For the beginnings in the U.K., see para. 3–15, above.

[48] "Compulsory licence" in this broad sense extends to the Crown use provisions discussed in the next section. Their similarity is stressed, for instance, in CPC, Art. 46(2).

curb tends to follow upon the success of particular patentees, frequently foreigners.

The meetings of Paris Convention countries have long been the field for exhausting battles over the principle of compulsory licensing. A stringent requirement of local working, for instance, would seem a means by which one country could give preference for its home inventors, while hoping for no corresponding handicap upon them abroad. In the industrial countries, however, what has seemed vital in an international forum has become purely token in domestic practice: compulsory licensing provisions are commonly enmeshed in such a net of procedures that it is only the threat of invoking them that carries any significant weight. Exceptionally, the compulsory licence has been used severely enough for a serious falling-off of patenting to occur. This led to the 1982 breakdown in revising the Paris Convention.[49]

The TRIPS Agreement signals an important reversal of direction on the **7–42** subject. It subjects the granting of compulsory licences (or any other use without the patentee's authorisation, including use by governments and their collaborators[50]) to a splay of conditions.[51] Each instance has to be considered individually, and must be preceded by attempts at voluntary negotiation. The scope and duration of the licence must be confined to its purpose[52] and must be open to review when circumstances change. The licence must be non-exclusive, non-assignable and predominantly for supply of the domestic market. Adequate remuneration must be required. Any decision, whether about authorisation or remuneration, must be open to judicial review. There are further conditions where a head patent is being licensed in order to permit exploitation of a subsidiary patent. The hostility of the United States to the very idea of compulsory patent licensing finds determined expression in these provisions.

(1) Compulsory licensing under the 1977 Act

(a) *Legal grounds*

Once a British patent has been granted for three years, the Comptroller has **7–43** power[53] to grant compulsory licences under it[54] on a number of grounds. He then settles the terms as he sees fit.[55] The elaborate provisions first give an

---

[49] See para. 3–17, above.
[50] For the effect of this on Crown use, see para. 7–51, n. 90, below.
[51] TRIPS, Art. 31.
[52] The are special limits here for semi-conductor technology patents.
[53] PA 1977, s. 48(1). An applicant may receive a licence in his own favour and in certain circumstances also in favour of his customers (see s. 49(1)). A government department may seek a licence for another.
[54] Or to enter a "licences of right" indorsement upon the register – as to which, see para. 4–25, above.
[55] PA 1977, s. 48(4). The licence may be exclusive even of the patentee and may revoke other licences: s. 49(2).

extensive list of grounds, and the applicant must show a case within one or more of them. But their breadth is qualified, not simply by the fact that the Comptroller's jurisdiction is discretionary, but by the enumeration of various policy considerations which he is expected to balance in assessing the particular case. Recently, as the result of decisions of the European Court of Justice,[56] it has also been necessary to ensure that compulsory licence rules do not result in discrimination against enterprises from other E.C. States which seek to export to Britain. Moreover, since the Comptroller may not make any order at variance with an international convention to which the United Kingdom is a party, he is obliged to observe the restrictive terms of TRIPs, Article 31.[57]

Under a special provision concerning food and drug patents, which was abandoned by the 1977 Act, compulsory licences were available save exceptionally. The general rules covering compulsory licences (which survive in that Act) do not raise the same expectation that once a ground is made out the public interest demands a licence unless there are special circumstances. It is this difference which is the first explanation of why the general provisions result in very few applications and even fewer grants.

7–44   Three principal motives have lain behind the creation of the present powers. They form useful heads under which to group the statutory grounds:

(1) It should not be permissible to hinder the exploitation of other new technology. Hence one ground for granting compulsory licences is that the working of another patented invention in the United Kingdom is being prevented or hindered through refusal to grant licences at all or on reasonable terms.[58] This could arise, for instance, where one patentee is refusing to licence a "head" patent to another who has a derivative patent for a selection or improvement. The ground is subject to the requirement that the compulsory licensee be prepared to cross-license his own patent on reasonable terms.[59] This power is easy to justify in the light of the overall objectives of the patent system.

(2) A patent should not be a pretext for refusing to exploit new technology at all. Thus one ground for compulsory licensing is that United Kingdom demand for a patented product is not being met on reasonable terms.[60] There is a perennial fear that inventions so

---

[56] *E.C. Commission v. Italy and v. United Kingdom* [1992] 1 E.C.R. 777, 829; and see the decisions concerning compulsory licences of right associated with extensions of patent term under the 1977 Act: *Allen & Hanbury's v. Generics (U.K.)* [1988] E.C.R. 1245; *Generics v. Smith Kline & French* [1992] 1 E.C.R. 5335; PA 1977, s. 46(3)(c) (as amended). *cf.* CPC, Arts 46, 77, 83. See also para. 18–06, below.

[57] PA 1977, s. 55(5); *Allen & Hanburys v. Controller of Patents (Ireland)* [1997] F.S.R. 1, ECJ.

[58] PA 1977, s. 48(3)(d)(ii). Note now the contents of the TRIPS Agreements, Art. 31(l).

[59] PA 1977, s. 48(7); *cf. Taylor's Patent* (1912) 29 R.P.C. 296.

[60] PA 1977, s. 48(3)(b) and see also the grounds mentioned under head (3) below.

efficient as to threaten the future of an industry (the long-life light-bulb or razor-blade, for instance) are patented in order to delay their introduction. If that fear is at all justified, this power ought to have some effect. But the effect may only be to make the industry more than ever determined to suppress the information entirely.[61] Only very exceptionally could compulsory licensing of patents help: the usual difficulty with inventions is to show that they are a success. Compulsory licence applications in Britain (few as they have been) have mostly concerned things that the patentee or his voluntary licensees have shown to have market potential.

Note that the ground just mentioned covers more than the case of suppression. Its terms are wide enough to support an attack on "unduly high" monopoly prices: of this, more below.

(3) A patent should result in the invention being worked in the United Kingdom or another E.C. State.[62] As the history of the Paris Convention shows, most countries have wanted to use the patent system to induce the actual working of the invention in their home territories.[63] Some countries used to provide harsh sanctions in this endeavour[64] and one role of the Convention has been to secure some moderation: by requiring that compulsory licensing should be tried before revocation, and that it should not be imposed within three years of grant.[65] For many inventions, the scale needed for cost-effective manufacture would make it absurd to expect plant to be established in each country where products are sold. However, it is in such cases that compulsory licences are least likely to be sought.[66] But in less obvious cases, patentees may feel that there is enough danger in failing to work in a country for them to set up facilities at least to finish their products there.[67]

The legal grounds in the British legislation, even after taking account of **7–45** E.C. law qualifications,[68] are couched broadly. The patent may be licensed:

---

[61] The fear is easily fanned in political debate on patents. Evidence on the matter is very hard to come by.

[62] See para. 7–41, above.

[63] See Ladas, *The International Protection of Industrial Property* (1930); Penrose, *The Economics of the International Patent System* (1951), pp. 78–87. The old notion of the "importer-inventor" reflected the same desire: see para. 4–06, above.

[64] See para. 3–15, above.

[65] PIP, Art. 5A. The Convention allows revocation as a sanction if compulsory licensing is ineffective, but this has been dropped from PA 1977.

[66] For the economic implications of compulsory working, see Penrose (n. 63, above), Chap. 8.

[67] Thus obscuring the question whether the patent is really being worked in the territory. Pharmaceuticals, for instance, can be conveniently transported in bulk and made into tablet form immediately for supply.

[68] For these, see *E.C. Commission v. U.K. and Italy* [1992] 1 E.C.R. 777; *Generics v. SFK* [1992] 1 E.C.R. 5335; note also *Allen & Hanburys v. Generics* [1988] E.C.R. 1275.

(1) if the invention is not being worked to the fullest extent that is reasonably practicable in the United Kingdom or the E.C.[69];

(2) if United Kingdom demand for a patented product is not being met on reasonable terms or is being met to a substantial extent by importation from outside the E.C.[70];

(3) if United Kingdom working is being hindered or prevented by importation from outside the E.C.[71];

(4) if refusal of licences (at all or on reasonable terms) prevents an export market from being supplied with United Kingdom products or prejudices the establishment or development of United Kingdom industry.[72]

(b) *The discretion*

7–46 Beside these grounds, the Comptroller must balance a variety of considerations in deciding whether and what licence to grant compulsorily. To some extent these make clearer what limits upon monopoly power Parliament considered that it was imposing. Thus, in addition to weighing such factors[73] as the nature of the invention, the time that has elapsed since grant, what the patentee or any licensee has already done to make full use of the invention and the ability of the applicant to work it to the public advantage and the risks to him, three purposes are stated to be the aim of the power: (1) to secure full use quickly, (2) to give the patentee "reasonable remuneration", and (3) to protect anyone working or developing an invention in the United Kingdom (or, probably, the E.C.) from unfair prejudice.[74]

This contemplates qualifying the patentee's potential market power in two ways. First, the pressure that it imposes upon him to establish manufacturing facilities in the E.C. may prevent him from producing where he can do so most cheaply and efficiently. Secondly, the requirement that working be to the fullest practicable extent appears to contemplate that price ought to be reduced to satisfy larger demand, even if the monopoly

---

[69] PA 1977, s. 48(3)(a); *Kamborian's Patent* [1961] R.P.C. 403; *Kalle's Patent* [1966] F.S.R. 112; *Therma-Tru Corp.'s Patent* [1997] R.P.C. 777.

[70] PA 1977, s. 48(3)(b).

[71] *ibid.*, s. 48(3)(c); this covers the direct products of patented processes.

[72] *ibid.*, s. 48(3)(d)(i), (iii), (e), where exports are concerned, the countries may be limited: s. 48(6). This provision must also now be regarded as qualified by the need not to create discriminatory conditions within the Single Market.

[73] *cf.* the list of factors in *Brownie Wireless' Application* (1929) 46 R.P.C. 457 at 473.

[74] See PA 1977, s. 50. The factors are to be weighed at the time of making the application; the patentee may not fudge the issue by hasty last minute activity: *McKechnie's Application* (1943) 51 R.P.C. 461 at 467.

profits will in consequence be reduced.[75] (On this front, the application will only take place if the patentee will not grant a voluntary licence on acceptable terms.)

But because the Comptroller must still leave the patentee with "reasonable remuneration", the licence must not venture too far in either of these directions. The courts have had little enough opportunity to indicate how far it is proper to go. As far as manufacturing in the E.C. is concerned, the patentee will not protect himself against any grant at all simply by showing that present costs of foreign manufacture abroad are lower; there must be an historical inquiry to see whether he "used his monopoly fairly as between home and foreign trade", that is to determine whether his efforts to build up foreign manufacture did not prejudice the chance of doing so in the E.C.[76]

As far as concerns "further markets", where the foreign patentees of **7–47** copying machinery had sold to a limited field of British customers, a compulsory licence was granted to a British company upon their prediction that they could sell to an extended range of customers.[77] Even when the Comptroller decides to grant the licence, its terms (particularly the rate of royalty) will influence the licensee's decisions about selling price and hence quantity; which in turn will affect the patentee's remuneration. The royalty rate, however, is most likely to be fixed by comparison with any relevant rate charged by the patentee or others in the industry for similar licences.

A compulsory licence system which is directed at one or other form of **7–48** insufficient exploitation, and which thus requires careful investigation of the circumstances before grant, is not likely to be much used. This is indeed borne out by British and other experience.[78] How far the threat of applying

---

[75] The unadorned case that the patentee's own prices in the U.K. are too high and that therefore a compulsory licence should be granted, seems rarely to have been presented: but note *Robin Electric's Petition* (1915) 32 R.P.C. 202 (minimum price clause in voluntary licence required licensee to charge higher prices in U.K. than abroad; held unobjectionable, since prices "not so high as to be a serious burden on the consumer or to be unreasonable"). Such an issue is examinable by the Monopolies and Mergers Commission, if the general conditions for a reference to it are satisfied. In essence such an issue was dealt with by the Commission in its report criticising the pricing by the Hoffmann-La Roche group of its tranquillisers trade-marked "Librium" and "Valium": Report on Tranquillisers (H.C. 197, 1973).

[76] Parker J., *Hatschek's Patent* (1909) 26 R.P.C. 228 at 243; see also *Johnson's Patent* (1909) 26 R.P.C. 52; *Bremer's Patent* (1909) 26 R.P.C. 449 at 465.

[77] *Kallé's Patent* [1966] F.S.R. 112. A number of grounds were alleged by the applicant. In a case where the circumstances were rather special (*Cathro's Application* (1934) 51 R.P.C. 75) it was said that demand must be actual not potential. But the Act now refers to "a" rather than "the" demand, and other cases, including *Kallé*, making nothing of the point: see also *Boult's Patent* (1909) 26 R.P.C. 383 at 387; *Fabricmeter's Application* (1936) 53 R.P.C. 307 at 312; *Kamborian's Patent* [1961] R.P.C. 403 at 405. As to sub-licensing, see *Hilti's Patent* [1988] R.P.C. 51.

[78] Between 1959 and 1968 an average of 1.5 were applied for in the U.K. per annum under the general provisions; only two were granted for the whole period; for the special food and drugs provision average applications were 4.1 per annum; four were granted in toto: Banks Report (Cmnd. 4407, 1970), App.D(d).

to the Comptroller enhances the bargaining position of would-be voluntary licensees cannot be measured. Neither can it be discounted.[79] But in many cases it will not be strong: for the licensee may also need know-how to get started: and the licensor cannot be obliged to provide that under the present rules.

4. CROWN USE

7–49 The British government has a special exemption from the exclusive rights of patentees. The Crown may make or sanction use of a patented invention without previous licence, subject only to an obligation to pay compensation for doing so. Originally the Crown was in no sense bound by Letters Patent: for one thing, classic theory relieved "the Crown"—not just the sovereign in person—of civil responsibility imposed by courts of justice.[80] Compensation for use of patented inventions was paid *ex gratia*. In 1883 came a change. In principle the Crown was made subject to patents, but was given the benefit of Crown use provisions that were the ancestors of the present law.[81] Compensation became a matter of legal entitlement; but the Crown could, of course, claim that it was not within the scope of monopoly or that the patent was invalid.[82]

The obvious justification for the Crown use provision lies in national security.[83] But central government acts in many other spheres besides defence and the wider potential of its powers were dramatically demonstrated in 1965: the House of Lords held that the Ministry of Health might authorise an importer to bring in drugs not made by the patentee for use in the NHS hospital service.[84] In the cases to which it is applicable, the Crown's ability to override the patentee's decisions on exploitation may prove a decisive counterweight to full monopoly power. Because of this, it tends to be viewed critically, particularly in the E.C. and other countries which do not allow their governments so wide-ranging a weapon.[85] In

---

[79] The Banks Committee thought there was enough indirect effect to justify retaining the provisions on compulsory licensing in general: *ibid.*, Chap. 12; but it shared the hostility of leading pharmaceutical firms towards the compulsory licensing provision (PA 1949, s. 41—abandoned in PA 1977) that allowed the grant of licences save in exceptional circumstances: Bank Reports, Chap. 14.

[80] *Feather v. R.* (1865) 6 B. & S. 257. For the political history, O'Dell, *Inventions and Official Secrecy* (1994). Printing of bank notes for a foreign Government is not a sovereign act. It may be a patent infringement justiciable in English courts: *A Ltd. v. B Bank* [1997] F.S.R. 165, CA.

[81] Patents, Design and Trade Marks Act 1883, s. 27.

[82] Today validity may also be challenged in proceedings for compensation: PA 1977, s. 74(1)(e).

[83] In times of national emergency, the Crown's powers become very wide indeed: see PA 1977, s. 59.

[84] *Pfizer v. Ministry of Health* [1965] A.C. 512, [1965] R.P.C. 261.

[85] See, *e.g.* Demaret, *Patents, Territorial Restrictions and EEC Law* (1978), pp. 12–17, 87–89. (On the "reasonable reward" theory also applied by British legislation to compulsory licensing, and on the impact of compulsory licensing and Crown use provisions in the *Sterling Drug* case [1972] F.S.R. 529. Note the limitations now imposed by the TRIPS Agreement, Art. 31.

response, it can be said that if a government department decides to take up an invention, it may well be providing an exceptionally large market for it, one that it might take much greater effort to establish in the private sector. As an incentive to invent and innovate, therefore, the prospect of securing compensation for Crown use may in many instances be broadly as attractive as full monopoly profits from other sources. Whether this sort of justification has a sufficient basis in historical fact deserves examination: this it has never had.

The special powers of the Crown to use and then pay compensation are **7–50** governed by three principal factors:

(1) The acts performed must be "for the services of the Crown".[86] They do not have to be done by a government department. Anyone authorised to act on the Crown's behalf is included,[87] but still the aim must be to fulfil a Crown service, whether the benefit goes to the Crown or to members of the public. By the Crown is meant the executive government of the United Kingdom and its services are those supplied by Crown servants under the direction of a minister.[88] This excludes services provided by other agencies of government or supported by public finance: the industries still in public ownership, independent authorities such as the Post Office, local government, universities and so forth. It does, however, cover the supply of anything for foreign defence purposes (that is arms to foreign governments), the supply of scheduled drugs in the Health Service, and research into, and supply of, atomic energy.[89] But why, it may be asked, central government and not the rest? Which leads back to the question: apart from defence, has central government (and through it the public) such a claim to cheap inventions that the incentive device provided by the patent system deserves to be substantially qualified?

(2) Not every act which would otherwise amount to infringement falls within the Crown use exemption. In particular, while acts of manufacture, use and associated activities of keeping and importing are within the exemption, selling and offering to sell fall outside, save exceptionally: as an incident of making, using or importing; in contracts to supply arms to foreign governments; in supplying scheduled medicines through the NHS pharmaceutical services; and in disposing of things no longer required.[90]

---

[86] PA 1977, s. 55(1).

[87] *ibid.* The authorisation must be in writing; but it does not have to be given until after the event: s. 55(6). Normally the patentee or an exclusive licensee needs no authority, and so obtains no right to compensation; but see the exceptions in s. 57(3), (4); Ency. PL, 9–18.

[88] *Pfizer v. Ministry of Health* [1965] R.P.C. 261 at 295, 301, 306.

[89] PA 1977, s. 56(2)–(4).

[90] *ibid.*, s. 55(1). Even so, it is hard to see how these distinctions satisfy the TRIPS requirement that each case be considered individually: see above, para. 7–42.

(3) The rate of compensation is not dictated by the Crown but will, if it cannot be agreed, be settled by the court.[91] The Crown is entitled to put itself in the position of a licensee. If it causes loss of manufacturing or other profit, it is obliged to compensate for this.[92] Other benefits from government departments have to be brought into consideration and there is a curious provision which possibly means that the patentee may have his compensation reduced if he would not accept a reasonable offer from the Crown.[93]

Where these rules cover the operation, there are a variety of provisions which override ancillary rights: terms in licences, assignments and agreements restricting working or requiring payments are of no effect[94]; copyright in certain models and documents is not infringed[95]; subsequent acquirers are treated as if the Crown were the patentee.[96] In addition, the Crown is made free of all obligations not only if it has undertaken prior use but even if the invention has been merely recorded for the Crown before the priority date of the patent.[97]

---

[91] *ibid.*, s. 55(4). The obligation may run from the date of publishing the application; or, if revealed without obligation of confidence to a government department before that, from the priority date. Note that the government department concerned is under (sanctionless) obligation to notify the patentee of use, unless contrary to the public interest: s. 55(7). See generally, *Henry v. Ministry of Defence* [1999] R.P.C. 442, CA.

[92] CDPA 1988, Sched. 5, para. 16, belatedly abrogating *Patchett's Patent* [1967] R.P.C. 237, CA.

[93] PA 1977, s. 58(3). There are a number of provisions limiting the right to compensation on grounds similar to those limiting claims to damages for infringment of rights in patents and applications: see s. 58(6), (8), (10).

[94] *ibid.*, s. 57(1), (2).

[95] *ibid.*, s. 57(1). By contrast, registered designs are subject to Crown use provisions, similar to those applying to patents: see Registered Designs Act 1949, s. 12, Sched. 1. Rights in confidential information cannot be overridden (PA 1977, s. 55(10)), save in the cases covered by the Defence Contracts Act 1958, ss. 2, 3.

[96] PA 1977, s. 55(8).

[97] *ibid.*, s. 55(4). As to the scope of this, see Ency. PL, para. 9–019.

Part III

CONFIDENCE

CHAPTER 8

CONFIDENTIAL INFORMATION

1. INTRODUCTION

(1) Nature of the liability

A person ought to keep a secret if he has said that he will do so. English **8–01** courts have translated this simple moral precept into a form of civil legal liability which is of considerable breadth.[1] The development runs counter to the judges' traditional reluctance to adopt broad propositions as ground rules for the imposition of liability, and they are now having to face some of the difficulties inherent in their unusual course.[2]

All sorts of information may be imparted or gathered in confidence; the degree of secrecy required may be partial or total. The fashioning of the law into more specific rules is accordingly difficult and much of what follows may appear as imprecise as the subject-matter is ephemeral. In contrast with many other legal systems, English law does not distinguish between types of information that may be protected against breach of confidence: technological secrets, such as chemical formulae and mechanical techniques,[3] commercial records such as customer lists and sales figures,[4] marketing, professional and managerial procedures,[5] and equally information of political significance[6] and about personal relationships, such

---

[1] The subject has generated a considerable literature. See esp. Jones (1970) 86 L.Q.R. 463; North (1971) 12 J.S.P.T.L. 149; Finn, *Fiduciary Obligations* (1977) Chap. 19 and (1984) 58 A.L.J. 497; Vaver (1979) 1 E.I.P.R. 301; English Law Commission, Report No. 110, *Breach of Confidence* (Cmnd. 8388, 1981); Gurry, *Breach of Confidence* (1984); Dean, *Law of Trade Secrets* (1990); Clarke, *Confidentiality and the Law* (1990); Coleman, *The Legal Protection of Trade Secrets* (1992); Meagher, Gummow and Lehane, *Equity: Doctrines and Remedies* (3rd ed., 1992), Chap. 41; Goff and Jones: *Law of Restitution* (5th ed., 1998), Chap. 34; Hull, *Commercial Secrecy* (1998)..

[2] As to the moral basis of the cause of action, see *House of Spring Gardens v. Point Blank* [1983] F.S.R. 213 at 253, [1985] F.S.R. 327 at 335, S.C. (Ir.).

[3] Many of the cases concern this variety of "know-how", as examples below will show.

[4] *e.g. Robb v. Green* [1895] 2 Q.B. 315; *Lamb v. Evans* [1893] 1 Ch. 218.

[5] *Stephenson Jordan v. McDonald and Evans* (1951) 68 R.P.C. 190 (but note the traditional reluctance to recognise that business management techniques deserve protection: Evershed M.R., same case (1952) 69 R.P.C. 10 at 14); *Thomas v. Mould* [1968] 1 All E.R. 963; *Interfirm Comparison v. Law Society of N.S.W.* [1975] R.P.C. 137.

[6] *Fraser v. Evans* [1969] 1 All E.R. 8, CA; *Att.-Gen. v. Jonathan Cape* (1976) Q.B. 752, DC (Cabinet papers); *Att.-Gen. v. Guardian Newspapers (No. 2)* [1990] A.C. 109 ("*Spycatcher*").

as the Duchess of Argyll's tales to the Duke of her earlier sentimental journeys[7]—all have been treated as protectable.

8–02   English law has proved unwilling to include a "right to privacy" among its pantheon of protectable values, fearing that so broad a concept would unduly prejudice competing interests in freedom of information and expression and in a free press. Some of the potential territory is covered by a breach of confidence action, which extends to personal as well as economic subject-matter. But even so, its keystone is the undertaking to preserve confidence, which is either given directly by the defendant, or by someone from whom the defendant derives his information. Invasions of privacy which lie outside this limit remain open to civil or criminal redress only if some general tort, crime or other wrong has been committed. Confidence protection thus plays an important role in achieving a sensitive political balance. We shall return to its relationship to the legal protection of privacy when we consider proposals for reform at the end of the chapter.[8]

In the United States, as in many Continental countries, in that branch of the subject which is concerned with trade secrets, the criminal law operates alongside the civil to provide sanctions against the most serious breaches of confidence and industrial spying. Under pressure from the Confederation of British Industry and others, the Law Commission has put out a Discussion Paper on the subject and there is some prospect that Britain may take an equivalent step. The concerns which the proposal evokes are also best reviewed after the scope and difficulties of civil liability in this sphere have been considered.[9]

(2) Confidence and patents

8–03   Given the range of subject-matter it is important to compare the protection of confidential information with that provided by patents and by copyright. In the realm of technical ideas confidence cannot play any long-term role unless the information can be put to commercial use without at the same time becoming public.[10] A mechanical device will almost always reveal its workings to experts once it is marketed; but a process of manufacture may not be similarly detectable. In the latter case, an inventor may secure a patent that gives him monopoly protection even against independent devisers of the same invention; but it is for a limited period, and on condition that the invention is sufficiently described in the specification. Accordingly, to keep this invention secret through obligations of confidence

---

[7] *Argyll v. Argyll* [1967] Ch. 302.
[8] See paras 8–54 *et seq.*
[9] See paras 8–61.
[10] In the short term—until a patent application can be filed—obligations of confidence prevent the danger that revelation of the invention will destroy its novelty: see para. 5–14, above.

is for him an alternative, not an additional, form of protection—an alternative that is not tied to specified time periods but which is good only against those who receive the information directly or (in some cases) indirectly from him.

Many countries have accepted that this choice should be provided, however much it may detract from the incentive to publicise that is one root purpose of the patent system. Even in the United States, where the matter has been extensively debated,[11] the outcome has been to permit the alternatives. For it was finally decided that industry must be assured the opportunity of conserving new technology that was not necessarily patentable by means of confidence; and to insist that patentable inventions should only be protected by patents would be to introduce a distinction that it would be difficult and cumbersome to draw.[12] In any case, in current European law, prior secret use is not an objection to a later patent on an invention.[13] A person who chooses to keep an idea confidential during his own exploitation of it runs the serious risk of someone else discovering and patenting it.

In particular the need to protect trade secrets (technical and commercial), not just as an aspect of contractual obligation but against infractions by direct and indirect recipients in non-contractual relationships, has not infrequently been neglected, even in legal systems which have the normal panoply of specific intellectual property rights.[14] Some countries have filled the void by statutory rules or a broad interpretation of unfair competition liability.

The increasing ease with which information can be despatched round the world electronically gives an urgency to pleas for greater legal security over confidential information.[15] Responding to this interest of creators and investors, the TRIPS Agreement now contains a broad provision requiring that persons who have secret information lawfully in their control be able to prevent its unauthorised disclosure, acquisition or use "in a manner contrary to honest commercial practices".[16] The liability is stated to arise

---

[11] In *Cadbury Schweppes v. FBI Foods* (1999) 83 C.P.R. (3d) 289, the SC of Canada gives this as one reason for not elevating confidential information to the status of property.

[12] In the wake of the *Sears* and *Compco* cases (para. 1–21, above) doubts about trade secrets protection were raised in *Lear v. Adkins* 395 U.S. 653 (1969), and finally disposed of by *Kewanee v. Bicron* 416 U.S. 470 (1974).

[13] See above, para. 5–06.

[14] Thus it took until 1990 for Japan (of all countries) to give special protection to secret knowhow and the like. The uncertain status of the liability in many systems has led to calls that trade secrets should be treated as property: Soltysinski (1986) 17 I.I.C. 331.

[15] Cross-border data flows pose private international law conundrums, which have not begun to be resolved. Their solution could soon become urgent.

[16] Art. 39: secret includes what is not generally known in interested circles. Art. 39(3) has a special provision on pharmaceutical and agricultural test data submitted in order to gain approval; these must be protected against "unfair commercial use". *Quaere* the position regarding the certification of rival products: *cf.* para. 8–52, below. See generally, Krasser in Beier and Schricker, p. 216.

"in the course of ensuring effective protection against unfair competition as provided in Article 10bis of the Paris Convention (1967).[17] Accordingly it must be confined to abuses of trade sercrets between competitors.[18]

8–04 In actual practice, patents are often secured for a central invention, while much that is learned in the process of bringing it into commercial production is tied up as secret "know-how" by means of confidence undertakings.[19] The distinction, as we have noted, is marked in licensing practice[20]—bare patent licences are very different from operational production packages. The question to be considered here is how far the non-patentable "know-how" is really capable of protection against those who seek to make use of it without consent, as distinct from those who will pay for a licence to obtain it. The problem commonly arises when managers and other employees of a concern seek to take the "know-how" off to a rival business. We shall see that the courts have been particularly reluctant to saddle ex-employees with obligations that will prevent them from disposing of their general knowledge and skill to their best advantage.[21] Against them, breach of confidence proceedings are hard to maintain, and in this way also the courts have checked the ability of breach of confidence protection to make real inroads into the territory of the patent system.

(3) Confidence and copyright

8–05 In principle copyright is capable of helping to resist invasions of privacy, but the intrusion must take the form of making at least one copy, or of giving a performance in public, or of doing one of the other acts specified as constituting infringement. Coupled with this, there must be a copying of the manner of expression and not merely use of the information contained in the copyright work. The proceedings, moreover, must be brought by those with title to the copyright.[22] Breach of confidence protection resembles copyright in that the information which the defendant seeks to deploy must derive from that which the plaintiff seeks to protect. But confidence protection is not generally tied to particular ways of using the material.[23] It is concerned with the information in substance and not in

---

[17] A footnote indicates that liability should extend at least to knowing and grossly negligent third parties.

[18] The formulation is designed to import into Art. 10bis an activity which is conspicuously absent from the examples which it gives. These relate to activities liable to mislead the public.

[19] The patent has, of course, to satisfy the requirement of sufficient disclosure: see paras 5–93 *et seq.*, above.

[20] See para. 7–21, above.

[21] Hence the fact that licensees may be willing to pay for know-how does not necessarily demonstrate that the know-how amounts to more than an employee is entitled to treat as general skill and knowledge: see *Potters-Ballotini v. Weston-Baker* [1977] R.P.C. 202, CA; *Yates Circuit Foil v. Electrofoils* [1976] F.S.R. 345; and see paras 8–24—8–30, below.

[22] See paras 12–04 *et seq.*, below.

[23] But where the confidentiality relates to the way in which ideas are expressed (*e.g.* in a set of precedents or a questionnaire), breach which does not result in use of the same expression may give rise only to nominal damages: *Interfirm Comparison v. Law Society* [1975] R.P.C. 157.

form,[24] and only the person to whom obligations of confidence are owed will be entitled to sue.[25]

Thus, if a secret society has rules written for it by a functionary, who does nothing to dispose of his copyright in them, a renegade member intent on "exposing" the society to the public may be in breach of confidential obligations to the society, however he chooses to summarise the rules. But he will infringe the author's copyright in the rules only if he substantially reproduces their content. If he pleads "public interest" in defence, the concept is probably the same in each case; but for copyright there are further statutory defences of "fair dealing" that may be apposite.[26]

(4) Historical and doctrinal

The jurisdiction to restrain breach of confidence has its roots in equity, **8–06** partly because the remedy most often sought has been the injunction, and partly because the subject-matter occupies the same moral terrain as breach of trust.[27] The scope of the modern law began to be settled around 1850 with *Prince Albert v. Strange*[28] (literary material, at once royal and private, on the borders of copyright) and *Morison v. Moat*[29] (recipe for a medicine). In both cases, injunctions were granted against indirect recipients of the confidential information, and the jurisdiction was said, rather prodigally, to arise by virtue of property, agreement, confidence, trust and bailment. But it was left uncertain then (as it remains now) in what circumstances direct and indirect recipients of information would have liability imposed upon them. In the period after the Judicature Acts, there were some attempts (typical of their time) to confine the equitable wrong to cases in which the original disclosee agreed by contract, express or implied, to respect

---

[24] Nor does the information have to exist in recorded form: see *Printers & Finishers v. Holloway (No. 2)* [1965] R.P.C. 239 at 255; *Fraser v. Thames Television* (n. 43, below).

[25] *Fraser v. Evans* [1969] 1 All E.R. 8, CA (see n. 96, below).

[26] For these defences, see *Hubbard v. Vosper; Beloff v. Pressdram; Commonwealth v. Fairfax* (nn. 70, 80, below).

[27] The old couplet, "Three things are to be helped in Conscience, Fraud, Accident and Things of Confidence", attributed to Sir Thomas More (see *Coco v. Clark* [1969] R.P.C. 41 at 46) suggests how long the connection has stood. As perhaps the latest creation of equity, it has indeed excited the protective instincts of Chancery traditionalists against modernising fusionists: as in Meagher *et al.*'s, denunciation of the New Zealand Court of Appeal's views on the subject as disentitled to "serious consideration": (n. 1, above) p. 888. See further, para. 8–17, below.

[28] (1849) 2 De G. & Sm. 652; Mac. & G. 25. Before this there had been a number of cases in which injunctions had been granted to prevent the publication of unpublished letters, plays and other literary works; these were based on a "common law right of property" that a majority of the judges found to exist in *Millar v. Taylor* (1769) 4 Burr. 2303, and *Donaldson v. Beckett* (1774) 2 Bro.P.C. 129; see para. 9–03, below.

[29] (1851) 9 Hare 241.

confidence,[30] with the apparent consequence that an indirect recipient, not being privy to the contract, would be liable only if he deliberately or recklessly induced breach of that contract.[31] Contract and tort would thus subsume the whole field between them.

8–07   More recently, contract has ceased to be treated as the universal touchstone of liability (though its role in determining what obligations of confidence exist may still be crucial).[32] Starting with *Saltman v. Campbell*,[33] the courts have recognised a wider equitable jurisdiction, based, it is said, "not so much on property or on contract, but rather on good faith",[34] and this approach is now reasonably well entrenched among the judiciary. As a justification for intervening, particularly at this intermediate stage of legal development, "good faith" has a certain forthrightness that is attractive. The issue is not hedged behind conceptual dogma which all too readily states legal results without properly considering their justification. But if the true measure is a simple moral yardstick, the courts have been tantalisingly vague in the matter of how it is calibrated. This casualness has excited scientifically-minded jurists to a rash of disputation: in favour of working out the implications of "good faith" more exactly[35]; in favour of a new tort of breach of confidence[36]; in favour of "equitable property" as the true basis of protection.[37]

8–08   In the account that follows we must isolate the points at which these differences of pedigree begin to matter. They are to be found at the fringes of the wrong, and concern in particular: (1) the liability of those who in some sense act innocently; (2) the circumstances in which damages may be awarded for breach; (3) the possibility of awarding damages for injury to feelings as distinct from economic loss; (4) the liability of indirect recipients; and (5) the effect of dealings that treat the information as property. The most pertinent question to ask about these problems is whether the

---

[30] Contractual language reaches a climax in *Vokes v. Heather* (1945) 62 R.P.C. 135, CA. *cf. British Celanese v. Moncrieff* (1948) 65 R.P.C. 165 at 167, CA. The approach produced nice conundrums: see *Triplex v. Scorah*, (1938) 55 R.P.C. 21. But *Robb v. Green* [1895] 2 Q.B. 315, CA, put the jurisdiction in both contract and equity and this conceptual casualness has been echoed more recently, *e.g.* in *Nichrotherm v. Percy* [1957] R.P.C. 207, CA, and *Ackroyds v. Islington Plastics* [1962] R.P.C. 97.

[31] *British Industrial Plastics v. Ferguson* [1940] 1 All E.R. 479, HL.

[32] As to this, see para. 8–29, below.

[33] (1948) 65 R.P.C. 203, CA; and see *Nichrotherm v. Percy* (n. 30, above) at 213–214. *Peter Pan v. Corsets Silhouette* [1963] R.P.C. 45 and *Cranleigh Precision v. Bryant* [1966] R.P.C. 81, are both cases in which jurisdiction is put solely in equity despite the presence of contract. See further Vaver (n. 1, above) at 303.

[34] Lord Denning M.R., *Fraser v. Evans* [1969] 1 All E.R. 8 at 11; and also in *Seager v. Copydex (No. 1)* [1967] 2 All E.R. 415 at 417. For a distinguished precursor see Holmes J., *Du Pont v. Masland*, 244 U.S. 100 at 102 (1917). In *Att.-Gen. v. Guardian Newspapers (No. 2)* (n. 6, above), the House of Lords eschewed the question, while accepting that the jurisdiction in equity extended beyond contract.

[35] Jones (1970) 86 L.Q.R. 463.

[36] North and Law Commission, n. 1, above.

[37] Ricketson, (1977) 11 M.U.L.R. 223, 289.

answers so far given justify basing the jurisdiction on "good faith"; or whether one of the other explanations, although enjoying little popularity with the judges at present, is in fact truer to the results which they wish to procure.

2. Requirements for Liability

Megarry J.'s listing of the requirements for an actionable breach of **8–09** confidence[38] makes a convenient starting-point for analysis:

> "First, the information itself . . . must 'have the necessary quality of confidence about it.'[39] Secondly, that information must have been imparted in circumstances importing an obligation of confidence. Thirdly, there must be an unauthorised use of that information [possibly[40]] to the detriment of the party communicating it."

Each of these heads will be treated in turn.

(1) Subject-matter capable of protection

(a) *Types of information*

The breach of confidence action, as already stated, lies in respect of **8–10** technical, commercial, personal and other information without distinction by subject. A general reservation has been expressed against covering "trivial tittle-tattle"[41]; and it has recently been accepted that scandalous or immoral material may be disqualified from protection, just as it is not accorded copyright.[42]

An idea for something yet to be elaborated may attract legal protection as confidential information where there is nothing that generates copyright. Thus, the idea for a television series about a female popgroup, which would draw upon the backgrounds and histories of three actresses intended for the parts, was held capable of protection. The requirements of copyright law to show specific expression of the idea in scenarios or scripts, in writing or other recorded form, were held not necessary in the law of confidence. It was enough that "the content of the idea was clearly identifiable, original, of potential commercial attractiveness and capable

---

[38] *Coco v. Clark* [1969] R.P.C. 41 at 47. Approved by the Court of Appeal in *Dunford & Elliott v. Johnston* [1978] F.S.R. 143 at 148, CA; *Jarman & Platt v. Barget* [1977] F.S.R. 260 at 276–277; and relied upon in many other cases.

[39] This expression is Lord Greene M.R.'s: *Saltman v. Campbell* (n. 33, above) at 215.

[40] For Megarry J.'s doubt about detriment, see para. 8–39, below.

[41] Megarry J., *Coco v. Clark* (n. 35, above) at 48. But trivia worth money are different: see *Argyll v. Argyll* (n. 7, above); cf. *Church of Scientology v. Kaufman* [1973] R.P.C. 635.

[42] *Stephens v. Avery* [1988] F.S.R. 510. However, a lesbian relationship is no longer so unmentionable a subject that it cannot be protected in confidence: *ibid.*

of being realised in actuality".[43] This recognises the considerable value that such initial inspirations may now have. Again, technical information does not have to be novel or attain any level of inventiveness[44]:

> "it is perfectly possible to have a confidential document, be it a formula, a plan, a sketch, or something of that kind, which is the result of work done by the maker on materials which may be available for the use of anybody; but what makes it confidential is the fact that the maker of the document has used his brain and thus produced a result which can only be produced by somebody who goes through the same process."[45]

(b) *Information and observation*

8–11 Typically, the subject of protection exists as information before the obligation of confidence is assumed. Some cases, however, have concerned events which the person bound by confidence has observed for himself.[46] So far the courts have shown no inclination to treat the two cases differently and indeed to do so would be highly artificial. The consequence, however, is to broaden the role of the confidence action in the field of privacy.

(c) *Public knowledge*

8–12 If information has been made freely and entirely public, either before it was given to the defendant in confidence, or else in the interval between that time and the trial of the action, then in many cases nothing protectable will remain,[47] at least if the defendant's breach of confidence is not the cause.[48]

---

[43] *Fraser v. Thames Television* [1983] 2 All E.R. 101; applying *Talbot v. General Television* [1981] R.P.C. 1, (SC, Victoria)—where the particular twist to the idea was merely that a programme series about millionaires would include interviews with particular exemplars. *cf. De Maudsley v. Palumbo* [1996] F.S.R. 447: "a considerable degree of particularity in a definite product needs to be shown ... That of course does not exclude simplicity ... Vagueness and simplicity are not the same" *per* Knox].

[44] But see *Nichrotherm v. Percy* [1957] R.P.C. 207 at 209, CA, where stating the technical problem that called for solution was treated as not protectable.

[45] Lord Greene M.R., *Saltman v. Campbell* (n. 33, above) at 215; and see *Ansell Rubber v. Allied Rubber* [1967] V.R. 37.

[46] This was the character of much of the information which the pop-stars were attempting to keep out of the press in *Woodward v. Hutchins* [1977] 2 All E.R. 751. The plaintiffs failed for other reasons: see n. 68, below. See also *Printers & Finishers v. Holloway* (para. 8–29, n. 15, below).

[47] See *Saltman v. Campbell* (n. 33, above) at 215; *John Zink v. Lloyds Bank* [1975] R.P.C. 385 at 389; *Harrison v. Project & Design* [1978] F.S.R. 81 (information becoming public). *Ocular Sciences v. Aspect Vision Care* [1997] R.P.C. 289 (information from public sources listed without selection). Note the readiness to take up this sort of explanation in an "unappetising" personal scandal case: *Lennon v. News Group* [1978] F.S.R. 573, CA; *cf. Argyll v. Argyll* (n. 7, above). See generally, Tettenborn [1982] 11 Anglo-Am.L.R. 273.

[48] If the publicity comes from the defendant, he may well be enjoined from making further or different disclosures of it: *Creation Records v. New Group* [1997] E.M.L.R. 444. The defendant's action may make an injunction purposeless, but damages and other remedies ought to be available. In *Harrison v. Project & Design* (n. 47, above), damages were awarded to the defendant for his production during a period of time until the information became public; it is not clear how this publicity came about, if it was not through the defendant's own activity.

308

(The possibility of publication occurring after the court's order goes to the scope of remedies and is discussed below).[49]

Where the revelation is by the defendant himself, he has been held to remain liable.[50] However, this problem has yet to receive the full judicial analysis it deserves. It may well be that even in this situation no subject-matter then subsists which can subsequently be the subject of obligation.[51] But there still remains the question of liability arising from the act of revelation, which is itself a breach. It will be seen later that relief may be granted against wrongful use quite independently of wrongful disclosure,[52] and accordingly an injunction to prevent future use may be appropriate. In addition, any pecuniary relief by way of damages, account or constructive trust should bring in the continuing consequences of the unjustified revelation.[53]

The issue is difficult when the relevation is in some sense only partial. If **8–13** not all the relevant information has been made public, the rest (if it can be adequately specified) remains capable of protection.[54] If the information has been given to some of those interested but not to others, there may remain some "relative secrecy"[55]; whether a Court will grant any form of relief in such cases seems to depend on the circumstances as a whole.

In this context, the "springboard" metaphor has enjoyed a vogue:

"A person who has obtained information in confidence is not allowed to use it as a springboard for activities detrimental to the person who made the confidential communication, and springboard it remains even when all the features have been published or can be ascertained by actual inspection by any member of the public. . . . The possessor of the confidential information still has a long start over any member of the public."[56]

---

[49] See para. 8–45, below.
[50] *Speed Seal v. Paddington* [1986] 1 All E.R. 91, CA.
[51] Lord Goff (*Att.-Gen. v. Guardian Newspapers (No. 2)* (n. 6, above)) at 285–286, criticises the *Speed Seal* case, particularly for its reliance on the view that only revelation by the plaintiff renders confidential information no longer open to protection—for which see n. 59, below.
[52] See para. 8–37, below.
[53] *Ocular Sciences v. Aspect Vision Centre* [1997] R.P.C. 289.
[54] Thus, in *Mustad v. Allcock and Dosen* (n. 61, below) the House of Lords only refused protection after noting that, on the evidence, the plaintiff's invention had been completely revealed in its patent specification (*cf. House of Spring Gardens v. Point Blank* [1985] F.S.R. 327, SC (Ir.)). The need to distinguish what is protectable as a secret is crucial where it must be specified in an injunction: see Ricketson (1977) 11 Melb. U.L.R. 223, 289 at 291 for the case law. The fact that a mixture of public and private information has been taken may lead to an award of damages; *cf. Seager v. Copydex (No. 1)* [1967] 2 All E.R. 415 at 417, CA.
[55] Cross J., *Franchi v. Franchi* [1967] R.P.C. 149; *cf. Dunford & Elliott v. Johnston* [1978] F.S.R. 143 at 148, CA, where the extent of revelation is given as one reason for refusing interlocutory relief. Note also *Foster v. Mountford* [1978] F.S.R. 582 (aboriginal tribal secrets); and the case law in n. 59, below.
[56] Roxburgh J., *Terrapin v. Builders Supply* [1967] R.P.C. 375 at 392; first approved in the Court of Appeal, *Seager v. Copydex (No. 1)* (n. 50, above) at 417. See also, *e.g. Cranleigh v. Bryant* (n. 63, below) and *Ackroyds v. Islington Plastics* [1962] R.P.C. 97.

8–14 But this is not an invariable rule which takes no account of subsequent developments and other circumstances: the "springboard does not last for ever".[57] Among other factors that a Court is likely to take into account are the following[58]:

(1) How truly did the information become public? Formal tests of publication drawn from patent law are not used.[59] Nor is it enough to show that a product has been marketed which, if dismantled or analysed, would reveal the information.[60] On the other hand, if the plaintiff includes all the information in a patent specification, he is taken to have made it public.[61]

(2) How likely was it that the defendant would in any event have discovered the information without impropriety, had he not received it in confidence from the plaintiff?[62] If it is in fact available in a third party's patent specification, the issue ought to be whether the defendant would have been likely to search for and discover that specification.[63]

(3) Did the plaintiff believe that he would be injured by release of the information, and that it was not yet in the public domain? According to Megarry J., if this belief was reasonable, the plaintiff ought to be entitled to protect it.[64] This approach may commend itself to future courts for dealing with cases where information has already got into a limited number of hands. There is some danger, however, that it will unduly favour plaintiffs.

---

[57] Lord Denning M.R., *Potters-Ballotini v. Weston-Baker* [1977] R.P.C. 202 at 205: *Harrison v. Project & Design* (n. 44, above) at 87. See generally, Barclay (1978) 26 U.C.L.A. Law R. 203.

[58] *cf.* the list in the American Restatement of Torts, Art. 757, referred to in a number of Australian decisions; see Ricketson (n. 54, above) at 228.

[59] *cf.* para. 5–13, above; *Yates v. Electrofoils* [1976] F.S.R. 345 at 387; *Interfirm Comparison v. Law Society* [1975] R.P.C. 137.

[60] See *Saltman v. Campbell* (n. 33, above) at 215; *Terrapin v. Builders Supply* (n. 52, above) at 26; *Conveyor v. Cameron* [1973] 2 N.Z.L.R. 38.

[61] *Mustad v. Allcock and Dosen* (1928) [1963] 3 All E.R. 416n., HL. See also *Lysnar v. Gisborne* [1924] N.Z.L.R. 13.

[62] On this problem, see especially Megarry J., *Coco v. Clark* (n. 38, above) at 49–50.

[63] In *Cranleigh Precision v. Bryant* [1966] R.P.C. 81 and *Franchi v. Franchi* (n. 55, above), it was said that the publication in a third party's patent specification should not be treated as bringing obligations of confidence to an end. But that seems too indiscriminate an approach. The former case, in particular, did not need to go so far; there were obvious breaches of fiduciary duty. The reasoning in the cases was criticised by Lord Goff: *Att.-Gen. v. Guardian Newspapers (No. 2)* (n. 6, above) at 661–662.

[64] *Marshall (Thomas) (Exports) v. Guinle* [1978] 3 All E.R. 193 at 209–210. Particular usage of a trade or industry might also make the information protectable: *ibid.*

(d) *Public interest* [65]

Free speech and freedom for the media are not under English law directly **8–15** guaranteed as fundamental legal rights.[66] They exist as political freedoms because censorship and fiscal inhibitions on the press were not able to survive the emergence of democracy, and they remain circumscribed by such limits as the law of defamation, the Official Secrets Act and proscriptions upon contempt of court.[67] Breach of confidence, now extended into the field of political and personal information, is the latest weapon in the armoury of those who wish to suppress items of embarrassing news. This development opens up a fundamental conflict of policies which the courts are still searching to resolve. It is well-settled that "there can be no confidence which can be relied on to restrain a disclosure of inquity",[68] and in this context "inquity" probably covers criminal, tortious and other legally wrongful conduct, at least if it is serious.[69] Some judges, clearly, consider that, save where the information concerns "misdeeds of a serious nature and importance to the country", they should intervene to preserve confidential obligations.[70]

There is now a broader approach which treats "iniquity" as merely one **8–16** instance of just cause for allowing confidence to be broken in the public interest. Lord Denning M.R., a principal proponent of this view,[71] has, for instance, held that, where pop-stars have deliberately promoted a glamorous image of themselves, it is permissible to present the less savoury truth about their style of life to the public, even if confidence has to be broken in the process.[72] This approach has much in common with the freedom of

---

[65] See Cripps, *The Legal Implications of Disclosure in the Public Interest* (2nd ed., 1995); Stuckey-Clarke in Clarke (n. 1, above) Chap. 8. See also the Public Interest Disclosure Act 1998, which adds a Part IVA to the Employment Rights Act 1996. This seeks to protect employees who blow the whistle on their employers from being victimised in consequence.

[66] The European Convention (for which see n. 8, above), guarantees the right of freedom of speech, subject *inter alia* to the preservation of confidence: Art. 10. In *Att.-Gen. v. Guardian Newspapers* (n. 6, above), Lords Griffiths and Goff considered the qualification discussed under this head to be in conformity with the Article: at 652, and at 660.

[67] See generally Cripps (n. 65, above).

[68] *Gartside v. Outram* (1856) 26 L.J. Ch. 113.

[69] But note Bankes L.J., *Weld-Blundell v. Stephens* [1919] 1 K.B. 520 at 527; *cf. Butler v. Board of Trade* [1971] Ch. 680; *cf. Hellewell v. Chief Constable of Derbyshire* [1995] 1 W.L.R. 804: police justified in showing known criminal's photograph to shopkeepers; *Bunn v. BBC* [1999] F.S.R. 70: accused's confession to police confidential but only until revealed in open Court.

[70] Ungoed Thomas J., *Beloff v. Pressdram* [1973] 1 All E.R. 241 at 260–261 (copyright proceedings, treated as subject to the same public interest considerations); and see Megaw L.J., *Hubbard v. Vosper* [1972] 2 Q.B. 84 at 100–101. Revelation of an agreement registrable under the Restrictive Trade Practices Act 1956 (*Initial Services v. Putterill* [1968] 1 Q.B. 396) could well fall within this restricted view of public interest. *cf.* also *British Steel v. Granada* [1982] A.C. 1096.

[71] *Initial Services v. Putterill* (n. 70, above) at 405; *Fraser v. Evans* (n. 34, above) at 11; *Hubbard v. Vosper* (n. 70, above) at 95–96; *Norwich Pharmacal v. Commissioners of Customs* [1972] R.P.C. 743 at 766, CA.

[72] *Woodward v. Hutchins* [1977] 2 All E.R. 751; Lawton and Bridge L.JJ. were equally convinced; *cf. Argyll v. Argyll* (n. 7, above) at 331–333; Wacks (1978) 41 M.L.R. 67.

speech defence to invasions of privacy in the United States: that by putting himself forward as a public figure, a celebrity must be prepared to suffer the exposure of truths about his personal life.

8–17 Other circumstances in which public interest may justify at least limited publication to an appropriate person to take action might include matters of public safety and the due administration of justice. Thus, in *Lion Laboratories v. Evans*,[73] a newspaper came by knowledge that a breathalyser used by the police on suspected drunken drivers gave inaccurate readings. It was held proper for the newspaper to publish this generally, because merely reporting the information to the police or the Home Office might have led to its suppression. However, it is not to be supposed that English Courts readily accept that there is a sufficient public interest, particularly to justify publication through the media, even if it is produced by a "whistle-blower" from inside an organisation who is moved by moral outrage and who may well be jeopardising a career rather than seeking any payment in return.[74]

8–18 In every case, whether the basis is "iniquity" or some other ground, the court has to balance the competing interests. For instance, the Court of Appeal restrained a newspaper from publishing allegations about a leading jockey's involvement in misleading the Jockey Club because the information had been obtained by private and unauthorised wire-tapping of a telephone conversation: the dissemination would be too wide, the breach of confidence too serious.[75] It is clear that Peter Wright could never have justified his "treacherous" breaches of confidence about his service in MI5 by a public interest in knowing that he and other officers attempted to prevent Harold Wilson's re-election and other unscrupulous operations.[76]

Many cases to do with newsworthy information are founded in copyright as well as confidence. In England, the tendency has been to treat public interest as having the same impact in respect of either cause of action. But,

---

[73] [1985] Q.B. 526, CA; and see *ex p. Smith Kline & French* [1989] F.S.R. 11, CA; *cf. X. Health Authority v. Y.* [1988] R.P.C. 379 (confidence in hospital records of doctors with AIDS outweighed public interest in knowing that there were doctors with the disease).

[74] Different attitudes have been expressed about the degree to which the moral scruples of the revealer are relevant in judging public interest: *cf.* esp. Lord Denning M.R.'s view that the use made of it by a person receiving the information is relevant, with Lord Fraser's rejection of that position: *British Steel v. Granada Television* [1981] A.C. 1096 at 1202. Even a professional may be entitled to break confidence in order to secure the safety of others: *W. v. Egdell* [1989] 1 All E.R. 1089 (psychiatrist disclosing violent character of patient to prison authorities); criticised by Meagher *et al.* (para. 8–01, n. 1, above) p. 883.

[75] *Francome v. Mirror Group* [1984] 2 All E.R. 408, CA; and see *Camelot Group v. Centaur Communications* [1998] E.M.L.R. 1, CA.

[76] This is made plain in *Att.-Gen. v. Guardian Newspapers (No. 2)* [1990] A.C. 109, HL Note the Court of Appeal's remarkable refusal to grant interlocutory relief to a newspaper which had bought the serial rights in the Downing Street memoirs of Mr. Wright's principal scourge against another, which got in ahead with the main revelations: *Times Newspapers v. Mirror Group* [1993] E.M.L.R. 442. The descriptions were said to include current events of public interest, and anyway they were intended for publication and so could not be confidential: see Nyman (1994) 3 Ent. L.R. 83.

as we shall see, in copyright there are other relevant defences provided by statute.[77]

(e) *Government secrets*

An opposite public interest arises when government seeks to protect **8–19** confidential information. For although it is relying on a private right, it does not have the same personal interest as an individual in preventing information from being released or used. It must show—and carries the burden of proof—that the public has an interest in the protection sought, "because in a free society there is a continuing public interest that the workings of government should be open to scrutiny and criticism".[78] Whether there is a sufficient public interest of this sort will depend on all the circumstances. Where the former minister, Richard Crossman, proposed to reveal Cabinet discussions recorded in his diaries, his publishers were not enjoined: the desirability of mutual confidence in Cabinet deliberations was not a sufficient interest when ten years had elapsed in the interim.[79] Where, apparently through a leak from a civil servant, Australian government documents concerning its relations with Indonesia over the East Timor crisis were about to be published, no sufficient reason for restraining their appearance could be found in national security, relations with foreign countries or the ordinary business of government.[80]

Where the *Guardian* and the *Observer* gave accounts of Australian proceedings to stop the publication of Peter Wright's *Spycatcher*, in which they disclosed some of Wright's allegations about wrongdoing in Britain's MI5, these publications did not amount to actionable breaches of confidence, even though they came through leaks of the book's contents at a time when it had been published nowhere.[81] Equally, after *Spycatcher's* publication in the United States, Australia and elsewhere, with the consequence that many copies and accounts had entered Britain, even the *Sunday Times*, which held "serial rights" to the book by "grant" from Wright's publishers,[82] could not be restrained from publishing it: the other events had rendered Wright's allegations too widely known for the public to have any further interest to protect.[83] An attempt to show continuing

---

[77] See paras 11–38 *et seq.*, below.
[78] Lord Goff, *Att.-Gen. v. Guardian Newspapers (No. 2)* [1990] 1 A.C. 109 at 283.
[79] *Att.-Gen. v. Jonathan Cape* [1976] Q.B. 752.
[80] *Commonwealth of Australia v. Fairfax* (1980) 32 A.L.R. 485; and see *Att.-Gen. v. Brandon Book Publishers* [1989] F.S.R. 37.
[81] *Att.-Gen. v. Guardian Newspapers (No. 2)* (n. 78, above); see Jones [1989] C.L.P. 49; Patfield [1989] E.I.P.R. 201.
[82] It seems that any such "licence" lacked subject-matter since Wright's breach of obligation left him without enforceable copyright: see para. 11–57, below.
[83] *The Sunday Times* had perpetrated an actionable breach by publishing a first episode of *Spycatcher* on the eve of U.S. publication, for which they were liable to an account of profits. From this no payment to Wright's publishers under the supposed "licence" would be deductible: *Att.-Gen. v. Guardian Newspapers (No. 2)* (n. 78, above), esp. at 262, 263, *per* Lord Keith.

damage to the operations of the Secret Services, if there could not be absolute assurance that its members would observe lifelong secrecy, was not accepted as sufficient in the circumstances.[84]

(2) Confidential obligation

(a) *Confidence in the receipt of information*

8–20 In the usual case, one person supplies information to another on condition that he will keep it secret. Equally the obligation to do so may arise where the first person employs,[85] commissions, or even requests, the second to acquire information and hold it in confidence for him. But—and here arises the whole case for founding the jurisdiction upon the requirements of "good faith"—whether recipient or acquirer, the second is bound only if he accepts that the information is to be treated confidentially. And yet this is tested objectively: "if the circumstances are such that any reasonable man standing in the shoes of the recipient of the information would have realised that upon reasonable grounds the information was being given to him in confidence, then this should suffice to impose upon him the equitable obligation of confidence."[86] Add to this that, once the obligation is assumed, it may be broken by conduct that is neither ill-motivated nor deliberate.[87] It becomes apparent that a somewhat diffuse notion of "good faith" is being employed.

8–21 There is no need to search for an implied contract, if none has been reached expressly: matrimonial and other personal confidences may give rise to obligations[88]; so equally when one party gives another information during negotiations towards a commercial agreement that is never reached[89]; or in circumstances where statute negates the existence of a contract.[90] On the other hand, it is unlikely that one person could oblige another to respect confidence by sending him unsolicited information in a

---

[84] Likewise in *Lord Advocate v. Scotsman* [1989] F.S.R. 580. Note also the refusal to impose a general obligation, not related to confidential information, which would bind secret services officers (however traitorous) not to write about their service; *A.G. v. Blake* [1996] F.S.R. 727.

[85] An instance is *Industrial Furnaces v. Reaves* [1970] R.P.C. 605.

[86] Megarry J., *Coco v. Clark* [1968] F.S.R. 415; and see *Yates v. Electrofoils* [1976] F.S.R. 345; *Interfirm Comparison v. Law Society* [1975] R.P.C. 137 at 151; *Delta Nominees v. Viscount Plastic* [1979] V.R. 167 at 191. If evidence of subjective intent is given, the Court should also bring it into account: *Carflow Products v. Linwood Securities* [1996] F.S.R. 424; Clark [1996] E.I.P.R. 632.

[87] See para. 8–43, below.

[88] *Argyll v. Argyll* [1967] Ch. 302 at 322, still spoke (unenthusiastically) of an implied contract, but demonstrated the unreality of such language.

[89] As in *Seager v. Copydex (No. 1)* [1967] R.P.C. 349, CA; *Coco v. Clark* (n. 86, above); *A.B. Consolidated v. Europe Strength* [1978] 2 N.Z.L.R. 520.

[90] *Malone v. Commissioner of Police* [1979] 2 All E.R. 620 at 645 (no contract between telephone subscriber and Post Office).

letter marked "Confidential". This is a practical problem of some importance: it is even said that one enterprise may try to foist confidential
material on another in order to put difficulties in the way of the latter using
it (or something similar), should it be discovered independently.[91] The
recipient of an unsolicited confidence should, for his own protection, return
the material at once, making it plain that he regards himself as being under
no obligation. If he goes on to use the information he is likely, under the
objective test, to be held bound.[92]

Of course, contracts continue to be of great importance. The circum- **8-22**
stances may be such that the reasonable man may freely use the information supplied to him in the absence of an express agreement to the
contrary. Thus, where a news agency provided stock-exchange and horse-
racing results to its subscribers, it was able to prevent the information being
passed on to non-subscribers precisely because the subscription contract
forbade this being done.[93] Equally, contract may prescribe the extent of the
obligation.[94] The purpose of a "know-how" licence is to permit the licensee
to make use of the information provided for the purposes of his own
business, but normally the agreement will limit the degree to which the
"know-how" can be imparted to others, and use by the licensee after
termination of the licence may also be circumscribed.[95] Again, contract may
settle that the plaintiff is not owed any duty of confidence, but instead owes
such a duty himself to a third party; in which case he has no qualification to
sue.[96]

(b) *Fiduciary duties*

The relationship between two persons may be such that equity imposes a **8-23**
duty upon one to act in the interests of the other rather than of himself. As
with contract, the proof of a fiduciary relationship may be the necessary

---

[91] See Law Commission (n. 1, above) paras 52, 72, 109–112; Turner [1976] CIPA 293. *Johnson v. Heat and Air* (1941) 58 R.P.C. 229 was a case where the defendant could show that he already knew the information when it was revealed to him.

[92] In complex situations, such as one in which businessmen are pooling private knowledge, the extent of any obligation to use the information only for the intended common purpose will depend on the particular circumstances: see *Murray v. Yorkshire Fund Managers* [1998] 1 W.L.R. 951, CA.

[93] *Exchange Telegraph v. Gregory* [1896] 1 Q.B. 147; *Exchange Telegraph v. Central News* [1897] 2 Ch. 48; *cf.* also *Paul v. Southern Instruments* [1964] R.P.C. 118, CA.

[94] For instance, by limiting the period during which the defendant is not to use the information: see *Potters-Ballotini v. Weston-Baker* [1977] R.P.C. 202; *cf.* the cases in n. 93, above.

[95] *National Broach v. Churchill* [1965] R.P.C. 61; *Torrington v. Smith* [1966] R.P.C. 285.

[96] *Fraser v. Evans* [1969] 1 All E.R. 8, CA, where the plaintiff prepared a report for the Greek government to which he owed a duty of confidence; the defendant editor procured the report from a Greek government source. Had it been improperly procured from the plaintiff he might have established the tort of inducing breach of his own contract of confidence. *cf.* the criminal proceedings in *D.P.P. v. Withers* [1975] A.C. 842; see para. 2–21, above.

foundation of an obligation of confidence.[97] This fiduciary duty may, for instance, exist between trustee and beneficiary, agent and principal, individual partner and partnership, director and company, responsible employee and employer,[98] secret service agent and government.[99] The list of relationships is not closed; but there is a reluctance to find it in commercial relationships, for example from franchisor to franchisee, or licensee to licensor.[1] Nor are the circumstances in which such fiduciaries are obliged to prefer the interests of their beneficiaries precisely defined.[2]

The moral impulse from which this fiduciary duty stems is very similar to that which requires confidence to be respected and often there is an overlap between the principles. But the difference needs to be observed. In the first place, a fiduciary responsibility may be the source of the duty to preserve confidence: the employee who removes a confidential report from his employer's desk[3] will break the confidence that already exists from his duty of fidelity; an outsider who did the same thing would commit a trespass, but he would not be in breach of confidence.[4] Again, the fiduciary duty may be wider in scope than a simple obligation to observe confidence: the fiduciary may, for example, be expected to continue using information for his beneficiary's advantage only, even after it has become public[5]; equally he may be obliged to hold the profits of his breach on trust for his beneficiary.[6] Equity's intervention is to prevent the fiduciary from taking a personal advantage from the possible conflict of interest and duty.

---

[97] *Moorgate Tobacco v. Philip Morris* [1985] R.P.C. 219, HC (Aust.).

[98] On employees, see *Canadian Aero v. O'Malley* (1973) 40 D.L.R. (3d) 371, SC (Canada). Amongst the category of agents, note in particular professional advisers such as doctors, lawyers and banks. The scope of the obligations of each category is worked out in case law: for which see, *e.g. Tournier v. National Provincial* [1924] 1 K.B. 461, CA (banker); *Hunter v. Mann* [1974] 1 Q.B. 767, DC (doctor); *Parry-Jones v. Law Society* [1969] 1 Ch. 1, CA (solicitor). For the relation between a solicitor's duty of confidence and his obligation not to reveal privileged communications in litigation without his client's consent, see *Lord Ashburton v. Pape* [1913] 2 Ch. 469; *Parry-Jones v. Law Society* (see above); *Butler v. Board of Trade* [1971] Ch. 680.

[99] *A.G. v. The Guardian Newspapers (No. 2)* [1990] 1 A.C. 109; it is a duty to preserve confidential information, but not a duty to remain silent about experiences in the service. *A.G. v. Blake* [1996] 3 All E.R. 903.

[1] *Jirna v. Mister Do-nut* (1973) 40 D.L.R. (3d) 303; *U.S.S.C. v. Hospital Products* (1984) 58 A.L.J.R. 587; *Moorgate* case [1985] R.P.C. 219, HC Aust. *Indata Equipment Supplies v. ACL* [1998] F.S.R. 248, CA.

[2] Readers unfamiliar with this important equitable duty will find good accounts, *e.g.* in *Goff and Jones: Law of Restitution* (4th ed., 1993), Chap. 33; Finn, *Fiduciary Duties* (1977) and on company directors, Farrer *et al. Company Law* (3rd ed., 1991), Chaps 25, 26.

[3] As in *Jarman & Platt v. Barget* [1977] F.S.R. 260 at 276, CA.

[4] On this problem, see paras 8–34—8–36, below.

[5] See *Cranleigh Precision v. Bryant* [1966] R.P.C. 81. The obligation extends equally to the personal use of property and to certain competitive activities.

[6] See para. 8–51, below.

(c) *Employer and employee*[7]

Where the relationship between supplier and recipient of information is **8–24** that of employer and employee, a further distinct policy has been pursued by the judges. They have struck a balance between the desire to accord every worker the freedom to dispose of his labour where and when he pleases and the wish to give some protection to valuable pieces of information that a particular employer may possess over his competitors and which an employee might give to a competitor or use himself in competition. While he remains in employment the employee must observe his "duty of fidelity". Once he leaves his employment, the balance rests largely in favour of the employee, who is entitled to make use of all the skill and knowledge that any employee of his kind would have acquired. He is only obliged to respect two specific "interests" of his employer: in "secret processes" that are in a strict sense "trade secrets"; and in the goodwill that exists between the employer and his customers.

(i) **The employee in service.** In a contract of employment, a term will be **8–25** implied (if it is not expressed) that the employee will act at all times during his service in his employer's best interests. This "duty of fidelity" embraces the protection of trade and commercial secrets, including both information which is given to the employee and that which he generates in the course of his work.[8] But it is wider than a matter of confidence and may, in some circumstances, embrace a duty not to engage, deliberately and secretly, in directly competitive work, either with another employer or on his own account. In *Hivac v. Park Royal*, the plaintiff company, which produced hearing-aids of advanced design, secured an interlocutory injunction to prevent a rival company from giving jobs to some of its technicians by way of "moonlighting" after hours. Since relief was apparently granted whether or not the technicians would be likely to impart confidential "know-how", the decision went a long way; but the plaintiff was constrained by war-time legislation from simply dismissing the technicians, and this condition made it a special case.[9]

---

[7] See Napier in Clarke (n. 1, above), Chap. 6. For a comparison with the position in the U.S., see Wilkof [1991] E.I.P.R. 269; and for Germany and other European countries, Beier in Leser and Isomura (eds.) *Wege zum japanischen Recht* (1992) 817.

[8] Employment being a contractual relationship, the implied term has been the legal device for imposing the obligation in question: see *Faccenda Chicken v. Fowler* [1986] 1 All E.R. 617 at 625. But clearly it bears an affinity to the equitable duty of good faith that is imposed on fiduciaries such as trustees, agents, partners and the like (for which, see para. 8–23, above). Accordingly, a tendency can be detected towards treating at least senior employees as fiduciaries: *Canadian Aero v. O'Malley* [1974] 40 D.L.R. (3d) 371; in England, see *Normalec v. Britton* [1983] F.S.R. 318. *cf.* the position concerning patents, para. 7–04, above, and copyright, paras 12–04—12–06, below.

[9] *Hivac v. Park Royal* [1946] 1 All E.R. 350, CA; see also *Reading v. Att.-Gen.* [1951] A.C. 507, HL; *Davies v. Presbyterian Church of Wales* [1986] 1 All E.R. 705, HL; *Missing Link Software v. Magee* [1989] F.S.R. 361. *Lancashire Fires v. Lyons*, below, n. 15; *Ocular Sciences v. Aspect Vision Care, ibid.* While there is no duty to report his own breaches of contract, the employee is under a duty to report those of a colleague: *Sybron v. Rochem* [1983] 3 W.L.R. 713, CA.

During the continuance of employment there is certainly an obligation to keep rival research staff from access to technical secrets,[10] and a duty not to provide the employee's own trade union with the employer's commercial information relevant to wage negotiations.[11]

There is an obligation not to extract information with a view to taking it away on departure, as for instance by copying it out or deliberately memorising it.[12] But information which would naturally be remembered, including even the names and addresses of customers, may be taken.[13] There is no general duty not to plan post-departure activities in advance.[14]

8–26 (ii) **The ex-employee.** In *Faccenda Chicken v. Fowler*,[15] the Court of Appeal contrasted the extensive duty owed during the continuance of employment with the more limited responsibility after termination. The principle that the employer may only seek to protect two interests—in his trade secrets and in the goodwill existing with his customers—was developed first in connection with express covenants. Undertakings by the employee that he will not, upon leaving the employment, set up or join a competitive business, solicit former customers or disclose or use trade secrets, are enforceable only if reasonably necessary to protect the employer; otherwise they are an undue restraint of trade and so are void as contrary to public policy. Such covenants by employees are scrupulously tested; they must be no wider in scope (taking account of the types of business excluded, duration and area of operation) than is reasonably necessary to give the employer protection of the relevant interest.[16]

Much detailed law has developed around this basic rule and it is easy to overstep the mark that it sets.[17] Nonetheless managerial, professional, sales and research staff are often required to enter such covenants. Not only does a covenant make the position a matter of express agreement (with attendant psychological effects) but it may give wider protection than if the employer seeks to rely upon rights arising by operation of the general law. Breach of a covenant not to compete is usually easier to establish than breach of an undertaking not to disclose or use confidential information: it is relatively easy to show that an ex-employee has joined a competitor or set up in business.

---

[10] *e.g. Printers & Finishers v. Holloway (No. 2)* [1964] 3 All E.R. 731.

[11] *Bents Brewery v. Hogan* [1945] 2 All E.R. 570 (where the covenant was express). See also paras 8–27 *et seq.*, below on the special problem of preparing to leave employment.

[12] *Baker v. Gibbons* [1972] 2 All E.R. 759.

[13] *Johnson & Bloy v. Wolstenholme Rink* [1989] F.S.R. 135, CA.

[14] *Balston v. Headline Filters* [1990] F.S.R. 385; *Ixora Trading v. Jones* [1990] F.S.R. 385.

[15] [1986] 1 All E.R. 617; *Lancashire Fires v. Lyons* [1996] F.S.R. 629, CA; *Ocular Sciences v. Aspect Vision Care* [1997] R.P.C. 289. See Hull, *Commercial Secrecy* (1998) Chaps 7, 8.

[16] Certain doubts about the scope of this doctrine, resulting from the *Faccenda Chicken* case, have been put to rest in *Lancashire Fires*.

[17] There is no room to review this important doctrine here. See especially Heydon, *The Restraint of Trade Doctrine* (1972) and, for an economic analysis, M. J. Trebilcock, *The Common Law of Restraint of Trade* (1986).

The employer who is not protected by covenant is not entirely without **8–27** remedy. If, for instance, he keeps a list of customers, he is entitled to stop an employee from deliberately memorising it or copying it out in order to make use of it himself once his employment ceases. This, indeed, is an aspect of the employee's implied duty of fidelity during his term of employment.[18] But he cannot stop an ex-employee from soliciting his customers in circumstances where the ex-employee merely remembers the customers' names in the ordinary course of events. If he had a valid express covenant, then he could.[19]

If there could not be an effective covenant, then, *a fortiori*, the law of **8–28** confidence cannot be relied upon. For this general law to apply, so the *Faccenda Chicken* case emphasises, a court must be convinced that the employee has departed with information that he ought not to take advantage of.[20] It is not enough to show that this special element was something that the employee was bound to keep "confidential" during his employment. He must have acquired "trade secrets or their equivalent". In investigating this, account will be taken of four factors: the nature of the employment (for example whether confidential information was regularly handled), the nature of the information at issue, the employer's view of its character, and the question whether it can easily be isolated from other, unprotectable information.[21]

Chemical formulae, details of technical processes, and hard commercial **8–29** information, such as prices, are considered examples of what, in the light of circumstances, may continue to be protected even after the determination of the job.[22] But within this category, a distinction is drawn between the discrete "trade secret", which any honest person of average intelligence would regard as such; and more incidental features or expedients, which were peculiar to the former employer's process or factory, but which are not to be separated from general knowledge and acquired skill. While information of the first kind continues to be protectable under the general obligation of confidence, that of the second calls for an express covenant. If a covenant has been taken, it is justifiable within the rule of public policy (provided that it is no wider than warranted by the ex-employer's interest).[23] Moreover, if a covenant is taken but it proves to be too widely drawn, there may still be a breach of general obligation to respect confidence if a

---

[18] See, *e.g. Robb v. Green* [1985] 2 Q.B. 315; *Baker v. Gibbons* [1972] 2 All E.R. 759; *Diamond Stylus v. Bauden* [1973] R.P.C. 675. It is difficult to prove the case if the defendant has not removed a copy of the list.

[19] *e.g. Coral Index v. Regent Index* [1970] R.P.C. 147.

[20] See also *G. D. Searle v. Celltech* [1982] F.S.R. 92, CA.

[21] See Purvis and Turner [1989] E.I.P.R. 3; Stewart [1989] E.I.P.R. 88.

[22] *Printers & Finishers v. Holloway (No. 2)* [1965] R.P.C. 239; and see *Under Water Welders v. Street* [1968] R.P.C. 498; *United Sterling v. Felton* [1974] R.P.C. 162; *Harvey Tiling v. Rodomac* [1977] R.P.C. 399, SC (S. Africa); *Yates v. Electrofoils* [1976] F.S.R. 345.

[23] This proposition in *Printers & Finishers*, is accepted in *Balston v. Headline Filters* [1987] F.S.R. 330; and *Lancashire Fires v. Lyons*, above, n. 15.

sufficiently significant trade secret is at issue.[24] Nothing, therefore, is lost by taking an express covenant, and if it proves valid, much may be gained.

8–30   A principle which distinguishes between discrete technical secrets (protectable even in the absence of covenant), incidental information known only to the ex-employee (protectable only by covenant) and general skill and knowledge (unprotectable), places a heavy burden of proof on any ex-employer who seeks to rely upon a general obligation of confidence. It is not enough, for instance, to show that others are prepared to pay for a package of know-how and associated rights if it cannot be shown that the defendant is taking a similar package to his new employer, but only rather general information about the kind of plant that both employers are operating.[25] The ex-employer also risks revealing, by his own pleadings and evidence, significant details which the defendant may not previously have appreciated.[26] Yet the courts can offer only limited help towards preserving the secrecy of what he is obliged to reveal.[27]

(d) *Government departments and agencies*

8–31   Government authorities—central, local and special—receive a mass of information, much of it, at least by implication, for limited purposes only. So far, the equity of confidence appears to apply to them as it would to other disclosees.[28] There may, however, be special reasons for allowing them to disclose or use the information in pursuit of some public interest, such as the enforcement of the civil or criminal law.[29] In this context the impact of the Official Secrets Acts should not be forgotten.[30]

(e) *The indirect recipient* [31]

8–32   If A gives B information in confidence and B passes it to C, C—the indirect recipient—may take it knowing that it is confidential; or the circumstances may be such that he ought to have known of the confidence; or he may

---

[24] *Wessex Dairies v. Smith* (1935) 2 K.B. 80, CA; *Triplex v. Scorah* (1938) 55 R.P.C. 21; *Marshall (Thomas) (Exports) v. Guinle* (n. 64, above).

[25] Thus evidence that visitors were not restricted in their inspections, or that the employee was never told of the secrecy is likely to tell against the employer: see *e.g. United Sterling v. Felton* [1974] R.P.C. 162; *Aveley/Cybervox v. Boman* [1975] F.S.R. 139 at 144.

[26] See *Yates v. Electrofoils* (n. 22, above) at 394–395; and see *Potters-Ballotini v. Weston-Baker* [1977] R.P.C. 202 at 206.

[27] In lieu of particulars, the Court may order that an independent expert be appointed to inspect the plaintiff's plant on condition that he reveals his findings only to the defendant's legal advisers and destroys any notes; in this procedure it is for the plaintiff to point out to the expert the features that he regards as secret: *Printers & Finishers v. Holloway* (n. 15, above) at 248. See also *Terrapin v. Tecton* (1968) 64 W.W.R. 129.

[28] This seems to be accepted, *e.g. in Butler v. Board of Trade* [1971] Ch. 680, *Norwich Pharmacal v. C.C.E.* [1974] A.C. 133.

[29] As in *Butler* and *Norwich Pharmacal.*

[30] See 11 *Halsbury's Laws of England* (4th ed.) paras 899 *et seq.*; Cripps (n. 65, above) pp. 148–170.

[31] See Stuckey (1981) 4 U.N.S.W.L.R. 73.

receive it without this knowledge, actual or imputed, only to be informed subsequently of the true position. In this last case, he may initially have purchased it or he may have had it as a gift. The courts undoubtedly wish to protect confidence to the extent of making indirect recipients liable in some of these circumstances; but which? It is here that doubts are thickest and doctrinal differences headiest.

The deliberate or reckless recipient would in many circumstances be liable under the general law of tort: for inducing or procuring breach of contract, unjustifiably interfering with business relations or conspiracy[32]; if not, his bad faith would easily justify equity's intervention.[33] Other recipients, who at most have only been negligent, are not themselves usually regarded as acting in bad faith. However, obligations of confidence are apparently imposed on direct recipients under an objective test and this may perhaps be justified by saying that it is too much to expect the plaintiff always to establish fraud.[34] The same approach might equally be applied to the indirect recipient. But if the non-negligent recipient is ever to be held liable, it cannot be because of his own default. It must either be because confidential information has been dignified with the status of "property", or else the court's intervention is to secure the information against breach of the obligation of good faith originally assumed by the first recipient.

Recent judgments touching the matter seem prepared to impose liability **8–33** on an innocent recipient from the time when he is informed of the breach of confidence.[35] In *Wheatley v. Bell* one defendant acquired confidential knowledge about franchising local business guides and proceeded to sell it to other defendants as franchisees in a different place. The latter, though initially innocent, were enjoined.[36] Assuming that it is the proper approach—and it seems sensible—then relief ought not to extend to damages for past innocent use; and it would be open to a court to refuse or limit any injunction in light of the extent to which the indirect recipient would be disadvantaged: taking account not only of whether he has paid a purchase price, but whether he could be reimbursed for that expenditure and any consequential investment intended to exploit the information.[37]

---

[32] For these torts, see paras 2–12 *et seq.*, above and esp. *British Industrial Plastics v. Ferguson* [1940] 1 All E.R. 479, HL.

[33] Thus in *Prince Albert v. Strange* (para. 8–05, above), stress is at one point laid on the duplicity of the indirect recipient: see 1 Mac. & G. 25 at 44. It is a breach of confidence knowingly to import products produced using the confidential information or through theft of documentary material: *Union Carbide v. Naturin* [1987] F.S.D. 538; *Beecham Group v. Norton Health Care* [1997] F.S.R. 81.

[34] See para. 8–20, above.

[35] *Stephenson Jordan v. MacDonald & Evans* (1951) 68 R.P.C. 190 at 195; *Printers & Finishers v. Holloway (No. 2)* (n. 22, above) at 253 (liability of Vita-Tex); *Malone v. Commissioner of Police* [1979] Ch. 344 at 634; *PSM International v. Whitehouse* [1992] F.S.R. 489, CA; *FBI Foods v. Cadbury Schweppes* [1999] (tbr), SC Canada.

[36] *Wheatley v. Bell* [1984] F.S.R. 16, SC (N.S.W.).

[37] See *Jones* (para. 8–01, n. 1, above) at 477–478; and note Evershed M.R. in the *Stephenson Jordan* case (on appeal) (1952) 69 R.P.C. 10 at 16.

If confidential information has become property, it is either property at common law which all must respect (save to the extent that the innocent are to be excused damages for past injuries)[38]; or it is property in equity, in which case the bona fide purchaser bears no responsibility but the innocent volunteer does. The difficulty with these stereotypes is that they each take a rather inflexible view of the defendant's circumstances. There is very little indication that English Courts wish to apply either theory to subject-matter of such varying character as is currently protectable in the name of confidence.[39]

(f) Absence of any relationship

8–34 In *Malone v. Commissioner of Police*,[40] an unsuccessful attack was made on the propriety of official wire-tapping (under the Home Secretary's warrant) in order to detect crime.[41] Megarry V.-C. took the view in principle that if one person told a second something in confidence, but a third overheard it, the last was under no legal liability to preserve the confidence. This is a point, so it was held, at which the moral constraints upon an honourable man outstrip those imposed by law. For this the only reason offered was that people (particularly those who use the telephone) know that they risk being overheard.[42] If the decision is followed strictly, only the recipient of the communication and those to whom he passes it directly or indirectly can be the subject of this equity. It cannot stretch to any form of surreptitious intervention by eavesdropping or other snooping, natural or technically aided.

Other courts have been readier to extend the scope of the equitable principle. In *Francome v. Mirror Group*,[43] held that where a person had tapped a telephone, privately and without official authority, in order to get discreditable information about a leading jockey, the action would in principle lie: apparently, a phone-user does not anticipate that form of

---

[38] Even if we are dealing with a new form of intellectual "property", the tendency to preclude such damages in other instances must be remembered: para. 2–42, above.

[39] Only the analogy to the tort of conversion as *one* method of assessing damages for breach of confidence (*Seager v. Copydex (No. 2)* [1969] R.P.C. 250) gives implied support to the common law property approach. Certainly in *Morison v. Moat* ((1851) 9 Hare 241), the bona fide purchaser was treated as exempt, but the proposition has not found clear echoes in England (*cf.* the cases in n. 35, above, which tend the other way). However, the bona fide purchaser has been treated as protected in Canada (*International Tools v. Kollar* (1968) 67 D.L.R. (2d) 386 at 391; *Tenatronics v. Hauf* (1972) 23 D.L.R. (3d) 60; *cf. Polyresins v. Skin-Hall* (1972) 25 D.L.R. (3d) 152).

[40] [1979] 2 All E.R. 620. See generally Wei (1992) 12 Leg. St. 302.

[41] The case reviews critically the present arrangement for supervising telephone tapping in Britain: "a subject which cries out for legislation": *ibid.*, at 649.

[42] *ibid.*, at 645–646. It is remarkable that this is the first occasion on which the general issue has been aired in a modern British case.

[43] [1984] 2 All E.R. 208, CA (see also above, para. 8–18); see also *Exchange Telegraph v. Howard* (1906) 22 T.L.R. 375.

bugging, whatever he may have to put up with from the police. In the Queensland case of *Franklin v. Giddings*,[44] one fruit-farmer stole budwood for a new variety of nectarine from his neighbour's orchard, built up his own stock of trees and then went into competitive marketing. His conduct was condemned as "unconscionable" and actionable in equity; destruction of his orchard was ordered.[45]

The Younger Committee on Privacy and the Law Commission both **8–35** favoured the creation of a separate form of civil liability which would encompass some activities of industrial and news spies. There are differences of view, however, about whether the improper conduct should be defined relatively specifically (for instance, by limiting only the use of technical devices)[46]; or whether some more general expression (such as "surreptitious obtaining") ought to be used, leaving more to be settled by the courts.[47] On so sensitive a matter, there is great virtue in being as specific as possible.[48] In the *Malone* case, Megarry V.-C. clearly appreciated the embarrassments that some all-embracing principle of liability might pose for official investigators.[49] Equally there are non-governmental interest groups (such as the press) who can justifiably demand specific guidance upon what they remain free to do.

If no liability can arise in equity for any form of spying or eavesdropping **8–36** the criminal law may impose its own form of sanction and from this may arise liability in tort. If there is a combination to procure information of economic value, it may well amount to a criminal conspiracy to defraud.[50] If pecuniary damage can be shown to follow, the conduct will amount to a conspiracy actionable in tort.[51]

---

[44] [1978] Qd R. 72.
[45] There has been held to be a breach of confidence where a journalist is allowed to remain on private premises on condition that he does not take photographs, yet he covertly proceeds to do so: *Shelley Films v. Rex Features* [1994] E.M.L.R. 134; *Creation Records v. News Group* [1997] E.M.L.R. 444. While there was a prior relationship in these instances, could a wholly evasive intrusion be differently treated? *cf.* instances of confrontational invasions, such as *Kaye v. Robertson* [1991] F.S.R. 62, CA; para. 16–52, below.
[46] The Younger Committee (Cmnd. 5012, 1972) favoured the creation of criminal offences relating to surreptitious surveillance by means of a technical device (paras 560–563) and that civil liability should depend upon proof of an unlawful act (para. 632).
[47] The Law Commission put up the alternatives for further discussion (Working Paper No. 58, paras 135–140).
[48] Note the warning against "wide and indefinite rights" in the *Malone* case (n. 35, above) at 643.
[49] Note however his criticism of the present administrative practice governing wire-tapping, and his plea for legislation: n. 34, above.
[50] Persons who combined to make surreptitious copies of films in breach of copyright were held to be conspiring to defraud the copyright owner, even though no one was deceived: *Scott v. Metropolitan Police Commissioner* [1975] A.C. 819; *cf. D.P.P. v. Withers* [1975] A.C. 842; See para 2–20, above. In this context it should be remembered that to borrow a copy of a film (in order to copy it) is not theft: *R. v. Lloyd* [1986] F.S.R. 138, CA. For the development of criminal sanctions against misuse of trade secrets in the U.S. and discussions in Canada, see Coleman (para. 8–01, n. 1 above), Chap. 7.
[51] For this tort, see para. 2–13, above; and note the other possibilities there canvassed.

(3) Unauthorised use

(a) *Wrongful acts*

8–37 The acts that constitute infringement of a patent or copyright are, in different ways, limited by relatively precise criteria: in the case of patents, by confining infringement to certain kinds of industrial use and commercial exploitation within the scope of the claims defining the monopoly[52]; in the case of copyright, by the requirements of reproduction or performance, copying of the manner in which ideas are expressed and the taking of a substantial part of the work.[53] The notion of breach of confidence is by comparison loosely defined. It may consist in any disclosure or use which contravenes the limited purpose for which the information was revealed.[54] If the question is one of misuse, it does not matter that the use will not disclose the information to further recipients.[55] Not all the information taken has to be used or disclosed before breach occurs, though doubtless the deployment of insubstantial amounts might be disregarded.[56] The information used must come from that disclosed in confidence and not from some other source. This may raise similar difficulties of proof to those arising in copyright; and, as there, courts may want to infer derivation of the idea from the similarity of end products.[57]

(b) *The defendant's state of mind*

8–38 The liability of a defendant may turn upon his state of mind both at the time when he receives the information and when he uses or discloses it. The former has already been discussed, since it goes to the question whether an obligation of confidence has been assumed or is to be imposed.[58] When it comes to breach, it appears not to matter that the defendant acts out of some misguided or well-meaning motive,[59] that he does not appreciate the confidentiality of a document from which he takes the information[60] or that he has forgotten the source of the information and

---

[52] See para. 6–02, above.
[53] See paras 11–03—11–20, below.
[54] But not where the information is no more than the knowledge, skill and experience that an employee must acquire in the course of his duties: *United Indigo v. Robinson* (1932) 49 R.P.C. 178 at 189; and more generally, *Worsley v. Cooper* [1939] 1 All E.R. 290 at 306–310.
[55] *Ocular Sciences v. Aspect Vision Care* [1997] R.P.C. 289: if the information contributes towards making of a product, the contribution must be sufficiently extensive and important: see at 401, 404.
[56] In *Amber Size v. Menzel* [1913] 2 Ch. 239 the defendant was restrained from misusing the whole or any material part of the plaintiff's secret process. Contrast the patent law principle which requires all essential integers of the claimed invention to be taken: para. 6–02, above.
[57] See para. 11–03, below.
[58] See paras 8–20, 8–32, above.
[59] *Nichrotherm v. Percy* [1956] R.P.C. 272 at 281.
[60] *National Broach v. Churchill Gear* [1965] R.P.C. 61.

thinks he has thought of it himself. *Seager v. Copydex*[61] was treated by the Court of Appeal as involving subconscious copying of this last kind: the defendant's employees were found to have worked out how to make a carpet grip embodying a basic idea which they had forgotten being shown by the plaintiff. A recent Australian decision,[62] however, has applied the notion of subconscious copying only with some reluctance. It must remain doubtful whether the law—particularly if it is based upon an obligation of "good faith"—needs to go so far.

(c) *Detriment to the plaintiff*

In *Coco v. Clark*,[63] Megarry J. questioned whether the plaintiff must show **8–39** that he has or will suffer detriment by the breach of confidence. The variety of information that may be the subject of confidence makes this a complex and difficult issue and one that remains unresolved. The motive for protecting technical and commercial information is normally to preserve its economic value for the plaintiff. In these cases is the plaintiff's interest like property[64] in the sense that he is entitled to decide if another may make use of it, whether or not he exploits the information himself? Or may he object only to misuses or disclosures of the information that injure him in trade competition?[65] The motive for protecting personal information may well be to prevent distress or embarrassment; though some people want privacy largely so that they can turn it to their own financial advantage.[66] In these cases, if there must be detriment, it may perhaps lie in the need to prove that the plaintiff's sensibilities will be disturbed; and that in turn raises the nice question whether an objective or a subjective test should be applied.[67] When it comes to governmental secrets, it is necessary to show a sufficient public interest in their protection,[68] and this may be expressed as the need to show detriment.[69]

It is tempting to say that liability ought to follow simply upon the breaking of the confidence without looking also for detriment. But one

---

[61] *Seager v. Copydex (No. 1)* [1967] 2 All E.R. 415 at 418; *cf.* "subsconscious copying" in copyright: para. 11–04, below.

[62] *Talbot v. General Television* [1981] R.P.C. 1. See also Ricketson (1980) 2 E.I.P.R. 149.

[63] [1969] R.P.C. 41 at 48; *Dunford v. Johnston* [1978] F.S.R. 143 at 148; and *Jarman Platt v. Barget* [1977] F.S.R. 260 at 277, assume that detriment is necessary. *cf. Nichrotherm v. Percy* [1956] R.P.C. 272 at 273.

[64] Talk of property may not seem very helpful in this context. *cf.* the discussion of whether passing off protected the property in a trade mark or only in the goodwill of the business in which it was used: see paras 15–05, 15–07, below.

[65] If the latter is the rule, what of the case where he wants to exploit a rival invention that he has also devised? *Seager v. Copydex* was such a case.

[66] Consider, *e.g. Lennon v. News Group* [1978] F.S.R. 573. CA.

[67] Law Commission (n. 47, above), paras 63, 65.

[68] See para. 8–19, below.

[69] So Lord Keith put the matter in *Att.-Gen. v. Guardian Newspapers (No. 2)* [1990] A.C. 109 at 258; and see Mason J., *Commonwealth of Australia v. Fairfax* (1980) 32 A.L.R. 485 at 492–493.

should remember that a very wide range of subject-matter is involved. Likewise there is always some public interest in the freedom to use information. Restriction of that freedom accordingly requires sufficient reason. In this connection, the caution exhibited in two areas of tort deserves mention: most economic torts are actionable only upon proof of damage[70]; and the tort of defamation is confined to statements which tend to lower the plaintiff in the eyes of right-thinking members of the public—an approach which imposes objective standards.

3. Remedies

(1) Injunction and other equitable remedies

8–40 The remedies available for infringement of intellectual property rights have been applied to breach of confidence without much difficulty, save in the case of damages.[71] Typically plaintiffs hope to contain the confidence before escape; hence the importance of injunctions. There has been no doctrinal impediment to awarding equity's ancillary forms of relief—account of profits[72] and delivery up or destruction on oath[73]—in appropriate cases.

To the general discussion of these equitable remedies[74] a number of supplemental points may here be added.

(a) *Interlocutory injunctions*

8–41 In cases where a defendant is seeking to stop general publication in a newspaper or elsewhere, the courts have to decide whether a special policy will apply. Interlocutory injunctions are not granted in proceedings for defamation if the defendant proposes to justify his statements (that is establish their truth) or to plead fair comment[75]; the press is thus left free to publish at risk of paying damages. In *Woodward v. Hutchins*,[76] the Court of Appeal considered that the alleged breaches of confidence were inextricably linked with defamation (though defamation was not pleaded) and so it refused to halt a newspaper story. But the case lays down no general principle equivalent to that for defamation.

8–42 In other circumstances, protection of confidence may override the preservation of free expression. In *Schering v. Falkman*,[77] for instance, a

---

[70] See paras 2–12—2–18, above.
[71] See paras 8–46, 8–48, below.
[72] As in *Peter Pan Mfg. v. Corsets Silhouette* [1963] R.P.C. 45.
[73] As in *Industrial Furnaces v. Reaves* [1970] R.P.C. 605, where the defendant was not trusted to destroy on oath.
[74] See paras 2–38, 2–43, above.
[75] *Bonnard v. Perryman* [1891] 2 Ch. 269; *Fraser v. Evans* [1969] 1 All E.R. 8 at 10, CA; the rule survives *American Cyanamid v. Ethicon* (for which see paras 2–32—2–35, above): *Woodward v. Hutchins* (n. 76, below).
[76] [1977] 2 All E.R. 751, CA; and see *Service Corp. v. Channel Four* [1999] E.M.L.R. 83.
[77] [1982] Q.B. 1.

man who had been hired to assist a drug company in countering adverse publicity about one of its products, Primodos, had subsequently become a journalist. He and a television company were about to show a programme in which the old controversy over the drug was resurrected. The idea came from his association with the company, though the material had mainly been recovered from public sources. The majority of the Court of Appeal gave interlocutory relief restraining the showing in terms which displayed their distaste for the journalist's lack of moral scruple in taking advantage of his earlier connection with the company. Only Lord Denning M.R., dissenting, gave higher value to the need to free the press and other media from prior restraint.[78] His position deserves to be remembered.

In the *"Spycatcher"* case, high indignation against the breaches of secrecy **8–43** by the former MI5 officer, Wright, led a majority of the House of Lords to continue and to strengthen interlocutory injunctions against three news-papers,[79] requiring them not to publish extracts or accounts from Wright's memoirs, even after publication abroad had made their contents widely known in Britain.[80] The object of this was to leave to the Attorney-General the practical possibility at the trial of arguing that general injunctions against further revelations by Wright or other confidential government officers should be granted in order to preserve the morale of the secret services.[81] In similar proceedings, shortly before the publication abroad, other newspapers had been obliged to respect the injunctions or Court liability for contempt.[82] Interlocutory decisions turn ultimately on the particular balance of convenience, and future courts may hesitate before finding it necessary to go as far as the remarkable circumstances of the Wright affair were considered to warrant. Nonetheless, it is now even clearer that in England the freedom of the press to publish is all too readily overridden by obligations of confidence. It is a very different situation from that which prevails in the United States under the First Amendment to the Constitution. There remains a serious question, which deserves airing under the European Convention on Human Rights, Article 10, whether the present state of the law is justifiable.

---

[78] He referred to a fine passage of Blackstone (*Commentaries*, IV, 151–152) on the subject, and to modern developments of the theme, including the European Convention on Human Rights, Art. 10, its interpretation in the *Sunday Times* case ((1979–1980) 2 E.H.R.R. 245), and the view of Lord Scarman in *Att.-Gen. v. B.B.C.* [1980] 3 All E.R. 161 at 183.

[79] They were strengthened by removing exceptions pertaining in part to reporting the contemporaneous proceedings in Australia.

[80] *Att.-Gen. v. Guardian Newspapers (No. 1)* [1987] 3 All E.R. 316. See also *Att.-Gen. v. Turnaround Distribution* [1989] 1 F.S.R. 169.

[81] An argument which ultimately failed: see para. 8–19, above.

[82] *Att.-Gen. v. Newspaper Publishing* [1987] 3 All E.R. 276; and ultimately *Att.-Gen. v. Times Newspapers* [1992] 1 A.C. 191, HL; Oliver (1989) 23 Israel L.R. 409; Cripps (para. 8–15, n. 61, above) at 244–253.

(b) *Discretion to grant injunction*

8–44 Courts consider a wider range of factors in deciding whether to grant a final injunction in a breach of confidence case than in patent or copyright cases.[83] Some judges have seen difficulties in imposing constraints on the defendant when the circumstances, particularly those arising after the confidential disclosure, make it unfair to go so far. In *Seager v. Copydex (No. 1)*[84] the Court of Appeal refused an injunction and left the defendant to relief in damages; in *Coco v. Clark*,[85] Megarry J. speculated upon a number of circumstances in which it might be appropriate to make the defendant pay only for what he had taken. A list of factors militating against an injunction might include: (1) the fact that the defendant was copying only sub-consciously or for some reason innocently; (2) the gratuitous manner of the plaintiff's communication; (3) the fact that he was not himself utilising the idea but was rather pursuing an alternative in collaboration with another producer; (4) the extent of the defendant's own contribution to the design of a successful product; (5) whether the information was economic or personal; (6) the relatively mundane or subsidiary character of what was taken; (7) the fact that the information had become public; (8) possibly even the patentable nature of the idea—thus requiring the plaintiff who wants a full right of property to apply for a patent.[86]

8–45 It would be possible for a court to limit the period of an injunction: for instance where it only wanted to deprive the defendant of his head start, or it wanted to leave the defendant free to use the information once it was put into the public domain. Limited injunctions to such ends have certainly been granted or accepted in principle in other jurisdictions.[87]

(2) Damages and other monetary relief[88]

8–46 Where a breach of confidence is also a breach of contract or a general tort such as inducing breach of contract, there is no difficulty in awarding damages in accordance with the normal principles applying to these

---

[83] *Cadbury Schweppes v. FBI Foods* (1999) 83 C.P.R. (3d) 289, SC Canada.
[84] See n. 61, above.
[85] [1969] R.P.C. 41 at 50. The learned judge's remarks are linked to the question of the extent of liability under the "springboard" doctrine: see paras 8–13—8–14, above. He shows some inclination to regard the liability as being to pay for information used, rather than not to use it. *cf. Terrapin v. Builders Supply* [1960] R.P.C. 128 at 135.
[86] Factors (1)—(4) and possibly (7) were relevant to the refusal of the injunction in *Seager v. Copydex*. Concerning (5), Megarry J. considered that personal information might be protectable by injunction, whether industrial or commercial was not. Factor (7), which is speculative, relates to the discussion of the question, para. 8–03, above.
[87] See *International Tools v. Kollar* (1968) 67 D.L.R. (2d) 386, CA Ont.; *A.B. Consolidated v. Europe Strength* [1978] 2 N.Z.L.R. 520; *Talbot v. General Television* [1981] R.P.C. 1, SC Vict.; *cf. Potters-Ballotini v. Weston-Baker* [1977] R.P.C. 202, CA.
[88] Gummow in Youdan (ed.) *Equity, Fiduciaries and Trusts* (1989) 57; Davies in Waters (ed.) *Equity, Fiduciaries and Trusts 1993* (1993) 297; Rickett and Gardner (1994) 24 Vict U. Well. L.R. 19.

common law wrongs. Where the liability arises only in equity, damages may be awarded "in lieu of or in addition to an injunction", in accordance with the principle of Lord Cairns' Act 1858, "against the commission or continuance of the wrongful act".[89] In other fields, the courts have shown little inclination to read this power in a limited way: such damages lie (1) where the wrongful act is purely equitable, and (2) whether the injury has already been committed or will be committed in the absence of an injunction.[90] There are also breach of confidence cases where damages were held available for injuries already caused, in addition to an injunction for the future.[91] But if the only likely breach has already occurred, it continues to be doubted whether damages under the Act can be given: there is then no case for the injunction to which the damages may be a substitute or addition.[92] One way of side-stepping such a narrowly historical view may be rely on Chancery's inherent jurisdiction on a "money bill" to award compensation for an equitable wrong—a notion which is currently enjoying a revival, particularly in Australia.[93] It has also recently been accepted that, where there is a pre-existing fiduciary duty, a constructive trust may be imposed on the fiduciary in appropriate circumstances.[94]

If damages are being given for future injuries in lieu of an injunction, it is **8–47** said, in *Seager v. Copydex (No. 2)*, that their assessment depends upon whether the information could have been acquired by employing a competent consultant, in which case his fee would be an appropriate measure[95]; or whether the information was special—for instance, inventive—in which case, by analogy to the tort of conversion, the sum should represent its price between willing seller and buyer.[96] In the latter case, however, a sale of all the rights (including the right to apply for a patent)[97] may not always be appropriate. Where the plaintiff is exploiting the information himself, or licensing others, a royalty, as if for a non-exclusive licence, may be the appropriate measure. Altogether, the analogy to damages for misappropriation of a single tangible article is inept, given in particular the more obvious

---

[89] *Saltman v. Campbell* (1948) 65 R.P.C. 203, CA.

[90] For a full review, see Jolowicz (1975) 34 C.L.J. 24; *cf.* Meagher, Gummow and Lehane *Equity: Doctrines and Remedies* (3rd ed., 1992), paras 2306–2321. See also *Elsley v. Collins* (1978) 83 D.L.R. (3d) 1 at 13, S.C. (Canada); *Talbot v. General Television* [1981] R.P.C. 1, SC Vict.

[91] *e.g. Peter Pan v. Corsets Silhouette* [1963] R.P.C. 45.

[92] *Proctor v. Bayley* (1889) 42 Ch.D. 390 at 401; *Nichrotherm v. Percy* [1957] R.P.C. 207 at 213–214; *Malone v. Commissioner of Police* [1979] 2 All E.R. 620 at 633.

[93] See, in addition to the citations in nn. 88, 90, above, Tettenborn (1987) 3 I.P.J. 183; Plibersek [1991] E.I.P.R. 283; Capper (1994) 14 Leg. St. 313.

[94] *Ocular Sciences v. Aspect Vision Care* [1997] R.P.C. 289, relying *inter alia* on *Lac Minerals* (below, n. 8).

[95] [1969] 1 W.L.R. 809; but only if the information is for sale: *FBI Foods v. Cadbury Schweppes*, n. 83, above.

[96] [1969] R.P.C. 250; followed in *Interfirm Comparison v. Law Society* [1975] R.P.C. 137 at 158.

[97] *Seager v. Copydex (No. 2)* (n. 95, above). The case has been treated as laying down no general principle: *Talbot v. General Television* (n. 90, above).

comparison to patents and copyright and the more flexible approach to damages which applies to their infringement.[98] Damages are awarded to put the plaintiff in the position that he would have been in, but for the breach of confidence. A person who loses his idea for a television series, because someone else misappropriates it, is entitled to a substantial sum even where his chances of having it taken up were uncertain.[99] So is a person whose business secret loses its commercial value because the misappropriator uses it irresponsibly.[1]

8–48 There remains the question, as yet unexplored in the case law, whether damages for injury to feelings are available for breach of confidence, as they are for defamation and copyright infringement.[2] All that can usefully be said is this. Breach of confidence is one of the ways in which the law accords protection to privacy and those aspects of personal reputation that are associated with it. Infringement of copyright and defamation fulfil the same function in ways that are differently limited. But since both allow damages for injured feelings, it would seem quixotic to bar this form of monetary compensation from the third field, for the sake of yet another historical point.

4. Confidential Information as "Property"[3]

8–49 The willingness of the courts to hold indirect recipients responsible shows that the obligation to respect confidence is not purely personal to the initial giver of the undertaking. Is it then, in any meaningful sense, "property"? The root difficulty of such a question is the flexibility of the property notion in English law and the many ends to which it is employed.[4] Clearly, those who deal in technical know-how often treat it as such. While noting this common usage, Lord Upjohn nevertheless denied that confidential information was "property in any normal sense, but equity will restrain its transmission to another if in breach of some confidential relationship".[5]

---

[98] cf. *Aquaculture Corp. New Zealand Green Mussel* [1990] 3 N.Z.L.R. 299, CA (N.Z.).

[99] *Talbot v. General Television* (n. 90, above). A plaintiff is entitled to fair compensation, but not to every potentially attributable loss: *Universal Thermosensors v. Hibben* [1992] F.S.R. 361.

[1] *Aquaculture* case (n. 98, above). The Court also accepted that exemplary damages might be awarded in an appropriate case: an "astonishing proposition" to Meagher *et al.* (n. 90, above) p. 888.

[2] Significantly, *Beloff v. Pressdram* [1973] 1 All E.R. 241, where this was the issue, was pleaded only in copyright.

[3] See para. 8–32, above; on the issue generally, cf. Ricketson (1977) 11 M.U.L.R. 223, 289; Stuckey (1981) 9 Syd.L.R. 402; Roberts (1987) 3 I.P.J. 209, Palmer in Clarke (para. 8–01, n. 1, above), Chap. 5.

[4] Thus in the *Boardman* case (n. 5, below), one question was whether a fiduciary broke his equitable obligation by using his principal's property (in information) to his own advantage.

[5] *Boardman v. Phipps* [1967] 2 A.C. 46 at 128, HL; *FBI Foods v. Cadbury Schweppes*, n. 83, above SC Canada. But cf. *Goddard v. Nationwide* [1987] Q.B. 670 at 685; *Att.-Gen. v. Guardian Newspapers* [1987] 3 All E.R. 316 at 337–338; *English and American Insurance v. Herbert Smith* [1988] F.S.R. 685.

This now predominant view is used by judges to support consequential conclusions in a variety of situations. These instances, taken as a whole, suggest the wisdom of shaping the obligation over such disparate and ephemeral subject-matter by reference to the requirements of conscientious behaviour, rather than by disposing of issues simply by attaching a "property" label.

First, the central significance given to the undertaking to respect **8–50** confidence makes liability turn on that initial personal obligation. This means that information otherwise obtained will not be protected just because it is in some sense private, and so a scrupulous respect for freedom of information and expression is maintained.[6] It means, moreover, that if a person with (say) technical know-how "assigns" it or "licenses" it exclusively to two different people in inconsistent dealings, the recipients are each left to their rights against the provider of the know-how, subject to any rights which may independently arise in law or equity directly against the other[7] (for an economic tort, or breach of fiduciary duty). Instead of the arbitrary rule that, as between owners of equitable interests, the first in time prevails, Courts are enabled to reach a resolution of a difficult three-cornered dispute which takes account of all the particular circumstances.

Secondly, if confidential information is *per se* classified as equitable **8–51** property, when it is misused so as to make a profit, the profit ought to be recoverable not just by the personal remedies of account or damages but by the proprietary remedy of a constructive trust in any traceable assets constituting the profit. In *Lac Minerals v. International Corona Resources*[8] the Supreme Court of Canada imposed this form of relief in a breach of confidence case. One gold-mining company had learned from another, during negotiations about collaboration on mining prospect No. 1, that the chances on No. 2 were good; the recipient thereupon secured No. 2 behind the informant's back, developed the mine and were obliged to hold it for the informant,[9] not merely to pay damages.

The decision is, however, difficult to interpret as a precedent, since a majority of the Court considered that the two parties were not in a fiduciary relationship, but a different majority favoured the constructive trust.[10] A view which would better fit the hierarchy of intellectual property rights would confine the constructive trust to fiduciary relationships apart from the mere receipt of confidential information.[11] At least it can be said that

---

[6] See para. 8–02, above.

[7] So held in *De Beer v. Graham* (1891) 12 L.R. N.S.W. Eq. 144, stressing that the obligation is one of good faith. But if the information provider undertakes to the first recipient not to give it to anyone else, the second recipient is liable to respect his breach of good faith once informed of it.

[8] (1989) 61 D.L.R. (4th) 14.

[9] Subject to being reimbursed for development costs. Damages would have been assessed at approximately one-quarter of the site value.

[10] Lamer J. found no fiduciary relationship, but held the undertaking of confidence enough to create a trust: see Hayhurst [1990] E.I.P.R. 30.

[11] See para. 8–23, above.

the Court was divided about the particular outcome, because its concern was with the consequences of a breach of good faith. On a property basis, the trust would have been imposed simply as a corollary.

8–52 Thirdly, when test material is submitted to a government authority for the licensing of a pharmaceutical product, can the authority take the information into account when considering the case of a rival submission relating to a generic version of the same drug? If it is property, this may of itself determine that the information may not be used for the second purpose. In an important Australian judgment, Gummow J. refused to uphold this line of argument and would have imposed liability only if in the circumstances the recipient authority had undertaken not to use the information in this way.[12]

8–53 Fourthly, if a person deliberately extracts confidential information and gains an advantage from it, the conduct is not theft within the Theft Act 1968.[13] This may be thought a disadvantage of refusing to accept that information can be property. Certainly deliberate spying and unscrupulous conduct of the kind in the *Lac Minerals* case[14] can be immensely damaging and some industrialists have long argued that criminal sanctions are badly needed. But, as English decisions on the subject have emphasised, it is not enough for theft that the information be characterised as property. There must also be an intention permanently to deprive the person entitled, and that cannot occur unless a sole record of the information is taken for good. If breach of confidence is to be made criminal, it should be by legislation which addresses the particular problem and defines the scope of the liability.[15]

5. CONFIDENCE AND PRIVACY

8–54 Privacy is the desire to be free of intrusion. At least for the fortunate, modern life has improved the chances of solitude and intimacy, while swelling the means by which they may be interrupted. Invasions of privacy

---

[12] *Smith Kline & French v. Department of Health* [1990] F.S.R. 617; Cornish in Leser and Isomura (eds.), *Wege zum japanischen Recht* (1992) pp. 843–850. In England, a public officer (of the Health and Safety Executive) was held entitled to pass information about the deceptive marking of a pharmaceutical product to the mark-owner, as a person to whom it was of mutual interest and concern: *Hoechst U.K. v. Chemiculture* [1993] F.S.R. 270; and see *Process Development v. Hogg* [1996] F.S.R. 45, CA.

[13] *Oxford v. Moss* (1979) 68 Cr.App.R. 183: the defendant temporarily extracted an examination paper in order to learn its content; followed in *R. v. Absolom* (cited in Coleman (para. 8–01, n. 1, above) at 96), where an employee attempted to sell off highly valuable oil exploration results. The same view was taken in Scotland (*Grant v. Procurator Fiscal* [1988] R.P.C. 41) and, after much argument, by the Supreme Court of Canada (*R. v. Stewart* (1988) 50 D.L.R. (4th) 1). See also Alderson (1992) 7 I.P.J. 1.

[14] Above, n. 8.

[15] As it is in numerous American states, and equally on the European continent (where in some states, by a good mercantilist twist, sending the information abroad is an aggravated offence): see Coleman (para. 8–01, n. 1, above), Chap. 7.

may involve personal confrontation, surreptitious physical presence, interference with personal property, or simply the acquisition and use of information. The variety of situations in which one person may seek to secure privacy against another are so considerable that there is the greatest difficulty in deciding when the law should provide an instrument of protection.[16]

Privacy does, as already noted, find a place in the European Convention **8-55** on Human Rights, Article 8 of which seeks to guarantee a right of respect for an individual's private and family life, home and correspondence. But the text recognises that there must be limitations to this. One is constituted by the countervailing guarantee of freedom of expression, which is specified in Article 10. In any case, the Convention is an instrument against public interference with privacy and not against such vociferous exposers of any-cost truth as the press.

Britain, with its reasonably proud and much trumpeted tradition of press **8-56** freedom, has erected only limited legal boundaries to investigative journalism, the most feared being the law of defamation. It does not include any general right of privacy. The recent readiness of tabloid and other newspapers to reveal the secrets of the mighty, the adulated and the humble, without count for the misery it will bring to the victims, has distended the patience of many beyond repair. The antic abandon with which editors seek to justify any and every exposé does their cause little good. But the root fact remains that what they reveal is more or less true; if it is misleading, the law already provides its defamation action. If we had a privacy law, the most disreputable would be among the first to flourish it aggressively.

So much for the dilemma. Left to itself, no British government seems likely to enact general sanctions against unjustified invasions of privacy. In 1993, after a term in which the press was set to secure adequate self-regulation and its Press Complaints Commission was found wanting,[17] Sir David Calcutt's Report to the National Heritage Minister[18] recommended:

(1) the immediate setting up of a statutory tribunal with powers of investigation, injunction, fining and compensation;
(2) the introduction of criminal penalties against various forms of physical intrusion for the purpose of obtaining personal information; and

---

[16] For reviews of a long debate, Seipp (1983) 30 J.L.S. 325, Wacks *The Protection of Privacy* (1980); *Personal Information* (1989). See also Lord Chancellor's Department and Scottish Office: Joint Consultation Paper on Infringement of Privacy (1993); National Heritage Committee, H.C. 1992–93, 294; *Privacy and Media Intrusion: the Government's Response*, Cm. 2918 (1993).

[17] A first Calcutt Committee on Privacy reported in favour of giving the self-regulatory body 18 months to prove its effectiveness (Cm. 1102, 1990). In just that period, a stream of revelations about the private lives of politicians and royalty (including "Dianagate" and "Fergietoes") suggested that the press were daring government to do its worst: hence the second Calcutt Report.

[18] Cm. 2135, 1993.

(3) further consideration of a tort of invasion of privacy.

The first was immediately rejected by government, and nothing has happened on the other fronts. The essential issue therefore remains the scope of judge-made law, and in particular the place of the breach of confidence action alongside that for defamation as the main tools for dividing the legally unacceptable from the intrusive but necessary. Indeed, it is striking how little has changed in a quarter of a century.

8–57 In 1972, the Younger Committee considered that a general right of privacy should not be introduced into the law: it might be used too readily to trespass upon the freedom to receive and make use of information and to express opinions.[19] Accepting this limitation, the Law Commission then undertook a review of the law of breach of confidence and published a Working Paper and then, in 1981, a Report and Draft Bill.[20] The latter proposed that the liability be expressed as a statutory duty, couched in the concepts and language of tortious wrong. There would be, first of all, a duty to preserve confidence arising initially out of a confidential relationship, and extending to indirect recipients once they knew the true position. There would also be a duty to respect confidence in information acquired in seven other specified circumstances, including unauthorised interference with anything containing the information, being in a place without authority, using devices for surreptitious surveillance and the like.

The recommendations as a whole were comprehensive and at several points they were rather more precise than the current case law. But at the really difficult junctures (for example, whether there is an overriding public interest in publication) much was left to the tribunal's particular sense of balance. Accordingly, the media hostility which prevents any substantial intervention in the field by the legislature leaves the judges to handle difficult cases without even the support of statutory authority.

8–58 Breach of confidence is a personal cause of action primarily to prevent the confidence from being broken, and secondarily to provide compensation or an accounting for profits where the damage has been done. It lasts only so long as the information retains a sufficient measure of secrecy and draws to a close as it becomes public, whether legally or illegally. It cannot, therefore, be treated as a continuing proprietary asset for which a licence to use is needed after that moment. In this respect confidence has a narrower potential than a right of privacy.

8–59 The experience of the United States shows just what is at stake. In that country a right of privacy was constructed out of more limited common law wrongs, including prominently the equitable action for breach of confi-

---

[19] Cmnd. 5012, 1972.
[20] English Law Commission, Working Paper No. 58 (1974); Report No. 110 (1981). *cf.* Canadian Institute of Law Research, Report No. 46, (1986); Coleman (para. 8–01, n. 1, above), esp. App. 2.

dence.[21] In a society hungry for commercial returns upon the exploitation of every aspect of personality, the right came to be conceived as a right to control personal information whether or not it was still withheld from the public. It developed into a distinct right of publicity. Those who have built up fame or notoriety, as indeed those who acquire either fortuitously, have a right to prevent others from using their name, their image, their voice and the characters they play.[22]

The shift from the defence of the individual against intrusion to control **8–60** over the exploitations of personality is a very considerable one. The property right which emerges can be subjected to the standard tests of intellectual property: is its purpose to promote the development of ideas or to protect a marketing association? If so, should it be restricted or indeterminate in length? What range of applications should constitute its infringement? What countervailing interests should give rise to a defence? One has only to pose such questions to realise what strangely amorphous stuff the publicising of personality is. Any country should think long and hard about competing values before it moves to a general protection of "personality" in commercial publicity. If it is convinced that diggers should have their gold, so be it; but it should not be led to that belief by crocodile tears about invasions of privacy.

6. TRADE SECRET MISUSE: CRIMINAL RESPONSIBILITY

Flagrant abuses of confidential commercial information can occur where **8–61** wrongdoer lets out the secret and then proves to have no assets. Civil liability can have no impact on such a situation. Accordingly the Law Commission has published a Discussion Paper on the desirability of making misuse of trade secrets a discrete criminal offence.[23] To do so would bring Britain broadly in line with Federal and much state law in the United States, and also with the law in many Continental countries.[24]

The paper demonstrates the complexity which such a law would have to assume. It is not able to propose any preferred definition of a "trade secret". Must the "owner" have indicated that it is to be kept secret? Is it to include professional and academic secrets? When will the information have come into the public domain? What will constitute the *mens rea* of the offence? What will be excluded? The employee's and independent contrac-

---

[21] Famously, it was declared in Warren and Brandeis' article (1890) 4 Harv. L.R. 193; and developed by Prosser, esp. in (1960) 48 Calif. L. R. 383.

[22] In the case of appearance and voice, the unauthorised adoption might be taken from the individual or come from an imitator, as in cases concerning a look-alike Jacqueline Onassis and a sound-alike Bette Midler. See generally on what is now a complex and shifting subject, esp. McCarthy, *The Rights of Publicity and Privacy* (1990); Goodenough [1992] E.I.P.R. 55, 90; paras 16–33—16–35, below.

[23] *i.e.* an offence other than conspiracy to defraud or theft (when some physical record is misappropriated): *Misuse of Trade Secrets*—Paper 150, 1997; see Hull [1998] Crim. L.R. 246.

[24] See Paper 150, App. B; and Coleman, *The Legal Protection of Trade Secrets* (1992), Chap. 7.

tor's personal knowledge, skill and experience, information aquired independently, by reverse engineering and from a third party—all are mentioned as possibilities (one would hope as a matter of course). So is publication which is justified in the public interest.

The discussion in the Paper reflects the difficulties which the civil law has faced in reaching reasonably clear limits to the scope of liability. Those who remain doubtful about the prospect of specific criminal sanctions are those who know the bitter self-justification often exhibited by each side in a breach of confidence dispute—not least in that familiar situation of the employee who leaves to further his own future. The danger of criminal sanctions—particularly if the offence is solely by indictment[25]—is that it unduly weights the balance in favour of the person asserting the misuse of a secret. The Law Commission seeks to deflect such criticism by limiting prosecutions to those brought by the Director of Public Prosecutions, or with his approval.[26] That at the least would be a necessary qualification. Even so, the issue is likely to continue to divide informed opinion.

---

[25] As is proposed: Paper 150, para. 5.11.
[26] Para. 5.15.

Part IV

COPYRIGHT AND DESIGNS

CHAPTER 9

RANGE AND AIMS OF COPYRIGHT

1. HISTORICAL INTRODUCTION

(1) The emergence of copyright[1]

The notion that an author should have an exclusive "copyright" in his **9–01** creation took firm shape at the beginning of the eighteenth century. It derived from a confusion of earlier strains and there was still a major evolutionary conflict to come before its modern form was finally fixed.

From the early years of the first copying industry—printing—a pattern of exploitation had been developing: an entrepreneur, whose calling was typically that of "stationer", became the principal risk-taker; he acquired the work from its author (if he was not reprinting a classic) and organised its printing and sale. The stationers (forefathers of the modern publisher) were the chief proponents of exclusive rights against copiers. Certainly their own practices—their guild rules and the terms on which they dealt with authors—insisted upon this exclusivity; their regime for "insiders" became a source of trade customs from which general rights against "outsiders" might be distilled.[2]

In this objective the stationers early found an ally in the Crown. In 1534 **9–02** they secured protection against the importation of foreign books; and in 1556, Mary, with her acute concern about religious opposition, granted the Stationers' Company a charter. This gave a power, in addition to the usual supervisory authority over the craft, to search out and destroy books

---

[1] The evolution of copyright has attracted scholars of formidable polish. The sketch that follows relies particularly on Scrutton, *Law of Copyright* (1883) Chap. 4; Birrell, *Seven Lectures on Copyright* (1898); Holdsworth, *History of English Law*, Vol. VI, pp. 360–379; Kaplan, *An Unhurried View of Copyright* (1967), pp. 1–25; Patterson, *Copyright in Historical Perspective* (1968); Feather, *A History of British Publishing* (1988); Feather (1989) 25 Pub. Hist. 45, and (1992) 10 Cardozo A.L.L.J. 455; Tompson [1992] Jur. Rev. 18; Saunders, *Authorship and Copyright* (1992); Ginsburg (1990) 64 Tul. L.R. and in Sherman and Strowel (eds.), *Of Authors and Origins* (1994) p. 131; Rose in *ibid.*, p. 23; Rose, *Authors and Owners* (1993); Davies, *Copyright and the Public Interest* (1994); Sherman and Bently, *The Making of Modern Intellectual Property Law* (1999); Seville, *Literary Copyright Reform in Early Victorian England* (1999).

[2] See Birrell, Lecture 3; Holdsworth, pp. 363–364 (both accounts being based on Arber, *A Transcript of the Stationers' Registers* (1875)).

printed in contravention of statute or proclamation. The company was thus enabled to organise what was in effect a licensing system by requiring lawfully printed books to be entered in its register. The right to make an entry was confined to company members, this being germane to the very purpose of the charter. The system of control was equally satisfying to Elizabeth and her Stuart successors, who supervised it through the Star Chamber and the heads of the established Church.[3] Governments determined to censor heterodoxy made concert with the established order of the publishing trade.

The royal predilection for granting special privileges might interfere with the interests of the stationers. Not only was the sole privilege to print Bibles, prayer books and laws claimed under the royal prerogative; much wider privileges—not confined to particular, or even new, works—were also granted by letters patent. In the long term, it was not the fact of individual grants which mattered,[4] but their cumulative effect. For they might bear the inference that, as with exclusive rights in technical inventions, it needed special authority from the Crown to secure legal protection against imitators.

So long as the licensing system survived, this line of argument was of no great significance. And Stationers' Company licensing had considerable vitality. It outlived the ignominy into which the Star Chamber fell, being kept up by the Long Parliament and confirmed in 1662 after Charles II's restoration. But he allowed it to lapse in 1679; and, while James II revived it for seven years in 1685, it could not last long in the political climate of his dethronement. Parliament finally refused to renew it in 1694. The stationers, who had argued forcefully against their loss of protection, were left with such claim to "copy-right" as they could make out of their own customary practices surrounding registration. As they also lost their search and seizure powers, and equity had not yet begun to grant injunctions to protect any interest that they might establish, their only hope was in common law and this they put to no decisive test.[5] Their needs were equally for definite substantive rights and for effective procedures to enforce them and these needs were reflected in the legislation that they secured in the reign of Anne, the Copyright Act of 1710.[6]

9-03   The "sole right and liberty of printing books" that the Act conferred was given to authors and their assigns; but it stemmed nonetheless from commercial exploitation rather than literary creation pure and simple.[7]

---

[3] The regulatory system was brought under a comprehensive Star Chamber decree of 1586; of this there was a new version in 1637.

[4] Many of the publishing patents naturally came into the hands of Stationers' Company members.

[5] Later judges and authors would engage in speculation disguised as assertion over "common law copyright" in this period: see, *e.g.* Scrutton, *op. cit.*, pp. 89–94.

[6] See Ransom, *The First Copyright Statute* (1956); Feather (1980) 8 Pub. History 19.

[7] See Copyright Act 1710, s. 1. Booksellers and printers were named as falling among the author's assigns.

Enforcing the right depended upon registering the book's title before publication with the Stationers' Company, "as hath been unusual"; and likewise it was enforceable by seizure and penalties.[8] The right lasted for 14 years from first publication "and no longer"; but if the author was still living at the end, the right was "returned" to him for another 14 years.[9] Other "copy-rights" were expressed to be unaffected by the Act. It was not difficult to argue that an author ought to have some protection over his work before it was published. Since this went uncovered by the Act, it could only lie in a right of literary property at common law.[10] But much more absorbing was the question whether any common law right survived in perpetuity the act of publication.

At first, in the view of a majority of judges, history and policy demanded the recognition of this complete property right.[11] The Act of Anne was treated as providing supplemental remedies during the period when unfair competition could most readily injure the first publisher.[12] In the end, the great case of *Donaldson v. Beckett*[13] narrowly settled the issue the other way: the statute was taken to delimit the scope of rights after publication absolutely. It was a most strategic victory for those who would insist that claims to trading exclusivity must be balanced against public interest in the freedom to exploit.[14] Had the case gone the other way, protection for other forms of intellectual endeavour against "misappropriation" would have been pressed in a host of analogies. Given *Donaldson v. Beckett*, new forms

---

[8] Copyright Act 1710, ss. 1, 2.

[9] *ibid.*, s. 11. For books already printed on April 10, 1710, the period was 21 years from that date: s. 1.

[10] The question was not actually decided before *Donaldson v. Beckett* (n. 13, below). But then, all but one of the judges had no doubt about its existence.

[11] Especially in *Millar v. Taylor* (1769) 4 Burr. 2303, where Lord Mansfield, a great champion of authors, led the majority. But the same assumption had been made in the 1730s when Chancery began to grant interlocutory injunctions concerning books no longer within the fold of the statute. And the booksellers found some favour from the King's Bench judges in an action (collusive and so ultimately abortive) begun in 1760. The tale is ebulliently told by Birrell (n. 1, above), Lecture 4; and see Walters (1974) 29 Library 290; Abrams (1983) 29 Wayne L.R. 1119; Feather (1987) 22 Pub. Hist. 5; Rose and Tompson (n. 1, above).

[12] There were other ways in which the Statute was read as protecting only the most serious invasions of the publisher's interests: thus neither translations nor "fair" abridgements at this stage constituted infringements: *Burnett v. Chetwood* (1720) 2 Mer. 441; *Gyles v. Wilcox* (1740) 2 Atk. 141, 3 Atk. 269; *Dodsley v. Kinnersley* (1761) Amb. 403. For the relation of these decisions to the scope of the common law right, see Kaplan (n. 1, above).

[13] (1774) 2 Bro. P.C. 129, 4 Burr. 2408, 17 Hansard Parl. Hist. 953. Lord Mansfield's failure to participate in the Lords suggests a dark secret: Tompson (n. 1, above).

[14] Its tone found sympathetic resonances in the century to come. A notable reiteration came in *Jeffreys v. Boosey* (1854) 4 H.L.C. 815. Here the issue took the form: if statute did not allow copyright to a foreign author, was he nonetheless protected at common law. On consulting the judges the House of Lords found that a majority of them favoured the common law right. But the Lords unanimously agreed with Pollock C.B.'s positivist view of copyright as "altogether an artificial right, not naturally and necessarily arising out of the social rules that ought to prevail among mankind, but . . . a creature of the municipal laws of each country, to be enjoyed for such time and under such regulation as the law of each state may direct": at 935.

of protection had to be secured from the legislature; and even if a lobby succeeded, the most that could be hoped for would be an exclusive right of limited duration.[15]

(2) Additions to copyright: nineteenth century experience

9-04 That process had indeed already begun. The engravers had succeeded in 1734 and 1766.[16] Textile designers secured some very temporary protection by statutes which were the precursors of the present registered design system.[17] In 1798 and 1814, sculptures were protected[18]; and eventually—as the technical possibilities for reproducing artistic works expanded—the Fine Arts Copyright Act 1862 brought in paintings, drawings and photographs.[19]

In 1814 the term of the statutory right in published books was extended to 28 years or the author's life, whichever was longer.[20] But Sergeant Talfourd's attempts to have it again extended—for a period of perhaps the author's life and 60 years—ran into the shoal of "economical" argument, put in particularly telling form by T. B. Macaulay.[21] His view of copyright as "a tax on readers for the purpose of giving a bounty to authors" meant that in 1842 the period was extended only to 42 years or the author's life and seven years, whichever was longer.[22] That compromise was to last until international pressures obliged Parliament to revise its views in Talfourd's direction.[23]

9-05 The commercial interests of book publishers had called for a "copyright"[24]; and much the same applied to artistic works. But in the arts of drama and music, exploitation occurred as much through performance as through the sale of copies. Playwrights, composers and their commercial associates sought a "use" right upon each public performance of the work. In 1833 this distinct performing right was given in dramatic works[25] and in

---

[15] *cf.* para. 8–05, above.

[16] Engraving Copyright Acts 1734 and 1766 (and further enactments in 1777 and 1836). The term was 28 years.

[17] An Act of 1787 gave protection against the printing, working or copying of an original pattern for certain types of textile. It lasted only for two months from publication (in 1794 extended to three)—giving at most a bare head-start.

[18] These Acts extended only to sculptures, etc., of the human figure; the term was 14 years from publication, with a further 14 years for authors who were living and had kept the copyright themselves.

[19] Here the term was the author's life and seven years.

[20] Copyright Act 1814, s. 4.

[21] Macaulay, *Speeches* (1866) pp. 109–122.

[22] Literary Copyright Act 1842, s. 3.

[23] See para. 9–06, below.

[24] There had been no difficulty in extending the Act of Anne to sheet music: *Bach v. Longman* (1777) 2 Cowp. 623. As for maps, see *Sayre v. Moore* (1785) 1 East 361n.

[25] Dramatic Copyright Act 1833; for its history, see McFarlane, *Copyright: the Development and Exercise of the Performing Right* (1980), Chaps 3–5; Peacock and Weir, *The Computer in the Market Place* (1975). Lectures in public were specially treated by the Lectures Copyright Act 1835.

1842 extended to musical works.[26] Despite the nature of the performing right, the wider term, "author's right", was never introduced into English usage, as it was in most other languages, in place of "copyright". The difference reflects the accretive historical process by which the British law developed. But equally it carries another overtone: a change to "author's right" might well symbolise some preference for creator over entrepreneur. That is something which has rarely attracted much ardour in Britain.

The same point is underscored in another way. The relation between author and exploiter offers many opportunities for tension and disagreement. In continental Europe the need to safeguard the artistic integrity of the author in the course of such relations was eloquently argued, particularly in the latter nineteenth century; and in many copyright laws the author was accorded moral rights which were entrenched by making inoperative any surrender of the rights in advance of the time when the author might want to rely upon them. These typically might include: the right to decide to make the work public; the right to be named as author; the right to object to revisions affecting honour or reputation. Some systems have gone to the extent of adding a right to have the work withdrawn upon payment of compensation; and the right to object to destruction.[27] In Britain, this sort of demand seems scarcely to have surfaced at all. Instead, in the high age of contractual freedom, relations were left to be determined by agreement, supported by such terms as the Court might imply in the name of business efficacy and subject to the torts of defamation, injurious falsehood and passing off.[28]

(3) International relations and the Act of 1911

Britain could not however afford to reject entirely the ideals of those for **9–06** whom copyright was a practical expression of reverence for the act of artistic creation. Her commercial position made her a considerable exporter of copyright material and she had a strong interest in reciprocal copyright arrangements with other countries and their colonies. On the question of protecting foreign works it was possible to take a number of attitudes: the French, for instance, granted protection to all authors of works published in France and to works of Frenchmen published anywhere. The Americans, by contrast, first underlined their independence from Britain by confining copyrights to citizens and residents; and, a century later, while conceding some place to foreign authors, country by country, Congress required all legitimate copies of various types of work to be produced in the United

---

[26] Literary Copyright Act 1842, s. 20; see further McFarlane (n. 25, above); Seville (above, n. 1).

[27] See, para. 11–64, below.

[28] There is no mention of the subject, for instance, in the Reports of the Royal Commission of 1875–1878 and the Committee of 1909.

States (under the controversial "manufacturing clause").[29] The British, true to their own tradition of giving first consideration to home publishers, admitted foreign authors to copyright upon condition that the work was first published within the country.[30]

9–07 With protectionist America, the hope of satisfactory mutual arrangements was slender; but with continental Europe and elsewhere the prospects were brighter. A number of bilateral arrangements were worked out.[31] Then, by the Berne Convention of 1886, a multi-national system evolved, under which either the personal connection of the author with a Member State, or first publication in a Member State, was to secure copyright in the other, under the principle of national treatment,[32] but this in turn raised questions about the scope of rights offered in each state. At the Berlin Revision of the Convention in 1908, Britain was obliged to accept the majority consensus on two matters: protection was to arise out of the act of creation itself, without any condition of registration or other formality—which obliged Britain to abandon even the traditional requirement of Stationers' Company registration before suing[33]; and the period of protection for most types of work was to be at least the author's life and 50 years—that quasi-proprietary right against which Macaulay had persuaded Parliament 70 years before.

9–08 These changes were adopted in the Copyright Act 1911, the first British legislation to bring the various copyrights within a single text, and at the same time to put rights, even in unpublished works, on a statutory footing.[34] There was, however, some concession to public interest arguments: in the later years of the copyright in published works there were certain provisions for automatic licences.[35]

---

[29] There were a series of later modifications to the manufacturing clause, see Nimmer, *Copyright* (1979 ed.), paras 722–723.

[30] For parts of this story, see Nowell-Smith, *International Copyright Law and the Publisher in the Reign of Queen Victoria* (1968), Chaps 1, 2.

[31] See Ladas, *The International Protection of Literary and Artistic Property* (1938) I, pp. 144–66.

[32] For the history of the Berne Convention, see Ricketson, Chap. 1; Cavalli, *La Genèse de la Convention de Berne* (1986).

[33] After 1842, registration was no longer required before publication, but only before suing on the copyright. Accordingly the requirement served no obvious function, and came in for a good deal of domestic criticism.

[34] Common law copyright in unpublished works was abolished: CA 1911, s. 31.

[35] CA 1911, s. 3, provided that, after 25 years from the death of an author of a published work, anyone might reproduce it for sale upon payment of a 10 per cent royalty to the copyright owner. Section 4 added a special power (first introduced in 1842) to seek a licence from the Privy Council, which in fact went unused. The Gregory Committee found that this machinery played no significant part in securing cheap republications. In order to satisfy the unqualified requirements of the Berne Convention in its 1948 revision (Brussels), the Committee recommended abandonment: see Cmd. 8661, paras 20–23. This was effected in 1956.

The provisions just mentioned were often linked with the reversionary interest rules introduced in 1911, though these were motivated by a concern for authors and their dependants *vis-à-vis* their entrepreneurs. Section 5 rendered ineffective an *inter vivos*

If the author gained by this intrusion of foreign ideals, the entrepreneur was by no means forgotten. The 1911 Act gave the producers of sound recordings their own exclusive right to prevent reproductions of their recordings (and, as the Courts later held, also to prevent public performances of them).[36] The right was indiscriminately labelled copyright, even though it was conferred not upon the executant artist whose performance was recorded but upon the business which organised the recording. It was thus not an author's right at all, but something which continental theory would scrupulously distinguish as a "neighbouring right". An important precedent was set for an age that was to see a great increase in the technical possibilities for artistic expression.

(4) Developments since 1945

(a) *The 1956 Act*

In the post-war period, there has been constant activity on the international **9–09** scene. However, alterations in domestic law have derived more from pressures at home and these may be dealt with first. The Copyright Act 1956 was a complex piece of draftsmanship which elaborated many rules at perplexing length while neglecting to spell out basic principles in the clear order appropriate to a real code.[37] The Act was most notable for adding three new forms of entrepreneurial copyright—in cinematograph films (hereafter "films" for short), broadcasts and the typographical format of published editions—to the 1911 copyright in sound recordings.

Equally significant in terms of new technique was the creation of a Performing Right Tribunal. In the inter-war period, it had been shown by the Performing Right Society (PRS) that joint action was a feasible method of turning the right of public performance in copyright music into something of real value[38]; and the record companies had followed suit, once they succeeded in establishing their own performing right,[39] by setting up the Phonographic Performance Ltd (PPL). The aggregation of copyrights that

---

assignment by an author of his copyright in a work, and equally his licence to publish such a work, so far as concerned the period from 25 years after his death. While this limited reversionary right was abolished after July 1, 1957, it continued to affect assignments and licences entered into before that date: CA 1956, Sched. 7, para. 28(3); Sched. 8, para. 6. Numerous musical works which have a recurrent popularity were dealt with in ways which allowed the legatees of composers (at least when moved by others to act) to claim back the last 25 years of the copyright. The precise impact of the reversionary right provision has accordingly been the subject of complex dispute: see *Redwood Music v. Francis Day* [1981] R.P.C. 337, HL; Harris [1983] 30 J. Cop. Soc. 544.

[36] CA 1911, s. 19(1); *Gramophone Co. v. Cawardine* [1934] Ch. 450.

[37] It was used as a text-book example of how not to proceed by Dale, *Legislative Drafting* (1976), Chap. 1.

[38] In the nineteenth century, the copyright owners of dramatic works had for some time run a Dramatic Authors' Society: see McFarlane (n. 25, above) pp. 65 *et seq.*

[39] See n. 34, above.

such organisations acquired brought a measure of power over their markets which, as the Gregory Committee found, was capable of being exercised in controversial ways: in particular PPL had been prepared to refuse or limit licences to, for instance, dance-halls, in order to sustain the employment of live musicians.[40] The Performing Right Tribunal was accordingly created to hear disputes over performing right licences from authors' collecting societies, and recording and broadcasting organisations.[41] Its services have been used on a number of important occasions and it is now being looked to as a model for controlling the activities of licensing bodies which have been or may be established to deal with reproduction rights, as distinct from performing rights.

9–10   Those who contributed to the production of recordings, films and broadcasts as performing artists gained no part in the proprietary rights of the Copyright Act 1956. It was argued that a performers copyright would make for disproportionate complexity in the handling of rights and that they could properly be left to protect themselves by contract.[42] However, even in 1925, it had been admitted that performers deserved some form of added help against strangers who misappropriated their performances: but they were only allowed the assistance of the criminal law.[43] The same system was continued in a series of statutes somewhat extending the original range. The Performers' Protection Acts 1958–1972 established summary offences against making non-private records or films of performances, performing them in public, and broadcasting performances, without the performers' written consent. As the volume of "bootlegging" (surreptitious recording of performances) grew, this half-way house became a much less satisfactory form of protection. There were attempts to persuade Courts that the Acts conferred civil rights of action. This produced only slow progress and the issue became one of the many pressures upon the government for the legislation which would eventually emerge as the Copyright, Designs and Patents Act 1988.

(b) *International developments*

9–11 (i) **The Universal Copyright Convention (UCC).**[44] The desire to bring the United States within a general network of international copyright relations was strong. So also was the wish to maintain the basic tenets of the Berne Convention; indeed its revision at Brussels in 1948 only served to strengthen its force. After that event UNESCO took the initiative by promoting the Universal Copyright Convention of 1952. This also guaran-

---

[40] See Cmd. 8862, 1952, paras 140–157.
[41] CA 1956, Pt 4; see paras 12–54 *et seq.*, below.
[42] See the Gregory Report (Cmd. 8662, 1952), paras 165–176.
[43] Dramatic and Musical Performers' Protection Act 1925.
[44] See Bogsch, *Law of Copyright under the Universal Copyright Convention* (3rd ed., 1972).

teed the principle of national treatment, but on less stringent conditions about the term of protection, the types of work protected and the extent of protection. There was, for instance, no mention of any moral right. The United States was able to join the new Convention, while retaining her copyright term of two periods of 28 years[45] and introducing a simple requirement of notice on published works of foreign authors not first published there: the symbol ©, together with the name of the copyright owner and the year of first publication.[46] Subsequently, in 1973, the U.S.S.R. joined the UCC and there are now a significant number of states which belong only to the less demanding of the two general Conventions.[47]

(ii) **The Stockholm and Paris Revisions of Berne and UCC: the developing** **9–12**
countries. Copyright was the first field of intellectual property which the developing countries sought to have their needs recognised as a special case. The shock waves of the initial confrontation were considerable: the concessions in favour of developing countries were originally moulded into a Protocol to the Berne Convention at the Stockholm Revision in 1967. These proved more than the traditional publishing states (led by the British) could take. The Protocol allowed developing countries to reduce the term of copyright in their national law; to authorise translations into their national languages; to authorise publishing for educational and cultural purposes and to exclude from the scope of infringement reproduction for teaching, study or research; and to limit the scope of the right to broadcast. As it became clear that the Stockholm version would not be supported, a further revision conference was called (in Paris, 1971).[48] This toned down the special concessions in a new Appendix to the Berne Convention.

The limitations which developing countries[49] are entitled to introduce **9–13**
into national law have been restricted to two. First, once three years have passed since first publication, a competent authority in the country may be empowered to license a national to translate a printed work into a national language,[50] and publish it, for the purpose of teaching, scholarship or research[51]; in the alternative, the country may take advantage of an older

---

[45] The UCC, Art. 4(2), provided for a minimum term of the author's life and 25 years, unless a country already measured by a term of years from publication; in that case the period had to be 25 years or more.

[46] This common marking is not needed to secure protection in any member state of the Berne Union, such as the U.K. For the recent adherence of the U.S. to Berne, see para. 9–21, below.

[47] A Berne member may not leave and then rely upon the protection flowing from the UCC, unless it is a developing country: see UCC, Art. 27 and Appendix Declaration, as revised in 1971.

[48] See now Masouyé, *Guide to the Berne Convention* (1978), Ricketson, Chap. 11.

[49] *i.e.* countries so regarded in U.N. practice: Appendix, Art. 1(1).

[50] *i.e.* one in general use there, or in use in a region or by an ethnic or governmental group or in education.

[51] Appendix, Art. 2. See also Art. 2(9) allowing a similar licence to a broadcasting organisation.

Convention provision[52] allowing the termination of the translation right, once 10 years from first publication have elapsed without the copyright owner publishing his own translation. Secondly, if the copyright owner or an associate does not publish the work in a country within a set period[53] after first publication, the competent authority can license a national to publish.[54] In both cases, the copies in both cases must be confined to the national market. Any licence must be upon terms of just compensation, judged by the standard of usual royalty rates between the two countries.[55]

9–14   At the same time, rather similar compromises were reached for the UCC. As far as translations are concerned, this Convention did not previously have the 10-year exception as in Berne, but instead allowed (in any country) a compulsory licence of a published "writing" after a seven-year period.[56] On top of this, the developing countries are permitted the post-three-year compulsory licence to translate as in Berne.[57] They also have equivalent rights to allow compulsory licences to reproduce.[58]

The process of reaching an international consensus on these points has become laborious and complex. The results may do something to colour the political climate in which publishing by foreign houses is conducted in developing countries. Yet even in those countries which have set up licensing procedures in pursuance of their Convention entitlements, there is little evidence that local publishers are taking advantage of them.[59]

9–15   (iii) **Protection of performers, recorders and broadcasters.** The 1956 Act strongly confirmed the United Kingdom's interest in supporting the entrepreneurs of the entertainment industry; and more guardedly the claims of performers were also acknowledged.[60] The country was accordingly a strong supporter of international collaboration against the piracy of performances, particularly through the media of records and broadcasts. A first drive resulted in the Rome Convention on the Protection of Performers, Producers of Phonograms and Broadcasting Organisations of 1961.[61] The Convention requires a member to provide[62]: (1) for performers,

---

[52] Convention, Art. 30(2), Appendix, Art. 5.
[53] These periods differ with the type of work, the period for scientific and technological works being as little as three years from first publication: Appendix, Art. 3(3).
[54] Appendix, Art. 3.
[55] *ibid.*, Art. 6; note the compromise on currency restrictions affecting compensation: Art. 4(6). There are a number of provisions on formalities and further qualifications; for which see Ricketson, Chaps 13, 14.
[56] UCC, Art. 5.
[57] *ibid.*, Art. 5*ter.*
[58] *ibid.*, Art. 5*quater.*
[59] For considerations of the future of the Berne Convention at its centennial point, see Ricketson, Pt. III; and the contributions of Davies, Phillips and Koumantos to (1986) 11 Col.-VLA J. 33, 165, 225.
[60] See para. 9–10, above.
[61] See Davies (1979) 1 E.I.P.R. 154; paras 9–29, 9–30, below.
[62] In each case, for the benefit of nationals of other Member States and for specified activities carried on in those states: see Convention, Arts 4–6.

power to prevent the fixation or broadcasting of their live performance (but not a recorded performance)[63]; (2) for record makers, the power to prevent reproduction of their records[64]; (3) for broadcasting organisations, the power to control re-broadcasting and public performance for an entrance fee (but not diffusion by wire).[65] It was indeed ambitious to try to secure international protection for rights of three groups who also have such evident conflicts of interest amongst themselves. The Convention has only attracted adherents slowly.[66] It proved necessary in 1971 to sign a second "Phonograms" Convention, dealing only with mutual protection against the unauthorised commercial copying of sound recordings.[67]

In the field of broadcasting likewise, separate links have been forged, **9–16** mainly through the activities of the European Broadcasting Union. In particular, the Agreement on Television Broadcasts 1960[68] goes some way in continental Europe towards limiting the freedom to pick up broadcasts from another member country and diffuse them by cable (Britain has been able to take advantage of an exception about this).[69] The Satellites Convention (1974) seeks to deal with people (particularly "pirate" radio stations) who might otherwise take the signals of transmissions from point-to-point satellites and broadcast or diffuse them locally. For various reasons Britain has not joined this arrangement.[70]

(c) *The new activism: from 1985*

(i) **The Copyright Designs and Patents Act 1988.** Just as technological **9–17** leaps began to demand international adjustments to copyright law, so the same bounds produced repercussions for national systems. Britain had been among the earliest countries to revise its Copyright Act in 1956 to meet the developments of the post-war decade. In 1988, equally, it made a further revision—in the Copyright, Designs and Patents Act ("CDPA")—which in another decade may be seen as having had a formative effect beyond its own territorial bounds. Even in the 1970s it was becoming clear that if copyright was to survive the impact of modern technology—photocopying, audio and video taping and computing—adaptations of British law and

---

[63] See, in full, *ibid.*, Arts 7–9.
[64] See *ibid.*, Arts 10–12.
[65] *ibid.*, Art. 13. The term must be at least 20 years from performance, fixation or broadcast: Art. 14.
[66] In 1998, it had 57 Member States, including the U.K.
[67] This convention now has 56 members. For its content, see Stewart, *International Copyright and Neighbouring Rights* (2nd ed., 1989), Chap. 8.
[68] Made permanent by a Protocol of 1965. Like the Agreement on Television Films of 1958, this agreement was secured by the Council of Europe through its expert committee on broadcasting.
[69] However, the Whitford Committee (Cmnd. 6732, 1977), paras 70–75 recommended that Britain should abandon this and most other exceptions that were inserted at her behest.
[70] See on this the Whitford Report, paras 76–81.

practice would be needed. At the same time, the unique, ill-considered experiment of using copyright to protect industrial design, was disturbing relations in a wide span of industries.[71]

In 1974 the Whitford Committee began the considerable task of reviewing the whole range of copyright and designs law in the United Kingdom. Its Report in 1977,[72] for the most part welcomed as an important step forward, nevertheless would remain in limbo for a decade while different parts of government produced their own views and reactions in a series of papers,[73] and the various interest groups engaged in a ferment of proposition and counter-proposition. They also secured a number of specific changes: to improve the remedies against pirates,[74] to provide copyright in cable-casts and to reinforce it in its application to computer programs.

Because, thanks to the adventure over industrial design, copyright has been drawn so far into the realm of industrial production, the question of reform fell to be assessed with the intellectual property regimes considered as a whole.[75] That is why the 1988 Act does a number of things. It restates the statutory law of copyright, on the whole in a plainer and more logical manner than the 1956 Act. At the same time it introduces a number of changes—in particular, the granting of a rental right in certain subject-matter, the creation of moral rights for authors and directors, the extension of control over collecting societies by means of a Copyright Tribunal, and the conferment of a quasi-copyright on performers and their exclusive contractors. The Act also completely revises the law affecting industrial designs.[76] Its details are the substance of the ensuing chapters.

So febrile is the condition of copyright that a statute only seven-years old is becoming pock-marked by subsequent alteration, giving the law a raddled physiognomy. In large measure this stems from harmonisation measures in the E.C.,[77] to which we turn next.

9–18 (ii) *Dirigisme* **from Brussels.** After laying its plans for Community patents and trade marks, the Community took a decade longer to begin serious intervention in the fields of copyright and industrial designs. An important study for the Commission by Dietz, exploring the prospects for harmonising the copyright in literary and artistic works, was published in 1977.[78] At that

---

[71] See paras 14–01 *et seq.*, below.

[72] *Copyright and Designs Law* (Cmnd. 6732, 1977).

[73] See esp. Green Paper, *Reform of the Law relating to Copyright, Designs and Performers' Protection* (Cmnd. 8302, 1981) and White Paper, *Intellectual Property and Innovation* (Cmnd. 9712, 1986).

[74] See esp. Copyright (Amendment) Acts of 1982 and 1983; Cable and Broadcasting Act 1984, esp. Sched. 5; Films Act 1985; Copyright (Computer Software) Act 1985.

[75] Note the Report of the Government Chief Scientist, *Innovation and Intellectual Property Rights* (Cmnd. 9117, 1984).

[76] The Act also varied details of patent law and administration, and extended the liabilities of trade-mark infringers, a process carried still further in the TMA 1994: see para. 2–20, above.

[77] Not, however, entirely: see para. 12–53, below (re-cabling).

[78] *Copyright in the European Community* (English version, 1978); and see Dietz [1985] E.I.P.R. 215.

period the differences of ideology were considered to be too firmly entrenched for practical progress to be made. But by the mid-1980s, the problems facing the traditional copyright industries—commercial piracy, home taping of recordings and films and reprography of text, music and design—were intermingling with demands to put copyright to new tasks, notably in providing coverage for mass-produced computer programs, for the design of semi-conductor chips and to deal with broadcasting and re-cabling between Member States.[79]

Various cases for action at Community level were rapidly increasing in strength. A Green Paper by the Commission, *Copyright and the Challenge of Technology*, discussed a programme of action at particular points on the juddering copyright compass.[80] It was an approach directed at the economic problems of producers, and it was soon re-oriented more in favour of authors, as the prime beneficiaries of copyright protection.[81] The conse-quence has been an outpouring of E.C. Directives, which improve the position of both creators and entrepreneurs across the entire stretch of the E.U.[82]

The course of E.C. legislation on copyright and designs will be listed here **9–19** chronologically, together with a note, concerning its incorporation into United Kingdom law. The detailed contents of the Directives will take their place in the discussion of the substantive law and practice in succeeding chapters.

(1) Directive on Semiconductor Topographies (December 16, 1986)[83]: requiring a regime for the protection of computer circuit layouts which is at least sufficient to meet the reciprocity requirements of U.S. legislation on the subject; implemented in the United Kingdom by Regulation, as from November 7, 1987.[84]

(2) Directive on Computer Programs (May 14, 1991)[85]: requiring pro-grams to be treated as literary works for copyright purposes and defining infringement extensively, while allowing special exceptions relevant to such novel and distinctive subject-matter among authors' rights, implemented in the United Kingdom from January 1, 1993.

(3) Directive on Rental, Lending and Neighbouring Rights (November 19, 1992)[86]: by way of response to the home taping problem,

---

[79] For the impact of the case law of the ECJ, see para. 13–57, below.
[80] COM (88) 172 final.
[81] Acknowledged in a Commission *Follow-up to the Green Paper* (COM (90) 584 final). See Cohen-Jehoram (1994) 25 I.I.C. 821; Karnell (1995) 26 I.I.C. 900; Davies (1995) 26 I.I.C. 964.
[82] Policy overall was epitomised in a Council Resolution (May 14 1992: [1992] O.J. C138/1) on increased protection for copyright and neighbouring rights; *cf.* Laddie [1996] E.I.P.R. 253.
[83] Directive 87/54; [1987] O.J. L24/36, for U.K. implementation, S.I. 1987 No. 1497; 1989 No. 1100.
[84] See paras 14–48—14–51, below.
[85] Directive 91/250, [1991] O.J. L122/42; for U.K. implementation, S.I. 1992 No. 3233; see paras 13–24 *et seq.*, below.
[86] Directive 92/100, [1992] O.J. L346/61; for U.K. implementation, S.I. 1996 No. 2967.

requiring rental rights for authors, performers and record and film producers, and in some measure, lending rights; and as a necessary precursor, introducing the three main neighbouring rights (for performers, phonogram producers and broadcasting organisations) in harmonised form throughout the E.U. The requirement of implementation by January 1, 1994 was not met by the United Kingdom, which has still not fashioned its regulations by May 1, 1996.

(4) Directive on Satellite Broadcasting and Cable Retransmission (September 27, 1993)[87]: dealing with the copyright aspects of a unified (and fortified) policy on broadcasting and the re-cabling of broadcasts within the E.U. This Directive has still not been implemented in United Kingdom law, despite the set date of January 1, 1995.

(5) Directive on Copyright Duration (October 27, 1993)[88]: in the supposed interest of unity, harmonising upwards the terms of various authors' rights and the three main neighbouring rights, to the highest factor operating in a Member State (authors, including film directors: life-plus-70 years; others: normally 50 years from exploitation). Since this goes to the essence of the economic rights, it will be discussed further in this introductory chapter.[89]

(6) Directive on the Legal Protection of Databases[90]: introducing a double form of provision, partly by copyright and for the rest by a short-term right against unauthorised extraction of the contents.

(7) Directive on the Harmonisation of Designs Law, affecting, as a correlative of a future E.C. Design Right, the national systems for registering designs.[91]

A Directive on Artists' Resale Right (*droit de suite*), requiring member states to adopt or adapt a right for visual artists to share in the proceeds from successive commmercial sales of their original works, has recently been abandoned.[92]

9–20 Beyond these again lie future projects: for instance, for a levy on copying machinery and blank tapes and other recording means; for the regulation of copyright collecting societies; perhaps, even for an alignment of moral rights. These initiatives, however, are either being side-tracked or put into different focus by the blinding prospect of super-highway communication

---

[87] Directive 93/83; for U.K. implementation, S.I. 1996 No. 2967.
[88] Directive 93/98; for U.K. implementation, S.I. 1995 No. 3297; 1996 No. 2967.
[89] See paras 9–54—9–55, below. See also paras 10–41—10–54, below.
[90] Directive 96/9; for U.K. implementation, S.I. 1997 No. 3032; paras 13–49—13–52, below.
[91] Directive 98/71, due for implementation by October 28, 2001. In reality this is likely to be delayed until the introduction of the Community Registered Design: for which, see below, paras 14–52ff.
[92] See below, paras 13–103—13–104.

and the digitised products which may pass down them (and in some cases, interactively back). On this re-direction of concern, the Commission issued a Green Paper,[93] and this has developed into a draft for a Directive on Copyright in the Information Society.[94]

(iii) **International agreements amid new technology.** By the 1988 Act the **9–21** United Kingdom put itself in a position to ratify the Paris Revisions (1971) of the Berne Convention and the UCC. This coincided with adherence by the United States to the Berne Convention, after a century of prevarication.[95] American accession, while exhibiting a measure of grudging suspicion,[96] nonetheless put international copyright relations into new focus. Other major states also joined: among them the Chinese and the Russian Republics.[97]

Increasingly, the U.S. is worried by the scale and sophistication of **9–22** international piracy, and it remains uncertain what a world transected by information superhighways will mean for traditional copyright industries and their earnings. It therefore continues its bullish offensive through a combination of Berne, TRIPS and its own trade legislation which imposes penal tariffs or embargoes on offending states. While not likely to go so far in the last direction, the E.U. will support the international initiatives, for it shares much of the basic economic concerns of U.S. policy.[98]

Whatever comes of these further developments it is plain that both the **9–23** Berne and the Rome Conventions are of increasing relevance to national copyright law, even in countries such as the United Kingdom which can at most treat the content of such Conventions as aids to the interpretation of municipal law. Accordingly, their present contents are summarised below, as are the obligations which are shafted alongside by TRIPS.

(d) *International conventions: current scope*

(i) **Berne Convention.** The Berne Union exists to protect the rights of **9–24** authors in their "literary and artistic works", an expression which is illustrated by a long catalogue of examples, and then a set of further

---

[93] Copyright and Related Rights in the Information Society (COM(95) 382 final). This came a year after its United States counterpart (*Intellectual Property and the National Information Infrastructure*, July 1994), but was much less instructive, on both the technical and the legal side.

[94] For which—including far-reaching proposals for amendment from the European Parliament, see below, para. 13–75ff.

[95] For which, see Brown (1988) 33 J. Cop. Soc. 196.

[96] The U.S. refused to introduce explicit provisions on moral rights in general implementation of Art 6*bis*, though it has subsequently (by the Visual Artists Rights Act of 1990) provided a measure of protection in one demanding sphere; and it has refused to extend protection to pre-accession works, despite the principle of the Berne Convention, Art. 18.

[97] Some 20 states, members only of the GATT, now assume Berne obligations and secure Berne benefits through TRIPS.

[98] It should not be forgotten, however, that the entire GATT renegotiation nearly foundered on an argument between France, seeking to preserve its own film industry as an expression of national culture by imposing quotas on the television showing of foreign films, and the U.S., seeking to get unlimited access to European channels.

explications and limitations.[99] The items in these provisions arise for discussion at various points in the next chapters, so they will not be listed here in full.[1] The aesthetic creations traditionally associated with copyright are the subject-matter of the Convention, and accordingly it covers literary, dramatic, musical and artistic works and also cinematogaphic films and analogous audio-visual works.[2] The rights arise by virtue of authorship. Although the Convention eschews any statement that an author must be a human rather than a legal person, or that the work must attain any defined level of originality, both these characteristics are commonly assumed to underlie the text.[3]

9–25 Berne's first requirement is that each Member State must follow the principle of national treatment, itself a product of the idea of territoriality.[4] This is organised through the concept of the "country of origin" of the work. Where possible this is the country of first publication, rather than that of any author's nationality or habitual residence, an approach which makes for simplicity, particularly where there is more than one author.[5] Where the country of origin is a Berne State, other members must accord to the work the same treatment as they offer their own nationals.[6] At this point, the Convention assumes that there will be differences in the scope of rights from one Member to another. And copyright remains the field in which jealousies over inequality of treatment most readily ignite.[7] The Convention itself, therefore, acknowledges a number of dispensations from national treatment, which include the well-known "principle of the shorter term".[8]

---

[99] The leading work on its history and scope is Ricketson, *The Berne Convention for the Protection of Literary and Artistic Works: 1886–1986* (1987). See also Masouyé, *Guide to the Berne Convention* (1978); Nordemann *et al.*, *International Copyright and Neighbouring Rights Law* (English ed., 1990) pp. 3–11; Stewart (ed.) *International Copyright and Neighbouring Rights* (2nd ed., 1989), Chap. 5; Nimmer and Geller (ed.), *International Copyright Law and Practice* (1988 ff.), Introduction; Sterling, *World Copyright Law* (1998).

[1] Berne Convention, Arts 2, 2*bis*.

[2] Adapting the Convention to the differing national approaches to copyright in cinematographic works has not been straightforward: see especially *ibid.*, Art. 14*bis*.

[3] *cf.* Ricketson, para. 5.2.

[4] Berne Convention, Arts 3–5. See para. 10–36, below; Ricketson, Chap. 5; Nordemann *et al.*, pp. 58–81; Vaver (1986) 17 I.I.C. 577, (1985) 16 I.I.C. 575, 715.

[5] Berne Convention, Art. 5(3), which also takes account only of publication in a Member State, if there has been simultaneous publication (*i.e.* within 30 days—Art. 3(4)) also in a non-Member State. There are special rules for films and architectural works.

[6] Including the rights guaranteed by the Berne Convention: Art. 5(1). The Convention does not impose obligations in relation to the protection of a work in its own country of origin (Art. 5(3)), but its requirement of national treatment applies independently of whether there is any protection in the country of origin (Art. 5(2)).

[7] See paras 9–06 *et seq.*, above.

[8] Berne Convention, Art. 7(8). See para. 10–56, below. This represents one example of so-called material reciprocity, as distinct from the formal reciprocity provided by (for instance) national treatment. For retaliation against non-Member States in certain circumstances, see Art. 6.

Because of legal differences and tendencies towards mutual suspicion,[9] the Berne Convention has gone further than any other intellectual property treaty to impose minimum standards on its Members. The Convention's requirements do not cover the whole field; and in any case they consist partly of mandatory requirements and partly of limits upon the potential scope of legislative measures in Member States. This exceptional movement towards standardisation of law has been of major influence upon a world made up mainly of importer, rather than exporter, countries. But, as already pointed out, the demanding nature of the Convention has made its progress uncertain throughout much of its existence, and the recent shift in its favour, supported as it is by the terms of the TRIPS Agreement,[10] is therefore the more remarkable.

What, then, does the Convention require of its Members by way of legal **9–26** guarantees? Since its Berlin revision, it has outlawed any form of registration as a precondition of legal right[11]; and it requires a minimum term of the author's life and fifty years thereafter.[12] It now gives some recognition to the moral rights of authors.[13] Otherwise its main substance is concerned with the scope of economic rights. Save in two exceptional cases, these are characterised as exclusive rights and not mere rights to remuneration.[14]

The right to authorise reproduction of a protected work[15] is subject to a strictly limited qualification: "in certain special cases" Members may allow such copying if it "does not conflict with a normal exploitation of the work and does not unreasonably prejudice the legitimate interests of the author".[16] By implication this limitation applies equally to the Convention's guarantees of rights to translate and to adapt works.[17] The Members may

---

[9] The British have tended to take a large view of international comity in the copyright sphere, and, therefore, do not always appreciate the longing for material reciprocity deep in hearts of other nations.

[10] See para. 9–31, below.

[11] Berne Convention, Art 5(2). It is, however, permissible, to require fixation in a material form: Art. 2(2).

[12] *ibid.*, Art. 7(1)—measured from the end of the year of the death: Art. 7(5); as to joint and unidentified authors, see Art. 7*bis* and 7(3). There are more limited terms for films, photographic works and works of applied art: Art. 7(2), (4). The rule of the shorter term (Art. 7(8)) arises because Members are free to exceed the minima (see Art. 7(6)). But the Convention adopts the general proposition that once a work falls into the public domain, rights in it should not thereafter be resurrected; regrettably this admirable principle is subject to overriding agreements between states: see Art. 18, and paras 9–54, 9–55, below. As to the retroactive effect of joining the Convention, see Gavrilov (1993) 24 I.I.C. 571.

[13] *ibid.*, Art. 6*bis*; see paras 11–63 *et seq.*, below.

[14] The Berne Convention avoids the word "property". The two instances of equitable remuneration which, under the Convention, Members may introduce concern (1) the broadcasting, etc., of works (Art. 11*bis*(2)) and (2) the mechanical reproduction of musical works and associated works (Art. 13). As an intermediate case, the Convention recognises (in a non-mandatory form) a *droit de suite* in original art works and manuscripts which, if it exists at all, is subject to national provisions on collection and actual amounts: see Art. 14*ter*; paras 13–103ff.

[15] *ibid.*, Art. 9(1), which includes sound and visual recording: Art. 9(3).

[16] *ibid.*, Art. 9(2); see further para. 9–31, below.

[17] *ibid.*, Arts 8, 12; see Ricketson, paras 9.64–9.68.

use this power by permitting a particular use of a work to be undertaken freely or subject to payment of equitable remuneration.[18] The Convention itself contains a number of more specific exceptions.[19]

9–27   Exploitation through new technologies has brought extensions to the Convention. Thus in addition to a general right of public performance and communication,[20] there must be protection for the broadcasting of a work, its wire and wireless transmission and public communication[21]; and also of works when they are adapted into films, so as to cover both reproduction of the result and also its public performance and communication.[22]

9–28   It is worth noting what the Convention does not cover: (1) it gives no right over the distribution and so does not address the vexed question whether copyright should be available to prevent parallel importation; (2) it attempts no legal regulation of collecting societies; (3) save in the case of films, it has nothing to say about initial entitlement to the ownership of copyright, or about other aspects of property rights; (4) the only aspect of remedies covered relates to the seizure of infringing copies; and (5) it does not touch the now significant issue of the transmission of works held in digitised form.

9–29   **(ii) Rome Convention for the Protection of Performers, Producers of Phonograms and Broadcasting Organisations.** The Rome Convention was achieved in 1961 at what now seems an early stage in the evolution of the entertainment industries. At that time neither sound recordings nor films could be routinely copied so as to produce a version just as good. Likewise, broadcasting frequencies were strictly limited, and extensions by cabling and by satellite relay lay in the future. Broadcasters had some copyright interests of their own, but *vis-à-vis* performers and record producers they were major users. It was a considerable achievement that the Convention went as far as it did; and no surprise that it attracted relatively few adherents.

9–30   After diplomatically stating that it leaves intact and in no way affects authors' rights,[23] the Convention requires each Member State to apply national treatment in respect of the rights which it accords to performers, record producers and broadcasting organisations.[24] In addition, Member States must offer those from other states who are protected by the Convention certain minimum rights. In the case of records (phonograms), these include an exclusive right to authorise all reproductions, direct or

---

[18] A logical deduction which has some express support: see Ricketson, paras 9.2–9.18.

[19] See para. 13–03, below.

[20] Berne Convention, Art. 11 (covering only dramatic and musical works); public recitation is separately guaranteed: Art.-11*ter*.

[21] *ibid.*, Art. 11*bis*.

[22] *ibid.*, Art. 14. Films are themselves works within the Convention: see para. 9–24, above.

[23] Rome Convention, Art. 1.

[24] *ibid.*, Arts 2, 3.

indirect; and also a right to equitable remuneration (which under national law could alternatively be paid to performers) for the use of records in broadcasts and public playing.[25] Broadcasters are to have exclusive rights over fixation, reproduction, re-broadcasting and public communication.[26] These two industries, however, withstood pressure from the often unionised performers (actors and musicians alike) that they also should have rights to "authorise or prohibit" equivalent acts. Performers acquired only the "possibility of preventing" various specified acts, a distinction which was thought to allow the United Kingdom, in particular, to continue its approach of only protecting performers by criminal sanctions.[27] The Convention guaranteed protection for a term of 20 years, from fixation, performance or broadcast as appropriate.[28]

(iii) **TRIPS and copyright.** The starting point of the TRIPS provisions on copyright is that all Members must comply with the substantive Articles (1–21) of the Berne Convention, other than the provision on moral rights.[29] At crucial points, these obligations affecting the works of authors, as defined in Berne, are extended or made more explicit. Three general and two special cases deserve note: **9–31**

(1) **General.** For the first time in an international instrument, the basic dichotomy of this branch of the law appears (in American form): "copyright protection shall extend to expressions and not to ideas, procedures, methods of operation or mathematical concepts as such."[30] This vital touchstone for balancing exclusivity against free access thus becomes part of international understanding. For all its difficulty of application, it must accordingly remain within our own law.[31]

TRIPS makes general the Berne principle restricting the extent of exceptions in national legislation to the reproduction right.[32] As to term, there is a new minimum of fifty years from the making of a work, where term is not measured by reference to a natural person's life.[33]

(2) **Special.** Computer programs are required to be protected as literary works "under the Berne Convention"; and so are some compilations of data.[34] A rental right is introduced for computer programs, and tentatively for films.[35]

---

[25] *ibid.*, Arts 5, 10–12.
[26] *ibid.*, Arts 6, 13.
[27] *ibid.*, Arts 4, 7–9; and see para. 9–15, above.
[28] *ibid.*, Art. 14.
[29] TRIPS, Arts 1–21 (omitting Art. 6*bis*); Correa (1994) 26 I.I.C. 543.
[30] TRIPS, Art. 9(2); for the U.S. version, see para. 13–28, n. 18, below.
[31] *cf.* para. 11–07, below.
[32] TRIPS, Art. 13; and for the Berne provision (in slightly varied language) see para. 9–26, above.
[33] TRIPS, Art. 12.
[34] See paras 13–22 *et seq.*, below.
[35] TRIPS, Art. 11.

9–32 By contrast, in the sphere of neighbouring rights there is no equivalent incorporation of the Rome Convention or the Phonograms Convention (though Members are allowed to adopt the Rome Convention's conditions, limitations, exceptions and reservations[36]). Instead the TRIPS Agreement has its own code of obligations relating to performers, sound-recording producers and broadcasting organisations:

(1) **Performers:** they must be provided with an exclusive right covering fixation, reproduction, wireless broadcasting and public communication of actual performances (as distinct from recordings of them). It must last for 50 years from the performance.[37]

(2) **Sound-recording producers:** they must have an exclusive right in the direct or indirect reproduction of their phonograms, and likewise (subject to certain limitations) to the rental of copies. It must last for 50 years from fixation.[38]

(3) **Broadcasters:** either broadcasting organisations themselves must have an exclusive right over fixation, reproduction and re-broadcasting of their (wireless) broadcasts, and a right of public communication in the case of television broadcasts; or else equivalent rights must be given to copyright owners of material broadcast. The minimum term is 20 years from the broadcast.[39]

9–33 These provisions impose considerable changes on many countries undergoing development, far less on the industrialised world. Neither the E.C. Directives of the earlier 1990s nor TRIPS make significant legal adjustments to cater for digitised information systems serving world networks, for information superhighways were too novel and shifting a phenomenon. Twenty years ago, this discriminating view of copyright's proper function could at least command some audience. Today it stands challenged by the unremitting lobbying of the copyright industries and by authors' associations, whether they rank as collecting societies or as labour unions.[40] Pleading their fears for a future of uncontrolled perfect copying (currently posed, in particular, by the Internet) they seek constantly to broaden and to intensify the grasp of copyright: by adding new suiject-matter, extending the range of infringing acts, imposing liability on general distributors such as telecommunication chains, removing or limiting traditional exceptions and insisting on draconian measures to support electronic management systems. Such legal changes would buttress, for instance, the E.U.'s commitment to a strong copyright regime.[41]

---

[36] See TRIPS, Art. 14(6).
[37] *ibid.*, Art. 14(1), (5).
[38] *ibid.*, Art. 14(2), (3), (5).
[39] *ibid.*, Art. 14(3), (5); *quaere*, whether the term relates only to a first broadcast.
[40] For their differing functions, see below, para. 9–49ff.
[41] See above, para. 9–18.

The movement to enhance the position of copyright owners draws basic support from Chicago-inspired theories of property rights.[42] This approach ranks copyright indiscriminately with other commodities and claims that its value will be most efficiently realised if it is placed in the hands of a single right-holder, either by initial allocation, or by ready, legally secure, bargaining over an exclusive right, rather than a mere right to remuneration or compensation. However much the right is the consequence of creative expression, what matters is that it should be exploited by the person most prepared to assume the investment risks of so doing. This, so it is argued, is the first object lesson of copyright's history and it leads away from the liberal view that the right is only justified to the extent that it encourages authorship and its initial marketing. Rather the law should give continued protection so that a work will be made available whenever an entrepreneur is prepared to re-issue a work. Free bargaining legally enforced, is an essential element in this process and it should not be constrained, save where absolutely necessary, by rules preventing a right-holder from taking more than copyright law itself allows him, by anti-trust rules applied to vertical restraints or by defences which in any way diminish the earning potential of the property right.

The drive behind such thinking can be taken far. Rights, whether **9–34** formally classified as economic or moral, should not be allowed to proliferate, so as, in particular, to exacerbate the transaction costs involved in procuring complex products such as films, databases and multi-media works and broadcasts. The law should therefore be ready to police copyright *ab initio*, not in the hands of the creator but those of the risk investor—certainly where the two are related by employment, and even where the work is otherwise "made for hire". Ultimately such thinking may sustain the case that copyright should be perpetual, like property in tangible things (taking one back to the "Battle of the Books")[43] *and* the case that the author should no longer be treated as the bearer of rights, only as their progenitor. In proclaiming the "death of the author", Turkevich, placardiste of the American record industry, found himself bearing the very banner of his Foucault-inspired denouncers.[44]

In actual practice, such extreme propositions are unlikely to hold sway. Copyright has emerged as an amalgam of differing passions and there is, more than ever, an international accord about its acceptable scope and effect. The functioning systems take account of, but are not determined, by economic arguments from either pole. Two other value systems contribute to the outcome. First, the ideal values which have been placed upon the

---

[42] For the theory in general, see above, para. 1–40ff.; in relation to copyright: Landes and Posner (1998) 18 J. Leg. St. 325; Goldstein, *Copyright's Highway* (1994); Gordon (1982) 82 Col. L.R. 1600, (1992) 21 J. Leg. St. 449; (1993) 102 Yale L.J. 1533; Cohen Jehoram (1990–92) 144 R.I.D.A. 80.

[43] Above, para. 9–03.

[44] Turkevich (1990) J. Cop. Soc. U.S. 41.

contribution of all arts to human culture, notably in Europe, have been an essential part of the rhetoric for copyright from the French Revolution onwards. In the last half-century, this has led to demands that authorship, far from being down-graded, in law should attract enhanced protection. So it is that moral rights have often been given guaranteed form in order that the author may be sure of being named and may object if its contents are deleteriously altered. So equally, in various countries, authors have been protected against the full force of "free contracting"; in some circumstances they are assured of equitable remuneration or fair compensation or protection against unconscionable bargaining.

9–35   Secondly, copyright's role in underpinning the democratic process is presented as a distinct and vital function.[45] Democracy can operate only upon a premise of free and open debate, and it is a basic element of the history which we have examined that modern copyright emerges only with the passing of a censorship run by bookseller power-brokers in league with church and state. By outlawing pirate copying in the marketplace, copyright fosters the presentation of arguments on social, political, religious and economic policy in highly significant ways. This perception gives its own emphases. It is likely to strengthen the view that copyright should last only for a limited period, since so far as possible the borrowing and exchange of ideas is itself crucial to a free society. Equally a social contribution can properly be demanded from copyright owners. In return for the valuable support which the state offers by conferring the rights, rightowners can be expected to contribute in limited ways to social policies on maintaining the stock of knowledge, fostering the processes of research and education, allowing the transmission of news and the expression of criticism and review. Hence the various exceptions for "fair dealing" which our law currently admits, in addition to the general principle that infringement requires substantial taking from a work.[46]

One step which straddles the analogue and the digital worlds has been the enactment (already mentioned) of the E.C.'s Database Directive.[47] This defines the extent to which copyright can exist in the creation of a database and giving a distinct right (*sui generis* or neighbouring, according to taste) to the financial organiser of a database, whether "creative" or not. The model has been examined in countries including the United States and in the councils of WIPO, but it has been treated with considerable suspicion.[48]

9–36   Over the last five years, the amazing potential of the Internet as a source of on-line services for education, information, entertainment, business and government has flamed around the world and its character has changed

---

[45] See, *e.g.* Elkin-Koren (1996) 14 Cardozo A&L.J. 215; Hamilton (1996) 49 Vand. L.R. 73; Netanel (1996) 106 Yale L.J. 283.

[46] See below, paras 11–41—11–42, 13–02ff.

[47] Above, para. 9–19; below, para. 13–50—13–52.

[48] At WIPO, the issue was raised during the 1996 Meetings which resulted in the two Treaties mentioned below. At that stage, the very idea was too new to be taken far.

rapidly. Parts of it are already being used to supply the stuff of the traditional copyright industries and much more is to come. The publishing, record and film industries face at least partial revolutions in their methods of delivery and they are each searching actively for secure techniques by which material can be obtained from authorised sites only on payment of a fee equivalent to the purchase or hiring of a hard copy of material. At the same time they fear the appearance of pirate sites, and the down-loading and distribution of illicit copies, which, on the worst prognostications, could amount to a complete undermining of their commercial positions. However, the possibilities within the new technology for monitoring the use of material is also considerable, and many do not take such a pessimistic view of the future.[49]

Major investigations of the position of copyright material on information superhighways were launched in the United States, the European Union and—internationally—at WIPO.[50] The Digital Millenium Copyright Act of 1998 introduced in the U.S. and the proposed Directive on Information Society Copyright which is moving its way through the E.U. institutions, will be discussed later.[51] But the developments at WIPO, which establish a first base for all that follows, deserve mention here. In December 1996, two international agreements were reached:

(1) **WIPO Copyright Treaty.**[52] As well as adding a number of general provisions to the range of the Berne Convention,[53] the Treaty deals with on-line digital services chiefly by requiring, for works within the Convention, a right of communication to the public (by wire or wireless means) which includes the making available to the public of their works in such a way that members of the public may access these works from a place and at a time individually chosen by them.[54] Since it was not previously clear in many copyright laws that communication to the public could take place in this piecemeal fashion the clarification makes sense.

---

[49] See, *e.g.* Goldstein, *Copyright's Highway* (1994); Crawford and Gorman, *Future Libraries* (1995).

[50] For the U.S. see the Information Infrastructure Task Force's Report, *Intellectual Property, and the National Information Infrastructure* (1995); for the E.U. the Green Paper, *Copyright and Related Rights in the Information Society* (COM(95) 382 final).

[51] Below, para. 13–68ff.

[52] This constitutes a Special Agreement under the Berne Convention, Art. 20 and is open for signature by any member state of WIPO, which must comply with Berne Arts 1–12 and Appendix: see Arts 1, 17. Note esp. Art. 3, extending the basic provisions of Berne to the new rights being accorded.

[53] Computer programs become literary works (Art. 4); databases acquire Berne protection to the extent that they constitute intellectual creations (Art. 5); a right of distribution is required, but not so as to affect national rules on exhaustion of right (Art. 6); a right of rental is created for computer programs, films and works embodied in phonograms (Art. 7); no special limitation is to apply to photographic works (Art. 9); and all national limitations and exceptions are confined by the requirements of Berne, Art. 9(2) (Art. 10).

[54] Art. 8.

Much more controversial, however, was the attempt to secure a right of electronic reproduction of extreme particularity. Internet placement and transmission involves constant steps of storage, some of them only transient, others more or less permanent. Rightowners hoped for a definition that would embrace them all, thus in principle making all providers of services liable for their roles in distribution. The campaign failed and no reproduction right was included in this Treaty by way of supplement to the Berne Convention, Article 9.[55]

Two technical questions are also addressed. First, the states concerned have to provide protection against anti-spoiler devices. This pertains to any circumvention which would allow the sidestepping of technical barriers to copying, when they are placed either in hard copy materials or in digital sites in order to restrict access and copying which is not authorised or permitted by law.[56] Surrounding this rather opaque language is a considerable controversy about the proper scope of such legislation.[57] Secondly, there is a generally accepted requirement that interference with "rights management information" (*i.e.* electronic identification of author, owner, terms and conditions of use, code numbering, etc.) should itself be a form of secondary infringement.[58]

(2) **WIPO Performance and Phonograms Treaty.**[59] While dealing only with the rights of performers and sound recording producers, this Convention makes some advances in their general protection. Both performers and record producers acquire a reproduction right, a distribution right and a rental right, as well as the right to single equitable remuneration for broadcasting and communication to the public—long a divisive issue in some countries.[60] Performers also acquire rights against the bootlegging of extempore performances and acquire certain moral rights.[61] On the digital front, equivalent provisions to those in the Copyright Treaty ensure that communication to the public occurs upon offer of access, and there must also be protection against anti-spoiler devices and of copyright management information.[62]

9–37 In the end the two Treaties made only cautious changes to the international law which will affect copyright on the Internet. That is a

---

[55] An Agreed Statement to Art, 1(4) states that digital storage—wholly undefined—within the reproduction right.

[56] Art. 11.

[57] See below, paras 13–85—13–87.

[58] Art. 12.

[59] A separate treaty which does not derogate from the Berne or Rome Conventions for states which are members of them: see Art. 1.

[60] See Arts 7–0, 11–13, 15. The power to introduce exceptions and limitations is subjected to the threefold Berne conditions: Art. 16.

[61] See Arts 5, 6.

[62] Arts 10, 14, 18, 19. The reproduction rights are subject to the Agreed Statement that they include digital storage as is the case in the Copyright Treaty.

desirable outcome, given that the technology is still so novel and its possibilities are constantly expanding.[63] Beneath the lobbying and in-fighting, lies a complex set of claims about the most efficient ways of eliminating piratical exploitation and about who should bear the costs of organising that process: rightowner and therefore legitimate customer, or those who pay for more general services—notably the customers of telecommunications services. At the same time there is concern that changes are being sought which will interstitially improve the position of rightowners against users across the copyright spectrum. This applies in particular to those (notably scholars, students and libraries) who in the past have been able to have free access and use of material. In the past owners have accepted (or at least conceded this) as a social contribution in return for the rights granted to them.

(e) *Copyright, unfair competition and industrial design*

An exclusive right which strikes only at copying is particularly suited to **9–38** claims that a person is taking something for nothing—that he is reaping fruits sown by the creativity of others. Nonetheless British copyright law has on the whole conformed to the prescription that new rights should not be conceded without making a reasoned case and securing legislation. Indeed, statute has increasingly been used to define not only the duration of the various copyrights, but their subject-matter, the exclusive rights to which they give rise and the exceptions that may be admitted. The refusal to allow any general principle of unfair competition that will extend to the misappropriation of ideas means, however, that no limited, short-term form of liability may be imposed upon even the most parasytic purveyor of other people's ideas and enterprise. Accordingly there is always some desire to press the existing concepts of copyright into service. Lord Devlin, for example, once said:

> "Free trade does not require that one should be allowed to appropriate the fruits of another's labour, whether they are tangible or intangible. The law has not found it possible to give full protection to the intangible. But it can protect the intangible in certain states, and one of them is when it is expressed in words or print. The fact that that protection is of necessity limited is no argument for diminishing it further, and it is nothing to the point to say that either side of the protective limits a man can obtain gratis whatever his ideas of honesty permit him to pick up."[64]

But this is not an attitude which has been maintained with consistency. There has been some tendency to look upon copyright as typically

---

[63] See Vinje [1997] E.I.P.R. 230; *cf.* Reinbothe *et al.* [1997] E.I.P.R. 171.
[64] *Ladbroke v. Hill* [1964] 1 W.L.R. 273 at 291; see further, para. 11–06, below. Contrast the thrust of these remarks with the well-known dictum of Dixon J., quoted in para. 1–16, above.

concerned with established forms of aesthetic activity; and so there are decisions making it difficult to use artistic copyright against the copying of a dress design, or to claim that a suite of furniture amounts to a "work of artistic craftsmanship".[65] In line with such caution, and very significant in its impact, was a tradition (reversed surprisingly in 1968) of excluding artistic copyright from the sphere of mass-produced goods, so as to leave the registered design system as sole occupant.

9–39   In a sense, the origins of registered designs stretch back to the earliest period of industrialisation in some parts of the textile industry.[66] However, the real impetus towards the modern system came in the 1830s. The poor quality of British industrial design, particularly when compared with the achievements of the French, incited middle-class radicals to press for a system of training designers, and manufacturers to demand a more substantial legal monopoly.[67] The system of registration that evolved under statutes of 1839 and 1842 gave a form of protection particularly directed towards preserving the original design-owner's headstart; the term was short but the design was kept confidential in the registry throughout the period.[68]

9–40   As we shall see, in 1911 artistic copyright was deliberately excluded from much of the industrial design field, and the same policy of preventing cumulative protection was pursued in 1956 under a rather more complete and satisfactory formula.[69] But the registered design system, with its patent-like preliminary examination and its requirement of novelty or originality, was too limited and cumbersome for many industries. They secured from the Johnston Departmental Committee in 1962 a recommendation of a simpler form of protection against copying. This would last for a relatively short period; but the interests of the rest of industry demanded as a prerequisite that a person claiming such a right should deposit his design in an official register.[70]

9–41   Even this balancing of interests was by-passed in the Design Copyright Act 1968, which was meant to secure such groups as makers of jewellery, furniture and toys against the unfair competition of free copying. The particular manner in which artistic copyright was introduced into the sphere of industrial production, however, was ill thought through. So in various respects it went much beyond the apparent intentions of its sponsors. Just what has happened must be left to be discussed later,[71] but the overall effect of allowing registered design and copyright protection to accumulate was

---

[65] See paras 10–17—10–22, below.
[66] See para. 9–04, above; Sherman and Bently (above, n. 1) Chap. 3.
[67] See Prouty, *The Transformation of the Board of Trade 1830–1857* (1957), pp. 18–27.
[68] Copyright of Designs Act 1842, s. 17; and for subsequent Acts and further details, see Johnston Committee on Industrial Designs (Cmnd. 1808, 1962), App. B.
[69] See paras 14–03—14–05, below; Laddie [1996] E.I.P.R. 253.
[70] Johnston Committee on Industrial Design (Cmnd. 1808, 1962), esp. paras 47–48.
[71] See para. 13–01, below.

very considerable. At least where a design originated from two-dimensional drawings or plans, to copy them (directly or indirectly) in three-dimensional products was likely to infringe copyright in them; and mostly it made no difference that shape is a consequence of function. Copyright invaded the sphere of technical design with an efficacy and simplicity that was truly dramatic.

As a form of protection against design misappropriation it was, for a number of reasons, extreme. The very substantial reduction in scope, embodied in the 1988 Act, is largely placed outside the frame of copyright and in the separate folds of registered and unregistered design right. One point of doing this, rather than adapting copyright, has been to avoid the international obligations which attach to the latter, given that most other countries have shown no inclination towards a reciprocal form of protection.

2. VALUES AND INTERESTS

Copyright sustains a triangle of relationships. While industrial property **9–42** tends to establish bi-polar linkages—between right-owner and user— copyright has, on the right-owner side, both creators and entrepreneurs. As against users, their interests are largely the same: to ensure that the use of works is licensed and that the returns on use are maximised. But between themselves, there will exist tensions over how works may be exploited and how returns are to be divided. This has indeed been so in every country from the moment when publishers and other investors have pressed for protection to be accorded in the name of their authors.

It is the cultural value attaching to authorship which provides such copious moral legitimacy for legal protection. Not only are authors given a longer-lasting right than could possibly be needed by way of economic incentive; entrepreneurs are also able to justify related rights which protect their own investments in cultural productions. The realm occupied by copyright is accordingly fed by society's deep desire for artistic creativity. The rights of authors in the true sense are reserved for categories—literary, dramatic, musical and artistic works, and now audiovisual works—where the best productions in the genre are considered to be of central cultural value. That is why film directors have now been accorded an author's right, while sound recording engineers have not,[72] and their employers are left with only a neighbouring right of more limited scope.

Over time these values change, and modern copyright systems have considerable capacity to embody that change once it is clearly established.

---

[72] Much to the chagrin of those who believe in the special structure of U.S. copyright law on the subject: this accords an author's copyright to sound recordings, and then vests that copyright from the outset in the entrepreneur who commissions it, whenever it is a work "made for hire".

However, authors' rights, as we know them today, do depend upon the experience that in the main it is only works of significant intrinsic value which survive in popularity for long. Our ever-growing appetite for the cultural trivia of previous generations may in the end upset this perception. Should it ever do so to a serious degree, it ought to lead to reductions in the scale of copyright protection.

9–43   The present balance, as it is widely perceived, allows copyright to protect both major cultural products for very substantial periods, and more ephemeral things for their temporary shelf-life. Its capacious nature also allows for the delayed appreciation of neglected figures or particular works. Likewise, through such concepts as joint authorship and copyright in adaptations, it is able to offer linked protection to those involved in complex productions—as today in films and multi-media products. This adaptable nature of copyright, which has characterised it from the outset, enables it to carry political conviction.

One glib commonplace has it that copyright was sired by the cult of the Romantic Author. But that makes no historical sense. Of course, among campaigners for copyright there have always been those who argue single-mindedly for the adequate recognition of genius. But from the Statute of Anne onwards, all concerned in shaping the law have appreciated that the demand for copyright is also directed towards protecting much more humble and transitory material from the trespasses of pirates and other free riders.[73] Copyright everywhere is open to those who cross a low threshold of creativity, and differences between national laws over the concept of originality operate only at this margin. No system reserves copyright only for those works which pass a substantial test of aesthetic merit.[74]

9–44   There are always those who are dissatisfied with prevailing views of copyright. Today's philosophic penchant for pointing up the relativity of artistic judgment, and for showing how dependent any creator is both upon his or her own intellectual inheritance and upon the perceptions of those who receive the work, is antagonistic to any idea of "greatness". Deconstructionist argument is among other things deployed to undermine the copyright of authors. Michel Foucault's questioning essay, "What is an Author?",[75] has sustained a school of writing about copyright and related rights which envisions a brave new world of freely co-operating writers and artists, each contributing to evolving work, each offering selfless support and accepting enlightened criticism.[76] At least in its beginnings, the Internet

---

[73] See esp. Ginsburg and Saunders, n. 1, above. In Britain and elsewhere, an immensely valuable product at the beginnings of copyright was the almanack, an assemblage of calendar, public information and mystic prognostication. Almanacks had the desirable quality of needing annual renewal, and should be ranked as the first commercial database.

[74] See further, para. 10–10, below.

[75] Harari (ed.) *Textual Strategies* (1979), p. 141.

[76] *e.g.* Woodmansee and Jaszi (eds.) *The Construction of Authorship* (1994); Rose, *Authors and Owners* (1993); and see Boyle, *Shamans, Software and Spleens* (1996), Chaps 6, 10, 11; Bettig, *Copyrighting Culture* (1996).

has seemed to offer a medium peculiarly suited to such an aetherial Academe.

The uncalculating exchange of ideas has long been part of scholarship and of shared interests of many kinds. If new technology enables that process to evolve, so much the better. But to suppose that it will supplant the need for informational, educational and entertainment material which is generated upon the expectation of a market return is the stuff of dreams. Copyright will remain because it provides necessary protection for the investment of intellectual effort and capital in material which is not produced in order to be freely shared. The law may have to be somewhat adapted, but its moral mainspring—that works should not be substantially copied or otherwise taken without authority—expresses a justification for legal intervention which will remain very widely accepted.

3. ECONOMIC AND PUBLIC INTEREST PERSPECTIVES[77]

(1) Market power and individual works

Even so brief an historical outline will suggest the range of industries that **9–45** copyright now serves. Starting from the production of books, it has moved out into the modern media of instruction and entertainment—through stage performances to recordings and broadcasting; and with its incursion into the field of computer programs it has provided a form of "industrial property" comparable in importance to the patent system and the protection of confidence. As with patents and confidential information, copyright may provide the legal foundation upon which monopoly profits can be generated, provided always that the market contains sufficient demand for the product. The ability of patented goods and processes to produce this effect largely depends upon their technical efficiency, judged in economic terms by comparison with any alternative products that are available. But many copyright works gain their uniqueness through the dictates of fashion, as moulded by advertising and other promotion, criticism, the reputation of the author's previous works, the shortage of new material[78] and other factors.

There are examples enough of the manner in which publishers and other **9–46** producers of copyright material have taken a monopolist's advantage of their exclusive position: the practice of publishing hard-back editions before

---

[77] Modern discussion of the economics of copyright began from a highly critical perspective: Plant (1934) 1 Economica 167 and *The New Commerce in Ideas and Intellectual Property* (1953); and see further Hart and Schuchman (1996) 56 Am. Econ. R. 421; Breyer (1970) 84 Harvard L.R. 281; countered by Tyerman (1971) 18 U.C.L.A. Law Rev. 1100, 19 Bull. U.S. Cop. S. 99. See Economic Council of Canada, *Report on Intellectual and Industrial Property* (1971), the Canadian White Paper, *From Gutenberg to Telidon* (1984); Davies, *Copyright and the Public Interest* (1994); Lunney (1996) 49 Vand. L.R. 483; Sterk (1996) 94 Mich. L.R. 1197.

[78] In his 1953 lecture (n. 77, above), p. 33, Plant commented upon the insatiable appetite of television programmers for expensive novelties.

paperbacks, for instance,[79] or that of showing films at expensive inner-city cinemas before allowing suburban release and then television showing.[80] That such practices should follow from the conferring of copyright is not of itself a ground for criticism. The first purpose of the protection is to allow recoupment for the initiative of creating the material and the investment risked in producing and marketing it. In most instances a copyist could produce a directly competing product at a much lower cost if copyright did not restrain him.[81] Nonetheless, the "tax upon the public" should be broadly commensurate with the objectives of conferring copyright. A first economic test of this is: what measure of protection is needed to bring about the creation and production of new works and other material within the copyright sphere? Since any answer must be a rough one, the issue is largely a matter of the duration of copyright. Should it last for the relatively short period for which a patent or registered design is thought to be needed as an industrial incentive? Or is there justification for the very much longer period currently allowed for copyright?

In seeking an answer, the original Statute of Anne has an interesting suggestiveness. As will be recalled, it first gave a copyright period that was clearly related to the entrepreneur's needs: its term of 14 years from first publication came from the analogy of patents for inventions. But the Act proceeded to distinguish a further interest of the author. It gave him a further 14 years copyright if he was still living at the end of the first period. In subsequent statutory developments, the usual pattern has been to provide an undivided period of entitlement; and the publisher has been left free to take an exclusive assignment or licence of the whole from the author.[82]

9–47 Economists who criticise the present approach stress the disadvantages to the consumer which flow from this ellision of the distinct interests of author and entrepreneur. Plant is surely correct in suggesting that few publishers (or, for that matter, record producers or film makers) calculate how much to risk in a particular venture by reference to likely returns over more than a few years.[83] To shorten the present copyright period is accordingly

---

[79] A practice which, in one instance, brought about the intervention of the E.C. Commission's Competition Directorate: see *Jonathan Cape—Penguin Books, "The Old Man and the Sea"* [1977] 1 C.M.L.R. D121. Examples of international price discrimination built upon copyright are to be found in the old British publishing practice of producing cheaper "colonial editions"; and in the pricing of books in Canada (see Economic Council of Canada n. 55, above) App. B) and in Australia (see the *Time-Life* case, [1978] F.S.R. 356, para. 12–15, below). Sometimes the organised power of a group of buyers may lead to raised retail prices, as was at one time the case with circulating libraries: see Plant (n. 77, above) pp. 186–187.

[80] See *Coditel v. Ciné Vog* [1980] E.C.R. 881, ECJ; which is based upon the assumption that such a system of exploitation is in principle legitimate.

[81] For examples relating to American book publishing, see Breyer (n. 77, above). In film production, comparable figures would be dramatic indeed.

[82] But note the reversionary right in published works that arose under the 1911 Act, s. 5.

[83] Plant (1953) (n. 77, above) p. 15.

unlikely to produce any noticeable effect upon the amount of copyright material which they are prepared to put out for consumption.[84] Instead, works which prove to have lasting popularity provide them with bonuses. One justification commonly offered for this is that it induces entrepreneurs to take greater risks in promoting works for which there may be no sufficient demand. That is an attractive argument so long as one restricts attention to things scholarly or acceptably cultural. However the copyright system leaves to the entrepreneur the choice of what to select from the pool of works otherwise uneconomic. A more satisfactory method of choosing what is most deserving (whatever the criteria may be) would be through some form of government or other subsidy, a technique which would prevent the cost having to be borne by the readers of successful books.[85]

The public is supplied with copyright material through the co-operation **9–48** of entrepreneur and author, and it may be that there are cases where the very long period of copyright makes it worth an author's while to embark upon a particular project. But this economic calculation can scarcely have stood high amongst the jumble of motives which have led to the current legal protection offered to authors. Their case has been borne along rather by special admiration for aesthetic creativity and the associated desire (often expressed in the rhetoric of natural justice) to provide authors with fruits for their labour which have the character of inheritable property.

(2) Collective enforcement

So far we have considered the market power that may stem from demand **9–49** for an individual copyright work. A different monopoly effect—and one that is likely to have graver impact—can arise if rights in a whole class of works come under single control. The markets for the distribution of copies of copyright works have not so far been subject to much "cornering" of this sort, at least in Britain.

The opposite is true for performing rights, as has already been mentioned.[86] Composers of most music, and their publishers, found it impossible to enforce their performing rights, work by work, against users such as concert promoters and theatre proprietors. The only practicable system was to found a single organ—in Britain the Performing Right Society—for the collective enforcement of rights. It then became possible to organise licensing schemes for the different categories of user and to set various rates for them.

---

[84] A far more likely way of inducing a successful author to keep writing would be to reduce the tax burden on his initial returns: see Plant (1953) (n. 77, above) p. 13.

[85] As it is, authors themselves, or learned societies or other patrons, often underwrite publishers in the pursuit of a risky venture.

[86] See para. 9–10, above.

9–50   While this accumulation of rights quite properly obliges users to respect copyright, it at the same time deprives them of the opportunity to object to the licence fee for one piece of music by playing another that is cheaper. The collecting society gains not only some power to set prices high but also to discriminate between users and to demand that performances be of a particular kind—for instance, that they be live rather than recorded. For the moment it is enough to draw attention to this type of problem. We shall return subsequently to the role that the Copyright Tribunal plays in disallowing practices by collecting societies it deems to be an abuse of their market position. Equally we shall see that the Tribunal fulfils the role of arbitrator in disputes where it cannot be said that there is much difference in the bargaining power of owner and user. For instance, PRS and PPL have as substantial a concern to see that their material is broadcast by the BBC and commercial stations as the broadcasting organisations have to secure the right to do so.

9–51   A number of developments are driving the collective administration of copyright beyond the traditional confines of musical performance rights. Photocopying technology has finally produced administrations in numerous countries which organise licensing schemes. In Britain this is now undertaken by the Copyright Licensing Agency, which is composed equally of authors' and publishers' interests.[87] In countries which have sought recompense for home audio-taping by a levy on equipment, it has again been necessary for authors to act corporately in order to organise a system for distributing the revenue collected.[88] Individual enforcement of copyright has been impossible in these cases because of the difficulty, if not the impossibility, of recording what material is being used. Collecting societies are obliged to offer blanket licences for the use of material in their "repertoire" and, in some cases, to make distributions of revenue to their members on the basis of sampling or other averaging techniques.

The new prospects of the Internet and other such services raise difficult issues, as yet unresolved, about payment for use of copyright material. However, it is the great hope of the medium that by electronic tagging the service can provide records of use accurately and very cheaply, so as to side-step the difficulties of monitoring which occur with juke boxes or home copying or public lending. Indeed, the ease with which information can be provided on such a service makes it possible to contemplate offering terms for use which distinguish one work from another. Consumers may then choose individually and their payments may be attributed to the particular authors, performers and entrepreneurs concerned. In this brave new world, there will be no need to resort to the averaging which has been part of collective administration of rights as we currently conceive it. If this can be eliminated, creators and producers will see more of the available revenue, and those whose work is most popular will be able to maximise its value.

---

[87] See paras 13–12 *et seq.*, below.
[88] See para. 13–70, below.

(3) Entrepreneurs and authors

Another type of collective organisation deserves to be noted. Various **9–52** commercial groups in the copyright industries have associations to watch over their mutual interests.[89] In the past at least, some of these associations have agreed that members would deal with outsiders only upon terms falling within certain limits. Thus publishers might agree upon the maximum rate of royalty that each would offer authors for certain types of copyright exploitation.[90]

Until quite recently creators have not had much reason for forming groups that will negotiate with entrepreneurial associations for collective guarantees of minimum terms in contracts to publish or use works.[91] Rather, successful authors and composers have negotiated better contracts individually, in some fields using agents, such as the literary agents who are so prominent a feature of English language publishing. This kind of practice probably explains why in Britain there has been relatively little demand that authors should have legal guarantees against unfair contract terms.

These conditions do not, however, prevail throughout all copyright **9–53** industries, and over the last 20 years, in cases involving pop-music composers and artists, instances of such oppressive, harsh and fraudulent contracting and dealing in the music industry have been demonstrated to English Courts that they have intervened on grounds of undue influence, unconscionability or undue restraint of trade. In Britain this has not led to general statutory protection, for instance, guaranteeing proportional remuneration to authors. But E.C. intervention at particular junctures makes an interstitial movement in that direction, which is viewed with considerable alarm by some investors.

To take one instance: throughout the Community performances on record which are then broadcast require the payment of a single equitable remuneration, and this must be split between the record producer and the performers in a proportion laid down, if necessary, by the Member State concerned. This is one element in conferring on performers their own exclusive right. Previously in Britain, despite the strength of performers' trade unions, performers, whose own right did not extend to the broadcast of recorded performances, were reliant upon payments from the producers

---

[89] For instance, at the national level in Britain, the Publishers Association, the British Phonographic Industry Copyright Association and the Music Publishers Association; at the international level, the International Federation of the Phonographic Industry. With the growth of commercial piracy, to these have been added organisations such as the Anti-Counterfeiting Group and the British Software Alliance.

[90] However, since the extension of the British trade practices legislation to services (see App. 1, para. A1–06, below), the legitimacy of such agreements is open to challenge.

[91] Which is not to say that mutual interest groups have not existed; witness, for instance, the Society of Authors, Playwrights and Composers and the Writers' Guild of Great Britain.

under contract or else *ex gratie*. The change of the law to meet the E.C. requirement[92] has meant that a wider range of performers are beginning to receive payments and that the proportion overall going to them has increased from one-third to one-half of receipts.

To a large extent authors and executant artists will gain a market price for their services which is not dependent on the extent of exclusive rights but will represent the outcome of negotiations. In that process those who join trade unions are likely to benefit from the combined pressure on employers which can then be brought to bear. But like all markets, expectations become settled over time, and the extent of copyright and neighbouring rights may well underpin the ordering of those expectations. As the example just given suggests, if the legal framework is changed, contractual benefits may be secured which union pressure had not by itself managed to achieve. This is the real significance of arguments over who should enjoy rights and what the scope of those rights should be. If authors and artists have been shortchanged in the past, their hope for the future must lie in a combination of collective labour negotiation and lobbying for legislative guarantees.

(4) The duration of copyright

9–54 The long term given to authors by copyright law stands in stark contrast to that for patents, industrial designs and other productive subject-matter such as plant variety rights and semi-conductor layouts. It is a provocative choice: why does the creativity of authors deserve this distinction? As already pointed out, the extensive term of copyright becomes possible because of the nature of what is protected and the limited scope of the rights granted. That, however, is not a sufficient explanation. The answer cannot lie in the economic incentive needed to secure the production of aesthetic work, for that is a question largely of entrepreneurial calculation and investors are concerned with returns that materialise over much shorter terms.[93] As to the authors, composers and artists themselves: it is true that they set out upon careers with high risks of failure or of only slight success in material terms. But the same can be said of inventors. Can one prognotisticate that either group is likely to be much swayed into greater productivity (particularly of quality, as distinct from quantity) by the distant prospect of returns to their successors? Authors' advocates sometimes make the claim, but they carry little conviction beyond their own coteries.

A rational policy concerned with such risks would look towards direct support for the most promising talent of each generation (and today much of that is provided through employment). One way of providing it, through

---

[92] See below, para. 10–43.
[93] See, *e.g.* Plant and Breyer, para. 9–45, n. 77, above; Ricketson (1992) 23 I.I.C. 753; Laddie [1996] E.I.P.R. 253; Parrinder and Cherniak (eds) *Textual Monopolies* (1997).

a link to returns on production, would be to institute a *domaine public payant*—a public fund into which royalties for use of works would be paid for (say) 20 years after the expiry of normal copyright.[94] In that way, successful authorship from two generations before would support the coming generation of literary and artistic producers. Living creators would benefit, rather than whoever has come to be copyright owner through the vagaries of commercial dealing, charitable instinct or personal inheritance.

The concept is an attractive one. But the funding of creators by grant-giving rather than by market-place returns is a process which may well attract prejudice, preference, jealousy and waste. Thereby hangs a tale. A plan for a *domaine public payant* was put to the West German legislature during the copyright revision of 1965; but antagonism towards its redistributive interventionism proved intransigent. Instead, by way of deflection, the term of authors' rights was extended by 20 years to their life plus 70 years. Out of this side-tracking of a serious policy initiative arose the central difference in copyright terms between E.C. States which, 30 years later, would be thought to require a Directive extending that term by the same amount throughout the E.U., and at the same time to dictate an upward levelling of the terms of the main neighbouring rights (in general to 50 years from first publication or public communication).

Upward levelling followed mainly from the need within the Common **9-55** Market to have a standard term and to achieve this at once, rather than waiting half a century for expiry of rights already granted, for a longer term existing in a few E.U. countries (reduction of a term already granted would be an unacceptable form of expropriation). Understood in these terms, the Directive is a once-for-all standardisation which implies nothing for the future. Unfortunately it was also justified by rhodomontade about a general Community policy in favour of copyright, and about the increasing longevity of E.U. citizens.[95] The former is in itself no argument and cannot justify whatever step pleases interest groups; the latter ignores the fact that measurement by the author's life already builds in some compensation for longevity; and that, so far as succeeding generations are concerned, what matters is whether people are having children later, rather than whether they are living longer.

Loose assertions of the type indulged in by the Community, however, pass for adequate justification and that in itself is interesting. Politicians and other arbiters of legislative "opinion" may know little enough of the inner workings of copyright, but they appear to accept that the archetypal forms of aesthetic work—the creation of great literature, music and art—deserve a market-based reward which should stretch over a long period.

---

[94] Occasionally, the idea has found British support: but proposals to both the Gregory and the Whitford Committees were rejected: Cmd. 8662, 1952, para. 24; Cmnd. 6732, 1977, paras 643–647.

[95] See the Directive on Duration (para. 9–19, above), Recitals 5, 10, 11.

They seem moved by a moral desire to give creators their due—a chance of reward somehow equating with the property rights which attach to the production of material things and the making of financial gains.

4. THE 1988 ACT AND PRE-EXISTING WORKS

9–56 One technical matter may serve as a link between this introductory chapter and the next. The current copyright law of the United Kingdom is now almost entirely contained in the Copyright Act 1988 and the case law pertaining to it. The 1988 Act repealed virtually all the 1956 Act, just as that Act had repealed the 1911 Act and the 1911 Act had largely replaced the common law and statutory rights that preceded it.[96] The commencement date of the 1988 Act was August 1, 1989; that for the 1956 Act, June 1, 1957; that for the 1911 Act, July 1, 1912.

The three Acts introduced basic changes. In particular, each added to the bundle of rights that constituted copyright. For instance, the 1911 Act specified that literary, dramatic and musical works were infringed by making a film, record or other "contrivance" for mechanical performance,[97] while the 1956 Act introduced infringement by broadcasting and by diffusing to subscribers.[98] The 1988 Act created a rental right in respect of sound recordings, films and computer programs[99]; and is noteworthy in particular for its introduction of moral rights for authors.[1] Again, statutory rules about initial ownership of the copyright were changed on each occasion,[2] as were the "qualifying factors" by which foreign publication or authorship might bring about the acquisition of British copyright.[3] Since then, the staged implementation of E.C. directives has introduced alterations each of which has its own commencement.[4] Since the duration of copyright is so substantial (particularly after the extensions of 1911), there remains a range of questions about works that were in existence before commencement of the 1988 Act, the 1956 Act, or even the 1911 Act. A work produced early in an author's life, which now acquires copyright until 70 years after his death, could well have a copyright life of 100 years and might last more than 120 years.[5]

9–57 The transitional arrangements in each Act for existing works must be separately considered. Both the 1956 Act and the 1988 Act operate upon the presumption that they apply to things in existence at commencement as

---

[96] See CA 1956, Sched. 9 and CA 1911, Sched. 2.

[97] CA 1911, s. 1(2)(d).

[98] See now, CDPA 1988, s. 20.

[99] CDPA 1988, s. 8(3), soon to be expanded, see para. 11–28, below.

[1] CDPA 1988, Pt. 1, Chap. 4, see paras 11–63 et seq., below.

[2] See CA 1911, s. 5; CA 1956, s. 4; CDPA 1988, s. 11, see paras 12–04—12–10, below.

[3] For "qualifying factors", see paras 10–36—10–37, below.

[4] See para. 9–18, above.

[5] For the term of copyright, see paras 10–43 et seq., below.

they apply to things brought into existence subsequently, subject to the particular modifications specified in Schedule 7 and Schedule 1 respectively.[6] Thus under the 1988 Act, the question of whether the work had copyright under the 1956 Act is not in issue.[7] To this, however, the prime exception is that subsistence of copyright in an existing work is determined by the legal position immediately before commencement.[8]

There are a considerable number of other qualifications and exceptions **9–58** spelled out in Schedule 1. During the immediate period of transition these are of particular importance and they will be mentioned at numerous points in the next four chapters. Where the new Act introduces enhanced rights, by and large it extends them to existing works. Where it alters or cuts down rights, the position under the 1956 Act may be conserved wholly or in part. Thus although the rules on first ownership of a work have changed in both the 1956 and 1988 Acts, the issue is determined by the law in operation when the work was made.[9] Equally, where the length of protection accorded to unpublished literary, dramatic and musical works, engravings and photographs is cut down by the 1988 Act, there are exceptions directed to eliminating any unfair prejudice to the owners of existing copyright.[10]

---

[6] CA 1956, Sched. 7, para. 45; CDPA 1988, Sched. 1, paras 3, 4.

[7] Under the 1911 Act, s. 24, subject-matter that was protected immediately before its commencement received the rights substituted by that Act, and this remains the position: CDPA 1988, Sched. 1, para. 2(2).

[8] CDPA 1988, Sched. 1, para. 5. For exceptions see para. 5(2).

[9] See para. 12–04, below.

[10] See para. 10–45, below.

CHAPTER 10

SUBSISTENCE OF COPYRIGHT

1. THE GENERAL PICTURE

The first task of the student of copyright law is to distinguish the different **10–01** types of copyright and to understand the essential questions surrounding them: Is the material of the kind that attracts copyright? If so, for what duration? Who initially is entitled to ownership? What acts constitute infringement? An overview is given in the Table on the following pages. This should be understood for what it is. It does no more than highlight the starting points in discovering the relevant legal rules. Some further factors (for example the various exceptions to infringement) are too complex to include conveniently. The Table must be read in conjunction with the text.

The previous Copyright Act (of 1956) was built upon a distinction between the Part I copyright of creators in literary, dramatic, musical and artistic *works*, and the Part II copyright, given in other *subject-matter* to entrepreneurs who produced sound recordings, films, broadcasts, cablecasts and published editions.[1] This adopted a strategic division between true authors' rights and the "neighbouring" or "related" rights of investors which was in the van for its time: German legislation, for instance, would adopt a similar pattern only in 1965. This division, however, has been obliterated in the 1988 Act. Instead—for better, for worse—the two types are listed indiscriminately. In each case the copyright is in a *work* and it is granted initially in most cases to an "author" who "creates" it. All is resolved in a grossly misshapen definition of the "creator" (see the Table, head 3). The shift is typical of that old strain of common law thought which sees no difference of kind between true creators and investors in the creations of others; and which is inclined to prefer the latter to the former.

The coming transformations of copyright for a digital future may have set the British approach again in advance: that is for the future to settle. In the meantime, the tensions between our "mixed" system and the worlds of "authors and neighbours" established in Continental Europe have still to be resolved. We shall see them reflected also in differing concepts of originality, different rules about initial ownership of rights, different attitudes to

---

[1] See para. 9–09, above.

moral rights and different approaches to legally guaranteed shares in economic returns.

10–02   The Table covers the various forms of copyright which arise under Part I of the 1988 Act. However, it does not include the following, none of which are "copyright":

(1) the rights given to performers and those with exclusive rights in performances, which are separately treated in Part II of the Act[2];

(2) the (unregistered) design right created by Part III[3]; or

(3) the publication right in long-secreted works which has been introduced in implementation of Article 4 of the Duration Directive.[4]

The Table gives a column each to the varieties of copyright "work", grouping together (a) literary, dramatic and musical works, and (b) broadcasts and cable-casts, because of the similarities in their treatment. It only summaries the law as it applies to works created now, and makes no reference to the qualifications which may affect works created under earlier rules which continue to apply to them.

10–03   Much of this chapter concerns the criteria for deciding whether a work attracts copyright. These criteria are of two principal kinds:

(1) The nature of the material (Table, head 1) and the intellectual or entrepreneurial activity that produced it (head 2). These factors, in certain respects closely interwoven, are analysed together in sections 2 and 3 below.[5]

(2) The qualifying factor, which brings into account international considerations stemming from the copyright conventions and similar arrangements (Table, head 4:, considered in section 4, below).[6] In part the qualifying factor depends upon what constitutes publication (Table, head 5:, discussed in section 5 below).[7]

Publication is also germane to the factors considered in the final section of this chapter, the duration of the copyright term (Table, head 6).[8] The other heads of the Table are taken up in succeeding chapters: the scope of copyright (Table, head 7) is dealt with in general terms in Chapter 11, and particular aspects are considered in Chapter 13. Authorship (Table, head 3) and initial ownership (Table, head 8) are discussed in Chapter 12.

---

[2] See paras 13–88 *et seq.*, below.
[3] See paras 14–33 *et seq.*, below.
[4] See para. 10–32, below.
[5] See paras 10–04—10–35, below.
[6] See paras 10–36—10–38, below.
[7] See paras 10–39—10–42, below.
[8] See paras 10–43—10–56, below.

BASIC STRUCTURE OF COPYRIGHT UNDER THE 1988 ACT

	Literary, Dramatic, Musical Work	Artistic Work	Sound Recording	Film	Broadcast; Cable-cast	Published edition
1. Nature of work	*Literary:* work that is written, spoken or sung, not dramatic or musical; includes table, compilation, computer program creative database *Dramatic:* includes dance or mime *Musical:* work consisting of music—not associated words or actions (s. 3(1)) Secondary activities (translating, editing, adapting etc.) may attract their own copyright	(a) "graphic work", "photograph", "sculpture", collage (b) work of architecture being a "building" or model thereof (c) work of artistic craftsmanship. Only works within (a) are protected "irrespective of artistic quality" (s. 4(1))	Reproducible recording of sounds or literary, dramatic or musical work (s. 5(1))	Recording on any medium from which a moving image may be produced (s. 5(1))	*Broadcast:* transmission by wireless telegraphy capable of lawful public reception or transmitted for public presentation (s. 6(1)) *Cable-cast:* cable programme service, by non-wireless telecommunication, for reception at 2 or more places or for public presentation (with exceptions) (s. 7(1), (2))	Typographical arrangement of a published edition of literary, dramatic or musical work (s. 8(1))
2. Originality or Equivalent	Work must be "original" (s. 1(1))	Work must be "original" (s. 1(1))	No copyright in recording that is a copy (s. 5(2))	No copyright in film that is a copy (s. 5(2))	Copyright in repeat expires at same time as in original (s. 14(2))	No copyright in reproduction of typographical arrangement of previous edition (s. 8(2))
3. Author	Creator of work (s. 9(1))	Creator of work (s. 9(1))	Person undertaking arrangements necessary for making recording (s. 9(2))	Person undertaking arrangements necessary for making film (s. 9(2)); and, since 1994, principal director	Person making the broadcast or providing the cable programme service (s. 9(2))	Publisher (s. 9(2))

BASIC STRUCTURE OF COPYRIGHT UNDER THE 1988 ACT—*continued*

	Literary, Dramatic, Musical Work	Artistic Work	Sound Recording	Film	Broadcast; Cable-cast	Published edition
4. Qualifying Factor	Unpublished work: status of author. Published work: either country of first publication or status of author at date of first publication or, if already dead, status at death (ss. 153–155)	As for literary etc. work	Status of "author" at date of making; country of first publication (ss. 153–155)	Status of "author" at date of making; country of first publication (ss. 153–155)	Status of "author" when broadcast or cable-cast; country from which broadcast or sent (ss. 153, 156)	Status of "author" at date of first publication; country of first publication (ss. 153–155)
5. Publication	Issue of copies to the public, making available to the public by means of an electronic retrieval system (s. 175)	As for literary etc. works; construction of architectural work or incorporation of artistic work into building is equivalent to publication (s. 175)	Issue of copies to the public (s. 175)	Issue of copies to the public (s. 175)	Issue of copies to the public (s. 175)	Issue of copies to the public (s. 175)
6. Duration	Until end of seventieth year from author's death (special cases: computer-generated works; unknown and joint authorship; Crown, Parliamentary and international organisation copyright) (s. 12)	As for literary etc. work	End of fiftieth year from making; or fiftieth year from release if release within fifty years of making (s. 13A)	End of seventieth year from the death of "persons connected with the film". (s. 13B)	End of fiftieth year from first transmission (s. 14)	End of twenty-fifth year from first publication (s. 15)

7. Scope of Monopoly (primary infringement)	(a) Copying; (reproducing in a material form, storing electronically); issuing copies to public; adapting; rental (computer programs only) (b) Performing in public; broadcasting, cable-casting (ss. 16–21)	(a) Copying; issuing copies to the public; (subject to exceptions) (b) Broadcasting, cable-casting (ss. 16–20)	(a) Copying; issuing, renting copies to public (b) Playing in public; broadcasting; cable-casting (ss. 16–20)	(a) Copying; issuing or renting copies to the public (b) Playing or showing in public; broadcasting or cable-casting (ss. 16–20)	(a) Copying; issuing copies to public (b) Playing or showing in public; broadcasting or cable-casting (ss. 16–20)
8. First Owner (subject to assignment of future copyright)	Author or, if made in course of employment, employer (ss. 9, 11)	As for literary etc. works	"Author" (ss. 9, 11)	"Author" (ss. 9, 11) (now including director)	"Author" (ss. 9, 11)

Making a facsimile copy of the typographical arrangement (ss. 16, 17)
Publisher (ss. 9, 11)

381

2. The Type and Quality of Subject-Matter

(1) Original literary, dramatic, musical and artistic works

10–04 Original literary, dramatic, musical and artistic works accorded copyright by the 1988 Act are further defined to some extent by statutory provisions or case law and this is discussed below. Behind this lies the root requirement that sufficient "skill, judgment and labour", or "selection, judgment and experience", or "labour, skill and capital",[9] be expended by the author in creating the work. In other words, not only must creative intellectual activity produce the right kind of work, but the input must satisfy a certain minimum standard of effort. Otherwise, there is nothing that can be treated as a work; or—closely associated with this—the work will not be regarded as "original". In the next paragraphs the application of these concepts to the four classical types of copyright work will be discussed. Another basic axiom is that copyright protects the expression of an idea rather than the idea itself. In the case of literary, dramatic and musical works this leads to difficult questions about the need to record the expression in some permanent form; these are also considered.[10]

Wherever possible, British copyright law treats the separate elements in a composite creation as having distinct copyrights: the words and music of a song are respectively literary and musical works, each with their own author and term. Particularly now that so much material may be held in digital form, distinctions of this kind are tending to elide. Yet the rights attaching to each type of work may differ. For instance, artistic works have the special advantage that they may be infringed by transposition from two into three dimensions and vice versa; yet so far as concerns industrial manufacture of the copyright in them may well be excluded, or at least limited to a 25-year period.[11] Neither of these rules apply to literary works. If, for instance, the design of some element of an industrial product is recorded partly by diagram (an artistic work) and partly in figures or language (a literary work), should the law adopt an exclusive or a cumulative approach? Should the work be placed in only one category, by reference to its main attributes?[12] Or may it always be separated into its constituents, each enjoying the relevant type of copyright to the extent allowed for that type?[13]

---

[9] This last formulation, employed by Lord Atkinson in *Macmillan v. Cooper* (1923) 93 L.J.P.C. 113 at 117, has particular point when facts have been amassed by "sweat of the brow": see para. 10–10, below.

[10] See paras 10–34—10–35, below.

[11] See below, Chap. 14.

[12] The approach preferred by Laddie J., *Electronic Techniques v. Critchley* [1997] F.S.R. 401 at 413.

[13] The approach preferred by Jacob J., *Anacon v. Environmental Research* [1994] F.S.R. 359; and Pumfrey J., *Sandman v. Panasonic* [1998] F.S.R. 651. See further, para. 11–24.

At first instance, the specialist judges are in dispute. The issue needs to be settled, not least because multi-media digital products are likely to have a considerable commercial future. That instance suggests that the cumulative solution is to be preferred.

(a) *Literary works*[14]

The expression "literary work", said Peterson J., covers: "work which is **10–05** expressed in print or writing, irrespective of the question whether the quality or style is high. The word literary seems to be used in a sense somewhat similar to the use of the word 'literature' in political or electioneering literature, and refers to written or printed matter."[15] As well as works embodying the fruits of considerable creative or intellectual endeavour, copyright has been allowed in such mundane compilations of information as a timetable index,[16] trade catalogues,[17] examination papers,[18] street directories,[19] football fixture lists,[20] a racing information service[21] and the listing of programmes to be broadcast.[22] The principle that there must be sufficient "skill, judgment and labour" accordingly operates as a proviso *de minimis*, excluding as insufficient only those cases where the degree of literary composition is slight. Thus in particular instances courts have refused to recognise as literary works a card containing spaces and directions for eliciting statutory information[23] and an advertisement consisting of four commonplace sentences.[24] In most cases, the titles of books—and equally of plays, films and the like—are treated as insufficiently substantial to attract copyright themselves.[25] The same is true of a trade mark or name. So copyright is not a means of preventing a well-known mark from being applied to an entirely different product or service.[26]

---

[14] See CDPA 1988, ss. 1(1)(a), 3. The expression is defined as any work which is written, spoken or sung, other than a dramatic or musical work, which does at least distinguish the separate copyrights in the words and music of a song (see para. 10–12, below). It includes tables, compilations and computer programs. For computer programs, see paras 13–25 *et seq.*, below.

[15] *University of London Press v. University Tutorial Press* [1916] 2 Ch. 601 at 608.

[16] *Blacklock v. Pearson* [1915] 2 Ch. 376.

[17] *Collis v. Cater* (1898) 78 L.T. 613; *Purefoy v. Sykes Boxall* (1955) 72 R.P.C. 89, CA.

[18] *University of London Press* case (n. 15, above).

[19] *e.g. Kelly v. Morris* (1866) L.R. 1 Eq. 697.

[20] *Football League v. Littlewoods* [1959] Ch. 637; *Ladbroke v. Wm. Hill* [1964] 1 W.L.R. 273, HL.

[21] *Portway Press v. Hague* [1957] R.P.C. 426.

[22] *Independent Television Publications v. Time Out* [1984] F.S.R. 64.

[23] *Libraco v. Shaw* (1913) 30 T.L.R. 22.

[24] *Kirk v. Fleming* [1928–1935] Mac. C.C. 44.

[25] See Lord Wright, *Francis Day v. Twentieth Century Fox* [1940] A.C. 112 at 123; Lord Hodson, *Ladbroke* case (n. 20, above) at 286. As a corollary, merely copying the title of a literary work would rarely be a substantial enough taking to constitute infringement: see generally, para. 11–06, below; and for newspaper headlines on the Internet: *Shetland Times v. Wills* [1997] F.S.R. 604; below, para. 13–77.

[26] *Exxon v. Exxon Insurance* [1982] R.P.C. 69, CA.

10–06   "Literary work" also covers secondary work on existing sources, provided that it in turn involves literary "skill, labour and judgment". The following may all suffice: translation,[27] editorial work that involves amendment,[28] critical annotation or explanation,[29] compilation,[30] selection and abridgment.[31] The same *de minimis* principle applies: gathering together existing tables for the front of a pocket diary was held insufficient in one House of Lords decision[32]; likewise the mere extraction of the time of local trains from a general timetable.[33] It makes no difference to the position whether the material taken from elsewhere is in or out of copyright.[34]

10–07   In deciding whether there has been sufficient skill, the courts take account not just of skill in literary expression or presentation, but also of commercial judgment. A fixed-odds football pool form attracted copyright even though it only consisted of a compilation of 16 known forms of bet. Account was taken of the skill deployed in selecting these particular forms of wager, as distinct from the simple labour of compiling them on the pool form.[35] The process was treated as analogous to that of the compiler of a selection of poetry, even though in that case there is literary skill in the selection.[36] Likewise in a random choice game in a newspaper where the only literary material comprised grids of letters printed on cards, some set out in each day's paper.[37]

10–08   The requirement that a literary work be "original" was only added to statutory copyright law in the Act of 1911. The adjective has been read in a limited sense. It is treated as bringing out one characteristic of the requirement of "skill, labour and judgment"—that the work must originate from the author and not be copied by him from another source. In a much repeated passage, Peterson J. said:

> "The word 'original' does not in this connection mean that the work must be the expression of original or inventive thought. Copyright Acts

---

[27] *Byrne v. Statist Co.* [1914] 1 K.B. 622; *Cummins v. Bond* [1927] 1 Ch. 167.

[28] *e.g.* an edited version of a trial transcript: *Warwick Film v. Eisinger* [1969] 1 Ch. 508.

[29] *Macmillan v. Cooper* (1923) 93 L.J.P.C. 113: the notes appended to a condensed text showed sufficient literary skill, taste and judgment, *cf. Cramp v. Smythson* n. 29, below.

[30] *e.g.* the football pool cases (n. 20, above); *Portway Press v. Hague* (n. 21, above).

[31] *Macmillan v. Cooper* (n. 29, above): condensation of a single text may not be sufficient, but collecting an anchology of verse would likely be: *Sweet v. Benning* (1855) 16 C.B. 459.

[32] *Cramp v. Smythson* [1944] A.C. 329; and see *Rose v. Information Services* [1987] F.S.R. 254.

[33] *Leslie v. Young* [1894] A.C. 335, HL; *cf. Blacklock v. Pearson* [1913] 2 Ch. 376.

[34] *Ashmore v. Douglas-Home* [1987] F.S.R. 553.

[35] The distinction drawn in *Purefoy v. Sykes Boxall* (n. 17, above) between the skill in selecting goods and in writing a catalogue of them needs to be read in context: the causal connection for infringement (see para. 11–03, below) was at issue; *cf. Ladbroke* case (n. 20, above) at 284, 287.

[36] *Ladbroke v. William Hill* (n. 20, above): "An anthology of saleable poems is as much entitled to protection as an anthology of beautiful poems": Lord Devlin at 290.

[37] *Express Newspapers v. Liverpool Daily Post* [1985] F.S.R. 306; and see *Mirror Newspapers v. Queensland Newspapers* [1982] Qd.R. 305; *Kalamazoo (Aust.) v. Compact* (1985) 5 I.P.R. 213.

are not concerned with the originality of ideas, but with the expression of thought, and, in the case of 'literary work,' with the expression of thought in print or writing. The originality which is required relates to the expression of the thought. But the Act does not require that the expression must be in an original or novel form, but that the work must not be copied from another work—that it should originate from the author."[38]

This has obvious significance for works that derive in some sense from an earlier source.[39] A piece of historical writing, a news report, a street directory and a selection of poetry all attract copyright once the choice and arrangement of source material is more than minimal. If the source or sources are still in copyright and they are reproduced to a substantial extent in the final work, a number of distinct copyrights will exist in it. If the rights are owned by different people, the permission of all will be needed for reproducing it and doing the other acts within the copyrights. This approach applies equally where a work evolves through a series of distinct drafts or other formations.[40] There is no implication that the copyright in the earlier drafts will merge or be subsumed in that for the final outcome.[41]

The strictly limited level of "original" achievement that is required in **10–09** order to attract literary copyright can be explained in two ways. First, it reduces to a minimum the element of subjective judgment (and attendant uncertainties) in deciding what qualifies for protection. Secondly, it allows protection for any investment of labour and capital that in some way produces a literary result: this is true equally of the compiler of mundane facts and of the deviser of a football pool form whose real effort is in the market research determining the best bets to combine. Here copyright is being used to compensate for lack of a roving concept of unfair competition.[42] It is noteworthy that in cases of this kind where copyright is found to exist, the defendant tends to be a direct business competitor. Where some other form of relief is available against the unfair competition (as in the case of titles), copyright tends to be denied.[43]

Authors' rights systems take as their starting point the intellectual act of **10–10** formulating a "work" and, therefore, tend to maintain in their law some initial criterion relating to creative expression. This differs in intent from the common law test that what is not copied is original.[44] It is, moreover, an

---

[38] *University of London Press* [1916] 2 Ch. 601 at 608.

[39] On derivative works in comparative perspective, Goldstein (1983) 30 J.Cop.Soc. 209.

[40] A topical example is the production of a computer program: from algorithm, through flow-chart and source code to object code: see below, para. 13–25ff.

[41] *Ray v. Classic FM* [1998] F.S.R. 622.

[42] On which theme, note Lord Devlin, *Ladbroke* case (n. 20, above).

[43] See *"Exxon"* case (n. 26, above).

[44] *e.g.* in *Van Dale v. Romme* [1991] Ned. Jur. 608 (also in Dommering and Hugenholtz (eds), *Protecting Works of Fact* (1991), p. 93, the Dutch Supreme Court required the selection of words for dictionary entries to express the selector's personal views, for there to be copyright in the list. The plaintiff succeeded: [1994] Ned. Jur. 58. *cf.* Schricker (1995) 26 I.I.C. 41.

issue which does not merely divide "copyright" and "authors' rights" systems, since the U.S. Supreme Court has been sufficiently moved by notions of "authorship" to hold that a "White Pages" telephone book cannot be copyright,[45] and the Canadian Supreme Court has applied the same philosophy to a "Yellow Pages" directory.[46]

The British approach, pragmatic and practical, is regarded by advocates of authors' rights as a hostage to fortune. It might, for instance, require the admission of sound recording producers into the pantheon of authorship—an American demand which has been stoutly resisted in the counsels of the WIPO. It might undermine the moral superiority of copyright over industrial property and so set in train the argument that copyright terms should be shortened, rather than lengthened. In consequence, there has been a campaign within the E.C. to scotch the "debased" common law test of originality in favour of a threshold that all works be the author's "own personal creation". As a formula, the phrase is decidedly ambiguous. It is meant to indicate that the creator has engaged in mental activity distinct from the humdrum that anyone else might produce.[47] This test is already supposed to apply to computer programs. This test was first applied to computer programs and now delimits the range of databases which may be the subject of copyright.[48] In consequence a separate *sui generis* right for investors in all databases, whether creative or not, has been introduced by Directive throughout the Community.[49]

Peterson J.'s exegesis on the notion of "originality" may lead to a peculiarly British outcome, but his words demonstrate some common foundation with both Continental and American approaches. For he makes clear that copyright is concerned with "expression of thought", rather than with "originality of ideas". Because of the limited approach to "originality", efforts to distinguish between idea and expression find only occasional place when addressing questions of whether works attract copyright at all. As with other systems, however, the dichotomy of expression and idea does play a necessary (if difficult) role in settling what amounts to substantial taking by a copier. It is accordingly in relation to infringement that we shall return to it.[50]

---

[45] *Feist Publications v. Rural Telephone* 499 U.S. 340 (1991); Weinreb (1998) 111 Harv. L.R. 1150. See further, para. 13–50, below.

[46] *Tele-Direct Publications v. American Business Information* (1997) 76 C.P.R. (3d) 296, FC Canada.

[47] Even Germany, which tends on occasion to take a serious view of minimum creativity, also witnesses a creeping down the scale, so as to give thin protection to "small change". Judges there, as elsewhere, prefer not to pass absolute aesthetic judgments against there being any copyright at all in a work. See also the Netherlands Copyright Law, Art. 10, which protects non-original "writings" in limited degree.

[48] CDPA 1988, s. 3A.

[49] See paras 10–31 and 13–42—13–49ff., below.

[50] See paras 11–06 *et seq.*, below.

(b) *Dramatic works*

Dramatic works must have movement, story or action; they cannot be **10–11** purely static.[51] Whether they must also be capable of being physically performed—a limitation which seems to exclude cartoon films—is much more dubious.[52] The 1988 Act defines "dramatic work" to include a work of dance or mime. They include the scenario or script for a film, the copyright in the film itself being separate.[53] The general principles concerning literary works apply to this closely analogous category. Nice questions can arise over the copyright entitlement of those who provide "secondary" contributions to scripts written by other playwrights. In *Tate v. Thomas*, for instance, a person who supplied a number of ideas, including key lines, which were to be worked out by others secured no part in the eventual copyright.[54] Scenic effects and costumes are only the subject of copyright if they are artistic works. Like literary works, dramatic works have to be "original" in the limited sense which that adjective has acquired in this context.[55]

The exclusion of most titles from the scope of copyright applies equally here.[56] This is linked with preclusion of any copyright in the names of characters or in the typical manner in which characters behave.[57] These can only be protected if sufficient trading reputation with the public gives rise to a form of passing off.[58]

(c) *Musical works: type and quality*

The term "musical work" is defined in the Act only as a work consisting of **10–12** music, exclusive of any words or action intended to be sung, spoken or performed with it.[59] It has long been accepted in British law that where words are set to music, the two remain distinct works for copyright purposes. If there is copyright in each, and lyric writer and composer are not the same person, the two copyrights will usually expire on different dates: Gilbert and Sullivan, for instance, were not commorient.

---

[51] *Creation Records v. News Group* [1997] E.M.L.R. 444: positioning of *objets trouvés* for a pop group photo.

[52] So held in *Norowziah v. Arks (No. 2)* [1999] F.S.R. 79: dance sequence subsequently edited on film by "jump cutting" held not then to be a dramatic work because no longer capable of physical performance.

[53] CDPA 1988, ss. 1(1)(a), 3(1), following Berne Convention, Art. 2(1). For this complex issue, see below, para. 10–46—10–47.

[54] [1921] 1 Ch. 503. See also *Tate v. Fullbrook* [1908] 1 K.B. 821, CA; *Wiseman v. George Weidenfeld & Nicolson* [1985] F.S.R. 525; *Ashmore v. Douglas-Home* [1987] F.S.R. 553.

[55] See para. 10–08 above.

[56] See para. 10–05, above.

[57] See, *e.g.* Maugham J., *Kelly v. Cinema Houses* [1928–1935] Mac. C.C. 362 at 368.

[58] *cf., e.g. Samuelson v. Producers' Distributing* ([1932] 1 Ch. 201, para. 16–44, below); *Shaw Bros v. Golden Harvest* ([1972] R.P.C. 559, para. 16–09, below).

[59] CDPA 1988, ss. 1(1)(a), 2(1).

Again general principles discussed in relation to literary and dramatic works will apply. "Secondary" activities which have been held to attract their own musical copyright include arranging music (by adding accompaniments, new harmonies, new rhythms and the like), and transcribing it for different musical forces. There has been little consideration of what minimum effort will suffice for musical copyright. Certainly, "secondary" activity such as selecting and arranging older tunes or scores,[60] orchestrating[61] or making a piano reduction[62] may qualify for its own copyright. But equally, there is very little content in what is sometimes said to be "arrangement",[63] and this may mean that the requirement of originality is not met.

(d) *Artistic works*

10–13 (i) **General.** Here the tension between different conceptions of copyright becomes marked. Some types of work are treated as artistic only if they bear a distinctive element of aesthetic creativity, others gain protection simply because labour and capital ought not to be freely appropriable.

Artistic works must be "original",[64] but as for literary works, this contemplates only that they will not be copied. In every case, the threshold measure of labour, skill and judgment must be present. Thus where the subject-matter was designs for "Lego" toy bricks, and those designs simply repeated earlier designs with indications of minor variations in words and figures (which are themselves not artistic works), the drawings did not have distinct copyright.[65] However, if artistic skill is required to make the copy, it seems that this may supply originality: as where a photograph is taken from a picture,[66] or a coin is engraved in three dimensions from a drawing.[67]

10–14 It is not therefore the requirement of originality which brings about the differences of approach so much as the manner in which the different categories of artistic work are listed in the Act.[68] These are: (1) irrespective of artistic quality, a graphic work,[69] photograph, sculpture or collage[70];

---

[60] *Austin v. Columbia* [1917–1923] Mac. C.C. 398.

[61] *Metzler v. Curwen* [1928–1935] Mac C.C. 127.

[62] *Wood v. Boosey* (1868) L.R. 3 Q.B. 223; *Redwood Music v. Chappell* [1982] R.P.C. 109.

[63] Claims by such arrangers may be excluded for not involving sufficient skill. But the argument that any copyright which they do attract adheres to that of the original composer runs counter to the whole development of British law on the subject: see Cornish [1971] J.B.L. 241; *cf. Performing Right*, November 1971, p. 34.

[64] CDPA 1988, s. 1(1)(a).

[65] *Interlego v. Tyco* [1988] R.P.C. 343, JC.

[66] *Graves' Case* (1869) L.R. 4 Q.B. 715.

[67] *Martin v. Polyplas* [1969] N.Z.L.R. 1046.

[68] CDPA 1988, s. 4.

[69] "Graphic works" includes (1) a painting, drawing, diagram, map, chart or plan; and (2) an engraving, etching lithograph, woodcut or similar work. "Photograph" means a recording of light or other radiation on any medium on which an image is produced (or from which it can be produced) which is not part of a film. "Sculpture" includes a cast or model made for the purposes of sculpture; see further para. 14–29.

[70] A collage has to be assembled for more than a few hours and has to be stuck: *Creation Records v. News Group* [1997] E.M.L.R. 444.

(2) works of architecture (buildings or models of buildings)[71]; (3) works of artistic craftsmanship not within category (1) or category (2).[72]

The requisite "skill, judgment and labour" is thus affected by the meaning of the various types of work and by the fact that only category (1) secures copyright "irrespective of artistic quality".[73] In the first category, most of the decisions set the minimal level of effort low: a simple drawing of a human hand showing voters where to mark their cross on a voting card,[74] the label design for a sweet tin,[75] the arrangement of a few decorative lines on a parcel label,[76] have all been accorded copyright. (We shall see that, by way of counterbalance, the scope of infringement is narrowly defined in such cases).[77] There was, moreover, a tendency to give very broad scope to the categories of artistic work included under this first head, in order to eliminate any consideration of "artistic quality". Upon such an assumption, a frisbee made from plastic was held to be an engraving because of the concentric rings on its body, and a model for its body was a sculpture[78]; a plastic mould for the heating plates of a sandwich-toaster was a sculpture[79] and so on. More recently, however, interpretation has been shifting towards everyday understanding of these terms; sculpture must have its ordinary, inevitably imprecise meaning of "a three-dimensional work made by an artist's hand[80]; it requires carving, modelling or similar activity, not merely the assemblage of things which are to be the subject of a photograph.[81] This greater realism is of much significance in the new law of industrial designs.[82]

As with literary works, judgment that does not go to the degree or amount of artistic skill may be brought into account in deciding whether the minimum requirement for copyright is satisfied. Even three concentric circles may suffice if they are drawn to precise measurements because they are a plan for a technical device.[83]

---

[71] Including any fixed structure—so this may cover a bridge or a dam.

[72] The concept is not further defined.

[73] This phrase, destined to produce unimagined consequences (Chap. 14, below), was inserted as a mild protection when maps, charts and plans were reclassified in 1956 as artistic, rather than as literary, works, as recommended by the Gregory Committee: see Fellner, para. 1.16.

[74] *Kenrick v. Lawrence* (1890) 25 Q.B.D. 99.

[75] *Tavener Rutledge v. Specters* [1959] R.P.C. 355, CA.

[76] *Walker v. British Picker* [1961] R.P.C. 57. An unreported decision held that there was artistic copyright in a signature, see Copinger, para. 2–23.

[77] See paras 11–13—11–14, below.

[78] *Wham-O v. Lincoln* [1985] R.P.C. 127, CA (N.Z.); and see *Plix Products v. Winstone* [1986] F.S.R. 92.

[79] *Breville Europe v. Thorn EMI* (1985) [1995] F.S.R. 77; and see *Arnold v. Miafern* [1980] R.P.C. 397.

[80] *Metix v. Maughan* [1997] F.S.R. 718: hence it could not include industrial results for making cartridges; see also *Greenfield v. Rover-Scott Bonner* (1990) 17 I.P.R. 417.

[81] *Creation Records v. News Group* [1997] E.M.L.R. 444.

[82] See below, para. 14–29.

[83] *Solar Thomson v. Barton* [1977] R.P.C. 537 at 558; and see *Ladbroke* case (n. 20, above).

10-15   The British have never scrupled to place every variety of photograph within copyright, however merely technical the procedure of pointing the camera at a subject and pressing the shutter may be in a particular instance. Authors' rights systems tend to give copyright only to "photographic works", that is the results of careful and distinctive arrangement (scene-setting, lighting, angle, etc.), involving an element of aesthetic judgment which is personal to the photographer (and/or to some "director", rather than the mere cameraman).[84] Since this will exclude not only casual snapshots (which occasionally—as when they show the shooting of a President—may have great commercial potential[85]) but also press photography, some form of related right for these lesser productions may be introduced, and with it much complicated law to distinguish the different categories.[86] Eventually Brussels may impose some such orthodoxy in the name of approximation of laws, but it is not on any priority list.

10-16   (ii) **Architectural works and models.**[87] An architect's plans fall within category (1) above.[88] It is the actual structure or a model of it which is separately treated in the second category. By implication, some consideration must be given to artistic quality. It may well be enough to show "something apart from the common stock of ideas".[89]

10-17   (iii) **Works of artistic craftsmanship.**[90] A considerable miscellany of artefacts—jewellery, furniture, cutlery, toys, educational aids and so on—may claim to rank as "works of artistic craftsmanship" within category (3).[91] As we shall see, the scope of this category has increased in importance under the 1988 Act.[92] The criteria which a Court should apply in deciding whether an article earns this description were intensively canvassed in *Hensher v. Restawile*[93] (where the subject-matter was a prototype for a suite of furniture of distinctly low-brow appeal).[94] However, the speeches in the

---

[84] Gendreau *La protection des photographies en droit d'auteur* (1994). A person who organises the objects to be photographed may be a joint author of the photograph then produced, but is not an author of another photograph of the objects, taken without authority: *Creation Records v. News Group* above, n. 81; Garnett and Abbott, [1998] E.I.P.R. 204.

[85] As to which, see para. 10–49, below.

[86] For another aspect of this controversy, see para. 10–48, below.

[87] See Greenwood (1986) 16 Queensland L.Soc.J. 221.

[88] See para. 10–14, above. *cf. Chabot v. Davies* (1936) 155 L.T. 525.

[89] For this distinction, *Blake v. Warren* [1928–1935] Mac. C.C. 268 (decided under the 1911 Act, s. 35(1) and concerned in any case with drawings).

[90] See R. G. Kenny (1984) 13 U. Queensland L.J. 206.

[91] See para. 10–14, above. For a recent example, the sets, costumes and latex prostheses for *Mary Shelley's Frankenstein*: *Shelley Films v. Rex Features* [1994] E.M.L.R. 134. Note that, if a three-dimensional object can be described as a "sculpture" or an "engraving", it comes within category (1): *cf.* n. 77, above.

[92] See Chap. 14, below.

[93] [1976] A.C. 64, [1975] R.P.C. 31.

[94] [1975] R.P.C. 31 at 62, 70, 72. There must be some craftsmanly activity, not mere assemblage: *Creation Records v. News Group*, above, n. 81.

House of Lords display no uniformity of approach. Three factors warrant attention: (1) Is it the craftsman's intention to create something artistic that counts or rather the perception by the public of artistic quality in the article? (2) What level of artistic aspiration or attainment must be shown? (3) Is it for the judge to make up his own mind on the question, or is his function to weigh the relative strength of expert and other testimony given to the Court?

Concerning factor (1), the House of Lords rejected the Court of Appeal's **10–18** approach. This was to ask whether the public would purchase the thing for its aesthetic appeal rather than its functional utility.[95] Lord Simon of Glaisdale drew attention to the English aesthetic tradition (stemming from Ruskin, Morris and the Arts and Crafts Movement) which eschewed any dichotomy between artistic appeal and functional value, seeking rather to derive the one from the other; indeed, the admission of "works of artistic craftsmanship" into the fold of copyright had been a response to that very movement.[96] Lord Reid, however, still attached first importance to the attitude of the public: a work of craftsmanship would be artistic if a substantial section of the public admired and valued it for its appearance.[97] Lord Kilbrandon, on the other hand, laid emphasis on the conscious intention to produce a work of art,[98] and Lord Simon took a similar starting point, though he also brought into account the result achieved.[99] Less specifically Lord Morris would give primacy neither to the intent of the artist nor the priorities of an acquirer, calling instead for a detached judgment of the thing itself. Viscount Dilhorne appears to take a similar view.[1] Walton J. has since held that, despite Lord Reid's reservation, the proper approach is to consider whether the maker of the object had the conscious purpose of creating a work of art.[2]

Concerning factor (2), at first instance Graham J. was satisfied that the **10–19** prototype furniture qualified for copyright because it had distinctive characteristics of shape, form and finish, and resulted in articles that were much more than purely utilitarian.[3] But since the House of Lords were unanimously of the opinion that it did not qualify, it seems clear that some higher level of artistic intent or attainment is necessary; this indeed is the

---

[95] [1975] R.P.C. 31 at 47.

[96] *ibid.*, at 65–67. One purpose of Lord Simon's disquisition was to emphasise that a work could not be excluded from consideration merely because it was machine-made, rather than hand-crafted. But Lord Reid seems to disagree: *cf.* at 53.

[97] *ibid.*, at 54. The same approach is found, *e.g.* in *Cuisenaire v. Reed* [1963] V.R. 719 (coloured sticks for mathematical teaching method neither craftsmanship nor artistic); *cf.* also *Cuisenaire v. South West Imports* [1968] 1 Ex. C.R. 493.

[98] [1975] R.P.C. 31 at 72.

[99] *ibid.*, at 70; see also *Hay v. Sloan* (1957) 16 Fox P.C. 185.

[1] [1975] R.P.C. 31 at 57, 62–63.

[2] *Merlet v. Mothercare* [1986] R.P.C. 115 (raincape not a work of artistic craftsmanship; point not at issue before CA).

[3] [1975] R.P.C. 31 at 40; taken by the CA to be the same test as whether there is novelty enough to secure a registered design: at 47. For this, see paras 14–10, 14–11, below.

real significance of the case. There must be sufficient craftsmanship as well as artistry. Accordingly, Lords Reid and Morris doubted whether a mere prototype, not intended to have value or permanence in itself, could count.[4]

10–20 Concerning factor (3), Lord Kilbrandon emphasised the place of the judge's own evaluation by treating the question as one of law.[5] But Viscount Dilhorne said that it was a question of fact to be decided on the evidence[6] and Lord Simon laid stress on expert evidence—from those who are acknowledged artist-craftsmen or who train such people.[7] Yet again, Lord Reid's view calls for proof that a substantial section of the public regard the article as artistic.[8] At least a person seeking to prove this form of copyright should be permitted to lead both kinds of evidence: expert and (if positive) non-expert.

10–21 One problem which the House of Lords judgment does not touch is the question whether there can be a work of artistic craftsmanship when one person supplies the artistic idea and another the craftsmanship. Clauson J. once considered that there could not then be copyright (the two people in question being the designer and the seamstress of a dress).[9] More recently other judges have shown some coolness towards this distinction.[10] Even if in itself it is a bad point, the *Hensher* decision nonetheless requires the designer's contribution to give serious aesthetic significance to the end product. This category of copyright is not a ready tool against unfair imitation.

(e) *Computer-generated works*

10–22 For the most part, the author of a literary, dramatic, musical or artistic work is its creator in a real sense. He or she (but not it) is the person who, by exercising labour, skill and judgment, gives expression to ideas of the appropriate kind. But even at this juncture, a certain notionalism begins to appear. For the 1988 Act acknowledges that works of all these types may be computer-generated; and it provides that, where the circumstances are such that there is no human author of such a work, the author shall be taken to be the person by whom the arrangements necessary for creation of the work are undertaken.[11]

---

[4] *ibid.*, at 53, 56.

[5] *ibid.*, at 72.

[6] *ibid.*, at 62–63.

[7] *ibid.*, at 69–70.

[8] See n. 93, above.

[9] *Burke v. Spicers Dress Designs* [1936] 1 Ch. 400; *cf.* Graham J., *Restawile* case [1975] 1 R.C.P. 31 at 40. And see Eder (1976) 5 CIPA 270; Gibbins and Hobbs [1979] 1 E.I.P.R. 8.

[10] *e.g.* Oliver J., *Spyrou v. Radley Gowns* [1975] F.S.R. 455; Fox J., *Bernstein v. Sydney Murray* [1981] R.P.C. 303; Walton J., *Merlet v. Mothercare* [1986] R.P.C. 115 at 123–124.

[11] CDPA 1988, ss. 9(3), 178 "computer-generated". This conception is difficult to apply. When a subscriber to a service such as "Lexis" has the results of a search printed out, is this "computer-generated", and if so by whom? See further para. 13–47, below.

(2) Films

Until the intervention of E.C. Directives, the copyright in a film (as distinct **10–23** from copyright in any dramatic, musical or other work incorporated into the film) was dealt with on an entrepreneurial basis. Under both the 1956 and the 1988 Acts the person who undertook the arrangements necessary for the making of the film (that is, normally, the film's producer, as financial and administrative organiser) was alone accorded the copyright in it. The 1988 Act continues to provide the crucial definition for the present law: "film" means a recording on any medium (including, therefore, celluloid, video tape and digital recording), provided that a moving image can be produced from it.[12] Thus the film is the recording and can be reproduced only by making a copy of that film, and not by re-filming it afresh.[13] In this it is more limited a right than the dramatic work which it may embody.[14]

However, for films made from July 1, 1994 onwards,[15] the Duration Directive requires the principal director of a film to be considered one of its authors.[16] Film-making has today acquired an irreversible status as an art-form and the Directive acknowledges the clear case of directors to be treated as authors. The acceptance of their case resolves one of the major conflicts between British copyright and Continental authors' rights. The British government has implemented this obligation by creating an admixed, author-cum-neighbour, copyright for films.[17] Copyright in a film is thus given jointly to the producer (in the above sense) and to the principal director. This must count as the ultimate hybrid among intellectual property rights, and it demonstrates a thoroughly British determination not to subscribe to the authors' rights-neighbouring rights dichotomy.

If one puts on one side the correlative enhancement of term[18] the **10–24** impending change in the director's copyright status may be of greater ideological than practical consequence. In the first place, the principal director's entitlement is subject to the general rule that works created in the course of employment are prima facie the property *ab initio* of the

---

[12] s. 5.

[13] *Norowzian v. Arks (No. 1)* [1998] F.S.R. 394.

[14] See below, para. 10–46.

[15] Earlier films will continue to be governed by the legal regime affecting them at the time they were made: Copyright and Related Rights Regs. 1996, S.I. 1995 No. 2967, reg. 36.

[16] Duration Directive (para. 9–19, above), Arts 2(1), 10(4). Arguably, a director who adds significantly to scenario or script of an acted film during filming in any case acquires copyright in the film as a dramatic work copyright for his or her life plus 70 years: Laddie *et al.*, para. 5.26; Kamina [1994] E.I.P.R. 319. However, there are difficulties in this approach for films made under the 1956 Act. Laddie *et al.*, para. 5.44, argue that the problems can be overcome.

[17] See the 1996 Regs (above, n. 15), reg. 17.

[18] For which, see paras 10–46, 10–47, below.

employer[19]; and, secondly, even directors who are commissioned rather than employed must normally expect to assign copyright to their producers. If they have an extraordinary reputation they may contract to do this on royalty-sharing or other special terms. The additional prestige which directors may derive from attaining the rank of author is subtle. Over time it may well contribute to their earning power as a class, but they are likely to be helped at least as much by collective action, either in the form of trade union pressure or the institution of collecting societies,[20] to enforce their rights directly against users.

10–25   Film is a field in which the law has needed to reflect highly significant technological advances. The 1956 Act was still conceived for an era of celluloid material and referred to "cinematographic films". The subsequent arrival of video taping, and now of digital recording, has added immensely to the ways in which filmed material can be produced and subsequently manipulated. The 1988 Act is much more up-to-date than its predecessor. It talks of "film", but defines it in a way which embraces audio-visual production in general, so as to include "a recording on any medium from which a moving image can be produced".[21]

Thus it would seem to cover many "multi-media" digital recordings. These may make much greater use of text, alongside visual images and a sound-track, than a traditional film, and they may include opportunities for interactivity; nevertheless, so long as moving images are part of their make-up, they fall to be treated as films. As with other films, the material which goes into their make-up will form distinct copyright subject-matter requiring a licence for use in any case where the subject-matter is substantially reproduced in the product. This will be true of any incorporated computer program (itself a literary work) which is needed to control interactivity, just as in a computer game.

(3) The entrepreneurial copyrights

10–26 The copyrights in sound recordings, broadcasts, cable-casts and typographical format, are all carried forward in updated form from the previous legislation. The *sui generis* database right is the product of the E.U. Directive on the subject[22]; and the publisher's right in long-unpublished works comes from the Duration Directive.[23]

The subject-matter in the first category has been re-defined to take account of major technological advances. "Sound recording" covers any

---

[19] CDPA 1988 (as amended), s. 11(2).
[20] For a presumption of assignment of rental rights in embodied material, and related rights to equitable remuneration, which will follow from implementation of the Directive on Rental Rights, see its Arts 2(7), (4).
[21] CDPA 1988, s. 5(1).
[22] Database Directive 96/9/E.C.; implemented by the Copyright and Rights in Databases Regs, S.I. 1997 No. 3032.
[23] Directive 93/98/EEC, Art. 4.

recording of literary, dramatic or musical work or other sounds (bird-song, the noises of a motor-race, etc.),[24] regardless of medium, and so will include disc, tape, compact disc, digital audio tape and future technical developments. There is, however, no copyright in any sound recording which is a copy of another, authorised or unauthorised.[25]

"Broadcast" is a transmission "by wireless telegraphy" of visual images, **10–27** sounds or other information which is capable of lawful reception by the public (in particular through use of decoding equipment made available through the person transmitting in encrypted form), or which is for presentation to the public.[26] This covers both terrestrial and satellite transmission and takes account of the forms of satellite broadcasting which may be directly received by individuals or may be received by subscribers who obtain a decoder. The definition, however, excludes the familiar satellite transmission that is only for reception and re-transmission by a local broadcasting station. For all these forms the place from where the signals are transmitted to the satellite (the "up-leg") is treated as the broadcasting.[27] Thus copyright arises in satellite broadcasts transmitted from the United Kingdom, extended territories and those countries with Rome Convention and other reciprocal connections to the United Kingdom. The notion of the "up-leg" is here used in order to identify the national system which determines whether it is copyright and accordingly to what extent. The "up-leg", as we shall see, also defines the act of broadcasting which requires a copyright licence from authors, film and record producers, other broadcasters, etc.[28]

"Cable-cast" is not a statutory term but is used here as a compendious **10–28** abbreviation for "any item included in a cable programme service" as elaborately defined in the 1988 Act.[29] Such a service is one which consists wholly or mainly in sending visual images, sounds or other information by a non-wireless telecommunications system, either to two or more places[30] or for presentation to the public. Excepted from this are interactive services; internal business services; individual domestic services; services on single-occupier premises otherwise than by way of business amenity; services for

---

[24] CDPA 1988, s. 5A(1). Both examples have a commercial value. Note that film sound-track now falls to be treated as a sound recording, rather than as part of the film, except when used to accompany the film: s. 5B(2), (3), (5). The rule applies to existing and new films: Sched. 1, para. 8. For the technology and its legal consequences, Sterling, *Intellectual Property Rights in Sound Recordings, Film and Video* (1992), Chaps 2, 3.

[25] CDPA 1988, s. 5A(2).

[26] *ibid.*, s. 6(1). The reception may be by means of a telecommunications system: s 6(4). Broadcasts made before June 1, 1957 acquire no copyright, though later repeats do so: Sched. 1, para. 9. Music played during a telephone "hold" is not broadcast: *APRA v. Telstra* (1995) 26 I.I.C. 578.

[27] CDPA 1988, s. 6(3).

[28] See paras 13–57, 13–59, below, which consider the impact of the E.C. Satellite Directive.

[29] CDPA 1988, s. 7. Cable-casts made before January 1, 1985 acquire no copyright, though later repeats do so: Sched. 1, para. 9.

[30] Not necessarily at the same time: *ibid.*, s. 7(1).

those running broadcasting or cabling services or programmes for them.[31] There is no copyright in a cable-cast that consists of reception and immediate re-transmission of a broadcast.[32] Neither a broadcast nor a cable-cast acquires copyright to the extent that it infringes another broadcast or cable-cast.[33]

This definition preceded the Internet and was intended to relate to cable services which were equivalent in essential respects to broadcasts (or at least of multi-casts to a net of subscribers). It has nonetheless been held that the definition does cover the placing of material on the World Wide Web for downloading by users—an interpretation which we examine at a later stage.[34]

10–29 The typographical-arrangement copyright arises in respect of a published edition of the whole or part of one or more literary, dramatic or musical (but not artistic) works, provided that it does not simply reproduce the typographical arrangement of a previous edition.[35]

10–30 As will be seen from the Table (head 3), the "creator-author" of these rights is not the person who by labour, skill and judgment puts the recording, broadcast, cable-cast or printed format into its particular form. He, or she, or (most likely) it, is the person in charge of the undertaking: the person who makes the necessary arrangements for a sound recording, the person making a broadcast or providing a cable programme service, the publisher of a typographical format. Despite their new guise, these remain in truth neighbouring rights.[36] They are accorded directly in order to protect investment, not creativity, and therefore do not depend upon any level of aesthetic achievement, such as the auditory skills of a recording engineer or the creativity of an editor in publishing. If the latter provides sufficient skill and labour in, for instance, selecting material for an anthology, he or she will be the author of a "literary work" and acquire copyright in that form.

10–31 The *sui generis* right in a database, deriving from the Database Directive,[37] has come into British law as a right separate from copyright (as have rights in performances). Nevertheless its subject-matter is so close to authors' copyright in compilations that the two need differentiation at this stage. A compilation is capable of being an original work of authorship for

---

[31] CDPA 1988, s. 7(2). The list is variable by order of the Secretary of State: s. 7(3), (4).
[32] *ibid.*, s. 7(5)(a); but this activity may constitute infringement of copyright in the broadcast, etc.
[33] *ibid.*, ss. 6(5), 7(6)(b).
[34] See below, para. 13–77.
[35] *ibid.*, ss. 8. The E.C. Directive on Copyright Duration, Art. 5, permits Member States to create a publishers' right in critical and scientific works which have fallen into the public domain. This may last for up to 30 years from publication. The U.K. has not so far taken advantage of this possibility, which for the works concerned, is not limited to a right against reprography.
[36] CDPA 1988, s. 9(2).
[37] Directive 96/9; above, para. 9–19.

copyright purposes.[38] However, most compilations will now fall within the definition of a "database":

> "a collection of independent works, data or other materials which (a) are arranged in a systematic or methodical way, and (b) are individual accessible by electronic or other means".[39]

The Directive has required that, for there to be copyright (literary—or, in appropriate cases, musical or artistic) in a database, the selection or arrangement of the independent material must constitute the author's own intellectual creation.[40] This is likely to exclude from copyright the listing of mundane information such as names and addresses in street directories, and telephone and Internet listings; what else will be cut away from former understandings of "originality" is hard to surmise.[41]

However that may be, the Database Right (the *sui generis* right), which **10–32** has been in operation for pre-existing as well as new databases of all kinds since 1998, applies without reference to any concept of originality. It is given instead to the investor who makes a substantial investment in obtaining, verifying or presenting the contents of a database.[42] It operates, at least when there has not been further investment in changing its contents, for a restricted term of 15 years from completion.[43] It thus ranks with the other entrepreneurial rights discussed under this head. The details of the right will be dealt with later.[44]

Also deserving comparison at this point is the publication right given to a person who "publishes" a work with authority for the first time after its term of copyright has expired.[45] Literary, dramatic, musical and artistic works and films are covered for 25-year term. Aimed particularly to secure the outlay on producing re-discovered manuscripts and art-works, it fills a gap which arose when in 1988 copyright in unpublished material ceased to have an indeterminate copyright.

---

[38] Above, para. 10–06, n. 30.
[39] Database Regs. S.I. 1997 No. 3032, reg. 6 (included in CDPA 1988, s. 3A).
[40] CDPA 1988, s. 3A(2).
[41] See below, para. 13–50.
[42] 1997 Regs, reg. 13–15.
[43] 1997 Regs, reg. 17.
[44] See below, para. 13–51, in particular for qualification, term and infringement.
[45] Copyright etc. Regs. S.I. 1996 No. 2967, regs. 16, 17. "Publication" includes, as well as making copies available to the public, renting, lending, performing, etc., in public, broadcasting and cable-casting, making the work available by means of an electronic retrieval system. The authority must be that of the owner of the physical record. Publication must be in the EEA or by an EEA national. Much of the detail follows provisions on copyright, including the requirement of copying for infringement. For a full account, see Copinger, Chap. 17, and for differences in implementation between member states, Burrell and Haslam [1998] E.I.P.R. 210.

3. FORMALITIES AND PERMANENT FORM

(1) Absence of formalities

10–33 Originally British copyright law required registration of works with the Stationers' Company as a condition, first of acquiring, later of enforcing, copyright in published works. But that had to be abandoned once the Berne Convention conceived copyright as a property flowing "naturally" and without formality from the act of creation.[46] Since the 1911 Act, neither registration nor any formal notification of the claim to copyright on copies of Berne Convention works has been a prerequisite either of copyright itself or of the entitlement to institute proceedings for infringement. As already explained,[47] the "copyright notice" on published works (©, name of copyright owner, year of first publication) appears in order to attract copyright in non-Berne countries—including, until recently, the United States—which accept this as a sufficient formality; they do so in general because they belong to the UCC which provides that this shall be sufficient.[48]

Since these Conventions only cover literary, dramatic, musical and artistic works and films, the same constraints do not apply to other copyright material. But sound recordings no longer require marking, as they did under the 1956 Act, in order to attract their own copyright.

(2) Permanent form for the work

10–34 Nonetheless it is an assumption of British copyright legislation that all subject-matter requires to exist in some permanent form before it gains copyright. It is possible to look upon this as a corollary of the principle that the protection goes only to the particular expression of ideas. Thus, in the case of most artistic works it is only when the particular painting, photograph or other work is executed that the idea for it is transmuted into expression; the act of creation and the "fixation" of the work are indivisible.[49]

But literary, dramatic and musical creativity admits of more stages. A man may conceive a speech in his mind and deliver it from memory without ever writing it down. Indeed, some composers, lacking musical literacy, can

---

[46] See paras 9–06—9–08, above; and note Berne Convention, Art. 5(2). Copyright does not depend upon the obligation of every publisher in the U.K. to supply a copy of a published book to the British Museum and five other libraries: see CA 1911, s. 15 (unrepealed).

[47] See para. 9–11, above.

[48] See UCC, Art. 3(1).

[49] Fixation and permanence can give rise to nice issues in the sphere of artistic activity. Adam Ant's face make-up did not have permanence enough for copyright: *Merchandising Corp. of America v. Harpbond* [1983] F.S.R. 32, CA; nor did a device containing sand and glycerine for making "sand pictures" by moving it: *Komesaroff v. Mickle* [1988] R.P.C. 204.

only get their works into permanent form by dictation or recording. So long as there is no fixation, they have no copyright and must seek legal protection elsewhere, particularly through performers' protection legislation and contract.[50]

The 1988 Act fills a previous lacuna in the statutes: it specifies that a **10–35** literary, dramatic or musical work is not the subject of copyright unless and until it is recorded, in writing or otherwise (for instance, by tape recording or filming)[51]; and that it is immaterial whether the author gave permission for the recording or not.[52] It has long been accepted that a person who arranges for a stenographer to take down his speech is the author of the resulting work, for it has merely been recorded by an amanuensis.[53] What, then, of a reporter who records a politician's speech, acting on his own initiative or that of his employer? The new provision treats the politician— the creator of the words—as the author of the literary work thus generated. The provision, however, is not to affect the question whether a distinct copyright exists in the record.[54]

If the reporter has used an audio-tape, clearly there is a sound recording that will be the subject of a separate copyright (with, of course, its own limited scope, probably not extending to acts of copying the speech as a written text).[55] But if the record was in writing—for instance, by shorthand—the old case of *Walter v. Lane*[56] still applies. This treated the reporter as entitled to literary copyright in the speech by virtue of his skill and labour in reducing it to permanent form. That decision was reached before the statutory requirement of "originality" was included in the law. How far it remains applicable has since been questioned and a distinction suggested between one who uses an aesthetic skill to make a record (for example the folk-song hunter) and one who uses a standard technique (certainly, the interviewer armed with a tape-recorder; more doubtfully, the stenographer).[57] More recently again, however, it has been held applicable:

---

[50] The copyrights in sound recordings, films and typographical format concern fixed subject-matter. Broadcasts and cable-casts, however, are essentially transient activities which are nevertheless protected as such.

[51] *Norowzian v. Arks (No. 2)* [1999] F.S.R. 49; the recording or filming relied upon must contain the earlier work.

[52] CDPA 1988, s. 3(2), (3). Previously a work was regarded as made when it was put in permanent form by writing or otherwise; choreographic works had, however to be notated: CA 1956, s. 48(1), 49(4). Accordingly, the wider scope of recording affects them in particular.

[53] Lord James of Hereford, *Walter v. Lane* [1900] A.C. 539 at 554. *cf.* the "ghost writer" who is the author giving expression to the teller's ideas: *Donoghue v. Allied Newspapers* [1938] 1 Ch. 106; and note *Evans v. Hulton* [1923–1928] Mac. C.C. 51. See also the entertaining cases on spiritual communication: *Cummins v. Bond* [1927] 1 Ch. 167; *Leah v. Two Worlds* [1951] Ch. 393.

[54] COPA 1988, s. 3(3).

[55] See para. 11–26, below.

[56] [1900] A.C. 539; *cf.* the copyright in a street directory, *e.g. Black v. Stacey* [1929] 1 Ch. 177; and see also *Sands McDougall v. Robinson* (1917) 23 C.L.R. 49 at 54–55, HC; *Gould v. Stoddard* (1998) 80 C.P.R. 93d) 161, CA Ont; *Hager v. ECW Press* [1999] (to be reported).

[57] *Roberton v. Lewis* (1960) [1976] R.P.C. 169.

a journalist who records a long interview and then selects brief extracts for a report shows the necessary skill and judgment.[58]

4. QUALIFICATION

10–36 One quintessential purpose of the Berne and UCC Conventions is to secure the principle of national treatment: the works of authors connected with any one Member State are to receive the same copyright under the law of each other Member State as do the works of authors connected with the latter state.[59] The same applies to the Rome Convention and now to TRIPS. The connection may arise by virtue of the author's personal relationship to a country—his status—or because the country is the place of first publication. While a work remains unpublished, of course, the connection can only concern personal status.

Accordingly, the United Kingdom Act first prescribes the factors (of status and first publication) that will give sufficient connection with Britain, and with the few dependent territories to which the 1988 Act is *extended*.[60] Then, as a consequence of British participation, the Act is *applied* to works and Part 2 subject-matter, which are connected by the same factors to other Convention countries. The legal machinery for this step is found in section 32 and the Orders in Council made in implementation of it.[61]

A complication arises because countries adhere to the Conventions at different dates. If a country is only a UCC Member, then works published before the country joined do not gain British copyright.[62] But the method of the Berne Convention is partly retrospective. Once a country joins, works that are connected with it and are still in copyright under its domestic legislation acquire British copyright. But persons who have incurred expenditure or liability for reproduction or performance of such a work before this copyright took effect can be enjoined only upon payment of compensation.[63]

---

[58] *Express Newspapers v. News (U.K.)* [1990] F.S.R. 359.

[59] Berne Convention, Arts 3–5; UCC, Art. 2. Both Conventions cover literary, dramatic, musical and artistic works and films: see Art. 2(1) and Art. 1, respectively.

[60] These include the Isle of Man, the Channel Islands and Colonies: see CDPA 1988, s. 157 and Orders in Council thereunder. Formerly the notion of extension was important since it was the foundation of "Imperial copyright" operating throughout the British Empire. But former British possessions, even if they have stayed within the Commonwealth, have not wished to preserve an essentially uniform copyright law. They are connected today only through the medium of the international conventions, if they have become members.

[61] In the 1988 Act, even the British have ceased to accord protection to authors who are "British Commonwealth citizens".

[62] But unpublished works already in existence may acquire copyright by virtue of personal connection with the UCC country.

[63] Berne Convention, Art. 18; Copyright (Application to Other Countries) Order 1993, S.I. 1993 No. 942, art. 7(2).

(1) Qualification by personal status

If the connection is directly to the United Kingdom, it is necessary to ask **10–37** whether the "author" is a "qualifying person": that is, he is (1) a British citizen or person within certain other categories of the British Nationality Act 1981[64]; (2) a person domiciled or resident in the United Kingdom; or (3) a body incorporated in part of the United Kingdom.[65] If the connection comes by application of the Act to Convention countries, it will be necessary to show the status, called for in the Copyright (Application to Other Countries) Order 1993 as amended in 1995 to take account of TRIPS: the relevant person must be a citizen or subject, domiciliary or resident, of a scheduled Convention country, or a company incorporated there.[66]

In either case, this question has to be asked at the "material time". For unpublished literary, dramatic, musical and artistic works, that is the date of making the work. Where the work has been published, it is the author's status at the date of first publication that is in issue; or, if the author died before publication, his status at the date of his death. By way of contrast, the material time for other copyrights does not change: it is the personal status of the "author" of a sound recording or film at the time of its making, that of the broadcasting or cable-casting organisation at the date of transmission and, for typographical format, that of the publisher at publication.[67]

(2) Connection by publication

First publication is not only a point in time for considering personal status; **10–38** it is also a connecting factor in its own right.[68] This is so both directly under the Act and through its application to the Convention countries.[69] If publication occurs in two countries within 30 days, the second may be treated as first publication, if this helps: the two are thus deemed simultaneous.[70]

In the past, when the United States and various other countries were not members of the Berne Convention, their citizens gained international protection achieved by first publication in a Convention country. In particular, Canada acted as the "Berne back-door" for the U.S., and so

---

[64] *i.e.* a British Dependent Territories citizen, a British National (Overseas), a British Overseas Citizen, a British Subject or a British Protected Person: see generally CDPA 1988, s. 154(1).

[65] In the last two categories, the connection may equally be to a country to which the Act extends.

[66] CDPA 1988, s. 154(2); S.I. 1993 No. 942; S.I. 1994 No. 263; S.I. 1995 No. 2987.

[67] CDPA 1988, s. 154(4), (5). For joint authors, see s. 154(3).

[68] For the meaning of "publication" see the next section.

[69] CDPA 1988, s. 155.

[70] *ibid.*, s. 153(3), following Berne Convention, Art. 3(4).

allowed the country which was rapidly becoming the greatest copyright exporter in the world to have the advantages of the Convention without such obligations as the long minimum term and the exclusion of registration. Today, the rush to join Berne has deprived this routine of much significance.

A different aspect of first publication under Berne should be noted here. Because it is an action which can be relatively easily proved, the Convention takes the country of first publication as the normal indicator of a work's "country of origin".[71] Only if first publication is not in a Berne Union country, will the nationality of the author determine country of origin. As we shall see, this has become important in imposing the rule of the lesser term on works originating outside the EEA.[72]

5. PUBLICATION

10–39 What amounts to publication can be significant in establishing a qualifying factor. "Publication" is also important in measuring the term of some kinds of copyright and it may occasionally be relevant at other points in the law.

In the law of defamation, "publication" means communication to any person other than the person defamed.[73] In the law of patents, it covers making information available to any person free in law and equity to use it as he wishes.[74] As a term of art in copyright law it comes closer to ordinary understanding: in general, it means issuing copies of the work to the public in quantities intended to satisfy reasonable public demand; and, in the case of literary, dramatic, musical and artistic works, it includes making the work available to the public through an electronic retrieval system.[75] It does not include performing a literary, dramatic or musical work, or broadcasting or cable-casting it; exhibiting an artistic work; or issuing graphic works or photographs of sculptures, works of architecture or works of artistic craftsmanship. Unauthorised acts are not brought into account.[76]

10–40 All this raises technical questions at the margins. Where the requirement is that copies be issued to the public, this refers to first putting them into circulation presumably by sale, hire or gift. Publication takes place wherever the publisher invites the public to acquire copies, not where the

---

[71] Berne Convention, Art. 5(4). Where there is simultaneous publication in more than one Berne country, that which gives the shorter term is the country of origin; where there is simultaneous publication in a Berne and a non-Berne country, the former is the country of origin.

[72] See para. 10–56, below.

[73] See, *e.g. Clerk and Lindsell on Torts* (17th ed., 1995), paras 21–61 *et seq.*

[74] See paras 5–12—5–13, above.

[75] CDPA 1988, s. 175(1). Construction of a building is the equivalent of publishing the architectural work it embodies: s. 175(3). There is also a definition of "commercial publication": s. 175(2).

[76] See *ibid.*, s. 175(6). Joint authors, etc., are not specifically dealt with, but probably all must consent before a publication is authorised.

copies are received.[77] To hold the contrary would make the country of first publication dependent on where shipments happen first to be received.[78] Whether publication is to be accounted more than "merely colourable"[79] depends primarily on the intent of the publisher at the date in question. The Court of Appeal held it enough to put six copies of the sheet music of a song on sale at a time when the song was not known—it was not necessary to promote it first.[80] Some account was taken of the publishers' readiness to fulfil demand when the song did become highly popular[81]; this is best viewed as confirmation of the original intention to supply whatever demand there was.

We shall see that the basic forms of copyright give the right not only to **10–41** stop unauthorised reproductions of the work in its original form but also in other "material" forms, and they give protection against adaptations (for example turning a book into a ballet, a novel into a play, a work in Polish into a work in English, a song into an orchestral number, a drawing into a three-dimensional object).[82] If the author, or someone with his permission, converts an unpublished work into one of these new forms and makes copies of the result available to the public, will this have the effect of publishing the original work? The Act gives no plain guidance; but the answer may well turn on the distinction between reproduction (in any material form) and adaptation,[83] publication being primarily concerned with issuing copies to the public. Thus it was held that a drawing was published by issuing three-dimensional embodiments of it to the public, because the definition of "reproduction" specifically included converting a 2D work into 3D and vice versa.[84] By parity of reasoning, it would seem that issuing a work on film or in any other "material" form of "reproduction" would suffice for publication.[85]

"Adaptation", which is distinguished from reproduction among the acts **10–42** restricted by literary, dramatic and musical copyright, is concerned with reworking material in a manner which normally involves enough to add a

---

[77] See Megarry J., *British Northrop v. Texteam* [1974] R.P.C. 57 at 67.

[78] *ibid.*, and see *McFarlane v. Hulton* [1899] 1 Ch. 884; *"Oscar" T.M.* [1980] F.S.R. 429.

[79] The phrase is used in CDPA 1988, s. 175(5) in contradistinction to an intent to fulfil the reasonable requirements of the public.

[80] *Francis Day v. Feldman* [1914] 2 Ch. 728, CA; and *see Bodley Head v. Flegon* [1972] 1 W.L.R. 680.

[81] In *Copex v. Flegon, The Times*, August 18, 1967, it was argued, but not decided, that there could be no publication of a work in its original Russian where the intent was merely to secure the copyright in subsequent translations. The two purposes, however, are not incompatible.

[82] The last instance is not strictly an "adaptation".

[83] See the definitions, paras 11–23, 11–25, above.

[84] *Merchant Adventurers v. Grew* [1973] R.P.C. 1 at 10; *British Northrop* case (n. 77, above) at 65. This question became significant once artistic copyright in industrial designs was recognised: see para. 14–05, below. Whether these decisions remain good in relation to design documents within the exclusion of CDPA 1988, s. 51, is a question of great obscurity.

[85] A further historical pointer is that, before 1911, publication consisted in principle of communicating a work to the public in any manner, including even by performance. The various specific exceptions operate to reverse this old presumption.

further adapter's copyright. This may well constitute sufficient reason for not treating publication of the adaptation as publication of the original. If this is right, consider its impact upon translations—an important form of adaptation. If a work is written by a resident a non-Convention country, and is then sent to (say) France for publication there in translation, only the particular translation will acquire Convention copyright. There will be nothing to prevent a British publisher from publishing a new translation from the original language.[86]

6. TERM OF COPYRIGHT

10–43 The question of duration is central to the justifications for authors' rights and neighbouring rights, and from that perspective the E.C. Directive on Duration has already been critically considered.[87] Here we turn to the practical effects of that Directive, for better or worse, under the amended Act of 1988.[88]

The term required by the Berne Convention for the classic forms of copyright is the author's life and 50 years thereafter.[89] Although this term is a minimum,[90] it has formed the root of British legislation from 1911 to 1988. Moreover, since 1956 it has been offered to nationals of other states connected with the United Kingdom by the Convention, even when their own terms of protection have been less (for example because they were only members of the UCC and not of Berne).[91] In other words, in 1956 and again in 1988, the United Kingdom did not take advantage of the "lesser term" qualification in Berne,[92] which allows a country to depart from national treatment to the extent of only giving a foreign claimant the shorter term of copyright operative in the "country of origin" of the work.[93]

---

[86] Hence the practice of publishing at least a limited edition of the original first, in order to provide a qualification through first publication for Convention copyright in it. This was the nub of the dispute in *Copex v. Flegon* (n. 81, above).

[87] Directive 93/98 (October 29, 1993); see paras 9–50, 9–55, above.

[88] See Adams and Edenborough [1996] E.I.P.R. 590.

[89] Berne Convention, Art. 7 (with exceptions for films, anonymous and pseudonymous works, photographs and applied art; see Ricketson (1987) Chap. 7; Berne Convention, Art. 7(5)), and in consequence the CDPA 1988, measures the duration of copyright from the end of the year in which a triggering event occurs, such as the author's death or the publication of a work or an edition. For brevity's sake, this added factor will be assumed throughout the text.

[90] Berne Convention, Art. 7(6); and see Rome Convention, Art. 14; Geneva Convention, Art. 4.

[91] Less includes non-existent: as for instance with snapshots, which are not protected at all in some countries, Berne's protection of "photographic works" being understood to mean only photographs which have some artistic element about them.

[92] Berne Convention, Art. 7(8). The Convention's own presumption is in favour of the lesser term principle.

[93] For simplicity and convenience of proof, the main criterion of "country of origin" is place of first publication, rather than nationality of author or authors: *ibid.*, Art. 5(4). This has an important effect in limiting the impact of the rule against discrimination on ground of nationality in the Rome Treaty: see para. 18–01, below.

Now, however, the Duration Directive not only requires longer periods for copyright than Berne and Rome Convention minima; it also adopts a reciprocal, "lesser term", approach to foreign claimants from outside the EEA—an issue to which we return after considering the rules for the different types of copyright.

(1) Classical works of authorship

Following the E.C. Directive, the general term for copyright in literary, **10–44** dramatic, musical and artistic works is the author's life and 70 years thereafter.[94] If there are joint authors, then the term is measured from the death of the longest living among those who qualify for United Kingdom copyright.[95] Special exceptions concerning term are dealt with below.[96]

The 20-year increase in term applies to works created before its **10–45** introduction date (January 1, 1996) as well as to those created subsequently.[97] This has the effect not only of *extending* the protection of works which are still in British copyright on the introduction date, but even of *reviving* copyright in works which in Britain had by then fallen into the public domain.[98] Copyright revives wherever a work is still protected in one EEA State on July 1, 1995, the most obvious point of reference being the German term of the author's life plus 70 years.[99] Both extension and revival of copyright raise questions about title and other interests during the new term, which we will deal with later.[1]

The main thrust of the changes to the duration of British copyright can be illustrated here:

The copyright of Puccini (died 1924) expired at the end of 1974, so it remains lapsed.

The copyright of D.H. Lawrence (died 1930) expired in 1980, so it revives from January 1, 1996 until the end of 2000.

---

[94] CDPA 1988, s. 12(1). Citations in what follows are to the Act as amended by the Duration of Copyright and Rights in Performances Regulations 1995, S.I. 1995 No. 3297 (hereafter, "Duration Regs. 1995"). Note that, in line with the Berne Convention, Art. 7(5), British terms are defined as being measured to the end of the year in which a death or other event occurs.

[95] CDPA 1988, s. 13(4); *cf.* Duration Directive, Art. 1(2). For joint authorship, a limited notion in U.K. law, see paras 12–19, 12–20, below.

[96] See paras 10–46—10–49, below.

[97] Duration Regs. 1995, reg. 16. On this the European Parliament insisted, overriding the Commission's better judgment.

[98] Moral rights are likewise extended: see para. 11–75, below.

[99] This follows the Duration Directive, Art. 10(2). The reference to the position in other states could in certain cases provide highly complex. It may well require an investigation of how another EEA country applies its rule of the lesser term to a particular case. At least that rule cannot be applied, in relation to an EEA citizen, so as to produce a discriminatory effect against him or her. That would be contrary to the Rome Treaty, Art 6 (revised): *Phil Collins v. Imtrat* [1993] 3 C.M.L.R. 773, para. 18–01 below; Cornish [1993] Y. Eur. L. 485.

[1] See para. 12–08, below.

The copyright of Picasso (died 1973) would have been due to expire in 2023, but will now extend until the end of 2043.

Since the 1988 Act, United Kingdom copyright has lasted for the specified term, whether or not the work has been published in that time. Previously copyright law had, in many cases, protected unreleased work without limit of time (thus acting to some degree as a blanket for privacy). It had allowed the copyright term in a work to run on until 50 years from whenever posthumously it was made available for the first time.[2] That approach was, however, deemed over-scrupulous and out of the European line, and so was abandoned even before the Duration Directive.[3] But the new approach leaves publishers without real protection against copying when they first bring out long-hidden, out-of-copyright, material. This unusual risk has led to the Directive's requirement of a 25-year publication right to cover the case.

(2) Films

10–46 Article 2(1) of the Duration Directive requires the principal director of a film made after July 1, 1994 to be given a copyright equivalent to that of other true authors and that has now been done. Thus so far as initial entitlement is concerned, "old" films are those made before that date, "new" films afterwards.[4] There is a separate obligation to increase the term of film copyright, previously confined to a neighbouring right period of 50 years from making or release, so as to become as 70 years from death. This operates for all films, old and new.[5] Moreover, the very considerable investment which goes into major film productions has been held to justify a special way of measuring lives. To guard against the consequences of the director's early death, the longest life among "persons connected with the film" is taken; and these include not only the principal director but the author of the screenplay, the author of the dialogue and the composer of any specifically created film score.[6] These latter are people who, according

---

[2] See, e.g. CA 1956, ss. 2(3), 3(4).

[3] Works existing on August 1, 1989, which would have enjoyed the longer posthumous period of the old law and were still not released on that date, enjoy copyright for 70 years from it: CDPA 1988, Sched. 1, para. 12(4) (as amended).

[4] CDPA 1998, s. 9(2)(ab); Copyright and Related Rights Regulations 1996, S.I. 1996 No. 2967, reg. 18, 36.

[5] The Duration Directive, Art. 3(3), requires that the lesser, neighbouring right, period should continue to be the period for the producer's right in the film (itself required by the Rental Directive, Art. 7). It is hard, therefore, to see that the British implementation complies with the Duration Directive. To the extent that the director can be regarded as already having copyright in the dramatic work made into the film (see para. 10–23, n. 16, above), this may have little practical significance, since the producer will normally acquire this dramatic copyright by assignment (thus aligning the U.K. with most other E.C. countries). But this argument is hard to sustain for some films.

[6] CDPA 1988, s. 13B(2). There can of course be more than one person in each of these categories.

to the Directive, do not have to be given a share in the film copyright.[7] Nonetheless they will each provide original copyright material for the films and the dramatic and musical works will have a duration measured by reference to their individual lives.[8] Film-makers need to employ assiduous obituarists, and also to make sure that one or two of the listed "lives" are young, healthy and, if promiscuous, then precautionary.[9]

Because the new term of copyright applies to existing films[10] it extends **10–47** the duration of those films in which copyright has not expired and revives copyright in those which have fallen into the public domain.[11] In either case the extension may be very considerable: in some cases, much more than the 20 years which is being added to authors' rights in general:

> A documentary film shot in the 1930s, which previously went out of United Kingdom copyright in the 1980s, will, as a film, gain revived copyright from November 1, 1995 until 70 years from the last death among its "connected persons".[12] A last death in 1980 would give copyright until 2050.[13] The director will not, however, become a joint author of it with the producer.

The current market for old films is so strong that these extensions are of prime economic importance. The risks undertaken in today's major productions are such that a studio needs a strong back-list to be sure of survival.

(3) Photographs

This type of artistic work calls for discussion because of the comparative **10–48** generosity which British law has long shown towards it.[14] Photographs have long attracted some measure of copyright protection, without the need to show that they meet any criterion of artistic quality: in contrast with the position in most systems of authors' rights, the work of the humble snapshot-taker stands in the same category as Beaton and Cartier-Bresson.

---

[7] Thus only the principal director has been given co-ownership of new films: above, para. 10–23.

[8] Normally the producer will have acquired their copyright by assignment or in consequence of employment and so is in any case interested in their dates of death.

[9] Each of the "lives" may consist of more than one person, where there is a collaboration.

[10] *i.e.* those existing at the date by which the Duration Directive should have been implemented: July 1, 1995.

[11] See Duration Directive, Art. 2(2).

[12] A pre-1956 Act film which was not a dramatic work could be protected only as a series of photographs—and they had copyright only for 50 years from making: see para. 10–23, above; and note Duration Regs. 1995, reg. 13. The increase will be equally substantial for most films made under the 1956 Act; it is less so (an extra 20 years, plus whatever bonus comes from the added lives) for those which were dramatic works under the 1911 Act.

[13] But, being a revived copyright, the owner is entitled only to equitable remuneration: see para. 12–08, below.

[14] See para. 10–15, above.

Occasionally, a casual photo will have a very considerable commercial value: it may reveal a celebrity's lies, or capture the winning goal. This continues to be the British approach, although the Duration Directive only requires its "life-plus-70" duration to be given to photographs which are "the author's own intellectual creation".[15]

10–49 Under earlier British law, photographs were given their own, limited term.[16] In 1988, they were placed on the level of other artistic works, by giving protection for the photographer's life and 50 years—a term which now increases to life plus 70 years.[17] While initially the increased term applied only to new photographs,[18] implementation of the Duration Directive has its general retroactive effect of both extending and reviving copyrights in existing work. As with films, the change for photographs can be very considerable:

> A child's snapshot of Mrs Thatcher riding high in 1979, not published until 1985, would have enjoyed copyright until 2035, but will now have it extended until the child's death (say in 2040), plus 70 years, that is to 2110. A photograph of a society wedding in 1930 kept British copyright until 1980, a term unaltered by either the 1956 or the 1988 Acts. Under the 1995 changes, it may re-acquire copyright from January 1, 1996 until the end of 70 years from the photographer's death. But in order to do so, it must still have been protected in an EEA State on July 1, 1995. This may well involve an investigation of its artistic quality under the foreign law in question.[19]

(4) Revived copyright: protection of third parties

10–50 The revival of lapsed copyright in works or films presents obvious difficulties for those who in the interim have invested in producing the work on the understanding that it was freely available. They have accordingly received some protection. First of all, anything done before January 1, 1996 cannot amount to infringement; nor can subsequent issuing of copies to the public if they were made before July 1, 1995. In addition where

---

[15] Duration Directive, Art. 6. Member States are left free to protect non-"creative" photos by some lesser right against misappropriation, as is relatively common. They are no longer allowed to reserve full copyright for photographs which measure up to some higher criterion than "own intellectual creation". Even that level of attainment is difficult to define (which is one reason for British avoidance of it). Carefully staged photography, both professional and amateur, is likely to satisfy it. But even press photography is much less easy to categorise.

[16] Under the 1911 Act, s. 21, this was 50 years from making; under the 1956 Act, s. 4, 50 years from publication.

[17] At the same time, the law abandoned a curious entrepreneurial preference. Under the 1956 Act, s. 48(1), the author of a photograph was deemed to be the owner of the material on which it was taken.

[18] CDPA 1988, Sched. 1, para. 12(2).

[19] Because of the limitation of copyright to "creative" photographs (however the foreign law defines this), mentioned in n. 15, above.

arrangements have been made, at a time before January 1, 1995 when the work was out of copyright, to do anything subsequently which falls within the revived copyright, the act in question is exempt from liability.[20] Moreover, if reasonable inquiry does not reveal the name and address of the person with power to license a restricted act under the revived copyright, permission is not required.[21]

Extensions and revivals of copyright raise inevitable questions about who is to enjoy rights in them. These have been dealt with in the British Regulations and are discussed in Chapter 12.[22]

(5) "Neighbouring" copyrights

The period now conferred for other copyrights is indicated in the Table **10–51** (head 6). For sound recordings this becomes 50 years from making, or if "released"[23] within that period, 50 years from release.[24] The copyright in broadcasts and cable-casts continues to endure for 50 years from first transmission in an EEA country.[25] That in typographical format for 25 years from first publication.[26] Computer-generated works, which are treated much like other entrepreneurial copyrights, have a term of 50 years from the making of the work.[27]

(6) Special cases

From the rules so far mentioned there are a number of important **10–52** variations:

(a) *Anonymous and pseudonymous works*

The Berne Convention imposes twin obligations on Member Countries: **10–53** first, an author of a work within the Convention should be entitled to copyright in a publication while preserving anonymity.[28] This moral

---

[20] Duration Regs. 1995, reg. 23(1), (2). There is also a provision (reg. 23(3)), almost impenetrable, which allows free exploitation, despite the revived copyright, of a work or film made or arranged for before July 1, 1995 which contains a copy or adaptation of the work whose copyright is revived. Thus, where a novel which went out of "old" copyright in 1990 is the subject of a film adaptation completed in June 1995, the film-maker may arrange (say) its broadcast at any time, even though it is back in copyright from 1996–2020. Not so, if the film was made in August 1995.

[21] *ibid.*, reg. 23(4). If there is no copyright infringement, there can be no infringement of moral rights: reg. 23(5).

[22] See paras 12–08, below.

[23] *i.e.* in an EEA country, first published, broadcast, cable-cast.

[24] CDPA 1988, s. 13A(2), following the Duration Directive, Art. 3(2).

[25] CDPA 1988, s. 14, following the Duration Directive, Art. 3(4).

[26] *ibid.*, s. 15.

[27] *ibid.* s. 12(7); for this copyright, see paras 13–47—13–48, below. For the terms of the "non-copyrights", see above, para. 10–32 (publication right); and below, paras 13–31 (database right); 13–97 (performance rights); 14–32 (design right).

[28] Berne Convention, Art 7(3). For the history of the provision, see Ricketson (1987) pp. 339–340.

imperative is not easily realised in a system which measures the copyright term by the life of the author. Hence the second requirement: the publisher of an anonymous work should be able to enforce the author's rights as his deemed representative.[29]

It is no precondition of British copyright that the author be named in any publication; and the Act includes a presumption, until the contrary is proved, that, if a work is published in the United Kingdom without attribution but with the name of a publisher, that person shall be taken to be the owner of copyright at the date of publication.[30] If someone other than the publisher then seeks to assert copyright in the publication, he must either show that his right derives from the publisher or else he must rebut the presumption. He will not succeed in the latter endeavour merely by showing an assignment from the alleged author.[31]

Moreover, as long as a literary, dramatic, musical or artistic work remains of unknown authorship,[32] its copyright is measured without reference to the author's date of death. Instead, the work enjoys copyright for 70 years from the date when it was made; or if, before that date, the work was "made available to the public", then for 70 years from this second event.[33] The duration may not be increased by revealing the author's name once the term thus measured has expired. By implication, if the name emerges before the end of the special term, the general rule of author's life and 70 years thereafter will apply, whether this results in a longer or a shorter term overall.[34]

10–54 The position established by implemention of the Duration Directive is at least an improvement on the former indeterminate copyright in unpublished material.[35] Previously, where there was no identifiable author, a potential user might have no means of securing a licence, yet could have no exemption in law—a blight for the scholarly in particular. At least under section 57 of the 1988 Act, a defence was introduced for the case where the author (though unknown) could be reasonably presumed dead for 50 years. That same defence continues (the period now being raised to 70 years), but it will now (with the limited periods) be applicable only in very unusual cases.

---

[29] Berne Convention, Art. 15(2).

[30] CDPA 1988, s. 103(4).

[31] *Warwick Film v. Eisinger* [1969] 1 Ch. 508. It must be doubted whether this truly gives effect to the Berne Convention, Art. 15(2), since the publisher is by no means necessarily representing the author and enforcing his rights. By confining the presumption to publication in the U.K., the Act may also be failing to fulfil the Convention.

[32] Once the identity of the author, or of one among joint authors, becomes known it cannot subsequently be a work of unknown authorship: CDPA 1988, s. 12(3)–(5).

[33] This implements the Duration Directive, Art. 1(3), and eliminates a curious survival of indeterminate copyright which was included in the Act of 1988.

[34] The Duration Directive, Art. 1(3), specifies this result.

[35] With only limited qualifications, "existing" anonymous works continue to be governed by their original regime: see CDPA 1988, Sched. 1, para. 12(3), (5).

(b) *Crown and Parliamentary copyright*

The Crown has a special copyright in works made by an officer or servant **10–55** of the Crown in the course of his duties, and in Acts and Measures. The Houses of Parliament have Parliamentary copyright in Bills and other works prepared under their direction and control. The 1988 Act has introduced substantial changes on this subject which will be discussed later. Here it should be noted that Crown copyright in literary, dramatic, musical and artistic works lasts for 50 years from publication or 125 years from creation, whichever is the shorter.[36] Parliamentary copyright in Bills covers only their duration as such, but in other works of the same type, it lasts for 50 years from making.[37]

(7) **Lesser terms outside the EEA**

The Duration Directive imposes its long periods of protection in favour of **10–56** rightholders from within the E.U. At the same time, following Berne,[38] it uses the concept of the "shorter term" to encourage other countries to adopt equivalent standards.[39] Accordingly, when the country of origin (in the Berne Convention sense[40]) and the nationality of the author lie outside the EEA, United Kingdom (and other EEA) copyright is reduced to the period of any shorter home term. Likewise with related rights, where the rightholder is not a Community national. So long as the U.S. grants an author's right of life plus 50 years, works by American citizens first published there, will have only that period of copyright in the United Kingdom and other EEA countries.[41]

The TRIPS Agreement, however, adopts a most-favoured-nation ("MFN") rule, as well as a requirement of national treatment, as a general basis of its obligations.[42] Moreover, the new GATT contains no explicit exception which would allow an economic union such as the Community to give preferences between its Member States, which would not be caught by the MFN requirement.[43] Nonetheless such an understanding may need to be implied. Otherwise, the U.S. could possibly claim under TRIPS against each Community state when that state gives a longer period of protection to other EEA nationals and "first publishers" than to those from the U.S.

---

[36] For transitional arrangements, see CDPA 1988, Sched. 1, paras 41, 43.

[37] Other points about Crown copyright are discussed in paras 13–105—13–106, below.

[38] Duration Directive, Art. 7(8).

[39] Duration Directive, Art. 7; implemented in the U.K. by CDPA 1988, ss. 12(6), 13A(4), 13B(7), 14(3).

[40] See para. 9–25, above, and CDPA 1988, s. 15A "country of origin".

[41] This, however, cannot operate so as to reduce the period of existing copyrights in non-EEA works: Duration Regs. 1995, reg. 15(1).

[42] See para. 1–32, n. 94, above.

[43] But the question is much complicated by the meaning of Exemption (d) in TRIPS, Art. 4.

CHAPTER 11

INFRINGEMENT OF COPYRIGHT AND MORAL RIGHTS

1. INFRINGEMENT: BASIC CONCEPTS[1]

The Copyright Act defines in some detail the types of activity which **11–01** constitute infringement of the various forms of copyright. As the Table (on pp. 330 to 331) indicates (head 7), the rights of the copyright owner may be roughly classified into "reproduction" rights and "performing" rights. The more detailed statutory categories that can be placed under these heads will be considered later,[2] as will certain special forms of infringement, defences and remedies.[3] But first, there are four basic matters to discuss: copyright must be distinguished from rights in the physical embodiment of the original work; then come two aspects of the subject-matter improperly taken—the need to show that the defendant has misappropriated the actual work and that this has been to a substantial extent; the last concerns the infringer—the degree to which he may infringe by authorising the acts of others.

(1) Ownership of the original work

Copyright in a work gives rights that are distinct from ownership of the **11–02** physical embodiment of the original work—the manuscript, letter, painting or whatever. When one person sends another a letter, he will normally be taken to intend a gift of the paper on which it is written and the recipient becomes its owner. Only if conditions of confidence exist can the author prevent it being shown, given or sold to others.[4] But sending a private letter implies no assignment or licence of the copyright in it and the recipient has

---

[1] Laddie *et al.* pp. 60–115, 210–248; Copinger, Chaps 7–9.
[2] See paras 11–21—11–39, below. Note that the new law of infringement applies to existing works in respect of acts done after commencement: CDPA 1988, Sched. 1, para. 14. There are special provisions affecting rental rights, subsequent dealings in copies made under an exception, typefaces, reconstruction of buildings, libraries, pre-1912 dramatic and musical works, statutory recording, and licences.
[3] Partly discussed in paras 11–38—11–62, below, and partly in Chap. 13, below.
[4] See, *e.g. Pope v. Curl* (1741) 2 Atk. 341; *Gee v. Pritchard* (1818) 2 Swans. 402; *Philip v. Pennell* [1907] 2 Ch. 577; Hauhart (1984) 13 U.Balt.L.R. 244.

no right to make copies or give performances of its content.[5] The same is true of artistic works. The artist's lack of rights in the original painting or sculpture, once he disposes of it, is often a considerable economic disadvantage and has led some legal systems to introduce a special right to share in the proceeds of certain re-sales.[6] But such a sale assigns no copyright unless this is separately expressed or can be implied from the purpose of the transaction.[7]

If the right granted is an exclusive licence of the relevant aspect of the copyright, the licensee is also entitled to sue an infringer.[8]

(2) Misappropriation

(a) *Causal connection*

11–03 The plaintiff must prove that, directly or indirectly, the defendant's alleged infringement is taken from the work or subject-matter in which he claims copyright.[9] This is fundamental to the whole concept of copyright, and distinguishes it from the "full" monopoly of the patent system. (Despite the very term, copyright, the legislation has, until 1988, mostly avoided reference to "copying". Now that word is used in relation to the making and marketing of reproductions. But equally there must also be copying in a general sense for infringement of the performing rights.) The owner must show that this causal connection is the explanation of the similarity between the work and the infringement—the other possibilities being that he copied from the defendant, that they both copied from a common source, or that they arrived at their results independently.[10] On the other hand, he does not have to show that the defendant knew that his copying constituted an infringement. As with other rights of property recognised at common law, the primary exclusive rights may be asserted against even the defendant who honestly believes that he purchased the right to reproduce the work.[11]

If the evidence shows that there are striking similarities between the two works, that the plaintiff's was the earlier in time and that the defendant had the opportunity to get to know the plaintiff's work, then a Court may well

---

[5] *cf.* a letter to the editor. Under a will a bequest of an unpublished manuscript or artistic work is now to be construed as including the copyright: CDPA 1988, s. 89. *cf.* the 1911 Act, s. 17(2), restrictively construed in *Re Dickens* [1935] Ch. 267 which still applies to wills that took effect before the 1956 Act: CDPA 1988, Sched. 1, para. 29.

[6] For this *droit de suite*, see paras 13–103—13–104, below.

[7] In any case a licence (exclusive or non-exclusive, according to circumstances) may be a more reasonable implication.

[8] CDPA 1988, s. 94, 101, 102; and see below, para. 12–12; *Michael O'Mara Books v. Express Newspapers* [1999] F.S.R. 49.

[9] *cf.* the "exclusive right" and the basic statement about infringement in CDPA 1988, ss. 2, 16.

[10] See Sargant J., *Corelli v. Gray* (1913) 29 T.L.R. 116; Diplock L.J., *Francis Day* case (n. 16, below) at 625. See also Learned Hand J., *Fisher v. Dillingham*, 298 Fed. 145 (1924) at 150.

[11] *Mansell v. Valley Printing* [1908] 2 Ch. 441; *Byrne v. Statist* Co. [1914] 1 K.B. 622. Innocent defendants may be protected from liability for damages: see para. 2–42, above.

find copying proved in the absence of any convincing explanation to the contrary by the defendant.[12] But the judges have hesitated to fetter the assessment of each case on its facts by the introduction of rules formally shifting the burden of proof from plaintiff to defendant at any stage of the trial.[13] Some subject-matter, such as factual and historical information, may well derive from independent effort or a common source.[14] Even if there has been some copying, whether there has been a substantial taking calls for separate evaluation; this is discussed later.[15]

(b) *Subconscious copying*

Particular difficulty arises when the defendant denies any intention to copy **11–04** and the Court believes him. Some judges have accepted that copying could occur subconsciously where a person reads, sees or hears a work, forgets about it but then reproduces it, genuinely believing it to be his own.[16] In such a case, proof of copying is said to depend on:

> "a number of composite elements: The degree of familiarity (if proved at all, or properly inferred) with the plaintiff's work, the character of the work, particularly its qualities of impressing the mind and memory, the objective similarity of the defendant's work, the inherent probability that such similarity as is found could be due to coincidence, the existence of other influences on the defendant . . . the quality of the defendant's . . . own evidence on the presence or otherwise in his mind of the plaintiff's work."[17]

(c) *Indirect copying*

It has long been accepted that a work may be copied by imitating a copy of **11–05** it: "to hold otherwise would be to open the door to indirect piracies, which I am not at all disposed to do."[18] If the plaintiff owns a copyright drawing

---

[12] If the question is whether the defendant's work has come from the plaintiff's or from independent sources, the defendant may find it difficult to explain the presence of the plaintiff's errors or idiosyncrasies in his text: see, *e.g. Harman Pictures v. Osborne* (n. 14, below).

[13] See especially the *Francis Day* case (n. 16, below).

[14] See, *e.g. Poznanski v. London Film* [1937–1945] Mac. C.C. 107 at 108; *Harman Pictures v. Osborne* [1967] 2 All E.R. 324 at 328.

[15] *Billhöfer v. Dixon* [1990] F.S.R. 105; *Ibcos v. Barclays Mercantile* [1994] F.S.R. 297; and see paras 11–06 *et seq.*, below.

[16] *Rees v. Melville* [1911–1916] Mac. C.C. 168; *Ricordi v. Clayton & Waller* [1928–1935] Mac. C.C. 154; *Francis Day v. Bron* [1963] Ch. 587, *per* Willmer L.J. (*cf.* at 622, and at 626–627, *per* Upjohn and Diplock L.JJ.); *Industrial Furnaces v. Reaves* [1970] R.P.C. 605 at 623. The notion has actually been applied in *Sinanide v. Kosmeo* (1927) 44 T.L.R. 371 and the breach of confidence cases, *Seager v. Copydex* and *Talbot v. General Television* ([1981] R.P.C. 1, para. 8–38, above).

[17] *per* Wilberforce J., *Francis Day v. Bron* (n. 16, above) at 614.

[18] Lindley L.J., *Hanfstaegl v. Empire Palace* [1894] 3 Ch. 109 at 127; and see, *e.g.* Blackburn J., *ex p. Beal* (1868) L.R. 3 Q.B. 387 at 394. The leading modern authorities are *King Features Syndicate v. Kleeman* [1941] A.C. 417; *British Leyland v. Armstrong* [1986] R.P.C. 279, HL The principle now has statutory force: CDPA 1988, s. 16(3).

and then turns it into a three-dimensional article and this is copied in three dimensions by the defendant, the "causal connection" for indirect copying of the drawing will be established.[19] Likewise if the defendant takes a photo of the plaintiff's three-dimensional article, or his own copy.[20] If a novel is turned into a play, which is in turn converted into a ballet, the same will apply. But the causal chain must run in the right direction. In *Purefoy v. Sykes Boxall*, P made a trade catalogue with illustrations of his products and D also published a catalogue with pictures of his own products, which were copied from P's products. In this alone there was no infringement of P's catalogue, for it was not that catalogue but the products which were the starting point in the chain.[21] On the other hand, if the plaintiff's parts were reproductions of copyright drawings, the defendant's illustrations would derive from those drawings. But to establish the linkage is not enough. It is also necessary to show that the defendant's ultimate use is a substantial reproduction of the plaintiff's work—this is simply the general requirement discussed in the next section. In providing that infringement may be direct or indirect, the 1988 Act also renders it immaterial that any intervening act does not itself constitute infringement.[22]

(3) Substantial taking

11–06 Where there has been copying and all or virtually all of a work is taken without emendation, the proof of infringement is straightforward; difficulties arise to the extent that this is not the case. The 1988 Act requires that a substantial part must have been copied.[23] This test is a major tool for giving expression to the court's sense of fair play. So "the question whether the defendant has copied a substantial part depends much more on the quality than the quantity of what he has taken".[24] Likewise it has often enough been insisted that the copying must be of the expression of ideas, rather than just of the ideas. But that is a distinction with an ill-defined boundary. Judge Learned Hand famously pointed out that, in any case which turns upon a taking of structure, rather than line-by-line (or note-by-note) detail:

> "[u]pon any work . . . a great number of patterns of increasing generality will fit equally well, as more and more incident is left out.

---

[19] The great significance of this example for the law of industrial design is discussed in paras 14–03 *et seq.*, below.

[20] *Dorling v. Honnor Marine* [1965] Ch. 1.

[21] (1954) 71 R.P.C. 227 at 232; 72 R.P.C. 89 at 99, CA, which found nonetheless against the defendant; a degree of both direct and indirect copying of the catalogue was proved.

[22] CDPA 1988, s. 16(3). It might have been better to say that the act need not involve the making of anything that could be a copyright work.

[23] CDPA 1988, s. 16(3)(a).

[24] Lord Reid, *Ladbroke v. William Hill* [1964] 1 W.L.R. 273 at 276; and see Lord Pearce at 293; *P.C.R. v. Dow Jones Telerate* [1998] E.M.L.R. 407.

The last may perhaps be no more than the most general statement of what the [work] is about, and may at times consist only of its title; but there is a point in this series of abstractions where they are no longer protected, since otherwise the [author] could prevent the use of his 'ideas', to which, apart from their expression, his property never extended . . . Nobody has ever been able to fix that boundary, and nobody ever can."[25]

The imprecision of any line between idea and expression causes our **11–07** leading authors to castigate the whole notion.[26] Why then does the distinction survive such disparagement? Why, indeed, is it seized on as the basis of international accord?[27] Copyright, by universal agreement, cannot be limited to straight plagiarism and there is no simple test by which to evaluate what taking, in terms of quality and quantity, is unacceptable. But courts are inevitably pressed with cases where the plaintiff's grievance is that he thought of the very first instance of a whole type of work (a detective story, a restaurant guide, a building of glass panels, and so on) and wants rights over all subsequent variants. In relation to infringement, the "idea/expression dichotomy" directs a necessary inquiry to restrict copyright to a taking from the protected work, and there seems no better indicator of the judgment called for. Undoubtedly it is too vague a distinction to offer more by way of general guidance. The answer in a particular case can only lie in the tribunal's innate sense of fairness.

One context in which judges who incline to the view that "what is worth copying is prima facie worth protecting"[28] may well stretch the notion of "expression" a considerable way. Once convinced that the defendant unfairly cut a competitive corner by setting out to revamp the plaintiff's completed work, they will not easily be dissuaded that the alterations have been sufficient.[29] In this approach the taking of ideas alone is confined to cases where the defendant does not start from the completed work at all, save in the sense that he goes through a similar process of creation: as where he paints for himself the scene that the plaintiff painted,[30] or draws his own cartoon for the same basic joke.[31]

---

[25] *Nichols v. Universal Pictures* 45 F (2d) 119 (1930)—stated with particular reference to an allegation that one play copied the plot of another. Note also, Lord Hailsham, in *LB Plastics v. Swish* [1979] R.P.C. 611 at 629: "of course, as the late Professor Joad used to observe, it all depends on what you mean by 'ideas'. What the respondents in fact copied from the appellants was no mere general idea."

[26] Laddie *et al.*, pp. 273–291.

[27] TRIPS Agreement, Art. 9(2); WIPO Copyright Treaty 1996, Art. 2; and see the E.C. Software Directive, Art. 1(2).

[28] Peterson J., *University of London Press* case [1916] 2 Ch. 601 at 610; quoted by Lords Reid and Pearce in the *Ladbroke* case (n. 24, above) at 279, 293. See Christie (1984) 10 Monash L.R. 175.

[29] For a striking example, see *Elanco v. Mandops* [1980] R.P.C. 213, CA.

[30] *cf. e.g. Krisarts v. Briarfine* [1977] F.S.R. 537; and see, as to indirect copying of a drawing for an object: *Ward v. Richard Sankey* [1988] F.S.R. 66.

[31] *McCrum v. Eisner* [1917–1923] Mac. C.C. 14.

The assessment of each case turns a good deal on its own circumstances. But there are some general considerations which may well have a bearing on the result. These are worth illustrating.

(a) *Unaltered copying*

11–08 If the defendant has copied without additions or alterations to the part taken, the proportion of that part to the whole of the plaintiff's work need not be large: a short extract from a poem, a recognisable segment of a painting, the refrain of a pop-song. The issue is not much contested, but, given the new copying technology, its practical importance is considerable.[32]

(b) *Extent of defendant's alteration*

11–09 Where the defendant has reworked the plaintiff's material there comes a point beyond which the plaintiff has no claim. Whatever may have been the position in the past, the fact that the defendant has himself added enough by way of skill, labour and judgment to secure copyright for his effort does not, under the present law, settle the question whether he has infringed; rather the issue is whether a substantial part of the plaintiff's work survives in the defendant's so as to appear to be a copy of it.[33]

11–10 Particular difficulty arises when the plaintiff's work is taken with intent to satirise—whether the butt in mind is the work itself or some quite different object.[34] In *Glyn v. Weston Feature*[35] a filmed burlesque (or, in today's language, "send-up") of Elinor Glyn's once notorious novel, *Three Weeks*, was held not to infringe because very little by way of incident was taken over from novel to film. Likewise in *Joy Music v. Sunday Pictorial*,[36] a song lyric had been parodied in pursuit of Prince Philip; but only one repeated phrase was taken, and that with pointed variation. Again there was no infringement. In both decisions it was asked whether the defendant had bestowed such mental labour on what he had taken and subjected it to such revision and alteration as to produce an original work.[37] This must be

---

[32] See paras 13–09 *et seq.*, below; equally in the field of performing rights.

[33] *Redwood Music v. Chappell* [1982] R.P.C. 109 (adaptation of song—generous view of difference). The matter is one on which an expert witness may express a view: *Designers Guild v. Williams* [1998] F.S.R. 803.

[34] The subject is a theoretical paradise: see, *e.g.* Gredley and Maniatis [1997] E.I.P.R. 339; Spence (1998) 114 L.Q.R. 594. Note that the European Human Rights Convention, Art. 10(1), guarantees the right to parody the work of another. This, however, does not justify defamation, passing off or false attribution of authorship: *Clark v. Associated Newspapers* [1998] R.P.C. 261.

[35] [1916] 1 Ch. 261. The plaintiff's claim also failed for its "grossly immoral" tendency: see paras 11–56, 11–57, below.

[36] [1960] 2 Q.B. 60.

[37] This derives from Lindley L.J., *Hanfstaengl v. Empire Palace* [1894] 3 Ch. 109 at 128; and the *Glyn* case (n. 35, above) at 268; *United Feature v. Star Newspaper* (1980) 2 E.I.P.R. D 43, SC (N.S.W.).

understood as a way of emphasising that nothing substantial must remain from the plaintiff's work.[38] While in the past, English judges have seemed loth to find sufficient copying in borderline parody cases,[39] they have now also to consider the moral right of integrity, which is discussed later.[40]

A rather similar difficulty relates to résumés—summarised plots of plays, **11–11** abridgments of novels, headnotes of law reports, and so on. There was a tendency, at least in earlier case law, to treat a really substantial précis of contents as permissible—because it was useful or because it did not seriously interfere with the plaintiff's interests.[41] To this end it has been asked whether the defendant has really produced a "new work".[42] In this context the phrase seems to indicate a very substantial condensation and revision of the material. With this should be contrasted the Court of Appeal's grant of an interlocutory injunction in *Elanco v. Mandops*.[43] The defendants first copied the plaintiff's instruction leaflet for a weed killer and had to withdraw it; they then produced a revision giving the same detailed information in other words. This was held to create an arguable case of infringement because the defendants were not entitled to make use of the plaintiff's skill and judgment in securing the information.

A nice question arises where a defendant engages in very small borrowings from a succession of the plaintiffs works. In *Cate v. Devon and Exeter Constitutional Newspaper*,[44] items of information were drawn from each day's newspaper and this was considered substantial taking, even though each extraction in isolation would not infringe. The correctness of this approach has recently been doubted: its logic dictates that the first few extractions become infringements *ex post facto*.[45]

(c) *Character of plaintiff's or defendant's work*

Certain types of work are treated as having a particular value; to appropri- **11–12** ate this feature is accordingly of qualitative significance. This is particularly true of dramatic works and films. In periods when stock dramas made the staple of so much English theatre, there were frequent allegations of

---

[38] *Schweppes v. Wellington* [1984] F.S.R. 210 ("Schlurppes" label intended as joke; plaintiff not amused); *Williamson Music v. Pearson Partnership* [1987] F.S.R. 97; Phillips (1984) 43 Camb. L.J. 245.

[39] Younger J., in the *Glyn* case (n. 35, above) at 268, notes the absence of decisions finding infringement in "burlesque" cases.

[40] See paras 11–75—11–82, below.

[41] Cases on the subject decided before the modern notion of infringement had fully appeared must be treated with caution. But see *D'Almaine v. Boosey* (1835) 1 Y. & C. Ex. 288; *Dickens v. Lee* (1844) 8 Jur. 183; *Tinsley v. Lacy* (1863) 1 H. & M. 747; *Valcarenghi v. Gramophone* [1928–1935] Mac. C.C. 301.

[42] Jervis C.J., *Sweet v. Benning* (1855) 16 C.B. 459 at 483.-

[43] [1980] R.P.C. 213; Dworkin [1979] E.I.P.R. 117.

[44] (1889) 40 Ch. D. 500; and see *Spectravest v. Aperknit* [1988] F.S.R. 161. The digital sampling of pop-songs provides a current example.

[45] *Electronic Techniques v. Critchley* [1997] F.S.R. at 408–410.

improper borrowing. After 1911, a series of cases[46] settled that "if the plot of a story, whether it be found in a play or in a novel, is taken bodily with or without some minor additions or subtractions for the purposes of a stage play or cinema film, there is no doubt about the case".[47] It was not necessary to copy the actual words used to work out the plot.[48] The same approach has now been applied to non-literal copying of computer programs.[49]

This approach shows the concept of mere ideas being confined to "starting point" conceptions—it would be no more than an idea, for instance, to conceive of a play about the return of a husband who has been presumed dead.[50] Where the works in question are both non-dramatic, probably more by way of detailed incident and language must be taken before there is substantial copying.[51] Where the works are artistic, and the Court is testing sufficient similarity by appeal to the eye, stress is sometimes laid upon the "feeling and artistic character" of the plaintiff's work,[52] an idea that can be extended to the screen displays of a computer.[53]

(d) *Nature of plaintiff's effort*

11–13 In some cases, the plaintiff's "skill, labour and judgment" form a distinct part of the whole result. This may well be so where the effort consists of such secondary work as editing, compiling or selecting material. A Court will treat the whole work as the subject of copyright.[54] But whether there is substantial taking falls to be judged by reference to the plaintiff's contribution. In *Warwick Film v. Eisinger*,[55] an author published an edited version of Oscar Wilde's trials, a transcript of which had earlier appeared. He acquired copyright in the whole by virtue of his work in selection and providing linking passages. But a defendant who took from it passages of the transcript but very little of the author's editing was held not to infringe. This neatly adjusts the scope of protection to the author's literary effort.

---

[46] *e.g. Corelli v. Gray* (1913) 30 T.L.R. 116, CA; Scrutton L.J., *Vane v. Famous Players* [1928–1935] Mac. C.C. 6 at 8 (particularly significant in the age of silent film). One earlier decision at least had required appropriation of actual dialogue; *Scholtz v. Amasis* [1905–1910] Mac. C.C. 216; *cf.* also *Chatterton v. Cave* (1878) 3 App. Cas. 483.

[47] Maugham J., *Kelly v. Cinema Houses* [1928–1935] Mac. C.C. 362; *Dagnall v. British Film* [1928–1935] Mac. C.C. 391.

[48] In *Fernald v. Jay Lewis* (1953) [1975] F.S.R. 499, even the taking of one episode out of a novel for a film was held to infringe when the literary characteristics of the episode were all copied and there were some startling similarities of dialogue.

[49] See paras 13–31—13–35, below.

[50] An example given by Scrutton L.J., *Vane* case (n. 46, above) at 8–9; and see *de Manduit v. Gaumont British* [1936–45] Mac. C.C. 292.

[51] Copinger, para. 480, suggests that the same may be true where a non-dramatic work is turned into a drama; but *cf.* the *Corelli* and *Vane* cases (n. 46, above); Lahore, para. 1144.

[52] *e.g.* Somervell L.J., *Bauman v. Fussell*, (1953) [1978] R.P.C. 485 at 487.

[53] See paras 13–43—13–45, below.

[54] *Ladbroke* case (n. 24, above).

[55] [1969] 1 Ch. 508; see also *John Fairfax v. Australian Consolidated Press* (1960) 60 S.R. (N.S.W.) 413.

The same approach can be seen to apply to some cases where the real skill lies in some commercial assessment distinct from the expressive content of the work: thus in the football pool coupon cases,[56] where it is the particular selection that is so significant, protection goes to taking the selection more or less as a whole. This correlation of protection with achievement is not easily made in all such cases. Where, for instance, the skill consists in recording someone else's performance,[57] it is arguable that there should be infringement only where some considerable part of the whole is taken. The same might be said of the entrepreneurial copyrights—particularly that for typographical format, since it is not associated with the artistic execution of performers, directors or the like. But this sort of consideration is at present speculative.[58]

(e) Extent of plaintiff's effort

If the plaintiff's labour, skill and judgment have only been just enough to **11–14** earn him copyright, infringement may arise only where there is exact imitation of such features as are of some individuality. In *Kenrick v. Lawrence*,[59] the plaintiff claimed copyright in a simple drawing of a hand, made with the intention of showing voters where to register their vote on a ballot form. But it was held that only an exact copy of the drawing would infringe, if the plaintiff were not to be conceded a monopoly in drawings of hands for this and other purposes. Through this consideration also the Court is able to take account of the overall merit of the plaintiff's work.

(f) Manner in which the defendant has taken advantage of plaintiff's work

Where the plaintiff's work records information, the use that a defendant **11–15** may make of it for his own purposes has been carefully circumscribed. The defendant is entitled to use the plaintiff's work as a source of ideas or information if he takes it as a starting point for his own collation of information or as a means of checking his own independent research.[60] However, he is not entitled to copy what the plaintiff has done as a substitute for exercising his own labour, skill and judgment. Moreover, he will not escape having his conduct so regarded merely by taking the plaintiff's work and checking that its contents are accurate. Thus it was improper to compile a street directory by sending out slips for checking, which contained entries from the plaintiff's directory.[61] Equally, it is wrong

---

[56] See para. 10–07, above.
[57] In so far as this is properly the subject of copyright: *cf.* para. 10–35, above.
[58] See further para. 11–40, below.
[59] (1890) 25 Q.B.D. 99. Contrast the cases on plays and novels: para. 11–12, above.
[60] See *Jarrold v. Houston* (1857) 3 K. & J. 708; *Pike v. Nicholas* (1869) L.R. 5 Ch. App. 251; *Hogg v. Scott* (1874) L.R. 18 Eq. 444.
[61] *Kelly v. Morris* (1866) L.R. 1 Eq. 677; see also *Morris v. Ashbee* (1868) L.R. 7 Eq. 34 (poacher turned gamekeeper). The Whitford Committee (Cmnd. 6732, 1977) paras 862–863 considered that new versions of the Ordnance Survey would be infringed if details were systematically copied onto other maps; see also *Sands & McDougall v. Robinson* (1917) 23 C.L.R. 49, HC (Aust.).

to adopt the same quotations which have been selected for a critical edition of a Shakespeare play,[62] or an account of historical incidents which digest the available sources.[63] In such cases, a defendant who is shown to have adopted the plaintiff's imaginative embellishments or plain errors will be in particular jeopardy.[64]

(g) *Whether the defendant's use will seriously interfere with the plaintiff's exploitation of his own work*

11–16 While infringement may occur even if there is no likelihood of competition between plaintiff and defendant, the possibility of such competition or its absence may nevertheless be treated as a relevant factor. This factor undoubtedly played a more significant role while copyright was still in the process of acquiring its character as a full right of property, and before substantial taking was distinguished from notions of "fair use".[65] Nonetheless the factor remains a practical consideration that courts are unlikely ever entirely to discount.[66] Thus it is referred to by Farwell J. in deciding that four brief lines from a popular song did not infringe when taken as a heading for a serial story in the *Red Star Weekly*.[67]

(h) *Reproduction by the original author*

11–17 Suppose that an author creates a work, and subsequently, at a time when he does not own the copyright,[68] he reproduces it in a second work. Some concession in his favour seems called for, in order to allow him to continue doing the kind of work at which he is proficient. But across the spectrum of copyright activity it is difficult to know how far judges would accord him any greater freedom than is permitted to others. In respect of artistic works, a special compromise is embodied in legislation: the artist may make substantial reproductions, even using the same mould, sketch or similar plan, provided that the subsequent work does not repeat or imitate the main design of the earlier work.[69] Where other types of work are

---

[62] Collins M.R., *Moffatt & Page v. Gill* (1902) 86 L.T. 465 at 471; and see *Blackie v. Lothian* (1921) 29 C.L.R. 396, HC (Aust.).

[63] *Harman v. Osborne* [1967] 2 All E.R. 324; *Ravenscroft v. Herbert* [1980] R.P.C. 193.

[64] *Harman* case (n. 63, above).

[65] Thus initially such activities as translation and abridgment did not count as infringement.

[66] *Chappell v. Thompson* [1928–1935] Mac. C.C. 467 at 471. Note also Parker J., *Weatherby v. International Horse Agency* [1910] 1 Ch. 297 at 305: ". . . the nature of the two publications and the likelihood of their entering into competition with each other is not only a relevant but may even be a determining factor in the case. But . . . an unfair use may be made of one book in the preparation of another, even if there is no likelihood of competition between the former and the latter. After all copyright is property. . . ."

[67] *Chappell v. Thompson* (n. 66, above); and see *Ravenscroft v. Herbert* [1980] R.P.C. 193.

[68] If he has given up rights by assignment, his freedom to copy the work may be governed by its express terms.

[69] CDPA 1988, s. 64, based upon *Preston v. Tuck* [1926] Ch. 667.

concerned, a similar approach might well be adopted: the relation between the two end products would be considered rather than the relation between the first work and what has been copied from it. The fact that the author made his reproduction unconsciously (if he can be believed) would probably enhance any claim not to have infringed.[70]

(4) Infringement carried out by others[71]

Infringement of copyright being a tort, in the ordinary run of things an **11–18** employer will be vicariously liable[72] for any infringement committed by an employee in the course of his employment and for the acts of independent contractors which he specifically requested. Under earlier law, these principles seem to have delimited the scope of one person's liability for infringements committed by another.[73] But, in contrast with the case of patents,[74] judges have more recently been ready enough to extend the scope of responsibility for the infringement of copyright committed by others.

In this they have been assisted by the legislature, which has introduced three forms of infringement: (1) "authorising" infringement by others[75]; (2) "permitting" a place of public entertainment to be used for performance of a work[76]; and (3) providing apparatus for performing, playing or showing a work, etc.[77] (Of these, heads (2) and (3) are now forms of secondary infringement which require proof of the defendant's complicity in ways which will be described later).[78]

"Authorise" has been read as bearing its dictionary meaning of "sanc- **11–19** tion, countenance or approve".[79] In line with these broad synonyms, it has been said that "indifference, exhibited by acts of commission or omission, may reach a degree from which authorisation or permission may be inferred".[80] Accordingly in a case concerning performing rights (which has

---

[70] On the difficulties of deciding this, see *Industrial Furnaces v. Reaves* [1970] R.P.C. 605 at 623–624.

[71] See Stuckey [1984] U.N.S.W.L.J. 77.

[72] For vicarious liability, see para. 2–09, above. To tell a servant not to infringe will not affect this liability if he defies instructions in the course of employment: *PRS v. Mitchell & Booker* [1924] 1 K.B. 762; *cf. PRS v. Bradford Corp.* [1917–1923] Mac. C.C. 309.

[73] See especially *Karno v. Pathé* (1909) 100 L.T. 260—film distributor did not "cause" representation of a play in public by supplying a theatre operator with film of it; only the operator infringed. *cf. Falcon v. Famous Players* [1926] 2 K.B. 474.

[74] See paras 6–17—6–19, above.

[75] Now CDPA 1988, s. 16(2).

[76] Now CDPA 1988, s. 25. This relates only to literary, dramatic and musical works; a defence concerning non-profit activities has been dropped.

[77] Now CDPA 1988, s. 26.

[78] See para. 11–37, below.

[79] Tomlin J., *Evans v. Hulton* [1923–1928] Mac. C.C. 51; Bankes L.J., *Falcon v. Famous Players* (n. 73, above) at 491.

[80] *PRS v. Ciryl* [1914] 1 K.B. 1 at 9; *Moorhouse v. University of N.S.W.* (1975) 6 A.L.R. 193, [1976] R.P.C. 151; Catterns (1976) 23 Bull. U.S. Cop. 213. The authorisation will be caught wherever it is given, provided that it is to infringe in the United Kingdom: *Abkco v. Music Collection* [1995] E.M.L.R. 449, CA.

been the commonest field of application for these provisions) both authorising and permitting may be alleged, and they amount to much the same
thing. "Permitting" performance is expressly stated to be subject to the
defence of reasonable belief that there would be no infringement[81];
"authorising" is not the subject of specific exceptions, but the meaning
given to the word excludes liability when the defendant could not reasonably expect that another would infringe.[82] It is also necessary to show an act
of infringement which has occurred as a result of the authorisation.[83]

To take some examples: people who organise public entertainments by
hiring musicians as independent contractors are likely to be authorising or
permitting infringement if they simply leave the choice of music to the
musicians.[84] Accordingly they ought to procure an appropriate licence from
the Performing Right Society themselves or require the musicians to do so.
Where the defendant is not the organiser of the entertainment, but only,
for instance, the owner of the hall, he is unlikely to be held culpable if he is
simply "indifferent" to the choice of music.[85]

11–20   In other fields, authorising may also occur by implication. A person who
transfers the serial rights in a book authorises their publication in that
form, since the specific intent is apparent.[86] An Australian university was
held to have authorised infringement by allowing library readers to use its
copying machine, without giving precise information about the limits to
copying within the copyright legislation and without attempting any supervision to prevent infringement: the degree of indifference was too blatant to
escape liability.[87] On the other hand, those who provide the copying
machinery or the material for home taping will rarely be found to have the
necessary control over what is then done, to be "authorised".[88] The
manufacturer of a twin-deck cassette recorder did not authorise infringement of particular copyrights, even though he advertised the capabilities of
his product, since he also drew attention to copyright obligations.[89]

---

[81] CDPA 1988, s. 25(1).
[82] See *Ciryl* case (n. 80, above).
[83] *RCA v. Fairfax* [1982] R.P.C. 91 (newspaper article suggesting the possibility of home taping); *WEA International v. Hanimax* (1988) 10 I.P.R. 349.
[84] *PRS v. Bradford Corp.* (n. 72, above); *Australian PRA v. Canterbury-Bankstown Club* [1964–1965] N.S.W.R. 138; *Australian PRA v. Miles* [1962] N.S.W.R. 405; *Australian PRA v. Koolman* [1969] N.Z.L.R. 273. *cf. Monaghan v. Taylor* (1885) 2 T.L.R. 685 (entrepreneur present); *PRS v. Bray UDC* [1930] A.C. 377 (entrepreneur approved list).
[85] *Vigneux v. Canadian PRS* [1945] A.C. 108 at 123. *cf. Winstone v. Wurlitzer* [1946] V.L.R. 338; *Adelaide Corp. v. Australian PRS* (1928) 40 C.L.R. 481 (despite knowledge that infringement likely); *Ciryl* case (n. 72, above) (defendant only managing director of entrepreneur company); *Performances (N.Z.) v. Lion Breweries* [1980] F.S.R. 1.
[86] *Evans v. Hulton* [1923–28] Mac. C.C. 51; and see *Falcon v. Famous Players* (n. 73, above).
[87] *Moorhouse* case (n. 80, above); in another context, see *Standen Engineering v. Spalding* [1984] F.S.R. 554.
[88] See *A. & M. Records v. Audio Magnetics* [1979] F.S.R. 1; *CBS v. Ames* [1981] R.P.C. 407.
[89] *CBS U.K. v. Amstrad* [1988] R.P.C. 567; and see para. 17–17, below.

2. CLASSES OF PROHIBITED ACT

The 1988 Act defines the "acts restricted by the copyright" in general **11–21** terms, each type applying to the various categories of work unless a specific exception is given. The 1956 Act, by contrast, took each category of subject-matter and listed the relevant acts of infringement. The current technique seems rather more straightforward. In the Table (head 7) (on pp. 330 to 331) the restricted acts are listed in two groups, the first being concerned with making reproductions, adaptations and the like, the second with transient activities involving a performance or broadcast.

In British patent law, as we have seen, the monopoly right was extended to use, as well as manufacture and sale, thus enabling the patentee and his associates to exercise whatever control over their own products seemed advantageous. In British copyright law, the same basic assumption has not been made.[90] The typical act of infringement has been the making of copies. Control over them and their contents once legitimately made has been conceded only on a case-by-case basis: the rights over public performance and broadcasting are one form of control over use; the rental right in sound recordings, films and computer programs is another.[91]

Often enough the various rights that make up copyright are separately assigned or made the subject of an exclusive licence.[92] The assignee or exclusive licensee is then entitled to sue only in respect of his own part and it may be necessary to decide just what his part is. If the division up has been made by reference to the different acts listed in the statute, then the question will turn on the meaning of the statutory words.[93] If some other, more specific right has been conceded (such as the right to translate into French, or the right to engrave a picture for a particular book) then the particular assignment or licence will require interpretation.

The 1988 Act distinguishes two broad categories of infringement: **11–22** restricted acts (or primary infringement) which occur without regard to the defendant's state of mind[94]; and secondary infringements which are committed only if the defendant knew or had reason to believe a defined state of affairs relating to infringement. Under each of the following heads primary and secondary infringement will be considered separately.

---

[90] The supposed *droit de destination* in French and Belgian copyright law fulfils much the same function as the British patent law doctrine; it allows, for instance, a rental right to be read into the law without specific provision: see E.C. Commission, Green Paper, *Copyright and the Challenge of Technology* (Com. (88) 172) 146.

[91] See paras 11–27—11–29, below, and consider also the special scheme for the public lending of books: paras 13–99—13–102 below.

[92] See paras 12–11 *et seq.*, below.

[93] See, *e.g. Chappell v. Columbia* [1914] 2 Ch. 124.

[94] Thus making the deliberateness or otherwise of the defendant's conduct not relevant to the assessment of infringement: Laddie J., *Electronic Techniques v. Critchley Components* [1997] F.S.R. 401 at 410.

(1) Rights concerned with reproduction and adaptation

(a) *Primary infringement: copying*

11–23 Copyright in a work may be infringed by copying it, issuing copies of it to the public, or by making an adaptation of it.[95] Copying a work, so far as concerns literary, dramatic, musical and artistic copyright, means "reproducing the work in a material form"—a formula originally introduced in the 1911 Act.[96] Some of the material forms are now specifically listed. These include: (1) storing the work in any medium by electronic means—which clearly covers computer storage and presumably extends to the incorporation of the work in a record or film[97] and the transcription into digital form; and (2) converting a two-dimensional artistic work into three dimensions, and vice versa.[98] But other changes of form may also count: for instance, turning a story into a ballet,[99] copying a photograph by painting,[1] making a knitting pattern into a fabric,[2] and turning a drawing, such as a cartoon, into a revue sketch.[3] Novel analogies can be made, subject always to the need to satisfy the test of substantial taking. The scope of "copying" is stretched to its very borders by section 17(6) of the 1988 Act which extends liability as far as the making of copies which are transient or are incidental to some other use. Yet it is now of great practical significance in the provision of electronic data in response to individual orders: and it raises questions about the limits currently placed upon performance rights.[4]

11–24 There are other important ramifications of this crucial idea as copyright questions develop around modern electronic techniques, particularly in the field of computerised design and manufacture. On the one hand, it may seem only appropriate to extend the range of the law to embrace a new technique for copying. On the other, there is an evident danger of going too far (particularly with a right so readily conceded and long-lasting as copyright) if it were to become infringement merely to carry out another person's instructions to do something (for example bake a cake[5]).

Although, as we shall see, the statutory provision that a 2-D artistic work can be reproduced in 3-D contributed crucially to the concept of copyright

---

[95] CDPA 1988, ss. 16–18, 21.

[96] *ibid.*, s. 17(2).

[97] *cf.* CA 1956, s. 48(1) "reproduction", which specified these cases; *Ocular Sciences v. Aspect Vision Care* [1997] R.P.C. at 418.

[98] CDPA 1988, s. 17(3).

[99] *Holland v. Van Damm* [1936–1945] Mac. C.C. 69.

[1] *Bauman v. Fussell* (1953) [1978] R.P.C. 485, CA; *Hanfstaegl v. W. H. Smith* [1905] 1 Ch. 519.

[2] *Lerose v. Hawick Jersey* [1974] R.P.C. 42; *cf. Dicks v. Brooks* (1880) Ch.D. 22 (pre-1911 legislation).

[3] *Bradbury, Agnew v. Day* (1916) 32 T.L.R. 349 (*cf.* the pre-1911 position in *Hanfstaegl v. Empire Palace* [1894] 2 Ch. 1). Note the absence of a general performing right in artistic works.

[4] See paras 11–32, 11–56, below.

[5] For some teasing on the subject, see Mout-Bouwman [1988] E.I.P.R. 234.

affecting industrial production, the courts have in the main refused to hold that a *literary* work (recipes, etc.) can be infringed by making an object in accordance with the work.[6] However, Jacob J. appears now to have departed from this by holding that if instructions about the component of an electrical circuit diagram (ohms for a resistor, etc.) were worked out into a "net list" and then reproduced in a circuit board without authority, there can be infringement of the literary copyright in the plaintiff's net list and even the literary aspects of the circuit diagram.[7] If developed, this line of thinking might provide literary copyright in structural information about the human and other genomes which would be infringed whenever the information was copied for use in genetic engineering.[7a] The general issue thus raised deserves anxious consideration, taking account in particular of whether the copyright laws of other countries are in the least likely to take a similar turn.

Quite apart from this, certain acts of adaptation constitute infringement: **11–25** turning a literary work into a dramatic work or vice versa; translating either kind of work or turning it into a picture form (such as a comic strip); arranging or transcribing a musical work (by, for instance, harmonising or orchestrating it); arranging or altering a computer program, or translating it into another computer language.[8]

The 1988 Act is not so specific as its predecessor about what acts of **11–26** "copying" infringe sound recording, film, broadcasting and cable-casting copyright. Presumably, as before, this includes making recordings or films that are substantial copies of those things. But it is not infringement of copyright to make it afresh. A film is the recording of moving images; it is not the dramatic work or other content embodied in it.[9]

Copying also includes specific cases. Making a photograph of the whole or a substantial part of any image forming part of a film, broadcast or cable programme—for instance for a post-card or poster—is such an infringement.[10] The publisher's copyright in typographical format is infringed solely by making a facsimile copy, even if it is enlarged or reduced.[11]

---

[6] *Brigid Foley v. Ellot* [1982] R.P.C. 433 (knitting pattern for machine); *Duriron v. Hugh Jennings* [1984] F.S.R. 1, CA (table of dimensions).

[7] *Anacon v. Environmental Research* [1994] F.S.R. 359; Reynolds and Brownlow [1994] E.I.P.R. 399. The circuit diagram was an artistic work, but the defendant, employing a computer to obtain its own layout, did not reproduce the physical form of the diagram. Accordingly, there was no infringement of the special design right in the topography of the circuit: for which, see para. 14–50, below. The line of argument has been accepted in *Sandman v. Panasonic* [1998] F.S.R. 651; but doubted in *Electronic Techniques v. Critchley Components* [1997] F.S.R. 401; see above, para. 10–14.

[7a] See esp. Laddie *et al.*, Chap. 21.

[8] CDPA 1988, s. 21. Section 21(5) suggests that these forms of infringement are closely related to infringement by reproduction in a material form: "No inference shall be drawn from this section as to what does or does not amount to copying the work."

[9] *Norowzian v. Arks (No. 1)* [1998] F.S.R. 394; *cf. ibid. (No. 2)* [1997] F.S.R. 79.

[10] CDPA 1988, s. 17(4), giving statutory effect to *Spelling Goldberg v. B.P.C. Publishing* [1981] R.P.C. 280, CA.

[11] CDPA 1988, ss. 17, 178 "facsimile copy."

(b) *Primary infringement: issuing copies, rental and lending*

11–27 Issuing copies of a work to the public[12] is a form of primary infringement which relates to the first release of the copies into circulation. When originally introduced in 1988, this form of infringement did not apply to the parallel importation of products legitimately marketed in other countries.[13] Under E.C. law, these could normally be freely imported from other Member States.[14] From non-Member States they also might give rise to liability for *secondary* infringement, if the requisite state of mind could be imputed to the defendant. This is discussed below.[15]

It is the intent of E.C. authorities that the exclusive right of reproduction should not be treated as exhausted by any distribution of copies outside the EEA as a whole.[16] In consequence, parallel importation of such copies into the EEA from beyond its borders should become a form of primary infringement. The matter has so far been dealt with in Directives only in relation to the literary copyright in computer programs, and the related rights given to performers, record and film producers and broadcasting organisations.[17] Even in these cases, the legal proposition is oblique: the Directives state that the rights are exhausted by first authorised sale within the Community, thereby raising the implication that there is no exhaustion of the right by sale outside the Community. (The ploy avoids drawing political attention to the parallel import bans.) In pursuit of this interpretation, the 1988 Act has been amended.[18] To import and sell legitimate copies of a work from a non-E.C. state counts as issuing the copies to the British public and so needs to be licensed.

11–28 Despite the general restriction of the primary distribution right to initial sale and other disposal, it has nevertheless been extended to cover important forms of renting copies. The object has been to secure some measure of return to copyright owners from material which is likely to be privately copied without practical redress. The 1988 Act introduced temporary-use protection only for the rental (not the lending) of sound recordings, films and computer programs—the three cases where renting was at all widespread. The E.C. Directive on Rental, Lending and Related

---

[12] CDPA 1988, s. 18; previously only first publication of the *work* constituted primary infringement: *Infabrics v. Jaytex* [1982] A.C. 1 (a narrow view of the 1956 Act provision).

[13] CDPA 1988 s. 18(2), which (save for computer programs) still states that issuing copies to the public is not concerned with copies previously put into circulation in the United Kingdom or elsewhere.

[14] By virtue of the Rome Treaty, Arts 30 and 36: see paras 1–51, 1–52, above, paras 18–02 *et seq.*, below.

[15] See para. 11–29, below.

[16] See para. 1–58, above, paras 18–17 *et seq.*, below.

[17] Software Directive 91/250, Art. 4(c); Rental, Lending and Related Rights Directive 92/100, Art. 9(2) and note Art. 1(4).

[18] CDPA 1988, s. 18(3); Copyright and Related Rights Regs. 1996, reg. 9(3), effective, December 1, 1996.

Rights, however, expands this[19] and British legislation now gives rental and lending rights in literary, dramatic and musical works,[20] most artistic works, and films and sound recordings.[21] Rental is broadly defined to cover the temporary provision of copies "for direct or indirect economic or commercial advantage", but this will be on terms that they will or may be returned—thus excluding any electronic provision. Lending relates only to loans through a publicly accessible establishment, such as a public library.[22] A protective element in the scheme requires that once authors and performers assign their rental rights in a sound recording or audio-visual work to a producer (a practice so much to be expected in the case of films that there is a statutory presumption in its favour),[23] they will remain entitled to equitable remuneration.[24] They have no power to waive their entitlement to equitable remuneration, although they can exercise it only personally or through a collecting society. This legal intervention has the merit of safeguarding the benefits of a new right which is being attached to existing works. Its long-term effects on the overall bargaining position of authors is much less easy to predict.

(c) *Secondary infringement: dealings with copies*

Infringement of all forms of copyright may be committed by a defendant **11–29** concerned in the commercial exploitation of copies, if he knows or has reason to believe that the copies were infringements when they were made.[25] In the case of imported copies this includes "notional infringements", that is copies that would have infringed if they had been made in Britain or would have constituted a breach of an exclusive licence agreement relating to that work.[26] The stages of exploitation in question are: importing, possessing in the course of a business, selling, letting for hire, offering or exposing for sale or hire, and exhibiting in public in the course of a business, and distributing either in the course of a business, or otherwise to an extent that prejudicially affects the copyright owner.[27]

---

[19] Directive 92/100; para. 9–18, above; Reinbothe and von Lewinski, *The E.C. Directive on Rental and Lending Rights and on Piracy* (1993). For the constitutionality of the Directive, see, *Metronome Musik v. Music Point Hokamp* [1997] E.M.L.R. 93, ECJ.

[20] *i.e.* other than architectural works and works of applied art.

[21] CDPA 1988. s. 18A (effective, August 1, 1996). Note that the section confers on producers of films.

[22] s. 18A (2)–(6). A number of exceptions include loans for performance, for exhibition and for on-the-spot reference; inter-library loans; and lending by an educational establishment (s. 36A). Public libraries which charge no more than operating costs engage in lending, not rental. Curiously, the original work is included within the notion of "copies". For the preservation of the Public Lending right scheme for books, see below, para. 13–101; and for the public lending of other material, para. 13–102.

[23] s. 93A, 191F.

[24] s. 93B, 93C, 191G, 191H. For the jurisdiction of the Copyright Tribunal, s. 117, 124.

[25] CDPA 1988, ss. 22–24, 27. As already noted, the person who first puts copies into circulation commits the primary infringement of issuing copies to the public: para. 11–27, above. For infringement by telecommunication of text (s. 24(2), see para. 13–55, below).

[26] *ibid.*, s. 27(3); see paras 12–14—12–18, below.

[27] CDPA 1988, s. 23. For parallel importation, see below, para. 12–14.

As to the defendant's state of mind in secondary infringement, the previous law required it to be shown that the defendant had knowledge that the copies in issue were infringements.[28] But that had been read as requiring only that he had "notice of facts such as would suggest to a reasonable man that a breach of copyright was being committed".[29] The new phrase, "knew or had reason to believe", has been understood in the same sense.[30] It is no defence genuinely to believe, or to rely upon legal advice, that what is being done does not, as a matter of law, amount to copyright infringement[31].

(2) Rights concerned with performance, broadcasting and cable-casting

(a) *Primary infringement: the various performing rights*

11–30 The extension of copyright from the making of copies to the giving of public performances began in 1833. With modern technology, this has grown into a bundle of related aspects of copyright that can be loosely grouped as "performing rights". These are listed in the Table (head 7: on pp. 330 to 331) performing, playing or showing a work in public; broadcasting it or including it in a cable programme (cable-casting).[32]

The possibilities of infringement in this field have become complex. If, for instance, a copyright musical work is performed to a public audience at the same time as being televised, both the performance and the broadcast require a licence. If the broadcast is received and shown publicly, this calls for licence of the copyright in the music, and (save where the showing is free) of that in the broadcast.[33] If the original performance was recorded this will be either in the form of a sound recording or a film with associated sound track (each of which will be a form of reproduction). If either the recording or the film is broadcast, this needs a licence. However, the owner of copyright in the sound recording or film (as distinct from that in the musical work) has no right in respect of free public playings or showings of the broadcast.[34]

11–31 Performance is too ephemeral a phenomenon for it to be easy for copyright owners to enforce their performing rights individually. Those who have copyright in musical works and associated lyrics have been leaders in

---

[28] CA 1956, ss. 5, 16.
[29] Harvey J., *Albert v. Hoffnung* (1922) 22 S.R. (N.S.W.) 75 at 81; followed by Whitford J., *Infabrics v. Jaytex* [1978] F.S.R. 451 at 464–465; and see at 467: was the defendant's selector "put on inquiry?" Did he turn "a blind eye to an inquiry which he should have known he ought to have made?" Once apprised of the truth he was allowed a number of days to make his own inquiries: *Van Dusen v. Kritz* [1936] 2 K.B. 176.
[30] *LA Gear v. Hi-Tec* [1992] F.S.R. 121, CA; *ZYX Music v. King* [1997] E.M.L.R. 319, CA.
[31] *Sillitoe v. McGraw-Hill Books* [1993] F.S.R. 545; *ZYX Music v. King*, above, n. 30.
[32] CDPA 1988, ss. 19, 20.
[33] *cf. ibid.*, s. 72.
[34] See *ibid.*, s. 72; para. 11–47, below.

establishing societies for the collective enforcement of their rights. The great proliferation in the exploitation of music through recordings and broadcasts has made this economically feasible in many countries, and an international network of performing right societies now exists.[35] In Britain, where record companies have performing rights in their recordings, they have a separate collecting society to assert their rights.[36] In various countries, the economic power of collecting societies has become suspect: the case for public surveillance is discussed in the next chapter.[37]

The potential ability of electronic data services to deliver a "showing" or **11–32** "hearing" down an individual line poses difficulties for the present range of copyright protection. Already copyright may be infringed by the most transient electronic storage[38] and by rental. Yet performance and similar acts do not infringe if they are not public.[39] To this novel problem, we return later.[40] The old categories may indeed be breaking down in the face of new technologies. What is important to preserve is the notion that copyright applies only to a defined set of circumstances and not to all uses to which its content might be put.

(b) *Performance in public*

It has been left to the courts to draw the line between performances in **11–33** public and in private. In 1884, the Court of Appeal characterised as "quasi-domestic"—and therefore private—an amateur performance of a play in Guy's Hospital to an audience of doctors and their families, nurses, attendants and students.[41] This was regarded (even in the decision itself) as marking the extreme outpost of free territory. To be in public a performance does not have to be to a paying audience or by paid performers[42]; it is enough that entertainment is being offered as an incident of some

---

[35] For the history, particularly of the British organisation, the Performing Right Society (PRS), see Peacock and Weir, *The Composer in the Market Place* (1975); McFarlane, *Copyright: the Development and Exercise of the Performing Right* (1980), Chaps 6–11. The PRS collects on behalf of foreign societies for British use of their repertoires, and it has arrangements to receive equivalent royalties from the foreign societies on its own members' behalf. The Confédération Internationale des Sociétés d'Auteurs et Compositeurs (CISAC) has played an important role in settling the terms of the international system of collection and distribution.

[36] Called Phonographic Performance Ltd (PPL). See para. 9–50, above.

[37] See para. 12–53, below.

[38] See para. in 12–23, below. The point is still doubtful in most other copyright laws.

[39] It has been argued that on-line supply should be treated as rental under the Rental and Lending Directive, even though no material copy is temporarily delivered: Reinbothe and von Lewinski, *The E.C. Directive on Rental and Lending Rights and on Piracy* (1993), paras 41–42. That sounds like drafters' wish-fulfilment.

[40] See paras 13–76ff., below.

[41] *Duck v. Bates* (1884) 13 Q.B.D. 843; under the 1833 Act, the requirement was in any case that the performance be in a "place of public entertainment".

[42] *PRS v. Hawthornes Hotel* [1933] Ch. 855; and see *Harms v. Martans Club* [1927] 1 Ch. 526 (dance club).

commercial activity (such as running a hotel, or even a shop that is seeking to sell the records being played)[43] or of industrial production ("music while you work").[44] Even such worthy institutions as the Women's Institute and a football club's supporters' association engage in public performance, whether they restrict audiences to their own members or allow in guests[45]; and the 1988 Act makes clear that a school play or other performance will not be exempt if parents or friends are present.[46] Greene M.R. laid particular stress on the need to consider the relationship of the audience to the owner of the copyright rather than to the performers.[47] This is one way of emphasising the primacy of the owner's entitlement to an economic return from his proprietary rights; the fact that an organisation is socially desirable does not normally give it a claim to free use of copyright material. The one general exception concerns the sound recording right (as distinct from copyright in music and words) where records are played at a charitable or similar club or organisation.[48]

(c) *Broadcasting*

11–34 The broadcasting of every type of copyright work, other than a typographical format, requires authorisation.[49] However, the copyright in a sound recording (as distinct from any copyright in works recorded) is subject to a statutory licence for broadcasting.[50] This limitation was adopted in Britain as the result of a critical report by the Monopolies and Mergers Commission concerning the demands of the record companies' collecting society, Phonographic Performance Ltd.[51] The rate will, if necessary be set by the Copyright Tribunal in accordance with a prescribed statutory procedure.

With the advance of satellite technology, broadcasting has become an increasingly international medium. A country may receive many more transmissions than would be made by its own network of sound and television broadcasts. Broadcasting organisations have accordingly insisted that, in the interests of simplicity and certainty, the "up-leg" of a transmission alone should require licensing. Under the present British approach, the licence will be under the law of the place where the "up-leg" occurs, and the fee will take account of the audience size in the various countries which may feel its footprint.[52]

---

[43] *PRS v. Harlequin Record* [1979] F.S.R. 233.
[44] *Ernest Turner v. PRS* [1943] Ch. 167.
[45] *Jennings v. Stephens* [1936] Ch. 469; *PRS v. Rangers Club* [1975] R.P.C. 626; *Australian PRA v. Commonwealth Bank* (1992) 25 I.P.R. 157.
[46] CDPA 1988, s. 34(3).
[47] In the *Jennings* and *Turner* cases (nn. 44, 45, above).
[48] So a PRS licence remains necessary, though a PPL licence is not: CDPA 1988, s. 67. Note also the special provision to allow adaptations of broadcasts and cable-casts for the deaf, hard of hearing and handicapped: s. 74, para. 11–49, below.
[49] CDPA 1988, s. 20.
[50] CDPA 1988, ss. 135A–135G.
[51] See para. 13–57, below.
[52] For amendment needed to adopt the Satellite and Cable Directive, see para. 13–48, below.

Broadcasting stands on the brink of a further revolution, since the **11–35** medium is about to shift from a purely analogue base to a digital one. It will become possible to transmit immense quantities of digital material via a single satellite, and thousands of channels may become available, some for their own programmes and others for interactive selection of material by individuals.[53] While this may well change the whole economic structure of broadcasting, it is not at present apparent that the British copyright law on the subject needs change to accommodate digital broadcasting, since it already carries its own copyright, as well as copyright in protected materials which it may transmit. What has to be introduced is electronic means for monitoring and recording all the myriad works which are being broadcast.

(d) *Cable-casting*

The act of "including a work in a cable programme" is a form of primary **11–36** infringement,[54] which is defined in the same manner as that activity when it attracts its own copyright.[55] Since the Internet involves cabled communication, it is often arguable that making material available for down-loading falls within this type of infringing act. In this context, we return to the issue later.[56]

(e) *Secondary infringement: performances*

As with dealings in copies, certain activities connected with public perfor- **11–37** mances give rise to secondary infringement. These are: (1) permitting premises to be used for an infringing performance,[57] and (2) providing certain apparatus (for playing recordings, showing films and receiving broadcasts, etc.).[58] The former of these is closely linked to the concept of authorising infringement and has been mentioned in that context.[59] The latter is allied to secondary infringement involving infringing copies, and depends upon showing that a defendant knew or had reason to believe that the act in question—provision of the equipment or premises for it—is likely to lead to use involving infringement.[60]

---

[53] See further, paras 13–53 *et seq.*, below.
[54] CDPA 1988, s. 20.
[55] s. 7: however, the exclusion of immediate re-transmissions of broadcasts applies only to the question whether copyright has been acquired, not to infringement: see s. 7(6)(a).
[56] Below, para. 13–77.
[57] CDPA 1988, s. 25.
[58] *ibid.*, s. 26.
[59] See para. 11–18, above.
[60] CDPA 1988, s. 26(2), (3).

3. "FAIR DEALING" AND LIKE EXCEPTIONS

(1) Fair dealing

(a) *General*

11-38 The requirement of "substantial taking" prevents the owner from objecting to minor borrowings from his copyright work. And, as we have just seen, the requirement that a performance be in public means that his licence is unnecessary for a private performance, even of the complete work. In the modern Copyright Acts, other exceptions from the scope of copyright have been specified and the 1988 Act now has a lengthy list. Some of them, such as those relating to education, concern important conflicts of interest, and they will be discussed in their own context in Chapter 13. Here they are listed in order that they can be compared in the round.

11-39 The three most important of these exceptions turn upon a qualitative assessment. They exempt copying for certain purposes if it amounts to no more than "fair dealing". In these cases the courts are left to judge fairness in the light of all the circumstances. The Court of Appeal has recently encouraged a liberal approach to their interpretation.[61] But other exceptions are more factual; for instance, unduplicated copying in the course of instruction is exempt irrespective of the amount copied.

Before the 1911 Act, the three main "fair dealing" exceptions were foreshadowed in the case law as forms of "fair use", a concept that was not clearly distinguished from "insubstantial taking". If there is substantial copying, it is a nice question today how far the use could nevertheless be justified for a reason beyond the confines of the statutory exceptions. Certainly this would be difficult if the case was closely analogous to one of the statutory exceptions but just outside it; the more so if the statutory exceptions are to be strictly construed as limitations upon property rights.[62] Nonetheless a "defence" of publication in the public interest has been recognised to exist and now has a place in the statute.[63] In Australia it has been suggested that it is less extensive than in a claim based on breach of confidence[64]; but in England the tendency has been to treat the two cases alike.[65]

By relying almost wholly on specified statutory limitations, British copyright law differs both from United States law, where the concept of

---

[61] *Pro Sieben v. Carlton UK TV* [1999] E.M.L.R. 109; below, para. 13–04.
[62] This approach was taken in *Hawkes v. Paramount* [1934] Ch. 593, CA, to a fair dealing exception in the 1911 Act.
[63] CDPA 1988, s. 171(3), preserving rules of law preventing or restricting the enforcement of copyright, on grounds of public interest or otherwise. See further para. 11–57, below.
[64] *Commonwealth of Australia v. Fairfax* (1980) 32 A.L.R. 485. See also *Kennard v. Lewis* [1983] F.S.R. 346 (right-wing criticism of C.N.D. pamphlet).
[65] *e.g. Hubbard v. Vosper* [1972] 2 Q.B. 84, CA; *Beloff v. Pressdram* [1973] 1 All E.R. 241.

"fair use" has a scope that is both general and central, and authors' rights systems, which tend to have a general defence of private use.[66] In United Kingdom law, while neither "fair" nor "private" use forms a general ground of excusal in relation to the reproduction and related rights, the limitation to public use is written into the very definition of the various forms of performing right. As already noted, there is here a puzzling issue for the exploitation of new electronic media. Significantly, it has recently been said that it may be proper to take one copy of a whole work if the purpose is to use extracts in a way that is legitimate.[67]

(b) *Research or private study*

The first fair dealing exception is that covering purposes of research or private study,[68] which now applies to the copyright in literary, dramatic, musical and artistic works, and published editions. With this must be read (1) the more specific exceptions covering certain librarians and archivists[69]; (2) the exception for the inclusion of short passages of literary and dramatic works in collections for schools,[70] and the exceptions for copying and photocopying works in the course of instruction and examination and performing, playing or showing works in certain circumstances at schools, etc.[71]; and (3) for recording broadcasts and cable-casts.[72] The role of these defences is particularly important in the field of education and it is in that context that they will be discussed in more detail.[73] It is plain from the Parliamentary evolution of this defence that it may in principle cover research in commerce, industry and government. What is "fair" will presumably vary to fit each case.

11–40

(c) *Reporting current events*

The second fair dealing exception permits all works, other than photographs, to be used for reporting current events.[74] Photographs have been differently treated in order to preserve the full value of holding a unique

11–41

---

[66] For views of the future structure of exceptions, see Copyright Law Review Committee (Australia), *Simplification of the Copyright Act 1968*, Part 1 (1998); and see Rothnie in Sherman and Saunders (eds.) *From Berne to Geneva* (1997) Chap. 6. For U.S. perspectives, Gordon (1982) 82 Col. L.R. 1600; [1997] 8 J.L. & Info. Soc. 7; Netanel (1996) 106 Yale L.J. 283.

[67] *Pro Sieben v. Carlton UK TV* [1999] E.M.L.R. 109, 127, per Walker J.

[68] CDPA 1988, s. 29; for its history, Merkin and Black, *Copyright and Designs Law* (1993ff.), paras 10–17—10–18.

[69] *ibid.*, ss. 37–44.

[70] *ibid.*, s. 33.

[71] *ibid.*, ss. 32, 34, 36.

[72] *ibid.*, s. 35.

[73] See paras 13–11 *et seq.*, below.

[74] CDPA 1988, s. 30(2), (3). This may be in a newspaper or magazine, in which case sufficient acknowledgement is required; or in a sound recording, film, broadcast or cable-cast, where acknowledgement is not called for.

visual record of some person or event. To come within the exception, the event itself must be current and not the pretext for reviving historical information: the death of the Duchess of Windsor did not justify an exchange of letters between her and the Duke being published without copyright licence.[75] The exception must be read in conjunction with a number of cognate provisions.[76] Together they are of particular importance to the public-affairs media and they will be related to that field later.[77]

(d) *Criticism or review*

11–42 It is the third fair dealing exception that is most general of all, allowing works to be used for purposes of criticism or review (of themselves or another work), one precondition of fairness being that the source should be sufficiently acknowledged.[78] Despite its potential range, the defence has not been much elucidated in the case law. The Court of Appeal has held that the criticism or review may concern the ideas expressed as well as the mode of expression.[79] It has also been said that it cannot be "fair" to publish an unpublished work for this purpose, at least if it is known to have been improperly obtained.[80] And the courts will not permit wholesale borrowing to be dressed up as critical quotation.[81] Lord Denning M.R.'s remarks stressing that fair dealing is inevitably a matter of degree can usefully be applied not only to this head but in spirit equally to the other two:

> "You must consider first the number and extent of the quotations and extracts. Are they altogether too many and too long to be fair? Then you must consider the use made of them. If they are used as a basis for comment, criticism or review, that may be a fair dealing. If they are used to convey the same information as the author, for a rival purpose, they may be unfair. Next, you must consider the proportions. To take long extracts and attach short comments may be unfair. But short extracts and long comments may be fair. Other considerations may come to mind also. But, after all is said and done, it must be a matter of impression."[82]

---

[75] *Associated Newspapers v. News Group* [1986] R.P.C. 515; *Newspaper Licensing Agency v. Marks & Spencer* [1999] E.M.L.R. 369 (current events do not include life-style articles, etc.).

[76] Especially CDPA 1988, s. 31 (incidental inclusion); s. 58 (record of spoken words); s. 62 (artistic works on public display).

[77] See paras 13–04, 13–06, below.

[78] CDPA 1988, s. 30(1); Display of a foreign TV station's logo can suffice for acknowledgement: *Pro Sieben v. Carlton* [1999] E.M.L.R. 109, CA, as to material initially published anonymously: *PCR v. Dow Jones Telerate* [1998] F.S.R. 170.

[79] *Hubbard v. Vosper* [1972] 2 Q.B. 84 at 94–95, 98. See also *Time Warner v. Channel 4* [1994] E.M.L.R. 1, CA; *Pro Sieben v. Carlton*, above, n. 78; and see further, paras 13–04, 13–06.

[80] *British Oxygen v. Liquid Air* [1925] Ch. 383 at 393; but *cf. Beloff v. Pressdram* [1973] 1 All E.R. 241 at 264.

[81] *Mawman v. Tegg* (1826) 2 Russ. 385; *cf.* Megaw L.J., *Hubbard* case (n. 79, above) at 98.

[82] *Hubbard* case (n. 79, above) at 94.

(2) Other exceptions

Beyond the statutory categories of "fair dealing" and the like, there are **11–43** numerous exceptions which, as a whole, are not easily classified.

(a) *Exceptions designed to encourage collective licensing schemes*

As a matter of practicality, the 1988 Act aims to foster the administration **11–44** of copyright through licensing schemes which are conducted for groups of right-owners. Of the five specific cases, three prescribe an exception to infringement which is to operate in the absence of a certified licensing scheme covering the proposed use. These are: (1) recording of broadcasts, cable-casts and material contained in them for the purposes of an educational establishment[83]; (2) copying and issuing copies of the published abstracts of scientific or technical articles in periodicals[84]; and (3) making and issuing copies of broadcasts and cable-casts with subtitling or other modifications for the special needs of the deaf and handicapped, where this is done by a body specially designated by the Minister.[85] In a fourth case— reprographic copying by educational establishments—the same result is achieved by conferring a limited freedom to copy if no certified scheme is offered.[86] In the fifth case—the rental right as it affects legitimate sound recordings, films and computer programs—the Minister has power to convert the exclusive right into a right to a reasonable royalty, set, if necessary, by the Copyright Tribunal.[87]

(b) *Exceptions concerning artistic works*

There are carried forward into the 1988 Act a number of provisions **11–45** affecting artistic works: sculptures, building models and works of artistic craftsmanship, if permanently situated in public, may be represented in a graphic work, photographed, filmed, broadcast or cable-cast without licence; likewise buildings, wherever situate.[88] An artistic work may be copied, and those copies issued to the public, when advertising its sale—an exception important to auction houses.[89] An artist may copy his own earlier work, provided that he does not repeat or imitate its main design.[90] A building may be reconstructed without infringing copyright in it or the original drawings or plans.[91]

---

[83] CDPA 1988, s. 35.

[84] *ibid.*, s. 60.

[85] *ibid.*, s. 74.

[86] *ibid.*, s. 36; see paras 13–14—13–15, below.

[87] *ibid.*, s. 66; this, however, is likely to be affected by implementation of the Rental Directive. See para. 13–22, below.

[88] *ibid.*, s. 62; extending to certain consequential acts: s. 62(3).

[89] *ibid.*, s. 63—not extending to subsequent dealings for any other purpose.

[90] *ibid.*, s. 64.

[91] *ibid.*, s. 65.

In addition there are exclusions and limitations which are crucial to the scheme of protection for industrial designs, which are reserved for discussion in Chapter 14.[92]

It is at this juncture that one meets the strictly limited rights recognised in a typeface as a form of artistic work.[93] The copyright is restricted to making, importing and dealing in machines and other articles specifically designed or adapted for producing material in the typeface. It does not extend to using the typeface itself. The right in relation to machines lasts for 25 years from the first marketing of the machines.[94]

(c) *Broadcasts and cable-casts*

11–46 (i) **Re-cabling.** Where a broadcast is immediately re-transmitted by cable within the area of reception for the broadcast, the cable-casting is not an infringement of the broadcast, provided that it is not encrypted or by satellite; nor is it infringement of any work included in the broadcast.[95] This exception, in its present version limited mainly to cases where poor reception is averted by cabling, is contested by some copyright owners as a derogation from the Berne Convention obligation to accord an exclusive right in the consequent cabling of a broadcast,[96] but that obligation may be conditioned by national legislation, as it is here.

11–47 (ii) **Free public showing.** Where a broadcast or cable-cast is shown or played to a non-paying audience,[97] there is no infringement of copyright in the broadcast or cable-cast, nor in any sound recording or film contained in them.[98] This exception extends to provisions for residents or inmates of a "place" (for example a hotel, holiday camp, hospital or prison) and for members as an incident of membership of a club or society.

11–48 (iii) **Time shifting.** By way of considerable variation on the former law, a broadcast or cable-cast may be recorded for private and domestic use (as distinct from research and private study) in order to view it or listen to it at a more convenient time; the exception extends to the works included in the transmission as well as the transmission itself.[99]

11–49 (iv) **Various.** There are also provisions covering: a compulsory licence for the broadcasting of sound recordings[1]; incidental recording in the course of

---

[92] CDPA 1988, ss. 51 and 52 which are discussed at paras 14–27—14–32, below.

[93] This is assumed in the Act from *Stephenson Blake v. Grant Legros* (1916) 33 R.P.C. 406.

[94] CDPA 1988, ss. 54, 55. The change enables the U.K. to ratify the so-far inoperative Vienna Convention on Typefaces of 1973.

[95] CDPA 1988, s. 73. There is also an exception in respect of material which the Cable Authority requires to be included in a cable-cast (*i.e.* those granted rediffusion licences), which in turn is subject to special provision on damages: s. 73(3).

[96] Berne Convention, Art. 11*bis* (1), (2); Ricketson, pp. 455–476.

[97] This concept is elaborately defined.

[98] CDPA 1988, s. 72. Note the counter-provision on damages: s. 72(4).

[99] *ibid.*, s. 70; see para. 13–19, below.

[1] *ibid.*, s. 135A.

making a licensed broadcast or cable-cast of a work[2]; recordings by the supervisory bodies for the purpose of controlling broadcasting and cable-casting[3]; the making of private photographs from television broadcasts or cable-casts[4]; the sub-titling of broadcasts and cable-casts to the deaf, hard of hearing and handicapped[5]; and archival purposes.[6]

(d) *Public administration*

The 1988 Act contains a much expanded list of excepted activities **11–50** connected with government. These include things done for the purpose of Parliamentary and judicial proceedings, Royal Commissions and statutory inquiries,[7] and extend to direct reports of any of them. In addition various public records and other types of official information may be copied without licence in given ways. The development is a counterpart to the new restriction in scope of Crown copyright, and will be discussed further in that context.[8]

(e) *Miscellaneous*

(i) **Anonymous and pseudonymous works.** There is an ultimate exception, **11–51** already discussed in relation to these types of work, where it is reasonable to suppose that copyright has expired.[9]

(ii) **Extracts in recital.** A solo reading or recitation of a reasonable extract **11–52** from a literary or dramatic work may be made in public with sufficient acknowledgment; and a recording, broadcast or cable-cast may be made of it, if mainly of material not covered by the exception.[10]

(iii) **Folksong recordings.** A designated non-profit organisation may **11–53** record a song for an archive, and make copies available for private study or research, even though there is copyright in the words or music, provided that the words are unpublished and of unknown authorship.[11]

---

[2] CDPA 1988, s. 68.
[3] *ibid.*, s. 69.
[4] *ibid.*, s. 71.
[5] *ibid.*, s. 74.
[6] *ibid.*, s. 75.
[7] CDPA 1988, ss. 45, 46.
[8] *ibid.*, ss. 47–50; paras 13–105—13–106, below.
[9] *ibid.*, s. 57; for joint authorship see s. 57(3), para. 10–55, above.
[10] *ibid.*, s. 59.
[11] *ibid.*, s. 61. This should be related to the special arrangements under s. 169 for according overseas protection authorities to exercise copyright in respect of folksongs that are part of their national heritage.

11–54 (iv) **Works in electronic form.** Where the purchaser of a legitimate copy of, say, a computer program is entitled himself to make further copies, he transfers this additional power when he transfers the copy to another, unless there are express conditions to the contrary.[12]

4. PUBLIC POLICY

11–55 In contradistinction to the statutorily defined defences just mentioned, the judges have kept the power to refuse protection to a copyright owner on public policy grounds,[13] and these we may divide into two kinds.

(1) Policy against legal protection

11–56 A line of cases justifies the refusal of relief on a variety of grounds which express disapproval of the content of the work: because it is obscene, sexually immoral, defamatory, blasphemous, irreligious, or seriously deceptive of the public.[14] Thus Elinor Glyn's *Three Weeks*, however opaque its voluptuousness may seem today, was condemned in 1916 as a "glittering record of adulterous sensuality masquerading as superior virtue".[15] A trade catalogue which contained misleading statements about the plaintiff's patents and the size of his premises was not protected.[16] While the power to refuse the assistance of the Court survives, it is likely to be exercised today only in clear cases; in particular, some of the early nineteenth-century decisions should be treated with caution.[17]

A work which satisfies the general criterion of originality does not lose its copyright, or cease to be enforceable, because it embodies another copyright work to an extent which requires a licence and that authority has not been obtained.[18] If A translates B's copyright novel without permission, B may obtain relief against any exploitation of the translation. But in turn no one without A's authority may infringe his rights in the translation.[19] If B

---

[12] CDPA 1988, s. 56; see para. 13–36, below.

[13] See now CDPA 1988, s. 171(3).

[14] See Phillips (1977) 6 Anglo-Am.L.R. 138; and for the same factors in breach of confidence, see para. 8–10, above.

[15] *Glyn v. Weston Feature Film* [1916] 1 Ch. 261 at 269–270; *cf.* now *Stephens v. Avery* [1988] F.S.R. 510; *Masterman's Design* [1991] R.P.C. 89.

[16] *Slingsby v. Bradford Patent Truck* [1906] W.N. 51, CA; and see *Wright v. Tallis* (1845) 1 C.B. 863 (book passed off as the work of a well-known author; no cause of action to protect copyright in that book).

[17] See Younger J., *Glyn's* case (n. 15, above) at 269. During Lord Eldon's Chancellorship, this form of "negative censorship" went particularly far: as in *Murray v. Benbow* (1822) Jac. 474n (Byron's "Cain" refused protection); *Lawrence v. Smith* (1822) Jac. 471. *cf.* also *Stockdale v. Onwhyn* (1826) 5 B. & C. 173 ("memoirs" of a prostitute). For further case law, see Laddie *et al.*, pp. 117–123.

[18] *Redwood v. Chappell* [1982] R.P.C. 109 at 120.

[19] *Ashmore v. Douglas-Home* [1987] F.S.R. 553, *contra*, is on this matter wrong: Laddie *et al.*, pp. 123–126.

recovers monetary compensation he will be obliged to account to A for the latter's due share.[20]

(2) Policy favouring dissemination

The ability to protect confidential information, it will be recalled, is **11–57** qualified by considerations of public interest.[21] The same considerations were held in *Beloff v. Pressdram* to affect copyright; they created a defence arising outside the statute and based on a general common law principle.[22] In that case, the work consisted of a journalist's private memorandum to colleagues about a Cabinet Minister's view on the succession to the leadership of the Conservative Party. A narrow view was taken of what might be justified in the public interest: it was necessary to show an "iniquity" or "misdeed" and so the defence did not succeed on the facts.[23] But some of the breach of confidence cases already discussed take a broader view of the general principle.[24]

5. ACTIONS FOR INFRINGEMENT

Copyright infringements give rise to a range of remedies, civil, criminal and **11–58** administrative as well as of self-help. These have been mentioned in the introductory chapter on the subject.[25] All are today important, particularly given the very considerable quantity of pirate copying that continues to plague the record, film and television industries; and none more so than the *Anton Piller* order for inspection.[26] The whole territory will not be traversed again, comment being restricted here to a number of special provisions affecting civil actions.

(1) Damages

Copyright is a property right invaded by the particularly unfair step of **11–59** copying. At the same time, to some extent it serves to protect an individual's desire to keep his affairs private. Until the 1988 Act this was reflected particularly in the exceptional entitlement to "conversion damages"—essentially for the value of infringing copies as property—as distinct from "infringement damages". This advantage came, however, to

---

[20] *ZYX Music v. King* [1995] E.M.L.R. 281.
[21] See above, para. 11–39
[22] [1973] 1 All E.R. 241 at 259; and see *Hyde Park Residents v. Yelland* [1999] R.P.C. 655: photograph may be published in press without authority if it shows that a prominent person lied about a fact affecting the future of an ex-member of the Royal Family.
[23] *ibid.*, at 261.
[24] See paras 8–15—8–19, above.
[25] See paras 2–28 *et seq.*, above.
[26] See paras 2–48 *et seq.*, above.

be considered too draconian, and conversion damages were abolished by the 1988 Act. The Act, however, expands the possibility of claiming "additional damages" and delivery up for disposal, both of which are discussed below.[27]

11–60 The usual basis for claiming substantial damages for infringement relates to the commercial value of the work[28]: as with patents, the claim is either for compensation for lost profits—because the defendant's infringements have lost the plaintiff his own opportunities for sale. How far this will be assumed from the very fact of the defendant's piratical sales depends on the particular circumstances.[29] Alternatively, the claim is for the misappropriation—because the plaintiff has lost the chance of licensing or selling his copyright to the defendant.[30] As part of such a claim, the plaintiff is entitled to show that the cheap or vulgar form of the defendant's piracy injured his reputation and so lost him sales,[31] indeed it has been presumed, in the absence of explanation from the defendant, that a film's lack of success was due to the existence of poor quality copies on the market.[32]

11–61 Injury to reputation may, however, have little or nothing to do with the commercial popularity of the work; the psychological effect, the injury to feelings, may be much more significant. The 1988 Act allows a Court to award damages "in addition to all other material considerations", having regard to the flagrancy of the infringement and any benefit to the defendant, and this is now possible without having to consider whether effective relief is otherwise available.[33] While the normal rule today is that damages must be compensatory rather than punitive,[34] "additional damages" under the Act have been held to include damages by way of example. The plaintiff must, however, opt for an award of damages, rather than an account of profits; otherwise there is no corpus to which the further damages can be added.[35] On this basis, "additional" damages may lie against a professional photographer for supplying the press with a wedding photo which included a man subsequently murdered, without any consent from the member of the man's family who owned the copyright[36]; or against a lampooning magazine which published a confidential memorandum

---

[27] See Whitford Report, paras 701, 702; CDPA 1988, Sched. 1, para. 30(2).

[28] But this approach may not always be followed: see Bowen C.J., *Interfirm Comparison v. Law Society* (1975) 6 A.L.R. 445 at 446–447.

[29] *Columbia Picture Industries v. Robinson* [1986] F.S.R. 367.

[30] See para. 2–41, above.

[31] Lord Wright M.R., *Sutherland v. Caxton* [1936] Ch. 323 at 336.

[32] *Columbia Pictures* case (n. 29, above).

[33] CDPA 1988 s. 96(2); *cf.* CA 1956, s. 17(3).

[34] See para. 2–38, above.

[35] *Redrow Homes v. Betts Brothers* [1998] R.P.C. 793, HL. The plaintiff is entitled to know the court's view of flagrancy before electing between damages and an account of profits: *Condé-Nast v. MGN* [1998] F.S.R 427.

[36] As in *Williams v. Settle* [1960] 1 W.L.R. 1072, CA, which, however, was decided as a case on exemplary damages. For ownership of copyright in these circumstances today, see para. 12–04, below, and for the consequential right of privacy, see paras 11–85, 11–86, below.

written by a journalist to her colleagues, thereby damaging her reputation as a Parliamentary correspondent.[37]

(2) Presumptions in copyright infringement actions

It is no longer provided in the 1988 Act that, if the defendant wishes to **11–62** dispute the subsistence of copyright or the plaintiff's title, he must put the matter in issue by pleading it. The question accordingly takes its place alongside all other assertions which the plaintiff makes and must, if necessary, prove. There are, however, statutory presumptions which throw the legal burden of proof upon the defendant to infringement proceedings. Where literary, dramatic, musical or artistic copyright is concerned these are:

(1) that a person named as author is the author of a work; and that he did not produce it in circumstances (such as in the course of employment) which would deprive him of the copyright initially.[38] If this does not apply, then:

(2) that if first publication of a work qualifies it for copyright, copyright subsists and was owned at first publication by the person named as publisher.[39] In any case:

(3) that, where the author is dead or unidentifiable when the action is brought, the work was original and was first published where and when the plaintiff alleges.[40]

As regards copyright in sound recordings, films and computer programs, there are presumptions that statements naming the copyright owner, or giving the date or place of first publication, are true.[41]

6. MORAL RIGHTS[42]

All systems of copyright protection have as their prime inspiration the **11–63** cultural value of authorship. The Romantic ideal, so ardently pursued two centuries ago, claimed for the creative artist a unique sensibility and

---

[37] *Beloff* case [1973] 1 All E.R. 241 at 264–272; but the plaintiff failed for want of title (para. 12–05, below).

[38] CDPA 1988, s. 104(2); and for the same presumptions in relation to each of joint authors, s. 104(3).

[39] *ibid.*, s. 104(4). This affects anonymous works: see para. 10–53, above.

[40] *ibid.*, s. 104(5).

[41] *ibid.*, s. 105. The statements are also admissible as evidence of the facts stated and may apply in relation to infringements occurring before the publication or similar act.

[42] For a wide-ranging review of the current situation in leading common law countries, see Dworkin [1994] Aust. I.P.R. 449; Anderson and Saunders (eds), *Moral Rights Protection in a Copyright System* (1992). And *cf.* Copyright Law Review Committee (Australia), *Moral Rights* (1988); Ricketson [1990] Ent. L.R. 76; Attorney-General's Department (Australia), *Proposed Moral Rights Legislation* (1994); Parliamentary Sub-Committee (Canada), *A Charter of Rights for Authors* (1985); Vaver (1987) 25 Osgoode Hall L.J. 749; Gibbens (1989) 15 Can. B.L.J. 441; Ginsburg [1990] Ent. L.R. 121; Nimmer [1992] Ent. L.R. 94; Stamtoudi [1997] I.P.J. 478.

foresight, and every age continues to regard with fascination those aesthetic achievements which it treasures as special contributions to the human condition. Indeed, whatever today's scepticism over objective values and universal truths, the arts receive serious and sustained study and participation on a scale previously unknown.

In countries where this complex social force presses urgently, it finds legal expression in a proprietary right which protects the personality of authors as expressed in their creations alongside their economic interests in exploitation. This separate element—the author's so-called moral right (from the French *droit moral*[43])—has been progressively enhanced in Continental systems of authors' rights over the past century.[44] In the legislative schemes of French and German law and their many derivatives, moral rights rank as a category at least the equal of economic rights. The two schemes in fact differ in basic assumption, since French law renders moral rights perpetual as well as (in some sense) inalienable, thus creating a necessary duality[45]; while German law, drawing upon the Hegelian perception of the work as the fulfilled expression of the author's personality, gives both moral and economic rights the same duration and treats them monistically as branches of the same tree.

In partial recognition of these developments, Article 6*bis* of the Berne Convention requires Member States to provide, in principle for as long as the economic rights,[46] independent rights to claim authorship and to object to modifications or other derogatory action in relation to a work which would be prejudicial to the author's honour or reputation.[47]

11–64 Each law within the fold of authors' rights countries differs over the precise content and scope of moral rights, but they are likely to include: a right to decide upon first publication or other release; a right to be named as author; a right to object to modifications of the work and to its presentation in derogatory circumstances. There may also be provision for an author to insist on completion of the original where that depends on the execution of others, to withdraw works of which he no longer approves and to object to destruction or removal of the original.[48]

One driving inspiration for moral-rights doctrine has been the belief that at least some great artists are unworldly prey to the vultures of copyright

---

[43] German law refers to the author's right of personality in his work, an expression which in English is better fitted to what is intended.

[44] For a current assessment of these developments, see esp. Dietz in ALAI. *The Moral Right of the Author*, p. 54; for a magisterial history, Strömholm, *Le droit moral de l'auteur* (1967). For comparisons between the U.S. and France, see Sarraute (1968) 16 Am. J. Comp. L. 465; Treece (1968) 16 Am. J. Comp. L. 487.

[45] And so the heirs of a classic playwright may object to a demeaning production of his work.

[46] In the Paris Act of 1971, there is a diplomatic exception allowing some countries to limit "some" (*sic*) of the moral rights to a lesser period.

[47] First introduced in non-compulsory form in the Rome version (1928), Art. 6*bis* became obligatory in the Brussels version of 1948 and was extended in the present Paris Act: Ricketson pp. 455–467; Plaisant (1986) 11 Col-VLA JLA 157.

[48] See further, paras 11–76—11–77, below.

industries: the voracious among literary and music publishers, recording, stage and film producers and art dealers. Moral rights seek at least to protect the integrity of a work and the author's connection with it. But once that step is taken, it is natural also to buttress the author's economic interest against unfair deprivation, particularly by the entrepreneurs who undertake to exploit the work. There is no simple dividing line between the purely "moral" and the purely economic. For every individual who insists unflinchingly upon his artistic integrity, there are many whose insistence can be compromised at a price. Equally, the innocent author abroad may well need more help in realising his economic potential than in protecting his essential relationship to his work.

Anglo-American tradition has manifested a certain scepticism towards **11–65** claims that authors deserve special protection in law. The attitude is part of a wider reluctance to subject the bargainings of the market-place to higher dictates of good faith, propriety and fairness. The Victorians' primary insistence upon sanctity of contract has today been to some degree modified by broader notions of fiduciary responsibility, duties of care and unconscionability. Indeed, as we shall see, this shift has been impelled particularly by sharp and harsh practices in the modern music industry. Given that shift, the question remains, what justifies a heightened protective regime for the moral rights of authors?

Argument on the subject remains intense, the representative voices of authors insisting that all systems should have a structured set of rules on moral rights in place, the entrepreneurial lobbyists claiming that these rights strengthen the position of authors unduly and lead to endless complications, particularly when it comes to complex collaborations such as audio-visual works or multi-media productions. This section returns to the root issue at its conclusion.[49] First, it must trace the course of development of British law on the subject, concentrating on those moral rights which were given explicit legislative form, very largely for the first time, in the 1988 Act, but in a scrupulously moderate version.

(1) Protection of authors under general legal rules

The common law may not have placed authors in any special sheepfold, but **11–66** it did not leave them at large in the wild. Since most of the practical problems arose between the author and those with whom he dealt in exploitation of his work, the author could provide much of what he might want by contractual stipulation. Beyond that he might be helped by the law of confidence, defamation, passing off, injurious falsehood, and the general economic torts. Thus, in *Humphreys v. Thompson*,[50] a jury found an

---

[49] See paras 11–87—11–89, below.
[50] *Humphreys v. Thompson* [1905–1910] Mac. C.C. 148; and see *Lee v. Gibbings* (1892) 67 L.J. 263; *Frisby v. B.B.C.* [1967] Ch. 932.

authoress to have been defamed by a newspaper serialisation of her story in which the names of the characters were simplified, passages of description were omitted and "curtains" were added at the beginning and end of each episode to whet readers' appetites. Her reputation had thus been lowered in the eyes of right-thinking members of the public. In *Samuelson v. Producers Distributing*,[51] the defendant put out a film of a revue sketch, wrongly claiming it to be the plaintiff's. Because the plaintiff's piece was well-known, thanks to its inclusion in a royal variety performance, this constituted a form of passing off.

11–67 Subsequently section 43 of the Copyright Act 1956, by creating a tort of misattribution, extended the range of such legal protection, since it eliminated the need to show any established reputation with the public.[52] Otherwise, the legislature in 1956 followed the Gregory Committee's view of *les droits moraux* as suspiciously foreign.[53] It felt no need to confer an explicit right to claim authorship or to preserve integrity, let alone to enshrine these rights, or other manifestations of the same idea, as inalienable and incapable of waiver in advance of actual publication or other use of the work. Yet the United Kingdom, unlike the United States at that juncture, was preparing to ratify the Brussels Act of the Berne Convention.[54]

11–68 In 1977, the Whitford Committee accepted that these moral rights should be translated into British legislation to a reasonable extent.[55] This proposal set in train the search for a formulation which would retain due respect for freedom and sanctity of contract and would protect entrepreneurs in their turn from being held to ransom as infringers of moral rights at a time when it would be difficult and expensive to rectify the wrong.[56] It was this overbearing potential in foreign laws which had for long fuelled the common law antagonism towards them.

In the upshot, the 1988 Act defines four distinct moral rights, the first two of which are in fulfilment of Berne obligations:

(1) the right to be identified as author or film director (the right of paternity);

---

[51] See para. 16–44, below. For a similar case in defamation see *Ridge v. English Illustrated Magazine* [1911–1916] Mac. C.C. 91.

[52] For the current version, see paras 11–83—11–84, below.

[53] See Cmd. 8662, 1952, para. 222.

[54] Later (in 1989) the U.S. would join Berne without explicit enactment covering Art *6bis*, in reliance upon the scope of general common law and statutory provisions which were arguably more extensive than those under English law. In 1990, limited moral rights would be conferred by Federal legislation in respect of visual art alone: see Ginsburg and Kernochan (1988) 13 Columbia-VLA JLA 1; Ginsburg (1990) 14 Columbia-VLA JLA 121; Tannenbaum [1991] E.I.P.R. 449; Appelbaum (1992) 8 Am.U.JILP 191.

[55] Cmnd. 6732, 1977, paras 51–57, drawing attention to the Dutch law as a model.

[56] As where a minor author of a film script might object to his omission from the credits on the eve of the premiere.

(2) the right to object to derogatory treatment of a work (the right of integrity);

(3) the right against false attribution of a work; and

(4) the right to privacy in private photographs and films.[57]

Each has its own incidents, but all adopt one basic characteristic of such rights in other systems: that they are inalienable to others while being transmissible on death.[58] Where they depart from more severely protective systems, is above all in the extent to which they may be compromised in advance by waiver.

(2) Right to be identified

(a) *Entitlement and duration*

The right to be identified as author is given to the creators of literary **11–69** dramatic, musical and artistic works, and also to the directors of films even though it is only for films made after July 1, 1995 that they are to enjoy copyright.[59] It is not accorded to other persons who are treated by the 1988 Act as "authors" for copyright purposes. Here is a first indication that the moral rights are not simply an aspect of copyright but instead fall to be treated separately. Subject to a number of exceptions, this moral right applies to works existing on August 1, 1989 in relation to publication, public exhibition and other acts done subsequently.[60]

The right inures only if the work itself is copyright—so the same qualification rules apply as for copyright. It lasts for the same period as the copyright.[61]

(b) *Assertion*

It is a pre-condition of the right to be identified that it be asserted. In **11–70** general, this may be done as a statement in an instrument assigning copyright in the work or by any other instrument in writing signed by the

---

[57] See further, Cornish [1989] E.I.P.R. 449; McCartney (1991) 15 Columbia-VLA JLA 161.

[58] CDPA 1988, ss. 94, 95.

[59] CDPA 1988, s. 77(1); for joint authors and directors, see s. 88(1), (5).

[60] *ibid.*, Sched. 1, paras 22, 23. The main exceptions are: the work of an author dead at commencement; works whose initial copyright invested in someone other than the author; films made before commencement; and anything done in pursuance of a licence or assignment by an author-owner. Because of the complete exclusion of pre-1989 films, there is no scope for using this right to object in the U.K. to their colourisation if originally black-and-white.

[61] *ibid.*, s. 86(1). The extensions of copyright terms (paras 10–44—10–51, above) accordingly affect the statutory moral rights. Any assertion of the right to be named and any waiver continue to affect extended and revived copyright works: Duration of Copyright, etc., Regulations 1995, S.I. 1995 No. 3297, regs. 21(1), 22(2), (3), 23(6): see para. 12–08, below.

author or director during the life of the right.[62] If it is made as part of an assignment, the assertion binds the assignee and anyone claiming through him, with or without notice; whereas if it is made by another instrument, it binds only those with notice of it.[63] Thus an assertion has in principle only to be made in the required form to any exploiter of the work for it to impose on him the obligation to identify the author or director; but delay in making the assertion is to be taken into account in determining whether an injunction must be granted and also, it seems, in settling damages and other relief.[64]

Assertion is a necessary preliminary to enjoyment of the right to be named, and so is arguably inconsistent with the requirement in Article 5(2) of the Berne Convention, so far as Convention nationals are concerned, that they should enjoy rights under British law without being subject to any formality. Assertion may have been necessary in order initially to secure the enactment of this moral right. Nonetheless it is a confusing complexity which achieves little. It should certainly be abandoned in any legislative revision. The author may still, after all, waive the right to be named, and that waiver may be given expressly or implied from the circumstances.

(c) *Preclusion*

11–71 In contradistinction with truly protective regimes of moral rights, it is possible for the person who would otherwise enjoy any of the four rights to surrender it in advance of the time when an issue actually arises—such as, for instance, a publisher's decision to exclude an author's name from a pending publication. The waiver may be by instrument in writing signed by the person giving up the right, and it may relate not only to a specific work in existence, but to a class of works or even works in general, and to future works. It may be the subject of a condition and it may be revocable.[65] Such express consent does not require contractual consideration. But an informal waiver may also be operative under general principles of contract or estoppel.[66] So conduct of an author or director on which another person relies in the belief that identification will not be insisted upon (whether or not there has already been an assertion) may well preclude any subsequent enforcement of the moral right.

(d) *Acts covered*

11–72 The occasions on which an author or director may insist upon identification are so defined as to incorporate a "disc-jockey" exception. Thus the author of most literary, dramatic and artistic works and directors of films may

---

[62] CDPA 1988, s. 78(1), (2). There are additional provisions concerning the assertion of the right in relation to public exhibition of an artistic work: s. 78(3).
[63] *ibid.*, s. 78(4).
[64] *ibid.*, s. 78(5).
[65] *ibid.*, s. 87(1)–(3).
[66] *ibid.*, s. 87(4).

require identification upon copies being published commercially, copies of a sound recording or film being issued to the public, performance or showing in public, broadcasting or cable-casting.[67] However, authors of musical works, and of words intended to be sung or spoken with music, do not have the right in respect of public performances, broadcasting and cable-casting. In each case, the identification has to be likely to bring the identity to the attention of those acquiring a copy, listening to a performance, etc.[68]

There are other special cases. In particular, although copyright itself does not extend to the public exhibition of artistic works, there is a right to be identified as artist at a public exhibition.[69] In this respect at least, protection is given to the original work itself, as well as to copies. For this purpose, moreover, the right is sufficiently asserted by attaching an identification to the work or a copy when the author or other first owner of copyright parts with possession of it, or the assertion is included in a licence to make copies of the work; in either case notice is not necessary in order to bind third parties.[70]

Equally, there is a substantial list of exceptions. There is no right of **11–73** identification in computer programs, computer-generated works, or typefaces, or works which are Crown or similar copyright.[71] Where a work or film is made in the course of employment, the employer, as first owner of the copyright, is not obliged to make the identification; nor is anyone else who acts with his authority.[72] Publication in a newspaper, magazine or periodical, or in an encyclopedia or similar work, is excluded.[73] A number of the exceptions applicable to copyright also apply to the right to be identified: fair dealing for the purpose of reporting current events in a sound recording, film, broadcast or cable-cast; incidental inclusion in an artistic work, sound recording, film, broadcast or cable-cast; the exclusion and limitation of artistic copyright in the sphere of industrial design; and other more specific cases.[74]

(e) *Impact*

The right to be identified is inherently more likely to be of importance to **11–74** those who have a reputation still to establish than those whose name will attract attention on a publication or through other exploitation. The right

---

[67] CDPA 1988, s. 77(2), (3).

[68] See *ibid.*, s. 77(7), for a full definition of sufficient identification: and s. 77(8) for the form to be adopted.

[69] *ibid.*, s. 77(4)(a). For works of architecture, sculptures and works of artistic craftsmanship, see s. 77(4)(c).

[70] *ibid.*, s. 78(3), (4)(c), (d).

[71] *ibid.*, s. 79(2), (7).

[72] *ibid.*, s. 79(3).

[73] *ibid.*, s. 79(6).

[74] *ibid.*, s. 79(4).

does, however, extend not only to failure to name anyone but also to plagiarism of work under the name of another, and here even the famous may have occasion to complain. In the film and television industries, the matter of screen credits (for performers as well as creators) is considered of such importance that detailed arrangements on the matter have been reached by collective agreement—initially in the Screenwriting Credits Agreement of 1974.[75] Precision of this order is far more satisfactory than a general obligation under legislation.

Among lesser authors and directors, it is those who provide work for others in some capacity, without becoming employees,[76] who are most likely to be aggrieved by non-identification. There will be some circumstances where by implication the right has been contractually excluded.[77] The person who is commissioned to act as ghost-writer for another would be presumed to accept the consequences. But that is not necessarily the implication between members of a research team in writing up results. Equally the photographer who supplies material for a book or a film may well have done nothing to raise the belief that he would not claim to be identified.

(3) Right to object to derogatory treatment[78]

(a) *Entitlement and duration*

11–75 As in the previous case, the right to object to derogatory treatment is given to authors in respect of literary, dramatic, musical and artistic works, and to directors in respect of their films, to the extent that they are the subject of, and remain in, copyright.[79] It is a right which draws upon Article 6*bis* of the Berne Convention, though it is in apparently narrower terms. Objection may be raised to "derogatory treatment" of the work, which requires demonstration (1) that the work is subject to addition, deletion, alteration or adaptation; and (2) that this "amounts to distortion or mutilation of the work or is otherwise prejudicial to the honour or reputation of the author or director".[80]

It may not be an infraction of this right to place a work in a context which subjects it to criticism or ridicule—for instance, using a painting in an exhibition deliberately to show up the superiority of other paintings or to

---

[75] See Cotterell, *Performance* (3rd ed., 1993) pp. 487–488; para. 12–48, below.

[76] In general, employees in any case do not have the right: n. 72, above.

[77] As the 1988 Act is less categoric than other systems, the question of which law governs, *e.g.* assignments and licences, will remain important; see the French Cour d'Appel's decision in *Rowe v. Walt Disney* [1987] F.S.R. 37; *Huston* case (n. 86, below).

[78] See Goldstein (1983) 14 I.I.C. 43; Smith [1992] Ent.L.R. 26.

[79] CDPA 1988, s. 80(1) for the term, see s. 86(1), and para. 10–45, above; and see n. 61, above. As to joint authorship and direction, see s. 88(2), (5).

[80] *ibid.*, s. 80(2). Berne Convention, Art. 6*bis* refers to "distortion, mutilation or other modification of, *or other derogatory action in relation to*, [the work]" (italics added).

cast aspersions on the artist's life-style. A sculptor may not even be able to object to the hanging of Christmas decorations on his work.[81] An extensive interpretation of "addition" to the work would, however, accord with the spirit and terms of Article 6*bis*. It would not give an author a cause of action if his publisher also published a piece critical of him or his work[82]; but then the law ought not to subject a publisher to a special degree of dependence beyond the need to observe the law of defamation.[83] There will, of course, be borderline cases: a production of a sentimental comedy in a vein of social criticism intended to deride the genre will offend, provided that the text is altered or explicit stage instructions are defied.[84]

Truly committed systems of moral rights may go further than the Berne **11–76** Convention in extending protection beyond cases where there will be injury to honour and reputation. Notably in France the subjective reaction of the author to the alteration or use of the work is generally the governing consideration: thus a French Court upheld Beckett's objections to *Waiting for Godot* being played by women; and another refused to permit the addition to a book of even a complimentary preface.[85] On the same basis the colourisation of a black-and-white film was actionable by the director's personal representatives.[86]

So unconditional a form of integrity right inevitably acts as a considerable constraint on the freedom of others to use the work as they in turn choose, and their motives may vary considerably. For instance, parody is for the most part a form of healthy social and artistic criticism: indeed in French law there is a special exception covering it,[87] as well as other

---

[81] Held actionable under the Canadian provision which more faithfully follows the language of the Berne Convention, Art. 6*bis*: *Snow v. Eaton Centre* (1982) 70 C.P.R. (2d) 105.

[82] A French Court granted damages to the estate of Albert Camus against his publisher, when the British sub-licensee produced a book which criticised not so much Camus' writing as his personal integrity: *Gallimard v. Hamish Hamilton* [1985] E.C.C. 574. It is considered an extreme and isolated decision.

[83] Fair dealing for purposes of criticism or review is a defence to copyright infringement: para. 11–42, above. It certainly should not be that a person who has no connection with the author cannot engage in selective quotation for such purposes just because the result is in some sense derogatory. Courts should be unwilling to find a sufficient degree of derogation (and see Laddie *et al.*, para. 27.27).

[84] *cf. Maske in Blau* (1971) 2 I.I.C. 209 (Germany).

[85] R.I.D.A. 1993, No. 155, 225; J.C.P. 1988 II 21062. These examples epitomise the normal approach. Occasionally, Courts react against oversensitivity: as when Salvador Dali failed to prevent his ballet costume designs from being added to: D.S. 1967 555, D.S. 1968 382; and note in Italy Giorgio Chirico's failure to stop an exhibition which he claimed gave too much attention to his early work: Foro ital. 1955 I 717.

[86] *Huston v. Turner Entertainment* (1992) 23 I.I.C. 702; Edelman, 23 I.I.C. 629; Gendreau (1992) 7 I.P.J. 340. So fundamental was the right adjudged, that it was applied (for France) to the John Huston film, "Asphalt Jungle", even though it was subject to American contractual arrangements allowing the addition of colour. The decision is considered a triumph for moral rights doctrine.

[87] Intellectual Property Code, Art. 41. *cf.* the refusal in Sweden to protect a surrealist lithograph against the addition of satirical instructions and comments: *Svanberg v. Eriksson* [1979] E.I.P.R. D-93.

exceptions which would allow for quotation by way of criticism. The British provisions must be interpreted in a creative way which will allow a balance to be struck between the evidently conflicting interests raised by even the limited integrity right introduced in 1988.[88] In this process, decisions from other jurisdictions make interesting comparisons. But they are frequently not based on the same legislative texts or underlying principles, and they do not necessarily have an outcome which would be regarded as sensible in this country.

11–77 Indeed under such systems, there is a concern to protect the work from conception to final solution. The stages may be characterised as follow:

(1) **Refusal to supply original**: in an early case in France, James McNeill Whistler was held entitled not to deliver a portrait with which he was dissatisfied to its commissioner, even though he had exhibited it.[89] The circumstance might be one in which an English Court of equity would make no order of specific performance, though it might award damages or repayment of an advance. It is not an issue addressed in the moral right provisions of the 1988 Act.

(2) **Completion of original to the author's design**: again in France, courts have ordered the commissioner of a space sculpture and the commissioner of a television series to complete work on the author's design or script, once execution has begun.[90] The extreme character of such decisions has, however, been criticised by leading authors.[91] In England it would be rare indeed for a Court to require the carrying out of a contract which would involve personal labour or extended supervision. However, if the incomplete work were publicly exhibited, there might be infraction of the moral right of integrity.[92]

(3) **Correction or withdrawal of a work after publication**: while this is recognised in, for instance, French law,[93] it is subject to an obligation to indemnify the publisher against loss, and so appears to be exercised rarely. No such power is conferred by the 1988 Act.

(4) **Maintenance of a work at a site**: if there is an obligation to complete a work, it would seem that commensurately it should be maintained in the site for which it was destined.[94] But that could impose very considerable burdens of cost and stultified use on those who own the object, and Courts everywhere are likely to be cautious in extending protection so far.

---

[88] As in the suggestion that *Carry On Cleo* would not injure the director of *Anthony and Cleopatra*'s honour and reputation: Laddie *et al.*, para. 17.18.

[89] *Eden v. Whistler* D.P. 1900 I 497; the artist had to return his fee and undertake not to exhibit the portrait himself.

[90] *Renault v. Dubuffet* [1983] E.C.C. 453 (even though the contract contained a provision for liquidated damages in case of non-performance); *Affaire TF1*, R.I.D.A. 1983 Apr. 172.

[91] Françon and Ginsburg (1985) 9 Col-VLA JLA 381.

[92] *cf.* Laddie *et al.*, para. 27.23.

[93] Intellectual Property Code L. 121–4.

[94] This consequence was one reason for the criticism cited in n. 91, above.

(5) **Prevention of destruction, particularly of an original artistic work**: This raises an even starker conflict with the position of the owner of the physical object. Out of distaste, physical encumbrance or financial difficulty, he or she may wish to reduce it to nothing (as distinct from turning it into something else[95]). Even in French law it is not settled that the moral right extends against destruction. Under British law, destruction leaves behind nothing which can be copied, performed or exhibited within the terms of section 80.

(b) *Exercise and preclusion*

The right to object to derogatory treatment does not depend upon any pre- **11–78** condition, such as assertion. As with the other moral rights, it can be precluded by consent or other waiver.[96] However, those who seek to achieve this, by an advance provision in a contract of exploitation, will need to express themselves in unequivocal terms; for it is inherently unlikely that an author or director will be wishing to expose himself to alterations which are prejudicial to his honour and reputation.[97]

The integrity of a work is most readily conceived where the work is the **11–79** discrete production of a single author. Difficulties are added once there is joint authorship, or the linked authorship of (say) Rogers and Hammerstein. When one reaches complex productions, such as audio-visual works, in which it is accepted that various secondary writers (of work to be adapted, scenario, script, music, etc.) will contribute to the final outcome, but that many decisions about content will be taken by the director of the production, participation in the venture must imply a considerable readiness to permit modification of a contribution. Certainly, industry agreements and practices which define the point at which a contributor either accepts the need for modification, or is paid off for work to date, must constitute operative waivers.[98] The costly process of production could not go on without such a measure of security.

(c) *Acts covered*

In general authors and directors may object to derogatory treatment **11–80** occurring in copies being published commercially, copies of a sound recording or film being made available to the public, performance, playing and showing in public, broadcasting and cable-casting.[99] So far as concerns

---

[95] As with the celebrated refrigerator, which Bernard Buffet decorated on all its panels; its owner was prevented from breaking it up in order to sell each panel separately: D. 1962 570.

[96] CDPA 1988, s. 87.

[97] See, *e.g. Frisby v. B.B.C.* [1967] Ch. 932.

[98] As, *e.g.* the Writers' Guild/PACT Collective Agreement for Films and Television Films, described in Cotterell, *Performance* (3rd ed., 1993), pp. 481–482.

[99] CDPA 1988, s. 80(3)–(6); and note s. 80(7) on parts of works previously treated by others.

artistic works, the right also covers public exhibition and in that respect extends to the original work itself.[1] There are, however, some major exceptions and limitations. The right does not apply in relation (1) to translation, or transposition of the key or register of a musical work[2]; (2) to computer programs or computer generated works; (3) to any work made for the purpose of reporting current events; (4) to publication in a newspaper, magazine or periodical or encyclopedia or similar work, or any unmodified subsequent publication therefrom.[3]

In the case of a work of architecture, the architect has no right other than to have his identification as architect removed from the building.[4] In the case of works made in employment, or which are Crown or similar copyright, an author or director who is identified may only insist upon a sufficient disclaimer of association with the work as altered.[5] The broadcasting authorities also have power to make excisions and alterations in order to stop the broadcasting of anything offensive to good taste and decency, or which could encourage or incite to crime, lead to disorder or offend public feeling.[6] In the clean new world of broadcasting, this may be a provision which is relied upon with some frequency.

(d) *Impact*

11–81 Many of the recurrent circumstances in which anxiety and objection arise over derogatory treatment have been excised or anaesthetised, so far as this right is concerned, particularly through the provisions relating to employment, the press, current affairs and, above all, translation: what can do more harm to reputation than an incomprehensible or distortive rendition in another language?[7] In the past, directors of films have complained about the manner in which producers, intent on maximising the commercial potential of their investment, have compromised the artistic integrity of the film by subsequent cutting or interpolation. Doubtless in the future producers will use express stipulations to procure their ability to do the same. However, to the extent that they do not, the director will have a power of objection more readily enforced than the vestigial possibilities at common law of suing for defamation, trade libel or some form of passing off. But at the end of the day in Court, he may secure no more than an order that the work be published with a disclaimer dissociating him from it.[8]

---

[1] CDPA 1988, s. 80(4)(a).

[2] *ibid.*, s. 80(2)(a). But "megamixing" samples from pop music sources may well offend: *Morrison Leahy v. Lightbond* [1993] E.M.L.R. 144; and possibly reducing cartoons in size: *Tidy v. Natural History Museum* (1995) 39 I.P.R. 501.

[3] CDPA 1988, s. 81(2)–(5).

[4] *ibid.*, s. 80(5).

[5] *ibid.*, s. 82.

[6] *ibid.*, s. 81(6) (and for the Independent Broadcasting Authority, see the Broadcasting Act 1981, s. 4(1)).

[7] Accordingly actionable in, *e.g.* France, *Zorine v. Lucernaire* [1987] E.C.C. 54.

[8] See CDPA 1988, s. 103(2).

Digital technology poses threats of a new order to the integrity of works. **11–82** Once they are recorded in digital form they can be shredded into components and then varied, particle by particle, with an ease inconceivable even with analogue recordings of audio and audio-visual material. These techniques are becoming the commonplace of filming, advertisements, illustration and music-mixing. The prospects are still in their infancy. Exotic locations can be added into film on demand. A few stills of an actor can be animated into an entire performance. Personalities can be given lives after death.[9]

The law will have to work towards an accommodation between originators and adaptors which allows these new techniques to flourish, while still inhibiting manipulation of digital material which is evidently unfair and unacceptable. In striking this balance, two features of British law—the fact that the integrity right is restricted to derogatory treatment, and the fact that the right may be waived in advance—are likely to be important elements in this adjustment. Above all, once an author has assented to the digital holding of his work, potential users should be able to know whether they can only use it in unaltered form, or can use it in any altered form or in an altered form of which the author approves. The last case requires permission case by case. Digital service providers will doubtless seek to prescribe arrangements for rapid decision-making. If authors regularly prove recalcitrant, it may be necessary to consider some form of compulsory licensing to aid the process.

(4) False attribution

The right to object to a false attribution is the converse of the right to be **11–83** identified. It is an amplification of rights contained in section 43 of the Copyright Act 1956. A person to whom a literary, dramatic, musical or artistic work is attributed as author, or to whom a film is attributed as director, has the right to object when that attribution is false.[10] The objection may be in relation to the issue of copies to the public, public exhibition of an artistic work (or copy of it), public performance or showing, broadcast or cable-cast of a literary, dramatic or musical work or a film.[11] Here there is also a secondary wrong (requiring proof of knowledge or reason to believe that there is false attribution) which consists in possessing or dealing with a copy of the work in the course of business: also in the case of an artistic work, dealing with it in business as the unaltered work of the artist, when in fact it was altered after leaving his possession.[12]

---

[9] Beard (1993) 8 High Tech. L.J. 101. At present, British legislation provides no moral rights for performers. However, they have been included in the Performers and Phonograms Treaty 1996, Art. 5, and so will in due course require implementation.

[10] CDPA 1988, s. 84(1); in relation to joint works, see s. 88(4), (5).

[11] *ibid.*, s. 84(2).

[12] *ibid.*, s. 84(3).

These rights enure for 20 years from the year of death of the person who is subject to the false attribution.[13]

11–84 There is now a considerable overlap between the attribution right and the derogatory treatment right. Before the 1988 Act, the former was sometimes used to object to work appearing which was very largely not that of the person named. Thus the singer, Dorothy Squires, obtained damages on account of a newspaper item allegedly by her, when she actually said only about 10 per cent of it to the journalist concerned.[14] Nonetheless false attribution turns upon the inaccurate naming of a person as author, while derogatory treatment must show prejudice to honour and reputation; the inflections are slightly different. If the attribution is misleading, it is no defence that satire was intended.[15]

(5) Right to privacy

11–85 This, the first acknowledgement in English law of any right to privacy, operates only in strictly delimited circumstances, and is a corollary of shifting the first ownership of certain artistic works from the person who commissioned them to the person who created them or his employer.[16] Under the 1988 Act, where a person commissions a photograph or a film for private or domestic purposes, and that work attracts copyright, he has the right to object to issuing copies to the public, public exhibition or showing, broadcasting or cable-casting.[17] To this there are certain exceptions which also apply to copyright, of which the most general is incidental inclusion in an artistic work, film, broadcast or cable-cast.[18]

The right lasts as long as the copyright in the photograph or film[19] and is given independently to each joint commissioner.[20] It will be of value in those cases where a wedding group or party picture contains someone who subsequently becomes newsworthy, and will be assertable both where copyright belongs to a commercial photographer or film-maker, and to a relative or friend who undertakes the task for nothing, since the commission does not here have to be for money or money's worth.

11–86 Like all rights accorded to protect privacy, it has the potential to become a right to share in the publicity value of the work; just as much as the copyright owner, the commissioner may consent to publication or other use. In a case under the 1956 Act, wedding photographs of a couple were sought

---

[13] CDPA 1988, s. 86(2).

[14] *Moore v. News of the World* [1972] 1 Q.B. 441; extended in *Noah v. Shuba* [1991] F.S.R. 14, to the addition of two misleading lines to the plaintiff's article on hygienic skin piercing.

[15] *Clark v. Associated Newspapers* [1998] R.P.C. 261.

[16] See para. 12–04, below.

[17] CDPA 1988, s. 85(1).

[18] *ibid.*, s. 85(2).

[19] *i.e.*, the photographer's life and 70 years.

[20] CDPA 1988, ss. 86, 88(6).

by newspapers when it was learned that the wife, after a brain haemor-rhage, was being kept alive in order to give birth. One issue then was whether the wife was a co-commissioner of the photographs. If so, a paper seeking exclusive rights of exploitation, which it could enforce against others, would need a copyright licence from her husband and herself.[21] Under the 1988 Act, the paper could itself get a proprietary right only from the photographer or his successor in title. But any paper which published, without waivers from the photograph's commissioners of their moral rights of privacy, could be sued by either of them individually. It is curious that this right is conferred on the commissioner, rather than the person whose image is subjected to publicity (unwanted, or wanted only at a price). It would, however, be hopelessly cumbersome to require permission of all in a group photograph, so the commissioner is put in their stead.

(6) Overall significance

The statutory moral rights, particularly the rights to be named and to object **11–87** to derogatory treatment, give the very concept a prominence which in some measure redounds to the benefit of authors. It is hard to assess how considerable this enhancement is, compared with the protection afforded in any case by contract and by torts such as defamation, injurious falsehood and passing off. At the very least the availability of these other bases of liability must not be forgotten.

The treatment of moral rights in the 1988 Act as interests distinct from **11–88** copyright has a number of consequences:

(1) The rights (other than that to privacy) have been accorded only to authors whose copyright rests on creativity rather than investment. The rights were extended to film directors at a time when they were not authors and it has aided their campaign for their own copyright.

(2) The rights are personal (and in that sense inalienable), but they are good against all who treat the work in a prejudicial manner falling within one of the provisions. They accordingly afford relief in circumstances which the author could scarcely control by express contract.

(3) The rights are not entirely tied to the acts of reproduction and performance which make up copyright. In particular, in the sphere of artistic works, moral rights cover public exhibition of the original as well as copying of it.[22]

In sum, the 1988 legislation has attempted from scratch to set out **11–89** detailed rules to govern complex problems, which Continental systems have been able to tackle incrementally through case law and statute in combina-

---

[21] *Mail Newspapers v. Express Newspapers* [1987] F.S.R. 90.
[22] See paras 11–72, 11–80, above.

tion. Because of this, our legislation needs imaginative interpretation. For all the exceptions and limitations in our texts, the rights have a considerable range, as has just been indicated. The courts will be assisted in keeping them within bounds by criteria in the rules which call for objective evaluation—and most notably with the concept of "derogatory treatment" which must prejudice "honour and reputation".

Because copyright endures for long periods and often covers a range of different exploitations, there is a real case for protecting the "moral" position of authors by guaranteed rights which extend beyond the potential of contractual agreement. Nonetheless, every infraction of a moral right hampers some other person's freedom of expression or freedom to do business. The rights must accordingly be confined to cases of real injury. Scope must be left for the parties concerned to reach reasonable agreements concerning moral interests, secure in the knowledge that the agreements are binding. Where this can be achieved by collective negotiation with authors' societies,[23] there is a good case for saying that an industry standard has been settled and is not open to alteration. Isolated Court decisions after the event are no adequate substitute for the hammering out of rights and procedures in advance.

---

[23] As in the instances cited in nn. 75, 98, above.

CHAPTER 12

PROPERTY RIGHTS AND EXPLOITATION

The previous two chapters have been concerned with the basic rules of **12–01** British copyright law as a whole. But copyright entwines itself in the workings of several major industries in ways which are distinct to each of them. In turning to the proprietary aspects of copyright we can begin to see something of this variable impact.

Copyright, like other intellectual property, is first and foremost an exclusionary right and the significance of that characteristic to industries faced with modern copying technology needs no reiteration at this juncture. But there are many enterprises, as well as individuals, who want to be able to take copies and develop derivative works, to give performances, to broadcast and so on. Licensing is the stuff of much copyright exploitation and devising practicable systems for it, such as the development of collecting societies, has been a distinctive characteristic of the copyright world. The challenge set by electronic information networks is the latest (and possibly most daunting) in a long train of difficulties.

At the same time copyright is unique in the extent to which its exploitation involves not uniplanar, but bi-planar, linkages. It depends for its effectiveness not just on the relationship between rightowner and user, but equally on the relationship between the creative author and the entrepreneur who undertakes exploitation of the material. From its earliest foundations, as we have noted, copyright has been the shared sword of author and entrepreneur as they march forth against potential users; at the same time each has sought to appropriate it for internal struggles over profit shares, payments for work and artistic integrity.

The ideological differences between "authors' rights" and "copyright" **12–02** systems stem from opposed views of how relationships on this internal plane should be governed in law. "Authors' rights" advocates demand with rising insistence that copyright law should set minimum standards, designed to protect individual creators against the superior bargaining knowledge, skills and sheer power of entrepreneurs. Partly these should protect the copyright work, as an expression of the author's personality, against infractions of "moral rights"; but beyond this there should also be controls which assure "equitable" or "proportional" renumeration to authors.

The Anglo-American approach to copyright reflects the strong (though not exclusive) commitment of the common law systems to the virtues of

459

free contractual bargaining. Accordingly, as we have already seen, the notion of guaranteed moral rights for authors, has found no natural and flourishing soil within these systems; Article 6*bis* of the Berne Convention, is an artificial fertiliser of still uncertain effectiveness. Much of the resistance to moral rights, however, expresses a fear that they will indirectly promote the growth of restrictions over freely bargained economic rights. The building of just such a provision into the E.C.'s rental rights for authors and performers is taken as proof of what is more generally afoot.

12–03 Authors' rights and copyright systems can exist together in an increasingly intermeshed world because they have a similar effect over the external plane of relationships with users. Yet even here the differing internal planes may produce difficulties. Users require quick and efficient systems for the acquisition of rights. If the law increases the range of individuals who can claim copyright and the territories over which they can claim it, the task of securing all the necessary licences may become intolerably burdensome. Objections of this kind have caused the E.C. to adopt the "up-leg" limitation on satellite broadcast licences, but that is only one case. The digitisation of information systems seems likely to force the major copyright systems into increasingly similar forms, so that multi-country uses can be accounted for on a single basis.

So much for the future. We must first consider the inherited British law on initial ownership and then the methods of dealing by assignment and licence, before turning to questions of contracting and the impact of the law upon the different copyright fields.

1. INITIAL OWNERSHIP

(1) Literary, dramatic, musical and artistic works; films

(a) *Legal framework*

12–04 Because copyright arises upon creation of the work, the question of initial ownership is not complicated, as is the case with patents and registered designs, by any need to apply for a grant. With literary, dramatic, musical and artistic works, first ownership rests in the author or co-authors unless the exception concerning employment applies.[1] This is a simpler rule than under the 1956 Act which also contained special provisions concerning employed journalists and certain artistic works made under commission.[2] It is not, however, the solution proposed by the Whitford Committee, since it

---

[1] CDPA 1988, s. 11; and for the concept of authorship (s. 9), see paras 10–04 *et seq.*, above. Crown and Parliamentary copyright is also subject to special rules: s. 11(3); see paras 13–105, 13–106, below. Co-authorship is discussed in paras 12–19—12–21, below. See generally Stephenson [1980] 2 E.I.P.R. 19.

[2] CA 1956, s. 4; preserved for works made before August 1, 1989, by CDPA 1988, Sched. 1, para. 11.

allows the copyright owner to have all the rights even when an unintended exploitation of the work materialises.[3]

Once the United Kingdom fulfils its obligation to accord copyright in a film to its principal director,[4] he or she should fall to be treated like literary and other authors. Currently the only person initially entitled to this form of copyright is the producer.[5]

(b) *Employment*

For all the types of work under consideration, an employer becomes the **12–05** initial owner of the copyright if it is made by his employee in the course of the employment and in the absence of contrary agreement.

What falls within the scope of the employment will depend upon the nature and terms of the job and the relation of the work to it.[6] But while it is often clear whether or not an invention relates to an employer's business, with copyright material the issue may well be obscure. A senior executive in a firm of management consultants wrote public lectures about the budgetary control of firms; he was held entitled to the copyright in them.[7] So also was a journalist who undertook a piece of translation and editing from the Portuguese as a special task outside his normal hours of employment; it made no difference that the piece was for an advertisement in his employer's newspapers.[8] But another journalist who wrote an internal memorandum to her colleagues about a possible article was held to be acting strictly within the course of her employment.[9]

The distinction between servants and independent contractors—between **12–06** those under contracts of service and contracts for services—is a familiar part of the principles governing vicarious liability (in which context it has already been discussed)[10] and it has become increasingly important with the growing variety of labour laws. It was in the context of copyright ownership that Denning L.J. suggested that the old test of whether the person contracting for the work could exercise control over how it was done was becoming obsolete; the question ought rather to be whether the person performing it was doing so as an integral part of the business.[11]

---

[3] See further para. 13–07, below.

[4] See paras 10–23—10–25, 10–46, above.

[5] CDPA 1988, ss. 9(2)(a), 11(1).

[6] CDPA 1988, s. 11(2). The distinction is essentially similar to that concerning patent rights: see paras 7–03 *et seq.*, above.

[7] *Stephenson Jordan v. McDonald & Evans* (1951) 69 R.P.C. 10, CA; and similarly *Noah v. Shuba* [1991] F.S.R. 14 (consultant epidemiologist in government service). In the *Stephenson Jordan* case the employer was allowed copyright in a chapter written as part of an assignment for a particular client of the employer. For application of this last case by analogy in the field of patents, see *Glasgow General* (para. 7–04, above). See generally, Monotti [1997] E.I.P.R. 715.

[8] *Byrne v. Statist Co.* [1914] 1 K.B. 622.

[9] *Beloff v. Pressdram* [1973] 1 All E.R. 241.

[10] See para. 2–09, above.

[11] *Stephenson Jordan* (case n. 7, above) at 22.

Under the former law, the employed journalist was permitted to have copyright in exploitations of his work beyond the purpose for which it was created, and there was some case for making this a general rule.[12] Instead, amid loud cries of "anomaly" from the newspaper industry, the 1988 Act cut away the exception and all employees were left to bargain for special arrangements or to demonstrate that they arise by implication.

(c) *Contracts to the contrary*

12–07 Where an employer is surrendering the initial copyright given him by law, the agreement does not have to be in any particular form and may therefore be deduced from conduct and surrounding circumstances. Where, however, an author is arranging that another person (such as a commissioner of the work) shall have copyright in it, to confer that legal title he must execute an assignment which complies with the formalities required for an actual or a future work.[13] However, an informal agreement, or indeed circumstances which give rise to fiduciary obligation, may have the effect in equity that the author from the outset holds the copyright in trust. Thus, in the "Spycatcher" case, the ex-MI5 officer, who wrote memoirs in flagrant breach of confidence owed to the Crown, was said by Members of the House of Lords to be under such an obligation.[14] In another context, work by a computer programmer as a partner has been treated as impliedly assigned in equity to the partnership,[15] and a similar conclusion is often appropriate where designs are specifically commissioned.[16] Nevertheless, such an implication is to be made only where it is necessary. Unless the commissioner can show that he needed to exclude the author from using the work and the ability to enforce the copyright against third party, he will only have an implied licence to use for the purposes of the commission.[17]

In applying these flexible rules, it may well be important to know whether the relevant presumption can be excluded by implication. If an employed teacher writes a textbook for his subject, he may be entitled to the copyright because he is employed to teach, not to write textbooks.[18] But if writing the

---

[12] CA 1956, s. 4(2); the Whitford Committee (Cmnd. 6732, 1977) para. 574, looked with favour on a scheme of "compensation" for authors, similar to that affecting inventors; for which, see paras 7–08 *et seq.*, above.

[13] For the requirements, see para. 12–12, below.

[14] *Att.-Gen. v. Guardian Newspapers (No. 2)* [1988] 3 All E.R. 545 at 645 (Lord Keith), at 647 (Lord Brightman); *cf.* at 604 (Lord Goff). Note, in the context of good faith, the moral right of privacy in certain photographs and films, paras 11–85, 11–86, above.

[15] *John Richardson v. Flanders* [1993] F.S.R. 497; Lea [1994] E.I.P.R. 152.

[16] *e.g. Merchant Adventurers v. Grew* [1973] R.P.C. 1.

[17] *Ray v. Classic FM* [1998] F.S.R. 622.

[18] It seems that university teachers (or at least Cambridge professors) are to be so regarded: Lord Evershed M.R., *Stephenson Jordan* case (n. 7, above) at 18. While today they are often employed also to undertake research, the work to be done is not specified, nor is any requirement to present the results. If copyright were to vest in the employing institution it could be used to prevent freedom of academic expression: see further, Cornish [1992] E.I.P.R. 13.

book is within the course of employment, he may nevertheless be able to show that an authority employing him has not claimed copyright from him in the past, or has not done so from other teachers who have written similar books. From such evidence an agreement that any copyright is to be the teacher's may be implied.[19]

(d) *Copyright extended and revived*

When the 1988 Act introduced the E.C.'s life-plus-70-years term for the major copyrights, it affected both works created before July 1, 1995 which were still in copyright and those which had expired but could enjoy a revival for the remaining portion of the added term.[20] The consequent proprietary issues were ducked by the Duration Directive and left to national provisions.[21] In the United Kingdom, ownership in the extended term of works still in copyright was given to the owner on December 31, 1995.[22] Where assignment had previously split title to different aspects of the copyright (say, mechanical reproduction as distinct from performing rights in music), each owner keeps its portion. Licences, including those imposed by the Copyright Tribunal, and assertions and waivers of moral rights are extended on a similar basis.[23] **12–08**

Where copyright has run out before January 1, 1996, but there would be some part of the new term still to run, the revived copyright goes to the owner at expiry. But if that person has died or ceased to exist before the revival date, the right goes to the author or film director or their personal representatives.[24] This may be particularly important for a film produced by a one-film company which was thereafter liquidated. **12–09**

With sensible circumspection, the right in revived copyright is in many cases restricted to a right to claim a reasonable royalty, set if necessary by the Copyright Tribunal. The would-be user of the work must give notice of his intention; once he does he is treated as licensed, even though the royalty is not settled until later.[25] The Directive contains nothing to preclude this solution.

---

[19] *Noah v. Shuba* (n. 7, above). See also paras 2–07, 7–04, above.
[20] See para. 10–50, above.
[21] See the Duration of Copyright and Rights in Performances Regulations 1995, S.I. 1995 No 3297, regs. 18–25; for rights in performances, see paras 13–88ff, below.
[22] Duration Regs. 1995, reg. 18. Where, however, the assignment is for a limited period, the extended term accrues to the owner of the reversionary interest.
[23] *ibid.*, reg. 21.
[24] *ibid.*, reg. 19. Pre-revival agreements to assign or grant licences in the revived term are given effect as if executed: reg. 20. Earlier waivers and assertions of moral rights are revived: reg. 22.
[25] *ibid.*, regs. 24, 25. The major exception arises where a licensing body (for which see paras 12–54 *et seq.*, below) could have granted a licence, under a scheme or otherwise.

(2) Entrepreneurial copyright

12–10 The copyrights in sound recordings, films, broadcasts, cable-casts and typographical format are conferred initially upon the "authors" who are responsible for organising production of the material (see the Table in Chapter 10 (pp. 377 to 379, heads 4 and 8). The management company for the skaters, Torville and Dean, commissioned the recording of music for one of the pair's skating routines. The company was held to be the "maker" of the resultant sound recording, rather than the person with whom it contracted to organise the writing of the musical arrangement, the hiring of musicians and technicians and the arrangements for the studio. It was the former who took the essential initiative and investment risk.[26]

2. ASSIGNMENTS AND LICENSING

(1) The distinction

12–11 The most lucrative copyright works are often exploited in a number of ways. Take a popular novel: there are the volume rights, the serial rights (in newspapers and magazines), the translation rights, the film rights, the dramatisation rights (play, opera, musical, ballet); now there will also be electronic rights to call it up from store in any one of its emanations. Add the fact that for some of these it may be desirable to split the rights of exploitation language by language; and there is the possibility of dealing with each national copyright separately. The result is an elaborate concoction of prospects.

As far as British copyright is concerned, the Act permits the various rights bundled together as copyright not only to be licensed but also to be assigned separately.[27] It is possible to assign for a limited term within the copyright period.[28] Often, therefore, there is a choice whether to grant rights by assignment or by exclusive licence. Provided that the contract in which the grant is made is clear about consequential matters, it makes no difference which type is used.[29] But if ambiguities are left, their resolution

---

[26] *A & M Records v. Video Collection* [1995] E.M.L.R. 25. The E.C. Database Directive (96/9) Rec. 41, adopts an equivalent approach in giving the maker of a database a *sui generis* right against extraction or reutilisation: see para. 13–50, below.

[27] CDPA 1988, s. 90. The right assigned can be part of one head (such as the right of reproduction or of publishing) in the list of exclusive rights. Thus the right to reproduce a book in French translation may be separately assigned. Terms purporting to give exclusive rights over acts beyond the scope of copyright can take effect only in contract.

[28] *ibid.*, s. 90(2)(b)—but no longer for part of the U.K.: an E.C. influence.

[29] A not uncommon practice has been to blur the boundary by "giving" (not "granting") the exclusive right to (say) publish. It is then a question of construction to decide which is meant. Failure to use an appropriate technical word does not preclude a finding of assignment: *Chaplin v. Frewin* [1966] Ch. 71 at 94, CA; and see *Orwin v. A.G.* [1988] F.S.R. 415, CA.

may be affected by the fact that an assignment is in essence a transfer of ownership (however partial), while a licence is in essence permission to do what otherwise would be infringement.[30] Thus a licensee's freedom to make alterations in the work may be more restricted than an assignee's.[31] The licensee may well not be entitled to assign or sub-license his interest,[32] while his licensor will retain the right to grant licences to others, unless he has granted exclusive rights to the licensee.

(2) Formal requirement

(a) *Statutory provisions*

Assignments of copyright (that is the legal right of ownership) only take **12–12** effect if they are in writing, signed by or on behalf of the assignor.[33] Once this is complied with the assignment is effective against all subsequent takers of conflicting interests. There is no public register of copyright transactions and any assignee takes the risk that there are no prior assignments of which he does not know. If there are, his only recourse may well be against his assignor.[34] Agreements to assign future copyright which are signed by or on behalf of the prospective owner have the effect of automatically vesting legal ownership in the assignee. However, there must be no other person with a superior equity.[35] On occasion, courts have been willing to imply an assignment in equity from the circumstances in which works have been produced to order.[36]

Licences do not in principle have to take any particular form. However, an exclusive licensee will have no right to sue infringers unless the licence complies with similar formalities to those for assignments.[37] Licences bind all successors in title[38] to the licensor's interest except a purchaser in good

---

[30] But if more than a bare permission, it will acquire some of the characteristics of a property right.

[31] See *Frisby v. BBC* [1967] Ch. 932.

[32] See para. 12–14, below.

[33] CDPA 1988, s. 90(3); *Roban Jig v. Taylor* [1979] R.P.C. 130, CA. Agreements which do not comply with the formal requirements may still be effective to transfer an equitable interest: see para. 12–07, above. But an assignment of a purely equitable interest must satisfy the formal requirements of the Law of Property Act 1925, s. 53(1)(c): *Roban Jig* case. Once the Rental Rights Directive is implemented, where works are incorporated into a film under agreements with the producer, the authors' rental rights are likely to be deemed assigned to the producer, subject to the guaranteed right of equitable remuneration, for which see para. 11–28, above.

[34] By way of action for breach of condition of good title or for money paid upon a total failure of consideration.

[35] CDPA 1988, s. 91(1), (2). The assignment probably has to be for valuable consideration; and see *Wah Sang v. Takmay* [1980] F.S.R. 303, CA (H.K.).

[36] See, *e.g. John Richardson v. Flanders* [1993] F.S.R. 497; *Ibcos Computers v. Barclays Mercantile* [1994] F.S.R. 275.

[37] CDPA 1988, ss. 101, 102; see para. 2–06, above.

[38] This does not clearly cover a later licensee, when one or other licence is exclusive; but he ought to be similarly treated.

faith for the valuable consideration and without notice (actual or constructive) and those who take from such a person.[39]

(b) *Implied licences*

12–13 Licences are frequently to be implied from the circumstances in which copyright material is handed over. A commission to prepare the work may well carry this inference, at least to the extent that is customary. In *Blair v. Osborne & Tomkins*,[40] an architect was hired to prepare plans for the submission of a planning application and was paid for the work to this point. After securing permission, the landowner built in a way that reproduced the plans, and was held to have an implied licence to do so even though he had not employed the architect to supervise construction of the building. But if the architect charges a nominal fee, rather than a proportion of the full scale fee, for his work up to the planning permission stage, and he makes it clear that no licence is being conferred for actual construction, he will not be held to have conferred one (at least in the absence of further factors).[41]

There may also be an implied licence without any initial commission from the licensee. A "letter to the editor" on a theme of public interest is taken to be intended for publication[42]; so also is a submission of material to a magazine, subject to any customary royalty.[43]

(c) *Trans-national movement of goods*

12–14 Expressly or impliedly, a licence may confer authority to produce copies of copyright works in one country and then to transship them to another, whatever the prohibitions in the copyright law of the second against importation. It will be recalled that in our copyright law, leaving aside the free movement requirements for the EEA, imports into the United Kingdom will infringe if, had the goods been made in Britain, they would have infringed copyright or breached an exclusive licence, to the importer's knowledge or reasonable belief.[44] Thus, provided that the goods are actually made outside Britain, it is not relevant to consider whether they were legitimately made under the copyright law of that place.

---

[39] CDPA 1988, s. 90 (4). Licences of future copyright are similarly treated: s. 91(3).
[40] *Blair v. Osborne & Tomkins* [1971] 2 Q.B. 78, CA; and see *Beck v. Montana Constructions* [1964–1965] N.S.W.R. 229.
[41] *Stovin-Bradford v. Volpoint* [1971] Ch. 1007, CA *cf.* also *Netupsky v. Dominion Bridge* (1969) 68 W.W.R. 529; *Barnett v. Cape Town Foreshore Board* (1960) [1978] F.S.R. 176.
[42] *Springfield v. Thame* (1903) 89 L.T. 242; the editor may also alter such a letter in order to fit it in. See further *Roberts v. Candiware* [1980] F.S.R. 352.
[43] *Hall-Brown v. Illiffe* [1928–1935] Mac. C.C. 88; *cf. PRS v. Coates* [1923–1928] Mac. C.C. 103; *Banks v. CBS Songs* [1996] E.M.L.R. 440.
[44] CDPA 1988, ss. 22, 27(3); see para. 11–29, above; and for the special position of computer programs, see para. 11–27, above.

The extensive scope of British patent rights (which in principle cover **12–15** even the subsequent resale and use of goods first marketed by the patentee) led, by way of counterbalance, to the presumption of a broad implied licence. If the patentee disposes of the goods without limiting the manner in which they may subsequently be dealt with, the implication is that there is no restriction on their circulation or use; but the contrary might be inferred from all the circumstances.[45]

What, then, of a sale abroad of "legitimate" goods embodying copyright? Since copyright does not embrace their subsequent sale and use in any general way, arguably the implied permission to export is the stronger. But in *Time-Life v. Interstate Parcel*[46] the High Court of Australia refused to draw this analogy. Time-Life was exploiting its Australian copyright in certain cookery books by licensing it exclusively to a Dutch subsidiary, which in turn sub-licensed an exclusive distributor in Australia. A parallel importer bought its copies in the United States which were first marketed there by Time-Life.[47] The unconditional sales in America were held to carry no implied licence to import into Australia.[48] It was not therefore necessary to show either an express limitation ("Not for sale in Australia" or the like) or surrounding circumstances (such as knowledge of the exclusive distributorship) which would negate the implied licence.

An English Court might well be persuaded to draw the analogy to the patent cases which the High Court rejected.[49] Even so, it will be seen that the argument is only about implied intent and the need to give sufficient notice that goods are not to be transferred from one national market to another. It is not about public policy rules overriding the copyright owner's wish to preserve price differentials between different countries by means of copyright.[50]

Once copies have been legitimately sold within the internal market of the **12–16** EEA, they must thereafter be free to circulate between Member States, following the basic requirement of free movement prescribed in Articles 30 and 36 or the Rome Treaty. However, at the perimeter borders of the EEA as a whole, the Commission believes that intellectual property of all kinds should prevent the importation of "legitimate" goods, even though they are

---

[45] See para. 6–15, above. For trade marks, see para. 17–123, below.
[46] [1978] F.S.R. 251.
[47] The parallel importers sold in Australia for just over half the exclusive distributors' retail price. For criticism by the Prices Surveillance Authority, see its *Inquiry into the Price of Books* (1989), and *Inquiry into the Price of Sound Recordings* (1990).
[48] An argument based upon the warranty of quiet possession got no further.
[49] Laddie *et al.*, paras 18.19–18.24, argue that the patent law rule should apply equally to copyright. Its effect, as they concede, would be at most to oblige an objector to place an express limitation on packaging. With a bit of effort any producer in the know could thus prevent parallel imports. In any case, *cf.* Walton and Laddie, *Patent Law of Europe and the United Kingdom* (1978), paras 948–950, calling *Betts* "illogical". See further, paras 17–114 *et seq.*, below.
[50] Note, however, Murphy J.'s reference to possible breaches of the Trade Practices Act 1974 (Commonwealth): [1978] F.S.R. 251 at 287–288.

initially marketed outside by the internal rightowner or an associated enterprise.[51] Whatever the difficulties of principle in translating this policy into trade-mark law, in respect of copyright law in the United Kingdom, the result will very largely be achieved in the course of implementing the Directive on Rental, Lending and Neighbouring Rights. As already explained, the "distribution right"—the primary right to issue copies to the public by first putting them into circulation—is intended to be excluded from operation only where there has already been a "putting into circulation" within the EEA[52]; releasing in another country is not to count.

12–17   Secondary infringement by importation for non-private or domestic use (with the requisite state of knowledge), so important and problematic a provision in the past in relation to parallel imports, now plays only a lesser role.[53] It will cover those cases where the importing is for some internal purpose of the importer or its associates, such as bringing in a film for showing in cinemas or a record for broadcasting.[54] In order to secure customs seizure against parallel imports, it will be necessary to show that the actual importation is of an infringing copy.[55] With the implementation of the Rental and Related Rights Directive, at least the primary distribution right in the entrepreneurial copyrights applies to the first sale or similar commercial act after importation. This simplifies considerably the task of those who pursue parallel importers, as well as pirates.[56]

12–18   There must remain the question, has the person entitled either to the distribution right or the importation right nonetheless consented to the importation or subsequent sale of goods initially marketed outside the EEA with that person's assent? The distribution of newspapers and magazines may well be an instance where it is natural to expect such freedom, at least if no express conditions are laid down.

(3) Co-ownership of copyright

12–19   Co-ownership may come about in two ways: (1) because the copyright material is produced by joint authors, or (2) because an interest is assigned to more than one person.[57] In each case, there are circumstances to be

---

[51] See paras 18–17 et seq., below.

[52] See para. 11–27, above, expressing doubts about the legal effectiveness of the proposals.

[53] Because this is now so, the precise import of the secondary infringement provision (CDPA 1988, s. 27(3)) will not be investigated. For a virtuoso discussion of the subject, see Laddie et al., paras 18.27–18.51. For the present at least, the original 1988 formulation will continue to apply to unregistered design right (CDPA 1988, ss. 227, 228): see para. 14–41, below.

[54] These may give rise to difficult fringe cases, such as importation in order to use in a way that is permitted: for instance, as an ephemeral recording for a broadcast (para. 11–49, above); Albert v. Fletcher [1976] R.P.C. 615, SC (N.Z.).

[55] CDPA 1988, ss. 111, 112.

[56] See para. 11–28, above.

[57] In the case of assignment, whether the co-owners become joint tenants or tenants in common depends on the terms of the assignment. Joint authors have interests as tenants in common: Lauri v. Renad [1892] 3 Ch. 402; Redwood v. Feldman [1979] R.P.C. 1.

distinguished. Joint authorship does not arise where a creative work is compounded of parts that demand discrete forms of mental activity: the text and music for a song or opera; script, scenery and costume design for a play; an original text and a translation of it.[58] In such cases there are distinct copyrights, each with its own duration measured by relation to the life of the relevant author, each requiring for its exploitation the assent of the owner of that particular right.[59]

Co-authorship occurs when collaborators have worked to produce **12–20** copyright work of a single kind "in prosecution of a preconcerted joint design".[60] Each must provide a significant creative input to the expression of the finished work (akin to penmanship), which is not distinct from the contributions of others.[61] It does not arise where one author writes a play, and another subsequently adds a scene to it; rather the first author brings into existence a copyright in what he has written, and likewise the second.[62] In the latter case, infringement of each copyright is a question whether there has been substantial copying of the work that each covers; neither derives advantage from the other's contribution.[63]

Co-ownership by assignment does not arise when different aspects of the **12–21** copyright (publishing rights, performing rights, film rights, etc.) are transferred to different people: each has the exclusive right over his apportioned subject-matter.[64]

In contrast with patents, it has been held that a joint owner of copyright or a part of it is not entitled to do acts within its scope without securing permission from his fellows.[65] Equally a licensee needs permission from all his owners.[66] This can cause problems when it is not clear how many authors contributed to a joint work; for one thing, nice distinctions may

---

[58] See CDPA 1988, ss. 3, 10.

[59] See also para. 10–12, above.

[60] *Levy v. Rutley* (1871) L.R. 6 C.P. 523 at 528, 529.

[61] *Cala Homes v. McAlpine (No. 1)* [1995] F.S.R. 623; *Fylde Microsystems v. Key Radio* [1998] F.S.R. 449; *Ray v. Classic FM* [1998] F.S.R. 623.

[62] Note the case of correcting and editing a text in the course of its production, which is treated as producing a joint work if the editor's contribution is sufficient to attract copyright at all: *Springfield v. Thame* (1903) 89 L.T. 242; *cf. Samuelson v. Producers Distributing* (1931) 48 R.P.C. 580 at 586.

[63] *e.g. Warwick Films v. Eisinger* (para. 11–13, above).

[64] See CDPA 1988, s. 90(2)(a).

[65] *Cescinsky v. Routledge* [1916] 2 K.B. 325; *Cala Homes v. McAlpine* [1995] F.S.R. 818; *Ray v. Classic FM* [1998] F.S.R. 623, *cf.* para. 7–18, above. The rule is thus the opposite of that for patents (for which, see para. 7–18, above). The difference may perhaps lie in the need to protect an author against an entrepreneur, when both have become co-owners.

[66] *Powell v. Head* (1879) 12 Ch.D. 686; *Mail Newspapers v. Express Newspapers* [1987] F.S.R. 90 (one co-owner clinically dead). As a corollary, one joint owner can sue without having to join others.

have to be drawn between authors who participated in actually expressing the copyright work and preliminary contributors who put up starting ideas.[67]

3. DEALINGS BASED ON COPYRIGHT

(1) Types of dealing

12–22 The worlds of information, education and entertainment, shaped as they are by copyright and rights in performances, are growing increasingly complex. As copying, storing and replaying technologies advance, the numbers and the variety of users, commercial, public and private, splay outwards, the search for ways of tying them to licences gains energy and, in some cases, desperation.

How then are these proprietary possibilities turned to effect? In this section, attention focuses primarily on the plane between creator and the exploiter with whom he or she collaborates. It has to be kept in mind that, thanks to advances in copying, storing and replaying technology, the plane of owners and users is often an elaborate maze. Old patterns of understanding would treat a work of (say) fiction as primarily a matter of book publication, and only secondarily as a text which might be anthologised, filmed or photocopied, but these attitudes are being replaced. A work goes forth to find its own best seeding-grounds. All prospects need to be dealt with in advance in contracts for exploitation.

On this creator-exploiter plane, the terms which are set for the exploitation of a particular work derive from three principal possibilities:

12–23 (1) **Individual negotiation:** leading to contractual arrangements for the rights and returns upon them within the framework of an employment relationship, a commission to undertake work or an agreement to commercialise work already done. The negotiation may be by the parties themselves, or either side may use agents. The terms may be hammered out from scratch, they may be presented on a "take-it-or-leave-it" basis by an exploiter armed with standard terms, or even by a successful creator strong enough to play the field. Whatever the particular mix, the deal is struck on the basis of the individual bargaining position of each party.

12–24 (2) **Collective negotiation:** trade union activity by creators and performers is common, particularly in the music and audio-visual industries; it may well be matched by association among

---

[67] *e.g.* if a ghost writer is commissioned to write up a celebrity's memoirs he alone is the author: *Evans v. Hulton* [1923–1928] Mac. C.C. 51; and see *Kenrick v. Lawrence* (1890) 285 Q.B.D. 99 (para. 10–14, above); *Tate v. Thomas* [1921] 1 Ch. 503. But remember now the copyright of the speaker who is recorded: paras 10–34, 10–35, above. As to film directors, see Kamina [1994] E.I.P.R. 319; Laddie *et al.*, para. 5.26.

entrepreneurs which aims to establish a countervailing force of equal significance. In many circumstances, the groups represent employees and employers, as in most labour relations; but even though many writers, composers and film directors operate as independent contractors, they may join guilds and associations which will negotiate terms collectively on their behalf. Following the standard pattern of British industrial practice, these collective agreements will acquire legal force to the extent that their terms are then written into individual contracts.

Between this second category and the first lies a no-man's-land of weaker collective action, in which a creators' association promotes model terms but does not have the strength to secure undertakings from exploiters that they will always abide by them.

(3) **Collecting society action:** with a collecting society the object of the **12–25** joint action shifts from the creator-exploiter plane to that of the owner-user. A typical collecting society aims to generate returns on repetitive uses of copyright material such as performances, photocopying and now electronic distribution, which it would be too costly for owners to demand on an individual basis. The first field in which it was demonstrated that collecting societies were not only necessary but could be made to work—and indeed to work on the basis of international collaboration—was in the performance of music. In that field, the necessary economies of scale came from broadcasting, with its dependence on live and recorded music. With this foundation, it was possible to maintain an often dogged policing of dance and concert halls, cinemas, bars and restaurants, shops, schools and so on.

The earliest among these societies—in Britain, the Performing **12–26** Right Society (PRS)[68]—had as members both composers and their publishers. It is quite possible to apply the collecting society principle to associations purely of creators, as is now occurring with film directors, or to associations purely of exploiters, as occurred once record producers were given sound recording rights, particularly when they extended to rights in performances as well as over reproduction.

One problem, which any society may have, is to prevent penetration of its ranks by users whose ultimate interest is to keep royalty rates low or otherwise undermine the society's objectives. A collecting society acquires very considerable market power by drawing together the rights in the whole repertoire of works sought by users. Another problem accordingly is to satisfy such arbiters of the public interest as competition authorities that this economic dominance is a

---

[68] See para. 9–49, above.

necessity.[69] This task, which never disappears for long, is made more difficult if cartels of producers seek to justify their joint economic action by posing as copyright collecting societies.

12–27 Recognising these three categories of contracting helps to explain two basic questions: why has modern copyright law tended to proliferate the number of authors' rights and neighbouring rights? And why have countries varied in their views of the extent to which the law must guarantee fair dealing between authors and their exploiters? The grandest authors, and even more, the most popular performers, are in a position to play entrepreneurs off one against another. The general run of creators, actors and musicians, are not, and this includes, of course, the famous before they become so.

To the extent that labour relations between these two sides have become settled, it is enough for collective agreements to define the terms on which work is done, and to leave exploitation of rights against users to the production organisers. But collectivisation of this kind is far from universal. One prospect, in order for authors and performers to improve their position, is to increase their property rights. This may give them some enhanced status in the direct bargaining process, whether this is individual or collective—and at least some of them may sooner or later be able to turn this to financial account.[70] But beyond this, a distinct right may well be necessary in order to form a society which will collect directly from users. Obviously, where collective bargaining or direct arrangements with users can succeed, the case for protective legislation is reduced.

(2) Legal controls on bargaining

12–28 In the United Kingdom the Acts of 1956 and 1988 have avoided provisions designed to protect the individual author or performer when he or she bargains from a position of economic weakness or inexperience. There is no provision to revise a royalty arrangement when a work becomes a best seller, nor is there any general guarantee of an "equitable" or "proportionate" share of earnings.[71] In part that is because general contract law provides means of intervening in egregious cases,[72] and in recent years the Courts have not hesitated to use this weaponry in entertainment industry

---

[69] Para. 12–53, below. See Ficsor [1985] Copyright 341; Kernochan [1985] Copyright 389; Freegard [1985] Copyright 443; Karnell [1986] Copyright 45; Report by the International Bureau, WIPO, "Collective Administration of Copyright and Neighboring Rights" [1989] Copyright 309; Karnell in *Festskrift till Lars Hjerner* (1990) p. 277.

[70] For an instance, following from an increase in legal rights, see para. 9–53, above.

[71] For the special case of the rental right of authors and performers, see para. 11–28, above.

[72] The determination of terms orally agreed in a publishing contract may result in a decision favouring an author against a publisher: as in *Malcolm v. Oxford University Press* [1994] E.M.L.R. 17, CA.

cases. Both the common law public policy against restraints of trade and the equitable doctrine of undue influence have been called in play.

(a) *Restraint of trade*

The common law treats as unenforceable any contractual term which is in **12–29** unreasonable restraint of trade, having regard both to the interests of the parties and the public interest.[73] The doctrine has been applied with some severity to covenants binding an employee not to work for a competitor or engage in competitive work once he leaves an employment; such covenants have to be strictly limited in terms of time and place if they are not to be regarded as unreasonable. The doctrine has been applied more cautiously to restraint clauses on the sale of a business, and to restrictive business agreements among competitors.[74] However, in the 1960s, alongside the development of a British system of competition control, the Courts used the restraint of trade doctrine against anti-competitive arrangements operating both horizontally and vertically.

It was at this juncture, in *A. Schroeder Music v. Macaulay*,[75] that the **12–30** House of Lords found an agreement between a young unknown pop composer and a leading music publisher to be unenforceable as being in unreasonable restraint of trade. The broader label, "unconscionable", was also used of the agreement, but there has since been some resistance against adopting this highly amorphous concept as the essential test of what is inoperative.[76] The objection in the *Schroeder* case was the evidently unbalanced character of the obligations in what was a standard term contract: by its terms a composer who generated a moderate flow of royalties (£5,000 over five years) was obliged to give his services exclusively to the publisher for 10 years without any escape clause. The publisher was to be granted copyright throughout the world in all songs written solely or jointly, the composer undertaking to "obey and comply with all lawful orders and directions" from the publisher. By contrast, the publisher could at any time give one month's notice of termination, and was in any case under no obligation to publish any of the songs, being merely obliged to pay royalties and to make modest advances against them. The House of

---

[73] See generally, *e.g.* Treitel, *The Law of Contract* (9th ed., 1995), pp. 401–424, 919–920; and for further details, Bagehot, *Music Business Agreements* (1989), esp. App. 3; Nelson, *Law of Entertainment and Broadcasting* (1995), Chap. 5.

[74] Note especially *Printers and Numerical Registering v. Sampson* (1875) L.R. 19 Eq. 462 (patent licensee's obligation to transfer rights in subsequent inventions to licensor held valid: celebrated statement of the virtues of sanctity of contract); *Morris v. Coleman* (1812) 18 Ves. Jr (Ch) 437 (author's undertaking not to engage in competing publication); and see Downey [1992] Int. Media L. 74.

[75] [1974] 1 W.L.R. 1308, [1974] 3 All E.R. 616.

[76] See citations in Treitel (n. 73, above) at pp. 370–373; Goff and Jones: *Law of Restitution* (5th ed., 1998) pp. 343–345.

Lords regarded such terms as manifestly unfair,[77] without considering the highly competitive nature of the music industry, with its relentless search for new talent.[78]

The prime concern of the law in intervening to end an unreasonable restraint of trade is to aid the individual who has been unduly tied. If, therefore, he is an established artist who, with professional advice, renegotiates the terms of an earlier agreement in ways that recognise his rise to stardom, he is likely to be held bound by the new agreement, even if it ties him to working for one record company exclusively for a considerable number of years. There is a policy which strongly favours upholding a renegotiated arrangement because it is a compromise.[79]

(b) *Undue influence*

12–31 In equity, relief has long been given against contracts, wills and other transactions which have been entered into under undue influence, that is in cases where the person entering the transaction is so influenced by the ideas and personality of another that he or she is unable to reach any independent decision about its desirability.[80] Indeed the courts will presume from the existence of certain relationships between two persons that undue influence affected their transaction, unless sufficient evidence is produced to show that after all there was a chance to exercise proper judgment— usually by demonstrating that independent advice was offered.

This relief typically takes the form of an order for rescission, which seeks, where possible, to put the parties back in an equivalent position to that which they occupied before execution of the transaction. Thus a contract made under undue influence is treated as voidable upon a Court order, but not void *ab initio*. Acts done in execution of the contract before it is avoided—and in particular where they have an effect on innocent third parties—may accordingly remain binding.

12–32 The relationship between a pop artist and his manager has been characterised as one capable of raising a presumption of undue influence. This will be so where, for instance, a young, inexperienced and unknown composer, librettist or performer enters publishing, recording or management agreements by virtue of which the manager master-minds the subsequent success of the artist (*Gilbert O'Sullivan v. Management Agency*

---

[77] In a decision which followed soon after, Lord Denning M.R., a leading protagonist of the concept of "unconscionability", condemned a similar agreement as having "some amazing provisions" which imposed a "stranglehold" on the composers concerned: *Clifford Davis Management v. WEA Records* [1975] 1 All E.R. 237. See also *Zang Tumb Tuum v. Johnson* [1993] E.M.L.R. 61; *Silvertone Records v. Mountford* [1993] E.M.L.R. 152.

[78] Hence the vigorous criticism by Trebilcock (1976) 26 U. Toronto L.J. 359. For a more realistic assessment of the economic pressures on pop music developers, see *Elton John v. James* (n. 82, below), esp. at 450–453.

[79] See *Panayiotou v. Sony* [1994] E.M.L.R. 229.

[80] See generally, Treitel (n. 73, above), pp. 377–387; Brownsword [1998] I.P.R. 311.

and Music[81]; *Elton John v. James*[82]). Subsequent events, such as failure to raise any timely objection, or later agreements made with independent advice, which assume that the earlier agreements are valid, may provide reasons for refusing rescission of the contracts. Even then, if there is secrecy which leads to the artist being paid less than his entitlement, this will amount to fraud for which damages will be awarded.[83]

There are cases in which both restraint of trade and undue influence **12–33** arise on the facts, in which case rescission may be ordered wherever it is appropriate. If there is only a finding of restraint of trade, it is by no means clear what effect this can have on assignments of copyright which have taken place before the Court declares the contract invalid. In *Clifford Davis v. WEA Records*,[84] the Court of Appeal held that, where copyright in songs was assigned under such an invalid agreement, the assignee could not assert any copyright in songs already assigned against a record company to which the composers concerned had subsequently granted rights of exploitation. But that decision arose at a very early stage in the evolution of these modern rules.

(c) *E.C. Competition Law*

Article 85 of the Treaty of Rome may also affect the contracts of leading **12–34** artists in entertainment.[85] If they have a significant share of the market for their type of service, then the effect of exclusivity deals upon that market will be judged from the perspective of public interest in maintaining competition, rather than from considerations of fairness to the parties. Such an argument was raised in the unsuccessful attempt by George Michael to avoid his exclusive recording contract with Sony.[86] The reasons for rejecting the argument—that the market was purely national, and that the long ties were "objectively necessary"—seem inadequate, but were at least related to the particular circumstances. In another case, the Rules of Competition could well apply.

(3) **The main copyright industries**

(a) *Publishing*

Among professional writers of fiction, biography and the like, established **12–35** authors tend to have literary agents, who have an insider's view of publishing. They do much to improve the competitiveness of the market,

---

[81] [1985] Q.B. 428; to some extent foreshadowed by Lord Denning M.R. in the *Clifford Davis* case (n. 77, above) at 241.

[82] (1985) [1991] F.S.R. 397.

[83] In the *Elton John* case (n. 82, above) rescission was refused for delay and acquiescence, but the levying of unjustified management charges led to an award of damages. It is one of the greatest difficulties in copyright businesses for authors and artists to ensure that they are receiving accurate accounts.

[84] [1975] 1 All E.R. 237.

[85] *RAI/Unitel* [1987] 3 C.M.L.R. 306.

[86] See *Panayiotou* (n. 79, above); Coulthard [1995] J.B.L. 414; and generally Fine [1992] Ent. L.R. 6.

and can guard authors against the dangers inherent in any relationship as complex as the modern publishing agreement. Significantly, it is often the agent who presents the draft contract to the publisher for negotiation.

While this practice, less known in non-English language publishing, has probably retarded the growth of collective action by writers, the practice has nonetheless advanced in the last two decades. Two major associations, the Society of Authors and the Writers' Guild of Great Britain, have indeed collaborated in producing "Minimum Term Agreements" (MTAs) which they seek to have accepted by publishers. These have not yet become trade standards, though some individual firms apply a version of them.

12–36 The MTAs specify the rights which are the subject of a publishing agreement, the minimum royalties to be paid for each right within copyright, the type of right granted (exclusive licence unless there is some specific justification for an assignment), and the various forms of exploitation covered. As to the forms of exploitation, these will today cover not only the primary forms of book publication in home and overseas markets, in translation, etc., they will also include "volume subsidiary rights", such as quotation, digest, book-club, later serial, periodical, educational-edition, large-print, strip-cartoon and reprography rights; and "non-volume subsidiary rights", such as first serial, dramatisation, merchandising and—suddenly now of high significance in many cases—electronic publishing rights. It will be appreciated that in today's rapidly changing world MTAs themselves need revision as new forms of exploitation develop.

As to the duration of the grant, the different versions of the MTA have tackled the question of a reversionary power in various ways: a maximum licence term of 20 years[87] or of a period to be fixed in the particular agreement; full- or part-term licences which in certain cases (such as cessation of production of the work) become capable of termination by the author; licences which after a specified period or in specified circumstances become capable of renegotiation.

12–37 For publishers in general, the Publishers' Association has its own voluntary Code of Practice and this acknowledges some of the claims of the MTAs.[88] Thus it calls for the clear statement of all obligations assumed by each side, with proper explanation of the terms to an author who is not professionally advised. It recommends that the publisher be granted only a licence unless there are special reasons for an assignment. There are certain reversionary arrangements and a statement that an author should have "proper opportunity to share in the success of a work" (though nothing more specific is said about the measure of this sharing). The manuscript should be handled promptly in accordance with a set timetable and the author should be informed about all important design, promotion, market-

---

[87] By 1992 five publishers had been prepared to include a 20-year limitation in their MTA: *The Author* (1992), p. 91.
[88] See Clark *et al.*, *Publishing Agreements* (5th ed., 1997), App. F.

ing and sub-licensing decisions. Cancellation by the publisher should occur only for sufficient reason. The author should receive regular and clear accounting. The publisher should respect the integrity of the work and "fullest possible credit" should be accorded to the author.[89]

(b) *Music*

(i) **Composition and initial publication, recording and performances.** The **12–38** writing of music is not a field in which collective negotiation has proceeded far. Composers now have an Association of Composers' Organisations, comprising representatives of the Association of Professional Composers, the Composers Guild of Great Britain and the British Academy of Songwriters, Composers and Authors. To some extent this umbrella organisation negotiates with the Music Publishers' Association, the Producers Alliance for Cinema and Television (PACT), the BBC and the PRS on rights and appropriate fee levels, but this falls short of general agreements on minimum terms. It was the absence of either composers' agents or collective protection among entrants into pop composition, coinciding with the sudden cult of the composer-performer, which 20 years ago led the courts to their resilient use of the doctrines of restraint of trade and undue influence.[90]

The consequence of this intervention has been to enhance the position of the composer. While it is still the practice for copyright to be assigned to the publisher, the transfer of rights is no longer always for the entire copyright term. There may well be clauses allowing for reversion of title in works which the publisher chooses not to promote; for termination of the agreement (including the assignment) after a limited term; for revision of royalties either in accordance with a scheme prescribed from the outset or through an obligation to renegotiate. In the past publishers have taken express power to make adaptations, arrangements and alterations to popular compositions, and to change the title. Such clauses will now constitute waivers of the composer's moral right of integrity in the circumstances to which they apply. One effect of the statutory statement of this moral right, however, may be to induce a scrupulous interpretation of any contract term which operates as a waiver.

(ii) **Consequential uses: mechanical right.** In the United Kingdom the **12–39** Mechanical-Copyright Protection Society (MCPS) is the principal body through which licences to record musical works are obtained by record

---

[89] Other provisions cover: liability to third parties, author's costs of preparation, calculation of direct costs and overheads, cost of corrections, option clauses, remaindering, changes of publisher and imprint, assistance to literary estate, and co-operation in general. For the text, see Clark, App. F.
[90] See paras 12–29 *et seq.*, above.

producers, film producers (other than for specially commissioned works), broadcasters and others from composers, lyricists and their publishers. MCPS is owned by the Music Publishers' Association and operates not as assignee of the relevant copyright but as exclusive management agent for the copyright owners. In music industry practice the composer will normally assign copyright to the individual publisher, save for the performing rights, which go to the PRS.

MCPS offers standard terms for membership to composers and to publishers without specifying any minimum level of activity as a pre-condition. To the Membership Agreement is annexed the Terms and Conditions of Business, which settle the commission charged by MCPS for its services and the basis for collecting and distributing royalties. Whatever becomes due is paid to the publisher, who alone will be responsible for distributing a share to composer and lyricist, in accordance with whatever contractual arrangements exist between them.

It is part of MCPS's role that it will negotiate with groups of users and individuals and it operates three main schemes: one for manufacture and sale of sound recordings, tapes and videos; one for recordings made by broadcasting organisations, suppliers of background music and juke-box contents, etc. (these take the form of blanket licences); and one for other recordings, including synchronisation of music in films. The operation of these schemes is further clarified by codes of practice which accompany the licence terms themselves. Since the 1988 Act these schemes are subject to the jurisdiction of the Copyright Tribunal.[91] The same Act abolished the statutory licence for the mechanical right in musical works which imposed a set royalty on the recording company.[92] Control over excessive demands for this copyright has accordingly passed to the Tribunal.[93]

12–40 (iii) **Consequential uses: performing and related rights.** The Performing Right Society acts on behalf of its two categories of members—composers and lyricists, publishers—to license the public performance,[94] broadcasting and cabling of music,[95] mainly by establishing tariffs for different categories

---

[91] See paras 12–54 et seq., above.

[92] See Copyright Act 1956, s. 8; the royalty was 6 1/4 per cent of the net selling price of records.

[93] For exercise of this jurisdiction, see para. 12–58, below.

[94] A well-established tradition leaves administration of "grand rights", i.e. the licensing of stage performances and the like of a dramatic-musical work or a ballet, to the authors or their publishers; while the "small rights" in other performances go to the PRS. The grand/small distinction is defined with some precision in the Directives of the PRS: for which, see Cotterell, *Performance* (3rd ed., 1993), pp. 508–510.

[95] As well as these performing rights, the PRS administers the synchronisation right in works commissioned for the soundtrack of a particular film, in order to secure royalties on cinema performances. There are provisions in its rules for the return of the rights in a work to a member in order to allow the licensing of performances in so-called "compilation shows": see Cotterell (n. 89, above) pp. 511–512. The PRS has, however, resisted the not dissimilar demand from the Irish pop-group, "U2", to acquire back the right to license performance of its own works in its concerts. This has led to a Decision of the Irish Competition Authority criticising the PRS's refusal: Decision No. 326, May 18, 1994.

of use.[96] These are often reached after negotiation with trade associations and other representative bodies of user.[97] The membership rules, which respect the requirement that there must be no discrimination against those who come from or operate in the other E.U. countries, prescribe minimum levels of activity to qualify for provisional, associate and finally full membership.[98]

The Society requires the assignment to it of the rights it administers, a **12–41** practice justified by its not infrequent need to back its system of inspection by litigation against those who refuse to take licences. Its licences are mainly granted to those who operate venues and to broadcasting organisations, rather than to performers or their agents. Information about works performed is gathered by a mixture of methods. In the case of major broadcasting, an accurate schedule is provided; but for many other circumstances (theatres, halls, clubs, cinemas, pubs, restaurants, shops, coaches, etc.) a more or less sophisticated scheme of sampling or indirect indication is used.

The revenue received (after deduction of administration expenses) is **12–42** divided principally by reference to a complex points system, which takes account both of characteristics of the work performed (principally its duration) and the nature of the performance (television or sound broadcast, live performance, recorded performance, background or foreground, etc). As between those who have a share in a particular work, there is a standard division of two-thirds to the composer and one-third to the publisher; or equal shares if there is also a lyric writer. This standard can be varied by the two sides, but never so as to allow the publisher more than half.[99]

While this distribution scheme aims to divide revenue in accordance with the actual use of works, there is a relatively minor departure which provides a measure of social benefit to older members. Those who are 50-years old or more and have completed 25 years of membership qualify for an allowance under the Earnings Equalisation Scheme.

The technology which has become available for the private copying of **12–43** sound recordings has made considerable inroads into the sales of recordings of music. Implementation of the Rental Right Directive will give the authors (and performers) of works recorded their own rental right. Both acquire an unwaivable right to equitable remuneration from the record producer or subsequent assignee of their rental right, to be assessed if necessary by the Copyright Tribunal. Although no contractual agreement can fix this amount so as to render it incapable of review, the payment may

---

[96] There are now more than 40 standard tariffs.
[97] Subject ultimately to the jurisdiction of the Copyright Tribunal.
[98] For associate and full membership, the main criterion is the earning of a prescribed minimum royalty from the PRS.
[99] The PRS must be notified of the special agreement. The division must be made in twelfths. There are numerous consequential rules: see Cotterell (n. 94, above), pp. 513–515.

take the form of one lump sum paid at the time of assignment. If such a payment is made, but the rental earnings then turn out to be unexpectedly large, there ought to be an entitlement to more: the right is, after all, "unwaivable".[1]

(c) *Screenwriting: film, television and video*

12–44 Production of audio-visual material in Britain takes place on many levels, from feature films, through television productions, to videograms, documentaries and promotional material. Much of it is produced on an "in-house" basis, in which case, most of the writing and other copyright contributions will be made by employees. The copyright will therefore belong to the employer from the outset unless some other contractual arrangement applies.

Production on commission is also important, particularly for television, since both the main broadcasting organisations—the British Broadcasting Corporation and the Independent Television Commission (for the two commercial channels)—are under statutory duties to commission 25 per cent of their broadcasts from independent producers. The effect of this upon the creators of material is that a production starts from a commission contract between the BBC or one of the 15 regional commercial licensees of the ITC and the outside producer.[2] It will be for the producer then to hire the writers and performers. The commissioner, as the main financier of the production, often has the right to approve the producer's selection.

The proprietary basis of the commission is that, once the film is complete and is transferred in return for final payment, all copyright is assigned to the commissioning broadcaster. This necessitates (1) that the producer has already secured all copyright in contributions, either through the rule on employee's copyright or by assignment; and (2) that all obligations (for example, to pay royalties) which arise under the contributors' contracts are assumed by the broadcaster upon transfer of the film. Since the producer remains contractually liable on the obligations, he must take an appropriate indemnity from the commissioner.

12–45 These arrangements have in the past been made within a copyright framework in which the material in the film has been protected for the relevant author's life and 50 years, and the film itself has had a producer's copyright, normally for 50 years from release. In implementation of the Duration Directive, as already explained, much changes. Even for existing films, copyright in the contributions extends to each author's life plus 70

---

[1] For the meaning of the term, see Reinbothe and von Lewinski, *The E.C. Directive on Rental and Lending Rights and on Piracy* (1993) p. 72. See also para. 11–28, above.

[2] On the commercial side, what is commissioned for the ITC network is a matter for negotiation between the 15 licensees, in itself a complex and politically sensitive matter: see Cotterell (n. 94, above), pp. 539–540; Nelson, *Law of Entertainment and Broadcasting* (1993), Chap. 28.

years and introduces the complex machinery for revival of rights. Copyright in the film itself changes, if it is made after July 1, 1994, to a right lasting for 70 years from the last death among the four "associated lives".[3] For films made after June 30, 1994 (subject to exploitation arrangements in a contract made before November 1992), this film copyright will belong initially to the producer and chief director jointly, unless the latter is in employment. So the producer must take the necessary assignment, on such terms as may be bargained. So far as rental rights are concerned (and this affects all the authors and also performers), the guarantee of equitable remuneration will provide one protected floor in the overall negotiations.

Writers' and other creators' contracts have accordingly to be understood **12–46** within larger frameworks of direct organisation and commission. The Writers' Guild of Great Britain, which is now the main representative body of screenwriters, has negotiated a range of collective agreements with British producers of cinema films, television productions and videos. These include:

(1) For commissions from independent production companies: the Writers' Collective Agreement for Films, Television Films and Videograms; the latest version (1992) is between the Writers' Guild and the Producers Alliance for Cinema and Television (PACT). Annexed to it is the Screenwriting Credits Agreement of 1974.

(2) For commissions from the broadcasting producers for television drama: the Writers' Collective Agreements (a) with the British Broadcasting Corporation[4]; and (b) with the fifteen programme companies which have regional licences from the Independent Television Commission (ITC) for the commercial television channels.

While varying in detail these agreements cover much common ground, **12–47** and the first of them, the agreement with independent production companies, will be referred to in a little detail here. Its prime object is to give structure to an arrangement by which fees will be payable as work progresses through different stages, while allowing the producer the option to reject the work and terminate the agreement. It therefore allows for a maximum of four stages: the preliminary stage of drawing a story outline; first draft script; second draft script; and principal photography script. For each stage an initial and a delivery fee are payable, which must not be below the minima prescribed. Upon completing payment for a stage, the

---

[3] Chief director, screenplay writer, dialogue writer, composer of commissioned music: see para. 10–46, above.

[4] In an allied field, note also the Collective Agreement of 1992 between the BBC and the Writers' Guild, together with the Society of Authors, for the commissioning of original or adapted drama for radio: see Cotterell (n. 94, above), pp. 476–480.

producer becomes owner of the copyright in the work thus far written, and becomes entitled to have another person develop the writing further—a provision which operates as a waiver of the author's moral right of integrity.

On completion of the film, the rights acquired by the producer vary somewhat with the nature of the film. To take the case of a feature film: if the budget is over £2 million, the producer will gain all rights except those for free (that is, non-pay) television broadcasting and videograms; if the budget is in the range £750,000–£2 million, the producer has either world theatre rights or two United Kingdom network television transmissions, plus in either case strictly limited theatre rights; for budgets below this, the same applies, save that the theatre rights are excluded. Further rights must accordingly be separately acquired and the agreement specifies minimum amounts payable for a considerable range of additional uses.

There are also provisions:

(1) for re-acquiring copyright, for example where the writing is completely original and two years have elapsed without the start of filming; there can be retrieval upon repayment of half the fees received;

(2) for publishing of the script in written form;

(3) for negotiating terms covering merchandising rights.

12–48 The Credits Agreement already mentioned deals with one moral right issue at a level of detail which would scarcely be conceivable in legislation on the subject. An author becomes entitled to have his name given as main or a subsidiary writer, following specified verbal formulae. There are also requirements for contributors of source material. Placement and size are prescribed for the film itself. Main writers must also be credited in most advertising and publicity material. There is provision for the negative moral right of non-association; but a writer must request that he should not be named at the outset or within 48 hours of the rough cut of the film being shown.[5]

(d) *Visual arts*

12–49 In the production of graphic and ceramic works, collective organisation has not yet progressed to the point of general agreements between artists and commissioners or employers. Characteristic of the field is the large number of separate associations in which artists collaborate. These distinguish between the creators of high art and the practitioners of workaday crafts (from the National Artists' Association and the Chartered Society of Designers to the Society of Picture Researchers and Editors); and equally between general and highly specific spheres of work (from the Association

---

[5] See Cotterell (n. 94, above), pp. 487–488.

of Illustrators and the Association of Photographers to the Institute of Medical Illustrators and the Association of Historical and Fine Art Photographers).

Many of these bodies are now able to offer their members support in negotiating individual contracts, at least by suggesting model forms or by offering advice on particular terms.[6] Thus, they stress not only on the dangers of assigning or granting exclusive licences in general terms (particularly in relation to the future), but also find occasion to advise on difficult issues of privacy, permission to use a subject (particularly a person) and copyright arising from secondary activities affecting artistic works, such as retouching, collaging, incorporation into advertisements, and so on. With the coming of digital libraries of visual art works, the scope for re-use, often after some form of re-working, is hugely enhanced.

Architectural work, which often takes the form of a professional commis- **12–50** sion, is likely to follow one of the Standard Forms of Agreement of the Royal Institute of British Architects, though these may always be varied expressly. The 1992 version of the Form for Appointment of an Architect[7] states that copyright in all documents and drawings prepared by the architect remains his or her property. However, the client is licensed to reproduce the design by building on the site or part of the site to which the design relates, provided that the architect has completed the scheme design or provided detailed design and production information and has been paid as agreed. Until a scheme design is complete, the client has no right to proceed without consent; but if the architect's services are limited to making and negotiating a planning application, consent may not unreasonably be withheld.[8]

4. CONTROL OF MONOPOLY

(1) The 1988 Act

As already noted, the chance of extracting monopoly profits from copyright **12–51** in particular works is less likely than from a patented invention. There is no longer any rule allowing for the grant of compulsory licences of copyright in general, equivalent to those for patents,[9] nor for that matter is the Crown permitted to use on special terms. In the early stages of sound recording, it

---

[6] Witness, for instance, British Photographers' Liaison Committee, *The ABC of Photographic Copyright* (1994), which warns against surrendering all economic and moral rights without careful consideration. *cf. Hutchinson v. Hook* [1996] F.S.R. 549.

[7] Conditions of Appointment, para. 1.7.1.

[8] *ibid.*, para. 2.3. The Form for Appointment of an Architect to Design and Build (para. 2.3.2) provides that, even if no scheme design has been completed, consent to use is not to be unreasonably withheld.

[9] But the general provisions for control by reference to the Monopolies and Mergers Commission apply to copyright, as they do to patents and to the design rights: CDPA 1988, s. 144; and see paras A1–11—A1–14, below.

was feared that the mechanical right to record copyright music might be used extravagantly. In the 1911 Act, a statutory right was given to others in certain circumstances to make their own recordings of such music upon payment of a set royalty. This was continued in 1956, but has now been repealed, there being no sufficient case for singling out the recording of music as suitable for "equitable remuneration".[10]

12–52 The most considerable danger of monopoly in the copyright sphere comes from the collective administration of rights, because their accumulation carries an ability to cut a user off from access to much of the material that he may wish to exploit.

After the Second World War, there was a current of resentment from major copyright users over the terms on which the performing right societies were prepared to do business. On the recommendation of the Gregory Committee,[11] the 1956 Act established a Performing Right Tribunal (PRT), specially charged with power to review the licences and schemes offered by collecting societies in this one field by reference to the criterion of "reasonableness". For this there was already a Canadian precedent; and in turn the lead was followed in other countries, for instance, Australia, the United States, and in some European countries, such as West Germany.

12–53 Now that new technology is so rapidly amplifying the ability to copy material, collective administration is spreading also to cover reproduction rights, and in turn this has raised the need for wider public interest controls. Following proposals of the Whitford Committee,[12] the PRT has been converted under the 1988 Act into the Copyright Tribunal. Contemporaneously with the passage of the Act, the overall justification for the existence of PPL was raised before the Monopolies and Mergers Commission at the behest of local radio stations. The Commission's report, while not uncritical,[13] has recognised the economic necessity of collecting societies in the performing rights field.[14] Nonetheless it considered that PPL's exclusive right over the broadcasting of recordings gave it unjustified market power. In 1990 the right was reduced to the statutory right to remuneration already noted.[15] If a royalty rate cannot be agreed, the

---

[10] For the abolition of the statutory licence to record a work bearing musical copyright, see CDPA 1988, Sched. 1, para. 21. Note, however, the sanction against abuse of rental right in s. 66; para. 11–44, above.

[11] See para. 9–09, above.

[12] Cmnd. 6732, 1977, Chap. 16.

[13] Report on Collective Licensing (Cm. 530, 1988).

[14] Essentially the same judgment informs the Commission's subsequent report (Performing Rights, Cm. 3147, 1996) on the workings of the Performing Right Society. But the management structure and attitudes towards membership were the subject of wide-ranging criticism and a considerable measure of remedial action is now in train. Among other things, the PRS failed to justify a claim that it must administer all performing rights of all members.

[15] See para. 11–49, above.

broadcaster may pay a self-assessed royalty until the Copyright Tribunal makes an award, which will, if necessary, be back-dated.[16]

(2) The Copyright Tribunal[17]

The Tribunal is composed of a chairman and two deputy chairmen, who **12–54** will be legally qualified, and between two and eight ordinary members.[18] It sits in panels of three and works according to rules which, more than in the past, encourage the use of written procedures.[19]

The Tribunal may consider two principal categories of case: licensing **12–55** schemes and licences. A scheme sets out "the classes of case in which the operator . . . is willing to grant licences" and the terms for doing so. Licences are permissions which fall outside this definition.[20] While a tariff offered by one of the performing right societies to all dance hall proprietors is typically a scheme, being "in the nature of a standing invitation to treat",[21] it is the government's view that the licence for reprographic copying in schools which the Copyright Licensing Agency now offers to local education authorities is not. The correctness of this assumption may one day fall to be questioned, since it is only in the case of schemes that representative bodies of users have the right to bring a case before the Tribunal.

The Tribunal's jurisdiction does not extend to all copyright licences; it would be contrary to the Berne Convention to place under public control the licences and licensing schemes offered by individual right-owners of literary, dramatic, musical and artistic works and films. Equally it has not been thought necessary to cover publishing, as distinct from copying, these works. Accordingly, in respect of these works, jurisdiction relates to licences and schemes of a licensing body—that is, a society or other organisation with a main object of negotiating or granting licences, including licences covering works of more than one author. In other cases—relating to neighbouring rights and the new rental rights—the licences and schemes do not have to be from a licensing body.[22]

The Tribunal does not act of its own motion but on a complaint by, or on **12–56** behalf of, licensees, actual or potential. They may raise objections before they enter a licence, or against the refusal to grant them one, but not afterwards, save in one special case concerning expiry[23]; sanctity of contract

---

[16] CDPA 1988, s. 135A, which also prevents PPL from demanding that a broadcaster limit its proportion of "needle time" broadcasts.
[17] Freegard and Black, *The Decisions of the UK Performing Right and Copyright Tribunals* (1997).
[18] CDPA 1988, Pt. 1, Chap. 8. The Lord Chancellor will appoint the legal members, the Secretary of State the others.
[19] Some proceedings of the PRT were criticised as being unduly lengthy.
[20] CDPA 1988, s. 117.
[21] *PRS v. Workmen's Club Union* [1988] F.S.R. 586.
[22] CDPA 1988, s. 116.
[23] See *ibid.*, s. 126 for this case.

is not to be compromised by giving an individual licensee the continuous power to seek a re-writing of his terms. As far as concerns schemes, so long as they are not yet operational, it is for a representative organisation of potential licensees to make the reference.[24] Once the scheme takes effect, the right covers both such an organisation and a person claiming a licence.[25] Once an order has been made, the scheme may be referred again by its operator, a claimant for a licence or a representative organisation.[26] As regards separate licences, it is the person seeking the licence who may refer the case.[27]

In the past there have been cases concerning schemes raised before the PRT by organisations of dance hall proprietors, cinema operators, and bingo-hall enterprises.[28] The second kind of application has been important for broadcasting organisations and there have been references by the BBC, Manx Radio, and the Association of Independent Radio Contractors.[29]

12–57 The legislation defines one main criterion by which the Tribunal is to decide whether it will confirm or vary a scheme, or vary or impose a licence—reasonableness in the circumstances. But it is obliged to take account of all relevant considerations,[30] and in every case it must have regard to the availability of schemes or the grant of licences to others in similar circumstances, and the terms offered them, exercising its power so as to prevent unreasonable discrimination in the scheme or licences of the organisation in question.[31] In various instances more specific matters are also listed for consideration: in respect of reprography licences,[32] educational taping of broadcasts,[33] conditions imposed by promoters of events,[34] payments in respect of underlying rights,[35] and works included in retransmissions.[36]

The actual orders of the PRT show that it often acted in a generally similar manner to a labour arbitrator who is dealing with a conflict about future terms and conditions of employment, rather than about existing legal rights. (Indeed, in so far as the PRS represents authors rather than entrepreneurs, their role is comparable to that of a trade union in negotiating on behalf of the labour force that it represents; the comparison becomes blurred because the Society also represents music publishers.)

---

[24] CDPA 1988, s. 118.
[25] *ibid.*, s. 119.
[26] *ibid.*, s. 120; but subject to limitations designed to prevent constant harassment.
[27] *ibid.*, s. 125.
[28] See Cases 1/1958, 9/1960, 11 and 12/1962, 13/1963, 21/1966, 23/1971, 27/1973 and 28/1975. On the scope of jurisdiction, see *Reditune v. PRS* (PRT Cases, 30–32/1977).
[29] See Cases 17 and 18/1964, 24/1971 and 35/1978.
[30] CDPA 1988, s. 135.
[31] *ibid.*, s. 129.
[32] *ibid.*, s. 130; para. 13–15, below.
[33] *ibid.*, s. 131.
[34] *ibid.*, s. 132.
[35] *ibid.*, s. 133.
[36] *ibid.*, s. 134.

Thus where the prime issue is a tariff—or in other words what the licensor ought to be able to demand for its members—the Copyright Tribunal's starting point will be the difference between asking-price and offer. It will then look to see what justifications can be offered for fixing upon one point rather than another between these poles. If there has been a previous agreement, comparisons with this tariff as the "fair price" for its own time will obviously have some relevance. Equally, it may serve a purpose to compare the rates agreed with other categories of user.[37] This, after all, is often as close as the Tribunal can get to a market comparison, and even so there will be no competing sellers.[38]

A few cases have raised issues of whose interests it is legitimate for a **12–58** licensor to protect; and these resemble questions about abuse of market power. Thus it was not proper for the PRS to offer film exhibitors licences at discriminatory discounts, depending on whether an exhibitor belonged to one or other trade association; the PRS got nothing in return that could justify this preference.[39] On the other hand, it was proper for PPL to impose some limit on a local radio station's proportion of "needle time" (the amount of records broadcast compared with the amount of live music): the record companies were found to have a legitimate long-term interest in the continued employment of live performers who would act as the source for their future business.[40]

(3) Dominant position in the E.C.[41]

The Copyright Tribunal is primarily concerned with the licensing activities **12–59** of the performing right societies rather than their constitutional arrangements. Yet there are numerous ways in which a society may want to strengthen its economic position through its rules and their effect on members. Take, for instance, the record companies: they have a performing right in their own records, exploited through PPL. They have an interest to see that the authors and publishers do not secure an undue proportion of what users will pay overall for performing rights in recordings of copyright music; and they may want to protect live performers against too high a

---

[37] Where the circumstances are similar, availability and terms must be taken into account: *ibid.*, s. 129. For a decision that there was no sufficient similarity, see Case 38/1978 (independent local radio/PPL).

[38] See also *PRS v. British Entertainment and Dancing Assocn.* [1993] E.M.L.R. 143; *British Phonographic Industry v. MCPS* [1993] E.M.L.R. 86; *Assocn. of Independent Radio Companies v. PPL* [1994] R.P.C. 143; *AEI Rediffusion Music v. PPL* [1998] R.P.C. 335; *British Sky Broadcasting v. PRS* [1998] R.P.C 467.

[39] Case 9/1960. Another case concerned the PRS's insistence that Southern Television pay royalties on emphemeral recordings made in the course of broadcasting despite the explicit exception of this activity from infringement (CA 1956, s. 6(7)); see now para. 11–49, above; the Tribunal disapproved: Case 2/1958. *cf.* the practice mentioned in the Whitford Report, paras 389–394.

[40] Case 18/1964; and see also Case 35/1978.

[41] Stamatoudi [1997] E.I.P.R. 289.

proportion of "needle time"—in broadcasting, dance halls or wherever. An authors-and-publishers' society like the PRS may, therefore, be significantly affected if record companies can become members of it, for instance by setting up a publishing operation. Not surprisingly, therefore, such societies tend to take counteractive steps at least to limit the rights of record-company members.[42]

12–60   The E.C. Commission, which can intervene only within the terms of its competition rules, investigated the organisational structure of the West German collecting society, GEMA,[43] and found a number of its restrictive rules and practices to constitute an abuse of its dominant position, contrary to Article 86 of the Rome Treaty.[44] The basic objectives of joint collecting societies were accepted to be legitimate—and in a later case, the European Court of Justice has agreed.[45] It is proper for individual members (composers, associated authors and publishers) to protect their interests against major music users (such as broadcasting organisations and record companies) by assigning rights to a joint association. But nevertheless anti-competitive arrangements must not be made if they are beyond what is required "for the association to carry out its activity on the necessary scale".

12–61   In particular, three aspects of GEMA's rules were criticised:

> (1) Rules which followed from the arrangement amongst national collecting societies that each would have only its own nationals as members were disapproved.[46] It is true that these rules limited members' ability to express dissatisfaction with their national society by joining the society of another E.C. state and taking whatever advantages it offered its members: the effect of such a transfer of allegiance would be to make the national society a mere collecting agency on its own territory for the foreign society which the author had joined. The Commission's decision amounts to an insistence that members should not be deprived of this measure of ultimate independence. In reality habit makes them unlikely to take advantage of such a power.[47]

---

[42] Thus the PRS has rules restricting the number of directors from "user-owned" publishers and foreign publishers. For the German society, GEMA, see para. 12–61, below.

[43] *Re Gema (No. 1)* [1971] C.M.L.R. D35. At the same time other national collecting societies within the then EEC were investigated, but no decisions were issued. In the U.S., similar collecting societies have had their activities circumscribed by anti-trust proceedings.

[44] For Art. 86 in general, see para. 1–53, above.

[45] *Belgische Radio v. SABAM* [1974] E.C.R. 51, [1974] 2 C.M.L.R. 238. However, imposing obligations on members which are not necessary may abuse the dominant position. Note also *Greenwich Film v. SACEM* [1980] 1 C.M.L.R. 629; *BEMIM v E.C. Commission* [1976] E.M.L.R. 97.

[46] See [1971] C.M.L.R. D35 at D47; and see *Gesellschaft für Verwertung von Leistungsschutzrechten* [1983] 3 C.M.L.R. 695. The international arrangements concerning performing rights are mentioned in para. 11–31, n. 35, above.

[47] Rules making it difficult for publishers with foreign connections to become ordinary members were criticised as tending to hinder the formation of a Community-wide market: [1971] C.M.L.R. D35 at D47–48.

(2) Since GEMA acted as licensor not only of performing rights, but also (among other things) of the mechanical right to record music, it required a transfer of exclusive rights of all aspects of copyright, at home and abroad. It accordingly had a strong interest in preventing individual authors from being drawn out of membership and into direct relationship with a user such as a record company. This objective it pursued by a variety of measures: requiring a long period for notice of withdrawal, taking the right to future works even after resignation, paying loyalty bonuses and paying out of its social fund only to members of 20 years' standing. The Commission insisted that the rules should not oblige members to assign rights for territories in which it did not act directly; nor should it take over all aspects of copyright in the territories in which it did operate.[48] Likewise it ought to be possible to resign at the end of any year—a demand which the Commission was later to soften to three years in return for further concessions on the range of rights transferable to the society.[49]

(3) GEMA had prevented record companies from acquiring influence by excluding them from membership as publishers.[50] This the Commission also objected to, while recognising that it would be proper to restrict the voting rights of such members when they had a conflict of interests (for example over the licence rate for the mechanical right to record musical compositions).[51]

A number of GEMA's commercial practices were also characterised as abusive: for example, the tariff on the mechanical right was found to discriminate in favour of German-produced records, and that on recording equipment in favour of German manufacturers[52]; and it was improper for the mechanical right fee in effect to require payments for works not under the society's control.[53]

The types of investigations that are conducted, on the one hand by the **12–62** Copyright Tribunal, and on the other by the E.C. Commission follow from the different powers with which they are invested. The case for the British approach is that an organised arbitral body, independent of governmental influence, provides a satisfactory means of controlling a monopoly that is in other respects efficient from the point of view of both owners and users.[54]

---

[48] [1971] C.M.L.R. D35 at D48–50.

[49] *ibid.*, at D50; *Re Gema (No. 2)* [1972] C.M.L.R. D115.

[50] *cf.* the rules of the PRS on the matter, mentioned para. 9–49, above.

[51] [1971] C.M.L.R. D35 at D51–52; and see the later negative clearance [1982] 2 C.M.L.R. 482.

[52] For this special levy on equipment, see para. 13–20, below.

[53] [1971] C.M.L.R. D35 at D53–55.

[54] Wallace (1973) 4 I.I.C. 280; see also Joliet [1973] Europarecht 17; de Freitas (1987) 34 J.Cop.Soc. 148; Deringer and Mestmäcker [1985] Int.Bus.L., 65, 71.

On the other hand the likelihood that many licensing negotiations will lead to a reference or application to the Tribunal has been criticised: the extra time and expense that are used up is said to distort the ability of the licensing societies to react to inflation, causing them to press cases earlier and harder than would probably be the case if voluntary bargaining were the sole route to settlement. The stand taken by the E.C. Commission has shown collecting societies that the manner in which they organise their activities is not above scrutiny in the public interest.[55] In a field where conflicts of interest are complex and the stakes are considerable, this makes a great deal of political sense.

---

[55] Later cases have investigated, *inter alia*, the range of rights for which charges are separately made (*Basset v. SACEM* [1997] E.C.R. 1747); royalty rates in comparison with those of other national societies—but only where this can be done objectively (*SACEM v. Lucazeau* [1989] E.C.R. 2811); and a refusal to licence only part of a society's repertoire (*Ministère Public v. Tournier, ibid.*).

CHAPTER 13

COPYRIGHT: PARTICULAR CASES

More than other types of intellectual property, copyright has burgeoned **13–01** into separate varieties, related but distinct. The preceding chapters have emphasised the principles that identify the species as a whole. It is important to start with these common characteristics. For one thing they focus attention on why copyright is so often the form adopted when new circumstances call for protection: a right against copying appears proof against unduly wide monopoly and it makes others accountable where the claim is most evidently justifiable. However, the point has been reached at which we must turn to the many differences of detail in the various copyrights.

This chapter is not intended to be exhaustive. Rather it takes up a number of subjects where the impact of copyright is currently significant and controversial. The first section deals with the role of copyright in the politically sensitive area of the news media. The following sections (2 to 6) are concerned with technological advances that affect the dissemination of information, culture and entertainment: visual and aural reprography; computers; databases; the diffusion of broadcasts and other material by wire and by satellite; multimedia products and the Internet. Sections 7 to 9 concern claims to forms of right: by performers; by writers against public lending; by artists for a share in resale prices. Finally, in section 10 the special position of Crown and Parliamentary copyright is treated. The limited role of copyright in the protection of industrial design is reserved for the next chapter.

1. The Media and the Public Interest in News

Producing the news of the day generates many tensions. Between rivals in **13–02** the media there is constant pressure to stay in the van, and if at all possible to get ahead with a scoop—whether it is the first story or the most captivating photograph. A journalist may meet all sorts of difficulties in extracting information, which will cost time and money to overcome. Obligations of confidence may hinder him even when he has acquired it. We have already seen that the judges have fashioned a defence of public interest which may limit rights in confidential information; the same general defence may be raised to claims of copyright.[1] In any country which seeks to conserve the independence and freedom of action of its press and other media there is a nice balance to be struck. Here we explore the extent to which copyright gives rise to exclusive rights in news reports; and the degree to which it can hamper the revelation of material by anyone other than its owner.

(1) Copyright in news

13–03 There will be no copyright in news until there is a work or other subject-matter capable of protection; and then only to the extent that the particular type of copyright may be infringed.[2] Once a story is turned into a literary work or illustrated by an artistic work there may be infringement in the form of reproduction in another paper or inclusion in a broadcast. This is equally so, where the literary work is the script of a news broadcast and the copyist works from the legitimate broadcast. But if a broadcast is verbatim and there is no initial work, the copyright in the broadcast may be of no help.[3] For this special copyright probably does not cover any literary or pictorial reproduction of its content as such[4]; and even the right to prevent rebroadcasting may well not extend to the case where the material is taken down and a different news-reader broadcasts it afresh.[5] In these cases, the broadcast copyright is clearly infringed only if the copyist can be shown to have made an intermediate recording.

In the *INS* case,[6] the Supreme Court of the United States was moved to provide a remedy against the systematic and damaging misappropriation of news by one agency from the newspapers supplied by a rival. At that time the limited scope of American copyright law made it impracticable to seek copyright protection. In any Berne Convention State, copyright arises upon the creation of a literary or artistic work and is enforceable without formalities: its potency is accordingly the greater and the need to qualify it in the public interest may be more pressing.

In England, *Walter v. Steinkopff*[7] illustrates the basic approach. The *St. James' Gazette* copied a number of extracts from *The Times* almost word for

---

[1] See paras 8–15—8–19, 11–55—11–57, above.
[2] The Brussels version of the Berne Convention (Art. 9(3)) allowed member countries to create exceptions from copyright for the "news of the day"; but the current Paris version does not go so far: *cf.* Art. 2*bis* (1) (political and forensic speeches), Art. 10(1) (fair quotation), Art. 10*bis* (public interest copying of media works; reporting of current events). Nor does British law.
[3] The broadcast copyright covers filming, re-broadcasting and certain types of public performance: see Table, pp. 330 to 331 above, head 7.
[4] The 1956 Act clearly excluded such forms of infringement; but the 1988 Act refers to "copying a work" (including a broadcast), without offering further definition, save that "reproduction in a material form" is not a form of copying that apparently applies to a broadcast: see para. 11–26, above.
[5] The new Act does not deal with the point specifically, nor did the old.
[6] See para. 1–15, above.
[7] [1892] 3 Ch. 489.

word, including some two-fifths of an article by Rudyard Kipling. This was held to infringe *The Times'* copyright in its pieces. It made no difference that *The Times* had itself borrowed some of the information, that the *St. James' Gazette* was not a direct competitor (since it gave the news only later), that the source was acknowledged or that the editor of *The Times* did not at once object. North J. sought to dispel any implication that copyright might confer exclusive rights in the news itself by stressing the dichotomy between unprotectable idea and protectable expression. In other contexts, the courts have shown some willingness to treat the taking of detailed information as infringement, even when the actual expression of the ideas has been worked out afresh.[8] Given the general interest in making news available through channels on which the public relies, it may well be that copyright in news is confined to substantial reproduction of the actual language used to write it up or the actual content of a broadcast.

It is of course a sphere in which digital communication is breaking up former modes of delivery. The monolithic presentations of newspapers and broadcasting channels are being challenged by interlinkings of information on specific subjects which users may select for themselves and pursue to a depth that suits them by consulting networked files of data. How far this goes will depend, among other things, on the availability of electronic accounting systems which accurately distinguish uses.[9]

(2) Fair dealing and recorded speech

The two forms of fair dealing that are germane to the news media[10] are: (1) **13–04** use of any work for purposes of criticism or review of it or another work or a performance of either[11]; and (2) use of any work other than a photograph for the purpose of reporting current events.[12] The exception for "on-the-spot" photographs leaves the law affecting them as it was previously.[13]

A Court must consider all the circumstances of the "dealing" in the light of the purpose for which alone it is permitted.[14] The proportion of the work that has been copied is one starting point. No question of fair dealing arises unless there has been "substantial taking"; but even when this point is passed, questions of quantity may well be less significant than quality. There may be occasions upon which it is proper to take the whole work.[15]

---

[8] See especially *Elanco v. Mandops* [1980] R.P.C. 213; see para. 11–11, above.

[9] See para. 13–85, below.

[10] The broadcasting media may also benefit from the exception concerning incidental inclusion: CDPA 1988, s. 31; para. 11–41, above.

[11] CDPA 1988, s. 30(1); "sufficient acknowledgment" (see s. 78) is a prerequisite: para. 11–41, above.

[12] CDPA 1988, s. 30(2). Again there must be "sufficient acknowledgment" save in a sound recording, film, broadcast or cable-cast: see Berne Convention, Art. 10*bis*.

[13] CDPA 1988, s. 30(2): see para. 11–41, above.

[14] As far as criticism or review is concerned, this may relate to the content, as distinct from the style, of a literary (or other) work; as for current events, they may not be a pretext for reporting something else: see *Commonwealth of Australia v. Fairfax* (1980) 32 A.L.R. 485.

[15] *Hubbard v. Vosper* [1972] 2 Q.B. 84 at 98, CA; *Beloff v. Pressdram* [1973] 1 All E.R. 241 at 263; *Pro Sieben v. Carlton UK TV* [1999] E.M.L.R. 109, CA.

Equally the precise manner in which the work is used for criticism, review or reporting current events will be important. Both expressions are of wide and indefinite scope, to be interpreted liberally[16]; but "the nearer that any particular derivative use of copyright material comes to the boundaries, unplotted though they are, the less likely it is to make good the fair dealing defence."[17]

> In *Pro Sieben Media v. Carlton*,[18] Carlton TV broadcast an exposé of "cheque-book journalism," illustrated by the furore whipped up over Mandy Allwood's pregnancy of eight embryos and the exclusive publicity organised for her, showing her determination to avoid abortion. For this clips were taken from one such interview, in which the broadcasting copyright was held by the German plaintiff. The Court of Appeal was prepared to apply the principle that permissible criticism could extend of ideas in a work and its social or moral implications so extensively that it could cover disapproval of a general media practice, of which the material was merely one illustration. Whether the criticisms were fair depended primarily on their objective impact, not on the motivations of those who made them. They did not have to present a balanced view of the source from which they were derived. In this case, fair dealing was held to have been made out.

13–05 Nevertheless, courts will remain astute again dressing unfair competition up as criticism or review.[19] A photograph cannot be taken in order to illustrate a news story simply by labelling it "review".[20] The contents of an interview with an ethnic poet cannot be taken in order to fill out a biography of her.[21] In some situations the fact that the work was private or was given to a person in confidence will be influential. This, however, is simply a further consideration, since the defences are not confined to published material.[22] As *Beloff v. Pressdram* emphasised, the press is accustomed to rely upon leaks of information in advance of formal publication. Ungoed Thomas J. refused to draw any distinction between leaks to a newspaper from another newspaper and from some other source. Since he found the publication of a memorandum to be unfair chiefly because it was not intended for publication and had been leaked in breach of confidence, a newspaper which publishes a leaked document of any kind

---

[16] See *Time Warner Entertainment v. Channel Four TV* [1994] E.M.L.R. 1, CA. (Extracts from "A Clockwork Orange" used to point up criticism of decision not to release the film in Britain.)

[17] Walker L.J., *Pro Sieben case*, below, n. 18.

[18] [1999] E.M.L.R. 109, CA.

[19] Henry L.J., *Time Warner* case, above, n. 16.

[20] *Banier v. News Group* [1997] F.S.R. 812. Photographs are excluded from the current affairs defence: above, n. 13.

[21] *Hager v. ECW Press* (1998) 85 C.P.R. (3d) 289, FC Can.

[22] *Beloff v. Pressdram* (n. 15, above) at 263, refusing to give any firmer meaning to Romer J., *British Oxygen v. Liquid Air* [1925] Ch. 383 at 393.

may have difficulty in making out such a defence.[23] Only if the publisher is able to rely on factors which pertain to the public interest—and which might be raised under that separate but related head[24]—will it be on surer ground. That might be so, for instance, if the document revealed criminal activities or a serious threat to public safety or health.

Economic considerations will include the amount of damage that the defendant may inflict on the plaintiff, and the extent to which the defendant will get for nothing something which in usual business practice he would expect to have to pay for. It was not infringement for a small satellite broadcaster to include in its sports bulletins short clips (14–37 seconds in length) showing highlights of World Cup soccer games, which were taken from the BBC broadcasts of complete matches. Audiences were not thereby diverted—a very significant element in the assessment.[25] On the other hand, for an enterprise to run a regular clippings service from newspapers for its employees, which covered not only news but other features, went much too far.[26]

The express acknowledgment in the 1988 Act that a speaker may acquire **13–06** copyright from the recording of his statement, if the result is an original work,[27] has an immediate importance to both the written and the broadcast media, since they make wide use of interviews. The media have an exception in addition to the general fair dealing provisions. Section 58 of the 1988 Act, provides for two distinct cases: a record of spoken words that is made for reporting current events may be used for doing so; and a record made for broadcasting or cable-casting may be used for that purpose. It must be a direct record, which is not an infringement of any other copyright; the use must not be prohibited by the speaker; and it must be a use permitted by the possessor of the record (not a leak). In any case, most of those who make public speeches (especially politicians) must be taken to be courting the media and so impliedly to be licensing journalistic use of the material.[28]

Particular circumstances may well import further legal considerations. If a celebrity gives someone an interview about his private life (not a current event), which is recorded verbatim, the speaker becomes the owner of the copyright.[29] He or she may therefore have a moral right to object to derogatory treatment by alteration or omission, though this will not

---

[23] *Beloff v. Pressdram* (n. 15, above) at 264. Whether it could make a difference that the information was secured by theft rather than by breach of confidence was left open.

[24] See para. 11–56, above.

[25] *British Broadcasting Corporation v. British Satellite Broadcasting* [1992] Ch. 141.

[26] *Newspaper Licencing Agency v. Marks & Spencer* [1999] E.M.L.R. 369; and see *Television NZ v. Newsmonitor* (1993) 27 I.P.R. 441; Sinclair [1997] E.I.P.R. 188.

[27] See para. 10–35, above.

[28] Laddie *et al.*, para. 2.190.

[29] Whether the interviewer has a recorder's copyright is a separate issue, which may turn on the recording means employed, together with editing and similar skills: *Express Newspapers v. News (U.K.)* [1990] F.S.R. 359.

normally extend to press publication. In this latter case, he might object by demonstrating breach of the moral right against false attribution.[30]

(3) Organisation and journalist

13-07 Since most of the material supplied to newspapers and news programmes comes from employed journalists and reporters, their copyright relationship to their employer is important. Previously newspaper journalists presumptively enjoyed a special division of the copyright, which went to the employer only for press use. It was the only instance in British law of statutory intervention, in authors' interests, to ensure that investors acquired (at least presumptively) only that part of copyright which related to the purpose of the transaction. Under severe pressure from press interests, this special case has disappeared in the 1988 Act. The entire copyright in the work of all employed journalists now resides initially in their employers, unless they can show a contract to the contrary.[31]

Where the material is submitted by a freelance writer or artist, the terms of any express assignment or licence of the copyright will govern. If there are none sufficient to meet the case, there will be an implied licence to publish in accordance with usual practice.[32] This would not include a licence to use the material in a new medium, such as the Internet, if no custom of conferring such an entitlement can be shown to have existed at the time.

13-08 Where the employer has the copyright, the employee will not enjoy the moral right to be identified.[33] Indeed, so great was the proprietors' fear of the need to name contributors that this moral right does not arise over any publication in a newspaper, magazine or similar periodical, even where the material comes from a non-employed person.[34] It does, however, apply to broadcasts, to the extent that the exception for fair dealing in reporting current events does not operate.[35] Doubtless waivers will be extracted in many cases. The moral right to object to derogatory treatment may not be claimed by an employed journalist, or by anyone else who is published in a newspaper, magazine or periodical, if the work was prepared for such a purpose.[36] These exemptions of the media do not apply in countries with a stronger tradition of moral rights and do not deserve a place in British law.

Where the material being used consists of a photograph or film, it may not be sufficient to secure the licence of the copyright owner. If the work was commissioned for private and domestic purposes, then the commissioner enjoys the special right of privacy given by section 85, and may, *inter*

---

[30] See paras 11–75—11–82, above; *Moore v. News of the World* [1972] 1 All E.R. 441.
[31] CA 1956, s. 4(2); *cf.* CDPA 1988, s. 11; see para. 12–05, above.
[32] *Joseph v. National Magazine* [1959] Ch. 14.
[33] CDPA 1988, s. 79(3).
[34] *ibid.*, s. 79(6).
[35] *ibid.*, s. 79(4). There must in any case be an "assertion".
[36] *ibid.*, s. 81(4).

alia, object to inclusion of the material in a newspaper, broadcast or cable-cast.[37]

2. Reprography and Recording: Educational and Private Copying

At the beginning of this century, the techniques for copying (except by hand **13–09** or typewriter) were still limited to laborious and technical procedures like printing. Even photography of the printed page or picture required the subsequent intervention of a person able to develop negatives and make prints. The vast improvement of reprographic techniques for producing copies of material written and drawn has been matched by an equally startling advance in simple means for recording musical and dramatic performances—in sound alone or in audio-visual form. Now the analogue techniques of the last three decades are fast being replaced by digital electronics which are remarkably efficient.

The characteristic of these developments which most threatens the copyright system is the ease with which one or more copies can be produced. The upsurge in commercial piracy of books, recordings, films, computer games and other programs directly undermines the economic interest of the original producers. It has had to be met by much more intensive policing of activities which for the most part constitute direct and incontrovertible imitation; sometimes, also, as where the entire get-up and trade-marking is also counterfeited, it is a source of ready deception to consumers. In the counter-attack, the Courts have made a distinct contribution, as in the development of the *Anton Piller* and allied orders; and so equally have administrative officers, as where trading standards authorities have taken action under the Trade Descriptions Act 1968.

Where individuals make single copies for their own use the balance of **13–10** conflicting interests between copyright owners and users is much more even. Each act, at least if viewed in isolation, is only a slight threat to the copyright owner's economic concerns; and the educational or personal value of being free to copy in this way is not to be discounted as insignificant.

This section is accordingly concerned with the proposals that have been pressed to deal with the phenomena of private copying and home taping; and with the solutions which the government saw fit to offer in the 1988 Act.

---

[37] See paras 11–85—11–86, above.

(1) Visual copies of literary and other material[38]

(a) *Fair dealing and other exceptions*

13–11 The world's early copyright systems naturally concentrated their fire upon the multiplication of pirated copies. In most, including the British, little attention was given to the question whether making a single copy counted as an infringement, or whether, on the contrary, a private use was an exploitation of knowledge and ideas which ought to be left free for all. In 1911, when the "fair dealing" exceptions were first spelled out in statutory terms, "private study" and "research" were included in the list of permitted purposes[39] without the problem having surfaced in previously reported litigation. Nor was there much consideration of the matter afterwards. It was held, not surprisingly, that a publisher could not justify an infringing book by saying that readers would use it for private study.[40] But otherwise the courts were not asked to say how much could be taken; nor what purposes constituted private study or research[41]; nor whether multiple copying could ever be justified under this head.

The 1956 Act left "fair dealing for purposes of research or private study" as an exception and added provisions concerning educational instruction and examination, the making of anthologies and, above all, copying in non-profit libraries.[42] There were a number of indications within them that the notion of fair dealing in this context was restricted to the taking of single copies by or for individuals and did not extend to multiple copying for (say) members of a class or choir.[43] The libraries exception, moreover, indicated that copying of a single article from a periodical was permissible, but that copying of substantial extracts from books required permission of the copyright owner where that could reasonably be obtained.[44] Beyond this, the British Copyright Council, on behalf of publishers and authors, issued statements of what it would regard as fair.[45]

(b) *The reprography problem*

13–12 For a long period, publishers in the United Kingdom contemplated possible solutions to the mounting tide of photocopying without arriving at any clear policy. The prospect of finding a technical device which would prevent

---

[38] See generally Kolle (1975) 6 I.I.C. 382; Kerever [1976] Copyright 188; Ricketson (1982) 10 Aust.B.L.R. 31; Nevins (1985) 7 E.I.P.R. 222.

[39] CA 1911, s 2(1)(i).

[40] *University of London Press v. University Tutorial Press* [1916] 2 Ch. 601; *Sillitoe v. McGraw-Hill* [1983] F.S.R. 545.

[41] Consider, for instance, copies for the professional information of businessmen or government servants.

[42] CA 1956, ss. 6(1), 6(6), 7, 9(1), 41.

[43] Esp. *ibid.*, s. 41.

[44] *ibid.*, s. 7.

[45] See para. 13–14, below.

machines from being used to reproduce copyright work mostly looked unpromising, and in any case would have led to an undesirable embargo on something which large numbers of readers wished to do. The field was not one in which government was likely to be persuaded that a levy on copying machines or the paper used in them should be introduced: for one thing much photocopying involves no copyright infringement.[46]

The Whitford Committee treated the question extensively and with considerable sympathy for the difficulties faced by authors and publishers, taking the view that the scholar had no better claim to the free provision of copies of intellectual material than he did to free pens and paper.[47] The Committee's solution was to propose the introduction of appropriate blanket licensing arrangements through collecting societies of right-owners. The government would supervise the establishment and organisation of these societies, using by way of sanction the withdrawal of reprographic copyright for any sector which failed to act. Where proper licensing arrangements were in place, the fair dealing exception for research or private study would no longer avail, so that the licence would be needed for single as well as multiple copying of copyright material in all institutions, organisations, offices and even private homes. This, however, proved too aggressive a disturbance of the existing compromise to be politically acceptable.[48]

During the 1980s, publishers began to press more vigorously for licensing **13–13** arrangements. Music publishers launched proceedings against a school and a local authority for substantial photocopying of scores which otherwise they would have had to purchase[49]; book publishers proceeded against a university for multiple copying. Authors and book publishers formed the Copyright Licensing Agency to license reprography by major users, either in the form of blanket permission or by granting specific licences.[50] It succeeded first with local education authorities and then with universities. Now it also has schemes in operation with government departments and local authority sectors and is securing co-operation from industry and the professions.[51]

The 1988 Act has a range of provisions designed to encourage this **13–14** evolutionary process by means of a relatively light legislative hand.[52] Fair dealing for purposes of research or private study remains a defence and it is

---

[46] Such a levy exists, however, in, *e.g.* Germany and Spain.

[47] Cmnd. 6732, 1977, Chap. 4.

[48] The libraries and educational organisations offered strong resistance to the idea.

[49] The effects of photocopying have been particularly hard on the publishers of sheet music.

[50] The CLA belongs equally to the Authors' Licensing and Collecting Society (itself representing two major authors' societies, but not graphic artists) and the Publishers' Licensing Society (representing three associations of publishers). It is a leading member of the International Federation of Reproduction Rights Associations (IFRRO), a forum which facilitates the distribution of royalties for foreign authors and publishers.

[51] See Clark, Owen and Palmer, *Publishing Agreements* (5th ed., 1997), App. E.

[52] See Laddie *et al.*, Chap. 19.

now specified that someone other than the scholar or researcher may copy on his behalf.[53] Since, after substantial debate, the government agreed that those in commerce and industry who undertake research or private study should not be excluded, it must be their view that the exception is of rather broad scope. But it remains for the courts to decide how far business, and for that matter government, should be able to take single copies without licence by claiming to need them for these purposes.[54]

The Act makes clear that "systematic single copying" (for instance all the members of a class requesting the same material at once) is not within the exception.[55] No more specific guidance is given on what measure of single copying is "fair" than under the previous Act.[56] As before, there are separate provisions concerning copying by the librarians of prescribed (that is, non-profit-making) libraries. Provided they are supplying individuals for research or private study at cost and in accordance with regulations, they may copy up to one article in an issue of a periodical and a reasonable extract from any other publication. In the latter case it is no longer necessary to seek permission of the copyright owner if that is reasonably obtainable.[57] These "library" arrangements are now essentially by way of supplement to the fair dealing provision, since any librarian or other person may also rely upon the fair dealing defence, when supplying a researcher or student. In its current guidance on photocopying, the British Copyright Council asserts (1) that prescribed librarians are given greater scope to photocopy than are individual scholars and those who act for them under the general fair dealing provision; and (2) in particular, prescribed librarians may copy single articles from journals while others may not, and prescribed librarians may normally copy 10 per cent of a work while others may only copy a chapter or 5 per cent.[58] This, however, is entirely an owners' concession. It in no way precludes a scholar from arguing, for instance, that in copying a single article he is not damaging the journal publisher's prospects since he would not subscribe to the journal.

13–15 Copyright accordingly is much more likely to be infringed by multiple copying (including colourable disguises for it). Only for purposes of examination are schools and other prescribed "educational establishments"[59] entitled to copy by means of a reprographic process.[60] But in order

---

[53] CDPA 1988, s. 29.

[54] *cf.* the disagreement over the legitimacy of government copying in *Williams & Wilkins v. U.S.* 487 Fed. 2d. 1345 (1973).

[55] CDPA 1988, s. 29(3)(b); applied to the library exceptions by s. 40.

[56] See paras 11–38—11–42, above.

[57] CDPA 1988, ss. 38–40. See also s. 41 (one library supplying, another); s. 42 (replacements); and s. 43 (copying by librarians and archivists of unpublished works); note also s. 44 (copy necessary before export of an article of cultural or historical importance).

[58] See Clark, *Photocopying* (1990), pp. 8–11.

[59] The category may be expanded beyond schools by Ministerial order: CDPA 1988, s. 174.

[60] CDPA 1988, s. 32(3)—even then there is an exception in respect of musical works, because of the widespread sale of examination pieces.

to encourage the organisation of general licences, the Act says this: until they become available, these institutions are permitted to copy very small amounts of literary, dramatic and musical works and typographical arrangements for purposes of instruction—1 per cent per quarter of the year.[61] The licences have to allow at least as much copying as this. Moreover their terms are subject to the jurisdiction of the Copyright Tribunal, which is specifically directed, in all cases dealing with reprography, to have regard to (1) the availability of the published edition, (2) the proportion being copied, and (3) the nature of the use.[62] It is not clear how far weight will be given to evidence that (say) students are unlikely to buy a book if they cannot have a photocopy of some section of it, but it is surely a highly relevant factor.

There are three other provisions which aim to assist the creation of licensing arrangements. First, reprography schemes and other licences are subject to a statutory implied indemnity by the licensor covering infringement of any work which the licence purports to cover in its "blanket" but which is in fact not within the licensor's authority to grant.[63] Secondly, in relation to instruction in educational establishments, the Secretary of State has power to order the extension of a licence or scheme to cover works which are similar and are unreasonably excluded.[64] Thirdly, also in respect of such instruction, the Secretary of State may establish an inquiry to decide whether a scheme or general licence should be established for a category of literary, dramatic, musical or artistic work not currently covered.[65] If the recommendation favours such a step, but it is not organised by right-owners within a year, a royalty-free licence takes effect.[66]

(c) *Rights for publishers*

In the 1950s the publishers saw the approaching revolution in reprography **13–16** and successfully lobbied for a distinct "publishers' right" to be included in the 1956 Act—the copyright in typographical arrangement of a published edition of a literary, dramatic or musical work.[67] While in this first form, much was left unsaid about the scope of protection, the version to be found in the 1988 Act is a considerable improvement. The right is given to the publishers for 25 years from publication of any edition of a literary, dramatic, or musical work, which is not merely a re-publication.[68] It is

---

[61] CDPA 1988, s. 36.

[62] *ibid.*, s. 130; and see paras 12–54—12–58, above.

[63] *ibid.*, s. 136.

[64] *ibid.*, s. 137; it is necessary to find that adding the works would not conflict with normal exploitation and would not unreasonably prejudice legitimate interests. For variation, discharge and appeal, see ss. 138, 139.

[65] *ibid.*, s. 140; again subject to the condition concerning normal exploitation and unreasonable prejudice.

[66] *ibid.*, s. 141.

[67] CA 1956, s. 15.

[68] CDPA 1988, s. 8. Artistic works are still not included, for reasons that remain obscure: Dworkin and Taylor 30. Electronic publishing is probably included.

infringed by making a facsimile copy of the typographical arrangement—the means of doing so is no longer limited by definition. The work that has been published does not itself have to be in copyright; indeed the particular value of the right is in relation to new editions of old works, where the publisher nonetheless has a setting cost to retrieve.[69] Where there is fair dealing for purposes of research or private study, this special copyright is not infringed: and that is likewise so in respect of the acts of copying permitted by librarians.[70]

13–17   In other countries of the European Community, as indeed in other parts of the world, various arrangements have been introduced to turn reprography to account. Belatedly they are beginning to generate serious revenue, just as the arrival of electronic delivery systems seem poised to reduce the extent to which hard copies are taken individually from a non-digital source. How quickly this change will manifest itself is unknowable and photocopying is likely to remain a cheap and simple way of getting much material to those who need it. Certainly the E.C. Commission has planned for the harmonisation of the arrangements for administering the reprographic rights of authors. However, the legal basis for Community intervention is doubtful, since there is little evidence that distortions of the internal Common Market are the result of different national dispensations.

So far as concerns a publisher's right, there remains considerable argument elsewhere in Europe, for such a neighbouring right is thought likely to diminish the position of authors. However, the Directive on Copyright Duration requires the establishment of a publication right in works first published after copyright has expired.[71] While it is a right reserved for that special circumstance, it is broader than the British right in the format of a publication, in that it protects the work whatever its form, and not merely the particular setting in which a publisher sets it. This is an important shift of emphasis at a juncture when works are become reproducible with endless variations of appearance, once they are put into digital form.

13–18   Publisher's right is an entitlement separate from copyright.[72] It is given to non-nationals only on a basis of strict reciprocity, and no moral rights are added to its economic protection. Nonetheless, the rules for copyright concerning rights, permitted acts, remedies, review of licences and copy-protection circumvention for the most part apply also to this new right. The new right deals with a somewhat obscure facet of publishing. Unlike some

---

[69] Once the 1988 Act abandoned the indeterminate term which applied to many works before their posthumous publication, this became more important.

[70] CDPA 1988, ss. 29(1), 38(1), 39(1), 41(1), 42(1).

[71] Art. 4; above, para. 10–32; *cf.* Art. 5, which is only permissive in form, and allows a 30-year maximum right in "critical and scientific publications of works". Presumably this may include not only original text versions of literature, music and art, but even school editions with notes.

[72] The treatment is similar to that of rights in performances and design right.

of the pro-copyright initiatives of the Commission after 1990, it should be regarded as essentially benign. In the main it will foster the publication of historical scholarship, which might otherwise be prey to simple, undercutting imitation.

(2) Audio and video copying

Audio- and video-cassette recorders are standard equipment for much of **13–19** today's population. What minute proportion of them have any idea how frequently they are infringing copyright by their copying? The legal position under the 1988 Act in the United Kingdom is that copying of most copyright material remains an act of primary infringement, even where it takes place in the home.

Very little home taping could be justified as fair dealing for research or private study, for that exception does not apply to sound recording and film copyright.[73] Some of the home taping of sound undoubtedly deprives recording manufacturers of sales that they would otherwise have made, but it is very difficult to determine how much; the claims of the manufacturers and the counterclaims of blank tape manufacturers show stark differences of opinion.[74] The same is true of the recording of broadcasts and cablecasts. Markets are now well-established for both the rental and sale of "home videos", which provide substantial slices of the returns on many popular films. How much of their revenue is lost through home taping at present can only be guessed.

Unlike the position with audio material, the technology available to the domestic user for copying audio-visual material is still largely restricted to the taping of broadcasts. Moreover, much of this copying involves the "time-shifting" of broadcasts for viewing at a more convenient moment, the copier then wiping the tape by recording something else. These differences between audio and video recording are important in assessing the impact of the Berne Convention, which appears to disallow any general exception for domestic copying if it would deprive the owner of just remuneration.[75]

Owners of copyright in audio and video material have striven to secure **13–20** an actual return by a sales royalty or levy on recording equipment or tapes or both. No copyright issue has been more hotly debated than this proposed royalty-cum-levy. In the years before the 1988 Act, on no other matter did the British government swing so evidently in the wind. Supporters promoted the royalty as the least compensation to which producers were entitled; but they succumbed to sharper critics who sensed the levy to

---

[73] See CDPA 1988, s. 29(1).
[74] For the debates, see Davies, *Private Copying of Sound and Audio-Visual Recordings* (1984); Home Taping Rights Campaign Office, *The Case for Home Taping* (1987). See generally, Davies and Hung, *Music and Video Private Copying* (1993); Davies, *Copyright and the Public Interest* (1995).
[75] Berne Convention (Paris Act), Art. 9(2); Ricketson, pp. 479–489.

be an interest-group tax and so a political danger. Britain, therefore, has not for the moment followed the lead set by Germany, Austria, France, the Iberian countries and most Scandinavian countries.[76] The government's refusal received contemporaneous support from the E.C.'s Green Paper on copyright issues, which blew hot and cold on the levy concept and warmed instead to the idea of spoiler devices.[77] The variations in approach between E.C. States may be a significant factor affecting the conditions of trade in equipment and recording media. There is accordingly a basis for reaching a standard approach throughout the Community and in the early 1990s the Commission was actively exploring the prospects for action.[78] But the issue is provocative both between the industries concerned and at a general political level. Intervention accordingly looks unlikely in the near future.

13-21 As we have seen, right-owners have been attempting to persuade Courts that those who supply recording equipment are authorising or inciting infringement. But in the celebrated "Betamax" case, a majority of the United States Supreme Court refused to find private recording from television, largely for "time-shifting", to be anything other than "fair use" (according to American doctrine).[79] In England, equally, in *CBS Songs v. Amstrad*, the House of Lords refused to find infringement or other wrong in marketing a twin-deck tape recorder, for all that it would likely be used for taping copyright music and sound recordings without licence.[80] Now, where material is copied from a broadcast or cable-cast, the 1988 Act has in any case introduced an exception for time-shifting, which affects all copyrights in the material transmitted as well as in the transmission itself.[81] Record and film companies will scarcely set about home copiers, requiring them to prove their intent to view or listen at a more convenient time; so this is very close to an exemption of all domestic copying, provided that it comes from a broadcast or cable-cast. The government thought that the Berne Convention allowed it to go so far.

13-22 With these avenues closed, right-owners in the United Kingdom have had to rest content with two provisions. The first was the introduction in 1988 of the rental right as part of the copyright in sound recordings, films and computer programs.[82] It is a right against the business activity of

---

[76] *cf.* the Government's pro-levy stand in White Paper (Cmnd. 9712, 1986), Chap. 6. Ten of the 15 E.C. states now have some levy: see, *e.g.* Kreile (1992) 23 I.I.C. 449.

[77] *Copyright and the Challenge of Technology* (Com (88) 172), Chap. 3.

[78] Consultation took place in 1991, leading to a public hearing.

[79] *Sony v. Universal City Studios* 104 U.S. 774 (1984); Ladd (1983) J.Cop.Soc. 421; Leete (1986) 23 Am.Bus.L.J. 551.

[80] [1988] R.P.C. 567; and see para. 11–20, above. *cf.* the position of a library which supplies a photocopying machine for use by readers: *Moorhouse v. University of NSW* [1976] R.P.C. 151, (1975) 6 A.L.R. 193.

[81] CDPA 1988, s. 70, covering private and domestic recording of a broadcast or cable programme solely for the purpose of enabling it to be viewed or listened to at a more convenient time.

[82] *ibid.*, s. 18(2) proviso.

making copies available for a payment in money (or money's worth) on terms that they will be returned.[83] Schemes and general licences are subject to the jurisdiction of the Copyright Tribunal[84]; and if they refuse to license rental shops they face the threat of a Ministerial order reducing their right to one of equitable remuneration.[85] Now that the United Kingdom has given effect to the E.C. Directive on Rental Rights, the scope of rental is extended to all relevant copyright. Moreover, while authors and performers are presumed to assign their rights to producers, they thereby become entitled to equitable remuneration from rental revenues. These at present form a substantial proportion of returns on films, though it is not clear for how long this will continue in face of growing demand for sale copies and the coming of digital broadcasting.

The second provision is aimed, in the coming era of highly efficient **13–23** copying equipment, to support the fitting of spoiler devices which will prevent the making of useable copies. Once such techniques are adopted the problem becomes the elimination of anti-spoiler devices. Section 296 gives a new right to a person who issues copies of copyright works to the public with built-in "copy-protection". He is entitled to proceed against anyone who "knowingly" makes, imports or markets equipment designed to circumvent the copy protection.[86] This is a civil right of action which may lead to an injunction, monetary relief, delivery up and direct seizure, as with copyright piracy. But it is not necessary for the right-owner to show that his own works were likely to be copied on the defendants' machines. In this respect, the protection is wide. It may become more extensive under the E.U. regime proposed in the Information Society Copyright Directive, in which case it may cap whatever defences are still left to users of copyright in digital form.[87]

3. COMPUTERS: SOFTWARE, OUTPUT, DATABASES

It is through copyright law that demands for property rights in computer **13–24** products have to date been most immediately satisfied. Something of that process has already been indicated in the general descriptions of copyright law. Necessarily so, since the adaptation of copyright to the computer has brought a range of influences to bear on basic concepts which are inducing their own sea-change. The impact of computer science on the patent system, for long dulled by caution, has certainly not penetrated so deep.[88]

---

[83] CDPA 1988, s. 179 "rental"; but the concept is extended to all lending of this material by public libraries: see para. 11–28, above.

[84] See paras 12–54—12–58, above.

[85] CDPA 1988, s. 66(1)–(4).

[86] It also extends to those who publish information intended to aid or assist such circumvention. See generally, Davies [1986] E.I.P.R. 155.

[87] Draft, Art. 6; for which see below para. 13–87.

[88] For which, see paras 5–63 et seq., above.

Although the manifold capacities of computers are such that they straddle the world between the technological and the informational and aesthetic, the adaptations required of industrial property are not so striking as those demanded of a system which has as its prototype the expression of literary and artistic individuality.[89]

In the 1970s, the arrival of computer products for mass markets—notably personal computers and computer games—put paid to "first generation" notions that functioning elements, and above all computer programs, could be adequately protected within the framework of contracts and associated confidence. In considering the intellectual property response, it is important not to forget the continuing significance of agreements within the framework of property rights. For particular terms, if only they can be made effective within the constraints of sufficient notification and of privity, remain a vital source of legal obligation, including definition of its scope.[90]

In this section we are first concerned with the application of copyright law to computer programs, in the light particularly of the E.C. Directive on the subject and its implementation by amendments to the 1988 Act.[91] Under this head, reference is also made to elements which interact directly with programs, such as "menus" displayed on screen and other "user interfaces". The second sub-section deals with computer output which can be regarded as the production of distinct works. In the third sub-section, we turn to data inputs, having in mind the massive stores of data which information super-highways are beginning to make available. This last sub-section deals in particular with the new E.C. protection of databases.

(1) Computer programs[92]

13–25 As in the working out of complete copyright works such as films or symphonies, the program which instructs a computer to perform the desired operation often goes through a series of evolutionary steps from preliminary conception to detailed and complex expression. In this process (which varies from case to case) a crucial stage in the conception is often the expression of the basic steps to be executed—the algorithm—in the form of a flow-chart or other logical flow diagram. Thereafter the statement

---

[89] See para. 9–17, above.
[90] See para. 13–36, below.
[91] For enactment of the Directive, see Dreier [1991] E.I.P.R. 319; Vinje in Tapper and Lehmann (eds), *Handbook of European Software Law* (1993, p. 39).
[92] For the position since enactment of the E.C. Directive, see Czarnota and Hart, *Legal Protection of Computer Programs in Europe* (1991); Carr and Arnold, *Computer Software* (2nd ed., 1992), Chaps 4, 5; Lehmann and Tapper (eds.) *Handbook of European Software Law* (1993ff.); Laddie *et al.*, Chap. 20; Rowland and Macdonald, *Information Technology Law* (1997). See also Australian Copyright Law Review Comm., Final Report on Computer Software Protection (1995). For the U.S., Sherman, Sandison and Guren, *Computer Software Protection Law* (1989ff.); and for a comparison, Drexl, *What Is Protected in a Computer Program?* (1994).

of instructions in a computer language is relatively unskilled though it may be very laborious. The detailed writing will likely be in a so-called "high level" language (such as Fortran or Cobol), giving the program in source code. The computer itself then converts this into operational terms of object code, by means of a separate "system control" program.

Since the advent of the micro-computer, producers of software, some of **13–26** it the result of very large investment indeed, have become most anxious to prevent imitations appearing on the mass market and to prevent down-line copying by legitimate purchasers. They have turned to copyright as the form of intellectual property most immediately adaptable to their purpose and have striven to establish, country by country, that the generation of a program is considered the creation of literary work. In some countries this result was first achieved by Court decision.

However, two hazards in particular emerged. First, there was a counter-argument that, at least when the program reaches electronic form, it has become a means of operating the machine and is no longer appropriate subject-matter for copyright protection.[93] This is a particularly damaging view, given that many programs are now written entirely on computer, rather than first on paper. Secondly, in countries which required a sufficient level of originality to be shown, there might be no protection for a program involving only humdrum writing skills.[94]

Partly because of these considerations, there have been contemporaneous attempts to procure legislation specifically incorporating programs into the copyright fold, mainly as literary works. While in the United Kingdom, the judges showed no tendency to resist this deployment of copyright,[95] an Act was nevertheless procured in 1985 which sought to forestall any lapse into apostasy.[96] In the 1988 Act, that position was reaffirmed and extended. Going even further down the same road, the 1991 Software Directive required a standard set of provisions in the national copyright laws of E.C. States and this has been adapted into the 1988 Act

---

[93] So the High Court of Australia by majority held in *Computer Edge v. Apple Computer* [1986] F.S.R. 537, joining in the revival of Davey L.J.'s dictum: "a literary work is intended to afford either information and instruction, or pleasure, in the form of literary enjoyment" (*Hollingrake v. Truswell* [1894] 3 Ch. 420; and see *Exxon v. Exxon* [1982] R.P.C. 69). But "instruction?" For the opposite view, in the U.S. and Canada: *Apple Computer v. Franklin* 714 F.2d 1240 (1984); *Whelan v. Jaslow* 797 F.2d 1222 (1986), [1987] F.S.R 1; *Broderbund Software v. Unison World* 684 F.supp. 1127; *Apple Computer v. Mackintosh Computers* (1986) 28 D.L.R. (4th) 178; Hoffmann *et al.* [1988] E.I.P.R. 337. See further, Laddie *et al.*, para. 20–18.

[94] See, for instance, the German Supreme Court's decision, *Inkasso-Program* [1986] E.I.P.R. 185. Now altered by the Software Directive, Art. 1(3), for which, see para. 13–28, below; Lehmann (1988) 19 I.I.C. 473; Lehmann and Tapper (n. 92, above) p. 167.

[95] Thus there were interlocutory decisions in which copyright protection was assumed: *e.g. Sega Enterprises v. Richards* [1983] F.S.R. 73; *Thrustcode v. W.W. Computing* [1983] F.S.R. 502.

[96] Copyright (Computer Software) Amendment Act 1985, applying the 1956 Act to programs as it applied to literary works.

by amendment.[97] The excruciating gestation of the Directive left it with strange marks, and its subsequent conversion into United Kingdom law has added others.

(a) *Existence of copyright*

13–27 "Literary work"—which in general is any work that is not dramatic or musical and which is written, spoken or sung—now explicitly includes a computer program and (separately) preparatory design material for a program.[98] The program must be recorded in writing or otherwise; but this is defined to include writing in code, not necessarily by hand, and "regardless of the method by which, or medium in or on which, it is recorded".[99] This is wide enough to embrace storage in a computer. There will still be the general copyright considerations: has there been sufficient labour, skill and judgment to satisfy the requirement that there is an "original literary work"? The mental input may therefore consist in the writing of the program from its first sketching in any detail, through source code to machine code.[1] It can also consist in compiling a suite of programs together.[2] Very simple programs may fail to embody sufficient "labour, skill and judgment"[3]; but, provided that they are not in substance copied, programs will mostly pass that threshold and be given a breadth of protection proportionate to the intellectual value of their content.[4]

13–28 British implementation of the Software Directive has made no alteration to these general principles. Note, however, that the Directive seeks to impose a test of originality for software which requires the program to be

---

[97] Copyright (Computer Programs) Regulation 1992, S.I. 1992 No. 3233: the complex result is severely analysed by reference to the unamended Act, the Directive and the Regulations, in Laddie *et al.*, paras 20.24 *et seq.*

[98] CDPA 1988, s. 3(1)(b), (c). Unlike the Australian and U.S. legislation, there is no definition of "computer program". The placing of preparatory material not within "computer program" (as required by the Software Dir., Art. 1(1)) but apart, means that the special defences do not apply to the material; but conversely the general "fair dealing provisions" may: see Chalton [1993] 9 Comp.L.S.R. 115.

[99] CDPA 1988, ss. 3(2), 178, "writing".

[1] What is a sufficient working out of an initial idea to count as copyrightable "expression" must be judged in the circumstances; but certainly source code may be copyright: *Ibcos* case (n. 39, below) at 296.

[2] *ibid.*, at 290.

[3] The process of converting a program for use on a different computer can be a complex business involving "translation" into a different source code language; this secondary work ought to attract copyright, even where it may also involve adaptation of the first version: *cf. John Richardson Computers v. Flanders* (n. 37, below) at 518.

[4] *cf. Autodesk v. Dyason* [1992] R.P.C. 575, where the High Court of Australia (by majority) found that a locking device needed to gain access to a popular design program had been infringed by an alternative device which, like the first, gave electronic instructions to "turn the key". It is, however, not easy to say either that there was a copyright program in the first device or that it had been substantially copied: see Prescott [1992] E.I.P.R. 191.

"the author's own intellectual creation".[5] For some Commission officials especially, the British implementation is defective in not introducing this wording.[6] The difference could affect such questions as whether there is copyright in microcode embodying simple functions,[7] in a programming language[8] or in identification codes for such things as drugs or the controls on a traffic-light system.[9]

The general rules for literary works also apply to questions of authorship, since this is permitted by the Software Directive.[10] So in United Kingdom law, the programmer or programmers will be author or joint authors. Their lives will therefore measure the term of protection, which, however inappropriately, follows the longest-life-plus-seventy-years rule.[11] Where the work is created in employment, first ownership must go to the employer, in the absence of a contrary contractual arrangement.[12] In all other cases the ownership trail starts with the author. If he or she is commissioned to write the program, there may be an implied undertaking (if there is no express term) to assign the right.[13]

(b) *Exclusive rights*[14]

The 1988 Act takes an embracing approach to the exclusive rights in a **13–29** program (and equally to works stored as data in a computer[15]) by defining "copying a work" to include storing the work in any medium by electronic

---

[5] Software Dir., Art. 1(3), so provided chiefly in order to oblige the German Courts to abandon the high standard of originality which they had adopted in *Inkasso-Program* (for which see n. 94, above). At the same time, the introduction of a personal creation test of originality has been seen as a bridgehead against the common law conception; which in turn makes the British omission provocative: see further para. 10–10, below.

[6] Of course, the phrase could be read to refer only to a "not-copied" test.

[7] Held to be protected in the U.S.: *NEC v. Intel* 645 F. Supp. 1485 (1985).

[8] Protectable like other codes under present British law: *Anderson v. Lieber Code* [1917] 2 K.B. 469.

[9] *cf. Flanders* case (n. 37, below); *Computer-Aided Systems v. Bolwell* (1989) I.P.D., April 1990, 15.

[10] Software Dir., Art. 2, which is a moderate concession away from strict author's right theory. Each Member State is left to approach these issues in accordance with its general law.

[11] The Commission's original intention to impose a limit of 50 years' protection was surrendered in order to show that the E.C. was treating programs as works within the Berne Convention. The Convention was last revised before their inclusion was a practical issue. Accordingly, countries wishing to foster their international protection have treated them as if within the Convention *pour encourager les autres*. Now their protection as literary works under Berne is required by TRIPS, Art. 10(1): see further Cornish in Lehmann and Tapper (n. 85, above) p. 183; *cf.* Burkill [1990] Comp.L.R.F. 114.

[12] The importation of this convenient presumption appears the thin end of a disruptive wedge for authors' rights theorists. The Directive restricts it to the "economic" rights. This is of no importance to U.K. law, since there are no moral rights in computer program copyright: see paras 11–73, 11–80, above.

[13] See para. 12–07, above.

[14] See generally, Copyright Law Review Committee, (Australia), *Final Report on Computer Software Protection* (1995); Drexl, *What is Protected in a Computer Program?* (1994); Bandey, *International Copyright in Computer Program Technology* (1996).

[15] See para. 13–49, below.

means. This includes the making of copies which are transient or are incidental to some other use of the work.[16] The Software Directive is more specific, but probably goes little further: it requires the exclusive right to cover any permanent or temporary reproduction of a program[17] by any means and in any form, in part or in whole,[18] to be authorised, including loading, displaying, running, transmission and storage. Programs have been the foremost form of digital record to have proved pre-eminently copiable. It is this capacity savagely to undermine major investment by developers of software that has driven the copyright in copies to a point where it virtually overlaps with the notion of performance (without, however, being tied to any concept of public availability).

So far as dealings in copies are concerned, particularly in relation to parallel importation across state boundaries, it is in the Software Directive that the Community has sought to enshrine in national copyright laws its formula for intra-EEA exhaustion, together with extra-EEA non-exhaustion.[19]

(c) *Substantial taking*

13–30 Major commercial programs are, almost inevitably, subject to direct, line-by-line copying. The software industry has had to tackle not only those who make a business of piracy but also private corporations, professional practices, government organisations and educational establishments which clone multiple copies of programs from a single purchase. It is the immense disparity between the costs of originally producing programs and those of direct accurate copying which has so much strengthened the political arguments for their protection.[20]

Copyright also covers selective, altered, summarised and otherwise varied versions of a work, where it still involves substantial reproduction of the original. Indeed, it is explicitly provided that adaptation, as an act of infringement, includes making an arrangement, an altered version or a translation (from one language or code to another) of a program.[21] Since programming is a sphere in which, for many reasons, derivation in some sense may be occurring in the course of evolving new programs, there is

---

[16] CDPA 1988, s. 17(1), (2), (6), which anticipated the requirements of the Software Directive on the matter: see Art. 4. The Act thereby pushes the notion of "reproduction" to the very boundary of passing uses and approaches those associated with performance: some forms of random access memory (RAM) involve only fleeting retention of computerised information.

[17] For the difficulties about transmission of data as part of an on-line service, see paras 13–76ff., below.

[18] Whatever this may imply, U.K. law operates in accordance with its general test of substantial taking of the "work": see para. 13–30, below.

[19] See para. 11–27, above. Its precursor in the matter was the Semi-Conductor Topographies Directive 87/54, Art. 5(5).

[20] So also for all digitally recorded material: see paras 13–60 *et seq.*, below.

[21] CDPA 1988, s. 21, amended to comply with the Software Dir., Art. 4(b).

endless scope for argument about what should amount to infringement. Successful programs invite the challenge of more or less competitive variants. With a form of protection as ubiquitous as copyright, it is particularly difficult to distinguish the inexcusably predatory from the acceptably competitive.

On this most central of all issues, the Software Directive has relatively **13–31** little to contribute—mercifully, since the essential judgment must be specific to each case and can only be made by courts. The question whether the program itself is infringed—as distinct from issues about copyright in related output, such as screen displays of "menus" and games—is likely to turn either upon analysis of actual program content (at the level of lines of source or assembly code), or else upon analysis of those elements which together make up the program. In copyright terms, these latter elements, often characterised as a compilation, form the "sequence, structure and organisation" of the program. An understanding of how the elements work together gives a "look and feel" to the program, and, if that can be said to have been re-created in another program, a finding of infringement may follow, even in the absence of line-by-line copying. The clearest analogy is to the plot of a novel or a play, which may be infringed if taken in detail, even where the dialogue or description is written afresh.[22] Some warning against too readily assuming that structure is protectable subject-matter occurs in the Software Directive which specifies that "expression" alone is protected, and not underlying ideas and principles, "including those which underlie its interfaces."[23]

It is a context in which copyright systems turn to the distinction between ideas and their expression, and this the Software Directive reiterates, insisting that "ideas and principles which underlie any element of a computer program, including those which underlie its interfaces, are not protected".[24] This proposition has been left unstated in the British implementation,[25] for the understandable reason that it is already there as a matter of common law principle applicable to the entire field of copyright.[26]

---

[22] See, *e.g.* the *Flanders* case (n. 37 below) at 519–520, quoting Learned Hand J., *Nichols v. Universal Pictures* 45 F (2d) 119 (1930) at 121 (see para. 11–06, above). U.S. law refers to the recurrence of stock material in this context as *scènes à faire*; these tend to be discounted in deciding whether copyright existed, and whether there was copying or substantial taking: *Caiq v. Universal Pictures* 47 F.Supp. 1013 (1942).

[23] Art. 1(2); and see *Powerflex Services v. Data Access* [1997] F.C.R. 490, FC Aust; *Creative Technology v. Aztech Systems* [1997] F.S.R. 491, CA Sing.

[24] Software Dir., Art. 1(2); for interfaces, see paras 13–37 *et seq.*, below.

[25] It is in the Directive only for the avoidance of doubt: Recital 13.

[26] It is applied, for instance, in *Ibcos* (n. 39, below) esp. at 305, with the embellishment that "general" ideas are precluded, while "specific" ideas are not: at 291–292.

13–32   In the United States, the Copyright Act of 1976 sets out the dichotomy.[27] In applying it to computer program cases, Courts there have shown the world what differences of attitude can emerge:

> (*Whelan v. Jaslow*[28]: dental laboratory program). The plaintiffs held the copyright in a program, "Dentalab", for organising the business of dental laboratories. The defendants, previously involved in commissioning and marketing that program, then prepared a similar program, "Dentcom", in a different computer language (BASIC, rather than EDL), which could be used on personal computers. The Third Circuit Court of Appeals upheld infringement. Line-by-line copying did not have to be shown. It sufficed that there were step-by-step similarities in the listings of the source code covering particularly significant subroutines. These were referred to as similarities of "structure".
>
> In rejecting an argument that all elements of "structure" must be excluded from consideration as mere "idea", the Court preferred the generalisation that "the purpose or function of a utilitarian work would be the work's idea, and everything that is not necessary to that purpose or function would be part of the expression of the idea".[29] Aiding the business of a dental laboratory was "idea", but how this was worked out in any particular program was expression, a crucial indicator being that various non-infringing dental laboratory programs were competing on the market.[30]
>
> (*Computer Associates v. Altai*[31]: computer job scheduling). The defendants' "Oscar" program, which controlled the order of computing tasks, contained an interface component which allowed use with different operating systems. The plaintiffs alleged that this element had been added by unlawful copying from its "Adapter" program.[32] Here, rejecting *Whelan*, the Court refused protection, applying an apparently scrupulous legal test. It first analysed the "levels of abstraction" of the plaintiff's program, starting from its final expression in object code. It retraced and mapped the program designer's steps back from imple-

---

[27] Section 102(b): "In no case does copyright protection for an original work of authorship extend to any idea, procedure, process, system, method of operation, concept, principle, or discovery, regardless of the form in which it is described, explained, illustrated, or embodied in such work".

[28] [1987] F.S.R. 1 (C.Apps., 3d Circ.).

[29] Derived from Learned Hand J.'s dictum on the subject (para. 11–06, above), this nonetheless went as far in favour of liability as "what is worth copying is worth protecting".

[30] [1981] F.S.R. 1 at 19, 21–22. For U.S. views highly supportive of embracing protection, see Clapes and Daniels (1992) 9 No. 11, Comp. Lyr. 11; Miller (1993) 106 Harv. L.R. 977.

[31] 982 F. 2d 693 (1992) (C.Apps. 2d Circ.); Karjala (1998) 68 Brooklyn L.R. 519.

[32] It was first added by an ex-employee of the plaintiffs, who did infringe. When the defendants found out, they removed his work and had the element reprogrammed independently.

mentation to formative conception.[33] It was then in a position to exclude from consideration those elements taken from the public domain and those which could be expressed only in one way (elements dictated by "efficiency" and by "external factors",[34] where expression must be regarded as confounded into idea—the "merger doctrine"). It thus arrived at a "core of protectable expression" and on the facts the defendant was found not to have taken this.[35]

The learning process evident in these and other U.S. decisions has had a **13–33** variable impact in English courts, notably in two cases concerning straightforward application programs. One shared characteristic of the English decisions was that the defendant's program in suit had been written by the programmer who earlier had a major responsibility for the plaintiff's program.[36]

(*John Richardson Computers v. Flanders*[37]: labelling and stock-taking program for pharmacies). Here the defendant programmer had written a competitive program in a different computer language from the plaintiff's and the plaintiff did not contend that detailed programming had been taken. Rather, as in *Whelan*, there was said to be infringement in building the program as a whole from various sub-units—the routine and information order for entering drugs, codes for doses, pre-printing options for labels, best day's stock control, etc. Ferris J. concluded that he should undertake the "abstraction, filtration and analysis" process prescribed in *Computer Associates*, though he found it difficult. Curiously, he then concluded that in the whole program there were seventeen apparently similar elements, but that of these only three constituted infringement, all of them aspects of the display to the user.[38] It has to be doubted whether he sufficiently heeded the House of Lords' injunction, particularly in a compilation case of this

---

[33] Again, the starting point is Learned Hand J.'s dictum. Subsequently, in *Gates Rubber v. Bando* 9 F.3d 823 (1993), the Tenth Circuit CA, identified six levels: from main purpose and program architecture through modules and algorithms to source code and finally object code. Only the last two would almost always be protected, those in the middle being a matter of judging the particular case.

[34] Sometimes referred to as *scènes à faire, i.e.*, "incidents, characters or settings which are as a practical matter indispensable . . . in the treatment of a given topic": *Atari v. North American Philips* 672 F. 2d 607 at 616. The *Whelan* judgment equally emphasises the need to exclude such matters: see [1987] F.S.R. 1 at 18–20.

[35] For U.S. views supporting this caution, see *e.g.* Karjala [1994] E.I.P.R. 13, 58, (1994) 13 U. Dayton L.R. 975; Gambrell, Hamilton and Hood (1994) 11, No. 7, Comp. Lyr. 9. The majority of Federal Circuit Courts continue to show allegiance to the *Computer Associates* formulation. Inevitably, however, in the constant stream of American case law, differences have emerged over its application.

[36] In both, there were arguments about that person's interest in the plaintiff's own program, which resulted in findings that all rights were held on trust for the plaintiff: see para. 12–07, above.

[37] [1993] F.S.R. 497.

[38] For this see paras 13–43, 13–44, below.

kind, to consider whether there had been the taking of a substantial part of the work as a whole.

(*Ibcos Computers v. Barclays Mercantile*[39]: packaged "suite" of accounting programs for agricultural dealership). In factually quite different circumstances, Jacob J. held that British copyright law did not demand a search for a "core of protectable expression", and he rejected the very concept of a "merger" of expression into idea, of which increasing use has been made in U.S. decisions.[40] The plaintiffs' program was found infringed by "over-borrowing". In the particular circumstances this was demonstrated partly by identifying copying of specific lines of code (the judge refusing to believe the programmer's protestations that he had not started from the plaintiff's program) and partly by transferring structures from the plaintiff's program.

13–34   The *Ibcos* judgment is right to point out some essential differences between British and American copyright doctrine. The former, deploying its strictly limited requirement of "originality", has not hesitated to protect compilations of information against copying, even where there is little real scope for alternative expression.[41] Likewise it has not feared to trespass on the territory of the "functional".[42]

Nonetheless the caution exhibited in *Computer Associates* is not without its resonances for the assessment of "substantial taking" under British law. That judgment focuses very firmly on the quality of what has been reproduced. Indeed all pronouncements on the subject underscore the importance of considering, in one direction, the unusualness, and, in the other, the ordinariness, of what is being taken. So standard programming, even if copied, may be given little weight, whereas a truly ingenious structural device may be found to infringe even when subsequently varied quite considerably. Long ago, it was held that a simple picture of a hand pointing to a square on a ballot paper could be copyright, even though its whole purpose was to tell the voter where to put a cross; but for such a simple, functional work only very close imitation would infringe.[43]

---

[39] [1994] F.S.R. 275; see Grewal [1996] E.I.P.R. 454. Applied in *Cantor Fitzgerald v. Tradition (UK)*, April 15, 1999.

[40] [1994] F.S.R. 275 at 289–291. Note the Whelanesque flourish, mentioned in n. 20, above. "What is worth copying is worth protecting" is, however, disparaged as a means of jumping to a conclusion.

[41] Hence the protection of street directories and TV programme scheduling: for which see para. 10–10, above; *cf.* esp. the *Feist* case there mentioned. Commissioner Bangemann, however, did not hesitate to assure the European Parliament that the merger doctrine was a general component of European copyright laws (Session, April 16, 1991, p. 83). How long can the British maintain their peculiarity in the matter?

[42] As in the protection of grid layouts for a competition (*Express Newspapers v. Liverpool Daily Post* [1985] 3 All E.R. 680) and engineering drawings against 3D reproduction. This contrasts notably with the U.S. doctrine stemming from the classic *Baker v. Selden* 101 US 99 (1877) (no copyright there in accounting forms); *Rosenthal v. Kalpakian*, 446 F.2d. 738 (1971).

[43] *Kenrick v. Lawrence* (1890) 25 Q.B.D. 99; on which, see the *Ibcos* case (n. 39, above), at 290–291.

It is true that the British experience with copyright in industrial design **13–35** established that the protection extended to the purely functional. However, as the Court of Appeal has stressed, what is necessarily functional should not for that reason be accorded any special weight in reaching a final judgment on whether there has been substantial taking of a drawing or other work which is accorded artistic copyright.[44] It remains to be seen whether an equivalent approach can be built into the assessment of literary "copying". Ultimately the Courts look to see if a defendant who is conversant with the plaintiff's work (whether he admits this or his denial is not believed) has nonetheless in large measure produced his own work as distinct from disguising his borrowings from the plaintiff.

Other limitations may equally apply: if the allegedly similar material or element in a compilation is a standard routine employed by programmers, there may well be no finding of copying. In cases where one programmer is responsible for both, there is the difficult question, how far may a person who has actually started afresh, use knowledge and training which, in such a functional task, are all too likely to lead him down the same paths?[45] In breach of confidence cases, the courts have been very protective of the right of an ex-employee to deploy his own skill and knowledge in competition with his former employer.[46] The same basic consideration arises in relation to copyright and suggests the following distinction: an ex-employee who starts from the program itself and sets out to vary it may well be found not to have done enough; the ex-employee who is alleged only to have taken structure should not be held to infringe unless it is clearly shown that he nevertheless worked in detail from the original program.

(d) *Exceptions*

(i) **Back-up copies.** The Software Directive, and so now the 1988 Act, **13–36** entitle lawful users of a program to make "necessary" back-up copies.[47] Making back-ups of programs as well as stored data is widely considered a matter of sensible practice; so it can only be hoped that what is "necessary" will be given reasonable scope. A contractual clause seeking to override the entitlement is void.[48] In addition, in order to correct errors in a program or

---

[44] *Johnstone Safety v. Peter Cook* [1990] F.S.R. 161 (traffic cones). The scope of such copyright is in any case much reduced under the 1988 Act: see para. 14–27, below.

[45] The same problem will arise in writing a history, composing a song, drawing a landscape: see para. 11–15, above.

[46] See paras 8–24 *et seq.*, above.

[47] Software Dir., Art. 5(2); CDPA 1988, s. 50A. At least under the Act, a "lawful user" can be not only a licensed purchaser but any successor in title or other reasonably anticipated user (employee, agent, inspector, etc.) Initially the government insisted that even the question of back-up be left to contractual terms; a "back-up" power was doubtless normally to be implied—or possibly imposed as "non-derogable" under *British Leyland v. Armstrong* (for which, see para. 14–06, below). See also, CDPA 1988, s. 56(2) on the implied transfer of back-up and adaptation rights to subsequent transferees of a copy.

[48] Software Dir., Art. 9(1), CDPA 1988, ss. 50A(3), 296A; not affecting agreements made before January 1, 1993: Copyright (Computer) Regulations 1992, S.I. 1992 No. 3233, reg. 12(2).

for any other purpose "necessary for . . . lawful use", there is power to copy or adapt the program; but this may be excluded by a contractual term which after all prohibits such interference and so sends the user back to the manufacturer or supplier for debugging and other maintenance.[49]

13–37 (ii) **Decompilation and other reverse analysis.** During the personal computing revolution of the last 20 years, the industry's leaders have explored, with varying degrees of commitment, the possibility of maintaining "closed" systems in which they would produce and maintain an entire complex of software, covering not only the basic input-output systems (BIOS) which link all other programs to the hardware, but programs for external connections and application programs of all kinds (word-processing, spreadsheets, etc.). Equally a buoyant explosion of independent producers, both of personal computers and of programs for them, have competed to supply a host of alternatives, ranging from the directly competitive to the wholly complementary. In the early 1980s, IBM established its P.C. as the dominant product and the great bulk of programs came to be written to operate on this machine. Not only had other software producers to ensure compatability with the IBM PC-BIOS but also computer producers (such as, in Europe, Olivetti and Bull) had to provide a BIOS which would function accurately with such programs. While IBM fostered this development,[50] Apple was able to build up a second, more closely tied, system.

13–38 All in all, the range of consumer choice spiralled. The E.C., looking to assist a European computer industry in third place behind the American and Japanese, saw the importance of open systems in which programs supplied from different sources are "interoperable". The technical key to interoperability has lain in the ability of the outsider to have access to the structure of the technical interface of software to which a connection is desired. For the interface is a set of electronic keys which, so far as structure is concerned, must be precisely emulated, in order to secure co-operation between programs.

After a contortionate wrestle, at least in Europe, the campaign for interoperability has to a significant extent succeeded. Even so, major providers may choose to reveal in full only the object code of their programs, keeping the source code a guarded secret. For an outsider to secure knowledge of the interface information in that code, it was in some cases necessary to engage in the tedious and often only approximate

---

[49] Software Dir., Arts 5(1), 9(1); CDPA 1988, ss. 50A(2), 50C; but *cf.* Dir. rec. 17; Smith (1990–91) 7 C.S.L.R. 148.

[50] At first, IBM published its BIOS source and object code (which made this a *de facto* standard); later it was choosier about how much program information it released, being obliged to give more by a competition dispute with the E.C. Commission which was settled on terms (E.C. Bulletin 10–1984). The subsequent confrontation over the content of the Software Directive expressed a renewed concern by IBM to prevent interoperability with its products: see Sucker and Wilkinson in Lehmann and Tapper (n. 92, above), pp. 11, 24.

business of "decompilation".[51] This required the conversion of machine code by means of a disassembly program back to a level which gave partial access to the source code. No automated system existed, however, from which to recapture the full source code. Indications which explained the intent behind the succession of steps could not be recovered because these comments would not have been transmitted into the machine code.[52] Without them, it requires highly skilled and laborious work even to approximate source code. It can, however, be done sufficiently well to provide both substitute and complementary programs and this ability has been vital to the way in which the industry has developed to date.

That is the crucial significance of Article 6 of the Software Directive, **13–39** which eventually took a comparatively broad form.[53] The Article was intended to give the industry immediate guidance on what decompilation was permitted, so as not to leave the issue to the vagaries of case law in the various jurisdictions.[54] It is essential to keep in mind the special circumstances in which the issue arises. Decompilation will become significant if it leads to the writing and production of a program which is not itself an infringement of the program decompiled. If it can be shown that the final product infringes then it can itself be attacked; in support of that, decompilation for the purpose of writing such a program cannot fall within the exception provided by Article 6.[55]

Decompilation is concerned with clear, line-by-line, copying and so does not raise questions about "substantial taking" of the kind discussed above. Those who argued against any exception took their stand partly on the difficulties of demonstrating infringement in re-written final products.[56] They claimed that they must be able to object to the one step in the evolution of those products which unequivocally involved straightforward copying. Their opponents riposted that other copyright works could be consulted and drawn upon in order to follow instructions or to make other works, provided that the results were not themselves infringements.[57] From

[51] Particularly in the production of compatible BIOS's. In other cases, it suffices to engage in "black box" techniques—test runs, communication line traces, storage media dumps, etc. These now receive some protection (see para. 13–36, above). In any case, they are distinct from decompilation in that they do not require the making of a copy of a version of the program by disassembly.

[52] Johnson-Laird (1992) 5 Software L.J. 331; (1994) 19 U. Dayton L.R. 843.

[53] For an analysis of the proposals for narrower and wider drafting of the Directive, see Vinje in Tapper and Lehmann, para. 13–25, n. 92, above.

[54] Thus, while it may be that "of course, an individual owner could interface his program with that of another" (*per* Jacob J., *Ibcos* case (n. 39, above) at 290), that does not settle how much can be reproduced in a search for interface specifications. Nor is it clear how far taking one copy at that stage could lead to an award of damages including losses from the competition of a non-infringing program: *cf.* para. 2–46, above.

[55] Software Dir., Art. 6(2)(c); CDPA 1988, s. 50B(3)(d).

[56] See esp. Lake *et al.*, [1989] E.I.P.R. 43; Hart [1991] E.I.P.R. 111; Miller (1993) 106 Harvard L.R. 977.

[57] See, esp., Colombe and Meyer [1990] E.I.P.R. 79, 325; Karjala (1994) 19 U. Dayton L.R. 975; Vinje [1994] E.I.P.R. 364.

this perspective it was merely a peculiarity of computer technology that a single copy had to be made before the step of consultation could take place.

13–40   The actual exception now inserted in the 1988 Act is an adapted version of Article 6 of the Software Directive. It might have been more discreet to tread this bloody and treacherous battlefield exactly in the footsteps of the Directive; but our valiant draftsman struck out for himself.

Under the new Section 50B of the 1988 Act it is not infringement of copyright for a lawful user to decompile a program for a "permitted objective", provided that a set of limiting conditions are satisfied. A term in an agreement, which seeks to prevent such decompilation, is void.[58] On the other hand, the defence of fair dealing for purposes of research or private study has no application to decompilation[59] (though it remains relevant to any other computer use which otherwise would constitute infringement).[60]

The section departs from the Software Directive at two basic points. It defines "decompiling" as converting a copy of a computer program expressed in a low level language into a version in a higher level language; or, incidentally while doing so, copying the program.[61] Moreover, eschewing entirely the concocted term, "interoperability", it defines the "permitted objective" of decompilation as: obtaining the information necessary to create an independent program which can be operated with the program decompiled or with another program.[62]

13–41   Of the limiting conditions, three are in the nature of corollaries to the basic definitions. The sole permitted purpose is to create an independent interoperable program; so (1) the information obtained must not be used for any other purpose, in particular (2) it must not be used in a program which infringes that decompiled,[63] nor (3) must it be supplied to any other

---

[58] CDPA 1988, ss. 50B(4), 296A; the contract must have been entered after January 1, 1993: Copyright (Computer Programs) Regulations 1992, S.I. 1992 No. 3233, reg. 12(2).

[59] CDPA 1988, s. 29(4).

[60] The Software Directive and its implementation set other conundrums about the relationship of the specific provisions to the general law: as for instance the preservation in Software Dir., Art. 9(1) of other intellectual property rights and those concerning unfair competition and trade secrets. Where a contractual term is specifically declared void, it would be strange indeed for a Court to find that its purported obligation nonetheless arose under an equitable duty to preserve trade secrets: see Dreier [1991] E.I.P.R. 319 at 325.

[61] The Software Directive wisely avoids any comparison in the level of languages. The British section may not apply to a "hex dump", which is the conversion of object code in binary form into hexadecimal code—not itself a higher level language.

[62] This is clearer than the Software Directive in defining the types of interoperable connection.

[63] This is expressed overemphatically in both the Software Directive and CDPA 1988, s. 50B (3)(d) as use "to create a program which is substantially similar in its expression to the program decompiled *or* to do any act restricted by copyright". The first is necessarily included in the second, and it is quite unclear what, if anything, may fall only within the second; so the "or" makes no appreciable sense.

   The Software Directive (Art. 6(3)) spells out the limits which the Berne Convention (Art. 9(2)) places upon national exceptions to the reproduction right: decompilation must not conflict with normal exploitation or unreasonably prejudice the rightholder's legitimate interests (mysteriously, these are put in reverse order). CDPA 1988, s. 50B makes no mention of this: rightly, since it must be taken to exemplify the Berne proposition.

person for a different purpose. Beyond these are two factors which are inherently adapted to provoke controversy:

(a) the lawful user must not have the necessary information "readily available to him"; and
(b) the lawful user must not decompile more than necessary to achieve the permitted objective.

Condition (a) will not be satisfied where the details of technical interfaces have been accurately published, for instance, with copies of the program: but in that case, who would wish to engage in the tedious treasure-hunt of decompilation? How far it also covers a case where the rightholder will provide details for a charge is entirely unsettled. But a decompiler who fails first to inquire whether the information is available and on what terms puts himself at risk.[64]

Condition (b) may create some hazard for those who have to search around a program for interface structures, bearing in mind that they may have been scrupulously hidden. A decompiler ought not to be held to have acted improperly unless it becomes clear that he went fishing for other things using interoperability as a pretext.[65]

In addition to the provision allowing this limited measure of decompila- **13–42** tion, section 296A of the 1988 Act also renders void any term or condition of an agreement which prohibits or restricts the use of any device or means to observe, study or test the functioning of a program in order to understand the underlying ideas and principles of any element in it—not just interface elements.[66] It covers acts, such as running the program, which fall outside decompilation. For these, fair dealing is in any case a defence. Section 296A may be regarded both as defining one form of fair dealing and ensuring that it is not displaced by exclusory contract. As such it acts as a reasonable complement to the decompilation section.[67]

(iii) **Screen displays.** We move here to elements in the complex of **13–43** computing which are closely allied to programs, but (at least for copyright purposes) must be considered something apart. The displays on a screen provide the crucial elements of the "user interface". They are the keys which allow the operator to instruct the computer what is wanted of the programs being run. The immense spread of computer usage, and the progress towards "open", mixed programming, make it vital that this

---

[64] See Krocker [1997] E.I.P.R. 247.
[65] cf. Walker L.J., *Pro Sieben v. Carlton UK TV* [1999] E.M.L.R. 109, 127.
[66] CDPA 1988, s. 296A(1)(c); see also n. 60, above.
[67] This is the only U.K. transposition of the Directive, Art. 5(3) and the correlative Recital 19. These provisions, tortured beyond meaning during their evolution, purport to state an exception to the restricted acts, while claiming not to operate where there would be copyright infringement. For a devastating analysis: Laddie *et al.*, para. 20.46.

process should be made as simple and easily memorised as possible. Nevertheless, each user builds up a fund of knowledge about a program or programs which turns upon familiarity with particular displays and their operation. At this stage of the evolving technology (as is typical of such developments[68]) the lack of standard usage may still tie the user to the system he or she knows.

At present, therefore, new software competitors may in effect need to emulate the screen displays of leading programs if they are to make much headway in the market. In the United Kingdom the question has so far been considered only in passing. There are, however, signs that displays may be treated either as artistic or literary works (depending on their content), which give exclusive copyright protection.[69] If this is so, it is irrelevant that the programming to achieve them is quite different.[70] Moreover, there seems to be no obvious basis in British law by which to place any curb on the exercise to prevent screen display imitation.

13–44   In the United States the issue has provoked a rash of litigation, which has turned in favour of defendants as Courts have come to appreciate the tying effect on users. Apple, for instance, failed in claims that Microsoft and Hewlett Packard had copied such user interface features as overlapping windows, menus and icons.[71] Lotus failed to protect the menu command hierarchy of its "1–2–3" spreadsheet against Borland, who replicated it (using its own code) and provided for the transmission of the user's own Macros[72] from the Lotus.[73] In both decisions much emphasis was placed (following *Computer Associates v. Altai*) on filtering out unprotectable elements which were functional, unoriginal or indispensable in the circumstances, or which produced mergers of expression into idea. There is no mistaking the strong antipathy which the courts felt towards so extended a reach for this new and strange application of copyright protection.

13–45   As already noted, British copyright law lacks any principle which places "functional" elements beyond copyright, just as it has no general concept of

---

[68] Compare car-driving, as did the U.S. Court in *Apple v. Microsoft* 24 U.S.P.Q. 2d 1081 at 1088–1089 (1992).

[69] In the *Flanders* case (n. 37, above), Ferris J. correctly distinguished a screen display as a product of the program, distinct from the program itself. He considered that the display might itself be a photographic work or a film; and that it might reproduce a drawing so that if copied there would be indirect infringement of copyright in the drawing: at 527. See also *Powerflex Services v. Data Access* (n. 23, above); Jew [1997] E.I.P.R. 732.

[70] As Ferris J. recognises in *Flanders*, similarity of displays does not prove that the program to produce each is the same. But this appears to be ignored in the finding that the *program* was infringed by three interface elements because they were the same in their presentation to the user: see Karjala [1994] E.I.P.R. 58 at 63–64.

[71] *Apple v. Microsoft* 35 F 3d. 1435 (1994), refusing a broad "look-and-feel" approach (of *Whelan* parentage) in favour of a scrupulous analysis to exclude non-protectable elements (out of *Altai*); leading to the conclusion that what was sought to be protected was functional and therefore not the subject of copyright: see Neville (1996) 61 Missouri L.R. 203.

[72] *i.e.* chains of commands which the user has linked so that all will be performed upon a single instruction.

[73] *Lotus Development v. Borland International* 49 F. 3rd 807 (1995), affirmed by S.C. (4–4).

fair use to call in aid. But, as already noted, similarities which are functional may be discounted in deciding whether there has been taking at all and in assessing whether that taking is substantial. If courts here were to become as indignant as their American counterparts about claims of this nature, they might well use these limitations robustly.[74]

If the claims could be said to affect trade between EEA countries, there might also be a prospect of challenging the assertion of copyright as anti-competitive. Conceivably, the practice might amount to abuse of a dominant position, under Article 86 of the Rome Treaty, because restrictions on an "aftermarket" are gained through controls obtained in the "fore-market". The "*Magill*" case has settled that in extreme circumstances, Article 86 may apply even to refusals to license intellectual property to a competitor and nothing else.[75]

(iv) **Standard terms.** Software providers, who sell physical embodiments of **13–46** the program and at the same time licence its copyright, frequently seek to impose limits on permitted uses through a set of standard terms. As already noted, terms which seek to preclude permitted back-up, decompilation and other observation have no legal effect. Other terms will be effective, subject only to the interpretation of their language, provided that they have indeed been incorporated into the contract.[76] Since the conditions are often complex and are actually in the licensee's hands only when he comes to unpack the product,[77] there are evident difficulties in making them a binding part of the sale-cum-licence. When an English Court faces such a problem, it may perhaps use the notion of collateral contracts in order to impose initial liabilities upon the licensor, while also subjecting the licensee to the prescribed terms (at least if they do not seem markedly unusual and unfair) from the time when he could be expected either to accept them or return the product. The Court would be most unlikely to find that a licensor who is proferring a set of conditions by subsequent notification can both bind the licensee strictly to a sale from the outset and expect the conditions to be effective from notification. Certainly in a Scots case where the

---

[74] There now seems little scope to apply the concept of non-derogation from grant in this context: see para. 14–06, below; and see *Creative Technology v. Aztech Systems* [1997] F.S.R. 491, CA Sing.

[75] See para. 18–16, below.

[76] Where copying for the purpose of correcting errors was precluded by contract, it was held that this was not permissible even when the errors were so gross as to render the program not of merchantable quality. It was enough to leave the licensee to a claim for damages for the breach of contract: *Fylde Microsystems v. Key Radio Systems* [1998] F.S.R. 449.

[77] Plastic sheathing gives us the problem, in American jargon, of the "shrink-wrap licence"; though equally a box-top, envelope, cross-reference or pre-loaded program could contain the conditions. See generally, Tapper in Lehmann and Tapper, *Handbook of European Software Law* (1993) 61, and in Rose (ed.) *Consensus ad Idem* (1996) 293.

licensor took that stance, he was unable to sue the licensee for rejecting the software before receiving the conditions.[78]

(2) Output

13–47 Where a computer is utilised to produce material that is recognisable as a "work" in any copyright sense, the question of copyright in that output can also arise. According to the Whitford Committee, "the author of the output can be none other than the person, or persons, who devised the instructions and originated the data used to control and condition the computer to produce the particular result. In many cases it will be a matter of joint authorship".[79] This analysis may fit expectations when an individual or an organisation is responsible for its own data and program. The outcome can be secured by express assignment, or, if it has to be assumed from the circumstances, by an assignment implied by a court.[80] It is a solution which preserves the essence of copyright even in this strange territory, and so accords with the tenets of an authors' right approach to the subject.

Abandoning any such purism, however, the 1988 Act introduced the "computer-generated work"—a work produced "in circumstances such that there is no human author".[81] Dazzled by ideas that computer-aided design and computer-aided manufacture (CAD/CAM) were lighting a road towards industrial and informational productions from the "intelligence" of computers, Parliament felt that this precautionary intervention was needed. Where it can be said that there was no human author, but where a software house is commissioned by a client to provide the program, it may well be reasonable for the client to assume that it holds copyright in the output.

13–48 The copyright endures for 50 years from making the work[82] and is accorded initially to "the person by whom the arrangements necessary for the creation of the work are undertaken".[83] These rules make plain the borrowing from ideas affecting the older neighbouring rights, particularly in films. But their transposition to this new field is less than happy. As between the provider of a database (such as "Lexis") and a user who extracts information from it, who undertakes the arrangements for creation? Perhaps this is a case of joint authorship, as Whitford suggested—but is there really a "common design"?

"Computer-generated works" have been part of the law for several years, but the uncertainties about when a human author can and cannot be

---

[78] *Beta v. Adobe* [1996] F.S.R. 367: issues of classification of the contract and of benefits to third parties under Scots law played a significant role in the judgment, though their relevance has been doubted: MacQueen in Edwards and Waelde (eds.), *Law and the Internet* (1997) 121.

[79] Cmnd. 6732 (1977) paras 514, 515; see also National Commission on New Technological Uses of Copyrighted Works (CONTU), Final Report 43–46; Hewitt [1983] E.I.P.R. 308.

[80] *cf.* similar implications in the program cases: para. 12–07, above.

[81] CDPA 1988, s. 178.

[82] *ibid.*, s. 12(3).

[83] *ibid.*, s. 9(3); for the exclusion of moral rights, ss. 79(2), 81(2).

identified remain as great as ever. In international circles the concept has been greeted with scepticism—partly because the idea is antipathetic to "authorship" and partly because there is no rush of actual cases where investment would otherwise go unprotected. The experimental concept has not so far proved successful and some consider that it should be abandoned.[84] But the next generation of advances of computing techniques—towards such fascinations as neural networks—may give it a usefulness that is currently hard to guess at.[85] It is probably better at the moment to wait and see.

(3) Databases

To shift from output to input is to open up a very different prospect. The **13–49** storage of data in computers and other electronic servers is a highly significant element in the new digital information systems. Yet it is unclear how far, in many legal systems, the twin steps of storage and extraction attract copyright protection. To create digital files of a hundred medical journals or a national art collection or the daily business of world stock exchanges is a costly business and an investment which could be shattered by free access for re-copying. Yet if control is not possible, they will become prey both to pirates who are looking to create rival services and to those who want to extract material for their own benefit (and perhaps that of a surrounding circle) without payment.

Where the material on the base is itself copyright that is in the hands of the database provider (say, a publisher or record producer), that enterprise is protected already against extractions which involve making a computer copy, even if it is only on a transient basis. More difficult are the cases of enterprises which collect information, including works which are not their copyright, for provision to subscribers. These providers act like anthologists or directory compilers or cataloguers.

Traditionally, if they contributed sufficient skill, judgment and labour to this compilation process, albeit entirely through collecting and recording mundane data, they were treated in British law as themselves having copyright in their database. Their right was infringed only if there was substantial reproduction (or other taking) of their contribution. They had rights against the pirate who took the whole base and against many who for commercial purposes extracted some significant part in order to re-utilise it, perhaps in re-edited form. But the hacker who extracted small amounts of the total, even if what he took (financial details, say, or a photograph) was itself a protected work, would not infringe the copyright in the database.

---

[84] *e.g.* Tapper, in Lehmann and Tapper (n. 77, above) at 150.
[85] See the introduction given by Laddie *et al.*, paras 20, 74–20.92.

13–50   The rapidly advancing importance of databases has been acknowledged in the Database Directive. This has been incorporated into British law from January 1, 1998 and affects both pre-existing and new databases.[86] The need for it is accentuated by the hard fact that most Member States refuse to abandon their test of originality in copyright, which requires a protectable work to be the product of personal intellectual creativity. The Dutch Supreme Court has, for instance, held that the compiler of a dictionary will have copyright in the words selected for entry (as distinct from the definitions supplied) only if there is shown to be sufficient individuality in choosing them; in similar spirit, the U.S. Supreme Court has ruled against copyright in a white pages telephone book which lists all subscribers. In Canada, the same exclusion has recently been applied to a yellow pages book, which categorises subscribers by business type.[87]

The Database Directive engages in a highly elaborate strategy in order to by-pass this difficulty. First, it defines what is meant by a "database": "a collection of independent works, data or other materials arranged in a systematic or methodical way and individually accessible by electronic or other means. Then it allows copyright[88] in a database (as distinct from its contents), but only on the basis of authorship involving personal intellectual creativity[89] (a new limitation, so far as common law countries are concerned, and one which must presage a raising of the standard of originality throughout British copyright law). Intellectual judgment which is in some sense the author's own must go either into choosing contents or into the method of arrangement (the selective dictionary will doubtless be a clearer case than the classificatory telephone directory, but each may have some hope; the merely comprehensive will be precluded—that is the silliness of the whole construct).

Where this copyright arises, it is an author's right. Accordingly it will last for life plus 70 years; so a couple of youngsters should be on the production team (with their "personal intellectual" contributions carefully recorded). The author's right will be available under the Berne Convention to Americans and others entitled to national treatment as qualified by a lesser term in the country of origin. The right covers a comprehensive list of copying and like activities, and of public communication and similar steps.[90]

---

[86] Directive on the Legal Protection of Databases, March 11, 1996 (96/9). Implementation in U.K. law is by the Copyright and Rights in Databases Regs. (S.I. 1997 No. 3032—hereafter "U.K. Regs"). For database copyright these amend the CDPA 1988. For the *sui generis* right of the database maker, the Regs. themselves prescribe the law in Parts III and IV and associated Schedules.

[87] For these cases, see para. 10–10, above.

[88] Database Dir., Art. 3; CDPA 1988 s. 3A(1).

[89] Dir., Art. 3(1); CDPA 1988, s. 3(1)(d), 3A(2).

[90] Dir., Art. 5; and for the exceptions which Member States may adopt: Art. 6; in the CDPA this follows from characterising an original database as a literary work.

In addition there is a separate *sui generis* right given to the maker of a **13–51** database (the investing initiator) against extraction or re-utilisation of the contents of the database.[91] Four essential points may be highlighted:

(1) It applies to databases whether or not their arrangement justifies copyright.[92]

(2) The focus upon contents, rather than organisational structure, is intended to give a right where the contents have been wholly or substantially taken out and re-arranged (generally by a computer) so as to provide a quite different organisation to essentially the same material—a re-organisation which would not necessarily amount of infringement of copyright in the original arrangement.[93]

(3) The database has to be the product of substantial investment (so that it cannot, for instance, consist merely of different works collected together on an ordinary CD[94]).

(4) The right lasts for 15 years from completion of the database, or 15 years from its becoming available to the public during that initial period.[95] However, further substantial investment in additions, deletions or alterations starts time running afresh.[96] This must mean that a living database (like a regularly re-vitalised textbook) in effect has indeterminate protection.

The *sui generis* right has its place in the Database Directive because there is no harmonised law of unfair competition as between E.U. states by which undue misappropriation of information could be attacked.[97] The four essential elements in the right constitute some attempt to define what is to count as unfair. In going beyond copyright (points (1) and (2)), yet confining protection to substantial investment in a roughly proportionate way (points (3) and (4)), it seeks the sort of balance which was, for instance, so signally lacking when the United Kingdom engaged in its extraordinary experiment with copyright in industrial designs (1968–1988).[98]

Courts around the Community will doubtless have difficulty in deciding what is an adequate minimum investment to justify this form of protection.

---

[91] By Rec. 41, the "maker of the database" is the person who takes the initiative and the risk of investing, not any sub-contractor (*cf.* the *A & M Records* case, para. 12–09, above).

[92] See Recs. 38–40, 45, 46.

[93] See Rec. 38; and see Cerina (1993) 24 I.I.C. 579.

[94] See Rec. 19: such a collation would give no compiler's copyright either.

[95] Art. 10(1), (2).

[96] Dir., Art. 10(3). For verification, see Rec. 55; this seems to have been wrongly omitted from the U.K. Regs. 17(3).

[97] See Dir., Rec. 6 *sui generis* right will be accorded to nationals, habitual residents and companies of non-E.C. countries only where there is a Community agreement, based presumably on sufficient reciprocity. This necessarily assumes that the new right does not already fall within the unfair competition provisions of the Paris Convention, Art. 10*bis*.

[98] For which, see paras 14–05—14–06, below; Laddie [1995] E.I.P.R. 253.

At the same time they will have to consider another element in the balance: what is to count as extracting or re-utilising "all or a substantial part" of the database contents.[99] In relation both to the plaintiff's investment and the defendant's taking, there will have to be a quantitative and a qualitative assessment.[1] Provided that courts take each element in the equation seriously, the results should prove broadly acceptable. It is essential that they intervene only when a clear case has been made out.[2] Business developments in competitive economies have always turned in large measure upon the borrowing of ideas: intellectual property, including rights of unfair competition, must be restricted to those exceptional cases where the borrowing is unequivocally parasitic.

13–52   The new rights will protect large compilations of data and indeed large collections of copyright works (such as digitised versions of the contents of an art gallery). In this there is a serious danger that a major source of information may fall into a monopolist's hands. The monopoly element may arise because there is a single producer of the information (as with, say, the production of official statistics) or because there is a single holder of sources (as with the art gallery example). Earlier drafts of the Database Directive provided for compulsory licensing in many of these cases.[3] The database industries lobbied successfully for the removal of this direct approach. What remains are (i) a very limited fair dealing defence which is open only to those who are already lawful users for illustration for teaching or research[4]; (ii) certain exclusions relating to parliamentary and judicial proceedings and other public administration[5]; and (iii) control by the Copyright Tribunal of licensing schemes and collective licensing of database right in terms corresponding to those for copyright.[6] Beyond this lie the corrective measures which may be taken against abuse of dominant position under Article 86 of the Rome Treaty. The "Magill" case authorises the imposition of compulsory licences where, exceptionally, it is found that intellectual property is being licensed only on unacceptable terms.[7] This power could prove to be of some significance in relation to database right.

4. CABLE AND SATELLITE TRANSMISSION

13–53 Broadcasting by Hertzian wave opened the first great opportunity of relaying performances to truly mass audiences. The resultant copyright issues were resolved over time, first, as with public performance, by treating

---

[99] "Extraction" means the permanent or temporary transfer of contents to another medium by any means or form; "re-utilisation" means making the contents available to the public by any means.

[1] Dir., Rec. 42; U.K. Regs. 12 "substantial"; and note reg. 16(2), providing that repeated and systematic extraction of insubstantial parts amounts to infringement.

[2] Note the burdens of proof imposed by *ibid.*, Recs. 53, 54.

[3] Dir., Second Draft (COM(93) 464 final), Art. 11(1)–(4).

[4] U.K. Regs. 20(1).

[5] U.K. Regs. 20(2).

[6] U.K. Regs. 24.

[7] *RTE v. E.C. Commission* [1995] E.C.R. I–743; below, para. 18–16.

broadcasting as an act of infringement—broadcasters as users of copyright works had therefore to seek copyright licences; and secondly, by making the act of broadcasting an activity which itself attracted copyright—those who relayed or re-transmitted the broadcast then needed a licence (unless they could claim some special exemption). By 1956, the use of wire to distribute broadcasts from a receiving antenna or to transmit other programmes was sufficiently advanced for cable-casting to be made a restricted act for literary, dramatic and musical works. A European Television Agreement of 1960, sponsored by the Council of Europe, aimed to prevent a person receiving a broadcast from another state in order to diffuse it by cable. To this the British have been parties, but subject to significant reservations.[8] A separate right in cable-casts that were not mere relays had to wait until 1984, when the technical possibilities of co-axial cable heralded a communication revolution in the United Kingdom as in other countries.[9]

Satellite transmissions now perform an increasing range of functions. In **13–54** part they concern broadcasting activities. Fixed satellite service (FSS) systems operate by securing that the transmission is received from the satellite by a station and the programme is then distributed (typically) through a cable system. Direct broadcasting by satellite (DBS) systems operate to individual receivers, such as dishes, without the intervention of earth station and cable. With the development of encryption techniques, an operator can limit direct reception so that it is available only to those who have the requisite decoding receiver. Other elements discriminating between recipients can be added, such as language and advertising. At the same time, the distinction between FSS and DBS has been blurred by the possibility of receiving the same broadcast directly or through a station. Mixed systems of this kind were licensed in the United Kingdom from 1985 onwards and are the basis of the pay-TV services, now operating in Britain and elsewhere in Europe.

Cable and satellite are between them opening many new communications prospects apart from broadcasting and cable-casting, such as relaying a meeting, speech or performance to limited numbers of people in a different place or places; transmitting the content of documents so as to produce facsimiles at the point of reception; and providing access to the global information services of which the Internet is the current harbinger.

In determining how far these activities should be the subject of copyright, **13–55** the 1988 legislation proceeds by reference to general precepts. The distinction between reproduction and performance rights is observed. Thus "faxing" involves copying upon reception, and a special provision makes it secondary infringement to transmit a work by telecommunication system knowing or having reason to believe that such a copy will result.[10]

---

[8] Some but not all of these were withdrawn after the 1988 Act.
[9] Cable and Broadcasting Act 1984, s. 57, Sched. 5, paras 6, 7.
[10] CDPA 1988, s. 24(2).

Broadcasting and cable-casting, however, are acts of performance which accordingly require dissemination to sufficient numbers before they are covered. Hence the definition of "broadcast" which requires a transmission by wireless telegraphy capable of being lawfully received by members of the public, but includes one in encrypted form for which the programme provider has made decoding equipment available to the public.[11] Hence also the definition of "cable programme service" which covers the sending of information by a "non-wireless" telecommunications system, either to two or more places on request or for presentation to the public, but excepting from this a variety of limited, "closed-circuit" possibilities, which have been mentioned earlier[12]; and also by excluding services (like tele-shopping) so far as they are inter-active.[13]

Beyond this, there are a number of crucial provisions determining the basis on which right-owners can assert economic interests. Thus "broadcaster" is defined (so as to affect both rights and liabilities) to cover those who share responsibility for programme content, but to exclude carriers who merely provide some part of the transmission service (such as satellite access).[14] Satellite broadcasting occurs at the stage of the "upleg" to the satellite, rather than the subsequent "down-leg" for reception—and this is so whether the primary arrangement is for FSS or DBS transmission.[15] Thus if the programme is transmitted from the United Kingdom, copyright licences are needed there and deserve to be rewarded at a rate which takes account of audiences wherever they are being reached.

13–56 The right of a copyright owner to a return in respect of the immediate re-transmission of a broadcast by cable within the United Kingdom is limited. In particular, diffusion service licensees in Britain do not need a separate licence of either copyright in the broadcast or in works, recordings or films transmitted, because of their statutory responsibility to carry all BBC and ITC programmes[16]; nor do those who provide cable services in the area intended for reception of the broadcast (where the object of cabling will normally be to overcome some reception difficulty).[17] In these cases, the right-owner of material broadcast must expect his return through the royalty paid by the broadcaster, subject only to an ultimate provision

---

[11] CDPA 1988, s. 6(1), (2). Note the provisions designed to reinforce the position of those who supply encrypted service; s. 297 makes it a summary offence fraudulently to receive such a programme; and s. 298 gives civil remedies against a person who makes or provides equipment for fraudulent reception: see para. 13–19, above.

[12] *ibid.*, s. 7; see para. 10–28, above. Note, however, that the cabling of broadcasts within hotels, institutions and the like is no longer an excepted activity. It needs its own licence: *cf.* CA 1956, s. 48(3).

[13] For the relevance of this to Internet access, see below, para. 13–77.

[14] CDPA 1988, s. 6(3).

[15] *ibid.*, s. 6(4). This accepts a solution which makes for commercial convenience, and is now required by the Cable and Satellite Directive: see para. 9–19 above.

[16] *ibid.*, s. 72(2), (3).

[17] *ibid.*; but this applies only if the transmission is not by satellite and is not encrypted.

concerning enhanced damages for any infringement in both the broadcast and the cable re-transmission.[18]

Within the E.C. broadcasting and cabling have largely remained matters **13–57** of national policy. But at a relatively early stage one Community issue presented itself somewhat peremptorily. In some Member States cable networks were building up rapidly and were being used not just for the transmission of original cable-casts and the better reception of national broadcasts but also for the re-transmission of broadcasts from other Member States.

In *Ciné Vog v. Coditel (No. 1)*,[19] a national German channel transmitted the French film, *Le Boucher*. A Belgian company received it and cabled it to subscribers in Brussels and West Belgium. The film was licensed for broadcasting in Germany but not yet in Belgium, in accordance with standard distribution arrangements designed first to exploit the cinema market for the film. The cabling, being unlicensed, was an infringement of Belgian copyright law, but the company argued that the initial broadcast in Germany exhausted any right in the material throughout the E.C.; the Rome Treaty's policy of free provision of services within the Community demanded that there could be no right over such further treatment of the material as re-cabling.[20]

The Court of Justice refused to interpret the Treaty in this way, holding **13–58** instead that restrictive distribution arrangements for films were in principle a justifiable method of maximising the economic potential of the copyright. Licences tended to be on a national basis for the practical reason that broadcasting was for the most part organised nationally. What had to be examined was whether the particular restrictions in the network of distribution agreements constituted an offensive practice under Article 85 of the Rome Treaty.[21]

This litigious history made the question of cross-frontier rights one of the factors in a wider range of broadcasting issues between Member States. The Commission accordingly intervened, first with a contentious Green Paper, *Television without Frontiers*,[22] arguing for policies which would in various

---

[18] See CDPA 1988, s. 73(3) proviso. Right-owners have argued that this limitation is inconsistent with the Berne Convention, Art. 11*bis* (1), which distinguishes acts of radio-diffusion and acts of communicating a radio-diffusion of a work to the public, "whether over wires or not". This position has considerable strength, given the specific language of the text, but the U.K. government has not agreed.

[19] [1980] E.C.R. 881.

[20] The thrust of the argument was that these services should be treated in the same way as goods bearing copyright material, once they were legitimately marketed in a Community country: for which see paras 18-04 *et seq.*, below.

[21] In a second *Coditel* case ([1982] E.C.R. 3381) the Court held that limited-term agreements for exclusive cinema exhibition were justifiable and did not infringe Article 85(1), but that other exclusive agreements for the distribution of films required to be examined to see whether their terms were artificial and unjustifiable, were for unfairly high fees or created distortions of competition within the Common Market by their geographical limitations.

[22] COM(84) 300 final.

ways reduce impediments to interstate broadcasting in the Community. On the acquisition of rights, it recommended that broadcasters should be able, if necessary, to obtain a statutory licence from all right-owners, including authors. This was fiercely criticised, the case being countered, in particular, by the claim that licences were already, or else could be, negotiated satisfactorily through the voluntary machinery of collecting societies. Other aspects of broadcasting, including the requirement of a minimum Community content which has so exercised the French against the Americans, had to be dealt with in advance of issues about rights. But in the end they too have been dealt with.

13–59   The Satellite Broadcasting and Cable Retransmission Directive achieves a triangular accommodation between right-owners of audio-visual and sound material, broadcasters and cable operators which has three major elements:

(1) It requires "communication to the public by satellite" to be part of the broadcasting rights given to authors and also those given to performers, sound recording producers and broadcasting organisations[23];

(2) As in the United Kingdom Act of 1988, it adopts the simplifying position that a satellite broadcast is deemed to take place from the Member State which is the "up-leg" country[24]; so that a licence is needed for that country alone and not for all the "down-leg" countries within the footprint[25];

(3) For cable retransmission of a broadcast[26] from another Member State, the Directive requires right-owners to exercise their rights collectively and authorises the appropriate collecting society to act on behalf of right-owners who refuse to participate voluntarily.[27]

In the main these requirements do not call for major readjustments of the position under United Kingdom law, but the necessary minor adjustments still await implementation.

---

[23] Satellite Directive 93/83, Arts 1(2), 2, 4. The neighbouring rights are specified in the Directive conferring them: Rental Directive 92/100.

[24] The "up-leg" concept is defined with acuity: if actual transmission is from a low-provision country outside the Community but either the signal originates in an E.C. country or is commissioned by a broadcasting organisation there, the latter country is treated as an "up-leg" state: Satellite Directive, Art. 1(2)(d). By retransmission, the Directive covers only simultaneous, unaltered and unabridged retransmission for public reception of a broadcast or cable-cast from another Member State: Art. 1(3).

[25] Within the E.C. it was considered acceptable to adopt this approach, rather than insisting, in accordance with theories much favoured by the Directorate of WIPO, that "down-leg" territories be licensed. The licence fee is expected to take account of the whole coverage.

[26] As defined n. 15, above.

[27] Upon a failure of negotiations, the Satellite Directive only requires mediation (Art. 11); but national laws regulating collecting societies (such as the jurisdiction of the Copyright Tribunal in the U.K.) are preserved, at least for eight years (Art. 12(2), *cf.* Art. 13, Recital 34).

5. DIGITISED MATERIAL: MULTI-MEDIA[28]

In the 1980s the telephonic linking of computers to provide e-mail services **13–60** and access to databases grew apace. By the early 1990s these extraordinary capacities were harnessed to form the Internet, which originated as an electronic dispersal of defence in formation to guard it from central attack. Scholars were soon enticed by the ready exchange of ideas which it offered; others with interests and obsessions, high and low, were drawn to its frenetic interchanging of information across continents. As ever in the history of education, entertainment and culture, a new technology for the expression of ideas soon enough began to be commercialised. The super-highways for information supplied by the Internet and other electronic channels now attract those who will supply only upon payment and who deal in products attractive enough to find customers at a price.

The fundamental technique which brings about this dematerialised Nirvana is digitisation—the power to reduce information of all kinds into the binary representation of 0s and 1s which is the essential function of all computerised technology. Information can be accurately recorded in a form which leaves it readily available to be seen or heard. It may be retrieved as written text, graphic display, moving images, spoken words, music or other sounds; and this retrieval may be purely temporary (as in a screen display accompanied by sounds) or it may be more permanent (as when a copy, electronic or otherwise, is taken). So long at least as digital recording is not compressed for purposes of transmission,[29] it can be endlessly reproduced without loss of quality. It may be transmitted in hard form, as in a CD-ROM, but equally it may be down-loaded directly onto screen.

It is still very difficult to know what products and services are going to be **13–61** generated by this technology in ways that attract the public on a major scale. The publishing, film, broadcasting and record industries look with nervous excitement at potentialities which may upset the whole structure of their present operations. They are frightened by the capacity for unlicensed copying, at both the commercial and the private ends of the scale, which could pose a threat far graver in degree than with the photocopying, faxing,

---

[28] The whole subject is under intense discussion at many levels. See the Report for the U.S. Government's Information Infrastructure Task Force (IITF), *Intellectual Property and the National Information Infrastructure* (1995) and the E.C. Commission's Green Paper, *Copyright and Related Rights in the Information Society* (1995); the proceedings of the WIPO Symposia, *The Impact of Digital Technology on Copyright and Neighbouring Rights* (1993) and *The Future of Copyright and Neighbouring Rights* (1994); and, in a surging literature, Reichman (1993) 21 I.I.C. 241, 446; Geller (1994) 25 I.I.C. 54; Olswang [1995] E.I.P.R. 215; Christie [1995] E.I.P.R. 522; Ginsburg (1995) 95 Col. L.R. 1466; Cameron [1996] E.I.P.R. 115; Kurtz [1996] E.I.P.R. 120; Löwenheim (1996) 27 I.I.C. 41; Gimeno (1998) 29 I.I.C. 907; Fitzgerald and Cifuentes [1999] Ent. L.R. 32.

[29] Highly complex works, such as film, need vast quantities of computer memory for full recording. Much of their quality can be retained by compression techniques which delete the least perceptible differences. Compression is the key to affordable digital broadcasting and is the subject of much experimentation by computer scientists.

sound taping and video recording of the last 20 years. At the same time, they see new possibilities of tracking the use of their material electronically and billing for use of particular works, each at their own price, without resort to such averaging techniques as blanket licensing or sampling of use. They also appreciate that out of the possibilities for making new kinds of work and new collations of material, consumer demand could be much heightened, as is also likely to follow from the ready availability and the on-demand transmission of which the technology is increasingly capable.

The appearance of each new technology for the creation or storing of literary and artistic works has led, in case after case, to claims that copyright has become irrelevant or unusable, its wasting away inevitable. What, therefore, is remarkable in the history of copyright is its resilience. With the arrival of photography, sound recording, filming and broadcasting one thing at least was plain: existing law would need rewriting if it was to embrace the products of the novel techniques. Sometimes, indeed, it has required a lot of persuasion to carry the point that the new techniques were close enough to creative activity to merit copyright protection: photography was the first, and most striking, example.[30]

The curious feature of digitisation is that it provides a homogenous medium for storing and transmitting a whole range of works which previously seemed distinct. There is accordingly no simple question of the old type. One has to ask, what is it that those who proclaim the death of copyright at the hand of digitisation want to see? Are they advocates of free access and circulation of all information in digital form? Do they, *per contra*, so fear the new medium that they would seek to stop their material from being placed upon it? Or do they see some characteristic of it which requires a different form of legal control in the interests of creators and investors? It is by now at least clear that policy-makers are focussing on the third of these concerns. We shall accordingly, in this section consider the creation of products in digital form. The next section deals with Internet distribution.

13–62   There seems no insuperable difficulty in using the constructs of copyright to protect material which is created and stored in digital form. This proposition can be explored by considering the various quantities in the copyright formula.

(1) Work[31]

13–63 Works which otherwise qualify under our definitions of literary, dramatic, musical and artistic works are nonetheless copyright for all that their fixation or recording occurs in digital form; likewise with sound recordings

---

[30] See para. 10–48, above.
[31] For an interesting examination of how copyright of the British form may need to be restructured, see Copyright Law Review Committee (Australia), *Simplification of the Copyright Act* Part 2 (1999).

and films. However, the range of material which may be combined together in digital recording (as in a multi-media product) is such that the result may not easily fit into any one of these relatively limited categories.

Where, for instance, does one place an electronic encyclopedia which can illustrate its basic text by films, recordings of music and of animal sounds, and which offers the user the capacity to re-draw and re-colour artistic works? Like songs and films before it, such a compendium can be conceived as a coalescence of different copyrights. In so far as it is a film, as well as constituting an accumulation of contributory copyrights, the digitised encyclopedia will also be a work in itself. But large parts of it may not produce moving images; the whole (or perhaps those parts) may therefore not fit within the definition of film. What the electronic editor does in assembling the whole seems akin in skill and judgment to the work involved in creating a printed encyclopedia and so ought to qualify for literary copyright, and, perhaps in appropriate cases, musical and artistic copyright as well. A Court would seek to find copyright in any substantial work of this kind so as to be able to stop substantial unauthorised borrowing. If there proves to be difficulties over this, it may be necessary to add some inclusive form of definition to the statute.[32]

As with other forms of collated material, what is described as "editor- **13–64** ship" may at one extreme call for highly sophisticated judgment and at the other be no more than indiscriminate assemblage, of the same order as choosing the titles for a newsagent's shelves. Legal systems use different tests of originality in order to settle where exactly copyright begins on the line between these poles. The common law approach takes a liberal view, but even it will exclude matter which fails to embody any sufficient labour, skill and judgment.[33]

The investment needed to put together factual information which is complete, rather than significantly selective, can be very considerable where the material is being collected in digital form. It is the rapid development of such databases, and the prospect that they could be commercially hijacked, that has led to the drafting of the E.C.'s Database Directive with its double tier of rights. Despite its considerable legal complexity, this should provide an ample basis for protecting database investment.[34]

(2) Author

Copyright law already has a highly flexible notion of authorship which **13–65** operates on twin planes: where a work within a particular category (literary, musical, etc.) results from the joint planning of two or more creators, they

---

[32] In 1994, New Zealand attempted this by defining "compilation", a form of literary work, to include compilations of works and/or other data of any kind. "Work" covers the same broad range of matter as in the 1988 Act.

[33] See para. 10–06, above.

[34] See para. 13–50, above.

become joint authors of a single work; if that is not the case, successive work can create successive copyrights. Where the works are in different categories (words and music of a song), or where a first work is in some way re-worked (translated, put into a comic strip, etc.) a succession of distinct copyrights is generated, each with its own authors, on whose lives the various terms will depend.[35] In detail these rules may vary between legal systems, thus bringing marginal divergencies in their train. But because copyright interests can be collected into a single hand for purposes of exploitation (by means of assignment, exclusive licensing or a presumption in employment), the law operates with considerable subtlety. There seems no strong reason for distinguishing multi-media products from other material equally complex in its constitution, such as operas and films.

Computer technology allows developments in the electronic treatment of material at a wholly new level. First, a program may be written to operate upon automatically recorded data so as to produce interpretations which have the appearance of a new work: the generation of weather reports from continual atmospheric monitoring is the common example; automatic translation will prove to be another. It has been with such instances in mind that the British legislation has introduced the concept of a computer-generated work, for products which have no sufficiently identifiable author. As we have seen, the character of this right is in the nature of a long-stop.[36] It has not as yet been taken up in most other legal systems, since it dispenses with authorship as the prime justification for copyright protection. That caution is possible partly because it is not yet clear that there is any strong demand in practice for protection of this sort of material. In most cases it is possible to assign authorship to some person or persons.

Secondly, programming can allow interaction by a person who receives material, so as to add to it or alter it, and this step can occur not only when a further commercial service (such as a database) is being generated but also when an individual user receives it. The circumstances in which this technique might be employed seem vast. Accordingly, the actual conditions in which intervention might confer significant added value on the original are still very hard to predict. As problems emerge an adequate legal solution can probably be fashioned within copyright law. It is hard to see that any *sui generis* alternative would produce surer justice, and as always it would be immensely cumbersome and time-consuming to develop.

(3) Adaptation

13–66 A digitised encyclopedia or other databank may well draw pre-existing works directly into its content, either in their original form or with alterations. The step of putting material into digital form for the first time,

---

[35] See para. 10–06, above.
[36] See para. 10–22, above.

as also of transferring it from one digital bank to another, amount to copying within the right of reproduction. The immense new capacity for combining and modifying works of all kinds may indeed give their first form a merely conditional quality but it will enjoy copyright nonetheless.

The relevant copyright test to apply to an adaptation is whether the result still contains a substantial reproduction of the original work.[37] This requires judgment and so leaves scope for considerable argument. One particular problem may prove to be the endless divisibility of digitally recorded material: for what, then, is the *work* from which assessment starts? Nonetheless the test seems as appropriate to this medium as to others, such as a film or broadcast. A rule which would instead ask, has there been sufficient addition or re-fashioning to create a "new work"?, might result in fewer claims, but it would be at least as uncertain in operation.[38] On the other hand, a rule which imposed liability for any provable borrowing, even when nothing of the original ultimately remained, would be unduly severe.

At present, there is much concern about the amount and complexity of "permissions" work for putting together elaborate digital collections. Mixed with it are complaints about the unreasonably high demands of copyright owners, when invited to grant licences. Some multi-media projects have been abandoned, so it is said, in face of such intransigence. The essential difficulty is that regular markets for the material are only slowly emerging, and owners have suspicions still to be overcome. It is a problem, however, for which a market solution would seem wholly appropriate. Electronic shops of copyright material are already opening with prices in their windows. Much photographic and other design material is available in this form. If a market fails to come into being, it would be possible for the law to subject owners of copyright works to statutory licensing requirements. But why should such a solution be imported for multi-media works, if it does not also apply to films or broadcasts?[39]

(4) Moral right of integrity

As for the original author's concern to protect the integrity of his creation, **13–67** the moral right against derogatory treatment supplies a reasonable basis for intervention. How it should be exerciseable in a digital environment has been discussed already.[40] It may be recalled that the writing of computer programs has been considered so technical an activity as to warrant the exclusion of moral rights in relation to them.[41] Quite different considerations ought to apply to the great variety of works which can be recorded digitally.

---

[37] See para. 11–06, above.
[38] *cf.* the fate of such a test in relation to lampoons: para. 11–10, above.
[39] There would in any case be grave difficulties in distinguishing such types of work, one from another.
[40] See para. 11–82, above.
[41] See para. 11–80, above.

6. MATERIAL ON THE INTERNET[42]

(1) Introductory

13–68 This section turns attention to the distribution of copyright material on the Internet. A series of sequential problems present themselves, which vary somewhat, depending on whether it is the Worldwide Web, a newsgroup facility or Email which is being deployed. The most complex problems arise with the Web and it is intended to concentrate on these. The other cases can be handled by analogy so far as this is relevant.

The discussion will follow the sequence of events from the placing of material on the Internet, through its provision to an ultimate user in response to that user's request for it ("accessing"), and the subsequent uses which may be made of it by that recipient ("downloading", etc.) The initial placing of the material will be by a content provider and it will be at the site of a host ISP ("Internet service provider").[43] The transmission of the content of a page or site will take place in packets through a variety of computer linkages, each belonging to a service provider, until it reaches the user's access provider and so can be supplied to the user (*i.e.* the person who has ordered the material and views or hears it). While one can distinguish the various functions along the chain which runs from content provision to final access, often enough a single enterprise may fulfil more than one role. It is vital to think in terms of the particular function in issue, and not of legal personality.

13–69 As more generally with computer technology, each step in transmission and storage, whether fleeting or retentive, involves the making of a digital copy. Whether each of those steps should be treated as "reproduction" for copyright purposes, and, if so, whether some of the steps should be made the subject of an exception to the reproduction right, are issues on which national laws may well differ. As already noted, the British legislation takes a particularly embracing view of the matter.[44] Since the Internet is an incorrigibly global phenomenon, such differences affect the search for liability and the securing of jurisdiction over defendants who can actually be made responsible for copyright infringements. That is the first reason for

---

[42] From a U.K. perspective, see MacQueen in Waedle and Edwards, *Law and the Internet* (1997), Chap. 5; Smith, *Internet Law and Regulation* (ed., 1997), pp. 13–33; Gringras, *The Laws of the Internet* (1997); Cameron [1996] E.I.P.R. 115. Generally, Hugenholtz, (ed.) *The Future of Copyright in a Digital Environment* (1996). For a celebrated squib, designed to explode any such prospect, Barlow in Moore, *Intellectual Property: Moral, Legal and International Dilemmas* (1997) Chap. 13.

[43] For Uniform Resource Locators and the Domain Name System which allows ready identification of material, see below, paras 15–21—15–23, 16–27.

[44] Above, 13–29. *Cf. Spiritual Technology v. Dataweb* (District Court of The Hague, June 9, 1999) holding that any copying onto or from a Home Page is by the content provider or user, not the ISP; the latter is therefore only liable to respect the generally accepted standard that it will remove infringing material when informed that it is there.

seeking international accords which will reduce the urge to seek out the best forum. It also explains why rightowners press for liability to be imposed on all those involved in placing and delivering material on the Internet.

(a) *International and regional law-making*

The TRIPs Agreement came too early to deal with Internet issues in its **13–70** current form (doubtless they will play a prominent part in the proposed revisions of WTO 2000). However, they became the chief focus of the consequent negotiations at WIPO of the two Treaties of 1996 already outlined.[45] Limited though those Treaties are, they require implementation in the E.U. The Commission has taken this as a stimulus for a more extensive set of proposals going well beyond the merely digital. (The result may prove to be a constitutionally dubious transposition of copyright law into the realm of E.U. law, despite the absence of any direct power to this effect in the E.U. Treaty.)[46]

At present there are two proposals in course of consideration by the Community Institutions, which dominate the future course of policy-making in Europe, but which appear to speak in different accents. The more embracing of them is the Draft Directive on Copyright in the Information Society[47] (hereafter the "InfoSoc. Directive"). This seeks: (i) to impose a definition of the reproduction right adapted to the digital environment[48]—including an assurance that the concept of exhaustion of right is not applicable to electronically delivered copies[49]; (ii) to implement the WIPO Treaties' definition of communication to the public so as to cover individual accessing[50]; (iii) to limit the liability of service providers in the chain of Internet transmission[51]; (iv) to restrict the range of exceptions and limitations which a member state may retain in its copyright law[52]; and (v) following the WIPO Treaties, to require support for the integrity of electronic management systems of copyright protection and to insist upon the introduction of measures against "anti-spoiler devices".[53] In February 1999, the European Parliament insisted on strengthening the Commission's proposals so as to favour copyright owners in many ways—above all in

---

[45] Above, para. 9–36. See further, Ficsor (1997) 21 Col.-VLA JLA 197; Reinbothe *et al.* [1997] E.I.P.R. 171; Vinje [1997] E.I.P.R. 230.

[46] On this theme, see further below, para. 13–84.

[47] Published by the Commission as COM (97) 628. For its precursors, see the Green Paper, COM (95) 382 final; and the Communication COM (96) 586 final; Dietz [1998] I.P.Q. 335; Dreier (1998) 29 I.I.C. 623.

[48] Art. 2.

[49] Art. 4.

[50] Art. 3.

[51] Art 5(1).

[52] Art. 5(2)–(4).

[53] Arts 6, 7.

relation to the various exceptions (*i.e.* in relation to (iii) and (iv) above). Even in its own terms, therefore, the InfoSoc Directive is far from settled.

13–71   At the same time the same Commission Directorate (XV: Internal Market) is responsible for a Draft Directive on Electronic Commerce (the "E-Commerce Directive").[54] This facilitates e-transactions and deals with various aspects of regulation. Amongst these latter, it contains detailed provisions aimed at protecting telecommunicators from certain liabilities for copyright infringement when they are unsuspecting conveyors of material which infringes copyright. It therefore touches the same territory as (iv) in the InfoSoc Directive.

(b) *Private international law and procedure*

13–72 Until the world eliminates all conflicts of substantive law and jurisdiction affecting copyright material on the Internet, the issues of private international law and procedure remain acute and plans for dealing with them proliferate. One school of thought argues, by general analogy to the satellite broadcasting solution in the European Union, that normally the sole applicable law governing Internet placement and transmission should be the law of the Host ISP's operation.[55] Users would thus have a clear point of reference in determining what licences are necessary. The opposite school of thought distances the satellite solution as a regional arrangement between responsible operators, quite unlike the utterly unregulated condition of the Internet.[56] Accordingly it is necessary to leave liability to be settled on a multi-country basis against the whole range of ISPs. Only in this way can it be ensured that hosts do not take their business off to small "havens" with only very limited copyright laws.[57] The argument over international liability underlies all that will be said about the position in the United Kingdom.

(2) British Law and its Amendment

13–73 The most useful primary division is between illicit and legitimate content, looking from a copyright perspective. The first question, in other words, is whether, at the moment when content is placed on an Internet site a copyright infringement occurs. Much else flows from that distinction.

(a) *Illicit material*

13–74 (i) **Initial infringement.** There are two main reasons why material may be illegitimate: it may be lifted from a source by an unconnected third party intent on piratical copying, or it may come from a person who is exceeding

---

[54] *Certain Legal Aspects of Electronic Commerce in the Internal Market*, November 18, 1998; for its precursor, COM (97) 157.
[55] See Ginsburg, WIPO Doct GCPIC/2, 1998.
[56] See Dreier in Hugenholtz (above, n. 42).
[57] See Lucas, WIPO Doct. GCPIC/1, 1998; *cf.* Dutson [1997] J.B.L. 495.

a limited licence. The first type of infringer may be copying from a traditional source, such as a book or record; or there may be a transfer from another Internet site—as where one newspaper proprietor lifts the main headlines from a rival's paper[58]; or the code-constructing elements of one Website are lifted for use in another[59]; or material may be extracted by an Internet search engine in order to give a reasonably detailed indication of contents in its own indexing system—an issue which has as yet been given little attention.

The second type of infringer may, for instance, be a person who is only **13–75** licensed to reproduce literary work in the medium of print and not in electronic form. Many copyright owners have been chary of granting electronic publishing rights, for fear that they will undermine their traditional forms of marketing. In many contracts written before the mid-1990s, the position was left unclear because the possibility went unappreciated. English courts will approach the matter as one of interpreting the particular language of the grant.[60] There may be some inclination, where the terms permit it, to exclude from the grant what the parties could not have contemplated; but there is no rule to this effect, as there is in some Continental copyright laws. In many countries, as electronic newspapers have come on stream, this has been a particularly acrimonious issue between journalists and proprietors.[61]

If there is no authority to place the material on the Internet site, then the content provider infringes by its own act of copying and by authorising the Host ISP's computer to make its copy. It is the host's machine which makes the copy and that equally amounts to primary infringement by copying. Accordingly, it is not usually necessary to consider whether the host is authorising infringement, either by the content provider or by any person who seeks access.[62] There does not seem room, under the present law, for the differentiation, which United States decisions suggest, between the complicit, organising host and the innocent provider of a site?[63] There is

---

[58] As was occurring in the *Shetland Times* case (Below, n. 73).

[59] As in Gringras' example (above, n. 42, at 180): in constructing a Website, a set of instructions (written as a Java applet) is copied without licence in order to make the site-holder's logo turn like a globe.

[60] If the term specifically assigns or grants a licence of rights including those arising in future through novel technical developments, it will be taken at face value: *Campbell Connelly v. Noble* [1963] 1 All E.R. 237.

[61] See, *e.g.*, Lindner [1998] E.I.P.R. 410.

[62] But in terms of territoriality, an authoriser need not himself act within the United Kingdom: see above, para. 11–19.

[63] Liability found: *Playboy Enterprises v. Frena*, 839 F. Supp. 1552 (1993): operator played active role in preparing *Playboy* pictures for storing on a girlie-pic bulletin board; *Sega Enterprises v. Maphia*, 857 F. Supp. 679 (1994): operators solicited the up-loading of Sega computer. games without licence onto bulletin board for free down-loading to others. Liability denied: *Religious Technology Centre v. Netcom*, 907 F. Supp. 1361 (1995): defector from Scientology movement loaded some of the movement's texts on to a critical newsgroup site provided by Netcom which had no knowledge of content. See generally MacMillan and Blakeney [1998] E.I.P.R. 52.

certainly a case for considering whether the law should incorporate such protection. If it does not, the host risks liability, in particular, for damages.[64] Against that prospect it can only fall back on a contractual indemnity from the content provider or monitoring the material itself—an enormous, probably quite impractical, task. In its E-Commerce Directive, the European Commission has proposed to introduce an exception against damage awards for innocent hosts.[65] To the contrary, its InfoSoc Directive initially contained an exception only for intermediate transmitters—a provision which in any case the European Parliament has since chosen to limit to cases where the user is entitled to rely upon some other exception.[66] The ultimate resolution of this conflict is not to be predicted.

13–76   The liability of the content provider and host falls to be considered both under the "reproduction" and the "performing" rights. So far as concerns reproduction, the 1988 Act pushed the concept a considerable distance by making even transient and incidental copying suffice.[67] The real issues for British legislation accordingly relate to the scope of counterbalancing exceptions—which ought to be correspondingly broad.[68]

Equally there may be liability arising out of the holding of the material in the Host site to be accessed by any person who requests it and who satisfies any conditions that there may be for access (such as an electronic payment).[69] Under the present U.K. law, this way of providing the material is unlikely to amount to performing, showing or playing the copyright work in public, since "in public" probably implies reception by a non-selected audience at a given time.[70]

13–77   However, it may well amount to "cable-casting", *i.e.* including in cable programme service (wired connection being the essential technique of the present Internet).[71] As the 1988 Act providentially specifies,[72] this type of infringement consists of sending the service containing the material either

---

[64] In this context, an injunction requiring removal of material from a site can be complied with without massive expense in advance.

[65] Art. 14, which is linked to a provision preventing member states from imposing any obligation ot monitor: Art. 15.

[66] Art. 5(1). The Commission at once indicated that it would not accept this limitation.

[67] s. 17(6), above, para. 11–23 *cf.* generally, Spoor in Hugenholtz (above, n. 42) 67. Because copying is so inclusively defined, there is little need to consider whether providing or hosting Internet content can amount to infringement by first publishing copies of works (under s. 18). Is making Internet content available to users the issuing of copies to the public? More likely s. 18 is confined to the delivery of material embodiments, such as books, records and films. This is even clearer in the case of the rental right, since rental requires return of the thing rented (s. 18A). Most of the acts of secondary infringement are probably not relevant to Internet activities for the same reason.

[68] See below, paras 13–82ff.

[69] Here it is the Host ISP which is performing the wrongful act; the content provider becomes equally liable for authorising the wrong: see above, n. 62.

[70] s. 19.

[71] CDPA 1988, s. 178. Accordingly Internet transmission cannot be broadcasting, since this involves wireless transmission.

[72] See above, para. 11–36.

for presentation to the public, or for reception by two or more persons simultaneously or at different times in response to requests—a provision which, not surprisingly, has been held to cover the ordering by the user which occurs when the Internet is accessed.

> In *Shetland Times v. Wills*,[73] the plaintiff newspaper established a Website for its news stories identified primarily by headline. *The Shetland News* created its own site on which hypertext links consisting of the plaintiff's headlines were available so that a user could click over to the relevant page of the plaintiff's site. One consequence was that such a user would avoid passing through the plaintiff's home page and so would not be confronted with any advertising placed there. Lord Hamilton granted an interim interdict (interlocutory injunction) accepting that there was a sufficient case for liability under section 20. As content provider, *The Shetland Times* might be responding to requests purely passively; but this could still be regarded as sending for receipt.[74]

Nevertheless, there is in our legislation a qualification which excludes **13–78** from "cable-casting" the case of an interactive service, provided that this amounts to more than interaction by signals sent for the operation or control of the service. In relation to some Internet sites, therefore, this form of infringement may after all not occur. In the *Shetland Times* case, however, a capacity allowing users to offer comments on the news service was discounted as secondary and little used.[75]

Subject to this one question, however, the reproduction and public communication rights in British copyright law seem already more than sufficient to meet the requirements of the two WIPO Treaties of 1996 and the proposed InfoSoc Directive. As with traditional infringement, making copyright material available for general consumption will fall within a "fair dealing" defence only in particular cases. In electronic news-services, the exception for the reporting of current events could have some role. On the other hand, the provision of educational material to others is not for purposes of private study or research, any more than giving large slabs of texts, accompanied by minimal comment, can be fair criticism or review.[76]

(ii) **Transmission of illegitimate material.** The accessing of initially **13–79** infringing material involves a series of copying steps. Accordingly it can be argued that each service provider engaged in the chain of transmission should be liable without consideration of its state of knowledge. Again the

---

[73] [1997] F.S.R. 604, CS, OH.
[74] Indeed, if this is not so, it is difficult to know what cabling on request in s. 20 does cover: *cf.* Gringras, above, n. 42, at 170–171; Campbell [1997] E.I.P.R. 255.
[75] *cf.* Gringras, above, n. 42, at 171.
[76] See above, paras 11–40, 11–42.

copyright industries have been pressing the case for imposing that liability and telecommunications corporations have been resisting the claim as wholly unreasonable. The draft E-Commerce Directive is clear that pecuniary liability is not to be imposed upon unwitting ISPs who do no more than transmit down the line—and specifically there is no obligation to monitor content. The case is stronger than that for Host ISPs.[77] In its draft InfoSoc Directive, using similar but less precise terms, the European Commission proposed that temporary acts of reproduction must be exempted from liability even in respect of illicit material, if the acts are an integral part of a technological process for the sole purpose of enabling use to be made of it and if they have no independent economic significance. Utterly at odds with this, the European Parliament has chosen to limit the application of the InfoSoc exception to reproduction "taking place within the context of the exercise of a contractual or statutory right"—a proposal which the Commission has not surprisingly rejected, but which illustrates the extreme nature of the Parliament's intentions.

13–80 (iii) **Reception by the access provider and viewer.** Even at the end-point of an Internet transmission, a copy is made, so there is a basis for liability when the material has come from an illegitimate source. It makes no difference whether the holding is purely temporary or is stored for a period in a cache in the receiver's computer. If the user afterwards transmits the material elsewhere, or uses it to make hard copies, those acts equally will infringe. Under the present law relating to exceptions from liability, it is unlikely that any excuse will be available in relation to material which from the outset has been taken without permission. That is a factor which in all likelihood prevents there being "fair dealing". Certainly the exceptions relating to computer programs apply only in relation to lawful users of the program.[78]

(b) *Legitimate material*

13–81 (i) **Constrictions on transmission and use.** The great bulk of copyright material which is placed on the Internet belongs to the content provider or has the licence of the copyright owner. Where, in consequence, access to the site is unlimited and the whole intention is to make the content available to anyone who may be interested, there must be at least an implied licence to transmit it and to authorise its downloading for anticipated uses.

> One enterprise provided software to another as "shareware" which the latter was entitled to bundle with its own software and distribute over

---

[77] See above, at n. 69. The thrust of the E-Commerce Directive is to bring E.U. law broadly into line with that prescribed in the U.S. Millennium Digital Copyright Act of 1997.
[78] s. 50A–50C,

the Internet. It was held to have an implied licence to do so, but only in its entire, unaltered form.[79]

The user who receives authorised material may well store it in a cache on his computer and that is likely to be considered a legitimate consequence. Where the ISP providing the user with access makes a so-called "mirror cache" of material the legal consequence is less clear. Because Internet access is often slow (particularly at popular times), an Access Provider may help its customers by retaining frequently consulted material locally. One deleterious consequence for the site owner is that upgrades to the material may be missed and these are highly important to "latest news" services. Courts are likely therefore to regard such mirror caching as not within any licence. It will therefore constitute infringement.

If the site-holder has imposed a limit upon access by password or other gateway—in order to secure a fee, or to restrict the range of recipients, or for any other reason—it is the technical constraint which in large measure gives the protection. Copyright is needed only against those who hack a way round that barrier. It is now widely accepted that, in general, where technical barriers are instituted they should be supported. The WIPO Treaties of 1996 accordingly require national systems to protect electronic rights management information, which identifies the work and the terms and conditions of its use; and to prevent circumvention.[80] There are, however, controversial issues about the perimeters of this common ground.

(ii) **Exceptions for users.**[81] Every copyright system provides a series of **13–82** exceptions to the general scope of the rights. The countervailing justifications for them in British law, and the way in which they are expressed, have already been explored in Chapter 11 and the preceding sections of this Chapter. With advances in copying technology, many of these exceptions are attacked as unfair deprivations of potential earning capacity by the copyright industries. Property rights supporters argue the case on the basis that electronic recording now makes it cheap and easy to grant licences for copyright use, where previously this would have been slow and invasive: accordingly market conditions are now able to operate and should therefore be allowed to govern. Putting it in down-to-earth terms, major copyright owners fear that exceptions which have the position of the individual as a starting point will come to undermine their commercial prospects in the new digital world. Many laws, for instance, provide an

---

[79] *Trumpet Software v. OzEmail* [1996] 18(12) I.P.R. 69.
[80] WIPO Copyright Treaty, Arts 11, 12; WIPO Performances and Phonograms Treaty, Arts 19, 20.
[81] See esp. Hugenholtz, Imprimatur Paper, October 30, 1997; Hart [1998] E.I.P.R. 169; *cf.* Samuelson in Poulin (ed.) *The Electronic Superhighway* (1995); ALAI, *Exceptions and Limitations to Copyright* (1999).

exception for private use.[82] The British Act, which proceeds more circumspectly through the categories of "fair dealing" and other nominate defences, also allows protection for a considerable range of cases which justify to some degree the same fears.

Are these fears nonetheless exaggerated? Are they not being expressed mainly as a pretext for upsetting the present balances of interest which the defences represent? Mutual suspicion between owner and user interests runs high. In its InfoSoc Directive draft, the Commission began from a relatively circumspect position which would leave the terms of exemptions to national legislators so far at least as the refinements of definition were concerned.[83] The European Parliament, however, whipped up by horror stories of the mass piracy of records, films and the like,[84] has taken a much more protective attitude. If the Parliament's view prevails, most exceptions will be reduced by E.C. Directive to entitlements to take copies and make other uses upon payment of a reasonable fee.[85]

13–83 (iii) **E.U. Law governing exceptions.** The debate is partly about public interests in freedom of expression—as represented, for instance, in the present British exceptions for fair criticism and review, and fair reporting of current events. It is also in part about the extent to which society may expect free use of copyright material (for research and private study, for education, for library provision, etc.) in return for the considerable boon which copyright protection confers over commercial exploitation. Appreciating this may help to bring a little light to the questions surrounding exceptions in an Internet context.

13–84   The arguments within the E.U. about the scope of exceptions and limitations are, at the time of writing, poised around the differing views of the Commission and the Parliament. The essence of their positions can be summarised as follows:

    (i) In the InfoSoc Directive, both organs seem intent on laying down, for national copyright law across the Community, the entire range of permitted exceptions. The Commission recognises that, where the particular issue does not have significant consequences for freedom of trade within the internal market, all that it can do is acknowledge that a matter remains within the purview of national law alone: this

---

[82] In Europe, countries which have such a defence have nonetheless introduced levies on equipment and recording media, such as tapes, by which to some degree to compensate right owners for private copying. The U.K. has long resisted the introduction of such a private interest "tax".

[83] But see below, para. 13–84.

[84] These belong to the category of illegitimate takings and are accordingly irrelevant to the problem of exceptions. The E.P. chose to add some high-sounding Recitals about the social virtues of the exceptions which it proceeded to curtail: See Recs. 2a, 6a, 10b.

[85] In the recondite apologetics used to describe extensions of rights, this is labelled "fair compensation".

is its position on photographic reprography. The Parliament, on the other hand, is seeking to lay down its own edict on all exceptions as a matter of Community law. It may be doubted whether even the Commission's view is within the Institutions' powers, since the E.U. Treaty still contains no general power over intellectual property law. With the Parliament's amendments, the constitutional question is much more serious, since the bid for exclusive authority is unequivocal and therefore questionable.

(ii) Any exception admitted by national law is to be conditioned by the Berne-TRIPS constraints[86]: it must be for certain specific cases[87]; it must not involve use in a manner which unreasonably prejudices the rightowner's legitimate interests[88]; nor must there be a conflict with the normal exploitation of the subject-matter. In general this has become a commonplace of international copyright law, though its interpretation needs to be read in the light of the not inconsiderable exceptions which were in existence in Berne countries when it was drafted and were not thereafter altered. There remains also the issue whether the formula merely sets the criteria which Member States must observe in formulating exceptions or whether it must be made a distinct element in the substantive law of the state.[89] Most immediately controversial, however, is Parliament's proposal to add to the tri-partite formula that rightowners must be left free to use technical shields to overrun the protection of users under any exception. This expresses a preference for any technical means which overrides the operation of defences, rendering them at most presumptions which a rightowner intent on absolute contractual arrangements would remain free to override. To this explosive issue we return below.[90]

(iii) Member States will be allowed to introduce exceptions to the reproduction right alone, (a) for reprography on paper[91] and for private, non-commercial copying on audio, and audio-visual media[92]; but, in the Parliament's view, in each case, subject to payment of fair

---

[86] See above, para. 9–26; Ricketson (1987) 482ff.; [1999] I.P.Q. 56.

[87] The two international Agreements say "certain special cases", which some argue imposes a higher standard. Which ever phrase is used, its scope is perplexing, since it was introduced into Berne for the reproduction rights at a time when most member states had general exceptions for private use or for fair uses or dealings. "Special/specific" cannot therefore be understood in the sense of requiring a decision separately upon each case, as may arise with compulsory licences for patents: cf. TRIPs, Art. 31a.

[88] The order of the last two points in the Berne formula is reversed in Community usage: for imperceptible reasons.

[89] See Mason [1997] E.I.P.R. 636; Rosenblatt (1997) 13 Comp. L. & S. Rep. 307; Quaedvlieg (1998) 29 I.I.C. 420.

[90] See para. 13–86.

[91] Art. 5(2)(a): the E.P. would allow no exception at all for published musical works.

[92] Art. 5(2)(b); the E.P. wants a severer regime for digital copying in this category; see above, para. 13–19ff.

compensation; (b) for non-commercial copying in public libraries and similar establishments, the Parliament adding that this must only be "for documentation or conservation purposes"—a phrase doubtless intended to exclude the supply of material to scholars or to allow them to engage in casual browsing.

(iv) Member States will be allowed to introduce exceptions to both the reproduction right and the right of public communication: (a) for the sole purpose of illustration for teaching or scientific research;[93] but in the Parliament's view, subject to payment of fair compensation[94]; (b) for people with disabilities; but in the Commission's view only for the blind and deaf[95]; (c) for the use of excerpts in connection with reporting current events[96]; (d) for quotations for criticism or review[97]; and for public security or proper performance or reporting of administrative, parliamentary or judicial proceedings.[98]

13–85 (iv) **Technical barriers, their reversal and exceptions.**[99] All these exceptions raise two types of issue: first, about access to the material at its Website or bulletin board; and secondly concerning uses made of the material once it has been downloaded. In the past, many of the actual concerns raised by the exceptions have related to the second situation: multiple reprography for classes and choirs, quotations in published reviews, news stories taken over by one newspaper from another. With the Internet, much more turns on the initial access and this heightens the clash of interests at stake, because the content provider may impose contractual or technical barriers in the way of obtaining the copyright material. As a result both the initial downloading and the subsequent deployment call for consideration.

The provider may set out contractual conditions to which a person seeking access must agree (by "click-on") before gaining access to the

---

[93] Art. 5(2)(c); the formulation was first used in the Database Dir. Arts. 6, 9. The E.P. wishes to add two further exceptions in this category: one for the facilitation of legitimate broadcasting, and the other for analogue news reporting in daily newspapers and on radio— a proposal probably more interesting for what is thereby excluded (cf. Art. 5(3)(b), below, n. 95).

[94] Art. 5(3)(a): the course must be indicated; the extent of copying must be justified by its non-commercial purpose (which is the language of fair dealing).

[95] Art. 5(3)(b): various limitations are added.

[96] Art. 5(3)(c): the source (if possible) must be indicated and the extent justified by the informatory purpose and (according to the E.P.) the objective of illustrating the event concerned. The E.P. want the excerpts to be "short".

[97] Art. 5(3)(d): the must related to a published work, source must (if possible) be indicated, the copying must be fair and to only to the extent required for the specific purpose (again, fair dealing).

[98] Art. 5(3)(e): this is the somewhat extended version favoured by the E.P., which added "reporting" and "parliamentary".

[99] Goldstein [1997] Wisc. L.R. 865; Vinje [1996] E.I.P.R. 431. [1999] E.I.P.R. 192; Samuelson and others (1998) 13 Berk. Tech.L.J. 1239ff; ALAI, *Limitations and Exceptions to Copyright* (1999), esp. papers by Spoor, Guilbault, Ginsburg, Sirinelli.

material. Unless there are arrangements for electronic negotiation, the terms offered will ordinarily be in standard form: take or leave. What if they seek to take away from the user a freedom which falls within one of the fair dealing or related exceptions in the national law? Suppose that they insist upon a fee before a scholar makes a permanent copy of even the smallest part of a work; or a fee for any quotation in an examination paper; or specific permission before using any part for criticism or review or for reporting current events?

One novel question is whether the exceptions should be raised to the **13–86** level of guaranteed rights of access and use, which cannot be by-passed by contractual provisions more protective of copyright owners. In the past, it has generally been assumed in British and other copyright systems that exceptions do have this character, though there has been only very occasional contest about it. If that is so, why should the approach change under a digital system? Why should not the former balances of interest continue under the new technology? Can it really be that, because there are the means of requiring payment, every transaction, no matter what its justification, should lead to that payment? If so, will there in the end be any purpose in imposing any limit even on the duration of copyright itself? In the counsels of the European Union there are few signs that these questions have received truly serious attention.[1]

If the limitations upon contractual restrictions are to be guaranteed against reversal by contract, then the same effect should not be attainable simply by a technical barrier. In particular, there should not be a technical barrier, which is supported by a legal ban on countervailing techniques which will prevent the barrier being by-passed in cases where there is a legitimate case for access under one of the guaranteed exceptions. Yet, as already noted, the European Parliament is pursuing an amendment to the InfoSoc Directive which will make sure that the technical constraint will prevail.

The provider may also build in to the site a technical device which is **13–87** designed, once material has been downloaded into a user's computer, to prevent further copies from being made. Again, an electronic check of this kind will have its desired effect so long as no counter-device (an "anti-spoiler" in the more traditional sense) is available to circumvent the protection. Again the core issue is how to leave room for those who are protected by a legal exception from infringement actually to secure access to material to which they are entitled.

The Commission's proposed Article on measures to prevent the circumvention of technical protection has allowed very little in order to overcome

---

[1] *cf.* the overriding provisions of the Software Dir., above, para. 13–36ff. In the U.S. the matter has been hotly debated in the context of the proposed Art. 2B of the Uniform Commercial Code, which aims to regulate E-commerce. For its relevance to Europe, see, *e.g.,* Grosheide and Boele-Woekli (eds.) *Europees Privaatrecht 1998* (1998), Pt. II (Samuelson and Opsahl, MacQueen *et al.*, Guibault, Grosheide).

this difficulty. It requires action in relation to all "circumvention" activities, which include the manufacture or distribution of devices and the performance of services "which have only limited commercially significant purpose or use other than circumvention of any effective technological measures design to protect any copyrights or any rights related to copyright as provided by law. . ."[2] This involved formula may still respect the freedom to engage in activities which allow access by users falling within an exception: it is difficult to tell. The European Parliament purports to do little more than re-order the language of this proposal. However, when read with its statement that exceptions and limitations must not only prevent the use of technical means to protect works but also must not prejudice the prohibition of circumvention devices, the true complexion of their intent becomes apparent. On this view there should be an invariate prohibition of circumvention, which will treat exceptions and limitations as providing no legitimising basis for reversing technical controls. It will be a legal wrong, for instance, to give a non-profit library advice on how to make the electronic copies it needs for documentation and preservation under the exception which allows this. Across the millennial divide, this issue needs most urgent and prominent debate.

7. RIGHTS IN PERFORMANCES[3]

13–88 Performers engage in activities which are more immediately artistic and re-creative than the entrepreneurs who enjoy copyrights in sound recordings, films, broadcasts and cable-casts. The greatest and the most charismatic interpreters of drama and music are deeply treasured and may therefore secure more for their services than the authors they serve. Yet there has been considerable reluctance to give performers an equivalent property right, and this has in the past been sustained by objections from these very entrepreneurs. It is said that performers are protected indirectly by the entrepreneurial rights, that those financially responsible are best placed to pursue imitators, and that to give copyright to all performers in a play, a film or an orchestra would lead to quite unnecessary complexity.[4] Besides, actors and musicians tend to form powerful unions; investors and authors alike tend therefore to resist additions to their armoury in the form of property rights.

However, some right to stop the unauthorised appropriation of performances has long been needed to cover "bootlegging", that is, the covert

---

[2] The definition is so wide that arguably it extends to a disassembling program which will effect the initial stage in decompiling a computer program from object to quasi-source code. Since the entitlement to do this is guaranteed in the Software Directive, as both sides of the computer industry apparently accept, it is vital that the position should not be compromised by the InfoSoc Directive.

[3] See Arnold, *Performers' Rights* (2nd ed., 1997).

[4] So the Gregory Committee were persuaded: Cmd. 8662, 1952, Pt 7.

recording of performances, which may well not be of copyright works or at least of works written by the performers; and which equally will not infringe the legitimate recording company's rights, since no copy is taken of its contemporaneous recording. This was originally achieved through the Performers Protection Acts,[5] which carefully restricted the available sanctions to criminal penalties and conferred no civil rights of action by their explicit terms.

Although the United Kingdom was a prominent proponent of the Rome Convention for the Protection of Performers, Producers of Phonograms and Broadcasting Organisations (1961), it made sure that the right guaranteed to performers in contracting states went only to the "possibility of preventing" a list of acts, and gave no "right to authorise and prohibit", as it did for sound recordings and broadcasts.[6] Thus the approach through the criminal law could continue to be justified. Eventually the Courts intervened: a civil action for breach of the duties defined in the Performers Protection Acts was accorded to performers, though not to the recording companies with which they had exclusive contracts.[7]

Over the last two decades, the bootlegging of performances by pop-stars **13–89** and others has grown considerably and parts of the music industry have become particularly concerned. The Whitford Committee was convinced that performers should enjoy a civil right of action to injunction and damages. It considered that this should not amount to copyright, even though it did not indicate with any certainty what differences there should be.[8] Loyally following this recommendation, the 1988 Act initially created two separate rights in performances: one for performers, which was a personal, non-assignable, right[9]; and one for their exclusive recording contractors, which could be transferred by contractual assignment.[10] This created a limited range of rights, in effect giving performers no entitlement of their own, distinct from that of their recording company, except in relation to bootlegging.

(1) The New Law

This position converted rights in performances into a form of neighbouring **13–90** right to copyright. Even so it has changed within a decade. The E.C. Directive on Rental and Related Rights has required that performers be

---

[5] Initially the Musical Performers' Protection Act 1925; subsequently the Performers Protection Acts 1958–1972.

[6] *cf.* Rome Convention, Art. 7 with Arts 10, 13.

[7] Initially, the Court of Appeal enthusiastically granted *Anton Piller* orders against bootleggers (*Island Records v. Corkindale* [1978] F.S.R. 505); but subsequent doubts (notably the House of Lords in *Lonrho v. Shell* [1982] A.C. 173) left a trail of uncertainty until *Rickless v. United Artists* [1987] F.S.R. 362, CA. *cf. RCA v. Pollard* [1983] Ch. 135, CA.

[8] Cmnd 6732, 1977, para. 412.

[9] See generally, CDPA 1988, ss. 181–184, 192.

[10] *ibid.*, ss. 185–188, 192.

given transferable property rights on a more general scale[11] and the Directive on Duration has added to their period.[12] The law is now to be found in the 1988 Act, Part II—as it has since been amended by the Duration of Copyright and Rights in Performances Regulations 1995[13] and the Copyright and Related Rights Regulations 1996.[14] The result is an extraordinarily impenetrable amalgam of provisions, in large measure because the Directives required changes to the 1988 position only in certain respects and implementing regulations could not take the further step of a full rationalisation. Some of the performers' rights are characterised as "proprietary", and so fully transferable, while others are "non-proprietary". The performer is not able to assign "non-proprietary rights" *inter vivos*, though they may be licensed and transmitted on death.[15]

13–91   As a consequence, performers now have rights in three main categories.

(i) *Rights in copies.* Performers have four basic *property* rights, giving exclusive rights to: reproduction, distribution, rental and lending.[16] These rights apply to a performance which is legitimately recorded but then improperly copied, and equally to a recording which is made without authority by an interloper, such as a bootlegger. The rights are equivalent to those given to literary and other authors in relation to tangible copies of their works (in contrast with the various performing rights).

As applies equally to authors, performers who transfer their rental rights to the producer of a sound recording or a film have a guaranteed right to equitable remuneration for the rental.[17] The right to remuneration is, however, qualified in character, since it may only be assigned by the performer to a collecting society which will act on the performer's behalf.[18] Here at least, it is clear that the law's intervention is paternalist, since the right to equitable remuneration cannot be abrogated by contract. Given that, in much of the E.U., rental rights were a novelty, there was a strong case for bolstering the performer's entitlement to a share in the earnings which are secured by this special protection.[19]

---

[11] Directive 92/100/EEC, Chap. II; Satellite and Cable Directive 93/83/EEC, Art. 4(1), applies these requirements to satellite broadcasting.

[12] Directive 93/98/EEC, Art. 3(1).

[13] S.I. (U.K.) 1995 No. 3297, effective on January 1, 1996, instead of the Duration Directive's requirement of July 1, 1995.

[14] S.I. (U.K.) 1996 No. 2967, effective on December 1, 1996, instead of July 1, 1994.

[15] Meanwhile, exclusive recording contractors continue to enjoy their own rights against bootlegging, mentioned in the previous paragraph.

[16] ss. 182A, 182B, 182C; 191A; s. 191G; see further below, para. 13–98.

[17] Nonetheless, the British Act characterises this as a "property right". In truth it is neither one thing nor the other.

[18] s. 191G(2). It is, however, a right which may be transmitted by testamentary disposition or operation of law; and once this occurs, a successor in title may treat it as a full right of property, ss. 182; 192A.

[19] But the case was stronger for performances which were already recorded than for future performances, undertaken when the rental right was known about.

(ii) *"Non proprietary" rights against bootlegging.* Alongside this new core **13–92** of protection, the "non-property" rights introduced in 1988 in relation to bootlegging survive. These are rights given to performers: (a) in the initial fixation and the live broadcasting of performances without the performer's consent; (b) in the public performance and broadcasting by means of recording made without consent; and (c) in dealings in illicit recordings.[20] It was over these activities that record and other producers had no neighbouring right of their own since the sound recording right applies only to copies of their own recordings yet they had a real need for protection. They accordingly have their own set of rights covering the same illicit activities.[21] Since they may by contract assign their interest it is "quasi-proprietary".

(iii) *Remuneration right in public uses.* Where a commercially published **13–93** sound recording of a performance is played in public or included in a broadcast or cable programme service, the performer is entitled to equitable remuneration from the owner of the copyright in the sound recording.[22] This is the special compromise in relation to performing rights for performers which the copyright producers and major users in the E.U. have been prepared or obliged to concede.

In addition to these three "primary" categories of right, there are certain forms of "secondary infringement". As in copyright, secondary infringements require it to be shown that the wrongdoer knew or had reason to believe that he or she was dealing with an illicit recording.[23] The acts of dealing which may amount to secondary infringement are: showing or playing the performance in public; broadcasting or cable-casting it; importing a recording or a copy (save for private and domestic use); selling, hiring, distributing or dealing in certain other ways with copies.[24]

From the introduction of performers' rights by the 1988 Act onwards, the entitlements have applied equally to pre-existing, as well as subsequent, performances, though subject to the limitation that no prior acts by others can amount to infringements.[25] This has led to an elaborate set of

---

[20] s. 182. Since, even in 1988, "recording" was defined to include making a copy of an existing recording (s. 108(2)), there was already a "reproduction right" at that stage: see *Bassey v. Icon Entertainment* [1995] E.M.L.R. 596. This "non-property" right must now be regarded as merged in the new "property right"; but what a muddle!

[21] ss. 185–188, 192.

[22] s. 182D.

[23] Under ss. 180(2) and 197, "illicit recording" covers recordings made without the performer's consent and inlcudes the copying of an earlier recording, whether or not that recording was authorised.

[24] ss. 183, 184.

[25] s. 180(3). The same principle is applied to the further expansions of rights by the 1995 and 1996 Regulations implementing the Directives.

transitional provisions, particularly concerning duration (mentioned below).[26]

(2) Other Characteristics

13–94 Now that in Britain performers' rights have inched so close to copyright, they are the subject of parallel conditions. A number of these may be noted.

13–95 (i) *"Performance."* The rights are given in dramatic performances (including dance and mime), musical performance, reading or recitation of a literary work and performance of a variety act or any similar presentation. Other activities which might be called performances, notably those of sportsmen, do not qualify for protection.[27] Some would argue that no such distinction should be drawn.[28] There is however no persistent lobby claiming that sports presentations cannot be adequately "commodified" under present contractual and associated arrangements.

The performance has to be a live one, although, as we have already seen, performers' rights may relate both to authorised and to unauthorised recordings of the performance. In other words, what is not protected is the use of a recorded performance in the course of another live performance.[29] The definition inevitably recognises that a single live performance may be given by more than one individual; but it seems that each individual performer gains a separate right and each must therefore assent to the use of the performance by any other person including the other performers.[30] It is the giving of the performance which brings the right into existence. No formalities of registration, deposit or notice have to be complied with.

13–96 (ii) *Qualifying Performances.* A performance qualifies for protection if it is either given by a qualifying individual (a citizen, subject or resident of a qualifying country) or takes place in a qualifying country. E.C. Member States and countries party to the Rome Convention, the TRIPs Agreement and bilateral arrangements, which are designated by a specific Order.[31]

13–97 (iii) *Duration.* The effect of the Duration Directive on performance rights in Britain has been to extend them from a period of 50 years from the

---

[26] The searcher for British legislation needs to know that, while Regulations implementing E.C. Directives make changes to the substantive provisions of the 1988 Act which appear in subsequent printing of the Act, transitional provisions are to be found only in the Regulations themselves.

[27] s. 180(2).

[28] See, *e.g.* Arnold, *Performers' Rights* (2nd ed. 1997), para. 1.105. He regards the distinction as one of pure "snobbery".

[29] s. 180(2).

[30] There is no conceptual equivalent of joint authorship in copyright law.

[31] ss. 206(1), 208(1). There are further definitions of what constitutes British performances and what amounts to British territory.

performance to a period of 50 years from the end of the calendar year in which the performance takes place, unless a recording of the performance is released during that period, in which case the rights expire 50 years from the end of the calendar year in which the recording is released.[32] In addition, the principle of the shorter term is applied in relation to performers from qualifing countries which nevertheless have a shorter term of protection.[33]

As with the further term for authors' rights, the addition to performers' rights in existing performances (*i.e.* those given before January 1, 1996) has required elaborate transitional provisions. These likewise distinguish between extended rights (those still under protection at the beginning of 1996) and revised rights (those already out of protection but being brought back in).[34]

(3) Remedies for infringement

These include, it would seem, injunction, damages and account of profits. **13–98** The rights are enforceable as breaches of statutory duty. Because this is territory where immediate remedies are needed, the right-owner is given similar powers to those conferred on copyright owners: to engage in seizure against traders without premises, to have orders which include delivery up and disposal, and to proceed by way of prosecution for a range of statutory offences.[35]

8. PUBLIC LENDING RIGHT

(1) Background

In Britain it was not the rental of copies but their lending by public libraries **13–99** which provided the first breach in the "exhaustion" idea. While in general copies legitimately made in the United Kingdom or imported here could not be controlled by copyright after disposal on the market, the special Public Lending Right Scheme provided a return to some authors when the copies were lent out by public libraries. The Scheme, established under the Public Lending Right Act 1979, was originally conceived for books.[36] It acknowledged that organised borrowing eliminates the sale of copies to some at least of the readers, and it increases the number of people who

---

[32] s. 191. "Release" occurs when, with authority, the performance is first published, played or show in public, broadcast or cable-cast.

[33] s. 191(4), (5). For the impact of the principle of non-discrimination (E.C. Treaty, Art. 6), see below, para. 18–01.

[34] 1995 Regs., r. 27–35.

[35] See general, *ibid.*, ss. 194–202; and paras 2–22, 2–27, above.

[36] The campaign for PLR was eloquent, but for two decades faced stubborn resistance: see Brophy, *Guide to Public Lending Right* (1983).

have access to the copies lent without bringing any additional return to author and publisher, over and above their earnings on the original sale.

The case was a particularly strong one in Britain because the use of public libraries is such a staunch tradition, more books being borrowed in much higher proportion to population than in most European countries or the USA. Because of this social importance, the Scheme has been financed by separate funding from central government, rather than by the libraries themselves. Accordingly, in 1979 there was no extension of authors' copyright to include public lending. Instead, those with protectable interests had to register their works with a public office, that of the PLR Registrar, which conducts sample surveys of borrowing in order to decide how to distribute the public grant. That grant currently runs at a rather modest sum fluctuating at or below the £5 million mark.

13–100 The Scheme for books thus retains a measure of common ground with copyright, both by relating entitlement to authorship and in apportioning payments, as nearly as practicable, to the lending of individual works. The Scheme is not one, for instance, in which grants are made to authors' welfare funds or in which a levy is imposed on initial sales to libraries.[37] Other countries have adopted a variety of solutions to the problem. In Germany, notably, the copyright model was adopted for the public lending of books. When pressure to extend the British Scheme to sound recordings, films and computer programs succeeded in the 1988 Act, these cases were put on a copyright basis. Books continue to be treated in their distinct and limited way, because they are the staple of public library lending. The strange outcome can be explained only by government parsimony.

Despite the different bases of their book schemes, reciprocal arrangements for payments to each other's authors exist between Germany and Britain. Now the Directive on Rental and Lending, read in conjunction with the Directive on Duration of Copyright, attempts to harmonise the law on public lending in Member States.[38] In reality, in addition to the two countries mentioned, only the Scandanavian countries and the Netherlands have any sort of scheme. The obligation to introduce any PLR is restricted to the need to provide equitable remuneration to authors; and even then "certain categories of establishments" may be exempted by national legislation. The whole question is supposed to be the subject of a Commission Report by July 1997.[39]

---

[37] An investigation in the 1970s found that a borrowings-based scheme would be not significantly more expensive than a sales-based scheme: Technical Information Group, Papers of 1975 and 1976.

[38] Rental and Lending Rights Directive 92/100 ([1992] O.J. L.346/61), Art. 2, stating that PLR shall be accorded to authors, performers, phonogram producers, audio-visual producers (but note the derogations allowed). Lending involves making copies available for limited periods and not for direct or indirect economic or commercial advantage: Art. 1. See Griffiths [1997] E.I.P.R. 499.

[39] *ibid.*, Art. 5, Sched. 5; para. 13–102, below.

(2) The PLR Scheme for books

The right created by the 1979 Act covers books lent out to the public by **13-101**
local library authorities[40] in the United Kingdom. It is given to the authors
of the books; but as it is assignable without restriction,[41] so that it is open to
publishers to negotiate an interest in it. Nothing is said about employed
authors, so common law principle may dictate that presumptively they hold
their interest in trust for their employers, where the work is prepared in the
course of employment. The entitlement lasts at most for the author's life
and 50 years.[42] The E.C. Directives on Lending and Duration together
make plain that the author's PLR must last for 70 years *post mortem*, but
implementation of this requirement is still awaited.

The Scheme itself now defines "books" to which it applies as printed and
bound publications, with at least one named author who is a natural
person.[43] Serials, musical scores and Crown copyright works are excluded.[44]
An author is a writer (including a translator or editor) or illustrator[45] and
must be qualified by having his principal home in the United Kingdom or
Germany[46] Although not strictly related to nationality,[47] this provision dices
with the prohibition in the Rome Treaty of all discrimination against E.C.
citizens on that ground.[48] Rights accrue from registration. They are
transmissible as personal property, but only as a whole.[49]

The manner of organising samples of borrowing is elaborately defined.[50]
An interest (whether of one or more authors[51]) attracts 2p. per borrowing,
up to a maximum on all books of the author of £6,000 in any sample year.
Some 60 authors a year reach this ceiling, which is imposed in order to
spread the strictly limited grant more broadly. For most of those 60, the
payment is a pourboire, their drink being champagne.

---

[40] As defined in PLRA 1979, s. 5(2).

[41] See *ibid.*, s. 1(7)(b); Scheme, para. 10.

[42] *ibid.*, s. 1(6), Scheme, para. 20. The PLR Scheme is set out in App. 2 of the Act.

[43] PLR Scheme, para. 6. They must have an ISBN and have been offered for sale to the public.

[44] Separate volumes and editions are treated as distinct books.

[45] PLR Scheme, para. 4, which lays down precise methods for identifying authors.

[46] PLR Scheme, para. 5, Sched. 5; *cf.* the *Phil Collins* case, para. 18–01, below. For
posthumous eligibility, see PLR Scheme, paras 5A, 6A.

[47] It excludes expatriate British authors, who enjoy fiscal or other sunshine elsewhere.

[48] *cf.* the Scandanavian schemes which make payments only upon books in national languages.

[49] See the PLR Scheme, paras 19–31 for details. The Registrar may remove an entry after 10
years of no payments: para. 34.

[50] PLR Scheme, Pt. 4. Altogether administrative costs absorb some 20 per cent of the
government grant.

[51] There are specified shares for translating (30 per cent), editing (20 per cent) and illustrating
(up to 50 per cent). Those jointly entitled to any share may notify the proportions of their
sub-interest: PLR Scheme, para. 9.

(3) Public "rental"

13–102 The 1988 Act created a rental right in sound recordings, films and computer programs, where the hiring is by a business for money or its equivalent.[52] By sleight-of-hand in an obscure Schedule, the government extended this right to lendings by public libraries of these types of material, not only where a charge is made but when the loan is free.[53] So the copyright owners of this material—by definition entrepreneurs, save in the case of the occasional computer program—have protection within the framework of copyright and may extract what they can from the libraries (who in turn must decide what charges they will pass on to borrowers), subject only to the threat of Copyright Tribunal proceedings, or the imposition of an equitable remuneration scheme[54] if these demands prove too strident. As already indicated, the Directive on Lending at present imposes no obligation to provide any PLR, save to authors. It is therefore open to our own government to continue to provide nothing for performers, and to reduce our existing non-book PLRs to rights to equitable remuneration. It is obliged to give authors at least equitable remuneration for copies of their work which are subject to public lending.[55]

9. ARTISTS' RESALE RIGHT: DROIT DE SUITE

13–103 The special value of some artistic works lies not in the capacity to multiply copies but in the uniqueness of the original. This is true of many paintings and sculptures. As artists acquire a reputation, works of this kind accelerate in value. Their deaths may add to the element of scarcity, and the effect will be marked in the resale prices of their works. Since artists, and their estates normally benefit only from the first sale of the work, they receive no return from subsequent increases in capital value. *A droit de suite*, which is provided by the laws of 10 E.U. states,[56] requires a proportion of resale prices[57] to be paid during the copyright period to the artist or his successors.[58] As an "author's right" it is the antithesis of "*copy*right"; but it shares the same moral justification.[59]

13–104 In the E.U. states with a *droit de suite*, the scope of the rights varies, particularly in relation to the types of work covered, the application to non-

---

[52] See paras 11–27—11–28, above.
[53] CDPA 1988, Sched. 7, paras 6, 8, amending the Public Libraries and Museums Act 1964, s. 8(6), and the Public Libraries (Scotland) Act 1955, s. 4.
[54] Under CDPA 1988, s. 66; see para. 11–44, above.
[55] Rental Directive 92/100 ([1992] O.J. L.346/61), Art. 5.
[56] In only eight of them is it operative. For the origins of the right in French law, see Pierredm-Fawcett, *The Droit de Suite in Literary and Artistic Property* (1991).
[57] Frequently there is a minimum value by way of starting point.
[58] See generally, Price (1960) 77 Yale L.J. 1333; Plaisant (1969) 5 Copyright 15; Lahore, *Copyright and the Arts in Australia* (1974), pp. 83–86.
[59] Hence it has attained a place in the Berne Convention (Brussels, Art. 14*bis*; Paris, Art. 14*ter*); but it is left to Member States to decide whether to confer it.

auction as well as auction sales, the percentage of the price to be accounted (one per cent to six per cent). There is, at least on paper, a distortion of trade within the Common Market. The great European centres for the sale of modern artworks are London and Switzerland, in neither of which the artist has any title to share in resale proceeds, and auctioneers are intent on extracting high commissions from sellers and buyers.

This justification has driven forward a plan for a harmonisation Directive, which would impose a standard version of artists' resale right in each member state.[60] In Britain, where the move is seen by many as an incitement to transfer sales of modern artworks to Geneva and New York, the plan has come under greatest critical scrutiny.[61] It has been argued strongly that no adequate evidence demonstrates that sales work goes to one Member State rather than another because of differing approaches to *droit de suite*.[62] It is the case, for instance, that differing rates of VAT have more effect on the proportion of sales revenue which actually goes to the seller than any which may go to the artist. It is also evident that, in such a specialised market, much depends upon the available expertise: for this London has built up an enviable reputation. The campaign to achieve the Directive has been very determined, but in June 1999 it was called off by agreement in the Council. For the future, with the prospect of electronic dealing in the market for modern art, the issue may be relevant only at a global level.

10. CROWN AND PARLIAMENTARY COPYRIGHT

Under the 1956 Act, there were sweeping provisions giving copyright in **13–105** literary, dramatic, musical and artistic works to the Crown if they were either made under its direction or control, or were so first published.[63] Thus, for instance, a patent specification, drafted by a patent agent for a client, ceased to be a copyright of either and became the Crown's when the Patent Office published it. The Whitford Committee criticised the reach of these provisions, but at first it appeared that the government was not to be shifted on the subject. However, more temperate attitudes in the end prevailed, and the Crown's claims have been largely aligned with those of employers.[64] In the wake of this it has been necessary to confer a separate

---

[60] For the Draft Directive in amended form, COM (1998) 78 final, [1998] O.J., E.C. C125/8. One sophisticated attempt to demonstrate the distortive effect of the present disparities is Doutrelepont, *Droit et l'objet d'Art* (1996).

[61] Some of the argument has been decidedly woolly: see, *e.g.* Whitford Report, Cmnd. 6732, 1977, Chap. 17. Objections that the result will be higher returns for those already over-rich, apply equally to the more distasteful excesses of pop-composers, film corporations and others blessed with copyright and neighbouring rights: *cf.* Merryman [1997] I.P.Q. 1.

[62] Jacob [1997] I.P.Q. 3; Booton [1998] I.P.Q. 165; Hughes in Bently and Maniatis, *Intellectual Property and Ethics* (1998) 147.

[63] CA 1956, s. 39. For egregious consequences, see, *e.g. Ironside v. Att.-Gen.* [1988] R.P.C. 197.

[64] CDPA 1988, ss. 163, 164; *cf.* para. 12–05, above. For the copyright which may by Order be conferred on international organisations, see s. 168.

copyright on Parliament in respect of documents and other material emerging from its proceedings[65]; and also to confer immunity from infringement where a public office or person in authority is producing information in which there is a special public interest.[66] In approaching the subject, the lawyer needs to remember that Crown and Parliamentary copyright remain distinctive creatures. Among their characteristics, those concerning duration of the rights have already been mentioned.[67]

Crown copyright under the 1988 Act arises where a work is made by an officer or servant of the Crown in the course of his duties.[68] Parliamentary copyright is, in the main, given to whichever House has, by its direction or control, had the work made; or to both, if they are jointly responsible.[69] But while the old formula of "under direction or control" is still used in respect of Parliamentary copyright, Crown copyright is explicitly limited to work made by an officer or servant of the relevant House in the course of his duties, and to any sound recording, film, live broadcast or live cable-cast of proceedings.[70] It is not sufficient that a House commissions a report from an outside person, such as specialist adviser to a Select Committee. These copyrights take effect without the need to comply with the usual rules for qualification.

13–106 As regards the acts permitted in the interests of public administration,[71] the Crown is entitled to make copies[72] of a literary, dramatic, musical or artistic work communicated to it in the course of public business, but only when it does so for the purpose of the communication to it, and only if no breach of confidence is involved.[73] By this, the Crown recovers some of the ground which it surrendered in accepting a more limited concept of Crown copyright. But not all: in particular, in the material that no longer belongs to it, it has no proprietary right to prevent publication, politically embarrassing though that may be. This perhaps explains (while it certainly does not excuse) the recent insistence of government departments that they be given contractual powers to decide if and when reports of research which

---

[65] CDPA 1988, ss. 165–167.
[66] *ibid.*, ss. 47–50.
[67] See para. 10–55, above.
[68] The old test (was the work made under the Crown's direction or control?) was in some respects wider. By the relevant transitional provision, it would appear that a work which was Crown copyright under the old law, but not under the new, ceases at "commencement" to be Crown copyright and becomes (presumably) that of the author, or his employer, or the assignee of either and has the duration of ordinary copyright: Sched. 1, para. 40.
[69] CDPA 1988, s. 165, and see s. 166 for the special copyright in Bills.
[70] *ibid.*, s. 165(4).
[71] Note also *ibid.*, s. 47, allowing the person duly authorised to permit copying of the content of a public register, but not for publication; similarly, under s. 49, for public records; and under s. 50 for acts specifically authorised by statute.
[72] And to issue the copies to the public.
[73] CDPA 1988, ss. 47, 171(1)(e).

they have commissioned shall be published.[74] The United Kingdom is not a country in which ideas of free access to, and free use of, government information flourish with any vigour.[75] Were this so, there would have developed, as in the United States,[76] much more embracing notions of public domain material in which no copyright may be claimed. As it is, in Britain, the Crown has copyright even in Acts of Parliament and Church of England Measures.[77] For these, as for delegated legislation and official reports, the government will doubtless continue to specify by Treasury Circular how far it will countenance free copying by others.

Of particular interest is the copyright in judgments and law reports. Under the previous law (which still affects judgments given before August 1989), the first test of whether they were Crown copyright was whether they were made under the direction or control of the Crown.[78] To take this view would be quite inconsistent with the independence of the judiciary. Under the 1988 Act, the question becomes whether judges are officers or servants of the Crown. Their independence means that they cannot be regarded as servants.[79] Yet, being Crown appointees, are they officers? An affirmative answer would mean that the Crown could control the publication and other copyright use of their judgments.[80] So long as that is so, it ought to be concluded that the judges are not officers appointed for the purpose of delivering any particular judgment[81]; accordingly a judgment remains personal to its author for copyright purposes.

It may be that the circumstances in which it is delivered amount to a waiver of any claim by the judge, at least to economic rights.[82] Those who make a business of transcribing and publishing judgments would themselves be free to act, and to claim any transcriber's copyright which may fall to them under *Walter v. Lane*.[83]

---

[74] Under the old law, where copyright lay in the Crown, the DHSS and some other departments nevertheless conceded in research contract conditions that the researchers should be entitled after notice to publish. One argument in 1987 for changing this provision, was that the Crown needed to control publication in order to "protect Crown copyright". So little is the nature and purpose of copyright understood that many must have been misled by this piece of self-serving mystification.

[75] *Pace* Lord Goff, *Att.-Gen. v. Guardian Newspapers (No. 2)* [1990] 1 A.C. 109 at 283; para. 8–19, above.

[76] For which see, Nimmer, *Copyright*, para. 5–06.

[77] CDPA 1988, s. 164.

[78] See n. 63, above; the second test was first publication.

[79] They can be ordered to undertake work, but not told how to do it; *a fortiori* university teachers and their research: see paras 12–06, 12–07, above.

[80] Control could involve suppression or alteration, though, in the latter case, the author would have a right to object to derogatory treatment which doubtless would not be side-stepped by any sufficient disclaimer: see CDPA 1988, ss. 80, 82. Even extempore judgments recorded by others will attract copyright under the 1988 Act: para. 10–34, above.

[81] *cf.* Laddie *et al.*, para. 22–37, avoiding the awkward "officer". See generally Taggart (1984) 10 Sydney L.R. 319; von Nessen (1985) 48 M.L.R. 412; Tapper (1985) 11 Monash U.L.R. 78; Monotti [1992] E.I.P.R. 305.

[82] See Laddie *et al.*, para. 22–40.

[83] See para. 10–35 above. Most Court reporting in England is undertaken privately, the R.P.C. series being an exception: see further, Laddie *et al.*, paras 22–41, 22–42.

CHAPTER 14

INDUSTRIAL DESIGN

1. BACKGROUND

So far as industry in general is concerned, easily the most significant **14–01** changes introduced into intellectual property law by the Copyright, Designs and Patents Act 1988 concern design elements in industrially produced articles.[1] Thanks to the history of this vexed question over the preceding 20 years in the United Kingdom and other Commonwealth countries, many industries, whether their production concentrated upon machinery or upon decorative articles, had come to rely upon copyright protection against imitations of the form and appearance of their products.

Under the 1988 Act, the law was cut back so that it is no longer extravagantly embracing in comparison with that in other industrial countries. As is all too evident, arriving at a balanced scheme of protection for industrial designs is an elusive goal, and all countries struggle in seeking to attain it.[2]

There are, for instance, disparities throughout the E.C.—Greece, indeed, has no registered designs system at all—and these have not escaped the glint of Brussels. There are well-advanced proposals both to create Community design rights and to engage in a co-ordinated harmonisation of the national laws of registered designs (though not of "informal" rights, such as copyright and the British unregistered design right). The Community design rights will comprise not only a Community registered design having effect throughout the Common Market but also (in a new outstretch of Community law) an informal three-year right, aimed particularly at trades in passing fashion: cosmetics, crockery, and above all clothing. This plan, which will be outlined briefly in its present form,[3] is destined to roll in a fog of new uncertainties.

---

[1] See Tootal, *Law of Industrial Design* (1990); Laddle *et al.*, Chaps 29 *et seq.*; MacQueen, *Copyright, Competition and Industrial Design* (2nd ed., 1995); Fellner, *Industrial Design Law* (1995); Copinger, Chap. 13; Howe, *Russell-Clarke on Industrial Designs* (6th ed., 1998). See also Lahore [1992] E.I.P.R. 428; Laddie [1996] E.I.P.R. 253.

[2] See, for comparisons, Reichman [1983] Duke L.J. 1143, 31 J.Cop.Soc. 267; Perot-Morel [1984] E.I.P.R. 129; Krüger (1984) 15 I.I.C. 168; Fellner, *The Protection of Industrial Designs in the EEC* (1985); Suthersanen in Sterling (ed.) *Intellectual Property and Market Freedom* (1997). For the emergence of an E.C. Design regime, below, para. 14–52ff.

[3] See paras 14–52 *et seq.*, below.

From the tortuous history of the subject in Britain certain salient features can be picked out.

(1) Origins of design registration

14–02 The registration system was the nineteenth-century answer to demands for protection of the design elements in articles mass-produced by an industrial process.[4] Initially it gave only a very short term of protection to cover the lead-time in introducing a new product onto the market.

(2) Copyright Act 1911

14–03 The 1911 Act introduced the concept of infringement of an artistic work by "reproduction in a material form", including the conversion of a two-dimensional design into a three-dimensional article.[5] In order to sterilise the potency of this new notion in the field of industrial design, section 22 excluded all copyright in designs capable of being registered under the registration system, which were used or intended to be used as models or patterns to be multiplied by any industrial process.[6] This had the effect of keeping copyright out of most industrial territory, though its effect did not extend to designs which were originally intended for a non-industrial process, such as comic-strip illustration. Because of this difference the section was eventually judged unsatisfactory, though it has continued to be the rule affecting pre-1957 designs.[7]

(3) Copyright Act 1956

14–04 The 1956 Act set out to eliminate dual protection by copyright as well as design registration on a different, highly complex basis. The essential feature of section 10 was that while copyright now subsisted in designs of all kinds, industrial application of them would not amount to infringement of the copyright if a registered right had been applied for, or if the copyright

---

[4] See para. 14–08, below; Sherman and Bently, *The Making of Intellectual Property Law* (1999).

[5] To be understood with its co-ordinate: infringement by indirect copying of the article legitimately made from the design: see *King Features* case (see para. 14–30, n. 24, below).

[6] For a long period there was little consideration of which designs were capable of registration. Latterly, it was held that, while they might not be registrable because solely functional (see para. 14–17, below), they did not lose this quality because in the particular case they were not "new or original": see *Interlego v. Tyco* [1988] R.P.C. 343 (and, for the equivalent point under the 1956 Act, *Interlego v. Alex Foley* [1987] F.S.R. 283). In the *Tyco* case the point was part of an argument of considerable audacity (which failed).

[7] See now CDPA 1988, Sched. 1, para. 6.

owner had used the design on industrially produced articles. In the regrettable decision of *Dorling v. Honnor Marine*,[8] the Court of Appeal chose to distinguish between designs capable of registration which were subject to section 10, and designs which were not registrable (chiefly because they were functional) and so bore full-term artistic copyright even in industrial applications.[9]

(4) Design Copyright Act 1968

The 1956 Act provision was modified in 1968, by a terse Act,[10] which in essence put off the moment for excluding copyright in industrial applications of a design until 15 years from first authorised marketing of articles bearing the design. Despite the best efforts of Whitford J.,[11] this was held to continue the *Dorling* distinction between registrable designs (now able to enjoy 15-year copyright) and non-registrable functional designs which had a copyright enduring for the designer's life and 50 years thereafter.[12] **14–05**

The 1968 Act highlighted the implications of the *Dorling* case and ushered in a merry litigious bonanza. Design copyright was held to exist in the copying of a vast range of industrial products, and indeed for every part of them, whether they were watches or atomic power-stations.[13] It had such a swamping effect by virtue of the general principles: (1) that a design would be an artistic work irrespective of artistic quality; (2) that an artistic work in two dimensions could be copied by reproduction in three; and (3) that a person who made his own product by copying another's product would indirectly infringe copyright in the production drawings.[14]

---

[8] [1965] Ch. 1.

[9] If the reason why a design was unregistrable was that it was not novel, this was eventually not treated as giving it full artistic copyright.

[10] Introduced as a Private Member's Bill, it was intended to improve the position of the designs of furniture, jewellery, toys and the like. Its impact on functional design went unappreciated during its enactment.

[11] *e.g. Hoover v. Hulme* [1982] F.S.R. 565; overruled (quite unnecessarily) by the Court of Appeal in *British Leyland v. Armstrong* [1986] R.P.C. 279. The issue was not taken to the House of Lords.

[12] A distinction labelled by the Whitford Committee, "bizarre": (Cmnd. 6732, 1977) para. 96. When in 1974, the House of Lords raised the level of "eye appeal" for a registered design (*Amp v. Utilux* (para. 14–09, n. 34, below)) the effect was to increase the range or functional designs which acquired full-term copyright.

[13] The existence in the then law of an entitlement to conversion damages, as distinct from infringement damages, meant that the material value of precious objects and complex machinery might be payable to a successful plaintiff. This outrageously oppressive consequence was abandoned in the 1988 Act, on the Whitford Committee's recommendation (Cmnd. 6732, 1977), para. 702.

[14] See para. 11–05, above. For the law before the 1988 Act, see Laddie *et al.,* paras 46.6–46.29; Fellner (n. 1, above), Chap. 1.

(5) *British Leyland v. Armstrong*[15]; *Canon v. Green Cartridge*[16]

14–06 Because this disproportion produced extreme results affecting so much industrial production,[17] the House of Lords were moved to intervene in advance of new legislation. In the *British Leyland* case they had to consider a copyright claim to the design of the exhaust pipes for certain BL cars, which was being asserted against spare-part manufacturers. Exhaust pipes had the characteristics (1) that they must assume a given shape in order to fit the particular contours of the underbody, and (2) that they needed quite regular replacement. The market was accordingly lucrative, and much more so to BL if its licence was needed for all pipes made to its designs.[18] The majority of the House of Lords were attracted by the notion that the sale of a car carried with it implied licence to use BL designs in the course of repairing the car.[19] But they saw the need to go beyond the idea of implied licences[20] and instead imported the land law concept that a person may not derogate from his grant. From this they drew the conclusion that BL could not object to anyone, including a spare-parts manufacturer, using the designs to make things which would go to repairing their cars.

To transplant so basic a notion into a new field raises various uncertainties about its potential, and the decision has since been severely criticised in the *Canon* case as constitutionally unacceptable.[21] Lord Hoffmann, for the Privy Council, considered that a head of public policy ought not to be created by judges in order to modify express statutory rights of property, however much those rights might result in the exercise of monopoly power in the after-market. The Judicial Committee refused to hold that the *British Leyland* doctrine could be applied to the design of cartridges which had regularly to be replaced in laser printers and photocopy.[22] *British Leyland*

---

[15] [1986] R.P.C. 279; Tettenborn [1986] Camb.L.J. 216.

[16] [1997] F.S.R. 817, JC.

[17] An equivalent result was reached under the laws of most Commonwealth countries, causing Thomas J. to cast an anathema upon all (including textbook writers!) who had allowed the law to get so out of hand: "Like ants in the forest, they have constructed a misshapen anthill of enormous proportions which is of no use or value to anyone or anything save other ants and the parasites that feed upon their indulgent labours" (etc.): *Franklin Machinery v. Albany Farm Centre* (1991) 23 I.P.R. 649, SC (N.Z.).

[18] The "Euro-defence" of abuse of dominant position (Treaty of Rome, Art. 86) was dismissed in the litigation in a manner amounting virtually to incomprehension: see the CA judgments (n. 11, above).

[19] Lord Griffiths' interesting dissent went so far as to deny that a design for a functional part could be infringed by three-dimensional, indirect copying. This solution would have prevented much artistic copyright from operating in the sphere of industrial production; the majority judgments are confined to cases of spare parts.

[20] The difficulties with "implied licence" were: (1) how could it extend to protect a parts manufacturer? and (2) how could its exclusion by express statement to the contrary in the initial contract of sale be prevented?

[21] Above, n. 16. See also *Flogates v. Refco* [1996] F.S.R. 874; *Creative Technology v. Aztech Systems* [1997] F.S.R. 491, CA Sing.

[22] See also *Creative Technology v. Aztech Systems* (above, n. 21).

was confined to parts needed for occasional repairs. So much apparently could be regarded as an inherent aspect of ownership—the entitlement to keep a thing in repair. The distinction is scarcely satisfactory and may lead to *British Leyland* being directly overruled.

(6) Order of the chapter

In tackling the 1988 Act, the new must be set alongside the continuing and **14–07** the old. The next section is a description of the traditional scheme for protecting designs by registration, which highlights both the inherited characteristics of that system and the modifications introduced by the 1988 Act. The following section outlines the succession of attempts to preclude or limit the role of artistic copyright in the sphere of industrial protection, as part of a policy which, until 1968, strove (not entirely successfully) to avoid cumulative protection. The final section deals with the new strategy of 1988: (1) the preclusion of artistic copyright once more from much of the field; (2) the introduction of an unregistered design right of strictly limited duration in the area vacated; and (3) the continuance of registered design partly in the territories of copyright and unregistered design, but partly in its own exclusive field.

2. Registered Designs[23]

The origins of design registration stretch back to the earliest period of **14–08** industrialisation in some parts of the textile industry.[24] The real impetus towards the modern system came in the 1830s. The poor quality of British industrial design, particularly when compared with the achievements of the French, incited middle-class radicals to press for a system of training designers and manufacturers to demand a more substantial legal mono- poly.[25] The result was a form of "head-start." protection. The term was short but the design was kept confidential in the registry for its duration.[26]

Although initially conceived as some form of copyright protection, the need actually to prove that an alleged infringement was copied was gradually obliterated. The history is rather obscure,[27] but it is one part of the process by which design registration acquired characteristics of the patent system. Both called for an initial application and grant of rights, and in 1875 the Patent Office took over the administration of designs. There-

---

[23] For detailed treatment, see Laddie *et al.*, Chaps 29–39; Fellner (1995), paras 2.01–2.119, 3.109–3.310, 4.60–4.75, 5.149–5.191.

[24] See para. 9–39, above.

[25] See Prouty, *The Transformation of the Board of Trade 1830–1857* (1957), pp. 18–27; Sherman and Bently, *The Making of Modern Intellectual Property Law* (1999), Chaps 3, 4.

[26] Copyright of Designs Act 1842, s. 17. For subsequent statutes and other details, see Cmnd. 1808, 1962, App. 8.

[27] CDPA 1988, s. 268, at last eliminates the confusing phrase "copyright in the design".

after the governing legislation was brought together in a single statute (the Act of 1883, maintained in 1907). Only in 1949 were the systems separated into parallel Acts. Designs are still protected under the Registered Designs Act 1949; but that Act was amended at a number of points in 1988, in order to fit the system into the new order.[28] The right is a legal monopoly not dependent upon proof of copying.[29]

(1) Requirements for a registrable design (validity)[30]

14–09 "Design"—the crux of the system—is defined thus:

> "features of shape, configuration, pattern or ornament applied to an article by any industrial process, being features which in the finished article appeal to and are judged by the eye . . ."[31]

The design is not something distinct from the article to which it is applied; nor does the manner in which it is applied affect the issue.[32] What is depicted and described in the registration is the article with the design incorporated. So the design must be registered separately for different kinds of article.[33] The features that are applied to the article must appeal to the eye, in the sense of catching or attracting the eye—particularly the eye of a potential buyer. They may be decorative elements ("pattern", "ornament") added to the article or they may be part of the very structure ("shape", "configuration").[34] To this basic definition, there are a set of exceptions. Among them it is important to distinguish those which were part of the original 1949 Act from those which have been added in 1988.[35] And in relation to the latter, it is useful to mark points of comparison with unregistered design right, since many designs qualify for both types of protection.

(a) *Novelty*[36]

14–10 Designs are not registrable unless they are "new". This is a 1988 variant of the 1949 requirement that the design be "new or original".[37] The concepts of novelty in patent law and originality in copyright law are quite distinct,

---

[28] Major amendments, and the transition to them, are contained in CDPA 1988, Pt. 4; further amendments are added by Sched. 3, and the RDA 1949 in its new form is given in CDPA 1988, Sched. 4 (but without the transitional provisions). References here are to the RDA 1949 in this amended version.

[29] See, *e.g. Gaskell & Chambers v. Measure Master* [1993] R.P.C. 76.

[30] See generally, Laddie *et al.*, Chaps 30, 31; Fellner, paras 2.01–2.87.

[31] RDA 1949, s. 1(3).

[32] For the boundary line with the ordinary exploitation of copyright works, drawn in the Registered Design Rules 1989, r. 26, see para. 14–12, below.

[33] See para. 14–20, below. The Community design will not be so constrained: para. 14–55, below.

[34] See especially *Amp v. Utilux* [1972] R.P.C. 103 at 107, 112, HL.

[35] Unless the contrary is indicated, references will be given to the amended version of the 1949 Act set out in CDPA 1988, Sched. 4.

[36] Laddie *et al.*, Chap. 31; Fellner, paras 2.87–2.119.

[37] RDA 1949, s. 2.

and the 1949 requirement never received a full analysis which would have demonstrated how near "new or original" was to either. The main emphasis in the prior case law was upon "new", and it is simpler, and probably no great change, to make "new" the sole criterion (Note, however, that the equivalent adjective in the unregistered design right is "original"—a distinction not without resonance).[38]

In the law of registered designs, the requirement of novelty is amplified by a number of matters. It is specifically stated that there will be no novelty where the only differences are in immaterial details or amount to no more than variants commonly used in the trade.[39] Protection is not justified, for instance, where a person has put together an old design for a rocking horse and another old design for a base.[40] The designer must have applied some further skill and labour of a draftsmanlike nature.[41] This was shown in a case where four features of a coffee-pot were brought together, even though each had precursors in different examples of prior art.[42]

In the law of registered designs, the requirement of novelty is amplified **14–11** in various further ways which suggest comparisons with the concepts of novelty and obviousness in patent law. Thus there is a "state of the art" test. This includes designs for any kind of article (not just articles for which registration is sought[43]); but the test is local, not universal, taking account only of those which have been published in the United Kingdom or registered there (including those for which there is a prior application).[44] Equally the publication may arise out of embodiment in an actual article. If the document or the article is made available to the public, rather than kept secret, it will anticipate.[45] Indeed, as for patents, it seems that to disclose the design to one specific person who is under no obligation of confidence to the discloser will amount to publication.[46]

Where the publication is in a document, there must, it seems, be clear and unmistakeable directions to make an article bearing the design. It is

---

[38] See para. 14–34, below, and, for the E.C. Directive, para. 14–56, below.

[39] RDA 1949, s. 1(4).

[40] *Sebel's Application* [1959] R.P.C. 12.

[41] Farwell J., *Re Calder Vale* (1934) 53 R.P.C. 117 at 125; and see Lord Moulton, *Phillips v. Harbro Rubber* (1920) 37 R.P.C. 233 at 240.

[42] *Household Article's R.D.* [1998] F.S.R. 676.

[43] Where the designs are for different articles, however, the degree of dissimilarity between them may well mean that the second is treated as novel: *Re Clarke's Design* (1898) 13 R.P.C. 351: "A design may be new for a coal scuttle, but not for a bonnet" (Lindley L.J.).

[44] RDA 1949, s. 1(4). Novelty is judged at the date of application, save that a Paris Convention applicant who first applied in another Convention country not more than six months before may claim priority back to the date of this application: ss. 13–16; *Deyhle's Application* [1982] R.P.C. 526. For the addition of designs containing non-essential variations, see RDA 1949, s. 4.

[45] See RDA 1949, s. 6(1); and note the further exceptions in s. 6(2), (3): *Mod-Tap W. Corp. v. BI Communications* [1999] R.P.C. 333.

[46] See *Car Flow Products v. Linwood Securities* [1996] F.S.R. 424; *Rapee v. Kas Cushions* (1989) 15 I.P.R. 577.

not enough simply that it is an artistic work.[47] Over and above this, where the application is to register a design corresponding to an artistic work, and it is made by or with the consent of the copyright owner, the fact that the artistic work itself has previously been used (and therefore published) is not of itself an anticipation. Only if the work had been applied industrially as a design to articles which were then marketed could it found an attack on novelty.[48] Here we meet three concepts which have been crucial in defining the relation between registered designs and artistic copyright[49]:

14–12   (1) **Corresponding design**: in relation to an artistic work, this means a design which, if applied to an article, would produce a copy within the terms of the 1988 Act[50];

(2) **Applied industrially**: an activity which is defined by rule; it means application of the design to more than 50 articles (not forming a set, as in a canteen of cutlery) or to non-hand-made goods manufactured in lengths or pieces, such as textiles and wallpaper[51];

(3) **Articles excluded from registration**: these too are prescribed by rule,[52] and cover much sculpture,[53] wall plaques and medals and printed matter primarily of a literary or artistic character.[54] It is to be expected that in any new definition of "applied industrially" these applications of artistic works will be excluded.

(b) *The whole article and parts*

14–13 The 1949 Act has always provided that an article for which a design may be registered includes "any part of an article if that part is made and sold separately".[55] In a severely limiting decision, *Ford Motor's Designs*,[56] the House of Lords has held that this excludes registration not only of parts which will only ever form part of a finished product, such as the face for an ammeter,[57] but also parts which are intended both as part of some larger object and as replacement spares for that object, such as the car body panels and similar parts which were the subject of the litigation. Anything within either category was characterised as having no "independent life as

---

[47] *Dean's Rag Book v. Pomerantz* (1930) 47 R.P.C. 485; *Rosedale v. Airfix* [1957] R.P.C. 239 at 244, 249.

[48] RDA 1949, s. 6(4), (5).

[49] See also para. 14–27, below.

[50] RDA 1949, s. 44(1).

[51] RDA 1949, s. 6(6) and see Registered Design Rules 1989, r. 35.

[52] Registered Design Rules 1989, r. 26.

[53] *i.e.* sculpture other than casts or models used or intended as models or patterns to be multiplied by any industrial process.

[54] A long list is given.

[55] RDA 1949, s. 44(1) "article".

[56] [1995] R.P.C. 167. *cf.* Groves [1993] Bus. L.R. 279.

[57] See *Sifam Electrical v. Sangamo Weston* [1973] R.P.C. 899.

an article of commerce".[58] The dual purpose of second category articles was said to create grave difficulties of interpretation. The House chose to ignore their use as spares, when it might as easily have said that such a use sufficed to make the design registrable. The decision is imbued with that same fear of undue monopoly that (more justifiably) informed the *British Leyland* case.[59] Its conclusion effectively overrides the more scrupulous limits upon design rights which were included in the 1988 Act by way of resolution of the spare-parts issue. These are mentioned under the ensuing sub-heads.

The Act deals with the "part-and-whole" question by providing for registration for the whole article with a statement of novelty. This draws attention to a particular feature for which design protection is claimed and effectively defines the scope of protection. More than one registration may be obtained for the same article where a different novelty is stated for each.[60]

(c) *Construction method*

Associated since 1949 with the exclusion of functional designs has been the exclusion of a "method or principle of construction".[61] The concept has received little interpretation in English Courts. In *Swain v. Barker*,[62] where the sides of a wire filing-tray were in half circles, making it impracticable to include corner supports, their absence was said to be a design feature that could not be considered as it arose from the construction adopted. **14–14**

(d) *"Must match"*

As equally with unregistered design right, the 1988 Act excludes considera- **14–15** tion of features of shape and configuration which are "dependent upon the appearance of another article of which the article is intended by the author of the design to form an integral part".[63] The scope of this formula will be discussed later.[64]

It was this provision that was intended in particular to lay down the limit to which design protection could apply to spares such as car-body parts. Its significance for registered designs is much reduced by the House of Lords'

---

[58] On the other hand, wing mirrors, wheels, seats, steering wheels, etc., were permitted to be registered (in the proceedings below), because they were subsidiary to the general shape of the car.

[59] See para. 14–06, above.

[60] At least where different types of design are involved, *e.g.* shape in the one case, ornament in the other. *Evered's Application* [1961] R.P.C. 105, where two applications for different aspects of shape were not permitted, is criticised by Laddie *et al.*, para. 30.31.

[61] RDA 1949, s. 1(1)(a).

[62] [1967] R.P.C. 23.

[63] RDA 1949, s. 1(1)(b)(ii).

[64] See para. 14–37, below. For registered designs, the question is largely eclipsed by the *Ford* case (n. 56, above). Separate designs will rarely have to match.

decision that these are not articles sold separately. If registrations are made for the whole article with limited statements of novelty, the "must match" exclusion will become relevant. When it refers to "article", it must include within that concept articles which are not meant to be sold separately. Otherwise it would have very little practical effect.

(e) *Immaterial appearance*

14–16 The 1988 Act also adds an exclusion where "the appearance of the article is not material, that is, if aesthetic considerations are not normally taken into account to a material extent by persons acquiring or using articles of that description, and would not be so taken into account if the design were applied to the article".[65] This double-forked exegesis on the notion of "appeal to the eye" aims to prevent judgments such as *Gardex v. Sorata*[66] where even the design of the underside of a shower tray was allowed. It is not, however, meant to overrule the approach which allows designs for the insides of things, such as chocolate sweets, which cannot be seen until after purchase.[67] It ensures that any judgment about aesthetic content is made from the perspective of a purchaser. It is not relevant—as it is for a work of artistic craftsmanship in copyright[68]—to consider the intention of the designer.

(f) *Functional features*

14–17 A registrable design does not include features of shape or configuration which are dictated solely by the function which the article has to perform. This 1949 provision was at one time thought to exclude only articles which assumed the sole shape possible for the particular purpose. If this were the rule, there would be very few cases indeed to which it could apply.[69] But in *Amp v. Utilux*,[70] the House of Lords extended its ambit by reading it together with the requirement of "eye appeal". An electrical terminal for washing machines was held unregistrable because a potential customer would decide to buy it solely for its utility and not because of any attraction in its shape. Strictly utilitarian articles were thus excluded from registration (with the curious consequence that the scope of full-term copyright protection was increased).[71]

The result was necessarily imprecise. In the earlier case of *Cow v. Cannon*,[72] a hot-water bottle was constructed with a series of thick ribs

---

[65] RDA 1949, s. 1(3).
[66] [1986] R.P.C. 623.
[67] *Ferrero's Application* [1978] R.P.C. 473.
[68] See paras 10–17—10–22, above.
[69] Note that it is such an exclusion which may have been attached to the Community design and the concurrent Harmonisation Directive: see para. 14–57, below.
[70] [1972] R.P.C. 103. See also *Kevi v. Suspa Verein* [1982] R.P.C. 173.
[71] See para. 14–27, below.
[72] [1961] R.P.C. 236.

which had an insulating function similar to that of a separate cover. The Court of Appeal upheld the design registered for diagonal ribs, because they might have been incorporated using different patterns—horizontal or vertical lines, for instance, or some more elaborate conformation. Under the *Amp* rule, it was necessary to test the motives of customers, looking to discover whether at least an appreciable proportion of them would buy partly because of the appearance of the ribs. This would doubtless be easier to conclude if the ribs formed a picture of a bed.

In *Interlego v. Tyco*,[73] it was held that attention must concentrate on the design as a whole. If it has eye appeal, then it will be registrable unless every feature of it is purely functional. Eye-appeal overall is a vague criterion which distracts attention from the non-functional features in which the novelty of the design is said to lie. The circumstances of the *Tyco* case were decidedly strange and its impact is probably diminishing.

(g) *Illegality or immorality*

The Registrar's general discretion to refuse a design or require modifica- **14–18** tion may be used to exclude illegal or immoral designs; but high horses are not so speedily mounted these days.[74]

(2) **Proprietorship and dealings**[75]

The commissioner of a design for money or money's worth[76] is the person **14–19** primarily entitled to apply for registration; if the design is not so created, the right is in the employer of the designer, where it is created in the course of employment; but otherwise the right belongs to the designer.[77]

These rules are the same for unregistered design right.[78] Indeed there is a presumption that any dealing with the latter also covers a registration relating to it[79]; and the Registrar is not to register a person's interest in a registered design unless satisfied that it is also held in the corresponding unregistered design rights.[80] The rules are not the same for copyright, where initial ownership is presumed to be in an employer but not in a commissioner. This difference, which makes it important to determine the matter by express agreement wherever possible, is also mediated by a provision of the 1988 Act, which exempts from copyright infringement

---

[73] [1989] 1 A.C. 217, JC. See Fellner, para. 2.042ff.
[74] *Masterman's (sic) Design* [1991] R.P.C. 89 ("Highlander" doll with what is beneath sporran held registrable: full frontal at 108).
[75] Laddie *et al.*, Chap. 33; Fellner, paras 3.123–3.127, 4.60–4.75.
[76] For an instance of money's worth: *Breville v. Thorn EMI* (1985) [1995] F.S.R. 77.
[77] RDA 1949, s. 2(1)–(1B). If the design is computer-generated without a human author, the arranger of its creation is treated as author: s. 2(4); and *cf.* para. 13–47, above.
[78] See para. 14–43, below.
[79] CDPA 1988, s. 224.
[80] RDA 1949, s. 19A.

anything done bona fide under an assignment or licence of a corresponding registered design.[81]

The right to apply may be transferred by assignment, transmission or operation of law. As with patents, access to the system is open to all, regardless of nationality. The preference accorded to nationals of Paris Convention countries is the six-month priority affecting the question of novelty. Here there is a direct contrast with the qualification conditions imposed on unregistered design right.[82]

(3) Registration and term[83]

14–20 It follows from the definition of "design" that the application must be to register for a specified article,[84] and registration can become expensive if the design is intended for a considerable range of goods. Where the articles are of the same general character ordinarily on sale or intended to be used together (for example cups and saucers) a single registration for the set of articles is permitted.[85]

The Registry searches through previous registrations to discover anticipations.[86] If the application is accepted,[87] the design is registered and made public.[88] An interested person may not oppose the application but may seek cancellation after grant before the Registrar[89] or the High Court.[90] From the Registrar appeal lies to the Registered Designs Appeal Tribunal[91] (which is similar to the former Patents Appeal Tribunal).

14–21 The term of a registered design is measured from date of application.[92] Under the 1949 Act, the duration was a maximum of three periods each of five years. In the 1988 Act, this has been extended to five periods, making a maximum of 25 years.[93] The term thus became broadly equivalent to that being given to industrial applications of artistic copyright.[94]

---

[81] CDPA 1988, s. 53.
[82] See paras 14–39, 14–40, below.
[83] Laddie *et al.*, Chaps 32, 34; Fellner, paras 3.009–3.122, 3.128–3.130.
[84] Registered Design Rules 1989, S.I. 1989 No. 1105, r. 13.
[85] *ibid.*, r. 12; and see RDA 1949, s. 144(1).
[86] RDA 1949, s. 3(2).
[87] The Registrar is left with an ultimate discretion: *ibid.*, s. 3(3) and note s. 43(1).
[88] See *ibid.*, ss. 17, 22–24; for secrecy directions in the interests of defence: s. 5. There is an obligation to register changes of ownership and grants of interest (licences, mortgages, etc.): ss. 17, 19.
[89] *ibid.*, s. 11(2).
[90] There is a special provision for a certificate of contested validity in High Court proceedings: *ibid.*, s. 25.
[91] *ibid.*, s. 28 (as amended).
[92] *ibid.*, s. 3(5).
[93] *ibid.*, s. 8. Provisions are added, equivalent to those in PA 1977, ss. 25(4), 28, allowing the restoration of a registration which has lapsed through non-payment of renewal fees: ss. 8(4), 8A, 8B. The lengthened term is equivalent to that for copyright in articles that are artistic works: see para. 14–32, below. Note that if the design derives from an artistic work, and is registrable only by virtue of s. 6(4), the registered design may last only as long as copyright in that artistic work: s. 8(5).
[94] See para. 14–32, below.

(4) Property rights

Once granted a registered design can be transferred by assignment, **14–22** transmission on death or operation of law, but only in respect of all the rights in it.[95] It can also be mortgaged and licensed. While formally an assignment is not required to be in writing,[96] it ought to be for the purpose of registration, which is needed for all proprietary interests if they are to bind those with subsequent interests.[97]

(5) Infringement[98]

Over time, the registered design right became recognised as a full **14–23** monopoly not dependent on any proof of copying, and subject to no defence of innocence.[99]

The exclusive right given by registration covers manufacture and commercial dealing in the United Kingdom, but not (in general) use. More specifically infringement may be committed by doing any of the following acts with an article bearing the design, or one not substantially different: (1) making, or (2) importing it for sale, hire or use for the purposes of a trade or business; (3) selling, hiring, or offering or exposing it for sale or hire.[1] One "contributory" step towards manufacture is also covered: making anything for enabling the article itself to be made.[2] This relates to moulds, plates, dies and the like that will directly produce the designed article, and, at least for designs applied for after August 1, 1989, this extends to a kit of parts for making the articles.[3]

In testing whether an article infringes a registered design for that article, **14–24** the normal starting point is the design as a whole. The protection is for the entire thing and not for its separate parts by themselves.[4] But in many cases, the applicant is required to file a statement of novelty,[5] drawing attention to the special features which form the kernel of the designer's conception.[6] In any case, particular attention is given to the design of the

---

[95] RDA 1949, s. 19(1).

[96] In contrast with unregistered design right.

[97] RDA 1949, s. 19(4).

[98] Laddie *et al.*, Chaps 35, 36; Fellner, paras 5.149–5.191.

[99] *Sommer Allibert v. Flair Plastics* [1987] R.P.C. 599 at 610. As with patents, innocence may be a bar to an award of damages: RDA 1949, s. 9.

[1] *ibid.*, s. 7(1), (2).

[2] *ibid.*, s. 7(3), which applies even if the thing will be used abroad, perhaps in a country where no protection arises.

[3] For the position regarding earlier designs, see Laddie *et al.*, paras 35.29–35.33.

[4] See Lord Westbury, *Holdsworth v. McCrea* (1867) L.R. 2 HL 380 at 388. The definition of "article" discussed above (para. 14–13, above) applies here.

[5] See Registered Design Rules 1989, S.I. 1989 No. 1105, r. 14. The exceptions are textiles and wallpapers.

[6] The Courts tend not to treat the statement as conclusive in the way they do a patent claim: see, *e.g. Kevi v. Suspa-Verein* [1982] R.P.C. 173; but *cf. Gaskell & Chambers v. Measure Master* [1993] R.P.C. 76: a statement of novelty confined to shape excludes consideration of ornament.

striking, or commercially significant, features of an article, such as the whistle of a whistling kettle.[7] A Court will compare the two side by side. Nevertheless, it is proper to take account of imperfect recollections that a consumer may have, provided that he is a person interested in design features.[8]

The comparison between design and alleged infringement determines whether or not there are substantial differences between them. It is an inquiry of the same order as that to decide whether the design is novel in light of the prior art.[9] Even if the registered design itself does pass this test, the extent by which it does so is important in deciding what infringes it. If the distance is a small one, a defendant will not infringe who introduces small variations himself.[10] Moreover, the two things are not solely to be compared side by side.[11]

(6) Control of monopoly

14-25 A compulsory licence of a registered design may be granted by the Registrar (that is the Comptroller) on one broad ground: that the design is not being applied in the United Kingdom to such an extent as is reasonable in the circumstances of the case.[12] No further formula is given by way of guide towards the proper exercise of this discretion. Some assistance may be available from the comparable provisions on patents,[13] though they are much more elaborate. The power is certainly more limited than the licences of right now available in respect of unregistered design right.[14]

(7) Crown use

14-26 The Crown is entitled to use (or authorise the use of) a registered design for the services of the Crown.[15] The conditions are similar to those applying to patents. Compensation must be paid unless the Crown had already

---

[7] *Best v. Woolworth* [1964] R.P.C. 232, CA The registration was for an "audible alarm kettle". Since the defendant's kettle did not include an alarm, he was not selling the article for which the design was registered.

[8] *Sommer Allibert v. Flair Plastics* [1987] R.P.C. 599, CA.

[9] But deciding whether differences are immaterial or common trade variations (for novelty) is not exactly the same as deciding whether the differences are insubstantial (for infringement).

[10] See Luxmoore J., *Dean's Rag Book v. Pomerantz* (1930) 47 R.P.C. 485 at 491; *cf. Gaskell & Chambers* case (n. 6, above).

[11] See, *e.g. Valor Heating v. Main Gas Appliances* [1972] F.S.R. 497 at 502; *Benchairs v. Chair Centre* [1974] R.P.C. 429 at 442, CA.

[12] RDA 1949, s. 10.

[13] See paras 7–46 *et seq.*, above.

[14] For control over abuse of monopoly, as with the other rights applicable to designs, see RDA 1949, s. 11A.

[15] RDA 1949, s. 12, Sched. 1, now amended to include compensation for loss of profit provisions, as with patents: see para. 7–50, n. 92, above.

recorded or applied the design otherwise than in consequence of the registered proprietor's communication before the date of registration.[16]

3. ARTISTIC COPYRIGHT[17]

(1) The exclusion of design documents and models

Under the 1988 Act, as before, copyright in a drawing arises irrespective of **14–27** artistic quality, provided that there is sufficient labour, skill and judgment to give originality. It may be infringed by reproducing it in a three-dimensional article; and it matters not whether the act of copying is direct or indirect.[18] The main object of section 51 is accordingly to limit the application of that principle, by cutting out the application of copyright to industrial products which are not themselves capable of being the subject of copyright. It accordingly states that the act of making an article from a "design document or model" which records or embodies a design cannot after all constitute infringement. This applies where the design is "for anything other than an artistic work or a typeface". "Design" has a restricted meaning: "the design of any aspect of the shape or configuration (whether internal or external) of the whole or part of an article, other than surface decoration". However, one point should be kept in mind: it is not copyright in the design, but copyright in the design document or model, which is affected by the new limitation.

Section 51 undoubtedly excludes from the sphere of copyright much of what, under the previous law, has been considered to fall within it: blueprints for pumps, car exhausts or taps must count as design documents for non-artistic works, and this is so whatever the form of record—whether it is "a drawing, a written description, a photograph, data stored in a computer or otherwise".[19] The material thus excluded can only be protected as a registered or an unregistered design, if the conditions governing those rights are met. Previously there was no such limitation and artistic copyright ranged across much of the industrial landscape. A degree of uncertainty infects the penumbra of section 51, as can be seen if each of its requirements is further examined.

(a) *"Design document or model recording or embodying a design for anything other than an artistic work . . ."*

If the design document is for a piece of jewellery, the design is in many **14–28** cases for a "work of artistic craftsmanship". It could accordingly be infringement of copyright in the drawing to make up the jewellery from it

---

[16] RDA 1949, Sched. 1, para. 1(2), (3).
[17] See Laddie *et al.,* Chap. 46; Fellner, paras 2.120–2.219, 3.54–3.108, 5.76–5.48.
[18] See para. .11–05, above.
[19] The reference to "design models" excludes prototypes and mock-ups for things, provided that those things are not themselves artistic works: a model for a cup may itself be a sculpture (see para. 14–29, below) but it is still a model for a thing incapable of bearing copyright. Contrast a model for a figurine.

(direct), or from jewellery made from it (indirect); and in the latter case it would also be infringement of copyright in the jewellery (and the authors of these two copyrights may well be different people: designer and silversmith respectively).

The category, "works of artistic craftsmanship", is a limited one, as the House of Lords demonstrated in *Hensher v. Restawile*.[20] Copyright is not in this case accorded "irrespective of artistic quality". But among those things which are protected without regard to artistic quality, as well as drawings, are sculpture, engravings and etchings. None of these artistic works is further defined, save that "sculpture" includes a cast or model.

14–29   In considering the impact of these broad notions, the key is to remember the governing consideration: what is the design *for*?[21] If a document is drawn for the purpose of making a sculpture, an etching or an engraving, then the exclusion of copyright from industrial infringement does not apply.[22] If, however, the design is for something which is not itself an artistic work—such as, designs for the Teletubby dolls beloved of children's television[23]—the mere fact that a three-dimensional model (itself counting as a sculpture) is made as a stepping stone towards final production will not exclude section 51. The intermediate version is not the end, only a means to it.

14–30   Here we look at the same phrase one step back. Concern shifts to another aspect of the preposition "for". It brings into consideration the intention or purpose for which the design was recorded. Take the classic example—the cartoon character, Popeye, and his merchandising as a doll.[24] Initially the drawings were *for* a comic strip, not for making articles. Read naturally, section 51 would appear not to touch such a case, leaving the merchandising of such a figure to the sphere of copyright (and thus in effect returning to a basic distinction under the 1911 Act). However, it would be possible, if strained, to read the section as extending to any subject-matter capable of being turned into an article. In which case, Popeye and his ilk would be covered by it, so far as concerns the production of articles.

(b) *"Any aspect of shape or configuration . . . other than surface decoration"*

14–31 It will be a nice question whether a feature of a design is for surface decoration, so that a design document embodying it may bear artistic copyright; or whether it is for some other element of shape or configuration, with the consequence that it is excluded by section 51. There is nothing to say that the surface must be flat. The result must, however, be

---

[20] See paras 10–17—10–22, above.
[21] Taylor and Dworkin [1990] E.I.P.R. 33.
[22] For these types of artistic work, see above, paras 10–13ff.
[23] *BBC Worldwide v. Pally Screen Printing* [1998] F.S.R. 665.
[24] *King Features Syndicate v. Kleeman* [1941] A.C. 417.

decorative. Hence a circuit diagram for an electronic mixer amounts to "configuration" and falls within section 51.[25] Since the copyright and design right provisions use exactly the same terminology, this interpretation ought to apply equally to copyright. What, then, of a dress? Are sleeves and pleats configuration, while buttons and bows mere surface decoration?

(2) The limitation of duration

In any case where section 51 does not apply to a design, copyright will **14–32** continue to be infringed by making three-dimensional copies of it. But once any artistic work has been used in industrial production with the copyright owner's authority, the duration of this aspect of the copyright is foreshortened by section 52.[26] It ceases to be infringement to make articles of any description (other than those of a primarily literary or artistic character)[27] which copy the copyright work, after 25 years from the end of the year in which industrially produced articles from the work were first marketed anywhere in the world by or with the authority of the copyright owner. The same concept of industrial application of a corresponding design is found here as applies to registered designs.[28] The section embodies the obligation under the Berne Convention to accord at least 25 years' protection to a work of applied art so far as it is copyright.[29] At the same time it rids copyright of its most egregious excess in entering the realm of industrial property.

Apart from this limitation of term in relation to industrial exploitation, copyright principles apply as before.[30] Qualification extends to persons connected by personal status to prescribed Convention countries—an important contrast, it seems, with unregistered design right. First ownership of a work made under commission belongs to the artist who creates the work (unless there has been an express assignment)—a contrast with both registered and unregistered design right.[31] The artist, moreover, will benefit

---

[25] *Mackie Designs v. Behringer* (January 22, 1999); and *cf.* the registered design cases, *Sommer-Allibert v. Flair Plastics* [1987] R.P.C. 599; *Cow v. Cannon* ([1961] R.P.C. 236, n. 72 above); and note the general reliance on Luxmoore J., *Kestos v. Kempat* (1936) 53 R.P.C. 139 at 152.

[26] *cf.* CA 1956, s. 10, after its amendment by the Design Copyright Act 1968: both the 1956 and 1988 Acts excluded one application of copyright from infringement; but the period before this happens is now 25, not 15 years; and there is no longer a distinction between designs that could, and could not, be registered.

[27] See para. 14–12, above.

[28] *ibid.*

[29] See the Paris Act of the Berne Convention (1971), Art. 7 (4); Ricketson, paras 6.44–6.54. *cf.* para. 14–39, below.

[30] For designs made before August 1, 1989, the previous law concerning design copyright continues in principle to apply, but subject to a series of restrictions which reduce protection to a level close to that of the new unregistered design right: see Laddie *et al.,* paras 46.46–46.48.

[31] *cf.* para. 14–19, above; para. 14–43, below. Note that the designer of material in a design document that has applications precluded from copyright by CDPA 1988, s. 51 has no moral right to be identified in those applications; but he does retain a right to object to derogatory treatment: *cf.* ss. 79(4)(f), (g), 80, 81; and see generally, paras 11–75 *et seq.*, above.

from the moral right to be identified (subject to the duration limit of section 52) and the right to object to derogatory treatment. These could be of some assistance to designers who are not employees.

4. (UNREGISTERED) DESIGN RIGHT[32]

(1) Subject-matter

14–33 The unregistered "Design Right" accorded by Part III of the 1988 Act co-ordinates with the terms which limit the scope of copyright in the sphere of industrial production. Nevertheless, the new right is a hybrid displaying characteristics both of copyright and registered design law. Accordingly one must be wary of transposing assumptions from either field without careful examination.

The right arises in an "original design", comprising "any aspect of the shape or configuration (whether internal or external) of an article" which is not "surface decoration."[33] In contrast with registered designs, there is nothing to require that the design should appeal to the eye, so as to evoke an aesthetic response; thus prostheses for women who have had a breast removed gain design right.[34] Indeed, the major purpose of the new right is to give relatively short-term, informal protection to technical designs. The right has been recognised in a slurry separator and its components, mobile phone cases and shape elements in transformers.[35] Indeed "design" is not confined to things that a human can see. The layout of a semiconductor chip is included within design right as a specially regulated instance of it.[36] The detailed dimensional shapes for contact lenses could in principle fall within the general scope of the right,[37] though they may face difficulties when it comes to the exclusory conditions mentioned below.

Could the structure of genetically engineered proteins, which are highly dependent on the manner in which they fold, therefore, attract design right?[38] For such a notion, kites have been flown.[39] They may well be earthed on the ground that what an electron microscope can detect is simply not what Parliament was considering when it employed the term "design" in this context.

14–34 To qualify for design right, the design needs to be original, while for the registered right it must be novel.[40] Design right, being informal, can be

---

[32] See Laddie *et al.*, Chaps 40–44; Fellner, paras 2.220–2.269, 3.04–3.53, 5.01–5.75; Bentley and Coulthard [1997] E.I.P.R. 401.
[33] CDPA 1988, s. 213(1), (2), (3)(c); see para. 14–31, above.
[34] *Amoena v. Trulife* [1995] S.R.I.S. C/72/95.
[35] *Farmers Build v. Carrier Bulk* [1999] R.P.C. 461, CA; *Parker v. Tidball* [1997] F.S.R. 680; *Electronic Techniques v. Critchley Components* [1997] F.S.R. 401.
[36] Below, para. 14–48.
[37] *Ocular Sciences v. Aspect Vision Care* [1997] R.P.C. 289 at 423.
[38] A naturally occurring DNA sequence would not pass the requisite test of originality.
[39] Hirde and Peeters [1991] E.I.P.R. 334; Laddie *et al.*, para. 21.41.
[40] *cf.* CDPA 1988, s. 213(1), (4); RDA 1949, s. 2(2), (4); para. 14–10, above.

infringed only by copying and it might be thought that "originality" bore no more than its copyright meaning of "not copied".[41] It includes that notion, but an all-important objective element is added: a design "commonplace in the design field in question at the time of its creation" is not to be regarded as original for the purpose of design right.[42] This excludes a design which is trite, trivial, common-or-garden, hackneyed or of the type which would excite no particular attention in the relevant art.[43] Compare with this the exclusion from registration of designs which differ from prior art only in "variants commonly used in the trade". The objective precondition for design right may be harder to satisfy than that for registered designs. A thing could be "commonplace" in a design field, without necessarily being one out of variants used in a trade. Nonetheless, the court will place weight on the number and closeness of other designs.[44] There is in the end, for both registered and unregistered design rights, a requirement of somewhat extended novelty.

The right is not restricted to designs applicable to the article as a whole **14–35** ("any aspect . . . of the whole or any substantial part").[45] However, as with registered designs, a method or principle of construction is excluded.[46] In addition there are two specific exceptions which were included to prevent the new right after all from applying to replacement parts in specified cases. These are: "features of shape or configuration which:

(1) enable the article to be connected to, or placed around or against, another article so that either article may perform its function, or
(2) are dependent upon the appearance of another article of which the article is intended by the designer to form an integral part."[47]

The first of these is a "must fit" exception, but in terms more limited **14–36** than the "purpose dictated solely by function" exception of registered design law.[48] The exception here requires that the article including the design must take its place "so that" one or other article may perform its function. This, however, can happen between components within complex machinery, such as a transformer.[49] It has even been held that one article

---

[41] *cf.* the EC Designs Directive, Art. 4, below, para. 14–56.

[42] This derives from the Semiconductor Topography Directive, Art. 2(2); below, para. 14–48.

[43] *Ocular Sciences v. Aspect Vision Care*, above, n. 37 at 429; *cf. Amoena v. Trulife*, above, n. 34; criticising the view that the test was that for novelty in patent law: *C & H Engineering v. Klucznik* [1992] F.S.R. 421.

[44] *Farmers Build v. Carrier Bulk*, above, n. 35.

[45] *cf.* registered designs, para. 14–13, above. It is for the plaintiff to set out in his pleadings what feactures give rise to design right. This determines the subject-matter which has to be shown to be "original" and infringed.

[46] CDPA 1988, s. 213(3)(a); 14–14 above. For this reason, the stitching on mobile phone cases was excluded: *Parker v. Tidball*, above, n. 35.

[47] *ibid.*, s. 213(3) (b).

[48] See para. 14–17, above.

[49] *Electronic Techniques v. Critchley*, above, n. 35, *cf. Baby-Dan v. Brevi* (to be reported).

may be a living organ: thus all those dimensional features of a contact lens which fixed it in place on the surface of an eye had to be discounted in a claim to design right. Moreover, the exception was not confined to the case where only one shape would do.[50]

14–37 The second exception—"must match"—has been added in the same terms to registered designs law.[51] The typical case was thought to be the panel for a car door, and in all likelihood that example is within the exception. The requirement that the shape or configuration be intended by the designer to form an integral part of something else was included in order to prevent the exception from extending to things intended to be made in sets, such as cutlery or glasses.[52]

14–38 It must be noted that, because of international obligations or in pursuit of reciprocity, the Secretary of State may make different provision for different descriptions of design or article or exclude acts from the scope of infringement.[53] This allows the special topography right to continue in the form prescribed by E.C. Directive at the dictation of the United States.[54]

(2) Qualification

14–39 One important motive in creating a separate unregistered design right has been to preclude foreigners from entitlement, in a way that was difficult to introduce while protection was accorded under copyright.[55]

The explicit provisions on qualification for unregistered design rights are expressed to relate to the United Kingdom, other Member States of the E.C., the colonies and like territories to which Part 2 may be extended, and countries which accord reciprocal protection to British designs.[56] "Qualifying individuals" are citizens, subjects or habitual residents of one of these countries; and "qualifying persons" are these individuals together with corporate bodies incorporated in, or carrying on substantial business in, such a country.[57] Qualification also turns on the circumstances in which a design is made. If not made under commission or in employment, the designer must be a qualifying individual (or qualifying person, where the work is computer-generated).[58] In the excepted cases, it is the commissioner

---

[50] *Ocular Sciences v. Aspect Vision Care* [1997] R.P.C., above, n. 37 at 425; *Parker v. Tidball*, above, n. 35. There comes a point where there is no sufficiently precise correspondence in the fit, *e.g.* between prosthetic breast and brassiere: *Amoena v. Trulife*, above, n. 34.

[51] See para. 14–15, above. For registered design law this exception has been deprived of much significance.

[52] There is, however, no exception for modular connectors in building toys and the like. *cf.* the new E.C. design plan: para. 14–57, n. 22, below.

[53] CDPA 1988, s. 245.

[54] See paras 14–48—14–51, below.

[55] Because of Berne Convention (Paris Act), Art. 2(4): para. 14–32, above.

[56] These countries are specified by Order under CDPA 1988, s. 256.

[57] CDPA 1988, s. 217. For an example of the consequences for a foreign claimant, see *Mackie Designs v. Behringer* (January 22, 1999).

[58] *ibid.*, s. 218; for joint designers, see s. 218(3), (4).

or employer who must be a qualifying person.[59] If there is no qualification according to these rules (and there may well not be), then it may arise from first marketing by a qualifying person with exclusive marketing rights in the United Kingdom, its extended territories, or the E.C.[60]

In this form, the qualification provisions amount to an attempt by this country to follow the path of reciprocity which it has long since abandoned in established fields of intellectual property, but to which it has recently been led in the cognate field of computer chip topography by pressure from the United States.[61] It is not clear what degree of reciprocity it is intent on securing. Will it treat as a reciprocating country one in which industrial designs are protected by an extension of unfair competition doctrine to cover the misappropriation of product ideas?[62] Or is it striving to tell the world that unfair competition protection is not direct enough? These uncertainties at least will be resolved in time. What must remain unsettled, since it is an inherent defect of the reciprocity approach to international relations throughout this field, is the train of reaction in other countries which may follow.

The Paris Convention for the Protection of Industrial Property, of which **14–40** the United Kingdom has been a member for more than a century, has as its object "patents, utility models, industrial designs . . ." and requires that "industrial property" be understood in its "broadest sense".[63]2 Accordingly it is arguable that, once the United Kingdom institutes a specific scheme for the protection of industrial designs, even though this does not require registration, it is obliged to provide equal treatment to nationals of Paris Convention States. The Government, it appears, is sufficiently uncertain of its position to have taken power to do this.[64] In the end, it may choose to by-pass the narrowly calculating approach of reciprocity. Such a step would improve its moral position *vis-à-vis* those countries which still refrain from joining the major intellectual property conventions and prefer to think in terms of bilateral negotiation. But it would make rather ridiculous the whole cumbersome edifice of unregistered design right.

(3) Exclusive right

The scope of design right bears important affinities to copyright, rather **14–41** than to registered design. However, design right has its own peculiarities. Primary infringement (which occurs irrespective of the defendant's culpability or innocence) consists either of making articles to the design for

---

[59] CDPA 1988, s. 219.
[60] *ibid*., s. 220.
[61] See paras 14–48 *et seq*., below.
[62] For the extent to which unfair competition laws give protection against "slavish imitation" in Western Europe, see Fellner, para. 14–01, n. 2, above.
[63] PIP, Art. 1(2), (3). For the obligation to protect industrial designs, see Art. 5*quinquies*.
[64] CDPA 1988, s. 221.

commercial purposes or making a design document in order to make such articles. What must occur is reproduction of the design, that is copying of the design, directly or indirectly, so as to produce articles exactly or substantially to that design.[65] The right given is only against copying, not against independent creation.[66] Much turns on what the design is alleged to be. In the *Klucznik* case,[67] it was for a pig fender of which the only element out of the ordinary was a round tube on top (to stop sows hurting their teats). Aldous J. compared the other party's fender as a whole; because it contained other features, notably an arrangement for stacking, there was no infringement. This is a more difficult test to satisfy than an inquiry to see whether there has been substantial reproduction in the copyright sense.[68]

Secondary infringement, which can occur only where the defendant knows or has reason to believe that he is dealing with an infringing article, may be constituted by unauthorised importation for commercial purposes, possessing for commercial purposes, and selling, letting for hire, or offering or exposing for sale or hire, in the course of a business.[69]

The right is akin to copyright infringement in that it has equivalent provisions concerning additional damages, delivery up, disposal of infringing articles, exclusion of damages for innocent infringement, exclusive licensees, and joint ownership.[70] There is, however, no right to engage in self-help seizure.

14–42   In design right cases, the plaintiff is given one exceptional advantage which is not accorded in copyright. Once he shows that an alleged "infringing article" has been made to a design in which the right subsists or has subsisted at any time, it is for the defendant to prove that the article was made at a time when design right did not subsist.[71] That seems a fair presumption when the duration of the right itself is not in issue and the only question is the date on which the defendant acted. If, however, there is contention over the date on which the plaintiff's design was first recorded, or on which the plaintiff first authorised marketing of articles to the design somewhere in the world—both of which will affect the duration of the right—the defendant is put to proof of matter which cannot be in his own knowledge. The inherent unfairness of the provision might be limited if the plaintiff were first obliged to show that his design was not copied from another source. This at least could oblige him to give details of its creation,

---

[65] CDPA 1988, s. 226.

[66] *ibid.*, s. 226(2); *C & H Engineering v. Klucznik* (n. 67, below) at 428. The functional purpose of the design may make proof of copying difficult: *Ocular Sciences*, above, n. 37; *Amoena v. Trulife*, above, n. 34; *cf.* Bently and Coulthard, above, n. 32.

[67] *C & H Engineering v. Klucznik* [1992] F.S.R. 421.

[68] When the design cannot be perceived by the eye, the test becomes particularly difficult to apply: *cf. Ocular Sciences*, above, n. 37 at 424.

[69] CDPA 1988, s. 227; s. 228 applies to unregistered design right the same rules concerning importation as have so far operated for copyright: but see paras 12–16—12–17, above.

[70] See *ibid.*, ss. 229–235.

[71] *ibid.*, s. 228(4).

if not of its first marketing. It is accordingly desirable that "original" should include this concept.

Unregistered design right is subject to Crown use on terms of compensation. The rules are as for registered designs.[72]

(4) Authorship and first ownership

The rules concerning authorship and first ownership run in tandem with **14–43** those for registered designs and differ from those for copyright. This has already been commented upon.[73] If a design is made under a commission for money or money's worth, first ownership is accorded to the commissioner[74]; if that is not the case, where it is made by an employee in the course of employment, it belongs to the employer; failing this, the designer—that is the creator—becomes the first owner.[75] If any of these persons are prospective owners of a design still to be created, they may assign their right by agreement in writing, signed by both parties, so as to vest the right on creation in the assignee.[76]

(5) Duration and licences of right

The period for which unregistered design right subsists has been limited so **14–44** as to make the right less valuable than that arising under copyright or the design registration system. The main thrust of the system is to give protection to functional objects and parts against imitation in the early years of their exploitation. Design right expires 15 years after first recording of the design in a design document or the first making of an article to the design, whichever is earlier; or—a further limitation—if articles to the design are legitimately marketed anywhere in the world within the first five years of recording or making, then the period is 10 years from first beginning this activity. The latter circumstance is likely to be the most usual.[77]

Moreover, during the last five years of the right—in most cases, after five years from first legitimate marketing—others are entitled to a licence of right to do anything within the scope of the right, its terms to be settled (if necessary) by the Comptroller, with appeal to the Designs Appeal Tribunal.[78] In exceptional cases, after reference to the Monopolies and

---

[72] CDPA 1988, ss. 240–244, 252.

[73] *cf.* paras 12–02, 14–19, above.

[74] The amount paid does not have to be adequate: *Farmers Build v. Carrier Bulk* (n. 35, above).

[75] CDPA 1988, ss. 214, 215. Normally the designer is the person who draws the design, but could conceivably be the person who describes what is to be drawn; *Parker v. Tidball* (n. 35, above). A person who arranges the production of a computer-aided design is the designer: CDPA 1988, s. 214(2).

[76] CDPA 1988, s. 223.

[77] *ibid.*, s. 216.

[78] *ibid.*, s. 237 *Bance's Applcn.* [1996] R.P.C. 667. Categories of design may be excluded from this provision by Order, because of a Convention obligation or in order to secure or maintain reciprocal protection of British designs: the obvious case is the topography right in semiconductor chips; for which see para. 14–58, below.

Mergers Commission and a finding by it that design right is being asserted in a manner contrary to the public interest, the Minister may order (*inter alia*) that licences of right be available even before the last five-year period.[79] In recent years, there have been two Reports of the Commission which have criticised aspects of design copyright exploitation by car manufacturers—reports which have been influential in settling the terms of the 1988 New Deal.[80] Now there is legislative machinery for giving effect to the Commission's decisions, whether they relate to patents, copyright, registered designs or unregistered designs.[81] The application for a licence of right in the final five years may be made up to one year before commencement.[82]

14–45   Once the final five-year period is reached, an alleged infringer who undertakes to obtain a licence of right cannot be the subject of an injunction or delivery-up order; and damages against him are limited to double the rate of royalty set in the licence of right.[83] In arriving at an appropriate royalty rate, the Comptroller will be seeking to evaluate the design element in the plaintiff's product as a contributory factor both to its development cost and to its success in the market.[84] In some circumstances, there may be evidence of royalty practices in voluntary licences and these may indeed burgeon as the new regime comes to be understood.

14–46   Behind the availability of licences of right may well lurk issues of subsistence of the right, its terms and first entitlement. Save in infringement proceedings and other actions where they arise incidentally, these issues can be raised only in proceedings before the Comptroller, subject to reference or leave by him, or appeal from him, to the High Court or proceedings brought there by agreement of the parties.[85] The controversial presumption in the plaintiff's favour which arises in relation to "infringing articles" does not seemingly apply in such proceedings, a matter which design copiers would do well to note.

(6) A brief comparison

14–47   By way of summary, let us conjure the vision of a table lamp consisting of a base modelled as a mermaid and a lampshade in the form of a water-lily. The whole lovely complement could be the subject of a registered design, claiming its novelty in aspects of shape and configuration, and perhaps

---

[79] CDPA 1988 s. 238.
[80] *Re Car Parts* [1983] F.S.R. 115.
[81] For the equivalent provisions, see CDPA 1988, ss. 144, 270.
[82] *ibid.*, s. 247.
[83] *ibid.*, s. 239; See also *Dyrlund Smith v. Turberville Smith* [1998] F.S.R. 403.
[84] In exercising his discretion-as to terms, the Comptroller is given little statutory guidance. Some of the considerations which have been brought to bear on patent licences of right (see paras 7–46—7–48, above) are treated as germane: *E-U.K. Controls' Licence of Right* [1998] R.P.C. 833.
[85] CDPA 1988, s. 246.

pattern and ornament as well. If the intention is to make the shade a separate article of commerce, then (but then alone) will it satisfy the test that it is to be sold separately, so as to be entitled to a design registration just for the shade. That right could endure for 25 years from registration.

Equally the lamp might attract artistic copyright: (1) as a whole, because it had the quality to rank among works of artistic craftsmanship; or because copyright can be traced back to a drawing that was not for an industrial design; (2) in part, because one or other element constitutes a sculpture or perhaps an engraving—the base or (particularly if it is moulded) the shade. In these cases the protection will last for 25 years from the first legitimate marketing of products embodying the copyright work.

Such copyright can subsist beside any registered design that there may be. But to the extent that there is copyright there can be no infringement of unregistered design right in any element of shape or configuration.[86] There may, however, be elements, such as the bulb-holder, which will at most attract this lesser form of protection (with its normal maximum of 10 years, subject to licences of right in the last five years). Moreover, the essentially utilitarian bulb-holder could not attract the lesser design right so far as it was commonplace in the trade, nor so far as its shape was formed to receive the bulb ("must fit"). The scope for discriminatory argument seems altogether without bounds.

(7) Topography right[87]

Finally in this section we reach a juncture where the special demands of **14–48** computer technology meet more general concerns over the protection of industrial design. The semiconductor chip gives effect to program instructions through a circuitry fixed on semiconductor material in layered form.[88] The familiar ROMs, RAMs and EPROMs that are the basis of software packages are forms of such chips. Their mass-production is frequently the result of major investment in design, so there has been great pressure for legal means to prevent their imitation.

In the United Kingdom, it was likely that, because design copyright under the 1956 Act (as amended) was such an extended notion, the layered circuitry, taken from a design, could be treated as copyright. This was arguable particularly where photography was used to produce the layout. In other countries even this prospect was not open and the sole chance lay in an extension of unfair competition law. The United States, with the largest investments at risk, insisted that there be rapid legislative intervention. Its

---

[86] CDPA 1988, s. 236. Since, thanks to the different rules about ownership of commissioned works, there may be disputes about ownership, the presence or absence of copyright may well fall to be tested.

[87] See generally Christie, *Integrated Circuits and their Contents: International Protection* (1995); Laddie *et al.*, Chap. 45; Fellner, para. 2.253.

[88] For a clear technical description, Christie (n. 87, above) App. A.

own Semiconductor Chip Protection Act 1984 created a *sui generis* right in original "mask" works.[89] At the same time it announced that, if other countries wished their nationals to enjoy this new protection in the United States, they must provide equivalent protection for American mask works in their own territories. The European Community, by Directive to Member States,[90] led the scramble to comply with this edict, though it has been far from clear why, in the then state of the computer industry world-wide, it should hasten to confer rights which overall would be of greater benefit to Americans than would the reciprocal benefits in the United States to its own firms.[91]

14–49   The obligation under the Directive was originally met in the United Kingdom by Regulations of 1987 creating a "topography right". These have since become a specially conditioned form of unregistered design right.[92] The subject of protection is the pattern fixed, or intended to be fixed, in or upon a layer of a semiconductor product, or in the arrangement of the layers of a semiconductor product; and a semiconductor product is:

> "an article the purpose, or one of the purposes, of which is the performance of an electronic function and which consists of two or more layers, at least one of which is composed of semiconducting material and in or upon one or more of which is fixed a pattern appertaining to that or another function."[93]

To acquire protection the topography must be "original", in the same double sense that applies to design right in general.[94]

The basic period of protection is also as for design right. However, no compulsory licences provision limit the range of topography right.[95] Qualification for it is dependent on close reciprocation, for which there are separate lists of countries, including, of course, the United States.[96] Rules giving first ownership to a commissioner, an employer or otherwise the creator of the design closely parallel those for design right. In this context, the provision for computer generated design, accorded to the person who arranges for the design to be created, may possibly have some scope for application.[97]

---

[89] So called from the masking technique which is one method of producing the circuitry on the chip surface. See Ladd *et al., Protection of Semiconductor Chip Masks in the United States* (1986); Rauch (1993) 75 JPTOS 93.

[90] Directive 87/54: [1987] O.J. L24/36.

[91] In 1989, a WIPO Treaty on Intellectual Property in Respect of Integrated Circuits was concluded; but given in particular its low term (8 years minimum), it was spurned by the U.S. and Japan (the two dominant producer countries, now being challenged in some measure by Taiwan). The TRIPS Agreement provides for 10 years of protection, on the lines of the U.S. model: see Arts 35–38.

[92] Design Right (Semiconductor Topographies) Regulations 1989, S.I 1989 No. 1100.

[93] Design Right (Semiconductor Topography) Regulations 1989, reg. 2(1).

[94] See para. 14–34, above.

[95] Design Right (Semiconductor Topography) Regulations 1989, regs 6, 7, 9.

[96] *ibid.*, reg. 4, Sched. Pts 1 and 2.

[97] See para. 14–43, n. 61, above.

The rules governing infringement are modified in a number of ways. **14–50** Thus, there is a defence for reproduction of the design privately for non-commercial aims.[98] More significantly, and in direct descent from the United States Act, there is a wide-ranging freedom to engage in reverse engineering. It is permissible to reproduce the topography for the purpose of analysing or evaluating it, or analysing, evaluating or teaching the concepts, processes, systems or techniques embodied in it; and as a result of such steps, it is permissible to create another original topography.[99] This in effect substitutes an older test of copyright infringement for the one that currently prevails in that sphere. For topography right, it would seem, the question is how much original work has been done in addition by the alleged infringer, not, as in current copyright law, how much of the old can be traced in the new.[1] Under similar legislation in Australia, it has been held that to shrink the scale of the plaintiff's integrated circuit is merely a reducing operation involving no "intellectual or unique design work". Not suprisingly the defence was not made out.[2]

It will be appreciated that much of the unregistered design right now **14–51** introduced in the 1988 Act derives from the Topography Regulation. The two main points of difference are the absence from the latter of licences of right in the last five years and the absence from the former of the reverse engineering defence. In these respects the topography right continues to keep its special contours, set according to the American mould.[3]

5. THE EUROPEAN FUTURE[4]

The 1988 Act introduced a novel and complicated structure for the **14–52** protection of industrial designs which sought to calm the turbulent seas of the previous law. The upsurge of the 1970s and 1980s had driven the tide of copyright to the farthest shores of technical shape, giving an informal, anti-copying protection of the physical form of products and their parts, even where that form had nothing to do with "eye-appeal". The unregistered design right of the 1988 Act has sought to provide a more restrained replacement for this extensive "artistic" copyright. In some considerable degree design right gives protection against the copying of technical novelties, which in other countries have been protected instead through a short-term patent or utility model.[5] Rights of that kind, however, require formal grant and are mostly good even against independent devisers.

---

[98] Design Right (Semiconductor Topography) Regulations 1989, reg. 8(1).
[99] *ibid.*, reg. 8(1), (4). See also Hart [1989] E.I.P.R. 111.
[1] The onus of making out the defence is probably on the defendant: Christie (n. 87, above), pp. 147–148, 153.
[2] *Nintendo v. Centronics Systems* (1993) 23 I.P.R. 119.
[3] Under CDPA 1988, ss. 221(2), 237(3), 245(1).
[4] For the international position in the light of TRIPs, see Kur in Beier and Schricker, p. 141.
[5] See paras 3–31 *et seq.*, above.

It is this difference of approach which poses a particular puzzle for the British in relation to the "Europeanisation" of designs law. The European Union's plans are now well advanced but only half complete. They are for:

(1) a Regulation establishing (a) a Community registered design, and (b) preliminary unregistered design right—this is still only in draft form[6]; and

(2) a corresponding Directive harmonising national laws on registered designs—this becomes law in 1998 and gives member states three years for implementation.[7]

What is in store follows broadly the lines of the new Community deal for trade marks. Stimulated by claims that "design concepts" are at the hub of modern marketing, particularly in luxury product sectors, and moved by the disparate nature of design laws around the still unifying Market, proposed Regulation is to provide a unitary design right for the Community.[8] This, to begin with, will be an alternative to national registration. The national systems are accordingly to be co-ordinated by an extensive, but not complete, harmonisation in the terms of the recent Directive.[9]

14–53 Registered rights, Community and national, will for instance, have the patent-like attribute of being enforceable against the world, whereas the French and German systems have till now required proof of copying. The new rights will apply to all designs which are not purely functional, thus carrying the protection a long way into the no-man's land where aesthetic and functional aspects of appearance overlap. This favours the unity of art and function, of which the French have made so much, as against the Italian preference for separability—the requirement of a distinct design element added to improve appearance.[10]

14–54 Registration is envisaged as the standard form of protection for durable designs. As an approach, it will suit the Germans, who currently register far more designs than any other nation.[11] One reason for this is that the level of

---

[6] COM(93) 342 final; Horton [1994] E.I.P.R. 51. An amended version, not making substantive proposals on spare parts, was published on June 22, 1999 (DN: IP/99/407).

[7] Directive 98/71/EC on the Legal Protection of Designs, [1998] O.J. 289/28; to be implemented by October 28, 2001; Speyart [1997] E.I.P.R. 603.

[8] For earlier stages, see the Commission's Green Paper, *The Legal Protection of Industrial Designs* (1991) and the influential draft regulation prepared by the Max Planck Institute, Munich, for which see (1991) 22 I.I.C. 523.

[9] As with trade marks, harmonisation of national laws has preceded enactment of the Community right. There is an element of political persuasion involved, but equally the member states must have time to adapt their own laws, where necessary. The Community Design Reg. has in any case to secure the unanimity required by enactment under the E.U. Treaty, Art. 235; see the E.C.J.'s *Opinion 1/94* [1994] I E.C.R. 5267.

[10] See further para. 14–56, below.

[11] The U.K. has about 8,000 registrations a year, Italy a tenth of that, France double and Germany twelvefold: *cf.* Phillips [1993] E.I.P.R. 431. An E.C. move towards registration might also aid the international community by increasing participation in the Hague Agreement for the International Deposit of Industrial Designs (1925). To this the U.K. has never been party. A new version is about to be agreed. See generally, Fryer (1992) 74 JPTOS 923, (1994) 76 JPTOS 91.

originality required for the copyrighting of works of applied art in that country is considerable.[12] As a campaign to that end, it suffers from the disability that other states have not been persuaded to give up types of protection which they currently apply to industrial designs, particularly on an informal basis. The British have only recently arrived at their dual copyright and unregistered design right scheme and are still testing its viability. Much more prominently, the French have insisted on continuing their wide use of artistic copyright to give protection in the industrial design sphere. The European design proposals, vaunted for their unifying effect, will actually leave in place strategic differences between Member States over the balance of formal and informal rights.[13] The consequences are all too likely to be a muddle, gradually resolved at the expense of users of the various systems.

Because the Directive is now enacted, much of the detail of the Community design system must be regarded as settled, even though a revision of the draft Regulation remains to be done.[14] The main features of the overall scheme are as follows.

(1) Subject-matter

The registered design right will protect the appearance[15] of any product, **14–55** that is any industrial or handicraft item, including parts.[16] Where a designed element is intended as part of a more complex product, it can be protected only if the design remains visible in the normal end use. Since it is not intended that the Community design should be registered for particular products individually,[17] this may produce great uncertainty.

(2) Novelty and individuality

As a condition, the design must be both new and of "individual character" **14–56** when compared with prior art,[18] unless it could not have reasonably become known to relevant Community business circles before the priority date.[19]

---

[12] It may be compared to the scrupulous attitude which the House of Lords took to the copyright of works of artistic craftsmanship in *Hensher* (paras 10–17—10–21, above); but not, of course, to drawings, engravings, sculptures, etc. (para. 14–21, above).

[13] Accordingly, they are severely criticised by Cohen Jehoram [1994] E.I.P.R. 514. See further, para. 14–66, below.

[14] Accordingly references here are mainly to provisions in the Directive above, n. 91.

[15] Design Dir., Art. 1, Recs. 11, 12. This extends to features of the lines, contours, colours, shape and/or materials of the product itself and/or its ornamentation"—wider than the present British law in such matters as colour and materials.

[16] Also including packaging, get-up, graphic symbols and typographic typefaces, but excluding computer programs. No exception is admitted for designs of primarily literary or artistic character (books, cards, sculptures, etc.), even though they will also have copyright against copyists: *cf.* para. 14–12, above. As to the admission of parts, *cf.* para. 14–13, above.

[17] *cf.* the British registration system, para. 14–09, above. Note also that the system is not tied to industrial production of a minimum number of articles.

[18] Designs Dir., Arts. 3–5.

[19] *ibid.*, Art. 6(1). This is a difficult evaluative idea, generally avoided in industrial property rules on novelty.

For there to be "individual character", the informed user must receive a different overall impression from what is already known. There will be a one-year grace period for designs published by the applicant or with his consent (during which the informal Community right will apply against copying).[20] This will afford a much needed opportunity to give designs some commercial exposure before making application to protect them by registration.

(3) Exclusions

14–57 Designs will be excluded if dictated solely by technical function[21]; if they fall within a "must fit" exception[22]; or are rude.[23] It will be recalled that the British registered design is subject to a "must match" as well as a "technical function" exclusion; and that the unregistered design right is excluded in both "must fit" and "must match" cases.[24] On present reckoning, the right under the Directive encompasses a range of designs which ends somewhere between the present British registered and unregistered design rights. The "must fit" exception is here narrowly confined to features "which must necessarily be reproduced in the exact form and dimensions" in order to fit for functional purposes.

These exceptions have been highly controversial, mainly because of the commercial antipathies between automobile manufacturers and replacement part producers. The community institutions accordingly imposed various formulae for further modifying the normal effect of registration. The first model for these proposals was the compulsory licence in the British UDR.[25] At one stage, the Draft Directive proposed such licence throughout the life of the design. In the event, political division has been so vociferous that the whole issue has been left out of the Directive. Instead member states' laws concerning "must match" considerations must either be maintained or else made more favourable to spare parts producers.[26] The Commission is to study the matter at some leisure and make recommendations.[27] During this period the Community Design proposal will have to reach its own resolution of the issue. Such a unitary scheme cannot be left to produce differing effects between one member state and another.

---

[20] Designs Dir., Art. 6(2); and see below, para. 14–63.
[21] Art. 7(1) This does not mean that an aesthetic quality must be shown, but excludes "mechanical fittings": Designs Dir., Rec. 14—a highly opaque distinction.
[22] Designs Dir. Art. 7(2). Toy-makers have adroitly secured a complete exception for multiple assembly connectors in modular systems, such as "lego" bricks: see Art. 7(3).
[23] The standard exception on grounds of public policy or morality: Art. 8.
[24] See above, paras 14–09 *et seq.*, 14–33.
[25] Above, para. 14–44.
[26] Designs Dir., Art. 14, and see the apology in Rec. 19.
[27] It must report by 2004 and make any recommendations for reform within a year thereafter: Art. 18.

(4) Duration

The rights will last (as now in the United Kingdom) for five year periods, **14–58** renewable up to 25 years in total.[28]

(5) Infringement

The design will be infringed by unauthorised use of any product which **14–59** incorporates the design: there is no limitation to specified articles, though some designs will inherently be limited to certain types of object. The basic test of infringement is defined principally in the negative: it does not cover a design which would produce on the informed user a different overall impression, taking into account the designer's degree of freedom in developing his design.[29]

(6) Scope

The wrongful acts include in particular: making, offering or marketing the **14–60** product; or importing, exporting or stocking the product for those pur-poses. The exhaustion rule, couched in terms of consent to marketing within the Community, is internal in effect and intended to imply that importing of "parallel" goods from outside that territory requires a licence.[30]

(7) Exceptions

There will be a set of exceptions, generally similar to the exceptions to **14–61** patent infringement in the CPC, but adding an exception for "fair" and not unduly prejudicial citations and teaching.[31]

(8) Property issues

For the Community design, there will be rules on ownership and dealing **14–62** which bear a family resemblance to provisions in the CPC and the CTM Regulation. First ownership of the right is presumptively in an employer, but not in a commissioner. Applications will be made to the Office for the Harmonisation of the Internal Market (OHIM, in Alicante) which is also handling CTMs. Jurisdiction over issues of validity, infringement and other matters will also follow the pattern for the CTM.

(9) Informal right

A design holder may well wish to launch the design during the one-year **14–63** grace period, and then apply for registration. Under the current Draft of the Community Design Regulation there will be a Community law right to

---

[28] Designs Dir., Art. 10.
[29] *ibid.*, Art. 9, Rec. 13.
[30] *ibid.*, Arts. 12, 15.
[31] *ibid.*, Art. 13; and see para. 6–11, above.

prevent copying and consequential exploitation. It will be a right which stems from creating the design, not from any deposit or registration. It will accordingly last for three years from first legitimate marketing of products bearing the design.[32] In the United Kingdom, it needs to be asked how such a limited informal right would operate in relation to (unregistered) Design Right. The conjuncture is undoubtedly perplexing.[33]

(10) Open qualification

14–64 The Regulation will impose no qualification requirements on those who seek either form of Community law protection. Non-Community nationals will contrast this with the strict reciprocity that is a condition of British unregistered design right: the latter was introduced in the hope of persuading other countries to create an equivalent right. The ploy must be regarded as a failure.

(11) Summary

14–65 To summarise: the E.C. aspires to create a system in which the major protection for designs will be a unitary registered right. To make this prospect as attractive as possible, the proposed system allows a grace period for trying out designs in public, and the preliminary three-year informal right against copying of the design. The Community design will get rid of many of the constraints in national systems, such as (in the British) the need to register separately for different articles and the exclusion of non-separate parts. Because it gives a legal monopoly good against independent devisers, the right is limited by requirements not only of novelty but also of "individual character".

Exclusions for technical character and "must-fit" have had to be admitted but they may be of very limited scope, leading in practice to overlap with national systems of petty patents and utility models as well as with the territory reserved for the British unregistered design right. Given this breadth, the failure to settle the question of spare parts makes the harmonisation noticeably incomplete. The political arguments about this remain so intense that unless they are settled, they may spoil the whole outcome.[34]

14–66 There will, moreover, continue to be competing modes of protection (and, in consequence, the temptation to offer everything practicable to registrants). The national registration systems for designs must adopt the

---

[32] See COM(93) 342 final, Arts 12, 20.

[33] See Cornish in Kabel and Mom (eds.), *Intellectual Property and Information Law* (1998), p. 253.

[34] The arguments emanate almost entirely from the automobile industry: see Beier (1994) 25 I.I.C. 840. See also Posner, Int. Bus. Lawyer (March, 1994) 108; Holden, *ibid.*, 116.

"level playing field" set by the Directive's substantive provisions. It remains for Member States to determine how far they bring procedural and administrative rules into line. According to country, there may also be protection for some designs from "second-tier" rights in technical novelties (as already mentioned), from artistic copyright and from trade mark law which has been extended to cover get-up and shapes, which are distinctive of the mark-owner.[35]

One effect of this competition will be pressure to subsidise the Community registration system: application and renewal fees are likely to be pared. So long, however, as copyright and registered design protection remains open, many design holders may prefer to rely upon one or other. The Community system could well attract only a modicum of interest; and in turn that may lead to a Community witch-hunt against informal modes of protection.[36] Those who consider that the latter are useful instruments in setting the bounds of unacceptable design copying should prepare to defend them.

The case in favour of these informal rights is primarily that they arise out of creativity, not out of state grant; and that accordingly they are limited in scope to copying, an activity which of its nature is more readily to be condemned than that of independent creation. The case against them is that there is no official record of their subject-matter which industry can consult, and there is no preliminary monitoring of validity. There is a natural lobby in favour of registration systems formed by the professionals engaged in processing applications. It is the counter case which may get less attention than it deserves.

One particular question for the British concerns the future of unre- **14–67** gistered design right. This will never attract the world interest it deserves, so long as strict reciprocity applies and designers from the United States, most of the Commonwealth and the Pacific Rim are all excluded. The government should accept that this right falls within the Paris Convention and accordingly extend national treatment to applicants from Convention countries. It would then offer time-limited "industrial" copyright to designs for artistic works and to surface decoration; beyond this it will offer unregistered design right, with its additional restrictions, to aspects of shape and configuration. It would thus offer informal protection which is somewhat more wide-ranging as to subject-matter, but (when it comes to design right) will be more limited in duration and will be subjected to compulsory licensing. It would become an attractive precedent for Europe in general.

---

[35] Below, paras 17–41ff.
[36] In its final form, the Directive allows copyright provision to continue to the extent that national law allows. This solution is no longer said to continue only "pending further harmonisation". Designs Dir., Art. 17; cf. Draft Reg. COM(83) 342, Art. 100 (2).

Part V

TRADE MARKS AND NAMES

CHAPTER 15

COMPETITOR AND CONSUMER

1. UNDERLYING THEMES

This Part focuses attention upon rights long associated with intellectual **15–01** property, which nevertheless are concerned with methods of promoting and selling goods and services. Once more the purpose of legal intervention is to give protection to information. But trade marks, names and other such symbols have a less finite character than the information protected by patents, copyright and confidence. In an economy where most goods and services come from competing enterprises, trade mark owners typically use their marks to distinguish their products and services from others on offer. Their hope is that this will trigger off an association in consumers' minds between origin and good value. But what consumers understand by the cypher depends on their previous knowledge and experience.

Where brands are well-established—and that today means supporting actual trade with heavy and continuous advertising across regions or continents—their valuation as assets will run into billions of pounds.[1] Trade marks and names are accordingly quite as significant in economic terms as patents and copyright; and their impact across industry is far wider.

Two themes underlie the detailed law that is the subject of the following **15–02** chapters. The first was raised in Chapter 1[2] and need not be dwelt upon at length at this point. It is the question, how far should traders be invested with power to sue upon the unfair business practices of their competitors? We have already noticed the traditional British reluctance to do more than give protection against promotional tactics that will harm one rival in particular, for instance by passing off goods as his. In varying degrees, the unfair competition laws of most European states go further, and the differences have noticeable repercussions when it comes to the "Europeanisation" of specific regimes of intellectual property protection.

The most directly relevant of those regimes concerns the registration of trade marks. European registration systems are now being substantially reshaped by the introduction of a unitary mark for the whole E.C. (giving rise

---

[1] Valuing brands as assets is now an important financial service, not least in take-over battles: for methods, see Smith [1990] E.I.P.R. 159.
[2] See paras 1–13 *et seq.*, above

to a Community Trade Mark or "CTM"). At the same time the national systems of registration—which continue as alternatives to the CTM—are being substantially harmonised by a Directive.[3] Even before the creation of this dual system, some progress had been made towards a harmonised law of unfair competition. There is already in existence a harmonisation Directive on Misleading Advertising; and proposals are being promoted for a complementary Directive on comparative advertising.[4]

As a consequence of all the present activity, there will be renewed concern over unfair competition law as a framework for the whole of intellectual property. What its outcome will be is hard to predict. Until it occurs, however, there will be an underlying disparity between the different European approaches, which is all too easily ignored. Some systems—such as the French and Belgian—provide that, in the great bulk of cases, marks must be registered if they are to enjoy legal protection. There is no secondary, cumulative form of action to protect aspects of an actual reputation built up in trade. Such an all-or-nothing approach operates to give industry advance information about what is and what is not protected. Among its disadvantages it encourages both legislatures and courts to expand the outer peripheries of registration and thereby to give early entrants rights which they may not have to work very hard to maintain.[5] A passing-off approach allows for a more discriminating balance of interests between first user and subsequent, perfectly honest entrants. It turns on the current facts of actual goodwill in trade; and the remedies granted can be limited in various ways.[6]

15–03 The second basic theme concerns the uses to which trade marks are put and the scope of legal protection that ought in consequence to be accorded to them. Over the last century these uses have increased in diversity, which has raised conflicts with policies directed towards the welfare of consumers. The historical section which follows will provide some introduction to the interplay between business demand and legal response in Britain and other countries. Then some attempt will be made to present the controversies surrounding trade mark protection at the present day.

2. HISTORICAL DEVELOPMENT

(1) Judicial protection

15–04 As modern capitalism has grown, the drive to sell products and services by means of some mark, brand or name has invaded more and more fields. Some foods and a few other staples are still frequently sold to the consumer

---

[3] See Chap. 17, below.

[4] See Council Directive 84/450: [1984] OJ L250/17; Proposed Directive COM(94) 151 final—COD 343; See also Schricker (1990) 21 I.I.C. 620; (1991) 22 I.I.C. 788; and also paras 16–16–56, 17–104—17–107, below.

[5] They must not fail to use it for five years or allow it to become generic in the trade: paras 17–69—17–75, below.

[6] See further, para. 16–12, below.

without branding, but the tendency is consistently towards labelling to indicate source.[7] Before industrialisation, there were, of course, instances of traders or trader-groups who deployed marks of various kinds to distinguish their products. The hallmarks of goldsmiths and silversmiths and the marks of Sheffield cutlers are English examples which have survived as distinct systems.[8] But the demand for general legal protection against unfair imitation of marks and names is a product of the commercial revolution that followed upon factory production and the growth of canals and railways. That demand has swelled immensely with the development of modern advertising and large-scale retailing. Most advertising teaches the consumer to buy by product mark or house name and it keeps reiterating its message in the hope of stopping buyers from defecting to rivals. Trade marks and names have become nothing more nor less than the fundament of most market-place competition.

In the English case law demands for legal protection against the **15–05** imitation of marks and names were being made and acceded to from the early years of industrialisation. The courts of equity took the lead because plaintiffs wanted injunctions. They intervened when one trader represented to the public that he was selling the goods or carrying on the business of another.[9] Soon afterwards, similar actions for damages at common law are found, the action on the case for deceit being held to lie at the instance of a competitor.[10]

That extension bore its own limitation, for deceit required proof of deliberate fraud.[11] The courts of equity, however, being concerned primarily with a forward-looking remedy, did not feel the same constraint. Impelled by their sense of the injury that could be caused by passing off, they would enjoin even a defendant who had adopted the mark or name in all innocence: the goodwill at risk was easily characterised as "property", the deception of the public was in itself "fraud".[12] Other potential limitations

---

[7] Even the "corner-shop" may now be run under a business name sufficiently impersonal that, if a rival copies it for his business, the public may think that a new branch has been opened.

[8] British hallmarks are now regulated by the Hallmarking Act 1973. A proposal for an E.C. hallmarking system has been abandoned. For cutlers' marks, see para. 17–03, n. 10, below; and for the history, see Schechter (n. 9, below), Chap. 5; Wadlow (para. 16–01, n. 1, below), para. 9–30.

[9] The possibility of such an action seems recognised by Lord Hardwicke L.C. in *Blanchard v. Hill* (1742) 2 Atk. 485. The older, obscure case at common law, *Southern v. How* (1618) Popham 144, is treated as allowing an action on the case for a fraudulent design "to put off bad cloths . . . or to draw away customers from another clothier" (*i.e.* a competitor's, as well as a consumer's, action); as indeed it was: see J.H. Baker, *Introduction to English Legal History* (3rd ed., 1990) p. 522. Thereafter see *Hogg v. Kirby* (1803) 8 Ves. 215; *cf. Longman v. Winchester* (1809) 16 Ves. Jun. 269; *Crutwell v. Lye* (1810) 17 Ves. Jun. 335. See generally Schechter, *The Historical Foundations of the Law Relating to Trade Marks* (1925), Chap. 6; Behrendt (1961) 51 T.M.R. 853; McClure (1979) 69 T.M.R. 305.

[10] *Sykes v. Sykes* (1824) 3 B. & C. 541 (the basic principle appears already to be established); *Blofeld v. Payne* (1833) 4 B. & Ad. 410.

[11] See *Pasley v. Freeman* (1789) 3 T.R. 51; *Derry v. Peek* (1889) 14 App. Cas. 337, HL.

[12] *Millington v. Fox* (1838) 3 My. & Cr. 338; *Edelsten v. Edelsten* (1863) 4 De G.J. & S. 185. But for the adventures of "property" in this subject-matter, see paras 16–01—16–06, below.

were by-passed: the common law courts had no scruple in holding it actionable for a manufacturer to supply a retailer with "the instruments of fraud"[13]; or for one trader to pass off goods as another's even if they were not of inferior quality.[14] Westbury as Lord Chancellor insisted that a mark or name was protectable even though the public did not know the producer as such but used the connection with a trade source simply as a sign of quality.[15]

15–06 By the 1850s, public agitation about the extent to which food, drugs and other commodities were sold in an adulterated state was beginning to run high. It mixed with the complaints of established competitors that they were being undercut by such practices, by cheap imports that did not declare what they were and by the false imitation of brands, marks and names.[16] To some extent, purchasers found a market remedy—by lending their custom to the new retailing co-operatives.[17] But there were also calls on their behalf for legal protection, the criminal law being envisaged as the principal machinery.[18]

Important commercial interests, however, wanted Britain to adopt a system of registering trade marks—after the model, for instance, of the French law of 1857.[19] In part their concern was domestic. The passing-off action, though useful, depended on proving in each case that the plaintiff had a trade reputation with the public. That could sometimes be costly and laborious. If there were a register, the issue could be reduced to the question: was the defendant imitating the mark in a manner liable to deceive? But in part it was from international trade that the demand arose. Prussian and American counterfeiters were said to be passing off their own "Manchester" textiles and "Sheffield" cutlery in various parts of the world.[20] The hope of stopping foreign imitations of British marks seemed to lie in also establishing a register. Mutual protection of foreigners' marks in Britain could then be offered as a *quid pro quo*.

15–07 There was considerable "liberal" suspicion of this idea for a new property right: a first entrant might be able to appropriate ways of marking his goods that could pose difficulties for later competitors. The Merchandise Marks Act 1862, which included "forging a trade mark" prominently amongst its prohibitions on the false marking of goods, was solely a criminal statute, and deliberately so.[21] A pattern of considerable moment was thus estab-

---

[13] *Sykes v. Sykes* (n. 10, above).
[14] *Blofeld v. Payne* (n. 10, above).
[15] *Hall v. Barrows* (1863) 4 De G.J. & S. 150 at 157.
[16] See, *e.g.* E. W. Stieb, *Drug Adulteration* (1966), Chaps 8–11.
[17] See, *e.g.* G. D. H. Cole, *A Century of Co-operation* (1945); C. R. Fay, *Co-operation at Home and Abroad* (5th ed., 1948).
[18] One record of this political activity is the Report of the Trade Marks Bill Select Committee PP 1862 (212) XII.
[19] For this step and its consequences in French trade-mark law, see Beier (1975) 6 I.I.C. 285 at 294–298.
[20] See the many complaints in evidence to the 1862 Committee (n. 18, above).
[21] See the Report of the 1862 Committee (n. 18, above), p. vii.

lished: the criminal law was to provide the general machinery against misdescription of wares. The normal principle that any citizen might prosecute was to apply—indeed in the 1862 Act it was encouraged by the old device of sharing the penalty between prosecutor and Crown. But competitors were not to have the weaponry of civil suits to deal with a wide range of misleading trade descriptions. The Merchandise Marks legislation grew in completeness with a revised statute of 1887. This was to continue in force (with amendments) until the Trade Descriptions Act of 1968.[22] But its actual enforcement was to remain extremely patchy. For unlike the neighbouring legislation on food and drugs and weights and measures, local authorities were not placed under any duty to provide inspectors and others who would see to observance. In practice competitors showed little interest in putting their resources to the task.[23]

(2) The Trade Marks Register

Traders kept up pressure to have the protection of trade marks made more **15–08** secure. In 1875 the campaign for a registration system succeeded so far as marks for goods were concerned.[24] But the new system acquired from the start a number of characteristics which stamped it as a special privilege conceded with some misgiving:

(1) for the first 30 years of the register's operation, only a limited range of symbols might be registered as trade marks[25];
(2) registration was not simply a matter of deposit but was subject to an official examination and open to opposition by third parties after advertisement of the application;
(3) not only prior registrations but also prior use of the same mark or one deceptively similar would prevent registration.

There was, however, no obligation to use the mark before registering it. This gave businessmen an important measure of security when launching a new product.

---

[22] Enacted in the wake of the Final Report of the Malony Committee on Consumer Protection (Cmnd. 1781, 1962).

[23] Occasional prosecutions reached the law reports, *e.g.* where a name of geographical origin was in issue: see *e.g. Holmes v. Pipers* [1914] 1 K.B. 57; *Corke v. Pipers*, referred to in *Vine Products v. Mackenzie* [1969] R.P.C. 1 at 18–19. The failure of criminal proceedings against the importers of "Spanish Champagne" (see *Bollinger v. Costa Brava Co. Ltd* [1961] R.P.C. 116 at 119) underlines the standard of proof required. For subsequent developments, see para. 16–38, below.

[24] Trade Marks Registration Act 1875; amended in 1876 and 1877 and then incorporated into the Patents, Designs and Trade Marks Act 1883.

[25] In 1875, these were: name of individual or firm specially printed, etc., written signature, distinctive device, mark, heading, label or ticket, to which certain other matter might be added: see s. 10, slightly expanded in the 1883 and 1888 Patents, Designs and Trade Marks Acts.

For a time it was not clear whether the registrable types of mark could be protected only after registration.[26] But the judges were sympathetic to the view that goodwill acquired through actual trading should have the first call on legal protection. Common law and equity were held still to give relief against passing off, even if it was effected through imitating a mark that might have been registered.[27] The methods of protection became cumulative, not alternative.

15–09   As quite recent developments in France and the Benelux countries have shown,[28] trade mark registration systems may work on different premises: registration may be allowed without any substantive examination for conflicting interests beforehand; and as a corollary protection is made conditional upon registration, so that industry has an official record of all marks already in existence. The British system has continued to build upon its Victorian foundations. The cumulative relation between common law and statutory rights and the existence of a pre-grant examination allowed the categories of registrable marks to be expanded. By the Act of 1905, where there was some inherent objection to a mark (particularly because, being a word, it had some other meaning), this might be overcome upon proof of sufficient use as a trade mark to distinguish the origin of goods.[29] Furthermore in 1919 the register was divided into Parts A and B in order that certain marks could be given not quite complete protection before they had been used enough to overcome all doubts.[30] But for a long period service marks were not brought into the system, thus leaving one whole field exclusively to common law protection.

The 1905 Act tied the statutory privilege to actual trading by making non-use for the previous five years a ground upon which a person with an interest could have a mark removed from the register.[31] In a different way, the courts insisted on the same connection: under the 1905 Act, they treated registration as expungeable if the mark had been licensed[32]; for that rendered obscure whether the mark indicated a connection in trade with the registered proprietor or the licensee. They would not consider the registered right as a discrete part of the trader's property which might be dealt with by him without reference to the public's understanding of its meaning.

15–10   The ever-increasing scale of business organisation in the twentieth century led to many shifts in trading practice. The spread of production, the

---

[26] The 1875 Act, s. 1 (and its amendments in 1876) provided that "proceedings to prevent the infringement of any trade mark" should not be brought unless the mark was registered.

[27] See especially *Great Tower v. Langford* (1888) 5 R.P.C. 66; *Faulder v. Rushton* (1903) 20 R.P.C. 477, CA. In the U.S.A. the existence of common law rights alongside the federal system of registration has also been important, though with somewhat different consequences: see McCarthy, *Trade Marks and Unfair Competition* (3rd ed.), Chap. 1.

[28] For which see Beier (n. 19, above) at 297–298.

[29] On this see further, paras 17–17 *et seq.*, below.

[30] A scheme given up in the 1994 Act.

[31] For the present law, see paras 17–69 *et seq.*, below.

[32] See paras 17–12 *et seq.*, below.

growth of a popular press with its immense prospects for advertising, the increase of trans-national business in successful products and the consequent need to shield high-priced markets against parallel imports from elsewhere were all characteristics of the inter-war years. Brand advertising on a large scale by manufacturers replaced goodwill that was principally associated with retail outlets, and this only increased the commercial significance of the trade marks around which it revolved. There was considerable pressure to be able to license and assign marks more freely than was possible under the British system. This stemmed from the spread of corporate groupings under parent holding companies and the increase in licensing of technology and business "packages". One particular advantage, it was hoped, was that, if the same trade mark was in legally distinct ownership in different countries, the rights could be employed to deter parallel importing.[33] An elaborate and not very satisfactory compromise over assignment and licensing was embodied in the Trade Marks Act 1938,[34] the Act which would carry the law through to its Europeanisation in 1994.

New advertising techniques also led to pressure on the registration **15–11** system to compensate for the absence of a general unfair competition law. The 1938 Act contained two concessions in this direction.[35] Very well-known trade marks became registrable "defensively" for goods in which the owner did not trade, in the hope of preventing others from annexing any of their notoriety. But the judges treated this arrangement coldly and it had little impact.[36] Owners of Part A trade marks were also enabled to object to comparative advertising and similar practices which attempted to take the benefit of the advertising without paying for it. Again, some judges found the expansion of the law unpalatable and the provision had an uncertain effect.[37]

In 1974, the Mathys Departmental Committee reported on the British **15–12** system under the 1938 Act in terms of general satisfaction with the British way of doing things.[38] The most significant proposal was to admit service marks onto the register; even that took a decade to implement.[39] But

---

[33] For the fate of this device in recent times, see paras 17–76—17–79, below.

[34] See paras 17–13, 17–15, below.

[35] Both following recommendations of the Goschen Committee (Cmd. 4568, 1934), paras 73–77, 184–185.

[36] See esp. *Ferodo's Application* (1945) 65 R.P.C. 111; and *Eastex's Application* (1947) 64 R.P.C. 142. Between 1938 and 1974 only 100 defensive registrations succeeded and the Mathys Committee (Cmnd. 5601, 1974), para. 102, recommended the abandonment of this special form of registration. In the 1994 Act this has come about because of a broader approach to "dilution": see paras 17–100—17–102, below.

[37] See para. 17–83, below.

[38] Cmnd. 5601, 1974, esp. para. 46.

[39] Service marks became registrable under the Trade Marks Amendment Act 1984 (with addenda in 1986); the form of this legislation, introducing separate Acts for goods and service marks, was unduly elaborate and sometimes inconsistent. Various other Mathys recommendations find a place in the "new deal" of 1994.

doubts soon enough began to surface. Their cause arose mainly from the use of marks in international, rather than domestic, trade. Trans-national business wants simple, certain and cheap registration without having to apply country by country using systems encrusted with individual idio-syncrasies. Within the European Community, a unitary mark for a single market became an attractive aim. On the world scene, new initiatives to secure an international system for registration were proposed.

As a result, twenty years after Mathys, basic changes have been intro-duced into United Kingdom law by the Trade Marks Act 1994.[40] This establishes the new Community order for trade mark registration. At the same time it allows access to international registration through the so-called Madrid Protocol. The background to these important changes is to be found in developments on both the international and the E.C. scenes.

(3) Trade marks in world trade

(a) *International agreements*

15–13 The case for a United Kingdom registration system succeeded largely because of the needs of British exporters. It had proved difficult to negotiate bilateral arrangements with other countries when their nationals could not be offered the protection of a registered right in Britain.[41] The 1875 Act gave British manufacturers the increasingly important hope of protection abroad, and there was then no difficulty in supporting the provisions on trade marks in the Paris Convention on Industrial Property of 1883. These were modest, consisting mainly of the principle of "national treatment",[42] and a short period of priority stemming from the filing of a first application in one Member State,[43] and an acknowledgment of the independence both of filing and registration in each country.[44]

At no stage has the Paris Convention itself provided any form of international application for registration in a number of countries. But as

---

[40] The Government's intentions were indicated in the White Paper, Reform of Trade Marks Law (Cm. 1203, 1990).
[41] See Schechter (n. 9, above) at 140.
[42] See para. 1–31, above.
[43] For international priority and trade mark applications, see para. 17–04, below. The Paris Convention now contains a number of other guarantees. The following must be protected: service marks, collective marks, business names, national emblems, official signs, hallmarks, etc. (Arts 6*ter*, 6*sexies*; 7*bis*, 8); marks well-known in a country through their international reputation (Art 6*bis*, see para. 16–17, below); and competitors against acts of unfair competition (Art. 10*bis*, see paras 15–19, 15–20, below). There are provisions on infringing imports, remedies and the right to sue (Arts 9, 10*ter*).
[44] There is no need to file first in a country of origin, validity does not depend on that in a country of origin (*cf.* n. 50, below), and nor does renewal (Art. 6). However registration in a country of origin restricts the objections which may be raised in other countries to those listed in Art. 6*quinquies* B: third party rights, lack of distinctiveness, objections on grounds of morality and public order and unfair competition; see further, below, para. 17–51.

early as 1891, some Paris participants were prepared to take this step in the subsidiary Madrid Agreement.[45] This allows an applicant who has registered a mark in his home or business country to deposit an international registration with an international office (now WIPO). The mark will then be registered in each other Member State designated by the applicant, unless that state raises an objection, under its national law, within 12 months. Independent national trade marks are thus procured, subject, in the original Madrid Agreement, to the qualification that if the home registration is invalidated within five years, all the international registrations fall victim to this "central attack".

For countries such as the United Kingdom, which have a full examina- **15–14** tion of applications, the Madrid Agreement in its original form has remained unattractive. It gives advantages to those with easier access to their home registers (notably if they have a simple deposit system); and as a consequence its fee structure has been unacceptable.[46] In 1989, however, a Protocol to Madrid was negotiated which offered an alternative method of using the Madrid Scheme. This Protocol has attracted British approval and is being given effect under the 1994 Act.[47] The old Madrid countries remain happy with their original arrangement, and some bravura drafting has been necessary in order to continue the original arrangements between them, while giving the Protocol effect between the old set and the new joiners.

The relaxations which the Protocol admits include the following: international registration can proceed from a home application, rather than a home registration.[48] The fee basis allows countries with full examining offices to receive charges reflecting the work which they do.[49] The hotly contested principle of central attack is modified: if the original registration in the home country is held invalid within five years, and the international

---

[45] Madrid Agreement concerning the International Registration of Marks. At the same time a second Madrid Agreement was also reached, covering the Repression of False or Deceptive Indications of Source of Goods (1891, revised 1911, 1934, 1958; additional act, 1967) to which the U.K. has not become a party: see App. 2, para. A2–01, below.

  The main participants in the original Madrid Agreement have been the non-Nordic countries of continental Europe and certain North African states.

[46] From time to time there have been attempts to bring more of the world's industrial countries into an international application scheme. Notably a Trademark Registration Treaty (WIPO) reached final form in 1974, but in the event attracted few signatories and became a lost cause. The Trademark Law Treaty (WIPO), adopted on October 27, 1994, is a more modest arrangement, designed to secure greater homogeneity in national procedures for trademark applications, changes of ownership and renewals. It contains some quite significant restraints on national legislation which might otherwise create special difficulties for foreign enterprises—for instance, regarding the need to produce evidence of actual use (see esp. Arts 3(7), 11(4), 13(4)).

[47] The expanded Madrid system is likely to be in operation in 1996. In addition to Britain, it is hoped to attract into it the Nordic countries, Ireland, Japan and possibly even the U.S. See Kunze [1994] E.I.P.R. 223.

[48] For what constitutes a sufficient domestic basis, see the Madrid Agreement, Art. 1; and for the six-month Paris Convention priority, see Art. 4(2).

[49] Madrid Protocol, Art. 8.

registration falls in consequence, conversion into national applications of equivalent priority date may occur.[50] And the time limit within which a country may raise its own objections to an international application is 18 months, with possibility of extension to take account of opposition proceedings.[51]

15–15   The TRIPS Agreement imposes an obligation on its participant states to apply the Paris Convention standards relating to trade marks.[52] It also cross-refers to those provisions at a number of points, supplements some of them in significant respects and imposes its own obligations in addition. Thus in adopting a broad definition of the signs capable of being marks, it requires trade mark registration to extend to marks for services.[53]

It strikes out on its own in defining the right in a registered mark: this is the exclusive right to prevent unauthorised third parties from using in the course of trade identical or similar signs for goods or services which are identical or similar to those in respect of which the mark is registered and there is a likelihood of confusion; this likelihood will be presumed where both mark and goods or services are identical.[54] As well as this, TRIPS extends the Paris Convention provision on the protection of well-known marks to service marks and to cases of dilution by use for different goods and services where that use is damaging.[55]

Use may not be made an automatic precondition of registration, though it is to be taken into account in assessing distinctiveness.[56] Removal for non-use can occur only after a period of at least three years.[57] The term of a grant before renewal of a registration must be at least seven years.[58]

While it is proper to require the use of a house mark in addition to a product mark, other incumbrances, such as use with another trademark, use in a special form or use in an manner detrimental to its capacity to distinguish, are forbidden, as is compulsory licensing.[59] Assignments, moreover, are to be permitted with or without the transfer of the related business.[60] Developing countries have sometimes sought to impose trade mark curbs with a view to controlling technology transfers involving trans-

---

[50] Madrid Protocol, Art. 9*quinquies*.

[51] *ibid.*, Art. 5. See para. 17–02, below.

[52] TRIPS, Art. 2(1).

[53] *ibid.*, Art. 15.

[54] *ibid.*, Art. 16(1). This does not go as far as the provisions in the new E.C. law: paras 17–87 *et seq.*, below.

[55] *ibid.*, Art 16.

[56] *ibid.*, 15(1), (3); registration is not to be refused on the ground that the mark has not been used for the first three years after the application date. On the other hand, the mark has to be published and an opportunity for opposition afforded: Art. 15(5).

[57] *ibid.*, Art. 19.

[58] *ibid.*, Art. 18. Renewals must be allowed indefinitely.

[59] Such licensing would seem to conflict with the prime object of marking, which is to indicate source connections. But it offers a remedy for monopolistic practices, which has tempted even U.S. antitrust jurisdictions.

[60] TRIPS, Arts 20, 21.

national corporations. These hopes have largely proved vain and have been curtailed or abandoned. TRIPS will help to bury them.

(b) *The Community mark and the E.C. Directive*[61]

The Mathys Committee reported shortly after the United Kingdom joined **15–16** the E.C. Already Community law was beginning to affect the national schemes of protection. It was clear that the Treaty of Rome imposed substantial limitations upon the deployment of trade marks so as to prevent the movement of "parallel" goods from one Member State to another. The European Court of Justice was indeed developing a highly sceptical view of the outreaches of trade mark protection and this led to intense debate.[62] One consequence of the Court's intervention was to revive an earlier proposal for an E.C.-wide mark.[63] This in its turn focused attention on the differing regimes operating in the Member States and posed difficult questions. How would conflicts between marks legitimately used in different parts of the market be resolved? What priority should be given to those who would use Community-wide media to promote their products throughout the whole territory or major parts of it? What registration system was best designed to hold the balance between effectiveness and due respect for competing interests, large and small? What place would remain for the legal protection of marks and names on the basis of use rather than registration, where national law so allowed?

Reaching accord took substantial, but not inordinate, time. As already mentioned, a measure requiring the considerable (but not complete) harmonisation of national laws was enacted in 1988 and has now been given effect in Member States.[64] At the same time preparations are at last under way for the opening of the CTM Register, operating from the Office for the Harmonisation of the Internal Market (Trade Marks and Designs) in Alicante (the CTM Registry for short).[65] It is these cognate E.C. initiatives, together with adherence to the Madrid Protocol, which has called forth the Trade Marks Act 1994, an Act which rewrites much of the form and some of the substance of trade mark law, after the fashion of the Patents Act 1977 in its domain.

---

[61] Kur (1997) 28 I.I.C. 1.
[62] See para. 18–06, below.
[63] A Working Party, chaired by De Haan, had reported in 1964 but this was published only in 1973, once the EPC was complete: see DTI, *Proposed European Trade Mark* (1973). In 1976 a small group of experts produced a Memorandum on the Creation of an EEC Trade Mark (Bull. E.C. Supp. 8/76). In 1980, when the Commission produced its First Draft for a Regulation, it added a Draft Directive which contained some highly contentious provisions to foster the single market concept (see on the two documents, House of Lords, E.C. Select Committee, Report 1982–83, p. 21). Revised drafts followed (Regulation 1984; Directive 1985) before the final enactments (nn. 63, 64, below).
[64] First Directive (December 21, 1988) [1989] O.J. L40/1.
[65] Regulation (December 20, 1993) [1994] O.J. L11/1; Jaffey (1997) 28 I.I.C. 153.

15–17   As with patents, the 1994 Act offers alternative routes by which to apply for trade mark registration, and indeed it confronts the applicant with even more choices. The entrance doors which will soon be open are:

(1)   At the British Registry, to apply for (a) United Kingdom registration in the old way; or (b) United Kingdom registration using the application as a basis for international registration through WIPO in such Madrid Protocol countries as are designated; or (c) following a Madrid application started in another country, international registration of a United Kingdom mark. In all these cases, so far as Britain is concerned, a United Kingdom registration is the object and the rights in it arise under the 1994 Act and are enforceable in British courts.[66]

(2)   At the CTM Registry, to apply for a CTM which is unitary in effect and is enforceable throughout the E.C. in accordance with the terms of the CTM Regulation.[67]

15–18   Business people seeking trade marks will need sophisticated advice. Any judgment on how to proceed will have to balance the appropriate geographical and economic spread for the particular mark (language will be a crucial factor in many cases), the likelihood of objections in various parts of the market and comparative costs. Preliminary private searching will often be required (computerised databases have already revolutionised the possibilities). As the trade mark world in Europe stands poised for change, it is a common expectation that the revamped Madrid system will provide a flexibility that will make it popular, while the Community system, with its built-in requirement of unity, may prove unwieldy. Plainly there is to be a measure of competition which will set at rest some of the sillier niggles of the old national registries. The danger, however, is of a rush to coddle applicants through to registration, regardless of all but the most implacable objections. In the confluence of trade mark laws, we can already sense considerable fluctuations of attitude as the different traditions of Member States wash against each other.

(c) *Unfair competition and consumer protection*

15–19   Over a long period there have been attempts to arrive at a common foundation of unfair competition law as a floor for the Common Market.[68] It is not likely to be laid in the foreseeable future: the job is too intricate. However, in 1978, the E.C. Commission, developing its role in the

---

[66] See paras 17–02 *et seq.*, below.
[67] See para. 17–11, below.
[68] See, in particular, the Max-Planck-Institute volumes, ed. Ulmer, on the legal position in each Member State; Beier (1985) 16 I.I.C. 139; Robertson and Horton [1995] E.I.P.R. 568.

protection of consumers, produced a draft Directive requiring the harmonisation of laws against misleading and unfair advertising.[69] Originally of very considerable scope, it came under sustained attack. The case put by the British advertising industry was that there existed voluntary mechanisms, such as the Advertising Standards Authority,[70] which were better able to achieve results than the compulsory sanction of legal regulation.[71] The actual Directive which emerged was of more modest proportion. In implementing it by regulation in 1988, the United Kingdom government has added to existing legislation on trade descriptions and related matters[72] only in relatively minor ways.

The Director General of Fair Trading is given the duty of considering **15–20** complaints about misleading advertisements in the press and in public generally.[73] In deciding how to act he has to bear in mind the interests involved and the desirability of encouraging control by voluntary bodies.[74] If, upon investigation, he is not satisfied, he may seek an injunction from the High Court against anyone concerned with publication of the advertisements. The court may require such a person to substantiate the accuracy of any factual claim. It may grant the injunction without proof of actual loss or damage and irrespective of the intention or negligence of the person responsible.[75] In the field of broadcasting and cabling, equivalent powers are given to the Independent Television Commission, which may refuse to broadcast an advertisement,[76] and to the Cabling Authority, which may issue a direction not to transmit the advertisement, or to transmit it only in modified form.[77]

What is made clear is that a ground of objection may arise from prejudice to competitors as well as consumers. An advertisement is misleading if in any way (including its presentation) it deceives or is likely to deceive its recipients, so as to affect their economic behaviour or to injure a competitor.[78] The latter have still not been given a general right of civil action against any misleading advertisement, let alone other unfair competition, which is likely to harm them. Only administrative mechanisms have been somewhat strengthened.

---

[69] See Schricker (1977) 8 I.I.C. 185; but *cf.* now (1991) 22 I.I.C. 788 and esp. [1994] GRUR Int. 586, questioning the wisdom of the severe German approach. See further, para. 18–13, below.

[70] See para. 2–24, above.

[71] See HL Select Committee, Report on Misleading Advertising (HL, 1978); but *cf.* Dir.-Gen. of Fair Trading, *Review of the Self-Regulatory System of Advertising Control* (1978), taking a less sanguine view of self-regulation.

[72] See para. 15–07, above.

[73] Control of Misleading Advertisements Regulations 1988, S.I. 1988 No. 915, reg. 4, subject to the exclusions of regs. 3, 4(2).

[74] *ibid.*, reg. 4(3).

[75] *ibid.*, reg. 6. Note also the Director's powers to obtain and disclose information: reg. 7.

[76] *ibid.*, regs. 8, 9.

[77] *ibid.*, regs. 10, 11.

[78] *ibid.*, reg. 2(2).

(d) *Source Indications and other Naming Systems*

15–21 The core consideration in this part is the use of signs and symbols in words, designs, shapes, colours and the like to indicate the trade origin of goods and services. We live today surrounded by systems for indicating specific contacts: telephone numbers, numbers for financial services and state support schemes, names for corporate and unassociated businesses, special welfare schemes, and so on. Ensuring that specific names and addresses remain distinct within some of these systems has been of such crucial importance that they have had to be regulated. An early instance was the hallmarking of gold and silver objects which underpins the value associated with the purity of the metal and the maker's identity. In this century, it was for some 60 years thought necessary to have a register of business names where those names differed from those of the natural or legal persons running the enterprise. Company names are subject to approval by the Registrar, who above all else has been concerned to ensure that identical or very similar names are not adopted by unconnected companies.

Over time it has been possible to ensure that these various systems operate in harness with the protection given to trade marks, names and get-up. Currently, the control over choice of company names is governed by the Companies Act 1985, ss. 26–34. A company which objects on the ground of similarity to its own name or mark must pursue the matter in private litigation. Relief akin to that in passing off will be granted against a deliberate squatter. Thus, anticipating a merger between the pharmaceutical companies, Glaxo and Wellcome, one registrant secured "Glaxowellcome" as a corporate name and in due course demanded £100,000 in order to be bought out. He was compelled by mandatory injunction to surrender the name.[79]

15–22 One conflict, however, which is still in process of resolution, has arisen out of the sudden popularity of Internet domain names.[80] The addressing system of the Internet has not been restricted to numbers, despite the underlying digital procedures. Each item has a numerical Uniform Resource Locator (URL). Yet, at the core of the identification of specific items—whether they are websites, web pages, email addresses or other indicators—full words and abbreviations are used alongside numbers and are popular because of their appeal and memorability.

With e-mail, for instance: on the pivot of the <@> symbol is—to its right—the top level domain (TLD: <usco.com>, <britcorp.co.uk>); and—to its left—the second level domain (SLD: <jasonsmith>, <wrc100>). The TLD identifies the general root system, the SLD the individual addressee. The TLD system has acquired a two-tier complication. First, because it was developed in the U.S. the responsible agency (from 1992–98, the Internet

---

[79] *Glaxo v. Glaxowellcome* [1996] F.S.R. 388.
[80] Bettinger (1997) 28 I.I.C. 508.

Assigned Number Authority (IANA)) admitted American domain names without any geographical suffix, simply on the basis of a rough division of purposes[81]: <.com> for commercial organisations, <.net> for networks, <.org> for other organisations—all of which are available to organisations from any country; plus, for American institutions: <.edu> for education, <.gov> for government, <.int> for international bodies, and <.mil> for the military.

Secondly, there are in other countries assigned agencies which register domain names for their country, as indicated by an additional country code: <.uk>, <.de>, <.fr>, etc.[82]

No matter how similar domain names may appear, in digital terms a **15–23** single symbol difference makes all the difference. Domain name registers have to date been constructed on the basis of first come, first served. Given further that the generic indicators are very general—with <.com> having a special attractiveness—it has been inevitable that misperceptions would arise, particularly once the commercial potential of the Internet began to be realised. Trade marks and names are protected in law in ways which are in some respects more impressionistic and in some respects more precise: a trade mark may not be imitated either exactly or in a manner so similar that it is likely to confuse a significant portion of the public—an imprecise factor. On the other hand, in most cases, the protection is limited to use of the mark in a trade for specified goods or services, and those which are similar. It is possible for one enterprise to use "Prince" as a mark for sports goods and another to have "Prince" for computer services, since it is considered more important to keep choice of marks open than to eliminate cases of any confusion at all at the absolute extremities of possibility. But both may not have <prince.com> as TLDs; the second comer would have to resort to <prinz.com> or <prince.co.uk> or another variant which was still available.[83]

This disparity in objectives leads to two core problems: on the one hand there is the "cybersquatter". He deliberately secures TLDs containing the names or marks of well-known enterprises or other organisations in order to sell them to the latter.[84] On the other hand, there are rival claims between those who each have a genuine reason for wanting a particular TLD: previous trading, geographical connection, personal association and so on. There is great activity—in the United Kingdom, the U.S. and at the European and international levels—to provide a more substantial system

---

[81] This is the generic TLD—gTLD.

[82] The ccTLD. In the U.K. Nominet U.K. Ltd grants <.co.uk>, <.ac.uk>, <.org.uk> and other domain names.

[83] Example based on *Prince v. Price Sports Group* (for which see Osborne [1997] E.I.P.R. 644 at 646). In the actual case, the second applicant for the TLD found itself liable to a threats action for alleged trade mark infringement.

[84] If he, or any third party assignee, were to trade in them, there would often be a breach of trade mark law.

for governing and regulating the Internet. The U.S. government is in the process of passing the basic administration from IANA to the Internet Corporation for Assigned Numbers and Names. As part thereof, there is a strong movement to provide methods of arbitrating conflicts between honest claims to TLDs which conflict either in Internet terms or in trade mark law terms. These difficult policy issues remain to be settled. As for the cybersquatter, like mark and company squatters before him, firm answers have been found to his pretensions—as much in the United Kingdom as elsewhere round the world.[85]

3. The Purpose of Protecting Trade Marks[86]

(1) Trade mark functions

15–24 Trade marks and names perform a variety of economic functions. Discussions of the proper scope for their legal protection often take these functions as a starting point. Let us state them, discuss the economic world which they seek to differentiate, and then return to them as tools in arguments about legal policy.[87]

Three functions of trade marks may be distinguished:

(1) **Origin function**: marks deserve protection so that they may operate as indicators of the trade source from which goods or services come, or are in some other way connected.

(2) **Quality or guarantee function**: marks deserve protection because they symbolise qualities associated by consumers with certain goods or services and guarantee that the goods or services measure up to expectations.

(3) **Investment or advertising function**: marks are cyphers around which investment in the promotion of a product is built and that investment is a value which deserves protection as such, even when there is no abuse arising from misrepresentations either about origin or quality.

(2) Information versus promotion

15–25 Rational judgment and emotional preference intermingle in the myriad choices confronting consumers. In consequence, trade marks become crucial elements in the process of reaching decisions about what to buy.

---

[85] Below, paras 16–27, 17–101.

[86] There is a growing body of literature on the economics of information which pertains to the following discussion. References to it, and an attempt to extract its relevance to the policy issues surrounding trade marks can be found in Cornish and Phillips (1982) 13 I.I.C. 41; Landes and Posner (1987) 30 J.L. & Econ. 265; Economides (1988) 78 T.M.R. 523.

[87] See Schechter (1927) 40 Harv. L.R. 813; Brown (1948) 57 Yale L.J. 1165; Hanak (1975) 65 T.M.R. 318; Shanahan (1982) 72 T.M.R. 233; Akazaki (1990) 72 JPTOS 255; Dreyfuss (1990) 65 Notre Dame L.R. 397; Martino, *Trade Mark Dilution* (1996); Maniatis in Sterling (ed.) *Intellectual Property and Market Freedom* (1997) 63; Spence (1996) 112 L.Q.R. 472.

With the immense growth in the scale of business and the advertising that accompanies it, modern customers rarely have that personal knowledge of suppliers which is the hallmark of a village economy. Even so, their interest in source of supply has not in essence changed. Information about origin is only a means towards an end: their main concern is in the quality of what they are buying.

In the case of some goods, part of that quality may be bound up with source in a specific way: as, for instance, when the goods will need servicing and the manufacturer or supplier is looked to for the service. But in a great many cases source, particularly when indicated by a cypher such as a product mark or get-up, does not have even this significance. What it does is to enable the purchaser to link goods or services to a range of personal expectations about quality which derive from previous dealings, recommendations of others, attractive advertising and so on. Nor should it be forgotten that, however persuasively the advertiser may seek to promote this sort of symbol, it retains a neutral character in one sense: once a consumer learns that he does not want particular goods, the mark, name or get-up becomes a significant warning signal.

It is a basic assumption in a competitive economy that the consumer **15–26** benefits by being able to choose among a wide range in the quality and price of goods and services. But once a range of alternatives is offered, he can choose rationally only if he knows the relevant differences. Acquiring all the appropriate information is in many cases too time-consuming and costly, so risks have to be taken. This is particularly so over qualities that cannot properly be checked or tested before purchase, but have to be taken on trust. How willing a purchaser is to take the risk of buying something unknown in place of something known will depend on many factors: for instance, how satisfied he is with the known, and how serious the consequences will be for him if the unknown turns out unsatisfactory. It is one thing to experiment with a washing powder, but another with a drug or with decaffeinated coffee.

The seller's interest is to emphasise qualities (including price) that **15–27** differentiate his product from those of his competitors. Inevitably, if those differences are in reality slight, he will be tempted to exaggerate them, or to bolster them with appeals to sentiment of one kind or another. There is a strong case for controlling the claims of advertisers in the interests of consumers. The approach may be by persuasion[88] or by legal prohibition. In either case, it will probably aim first to eliminate factual inaccuracies, then points of spurious differentiation and ultimately the more oppressive manipulations of feeling—naked appeals, for instance, to fear or aggression.

---

[88] As in the self-regulation systems so characteristic of British business, such as the Advertising Standards Authority: for which see para. 15–19, above.

15–28   In such laudable pursuits, the continuing importance of being able to distinguish the source of goods and services should not be forgotten. To remove the possibility of differentiation (save for goods that can be tested by inspection) is, indeed, to eliminate the incentive to provide goods of superior quality.[89] If the consumer cannot trust the information that he receives he will tend to buy things of lower quality, although overall he may be less satisfied with the results. He may even feel compelled into extraordinary measures in his own defence. To take an extreme but telling example: developing countries have become alarmed by the high price of pharmaceuticals and the amount of advertising—filled with claims difficult to check—which accompanies their marketing. There has accordingly been a temptation to outlaw the sale of drugs by trade mark. Where this has been tried, however, without at the same time giving the state control over quality in the market, suspicion of the efficacy and genuineness of what is on offer soon runs high. So do black-market prices for products still bearing trustworthy trade marks.[90]

15–29   A law protecting marks, names and get-up accordingly seems unavoidable in a capitalist economy. In various aspects, however, these laws have tended to develop in a manner that may appear to confer power without responsibility. The trade mark owner acquires the all-important right to stop imitations of his indication of source, but his own use is conditioned by few limitations or positive requirements. It is perfectly possible for the public to be taught that a box bearing a particular mark and get-up contains 500 grams of chocolates and then, by discreet expansion of the packaging, to reduce that amount to 475 grams. Customarily the way of providing against such conduct, if it is shown to mislead the public, is to penalise it through criminal laws, such as those in Britain against false and misleading trade descriptions; or to enjoin it through laws on unfair competition (if they extend to such cases).[91]

As part of its quality function, should such a trader be deprived of his trade mark, or refused the right to enforce it? The main consequence of doing so would be to open the door to imitators of the mark,[92] thus compounding the existing confusion by the prospect of other imitators. Moreover, when uncovering the deception had led to adverse publicity, there will then be sectors of the public who want the mark to continue in use in order to know what to avoid.

---

[89] On this, see especially Akerlof (1970) 84 Q.J. Economics 488; Heal (1976) 90 Q.J. Economics 499 (with reply by Akerlof); Shapiro (1983) 98 Q.J. Economics 659.

[90] The country in question was Pakistan: see UNCTAD Secretariat, "The Impact of Trade Marks on the Development Process in Developing Countries" (TD/B/C/, 6A/C3.3, 1977) at 266.

[91] It would of course be possible to include such powers in trade mark statutes, if it were thought important enough to insist upon.

[92] Theoretically, it would be possible to enjoin the misuser from all uses of the mark in future, not just misleading ones. But that would be extreme.

In practice it is difficult to show that conduct of the kind just illustrated is definitely misleading. The qualities indicated by a trade mark are rarely definable with sufficient precision for it to be possible to say that if they are changed there is definite deception. The best hope of securing more reliable and relevant information for the buying public is by specifying the characteristics that must be given in labelling and advertising. Marketing which does not comply with the requirement can then be directly penalised or prohibited. To threaten deprivation of trade mark rights will in practice rarely be of assistance.

(3) Functions and rights

How serviceable, then, is it to distinguish between the origin, quality and **15–30** investment functions of trade marks, when deciding the proper extent of legal protection for them? Among those who seek to justify their position by reference to functions, it soon ·becomes apparent that there is no agreement about what these "functions" are and that disagreements often reflect the underlying commitment of the proponent.

First and foremost, the "origin function" is understood in two quite different ways. Supporters of a limited and cautious approach to trade mark protection tend to argue that the law should concern itself only with their "origin function". By this they mean both the use of marks actually to tell consumers specifically where goods or services come from, and also a looser usage to distinguish one line of goods or services from another on the market, in cases where consumers have no interest in source as such but only as the key to qualities.

Radicals who strive for a broader, more "modern", approach, on the other hand, tend to denigrate "origin" theories, by understanding them only to cover the first, specific usage; it can then be said that, plainly, trade mark law covers a second, "differentiation", or "identification",—or "communication" function, which is something more elusive—something quite as much concerned with the feelings and subconscious appreciations of consumers as with the rational evaluation of information. Because this is already so, goes the argument, there is an equal case for protecting the guarantees of quality and, indeed, all investment values which develop in a mark, name or similar sign as an essential element of business goodwill.[93]

Arguments along this divide have been with us since the birth of today's advertising practices.[94] The conflicts between them have nowhere been resolved to the complete satisfaction of one side or the other because they address attitudes towards marketing and promotion about which many people are ambivalent. Competitors in developed economies are dependent

---

[93] Indeed, "differentiation" may well be a sub-set of "quality", rather than of "origin", function.
[94] Carty (1996) 112 L.Q.R. 632; [1997] E.I.P.R. 684.

on these processes for establishing and maintaining market share. Some would claim that today it is often the mark, rather than the product, which has an autonomous image, deriving from the promotional aura; it has even been claimed that this enhances the consumer's rational choice.[95] Yet many observers are repelled by the manipulative persuasion of so much advertising, with its images of glamour and success (even in kitchen and laundry), or its more or less cynical appropriation of the shocking and pitiable, particularly when contrasted with its thin or non-existent measure of information.[96]

15–31 Not surprisingly, then, legal systems have taken up different positions between the poles of restricted and extended protection. The matter is complicated by differences in the relationship between registered marks and unfair competition or passing-off protection.[97] Jurisdictions under British influence, and to some extent those in the United States as well, have tended in the main towards caution. Pointers in the other direction, whether they come from statute or from case law, have often been ignored as sign-posts.[98] On the other hand, Continental jurisdictions, in some cases through an eager deployment of unfair competition rules, have gone a considerable way towards eradicating competitive behaviour which undercuts a market position built through the advertising of brands, whatever form that behaviour takes.

15–32 It is this opposition of attitudes, which makes the recent changes in statutory structures within the European Community so intriguing. New trade mark laws have taken largely standardised form. The Harmonisation Directive states that "the function of [legal protection] is in particular to guarantee the trade mark as an indication of origin" (plainly here, "origin" in a broad sense).[99] At the same time there have been some judiciously phrased hints that the Benelux Trade Mark Act was influential in shaping the new European law[1]; from this it can be argued that the supposedly embracing approach of that law should be a particular point of reference in interpreting the CTM Regulation and national rules derived from the Directive. But courts are not compelled to adopt any one precedent as the source of proper interpretation and there is no compelling argument why they should do so.

At the present juncture, the measure of whether the new E.C. law protects the "investment function" of marks is likely to turn upon one

---

[95] See *e.g.* Kur (1992) 23 I.I.C. 218; Martino, *Trade Mark Dilution* (1996); Mostert, *Famous and Well-Known Marks* (1997).

[96] Note particularly Schechter, n. 9, above.

[97] A striking example is provided by German approaches to the question of dilution: first, "famous" marks were given wide protection within the registered trade-mark law; then this was abandoned in favour of protecting "well-known" marks through unfair competition law: see Schricker (1979) 11 I.I.C. 166; Lehmann (1986) 17 I.I.C. 746; Kur (1992) 23 I.I.C. 218.

[98] Some sign-posts, of course, have pointed both ways at once: see para. 16–17, below.

[99] Dir. Rec. 10; CTM Reg. Rec. 7.

[1] A nudging which has proved of little avail, either in U.K. Courts or the E.C.J: see para. 17–95, below.

leading question: can a trade mark be regularly used to prevent the importation of goods into an E.U. State when they were originally marketed in a country from outside the E.E.A. by or with the consent of the relevant trade mark owner? If that is so, then marks shore up higher prices for a given product within the E.U. than outside—a differential which consumers often resent and politicians find it convenient to denounce. There may be reasons justifying the price discrimination—for instance, higher labour or advertising costs—and we will discuss them, together with the state of the law, at a later juncture.[2] The new law may be read as impliedly giving the trade mark this exclusory function against parallel importing from the E.C.; or it may be treated as passing the whole issue to the courts to settle. Because the question is of high practical importance, it cannot be long before the European Court of Justice is called upon to determine it on one or other basis.

The Court's decision will likely influence a range of issues about **15–33** "function", such as the extent to which there should be protection against dilution,[3] protection of what are essentially design elements in products,[4] and protection against comparative advertising.[5] In approaching the issue of "external" parallel imports, the Court accordingly needs to be aware of the distinct function of trade mark protection in law (dissociating it from patents and copyright), and of the reactions against over-generous trade mark rights which over time have occurred in many countries as well as in the E.C. itself.[6]

---

[2] See paras 17–120 *et seq.*, below.
[3] See paras 16–37—16–41, 17–100—17–102, below
[4] See paras 17–41—17–46, below.
[5] See paras 16–54, 17–104—17–107, below.
[6] See para. 18–13, below.

CHAPTER 16

COMMON LAW LIABILITY

1. PASSING OFF[1]

The passing-off action was first developed to meet a classic case. As Lord **16–01** Halsbury put it: "nobody has any right to represent his goods as the goods of somebody else".[2] The same has been held of representations about services; and a defendant may also be liable for passing off one class of the plaintiff's goods as another.[3] His means may consist of misappropriating the plaintiff's mark, business name or get-up; or he may simply supply his own goods when he receives an order for the plaintiff's.[4] In all such cases the plaintiff loses the customer because the latter is misled by a competitor. The seriousness of such a threat is recognised in legal principle: the action will lie even where the defendant is innocent[5]; and relief may be granted without proof of actual damage, but simply because of the likelihood of future injury.[6] This, as we have seen, carries passing off further than most other economic torts.[7] Because it is in this sense a wide-ranging form of liability, the judges have in the past been careful to ensure that it is not applied indiscriminately to analogies which fall outside the classic cases.

This caution is, for instance, expressed in the refusal to treat rights **16–02** arising from use of a trade mark as giving a fully-fledged right of property in that mark. All that the common law protects through its passing-off action is the goodwill between a trader and his customers which the mark

---

[1] See, generally, Wadlow, *The Law of Passing Off* (2nd ed., 1995); Kerly, Chap. 14; Young, *Passing Off* (3rd ed., 1994); Drysdale and Silverleaf, *Passing Off* (2nd ed., 1992); Morison (1956) 2 Syd. L.R. 50; Cornish (1972) 12 J.S.P.T.L. 126; Gummow (1974) 7 Syd. L.R. 224; Dworkin [1979] 1 E.I.P.R. 241; Naresh [1986] C.L.J. 97; Spence (1996) 112 L.Q.R. 472. For the history of the action, see paras 15–04—15–06, above.

[2] *Reddaway v. Banham* [1896] A.C. 199 at 204, 13 R.P.C. 218 at 224; echoing Lord Langdale M.R., in *Perry v. Truefitt* (1842) 6 Beav. 66 at 73. For the latter, see Lord Jauncey, *Reckitt & Colman v. Borden* [1990] R.P.C. 340, HL.

[3] See para. 16–11, below.

[4] As in *Bostitch v. McGarry* [1964] R.P.C. 173.

[5] See para. 16–22, below.

[6] See paras 16–29—16–35, below.

[7] See paras 2–12, 2–18, above.

helps to sustain; there is no property in a name as such.[8] His rights against imitators last only so long as he does not abandon his business; and he cannot by assignment give another trader the power to sue for passing off unless he assigns his business at the same time.[9] Moreover, this principle restricts the tort to injury in the course of trade. One person cannot object if the name by which his house is known is used on the house next door.[10]

16–03 Even if attention is confined to cases where customers are misled, there are forms of unfair competition which are not yet known to give a competitor a civil right of action. In particular, if one trader misdescribes some physical quality of his own goods in a way that brings in customers, this may well expose him to criminal sanctions and to contractual or even tortious liability to those actually deceived, but not to an action by other members of the trade.[11] One explanation for this may be that none of them suffers in a special degree more than the others. But we shall see that this has ceased to be a categorical point of distinction. For in *Erven Warnink v. Townend* (the "Advocaat" case)[12] the House of Lords accepted that where a group of traders share a reputation in a trade name that describes a type of product, any one of them may sue an outsider who uses it for goods which are not properly so described. For this Lord Diplock offered a broad justification in terms of policy. After noting the wider ambit of criminal offences in the Merchandise Marks Acts and now in the Trade Descriptions Act 1968 and associated legislation, he said:

> "Where over a period of years there can be discerned a steady trend in legislation which reflects the view of successive Parliaments as to what the public interest demands in a particular field of law, development of the common law in that part of the same field which has been left to it ought to proceed upon a parallel rather than a diverging course."[13]

16–04 Yet on the heels of this encouragement came a warning. In *Cadbury-Schweppes v. Pub Squash*,[14] unfair trading was alleged to lie in the defendant's advertising which had adopted the general tenor of the plaintiff's successful campaign to stress both the masculinity and the nostalgia attending the drinking of lemon squash. But there was no

---

[8] See especially *per* Lord Parker, *Burberrys v. Cording* (1909) 26 R.P.C. 693 at 701; *Spalding v. Gamage* (n. 33, below) at 284; and see *Singer Mfg. v. Loog* (1882) 8 App. Cas. 15; *Reddaway v. Banham* (n. 2, above); *Star Industrial v. Yap* [1976] F.S.R. 256, J.C.; *Erven Warnink v. Townend* (n. 12, below); *Harrods v. Harrodian School* [1996] R.P.C. 697, CA; *Harrods v. Harrods (Buenos Aires)* [1999] F.S.R. 187, CA.

[9] See paras 16–19—16–21, below.

[10] *Day v. Brownrigg* (1878) 10 Ch.D. 294. The same notion is expressed in the requirement of likely damage: see *Street v. Union Bank* (1885) 30 Ch.D. 156; *Hall of Arts v. Hall* (1934) 51 R.P.C. 398; and see paras 16–29 *et seq.*, below.

[11] See para. 2–19, above.

[12] [1979] F.S.R. 397, [1980] R.P.C. 31.

[13] [1979] F.S.R. 397 at 405–406 and see *Clark v. Associated Newspapers* [1998] R.P.C. 261.

[14] [1981] R.P.C. 429, J.C.; and see *Adidas v. O'Neill* [1983] F.S.R. 76, SC (Ir.); but *cf. Elida-Gibbs v. Colgate-Palmolive* [1983] F.S.R. 95.

confusion between the trade marks or the get-up of the actual products themselves and so no passing off, Lord Scarman remarking on the importance of not stifling competition by undue redress, and refraining from deciding whether any cause of action could lie in the absence of such confusion.[15] Accordingly there are some difficulties in describing the present scope of the cause of action.

In the "Jif Lemon" case, Lord Oliver elaborated the three elements **16–05** which a plaintiff must show in order to make a case of passing off:

> "First, he must establish a goodwill or reputation attached to the goods or services which he supplies in the mind of the purchasing public by association with the identifying 'get-up' (whether it consists simply of a brand name or a trade description, or the individual features of labelling or packaging) under which his particular goods or services are offered to the public, such that the get-up is recognised by the public as distinctive specifically of the plaintiff's goods or services. Secondly, he must demonstrate a misrepresentation by the defendant to the public (whether or not intentional) leading or likely to lead the public to believe that goods or services offered by him are the goods or services of the plaintiff. . . . Thirdly, he must demonstrate that he suffers, or in a *quia timet* action, that he is likely to suffer damage by reason of the erroneous belief engendered by the defendant's misrepresentation that the source of the defendant's goods or services is the same as the source of those offered by the plaintiff."[16]

These three requirements are the basis of the analysis which follows. In **16–06** judgments much use is also currently made of Lord Diplock's enumeration, in the "Advocaat" case, of five minimum requirements for the action:

> "(1) a misrepresentation (2) made by a trader in the course of trade, (3) to prospective customers of his or ultimate consumers of goods or services supplied by him, (4) which is calculated to injure the business or goodwill of another trader (in the sense that this is a reasonably foreseeable consequence) and (5) which causes actual damage to a business or goodwill of the trader by whom the action is brought or (in a *quia timet* action) will probably do so."[17]

---

[15] [1981] R.P.C. 429 at 490–491, PC. The caution in this opinion has been reflected in the unwillingness of Australian judges to use a statutory tort of deceptive trading (Trade Practices Act 1974, s. 52) as a vehicle for overrunning the bounds of passing off. This result is lamented by Blakeney (1984) 58 A.L.J. 316, but rather approved by Cornish (1985) 10 Adelaide L.R. 32.

[16] *Reckitt & Colman v. Borden* (n. 2, above) at 499.

[17] Above, n. 12, at 93. See also Lord Fraser at 105–106, who adds that the reputation must be with the English public as the result of trading in England (see paras 16–16, 16–17, below), Lord Fraser's formulation has been regarded as made "in the context of the case he was considering": Ralph Gibson L.J., *Bristol Conservatories v. Conservatories Custom Built* [1989] R.P.C. 455 at 466. Nourse L.J. expressed a decided preference for Lord Oliver's triptych over Diplockian neo-classicism: *Consorzio del Prosciutto di Parma v. Marks & Spencer* [1991] R.P.C. 351 at 368–369. But the formulations of Lords Diplock and Fraser were relied upon once more in *Chocosuisse v. Cadbury* (February 25, 1999), CA; and see further, para. 16–22, below.

However, these requisites are not to be taken as unduly confining the action. It must evolve so as to deal with changes in methods of trade and communication.[18]

(1) The plaintiff's reputation

(a) *Not just confusion*

16–07 In the normal case of passing off, the plaintiff has to prove a reputation sufficient for members of the public to be misled by the defendant's conduct into thinking that they are securing the goods or services of the plaintiff. It is not enough for the public simply to be confused about whether it is getting the plaintiff's or the defendant's goods: such might be the case, for example, where both start trading at virtually the same time with confusingly similar names[19]; or where a mark will not suggest either of them to the public because instead it carries an association with some third party. The makers of "Evian" water-bottles (for their "Evian" bicycles) could not stop a rival from selling bottles under the same name; the mark on the bottles was likely to be understood as referring to a third party, the marketers of "Evian" mineral-spring water.[20]

Accordingly, the plaintiff will demonstrate the volume of his sales and advertising expenditure and will supplement this by evidence from traders and the public of the meaning that they attach to the distinguishing features of the plaintiff's goods or business: saying, for instance, that they have long understood the trade mark "XXXX" to denote goods of the plaintiff's manufacture. At the end of the day, the plaintiff must show that it is his reputation that is being misappropriated by the defendant. Otherwise it may well be a case of "the unknown seeking remedies against the known".[21]

(b) *Distinguishing feature*

16–08 The plaintiff must have some badge of recognition upon which to found his reputation. Commonly this is a trade mark (whether it be a word, or a symbol such as a "logo") or a corporate, business, professional or philanthropic name specially adopted. But it need not be: it may simply be a personal name—in full or abbreviated, actual or assumed[22]; or the name of

---

[18] *British Telecommunications v. One in a Million*, [1999] F.S.R. 1, CA.

[19] But a head-start of three weeks was enough to secure an interlocutory injunction against a deliberate imitator in *Stannard v. Reay* [1967] R.P.C. 589. *cf. Compatibility Research v. Computer Psyche* [1967] R.P.C. 201 (logo for computer dating not sufficiently established in short period of use).

[20] *Evian v. Bowles* [1965] R.P.C. 327 and see *Rolls Razor v. Rolls (Lighters)* (1949) 66 R.P.C. 137 (suggesting, in the case of each product, "in the Rolls-Royce class").

[21] Harman J., *Serville v. Constance* (1954) 71 R.P.C. 146 at 149.

[22] Thus journalists and performers have protected their noms-de-plume and stage names: *e.g. Landa v. Greenberg* (1908) 24 T.L.R. 441 ("Aunt Naomi"); *Hines v. Winnick* [1947] Ch. 708 ("Dr. Crock and his Crackpots"); *Marengo v. Daily Sketch* (1948) 65 R.P.C. 242 ("Kem" the cartoonist); *Sykes v. Fairfax* [1978] F.S.R. 312, S.C. (N.S.W.). Note also cases where the name of someone else is used, as in *Franke v. Chappell* (1887) 57 L.T.(N.S.) 141 (impresario protected "Richter Concerts," named after the great conductor).

a place where the person does business; or the "get-up" in which goods or documents are packaged,[23] or, of course, any combination of mark, name and get-up. In one extreme case, the very shape of the product itself (laundry blue with a stick in it) was held to have come to indicate the plaintiff's goods.[24] In another, extreme in a rather different way, the plaintiff company was held to have a trading reputation in lemon juice sold in life-size plastic lemons, even though these also bore labels with its mark "Jif"; and the defendants' lemon containers amounted to passing off even though they bore the mark, "ReaLemon".[25] Also controversial has been a decision that the green-and-black colouring given to a well-known patented tranquilliser could not be imitated by a compulsory licensee because the public recognised it as a brand rather than an indicator of type.[26] There have been others, which can be kept for later discussion, in which the reference to the plaintiff is decidedly indirect.[27]

In the case of literary and other artistic works, and of performances, the **16–09** reputation may lie in the work or performance itself, or in a "character" drawn from either. In this way, subject-matter which may have no copyright receives protection: thus for a defendant to suggest that his film was yet another in a successful series concerning the "One-armed Swordsman" was held actionable at the suit of the producer of the series.[28]

It is the plaintiff's reputation as a source of goods or services that is in **16–10** issue. The courts have not required that he make his identity plain by, for instance, giving full name and address. It is enough that a trader uses a

---

[23] This may even consist of the colouring of a container: *Sodastream v. Thorn Cascade* [1982] R.P.C. 459, CA.

[24] *Edge v. Niccolls* [1911] A.C. 693, HL—despite the possible effect of raising the cost of production for any other competitor: see at 709. But that is an unfortunate consequence, avoided in other cases by making it difficult to prove the necessary reputation, *e.g. Williams v. Bronnley* (1909) 26 R.P.C. 765; *Hawkins v. Fludes Carpets* [1957] R.P.C. 8; *British American Glass v. Winton* [1962] R.P.C. 230; *Gordon Fraser v. Tatt* [1966] R.P.C. 505; *Jarman & Platt v. Barget* [1977] F.S.R. 260 at 272, CA; *Rizla v. Bryant & May* [1986] R.P.C. 389; *Hodgkinson & Corby v. Wards Mobility* [1995] F.S.R. 169. But note *Combe International v. Scholl* [1980] R.P.C. 1; *Weber-Stephen v. Alrite Engineering* [1992] R.P.C. 549, SC (S.A.). See also Evans (1968) 31 M.L.R. 642; Walton [1987] E.I.P.R. 159. *cf.* now the protection of industrial design by copyright and registered and unregistered design rights: Chap. 14, above.

[25] *Reckitt & Colman v. Borden* (n. 2, above); Christie [1990] C.L.J. 403. Although the defendant's mark was very well-known as such in the U.S., there was evidence that in the U.K. shoppers took it to be descriptive of the product.

[26] *Hoffmann-La Roche v. DDSA Pharmaceuticals* [1972] R.P.C. 1. Since this is a substantial barrier against a policy of encouraging generic substitutes for original proprietary drugs, it is important to note a certain readiness to distinguish the case: *e.g. Roche Products v. Berk Pharmaceuticals* [1973] R.P.C. 473—colouring of pills not distinctive of plaintiff's product; *John Wyeth v. M. & A. Pharmachem* [1988] R.P.C. 26—colouring denoted different dosages; *Boots v. Approved Prescription Services* [1988] F.S.R. 45—quality differences prevented through Medicines Act approval, so no argument for interlocutory relief; and *cf. Smith Kline & French v. K. V. Higson* [1988] F.S.R. 115—arguable that colouration not likely to be taken as use of a registered trade mark. See also Llewelyn (1981) 12 I.I.C. 185.

[27] See paras 16–37—16–40, below.

[28] *Shaw Bros. v. Golden Harvest* [1972] R.P.C. 559 SC (H.K.). *cf. Producers' Distributing v. Samuelson* [1932] 1 Ch. 201, para. 16–44, below.

mark, name or device of any kind as a cypher by which to teach the public how to get his goods.[29] Nor have the courts required that this connection be of any particular kind: he may be the manufacturer, wholesaler, retailer, selector or distributor of goods.[30] For example, a supermarket chain which offers its "own brand" lines has a reputation in both the goods and the business. An importer who provides all the advertising, sales and servicing for a product in his own name may well acquire the reputation even against the manufacturer.[31] If the plaintiff's reputation is adequate for the purpose, even to suggest that goods are made under his licence or some other trading arrangement giving him a means of control over them would be actionable.[32]

16–11 Accordingly the starting point for deciding whether there has been a misrepresentation amounting to passing off is the understanding that the plaintiff has built up with the public. Thus if his mark is used on one product of a particular quality, the defendant may not use the mark in trade for other goods, even if they emanate from the plaintiff. In *Spalding v. Gamage*,[33] for instance, the defendant was held not entitled to sell the plaintiff's "Orb" footballs as his "New Improved Orb" footballs. But in such cases it has been said that there must be two distinct classes of the plaintiff's goods: a songwriter could not prevent an early work from being passed off as a new work where the Court could draw no clear dividing line in quality between the older and the more recent.[34]

However, where a mark (whether it is a product or a house mark) is built up by an international group of companies, it may well signify the group as a whole, rather than individual members of it. This may limit the opportunity of using passing-off proceedings to prevent the parallel importing of the group's products. To this we return later.[35]

(c) *Secondary meaning*

16–12 If the plaintiff has used a mark or name which has some other connotation for the public, then he faces the special difficulty of establishing that the public does understand the word or symbol to indicate that goods or

---

[29] *Powell v. Birmingham Vinegar* [1897] A.C. 710, 14 R.P.C. 720; *Reckitt & Colman v. Borden* (n. 2, above). cf. *Politechnika v. Dallas Print Transfers* [1982] F.S.R. 529 ("Rubik's cube").

[30] In Hong Kong, reputation as a buyer has been protected: *Penney v. Punjabi Nick* [1979] F.S.R. 26; *Penney v. Penneys* [1979] F.S.R. 29.

[31] For the problems that arise between rival claimants to a single reputation, see para. 16–14, below.

[32] So said in *H. P. Bulmer v. Bollinger* [1978] R.P.C. 79, CA. But a majority of the Court refused to believe that the use of "champagne perry" led to the belief either that the drink was champagne or was indorsed by any champagne house.

[33] (1915) 32 R.P.C. 273, HL, and see *Robinson v. Wilts United Dairies* [1958] R.P.C. 94, CA; *Colgate Palmolive v. Markwell* [1988] R.P.C. 283, CA. The same applies where secondhand goods are called new, or imperfect goods perfect: see Kerly, para. 16–28.

[34] *Harris v. Warren* (1918) 35 R.P.C. 217; cf. Dworkin (1979) 1 E.I.P.R. 241 at 245.

[35] See paras 17–120ff.

services come from him. The other meaning may exist quite independently before he starts to trade: it may be a word or phrase which describes the goods or services, in particular or in general, or it may have a geographical significance. The plaintiff must then establish that his use of the term as an indicator of source has given it a "secondary meaning". How difficult it will be to do this depends on the particular circumstances. If the term precisely describes the product, then the secondary meaning has to be proved up to the hilt. In *Reddaway v. Banham*,[36] for instance, the mark "Camel Hair Belting" had just this character. However, as the House of Lords insisted in that case, there is no absolute rule that traders are not entitled to protection if they use such terms. Equally, in the "Jif" lemon case already mentioned,[37] there was surprising but incontrovertible evidence that considerable numbers of the public took a plastic lemon container to indicate the plaintiff's lemon juice. Other traders' interests are considered to be sufficiently protected by the form of injunction that will be granted. This requires the defendant not to use the descriptive term in such a way as to mislead the public into thinking that it is getting the plaintiff's goods or services.[38] Where the plaintiff is the first to develop a market, or has a legal monopoly of it (for instance, through a patent), the courts show great reluctance to treat the name of the product or service offered as bearing a secondary meaning: "oven chips", "Chicago pizza" "The Gold AM" (for a morning broadcast of "golden oldies") have provided recent examples.[39]

The same approach applies to geographical names. The makers of "Glenfield" starch sued a defendant who set up his starch-making business in Glenfield and then used the name as a trade mark. They secured an injunction in similarly qualified terms.[40] Again, where one trader has had the field to himself and has built up quality associations as an element in his get-up—such as different packet colouring for different qualities of cigarette paper—he cannot prevent a second entrant into his market from adopting the same indicators together with a different trade mark.[41]

(d) *Personal names*

Special considerations apply when the plaintiff establishes a reputation in a **16–13** word that is the defendant's personal name. It is the present rule "that a man must be allowed to trade in his own name and, if some confusion

---

[36] *Reddaway v. Banham* (n. 2, above); *cf. Cellular Clothing v. Maxton* [1899] A.C. 326, 16 R.P.C. 397, and for further case law, Kerly, paras 16–34 *et seq.*

[37] See para. 16–08, above.

[38] *Reddaway v. Banham* (n. 2, above) at 221, 231, 234. It may not provide much help to the defendant: see Lord Bridge's regret in the "Jif" case (n. 2, above) at 402: "The result gives the plaintiffs a *de facto* monopoly of the container as such which is just as effective as a *de jure* monopoly."

[39] See *McCain International v. Country Fair Foods* [1981] R.P.C. 69, CA; *My Kinda Town v. Soll* [1983] R.P.C. 407, CA; *County Sounds v. Ocean Sound* [1991] F.S.R. 367, CA.

[40] *Wotherspoon v. Currie* (1872) L.R. 5 HL 508, HL, where Lord Westbury first used the phrase "secondary meaning" (at 521). *cf.* the special facts of the "Stone Ale" case: *Montgomery v. Thompson* [1891] A.C. 217, HL.

[41] *Rizla v. Bryant & May* [1986] R.P.C. 389.

results, that is a lesser evil than that a man should be deprived of what would appear to be a natural and inherent right"[42]; but he must act honestly,[43] not setting out deliberately to take advantage of another's reputation. Moreover, the exception is confined to the naming of a business. It does not justify the use of a personal name as a mark for goods, if the result will be confusion with the established reputation of another.[44] In modern times most judges have felt that some other mark can always be found for goods.[45]

Company names are deliberately adopted in a way that personal names are not (unless they are assumed).[46] Nevertheless if a company originally takes its name honestly and then conducts business under it for a period, it will be entitled to continue using it for the business (but not as a mark for goods) as if it were an individual using a personal name.[47] A new company cannot claim this privilege, even if its name is taken chiefly from that of a person, unless it has taken over an existing business and is continuing to use its name.[48]

(e) *Mark becoming descriptive*

16-14 A mark may initially be used to distinguish the origin of goods; but if it proves highly successful the public may begin to use it as a generic term for the kind of article to which it has been applied. Marks of this sort—the

---

[42] Lord Simonds, *Marengo v. Daily Sketch* (1948) 65 R.P.C. 242 at 251. See also Lord Greene, M.R., reported at [1992] F.S.R. 1 at 2, 3. But first names and nicknames are not specially privileged: *Biba Group v. Biba Boutique* [1980] R.P.C. 413.

[43] Seeking out an individual with an appropriate name in order to lend colour to the imitation of a rival's name is not likely to be found honest. Likewise where the name of a person genuinely associated with an enterprise is nevertheless used as part of a scheme to suggest an association with the plaintiff which does not exist: as in *Bentley v. Lagonda* (1947) 64 R.P.C. 33. A scion of a family may not use the family name deliberately to set-up a breakaway business: *Tussaud v. Tussaud* (1890) 44 Ch.D. 678; *Gucci v. Gucci* [1991] F.S.R. 89.

[44] The distinction was clearly drawn by Romer J., *Rodgers v. Rodgers* (1924) 41 R.P.C. 227 at 291, and accepted, *e.g.* in *Baume v. Moore* [1958] R.P.C. 226, CA, and by a majority of the House of Lords in *Parker-Knoll v. Knoll International* [1962] R.P.C. 265 at 279, 284, 287.

[45] The earlier case law tended to treat the right to one's name as a higher right even in relation to selling goods: see, *e.g.* *Burgess v. Burgess* (1853) 3 De G.M. & G. 896; *Turton v. Turton* (1889) 42 Ch.D. 128. A turn in the tide is discernible in Buckley L.J.'s judgment in *Brinsmead v. Brinsmead* (1913) 30 R.P.C. 493 at 507–509; but there have been modern supporters of the older approach: Lord Greene M.R., *Wright v. Wright* (1949) 66 R.P.C. 149 at 151–1152; Lord Denning, *Parker-Knoll v. Knoll* (n. 44, above) at 277.

[46] Curiously, some uncertainty surrounds the question whether a person who has honestly taken up an assumed name can continue to use it for his business: see Kerly, para. 16–88.

[47] *Parker-Knoll v. Knoll* (n. 44, above); *Anderson & Lembke v. Anderson & Lembke* [1989] R.P.C. 124. But *cf.* cases where there is a dispute over entitlement to the reputation of a single business: para. 16–15, below.

[48] *Dunlop Pneumatic v. Dunlop Motor* (1907) 24 R.P.C. 572, HL; *Waring v. Gillow* (1916) 33 R.P.C. 173; *Hawtin v. Hawtin* [1960] R.P.C. 95; *Fine Cotton Spinners v. Harwood Cash* (1907) 24 R.P.C. 533; *Kingston Miller v. Kingston* (1912) 29 R.P.C. 289; *Fletcher Challenge v. Fletcher Challenge* [1982] F.S.R. 1.

advertiser's dream so long as they remain within the range of protection—are most commonly associated with products that have some really novel property or technical construction.[49] The company making "Corona" cigars proved that some purchasers treated this as a brand, others as an indication of size and shape. The plaintiff was entitled to a limited injunction against selling cigars not made by the plaintiff without making clear that this was so; only if the defendant proved that the word had wholly lost its original meaning, it seems, would he be entirely free to use it. But if the way in which he uses the term makes plain to his customers that he is adopting the descriptive sense, he will not be enjoined.[50]

(f) *Concurrent reputation*

If two separate businesses have honestly acquired a reputation in a single **16–15** mark or name, some of the public may associate it with the one, some with the other, some with both. This has not prevented the Courts from holding that each has a sufficient reputation to take action against an outside interloper who attempts to take advantage of it.[51] The same principle has been extended to the case where numbers of manufacturers have a joint reputation in the name for a product with particular qualities. The question, according to the House of Lords, is whether the class of traders can be defined with reasonable precision. The test can be satisfied by showing that a word connotes recognisable and distinctive qualities in goods. All who supply them then share in the reputation[52]; "champagne", "sherry", "Scotch whisky" and "advocaat" have all been held examples.[53] In the first of these instances there were at least 150 shippers, each of whom was entitled separately to sue.[54]

---

[49] For instance, in English Courts, "Linoleum" was found non-distinctive (*Linoleum Co. v. Nairn* (1878) 7 Ch.D. 834); but the registration of "Vaseline" as a trade mark survived (*Cheseborough's T.M.* (1901) 19 R.P.C. 342, CA).

[50] *Havana Cigar v. Oddenino* [1924] 1 Ch. 179, CA.

[51] *Dent v. Turpin* (1861) 2 J. & H. 139 (single business divided among successors); *Southorn v. Reynolds* (1865) 12 L.T. 75. Neither can sue the other: see below, para. 16–20. An association of the trade may have no trading activity on which it can sue in its own right, and there is presently no entitlement to sue in a representative capacity: *Chocosuisse v. Cadbury* (February 25, 1999), CA.

[52] *Erven Warnink v. Townend* [1980] R.P.C. 31 On the nature of the reputation raised in these cases—an issue at the frontier of passing off—see paras 16–38, 16–39, below. For the relation to other forms of protection, see App. 2, below.

[53] *Bollinger v. Costa Brava* [1960] R.P.C. 16, [1961] R.P.C. 116; *Vine Products v. Mackenzie* [1969] R.P.C. 1; *Walker (John) v. Ost* [1970] R.P.C. 489. See also *Pillsbury Washburn v. Eagle* 86 Fed. Rep. 608 (1898).

[54] "The larger [the class] is, the broader must be the range and quality of products to which the descriptive term used by the members of the class has been applied, and the more difficult it must be to show that the term has acquired a public reputation and goodwill as denoting a product endowed with recognisable qualities which distinguish it from others of inferior reputation that compete with it in the same market.": Lord Diplock, *Warnink* case (n. 52, above) at 95.

Contrast with these cases of shared reputation, the difficulties that may arise between two traders each of whom has built up an independent reputation quite honestly in the same or a similar mark. If one can show that he has the reputation in a business name for a particular area, the other will not be permitted to use the name in that area, however much he may enjoy a reputation in the name in some other part of the country.[55] But if each has built up his reputation in his own locality and argument arises because both are expanding business into intermediate territory, neither may be able to show that the public there associates the name with him so as to lead to passing off by the other.[56] Likewise if two companies have previously enjoyed a shared reputation through an element of joint ownership, and that connection is severed, for instance, by the nationalisation of one of them.[57]

(g) *Geographical considerations*

16–16 In the ordinary case, the plaintiff's reputation lies with the public within the jurisdiction and the defendant's passing off is directed at that public. But English courts have not hesitated to extend their protection to certain aspects of foreign trade: relief will be granted against supplying the "instruments of fraud" in Britain for the purpose of deceiving a foreign populace.[58]

A more difficult case arises where the plaintiff's business is one which is run abroad but has an international reputation which extends to this country. In the past, some Courts have insisted that what is in issue is the plaintiff's reputation with the English public bred from business conducted in England.[59] The proprietor of the internationally known "Crazy Horse Saloon" in Paris was thus unable to enjoin an imitator in London from cashing in on the reputation of the name and "get-up".[60] Some decisions have treated this dividing-line as too categorical. But it was re-affirmed in the "Budweiser" case, where the American and Czech enterprises, which each traded under this mark in selling lager in their domestic and other markets, were seeking to launch their own products in Britain at much the same time. The Americans sought to claim prior reputation by virtue of sales in service-base shops to United States forces; but the Court of Appeal

---

[55] *Cavendish House v. Cavendish-Woodhouse* [1970] R.P.C. 234, CA; *Levy v. Henderson-Kenton* [1974] R.P.C. 617.

[56] *Evans v. Eradicure* [1972] R.P.C. 808; *City Link v. Lakin* [1979] F.S.R. 653.

[57] *Habib Bank Ltd v. Habib Bank AG* [1982] R.P.C. 1; *Gromax v. Don & Law* [1999] R.P.C. 367.

[58] *Johnston v. Orr-Erwing* (1882) 7 App. Cas. 216, HL; *Walker (John) v. Ost* (n. 53, above).

[59] See esp. *Erven Warnink v. Townend* (n. 52, above) at 105, 106, *per* Lord Fraser; *Anheuser-Busch* case (n. 61, below).

[60] *Bernardin v. Pavilion Properties* [1967] R.P.C. 581.

refused to bring this reputation into account: it did not amount to carrying on a business in the country.[61]

However, under section 56 of the Trade Marks Act 1994, Article 6*bis* of **16–17** the Paris International Convention has been expressly made part of British law. A plaintiff must show that it is a Convention proprietor,[62] and that its mark is "well-known" (in the Paris Convention sense) in the United Kingdom. Then, irrespective of whether it carries on business or has any goodwill in Britain, it may enjoin use of an identical or similar mark, in relation to identical or similar goods or services, where the use is likely to cause confusion.[63] Though of wider ambit,[64] the main impact of this provision in Britain will be to override the scruple requiring, for passing off, a business base in the country, which is found in the case law just mentioned.

Two main limitations need to be observed: the first is that "well-known" in the Convention sense requires proof of a substantial degree of recognition, though how high a degree is not defined.[65] This country is unlikely to take as methodical an approach to the matter as the Germans, who require 80 per cent recognition in an adequate market survey[66]; but the courts are likely to think in broadly equivalent terms. Secondly, the Convention requires that the mark be well-known in the country where the injury is occurring, not in some other country. It is, therefore, only an occasional weapon against the "kidnapper" who seeks to appropriate a mark well-known abroad before it is introduced into a particular country. The lack of any Convention obligation relating to a foreign reputation is not a major problem in respect of a market such as the United Kingdom. But it is a serious matter in countries where free markets are being rapidly introduced, as today in Central and East Europe.

---

[61] *Anheuser-Busch v. Budejovicky Budvar* [1984] F.S.R. 413, CA. In another circumstance, it could be enough that a Californian company responded to an unsolicited order from England, for there to be British goodwill: *Jian Tools v. Roderick Manhattan* [1995] F.S.R. 924.

[62] *i.e.* if a natural person, a national or domiciliary of a Convention State (other than the U.K.); if a legal entity, having a real and effective industrial or commercial establishment in a Convention State: TMA 1994, ss. 55(1), 56(1). PIP, Art. 6*bis* only applies to marks for goods when applied to goods: Bodenhausen, *WIPO Guide to the Paris Convention* (1968) 90–91. It may be, therefore, that TMA 1994, s. 56 is similarly limited, since it applies to "trade marks entitled to protection under the Paris Convention as a well-known trade mark"; but it at least allows confusing use for goods or services to be taken into account: s. 56(2). See also Blakeney [1994] E.I.P.R. 481.

[63] Relief is apparently limited to an injunction; but possibly an account or delivery up could be ordered (as of old) by way of support for that order; an application for registration can be objected to on the same ground: TMA 1994, s. 5(4)(a).

[64] Introduced into the Paris Convention in 1925, its prime aim was to give well-known but unregistered marks protection in countries which otherwise required registration as a prerequisite. In the U.K. and elsewhere, the passing-off action largely fulfilled the Convention obligation.

[65] In French "marque notoire"; *cf.* the German distinctions between "famous" and "well-known" marks in relation to dilution onto other products: see para. 15–31, above.

[66] See esp. Kur, para. 15–31, n. 97, above.

(h) *Temporal considerations*

16–18 Again, in the straightforward case, the plaintiff's reputation arises from trade or business that he has built up and is continuing. If his business has ceased, his reputation may nevertheless survive. He will, however, only be able to succeed if he can also show that he has not abandoned the name or mark[67]; in other words that he intends to do business with it again in the future.[68] So the name-owner may preserve his interest while his business is temporarily closed during a change of premises.[69] The owner of the "Ad-Lib Club" was able to assert its notoriety even though it had been closed for five years (because of an injunction against noise); no alternative premises had since been found on which to re-open it, but that remained his intention.[70] The reputation must survive, however. Use at one period gives no property right of indefinite duration.[71]

From the other end of the spectrum, a sufficient reputation through publicity may be shown even before the plaintiff starts trading. The BBC succeeded in demonstrating such a reputation from the media interest in its "Carfax" traffic information system for cars.[72]

(i) *Dealings in trade reputation*

16–19 In different ways the preceding paragraphs have drawn attention to the fact that in a passing-off action what is being protected is the trading reputation built with the public, not some larger and more permanent right of property. This factor becomes specially significant when we turn to attempts to assign and to license "common law" marks.

First consider a common occurrence in international trade: a foreign enterprise sets up a distributing agency in Britain[73]; success makes it desirable to manufacture here[74]; eventually the British enterprise, for whatever reason, acquires independence that is economic as well as legal. At different stages the question may arise, which has the better right to the marks and names: foreign "originator" or local trader? A prime issue is: what has the British public been taught to understand by the reputation? If the mark is built up as the original manufacturer's mark and the goods still come from him, then the reputation must be his[75]; but the contrary is true

---

[67] *Maxims v. Dye* [1977] F.S.R. 321; *C & A Modes v. C & A (Waterford)* [1978] F.S.R. 126.
[68] *Star Industrial v. Yap* [1976] F.S.R. 256, JC.
[69] *Berkeley Hotel v. Berkeley International* [1972] R.P.C. 673.
[70] *Ad-Lib Club v. Granville* [1972] R.P.C. 673.
[71] *Norman Kark v. Odhams* [1962] R.P.C 163 ("Today" as a magazine title held not to survive seven years' non-use).
[72] *BBC v. Talbot* [1981] F.S.R. 228; but note *My Kinda Bones v. Dr. Pepper's Stove* [1984] F.S.R. 289.
[73] The agency may not start as a distinct legal entity; or it may be a subsidiary; or it may be an independent entity taking its own commercial risks.
[74] Or add to the product range from local manufacture: *cf.* Scandecor.
[75] *e.g. Imperial Tobacco v. Bonnan* (1924) 41 R.P.C. 441, JC (not passing off to import genuine "Gold Flake" cigarettes into India, despite the creation of an exclusive distributorship there); *Sturvenant Engineering v. Sturvenant Mill* (1936) 53 R.P.C. 430 (end of market-splitting agreement).

where it becomes known as the importer's or local manufacturer's, however much the originator may have desired and supposed that the mark would remain his.[76] There is no general principle that any goodwill accruing during the cooperation must belong to him at its end.[77]

If the marks have been transferred together with the business that uses **16–20** them then they must belong to the transferee. An extreme case is this: where the marks of a German company's British subsidiary were transferred to an unconnected entity as a measure of wartime expropriation, the new owner was able to restrain passing off by the German company.[78]

If the original owner believes it advantageous to "transfer" the marks without the accompanying business, he may instead create grave jeopardy: he himself will have abandoned his interest, however much his reputation lingers[79]; the "assignee" will have no reputation of his own on which to sue.[80]

Before the Trade Marks Act 1938, these sorts of difficulties affected **16–21** registered trade marks as well as unregistered.[81] The Act accordingly allowed the originator to license (and thus keep ultimate control of) registered marks and to assign them even without goodwill.[82] The Courts have not, however, been prepared to adapt the law affecting "common law" marks in order to bring about a comparable development. In *Star Industrial v. Yap*, a company manufacturing "Ace Brand" toothbrushes in Hong Kong stopped importing them into Singapore after an import duty was imposed on them, and it abandoned its business there. The Privy Council held that it could not, three years later, assign its Singapore rights in the mark to a part-owned subsidiary; nor, more than five years later, could it secure relief against passing off by a competitor.[83]

To businessmen who have not secured registration for a mark, this rule may present an unexpected obstacle to a profitable transaction. But the rule

---

[76] *Oertli v. Bowman* [1959] R.P.C. 1, HL (manufacturing licensee); *Diehl's T.M.* [1970] R.P.C. 435 (distributor's registered mark—unregistered mark should be similarly treated); *Fender Australia v. Bevk and Sullivan* (1989) 15 I.P.R. 257. In the context of interpreting the duration of a licence to use a mark, see *Harrods v. Harrods (Buenos Aires)* [1997].

[77] *Scandecor Development v. Scandecor Marketing* [1998] F.S.R. 503.

[78] *Adrema v. Adrema-Werke* [1958] R.P.C. 323; if the two concerns remain connected, the contrary may well be true. If both share the British goodwill, then neither may sue the other for passing off: *Scandecor Development v. Scandecor Marketing* [1998] F.S.R. 503. If the goods are being imported into the U.K. from another E.C. State, the result of the *Adrema* case will now be affected by the Rome Treaty, Arts 30, 36.

[79] See para. 16–18, above.

[80] At least until he builds up his own trade: see *Pinto v. Badman* (1891) 8 R.P.C. 181.

[81] Hence cases on registered and unregistered marks were decided on a similar basis. *Pinto v. Badman* in fact concerned the former. Probably the marks associated with a distinct part of the business could be assigned with that part alone; but this could not give cover to the assignment of one out of several marks with which the assignor labelled a single type of goods: see *Sinclair's T.M.* (1932) 49 R.P.C. 123; Kerly, paras 13–02—13–09.

[82] But subject to certain controls discussed in para. 17–13, below. To a limited extent it also became possible to assign unregistered marks together with those that were registered; but the effect of the provision was obscure: TMA 1938, s. 22(3).

[83] [1976] F.S.R. 256; *cf. Coles v. Need* [1934] A.C. 82, JC.

only emphasises a policy to which the Courts have consistently adhered: the passing-off action should extend only to the protection of subsisting goodwill; beyond this other traders should be free to use the names and marks that are to their best advantage.[84]

(2) Defendant's representation

(a) Defendant's state of mind

16–22 Where a defendant is perpetrating the passing off personally, the fact that he does not realise it is no defence to the grant of an injunction. Nineteenth-century Chancery had no qualms about imposing its future-regarding remedy even on those who started on a course of business without appreciating its injurious effect. For a long period, however, it was not clear that more than nominal damages would be awarded for the period before notification of the passing off to the defendant.[85] In historical terms passing-off liability derived from the action on the case for deceit, and so could be said to contain the same restriction to intentional and reckless conduct.[86] As a solution, moreover, it resembled the results fashioned for some other forms of intellectual property by precedent or statute.[87]

Now, in *Gillette v. Edenwest*,[88] Blackburne J. has held that passing off gives rise to damages regardless of the defendant's state of mind, just as with infringement of a registered trade mark (he took no account of the ability, in the latter case, to consult a public register).[89] So now the only remedy excluded for innocence (in respect of both forms of liability) is equity's account of profits.[90]

Where the defendant has supplied others with products which they then use to perpetrate passing off upon ultimate consumers, he will be liable for the misrepresentation if, in Lord Diplock's phrase, "it is calculated to injure [the plaintiff] (in the sense that this is a reasonably foreseeable consequence)".[91] It is one thing to put "instruments of fraud" into the hands of a collaborating distributor.[92] It is another to supply packaging intended for

---

[84] If they do so in a way which misleads consumers into connecting their goods with a former user of the mark, the public interest may be protected through the Trade Descriptions Act's machinery.

[85] See Lord Westbury L.C. *Edelsten v. Edelsten* (1863) 1 De G. J & S. 184 at 199 (refusing an equitable account or other compensation, while granting an injunction); *Draper v. Trist* (1939) 56 R.P.C. 429, esp. at 443 (Goddard L.J.); *Marengo v. Daily Sketch* (1948) 65 R.P.C. 242, HL In favour of substantial damages, *e.g.* Lord Parker, *Spalding v. Gamage* (1915) 32 R.P.C. 273; Greene M.R. in the *Draper* case (at 434); Cairns, *The Remedies for Trade Mark Infringement* (1988).

[86] See para. 15–05, above.

[87] See para. 2–42, above.

[88] [1994] R.P.C. 279 (innocent importation of counterfeit razor cartridges).

[89] For infringement of a registered mark, see paras 17–85 *et seq.*, below.

[90] See, *e.g.* the *Edelsten* case, (n. 83, above).

[91] *Erven Warnink v. Townend* [1979] F.S.R. 397.

[92] It is in just such a case that the Courts have extended the tort to cover English suppliers of counterfeit goods intended for marketing abroad: see para. 16–16, above.

the plaintiff's product, only to have a person down the chain of distribution replace the real thing with a substitute.

(b) *Form of passing off*

As already noted, it does not matter what means the defendant uses to **16–23** represent his goods or business to be another's. He may simply supply his own in response to an order for the plaintiff's, without ever making a positively misleading statement. Or he may imitate the badge which the plaintiff has used to implant reputation in the public mind. Nor does it matter what misrepresentation about trade is made: falsely to claim to be a manufacturer's authorised agent may be actionable.[93]

Confusion may occur only after sale—for instance, because the goods themselves will only be seen upon removal of packaging, or when taken to pieces, or when some distinguishing tag is seen without accompanying labels. So far, English Courts have shown some reluctance to take "post-sale confusion" into account, notably in relation to the "look-alike" elements of get-up.[94] But, at least in Lord Diplock's characterisation of passing off, consequent confusion appears to be a relevant factor. Where, therefore, actual or truly likely injury can be shown to arise in this way it ought to be actionable.[95]

(c) *Likelihood of confusion*

In a case where there is something to be said in the defendant's favour, the **16–24** most frequent issue is whether his way of doing business is sufficiently likely to confuse the public. If he has imitated the plaintiff's mark or other badge exactly, the only question left is whether he has done enough else to dispel the otherwise misleading effect of his imitation: has he said with sufficient prominence "No connection with the plaintiff"? It is an unusual case in which a trader attempts to do this; even more rarely will he do enough.[96] "Thirsty people want beer not explanations."[97] Despite which, judges and

---

[93] *Sony v. Saray Electronics* [1983] F.S.R. 302, CA.

[94] *Bostik v. Sellotape* [1994] R.P.C. 556 (substitute for "Blu-tak", differently labelled but also coloured blue); *cf. Levi Strauss v. Kimbyr* [1994] F.S.R. 335, HC (N.Z.) (red tag on jeans found confusing after sale); Prescott [1990] E.I.P.R. 241; Karet [1995] E.I.P.R. 3.

[95] A similar issue arises over infringement of non-identical registered marks: TMA 1994, s. 10(2), calls for confusion to exist when the defendant uses his sign in the course of trade. This may be held to exclude consideration of post-sale confusion: see para. 17–35, below.

[96] One instance is where the defendant is understood to be using the plaintiff's mark only to indicate that he is selling the same sort of product: "a substitute for 'Yeastvite'", "Claret style", and a host of nicely nuanced variants. On this sort of comparative reference, see paras 16–54—16–56, below.

[97] Lord Macnaghten, *Montgomery v. Thompson* [1891] A.C. 217. And see *McDonald's v. Burgerking* [1986] F.S.R. 45 ("It's not just Big, Mac"—taken to arouse confusing associations with plaintiff's product); *Neutrogena v. Golden* [1996] R.P.C. 473; *Kimberley-Clark v. Fort Sterling* [1997] F.S.R. 877.

legislators sometimes treat the ability to add distinguishing information as a practical possibility.[98]

If the defendant's marking or naming is not an exact imitation, the first question is whether he has sailed too close to the wind, or has shown a true mariner's judgment. This has to be decided largely in light of the particular circumstances. But the comparison to be made must be emphasised: it is between the manner in which the plaintiff's reputation has been acquired in actual trade and the trading practice in which the defendant is indulging or threatens to indulge.[99]

16–25 The question is: what impact would the defendant's mark be likely to have on probable customers, given the expectations they already have and the amount of attention that they will pay.[1] All the circumstances in which goods are actually sold, or business conducted, will be considered: will an appeal be made to the same set of customers? Will orders be in writing or by word of mouth? Will there be sales among ill-educated or illiterate customers?[2] Will marks be used in clearly legible and striking form?[3] If the goods themselves can be inspected before purchase, will this reveal a difference in kind?[4] The customer must, moreover, be led to think that the plaintiff had assumed responsibility for the quality of the defendant's goods or services, not merely that the plaintiff had sponsored or given financial support to the defendant: as where there is a misrepresentation about sports or arts sponsorship. Thus Harrods department store could not object to The Harrodian School being set up nearby, when at most this suggested that the store approved or gave some support to it.[5]

Normally the customer will not have the opportunity of seeing the two marks side by side. So, in comparing their visual appearance, it is necessary to allow for imperfect recollection by a person of ordinary memory.[6] A Court will concentrate on the aspect of the mark that is most likely to be

---

[98] It was the justification for introducing Part B to the Register between 1919 and 1994.

[99] Compare the test of whether a registered trade mark has been infringed: paras 17–87 *et seq.*, below. In general the principles here discussed apply equally in comparing marks on an application to register and in deciding upon infringement of a registered mark. For greater detail, see Kerly, Chap. 17.

[1] Good examples may be found in the cases concerning newspaper titles: *e.g. Borthwick v. Evening Post* (n. 25, below); *Morning Star v. Express Newspapers* [1979] F.S.R. 113 (see especially at 117; if "only a moron in a hurry would be misled" the case is not made out); *Morgan-Grampian v. Training Personnel* [1991] F.S.R. 267; *Tamworth Herald v. Thompson* [1991] F.S.R. 337; *Management Publications v. Blenheim Exhibitions* [1991] F.S.R. 550, CA; *The European v. The Economist Newspaper* [1998] F.S.R. 283, CA.

[2] *e.g. Edge v. Niccolls* [1911] A.C. 693, HL; *Johnston v. Orr-Ewing* (1882) 7 App.Cas. 219, HL (yarn for the "natives of Aden and India"); *Bollinger v. Costa Brava Wine* [1960] R.P.C. 16.

[3] Think of signs on petrol stations and marks on watches: *e.g. British Petroleum* [1968] R.P.C. 54; *"Accutron" T.M.* [1966] R.P.C. 152 at 155.

[4] Thus, in *Island Trading v. Anchor Brewing* [1989] R.P.C. 287 "Steam Beer" was enjoined for sales of draught, but not for bottles, beer.

[5] *Harrods v. Harrodian School* [1996] R.P.C. 697, CA.

[6] See especially *Aristoc v. Rysta* [1945] A.C. 68, HL; and Luxmoore L.J. in (1943) 60 R.P.C. 87 at 108, CA (registration case).

memorable—the "idea of the mark" as it is sometimes called. Thus to mark cigarettes "99" was held not to pass them off as "999"; the idea of the latter was triplication.[7] But to use a lion's head on a soap wrapper may well be actionable if someone else is already known for his "Lion" or "Red Lion" soap.[8] If phonetic similarity is important, account must be taken not only of the different ways in which customers and sales staff might pronounce a word but also of slovenly speech: consider, for example, the possibilities inherent in "Rysta", when compared with "Aristoc", for stockings[9]; or "Piquant" and "Picot" for cosmetics.[10]

(d) *Descriptive connotation*

Where the key to the plaintiff's reputation is alleged to lie in a word or **16–26** other symbol that describes some quality of the goods or services, the defendant may avoid liability by relatively minor differentiation. Thus, in a leading case, "Office Cleaning Association" was held sufficiently distinct from "Office Cleaning Services".[11] There has been much concern to ensure that a plaintiff is not unfairly inclosing part of "the great common of the English language".[12] Accordingly, whether the action succeeds is likely to depend on proof of actual passing off—proof that there were people who both took the word or phrase as indicating the plaintiff and were misled by the defendant's imitation; or at least that the defendant adopted his name in the hope of producing this result.

(e) *Responsibility upon the defendant*

In the context of passing off, the Courts have felt no hesitation in pinning **16–27** responsibility upon a person who enables the injury to occur.[13] A manufacturer or wholesaler who provides retailers with the means of deception will be liable without proof either that the retailers knew that they were passing

---

[7] *Ardath v. Sandorides* (1824) 42 R.P.C. 50. *Johnston v. Orr-Ewing* (1882) 7 App. Cas. 219, HL, provides a good example where the mark is compounded of picture and words. *Lever v. Goodwin* (1887) 36 Ch.D. 1, CA, is useful on general get-up. Whether there are similarities in colour may be important in passing-off cases, because the actual usages are being compared; *cf.* the position with a registered trade mark: para. 17–34, below.

[8] *Hodgson v. Kynoch* (1898) 15 R.P.C. 465 (note that the evidence was held to establish passing off but not trade mark infringement).

[9] See, n. 6, above.

[10] *Picot v. Goya* [1967] R.P.C. 573.

[11] *Office Cleaning Service v. Westminster Cleaners* (1946) 63 R.P.C. 39, HL. For further examples, see Kerly, para. 16–51. Likewise if the plaintiff's mark is close to a descriptive word, the Courts look with care at evidence of actual confusion, particularly if it is secured by a trap.order: *Fox's Glacier Mints v. Jobbings* (1932) 49 R.P.C. 352 (local use of "glassy mints").

[12] Cozens Hardy M.R., *Crosfield's Application* (1909) 26 R.P.C. 837 at 854.

[13] *cf.* the position over patents (paras 6–17—6–19, above) and copyright (paras 11–18—11–20, above).

off or that actual passing off was taking place.[14] The general test is whether the passing off is a reasonably foreseeable consequence of the misrepresentation.[15] Thus test was given an extended reading in a case of "cyber-squatting". The defendants made a practice of acquiring Internet top level domain names which included the names of well-known British companies ("bt.org.marksandspencer.com", etc). Each company had then to buy off the defendants if it wanted the name for itself. That was the defendants' main object; neither they nor any other "purchaser" from them could lawfully use the name in trade, *e.g.* on an advertising Website. Even so, there was held to be passing off in threatening to provide others with such a "instrument of fraud".[16] The defendants were ordered to surrender the domain names to those "rightfully" entitled.[17] In essence the decision is likely to stand. Much the same result has been reached in other countries.[18]

But the plaintiff, rather than the defendant, may be primarily responsible for the confusing state of affairs, as when he puts similar labels on products of different quality. In *Champagne Heidsieck v. Buxton*,[19] the plaintiff sold different types of champagne in France and England under similar labels. It was not open to him to say that an importer who brought the French goods into England for resale passed them off. It was for the plaintiff himself to make the difference plain. This concept would seem to place a particular difficulty in the way of using the passing-off action against a parallel importer and in that context we shall return to it.[20]

(f) *Proof of likely deception*

16–28 The plaintiff is not required to show actual deception in order to succeed, but if he can do so, his case will be much advanced.[21] Likewise he is not obliged to show that the defendant was acting dishonestly.[22] But if there is a question whether the public will be deceived, proof of actual fraud carries him a long way (without being necessarily conclusive): "Why should we be astute to say that [the defendant] cannot succeed in doing that which he is straining every nerve to do?"[23]

---

[14] *Singer v. Loog* (1882) 8 App Cas. 15; *Lever v. Goodwin* (1887) 36 Ch.D. 1, CA; *Draper v. Trist* (1939) 56 R.P.C. 429, CA; and see para. 16–22, above. It is different when goods leave the defendant in "innocent" condition and a subsequent seller misuses them.

[15] See Lord Diplock, "*Advocaat*" case (para. 16–06, above).

[16] *British Telecommunications v. One in a Million* [1999] F.S.R. 1, CA; Osborne [1997] E.I.P.R. 644; Meyer-Rochon [1998] E.I.P.R. 405. For the domain name registration system on the Internet, see above, para. 15–21—15–23.

[17] A questionable procedure when there could be more than one genuine claim—as was the case with <virgin.com>.

[18] See Bettinger (1997) 28 I.I.C. 508.

[19] [1930] 1 Ch. 330; *cf. Champagne Heidsieck v. Scotto* (1926) 43 R.P.C. 101.

[20] See paras 17–120 *et seq.*, below.

[21] See Kerly, paras 16–77, 17–38.

[22] See para. 16–22, above.

[23] Lindley L.J., *Slazenger v. Feltham* (1889) 6 R.P.C. 531 at 538 and see Kerly, paras 16–87, 17–39.

There has been very little discussion of how many people must likely be deceived.[24] It seems that their number must be "substantial"; even 20 cases of actual deception were once disregarded, where the plaintiff's case went to loss of reputation rather than to direct competition.[25] The Court of Appeal has been prepared to take account of a survey of opinion, after allowing for expert criticism of the manner in which it was conducted.[26] Clearly there are difficulties in devising investigations that are not biased, particularly if left to the parties; they are also expensive. But they can bring an element of objectivity into an inquiry that otherwise leaves a judge to his own hunch amid a welter of conflicting affidavits.

(3) Likelihood of damage

(a) *Likely damage*

Because the "property" is in the goodwill or business of the plaintiff, and **16–29** not in his mark, name or get-up, he has to show, if not actual injury, then at least some likelihood of injury that is more than mere imitation. The mark or other symbol, in other words, is not simply a licensable commodity. In "ordinary" passing off between competitors who are selling the same or substitutable products or services, likelihood of damage is the corollary of demonstrating likelihood of confusion. This third element assumes a distinctive role when the case is not one of simple diversion of customers from one rival to another.

(b) *Goods or business not the same*

In *Walter v. Ashton*,[27] the defendant, who had been responsible for a **16–30** successful sales campaign to sell "Daily Express" bicycles with the co-operation of that newspaper, launched a new campaign to sell "The Times" bicycles, but without having any connection with "The Times". Byrne J. required the existence of a "tangible probability of injury" to the plaintiff's property and found it thus: the representation that "The Times" had a business responsibility for the sale of the cycles exposed it at least to the risk of litigation and possibly (if the newspaper did not take steps to disconnect its name) even to liability. This test, though occasionally criticised,[28] has often been the touchstone of later cases.[29]

---

[24] *e.g. Globelegance v. Sarkissian* [1974] R.P.C. 603; *Wienerwald v. Kwan* [1979] F.S.R. 381.

[25] *Borthwick v. Evening Post* (1888) 37 Ch.D. 449, CA.

[26] *"GE" Trade Mark* [1970] R.P.C. 339 at 370, 383, 386 (not the subject of comment on further appeal); *cf.* Graham J. [1969] R.P.C. 418 at 446–447; *Stringfellow v. McCain Foods* (n. 35, below). See Morcom [1984] E.I.P.R. 6; Fellner (1985) J. Media L. 273; Pattinson [1990] E.I.P.R. 99; Wadlow (n. 1, above), paras 8–45—8–50.

[27] [1902] 2 Ch. 282.

[28] *Harrods v. Harrod* (1924) 41 R.P.C. 74 at 78; *cf.* at 86–87.

[29] The requirement is strongly reaffirmed in *Erven Warnink v. Townend* and *Reckitt & Colman v. Borden* (see paras 16–05, 16–06, above).

Another form of probable injury is damage to trade reputation from the assumed connection, such as suggesting that a nightclub had begun an escort agency[30] or that the Queen of department stores had stooped to moneylending (as conducted by the defendant).[31] Again, the plaintiff may be injured by losing the chance to expand his business into the field that the defendant has occupied, if the latter is not restrained. A plaintiff who sold "Marigold" rubber gloves and the like secured an interlocutory injunction against a defendant who began using the mark on toilet tissues, the plaintiff stating that he was planning to use the mark upon very similar goods.[32] In contrast, there have been numerous cases in which, because the goods or businesses are not the same, the plaintiff has failed, either at the interlocutory or the final stage. For instance, the "Albert Hall Orchestra" (organised by Albert Edward Hall) was allowed to continue using this name over the objection of the proprietor of the Royal Albert Hall, there being no actual or reasonable danger of damage.[33] The makers of "Zoom" iced lollipops could not obtain interlocutory relief against the marketing of "Zoom" bubble gum.[34] The night-club "Stringfellows" could not object to oven chips sold by that name.[35] The copyright owners of the "Wombles" books and television series had no "merchandising rights" that were good against a company that leased "Wombles" rubbish skips.[36]

(c) *Not trading in the same geographical area*

16-31 The same considerations apply when the plaintiff establishes a business reputation in one place and the defendant then sets up a similar business in another so as to suggest that the plaintiff has opened a new outlet. In *Brestian v. Try*, for instance, the plaintiff had hairdressers' shops in London, Wembley and Brighton; the defendant was restrained from using the same name for hairdressing in Tunbridge Wells. But Jenkins L.J. was careful to find "that damage would probably ensue" because customers might go to the defendant instead of the plaintiff; and Romer L.J. pointed to evidence that the plaintiff's credit and reputation might be endangered.[37] More

---

[30] *Annabel's v. Shock* [1972] R.P.C. 838.

[31] *Harrods* case (n. 28, above). See also *Hulton Press v. White Eagle* (1951) 68 R.P.C. 126.

[32] *L.R.C. v. Lilla Edets* [1973] R.P.C. 560. An extreme example is *Eastman Photographic v. Griffiths* (1898) 15 R.P.C. 105 ("Kodak" for bicycles, when cameras were being specially sold for bicycles: the prospect of the plaintiffs actually applying their mark to bicycles seems to have been supposition). Another is *Lego System v. Lego M. Lemelstrich* [1983] F.S.R. 155 (plastic gardening equipment likely to be associated with the well-known "Lego" toys; defendant's name adopted perfectly properly in Israel and elsewhere).

[33] *Hall of Arts v. Albert Hall* (1934) 51 R.P.C. 398.

[34] *Lyons Maid v. Trebor* [1967] R.P.C. 222.

[35] *Stringfellow v. McCain Foods* [1984] R.P.C. 501.

[36] *Wombles v. Womble Skips* [1977] R.P.C. 99. See paras 16-44—16-47, below.

[37] [1958] R.P.C. 161, CA; and see also *Outram v. Evening Newspapers* (1911) 28 R.P.C. 308 (papers of same name in Glasgow and London: no likelihood of pecuniary loss from confusion); *The Clock v. Clock House* (1936) 53 R.P.C. 269 (confusion of road houses, the proximity (five miles) being stressed).

recently a business with "Chelsea Man" shops in three cities was held entitled to a country-wide injunction, because of its intention to extend business beyond these places.[38]

This ought to be the appropriate principle for dealing with cases where a plaintiff has built up a reputation by business abroad and the defendant imitates him so as to lead customers to believe that the plaintiff has come to Britain.[39] If there is a tangible risk that the plaintiff's good name will be hurt by the poor quality of what the defendant provides or adverse publicity about him,[40] or if the plaintiff has plans to come to Britain which will be jeopardised,[41] these should provide a sufficient basis for his claim. But it would be a new departure to give such a plaintiff relief merely because the defendant was taking advantage of his reputation.[42] If the plaintiff has a reputation in Britain in advance of any trading, relief may now be available under section 56 of the Trade Marks Act 1994.[43]

(d) Not trading: other sufficient reputation

Professional and charitable institutions may have a reputation that will be **16–32** protected in passing-off proceedings if it is likely to be injured by the defendant's activities. Again Courts have been careful to state what it is that creates a tangible probability of injury: in the case of a professional association it may be that the passing off will induce members to leave and potential members not to join[44]; in the case of a charity that regularly appeals for funds, it may be the danger to its reputation, should the defendant ever fall into financial difficulties.[45]

---

[38] *Chelsea Man v. Chelsea Girl* [1987] R.P.C. 189, CA.

[39] *cf.* the discounting of foreign reputation in *Bernardin v. Pavilion Properties* [1967] R.P.C. 581 and *Anheuser Busch v. Budejovicky Budvar* [1984] F.S.R. 413, CA.

[40] *cf. Annabel's v. Shock* (n. 30, above).

[41] A nice question is, how definite must the plaintiff's plan to expand be? What is to be done about the business which tries to secure the name or brand of a trans-national company before the latter moves into a particular market? Note that in the *Bernardin* case, the proprietors of the French business had no plans to set up in Britain, so the refusal of relief may well have been correct on the facts.

[42] *Maxim's v. Dye* [1977] F.S.R. 321 appears to come close to this; but the defendant did not appear at the hearing. *cf. C & A Modes v. C & A (Waterford)* [1978] F.S.R. 126, S.C. (Ir.), where it was insisted that "goodwill does not necessarily stop at a frontier", but that the plaintiff's goodwill must nonetheless be liable to be damaged by the passing off. Both decisions were criticised in *Athletes Foot v. Cobra Sports* [1980] R.P.C. 343, which held that the plaintiff must have at least a customer in Britain. See also *Metric Resources v. Leasemetrix* [1979] F.S.R. 571; *Lettuce v. Soll* (see (1980) 2 E.I.P.R. at 170–171).

[43] See para. 16–17, above.

[44] *e.g. Society of Accountants v. Goodway* [1907] 1 Ch. 489, 24 R.P.C. 159; *B.M.A. v. Marsh* (1931) 48 R.P.C. 565; *Law Society v. Society of Lawyers* [1996] F.S.R. 739. *cf. British Assoc. of Aesthetic Plastic Surgeons v. Cambright* [1987] R.P.C. 549.

[45] *British Legion v. British Legion Club* (1931) 48 R.P.C. 555; *Dr. Barnardo's v. Barnado Amalgamated* (1949) 66 R.P.C. 103; *British Diabetic Association v. Diabetic Society* [1996] F.S.R. 1.

(e) *Not trading: sponsorship and personality association*[46]

16–33 The practice of having celebrities lend their names to the indorsement of products or services is an advertising device with a long history. For the most part this kind of sponsorship is arranged by contract, and in the advertising industry is considered improper to use a person's name without his consent for this purpose.[47] However unethical it may be, it is not settled how far it is actionable. Consider two cases:

(1) The value in taking the alleged "sponsor's" name lies in his expert knowledge of the product or business in question and it can be shown that his professional reputation will be damaged by the association that is wished upon him. Typically a doctor's name is taken to promote a medicine. In such a case there should be no obstacle to the grant of relief. The bulk of dicta seem to be in favour, though there is no authority clearly in point.[48]

(2) The value in taking the alleged sponsor's name lies either in his own expertise or simply in the glamour of the association; but there is no evidence that any professional reputation will suffer or that there will be any other form of financial loss.[49] It was in this context that Wynn-Parry J. insisted that, for the grant of an injunction, there be "a common field of activity in which, however remotely, both the plaintiff and the defendant were engaged".[50] In *McCullough v. May*, he held that "Uncle Mac", the children's broadcaster, could therefore not restrain the use of "Uncle Mac" as a trade mark for shredded wheat.

The appearance of certainty about this test has appealed to some judges as a reason for refusing relief[51]; to others it has seemed unduly mechanical,

---

[46] See Murumba, *Commercial Exploitation of Personality* (1986) Pt. II; Frazer (1983) 99 L.Q.R. 281; Van Caenegem [1990] E.I.P.R. 452; Phillips [1998] E.I.P.R. 201.

[47] See, paras 2–25, 2–26, above.

[48] See, *e.g.* Lord Cairns, *Maxwell v. Hogg* (1867) L.R. 2 Ch. App. 307 at 310; Maugham J., *B.M.A. v. Marsh* (1931) 48 R.P.C. 565 at 574; Sugerman J., *Henderson v. Radio Corp.* [1969] R.P.C. 218 at 221. In the old case of *Clark v. Freeman* (1848) 11 Beav. 112, a doctor, who objected to being associated with a quack medicine, failed to secure an injunction before his case had been put to a jury in a trial at law. But that only reflected the general practice before the Chancery reforms of the 1850s; Lord Langdale M.R. expressly left open the possibility of an injunction after a verdict for the plaintiff. But *cf. Dockrell v. Dougall* (1899) 80 L.T. 556; and see McClelland (1961) 3 Sydney L.R. 525, Mathieson (1961) 39 Can B.R. 409; Treece (1973) 51 Texas L.R. 637.

[49] Exceptionally, the use of a person's name as a sponsor may be found to carry an innuendo that will support a defamation action: the suggestion, for instance, that an amateur sportsman was in fact taking money for his sponsorship: *Tolley v. Fry* [1931] A.C. 333, HL. If a popular personality has already contracted exclusively to sponsor another trader's product and this is known, the tort of interfering with business relations might apply.

[50] (1948) 65 R.P.C. 58.

[51] See, *e.g.* Walton J., *Wombles v. Womble Skips* (n. 36, above); *Nice and Safe Attitude v. Flook* [1997] F.S.R. 14; *cf.* Millett L.J., *Harrods v. Harrodian School* [1996] R.PC. 697 at 714–715, treating the absence of a common field of activity as highly relevant to the question whether there was a likelihood of confusion.

leading apparently to a denial of relief even where it is likely that the plaintiff has, or will, suffer damage.[52]

At root the question is whether the right to one's own name (and to such other indicia of personality as sound of voice and appearance)[53] deserve to be a full property right. In *Henderson v. Radio Corporation*, the Supreme Court of New South Wales considered that a professional dancing couple could enjoin the unauthorised use of their photograph upon a record sleeve without proof of any likely financial loss[54]; the Ontario Court of Appeal has recognised that a professional player may sue for the "appropriation of his personality".[55] No English Court has been prepared to go even so far,[56] let alone to address the question whether an unknown person can object to the use of his "personality" (name, photograph, etc.) in commercial or other propaganda without his permission.

In cases like "Uncle Mac" and *Henderson*, the person's name or image is **16–34** being used in a way which offers or at least suggests indorsement or sponsorship of the product. It does not indicate trade origin, but it creates a connection which is meant to promote a particular product or service. Famous individuals are also associated with products without any direct element of commendation: the products become attractive simply because of the image or the name on them. Exploitation of living personalities then takes its place alongside all the other names and images which today are the subject of merchandising: fictional characters, names, pictures and crests of buildings, cities, sites and institutions, famous trade marks and so on.

Today the use of names and images is frequently, but by no means universally, the subject of a publicity contract with the individual or the organisation which has "manufactured" the fame or been closely associated with it. In order to give some association with the commercial usage being "licensed", it is a standard practice for the grantor to be given power to control the quality of the grantee's goods bearing the name or image; whether that power is actually exercised is, however, a highly variable quantity. As we shall see later,[57] for all these types of sign, the same difficulty arises of identifying any underlying right of protection which calls

---

[52] *e.g.* in *Henderson v. Radio Corp.* (n. 54, below); *Totalizator Agency Board v. Turf News* [1967] V.R. 605.

[53] Such as the voice of a well-known actor: *Sim v. Heinz* [1959] R.P.C. 75; Lloyd [1961] C.L.P. 39.

[54] [1969] R.P.C. 218.

[55] *Krouse v. Chrysler* (1973) 40 D.L.R. (3d) 15 (claim failed on facts); *Athans v. Canadian Adventure Camps* (1978) 80 D.L.R. (3d) 583.

[56] *cf. Lyngstad v. Annabas* [1977] F.S.R. 62 (doubt in interlocutory proceedings whether real prospect of the pop-group Abba succeeding at trial in preventing use of their name and likenesses on T-shirts, jewellery, etc.); *Harrison v. Polydor* [1977] F.S.R. 1 (no real prospect of preventing use of photos of The Beatles on the sleeve for a recording of interviews with them).

[57] See paras 16–44 *et seq.*, below.

for a contractual licence; and this may well make a merchandising contract more a matter of convenience than legal necessity. Moreover, the missing link is unlikely to be a registered trade mark, unless the public has been taught by extensive trading that the name or image distinguishes the source of goods. If not, it will only conjure up the personality on account of his or her actual fame—as athlete, popstar, actor, or consort of the powerful.[58]

English law has steadfastly refused to adopt any embracing principle that a person has a right to his, or her name, or, for that matter to identifying characteristics, such as voice or image.[59] An entitlement simply to demand that such characteristics without more amount to property in personality is highly regarded as a commodification too far. Its tendency would be to prevent others from making reference to the person in too varied a range of circumstances to be socially or economically justified.[60] The recent attempt by the trustees of the Princess Diana foundation to appropriate her name and memory is just the demonstration of how far this process could extend. English courts have signalled clearly that only a much more discriminating approach is justifiable. There may be a case for affording somewhat greater protection to personal privacy than at present.[61] That, however, is itself a more limited thing; and it is the obverse of a right to annexe all value flowing from publicity.

16–35   To some degree, copyright will prevent the misappropriation of the various elements of personality. Photographs and extracts from sound or video recordings, if taken without licence for another's advertising or products, may well be sufficiently substantial to amount to infringement of the relevant copyrights or performance rights.[62] The demand for a separate right of publicity goes to cases beyond this range: those where, for instance, advertisers use an imitator to produce a "look-alike" or a "sound-alike" of a political personality or an actress.[63]

The leading commercial jurisdictions in the United States have been active in establishing a "right of publicity" within a common law frame of reference.[64] In doing so they have had to face all the difficulties of attempting to define and delimit a novel exclusive right in intangible subject-matter which Brandeis J. famously insisted must be a matter for legislatures rather than case law.[65] With organisations such as the Elvis

---

[58] *"Elvis Presley" Trade Marks* [1999] R.P.C. 567, CA, *cf.,* below, para. 17–46A.

[59] *ibid.*

[60] The person might be a municipality, a charity, a university, a government agency; *cf., e.g.* the use by a business of the NASA logo in the *Flook* case, n. 51.

[61] For which, see paras 8–54 *et seq.,* above.

[62] See also paras 16–45, 16–46, below.

[63] The right of publicity in the U.S. has advanced by virtue of these forms of misappropriation: thus a Jackie Onassis look-alike in an advertisement, and a Bette Midler sound-alike, have both been held actionable; *Onassis v. Christian Dior* 472 N.Y.S. 2d 254 (1984) (affd. 488 N.Y.S. 943); *Midler v. Ford Motor* 849 F. 2d. 460 (1988).

[64] See McCarthy (1989) 79 T.M.R. 681; Goodenough [1992] E.I.P.R. 55, 90.

[65] In the *INS* case 248 U.S. 215 (1918), SC (U.S.).

Presley and Martin Luther King Estates resorting to litigation in pursuit of publicity revenues, it has been necessary to consider to what extent the new right survives the individual him- or herself.[66]

These difficulties are doubtless one reason why British judges have not encouraged a right of personal publicity any more than they have welcomed claims to merchandising rights in characters and other signs. If a right against the misappropriation of personality for the purpose of advertising or dressing-up products and services, its conditions would need to be carefully defined by statute. To date, however, the British have chosen to limit the misappropriation of personal images to cases of advertising through controls which in the print media are organised voluntarily and which in broadcasting result from a statutory system of approval.[67] This practical approach avoids the excesses that may follow from conferring a private proprietary right in name, appearance and voice.

(4) The proper scope of passing off[68]

The action labelled passing off is not confined to misrepresentations that **16–36** the defendant's goods or services are those of a trade competitor. Expansion of the tort is aided by the unspecific terms in which the elements of reputation, confusion of customers and likely damage are indicated in Lord Diplock's five characteristics.[69] A number of key issues deserve to be reviewed, some connected with cases already decided, others of a more speculative nature.

(a) *Nature of the deception*

Trade marks and names, which traders employ as indications of origin, are, **16–37** so far as customers are concerned, a means of identifying qualities that they more or less consciously link with origin.[70] Because of this, it seems natural to allow passing off to be extended to other indications which give consumers similar information about quality, either *in toto* or in some specific respect. While there have been cases which have confined passing off to misrepresenting indications of origin, a number of other decisions have been more liberal. For instance, the following have been treated as actionable: inserting pages of advertisements into a magazine, thus making

---

[66] It is extremely difficult to arrive at a reasonable answer to such a question by judicial decision; accordingly some states have intervened with legislation.

[67] See paras 2–25, 2–26, above.

[68] See Ricketson (1984) U. NSW L.R. (Special Issue) 1; Terry (1988) 51 M.L.R. 296; Morcom [1991] E.I.P.R. 380; Meyer-Rochow (1994) 84 T.M.R. 38; Kamperman Sanders in Sterling (ed.) *Intellectual Property and Market Freedom* (1997) 131 and *cf.* Kaufmann, *Passing Off and Misappropriation* (1986); Stephens (1990) 99 Yale L.J. 759.

[69] *cf.* the remark of Romer L.J., para. 16–44, below.

[70] See paras 15–24 *et seq.*, above.

it less attractive to other advertisers and exposing the publisher to claims of responsibility for inaccuracy[71]; claiming that pictures of the plaintiff's products are the defendant's (a trick of newcomers into the building trade)[72]; "misappropriating" commendations from customers of another trader's goods[73]; advertising goods to be "as shown on television", when it was really the plaintiff's goods that had been shown.[74] Contrast with these the decision (now of doubtful standing) that no action lay against selling one collection of Hazlitt's Essays as the book set for a particular examination, when in fact it was another collection (the plaintiff's) that was set.[75]

16–38   The line between quality and origin is also blurred in cases where plaintiffs share a reputation in a name that is descriptive such as "champagne" or "Scotch whisky". In its "Advocaat" decision, the House of Lords refused to confine the kind of description that would suffice to special cases, such as appellations of origin which indicate that a product has physical properties associated with its place of primary production.[76] But there is another, even more striking, respect in which these cases have extended the notion of deception. In the cases concerning the defendant's use of "Spanish Champagne," "British sherry" and the like,[77] the addition of the national adjective must have told the cognoscenti that they were getting a substitute; only those who wanted "the real thing" without knowing what it was would not pick up the distinction.[78] Relief was given in order to protect the proper meaning of the words against dilution even by an expression which would confuse only those with little idea of that meaning and so of the plaintiff's reputation.[79] The Court of Appeal has accepted the sufficiency of this approach and held that it was applicable in a further "champagne" case, where the defendant's product, "elderflower champagne", was a non-alcoholic fruit cordial. The plaintiff champagne

---

[71] *Illustrated Newspapers v. Publicity Services* (1938) 55 R.P.C. 172; and see *Associated Newspapers v. Insert Media* [1991] F.S.R. 380, CA.

[72] *Bristol Conservatories v. Conservatories Custom Built* [1989] R.P.C. 455, CA; *John Robert Powers School v. Jessensohn* [1995] F.S.R. 947, CA (Sing.); Carty [1993] E.I.P.R. 370.

[73] *Plomein Fuel v. National School of Salesmanship* (1943) 60 R.P.C. 219.

[74] *Copydex v. Noso* (1952) 69 R.P.C. 38.

[75] *Cambridge University Press v. University Tutorial Press* (1928) 45 R.P.C. 335. A similar attitude is to be found in older cases in which the defendant laid claim to prizes, medals or patents properly belonging to the plaintiff, but the latter could not prove that the public therefore thought that it was getting his goods: see *e.g. Batty v. Hill* (1863) 1 H. & M. 264 (where the transient value of the reputation was stressed); *Tallerman v. Dowsing Radiant* [1900] 1 Ch. 1; *Serville v. Constance* [1954] 1 All E.R. 662. They might be differently decided today: see Kerly, para. 16–26.

[76] Thus "advocaat" was properly described a liqueur, wherever made, which contained spirit, but not fortified wine. In *Chocosuisse v. Cadbury* (February 25, 1999) CA, this was even extended to "Swiss Chocolate" because of its recognised creamy smoothness. In some desperation, the court's order defined this in terms of the ingredients which secured the quality (percentage of fats, particle size).

[77] See para. 16–15, above.

[78] See *Bollinger v. Costa Brava Wine* [1961] R.P.C. 116; *Vine Product v. Mackenzie* [1969] R.P.C. 1.

[79] See especially [1969] R.P.C. at 23.

house succeeded on evidence that some people in England would confuse the defendant's product with the wine, and also on the ground that the singularity and exclusiveness of "champagne" would be eroded, leading to "insidious but serious" damage to the champagne houses' interest in the name.[80]

This latter finding should be linked with certain other cases where an **16-39** interest outside the normal range of "reputation" has been treated by the Courts as a protectable part of business "goodwill". This is the basis on which the Court of Appeal has protected an author's connection with his work, a manufacturer's connection with commendations of his product and a builder's connection with the appearance of his conservatories.[81] The interests in question are such that their misappropriation by a defendant is treated as of itself damaging: proof of loss in trade as the result of confusion among customers is not required. The interests, it could be said, have the status of property, in the sense that their taking by others requires to be licensed.[82] Since a pragmatic approach prevails, the judges may accept other interests as entitled to be similarly treated. As already argued, there is a good case for so treating personal attributes of living people—name, likeness, voice and so forth; borrowing them directly or imitating them by means of a look- or sound-alike for advertising and similar commercial purposes should be tortious in itself. A similar argument can also be put in relation to the merchandising of characters and names, though it is inherently less compelling. To this we will return under a separate head below.[83]

The judges are not, however, prepared to allow any wholescale abandonment of the need to show confusion of customers leading to damage in favour of some loosely defined wrong covering cases where all it can be said is that a defendant derives some tangential advantage from imprecise recollection and association. This the Privy Council signalled in the "Pub Squash" case, over a general similarity of tone in advertising and packaging.[84] Since that decision, there have been a succession of attempts to base passing off on similarities of packaging get-up where the trade marks used are clearly distinct. Similar blue tubs for baby wipes, similarly ridged pots for "pot noodles", pink pages in newspapers, similarly wrapped digestive

---

[80] *Taittinger v. Allbev* [1993] F.S.R. 641, esp. at 668–670, 674, 678; and see Wadlow (para. 16–01, n. 1, above), para. 3.24; *Scotch Whisky Assoc. v. Glen Kella* [1997] E.T.M.R. 470. In *Harrods v. Harrodian School* [1996] R.P.C. 697, CA, the extension of liability to cases where there is no proof of confusion is rejected by Millett L.J., though accepted by Sir Michael Kerr (dissenting). The injunction also restrained breach of E.C. Regulation 823/87 on wine labelling; see Carty [1996] E.I.P.R. 629; *cf.* Murray [1997] E.I.P.R. 345.

[81] See, para. 16–37, above.

[82] As to which, see para. 16–44, below.

[83] See paras 16–44 *et seq.*, below.

[84] See para. 16–04, above.

biscuits[85]—in all these instances, the distinct trade marks were enough to dispel any possible confusion as to source.

16–40   Occasionally, the "look-alike" element in packaging has been held to overstep the line so as to cause likely or actual confusion. Such as a case was *Reckitt & Colman v. Borden*, where the English public was shown to be very familiar with the plastic lemon as an indicator of the plaintiff's juice— so familiar that they would not take account of the defendant's attached label giving its own name.[86] But since "look-alikes" are generally quite sophisticated, most escape legal censure. It is not enough that the public calls the established product to mind through some loose form of "association".[87]

(b) *Nature of the injury*

16–41 The other direction in which the "drink" cases extend concepts concerns the likelihood of damage. "Classic" passing off involves a plaintiff who is peculiarly injured because it is his exclusive goodwill which is misappropriated. But in the cases concerning a shared reputation it is not necessary to show that the plaintiff suffers more than others with whom he shares the goodwill.[88] This carries passing off some way towards providing a general unfair competition action against all misdescriptive promotion of products and services. It would seem no substantial step after these cases to allow any one trader whose goods have a particular quality from objecting when another advertises his goods as having the quality when they do not. In the "drink" cases, it is true, qualities were subsumed within a word describing the product as a whole. But "advocaat" was held properly to describe an egg-and-spirits drink, whereas the defendant's product was composed of egg and fortified wine. A similar outcome might well have been reached if the misdescription had been directly of the contents of the drink.

It would be going further again to give a competitor an action where his product does not contain the quality which the defendant inaccurately claims for his own. This would indeed make the mere fact of being a competitor a sufficient ground for objecting to misleading advertising. This is often permitted in legal systems which have a general concept of unfair

---

[85] *Scott v. Nice-Pak* [1989] F.S.R. 100, CA; *Financial Times v. Evening Standard* [1991] F.S.R. 7; *United Biscuits v. Burtons Biscuits* [1992] F.S.R. 14; *Dalgety Spillers v. Food Brokers* [1994] F.S.R. 504; Mills [1995] E.I.P.R. 116. *A fortiori*, in the case of the product itself: *Cadbury v. Ulmer* [1988] F.S.R. 385 ("Flake" chocolate sticks).

[86] Above, para. 16–06. For a similar outcome, *United Biscuits v. Asda Stores* [1997] R.P.C. 513 ("Puffin" biscuits which resembled "Penguin' Biscuits).

[87] For the failed attempt to secure protection of registered trade marks against "association" which lies beyond "confusion", see below, para. 17–95. Nothing has come of pressure upon the U.K. government to extend the protection for look-alikes: see *Hansard*, H.L., Vol. 553, cols. 78–83. *cf.* Annand (1996) 84 T.M.R. 142.

[88] See para. 16–15, above.

competition,[89] and the traditions of other E.C. States in the matter may eventually exert their own influence upon developments in Britain.[90]

Many would treat competitors and consumers as having the same interest **16–42** to prevent misrepresentative marketing. Accordingly they would welcome the provision of competitors' actions as an effective method of policing from within an industry. But before accepting this unthinkingly, it is as well to reflect upon the reasons that may in the past have led the judges to move with circumspection in this field. Competitors furnished with a right of civil action which includes the chance of stopping a rival by injunction have a powerful weapon at their command. Some indication of that power has already been outlined in Chapter 2. In the cut and thrust of competitive marketing, the threat of intervening when a rival is launching an advertising campaign can inflict grave injury. That, of course, is justified when the defendant is plainly in the wrong. But there will be many cases when the issue is not easily determined; and others again when the plaintiff's concern for the welfare of the consumer might seem rather heavily spiced with self-interest. No one can weigh in advance the respective benefits and costs of making the content of each competitor's advertising and labelling the subject of actionable criticism by the rest of his industry. No one can predict how far a penchant for competition by litigation might develop. With the growth of European and other foreign penetration of the British market, the predispositions of non-domestic enterprises in this direction might have a significant influence.

The British approach to date has been largely to rely upon a set of **16–43** criminal sanctions aimed directly at protecting the consumer, and, since 1968, enforced principally through the trading standards departments of local authorities.[91] The procedures of the criminal law do not normally allow for rapid preventive action and they require a high standard of proof. At least in England, competitors are as free as other private citizens to launch such prosecutions. However, it seems that they do so only occasionally when they feel their own interests to be particularly threatened. Accordingly, as these laws operate in their modern context,[92] they provide a reasonably adequate means of combatting the serious cases of malpractice. There is certainly some wisdom in the Courts' reluctance to give competitors the additional chance of bringing a civil suit, with the inherent danger of self-serving interference that this would import.

---

[89] In the U.S., see *ALI Restatement of Torts*, para. 761; Lanham Trade Mark Act 1946, s. 43(a).
[90] However, the Directive on Misleading and Unfair Advertising (84/450: [1984] O.J. L.250/17) did not in the end require that competitors be accorded such a right of action.
[91] See para. 2–24, above.
[92] See paras 15–19, 15–20, above.

(c) *Character merchandising*[93]

16-44 The limited protection currently available for the commercialisation of personality has already been outlined. Here we move to the general issue of merchandising. Again, we should begin with what can be legally protected. Merchandising of fictional characters may make prominent use of images of them. If those images—drawings, photographs, film clips—are copyright material which is owned by the person seeking to assert a right in them, and if they are being copied to a substantial extent without licence, then infringement occurs. However, there is no copyright in a fictional character or a performer's act outside the confines of the particular texts or scenarios in which the character or act is developed. Copyright does not extend to Biggles, or the character repeatedly played by Charlie Chaplin, whatever they are made to do or say.

Nevertheless passing off may sometimes be used in aid of copyright. In *Samuelson v. Producers Distributing*,[94] the defendant held out his film as containing a popular revue sketch written by the plaintiff, when in fact it did not. (If it had, liability in copyright would have arisen.) The plaintiff's copyright included the exclusive right throughout its duration to authorise filming of the sketch. In granting relief, the Court of Appeal in effect treated this aspect of the property as equivalent to goodwill built up through trade. Romer L.J. pointed out that injunctions granted to restrain "classic" passing off were "merely instances . . . of a much wider principle . . . that the Court will always . . . restrain irreparable injury being done to the plaintiff's property."[95] So where a fictional character is put into a new book, play or film an action may be grounded on injury to goodwill. A publisher, impresario or producer who shows that he is likely to lose sales of his own books or theatre seats in consequence will have a cause of action.[96] However, where the character is deployed in some way that does not compete with the publishing or audio-visual business of the original exploiters—as when its name (as distinct from any visual image) is used on T-shirts, toys, sweets, badges or what you will—the difficulty of demonstrating damage or its likelihood stands in the way of a passing-off claim. Thus the developers of those once-popular denizens of children's television, the Wombles, could not secure relief against a person using "Wombles" on

---

[93] See generally Adams, *Merchandising Intellectual Property* (1987); Vaver [1978] 9 I.I.C. 541; Wood and Llewelyn [1983] E.I.P.R. 298; Mostert (1986) 17 I.I.C. 80; Ricketson (1990) 1 Aust. I.P.J. 191; Pendleton (1990) 1 Aust. I.P.J. 242; Howell (1990) 6 Aust. I.P.J. 197; Poulter and Stephens (1991) 3 I.P.B.R. 7; Holyoak [1993] J.B.L. 444; Carty (1993) 13 L.S. 289; Jaffey [1998] I.P.R. 240. WIPO has made an international comparison: reviewed by Ruijsenaars (1994) 25 I.I.C. 532.

[94] [1932] 1 Ch. 201. *cf. Ormond v. Knopf* (1932) 49 R.P.C. 634.

[95] *Samuelson* case (n. 94, above) at 210. This dictum was used in cases such as "Champagne" to justify a broad view of passing off.

[96] Illustrations are *Shaw Bros v. Golden Harvest* [1972] R.P.C. 559 and *Marengo v. Daily Sketch* (1948) 65 R.P.C. 242, HL (cartoonist's nom-de-plume).

rubbish skips.[97] Arguments that the relevant goodwill arises from the public's belief that originators do grant licences and that this acts as a guarantee of quality have been dismissed in cases concerned with the merchandising of a name alone, whether the name is of an entirely fictional character (such as the Wombles), a television character associated with a particular actor (such as Kojak[98]) or a pop group (such as Abba[99]).

Of these instances, the last takes us squarely back to the protection of an **16–45** aspect of personality,[1] and the second suggests that there is an important intermediate case where actor and role elide to such an extent that the buying public may simply not distinguish between the two. In Australia, the commercialisation of personality has been more readily protected in the latter case as well as the former: the taking of the character, Crocodile Dundee (played by the highly personable Paul Hogan), for use in spoof advertisements was held to amount to a form of passing off.[2] Moreover, in a case concerning toys which were shoddy versions of the "Muppet" characters from *Sesame Street*, an Australian Court found (on strong evidence) that the public did think that such toys were made under licence of the originators.[3]

England has had one interlocutory decision which follows this Muppet precedent. Teenage Mutant Ninja Turtles—cartoon characters, who appeared in comic strips, videos and films—were such a success that their worldwide merchandising value ran to hundreds of millions of dollars.[4] The defendant had his own drawings done of turtles with similar characteristics and was licensing these to T-shirt makers. While no sufficient case of copyright infringement was made out for interlocutory relief, passing off succeeded.[5] Browne Wilkinson V.-C. saw this as a case in which the plaintiff was merchandising copyright drawings on a large scale and would lose the royalties if the defendants could continue "misrepresenting to the public that his drawings are the drawings of the plaintiffs or are licensed by the

---

[97] *Wombles v. Wombles Skips* [1977] R.P.C. 99.

[98] *Tavener Rutledge v. Trexapalm* [1975] F.S.R. 479, esp. at 485–486: unassociated sweet manufacturer built up substantial trade in "Kojakpop" lollipops; it was entitled to prevent a "licensee" of the owner of the television series from entering the same market.

[99] *Lyngstad v. Annabas* [1977] F.S.R. 62.

[1] See paras 16–33—16–35, above.

[2] *Pacific Dunlop v. Hogan* (1989) 87 A.L.R. 14; and see *Hogan v. Koala Dundee* (1988) 83 A.L.R. 187 (a very broad view of misappropriation of personality); Shanahan (1991) 81 T.M.R. 351; Burley [1991] E.I.P.R. 227; Duxbury [1991] E.I.P.R. 426.

[3] *Children's Television Workshop v. Woolworths* [1981] R.P.C. 187—a case in which the plaintiff did exercise carefully its quality control powers over licensees; and see also *Fido Dido v. Venture Stores* (1981) 16 I.P.R. 365. *cf. Lorimar Productions v. Sterling ("Dallas")* [1982] R.P.C. 395, SC (S.A.); *Grundy Television v. Startrain ("Neighbours")* [1988] F.S.R. 581. The refusal, in the related aspect of registered trade mark law, to accept that use of a pop star's name suggests a licensing arrangement strengthens the continuing British scepticism: *Re Elvis Presley Enterprises Applcns* [1999] R.P.C. 567, CA.

[4] Licensing was accordingly well-organised on terms which gave the licensors the right to control the quality of products bearing the designs and names.

[5] *Mirage Studios v. Counter-Feat Clothing* [1991] F.S.R. 145.

plaintiffs". It sufficed to show that the public believed that the Turtle characters would not appear without the plaintiffs' licence. It was not necessary—so he held, though this must surely be controversial[6]—to demonstrate that they would rely on this misrepresentation when buying the products.

16–46   The interlocutory nature of the decision makes it hard to pin down as a precedent. It is best regarded as a variant of the *Samuelson* case, in which the defendant is condemned for claiming to provide a known copyright work, when in fact he is offering something else.[7] Accordingly, it cannot be taken as instituting any radical departure from the previous law. With a certain reluctance, the Vice-Chancellor accepts the earlier authorities which give no protection to the merchandising of mere names.[8] No British Court has yet been prepared to take the major step of saying that names of characters deserve protection, not as indications of origin or of advertising support, but simply as names.

To draw the line at this point may seem cautious pragmatism—a distinction which has about it a distinct tinge of arbitrariness.[9] It does, however, place a barrier in the way of claims to exclusive rights for any product which bears a name or image popularised by someone else. For if the law is as wide as that, then potentially the act of publicising or popularising anything would appear to give exclusive rights in all signs and symbols which identify that thing; for a term, moreover, which is unlimited. Who knows whether that right is restricted to the business which does the initial popularisation, or is a piece of property which may be transferred independently; and whether this imports the other rights and liabilities that attach to property. If there is to be such a broad development, it is surely of the kind (following Justice Brandeis) which should be given concrete form in legislation.

16–47   English law is more limited in scope than many jurisdictions that actively foster a law of unfair competition. In arguing the case for extension, Vaver claimed that this would "reflect the habits of fair commercial men and public expectations, without any recognisable public interest weighing against it".[10] The case can of course be put attractively. The desire to exploit a character on merchandise stems from its success with the public in the original fictional entertainment. For that success the author or performer and his associates are responsible and they claim in effect that merchandising rights should become part of their property.[11]

---

[6] See Wadlow, *The Law of Passing Off* (2nd ed., 1994), paras 5.44–5.46, contrasting, in particular, the *Fido Dido* case (n. 3, above), which calls for proof of a causal relation between the misrepresentation and purchases.

[7] See para. 16–44, above.

[8] See nn. 97–99, above.

[9] The matter looks even more casuistic when it is realised that public authorities and personages often secure special protection of their own names and images: see para. 17–51, below.

[10] See n. 94, above.

[11] The manner in which other jurisdictions approach the question is described in several articles in [1978] Ann. I.P.L.

But the corollary of property is potential market power. The claim to merchandising rights is made at a time when the popularity of the character would give an opportunity to charge monopoly prices if the rights were conceded. Far from there being no public interest against according the rights, there seems to be a strong case for preserving competition. At least the argument is close enough to militate against extending the law by judicial decision. Major additions to copyright are today generally made by Parliament and, as we have seen, this is the way in which some forms of reaping without sowing have recently been made actionable.[12] The same ought to apply to the claim to merchandising rights.[13] If such a change were introduced, it would presumably also include merchandising rights in the names and pictures of real people such as pop stars. As already suggested, their claim seems rather stronger.[14]

What ought to be of concern is that someone who does not trade should have the right nevertheless to license. The law should let all competitors come onto the market until such time as one of them shows that the name definitely indicates goods originating from him to a substantial sector of the public. This is partly a question of preventing registered trade mark rights from being too readily acquired—an aspect that will be reviewed later.[15] But if the issue is raised in passing-off proceedings, a question of secondary meaning arises, since the character's name has non-trade mark associations.[16] This, equally, deserves to be dealt with by demanding clear proof that the name has nevertheless come to be recognised as indicating a trade connection.[17]

2. Injurious Falsehood[18]

(1) Elements of the tort

The tort of injurious falsehood is sometimes available to deal with forms of **16–48** unfair trading that do not amount to passing off. These may consist of false claims to legal rights (including, of course, intellectual property rights) and

---

[12] Attempts to include a merchandising right in CDPA 1988 did not succeed.

[13] Though not, presumably, in copyright legislation, since characters have not been thought an appropriate subject-matter for copyright; certainly the Whitford Committee (Cmnd. 6732, 1977) para. 909, thought an unfair competition law was the appropriate framework for any development, rather than copyright.

[14] See para. 16–17, above.

[15] See paras 17–24 et seq., below.

[16] cf. "Tarzan" T.M. [1970] R.P.C. 450.

[17] On this, note the facts of the "Kojakpops" case ([1975] F.S.R. 479) where initially there were a number of competitors exploiting the name, but they all faded away save the plaintiff, who proved very substantial goodwill.

[18] See generally, Wood (1942) 20 Can.B.R. 296; Prosser (1959) 59 Col. L.R. 425; Morison (1959) 3 Sydney L.R. 4.

other false statements, such as disparaging criticisms of a competitor's goods or business. But, in contrast with passing off, at the end of the nineteenth century, the Courts deliberately confined this tort to those circumstances which were most incontrovertibly unjustifiable. Their caution stands as one of the chief barriers to the adoption of any broad conception of unfair competition.[19]

In *Ratcliffe v. Evans*, Bowen L.J. declared written or oral falsehoods to be actionable "where they are maliciously published, where they are calculated in the ordinary course of things to produce, and where they do produce, actual damage".[20] This formulation, which encapsulates the tort in its modern form, is broad so far as types of falsehood are concerned, but narrow in its requirement of malice and special damage (the latter being now modified by statute in many cases). Each of these elements calls for separate consideration.

(a) *The falsehood*

16–49 The first actionable falsehoods concerned slanders of title to land. In the course of the last century, the tort came to cover other misstatements—especially about property and business—until any falsehood was encompassed; but the requirement of pecuniary damage has served to limit successful claims mainly to falsehoods about property, profession, trade or business. The plaintiff must show that the statement is false: true statements, however disparaging and harmful, are not actionable.[21]

The damaging untruth may arise by implication from what is actually said.[22] To state, for instance, that a man is working for a particular organisation may suggest to the hearer that he is no longer working in his former business and so deprive him of orders.[23] Equally, for a defendant to claim to be the sole agent for particular machinery may imply that the plaintiff is no longer, or never was, such an agent.[24] If a statement is not explicitly about the plaintiff, whether it must nevertheless be taken as referring to him depends on the particular circumstances. In this connection, the Courts have held that an untrue claim to a title of any kind, or to

---

[19] For its relation to the registered trade mark system, see paras 17–79 *et seq.*, below.
[20] [1892] 2 Q.B. 524 at 527.
[21] The onus of proof, moreover, lies upon the plaintiff: see *Burnett v. Tak* (1882) 45 L.T. 743; *Anderson v. Liebig's Extract* (1882) 45 L.T. 757; *cf. Hargrave v. Le Breton* (1769) 4 Burr. 2422 at 2425.
[22] As in defamation law, in the absence of intrinsic knowledge from which to draw an innuendo, the courts will look for the natural and ordinary meaning (including inferential meaning) which the words would convey to the ordinary, reasonable, fairminded, reader: *Charleston v. News Group* [1995] 2 All E.R. 313 at 317 (Lord Bridge); *Vodafone v. Orange* [1997] F.S.R. 34.
[23] *cf. Balden v. Shorter* [1933] Ch. 427.
[24] *Danish Mercantile v. Beaumont* (1950) 67 R.P.C. 111. Consider also *Liebig's Extract v. Anderson* (1886) 55 L.T. 206.

be an inventor or designer, is a falsehood that may be actionable at the instance of the person properly entitled, which forms a link to what is sometimes called "inverse" passing off.[25] But there must be some reason to associate the statement with the particular plaintiff, rather than with all traders of his class.[26]

(b) Malice

There are occasions when "malice", as a legal term of art, has a broad **16–50** objective sense, indicating circumstances when a person has done something which has no sufficient justification or excuse; and there have been suggestions that this is what the term means in the law of injurious falsehood.[27] But most modern decisions agree that here it refers to the defendant's state of mind. Did he know his statement to be false? Did he act with some "by or sinister purpose"[28] or (to put it less pungently) some "indirect or dishonest motive".[29] Stable J. has summarised the case law thus: if the defendant knows the statement to be untrue, it is malicious whether or not the defendant intended to benefit himself (or someone else) rather than injure the plaintiff. If, however, the defendant does believe his untrue statement, but nevertheless he makes it for the purpose of injuring the plaintiff, that too will suffice.[30]

(c) Special damage

Until Parliament intervened, the Courts required proof of special **16–51** damage—proof, for instance, that property had lost its value, or a business its custom or a source of supply, as a consequence flowing naturally from the false statement.[31] But, in trading cases at least, they did not always restrict this to unequivocal proof that the plaintiff had lost particular transactions or profits. Where a defendant said in a press report that the plaintiff had gone out of business, then it might well be sufficient for him to prove that his sales overall had forthwith fallen, if his customers were normally unknown and changing; but not if they were regular and known.[32] What evidence will suffice must depend on the whole circumstances; a

---

[25] e.g. *Serville v. Constance* [1954] 1 All E.R. 662; *Customglass Boats v. Salthouse* [1976] 1 N.Z.L.R. 36, [1976] R.P.C. 589 and see para. 16–37, above.

[26] cf. cases cited in para. 16–15, above.

[27] e.g. Lord Davey, *Royal Baking Powder v. Wright Crossley* (1900) 18 R.P.C. 95 at 99; and see Newark (1944) 60 L.Q.R. 366; Wood (n. 7, above) at p. 319.

[28] Harman I., *Serville v. Constance* (n. 25, above) at 665.

[29] Scrutton L.J., *Greers v. Pearman* (1922) 39 R.P.C. 406 at 417; *Balden v. Shorter* [1933] Ch. 427; cf. earlier, less stringent views: *Royal Baking Powder v. Wright, Crossley* (1901) 18 R.P.C. 95.

[30] *Wilts United Dairy v. Robinson* [1957] R.P.C. 220 at 237.

[31] *Haddan v. Lott* (1854) 15 C.B. 411.

[32] e.g. *Ratcliffe v. Evans* (n. 20, above); *Greers v. Pearman* (n. 29, above).

plaintiff who fails to follow up a reasonable prospect of furnishing concrete proof may severely weaken his case.

Section 3 of the Defamation Act 1952, has abrogated the need to prove special damage if the words in question (1) were calculated to cause pecuniary damage to the plaintiff and were published in writing or other permanent form, or (2) were calculated to cause pecuniary damage to the plaintiff in respect of any office, profession, calling, trade or business, held or carried on by him at the time of the publication.[33] The pecuniary damage must be likely as a natural and probable consequence of the wrongful act.[34] It is not, in other words, a specific part of the requirement of malice, but is akin to the requirement of likely damage in the tort of passing off.[35]

(2) Particular aspects

(a) *Relation to other torts*

16–52 If the defendant's statement represents that his goods or business are those of the plaintiff, it is an injurious falsehood that amounts to passing off. So it is actionable despite lack of malice.[36] If the statement tends to lower the defendant personally in the eyes of right-thinking members of society then it is actionable as defamation: proof of intent to defame is then, in principle, irrelevant; and it is for the defendant to excuse himself by proving the truth of the statement or establishing some other defence such as fair comment on a matter of public interest or one of the forms of privilege. It is not defamation, but only injurious falsehood, to disparage a trader's goods, business or property, save where there is also an imputation of undue "carelessness, misconduct or want of skill".[37] This may, of course, be the innuendo behind a statement about the goods or business. Unless this is so, honest disparagement is not actionable at common law.[38]

---

[33] This was recommended by the Porter Committee on the Law of Defamation (Cmd. 7536, 1952), paras 50–54. A defamatory statement that is in the same form or of the same character as the cases covered by s. 3 is actionable in defamation without proof of special damage. The Faulks Committee on Defamation (Cmnd. 5909, 1975), paras 584–589, recommended that the distinction between the written and the spoken word should be abolished.

[34] *Lynch v. Knight* (1861) 9 H.L.C. 577; *Stewart-Brady v. Express Newspapers* [1997] E.M.L.R. 192; *Customglass* case (n. 25, above) at 603.

[35] See paras 16–29 *et seq.*, above.

[36] An instance where both were successfully pleaded in the *Wilts United Dairy* case (n. 30, above).

[37] *Linotype v. British Empire Type-Setting* (1899) 81 L.T. 331; *Griffiths v. Benn* (1911) 27 T.L.R. 346.; *Kaye v. Robertson* [1991] F.S.R. 62, CA; *CHC Software v. Hopkins & Wood* [1983] F.S.R. 241. Each must in consequence be separately pleaded: *A & M Records v. Audio Magnetics* [1979] F.S.R. 1 at 9. The distinction nonetheless did not appeal to forthright minds: see Lord Halsbury in the *Linotype* case at 333.

[38] Defamation of a private corporation is in principle actionable (*South Hetton Coal v. North-Eastern News* [1894] 1 Q.B. 133); but not of a local authority (*Derbyshire C.C. v. Times Newspapers* [1993] A.C. 534, HL.)

Because injurious falsehood requires it to be shown that there was a misrepresentation of the truth, it will not be committed if a statement is made in corrected form, and an injunction may be limited to exclude this. In one distasteful example, newspaper reporters broke into the hospital room of an actor who was recovering from a serious head injury. They insisted on "interviewing" and photographing him despite his poor condition. They could be enjoined from publishing the interview as an "exclusive" granted to the paper, since this lie prejudiced the victim's undoubted chances of selling his story later to others. But they could not be stopped from publishing an account and picture which stated truthfully how the material was come by.[39]

(b) *False claims of infringement*

Because intellectual property is protectable by litigation alone, and not also **16–53** by possession, the ability to assert rights is crucial. And equally, as earlier noted,[40] because it often takes time and expense to settle whether there has been infringement of a valid right, a threat to sue can do immense commercial harm, particularly to a manufacturer whose customers receive the threats. In this connection, the limited scope of injurious falsehood deserves special note. For it is only if a person untruthfully and maliciously asserts to a rival's customers that they are receiving infringing goods that the rival has any cause of action under the general common law. Hence the introduction of the special statutory action for threats of patent, registered design and registered mark infringement; and the question whether the same should apply to other threats of litigation. These have already been discussed.[41]

(c) *Comparative advertising*

Comparison—explicit or implied, specific or vague—lies at the root of **16–54** modern advertising. Where there is price competition, the cheaper rival may seek to stress similarities in his comparison with the more expensive;

---

[39] *Kaye v. Robertson* [1991] F.S.R. 62, CA: no other cause of action was presented which justified interlocutory relief: there was no trespass to the person merely from a flashlight which caused no reaction; no passing off, because the plaintiff was not a trader (though he had a story to sell!); and there was no defamatory innuendo clear enough—not even the suggestion that he was treating with the *Sunday Sport*—to justify an injunction till trial. For a demand that there should be statutory intervention on German lines to prevent such invasions of privacy, see Markesinis (1990) 53 M.L.R. 802, (1992) 55 M.L.R. 118; or instead, for a more imaginative use of existing tort law and its remedies, see Prescott (1991) 54 M.L.R. 451; and note Bedingfield (1992) 55 M.L.R. 111. See also paras 8–54 *et seq.*, above.
[40] See para. 16–42, above.
[41] See paras 2–91—2–94, above. Note that one effect of emphasising the balance of convenience in proceedings for an interlocutory injunction may be to undermine the requirement of malice in injurious falsehood: see *Jaybeam v. Abru* [1976] R.P.C. 308. But *cf. Polydor v. Harlequin Records* [1980] F.S.R. 26, CA; *Crest Homes v. Ascott* [1980] F.S.R. 396.

where there is not, he may emphasise some point of differentiation, more or less genuine and useful to the consumer. In the absence of passing off, the only weapon which the common law provided against any sort of comparative advertising was restricted to disparagements that amounted to injurious falsehood. And at an early stage of both the modern tort and modern advertising, the Courts showed particular reluctance to allow such actions to succeed.

Not only must there be malice and untruth in the comparison, but, where the two are distinct, the misstatement must be about the plaintiff's goods and not about the defendant's.[42] In *White v. Mellin*[43] the House of Lords held it not actionable for a retailer to attach stickers puffing his "own brand" to tins of the plaintiff's baby food; all the stickers said was that the "own brand" was "far more nutritious and healthful than any other preparation". Lord Herschell, in particular, feared a flood of litigation over the rival merits of products and the deployment of judicial decision as a means of advertisement.[44] In *Hubbuck v. Wilkinson*[45] the Court of Appeal treated even an advertisement purporting to set out the results of chemical tests as no more than a statement that the defendant's paint was equal to, or somewhat better than, the plaintiff's.

16–55   Actions have occasionally succeeded for specific and damaging lies, such as that the defendant's newspaper circulation was 20 times that of any local paper (that is the plaintiff's).[46] The present test has been stated thus: there must be a real disparagement or untrue statement that a reasonable man would take to be a serious claim.[47] Hyperbolic puffing, in other words, will be discounted for what it is.[48] There has been very little chance to see whether, in an age of consumer testing, the judges remain as reluctant as their predecessors to find that the "reasonable man" takes comparisons seriously. But the stress on an objective test should be noted.

16–56   Over the last half-century, the common law could often be left on one side, because under section 4(1)(b) of the Trade Marks Act 1938, comparative advertising constituted infringement simply upon proof that a registered mark had been used to "import a reference" to the registered proprietor or his goods, whether that reference was true or false, flattering

---

[42] *Canham v. Jones* (1813) V. & B. 218; *Young v. Macrae* (1862) 3 B. & S. 264. *cf. Western Counties Manure v. Lawes* (1874) L.R. 9 Ex. 218, which was criticised in *White v. Mellin* (n. 43, below) at 164.

[43] [1895] A.C. 154, HL.

[44] *ibid.*, at 164; an idea recently stressed in the context of passing off: *Consorzio del Proscuitto di Parma v. Marks & Spencer* [1996] R.P.C. 351.

[45] [1899] 1 Q.B. 86; and see *Alcott v. Millar's Karri* (1904) 21 T.L.R. 30.

[46] *Lyne v. Nicholls* (1906) 23 T.L.R. 86. At the interlocutory stage, the judge will ask whether there was any likelihood of a jury finding the misstatements to be true: *Compaq v. Dell* [1992] F.S.R. 93.

[47] *De Beers Abrasive v. International General Electric* [1975] F.S.R. 323.

[48] "Advertisements are not to be read as if they were some testamentary disposition in a will": Whitford J., *McDonald's v. Burger King* [1986] F.S.R. 45 at 58.

or disparaging. Parliament somewhat cavalierly conceded that this aspect of a mark's "investment function" should be protected without qualification.[49] Under pressure from Europe, the 1994 Act takes a more cautious view of the misuse of comparative advertising by means of registered trade marks. In its role of consumer protector, The E.U. has also adopted a Directive on the subject.[50] It takes a circumspect view of permissible comparative advertising which to some degree seeks to curb certain muscular applications of Continental unfair competition laws to them in the past. The British government apparently considers that the Directive's terms require no alteration even to our common law principles. That, however, is a question to which we revert when comparing the position on registered marks.[51] But that is most unlikely to presage any new dawn for injurious falsehood in comparison cases.

Overall the law seems to have played a surprisingly minor role in the matter. Even before the new strictness of 1938, there was not much comparative advertising: very largely a "dog-bites-dog" attitude among advertising agencies and their clients kept "knocking copy" out of the British press. In the new atmosphere of "consumerism", the advertisers and the media found it circumspect to agree in principle that "fair" comparisons ought to be allowed,[52] and (despite the 1938 Act provision) they are now a regular feature of some industries' advertising. This only strengthens the case for returning the law to the discriminating attitude found in the cases on injurious falsehood.

---

[49] Some judges looked decidedly askance at this departure from the "origin function" of the mark: see esp. *Bismag v. Amblins* (1940) 57 R.P.C. 209, where the judges were divided about an advertisement to sell both lines of product compared; and *Aristoc v. Rysta* (1945) 62 R.P.C. 65 at 77, 79, 85.

[50] Directive 97/55, amending the Misleading Advertising Directive, 84/450.

[51] Below, para. 17–104—17–107.

[52] What is regarded as unjustifiable is outlined in the British Code of Advertising Practice (1995 ed.) II, 11–14.

CHAPTER 17

REGISTERED TRADE MARKS

1. REGISTRATION SYSTEMS

From the initial adoption of a registration system in 1875, the British **17–01** approach has been to treat common law protection and registration cumulatively, the common law giving root protection wherever trading reputation justified it and registration providing surer, more straightforward, protection when an official grant had been secured. As already outlined, the European scheme aims to make registration the regular form of protection, either through the national registries or the CTM Office. Common law protection will in consequence move to the sidelines. The catalytic effect of competition among registration systems may be considerable, and even more the dictates of electronic commerce on an international scale. In the interim, in a country such as Britain, where registration has not previously been a *sine qua non* to any marketing project, it may well be that the passing-off action will retain much of its present usefulness.[1]

This chapter is concerned with the new registration systems for the United Kingdom and for the E.U. and with the substantive law which, in large measure, is in common form for them all.[2] The interpretation of these standard statutory provisions will, at least initially, reflect inherited traditions and attitudes of the various countries.[3] These vary at two levels:

(1) **as to the extent to which legal protection of any kind should go**: some countries have been readier than others to carry the protection

---

[1] See generally, Annand and Norman, *Blackstone's Guide to the Trade Marks Act 1994* (1994); Firth, *Trade Marks; the New Law* (1995); Kitchin and Mellor, *The Trade Marks Act 1994* (1995); Morcom, *Guide to the Trade Marks Act 1994* (1994). For the CTM, see Tatham and Richards, *ECTA Guide to EU Trade Mark Legislation* (1997).

[2] For transitional arrangements, establishing the extent to which the old law still applies, see TMA 1994, Sched. 3; Annand and Norman, pp. 51–54. The 1994 Act deals with marks for goods and for services together, in contrast to the 1938 Act, as amended in 1984 to introduce service-mark registration: it then acquired parallel texts for goods marks and service marks.

[3] The final arbiter of their meaning is the E.C. Court of Justice. Interpretation of provisions deriving from the CTM Regulation or TM Directive depends upon them and not upon explanations offered in the U.K. White Paper or Parliamentary debates: *British Sugar v. James Robertson* [1996] R.P.C. 281 at 292.

of marks for goods and services beyond any mere origin function, so as to protect a variety of "investment functions" associated with matters such as dilution, comparative advertising and parallel importation. A strongly protectionist country is likely to have an engrained belief (at least among its judges) in the gullibility of its consuming public and of the need to protect established businesses from encroachments into their markets which play upon this naivety. What other explanation can there be of the obsessive policing of potential misrepresentation under the German Law of Unfair Competition?[4]

(2) **as to the type of legal protection to be employed**: even where there is general accord that certain conduct should not be permitted, countries differ over whether to impose liability through underlying principle, such as is provided by a law of unfair competition or (in common law jurisdictions) by torts of passing off and the like, or as a consequence of registering a trade mark; or both. A law, which requires almost all protection of marks to be given within it, will be likely to strain registration law to impose liabilities which other systems deal with through the inherently subtler medium of tort or unfair competition law.

This difference is significant, since delegates from Benelux countries secured certain extending provisions in the E.C. Directive and Regulation which to some degree reflected their own unified law; and in consequence there has been a drive to recognise Benelux law as a prescient source of interpretation of the E.C. texts.[5] English courts were quick to discountenance this presumption.[6]

2. THE PROCESS OF REGISTRATION

17–02 This section outlines the steps involved in applying for a registered trade mark by virtue of the Trade Marks Act 1994.[7] It takes, first of all, the case of an application under national law to the British Registry. Where an applicant is interested only in the national market, his sole objective will likely be a British registration. But through United Kingdom participation in the Madrid Protocol,[8] those with wider horizons may use an application to the British Registry as the basis for an "international registration" in

---

[4] Now recognised as such by a leading authority: Schricker [1994] GRUR Int. 586.
[5] *e.g.* the content of unpublished Minutes of the Council Meeting adopting the E.C. Directive: para. 17–95, n. 98, below.
[6] See Laddie J., *Wagamama v. City Centre Restaurants* [1995] F.S.R. 713; discussed in para. 17–92, below (concerning "association" of marks—a central issue).
[7] For fuller accounts, see the works cited in n. 1, above.
[8] For the genesis of the Protocol, see para. 15–14, above. The CTM system may also join Madrid, but currently there are objections, on linguistic grounds, from Spain and Belgium.

TRADE MARK APPLICATIONS
FOR AND FROM THE UNITED KINGDOM

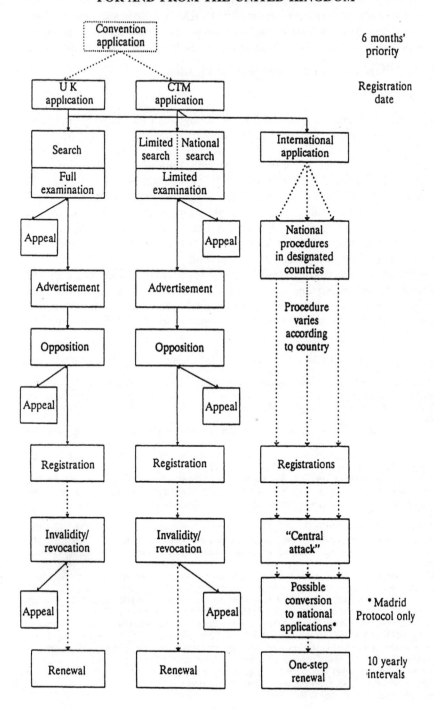

Protocol countries. This addition is dealt with next. Finally, within the E.C., it is possible to apply to the Office for the Harmonisation of the Internal Market (Trade Marks and Designs) ("OHIM") in Alicante for a Community Trade Mark having effect throughout the whole market.[9] A simple diagram on p. 571 indicates these alternatives and their inter-relationships.

(1) Procedure for a United Kingdom application

(a) *Applicants*

17–03 Any person, natural or legal, who is intending bona fide to use a mark for the goods or services specified in the application, may apply to the Trade Marks Registry of the Patent Office[10] to register it.[11] There is no requirement to have used the mark before applying. One of the great advantages of registration is to be able to secure legal protection before launching the mark itself.[12] If it can be shown that there was no such intention, then the application will have been in bad faith and can be rejected for that reason, or expunged after registration.[13] It has been the practice of the British Registry to query applications for very wide lists of goods or services.[14] This provides some hedge against pure stockpiling.

Applications which are in bad faith for some other reason must also be rejected. If an importing distributor deliberately seeks to register the foreign manufacturer's mark for itself, against the will of the manufacturer, it ought to fail[15]; the same applies as between employee and employer.[16]

---

[9] For the evolution of OHIM, see para. 15–16, above. It began to receive applications from April 1996, with a view to processing them from the autumn of 1996.

[10] The Manchester Branch of the Registry has now been fully absorbed; the Cutlers' Company continues to maintain the Sheffield Registry of Cutlery Marks. For current legislation on hallmarking, see *Butterworth's Trading and Consumer Law* (1976ff.), Div. 3, paras 2501–2956.

[11] Under the TMA (1994) s. 32(2), the application must: (1) request registration; (2) state the name and address of the applicant; (3) state the goods and/or services to be covered; and (4) set out a representation (or description) of the mark. For conversion of a pending 1938 Act application, see TMA 1994, s. 105, Sch 3, para. 11.

[12] Federal registration in the U.S. was for long dependent on use. But the use requirement there has been changed; and indeed the TRIPS Agreement precludes any prior use requirement, or indeed any requirement to show use within three years of the application date: Art. 15(3).

[13] TMA 1994, ss. 3(6), 32(3), 47(1); TM Dir., Art. 3(2)(d) (permissive); *cf.* CTM Reg., Art. 51(1)(b) (post-grant invalidity only). And *cf. Unilever v. Cussons* [1998] R.P.C. 369, JC. The objection goes only to bad faith; for other objections to registration, see paras 17–41 *et seq.*, below.

[14] Under the 1994 Act, a mark may be infringed by use upon similar goods or services, whereas previously the goods or services had to be within the registration: see para. 17–87, below. This gives added reason for restricting the scope of the registration itself: *Mercury Communications v. Mercury Interactive* [1995] F.S.R. 850; and see para. 17–91, below.

[15] Equally, any registration obtained by the agent should be expungeable: see, *e.g. "Sabatier" T.M.* [1993] R.P.C. 97. In the case of a Paris Convention national or corporation, rights against the agent's registration and use are conferred by the TMA 1994, s. 60 (in implementation of the Convention's Art.) *cf.* the case where the mark becomes an indication of the agent (*e.g.* as repairer and source of replacement parts): see, *e.g. Diehl's T.M.* [1970] R.P.C. 435; *"Al Bassam" T.M.* (n. 24 below).

[16] *e.g. "Zoppas" T.M.* [1965] R.P.C. 381.

This requirement should also be available against pre-emptive bids which seek:

(i) to stockpile marks because others may want them[17];
(ii) to misappropriate marks with a strong reputation elsewhere[18]; and perhaps even
(iii) to acquire without consent other "merchandisable" signs, such as the names of pop stars and film characters.[19]

All these objectives have their merits. The courts are only beginning to indicate how ready they are to pursue them. It is not settled whether in this context "bad faith" is a broad concept covering insincerity, artificiality or lack of genuine intention to use; or is narrower in requiring proof of actual dishonesty.[20] The latter view would render many "stockpiling" applications valid; and, moving in that direction, courts have so far refused to interfere with applications where there is a real intention to use the mark on some of the goods included in the specification.[21]

The practice of trade mark "squatting" has long been known[22]: a mark becomes well-known abroad before being extended to use in the U.K. An adventurer registers it in advance, expecting then to be bought off by the foreign owner who has built up the reputation.[23] Under the previous legislation, the courts refused applications on the ground that copying the foreign mark meant that the copier could not honestly claim to be its proprietor.[24] It is desirable that this conduct should be treated as "bad faith" under the new law since the concept distinguishes between cases where the registrant does and does not have sufficient ground for his claim.[25]

---

[17] As in *Imperial Group v. Philip Morris* [1982] F.S.R. 72, CA: one motive in seeking to register "Nerit" for cigarettes was to stop a rival from using "Merit".

[18] As in *Brown Shoe's Application* [1959] R.P.C. 29: "Naturaliset" for shoes refused in the U.K., given that it was deliberately derived from "Naturaliser", well-known for shoes in the U.S. A competitor whose mark is being misappropriated may need to bring opposition proceedings in order to demonstrate the bad faith involved: TMA 1994, s. 5(4) may need to be broadly interpreted in order to give a relative ground of objection covering all these cases.

[19] See TMA 1994, s. 3(6), and note in relation to "well-known" Convention country marks, s. 56 (para. 16–17, above).

[20] See *Roadtec v. Unison* [1996] F.S.R. 805.

[21] *Second Sight v. Novell* [1995] R.P.C 423; *Roadtec v. Unison* above, n. 20.

[22] It is more expensive and laborious than the recent "domain name squatting" but it involves the same parasitic instinct which Courts everywhere seek to combat as evidently and inexcusably unfair: see above, para. 15–21.

[23] See, *e.g. Brown Shoe's Appln* [1959] R.P.C. 29.

[24] *Brown Shoe's Application*, (n. 23, above). There was more hesitation about character merchandising (*"Rawhide" T.M.* [1962] R.P.C. 133). *cf.* also cases where the application was bona fide and any British goodwill was the applicant's: *"Genette" T.M.* [1968] R.P.C. 168 CA; *"Al Bassam" T.M* [1995] R.P.C. 511, CA.

[25] In the nature of things, the issue is likely to be raised only in opposition or invalidity proceedings, and under the CTM only the latter are possible (see CTM Reg. Art. 51(1)(b)). Owners of famous marks accordingly campaign for some form of international register from which national systems would derive proof and so be enabled to reject the application of their own motion at an early stage.

A more refined issue which goes to bona fides is the question whether the mark is to be used for the goods or services specified or really as a mark for something else. Under the old law, the owners of the famous mark, "Kodak", lost their registration of it for clothing, when their only use of it was to advertise cameras and films on T-shirts.[26]

An application must contain the following elements: a request for registration, the applicant's name and address, a statement of the goods and/or services to be included in the registration and a "representation" of the mark.[27] If complete it will be given a filing date—a vital factor in determining its claims as against competing applications and uses.[28]

(b) *Priority*

17–04 Sometimes independent parties will be seeking the same or similar marks without either of them being able to claim seniority from prior use. Then the issue will turn on which application has the earlier filing date, and priority arrangements under the Paris Convention may be important. These allow an applicant[29] in (say) the United Kingdom to claim up to six months priority from an application in another Convention country.[30] If there has been more than one earlier application, it is the first that counts, subject to the exception that an application which has been abandoned without publication may be discounted.[31]

(c) *Classification*

17–05 The Trade Marks Register is divided into 42 Classes, 34 for goods and 8 for services, in accordance with the Nice International Arrangement on the subject.[32] This classification is an administrative measure, designed to aid the process of searching. An applicant needs to name all the goods and services for which he wants the registration from the outset, since no amendment is allowed on this score.[33] Since many Classes are wide, the

---

[26] *"Kodak" T.M.* [1990] F.S.R. 495; and see *"Wells Fargo" T.M.* [1997] R.P.C. 503; *"Visa" T.M.* [1985] 323; *"Wild Child" T.M.* [1998] R.P.C. 455.

[27] TMA 1994, s. 32, which also requires a declaration of actual or intended use. For "representation", see para. 17–21, below.

[28] *ibid.*, s. 33.

[29] The applicant must have Convention nationality or establishment.

[30] The same principle applies in relation to dependent British territories and to other countries (*e.g.* Taiwan) with which Britain has a bilateral agreement on the matter; but not in relation to an earlier British application (which may, however, be the subject of a merger under TMA 1994, s. 41). See in general s. 35, which allows partial priorities to be claimed: see Annand and Norman, pp. 44–45.

[31] At the U.K. filing date the earlier application must have been withdrawn, abandoned or refused without publication or any rights remaining outstanding: TMA 1994, s. 35(4), following the Paris Convention, Art. 4C(4).

[32] Originally of 1957 and now in its sixth edition. See TMA 1994, s. 34; TMA 1994 Rules, Sched. 4; r. 40 allows the Registrar to re-classify pre-1938 (Sched. 3) registrations.

[33] See TMA 1994, s. 39(2) for the very limited ability to amend applications.

applicant will often specify the goods or services within a Class for which registration is sought. The Registrar has a final power to decide the Class in which particular goods or services are to be placed.[34] Classification does not directly affect the validity or the scope of protection of a mark.[35] It does not, for instance, settle what goods or services shall or shall not be treated as "similar".[36] Under the 1994 Act (for the first time) a single application may be made in respect of goods or services in different classes, though still with supplementary fees for each class.[37] Moreover, there is provision for filing a single application covering a series of marks which differ only in non-essentials.[38]

The new law no longer requires that, for a defendant to infringe, he must be using the mark for goods or services strictly within the registration: the right now extends to similar goods or services and, for marks with a reputation, sometimes beyond. So it has been said that wide scope for the registration is no longer justified.[39] Moreover, in construing the registration it is the core meaning which should be used.[40] Since service marks became registrable, there has been a persistent campaign from supermarkets and chain stores to secure the registration of their name as a mark for "retail services".[41] If such a registration could be obtained without limitation, it might cover all goods sold in the store under the store's own brand name. It could have the convenient effect of avoiding having to seek registrations in the various goods Classes for the different items sold and would expand to cover new lines as they were introduced. So long as not challenged for non-use, it might indeed cover services for goods of any kind, thereby providing a form of "dilution" cover which is not available to manufacturers.[42] Certainly it would have the cost-saving effect of permitting a single registration fee without class supplements, but that is by no means the only

---

[34] TMA 1994, s. 34(2).

[35] However, a reference in the description of goods or services to the classification (as, for instance, "syrups in Class 30") will exclude those goods under another class (as, for instance, syrups constituting jams, which fall under Class 29): *British Sugar v. James Robertson* [1996] R.P.C. 281 at 288–290.

[36] However, the fact that a registration is limited to a type of goods "within Class X" is likely to restrict the range of goods outside Class X which can be regarded as "similar": see *British Sugar v. Robertson*, [1996] R.P.C. 281, below, para. 17–35.

[37] TMA 1994 Rules, r. 5.

[38] TMA 1994, s. 41(1)(c)—this allows variations in script, hyphenation and non-distinctive suffixes, such as model numbers, to be covered in one application, for which only a single fee is payable. In this connection, particularly, the Registry's power to allow division or merger may be useful: TMA 1994, s. 41(1), TMA 1994 Rules, rr. 19, 20. There is also power in TMA 1994, s. 41(1) to merge or divide applications.

[39] *Mercury Communications v. Mercury Interactive* above, n. 14.

[40] *Avnet v. Isoact* [1998] F.S.R. 16 (running an Internet service for other advertisers is not providing "advertising and promotional services").

[41] They are allowed this form of registration in some other countries, notably the United States.

[42] Presumably a multiple manufacturer would fare no better if he sought to register for "production services".

issue at stake. The claim failed under the old law,[43] and it has found no recognition in the new regime.[44]

(d) *Search and examination*

17–06 An intending applicant will in all likelihood have a search undertaken for prior conflicting marks. Whether or not this happens, upon receipt with the necessary fee, the Registry will, as in the past, conduct a search of earlier marks, to the extent that is considered necessary.[45] It will then examine the application in the light of both the absolute and relative grounds of objection discussed below.[46] If it finds the mark not registrable, it must inform the applicant and allow representations and, if permitted, amendments.[47]

Once the Registrar is satisfied that the application meets the conditions specified in the Act, it must be accepted.[48] There is no longer any additional discretion in the matter.[49] Advertisement of the application follows in the Trade Marks Journal.[50] Once this occurs, the file becomes open to public inspection[51]—a change from the previous law, and one which could provide opponents with ammunition.

(e) *Opposition*

17–07 Any person may then within three months launch a formal opposition,[52] or in the alternative submit observations informally.[53] An opposition must allege at least one of the substantive grounds of objection, absolute or relative.[54] It may be supported by evidence, normally in the form of

---

[43] *Dee's Application* [1990] R.P.C. 159, CA; and for the same attitude, *Tool Wholesale v. Action Bolt* [1991] R.P.C. 251, SC (S.Af.); *cf.* Morcom [1989] E.I.P.R. 417.

[44] In one of their secret minutes, the E.C. Council and Commission showed a similar reluctance: see Morcom (n. 1, above), para. 2.5. An amendment seeking to admit marks for "retail services" was rejected in Parliament: *Hansard*, HL, Public Bill Committee, January 13, 1994, cols. 3–10.

[45] For the prospect of eliminating the official search after 2004, see para. 17–11, above.

[46] For the role of disclaimers, see para. 17–60, below.

[47] TMA 1994, s. 37(4). Amendment may restrict the specification of goods or services; beyond this, only name and address, errors of wording or copying and obvious mistakes may be corrected: s. 39; TMA 1994 Rules, r. 18.

[48] The former law allowed him an ultimate discretion to refuse acceptance.

[49] As there was under the TMA 1938, s. 17(1). The difference is more than a semantic one: *cf.* Annand & Norman, p. 41.

[50] TMA 1994, s. 38. There is no longer a power to advertise before formal acceptance.

[51] TMA 1994, s. 67.

[52] *ibid.*, s. 38(2). The period is no longer extendible on payment of a fee. For one thing, the Madrid Protocol imposes strict time limits on the processing of international applications. The applicant will receive notice of opposition or observations, and may respond to the former by a counter-statement, leading to the filing of evidence, a hearing (if requested) and a reasoned decision. For details, see TMA 1994 Rules, rr. 13, 14.

[53] TMA 1994, s. 38(3); this may lead to the Registrar reopening the case; *cf.* the more limited effect of observations under the CTM Reg., Art. 41.

[54] For which, see paras 17–23 *et seq.* below.

statutory declarations. There is now provision for discovery. Accordingly the power to call and cross-examine witnesses may acquire greater usefulness.[55]

(f) *Appeal*

A decision by the Registrar, either at the *ex parte* or *inter partes* stage, is **17–08** subject to appeal either to the High Court or to an "appointed person".[56] Appeals must be notified within one month of the decision.[57] Costs may be awarded in all proceedings and security for costs required.[58]

(g) *Registration and term*

Once an application has succeeded in overcoming whatever objections have **17–09** been raised to it,[59] it will be registered as of the filing date of the application.[60] From this "date of registration" the right will last for ten years and will then fall due for renewal at ten-yearly intervals for as long as the mark does not become liable to revocation, particularly for non-use.[61] The registration may be voluntarily surrendered, in whole or in part[62]—an important provision in the negotiation of compromises with others who have or want potentially conflicting marks. While the registration continues it may be amended or otherwise rectified only in strictly limited ways.[63] Registration creates a prima facie case of validity.[64]

Registrations under the previous legislation become registrations under the 1994 Act on October 31, 1994; only attacks on their validity which have been commenced by proceedings before that date will continue to be governed by the 1938 Act.[65]

---

[55] TMA 1994, s. 69(b).

[56] The latter is an individual similar to the senior barrister appointed to hear *ex parte* appeals (only) under the former law. But the appointment is now by the Lord Chancellor, not the President of the Board of Trade: *ibid.*, s. 77. From this person, no further appeal lies, though on issues of Community law, questions may be still be stated to the ECJ.

[57] *ibid.*, s. 76.

[58] *ibid.*, s. 68.

[59] Even after disposal of oppositions, the Registrar may refuse to register the mark if it was accepted in error: *ibid.*, s. 40(1). The fee for registration must be paid: s. 40(2).

[60] *ibid.*, s. 40(3). However, infringement proceedings can only be initiated after actual registration—though they may claim damages retrospectively; and criminal proceedings under s. 92 can only relate to things done after actual registration: s. 9(3). Rectification of the Register is permissible only to the limited extent allowed by s. 64; the mark itself may be changed only to alter a name or address, if it does not substantially affect the mark: s. 44.

[61] Previously U.K. grants were for seven years at a time, a term which applies across the transitional divide (*ibid.*, Sched. 3, para. 15). For renewal, see s. 43, which allows for a request up to six months late, upon payment of a supplementary renewal fee. A trade mark which lapses for failure to renew may be restored under certain conditions: TMA 1994 Rules, rr. 29, 30.

[62] TMA 1994, s. 45, TMA 1994 Rules, r. 26; Firth (n. 1, above), Chap. 9; *cf. Second Sight v. Novell U.K.* [1995] R.P.C. 423.

[63] See TMA 1994, s. 44.

[64] *ibid.*, s. 72.

[65] TMA 1994, Sched. 3, para. 2.

One way in which trans-European businesses may make use of the Community system, even for their established marks, is by obtaining a Community registration and then surrendering their equivalent national marks. This they can do while retaining the "seniority" of the national mark[66]; and they will do so if the advantages from fee reductions and unified infringement proceedings prove sufficient.

(2) Madrid Protocol: international application

17–10   Britain is now introducing the Protocol version of the Madrid Agreement concerning International Registration of Marks.[67] Something has already been said of the complexities which will result from maintaining the old Madrid Agreement for its original countries in parallel with the Protocol for relations between them and the Protocol countries. Since the United Kingdom will only participate in the Protocol, attention may be confined to it.

The Protocol, like the original system, is "closed", in the sense that it can be used only by persons who are vested in a Protocol country or "organisation".[68] Vesting can arise by nationality, domicile or—most importantly—by having a "real or effective industrial or commercial establishment" in a country. The first step is to make a "home" application for the mark.[69] On fulfilling this pre-condition, an international application, in English or French, can be made to WIPO as the administrator of the Madrid and Protocol systems, seeking registration in as many other Member States of either as are designated.[70] After a formal examination, it is passed to the national offices of those States for treatment in the same manner as national applications there.[71] The national offices have a limited period in which to find the application unacceptable: 18 months or such longer period as it takes to determine an opposition.[72] For this a fee equal to the ordinary national fee may be charged.[73]

There is a limited form of "central attack". If, say, a British applicant makes an international application for five other countries and then fails to

---

[66] CTM Reg., Arts 34, 35; but subject to attacks on the validity of the prior national marks: see TMA 1994, s. 52(2)(b).

[67] TMA 1994, ss. 53, 54. See Gevers (1991) 3 IP in Bus. No. 6, p. 19; (1992) 4 IP in Bus. No. 1, p. 27; Kunze [1994] E.I.P.R. 223; Annand and Norman, Chap. 15.

[68] "Organisation" refers to an organisation of states together, notably the CTM system.

[69] Madrid Protocol, Art. 2. The original Madrid requires a home *registration* as first base— which created difficulty for a system with full examination such as the British.

[70] Madrid Protocol, Art. 3ter. Further designations can be made subsequently as required. One application may cover as many classes of the Nice classification system as are required.

[71] At this point, it remains generally desirable to use a local trade-mark agent.

[72] Madrid Protocol, Art. 5. With the opposition addition, this is much longer than the 12 months allowed under original Madrid.

[73] Madrid Protocol, Arts 7(1), 8(7), 9ter. Original Madrid fees are noticeably lower, and there is some potential for discrimination against those who do not use the international system for their non-home applications; but there are not likely to be many such cases.

secure or to keep his British application within its first five years, then all the other applications-cum-registrations fall as well; but (unlike original Madrid) they may be converted into national applications in any of the other countries, holding the priority date of the British application for the purpose.[74] Registration lasts for 10 years,[75] and is renewed at WIPO for all the designated states. Assignments may also be registered centrally as may various formalities, such as changes of name.[76] Advertisement of the registration is undertaken by WIPO in *Les Marques Internationales*.

(3) Community trade marks[77]

Applications for a CTM are made to OHIM in Alicante.[77a] In many **17–11** respects, applications for a Community mark follow a similar course to the British route. Details will therefore not be given here, but can be found in the CTM Regulation, Title IV (registration procedure), Title V (duration, renewal and alteration), Title VII (appeals) and Title IX (procedure).

The one substantial difference is the more limited Community system of official search for conflicting earlier marks and other rights. There were very considerable arguments over whether, and if so to what extent, there should be any official searching and examination built into the new system, reflecting the obvious differences in national approach. A conditional compromise has found its way into the Regulation, which must be the subject of a Commission review after five years of operation. To begin with, the CTM Office will search its own Register and will make arrangements for searches of national registries with any Member State that is willing to co-operate. This does not lead to an *ex officio* examination on relative grounds. Instead owners of cited registrations are notified, so that they may oppose if they wish. Smaller businesses in countries which contribute national searches will be particular beneficiaries of this. There is inevitably an additional expense. This is not welcomed by large industry in Europe and eventually all searching may become private. In contrast, the British legislation guarantees continuance of search and official examination on relative grounds until 2004.

The range of objections which may be raised encompass rights both in earlier marks throughout Community countries and earlier rights, protected

---

[74] Madrid Protocol, Art. 9*quinquies*.
[75] *ibid.*, Art. 6; the initial registration under Madrid is for 20 years.
[76] Madrid Protocol, Arts 9, 9*bis*.
[77] See Tatham and Richards, Chaps 23–26; Elzaburu and Baz in Franzosi (ed.), *European Community Trade Mark* (1997), p. 341; Pagenberg (1998) 29 I.I.C. 406.
[77a] The issue of languages has created tensions and produced a complex result. Applications may be in any of the twelve official languages of the E.U.; and publications of the CTMO and Registry entries will be in those languages. Oppositions and cancellation proceedings must be in one of the Office's official languages: English, French, German, Italian and Spanish: CTM Reg., Arts 115–117.

through passing-off or unfair competition actions or through other intellectual property and associated rights. It remains to be seen whether the Community system can bear the burden that this imposes. More will be said of it in relation to the relative grounds of objection. When hearing an opposition, the Office has the power to invite the parties to make a friendly settlement—a provision which has no explicit counterpart in British procedure.[78] Long disputed, this compromise provision is feared by some as a tool which will indirectly force bureaucratic solutions, involving reductions in the range or degree of exclusivity attaching to marks which in some degree conflict with one another.

3. PROPRIETARY INTERESTS AND LICENCES

17-12 As with the other main forms of intellectual property, registered trade marks are now declared to be a personal property right under English law.[79] Trade marks are protected in law primarily in order that they may serve the function of distinguishing the "origin" of goods and services. As already explained, there has in the past been considerable resistance to the idea that marks may be treated simply as independent items of property capable of joint ownership, assignment, licensing and security interests as suits the registered proprietor. However, this concern has weakened progressively over time in many legal systems. Such marketing practices as the merchandising of popular characters and the franchising of business packages, whether for production or distribution of goods, or for the provision of services, have led to demands that rights in marks be more readily capable of being shared, divided and transferred.

The new European law meets this demand.[80] The rules on property and dealings are freed from fetters which were still present in the 1938 Act. There is now no limit on the persons who may be co-proprietors of trade marks: no legal relationship or business association has to be demonstrated.[81] Presumptively co-owners have equal undivided shares in the mark. Each has the right to use the mark personally or through an agent. But the consent of all other co-proprietors is needed in order to license, assign or charge the share.[82]

---

[78] CTM Reg., Art. 43(4) (and for revocation and invalidity, see Arts 56(4), 96(5)).

[79] TMA 1994, ss. 2(1), 22 (in Scotland, incorporeal moveable property). This applies also to applications to register, as in general do the other provisions on proprietary effect: s. 27. For Community marks as "objects of property", see CTM Reg., Arts 16 *et seq.*

[80] For the equivalent position under the CTM, see Tatham and Richards, Chap. 21; Kunze in Franzosi (ed.), *European Community Trade Mark* (1997), p. 243.

[81] *cf.* TMA 1938, s. 63, requiring joint use and joint connection. The change is not however from joint tenancy to tenancy in common as those terms are understood in property law generally: *cf.* Annand and Norman, pp. 188–190. For transitional arrangements, see TMA 1989, Sched. 3, para. 7.

[82] TMA 1994, s. 23(1)–(4). On bankruptcy, the share passes to the trustee in bankruptcy (see *Hansard*, HL Vol. 552, col. 745). In infringement proceedings, after the interlocutory stage, all co-owners must be joined as plaintiffs, or else as defendants: TMA 1994, s. 23(5).

(1) Assignment

Previously assignments of registered marks were subject to public interest **17–13** controls exercised by the Registrar. An assignment, together with a transfer of the business in which the mark was used, was of course permissible.[83] But if there was no transfer of goodwill, a special procedure had to be followed, which was intended to eliminate any serious prospect of resultant confusion. It involved notification to the Registrar, and, if the Registrar required it, advertisement of the assignment.[84]

Under the 1994 Act, there is no such supervision of assignments of registered United Kingdom marks without goodwill. A written instrument signed by the assignor or a personal representative is needed. It will then be registrable and will be subject to essentially the same rules concerning registration and failure to register as are patents and registered designs.[85]

The mark may indeed be assigned in whole or in part, for all or some of the specified goods or services, or for the use of the mark in a particular manner or a particular locality.[86] These provisions are notably more liberal than those applying to Community marks, for the principle of unity dictates that a CTM can only be dealt with in its entirety and for the whole area of the Community (though it may be the subject of split licensing).[87]

An assignment of either a British or a Community mark is subject to the overriding consideration that the use made of it in consequence must not be liable to mislead the public, particularly as to the nature, quality or geographical origin of the specified goods or services.[88] This controlling device may assume greater significance, now that assignment is little controlled in the course of registration. The matter is discussed below.[89]

---

[83] Before the 1938 Act, assignments without goodwill were treated as inherently prejudicing the validity of the registration: see esp. the *Bowden* case (para. 17–79, below) and Kerly, paras 13–02—13–09.

[84] TMA 1938, s. 22(4)–(7). A special provision (of uncertain scope) permitted the assignment of unregistered marks along with registered marks even though there was no corresponding transfer of goodwill. It is not repeated in the 1994 Act, but it is hard to know what difference this makes.

[85] See para. 7–17, above. Registration of an assignment, as of a licence, creates a presumption of validity of the transaction: TMA 1994, s. 72. Assignments of Community marks, if not part of a transfer of goodwill, must be in writing signed by both parties: CTM Reg., Art. 17(2), (3). There are several consequential provisions on assignments, secured interests, execution of judgments, bankruptcy and conflicts with third parties: see Arts 17(5), (6), 18–21, 23.

[86] TMA 1994, s. 24 (going further than the 1938 Act, s. 22(2) as regards locality and manner of use). There may also be transmission by will or operation of law. These provisions do not derive from the TM Directive.

[87] CTM Reg., Art. 16, which, subject to further provisions of the Regulation itself, makes them subject to the national law of the state of the registered proprietor's seat or domicile, or otherwise, establishment; failing which, the law of Spain (as seat of the Community Office).

[88] TMA 1994, s. 46(1)(d), derived from the TM Dir., Art. 12(2)(b); CTM Reg., Art. 50(1)(c). And note CTM Reg., Art 17(4), allowing refusal of registration when a particular objection is apparent on the transfer documents. An unjustified assignment is no longer void: *cf.* TMA 1938, s. 22(7).

[89] See para. 17–79, below.

(2) Licensing[90]

17–14 Licence to use a registered mark does not of itself confer any proprietary interest but amounts to permission to use which prevents any allegation of infringement.[91] However, concurrently with the rights of the registered proprietor, an exclusive licensee is given rights and remedies as though he were an assignee.[92]

In principle the 1994 Act permits licences, like assignments, to be general or limited as to the goods or services covered, the manner of use and the locality.[93] A licence must be in writing, signed by or for the grantor.[94] This should not, however, be taken, as between licensor and licensee, to preclude the effect of any contract in equity, estoppel or acquiescence.

17–15 Previously the licensing of a mark was thought liable to muddy it as an indication of source; and this despite an irresistible growth of trade mark licensing in practice. The 1938 Act set up a system of registered use, under which a licence was acceptable only if it was (1) part of a patent licensing scheme; (2) an arrangement between linked companies in a parent-subsidiary network; or (3) subject to the licensor's power to control the quality of the goods or services for which the licensee used the mark.[95]

This last relationship in particular made clear that the licensor needed to retain a continuing trade mark connection, if the licence was to be justifiable. Once a user agreement was registered, use by the licensee was deemed to be use by the licensor. In consequence the licensee's use could counter allegations of non-use (the 1994 Act has the same effect) and it could meet an argument that something done by the licensee made the mark deceptive. In the end the courts even accepted that a user agreement which was not registered was nevertheless effective and justifiable if a quality control relationship existed between the licensor and the products or services in question.[96]

17–16 However, the 1938 Act did contain a ban on "trafficking" in marks. In *"Hollie Hobby" T.M.*,[97] the House of Lords held that this prevented wholesale registration of a mark for many types of goods by a company whose business was to exploit the merchandising potential of the mark, rather than to produce or market any products. Certainly the applications were accompanied by registered user agreements for each category, which contained quality control clauses; but this control appeared to be a matter

---

[90] See Wilkof [1996] E.I.P.R. 261; *Trade Mark Licensing* (1999).
[91] See now *Northern & Shell v. Condé Nast* [1995] R.P.C. 117, commenting on the position under the 1938 and 1994 Acts.
[92] See para. 17–16, below.
[93] TMA 1994, s. 28; and for Community marks, CTM Reg., Art. 22.
[94] TMA 1994, s. 28(2).
[95] TMA 1938, s. 28, esp. s. 28(4); *"Molyslip" T.M.* [1978] R.P.C. 211; *"Job" T.M.* [1993] F.S.R. 118.
[96] *"Bostitch" T.M.* [1963] R.P.C. 183; *"GE" T.M.* [1970] R.P.C. 339 at 372, 392–395, CA.
[97] [1984] R.P.C. 329.

of form only, since the applicant did not have the personnel or equipment to exercise meaningful supervision.

In the 1994 Act the ban on trafficking in a mark has gone; but the teasing smile of the licensing question remains. The essential issue, discussed later, is: in what circumstances could licensing mean that a mark has become liable to deceive and so to be revocable?[98] If it is made a term of an exclusive licence, the licensee may sue an infringer as if he were an assignee.[99] Even without this, any licensee can require the proprietor to proceed against an infringer affecting him; and, upon a lapse of two months without action, he can then sue as though he were proprietor.[1]

A trade mark licence may be subject to conditions which have the effect of distorting competition between Member States of the E.U. They are then subject to Article 85 of the E.C. Treaty, but have not so regularly given rise to difficulties as to merit any form of Block Exemption.[2]

4. CONDITIONS FOR SECURING REGISTRATION: ABSOLUTE GROUNDS

(1) "Trade mark"

(a) *European definition*

Only a "trade mark" may be registered, and anything which is not a trade **17–17** mark must be refused registration, or if necessary removed from the register.[3] The 1994 Act defines a "trade mark" in the same embracing terms as the Regulation and the Directive. The term covers:

> "any sign capable of being represented graphically which is capable of distinguishing goods or services of one undertaking from those of other undertakings."[4]

It includes "words (including personal names), designs, letters, numerals or the shape of goods or their packaging".[5] The definition is intended to

---

[98] See para. 17–79, below.

[99] TMA 1994, s. 31, normally requiring joinder of the proprietor as plaintiff or defendant for stages after interlocutory relief (s. 31(4)). There are certain limits on monetary remedies and delivery up: s. 31(6), (7); *cf.* CTM Reg., Art. 22(4). Exclusivity requires exclusion even of the licensor: TMA 1994, s. 29(1).

[1] TMA 1994, s. 30; *cf.* CTM Reg., Art. 22(3).

[2] See Galandi [1997] E.I.P.R. 723.

[3] TMA 1994, ss. 3(1)(a), 47(1).

[4] The inclusion of the shape of the goods themselves suggests that the generic class of "signs", to which all trade marks must belong, is to be read broadly; it is not to be confined to something discrete which is added to or attached to the product by way of representation or point of distinction.

[5] TMA 1994, s. 1(1); TM Dir., Art. 2; CTM Reg., Art. 4. *cf.* the TRIPS Agreement, which is in generally similar terms, but adds specifically, "figurative elements and combinations of colours". For collective and certification marks, see paras A2–05—A2–07, below.

open registration to as wide a range of potential marks as is practicable.[6] Some earlier limitations on the scope of the British system will accordingly be overcome. In varying measures, the same process will be occurring in other E.C. states.

The changes can be associated with three main elements in the new definition: "capacity to distinguish", "graphic representation" and "undertaking".

(b) *Capacity to distinguish*

17–18 The inclusion of capacity to distinguish in the very definition of a trade mark ties the system for the most part to its historic basis: that the law's purpose is to protect marks as, in a broad sense, indicators of origin.[7]

Previously there was a certain niggardliness over what could be a trade mark—in relation, for instance, to slogans, get-up and coloration.[8] Greater liberality is now to be expected, but still subject to the governing consideration of distinctiveness. Under the former law, the House of Lords refused to treat the shape of the "Coca-Cola" bottle as a trade mark for non-alcoholic beverages in Class 32.[9] But at least that shape ought now to fall within the general concept of a mark: it is capable of being represented graphically, and must surely be "capable of distinguishing" the Coca-Cola Corporation's product, since the bottle is one of the most famous symbols of source in all marketing. The danger that as a trade mark it will become a "perpetual monopoly"[10] is separately addressed, because a mark has also to pass the "absolute" tests of distinctiveness in section 3 (including those specifically concerned with shape[11]).

17–19 Signs will be held to lack a capacity to distinguish so as not even to be trade marks, only in the plainest cases.[12] The same phrase was employed under the 1938 Act to determine whether a mark could be admitted to Part B of the old Register: "capable of distinguishing" was the relatively weak test for that Part, in contrast with "adapted to distinguish", which was the severer test for Part A. These two phrases bred an encrustation of case law, which treated the test for both Parts as being in some respects equally

---

[6] See Explanatory Memorandum to Draft CTM Regulation COM (80) 635; White Paper, Reform of Trade Marks Law (Cm. 1203, 1990), para. 2.06.

[7] See equally the relevant Recitals of the Regulation and Directive.

[8] *e.g.* "Have a Break" was not registrable by itself, because it was to be followed by "Have a Kit-Kat", which was the real trade mark use: see [1993] R.P.C. 217; however, "I Can't Believe It's Yogurt", intended as an independent mark, was allowed: [1992] R.P.C. 533.

[9] *Coca-Cola T.M.* [1986] R.P.C. 421; *cf. Smith, Kline & French's T.M.* [1976] R.P.C. 511, HL (where the House of Lords allowed the registration of a colour combination added to a drug capsule as a trade identification).

[10] This was the fear expressed by Lord Templeman in the *Coca-Cola* case (n. 96, above) at 457.

[11] TMA 1994, s. 3(2): paras 17–41—17–43, below.

[12] *Allied Domecq's Appln.* ("AD2000") [1997] E.T.M.R. 253; *Philips Electronics v. Remington* (to be reported, CA).

cautious. Thus geographical, laudatory and directly descriptive words were denied registration even in Part B, despite evidence that in fact they had been exclusively recognised as trade marks.[13]

That case law may still have some relevance to questions of distinctiveness arising under section 3 of the 1994 Act.[14] But the most general of the grounds under that section, is that a mark is not to be registered if it is "devoid of distinctiveness". Lack of capacity to distinguish—as an element in the initial definition of what is to count as a trade mark at all—must pertain to objections even more fundamental (and therefore less likely to arise) than "devoid of distinctiveness". The old measure for Part B should not be regarded as the same criterion and the case law on it is, therefore, not in point.

This is not to say that "capacity to distinguish" is entirely without **17-20** content. Most geographical and descriptive words are now to be "capable" of being marks and are now to be tested for the acquisition of that secondary meaning. But some words must remain totally incapable of ever being marks. Thus "Soap" could never now be registered for soap.[15] More significantly, "Jeryl Lynn" has been held wholly incapable of being a registrable mark, given that for twenty years it had been used in medical biology to describe a manipulated strain of the mumps virus which was a successful vaccine.[16] Because of the increased scope of eligible subject-matter, there will in particular be attempts to turn into trade marks what are primary characteristics of products themselves. When these are functional (as with the shape of an electric razor head[17]) the inappropriateness of their being marks will be plain. That could also be the case where the product element is essentially decorative (designs on a picture frame). Likewise for those new prospects, sound and smell trade marks. The fragrance of a scent surely cannot be a trade mark: it is the essence of the product itself. The smell incorporated in a detergent, however, is a non-essential additive.[18] A similar comparison arises between sounds for records and sounds for a petrol advertisement.

Because the objection excludes the mark from registration *in limine*— even where there is very strong evidence that it has secondary meaning—it will be cautiously applied. That famously descriptive mark, "camel-hair

---

[13] See para. 17–29, below.
[14] See paras 17–30—17–35, below.
[15] Jacob J., Philips Electronics v. Remington, [1998] R.P.C. 283 at 299–302.
[16] *"Jeryl Lynn" T.M.* [1999] F.S.R. 491. The name was that of the six-year-old, from whose throat the research began its course.
[17] *Philips*, above, n. 12 the primary message conveyed by the shape of the head to be: " 'here is a three headed rotary shaver—from what you see you know how this device works' ". For the contrary conclusion in the equivalent Swedish litigation, see *Ide Line v. Philips Electronics* [1997] E.T.M.R. 377 (Stockholm DC).
[18] The discussion of smell marks in the U.S. has drawn this basic distinction: see esp. Elias (1992) 82 T.M.R. 475; and see Burton [1995] E.I.P.R. 378; para. 17–35, below.

belting", which was long ago protected against passing off because of unimpeachable evidence of secondary meaning, might now qualify for registration[19]: the evidence of secondary meaning would satisfy distinctiveness for purposes of section 3, and there would be no sufficient reason for excluding registration under section 1 because the mark was (utterly) incapable of being a indication of origin.

(c) *Graphic representation*

17–21 The ways in which a trade mark may be infringed are no longer constricted to visual uses.[20] As one corollary, if a mark consisting of sound or smell can be "graphically represented" (and it has "capacity to distinguish"), it is in principle registrable. (The question then becomes whether on balance the particular sign meets the various criteria of distinctiveness set out in section 3.[21]) Advertising jingles can be written in musical notation,[22] non-musical sounds can be described ("the roar of a lion"[23]), smells can be defined in terms of chemical components, by chromatographical analysis or even by reference to elements in the product which cause them.[24]

"Graphic representation" may well be limited to clear and easily determined means of describing sensations which can be appreciated by hearing or smell. For CTMs, OHIM is manifesting a remarkably accommodating attitude: "the smell of fresh-cut grass" has been allowed for tennis balls.[25] Whether signs which are sensed by taste or touch ("strawberry flavour", "the feel of velvet") could ever be satisfactorily represented in graphic form cannot be predicted.[26]

(d) *Undertaking*

17–22 Under the previous law, trade marks had to indicate "a connection in the course of trade". This was read as imposing a number of limitations:

(1) the connection with goods had to be during their initial production and distribution (for example by a manufacturer, contributor of material, wholesaler, importer or retailer), rather than subsequently

---

[19] See para. 16–12, above.

[20] See para. 17–86, below.

[21] See paras 17–25 *et seq.*, below.

[22] Or some written description of that notation.

[23] An example debated in the House of Lords: see *Hansard*, HL (Committee, January 18, 1994), cols. 34, 35, Lord Oliver (18.1.94).

[24] See Lyons [1994] E.I.P.R. 540; Burton [1995] E.I.P.R. 378.

[25] *Senta Aromatic's Applcn* [1999] E.T.M.R. 429.

[26] The White Paper (Cm. 1203, 1990), referred only to the inclusion of sound and smell marks: para. 2.06.

(for example as a repairer or secondhand dealer);[27] nonetheless, the latter might obtain a service mark for his activities[28];

(2) the connection had to be with the goods or services registered and not with other things[29];

(3) the connection had to be that of a trader, and not for instance that of a charity which supplied things for free use or consumption.[30]

The new law refers to the capacity to distinguish goods or services of one undertaking from those of other undertakings. In the course of the Bill, the government insisted that this wording (from the Directive) implied that the mark must be used in a commercial context and therefore refused to accept an amendment which would have said so explicitly.[31] All in all, the former case law requiring a trade connection is likely to remain applicable.[32]

(2) Absolute and relative grounds

The grounds upon which an application to register a "trade mark" may be **17–23** refused have now been harmonised by the TM Directive so as to follow those for the CTM.[33] These divide into two main categories:

(1) the *absolute grounds*, which relate to inherent objections to distinctiveness and certain public interest objections; and

(2) the *relative grounds*, which arise because some other trader or proprietor has an earlier conflicting right.

The absolute grounds are by their nature not open to waiver by another person, but the relative grounds are. These various objections are familiar from the previous law, but the way in which they are now stated varies in detail and in emphasis. In general there is an apparent tendency to make the objections less unbending and so to make registration somewhat easier at the boundaries. This is so, even though the United Kingdom system has given up its secondary (Part B) category of registration for marks of doubtful distinctiveness.[34]

---

[27] *Aristoc v. Rysta* (1945) 62 R.P.C. 65, HL: "Rysta" refused as a mark for stockings when it was to be applied to their repair (at a date before registration of services).

[28] The White Paper (Cm. 1203, 1990), para 2.22 recognises the entitlement of a repairer to a service mark and contemplates the continuance of this distinction.

[29] A matter equally germain to the applicant's intention to use: see para. 17–03, above.

[30] As in *"Wells Fargo" T.M.* [1977] R.P.C. 503; *"Gideons International" S.M.* [1991] R.P.C. 141 (the definition of "service mark" at that time made it clear that the services required valuable consideration—a factor which has been dropped). *cf. "Golden Pages" T.M.* [1985] F.S.R. 27, SC(Ir.)

[31] *Hansard*, HL Vol. 552, cols. 732–733, confirming the view of the White Paper (n. 9, above).

[32] See para. 7–03, n. 20, above.

[33] TM Dir., Arts 3, 4; CTM Reg., Arts 7, 8.

[34] See *British Sugar v. James Robertson* [1996] R.P.C. 281 at 302.

(3) Absolute grounds: general categories

17–24 Section 3 of the 1994 Act, lists the absolute grounds of objection, first in a list of general objections; then in subsections which deal with (1) shapes of goods, (2) public interest, deceptiveness and illegality, and (3) bad faith on the part of the applicant.[35]

(a) *Statutory provisions*

17–25 The statutory provisions begin with signs which do not even fall within the definition of a trade mark (section (1)(a)).[36] As just noted, the main criterion of a trade mark, apart from the need of graphic representation, is its capacity to distinguish the source of goods and services.

There follow three categories of trade marks to which absolute objection may be taken:

(1) trade marks which are devoid of any distinctive character (section 3(1)(b)—the "devoid of distinctiveness" objection);

(2) trade marks which consist exclusively of signs or indications which may serve, in trade, to designate the kind, quality, quantity, intended purposes, value, geographical origin, the time of production of goods or rendering of services, or other characteristics of goods or services (section 3(1)(c)—the "characteristics" objection);

(3) trade marks which consist exclusively of signs or indications which have become customary in the current language or in the bona fide and established practices of the trade (section 3(1)(d)—the "customary usage" objection).

The need for distinctiveness accordingly operates at three levels: for there to be a trade mark at all; under the undefined "devoid of distinctiveness" objection; and in relation to the more specific "characteristics" and "customary usage" objections. These levels overlap and their operation is cumulative.[37] In practice many challenges will be raised under the "characteristics" objection, but there will also be important cases under "customary usage" and "devoid of distinctiveness".

(b) *Countervailing evidence*

17–26 There is another basic consideration to bring into account. Once a sign qualifies to be a trade mark, the "devoid of distinctiveness", "characteristics" and "customary usage" objections are subject to a counterbalancing

---

[35] As to bad faith, see para. 17–03, above. *cf.* CTM Reg., Art. 38(2), giving the CTM Office power to request a disclaimer as a condition of grant.

[36] See paras 17–17—17–22, above.

[37] In the TRIPS Agreement, the obligation to protect trade marks depends upon a definition which is derived from the new E.C. formula; but it omits the category, "devoid of distinctiveness": Art. 15.1. The same provision permits Member States to require, as a condition of registration, that signs be "visually perceptible"; this has not been included in the CTM Reg.

factor. If, before the application date, the mark "has in fact acquired a distinctive character as a result of the use made of it",[38] then it shall not after all be refused registration (or subsequently removed). Within the E.C., national and regional registries which regularly assess questions of distinctiveness before registration have a set of rules, guidelines and know-how about this evaluation as it affects different types of mark. In all of them, including the British, past practice is having its influence during the early stages of the new system.

In Britain, Lord Parker's well-known guidance remains pertinent: the **17–27** right to register will "largely depend on whether other traders are likely, in the ordinary course of their business and without any improper motive, to desire to use the same mark, or some mark nearly resembling it, upon or in connection with their own goods".[39] Registration will be denied not only where other traders would be under an intolerable burden, but also where they would be hindered or embarrassed. Not being able to register a particular mark does not keep an applicant out of the market; and, as has been wisely said: "the power of a trade mark monopoly should not be granted where it would require honest men to look for a defence to an infringement action."[40]

Given the territorial range of Community marks, it is particularly to be **17–28** hoped that this attitude will prevail in relation to them. The Community Office faces a difficult task in balancing whatever evidence there is of use— it may well be for only a small part of the whole territory, but may perhaps be intensive there—against the strength of the inherent objection. Altogether there is likely to be a considerable range of different objections, absolute and relative, to Community applications. The first reported decisions show a definite desire to let through borderline cases. It remains highly important that the accommodating of applicants should not become the dominant pressure behind the Office's decisions. To move too far in this direction invites collisions with national courts hearing invalidity claims after grant.

There is a general issue about evidence of distinctiveness which deserves a common approach. May a tribunal or Court considering an absolute ground of objection receive evidence of the registration of generally similar marks for the same register? May it take account of the registration of the same or a similar mark on the CTM or another register within the E.U.? Where the balance between the inherent objection and distinctiveness is being weighed by reference to the degree of trade mark use, such comparisons can be of little value. But when the question is of registration

---

[38] TMA 1994, s. 3(1) proviso.
[39] *Registrar v. W & G Du Cros* (1913) 30 R.P.C. 660 at 672. In the context of a geographical name, the E.C.J. has insisted that not only the present, but also the probable future, must be considered: *Windsurfing Chiemsee v. Huber* (May 4, 1999); see below, para. 7–38.
[40] *"Colorcoat" T.M.* [1990] R.P.C. 511; *Cheng Kang v. Sze Jishian* [1992] F.S.R. 621, HC (Singapore).

without such evidence, there is a case for allowing comparisons in order to show the prevailing standards. To admit them however, adds complexity and Jacob J. has therefore refused to engage in the exercise.[41] OHIM and other registries may well take a more liberal attitude.

(c) *Indefeasible objections*

17–29 As already noted, under the former law it was decided that certain marks were so inescapably descriptive, or geographical, that they could not be registered even if there was conclusive evidence that in trade they were understood to be the applicant's trade mark or (as it was inelegantly put) "100 per cent. distinctive in fact". Accordingly "Yorkshire" was refused for copper pipes, "Electrix" for vacuum cleaners and "York" for freight containers.[42] These decisions were over-scrupulous; the 1994 Act leaves the question of distinctiveness in such doubtful cases to be balanced by the Registry and the courts.[43]

The objection that a mark is not even a trade mark, which is not open to any counterbalancing, should be kept for objections to subject-matter which lacks any significative quality at all.[44] Some of these are dealt with specifically in the later sub-heads of section 3—notably that relating to the shape of products. But there will be similar cases, which do not fit within that exception, but which deserve to be excluded because of their ability to keep other traders from marketing something, however it is otherwise marked. Marks claiming fungibles—say a new type of drink or a new fruit— might fall to be excluded in this way, however overwhelming the evidence of their connection on the market with a single source. Consideration may also have to be given to the name of a novel product which has initially been patented and in consequence marketed by a single source.[45]

(d) *"Devoid of distinctiveness"*

17–30 (i) **General.** Many marks are inherently distinctive because no other meaning, at least in the context of marking goods and services, attaches to them. There are a host of devices, including logos, which have no pictorial content to conjure up other associations. Likewise there are invented words aplenty, like "Kodak" and "Exxon", which have the same naturally

---

[41] *British Sugar v. Robertson* [1996] R.P.C. 281 at 305.

[42] *Yorkshire Copper's Application* (1953) R.P.C. 71, HL; *Electrix's Application* [1959] R.P.C. 283, HL; *"York" T.M.* [1984] R.P.C. 231, HL. The principle was applied equally to registration in the lesser Part B under the 1938 Act.

[43] *British Sugar v. James Robertson* [1996] R.P.C. 281 at 305; this view is confirmed by *Windsurfing Chiemsee v. Huber* (May 4, 1999, ECJ); see below, para. 17–39.

[44] *ibid*; and see above, para. 17–19.

[45] This situation was previously the subject of a special provision: TMA 1938, s. 15(1)(b); and note s. 15(3).

distinctive character. Under the former law, one class of immediately admissible marks were "invented words" and there has been a long history of case law distinguishing between truly invented words and words which remain descriptive, such as the grossly misspelt "Orlwoola", and so-called portmanteau words like "Trakgrip" and "Weldmesh".[46] The objections now being considered go, in a variety of ways, to connotative factors which derogate from the distinctiveness of a mark as a trade mark.

Under the head "devoid of distinctiveness" will fall objections to distinctiveness which find no place in the two subsequent categories. "Devoid" may suggest a very limited criterion for objection. But it must be remembered that to be a mark at all, the sign must be capable of distinguishing. It is likely that "devoid of distinctiveness" will be read to cover signs which have potential ability to become trade marks, but need supporting evidence that they are known as such.[47] Under this intermediate head will fall signs which are also surnames, image-promoting words, letters, numerals, colours and smells.

(ii) **Surnames and Forenames.** The type of objection which will most **17–31** regularly arise under "devoid of distinctiveness" will be to the use of names, particularly surnames. The former law specifically allowed names to be registered when written in a special manner, such as a flowing script.[48] Such a case now falls under the general criteria. The king of rock-and-roll's signature, "Elvis Presley", was held to have some little capacity to distinguish from the manner in which it was written, despite the ordinariness of the handwriting.[49] Registration of a name without further limitation means that infringement may occur however the name is written. This should continue to be inherently objectionable so long as there is no countervailing evidence to tip the balance in favour of registration.

According to previous practice, names such as "Dabner" or "Crossingham" have no other meaning and the balance is straightforward. Unusual names may be registered with modest evidence of use; much more will be needed in cases like "Thompson" or "Jones". But even very common surnames can eventually succeed.[50]

Many surnames have another meaning either in English or another language. The practice has been to raise an inherent objection unless that other meaning was overwhelming commoner and better known: exceptional examples might be "Coup" and "Cheer"; whereas "Swallow", "Jury" and "Bugler" would fall to be treated as surnames.[51] In the past the British

---

[46] For details, see Kerly, paras 8.26 *et seq.*
[47] See *British Sugar* case, n. 34, above.
[48] Likewise for the signature of the applicant or a business predecessor: see TMA 1938, s. 9(1)(a), (b).
[49] *"Elvis Presley" T.M.s* [1999] R.P.C. 567, CA.
[50] See Kerly, paras 8–53, 8–54.
[51] See *Swallow Raincoats' Application* (1947) 64 R.P.C. 92 at 94; also *Burford's Application* (1919) 36 R.P.C. 139, CA—the test then being whether the word was "according to its ordinary signification" a surname.

Registry has sometimes referred to foreign telephone directories, as well as British, in pursuit of surnames.[52] It has recently been emphasised that the inquiry, even in relation to a mark for export goods, must be as to distinctiveness in the United Kingdom.[53] Nonetheless, in the current European environment, foreign usage may in future attract growing significance. The Community Office must needs be even-handed, given that a Community mark is for the entire E.U.

In judging the balance, one root issue is the likelihood of the public treating the mark and its use as a trade mark.[54] So it has been held that, as "Elvis Presley" comes to be known as the singer's name, the less likely is it that it will be taken as a *mark* for merchandise. Neither modern merchandising practices nor any notion of an inherent commercial right in a natural person's name has been allowed to affect the approach, here as elsewhere.[55]

17–32 (iii) **Other cases.** Past practice suggests that a motley collection of other considerations will also fall under "devoid of distinctiveness", for there are many circumstances in which Lord Parker's properly motivated businessman may wish to use some mark or a variant of it.[56] Words which promote the image of a product, however imprecisely, are of this kind. In a classic case, "Perfection" was not allowed for soap; recently "Magic Safe" was refused for safes; and even "Madame" was refused for food, where there was no countervailing evidence of use.[57]

17–33 Letters and numerals raise similar difficulties.[58] In the past, a single letter or number was treated as inherently unregistrable, two only upon very substantial evidence indeed of use as a mark, three and more with proportionately less difficulty. In the new system, a more relaxed approach is being established.[59]

17–34 Colour has also been treated cautiously in the past. Any registration for a single colour is likely to cover a relatively wide portion of the spectrum (red, blue, etc.) and it could well be that relatively few applications could between them cover all the useable colours for a particular product, thus preventing other competitors from marketing in anything other than a clear

---

[52] The London Directory has nevertheless been the most important.
[53] *"Al Bassam" T.M.* [1995] R.P.C. 511, CA, applying esp. *Bagots Hutton's Application* (1916) 33 R.P.C. 357 at 369.
[54] *British Sugar v. Robertson*, [1996] R.P.C. 281; and see *Car Wheel Trim T.M.* [1998] E.T.M.R. 584 (German SC).
[55] *"Elvis Presley" T.M.*, [1999] R.P.C. 567. See above, para 16–34.
[56] Trade marks consisting of the shape of products or their packaging have, first of all, to be judged under this and the next head, before being tested by the additional criteria of s. 3(2): see below, para. 17–41ff.
[57] *Crosfield's Application* (1909) 26 R.P.C. 837, CA; *"Magic Safe" T.M.* [1993] R.P.C. 470; *"Madame" T.M.* [1966] R.P.C. 415, see now *Lombard's Application* [1997] E.T.M.R. 500 ("Wellink" for Internet software); *Warnaco's Application* [1997] E.T.M.R. 505 ("The Perfectionists" for underwear).
[58] Likewise Chinese characters: *Yomeishu-Seizo v. Sinma Medical* [1991] F.S.R. 278.
[59] See, *e.g.* the OHIM Examination Guidelines, para. 8.

wrapper. For this reason red and white striping for toothpaste was refused registration: the red had the particular function of carrying a mouthwash and was one of the few colours which could do so.[60] On the other hand, a complex of different colours in a pharmaceutical capsule was held registrable upon proof that it was widely recognised as a trade mark.[61]

Smell marks are likely to face even greater difficulties. When the smell is **17–35** the main object of the product (as with scent or an air freshener) it should not be capable of being a trade mark at all.[62] Even when it is a secondary additive (detergent, shampoo, notepaper), it should be registrable only on very strong evidence of recognition as a trade mark. Given that there are likely to be other more evident visual marks used at the same time, it may indeed be difficult to show that the public had come to consider the smell as an indicator distinguishing source.[63] Moreover, secondary additives can rarely be smelled at the point of sale (compare trial bottles at perfume counters). In the past post-sale identifiers have been regarded as totally irrelevant in assessing distinctiveness, and even if given some role are not likely to be of much weight in making out a special case of distinctiveness in fact.[64]

(e) *"Characteristics"*

The head, "characteristics", set out above, deals with relatively specific **17–36** indicators of one or other quality of a product or service. Typical cases which are likely to arise include the following.

(i) **"Kind, quality, quantity, intended purpose, value, . . . the time of 17–37 production of goods or of the rendering of services, or other characteristics of goods and services."** The old law used the phrase, "direct reference to character or quality"[65] and that continues to be a fair indicator of what is now excluded under this longer list of factors, with its catch-all, "other characteristics", at the rear. Thus in the past "Tastee-Freez" for ice-cream, "Weldmesh" for wire mesh, and "Tarzan" for films and toys have been held at least prima facie unregistrable.[66] By contrast, "Brownie" and "Bullseye" for cameras and films, "Oomphies" for shoes, "Tub Happy" for clothing

---

[60] *Unilever's (Striped Toothpaste No. 2) T.M.* [1987] R.P.C. 13.

[61] *Smith Kline & French's Application* [1976] R.P.C. 511, HL. OHIM has proved willing to accept a colour mark without evidence of use only if it is "unique and unusual": *William Wrigley's Appln* [1999] E.T.M.R. 214—an elastic standard, perhaps.

[62] See para. 17–20, above.

[63] In the U.S., where smell marks have been registrable since 1946, the first registration succeeded only in 1990: *Re Clarke* 17 USPQ (2d) 1238 (fragrance of plumeria blossoms for embroidery yarn—in a "Scented Skunk" kit!); see esp. Elias (n. 18, above).

[64] See, *e.g. Bostick v. Sellotape* [1994] R.P.C. 556. But *cf. Levi-Strauss v. Kimbyr* [1974] F.S.R. 335 (N.Z.); Prescott [1990] E.I.P.R. 241.

[65] TMA 1938, s. 9(1)(d).

[66] *Tastee Freez's Application* [1960] R.P.C. 255; *"Weldmesh" T.M.* [1966] R.P.C. 220, CA; *"Tarzan" T.M.* [1970] R.P.C. 450, CA.

and even "Dustic" for adhesives have been allowed registration with varying amounts of evidence of use.[67]

Under the present legislation the following have been refused registration without use: "Bonus Gold" for financial investment services; "Automatic Network Exchange" for certain business information; "Coffeemix" for coffee and the like; "Frost Loops" for cereals; "Eurolamb" for that meat. "Xpresslink" for telecommunication equipment; "Polypad" for saddles because of "pony".[68]

A word which requires translation for its descriptive significance to be appreciated in the British Isles has been held inherently registrable. But it was "Kiku" for perfumes, which is Japanese for chrysanthemum.[69] Greater knowledge of the main European languages may now begin to be attributed. In the Community Office, the issue of meaning in at least all the Community languages, official and unofficial, is likely to be of importance and difficulty. It could prove to be a major reason why word marks, including words which applicants think they have invented, cannot be registered, at least without considerable evidence of distinctiveness in fact.

17–38 (ii) **"Geographical origin."** As with words describing qualities of the goods or services, the legitimate interests of other traders, present and future, dictate that no one person should acquire exclusive rights in a geographical name without convincing evidence that the name has been appropriated to trade mark purposes by actual use. In *Windsurfing Chiemsee v. Huber*,[70] the European Court of Justice has refused to confine the scope of this objection to cases where there is a real, current or serious need to leave mark free for use by others.[71] Rather, if the relevant public, in all the particular circumstances, would (or could later) take use of the name to indicate the locality from which goods come, or in which they were conceived or designed, the objection to registration must in principle arise. Thus "Chiemsee" for clothing was open to objection, since the Chiemsee is a large and well-populated lake in Bavaria.[72] In addition, the geographical word must not be allowed to mislead the public over where the goods or services come from: a company with no business in Switzerland could not therefore register "Swiss Miss" for its chocolate products.[73]

---

[67] *Kodak v. London Stereoscopic* (1903) 20 R.P.C. 337; *La Marquise's Application* (1947) 64 R.P.C. 27; *Mark Foys v. Davies Coop* (1956) 95 C.L.R. 190; *Dundas's Application* (1955) 72 R.P.C. 151. As to "Tub Happy", the High Court of Australia pronounced that it suggested only "in a vague and indefinite way a gladsome carelessness à propos the tub".

[68] *"Bonus Gold" T.M.* [1998] R.P.C. 859: *Automotive Network Exchange" T.M.* [1998] R.P.C. 885: *"Coffee Mix" T.M.* [1998] R.P.C. 717; *"Frost Loops" T.M.* [1998] R.P.C. 240; *"Eurolamb" T.M.* [1997] E.T.M.R. 420; *Siemens' Applicn* [1999] E.T.M.R. 146 (OHIM); *Penny McKinnon's Applcn* [1999] E.T.M.R. 234 (OHIM—note the necessity to consider various languages there).

[69] *"Kiku" T.M.* [1978] F.S.R. 246, Full SC(Ir.).

[70] [1999] E.T.M.R. 690.

[71] Thus rejecting the German doctrine of *Freihaltebedürfnis*, raised by the referring court.

[72] As to countervailing evidence, see text at n. 81, below.

[73] *"Swiss Miss" T.M.* [1998] R.P.C. 889, CA.

Commercially valuable associations between a place and type of goods or services are not infrequently built up by use of a place name. The association may derive from the physical conditions for production of raw material (for example grapes for wine) or for carrying out a manufacturing process (for example Roquefort cheese) or from an established tradition of local craftsmanship. In these cases, once a number of traders have come to share the use of the name, they will together be entitled to the special protection now accorded to appellations of origin and indications of source; and one way of achieving this is now through the registration of certification marks and collective marks.[74]

Where this process is only just initiated, it may be possible for one producer to get such a headstart that no one else could honestly claim to be entitled to use the name. The first user will be entitled to an exclusive registration—but only in special circumstances. Under the old law, the producers of "The Glenlivet" whisky not only succeeded in registering that name for whisky, their distillery being in the small Glen Livet; they also procured the mark for mineral water before using it on that product, on the basis of evidence that the public would think water so marked not only came from a source in the valley but also from them.[75] The decision emphasises the close association between water and whisky as a source of likely confusion and also emphasises that other traders could not honestly adopt the particular geographical name. Its thinking, therefore, seems closely in line with concept of confusing "association" in the 1994 Act.[76]

The question whether a word is to be treated as geographical has in the **17–39** past been judged by reference to the normal understanding of British people.[77] If the geographical usage is very little known, the word is likely to be treated as invented or to have some other meaning, according to circumstances. In the classic example, "Magnolia" was allowed for a metal alloy, even though several towns in the U.S. bore that name—a fact unknown to the average person in Britain.[78] Equally, fanciful uses of place names will be permitted: the classic examples have been "North Pole" bananas and "Monte Rosa" cigarettes.[79] On the other hand, if a word has suddenly

---

[74] For this issue, see App. 2, below.

[75] *"The Glenlivet" T.M.* [1993] R.P.C. 461.

[76] See TMA 1994, s. 3(1) proviso, and s. 5(2): paras 17–92 *et seq.*, below.

[77] Under the 1938 Act, the word had to be geographical "according to its ordinary signification", a formulation which stressed the objective nature of the inquiry. If a word was actually concocted, this did not prevent it being geographical: thus "Livron", invented for a liver and iron tonic, turned out to be the name of a French town sufficiently well-known to count as geographical: *Boots' T.M.*, (1937) 54 R.P.C. 327, CA. This approach is likely to continue in the British Registry. Note also cases where a word has acquired geographical connotations: *e.g. "Advokaat" T.M.* [1978] R.P.C. 252 (mark refused for Belgian advocaat because associated with Holland).

[78] The product was not made in any of them—often a significant factor: *Magnolia Metal's T.M.* [1897] 2 Ch. 371, 14 R.P.C. 621, CA; *"Tijuana Smalls" T.M.* [1973] F.S.R. 235. As to the degree of rarity, see *"Farah" T.M.* [1978] F.S.R. 234, SC(Ir.).

[79] In *Windsurfing Chiemsee* (above n. 70) the E.C.J. refers to the names of a mountain or lake as an example of this exceptional category; scrupulously, this is said not to include a case where the lakeshore or surrounding area would be thought to be included: paras. 33, 34.

become geographical—even between application and hearing—objection has been taken; as where "Avon" became the name of a new local authority.[80]

As to countervailing evidence of use of the geographical name as a mark, *Windsurfing Chiemsee*[81] provides important, if somewhat opaque, guidance. Where a geographical name is very well-known as such, proof of trade mark use has to be longstanding and intensive; the more so, if the word has been used to indicate the geographical origin of the category of goods in question.[82] The overall assessment must take account of promotional expenditure on the mark; the proportion of the relevant public who recognise it as distinctive; and statements from chambers of commerce and industry, and other trade and professional associations. While recognising the value of opinion poll evidence, the Court of Justice wisely refused to lay down numerical degrees of recognition as a test.

(f) *"Customary usage"*

17–40 Two cases are covered: signs or indications which have become customary (1) in the current language, or (2) in the bona fide and established practices of the trade. The expression, "signs . . . customary in the current language" is not clear, but most likely refers to words and other symbols (such as numbers, letters of an alphabet and punctuation) which have some meaning other than as a trade mark.[83] "Sheen" for sewing cotton is perhaps a sign which would be open to objection here, while not being precise enough to fall under any head in the "characteristics" objection.[84] Likewise, to take more recent examples: "Network 90" for telephones and the like; "Moneysworth" over a dollar sign for magazines; a simple pastoral scene on dairy products.[85] Pictures of a clothed woman on clothing, or of striped toothpaste on its packaging, would fall to be excluded as customary uses in trade practice, where the evidence justified the conclusion.[86]

---

[80] *"Avon" T.M.* [1985] R.P.C. 43.

[81] Above, n. 70; Judgment, paras 38–54.

[82] As on the first question in the case (above, at n. 70), the Court rejects any use of the German *Freihaltebedürfnis* test as a means of favouring the mark-owner at the expense of other trading interests: Judgment, paras 38, 48.

[83] It is not clear whether the phrase "of the trade" qualifies "the common language" as well as "the bona fide and established practices"; the repetition of the definite article rather suggest that it does; so may the CTM Reg., Art. 7(1)(d), which in employing the same expression must be referring to all Community languages. *cf.* the equivalent ground of revocation, paras 17–74, 17–75, below, which is confined solely to trade usage.

[84] Contrast, say, "Matt" for photographs.

[85] *"Network 90" T.M.* [1984] R.P.C. 549; *"Moneysworth" T.M.* [1976] R.P.C. 317; *Union Laitière's Application* [1993] R.P.C. 87.

[86] *Pantino's Application* [1966] R.P.C. 527; *Unilever's T.M.* [1984] R.P.C. 155. In a classic instance, *James' T.M.* (1886) 33 Ch.D. 392, the Court of Appeal upheld the registration of a picture of black lead (for stoves) in the form of a dome, given considerable evidence of use. The decision has been treated with great circumspection since; but *cf.* now *Absperrpoller* [1997] E.T.M.R. 176 (German Pat. Ct.).

(4) Absolute grounds: specific categories

(a) *Shapes*

With the growth of design variations as major keys to marketing success, **17–41** the desire to protect them as trade marks has also strengthened. Hence the specific enumeration in the definition of a "trade mark" of "the shape of goods or their packaging".[87] If a valid trade mark can be procured for an element of design shape, the protection may continue as long as the registration is renewed and so is not limited in the same way as copyright and design rights in the design elements.

In the past the particular danger of creating a continuing right in design features which will block the legitimate use of similar elements by others has been appreciated by excluding the shape of packaging as well as products from the range of the registration system[88]; and, in the law of passing off, by making it very difficult to demonstrate that shape, particularly of articles themselves, has acquired a secondary meaning as an indication of source.[89] In the 1994 Act, a list of shape marks which are inherently objectionable is given.[90] Shapes within this list are treated as are other signs that have no "capacity to distinguish" and so do not qualify as trade marks at all.[91] This list is intended to apply to the shape of packaging as well as products themselves (even though it does not say so).[92]

Before considering the list of exclusions, the position of other shapes— **17–42** those not excluded—must be understood. All shapes must satisfy the general tests of distinctiveness, under which inherent objections are balanced against evidence of use as a mark. Shape, just as much as other product ingredients such as colour, patterning or smell, is not inherently distinctive as a mark. Whatever form it takes, it will usually require considerable evidence of use before it can be registered.

> Philips sought to register the shaving-head shape of its "Philishave" electric razors, in which three circular cutters are placed within an equilateral triangle. There was evidence: (1) of widespread, but not universal, recognition of this as an indication of trade source; and (2) of the efficacy of this formation for the design of a three-cutter head. The Court of Appeal accepted that there was no sufficient case to

---

[87] TMA 1994, s. 1(1): para. 17–17, above; see Henning-Bodewig and Ruijsenaars (1992) 23 I.I.C. 643.

[88] See para. 17–18, above.

[89] See para. 16–08, n. 23, above.

[90] A European precursor of the list is to be found in the Benelux Trade Mark Law, Art. 1(2) though its language is more restricted. For the Benelux case law, see Strowel [1995] E.I.P.R. 154.

[91] See paras 17–18, 17–19, above.

[92] Non-citable Minute of Council and Commission on CTM Reg., Art. 7(1)(e).

overcome either the "devoid of distinctiveness" or the "characteristics" objections (section 3(1)(a) and (b).[93]

The presence of the excluded list implies that there must be some tempering of the position previously taken by the House of Lords over the Coca-Cola bottle—that, within the registration system, all traders must be left free to choose to sell containers or articles of similar shape.[94] But since labelling exists as the first and obvious technique for distinguishing source, it should only be where secondary meaning is clear from usage that any registration of shape could be allowed.[95]

17–43   In principle, then, the exclusionary list becomes relevant only when a shape is so well-established as a mark that it is on balance distinctive.[96] The list then imposes its overriding denial of registration.

The list of signs unregistrable because they consist exclusively of certain shapes is as follows:

(1) shapes resulting from the nature of the goods themselves;
(2) shapes of goods necessary to obtain a technical result;
(3) shapes which give substantial value to goods.

This statutory formula contains a number of indications that shapes on the prohibited list arise only in strictly limited cases: in all cases, the objection must go exclusively to the listed shape; head (2) turns on the adjective, "necessary", head (3) on "substantial". Moreover, the cases listed are precisely those in which it is least likely that sufficient distinctiveness can be made out. This will serve to give a sense of proportion in considering the list, which employs terms which have broad penumbrae.

17–44 (i) **Nature of the goods or packaging.** This first category leads one at once into a contemplation of the essence or the identity of things. One can be sure that an apple cannot be registered either for apples or for packaging in the shape of an apple. But what about packaging designed to hold kiwi-fruit safely? What about a pear-shaped balloon? Is its essence just its balloon-ness, or also its shape? In determining what the goods are, the Court should have regard to how they are considered in commercial terms. The question is not to be determined by the scope allowed in the registration.

Once the goods are identified, then the registration of a shape which forms only part of them is unlikely to result from their "nature". *In Philips*

---

[93] *Philips Electronics v. Remington* (CA, 1999, to be reported); Helbling [1997] I.P.Q. 413. The decision is currently the subject of a reference to the ECJ. See also *Procter & Gamble's Applcns* [1999] E.T.M.R. 375, CA (shapes and colours of cleaning product bottles not registrable without evidence of use).

[94] See para. 17–18, above.

[95] *Philips Electronics v. Remington* above, n. 93, emphasising that each party sold its razors under internationally known word marks. The shape was thus at best "a kind of limping mark" (at p. 312).

[96] A Court may turn to the list of exclusions as an aid in determining distinctiveness.

Electronics v. Remington, the goods were found to be electric shavers (rather than either shavers, or three-headed shavers) and the registration of the particular head-formation was not impermissible under this head.[97] More extreme is the decision in The Netherlands that the particular shape of "Lego" toy bricks is not part of their nature, apparently for the reason that there were other shapes which could be used to make toy building systems. This must be regarded as a dramatic invasion of a registered trade mark system into the sphere of product design, and accordingly highly controversial.[98] It reduces the "nature of the product category" to cases where there is no realistic alternative shape for the product and so opens the prospect of unending trade-mark protection for the appearance of many popular products.

(ii) **Technical necessity.** This objection overlaps to some degree with the **17–45** first, and equally suggests the extent to which trade-marking is annexing the sphere of design. The law of design protection has long known the exclusion of exclusively technical design, and has, therefore, grappled with the same sort of problem. Is a shape to be regarded as exclusively technical only if no other shape will perform its function (of this there are probably very few examples); or does it cover all cases where the functional purpose is the main reason for an object having the shape which is claimed as a mark? In the two cases over "Philips" rotary shaver, a majority of the Stockholm District Court took the first, limited view of the exclusionary ground. In England, however, Jacob J. and the Court of Appeal preferred the dissenting view in Sweden, that of Judge Nilsson: where the purpose of the shape is solely to produce a technical result it is not registrable.[99] One difficulty about adopting the first, highly restricted, meaning[1] is that it is hard to imagine any case of that kind which would not also be objectionable under the first heading (consider, for instance, the kiwi-fruit packaging). Yet something more must presumably have been intended by the second head.

(iii) **Substantial value.** The third category seems particularly opaque. It **17–46** asks the question: assuming that a shape has acquired distinctiveness in the trade mark sense, is that shape nonetheless somehow so substantial an element in its value that nevertheless registration should be ruled out? In the *Philips* case in England the Court of Appeal found that such added value did not result from the shaving-head despite its technical importance.[2]

---

[97] Above, n. 93.
[98] *cf. Interlego's Applications* [1998] R.P.C. 69: registration refused under the 1938 Act (U.K.).
[99] *Ide Line v. Philips Electronics* [1997] E.T.M.R. 103; *Philips Electronics v. Remington,* above, n. 93.
[1] Gielen and Strowel Mitt. d. Patentanwälte 198, however, argue for just such an approach. The Benelux case law provides instances of both approaches; *cf. Alfred Ritter v. Ion* [1997] E.T.M.R. 103 (Danish SC): an element of product shape which results from the method of packaging is unprotectable.
[2] The one point of difference from Jacob J.: *cf. Philips Electronics v. Remington,* [1998] R.P.C. 283 at 309–310.

Apart from that consideration, it is easiest to say that there is added value in the shape element can be regarded as a "capricious addition or feature"—say, the incorporation of animal figures into a lamp base. But there will be great difficulty over features of "good" design which, wittingly or (possibly) not, make functional elements at the same time beautiful or handsome or at least striking (to consumers? or to art critics?).

Inevitably, there will be questions about the type of value which may be brought into account. Under the equivalent provision of the Benelux law, the Dutch Supreme Court held, in different cases, that the round shape of one biscuit was unregistrable, while the spiral shape of another was registrable.[3] The first shape added too substantial an element of value, there being little distinction of taste between competing products; the second was said to add only to market value, whereas what mattered was "intrinsic" value. Such mysteries, which already haunt our copyright law on works of artistic craftsmanship,[4] seem destined to enshroud trade mark law across the E.C.

As fluctuating United States case law on the same subject shows all too plainly, courts will be drawn into asking why customers buy for the shape: is it because they like it as a shape or because they treat it as a distinguishing sign for a product line. So far as liking it as a shape, their judgment may be affected by aesthetic sensibilities or functional concerns, or these two factors may merge in their minds. It is an issue which arises initially in considering whether the shape has acquired secondary meaning; and then again if it proves necessary to address the strict exclusion for "substantial value".

(b) *Personality and Character merchandising*

17–46A English courts are reluctant to hold that sportsmen, actors, pop-stars and the like have an inherent right of publicity in their names, images or voices, and they adopt essentially the same approach to fictitious characters. At root, they continue to recognise only the origin function of trade marks and endorsements. Moreover, in their view the public do not assume that there is necessarily any licensing arrangement in place, let alone one under which the personality or promoter produces or guarantees the quality of the product or service bearing the name. The strenuous, but unsuccessful, attempts to monopolise the name and image of Diana, Princess of Wales, has sharpened this attitude in respect of memorabilia. When Elvis Presley died, he left his estate without any real organisation for exploiting his

---

[3] *Bacony Snack* [1989] E.I.P.R. D-122; *Wokkels* [1986] Ned. Jur. 285. The Benelux Court of Justice ruled that commercial value was the relevant factor in *Burberrys I* [1989] Ned. Jur. 834, [1989] E.I.P.R. D–122; but approved of *Wokkels* in *Burberry II* [1992] Ned. Jur. 567, [1992] E.I.P.R. D–140. So much for precedent in the Benelux system.
[4] See paras 10–17—10–22, above.

personality; this came only later. (Today, doubtless, there would have been much sharper attention to merchandising). In the United Kingdom, in consequence, marks could not be registered in Class 3 for his names or signature without actual proof that the public recognised them as the estate's trade mark, rather than merely as an association with their hero.[5]

(c) *Public interest*

Three "absolute" grounds of objection exist by way of protecting general **17–47** public interests. A mark is not registrable:

(1) if it is contrary to public policy or to accepted principles of morality;
(2) if it is of such a nature as to deceive the public (for instance as to the nature, quality or geographical origin of the goods or services); or
(3) if or to the extent that its use is prohibited by United Kingdom or Community law.[6]

(i) **Public policy or morality.** Of the grounds of objection the public policy **17–48** or morality ground will doubtless find an occasional use where it can be said that the mark would offend the generally accepted mores of the time. In the past the Registrar has refused "Hallelujah" for women's clothing out of religious scruple over its likely positioning.[7] But the trend is to allow greater frankness in sexual matters[8]; and in any case, the Registrar no longer has an additional discretion to police marginal cases.[9]

(ii) **Likely to deceive.** The most important of these grounds of objection **17–49** will be the second. Marks which evoke some connotation other than source may not only lack distinctiveness (as already indicated) but may be positively deceptive. The following illustrations arose under the former law:

> "Instant Dip" was refused for cleaning materials in general because it could be used to cover materials which were not dips.[10]

---

[5] *Re Elvis Presley Enterprises' Applcns* ([1999] R.P.C. 567, CA). Arising under the 1938 Act, it applied the character merchandising case, *"Tarzan T.M.* [1970] F.S.R. 245, CA. Sid Shaw, who ran an independent business in "Elvisly Yours" memorabilia, had registered that mark already in Class 3. Since this could not be attacked, its similarity gave rise to a conflict which rendered the applications at issue unregistrable.

[6] TMA 1994, s. 3(3), (4). Under the TMA 1938, s. 11, the equivalent objection was to matter contrary to law or morality, or any scandalous design.

[7] *"Hallelujah" T.M.* [1977] R.P.C. 605.

[8] *cf.* the registration of the beneath-the-kilt design: para. 14–18, n. 61, above.

[9] *cf. La Marquise's Application* (1947) 71 R.P.C. 52 ("Oomphies" for shoes allowed).

[10] *Seligmann's Application* (1954) 71 R.P.C. 52; and see *"China-Therm" T.M.* [1980] F.S.R. 21 (that mark for plastic containers). Now that a registered mark may be infringed by its use on similar goods or services to that for which it is registered, the actual registration can be limited to proper uses. The former more constricted law required more sophisticated handling.

"Livron", invented as a mark for a tonic of liver and iron, could be taken to mean that it came from the French town of Livron (where the opponent produced pharmaceuticals).[11]

An applicant proposed to apply the same mark to new and secondhand goods (stockings—at a time of shortage). The danger that the public will mistake the one for the other gave rise to objection.[12] Presumably, as in the past, a mere intention to change a previous connection with goods, as where a manufacturer is deciding for the future to become an importing agent of goods made by another concern, will not be prejudicial.[13]

A mark which was persistently used on pool coupons in breach of the Betting and Lotteries Acts was refused registration because that might appear to confer official approval upon the whole operation.[14]

17–50 (iii) **Use contrary to law.** The third ground allows objection to be taken to the use of marks in ways which contravene consumer protection legislation—notably the Trade Descriptions Act 1968.[15] If, moreover, Parliament chooses, as a public-health measure, to enact that (say) cigarette marks may not be used in relation to other goods or services—as has happened in a number of countries—then this ground would prevent registrations of the marks.

In this connection, it has been argued that such a rule would be contrary to Article 6*quinquies* of the Paris Convention.[16] This *"telle quelle"* provision requires, with only limited exceptions,[17] the registration and protection of marks as they are registered in their Convention "country of origin". The basic misconception in this argument is the assertion that trade marks are protected in order to guarantee the proprietor's own freedom to use the mark.[18] In truth that protection, to which the *telle quelle* Article contributes its particular buttressing, is aimed at misuse of the mark by others.

---

[11] *Boots' T.M.* (1937) 54 R.P.C. 327, CA; and see now "Swiss Miss" T.M. [1998] R.P.C. 889, CA.

[12] *Aristoc v. Rysta* [1945] A.C. 68, 62 R.P.C. 65, HL.

[13] *cf.* the acceptance of such situations in the TMA 1938, s. 62.

[14] *Fairest's Application* (1951) 68 R.P.C. 197, where it was said that this class of objection covered only "something intrinsic or inherent" in the mark itself. Similarly, *"Vitasafe" T.Ms.* [1963] R.P.C. 256 (suggesting official guarantee of vitamin preparations).

[15] For which see paras 15–19, 15–20, above; likewise legislation protecting hallmarks (Hall-marking Act 1973) and joint interests in marks and names: see para. A2–04, below.

[16] Bernitz [1990] E.I.P.R. 137; Kur (1992) 23 I.I.C. 31; [1996] E.I.P.R. 198.

[17] These exceptions, however, include morality and *ordre public*, the latter an expression which may well encompass consumer health measures.

[18] See Karnell [1990] E.I.P.R. 305.

(d) *State, official and royal emblems and other indicia*

As in the previous law, it is not possible, without authorisation, to register **17–51** various coats of arms, flags, crests and representations of the Royal Family.[19] The flags and emblems of Paris Convention States and of international organisations are similarly treated, in most cases after due notification.[20] Also following from that Convention, official signs and hallmarks which are used in other Member States to indicate control and warranty, may not be registered for the goods in question or similar goods. Again there has to be due notification.[21]

Royalty may be regarded as the first great merchandisers of their images and connections; the obtaining and brandishing of a warrant to purvey to royal personages has long been recognised as *the* form of snobbish sponsorship. Governments and international organisations have not been slow to follow suit in securing exclusive rights in their names and insignias. Why then should there be such qualms over according general merchandising rights to private claimants? Is it because public bodies are assumed not to take any return for the licensing of their signs, or that, if they do, it redounds to the benefit of the public? Even if true, should this make any difference?

5. CONDITIONS FOR SECURING REGISTRATION: THE RELATIVE GROUNDS

The relative grounds concern conflicts between marks and other signs. In **17–52** the CTM Office they may accordingly be raised only by an opponent; but for the moment the British Registry continues its former practice of searching for conflicting registrations and examining them *ex officio*.[22] The conflicts in question are between the mark applied for and both "earlier trade marks" and "earlier rights".

> "Earlier trade mark" covers: (1) British and Community marks with an earlier registration date (after bringing any priority dating into account[23]); (2) Community marks with seniority derived from an earlier British mark; and (3) earlier "well-known" marks within the meaning of Article 6*bis* of the Paris Convention.[24]

---

[19] TMA 1994, s. 4. With some foresight, no objection succeeded in *"Queen Diana" T.M.* [1991] R.P.C. 395.

[20] TMA 1994, ss. 57–59. There is an exception in respect of international organisations: see s. 58(2).

[21] *ibid.*, ss. 57, 59.

[22] See para. 17–06, above. Under the 1994 Act, an opponent does not have to be the person entitled to the conflicting right: *"Wild Child" T.M.* [1998] R.P.C. 455.

[23] See para. 17–04, above.

[24] TMA 1994, s. 6(1), here includes both U.K. registrations and international marks (U.K.) under the Madrid Protocol. It also covers an application still being processed but subsequently registered (s. 6(2)), since on registration the right dates back to the date of application (s. 9(3)). It also includes an expired mark for one year after expiry, unless there had been two years of non-use immediately before expiry (s. 6(3), implementing TM Dir., Art. 11(1), but going further). For Paris Convention, Art. 6*bis* protection, see para. 16–17, above.

"Earlier right" covers: (1) the entitlement to protect an unregistered right or other sign used in the course of trade (in particular by passing-off proceedings); and (2) other entitlements to object, in particular by virtue of the law of copyright, design right or registered designs.[25]

These two types of objection will be separately discussed. It is also necessary to have in mind a number of additional factors which affect the assessment of the objection: consent by third parties, onus of proof, absence of power to require a disclaimer, and honest concurrent use. These are referred to subsequently.[26]

(1) Earlier marks

17-53 The relative grounds of objection relating to "earlier trade marks" divide into three types[27]:

Type 1: Where the marks being compared are identical and the goods or services are also identical, no likelihood of confusion need be shown.[28] Because of the identity on both fronts, it is assumed that confusion must be sufficiently likely to raise a bar to registration of the second sign. Because Type 1 gives such embracing protection, its scope ought to be limited. Yet difficulties inevitably arise over what is identical, and none more then where one or both of the marks is used with associated matter. In *British Sugar v. Robertson*,[29] the defendant's later mark, "Robertson's Toffee Treat" fell to be considered beside the plaintiff's registered mark, "Treat", used in practice with its well-known mark, "Silver Spoon". Jacob J. would have been prepared to say that the marks were identical, because it was relevant to consider "Treat" separately in each case. That may lead to simplicity, but only of a kind which seems artificial.

Type 2: Where the goods or services are only similar and not identical; or the marks are only similar (for identical or similar goods or services), it must be shown that "there exists a likelihood of confusion on the part of the public, which includes the likelihood of association with the earlier trade mark".[30] The ECJ has accepted that "association" is one form of "confusion", not an independent concept.[31]

In *Lloyd Schuhfabrik Meyer v. Klijsen*,[32] the Court has also stressed that it is for the trade mark office or national court to assess the

---

[25] TMA 1994, s. 5(4). For marks which infringe other rights, see para. 17–54, below.
[26] See paras 17–58 *et seq.*, below.
[27] There is an equivalent division relating to infringement: see paras 17–85 *et seq.*, below.
[28] TMA 1994, s. 5(1).
[29] [1996] R.P.C. 3281 at 293–294; and see *Avnet v. Isoact* [1998] F.S.R. 16.
[30] TMA 1994, s. 5(2).
[31] *Sabel v. Puma* [1998] R.P.C. 199. The Formulation comes from the CTM Reg. (Art. 8(1)(b)) and TM Dir. (Art. 4(1)(b)), not from the Benelux Trade Mark Act, Art. 13. See below, para. 17–96.
[32] (June 22, 1999, to be reported): "Lloyd" for shoes, opposed by "Loints", also for shoes.

likelihood of confusion on the totality of evidence. It accordingly refused to lay down detailed rules about either the degree of similarity needed between one-syllable word marks or the effect of any given level of public recognition of the earlier mark. Rather it is for the court or office itself to consider whether there is a genuine and properly substantiated likelihood of confusion on the part of an average consumer.[33] That person is not the "moron in a hurry", but rather one who is "reasonably well informed and reasonably observant and circumspect". However, the chance to make a direct comparison is rare, so that imperfect recollection must be given account, bearing in mind that the average consumer's level of attention will vary for different types of goods and services.[34] It is necessary to consider visual and conceptual similarity, and also whether there is a danger of aural confusion, for that in itself may suffice. Likewise the more distinctive the prior mark has become through use, the more probable that there will be confusion. Where both marks are characterised by some unusual or original feature, this also increases that risk;[35] whereas, the presence of a descriptive element will lessen it.[36]

Type 3: In addition, where the marks are identical or similar, but the goods or services are not, an "anti-dilution" provision operates. A relative objection arises where an earlier similar mark for non-similar goods or services has a reputation in the United Kingdom—or, where it is a Community mark, in the European Community—and the use of the later mark without due cause would take unfair advantage of, or be detrimental to, the distinctive character or repute of the earlier trade mark. Observe that this type of objection arises not only where there is a danger of confusion, including association (as in Type 2) but also in circumstances apparently more embracing: the ground covers any use of another mark which can be characterised as affecting distinctive character or repute, not only so as to cause detriment to, but equally to take unfair advantage of, that character or repute. Making out such a case where there is no confusion is likely to prove difficult. This deployment of the registration scheme to protect aspects of "investment function" is further explored below.[37]

Precisely this three-fold typology is applied to the later question, what constitutes infringement of a mark once registered? Each issue—relative objection to registration and infringement—is accordingly treated as one of

---

[33] *Sabel v. Puma*, n. 31, above; *Gut Springenheide* [1998] I E.C.R. 4657; *Windsurfing Chiemsee v. Huber* (May 4, 1999, to be reported), para. 17–38, above.

[34] *Lloyd v. Klijsen*, n. 32, above; and cases on unfair competition and free movement, *e.g. Verband Sozialer Wettberwerb v. Clinique Laboratories* [1994] I E.C.R. 317, para. 18–11.

[35] *Sabel v. Puma*, n. 31 above; *Lloyd v. Klijsen*, n. 32, above.

[36] *Windsurfing Chiemsee v. Huber*, n. 33, above.

[37] See paras 17–96 *et seq.*, below.

seniority in entitlement: which of the contestants has the prior right to marks which overlap in one of the three ways? Some of the many difficult issues which arise in interpreting the three Types are accordingly left for the discussion of infringement. Here the footnotes refer the reader forward to the relevant passages.

Article 43(2) of the CTM Regulation provides, and Article 10 of the TM Directive requires, that the earlier mark should, if necessary, be shown to have been put to genuine use in the previous five years. Under the 1994 Act this can only be achieved by seeking revocation of the mark used in attack.[38]

(2) Earlier rights

17–54 In this category the definition of "earlier rights" itself delineates the scope of the objections. In the British legislation there are two sub-types:

> **Sub-type (i)**: Where use in the United Kingdom of the mark applied for is liable to be prevented by any rule of law protecting an unregistered trade mark or other sign used in the course of trade. This relates in particular to passing-off proceedings and may, therefore, cover conflicts with unregistered marks which are identical or similar, for goods or services which are the same or similar, or other circumstances where the three main requirements for passing off exist: a sufficient reputation in the country, a relevant misrepresentation and likelihood of damage.[39] Purely local rights are as relevant as those with coverage throughout the jurisdiction.[40]

> **Sub-type (ii)**: Where use in the United Kingdom of the mark applied for is liable to be prevented by virtue of some other right, in particular a copyright, design right or registered design.[41]

(3) Anti-dilution measures[42]

17–55 Thus, a plethora of objections may be raised on the basis of "earlier trade marks" and "earlier rights" in unregistered marks. Under the new dispensation, the first to acquire rights appears entitled to have them protected not only in respect of their "origin" function, but also in respect of other less

---

[38] For which, see TMA 1994, s. 46(1), para. 17–69, below.

[39] Within this head will fall the special right given to a principal mark-owner in a Convention country to enjoin use of his trade mark by his British agent, where the use is unauthorised and unjustified: TMA 1994, s. 60(4), (5), implementing the Paris Convention, Art. 6*septies*. See *"Travelpro" T.M.* [1998] R.P.C. 864.

[40] *cf.* the CTM: para. 17–67, below.

[41] As under the previous law: *e.g. "Karo Step" T.M.* [1977] R.P.C. 255 at 276 (trade name in logo-like presentation an artistic work); *"Oscar" T.M.* [1979] R.P.C. 173 (picture of the famous statuette); Lyons [1994] E.I.P.R. 21.

[42] See further para. 17–100 below.

specific values, including those involved in one or other notion of "dilution". In the early stages of evolving the CTM Regulation and TM Directive, the emphasis was on confining the scope of rights so as to enable as many legitimate traders as possible to use their own marks. The main test of objection then proposed was that there be a "serious danger" of confusion. But this severity has dissipated in a final outcome which seems more anxious to catch everything than to display any logical clarity about doing so.

One major distinction is between registered and unregistered trade **17–56** marks. For the most part, the latter give rise to objection only if they qualify to be treated as "earlier rights" and that depends largely upon whether the objector could sue for passing off. This distinction would be straightforward, were it not for the fact that unregistered as well as registered rights may fall to be treated as "earlier trade marks" when they acquire sufficient notoriety to be classified as "well-known" within the Paris Convention.[43] This circumstance should be treated as a special case, for most marks of this degree of fame will be registered in the British or Community Register. Dilution may cause difficulty here:

"Macy's" is famous throughout America as a department store and, if evidence can show it, will also be "well-known" in Britain for goods that such stores sell.[44] Another applicant, even one with substantial British trade under that mark, could not register it, or any close variant ("Macey", "Maty's"), for any department store goods or services. For dissimilar goods or services (tractors, office cleaning), New York Macy's could oppose if they can show (1) "a reputation in the United Kingdom" (which may call for a lower level of recognition than being a "well-known mark", but may be held to refer only to a trading reputation in the United Kingdom); and (2) the taking of unfair advantage or causing of detriment referred to in section 5(3) of the 1994 Act.[45]

If the mark is not so internationally famous as to be "well-known" in Britain, then the application can be prevented only by showing a British reputation sufficient to establish a right to prevent passing off.[46]

The other main distinction affecting "earlier trade marks", turns on **17–57** whether or not there is evidence of trading reputation. If the marks and/or the goods or services are similar, objection arises where the public is likely

---

[43] For the meaning of "well-known" in the Paris Convention, and for a comparison with the various refinements of the same general idea which over time have plagued German jurisprudence, see Kur (1992) 23 I.I.C. 18.

[44] An example sparked by *Macy's T.M.* [1989] R.P.C. 546. But under the old law, Paris Convention fame could not be brought into account. Unless the British user was shown to have copied the mark improperly, Macy's could object only on the basis of its own use of the mark in Britain and not from any reputation in Britain stemming from extensive trade abroad.

[45] *cf.* under the old law, *"Laura Ashley" T.M.* [1990] R.P.C. 539.

[46] *cf.* the less stringent test under the 1938 Act, illustrated in *Macy*, n. 44, above.

to be confused between them. If the earlier mark has a relevant reputation from trade use, the grounds of objection broaden to cover improper advantages or detriments which would arise from use of the later mark on non-similar goods or services. *A fortiori*, one would suppose, these broader grounds of objection should apply when the marks are being applied to *similar* goods and services, though this is not clear on the face of the text.

A reasonable balance would be preserved if (1) the notion of "association"—included within likelihood of confusion test for Type 2—is read to cover cases where it is difficult to be sure that there will be confusion about origin but it is quite plain that there will be some other form of detriment or else of unfair advantage from use of the later mark; and (2) the test for Type 3 is given the same general scope.

(4) Other factors

(a) *Consent of other party*

17–58 As already emphasised, the new legislation makes objections on these relative grounds subject to the view of the third party concerned. If that party consents to the registration, the objection falls. The Registrar has no residual power to consider the matter in the public interest, being now deprived of any ultimate discretion to refuse registration on any sufficient ground. In the past, for instance, the Registrar refused "Jardex" for poisonous disinfectant, given an existing registration of "Jardox" for meat extract, because of the particular danger which might ensue from muddling the two on the shelf.[47] It seems that such a consumerist objection would now fall within the Registry's remit only if it could be brought within an absolute ground, such as that the mark is likely to deceive or its use could be prohibited by law.[48]

(b) *Scope of objections*

17–59 There are other, quite subtle indications that the Registry must now be less scrupulous than previously. For example, the "earlier rights" objection arises only where there is indeed an actual right to protect.[49] More generally, there is no longer an onus on the applicant to overcome all objections to registration: on the contrary, it is now for the Registrar or an opponent to make out a sufficient objection.

At the same time, two moderating techniques of the earlier British law are now reduced in effect, just at the time when the need to accommodate

---

[47] *Edwards' Application* (1945) 63 R.P.C. 19. Or see *"Fingals"* T.M. [1993] R.P.C. 21, where, under the old law, the mark was refused for wines and spirits in face of an existing registration for restaurant services, even where the latter owner consented.
[48] See paras 17–49, 17–50, above.
[49] See para. 17–63, below.

competing users is likely to be particularly strong. These are, first, registration with disclaimer, and, secondly, registration upon proof of honest concurrent use.

(c) *Disclaimer*

There has long been a practice of registering marks subject to disclaimers **17–60** of exclusive right in some part of the whole, or subject to other limitations. In this way the Registry has been empowered to give the applicant some part of what it seeks, while taking sufficient account of an objection to the distinctiveness or deceptiveness of the mark.[50] The scope of disclaimers and limitations can be the subject of extended discussion between Registry and applicant. Under the former law, the Registry could, if it thought fit, impose them; now they have to be accepted by the applicant. This may shift the balance in the applicant's favour, but probably only to a marginal degree; for ultimately the Registry decides what is registrable within the law.

It is now explicitly stated that the rights in the mark are restricted in accordance with the disclaimer or limitation.[51] The correct approach is, first, to consider whether the mark is registrable apart from any question of disclaiming[52]; and then, if necessary, to consider whether, after discounting what is disclaimed, enough will remain of independent substance to deserve registration.[53]

(d) *Honest concurrent use*

Under the previous law, the Registrar had a discretion to register a mark **17–61** which posed some probability of confusion with an earlier registered mark, if the applicant could make out a sufficient case of "honest concurrent use". At the margins, the interest of competitors was thus preferred to that of consumers.[54] The concept has not found a place in the new Community regime. This is perhaps surprising, given the likely toll of such cases within an expanding Common Market.

In a curious legislative frolic, however, Parliament preserved for the British Registry a power to take account of honest concurrent use, which may occasionally be of help in dealing with ambivalent situations.[55] If the

---

[50] Formerly, conditions could also be imposed. These might, for instance, restrict the proprietor's own use so as to prevent potential deception. This power has now disappeared, but so too has the need to acquire a specification of goods or services that is as wide as possible: see para. 17–91, below.

[51] TMA 1994, s. 13. It is for the applicant to agree to a specified territorial or other limitation.

[52] *"Superwound"* T.M. [1988] R.P.C. 272.

[53] *"P.R.E.P.A.R.E."* T.M. [1997] R.P.C. 884: that mark not registerable even with a disclaimer of the word without the full stops.

[54] See Lord Diplock, *"GE" T.M.* [1973] R.P.C. 297 at 325, 326.

[55] If the *British Registry* ceases to examine *ex officio* on the relative grounds, then the provision on honest concurrent use will disappear: TMA 1994, s. 7(3); the CTM system, which depends upon opposition, has no place for it. Nor is it admitted into the Directive's exhaustive list of relative grounds of objection: see Art. 4 and Rec. 7.

Registry finds a possibility of confusion, but also that the later applicant has engaged in "honest concurrent use", then:

> "the registrar shall not refuse the application by reason of the earlier trade mark or earlier right únless objection on that ground is raised in opposition proceedings by the proprietor of that earlier trade mark or earlier right."[56]

It has been confirmed in *Road Tech Computers v. Unison Software*[57] that in an opposition honest concurrent uses raises no defence. Accordingly, no essential conflict with the E.C. Directive arises.[58]

17–62   Honest concurrent use is applicable in proceedings between applicant and Registrar before publication.[59] The concept is the same as in the previous law.[60] Accordingly it is necessary to consider:

(1) the degree of likely confusion;
(2) the honesty of the original adoption and subsequent use of the mark;
(3) the length of the applicant's use;
(4) evidence of confusion in actual use; and
(5) the comparative size of trade in the two marks.[61]

The earlier case law has shown considerable caution: a long period of concurrent use (upwards of seven years) was usually required[62]; and concurrent registration was refused where there was "triple identity"—of (a) marks, (b) goods or services, and (c) area of sale or service.[63] Perhaps the Registry can now afford to take a more generous view, given the purely provisional role which honest concurrent use appears to play under the 1994 Act.

(5) Comparison between marks

(a) *The basis for comparison*

17–63 Where the comparison between marks is being made before the Registry *ex officio*, account must be taken of any manner in which each mark as registered could be used in a normal and fair way. But where in fact there

---

[56] TMA 1994, s. 7(1).
[57] [1996] F.S.R. 805.
[58] *cf.* the explanation offered to Parliament of the scope of s. 7: Hans. HL, Vol. 550, cols. 70–72.
[59] An indication that it is restricted to those proceedings comes from the fact that honest concurrent use will disappear, if it is decided to get rid of *ex officio* examination on the relative grounds: TMA 1994, s. 7(5).
[60] TMA 1994, s. 7(3) says so.
[61] Lord Tomlin, *Pirie's Application* (1933) 50 R.P.C. 147 at 159–160; *Holt's Application* [1957] R.P.C. 289; *"Bali" T.M. (No. 2)* [1978] F.S.R. 193. See generally Faulkner, *Elements of Trade Mark Law and Practice* (3rd ed., 1971) pp. 13–14.
[62] *cf.* however, the special circumstances in *Peddie's Application* (1944) 61 R.P.C. 31, and *"Granada" T.M.* [1979] R.P.C. 303.
[63] But even in this case, there may be exceptions—*e.g.* affectionate abbreviation in *"Bud" T.M.* [1988] R.P.C. 535.

has been use of the other mark, it is that actual use which must be compared with any normal and fair use of the mark applied for.[64]

Where an objector is relying not upon a registration but upon an unregistered mark protected by passing off, then the comparison is with the actual reputation of the earlier mark derived from trading. Here, as already noted, the law is harder on objectors than formerly. The previous approach was to consider whether there was likelihood of confusion between the two marks.[65] Now it is necessary for the person claiming priority to show that he has a legal right to prevent use of the mark applied for, in particular because of passing off. This means demonstrating a sufficient reputation with the public and not merely that the public will be muddled about source. As before, it is for the tribunal, rather than witnesses, to determine whether a relative ground of objection is made out.[66]

(b) *Factors in the comparison*

Where words are involved, the proper approach was stated in classic form **17–64** by Parker J. in *Pianotist's Application*[67]:

> "You must take the two words. You must judge of them, both by their look and by their sound. You must consider the goods to which they are to be applied. You must consider the nature and kind of customer who would be likely to buy those goods. In fact, you must consider all the circumstances; and you must further consider what is likely to happen if each of those trade marks is used in a normal way as a trade mark for the goods of the respective owners of the marks."

At the same time, Farwell J.'s warning against artifice in the "Erectiko" case[68] must not be forgotten:

> "I do not think it is right to take a part of the word and compare it with a part of the other word; one word must be considered as a whole and compared with the other word as a whole . . . There may be two words which in their component parts are widely different but which, when read or spoken together, do represent something which is so similar as to lead inevitably to confusion."

If the mark is not just a word, but a word or words in a given format, a symbol, colour, ideogram, picture, shape or a combination of some or all of these, then the comparison is between the two, taking account particularly

---

[64] *Smith Hayden's Application* (1946) 63 R.P.C. 97 at 101 (though in opposition proceedings the onus may now be on the opponent, rather than, as previously, on the applicant).

[65] See *"Bali" T.M.* [1969] R.P.C. 472 at 496–497.

[66] *"Kidax" T.M.* (1933) 50 R.P.C. 117.

[67] (1906) 23 R.P.C. 774 at 777. There is a family resemblance in the approach to comparison of marks with that in a passing-off action: for which see paras 16–23—16–25, above.

[68] *William Bailey's Application* (1935) 52 R.P.C. 136 at 151–152.

of the features which make them memorable. Obviously, if it is only capable of being seen and not spoken, it is only visual comparison which is relevant.

17–65   The case law provides a lava-flow of illustrations. Some deal with the issue at the stage of application, others with infringement. In each case the essence of the inquiry is the same. Here are a few:

> "Rysta" for stockings was disallowed in face of "Aristoc" for the same goods: in over-the-counter sales, there would likely be careless and slurred pronunciation, imperfect recollection, and limitation of the knowledge of customer and shop assistant to one only of the marks.[69]

> Registration was granted of "Flowstacka" for lifting machines, despite its descriptive content and absence of any use, because the applicant already held a series of "Flow-" marks for the same machines. This meant that those in the industry would at once *associate* it with the applicant—an instance of "association" being held liable to cause confusion, which now has novel resonance.[70]

> An applicant was allowed to register "Ovax" for a cake ingredient over an objection from the owner of "Hovis", well-known for flour and bread. The contrary conclusion would have been to give the opponent in effect a monopoly in short words starting "Ov-", many deriving from *ovum*.[71]

> "Skin Dew" for cosmetics survived an attack by "Skin Deep" because the "idea" of the two marks was considered different; and because, there being various other "Skin . . ." marks on the market, customers were likely to pay attention to the differences of detail.[72]

(6) Community trade marks

17–66 The relative grounds affecting the registration of CTMs are largely in correlative terms to those for national marks. The consequential difficulties that this presents are considerable. Under the Community system there is to be no *ex officio* examination on these grounds and everything will accordingly turn on oppositions by third parties.[73] Practice in Germany under such a remit suggests that the list of cases will soon be a long one.

These opponents may succeed by showing a senior mark or right within the three types of objection found also in the Trade Marks Act.[74] But that

---

[69] *Aristoc v. Rysta* [1945] A.C. 68, HL. Comparison of sound is important where, for instance, telephone ordering is likely: *Philips' T.M* [1969] R.P.C. 78. Otherwise today sound may be less significant than it used to be: *"Lancer" T.M.* [1987] R.P.C. 303.

[70] *"Flowstacka" T.M.* [1968] R.P.C. 66; equally with such repeated suffixes as the "King" marks in *"Frigiking" T.M.* [1973] R.P.C. 739. For "association" see para. 17–95, below.

[71] *Smith Hayden's Appln* (1946) 63 R.P.C. 97.

[72] *Helena Rubenstein's Application* [1960] R.P.C. 229.

[73] CTM Reg., Art. 8. Where the earlier right is a registered mark, owners and licensees are both entitled to oppose.

[74] See para. 17–53, above. Note also CTM Reg., Art. 8(3), allowing an opposition by a principal to an unauthorised and unjustified application by his agent. *cf.* TMA 1994, s. 60 confining this ground to Paris Convention nationals, in implementation of that Convention, Art. 6 *septies*.

earlier mark may be a CTM or a mark registered in any Member State[75]; also brought into account are earlier unregistered rights. It was particularly important to the British and Irish, with systems which traditionally obliged many traders to rely on passing-off rights for a substantial part of their protection, to secure this last ground of opposition; it was heavily resisted by the German government from a fear that the pre-grant procedure will become hopelessly over-burdened.[76] One reason, of course, why their fears may not be realised is that the possibility of raising registrations from any of the national or regional registers of the entire Community may of itself make a CTM on balance unattractive. On the other hand, a CTM application allows a trader who needs a Europe-wide or international mark to discover conflicts, and negotiate solutions to them, at an early stage.

There is, however, one limit to the scope of objections to a CTM, which **17–67** does not affect national applications to the same extent: non-registered rights which are of "mere local significance" are not brought into account either in opposition or in subsequent invalidity proceedings.[77] They may, however, be asserted against the CTM holder for passing off in the particular locality until acquiescence has run for five years; and even thereafter the CTM owner has no right to stop the earlier user from continuing his marking in the locality.[78]

What is to count as merely "local" is not defined. Given the context just mentioned it is possible that fairly wide areas within Community countries will be treated as localities: England, Wales, Scotland, Northern Ireland in the British situation? Belgium, Netherlands and Luxembourg, given that they have a Benelux mark system in operation? Or is it really a reputation confined to a town or city, or perhaps a county, that is in issue—something that is confined by an acreage or population of comparatively modest proportion? National attitudes are likely to vary and the Court of Justice may find itself wrestling with the question.[79]

6. REVOCATION AND INVALIDITY

A British trade mark registration is open to attack on two major fronts: **17–68**

(1) Revocation proceedings may be brought in relation to grounds which have arisen since the date of registration—notably because of non-use or because the mark has become descriptive or misleading. A revocation order will operate from the date of the application to revoke or the date on which the ground for revocation existed, if earlier.[80]

---

[75] Including registrations procured internationally and prior applications which succeed.
[76] See von Mühlendahl (1989) 20 I.I.C. 583; Pagenberg (1989) 20 I.I.C. 595.
[77] CTM Reg., Arts 8(4), 52(1)(c).
[78] *ibid.*, Art. 107.
[79] Earlier "local" right can also provide a defence to an infringement action under the 1994 Act, s. 11(3); see para. 17–113, below.
[80] TMA 1994, s. 46, implementing the TM Dir., Arts 12–14.

(2) Proceedings to have the registration declared invalid may be brought on absolute or relative grounds which existed at the time of registration and which cannot be excused by subsequent events. If they succeed, the registration will be deemed never to have been made.[81]

A Community trade mark is open to attack on equivalent grounds.[82] But because of its unitary character, the objections have to be considered on a Community basis. It is far from clear what precisely this means. Discussion here will consider the position as it relates to British trade marks, but will draw attention to this special characteristic of Community marks.[83]

One apparent difference may be noted at once. If a Community ground for revocation or declaration of invalidity is made out, there is no discretion left to the tribunal concerned over whether to take consequent action: it is mandatory.[84] Under the British Act, perhaps following the TM Directive,[85] the matter is apparently left to the tribunal's discretion. But it should be recalled that similar wording concerning non-use under the 1938 Act was interpreted to leave virtually no scope for any discretion.[86]

(1) Revocation for non-use

17–69 The conception of a trade mark registration as an entitlement dependent upon need—which has always underpinned the British approach to the subject—has become a major element in the new European arrangements.[87] Accordingly the applicant for registration must intend bona fide to use the mark—a requirement already discussed.[88] After registration the proprietor or a licensee must put it to genuine use.[89] Registrations should not be stockpiled, either in their entirety or for certain goods or services; and it makes no difference whether the stockpiling is primarily for some future use by the person registered or a licensee, or is done to prevent competitors from obtaining desirable marks for themselves.

It is hard to eliminate stockpiling. In an effort to do so, the United States and Canadian systems require positive evidence of use to accompany each

---

[81] TMA 1994, s. 47, implementing the TM Dir., Arts 3, 4, 13, 14.
[82] CTM Reg., Arts 50, 51.
[83] Since the validity of a mark may be raised in infringement proceedings before national Courts, they will be obliged to decide such questions: see CTM Reg., Arts 50(1), 51(1).
[84] CTM Reg., Arts 50, 51—"shall be declared revoked/invalid".
[85] TMA 1994, ss. 46, 47—"may be revoked/declared invalid"; TM Dir., Arts 3, 4, 12—"liable to be revoked/declared invalid". *cf.* Annand and Norman, p. 141.
[86] TMA 1938, s. 26(1); *Lyons' Application* [1959] R.P.C. 120.
[87] TMA 1994, s. 50(1)(a) and (b), embodies the TM Dir., Art. 10, so far as it is relevant to the country. For the equivalent provisions in the CTM Reg., see n. 62 below. For a review of the position around the world, see Taylor (1990) 80 T.M.R. 197.
[88] See para. 17–03, above.
[89] For licensing, see para. 17–79, below.

application to renew the registration. It was initially proposed that there be a similar requirement for Community marks[90]: but protests from European industry led to a much less demanding approach, akin to that which, for instance, already operated in the British system. The new law accordingly shows no marked change over previous British practice. However, it does place the burden of proving use on the mark owner.[91] This is a significant exception to the general presumption of validity upon registration and an important change over previous practice.[92]

(a) *Scope of the ground*

Subject to certain exceptions, a registration is to be revoked for failure by **17–70** the proprietor, or any person with his consent,[93] to make genuine use of the mark in the United Kingdom in relation to the specified goods or services:

(1) in the five years from completion of registration[94]; or
(2) in any later uninterrupted period of five years.[95]

An application to revoke may be made by any person and not just a "person aggrieved", as under the previous law.[96] It is not therefore necessary for an objector to establish a sufficient interest in the mark. To this extent the objection has acquired a colouring of public interest. If the objection is made out only for some of the goods or services specified, there will be revocation for them alone.[97]

It is expressly stated that affixing the mark to goods or packaging purely **17–71** for export from the United Kingdom is sufficient use.[98] What else may suffice has yet to be defined. Earlier case law on this issue sought to

---

[90] See the first Draft CTM Reg., III/D/753/78, Art. 43.

[91] TMA 1994, s. 100.

[92] See Morcom [1990] E.I.P.R. 391 at 395.

[93] Use with the proprietor's consent is meant to include use by a licensee: *Hansard,* HL (Committee, January 19, 1994) col. 76.

[94] *i.e.* the actual date on which registration is complete, not the "date of registration" which involves a notional back-dating to filing of the application. The CTM Reg. omits reference to the first of these grounds: Art. 50(1)(a).

[95] TMA 1994, s. 46(1)(a), (b). The registration *may* be revoked on these grounds. Accordingly there is a discretion not to do so where sufficient reason exists: *Glen Catrine's T.M.* [1996] E.T.M.R. 56 (ch). In addition, the grounds themselves allow a mark to be saved where there are proper reasons for non-use: see para. 17–72, below. There seems no reason in principle why the same mark may not be registered by the same proprietor for identical goods. The second registration will then have its own five-year term for use to begin; but there will be a question whether initially it is registered in good faith (s. 3(6)), or in order to repair the lack of use of the first registration: *cf. Unilever v. Cussons (New Zealand)* [1998] R.P.C. 369.

[96] The same applies to the other grounds for revocation and declaration of invalidity. The application may be made to the Registrar or the High Court, unless the issue is already pending before the latter. The Registrar may refer the application to the Court at any stage: TMA 1994, s. 46(4).

[97] *ibid.*, s. 46(5); as in *Lyons' Application* [1959] R.P.C. 120, CA; *Unilever v. Johnson Wax* [1989] F.S.R. 145.

[98] TMA 1994; s. 46(2); as in the previous law: *Fisons v. Norton* [1994] F.S.R. 745.

distinguish between genuine efforts to start trading and purely colourable use designed to keep rights alive. It is likely still to apply.[99] If the proprietor falls in the former category, then to supply goods under the mark on a single occasion, or to make some other definite marketing effort, may amount to use.[1] It may even suffice to show that the mark has been used purely in brochures or advertisements, though such a case will be looked at with suspicion.[2] Use merely to endorse the products of others—for instance, by a chain store or a magazine—is not enough.[3]

If there is substantial use in actual trade, it will not cease to be genuine because it was undertaken in order to improve the user's position in a conflict with a competitor.[4] On the other hand, if the underlying motive is to keep up a "ghost" registration, so as really to protect another unregistrable mark, even quite high sales for a limited period may be deemed colourable, rather than genuine. For example, cigarette manufacturers who wished to use the laudatory mark, "Merit", and hoped to gain protection by registering and actually using for a while the mark "Nerit", were unable to show that this amounted to genuine use.[5]

So far as concerns British marks, it is only use of the mark in the United Kingdom which is relevant. But for a Community mark, "use in the Community" is the criterion.[6] This may be read as referring to use in more than one Member State. A Community registration, after all, gives a right of wide scope and should arguably be reserved for marks which are being used for trade between Member States. It is expressly provided that a CTM may be converted into a national mark where it has been revoked for non-use "in the Community", provided that it has been genuinely used in the state concerned.[7] This implies that a higher level of use needs be shown in the Community system than in national systems. Of course it may prove difficult to persuade Community tribunals to take any determined line on this. But the matter can equally be raised in a counterclaim before a national Court hearing infringement proceedings; and that could be a Court in a country where the CTM proprietor had not used the mark.

(b) *Exceptions*

17–72 For both British and Community marks, there will be no revocation if any of the specified exceptions apply:

---

[99] See the White Paper (Cm. 530, 1990) para. 4.29. Genuine use surely implies use as a trade mark for the goods or services registered, and not for some other purpose: *cf.* Annand and Norman, pp. 126–127.

[1] *"Nodoz" T.M.* [1962] R.P.C. 1; *"Hermes" T.M.* [1982] R.P.C. 425; *"Bon Matin" T.M.* [1989] R.P.C. 537—the latter two were cases where genuine preparation to market sufficed, without evidence of actual sales.

[2] *"Concord" T.M.* [1987] R.P.C. 209.

[3] *Safeway Stores v. HFP* [1997] E.T.M.R. 352; *"Elle" T.M.s* [1997] F.S.R. 529.

[4] *Electrolux v. Electrix* (1954) 71 R.P.C. 23 at 42, CA.

[5] *Imperial Group v. Philip Morris* [1982] F.S.R. 72, CA.

[6] CTM Reg., Art. 50(1)(a).

[7] A matter which would be assessed by the national registry considering the application for conversion: see CTM Reg., Arts 108–110.

(1) There has been use of a mark which differs only in elements which do not alter the distinctive character of the mark registered[8]; earlier case law shows that there may be a material difference between closely similar words if one spells something descriptive while the other does not: as in "Huggers", as opposed to "Huggars" for shoes.[9]

(2) There has been a subsequent resumption of use before the application to revoke is made. But here resumption within three months of that application does not count; this enables an attacker to give warning of his intention without inducing a repellent spurt of use.[10]

(3) There are proper reasons for non-use.[11] Under the former law, there was an exception for "special circumstances in the trade." Our Registry has held that this means any reason which is "apt, acceptable, reasonable, justifiable in all of the circumstances." Thus where there had been preparations to license the mark but these had been put in suspense by the revocation proceedings, this was held sufficient justification.[12] However, a trader's own business difficulties would not suffice.[13]

It is not an excuse that the mark has been used on similar goods or for **17–73** similar services.[14] This strictness appears appropriate, given that the scope of right granted under the law extends not only to specified goods and services but also to those which are similar.[15]

> Suppose that A has "Deft" registered for ice cream and jellies, but for the last five years has only used it on ice cream and not on jellies. Suppose then that B wants "Deft" for cakes, and cakes are considered similar to jellies but not to ice cream, even though jellies and ice cream are themselves similar. B could have A's registration for jellies revoked, thus removing any relevant objection.

(2) Mark becoming generic

When a new product appears on the market, and particularly when patent **17–74** protection eliminates direct competition for some initial period,[16] the

---

[8] TMA 1994, s. 46(2). The concept of "associated marks" has now gone from the law, and with it the possibility of taking account of the use of such marks.

[9] "Huggars" T.M. [1979] F.S.R. 310—another failed attempt at "ghosting".

[10] TMA 1994, s. 46(3).

[11] *ibid.*, s. 46(1)(a), (b).

[12] "Invermont" T.M. [1997] R.P.C. 125; Worth T.M.s. [1998] R.P.C. 875. For "special circumstances" under the TMA 1938, s. 26(3), see Kerly, paras 11–47, 11–48.

[13] Hansard, HL. (Committee, January 19, 1994) cols 84, 94. cf. Mouson's v. Boehm (1884) 26 Ch.D. 398 at 406.

[14] The TMA 1938, s. 26, did at least count use on goods or services "of the same description".

[15] For this rule, see para. 17–91, below.

[16] Under the former law, the naming of patented products was the subject of special treatment (TMA 1938, s. 15(2)) but this has now gone.

producer may find that the mark which he gives it comes to be used as a description of the product itself. Names which have gone through this process to a greater or lesser extent include aspirin, shredded wheat, thermos, hoover, frigidaire, sellotape, terylene and formica.

In some cases, the trade mark owner takes regular steps to emphasise that there is a separate generic name for the product, and to encourage those in trade to use the trade mark only for its own products, the generic name for substitutes (as, for instance, "adhesive tape" rather than "Sellotape").[17] If they take considerable care, then they are likely to be able to show that the distinct meanings remain understood. As well as ensuring that their own usage does not slide in a descriptive direction, they ought actively to pursue others who are careless.[18] They are then likely to have a preservable trade mark which is of great value. If generic use of the mark becomes widespread, however, they may not be able to show a sufficient reputation to support passing off,[19] and equally they may face revocation of their trade mark registrations.

17–75 The ground of revocation, replacing much more elaborate provisions under the former law, is that, in consequence of acts or inactivity of the proprietor, the mark has become the common name in the trade for a product or service for which it is registered.[20] The question (as under the 1938 Act) is what the relevant trade understands by the mark, and not what the general public or any sector of it thinks.[21] Since traders tend to be more sensitive to the distinction between marks and generic names than do the public, the test for removal is a limited one which will apply only in unusual cases.

Moreover, what now matters is the naming of products or services specified in the registration and not the naming of similar products or services. In a former leading example, "Daiquiri Rum", registered for rum, was expunged upon proof that "Daiquiri" had become the generic name among bartenders (the relevant trade) for a rum-based cocktail.[22] But under

---

[17] In the pharmaceutical industry, where patenting of new drugs gives opportunities for being the sole producer on the market and hence for a mark to become a generic name, there is a standard practice: the substance will be given an often abbreviated chemical name. The patentee's product will have a separate mark, often easier to remember and scribble on a prescription pad. The mark will then be advertised emphatically with a modicum of attention to the generic description.

[18] A particular danger arises if a trade mark is given a generic description in a dictionary. In the case of a Community trade mark, a dictionary or reference work publisher who has done this can be ordered to indicate in the next edition that the word is a registered trade mark: CTM Reg., Art. 10. The TM Directive did not require such a provision in the 1994 Act and none was introduced; it might well have been.

[19] See para. 16–14, above.

[20] If a mark was not distinctive at its date of registration, it will be declared invalid *ab initio* under TMA 1994, s. 47; but that ground applies only to non-distinctiveness at that date, not subsequently.

[21] The U.S. by contrast, takes account of public use: see McCarthy, Chap. 12.

[22] *"Daiquiri Rum" T.M.* [1969] R.P.C. 600, HL.

section 15 of the 1938 Act, it was enough that the descriptive use in the trade was applied to "goods of the same description".[23] Now it would be necessary to show that the cocktail was essentially rum. Moreover, if the use is of the identical mark, there is no need to show that it leads to trade mark confusion. So the registered proprietor can by means of an action now object to descriptive use unless the user can justify what he is doing as an honest commercial practice.[24] Its corollary ought to be that mark-owners should be active guardians of such marks or else risk the consequences.

(3) Mark becoming deceptive

Just as a mark may lose its distinctiveness after registration by becoming a **17–76** general description of a product, so it is possible (though doubtless rare) that it will become deceptive through some subsequent event. In the former British law, it was for a long time uncertain what circumstances of this character would justify expunging a registration. Eventually it was settled that only where the registered proprietor had been guilty of "blameworthy conduct" would there be a substantive reason for removing the mark from the register.[25]

Some echo of this approach resounds in the 1994 Act, which gives as a ground for revocation that, "as a consequence of use made by the proprietor of the registered trade mark or by any third party with the proprietor's consent, such use is liable to mislead the public, particularly as to the nature, quality or geographical origin of those goods and/or services". This, however, refers only to "use" and so omits the element of moral culpability inherent in "blameworthy".

Obvious examples of what is caught can easily be conceived: for instance, to use the mark "Orlwoola" on cloth with a polyester component; or to use "California Syrup of Figs" on a syrup not made from figs or not coming from California.[26] Such misleading deployments of the mark itself could come about either when it is put to use for the first time, when a change in use occurs, or as a result of an assignment or licensing.

---

[23] The House of Lords considered that this placed the mark-owner in a precarious position about which he could do nothing, since the 1938 Act only permitted him to sue infringers who used the mark on goods within the registration. But this ignores the broader possibilities in the passing-off action, which would lie so long as some part of the public still thought the mark an indication of origin: see para. 16–18, above.

[24] TMA 1994, ss. 10(1), 11(2): see paras 17–88, 17–112, below.

[25] *"GE" T.M.* [1973] R.P.C. 297 at 334, HL, *per* Lord Diplock. His speech also untied a complex knot of difficulties about jurisdiction under the 1938 Act to remove a deceptive mark. See further *New South Wales Dairy v. Murray Goulburn* [1991] R.P.C. 144, HC(Aust.); *Riv-Oland v. Settef* (1988) 12 I.P.R. 321.

[26] See *Crosfield's Applcn* (1909) 26 R.P.C. 837, CA. In *Unilever's Applcn* [1999] E.T.M.R. 406, "Mr Long" was registered for ices, on the condition that it would be used only on elongated products.

17–77   More equivocal issues will arise where public understanding of the mark's significance comes from its manner of past use, and where something occurs which misleads as to source (not of itself a factor specifically listed in the ground of revocation).

Consider a Canadian case: "Wilkinson Sword" for razor blades had been promoted in that country as a mark suggesting British manufacture—though this was not something inherent in the mark itself. Deception justifying removal from the Register was held to arise when the mark was assigned to a manufacturing subsidiary for use on blades manufactured in Canada, the assignment being a tool to prevent parallel importation of the British originals. Under the 1994 Act, this ought to be treated as use of the mark by the proprietor or with his consent. The issue is thus whether, on the evidence, the public is liable to be misled.[27]

17–78   So far as source is concerned, the provision does not refer directly to it as a relevant form of deception, but does not exclude consideration of it. It is possible for a mark to become confusing with another only after its registration. Take the well-known *"GE"* case:[28] in 1907, General Electric of America registered "GE" as a monogram in a rondel for various electrical goods but it made no use of the mark for decades. During that time the English General Electric Company—an entirely separate concern—made wide use of "GEC" in a flowing script as a mark for much the same goods. The House of Lords held that, when the American company at last began to use its own registration in Britain,[29] this could lead to a form of confusion with "GEC".[30] But merely to begin using a mark already registered was not regarded as "blameworthy".[31] Now, however, since blame is apparently not relevant, the mark may fall to be expunged.[32]

17–79   Assignment or licensing of a mark by one enterprise to another has some potential for causing confusion about source. As we have seen, the Registrar no longer plays any role in ensuring that either type of transaction is proper. This provides some indorsement for the view that businesses need the ability to engage in these transactions in a whole range of circumstances and that the great majority of them are perfectly

---

[27] *Wilkinson Sword v. Juda* (1967) 59 D.L.R. (2d) 418; *cf. Manus v. Fullwood & Bland* [1949] Ch. 208 (Swedish manufacturer's mark for milking machines used by British agent on British goods in order to keep the mark alive in wartime held to be no jeopardy; public not shown to attach particular significance to Swedish origin). There is no presumption or requirement that the established connection with a mark is that of a manufacturer, rather than distributor: *Growmax v. Don & Low* [1999] R.P.C. 367.

[28] See n. 11, above.

[29] As a proprietor is entitled to do, so long as the registration remains operative: see now TMA 1994, s. 11(1).

[30] Through a particular form of "association", for which see para. 17–95, below.

[31] See also *New South Wales Dairy* case, n. 11, above.

[32] In the *"GE"* case, the trial judge and the House of Lords could find nothing to blame; to the contrary, the Court of Appeal seized upon certain arrangements between the two companies to split the market. If nothing else, this demonstrated what an uncertain investigation the search for fault could be.

acceptable. At the same time there are serious hazards in restructuring relationships without clarifying the trade mark position so that it reflects the actual reputation derived of trading.

> Scandecor was a successful art poster business whose international operations were centred in Sweden. Its U.K. marketing subsidiary registered "Scandecor" in the forms for posters and similar products. Subsequently the marks were transferred to the Swedish parent company. Due, at least initially, to incompatibilities between the two originators of the business, the operation of distributing the Swedish posters in the U.K. and other non-Continental countries passed to an independent company directed by one of them, which also began to produce its own material and sell it under the mark. Even though the marks had been used by the international company to indicate a connection with Swedish production, the goodwill in Britain was found, in the light of the whole complicated history, to belong to it. Use of the marks by the registered Swedish owner accordingly amounted to passing off. The registration had therefore to be revoked under section 46(1)(d).[33]

In such circumstances there can be no absolutely compelling resolution to the dispute. A different view of the factual situation might have resulted in victory for the Swedish manufacturers.

7. INVALIDITY OF A REGISTERED MARK

The courts and tribunals which determine revocation proceedings also have **17–80** power to make declarations of invalidity concerning the original registration.[34] If such a declaration is made, the registration will be invalid from the outset.[35] The grounds are accordingly the absolute or relative grounds of objection to an application, and the case for applying them will only arise where an application has wrongly slipped through the initial net and reached registration. The time to which they refer is that of registration, not any later date.[36] If it were otherwise, the relative validity of marks could be the subject of continual contest as their comparative reputations on the market varied with use.[37]

---

[33] *Scandecor Development v. Scandecor Marketing* [1997] F.S.R. 26, CA, criticised for its assumptions about goodwill by Wilkof [1998] E.I.P.R. 386.

[34] The substantive grounds are found in TMA 1994, s. 47; CTM Reg., Art 7 s 51, 52. The application may be made by any person; and in the case of a registration in bad faith, the Registrar may apply to the Court for a declaration of invalidity: TMA 1994, s. 47(4).

[35] TMA 1994, s. 47(5), (6); CTM Reg., Art. 54(2); for the consequences, see para. 17–68, above.

[36] Note, however, the different tenses used in formulating the absolute and relative grounds of invalidity.

[37] The danger of such an investigation must increase under the *Canon* principle, which extends the scope of protection as reputation grows: see below paras 17–92—17–93.

(1) Absolute grounds

17–81 So far as the absolute grounds are concerned, those objections to a sign which is a trade mark, but which lacks distinctiveness under section 3(1)(b),(c) or (d) of the 1994 Act, will not operate if there is countervailing evidence that the mark has become distinctive since registration in relation to the specified goods or services. This qualification introduces the equivalent balancing process to that which applies during the application stage.[38]

(2) Relative grounds: acquiescence

17–82 As for the relative grounds, no owner of a senior mark or other right can object to a registration after consenting to it.[39] And even without any positive assent, the right to object may be lost through inaction which falls within the limits of statutory acquiescence.[40] This arises only when the person with the prior right has been aware that the later registered mark has been used in the United Kingdom for a continuous period of five years.[41] There is no acquiescence, however, when the later registration is obtained in bad faith: this might occur when a renowned foreign mark has been improperly "misappropriated".[42] Curiously, once an earlier owner has acquiesced, the later owner cannot "oppose" that person's use of its own mark or unregistered right.[43] But there may be proceedings, it seems, to revoke it for (say) non-use or deceptive use.

In relation to a Community mark, the same rules apply. If the earlier owner has a Community mark, the acquiescence relates to any use of the later mark within the Community of which that person was aware; and to any use within the national territory concerned so far as there are earlier national registrations.[44] This quite moderate position is the outcome of a

---

[38] See TMA 1994, s. 3(1) proviso; and note the power given by the TM Dir., Art. 3(3). A laudatory word like "Treat" will not acquire distinctiveness by evidence that less than 60 per cent of the public treat it as a trade mark: *British Sugar v. James Robertson* [1996] R.P.C. 281 at 306.

[39] No particular form is required for this consent, which could in an appropriate case be implied from conduct. A person who maintains that he is licensed under a mark, is estopped from seeking its removal from the register: *"Job" T.M.* [1993] F.S.R. 118.

[40] The rule applies equally in relation to proceedings attacking the use of the later mark. The statutory definition now given to acquiescence in this context must be taken to replace the less definite concepts of acquiescence and laches in equity: for which see para. 2–64, above. See *Kerly*, paras 15–43—15–49.

[41] Where the objection is by a Convention country principal against conflicting action by an agent (see para. 17–03, n. 15, above), the period of acquiescence is three years: TMA 1994, s. 60(6).

[42] See para. 17–03, above.

[43] TMA 1994, s. 48(2).

[44] TMA 1994, s. 48; CTM Reg., Art. 53: a person who acquiesces may not secure a declaration of invalidity or enjoin use of the mark—a consequence which follows anyway so long as the later mark remains registered: see para. 17–111, below.

long debate in the evolution of the CTM. Initially it was proposed that a Community mark should in general become incontestable after five years; but that concept was watered down in stages.[45] The rule concerning acquiescence, as finally agreed, makes registrations noticeably less secure than they would have been with an incontestability rule, for acquiescence will preclude an objection only in cases of supine passivity on the part of the senior rightholder.

8. INFRINGEMENT

The typical infringer uses another's registered mark, or some confusingly **17–83** similar sign, as a trade mark to indicate the source of goods or services. In a market of competitors, if this conduct is not prevented, not only will the mark-owner lose out but consumers will not be able to trust the marks they see and possibilities of product differentiation will disintegrate. Preventing such direct harm remains the prime object in defining infringement and much is quite rightly heard of the "origin" function of marks, both from policy-makers and from courts.[46]

Modern legislators, however, cannot resist calls to expand the range of rights stemming from registration so that it may give protection to some at least of the more controversial elements of value in marks. The British Parliament did so in 1938.[47] It created the special category of "defensive" registrations, designed to prevent "dilution". These were confined to "invented" words which had become so well-known as to deserve protection against use on other goods than those traded in by the registered proprietor.[48] In the event the judges proved unwilling to allow that additional penumbra of goods to extend very far[49] and few marks were ever registered defensively.[50]

Again in 1938, alongside infringement by using another's mark as one's own, the legislature added the separate notion of infringement by "importing a reference" to the registered proprietor or its goods—as typically occurs in a comparative advertisement. Since this applied to comparative advertising whether it was true or false, disparaging or sycophantic, it gave undiscriminating protection in one particular respect to investment in advertising and goodwill. Section 4 of the 1938 Act, which produced this

---

[45] A limited notion of incontestability arose under the TMA 1938, s. 13.

[46] See, *e.g.* the TM Dir., Rec. 10: "the function of [the protection afforded by the registered trade mark] is in particular to guarantee the trade mark as an indication of origin . . .".

[47] The Goschen Committee, whose Report (Cmd. 4568, 1934) had spoken of the modern need to move beyond notions of origin, provided the basis of the legislation.

[48] TMA 1938, s. 27.

[49] See esp. *Ferodo's Application* (1945) 62 R.P.C. 111; *Eastex's Application* (1947) 64 R.P.C. 142.

[50] Only 100 by 1974, which led the Mathys Committee to recommend abolition of the provision (Cmnd. 5601, 1974), para. 102. The 1994 Act abandons it.

result, was notorious for its "fulginous obscurity"[51] and its application was for long thought to be questionable.[52]

17–84 The 1994 Act, drawn in accordance with the TM Directive and influenced by the CTM Regulation, also seeks to stretch the ambit of the registration system beyond the protection of source indications. There are new provisions both on the dilution of marks with a reputation and on the use of marks in comparative advertising; and these too have penumbra which will cast uncertainty over a wide periphery. Their obscurity stems in part from unresolved tensions between the advocates of greater protection for modern advertising and promotion and the European integrationists (well represented in the E.C. Commission) who wanted to prevent trade marks from acquiring unnecessary power to impede the movement of products and the provision of services within the Common Market.[53]

A particular complication of the new trade mark order is that the law of infringement laid down in the 1994 Act for British marks does not coincide exactly with that applying to CTMs under the Regulation. This section will first discuss the 1994 Act provisions, noting in the process the extent to which they derive (via the TM Directive[54]) from Community law provisions and are therefore subject to interpretation ultimately by the E.C. Court of Justice. The different extent of rights in a Community mark will then be separately outlined.

One structural aspect of the new law represents a change over the previous British approach. As already noted, there is now a direct correlation between the relative grounds of objection which a prior trade mark owner may bring against later applications to register[55] and the definition of infringement. It is not a mirror image, since at the application stage, prior unregistered rights have also to be brought into account. But to a very substantial extent there is an overlap and much of the case law is likely to be transferable from the one sphere to the other: in large measure what is an objection to validity by a person with a "senior" claim will amount to infringement by a "junior".

(1) Infringement of a United Kingdom registered mark

17–85 The basic definition of infringement is compounded to two elements: (1) the types of use of a mark which can amount to infringement; and (2) the definition of the wrong *vis-à-vis* the registered mark.

---

[51] Mackinnon L.J., *Bismag v. Amblins* (1940) 57 R.P.C. 209 at 237; he was not alone in the harsh things he had to say on the subject.
[52] See the doubts expressed in *Aristoc v. Rysta* (1945) 62 R.P.C. 65 at 77, 79, 85.
[53] See para. 15–16, above.
[54] Even the provisions of the TM Directive have been copied only in most respects; the small differences could eventually lead to uncertainties, though the *Marleasing* principle of conforming interpretation will doubtless be a considerable influence (para. 1–27, above). It has been suggested that the Directive permits a wider exclusive right than its specifically enumerated cases; but since one of the latter is only optional, it is hard to see how logically this could be: *cf.* Annand and Norman, pp. 145–146.
[55] For which, see paras 17–23 *et seq.*, above.

(a) *Types of use amounting to infringement*

The list of activities which may constitute trade mark infringement in **17–86**
British law is now a more extensive one than ever before. The 1994 Act
includes within infringement a use "otherwise than by means of a graphic
representation", and so in principle could include renditions of the trade
mark (or a close approximation of it) through sound or smell.[56]

The most likely forms of infringement involve use of a sign in some
material form. The 1994 Act lists the actions which "in particular"
amount to using a sign[57]: affixing it to goods or packaging; trading in
goods[58] or supplying services[59] under it; importing or exporting goods
under it; using it on business papers[60] or in advertising.[61] There is a form
of contributory infringement affecting anyone who applies a mark to
material for labelling, packaging, business paper or advertising, and who
knows or has reason to believe that the use is not authorised by the
proprietor or a licensee.[62]

Merely to apply for an Internet domain name[63] which consists of, or
contains, another's mark, is not close enough to the trading activities in
this list of itself to amount to trade mark infringement. But use of the
domain name in advertising or a business document, including references
on the Internet itself, will be acts which are capable of infringing the trade
mark registration. Likewise, against "cyber-squatters", the Court of
Appeal has not hesitated to hold that their conduct (offering to assign,
including possible assignment to a third party) creates the likelihood of
infringing activity then occurring. It has therefore granted *quia timet* relief
which orders the transfer of the domain names to the various targetted
enterprises.[64] The reasons offered for this aspect of the decision are far
from pellucid; but the result resembles that reached in courts across the
world.[65]

---

[56] TMA 1994, s. 103(2). This clarification does not apply expressly to CTMs, since it is not
included in the CTM Regulation (nor is it in the TM Directive); it might be read into the
definition of those trade mark rights as a necessary counterpart to the granting of marks of
this character.

[57] TMA 1994, s. 10(4), reproducing the same non-exclusive lists in the TM Dir., Art. 5(3),
CTM Reg., Art. 9(2).

[58] *i.e.* offering or exposing goods for sale, putting them on the market or stocking them for
these purposes: TMA 1994, s. 10(4)(b). "Infringing goods", "infringing material" and
"infringing articles" are defined in equivalent terms in s. 17: the first of these includes goods
proposed to be imported into the U.K., other than those which may be imported by virtue
of an enforceable Community right: see para. 18–02, below.

[59] *i.e.* offering or supplying the services: *ibid.*, s. 10(4) (b); and see s. 17(4) "infringing
material".

[60] TMA 1994, s. 10(4)(d), covering letters, orders and invoices; even perhaps letters containing
the actual mark which are sent by customers to an infringing manufacturer or supplier. *cf.*
"*Cheetah*" *T.M.* [1993] F.S.R. 263.

[61] The same applies to the CTM: CTM Reg., Art. 9(2).

[62] TMA 1994, s. 10(5).

[63] Likewise for a company name registration.

[64] *British Telecom v. One in a Million* [1999] F.S.R. 1 (and see above, para. 16–34).

[65] Bettinger (1997) 28 I.I.C. 508.

(b) *The wrong to the registered mark*

17–87 The 1994 Act defines four types of infringement.[66] Through this typology runs a set of distinctions relating to the identity or similarity of marks and of goods or services, which for the most part parallels the relative grounds of invalidity[67]:

> **Type 1**: It is infringement to use, in the course of trade, a sign identical to the trade mark in suit for identical goods or services to those within the specification.[68] Under this head, unlike the next, it is not necessary to show any likelihood of confusion.[69] For a plaintiff, accordingly, this is the most straightforward case, though there can easily be questions about whether the marks are identical[70] and whether the goods or services for which the defendant is using the mark fall within those specified in the registration.[71] For the latter it is necessary to consider the "core" content of the specification:
>
> A company supplying electronic components and software registered the mark "Avnet" for advertising and promotional services. Aviators Network, the provider of an Internet service comprising a discussion forum for aviation and within it a sector where others could advertise products and services, did not infringe the first mark by using and having others use the domain name, >avnet.co.uk<.[72]
>
> Because Type 1 exempts a claimant from the need to prove likelihood of confusion, there is good reason to require that the twin identities are strictly proved: thus words ought to be the same both in spelling and sound.[73]
>
> **Type 2**: Where there is only similarity rather than identity between goods or services, and/or similarity between the defendant's sign and

---

[66] In addition, the special protection accorded a Convention principal against unjustified acts of a British agent (for which see para. 17–03, n. 15, above) can arise in relation to a mark already registered.

[67] For which, see paras 17–23 *et seq.*, above.

[68] TMA 1994, s. 10(1).

[69] Compare the "absolute" test of infringement applied under the old law to marks registered in the former Part A of the Register: Greene M.R., *Saville Perfumery v. June Perfect* [1941] R.P.C. 147 at 161; relied upon by Jacob J. in *Origins Natural Resources v. Origin Clothing* [1995] F.S.R. 280, 284.

[70] Thus in the case of a registration of the shape of an electric shaver-head, if the alleged infringement differs in detail it is not "identical": *Philips Electronics v. Remington* (above, para. 17–19, n. 12) (note also the etiolating view that registration of a picture of a shape cannot be identical with the actual shape of a product).

[71] In *British Sugar* (below, n. 72), Jacob J. refused to find a bread spread to be a "desert sauce or syrup" merely because it was occasionally used as such.

[72] *Avnet v. Isoact* [1998] F.S.R. 16; *c.f. British Sugar v. Robertson* [1996] R.P.C. 281 at 293, where regard was (surprisingly) given only to "Treat" in the phrase "Robertson's Toffee Treat", leading to a wide finding of identity.

[73] *cf. Canon KK v. MGM* [1999] E.T.M.R. 1, ECJ, where the marks were "Canon" and "Cannon".

the plaintiff's mark, then the plaintiff must prove that "there exists a likelihood of confusion on the part of the public, which includes likelihood of association with the trade mark".[74]

Type 3: Over and above this, where a trade mark has a "reputation" in the United Kingdom, it is infringement to use an identical or similar sign for *dissimilar* goods or services, where "the use of the sign, being without due cause, takes unfair advantage of, or is detrimental to, the distinctive character or the repute" of the mark.[75]

Type 4: Beyond again, it is infringement to use a trade mark to identify goods or services as those of the proprietor or a licensee, "otherwise than in accordance with honest practices in industrial and commercial matters", when "the use without due cause takes unfair advantage of, or is detrimental to, the distinctive character or repute" of the mark. This Type (to be found in the proviso to section 10(6) of the 1994 Act) may serve to outlaw unacceptable comparative advertising involving a registered trade mark.[76] Its obverse is that use of a trade mark without dishonesty, etc., actually to identify the goods or services of the proprietor or a licensee is not infringement. This is a highly significant defence, given the breadth of Type 1 infringement (where there is no need to show likelihood of confusion) and it must be discussed in relation to parallel importation from outside the EEA.[77] It has no parallel in the CTM Regulation,[78] and it is not clearly sanctioned by the TM Directive.[79]

At least five patches of obscurity lie within these definitions. They concern (1) the defendant's use of a "sign"; (2) similarity of goods or services; (3) association as a form of confusion; (4) the extended protection of marks with a reputation; and (5) dishonest reference to the proprietor's or licensee's goods or services.

(i) **The defendant's use of a "sign".** The first three types of infringement **17–88** require that the defendant use "in the course of trade a sign". It is no longer an explicit requirement that this use be "as a trade mark".[80]

Signs may well be used in trade for descriptive purposes or for identification not concerned with origin and to a large extent this is

---

[74] TMA 1994, s. 10(2), implementing the TM Dir., Art. 5(1); see further, para. 17–95, below.

[75] TMA 1994, s.10(3), as permitted by the TM Dir., Art. 5(2); see further, para. 17–100, below.

[76] TMA 1994, s. 10(6), as permitted by the TM Dir., Art. 5(5); for the position under the CTM Reg., see para. 17–104, below.

[77] See paras 17–120 *et seq.*, below.

[78] See para. 17–117, below.

[79] *cf.* TM Dir., Art. 5(5), which permits provisions in national law "relating to the protection against the use of a sign other than for the purposes of distinguishing goods or services".

[80] TMA 1994, s. 11(2)(b); see para. 17–112, below; and see Jacob J., *British Sugar v. James Robertson* [1996] R.P.C. 281 at 296–297.

permitted by explicit exception, treated below.[81] For instance, the use of the pop-group, "Wet, Wet, Wet's" name, registered as a mark, in a book-title would fall within the exception for indications of the actual character of the book itself.[82]

17–89 In addition, however, courts may confine infringement to trade mark uses of the mark because this is taken to be inherent in the notion of using a sign in the course of trade. Already there are indications of this tendency set out below.

(1) In the "Philishave" shape–mark case, the defendant, Remington, argued (*inter alia*) that, when they incorporated a similar shaving-head in their product, their use was functional and would not be understood as a trade mark. The point did not need to be decided and Jacob J. left it for consideration on a subsequent occasion.[83]

(2) The Football Association sought to prevent a well-known sweet manufacturer from putting cards in the products which showed England team players in shirts which bore the Association's registered logo. The Court refused to find that the sweets were put out under that sign; so there was no "use in relation to goods."[84]

(3) The French Cour de Cassation refused to find that the slogan "Visa pour le Muscle," when used on printed material, infringed the well-known credit card mark. It held that "Visa" was here used in the sense of a passport.[85]

(4) In dealing with an allegation that one bank's German company name, "Europabank", infringed another bank's registration of that word as a mark for its products and services, the Benelux Trade Mark Court advised that the first bank would infringe the mark only if it used the mark to distinguish the services which it offered. This it would not do merely by giving its business name.[86]

In these cases, the courts display a natural reluctance to prevent one trader from employing a word or other sign which corresponds to another's mark in where potential damage and undue misappropriation appear equally slight. They display a firm sense that marks are to be protected for their value as indications of origin.

17–90 Where (in relation to Type 3) the mark has a reputation, the consequent liability in relation to use on dissimilar goods could encompass a non-trade

---

[81] s. 11(2).

[82] *Bravado Merchandising v. Mainstream Publishing* [1996] F.S.R. 208; T.M.A. 1994, s. 11(2).

[83] *Philips Electronics v. Remington* [1998] R.P.C. 283 at 312 (above, para. 17–46); *cf.* the judge's earlier view that there was no requirement of use as a trade mark, as there had been under the former law: *British Sugar v. Robertson* [1996] R.P.C. 281 at 292–293, criticising the concession to the contrary in *Bravado Merchandising* (above, n. 82).

[84] *Trebor Bassett v. Football Association* [1997] F.S.R. 211.

[85] *Visa International v. Editions Liberna* [1998] E.T.M.R. 380.

[86] *Europabank v. Banque pour l'Europe* [1997] E.T.M.R. 143: the relevant provision was the Uniform Benelux Trade Mark Act, s. 13A; *cf. Tanderil* [1985] B.I.E. 50.

mark use. Giving a mark a generic description in a dictionary would be detrimental to distinctive character and might possibly be regarded both as a use in trade (as distinct from a "trade mark use") and "being without due cause" in that its character as a mark was ignored. This, however, is to scrape for some equivalent to the explicit "dictionary" protection given to Community marks but omitted from the TM Directive.[87]

(ii) **Similarity of goods or services.** This factor represents a definite **17–91** expansion of scope compared with the previous United Kingdom law. Formerly, infringement of a registered mark could occur only where the defendant's use related to goods or services within the registered specification. It was therefore important to procure registration for goods or services "of the same description" (which could normally be retained despite non-use).

In the 1994 Act, Type 2 infringement extends beyond the specified goods and services to those which are "similar", provided also that the public are likely to be confused.[88] "Similarity" has been held to import much the same considerations as the question under the former law, are goods or services "of the same description"? Six factors may need to be considered:

(1) the respective uses of the respective goods or services;
(2) the respective users of the respective goods or services;
(3) the physical nature of the goods or acts of service;
(4) the respective trade channels through which the goods or services reach the market;
(5) whether in self-service stores they are found together or apart;
(6) the extent to which the respective goods or services are competitive (for instance, in the eyes of market research companies).[89]

Applying these criteria, in *British Sugar v. Robertson*, Jacob J. found that **17–92** spreads for bread were not similar goods to dessert sauces and syrups (ice-cream toppings and the like).[90] The law was being interpreted in a severe fashion which imported much of the former restricted concept of "goods

---

[87] CTM Reg., Art. 10.
[88] Jacob J., *British Sugar v. James Robertson* [1996] R.P.C. 281 at 294, 295.
[89] *ibid.*, at 296, 297.
[90] *ibid.*, at 296, 297. As the judge separately found, the registration was specifically for "dessert sauces and syrups in Class 30", yet spreads for bread were in Class 29. If the goods were nonetheless similar, the limitation in the registration would be ineffective, even if it had for any reason been required by the Registry as a condition of registration. This aspect of the decision may lead to it being distinguished in future as a special case. There is no general requirement that the goods or services be in the same class: *Growmax v. Don & Low* [1999] R.P.C. 367.

and services of the same description".[91] It has to be doubted whether such a scrupulous approach can survive long in the new European ambience.

Equivalent caution was shown in resolving a separate problem. Jacob J. held that the question whether goods or services were "similar" was a distinct issue, which had to be settled before turning to the question whether the two marks were confusingly similar. This makes the question of similarity an objective issue, in the sense that no account is taken of the existing reputation of either mark. Controversially, however, in *Canon KK v. MGM*,[92] the ECJ has since held that this is the wrong approach. In Germany, MGM was seeking to register "Cannon" for films and related services but faced the earlier registration of "Canon" for cameras and various television devices. Responding to a direct question on the legal issue, the Court held that:

> "marks with a highly distinctive character, either *per se* or because of the reputation they possess on the market, enjoy broader protection than marks with a less distinctive character".

17–93   Once a mark has been registered, little is left of the traditional common law distinction between the core protection of infringement which was relatively straightforward to prove and a surrounding periphery of passing off which, when the mark was not naturally distinctive, required a strong case to be made out. The two now meld into one and an effect is achieved which may do a good deal for the harmonising of different European approaches to the scope of trade mark protection.

For that reason, the Court of Justice will doubtless stick to its opinion that registered marks with a reputation extend to a wider range of similar goods and services. What will be necessary, however, is that the rule should be applied only with care. The effect of the ECJ's ruling is to bring oppositions to applications for registration very close to passing off actions, not just where the senior mark is unregistered, but equally where it is registered for different, but somewhat related, goods. This may impose considerable burdens.

17–94   So far as infringement is concerned, the following may occur: a senior mark is not yet very well-known when a junior mark is allowed on the register as being for dissimilar goods. The senior mark becomes popular: the junior mark comes to be for similar goods, and therefore in principle becomes a Type 2 infringement. So long as the junior mark remains

---

[91] See also the application of *British Sugar* in *Baywatch Production v. Home Video Channel* [1997] F.S.R. 22, where it was held unarguable that video tapes and discs were similar to television programmes (with an "adult content"). The degree of proximity in the two cases seems much the same. However, in *British Sugar* there was the added factor that the plaintiff's mark was restricted to goods in Class 30, while the defendant's product fell within Class 29. *cf.* also *"Balmoral" T.M.* [1999] R.P.C. 297: whisky similar to wine.

[92] [1999] E.T.M.R. 1. In refusing to find similarity, the lower courts in Germany had shown a caution equivalent to that in the English decisions.

registered, however, U.K. law provides a defence to an action for infringement of the registration[93] and the senior owner would after all be obliged to sue for passing off. The registration itself would not be open to attack, since no relative ground of objection existed when it was made, and subsequent likelihood of confusion could only in the rarest cases suffice for revocation.[94]

(iii) **Likely confusion including association.** In infringement actions of the 17–95 first two types the essential comparison is between the plaintiff's mark as registered and the defendant's actual practice. It is one object of the registration system to provide advance security by foreshortening investigations (by survey, trade or consumer evidence) into actual comparisons between the way in which the plaintiff's goods or services are marketed, as well as those of the defendant. Of course, as in the past, courts will consider the features of the markets for the goods or services in question, and, as appropriate, will take account of confusions arising in both written and oral usage; consumers' knowledge about origins; the nature of consumers affected, and so on. The considerations which arise on a comparison of marks at the application stage are in general terms equally applicable here.[95]

In the former law, it was necessary to show that the defendant's use of the mark was "as a trade mark", to indicate the source of goods or services. Once that was done, so far as concerned Part A marks, "no amount of added matter intended to show the true origin of the goods" could affect the question whether there was infringement (while it would, of course, be relevant to passing off).[96] Under the 1994 Act, where the two Parts have become one, the courts may not take quite so categorical approach; but they are still likely to view attempts to explain away prima facie confusion with considerable scepticism.

Such an attitude must complement the now notorious statement (in section 10(2) of the 1994 Act) that "a likelihood of confusion on the part of the public . . . *includes* the likelihood of association with the trade mark". This is a factor which has also to be taken into account in considering the relative grounds of invalidity, and the discussion here is equally relevant in

---

[93] TMA 1994, s. 11(i). See below, para. 17-112.
[94] TMA 1994. s. 46(I)(d); above, para. 17–78.
[95] *Origins Natural Resources v. Origin Clothing* [1995] F.S.R. 280; *Neutrogena v. Golden* [1996] R.P.C. 473, CA; see above, para. 17–53. For survey evidence in different jurisdictions, see Knaak (1990) 21 I.I.C. 372.
[96] Greene M.R., *Saville Perfumery v. June Perfect* (1941) 58 R.P.C. 147 at 162, CA. Part B marks resembled those protected at common law precisely because a defendant might show that after all there would be no confusion.

that context.[97] The concept has been said to derive from Benelux trade mark law as it stood before implementation of the Directive.[98]

However, the Benelux Act referred only to proving similarity (it does not require likelihood of confusion); and the Benelux Court of Justice had ruled that confusion and association, which in Benelux law are separate concepts, were each of them sufficient to give rise to liability.[99]

17–96   In *Sabel v. Puma*,[1] the ECJ refused to interpret the Type 2 form of conflict between marks in the Registration and Directive so as to give "association" a distinct conceptual standing. On the contrary "association" was treated as a sub-set of "confusion". This was considered the correct approach, both because of the legislative language and because the origin function of trade marks remains the primary purpose of legal protection and it deserves to be tested by the criterion of likelihood of confusion.

Accordingly the senior mark, a drawing of a springing puma, did not give rise to an objection on relative ground to registration of a junior mark, comprising a springing cheetah with the word "Sabel". No danger of confusion to the relevant public could be found, and it was not enough to find that that public might assume an "association" between the two.

The Court issued significant guidance on the application of Type 2, both to registration and to infringement. Attention must be directed to "the perception of marks in the mind of the average consumer of the type of goods or services in question". There has to be a "global appreciation of the likelihood of confusion. The average consumer normally perceives a mark as a whole and does not analyse its various details." The Court then continued:

> "In that perspective, the more distinctive the earlier mark, the greater will be the likelihood of confusion. It is therefore not impossible that the conceptual similarity resulting from the fact that two marks use

---

[97] See para. 17–53, above.

[98] An unpublished (but well-known) Council and Commission Minute records cryptically that "'likelihood of association' is a concept which in particular has been developed by Benelux case law". In *Wagamama v. City Centre Restaurants* [1995] F.S.R. 713, Laddie J. refused to consider it because of its non-public nature (see para. 17–91, above). Even if it could be given account in English proceedings, it does not resolve how Benelux understandings should be applied to a quite different statutory formulation, however "strange" that difference may appear to Benelux lawyers: *cf.* Gielen and Strowel, [1995] Mitt. d. Patentanwälte 198. In truth the Minute echoed the considerable reluctance among other Member States to adopt the Benelux approach, as the Benelux negotiators recorded: Fürstner and Geuze, ECTA Newsletter, March 1989, 215, referred to in *Wagamama*.

[99] *Union/Union Soleure* [1984] Ned Jur. 72.

[1] [1998] R.P.C. 199; Davies and Annand (1998) 103 Tm. Wld. 18; Gielen [1998] E.I.P.R. 109; Gevers *et al.* (1998) 106 Tm. Wld. 18; Norman [1998] E.I.P.R. 310; Torremans [1998] I.P.R. 295. The issue was first confronted, somewhat dramatically, in *Wagamama v. City Centre Restaurants*, above, n. 98, where Laddie J. refused to find infringement of the mark "Wagamama" for restaurants by "Rajamama" on any separate ground of "association", though he did find sufficient likelihood of confusion for Type 2. For polarised reactions, see Kamperman Sanders [1996] E.I.P.R. 3, 521; Prescott, *ibid.*, 317; [1997] E.I.P.R. 99.

images with analogous semantic content may give rise to a likelihood of confusion where the earlier mark has a particularly distinctive character, either *per se* or because of the reputation it enjoys with the public."[2]

This appears substantially to reflect previous British understandings of what can constitute a likelihood of confusion between marks[3]:

(1) A plaintiff had one mark consisting mainly of a picture of a milkmaid, and another of a similar picture with the words "Milkmaid Brand", both registered for condensed milk and similar goods. The defendant's later registration of a different picture, with the word "Dairy-maid", was rectified to exclude condensed milk from the goods specified. There was evidence that purchasers commonly called the plaintiff's condensed milk, "Dairymaid".[4]

(2) Plaintiffs had used a registered mark "Rus" for bricks and tiles. They were entitled to object to the use of "Sanrus" for brick facings, not because the words would be confused, either in written or oral form, but because a purchaser would be likely to think that "Sanrus" was a mark being used by the plaintiffs.[5]

(3) Plaintiffs had well-known marks for portable buildings, beginning "Porta-" and held one relevant registration for this prefix alone. It was held infringed by the defendant's use of "Portoblast" (for a portable shot-blasting unit) because this took the essential features and idea of the plaintiffs' mark.[6]

(4) In the "*GE*" case;[7] the likelihood of confusion was not that a customer seeing "*GE*" would think that he saw "*GEC*"; it was that when he saw "*GE*" he would assume that it stood for General Electric and would take that to be the English and not the American General Electric Company.

Just as *Sabel v. Puma* requires, these decisions all looked at the **17–97** circumstances overall in order to determine whether there was, in a realistic sense, some likelihood of confusion. It was not enough that an average consumer might be attracted to choose goods or services under the second mark because some loose, non-confusing, association might be made to the first. In an attempt to re-kindle the former Benelux doctrine on the subject, the Dutch Supreme Court has asked whether a sufficient presumption of

---

[2] [1998] R.P.C. at 224.
[3] For which, see generally, paras 17–63—17–65.
[4] *Metcalf's T.M.* (1886) 31 Ch.D. 454.
[5] *Ravenhead Brick v. Ruabon Brick* (1937) 54 R.P.C. 341; relied upon in *Wagamama* (n. 98, above).
[6] *Portakin v. Powerblast* [1990] R.P.C. 471.
[7] See para. 17–78, above.

confusion can be constructed from proof that the first mark was well-known and that the public would, in the loose sense, associate the second with the first[8]; It has to be acknowledged that much of the difficulty about drawing this legal margin stems from a lack of agreement over what is meant in the first place by "confusion". Given that the EJC has indicated that confusion is not just about direct visual or aural mistakes, it can only be hoped that it will not weaken the approach which was adopted in *Sabel*. There may remain nuanced differences about the meaning of "confusion", but they are as nothing compared with those surrounding "association". The latter word is a passport to clever speculation about the possible psychological impact of marking or get-up on this or that social group. Much has been made in this context of actions by the owners of the mark, "Monopoly" (for the townscape acquisition board-game) against "Anti-Monopoly"—an anti-capitalistic counter-production. In the Dutch proceedings on the subject, the Court actually found on the evidence that a significant portion of the public would be confused between the two.[9] It has, however, since been claimed of that decision that consumers could not confuse the two because of their obverse qualities as games; liability should therefore be regarded as arising from a supposed likelihood of association which was distinct from confusion. But why? Anyone with wit enough to work out the difference between the games would surely dissociate, not associate.

A good instance of the danger inherent in allowing "association" to float free of "confusion" is provided by the Dutch action alleging infringement of "Isoglass" by "Isover" for building insulation. A survey demonstrated that some 15 per cent of consumers "associated" the two; but then over half that number also associated "Rockwool"![10]

17–98 Courts everywhere would do well to recall the need, in building a European Community system of registration, to adopt a moderate approach to protection and intervene only where the plaintiff faces substantial, rather than fancied, injury.[11] To do so would certainly reflect an established tradition in British trade mark law, which insists that there must be "a real tangible danger of confusion", and not merely "a possibility of confusion".[12]

17–99 Because association is stated to be one form of likely confusion, it cannot arise in most cases of comparative advertising. The point of such advertisements is to set the protected products or services apart from those of the competitor making the comparison, in order that the advantages of the

---

[8] *Marca Mode v. Adidas* (proceedings pending).
[9] *Edor v. General Mills Fun* [1978] Ned. Jur. 83. In U.S. proceedings (*Anti-Monopoly v. General Mills Fun* 611 Fed. Rep. 2d 296 (1979)), the Court of Appeals remitted the case for a finding whether the public understood the titles as trade-marks or as descriptive game-names.
[10] [1989] Ned. Jur. 836. Given such evidence, the court could scarcely find infringement.
[11] An objective clearly sought in early drafts of the CTM Reg.: see para. 15–17, above.
[12] See, *e.g.* Farwell J. in *William Bailey's Application* (1935) 52 R.P.C. 136 at 153.

latter can be demonstrated. Once the comparison is made plain,[13] there is no scope for confusion, even though, at least in sycophantic advertising, there is association, rather than dissociation, between the things compared. Comparative advertisements can accordingly give rise to liability only under the fourth type of infringement.[14]

(iv) Use of mark for dissimilar goods or services. The third type of **17–100** infringement, where there is use by the defendant of the same or a similar mark for *dissimilar* goods or services, can arise where:

(1) the plaintiff has a registered mark with a "reputation"; and
(2) the use by the defendant is without due cause, which takes unfair advantage of or is detrimental to, the distinctive character or repute of the mark.

This derives from the CTM Regulation.[15] The alternatives posited by its language—unfair advantage or detriment, distinctive character or repute—give it an apparently broad impact, since they must be presumed not to be co-terminous. The provision is intended to allow protection against "dilution" by the use of an established mark on different goods by persons not connected with the proprietor.

It draws particular support from Article 13A of the Benelux Trade Mark Law, but it is also sustained by the manner in which countries such as Germany and France give far-reaching protection against this type of dilution of famous trade marks under their unfair competition laws.[16] Thus under Benelux trade mark law, Colgate could not call a face cleanser, "Klarein", in face of the famous Dutch gin, "Claeryn";[17] in Germany it was unfair competition to advertise "Perrier" as "the Champagne of mineral waters"[18] and in France for Yves St. Laurent to use "Champagne" for scent.[19]

The incorporation of such liability within the CTM regime makes some sense for Member States where unfair competition laws are substantially precluded from the sphere of trade marks. Whether it is so wise to extend national trade mark law in the same way in countries where there is already

---

[13] An initial question is always whether the "comparison" is actually being used as a guise to deceive consumers into thinking that they are getting the products compared, rather than the defendant's products.
[14] For which see paras 17–104—17–107, below.
[15] CTM Reg., Art. 9(1) (c); it is permitted in national legislation by the TM Dir., Art. 5(2). All Member States have taken advantage of the Directive's permission.
[16] In Benelux law unfair competition rights are severely limited in the field of trade marks: see para. 17–01, above.
[17] (1976) 7 I.I.C. 420. The two marks were pronounced the same. The court was sensitive to the prospect of gin jokes.
[18] (1988) 19 I.I.C. 682.
[19] [1994] E.I.P.R. D–74.

coverage under these general principles is less clear. What matters is that "dilution" under either type of legal provision should be prevented only in cases where there really is sufficient cause for interfering with the freedom of all traders to promote their goods and services as best they can.

17–101 There have long been those who consider trade mark dilution an insidious and dangerous threat to advertising reputation. In America individual states enacted special statutes to bring diluters to heel.[20] These laws seem not to have made much headway, because they are met with a general scepticism: "Champagne" will survive being applied to scent because the public will appreciate what is going on and will, if anything, think the more and the better about the wine. Recently, a Federal Trademark Dilution Statute of 1996 has introduced measures against the tarnishment and blurring of trade marks,[21] which has proved valuable in dealing with one special problem: that posed by the cyber-squatter who has secured domain names embodying the business names or marks of famous corporations with a view to selling them over at a ransom price.[22] It is far from clear that the new Act will be much used when a well-known mark is taken over by an unconnected trader for his significantly different line of goods or services. Without being driven round a statutory course of this kind, the Courts in Britain have used the passing-off action against occasional instances of "dilution", such as the application of "Lego" to plastic gardening accessories and "Champagne" to elderflower cordial— cases where some prospect of confusion is considered to give rise to a sufficient likelihood of damage.[23] But these have been exceptional instances and similar cases ought to be approached in like spirit in future. Type 3 infringement exists, after all, in order to give a form of passing-off law to jurisdictions such as the Benelux, which normally insist that registration should be the basis of any protection.

17–102 Two elements in the statutory wording may suggest that liability should now be more readily imposed. The first is that a registered proprietor may sue for Type 3 infringement where the mark has a "reputation"; it does not have to be "well-known" or "famous".[24] In emphasising this, Jacobs A.G. has proposed to the Court of Justice that the reputation need exist only in part of the geographical area for which the registration pertains—as, for instance, a part of the Benelux.[25] The second is that it is enough to show

---

[20] Stimulated in particular by Schechter (1927) 40 Harv. L.R. 813, drawing upon German theory; for the history, see McCarthy (3rd ed., 1989), Chap. 24, Pt. 2.
[21] The Act adds a further case to the unfair competition provisions of the Lanham Act 1946, s. 43: see 15 U.S.C. s. 1125(c).
[22] Since the dilution liability does not require likelihood of confusion, defences cannot centre on the fact that the domain name is not for given goods or services. See the similar result reached in England in *British Telecommunications v. One in a Million* [1999] F.S.R. 1, CA; above, para. 16–27.
[23] See paras 16–30, n. 26, 16–38, n. 70, above.
[24] See para. 16–17, above.
[25] *General Motors v. Yplon* ("Chevy"—affectionate nickname for Chevrolets) [1999] E.T.M.R. 122.

that a defendant is taking unfair advantage, without showing that the proprietor is suffering detriment.

Despite these considerations, Type 3 must be seen in the context of other forms of infringement, and in particular Type 2. Under the latter, where the goods or services are similar, there is infringement only if there is likely confusion, including association. It cannot be that, when it comes to *dissimilar* goods and services, a mark-owner with a reputation has a right of action even where there is no likely confusion (including association), just because he has a reputation. What about the mark-owner for similar goods who has a reputation? The fact that he has that reputation does not exempt him from having to show the confusion element required under Type 2; it simply aids his task.[26] This would at least help to resolve a logical lapse in the legislation, which has arisen because passing-off considerations (based on reputation) have been roughly grafted onto legislation concerned with rights stemming from registration.

Type 3 can be treated consistently only if the further conditions on which **17–103** it depends—lack of due cause, unfair advantage or detriment—are given substantial meaning and are not assumed to be present whenever there is "dilution" onto other products. Causing confusion as to source should be treated as the most likely circumstance to satisfy the condition. It should be sufficient confusion to lead the public to believe that the owner of the mark with a reputation is extending its lines of business; that will occur most readily when the extension is an inherently likely one. Some British judges have indeed favoured the view that a measure of confusion is needed for Type 3, if it is to be congruently treated with Type 2.[27] In an obiter dictum, the European Court of Justice has suggested that it would not accept so circumscribed an interpretation. There may be other cases of truly serious tarnishment: perhaps the supposed mockery of "Claeryn" gin from "Klarein" face cleanser amounted to an instance.[28] And there may be cases of wholly unacceptable misappropriation of goodwill, which might occasionally fit within the provision. What ought not to happen is that the owner of a mark, which has a trading reputation with (say) 50 per cent of a public, should acquire a monopoly on that mark for all trading uses, including passing comparisons of a vaguely associative kind.[29] There is no sufficient case for interfering so sweepingly with the general freedom of an enterprise to adopt attractive marks whose use will do no clear harm to any other

---

[26] On this limited view of Type 3, it may be asked: what is the relevance of "without due cause" if there has to be "confusion . . . including association"? In dilution cases there may well be some element of confusion, but also honest concurrent use, particularly given that the goods or services are by definition dissimilar—as for instance in the foreign trading in the British "Lego" case [1983] F.S.R. 155, see para. 16–30, above. That use might provide "due cause".

[27] *e.g. BASF v. CEP(U.K.)* [1996] E.T.M.R. 51; *Baywatch v. Home Video* [1997] F.S.R. 22.

[28] Above, n. 99.

[29] This is the approach taken in *Oasis Stores, Application* [1998] R.P.C. 634.

mark. Nor in Britain is there likely to be much sympathy for attempts to stop the deployment of trade marks in parody advertisements,[30] counter-cultural advertising or other forms of critical comment.[31] Strong marks should be able to survive such knocks: they may even emerge the stronger.

17-104 (v) **Unfair reference to the proprietor or that a licensee: comparative advertising.** As already noted, comparison (provided that it is made plain) is the obverse of confusion, and those who seek to protect marks against use in comparative advertising have no complaint that the origins of goods or services are being muddled together. What is at stake is a different annexation of goodwill. In this field the common law offers protection only against injurious falsehood. So it leaves considerable freedom to pursue true, or at least honest, comparisons with the products and services of other traders.[32] The law of registered trade marks suddenly veered in 1938 towards sweeping protection wherever the comparison employed a Part A registered mark.[33] Type 4 infringement in the 1994 Act reaches a halfway house, which for the United Kingdom has been reasonably clearly positioned. How far, if at all, the Court of Justice may require a re-siting more in line with stricter European traditions is unfathomable.[34]

Some argue that no comparative advertising by one trader against another (as distinct from comparisons made by consumer organisations, etc.) can be regarded as an honest practice in industrial and commercial matters. Those who take this view either treat it as self-evident or else claim that the advertising will inevitably be selective in content (and so distortive) so as to favour the advertiser.[35] The opposite opinion is that comparisons which are truthful so far as they go are helpful to consumers in making choices. There should, therefore, be a prohibition only where there are misleading statements either about particular qualities of the products (that they are the same when they are not, or that they differ in some respect

---

[30] *cf.* Gredley and Maniatis [1997] E.I.P.R. 412; Spence (1998) 114 L.Q.R. 595; *Felix/Loesje* [1993] I.E.R. 56: "Ooh, that's tarty" (catfood marks) permitted in Netherlands for satirical political cartoon.

[31] *cf.* the Dutch cases disallowing (i) a film showing a girl doing something dirty with a "Coca-cola" bottle *(CocaCola/Alicia* [1997] Ned. Jur. 59); and (2) incorporation into the Philips logo of a swastika in an article illustrating the company's wartime activities *(Philips/Haagse Post* [1982] B.I.E. 41).

[32] See para. 16–54, above. Injurious falsehood remains the only possibility where comparisons are made by reference to an unregistered mark or other sign outside the scope of the registration system. A question will remain whether a business name which contains a registered trade mark as a major feature can have the statutory protection: see n. 83, below.

[33] See para. 16–55, above.

[34] See esp. Mills [1995] E.I.P.R. 417, contrasting also the liberal U.S. and the severe Continental approaches to the subject; and for the German approach, Steckler and Bachmann [1997] E.I.P.R. 578.

[35] Thus German law has traditionally been antagonistic to any comparisons, since they make the advertiser a judge in his own cause, rather than leaving comparison to the consumer: Steckler and Bachmann [1997] E.I.P.R. 578, *cf.* Wilkie and Farris (1975) 39 J. Marketing 7.

when they do not) or about such factors as price or after-sale services.[36] Plainly the new legislation accepts the latter approach; Laddie J. and Jacob J. have so held.[37]

The starting point for Type 4 infringement is that, in the case of **17–105** infringement of Type 1—the most likely category where comparisons are being made[38]—any use in trade, even one which does not cause confusion, is an infringement unless a specific exception operates. In the 1994 Act, section 10(6), there is an exception where the use of a registered mark is "for the purpose of identifying goods or services as those of the proprietor or a licensee". This exception prima facie excuses the use of another's trade mark when making comparisons. However, the elaborate qualification which follows after all imposes liability, if the reference to the proprietor or a licensee:

(1) is otherwise than in accordance with honest practices in industrial and commercial matters;
(2) is without due cause; and
(3) takes unfair advantage of, or is detrimental to, the distinctive character or repute of the mark.

Laddie J. has pointed out the virtually tautologous character of these cumulative strands, but refused to hold that a plaintiff would succeed merely by showing that the defendant was taking an unfair advantage of the mark at stake.[39] Since the sub-section was clearly intended to permit comparative advertising unless it was shown to be unjustifiable, a case of material dishonesty had to be made out which went beyond mere puffery. In the case before him, he refused interlocutory relief to "Barclaycard", when another bank's credit card venture both claimed to have 15 particular advantages and to fare well in a chart of charges which compared eight other credit cards by name, including "Barclaycard". It is a decision which suggests that, for the registration system to prevent comparisons, there must be a misleading usage of the mark registered, which is of the same order as that required for the tort of injurious falsehood.[40]

---

[36] The TM Directive has left it to Member States to decide whether to use trade mark law against some comparative advertising; a provision in the terms of Type 4 above, is not mandatory. *cf.* the CTM, para. 17–116, below.

[37] *Barclays Bank v. RBS Advanta* (n. 39, below).

[38] A comparison which involves only similarity of marks or of goods or services, unless for some reason it induces confusion about source, does not constitute an infringement of a registered mark: see para. 17–95, above. As to passing off in such circumstances, see, *e.g. McDonald's v. Burger King* [1986] F.S.R. 45: defendants liable for saying of their "Whopper" burger, "Not just Big, Mac . . .".

[39] *Barclays Bank v. RBS Advanta* [1996] R.P.C. 307 at 313–315, drawing attention to the different formulation of similar tests in TMA 1994, ss. 10(3) and 11(2).

[40] See para. 16–49, above. The common law liability, however, requires proof of malice.

17–106   The developing case law now demonstrates how section 10(6) (aided by reference to section 11(2)) should be applied to comparative advertising.[41] In contrast with the strict embargo apparently contained in the 1938 Act, Section 4, the primary objective is to permit honest comparative advertising, there being nothing inherently wrong in informing the public of the relative merits of goods or services by reference to registered marks. The onus of proving non-compliance with the conditions laid down in section 10(6) lies with the mark-owner whose mark has been taken for comparison. Above all he must show that the advertisement is not in accordance with honest practices.

This imposes an objective standard, tested by reference to the reasonable reader of the advertisement[42]: once that reader is given the full facts, would he say that the advertisement is not honest?[43] The general public is taken to know the ways of advertisers and to expect hyperbole. Accordingly, dishonesty is likely to be found only where an advertisement is significantly misleading, judging it as a whole, without more minute textual examination than the public would make and without imposing a more puritanical standard than the average reader's. While the standard is objective, it has also been said that an advertiser who does not know of the misleading element, may become liable only when he is made aware of it.[44]

> In comparing the costs of mobile-phone services, one of the intense competitors in that industry stated, "on average, Orange users save £20 every month". It was held that this would be read at face value. It would be taken to refer to the saving to a customer at the arithmetical mean, rather than to every customer across the range, averaging out the months, but irrespective of how much use they made of the service. Equally there was no injurious falsehood.[45] The complexity of comparing prices for these services means that each side will have greater knowledge about its own services, less about its rival's. Imposing the burden of proof of dishonest practice on the person objecting to the comparison may have considerable influence on the outcome of the proceedings.

---

[41] See esp. *Barclay's Bank v. RBS Advanta*, n. 39, above; *Vodafone v. Orange* [1997] F.S.R. 34; *Cable & Wireless v. British Telecom* [1998] F.S.R. 383, esp. p. 389–390 and *cf. Emaco v. Dyson Appliances*, *The Times*, February 8, 1999; Saltzmann and Algrove [1997] Ent. L.R. 11.

[42] In the context of registered marks at least, the Court may consider the impact of the advertisment upon different sectors of the public, provided that they are substantial. There is no need to arrive at the "single meaning" which the tort of injurious falsehood has apparently borrowed from defamation law: *Vodafone v. Orange*, above, n. 41, and see para. 16–49, above.

[43] Both the Advertising Standards Authority, in its Code of Conduct (mainly for press publication), and the Independent Television Commission, in its Rules for TV advertising, seek to regulate comparisons so as to ensure that they are fair. However, in litigation reference to statutory or industry codes has been treated as unhepful: *Cable & Wireless v. British Telecom*, above, n. 41.

[44] *ibid.*, at 390–391.

[45] *Vodafone v. Orange*, above, n. 41.

Much of Continental Europe views comparative advertising from a **17–107** protectionist perspective which has sometimes held little appeal in Britain. Not only are the results of cases likely to vary between E.C. countries as in the past, but the differences have spurred the Community to enact a Directive on Comparative Advertising. The initial consumerist bias of the proposal for this Directive has, in its final version, been replaced by an attitude much more censorious.[46] Under it, both direct and implicit comparison would be permitted in advertising only if (i) it is for goods or services meeting the same needs or purposes; (ii) it objectively compares one or more material, relevant, verifiable and representative features, which may include price[47]; (iii) it is not misleading, confusing as to source, discrediting or denigrating; and (iv) it does not take unfair advantage of the reputation of a mark, name or designation of origin.[48]

Inevitably, these requirements will be differently interpreted even when they become part of the law of member states. The European Court of Justice will find it difficult to provide such further clarification of them as will prevent evident variations when national courts apply them to particular advertisements. This may become most apparent when the diffusion of material—whether in the press, through broadcasting or on the Internet—leads to cross-border litigation.[49]

As to implementation of the Directive in British legislation, there appears little need to alter the law of registered trade marks The introduction of section 10(6) into the 1994 Act has provided adequate compliance in that sphere. More difficult is the protection afforded particularly to unregistered marks, business names and other signs apart from the registration system. As earlier noted, the tort of injurious falsehood is less protective than section 10(6). The tort requires proof both of a sufficient falsehood and of malice on the part of the defendant, in the sense of deliberate or reckless conduct, rather than mere negligence.[50] As far as falsehood is concerned, section 10(6) has been robustly interpreted so as in effect to impose the same objective test of misleading the public as is laid down for injurious falsehood in *De Beers Abrasive Products v. International General Electric.*[51] As to malice, in the context of comparative

---

[46] Directive on Comparative Advertising, 97/55/E.C.; to be implemented in national law by April 6, 2000. The Directive introduces amendments to Directive 84/850/EEC on Misleading Advertising. References are to that Directive as amended.

[47] Special offers have to be clearly dated: see Art. 3a(2).

[48] No statement may present goods or services as an imitation or replica or marked goods or services—so out goes "a substitute for Yeast-Vite": see Art. 3a(1)(h). At present in Britain, copyright material may not be inserted in a comparative advertisement without licence: *IPC Magazines v. Mirror Group* [1998] F.S.R. 431; but this may be excluded by the Directive: see Art. 7(1), (2).

[49] By April 2002, the Commission must report on the feasibility of a complaints system for cross-border comparative advertisements: Directive 97/E.C. Art. 2.

[50] See above, para. 16–50; for the difference from s. 10(6) infringement, see esp. *Emaco v. Dyson Appliances* (n. 41, above).

[51] [1975] F.S.R. 323, relied upon in relation to. s. 10(6) in *Cable & Wireless v. British Telecom*, above, n. 41 at 390. The "single meaning" doctrine should not, however, be imported into injurious falsehood from defamation law: see above, n. 42.

advertising the test should become one of advertising which is contrary to honest commercial practices. This should then be interpreted in the same manner as that which has developed under section 10(6). Unless this rather more flexible approach can be introduced through timely case law, legislative amendment would seem called for.

(c) *Scope of infringement: other factors*

17–108 (i) **Positive and negative definitions.** Under the 1938 Act, the rights given to the registered proprietor of a trade mark were defined both positively as an exclusive right of use and negatively by statements of what constituted infringement.[52] The positive statement was very occasionally used to carry the range of protection beyond the actual language concerning infringing acts. While the 1994 Act contains both positive and negative statements, it now seems clear that rights are determined by the various types of infringement discussed above.[53]

17–109 (ii) **Time factors.** Registration is back-dated to the date of application, but proceedings for infringement may not be begun until actual grant.[54]

17–110 (iii) **Contributory infringement.** For the first time, the 1994 Act lays down that a person (such as printer or packager) who actually applies a trade mark will be party to any subsequent infringing use of the mark if he knew or had reason to believe that the application of the mark was not authorised.[55]

(d) *Limitations upon infringement*

17–111 (i) **Conflicts between marks.** The new law preserves the former principle that, so long as a mark remains registered, use of it in its registered form cannot amount to infringement of any other mark.[56] The owner of the conflicting mark may still be able to bring proceedings for passing off, if he can make out the requirements of that tort.[57] It may be hard to make out

---

[52] See *per* Lord Greene M.R., *Bismag v. Amblins* (1940) 57 R.P.C. 209, CA, criticised by Kerly, para. 14–05.
[53] TMA 1994, s. 9(1), (2); *British Sugar v. James Robertson* [1996] R.P.C. 281 at 290, 291.
[54] TMA 1994, ss. 9(3), 40(3). Criminal proceedings under s. 92 may only relate to events after actual registration.
[55] *ibid.*, s. 10(5).
[56] *ibid.*, s. 11(1). This provision, which does not derive from the TM Directive or CTM Regulation, had a protective purpose under the former law, which allowed honest concurrent usage to justify a registration. The Government's minor detour down the same path in 1994 (see para. 17–61, above) does not give rights which survive opposition or invalidity proceedings. So TMA 1994, s. 11(1) appears merely to require a counterclaim, rather than a defence (each carrying the onus of proof). For what it is worth, it would seem to operate in the same way for a CTM: see CTM Reg., Art. 106(2).
[57] This is one effect of the preservation of passing off: see TMA 1994, s. 2(2).

the necessary reputation for passing off in cases where both parties have been trading in overlapping areas from much the same point in time.[58] Alternatively, the latter owner may proceed for a declaration of invalidity on the relative ground of a prior mark at the time of registration. The ability to invalidate a registration by showing a prior right at the time of application is subject to the twin limitations of the proprietor's consent to the conflicting registration and subsequent acquiescence in the registration by not objecting to known use.[59]

A different type of consent occurs where it is the proprietor or a licensee who has been responsible for marking particular goods. As already noted in connection with comparative advertising, no accurate and honest use of a mark to identify goods or services as those of the proprietor or a licensee will infringe. This principle continues to limit the usefulness of trade marks as a means of controlling parallel imports, a matter to which we return later.[60] We will then consider it together with the statutory rule on exhaustion of rights within the European Community,[61] and the specific question, how far (as a matter both of United Kingdom and of E.C. law) this provision can justify a recipient of the proprietor's goods or those of a licensee in repackaging them or relabelling them.

(ii) **Legitimate uses of the mark by an unauthorised user.** Certain uses of **17–112** a mark have always been permitted as legitimate forms of trading. Now, particularly in cases involving identical marks on identical goods or services,[62] a new significance attaches to such exceptions. The Act[63] permits the use, in accordance with honest practices in industrial and commercial matters, of the following:

(1) a person's own name or address[64];
(2) indications of kind, quality, quantity, intended purpose, value, geographical origin, time of production or rendering, or other characteristics of goods or services[65];
(3) the mark itself, where this is necessary to indicate the intended purpose of a product or service—in particular, as accessories or spare parts.[66]

---

[58] See para. 16–31, above.
[59] See para. 17–82, above; and also the CTM Reg., Art. 106(1).
[60] See paras 17–120 *et seq.*, below.
[61] TMA 1994, s. 12; CTM Reg., Art. 13.
[62] Use on similar goods or services, or use of a similar mark, first requires proof of confusion and this of itself may prevent a descriptive use of the mark from infringing; no such question arises in relation to an identical mark for identical goods or services: para. 17–87, above.
[63] TMA 1994, s.11(1), (2). The list applies equally to CTMs: CTM Reg., Art. 12.
[64] A Council Minute on the equivalent CTM Regulation provision (Art. 12) confines this exception to natural persons.
[65] The equivalent list to that in the absolute grounds of objection: see para. 17–23, above.
[66] TMA 1994, s.11(2)(c).

The defendant's use may be excepted whether it is purely descriptive or when it involves use of a trade mark as such for some honest descriptive purpose. On this basis the name of a pop group may be used as the title for a book about them,[67] and a mark-owner's own product may be referred to in a comparative advertisement.[68] Even if there is no separate requirement that the infringement involve "use as a trademark",[69] a use by the defendant which is not of this character is the more likely to be excused under section 11.[70] It is hard however to see that exemption applying to the mere decorative use on clothing of a name which turns[71] out to be another's mark. Hence the need for the broader requirement.

Previously such uses of a mark were excused if they were bona fide. The new reference to "honest practices" refers to objective standards, rather than subjective decision.[72] It is true that, in this context, bona fides was held to mean that the defendant acted "without any intention to deceive anybody or without any intention to make use of the goodwill which has been acquired by another trader".[73] That could indeed mean that if a defendant started out in ignorance of the conflicting mark, he could continue his use when he came to know of the conflict. At the same time, the Courts paid attention to the likely effect of the defendant's marking in order to judge whether the action was honest. The issue is according likely to be settled in much the same way as before.

Of these three defences, the third is needed on a regular basis, since traders must be permitted to advertise their films as useable in a "Kodak" camera, or as a replacement cartridge for a "Xerox" copier. However, if the statement being made is misleading, the use of the mark would not be honest and could therefore be the subject of proceedings for infringement.

17–113 The 1994 Act adds a different exception for purely local use of an unregistered mark or other sign which is itself protectable as an "earlier right".[74] But the mark or sign must have been in continuous use since a

---

[67] *Bravado Merchandising v. Mainstream Publishing* [1996] F.S.R. 205.

[68] This gives rise to an overlap with TMA 1994, s. 10(6): *British Sugar v. Robertson* (n. 70, below); *cf. Mothercare v. Penguin Books* [1998] R.P.C. 113, CA.

[69] See above, para. 17–89

[70] *British Sugar v. Robertson* [1996] R.P.C. 281 at 299, 300, holding that "treat" in the phrase "Toffee Treat" on the label for a spread would not be taken as a trade-mark use (despite the defendant's efforts to achieve this); *cf.* under the 1938 Act, *Mars v. Cadbury* [1978] R.P.C. 387 ("Treat size" chocolate bars not a trade mark use and so not an infringement of "Treat" for chocolate).

[71] *cf. Unidoor v. Marks & Spencer* [1998] R.P.C. 275: "Coast to Coast" featured on T-shirts—under the 1938 Act, held not to be "use as a trade mark".

[72] *cf. Barclays Bank v. RBS Advanta* [1996] R.P.C. 307 and see *Hansard*, HL (Com, January 18, 1994) cols 44–45.

[73] Danckwerts J., *Baume v. Moore* [1957] R.P.C. 459 at 463; and on appeal see Romer L.J., [1958] R.P.C. 226 at 235, stressing that "there is no such thing . . . as constructive dishonesty". *cf. Provident Financial v. Halifax Building Society* [1994] F.S.R. 81 at 93.

[74] TMA 1994, s. 11(3), rendering into English the gibberish of TM Dir., Art. 6(2). For the equivalent limitation upon a CTM, see CTM Reg., Art. 107, which—in a form of little-and-large co-existence—allows the defence to continue even after acquiescence by the local right-holder prevents him from objecting to the use of the CTM in his locality.

date before the registered mark was used or registered. A person entitled to such an earlier right may take advantage of this defence where his right to protection (most likely against passing off) applies only "in a particular locality", a phrase which it is left to Courts to define more precisely. This exception is related to the exclusion of purely local "earlier rights" from the relative grounds of objection to a CTM, where the same question arises.[75] Those whose rights extend to larger areas must take positive steps to attack the registration being asserted against them; and if they fail to act, they risk being held to have acquiesced in that registration.[76]

(2) Exhaustion of right

As noted elsewhere, the concept of exhaustion of right is relevant to goods **17–114** which emanate initially from an intellectual property owner or associated enterprises (other subsidiaries, licensees, distributors, etc.).[77] Its particular relevance over the last thirty years has been in relation to the parallel importation of goods between different states of the European Union. In that context, the European Court of Justice has established, through interpretation of the E.U. Treaty, that the exhaustion of trade mark rights applies on a Community-wide basis, rather than a purely national one.[78] The expression of this rule in the CTM Regulation and the Trade Marks Directive, applies to exhaustion within a single State as well as between Member States: the right may not be asserted "in relation to goods which have been put on the market in the Community under that trade mark by the proprietor or with his consent".[79] That general exemption from liability, however, does not apply "where there exist legitimate reasons for the proprietor to oppose further commercialisation of the goods, especially where the condition of the goods is changed or impaired after they have been put on the market".[80]

The consequence is that the courts have some scope for deciding what forms of "interference" with, or other "improper" reference to trademarked parallel imports is to amount to an act of infringement. Accordingly the European Court of Justice has held that a distributor may not repackage legitimate goods, or label them with a different trade mark, unless the practice complies with the special conditions which the European Court of Justice has already laid down for parallel importation from another member state.[81]

---

[75] See para. 17–67, above.
[76] The CTM Reg., Art. 107 has a similar provision, which continues to operate even when the proprietor of the earlier right has through acquiescence lost his power to prevent use of the CTM in his locality.
[77] Above, esp., para. 1–49.
[78] See below, para. 18–04 for fully "international" exhaustion, as it affects products initially marketed outside the E.E.A. see below, paras 17–120 et seq.
[79] CTM Reg. Art. 13; Dir. Art. 7; from which comes TMA 1994, s. 12. The rule applies equally to goods first marketed within the same state.
[80] TMA 1994, s. 12(2) following the language of the CTM Reg., Art. 13 and the Dir., Art. 7.
[81] For the case law, see below, para. 18–09. This rule is stricter than the regime which operated under the TMA 1938, s. 6.

17–115   In the context of parallel importing from elsewhere in the EEA, the Court has given two formative decisions:

> (1) In *Parfums Christian Dior v. Evora*,[82] the plaintiff perfume-house sought to prevent a supermarket chain from advertising genuine "Dior" perfumes in a Christmas promotion alongside other more common brands. The Court advised that they could not do so unless it could show that such a use of the mark would seriously damage its reputation. Where the advertising followed the customs of the retailer's sector of the trade, sufficient damage could be made out only in quite specific circumstances.
>
> (2) In *Bayerische Motorenwerke v. Deenik*,[83] the plaintiff car-maker sought to object to the use of its Benelux "BMW" mark by a garage-owner in Holland who specialised in selling secondhand BMWs and in servicing and repairing them. He was not an authorised dealer, but it was alleged that he was holding himself out to be one, or, that, by annexing the aura of high quality associated with the marque, he was infringing the plaintiff's rights. The European Court indicated that the exhaustion of right principle must apply to the cars, once sold in the Community. No exception to that principle could apply where the trade was informing the public of his wholly legitimate business in BMW repairs, servicing and resales. Only statements designed to suggest that he was an authorised dealer would infringe.[84]

In these decisions, true to its insistence that the "origin" function normally delimits the proper scope of the trade mark right, the Court has refused to allow it to become a general prop for marketing strategies merely because they seek to confine the choices of distributors and therefore the opportunities for consumers. That is not an investment value which the law of trade marks exists to support.

(3) Infringement of a CTM

17–116 The "effects of Community trade marks" are determined solely by the CTM Regulation, whereas other aspects of their infringement are in the main governed by national trade mark law.[85] By "effects" the Regulation

---

[82] [1998] R.P.C. 166. The goods were obtained by parallel importation from elsewhere in the E.C., but the same principle ought to apply where they are purchased in the home market.

[83] [1999] E.T.M.R. 339.

[84] The same approach had to be adopted in deciding whether there was an act of infringement of type 2 (likelihood of confusion in use of mark for cars and for servicing them); and in deciding whether any exception arose under the Directive Art. 6, TMA 1994, s. 11(2).

[85] CTM Reg., Art. 14. *cf.* Art. 97, which brings into account, where appropriate, the private international law of a state; also Arts. 98–103 on sanctions, provisional measures, jurisdictional conflicts, appeals, and other disputes. Art. 14(2) preserves rights under the general civil law and unfair competition law (in common law terms, the torts of passing off, injurious falsehood, etc.). For a comparative perspective, Bastian and Knaak (1995) 26 I.I.C. 149.

means the content of Articles 9–13, since they are placed under this general heading. These Articles cover the rights conferred by a CTM[86]; reproduction in dictionaries[87]; prohibition on unauthorised use of a mark by an agent or representative in whose name it has been registered[88]; defences of honest use[89]; and exhaustion of rights.[90]

In the main Community law corresponds to national law so far as concerns the definition of acts constituting use of the mark[91]; and the limitations allowing honest use of name, address, descriptions and indications of intended purpose.[92]

So far as concerns the four *types* of infringing activity set out above,[93] there are interesting questions concerning Type 4. As noted earlier, the CTM Regulation, unlike section 10(6) of the 1994 Act, does not have any explicit exception for using a mark to identify the goods or services of the actual proprietor, nor any qualification where such a use of the mark falls outside the sphere of honest trade practices.[94]

There are two consequential issues which go directly to the competing **17–117** views of trade mark functions:

(1) Use of a Community mark to identify the proprietor's or licensee's own goods or services in the course of comparative advertising could arguably be actionable in all cases: the reference in the advertisement will be to the very mark for the very goods or services and so in principle an "absolute" Type 1 liability. There will be no requirement to show the dishonest practice, etc., which section 10(6) of the 1994 Act requires in the British system. It is to be hoped that courts will not read Article 9(1)(a) of the CTM Regulation in this automatic sense. The issue should be dealt with explicitly in legislative provisions on comparative advertising.[95] If a different interpreta-

---

[86] CTM Reg., Art. 9.

[87] *ibid.*, Art. 10, a special provision, with no equivalent in U.K. law. It requires a dictionary publisher who has created the impression that a trade mark is a generic name to correct that impression at least by the next edition. Presumably this imposes a statutory duty under Community law, enforceable if necessary by a mandatory injunction.

[88] *ibid.*, Art. 11, implementing in part the Paris Convention, Art. 6*septies*. This Convention provision is now fully imported into U.K. law by the TMA 1994, s. 60, which also provides the "proprietor of the mark" with the right to oppose the agent's application to register and the right to be substituted as named proprietor. There are certain three-year limitation periods: see s. 60(6): see para. 17–03, above.

[89] CTM Reg., Art. 12, see para. 17–112, above.

[90] See para. 17–120, below.

[91] See para. 17–87, above; but note paras 17–100, 17–111, above.

[92] See para. 17–112, above; but note para. 17–113, above.

[93] See para. 17–87, above.

[94] See para. 17–100, above. It is not possible to treat TMA 1994, s. 10(6) as itself applying to CTMs because it deals with one of their effects. The matter must be entirely a matter for Community law. In this context, the stress in CTM Reg., Recital 10, on "origin theory" may provide an important clue.

[95] As in the proposed Directive on Comparative Advertising: see n. 46, above.

tion of the current Regulation is to be adopted, however, it may be necessary to hold that that Article does not cover references to "genuine" goods. If this is so, it must influence the outcome on the other consequence.

(2) Use of a Community mark to identify the goods of the proprietor or a licensee may arguably be objected to where a parallel importer, who has acquired them in a non-EEA country, seeks to bring them into any EEA country from outside. This has been taken by many to be a necessary implication of the "standard exhaustion formula"— for trade marks as much as for rights protecting one or other type of idea. It is a subject of pressing concern, to which we return below. Suffice it for the moment to notice the considerable difference that the presence of Section 10(6) may make to the interpretation of British, as distinct from Community law.[96] And to observe that it would make no sense that the results in the two systems should on this matter be different.

17–118   As to other aspects of infringement of a CTM, the concepts which leave a considerable range of judgment to courts—questions of what marks and goods or services are similar, of what amounts to confusion (including association), of what dilution of well-known marks is unacceptable—will fall to be developed in a "Community" context. There ought to be comparison of precedents from all Member States, and not just those of the Benelux Trade Marks Court. In that way, the competing flavours of the initial dish will gradually be blended into some blandishment acceptable to the mid-Union palette. It will be for the European Court of Justice to maintain a balance between its interpretations of the CTM Regulation and of equivalent provisions in the TM Directive as they apply in the context of national laws. In the nature of things the Court is likely first to receive references of the latter kind, some of which are already in process.

17–119   The CTM Regulation contains a set of provisions on jurisdiction to hear infringement actions and related matters, which establish an important precedent for Community forms of intellectual property.[97] Each Member State is required to nominate certain courts as Community trade mark courts of first and second instance (with further rights of appeal in accordance with general national rules). In Britain this will allow CTM jurisdiction to be exercised in the same courts as deal with national trade mark disputes. These courts alone may try:

(1) infringement proceedings;

---

[96] For which, see para. 17–87, above.
[97] These provisions were first drafted in relation to the Community patent (see CPC, Protocol on Litigation, Art. 14), but will first take effect in relation to the CTM, which is why they are described here).

(2) actions for a declaration of non-infringement;

(3) actions for compensation for acts done during the application period; and

(4) counterclaims for revocation of Community registrations or for declarations of their invalidity.[98]

A Germanic school of thought considered that attacks upon a registration should be a matter for tribunals within the CTM Office, as granting authority; but this approach has not prevailed.[99]

The heirarchy of jurisdictions between Member States follows a standard model. In order to secure relief throughout the E.C., actions are to be brought:

(a) first, in the Member State of the defendant's domicile or else establishment; if that is not in an E.C. State,

(b) in the Member State of the plaintiff's domicile, or else establishment; and failing either,

(c) in Spain (since the Office is there).[1]

The Brussels Judgments Convention is applicable, with certain modifications.[2] The relevant court may make orders relating to activity within any Member State, which are enforceable there without further proceedings. This is the essential practical advantage of a CTM registration.[3]

There is a separate jurisdiction given to national CTM courts in respect of wrongful acts occurring in that Member State, but orders are then confined to activities within that territory.[4]

(4) Trade marks and parallel importing

As we have noted, Community law imposes an exhaustion of trade mark **17–120** rights throughout the EEA.[5] Accordingly the activities of a parallel importer who operates between one EEA State and another cannot in most

---

[98] CTM Reg., Art. 92, the mark being presumed valid unless the defendant puts the matter in issue: Art. 95(1). For other proceedings involving Community marks, see Art. 102; the mark must in these cases be treated as valid: Art. 103. As to sanctions, including interlocutory relief, in the main national law applies; but injunctions against infringements or threats to infringe must be granted unless there are special reasons: Arts 98, 99. For interlocutory relief, courts other than CTM courts may have jurisdiction: Art. 99(1).

[99] The dispute was first raised in the context of the CPC, and resolved in the same way: see para. 3–27, above. Validity may not be put in issue when a declaration of non-infringement is sought: CTM Reg., Art. 95(2). For the determination of counterclaims, and the consequent registration of any judgment at the CTM Office, see Art. 96.

[1] Subject to agreement to submit to another Community trade mark court, or appearance in such a court by the defendant: CTM Reg., Art. 93(1)–(4). The Court empowered under this heirarchy may make interlocutory orders having Community-wide effect: Art. 99(2). See generally, Curley [1998] Apr. Man. I.P. 14.

[2] CTM Reg., Arts. 90, 104. The modifications are spelled out in Art. 90(2).

[3] *ibid.*, Art. 94(1).

[4] *ibid.*, Arts. 93(5), 94(2). It does not extend to declarations of non-infringement.

[5] Above, para. 17–114. For greater detail in the context of the E.C. Treaty, below, para. 18–04ff.

cases be controlled by trade mark rights in the country into which he imports. The working out of this general principle has proved particularly difficult in relation to trade marks, but its scope has now been clearly delineated by the European Court of Justice[6]; and it has been encapsulated in both the CTM Regulation and the TM Directive. Subject to certain exceptions, neither a CTM nor a national mark may "entitle the proprietor to prohibit its use in relation to goods which have been put on the market in the Community under that trade mark by the proprietor or with his consent".[7]

While this exhaustion rule operates in respect of goods which have been put on the market within the Community, nothing is said explicitly about importing goods from outside into the EEA. Originally it was proposed to introduce into the CTM Regulation a rule of fully international exhaustion, bringing national trade mark rights to an end in respect of marked goods marketed anywhere in the world by the right-owner or with its consent.[8] This was a particularly pronounced expression of the desire to draw trade mark protection back to its origin function. It would have coincided with the scope of rules then operating at the national level in some, but not all, EEA countries. Germany, for instance, had adopted international exhaustion in relation to all economically connected enterprises.[9] At the other end of the scale, Italy appears to have permitted marks to act as national barriers, whether they were held by the same or different legal persons (however closely connected) in the countries of export and import.[10]

In the United Kingdom, the law apparently took a midway position, though its scope was far from settled or complete. In *Revlon v. Cripps & Lee,*[11] the products of an internationally known corporate group could not be prevented from parallel movement into Britain from the United States. There was nothing about the product (shampoo) which would mislead an ordinary British consumer about the American product's qualities. Accordingly there was neither passing off nor infringement of the mark, as registered under the 1938 Act. On the other hand, if, as in *Colgate-Palmolive v. Markwell,*[12] the British consumer would expect, from his prior

---

[6] See paras 18–04 *et seq.*, below.

[7] CTM Reg., Art. 13; TM Dir., Art. 7; for the exceptions, see para. 18–09, below.

[8] See para. 15–17, above.

[9] See esp. *Cinzano v. Java Kaffeegeschäfte* [1974] 2 C.M.L.R. 21 (BGH): Cinzano Germany held not entitled to use its trade mark rights to prevent importation of "Cinzano" vermouth made by Spanish subsidiary or French exclusive licensee, each with taste variations designed to flatter local palates. For the history, Beier (1970) 1 I.I.C. 48. At least some degree of international exhaustion applied under the Benelux system and in the Scandanavian countries, Ireland and Austria, as well as the U.K. For a recent survey, see Klaka [1994] GRUR Int. 321.

[10] See the Survey by Beier and von Mühlendahl [1980] Mitt. d. Patentanwälte 101.

[11] [1980] F.S.R. 85, CA.

[12] [1989] R.P.C. 49, CA. The case sought to distinguish the *Revlon* case, but so far as it is based on the strict territorial conception of marks, it is hard to see that both could stand together.

knowledge of goods sold under the mark at home, that the imported products were of much higher quality than they in fact were, both forms of liability would arise. An express prohibition against export to Britain on the particular goods was probably a distinct ground for preventing their entry.[13] The position where the foreign marketer was not a subsidiary, but a licensed manufacturer for a limited territory, remained unsettled.

There was considerable pressure from European industry to retain trade **17–121** marks as a means of preventing parallel importing, in cases where no question of internal Community policy arose. The CTM Regulation and TM Directive were accordingly re-drafted in their final, less embracing terms, as set out above. The Commission announced that this text imposes a ring of non-exhaustion around the EEA.[14] This has been important, for instance, in dealing with the cheap labour markets of Central and Eastern Europe.

If such a blanket rule was to be, it could easily have been stated. It was left to be implied, because there was as little certainty about what was being agreed or should be agreed when the text was settled.[15]

The issue is incurably divisive:[16] consumers object to paying high prices for goods which they are told are cheaper in another country and politicians are ready enough to share their concern. From the opposite redoubt, manufacturers point to various reasons why the price differential is justifiable and should be supported by a trade mark right which prevents parallel importation internationally. They may have to invest more in order to launch and maintain a product in the higher-priced market; or it may be of different, superior quality there; or it may not be put on the less developed, cheaper market in the first place if parallel importation is the consequence: ideas of quality guarantee and investment protection underlie such pleas.

However, one frequent explanation of price differentials for a product as **17–122** between roughly equivalent markets is the fluctuation of exchange rates—a general risk affecting profitability which has very little to do with the marketing of particular product lines. Yet branding is now a crucial factor in selling virtually all finished products, and trade marks are not protected

---

[13] See, *e.g. Castrol v. Automotive Oil* [1983] R.P.C. 497; *Yardley v. Higson* [1984] F.S.R. 304, CA.

[14] See its Statement 94/C340/37 (December 12, 1994). By contrast, the EFTA Court ruled that the issue of international exhaustion remained a matter for each participant state: *Mag Instrument v. California Trading* (1998) 29 I.I.C. 316; Baudenbacher (1999) 22 Fordham Int. L.J. 645.

[15] For the range of views, compare, *e.g.* Beier (1990) 21 I.I.C. 131; Verkade [1992] GRUR Int. 92; von Gamm [1993] WRP 793 (all against the Commission's position); Shea [1995] E.I.P.R. 174; Rasmussen [1995] E.I.P.R. 174. Weekblad 232 (all for); and again Van Bunnen in *Jura Vigilantibus* (1994) 285 (favouring freedom of entry as a result of delictual liability).

[16] See the study, *Economic Consequences of the Choice of Regime of Exhaustion in the Area of Trade Marks* (1999), written by NERA *et al.* for the European Commission in the wake of the *Silhouette* case; *cf.* Van Melle [1999] E.I.P.R. 63.

as any special incentive to production (as are patented inventions or copyright works). Marks serve the primary function of distinguishing origin.[17] It is accordingly hard to accept that the law should adopt so wide-ranging a protective measure as an undiscriminating non-exhaustion of trade mark rights at the international level.

Nonetheless, in reading Article 7 of the Trade Market Directive[18] as necessarily implying exactly this, the Commission and its Member State supporters considered that they had found a technique for sealing off "Fortress Europe," which would operate across most trades as a matter of private right, rather than as a state measure imposed in a trade agreement and open therefore to re-negotiation. The legal question, accordingly, has been whether Article 7 does indeed achieve this effect. The Court of Justice has returned a first answer in *Silhouette v. Hartlauer*.[19]

> The case concerned a superior range of spectacle frames, manufactured and sold internationally under the mark "Silhouette" by the Austrian plaintiffs. A batch of the previous season's "Silhouette" spectacle frames were offloaded in Norway and sold on into Bulgaria on condition that marketing would occur only in former East Block countries. Through further deals, however, the frames were imported into Austria by the defendant and sold through its chain of outlets, which were no part of Silhouette's distribution system there. If the former Austrian law still applied, an extensive rule of international exhaustion would protect the defendant. The general question which the Austrian Supreme Court put to the European Court of Justice was accordingly whether Article 7 of the Trade Mark Directive, by sufficiently clear implication, required Member States to give up their national doctrine on the subject in favour of the Community Law rule laid down in that Article. The Court, having reworded the question so as to make plain that this was the only question which it was deciding, held that indeed there was no room for the continuance of the national law, whatever it might be. If some countries were free to maintain international exhaustion, while others did not, there would be an immediate difficulty in maintaining free movement within the internal market.[20] While Jacobs A.-G. was clear that Article 7 introduced an unbending rule that a registered right could be used to prevent the movement of genuine goods into the EEA from outside, the Court

---

[17] A policy which is stated in the Trade Mark Harmonisation Directive, Rec. 10, as the ECJ has repeatedly emphasised: *e.g. CNL-Sucal v. Hag* [1990] E.C.R. 3711; *ITH v. Ideal Standard* [1994] E.C.R. I–2789.

[18] Together with its equivalent in the CTM Regulation, Art. 12.

[19] [1998] E.C.R. I–4799; *cf.* Cornish [1998] E.I.P.R. 172.

[20] Moreover, since national rights and the CTM must be subject to an equivalent rule, and since the CTM is governed exclusively by E.U. law, it could make no sense to preserve differing national principles for the former: *cf.* Abbott and Verkade [1998] B.I.E. 111.

itself refrained from going so far.[21] Arguably, it has left itself the freedom to develop E.C. law so as to distinguish between cases where non-exhaustion is and is not justified.

As we shall see, the Court has limited the rule of exhaustion in the **17–123** internal market of the EEA so as not to apply where the trade mark function is unavoidably compromised, notably where there has been relabelling or repackaging of goods by a parallel importer, which fails to meet the strict limits which the Court itself has defined.[22] It must therefore be open to the Court to introduce limits, defined by Community law, to the Article 7 rule of non-international exhaustion. There are two directions in which it might be drawn to impose qualifications upon that rule.

First, there must remain scope for the mark owner to consent to parallel importation from outside the EEA, since that consent must be binding. The issue is whether such consent can be implied from the course of dealing. In *Silhouette*, the Bulgarian re-sellers knew of the express embargo against export to Austria and the Court was asked no further question about whether this bound subsequent purchasers. However, in *Zino Davidoff v. A & G Imports*,[23] Laddie J. refused summary judgment to the owner of "Cool Water" trade marks for perfumes against the parallel importer of its products from Singapore into Britain. He found it inherent in the nature of ownership of a thing that the owner is free to use it and deal with it as he wills, subject to any agreement to the contrary; a person may export what he owns, save where he has been made sufficiently aware on purchase that this is forbidden. As an approach Article 7 of the Directive is treated as in no way displacing this implication from the rightholder's conduct— inevitably a controversial proposition. In any case, as an approach, this view puts the mark owner to some effort in order to impose non-export terms and to alert subsequent purchasers sufficiently. At root, however, it would leave the mark owner a free choice after all to effect a legal barrier against parallel imports from outside.[24] Accordingly, it is scarcely a satisfactory means of securing a predominant place for international exhaustion. However, in some circumstances competion law may impose its own inhibitions on express notices limiting exportation to EEA countries. This possibility we explore in the next Chapter.[25]

---

[21] Jacobs A.G. continues to maintain that the issue has been settled: *Sebago v. GB Unic* [1999] E.T.M.R. 467, *cf., ibid.* 681. A second question in *Silhouette* concerned whether Austrian law alone governed the remedies available against the defendant. If so, in a case where customers were not being deceived about the goods (since they were genuine), no injunction might be available. While Jacobs A.G. considered that the Directive, Art. 7, overrode this, the Court held that the matter remained one for Austrian law, as interpreted in light of the Directive's objectives.

[22] Below, para. 18–09.

[23] May 18, 1999. Laddie J. has referred the correctness of his view to the ECJ.

[24] There may, of course, be commercial reasons for not using an express notice.

[25] Below, para. 18–21.

Secondly, the Court of Justice might follow the precedents currently prevailing in United States law on the subject. It could distinguish between cases where the parallel imports are in no relevant way distinguishable from those being sold directly in the home market and cases where the goods are different in quality and home consumers could be confused about them. As already noted, the latter case is one where there is a particular justification for preventing the entry of the parallel imports. In the inevitably rough distinctions to which the law is driven on this question, the line is one which could be used to maintain a reasonable balance of interests. It is in Europe's longer term interests that it should move in this direction.

Part VI

THE EUROPEAN DIMENSION

CHAPTER 18

INTELLECTUAL PROPERTY IN THE EUROPEAN ECONOMIC AREA

The world's trade is being transformed by the breakdown of old East-West **18–01** hostilities and by the emergence of rapidly developing industrial economies out of what passed, even recently, as a stagnant Third World. The long-standing industrial states see labour-intensive production moving away, leaving them to count increasingly on their sophisticated skills in servicing, marketing, financing and intellectual advances of many kinds. For developed and developing countries alike, there are new reasons to attach major importance to the shoring-up of value which intellectual property rights can provide. As a consequence it was possible to include an embracing panoply of protection in the TRIPS Agreement. A first step may well have been taken towards the true internationalisation of intellectual property as a framework for fair dealing within a world of free trade.

Nonetheless full integration of intellectual property on that scale is likely to be a slow and difficult process. Even within so committed an association of states as the European Community and its adjunct Economic Area, movement towards the ideal of a standard set of rules applicable on a unitary basis throughout the whole territory has been bumpy and difficult, as so many chapters of this book have indicated. This has often been because intellectual property forms a central barrier along the boundary between fair and unfair competition, and ideas about where that boundary should be drawn undoubtedly vary. These ideas are about basic values, which, in being converted into practical policies and legal rules, need to build on shared experiences as well as respecting differences of national attitude.

The Community is obliged to settle the place of intellectual property in relation to a variety of its quintessential objectives, which include (*inter alia*) the elimination of: internal restrictions on the import and export of goods; a common commercial policy; an internal market without obstacles to the free movement of goods, persons, services and capital; non-distortion of internal market competition; approximation of national laws required for the functioning of the Common Market; promotion of research and technological development; encouragement of trans-European networks; and the strengthening of consumer protection.[1]

---

[1] Treaty of Rome, Maastricht version, Art. 3.

There are points at which details of intellectual property rules have had to adapt to fundamental tenets of the Treaty. One basic guarantee of integration is that there shall be no discrimination on ground of nationality between citizens of Member States.[2] This had a dramatic impact on the performer's right in German law, which was accorded to German nationals wherever they performed, but to citizens of other countries (including other Community States) only if the performance took place in a Rome Convention country (as that Convention required). By German law, a British pop singer, Phil Collins, was thus not entitled to the performer's right in a performance recorded in the United States—a non-Rome Convention country—whereas a German singer would have been.[3] The European Court of Justice held that he must equally be accorded the right.[4]

1. THE INTERNAL MARKET: "INTELLECTUAL PROPERTY"[5]

(1) Free movement of goods

18–02 After nearly 40 years of striving towards a unified internal market, the elimination of price differentials for goods as between Member States still remains a future prospect. Differences in national tastes and other priorities, differences in the cost of establishing new products on particular parts of the whole market, differences in the way in which government influences or controls prices in certain sectors (notably pharmaceuticals), fluctuations in rates of currency exchange—any one of these may cause price differences. In consequence parallel importation is likely to occur and that practice acts, within the market itself, as an adjustment mechanism which drives towards price uniformity. The activities of the parallel importer are thus of singular importance to achievement of the common internal market and have been supported, wherever possible, by Community institutions—not least by the Court of Justice.

In the formative years of the EEC, the question soon arose: how far could intellectual property in one Member State (Country Impo) be used to stop the movement into that country of the "same goods" from another

---

[2] Treaty of Rome, Maastricht version, Art 6.

[3] *Collins v. Imtrat* [1993] E.C.R. I–5145. In a conjoint case, Cliff Richard had no right under German law because his performance was recorded in Britain before Germany assumed Rome Convention obligations. Accordingly, he was subject to discrimination under the E.C. Treaty.

[4] Community law thus affected the scope of the right within its own national territory; no cross-border issue arose over moving goods or providing services. For the impact of the case on implementation of the Directive on Copyright Term, see para. 10–45, above.

[5] Of the large literature on this topic, note esp. Joliet [1975] C.L.P. 15; Demaret, *Patents, Territorial Restrictions and EEC Law* (1978); Oliver, *Free Movement of Goods in the EEC* (3rd ed., 1995), pp. 247–300; Rothnie, *Parallel Imports* (1993); Marenco and Banks (1990) 15 Eur.L.R. 224; Beier (1990) 21 I.I.C. 131; Ullrich in Gijlstra and Murphy (eds.), *Competition Law of Western Europe and the USA*, C-491; Loewenheim (1995) 26 I.I.C. 829.

Member State (Country Expo)? What was the situation, in particular, when the goods had first been marketed in the other Member State (Country Expo) and had been acquired there by a parallel importer who would take them to Country Impo, only to be met by proceedings for infringement of the intellectual property right there? Specifically, could the action in Country Impo succeed when the initial marketing in Country Expo was by the owner of the right in Country Impo, or by a person connected with that owner—through a corporate grouping, manufacturing licences or a distribution network?

As already outlined in Chapter 1, the Court of Justice reached answers which in considerable measure favoured the parallel importer.[6] At the beginning the Court applied the Rules of Competition (notably Articles 85 and 86 of the E.C. Treaty); but increasingly it relied upon the principle of the Free Movement of Goods (notably Articles 30 and 36). For an outline of these provisions of the Treaty, the reader should return to the discussion in Chapter 1, where in particular their differing scope is noted.

(a) *Preliminary factors*

Over time the Court of Justice has laid down a number of basic tenets **18–03** concerning the impact of the free movement of goods principle on intellectual property. These can be listed in short order:

(1) An action in a national Court, founded upon a national intellectual property law, which prevents the importation of goods is a measure "having equivalent effect" to the quantitative restrictions on imports between Member States which are prohibited by Article 30.[7]

(2) Article 30 can be relied upon directly by a defendant to an intellectual property action. The Article therefore overrides the national right unless the latter can be maintained as an exception under Article 36.

(3) Article 36 obliges the plaintiff to show (a) that the right was a provision for "the protection of industrial or commercial property", and (b) that in the circumstances it does not amount to "a means of arbitrary discrimination nor to a disguised restriction on trade between Member States".

(4) Not only patents, trade marks and design rights but also authors' rights, neighbouring rights, plant variety rights[8] and even joint rights in geographical denominations[9] are treated as within the notion of

---

[6] See para. 1–51, above.

[7] It is with the state's intervention that the free movement policy is concerned, not with any act of an undertaking, such as selling with a prohibition against export: see, *e.g. Bayer v. Süllhöfer* [1988] E.C.R. 5249; *Ministre Public v. Tournier* [1989] E.C.R. 2521. The latter falls to be considered under the Competition Rules: see para. 18–14, below.

[8] As in *Nungesser* [1981] E.C.R. 45, para. 7–34, above.

[9] *Exportur v. Lur* [1992] E.C.R. I–5529.

"industrial or commercial property".[10] Much has come therefore to turn upon the derogations for arbitrary discrimination and disguised restrictions on trade in the second sentence of Article 36, which the Court has, by and large, treated as invitation for judicial policy-making.

(5) Some of the most difficult cases have arisen because of the absence or more limited scope of intellectual property rights in Country Expo than in Country Impo. The Court has very largely refused to enter upon any critical evaluation of such differences. Until there is a relevant harmonisation Directive, or a Community right becomes a complete substitute, it is for national law in each state to determine the content and scope of the rights and the conditions for obtaining them.[11]

(6) Where Community legislation does express the role of exhaustion across the internal market it will be interpreted in the sense already developed in the Court's decisions on Articles 30–36.[12]

(b) *Basic rule and its application*

18–04 Despite the obscurities of Article 36 in relation to intellectual property, the Court of Justice reached a basic proposition on the free movement of goods policy:

"The exercise, by a patentee [or other intellectual property owner], of the right which he enjoys under the legislation of a Member State to prohibit the sale, in that State, of a product protected by the patent [or other right] which has been marketed in another Member State by the patentee [or other owner] or with his consent is incompatible with the rules of the E.C. Treaty concerning the free movement of goods within the Common Market."

---

[10] Arguments were made in the 1970s that authors' rights, because of their moral ascendancy, must be treated apart; but that would require finding an even broader exception somewhere within the E.C. Treaty. In the event they were not distinguished: *Membran* (n. 44, below); *Dansk Supermarked* (n. 15, below). It has been argued, contrary to the Court's approach, that "unfair competition" laws should be similarly treated, because they are included within the Paris Convention: see Beier (1990) 21 I.I.C. 131 at 159, 160. Given their multifarious scope in, for instance, German law, this view is unlikely to gain acceptance.

[11] See, *e.g. Terrapin* (n. 27, below) (scope of protection for well-known marks in Germany); *Nancy Kean Gifts* [1982] E.C.R. 2853 (entitlement of applicant to Benelux design right); *Volvo v. Veng* [1988] E.C.R. 6211, and *CICRA v. Renault* [1988] E.C.R. 6039 (both concerning design rights applicable to car spare parts); *Thetford v. Fiamma* [1988] 3 C.M.L.R. 549 (narrower test of novelty in U.K. patent law meant patent maintainable there while not in Italy); *Generics v. Smith Kline & French Laboratories* [1997] R.P.C. 801, ECJ, (generic drug manufacturer infringed patent in course of obtaining authorisation to market after its expiry; remedy could include an injunction leasing 14 months after expiry). See also *Deutsche Renault v. Audi* [1993] 1 E.C.R. 6227.

[12] The most prominent example is the exhaustion provision in the Community Trade Mark Regulation, Art. 12, and the First Trade Mark Harmonisation Directive, Art. 7: see above, paras 17–114, 17–120.

What is relevant is consent to the act of first marketing of the specific goods,[13] not to the act of manufacture, whether that occurs within the E.C. or outside it.[14]

Note at once that, in this formulation, the Community Policy only has its overriding effect where national law would otherwise empower the right-owner to prevent the parallel importation—so the starting point is always the scope of the national law of Country Impo.[15] Note also that the Policy provides a rule of "Community-wide exhaustion"—it operates when the right-owner has marketed the goods, or consented to their marketing, in Country Expo and thereby has brought his rights (in Country Impo) to an end; it is not normally concerned with the direct access of the manufacturer or initial distributor in Country Expo to the market in Country Impo.

The Court applied the principle, for instance, to the following circumstances:

> (*Deutsche Grammophon v. Metro*[16]: parent and subsidiary). Records marketed by the French subsidiary of Deutsche Grammophon in France were bought there and exported indirectly to Germany for sale at a price less than that set under the then operating rules for resale price maintenance. Deutsche Grammophon's neighbouring right in the sound recording under German law could not be used to stop those sales, even though their effect was to destroy the maintained price at all retail outlets. France then had no equivalent neighbouring right and no price maintenance system, which may have explained the fact that French prices were much lower than the German. These factors did not, however, affect the outcome, since Deutsche Grammophon had consented to the initial sales by its subsidiaries.

> (*Centrafarm v. Sterling Drug*[17]: same right-holder, different subsidiaries in a group). A urinary infection drug, patented and marketed under the registered mark, Negram, was produced in the United Kingdom by the parent patentee, Sterling Drug, and marketed there by a Sterling subsidiary, registered proprietor of the mark. Its parallel importation into the Netherlands was opposed by Sterling as owner of the equivalent Dutch patent and a different subsidiary as owner of the Dutch trade mark. The Dutch price was much higher, chiefly because of improvements in the exchange rate of the guilder against the pound; but also possibly because the major purchaser in the United Kingdom,

---

[13] It is not enough that other batches of the same product have already been placed on the first market: *Sebago v. GB-Unic* [1999] E.T.M.R. 681, ECJ.

[14] *Phytheron v. Jean Bourdon* [1997] I E.C.R. 1729, ECJ.

[15] Sometimes, however, the Court of Justice is asked to advise on the Treaty of Rome question, upon the assumption that the national law would otherwise set up a barrier within the Common Market.

[16] [1971] E.C.R. 487.

[17] [1974] E.C.R. 1147 (patent) and *Centrafarm v. Winthrop* [1974] E.C.R. 1183 (trade mark).

the Department of Health, could buy at reasonable royalty rates as a Crown user, and because of the Department's strong assertion of its buying power. These various factors did not justify the use of either the patent or the trade mark to block free movement between Member States: all that mattered was the consent to the United Kingdom marketing by a member of the group.

(*Dansk Supermarked v. Imerco*[18]: manufacturing licence). Imerco, a Danish hardware firm, commissioned Broadhurst to manufacture china services in the United Kingdom, subject to strict quality standards, for sale in Denmark in celebration of Imerco's Fiftieth Anniversary. 300 sub-standard sets were rejected but Broadhurst were permitted to sell them off, subject to the condition that they were not to be brought onto the Danish market. When a parallel importer did just that, Imerco was not permitted to assert its copyright in the designs, nor its trade mark, against their sale; nor could it make a difference that the breach of condition rendered the conduct a form of unfair competition.[19]

(*Merck v. Stephar*[20]: manufacturer operating in unprotected and protected market). Merck held no patent on a hypertension drug, "Moduretic", in Italy but did have a patent for it in the Netherlands. It marketed the drug in Italy, where a parallel importer acquired it and exported to the Netherlands. Even though Merck had had no opportunity at all in Italy to profit from patent protection, the fact that it had itself undertaken the marketing there was treated as exhausting the Dutch patent right.

(c) *Justifications*

18–05 These decisions were justified primarily in terms of policy. For example, the Court of Justice said of the subject-matter of *Deutsche Grammophon*:

"If a right related to copyright is relied upon to prevent the marketing in a Member State of products distributed by the holder of the right or with his consent on the territory of another Member State on the sole ground that such distribution did not take place on the national territory, such a prohibition, which would legitimise the isolation of national markets, would be repugnant to the essential purpose of the Treaty, which is to unite national markets into a single market."

Underlying this justification is an assumption that, had the product first been sold in Country Impo, the right would thereafter have been treated as

---

[18] [1981] E.C.R. 181.
[19] Specifically, in breach of the Danish Marketing Act of 1974. For the application of similar principles to unfair competition laws, see paras 18–11 *et seq.*, below.
[20] [1981] E.C.R. 2063. Now re-affirmed in *Merck v. Primecrown*, below, para. 18–45.

exhausted and could not affect subsequent sales.[21] But because that exhaustion was applied only within the domestic market and not internationally, the parallel importer from elsewhere in the Community was discriminated against. The Court of Justice might have taken its stand explicitly upon the discrimination provision of Article 36. But it was here dealing with *property*; and Article 222 prescribes that the "Treaty shall in no way prejudice the rules in Member States governing the system of property ownership".[22] Uneasy that it risked trespassing on this special preserve, the Court ventured upon legalistic distinctions whose obscurity served only to disguise their essential banality.

The first of these is the supposed distinction between the existence of a right and its exercise:

> "... it is clear from [Article 36], in particular its second sentence, as well as from the context, that whilst the Treaty does not affect the existence of rights recognised by the legislation of a Member State in matters of industrial and commercial property, yet the exercise of these rights may nevertheless, depending on the circumstances, be affected by the prohibitions of the Treaty."[23]

Since a right exists to the extent that it can be exercised, this amounted to superior eye-wash and the Court soon chose to go further (probably in the hope of identifying "existence") by holding that the derogations from free movement permitted by Article 36 can be made only "where such derogations are justified for the purpose of safeguarding rights which constitute the specific subject-matter of this property".[24] While the Court has from time to time attempted some elucidation of what the specific subject-matter of various intellectual property rights is, in most instances the only real content of this "definition" concerns the scope of exhaustion. For instance:

> "In relation to patents, the specific subject matter of the industrial property is the guarantee that the patentee, to reward the creative effort of the inventor, has the exclusive right to use an invention with a

---

[21] Subsequently, the Court seems not to have considered whether the national right was subject to exhaustion. Had it done so in *Sterling Drug*, it would have found that U.K. patent law held no doctrine of exhaustion (see paras 6–15, 6–16, above). Its result could not, therefore, have depended on discrimination under Article 36; instead there must have been "disguised" (*i.e.* unjustifiable) restriction on trade.

[22] The reference to "property systems" expressed the intention to preserve whatever degree of socialisation existed in Member States. Accordingly, the impact of Art. 222 on a conflict between a Treaty policy and national intellectual property was not clear and produced starkly opposed views: see Ladas (1974) 5 I.I.C. 302; Mann (1975) 24 I.C.L.Q. 31; Mak (1975) 6 I.I.C. 29; Waelbroeck (1976) 21 Antitrust Bull. 99; Jacobs (1975) 24 I.C.L.Q. 643; Johannes and Wright (1976) 1 Eur. L.R. 230.

[23] *Centrafarm v. Sterling Drug* [1974] E.C.R. 1149, Judgment, para. 7. The formula has been much recited, though less of late: Marenco and Banks (n. 5, above) at 224–225.

[24] *Sterling Drug*, Judgment, para. 8.

view to manufacturing industrial products and putting them into circulation for the first time, either directly or by the grant of licences to third parties, as well as the right to oppose infringements."[25]

As a proposition, this too provides little by way of justification or even clarification. It might acquire body if it were a statement, made in the light of a comparative study, that all the Member States accepted as a matter of policy that the intellectual property right deserved to cover only first marketing. In fact the position in Member States is not uniform, and anyway differs from one type of intellectual property to another. The proposition, therefore, does little other than reiterate the very policy decision which the Court of Justice is seeking to justify.

The most that can be said for the "boot-strapping" character of this core reasoning is that the Court is left free to adopt a pragmatic approach to other related issues reviewed below. This pragmatism is apparent in the examples which follow. From it looms the question whether the decisions show an acceptable consistency; and whether, therefore, there are arguments which could persuade the Court to change its position, at least on particular applications.

(d) *The "common origin" adventure*

18–06 In one spectacular instance in this sphere, the Court of Justice has indeed reversed itself. While the result is now an historical diversion, it is not therefore to be ignored. In 1973, at the height of its determination to free the internal market of intellectual property sub-divisions, the Court developed a second principle, the so-called doctrine of "common origin", which was quite distinct from the principle concerning exhaustion by first marketing with consent.

(*Van Zuylen v. Hag*[26] ("Hag I")). The "Hag" trade mark for decaffeinated coffee, originally held by a single enterprise in Germany and Belgium, had passed in the latter country into entirely separate ownership as a measure of wartime sequestration. The original common ownership of the mark was held to entitle the German producer to market his marked product—either through a parallel importer or even directly—in the Benelux territories. Reflecting a disdainful view

---

[25] *Sterling Drug*, Judgment, para. 9. The specific subject-matter of the trade mark was first described as "the guarantee that the owner of the trade mark has the exclusive right to use that trade mark, for the purpose of putting products protected by the trade mark into circulation for the first time, and is therefore intended to protect him against competitors wishing to take advantage of the status and reputation of the trade mark by selling products illegally bearing that trade mark": *Centrafarm v. Winthrop* [1974] E.C.R. 1147, Judgment, para. 8. This was somewhat developed in later cases: see esp. *American Home Products* [1978] E.C.R. 1823 and "*Hag II*" (n. 28, below). It took temerity to attempt such a formulation for copyright, but the CFI tried in "Magill": [1991] E.C.R. II–485, paras 54–56.

[26] [1974] E.C.R. 731.

of the purpose and value of marks, the Court indicated that other means must be found for informing the Benelux public that they were obtaining the German, and not the Belgian, product.

The decision provoked an outcry from industry, for, if the Court of Justice would go so far, why not apply the same result even to marks of unconnected enterprises in different Common Market countries which had never had an original connection? That too would liberate the internal market. In the event, the Court soon drew back from this further step, holding in *"Terranova"*[27] that common origin was a special case.

Eventually, the Court would hear the counter-case between, in effect, the parties to the first "Hag" decision, and would reverse itself. Now showing an adequate appreciation of trade marks as necessary indicators of the source of goods and services, the Court held in *CNL-Sucal v. Hag GF* ("Hag II") that the Belgian business had no right to go into the German market, directly or indirectly, because in that territory the mark designated the German enterprise.[28] The same must apply to imports into Benelux (despite the first decision); it could not be said that the German firm deserved greater protection because it had never lost or changed its rights at home.

The ensuing decision in the *Ideal Standard* case[29] removed the last vestiges of "common origin" by holding that, even where trade marks were split within the Common Market between separate enterprises by a voluntary assignment, rather than by government expropriation, this of itself did not entitle either of the consequent owners or parallel importers to go into the other country. However, given the voluntary character of the assignment, that transaction and the surrounding conduct of the parties would fall to be assessed under the Rules of Competition.

The *affaire "Hag"* shows how far the Court has progressed in its appreciation of the objectives of intellectual property. For the scope of national laws to be limited by virtue of Article 30, it appears that there must generally have been a consensual act in Country Expo bringing about an exhaustion of right in Country Impo which frees parallel imports. The main addition to this arises when there is some provision in a national law which disadvantages imported goods in comparison with domestically-produced goods.[30] This attitude is much more scrupulous than in related legal fields where Article 36 is held not to apply.[31]

---

[27] See [1976] E.C.R. 1039.
[28] [1990] 1 E.C.R. 3711. Note the eloquent appreciation of the issue by Jacobs A.-G.
[29] *IHT v. Ideal Standard* [1994] 1 E.C.R. 2789; Gagliardi [1998] E.I.P.R. 371. See also the writings of its *juge rapporteur*; Joliet (1983) 5 N.W.J Int. L. 755; (1984) 15 I.I.C. 21.
[30] As for instance, the less favourable conditions of compulsory patent licences when granted for imports from another E.C. country than when manufactured in the domestic market: *Allen & Hanburys v. Generics* [1988] E.C.R. 1275; *E.C. Commission v. United Kingdom and Italy* [1992] 1 E.C.R. 829.
[31] See paras 18–11 *et seq.*, below.

(e) *Absence of consent*

18–07 By necessary implication, if a person other than the right-owner in Country Expo (or someone acting with its consent) placed the goods on the Expo market, there would be no exhaustion of the right in Country Impo.

> (*Terrapin v. Terranova*[32]). The owner of "Terranova" and other "Terra . . ." marks (for construction materials) in Germany could assert them against the importation of prefabricated housing made by a British firm and bearing its house mark, "Terrapin". Because there had never been any connection between the firms and the marks had been acquired quite independently in the two countries, the German firm's action could be maintained.[33]

> (*Keurkoop v. Nancy Kean Gifts*[34]). The owner of a Benelux registered design[35] for a handbag could object to the importation of bags bearing the design from another Community country into Holland, if they were not marketed in that other country "by, or with the consent of, the proprietor of the right or a person legally or economically dependent on him".[36]

> (*EMI Electrola v. Patricia*[37]). The sound recording right in Cliff Richard's recordings had expired in Denmark but not in Germany, where it was still owned by EMI. The defendant, an unconnected company, organised the marketing of its own version of the recordings by a Danish company in Denmark, and it re-purchased them for export to Germany. It was unsuccessful in claiming the freedom to ignore the German neighbouring right.[38]

> (*Pharmon v. Hoechst*[39]). Hoechst held patents on the drug, frusemide, in the United Kingdom and the Netherlands. DDSA obtained a compulsory licence to manufacture and sell the drug in the United

---

[32] [1976] E.C.R. 1039.

[33] The case raised concern over the scope of German trade mark and unfair competition rights: for this aspect, see para. 18–11, below, It had also to deal with the separate doctrine of "common origin" of trade marks, on which it is now otiose: see para. 18–06, above.

[34] [1982] E.C.R. 2853.

[35] Under Benelux Design Law, a person other than the designer could apply for the design unless the designer objected—a common enough formula in intellectual property law. The Court treated this rule as a matter purely for national law, and not one which could be the subject of an attack under the proviso to Art. 36.

[36] There must be no anti-competitive agreement or concerted practice or co-ordinate registration of the design under separate names in different states, but it was for national Courts to assess this.

[37] [1989] E.C.R. 79; Strivens [1989] E.I.P.R. 297.

[38] It was this case which provided justification for the Duration Directive, equating (and in many cases extending) the term of authors' and neighbouring rights: paras 10–43 *et seq.*, above.

[39] [1985] E.C.R. 2281.

Kingdom, subject to a prohibition against export.[40] DDSA nonetheless claimed the right under Article 30 to sell the British drug in Holland.[41] Because the manufacturing licence was compulsory, the Court of Justice found that Merck did not consent to DDSA's activities and so could still rely upon its Dutch patent.

In *Pharmon* the Court repeated its definition of the specific subject-matter of a patent, and held it "necessary to allow the patent proprietor to prevent the importation and marketing of products manufactured under a compulsory licence in order to protect the substance of his exclusive rights under his patent".[42] In doing so it referred to *Merck v. Stephar*[43] without concern. But its remark appears to cast doubt on the outcome of that case, raising the questions which have so frequently been adumbrated by commentators[44]: if a right-holder had no equivalent right in Country Expo from which to extract a benefit there, why should its mere consent to first marketing deprive it of the enhanced value of the product in Country Impo where it does have a right? Does not the *Merck* decision make it hard for the right-owner to market in Country Expo, since to do so threatens to reduce the Country Impo price towards that in Country Expo? May that not deprive Expo consumers of a novel and desirable product?

The markedly low prices of patented pharmaceuticals in Spain and **18–08** Portugal made the problem particularly pressing once those countries passed beyond the transitional stage of their entry into the E.U. In a case aimed against the export of parallel drugs from Spain to Britain, the manufacturer—again Merck—sought to show that its moral responsibility to supply an important drug even to low-profit countries fettered their "consent" as much as if they had been subjected to compulsory licensing. The Court, however, refused to alter its position and required that no injunction in Britain should prevent the movement of the patented goods.[45] It did so, despite the fact that, as cases such as "Hag II" and "Ideal Standard" demonstrate, the Court of Justice now attaches a great deal more significance to the objectives of the different forms of intellectual property than formerly it did.

---

[40] Granted under the PA 1949, s. 41, repealed in 1977.
[41] Direct exports were therefore at issue, but the Court considered the case as if they were by a parallel importer.
[42] [1985] E.C.R. 2281, Judgment, para. 26.
[43] See n. 20, above.
[44] Led by Joliet [1975] C.L.P. 15. Where statutory licensing powers exist (for instance, under Crown use provisions, or an entitlement only to fair remuneration in copyright), but the licensor has nonetheless entered voluntary licences, it may be that *Pharmon* will apply: *cf. Sterling Drug* (above, n. 17), *Musik Vertrieb Membran v. GEMA* [1981] E.C.R. 147.
[45] *Merck v. Primecrown* [1997] F.S.R. 237, *cf.* the opposite conclusion of Fennelly A.G. The decision is criticised by Fernandex Vicién [1996] E.C.L.R. 219; Korah [1997] E.C.L.R. 265; Kon and Schaffer [1997] E.C.L.R. 123; Torremans and Stamatoudi [1997] E.I.P.R. 545.

(f) *Repackaging and relabelling*

18–09 In the sphere of trade marks, some particularly nice issues arose over repackaging and relabelling with a different mark. These special principles, first developed by the Court under Articles 30–36, have been give explicit legislative expression in the Trade Marks Directive and Regulations.[46] In many E.C. States, it is considered an infringement of the mark to deal in marked goods which have been re-packed, re-marked or otherwise interfered with, because the mark no longer accurately indicates that the goods come unaltered from the originating enterprise. In the pharmaceutical field, this aspect of the right was turned against parallel importers in two ways:

(*Hoffmann-La Roche v. Centrafarm*[47]: repackaging). The practice in Germany was to supply certain drugs in packages of 1,000, while in Britain sales were in lots of 100 or 250. A parallel importer from Britain accordingly repacked the smaller lots into the larger, re-using the mark and indicating that it was the importer. Although the essential function of the mark as a guarantee of origin "would in fact be jeopardised if it were permissible for a third party to affix the mark to the product, even to an original product", nonetheless it had to be asked whether a particular assertion of the right amounted to a "disguised restriction on trade". This would after all occur in a case where a new larger pack showed that the original packs had not been interfered with, or where a public authority supervised the repackaging; but to act within this exception, the parallel importer must warn the right-owner in advance and indicate on the packaging what had been done.[48]

The Court has recently affirmed the conditions under which an importer may repackage goods where that is necessary in order to emulate the manufacture's own practices in different markets.[49] It adds, as instances of permitted conduct, the fixing of self-adhesive labels to the inner packaging of a product, the addition of new instructions or information, and the insertion of an additional article. The national Court must determine whether any of these acts omits information or misleads consumers or does not comply with the manufacturer's method of use or dosage.

---

[46] TM Dir., Art. 7, CTM Reg., Art. 12, for which see above, para. 17–122. Within the EEA, exhaustion of trade marks must apply unless E.U. law admits an exception.

[47] [1978] E.C.R. 1139. An attempt is in progress to reverse this decision upon the argument that the exhaustion rule now embodied in the TM Directive, Art. 7, allows exceptions to be made for legitimate reasons. Jacobs A.-G. has refused to upset the earlier decision: *Bristol-Myers Squibb v. Paranova* [1996] F.S.R. 225.

[48] In *Pfizer v. EurimPharm* [1981] E.C.R. 2913, the parallel importer was held by the Court to have satisfied the conditions.

[49] *Bristol-Myers Squibb v. Paranova* [1996] I–E.C.R. 3457. Sometimes the packaging arrangements in a country are determined or recommended by government.

(*American Home Products v. Centrafarm*[50]: applying a different mark). The plaintiff marketed essentially the same tranquilliser as "Serenid D" in Britain and as "Seresta" in the Netherlands; there was, however, some difference in taste. The parallel importer repackaged the British product as "Seresta" and sold it in Holland, indicating its own role as importer. While considering it of the essence that trade mark law should prevent use of a trade mark by a person not the "originator" of the goods, the Court of Justice considered that "exercise" of the right to that very end could nonetheless be a disguised restriction on trade. It would be so if the owner of the different marks had adopted them with the intention of dividing parts of the Common Market.[51]

The Court is also likely to continue to allow relabelling where the different marks contribute to an artificial partitioning of the internal market, whether or not this is the manufacturer's intention and the conditions prescribed for repackaging are followed.[52] The reputation of the trade mark must not be liable to damage[53]; but this does not mean that the manufacturer's own code for country of origin may not be removed—an important factor in the complex battles over the sourcing of parallel imports.[54]

In disposing of the re-labelling and re-packaging cases, the Court faced practices which posed a peculiarly provocative constraint on free movement. It could only provide awkward answers which have not proved easy to apply in subsequent practice. There may, for instance, be various explanations of why different marks were adopted in different countries: different prior rights in each of them, different relations to national languages, and so on. The Court's discomfort is marked in its reasoning. In particular the "essence/exercise" distinction is wrung dry of identifiable content.

(2) Rights in performance and other temporary use

The Court of Justice developed its main doctrine around the primary **18–10** activities of the parallel importer: the actual importation or the subsequent sale of goods embodying or bearing the protected subject-matter. But intellectual property may be employed against other activities. When these

---

[50] [1978] E.C.R. 1823.
[51] Banks and Marenco (n. 5, above) at 253–254, claim that this is an unacceptable application of Article 30 to private acts, rather than to state intervention. But, for all the crucial significance of the proprietor's intention, it was nonetheless bringing an action under state law.
[52] So proposed by Jacobs A.G., in *Upjohn v. Paranova* [1999] E.T.M.R. 97. In the pharmaceutical field, the European Medical Evaluation Authority is seeking to impose the requirement of a single mark for the whole E.U. The opposition remains vociferous.
[53] Using the mark in chain-store advertising is not a sufficient injury to its reputation: see *Christian Dior Parfums v. Evora* [1998] R.P.C. 166, ECJ; para. 17–115, above.
[54] *Loendersloot v. George Ballantine* [1998] F.S.R. 544, ECJ In this instance also, the manufacturer's intention is treated by the Court as irrelevant. See Clark [1998] E.I.P.R. 328.

too began to be challenged as contrary to Rome Treaty principles, the Court showed an essential sympathy for the objectives of intellectual property protection.

(*Coditel v. Ciné Vog (No. 1)*[55]). The owner of copyright in the film, *Le Boucher*, granted cinema and television rights in Belgium exclusively to Ciné Vog for seven years. Under another licence, the German television channel, ARD, broadcast the film. The Coditel companies received it off-air and transmitted it to their cable subscribers in Western Belgium. Under Belgian law this was an infringement of Ciné Vog exclusive rights for which they claimed damages. Coditel relied on the principle of Free Provision of Services in the Rome Treaty (Articles 59 to 66) for the proposition that their conduct could not be a breach of Ciné Vog's rights.

While the Court was prepared to treat those Articles as overriding the claim if it involved arbitrary discrimination or a disguised restriction on trade,[56] it could find neither in these circumstances. It accepted that the exploitation of performing rights by geographically limited licences was a necessary element in such copyright; and that because broadcasting was organised nationally, any other unit for dividing television rights would be impracticable.[57] Inevitably the case left floating the question, is the movement of goods between Member States really so different?

(*Warner Bros v. Christiansen*[58]). At a stage when a rental right for films had been introduced into Denmark but not yet into the United Kingdom, a Dane purchased a video-cassette of *Never Say Never Again* in London and hired it out from his video shop in Copenhagen. The owner of copyright in the film, together with the exclusive manager of its video rights in Denmark, succeeded in obtaining an injunction under Danish copyright law. The Court of Justice found that the Danish rental right applied equally to Danish and to imported videos and, being thus non-discriminatory, Article 36 allowed the rental right to be asserted against the imports. The Court's view that the introduction of rental rights as a proper addition to the range of copyright protection led to the Directive on Rental, Public Lending and Related Rights.[59] In turn the Court has upheld the constitutionality of that Directive's imposition of a standard rental right across the E.U. Rental is not an activity which conflicts with the right of unfettered disposition guaranteed by the free movement of goods policy.[60]

---

[55] [1980] E.C.R. 881.
[56] There is no express reference to these Art. 36 expressions in the Articles.
[57] There was a separate question whether the territorial licences were unduly restrictive of competition: see para. 13–57, n. 93, above.
[58] [1988] E.C.R. 2605; Defalque [1989] E.I.P.R. 434.
[59] See para. 9–18, above.
[60] *Metronome Music v. Music-Point-Hokamp* [1997] E.M.L.R. 93.

(*Basset v. SACEM*[61]). At the relevant time, French law did not grant a neighbouring right to a sound recording producer for the public performance or broadcast of a record. However, the composer's reproduction right in music is not limited by any exhaustion upon first sale even in France; instead subsequent uses may be controlled (if notified) through a *droit de destination*. On this basis, the French collecting society for composers, SACEM, charged discothèque owners and others a supplementary "mechanical reproduction" fee (1.65 per cent of receipts) in addition to its performing right fee (6.6 per cent). It levied this charge equally on records originating from the legitimate producer in other E.C. States and imported into France. The Court of Justice refused to view the different fees as more than subdivisions of a total charge for a normal exploitation of copyright, a charge which applied indiscriminately to French records and imports and was therefore not contrary to Articles 30 to 36.

2. INTERNAL MARKET: UNFAIR COMPETITION

In settling the impact of the free movement of goods policy on the major **18–11** intellectual property rights, the Court of Justice has inevitably been much influenced by the terms of Article 36. But "intellectual property" shades off into surrounding forms of civil liability. This includes, in the British approach, such non-statutory liability as that for passing off and breach of confidence; and in Continental thought it touches at least some aspects of unfair competition. In these spheres, likewise, the free movement policy has produced conflicts with national rights of action and here the Court has developed interpretations of Article 30 itself, which require a balancing of factors. But under Article 30 the weighting of the scales is not the same.

In particular, in the *"Cassis de Dijon"*, *Irish Souvenirs* and subsequent cases,[62] the following principle was established: in the absence of common rules relating to the production and marketing of products, obstacles to movement within the Community resulting from disparities between national legislation must be accepted in so far as such legislation, applying without discrimination to both domestic and imported products, may be justified as being necessary in order to satisfy mandatory requirements relating in particular to the protection of consumers and fairness in commercial transactions. In some recent cases, moreover, the Court of Justice was not prepared to leave the assessment involved in its application to national Courts (as sometimes it will). Since that is a controversial new step for it to take, the intensity of its mistrust will be apparent.[63]

---

[61] [1987] E.C.R. 1747.
[62] *Rewe v. Bundesmonopolverwaltung* [1979] E.C.R. 649; *E.C. Commission v. Ireland* [1981] E.C.R. 1625; see generally, Wyatt and Dashwood, *European Community Law* (3rd ed., 1993), pp. 221–233.
[63] *cf.* Schricker [1994] GRUR Int. 586, arguing the need for some deregulation of German Unfair Competition Law, given its relentlessly protective drive.

Illustrations of this principle in operations which border upon intellectual property include the following:

(*Pall v. Dahlhausen*[64]). Dahlhausen produced blood filters in Italy using its Italian mark, "Micropore", and indicating registration of the mark there by the symbol (R). The mark was not registered in Germany and a competitor objected that the (R) might therefore mislead German consumers and competitors, contrary to the Unfair Competition Law of 1909, Article 3. Applying *"Cassis de Dijon"*, the Court found that removal of the (R) would be a disproportionate burden, compared to the very doubtful alleged dangers: consumers were more interested in qualities of the product than place of registration of the mark; and other traders could consult the public register.

(*Verband Sozialer Wettbewerb v. Clinique Laboratories*[65]). Estée Lauder marketed a line of cosmetics under the mark, "Clinique", save in Germany, where an unfair competition objection had been raised: the mark might lead an appreciable proportion of consumers into thinking that the product had medical properties. The firm, obliged to package the goods destined for the German market as "Linique", objected to the additional cost involved. The Court, applying *"Cassis de Dijon"*, laid prime emphasis on the fact that no objection to the use of "Clinique" arose under the laws of other Member States, and proceeded to hold that the German prohibition displayed unnecessary scruple for consumer protection and human health.

(*Industrie Diensten Groep v. Beele*[66]). Dutch Unfair Competition law would enjoin the slavish imitation of the appearance of a product (pipe housing for ships), where its distinctive shape was not dictated by functional considerations. Here, there being no discrimination between domestic and imported products, the operation of the law was considered justified in the interest of consumer protection and fair trading.

18–12   The same principle operates not only in respect of consumer confusion over a particular competitor's individual products or identifying marks, but also with names and get-up associated with groups of traders. It has been applied also to descriptions shared at a national or regional level—thus Article 30 overrode the restriction of "Sekt" and "Branntwein" to German products.[67] It has also been held to override a range of other protection

---

[64] [1990] E.C.R. 4827.
[65] [1994] E.C.R. 317.
[66] [1982] E.C.R. 707.
[67] *E.C. Commission v. Germany* [1975] E.C.R. 181 (applying Directive 70/50, Art. 2(3)); and equally the German reservation of the "Bockbeutel" winebottle to certain national products, when that shape had long been legitimately used for wine in other Member States: *Prantl* [1984] E.C.R. 1299; *cf.*, *Exportur* [1992] I E.C.R. 5529; Cornish [1992] Y.Eur.L. 635.

measures where interstate trade is affected. Cases cover rules preventing free gifts as part of sales,[68] rules constraining the advertising of price cuts,[69] and powers conferred on a monopoly corporation to exclude others from markets in attachment products without appeal.[70]

The *Cassis de Dijon* principle applies whether or not there is explicit or implicit discrimination operating across a border. The degree to which this might lead to curbs being placed on local unfair competition rules caused the Court at one stage of draw back. In *Keck and Mithouard*,[71] a French law making it unlawful to sell off goods below cost as "loss-leaders" was held to be properly applied to imports from Germany. The law was not overtly discriminatory and constituted a "mere selling arrangement." It can nonetheless be very difficult to determine what falls into this amorphous category.

> (*Fratelli Graffione v. Ditta Fransa*[72]) In Italy the plaintiff was ordered not to use "Cotonelle" as a mark for toilet paper and disposable handkerchiefs, lest the public think them made from cotton. It was able to continue to use the mark in France and Spain and parallel importing of the products into Italy then occurred. Here the Court of Justice left it to the national courts to estimate whether the danger of misleading the public was sufficiently serious to justify an injunction against free movement

> (*Vereinigte Familiapresse v. Heinrich Bauer Verlag*[73]) An Austrian law designed to protect local products forbade the inclusion of crossword competitions for prizes in magazines: its impact was mainly on major publishers in Germany. The Court of Justice held this not be a "mere selling arrangement" and left it for the national tribunal to assess whether, given the desirability of press diversity, the measure was proportionate and non-discriminatory.

In applying Article 30 to cases not within Article 36, the Court has often **18–13** evaluated the merits or otherwise of the national rule in its application to the particular case, making much of the equivalent position in other Member States. It has refused to wait for harmonisation measures, sensing doubtless that there are differences of national attitude here which run too deep for any early bridging. It emerges from the comparative readiness to set aside the interstate operation of over-enthusiastic unfair competition rules, that, give or take the odd false step,[74] the Court has been comparatively careful to respect the policy objectives of intellectual property.

---

[68] *Oosthoeks Uitgeversmaatschappij* [1982] E.C.R. 4575.
[69] *GE-Inno-BM* [1990] 1 E.C.R. 667.
[70] *Regie des Télégraphes v. GB-Inno-BM* [1991] 1 E.C.R. 5941.
[71] *Keck and Mithouard* [1995] 1 C.M.L.R. 101, ECJ; and see *Hünermund* [1994] GRUR Int. 170.
[72] [1997] E.T.M.R. 71.
[73] [1997] I E.C.R. 3689.
[74] Most famously, *"Hag I"*, para. 18–06, n. 26, above.

Its attitude is in line with the growing awareness of intellectual property as a necessary condition of industrial and commercial prosperity. That it should not change its approach needs to be stressed in the light of the somewhat ominous formulation of its judgment in *Deutsche Renault v. Audi*.[75] The validity of a German trade mark comprising a single foreign number ("Quattro" for cars) and its application to exclude imports of the "Espace Quadro", were both challenged as unnecessary extensions of trade mark rights. While insisting that it was for national law to set the bounds on both these characteristics of the industrial property, the Court nevertheless spelled out why it thought the law's application to these facts was not excessive. Must we, therefore, anticipate cases where the Court is provoked into finding excess? Down that road lies incessant second-guessing about the correctness of intellectual property laws, based presumably on intra-Community comparisons. The temptation to open up this difficult route should be resisted.

The Court of Justice's restraint so far has been aided by the willingness of Member States to make progress towards the ideal of unified Community rights, or at least harmonised national laws. That movement is indeed coursing as never before and for this the Court may have reason to be pleased. When it is beset with appeals to unravel the complexities of the new Regulations and Directives, it may experience some discomfort. But at least it has shared the wisdom of Brandeis J.,[76] that intellectual property is subject-matter too complex to be fashioned out of case law.

3. THE RULES OF COMPETITION

18–14 The Rome Treaty makes plain that, complementary though they undoubtedly are, free movement and the fostering of competition are separate objectives, secured by different legal means.[77] The licensing of intellectual property must comply with the Competition Rules, and those Rules have been applied not only to horizontal arrangements to divide markets but also to vertical arrangements which restrict competition in unnecessary ways. We have already considered their impact in relation to patent and know-how licences and noted the shifting attitudes which have changed the application of the Rules to that subject-matter.

Parallel importation between Member States is undoubtedly one matter which a restrictive agreement may seek to prevent. But the practice is central to the dominant objective of a unified single market and that is why the cases just reviewed have mainly been dealt with under free movement policies, notably Articles 30 to 36 on goods. By comparison the Competition Rules pose the difficulty that their application must be related to the

---

[75] [1993] 1 E.C.R. 6227.
[76] See the *INS* case 248 U.S. 215 (1918), para. 1–15, above.
[77] See paras 1–51—1–57, above.

impact of the particular trader or concerting group of traders in the relevant market.

The impact of the Competition Rules on internal movement[78] should, however, not be forgotten. For one thing, the Rules operate upon agreements and other actions which do not necessarily involve enforcement through litigation.[79] For another, breach of the Rules may result in investigations by the Commission, E.C. fines and the abnegation of contracts in national courts. Equally the Competition Rules affect both parallel importation and direct territorial licensing. The two policies lock together over the matter of parallel imports: it is not possible, through use of the exemption powers in Article 85(3), for the Commission to approve contractual terms aimed at keeping out the independent transporter of goods around the Community: Articles 30 to 36 settle the overriding importance of such activity and Article 85 is similarly interpreted.[80]

However, as the discussion of patent and know-how licensing has already **18–15** demonstrated,[81] agreements which carve out exclusive territories for manufacturers or their own distributors raise different issues, which are not affected by Articles 30 to 36. Exclusive licences of all intellectual property (including know-how) have to be considered, first to decide whether they create any inhibition on competition at all, and, if they do, whether there are countervailing benefits which would justify the Commission in granting an individual or a block exemption.

It is accepted that once an intellectual property right is exploited by means of a licence or some equivalent consensual agreement or arrangement, the effect on trade is properly a matter for competition law. Within the E.C., this is so whether the attack is upon an agreement or a concerted practice (Article 85) or goes to the acquisition and exercise of market power (Article 86). At both the national and the international level, the general issue is likewise conceded.[82]

Where, however, an intellectual property owner does nothing apart from **18–16** refusing licences to those who seek them, serious controversy arises, in which the Court of Justice is embroiled.

(*Volvo v. Veng*[83]: registered design for car spare parts). Volvo was registered proprietor in the United Kingdom of designs for the front

---

[78] For external effects, see paras 18–17 *et seq.*, below.

[79] See n. 7, above.

[80] *Nungesser v. E.C. Commission* [1982] E.C.R. 2015. For the position regarding imports from outside the E.E.A., see below, paras 18–17 *et seq.*

[81] See paras 7–32—7–40, above.

[82] For British competition law, see App. 1, below. In the TRIPS Agreement, Art. 40(2) allows for the adoption of measures against "licensing practices or conditions that may in particular cases constitute an abuse of intellectual property rights having an adverse effect on competition in the relevant market"; and note the provisions for consultation between states towards enforcement: Art. 40(3), (4).

[83] [1988] E.C.R. 6211.

wings of its Series 200 cars. It was entitled to assert those rights against an independent importer of front-wing panels from elsewhere in the E.C. The Court considered the relevant market to be that in Volvo spare parts. Volvo accordingly held a dominant position, which it could abuse. This it would do if it refused arbitrarily to supply spare parts to independent repairers, fixed prices for them at an unfair level or gave up supplying them when many cars of the model in question were still in circulation.[84]

(*RTE and ITP v. E.C. Commission* ("*Magill*"))[85]: TV programme listings). In Ireland and Northern Ireland, the public and commercial broadcasting authorities each refused to license newspapers and magazines to print week-long listings of their forthcoming programmes, thus obliging viewers to purchase their own separate periodicals. Under Irish law, as in the United Kingdom, the material was copyright. So Magill, a firm which began independently to publish the week's listings from all channels, was enjoined in the Irish High Court.

The Court of Justice found that the broadcasters were perforce monopoly suppliers of information about their programmes and inferred from the extent to which each authority's broadcasts were received in the other Member State that there was a market for a joint listings magazine which was being denied by the refusal to licence. Exercise of an exclusive right in this fashion could exceptionally constitute a breach of Article 86. These circumstances were within that exception. Each broadcaster was subjected to a compulsory obligation to supply programme content against payment of a reasonable royalty.[86]

This Article 86 control over monopolists who refuse to license their intellectual property is a weapon which could ultimately be turned upon any enterprise with a major intellectual property success on its hands as the basis for requiring a licence. But although the case law to date does not attempt to define what circumstances will give rise to this "exceptional" jurisdiction, two factors about "Magill" suggest that the intervention is justified only in unusual and special cases.

First, the right which underpinned the broadcasters' position was an extension of copyright to subject-matter (straightforward factual informa-

---

[84] These forewarnings reflected the considerable battles already fought in Europe between major car manufacturers and competition authorities over spare-parts exclusivity: for which, see para. 14–61, above.

[85] [1995] 4 C.M.L.R. 718, [1995] F.S.R. 530; and see *Biotrading & Financing v. Biohit* [1998] F.S.R. 109, CA; and see Korah [1997] I.P.J. 395; Greaves [1998] E.I.P.R. 370.

[86] In the U.K., this solution had already been introduced by statute: Broadcasting Act 1990, s. 176, following upon Report on the subject by the Monopolies and Mergers Commission (Cmnd. 9614, 1985). Jurisdiction under the Act is given to the Copyright Tribunal: see *News Group v. ITP* [1993] R.P.C. 173; Laddie *et al.*, paras 14.46–14.48.

tion) which many Member States would consider not to justify intellectual property protection in the first place. In a period when intellectual property rights are being rapidly expanded, it must be wise for competition authorities to retain some ultimate means of curbing their range in egregious cases which, in the scramble to satisfy industrial lobbies, legislatures may not have sufficiently cogitated.

The other is that in *Magill*, the power over the listings market was an ancillary product of the entire system of broadcasting control. Once that primary market becomes itself competitive (as seems inevitable with the expansion of scope made possible by digital technology) the broadcasters will clamour to have their schedules publicised wherever possible. The decision does not stress sufficiently the barrier to entry in the "pre-market" which was the cause of unjustifiably monopolistic behaviour in the "after-market". An adequate emphasis upon this factor would help to identify what it was that made the dominant actors' refusal to license an abuse of their position.

Certainly a British Court has insisted that the *Volvo v. Veng* principle defines the norms in intellectual property owner who refuses to grant licences on reasonable terms is not therefore in breach of Article 86; there must be additional monopolistic behaviour of an unacceptable kind, if the *Magill* exception is to prevail.[87]

4. PARALLEL IMPORTATION FROM OUTSIDE THE EEA[88]

The rapidly changing conditions of world trade have thrown countries into **18–17** a quandary about the potential of parallel importation, when considered on a global scale. The European Community, its Member States and associated countries of the EEA, are affected by this as much as others. Large industrial producers which are likely to be placing their products on advanced and developing markets at differentiated prices are pressing for general barriers which will allow the higher price levels to be maintained. Consumers in those higher priced markets are likely to become suspicious when they find that the same article (or one virtually the same) can be bought more cheaply abroad. There is no easy resolution of the problem.

At various stages this book has examined the extent to which intellectual property rights may be drawn in service to create barriers to parallel movement. It has been argued that the justification for deploying them in this way varies with the fundamental purpose of the right. In particular, rights in forms or expressions of ideas—patents, copyright, designs and so forth—are granted essentially as a stimulus to their creation and exploita-

---

[87] *Philips Electronics v. Ingman.*
[88] See Abbey [1992] ECL Rev. 231; Stragier [1993] ECL Rev. 30; Prändl [1993] ECL Rev. 43; Diem [1994] ECL Rev. 263; Rasmussen [1995] E.I.P.R. 174; Abbott and Verkade [1998] B.I.E. 111; Cornish [1998] E.I.P.R. 172.

tion. That incentive may be heightened if price differentials between geographical markets can be maintained and the potential profitability of each can thus be extracted.[89] In these cases, there is a good argument for extending the right to cover parallel importation from cheaper markets (if necessary, upon condition that notice of the limitation is given).[90]

18–18   The approach in trade mark law is much more controversial, since marks are protected primarily as symbols for ascertaining the origin of products and to some extent for guaranteeing their qualities when these are associated in the public mind with their source. That moderate position may suggest that, where the mark-bearing goods of an enterprise or group differ in quality between one market and another, it may be reasonable to use trade mark rights to protect each market from parallel importation of the goods from the other. On the other hand, it would not be reasonable to do that when the goods are in no wise different and the mark exactly performs its origin-cum-quality function to the extent that policy demands. That, for instance, is the position presently prevailing in the law of the United States.

18–19   However, those who argue for a general measure against parallel importing in world trade, demand that marks be recognised as primary marketing tools and that therefore the investment in them be accorded much more embracing legal protection. On this view (which generally proclaims itself to be "modern"), trade mark rights should be automatically available to prevent the movement of legitimate goods by a parallel importer into markets for which they are not intended. As we have already seen, the European Court of Justice treats the legal question as having been largely settled by the terms of the First Harmonisation Directive, Article 7 and the Community Trade Mark Regulation, Article 12. These, it has been held, make it necessary to imply into the statement of the internal exhaustion rule that Member States may not maintain, as part of their own law, a rule of world-wide exhaustion. The Court believes that the political choice in favour using trade marks, both CTMs and national rights, as buttresses of a "fortress" EEA, has been expressed with sufficient clarity by E.C. legislation. Whether that belief will admit of exceptions as matters of E.U. law has yet to be seen; at least the precedent for admitting judge-made exceptions in the law pertaining to the internal market is well-established. The hope has already been expressed that the Court will consider what room there is for modifying an apparently impacable rule of non-exhaustion at the EAA borders.

---

[89] Even so, one must speak conditionally: price differentials come about through such external causes as currency shifts, and are scarcely something on which an investor or researcher counts in advance.

[90] If a product is manufactured outside the EEA (and, *e.g.* marked there), but then sold to an independent trader inside the EEA, it must thereafter be left free to circulate in the whole market: *Phytheron v. Jean Bourdon* [1997] E.T.M.R. 211, ECJ; *cf. Re Tylosin* [1977] 1 C.M.L.R. 460; and see *Re Patented Bandaging Material* [1988] 2 C.M.L.R. 359.

At this point, let us pursue a different line of observation. In legal terms, **18–20** it is not just from an intellectual property law perspective that the matter has to be approached. There is also the question of the impact of the Rules of Competition. It has long been accepted that, for instance, agreements between manufacturers which divide the external market from the Community market can infringe Article 85. *CBS U.K. v. EMI Records*,[91] dealt with the separation of the mark "Columbia" for records. Achieved in 1922, this gave the mark in E.C. countries to EMI, and in the Americas to CBS. National trade mark law in the United Kingdom, Denmark and West Germany could be used by EMI to prevent imports of CBS "Columbia" records by a CBS subsidiary and an independent importer, and the free movement of goods policy could have no application for the reason that it is stated to operate only upon trade between Member States. But the Court of Justice went on to warn that if the trade mark barrier to entry to any part of the Common Market was "the subject, the means, or the consequence of a restrictive practice", Article 85 could be breached; and this might occur if a formally abandoned agreement nonetheless continues to have practical effect. But if the external manufacturer has other marks which he could use, then it is permissible to require him to change the labelling.[92]

It has become clear that Article 85 can apply to vertical agreements down **18–21** the chain of distribution which affect parallel importation. In *Javico v. Yves Saint-Laurent*,[93] the Court of Justice dealt with an importation of "YSL" products from East Europe, which had been sold there under an express condition that the purchaser was to resell only in Russia and the Ukraine. While this contractual prohibition was not necessarily prohibited under Article 85, it would be in breach in any case where

> "Community market in the products in question is characterised by an oligopolistic structure or by an appreciable difference between the prices charged for the contractual product within the Community and those charged outside the Community and where, in view of the position occupied by the supplier of the products at issue and the extent of the supplier's production and sales in the Member States, the prohibition entails the risk that it might have an appreciable effect on the patterns of trade between Member States such as to undermine attainment of the objectives of the common market."

With leading brands of luxury goods, high prices in Community markets tend to be buttressed by selective distribution systems, and these may create the conditions for breach of Article 85 under the *Javico* test. Equally the principle could be applied to prohibitions on the re-sale of products

---

[91] [1976] E.C.R. 811; para. 1–56, above.
[92] *ibid.*, Judgment, paras 26–34. See also *Ideal Standard* (n. 29, above), Judgment, para. 59.
[93] [1998] I E.C.R. 1983.

protected by patents, copyright and other intellectual property.[94] As this book has been at pains to stress, attitudes towards the practice of parallel importation continue to be as divided as ever and no lasting resolution can be expected. *Javico* exhibits an underlying hostility towards restrictions on the practice, which is the opposite of the non-exhaustion policy set for trade marks by *Silhouette*. Which view is in the end to prevail? If a dominant firm avoids an Article 85 breach by not imposing an express ban on imports from outside the EEA into the Area, is the implication that it is consenting to the movement of the goods? Is it therefore conceding a licence which prevents it from afterwards relying on the trade mark barrier accepted in *Silhouette*? Or must a licence to import be in express terms before it is effective? Can the manufacturer rely on his trade mark to prevent entry while at the same time running no risk of breaking the Rules of Competition?

18–22 The dilemma is acute and the Court of Justice will undoubtedly be called upon to resolve it. However, it is only one more instance of the great difficulty with the very idea of intellectual property: in broad terms there is a good case for its various instances in the need for particular incentives and protection against unfair imitation. But arguments justifying the boundaries between protection and freedom to engage in competition are difficult to state convincingly. The law's actual limits often reflect political and social allegiances of an imprecise kind. When it comes to detail the present intellectual property systems have much about them that is arbitrary. Accordingly, they are with us for better, for worse. The luckiest rightowners emerge very much the richer, the mass of users and consumers are left rather the poorer, but with some enhancement of their opportunities. We do best by continuing to recognise a basic presumption in favour of competition. To it intellectual property operates as an exception which always needs a sufficient justification.

---

[94] In this connection, one should recall not only the *Nungesser* case (above, para. 7–34), but also the decisions of the Commission concerning territorial limits in patent licences for countries outside the E.C.: *Raymond/Nagoya* [1972] C.M.L.R. D45; *Kabelmetall/Luchaire* [1975] 2 C.M.L.R. D40. See paras 7–32 *et seq.*

APPENDICES

CONTROL OF MONOPOLIES AND RESTRICTIVE PRACTICES: NOTE ON INSTITUTIONS AND SOME SUBSTANTIVE RULES

The purpose of this Appendix, as explained in Chapter 1, is to give a brief **A1–01** introduction to certain aspects of the competition laws of the E.C. and the United Kingdom which have not found a place in the main text. The relation between intellectual property rights and E.C. policies has assumed such significance that it has already been dealt with at various points.[1] It remains to say something about the institutional framework for operating the E.C. rules. By contrast, the rather pragmatic British system of control has not given rise to the same degree of tension. So it has been left to this note to indicate the legal reasons for this. The discussion of the British legislation concerning restrictive practices in particular is concerned with substance rather than procedure.

1. E.C. INSTITUTIONS FOR IMPLEMENTING COMPETITION POLICY[2]

As we have seen, the Rome Treaty's Rules of Competition hinge on two **A1–02** complementary articles: Article 85 is directed against agreements and equivalent practices which prevent, restrict or distort competition; Article 86 against abuse of a dominant position; and in each case it is the effect on trade between Member States which is to be considered. The institutions which decide whether a particular case is to be condemned may have to consider it under both Articles: there is no division of authority such as is found in the United Kingdom system[3]; nor are the two Articles mutually exclusive—a practice may offend both.

The principal authority charged with securing observation of the Rules of Competition is the E.C. Commission, acting through its Competition Directorate. But the Articles have direct effect in the sense that the rights

---

[1] See paras 1–48—1–58, 6–15, 6–16, 7–36 et seq., 12–59—12–62, 18–01 et seq., above.
[2] See generally Bellamy and Child, *Common Market Law of Competition* (4th ed., 1993): Merkin (ed.) *Encyclopedia of Competition Law.*
[3] See para. A1–05, below.

of private citizens in Member States are affected by them without the need for further legislation. Accordingly, national courts may be obliged to consider their effect when deciding private suits. An agreement may be held void as restrictive of competition in the Common Market[4]; and action to enforce intellectual property (or other) rights may be lost because the rights are being asserted in pursuance of a restrictive practice or in abuse of a dominant position.[5]

(1) The E.C. Commission

A1–03 The following features mark the executive role of the Commission:

(1) It is armed with considerable powers of investigation into circumstances where it suspects an infringement of either Article.[6] These include powers of entry to examine records and to ask for immediate explanations.

(2) When the Commission does find an infringement of either Article it can require the parties to put an end to it, or to undertake to do so. And for an intentional or negligent infringement it can impose a fine of up to one million units of account or 10 per cent of an undertaking's turnover, whichever is the greater.[7]

(3) In order to induce the submission of information to it voluntarily, there is a system (prescribed in Council Regulation 17 of 1962) for notifying agreements, etc., either for negative clearance (that is a declaration that an agreement is not caught by Article 85(1)) or for exemption under Article 85(3). Where it is exemption that is sought, notification carries protection from being fined for implementing the agreement during the interim period (which frequently is substantial)[8]; only if the Commission takes the positive step of indicating, after a preliminary examination, that it considers the agreement to infringe, does this protection cease to operate.[9] Some agreements of relatively minor significance do not even require notification in order to attract the benefits that attach to that step. These include two-party agreements under which an assignee or user of industrial property rights or manufacturing know-how is bound by restrictions, and two-party agreements solely for joint research and development.[10]

(4) The task of granting individual exemption under Article 85(3) to agreements, etc., which contain restrictions indispensable in securing

---

[4] Rome Treaty, Art. 85(2).
[5] Bellamy and Child, Chap. 10; Merkin, paras 1–020 *et seq.*
[6] See generally Bellamy and Child, Chaps 11, 12.
[7] See Bellamy and Child, paras 62 *et seq.*, especially the Table of Fines Imposed.
[8] Regulation 17/62, Arts 2, 4, 5, 15(5), (6); Bellamy and Child, Chap. 11.
[9] *Bronbemaling v. Heidemaatschappij Beheer* (para. 7–32, n. 96, above) is an example of this sort of preliminary decision.
[10] See Regulation 17/62, Arts 4(2), 5(2).

countervailing benefits, is reserved exclusively to the Commission. This power is fundamental to the whole conception of Community competition policy.[11] Enterprises which are prepared to play the game may consult the Commission before ever entering their agreements, or they may notify an agreement already reached and then negotiate the removal or modification of clauses as a precondition to exemption. Exemption is always for a defined period, though it may be renewed in the light of conditions prevailing at the later time.[12]

(5) By its Regulation 19 of 1965, the Council of Ministers gave the Commission power to deal with exemptions on a group basis by specifying in regulations different categories of agreement which would qualify *en bloc*. The Block Exemptions for Technology Transfer and for Franchising Agreements fall under this power.

(2) National Courts

The question of infringement of either Article may well be raised in **A1–04** national Court proceedings, before the Commission has had time to rule upon the agreement or practice in question. If the agreement is "old" and has been duly notified to the Commission it is to be treated by national courts as valid until the Commission decides otherwise. But "new" agreements are not provisionally valid in this sense.[13] This rule was laid down by the European Court of Justice in order to deal with the considerable uncertainties that existed during the early stages of introducing the competition policy. If it does not give preliminary protection, the national Court must itself consider the question of infringement and, to this end, it may be obliged to analyse the structure and operation of the relevant market,[14] a task which cannot be easy for non-specialist tribunals. Behind these basic rules lie many uncertainties of considerable practical importance.

---

[11] *Davidson Rubber* [1972] F.S.R. 451 and *Raymond/Nagoya* (para. 7–32, n. 96, above) are examples.

[12] See generally Regulation 17/62, Arts 6–9, Bellamy and Child, Chap 3. Normally the period of exemption can run only from the date when the agreement is put into a form acceptable to the Commission.

[13] *Brasserie de Haecht v. Wilkin* (No. 2) [1973] E.C.R. 77. "Old" agreements were those in existence on March 13, 1962. "Pre-accession" agreements, which come within the Rules of Competition only by virtue of the accession of a state to the Rome Treaty, are probably to be treated as "old" agreements here.

[14] *Belgische Radio en Televisie v. SABAM* [1974] E.C.R. 51. The parts of an agreement that are absolutely void under Art. 85(2) may be severable; the rest of the contract will then remain enforceable: see *Chemidus Wavin v. S.p.r.l. Transformation* [1977] F.S.R. 181, CA.

2. UNITED KINGDOM COMPETITION LAW

(1) The Changing Law

A1–05 Since 1948, the United Kingdom has developed its own competition law, occupying (for the United Kingdom) the same legal territory as the Rules of Competition under the E.U. Treaty. United Kingdom competition law has been contained in a set of statutes, comprising latterly the Fair Trading Act 1973, the Restrictive Trade Practices Act 1976, the Resale Prices Act 1976 and the Competition Act 1980. The first of these, the Fair Trading Act, provides both for the Office of Fair Trading and the Monopolies and Mergers Commission and continues for the most part in force, the latter institution being broadened and renamed as the Competition Commission.[15] The other Acts are now to be replaced by the Competition Act 1998, which will take effect in 2000. A major aim of this legislation is to provide for the competitiveness of the British market in terms parallel to E.U. competition law. Issues which affect trade between Member States of the E.U. will be left to the European Commission, the British authorities being concerned with purely national trade.

Until the Competition Act 1998, United Kingdom competition law had an impact on the practices of intellectual property owners in the following main ways.

A1–06   (i) Under the Restrictive Trade Practices Act 1976, agreements and the like between suppliers of goods and services, under which at least two of them accepted restrictions on their freedom to trade, were registrable. The main impact was on horizontal agreements between competitors at the same level of trade. If not justifiable, these agreements could be held to be contrary to the public interest, bringing various consequential remedies in train. Patent and other intellectual property licences, however, were excepted, if only one party (normally the licensee) undertook restrictions, and so were agreements where two (but no more than two) parties undertook certain restrictions. The extent of these exceptions was ill-defined and their objectives somewhat obscure.

(ii) Under the Fair Trading Act 1973, normally upon a reference by the Director-General of Fair Trading, the Monopolies and Mergers Commission would report on whether the public interest was affected by a "monopoly situation," and upon an adverse report the Minister would take action, if necessary by statutory order, to secure a remedy. In addition, the Competition Act 1980 gave power to the Director-General to intervene against "anti-competitive practices,"

---

[15] For this body, see the Competition Act 1998, s. 45.

in particular, where they operated vertically down the chain of distribution (exclusive distribution, etc.). Where a patent placed its owner in a position to dominate a market, the refusal to follow general pricing practice in the industry could be treated as wrongful, though this was extreme and happened only on one contentious occasion.[16]

(iii) The Resale Prices Act 1976, in outlawing the practice of minimum resale price agreements, specifically provided that patent licences could not in most circumstances be used to justify the practice.

(2) Competition Act 1998

The Competition Act 1998 introduces provisions on restrictive agreements, **A1–07** arrangements and concerted practices in terms equivalent to Article 85 of the E.U. Treaty[17] and provisions on abuse of dominant position equivalent to Article 86.[18] The executive functions, equivalent to those of D.G. IV of the European Commission, are given to the Director-General of Fair Trading. He has extensive (indeed draconian) powers of investigation and, on finding a breach, may require alteration of agreements, termination of restrictive practices and abuses of dominant position, and the payment of fines.[19] For restrictive agreements, the Director-General also has powers to grant clearances, individual exemptions and block exemptions.[20] Where there is an E.C. block exemption, such as exist for technology transfer, joint ventures, research and development and specialisation agreements, its terms will be treated as applicable to the internal British market.[21] From the Directior-General's decisions over agreements and abusive practices, an appeal will lie to a Competition Commission Appeal Tribunal and from there, on a question of law, to the Court of Appeal.[22]

(3) Consequences of breach

Agreements which offend these provisions are void.[23] It must be assumed **A1–08** that this effect operates between the parties and so can be pleaded in defence to an action alleging their breach. More generally, the principles applicable to Article 85 and 86, notably as developed by the E.C.J., are to apply equally to the new British provisions. However, what the Competition

---

[16] Tranquillisers Report, H.C. 197, 1973.
[17] Competition Act 1998, Part I, Chap. I.
[18] Part I, Chap. II.
[19] Part I, Chap. IV.
[20] ss. 4–16.
[21] s. 10.
[22] Part I, Chap. IV.
[23] Note that the 1998 Act is to abolish the two "abuse of monopoly" provisions which survived in the Patents Act 1977, s. 44 ("tie-ins") and s. 45 ("tie-ups after expiry); for which see paras 7–27, 7–31, above.

Act does not introduce is a parallel principle requiring the free movement of goods, which has been one of the foundations of the Treaty of Rome. This could mean that there is now a doctrine of exhaustion of intellectual property rights in United Kingdom competition law which operates on parallel principles to that worked out for trade between Member States by the Court of Justice. But it must be doubtful whether the United Kingdom law goes so far. Be that as it may, where a "closed" restrictive agreement is in operation which is designed to prevent the parallel movement of goods from one part of the United Kingdom to another, this must be void, as incontrovertibly offending the prohibition on such agreements.[24]

---

[24] For "closed" and "open" agreements granting exclusive territorial licences of intellectual property, see *Nungesser v. E.C. Commission* [1982] E.C.R. 2015; and for the application of the principle to agreements not to import from outside the E.E.A., *EMI v. CBS UK* [1976] E.C.R. 811; *Javico v. Yves Saint Laurent* [1998] I E.C.R. 1983, above, para. 18–21.

JOINT INTERESTS IN MARKS, NAMES AND SYMBOLS

As the main text illustrates, there are words and symbols which groups of **A2–01** independent traders, rivals amongst themselves, nevertheless all use to distinguish their products from those of outside competitors.[1] Tradition, fashion or advertising may impart great drawing power to these signs. They cover a whole spectrum of types, of which it is useful to isolate the following examples:

> **Type 1: Geographical names from products which acquire their particular qualities from being produced in the place designated ("appellations of origin", "geographical denominations of source").** This category is largely confined to wines ("Champagne" "Sherry"), though other examples occasionally arise ("Roquefort" cheese, produced in caves of a particular natural formation). The special cachet of these denominations leads to the practice (particularly in countries other than that of production) of selling generally similar products with associative tags of the "Sherry-type", "British sherry" variety; or even to the adoption of the basic name without qualification.[2]

> **Type 2: Geographical names for products whose qualities are not particularly associated with the place designated (sometimes distinguished from the previous category as "indications of source").** A wider range of food, drink and other products are sold under the name of a town or region with which they have become associated, even

---

[1] See esp. paras 16–36—16–40, above.

[2] International agreements on the subject stretch back to one of the Madrid Arrangements of 1891, entered into by a few parties to the Paris Convention. In 1958, an Agreement for the Protection of Appellations of Origin and their International Registration was signed in Lisbon, but has not attracted wide support. There has, however, been increasing activity on the subject within the E.C., the present results of which are mentioned below (para. A2–04). On the international scene, there have been accords between countries and regional groups concerning the naming of various products. In TRIPS, Member States undertake in general terms to protect geographical indications in a narrow sense (Art. 22), an obligation which is made more specific in the case of wines and spirits (Art. 23). There is also an undertaking to negotiate about the strengthening of Art. 22, which is subject to elaborate conditions (Art. 24). The subject remains divisive: See Knaak in Beier and Schricker, 117; Lackert [1998] Aug. TM Wld 22.

though this association depends on local skills rather than on geographical peculiarities.

Type 3: Names or symbols associating goods with production in a particular country or region. Most obviously the name of a country as a whole, or of a region, may influence a customer's choice; and other words or symbols may suggest similar associations: tartan with Scotland, Eiffel Tower with Paris, etc.[3]

Type 4: Non-geographical names or symbols for products of a particular composition or quality. Hallmarks for metals are one instance[4]; "advocaat" for a concoction of brandwijn, eggs and sugar is another.

Type 5: Name or symbol of a trade association or group. A well-known example is the "Woolmark". The motive force of such a group will be the mutual self-interest of members. The extent to which they perceive their joint goodwill in the name or symbol to be a substantial weapon in the battle against outside competition will vary; so will their readiness to allow newcomers also to use it.

Type 6: Mark of an agency not directly connected with trading interests which is used to signify that goods have met a standard. This may be more or less specific. Design Council awards, for instance, recognise good design in British products of all kinds. BSIs (standards of the British Standards Institution) are much more precise.

There are three important ways in which words and symbols of these types may be legally protected against misappropriation by a trader who is not entitled to use them. These are discussed in the following paragraphs.

1. Criminal Proceedings

A2–02 The Trade Descriptions Act 1968[5] lays down a number of offences relating to misstatements about goods which are germane to the kinds of mark under consideration. Section 1 creates criminal liability for applying a false trade description, or selling goods to which such a description has been applied.[6] A false trade description may concern: (1) quantity, size or gauge; (2) method, place or date of manufacture, production, processing or reconditioning; (3) composition; (4) fitness for purpose, strength, perfor-

---

[3] For an example of the sort of conflict which may arise with the interest of an individual trader, see *"Welsh Lady" T.M.* [1964] R.P.C. 459.
[4] See also para. 15–04, n. 8, above.
[5] See also paras 2–19—2–22, above.
[6] This offence imposes strict liability, though there are important defences contained in Trade Descriptions Act 1968, ss. 23, 24; for which, see, *e.g.* Lowe and Woodroffe, *Consumer Law and Practice* (4th ed., 1995), pp. 243–249.

mance, behaviour or accuracy; (5) other physical characteristics; (6) testing by any person and its results; (7) approval by a person or conformity with a type approved by any person; (8) person by whom manufactured, produced, processed or recondition; (9) other history.[7] The somewhat narrower provisions on false statements relating to services[8] expressly include the examination, approval or evaluation by any person of services, accommodation or facilities provided in the course of trade or business. The range of these offences is extended by a number of definitional provisions,[9] and false statements in advertising are covered.[10]

Other more specific legislation may also be in point. Thus the Food Safety Act 1990 makes it an offence to display a label or publish an advertisement which falsely describes the food, or is calculated to mislead as to its nature, substance or quality.[11] Where the safety, life or health is at risk, the procedures of Part II of the Consumer Protection Act 1987,[12] may be brought into play. These depend upon the Secretary of State making an order covering the type of goods in question. *Inter alia* these orders may require a type of goods to meet a prescribed safety standard, such as one laid down by the British Standards Institution (BSI). It then becomes an offence to deal in goods which do not meet the standard.[13]

In general, these criminal statutes do not directly prescribe any statutory duty for breach of which civil proceedings may be instituted.[14] The possibility of seeking compensation in the criminal proceedings and of suing under the general law of tort should, however, be recalled.[15]

2. CIVIL PROCEEDINGS AT COMMON LAW

It will be appreciated, from the discussion of passing off in the text, that a **A2–03** right of action lies in any case of the above types where traders can show a joint reputation that is being misleadingly adopted by a stranger. The

---

[7] Trade Descriptions Act 1968, s. 2(1), there being special provisions relating to animals, plants and seeds, and food and drugs. Examples include labelling a Danish turkey, "Norfolk King Turkey" (*Beckett v. Kingston* [1970] 1 K.B. 606); labelling wine not from Portugal or Madeira, respectively "port" or "madeira" (Anglo-Portuguese Commercial Treaty Acts, 1914, 1916).

[8] Trade Descriptions Act 1968, s. 14(1): the offence must be committed knowingly or recklessly: *Wings v. Ellis* [1984] 3 All E.R. 577. See further, Lowe and Woodroffe, pp. 235–242.

[9] See especially Trade Descriptions Act 1968, ss. 3, 14(2), (3).

[10] For goods, by *ibid.*, s. 5; for services by the general terms of s. 14(1). Note the special defence in s. 25.

[11] Food Safety Act 1990, ss. 13 *et seq.*

[12] See also General Product Safety Regulations 1994, S.I. 1994 No. 2328. See generally, Lowe and Woodroffe, Chap. 14.

[13] Consumer Protection Act 1987, s. 2.

[14] See para. 2–22, above. The Consumer Protection Act, however, is the exception, giving a right of action to any person "affected by" failure to perform an obligation (such as carrying out a test) prescribed under its machinery. A certifying body or competitor might claim to be a person "affected": the issue has not been tested.

[15] See paras 2–12—2–18, above.

"Champagne" and "Sherry" cases were of Type 1; but the "Advocaat" decision, with its somewhat broadening dicta on the scope of passing off, was a case of Type 3.[16] Those dicta might now allow a Court to give civil protection to a certifying agency of Type 5 but only in an appropriate case.[17]

3. E.C. REGULATIONS

A2–04 The E.C. has progressively extended Community-wide provisions which aim to protect specific geographical designations on a uniform basis. These are limited as to product type, and in each case depend upon listing, under one of three Regulations:

(1) geographical designations of origin for wines[18];
(2) geographical designations of origin for spirits[19];
(3) geographical designations of origin (Type 1) and geographical indications (Type 2) for other agricultural products and foodstuffs.[20]

In the third, most general, case, listing is secured through the auspices of the national government concerned,[21] which is also charged with inspecting products bearing the name to ensure that they meet the standards set in the specification of the registration. A person entitled to use the indication may prevent its direct or indirect commercial use on all products comparable to those for which it is registered, as for instance in the "Elderflower Champagne" case in England.[22] There is thus no wide right against dilution onto other products.

This stepwise intervention is French in style and contrasts with a German preference for a general provision against the confusing use of such

---

[16] See para. 16–41, above. "Swiss Chalet" goes a remarkable way down this route: see para. 16–38, above.

[17] The Court of Appeal scornfully dismissed the attempt by the Italian association of Parma Ham produces to establish passing off where a chain-store refused to use certified Italian tradesmen to carve the ham: *Consorzio del Prosciutto di Parma v. Mark & Spencer* [1991] R.P.C. 351.

[18] Regulation 2392/89, Art. 40.

[19] Regulation 1576/89, Annex II, lists the protected names; the spirit in question must have acquired its character and definitive qualities in the place named.

[20] Regulations 2081/92; 1107/96; not extending to the slicing and packaging requirements for Parma Ham, which the producers' association have been trying to secure as a distribution restraint: *Consorzio del Prosciutto di Parma v. Asda Stores* [1999] F.S.R. 563, CA; *cf.* n. 17, above. For the definitions of the products and the names covered, see Arts 1(1), 2(2), Annex II; Rome Treaty, Annex 1. In this category the Regulation contemplates the grant of co-existent rights in the name and a trade mark, but only where there is no conflict with a prior right in the one or the other. See *Consorzio per Formaggio Gorgonzola v. Champignon Hofmeister* [1999] E.T.M.R. 454; *Denmark v. Commission, ibid.,* 478 (long use of "Feta" for non-Greek cheese); Schwab [1995] E.I.P.R. 242.

[21] In the U.K., the Ministry of Agriculture is responsible.

[22] *Taittinger v. Allbev* [1993] F.S.R. 699, CA.

indications as amounts to unfair competition.[23] By being specific, it can be unequivocal. It also allows a line to be drawn fairly precisely between cases of local marks deserving protection (Types 1 and 2) and general marks or symbols with some national or semi-national connotation which, as between E.C. States, may have an undesirably discriminatory effect (Type 3).

The latter have been regarded as indirect inhibitions on free movement under Article 30 of the Rome Treaty, for which there is unlikely to be sufficient justification. This the European Court of Justice has forbidden in the context of national legislation giving exclusive rights in a word or a packaging shape to producers in the country concerned or a large part of it: as with "Sekt" and "Weinbrand" for German wine and spirits,[24] or the Bocksbeutel bottle for Franconian wine, in circumstances where wine in other Community countries had traditionally been marketed in similar bottles.[25]

By contrast, the Court has upheld French legislation which outlawed the sale in France of French-made "Turron de Alicante", a sweet associated with the Spanish town, even though it had no quality with a particular geographical connection.[26] It was prepared to characterise this sort of marking as "industrial and commercial property" within Article 36 of the Rome Treaty, while still, it seems, treating the Bocksbeutel differently.[27] The Court is obliged to assess for itself whether the joint interest justifies its special status by considering the number of enterprises claiming to share in the goodwill, the size of the area concerned and the extent to which traders from other parts of the E.C. will have their traditional trading practices disturbed if exclusivity is allowed to prevail against them.

4. CERTIFICATION AND COLLECTIVE TRADE MARKS

There are two special types of registration which cover cases distinct from **A2–05** registration by particular applicants in relation to their own goods and services. *Certification marks* are given to those who do not themselves trade but who certify that goods (or services) satisfy prescribed standards concerning origin, material, mode of manufacture, quality, accuracy, or

---

[23] For the view, expressed with a fervour rare among the disinterested, that this sectoral creep is at the least misguided, see Beier and Knaak (1994) 25 I.I.C. 1. The authors also advance the remarkable argument that only general Community legislation is consistent with the ECJ's recognition of indications of source as industrial property within the permitted exceptions to the Rome Treaty, Art. 36.

[24] *E.C. Commission v. Germany* [1975] E.C.R. 184 (denounced by Beier in Cohen Jehoram (ed.) *Protection of Geographical Denominations of Goods and Services* (1980) p. 18).

[25] *Prantl* [1984] E.C.R. 1299.

[26] [1992] 1 E.C.R. 5529; legal protection arose from a Treaty between Spain and France, which was here taken as the source of legitimacy; see Cornish [1993] Y. Eur. L. 635. *cf.* also, *Delhaize v. Promalvin* [1992] 1 E.C.R. 3669 ("Rioja" as a geographical denomination for wine).

[27] See Oliver, *Free Movement of Goods in the European Community* (3rd ed., 1995) pp. 291–300, esp. p. 296.

other characteristic.[28] Often the proprietor is an association established by those with commercial interests in the mark. These marks are particularly appropriate for activities of Type 6, but cases under any of the other Types could become the subject of certification by an appropriate body. "Stilton" is a well-known example, the mark being available to all who manufacture cheese to defined standards within a given area.[29] Certification marks have long been a special part of the British registration system.

A2–06   *Collective marks* are new to the British Register,[30] though they are well-known in other European countries. Community trade marks may be collective.[31] They are given to an association of traders, not in order to indicate anything about quality, but in order to show that a member belongs to the association. They belong to Type 5, though the association may be formed mainly to protect designations of Types 1 to 4.

A2–07   Both certification and collective marks will be accepted only if the Registry is satisfied that they provide appropriate delineations of their purpose. They must be open to no objection, either on the absolute or the relative grounds applying to trade marks in general. Correspondingly, once they are registered the rights are the same as those given to individual marks.

---

[28] See TMA 1994, s. 50, Sched. 2. See also Dawson, *Certification Trade Marks* (1988).
[29] Which by historical anomaly does not include the town of Stilton itself: *"Stilton" T.M.* [1967] R.P.C. 173.
[30] TMA 1994, s. 49, Sched. 1.
[31] No provision is made for Community certification marks.

APPENDIX 3

PROTECTION OF PLANT VARIETIES

The scientific breeding of new plant varieties raises ecological issues that **A3–01** rank in difficulty beside the genetic engineering of animal tissue. Nonetheless it is now carried on by important commercial organisations which have secured legal protection for their substantial capital investment. In the United States the creation of a legislative shield began as long ago as 1930, when plant patents became available for a-sexually reproducing varieties.[1] In the United Kingdom, the Plant Varieties and Seeds Act 1964 introduced an elaborate form of intellectual property right designed to fit the particular case. This was part of a movement in various West European countries which also led to the establishment of the UPOV Convention mentioned below.[2] In the wake of revisions to the UPOV Convention in 1991,[3] admitting intergovernmental organisations such as the European Union, a unified Community Plant Variety Right (PVR) has been created.[4]

1. A SPECIAL SYSTEM

The 1964 Act provides for the grant of a full monopoly right, not **A3–02** dependent upon proof of copying, to breeders or discoverers of plant varieties.[5] It is not part of the patent system: the grant of rights is made by the Plant Variety Rights Office which has its own Controller.[6] This is in contrast with the United States and some West European countries. As succeeding paragraphs will suggest, there are a number of basic points at

---

[1] See 35 U.S.C., para. 161. Sexually reproducing varieties are now covered by the Plant Variety Protection Act 1970 (U.S.).
[2] For further discussion see Dworkin [1983] E.I.P.R. 270; and Jouffray [1984] E.I.P.R. 283.
[3] See Greengrass [1991] E.I.P.R. 466.
[4] See n. 8 below. There has been no equivalent Directive on the harmonisation of national laws.
[5] Plant Varieties and Seeds Act 1964, s 2(2), (4). As far as concerns priorities, the basic principle is that the first to apply has the better right; but there are arrangements to accord 12 months' priority to applications in countries of the Convention (see next note) in certain circumstances: Sched. 2, Pt 1.
[6] Plant Varieties and Seeds Act 1964, s. 1(2), Pt 2. The responsible department so far as concerns England and Wales is the Ministry of Agriculture. Decisions of the Controller are subject to appeal to the Plant Variety Rights Tribunal (s. 10, Sched. 4). The Plant Breeders Rights Regulations 1969 provide that any person with a substantial interest may intervene in applications for rights and most other proceedings.

which simple adherence to the patent model is unsatisfactory, and it is not easy to judge whether it is better to take that model, varying it where necessary, or to start afresh, in establishing protection for plant varieties. Advocates of the former approach tend to be strong protagonists of effective international protection who see the political advantages of bringing plant variety rights within the structure of the Paris Convention network, and who object to the limited scope of the current schemes. As the matter has so far developed, there has been an international convention in the field since 1961, when national legislation was beginning to spread,[7] but this convention is separately administered, being merely associated with WIPO.

Contemporaneously with the creation of a Community Trade Mark comes the Community PVR.[8] It too provides an alternative route to protection and gives rise to a unitary right throughout the Community, but it excludes the protection of plant variety by a national right where there is a Community PVR.[9]

2. OFFICIAL TESTING

A3–03 A basic point on which both the 1964 Act and the CPV Regulation depart from the patent system is that protection is granted only after official testing. This trial is designed to show that the variety has the requisite properties mentioned below.[10] The Plant Variety Rights Office continues its testing so long as the variety right endures, and it can revoke the grant should the variety lose its distinctiveness. Several West European systems (whether "patent" systems or not) also have similar testing and this has led to collaborative arrangements between the different countries.[11] There is a saving of effort which is increasing in significance as the number of applications grows. The United States system does not provide for the same tests on a regular basis, and this makes international co-operation difficult.

The process of testing is needed not only to obtain variety rights but also to secure government approval for the marketing of seed: the two requirements thus run in tandem.

---

[7] Convention for the Protection of New Varieties of Plants (UPOV) 1961; signed initially by several European states (including the U.K.) and ratified by the U.K. on September 17, 1965; a revised text was signed in October 1978, which in particular allowed countries to offer both patent and variety right to the same invention if this was part of their law upon ratifying. Thus the U.S. was able to join.

[8] Regulation 2100/94, operative on April 27, 1995 ("CPV Reg"); See van der Krooif, *Introduction to the E.C. Regulation on Plant Variety Protection* (1996).

[9] CPV Reg., Arts 2, 92.

[10] See para. A3–05, below. Because these trials will take at least two growing years, an applicant for variety rights may apply for a protective direction from the Controller of Plant Varieties: s. 1(3) under the 1964 Act, Sched. 1. This gives the applicant the right to prevent others from doing anything that would amount to infringement or wrongful use of the variety name if the rights had been granted; but the applicant must also undertake not to market the variety during the same period: Sched. 1, para. 2.

[11] Provided for by the Convention (n. 7, above), Art. 30(2).

3. GRADUALISM WITH VARIATIONS

Under the British system protection is available only when a scheme has **A3–04** been made by the relevant ministers for the genus or species to which the variety belongs.[12] The point of proceeding by schemes is that adaptations can be made to take account of particular characteristics and requirements. Thus, the term of the rights varies from scheme to scheme, being between 15 and 25 years in length[13]; and the scope of the exclusive right is in some schemes specially extended.[14]

The Community Scheme has similar flexibility: the general period of 25 years (30 years for trees and vines) may be extended by the Administrative Council by up to five years for certain genera and species.[15]

4. CRITERIA OF VALIDITY

A protectable variety must be new, distinct, uniform and stable. It is the last **A3–05** three of these characteristics that are officially tested. *Novelty* has a carefully limited meaning, different from that of patent law.[16] Only "prior commercialisation" counts against the applicant. This may be performed by anyone anywhere before the relevant scheme is introduced. But once the scheme exists, only prior sales and offers for sale by the applicant count against him, and even so his sales abroad in the previous four years are disregarded. To be *distinct*, the variety must have one or more important morphological, physiological or other characteristics that differ from other varieties according to common knowledge.[17] Whether the variety is sufficiently *uniform* has to be judged by reference to the particular features of the variety's sexual reproduction or vegetative propagation.[18] It will be *stable* if it remains true to its description after repeated reproduction or propagation. Where the applicant specifies a particular cycle of reproduction, the variety must keep its essential characteristics at the end of each cycle.[19]

---

[12] Plant Varieties and Seeds Act 1964, s. 1(1). The first five were introduced in 1965; the number has now greatly increased.

[13] *ibid.*, s. 3. For fruit, forest and ornamental trees the term must be at least 18 years. There is a provision allowing the Controller to make one extension (up to a maximum of 25 years) on the ground of inadequate remuneration: s. 3(5), (8), *cf.* PA 1949, s. 23. For surrender of rights, see Plant Varieties and Seeds Act 1964, s. 3(6).

[14] See para. A3–07, below.

[15] CPV Reg., Art. 19.

[16] Plant Varieties and Seeds Act 1964, Sched. 2, Pt 2, para. 2; *Elizabeth of Glamis-Rose* [1966] F.S.R. 265: see Lesser [1987] E.I.P.R. 172.

[17] Plant Varieties and Seeds Act 1964, Sched. 2, Pt 2, para. 1; see *Maris Druid-Spring Barley* [1968] F.S.R. 559.

[18] Plant Varieties and Seeds Act 1964, Sched. 2, Pt 2, para. 4; *Zephyr-Spring Barley* [1967] F.S.R. 576; *Moulin Wheat* [1985] F.S.R. 283.

[19] Plant Varieties and Seeds Act 1964, Sched. 2, Pt 2, para. 5; *Zephyr* case (n. 18, above); CPV Reg., Art. 9.

The Community Scheme imposes similar conditions. The impact of genetic engineering on plant breeding is shown by the requirement that there be distinctiveness, uniformity and stability in the expressed characteristics stemming from a particular genotype.[20]

A3–06 If rights have been granted, the Controller must revoke them if he is satisfied that: (1) there was prior commercialisation; (2) the variety is not distinct[21]; (3) the right-holder is no longer able to supply him with reproductive material for the variety; (4) prior rights existed in another persons; or (5) he was given incorrect information.[22] In addition he has a discretion to revoke on certain grounds concerning the maintenance of stocks, compulsory licences, protective directions and fees.[23] In proceedings for revocation, third parties may intervene, but they have no statutory right to initiate them. Moreover, there is no explicit power to plead invalidity as a defence to infringement; nor may a counterclaim for revocation be made.

5. Rights over Reproductive Material

A3–07 The rights given by the 1964 Act were deliberately limited in ways which sought to curb the right-owner's power to make monopoly profits. Two principles were accordingly adopted:

(1) the rights should extend only to the marketing of reproductive material (seed, tubers, cuttings, etc.) intended for reproduction and not for consumption (for example grain for milling);

(2) farmers and others should not have to procure a licence to make their own seed and other material from their previous crop. The exclusive right accordingly covers selling reproductive material and producing it for purposes of sale.[24] Only exceptionally—where plant breeders will not otherwise receive adequate remuneration—may a scheme extend the exclusive right so as to cover producing or propagating the variety for the purpose of selling cut blooms, fruit and some other parts of the product.[25] It is expressly provided that if the material is bought abroad (something which is not itself restricted), it is an infringement thereafter to use it for reproduction, or to sell it as such, in Great Britain.[26]

---

[20] CPV Reg., Arts 7–9.

[21] But not that it is not uniform or stable: *cf.* CPV Reg., Art. 20(1)(a).

[22] Plant Varieties and Seeds Act 1964, ss. 3(7), (8), 6(4), Sched. 2, Pt. 1, para. 2(b). See equally under the CPV Reg., Art. 20; for appeals, Arts 67, 68, 73, 74.

[23] Plant Varieties and Seeds Act 1964, ss. 6(3), 7(7), Sched. 1 para. 4(1); Plant Breeders' Rights Regulations 1978. S.I. 1978 No. 294.

[24] Selling is defined in Plant Varieties and Seeds Act 1964, s. 4(6).

[25] *ibid.*, s. 4(1)(c), Sched. 3, para. 3. This has been done, *e.g.* in the case of roses, chrysanthemums and carnations.

[26] Plant Varieties and Seeds Act 1964, s. 4(2). Where cut bloom reproduction has been covered by a scheme, there is no equivalent provision affecting the importation for sale of blooms grown abroad. But consider the analogy of the *Saccharin* rule for patents: para. 6–14, n. 60, above.

The CPV Scheme applies to the geographical area of the Union and in other ways it goes somewhat further. First, the possibility of genetic modification of a variety is recognised: the scope of the right extends to "essentially derived varieties".[27] Secondly, the "farmers' right" to free use of propagating material has been restricted to specially defined cases. In other instances, the right extends to harvested seed and other propagating material.[28]

6. The Registered Name

For any variety in which rights are granted, the Controller may require a **A3–08** name to be proposed. The name is intended to be descriptive of the variety and not distinctive of commercial source in the trade mark sense. The Controller may accordingly refuse to accept a proposed name because of its ability to cause confusion, including confusion with a trade mark or name.[29]

A similar system operates for the CPV Right.[30] The varietal name, once registered, carries its own right. The proprietor may bring a civil action against anyone who uses the name (or one confusingly similar) for selling any other variety within the same class.[31]

7. Licensing

The British Act and the CPV Regulation permit conditions, limitations and **A3–09** restrictions to be attached to licences, in the same way as is possible for other propriety rights.[32] The Community right is subject to the usual provision of intra-E.C. exhaustion, which follows from Article 36 of the Rome Treaty. There are, however, specified cases to which exhaustion does not apply: acts involving further propagation or the export of variety constituents to a third country which does not protect varieties.[33] The British right must equally be subject to the general principle of Community law,[34] and it appears to create a similar exception by permitting express embargoes to be placed on the resale of authorised reproductive material.[35] It is necessary to determine whether the various conditions of exclusivity

---

[27] CPV Reg., Art. 14(5), (6); Plant Varieties and Seeds Act 1964, s. 5; Plant Breeders' Rights Regulations 1978, reg. 18. For the relation to the Indices of varietal names generally, see 1964 Act, ss. 5(3), 20, 21.

[28] CPV Reg., Art. 14. *cf. Wheatcroft's T.M.* [1954] Ch. 210.

[29] Plant Breeders' Rights Regulations 1978, reg. 18(2).

[30] CPV Reg., Art. 63.

[31] Plant Varieties and Seeds Act 1964, s. 5(6), with a defence of reasonable innocence to a claim to damages. Note also s. 5A, making it an offence, save in specified circumstances, to sell reproductive material by a name other than its registered name.

[32] *ibid.*, s. 4(4). There is an implied licence (unless expressly negated) on a legitimate sale of reproductive material to re-sell, but not to produce reproductive material for sale: s. 4(5).

[33] CPV Reg., Art. 16.

[34] See *Nungesser v. E.C. Commission* ([1982] E.C.R. 2015, para. 7–34, above).

[35] See Plant Varieties and Seeds Act 1964, s. 4(4), (5).

provided for in a licence amount to distortions of competition or means of promoting the exploitation of the new variety.[36]

Given the importance of new plant varieties and the Act's determination to qualify the ability to make monopoly profits out of rights, it is no surprise to find a fairly extensive regime for compulsory licensing in the British Scheme.[37] After a period of years, which varies from scheme to scheme, the Controller must grant a non-exclusive licence if he is satisfied either that the right-holder has unreasonably refused to grant a voluntary licence or has proffered only unreasonable terms, unless there is good reason to the contrary.[38]

There is a vestigial power, under the Community system, to grant compulsory exploitation rights. When it is exercised it must be on grounds of public interest and after consulting the Administrative Council. The difficulty will always be to discover whether the public interest of the Community as a whole demands such intervention. As in Union affairs in general, there will often be differences of interest between Member States.

---

[36] *Nungesser v. E.C. Commission* (n. 34, above).
[37] Plant Varieties and Seeds Act 1964, s. 7.
[38] For the various criteria to be balanced by the Controller, see *ibid.*, s. 7(3), (6); *Cama-Wheat* [1968] F.S.R. 639. There are arrangements to give *locus standi* to collective organisations which represent right-holders: 1964 Act, s. 7(5).

INDEX

(All references are to paragraph number)